ADMINISTRATIVE LAW
IN IRELAND

THIRD EDITION

BY

DAVID GYWNN MORGAN, LL.M. (LOND.),
Ph.D.(N.U.I.)
of the Middle Temple, Barrister
Professor and Head of the Law Department,
at University College, Cork

and

GERARD HOGAN, B.C.L. LL.M., LL.M. (PENN.),
M.A. (DUBL.), LL.D.,
Senior Counsel,
Fellow of Trinity College, Dublin
Lecturer in Law, Trinity College, Dublin

ROUND HALL SWEET & MAXWELL
DUBLIN
1998

Administrative Law (Irish Law Texts)
First Edition 1986
Administrative Law in Ireland
Second Edition 1991

Published in 1998 by
Round Hall Sweet & Maxwell
Brehon House, 4 Upper Ormond Quay,
Dublin 7.
Typeset by
Carrigboy Typesetting Services, Durrus, County Cork.
Printed in Great Britain by
Antony Rowe Ltd, Chippenham, Wiltshire

ISBN 1-899738-67-3 (Paperback)
ISBN 1-899738-76-2 (Hardback)

A catalogue record for this book
is available from the British Library.

To Deirdre, Declan, Gwendolen, Daniel and Gareth

(D.G.M.)

In memory of Niall
and to Karen, Hilary and Hugh

(G.H.)

PREFACE

It is impossible to doubt the large and growing need for administrative law in this jurisdiction. The prevalence of Leviathan in all our lives can be demonstrated, for instance, both by the large sums of money of which he disposes and the presence of a huge corpus of regulatory legislation. Moreover, state authority in its multivarious forms looms especially large in any small country such as Ireland, which hitherto traditionally lacked any significant private institutions (like, for instance, the City of London) which would act as a counter-weight. Yet pulling in the opposite direction is a strong national preference for individualistic rights such as private property, political freedom and privacy: a preference which is conveniently implemented via a written Constitution containing an entrenched Bill of Rights, administered by a largely activist judiciary.

Taken together, these (and earlier) authorities represent a largely successful attempt to up-date the system of judicial control of governmental actions which has been shaped by such adventitious factors as: the King's defeat in the mid-Seventeenth Century English Civil War, Dicey's dislike of specialist regimes of law, even for the State; the pre-occupation of professional lawyers with procedure; and the nationalist feelings of some judges.

In the previous edition of this book, we bemoaned the failure, which we thought we had seen in some areas, to follow precedent – that most basic of judicial – craft. For justice may be a hobgoblin but certainty is possible and precedent remains the classic tool which the common law has fashioned to achieve it. Happily, the case law of the 1990s shows a return to this eternal verity.

In spite of this rich raw material, lawyers have hitherto been slow (for reasons examined briefly in Chapter 1) to admit administrative law to the charmed circle of blocs of law which are officially regarded as discrete legal subjects. Even in Britain, the sounds of self-congratulation celebrating the coming of age of administrative law have only recently died down. In this jurisdiction, the renaissance of administrative law – which may be said to have begun with the seminal trilogy of cases, *East Donegal Co-Operative Livestock Marts Ltd. v. Attorney General* [1970] I.R. 317; *Re Haughey* [1971] I.R. 217 and *Byrne v. Ireland* [1972] I.R. 241 – has now flowered almost to full bloom. Inevitably, perhaps, the volume of recent case law and legislation has been enormous. Thus, in 1997 alone the Supreme Court gave judgment in cases such as *Radio Limerick (One) Ltd. v. Independent Radio and Television Commission* [1997] 2 I.R. 291 (test for bias); *O'Reilly v. O'Sullivan*, unreported, Supreme Court, February 26, 1997 (extent of powers of County Manager); *Emerald Meats Ltd v. Minister for Agriculture & Food* [1997] 1 I.R. 1 (extent of damages for breach of statutory duty and European Community law); *Walsh v. Irish Red Cross Ltd* [1997] 2 I.R. 479 (scope of public law); *Duff v. Minister for Agriculture & Food* [1997] 2 I.R. 22 (reasonableness and damages for *ultra vires* actions); *Central Bank of Ireland v. Gildea* [1997] 1 I.R. 160 (status of Central Bank employees) *Skeffington v. Rooney* [1997] 1 I.R. 22 (executive privilege and discovery);

O'Malley v. An Ceann Comhairle [1997] 1 I.R. 428 (whether parliamentary rulings are amenable to judicial review); *Mooney v. An Post*, unreported, Supreme Court, March 20, 1997 (constitutional justice as applied to employment law); *O'Neill v. Minister for Agriculture & Food* [1997] 2 I.L.R.M. 435 (exclusive licensing schemes and *ultra vires*); *Malahide Community Council Ltd. v. Fingal County Council* [1997] 3 I.R. 383 (judicial review of a development plan); *Georgopulous v. Beaumont Hospital Board*, unreported, Supreme Court, June 4, 1997 (constitutional justice as applied to employment law); *McDonnell v. Ireland*, unreported, Supreme Court, July 23, 1997 (retroactive effect of a finding of invalidity and actions for breaches of constitutional rights); *Killeen v. Director of Public Prosecutions* [1998] 1 I.L.R.M. 1 (nature of errors of law affecting jurisdiction); *Farrell v. Attorney General* [1998] 1 I.L.R.M. 364 (statutory interpretation, *vires* and unreasonableness); *Riordan v. An Tánaiste* [1997] 3 I.R. 502 (*locus standi*); *Devanney v. District Judge Shields* [1998] 1 I.L.R.M. 81 (extent of *Carltona* doctrine); *Anisimova v. Minister for Justice*, unreported, Supreme Court, November 28, 1997 (judicial review of non-statutory scheme); *Henry Denny & Sons (Ire.) Ltd. v. Minister for Social Welfare*, unreported, Supreme Court, December 1, 1997 (nature of appellate jurisdiction from decisions of specialist tribunals). All of these judgments could justly be described as decisions of major importance and they collectively demonstrate once again the extent to which public law dominates the Supreme Court's agenda. How many decisions of comparable importance has the Supreme Court given in recent times in such traditional areas of the law as conveyancing or contract law?

What has been the effect of these developments in this decade? On the whole they have served to rationalise, develop and clarify the law, so that we can say that modern Irish administrative law is at once clearer and more coherent – although necessarily more complex – than it was at the start of this decade. And while many of these recent judgments both in the High Court as well as the Supreme Court – display a mastery of language as well as much creative thinking, some uncertainties still remain and some contemporary pronouncements may have to re-considered afresh. "In a case in which a court has decided that judicial intervention is inappropriate" Lord Hoffmann has written "there is a temptation to emphasise in the most general terms the reluctance of the courts to intervene. And there is always a tendency to reductionism, to trying the squeeze the diversity of life into a single formula which can be made to yield an answer in every case" ("A Sense of Proportion" (1997) 32 *Irish Jurist* 49 at 53–54). This is as at least as true of the Supreme Court as of the House of Lords. And thus in cases involving challenges based on reasonableness and irrationality, there has been an unfortunate tendency unthinkingly to invoke – without further analysis – the appropriate passages from the judgments of Henchy J. in *The State (Keegan) v. Stardust Victims' Compensation Tribunal* [1986] I.R. 542 and Finlay C.J. in *O'Keeffe v. An Bord Pleanála* [1993] 1 I.R. 39 when refusing relief on this ground. The real challenge here is to find a via media where the courts pay appropriate deference to the decisions of expert tribunals; yet at the same time ensure their supervisory jurisdiction is meaningfully exercised.

If we leave the consideration of judicial review on its own terms and instead consider it in the context of the political and constitutional framework within which it operates and against whose needs and values it must be judged, it may be legitimate to question, briefly, whether this is entirely a good thing. For on the plan of practicality it is a striking limitation on the value of judicial law-making that the only facts and considerations which will be properly before the court will be those relevant to the individual case. These may well omit matters which are significant in considering the wider ramifications of the law which is laid down in the case. It is significant, too, that other areas of the law with major effects on the balance between the community and the individual, for instance, Tax Law, Social Welfare Law or Criminal Law, are made mainly by way of legislation. And legal areas with swathes of judge-made law comparable to administrative law are to be found mainly in the private law field, where the rate of change has been far slower. Or they concern procedural or pre-trial law, areas in which the judiciary (from their experiences, as judges or barristers) correctly believe themselves to be peculiarly experienced. Worst of all, perhaps, if certain issues are in effect left to the courts then if no litigant with the appropriate case has the resolution to take the hard road to the High Court, then the matter will be left unresolved.

At a more political level, it has also been suggested that over emphasis upon the constraints upon political power has militated against good administration and pushed the balance between the needs of the community and the rights of the individual too far in favour of the individual. This debate has been characterised as a controversy between "red-" and "green-light" theorists (see Harlow and Rawlings, *Law and Administration* (1984) and Richardson and Genn (eds.) *Administrative Law and Government Action* (1994)). Here the imbalance between the present, largely individualistic temper of the Irish judiciary ("*fiat justitia, ruat coelum*") and, on the other, the rather conservative public service may be in danger of creating a lopsidedness at some points in our system of administrative law. Indeed, we have reached the position where – in contrast to the privileges traditionally enjoyed by the State in litigation – the State and public authorities is actually at a disadvantage. Thus, for example, there have been examples of cases (see, *e.g. Deane v. Voluntary Health Insurance Board (No. 2)*, unreported, High Court, April 22, 1993) where semi-state bodies have been exonerated from charges of anti-competitive behaviour, but the same conduct has nonetheless been characterised as amounting to the unfair use of statutory powers. There may be other areas – aspects of constitutional justice and state liability readily come to mind – where the law has have tilted too much against the State.

It would be easy to make two responses to this line of argument. First, it may be said that in the past the judges were more or less forced to introduce certain changes simply because of complacency in the case of the executive and inertia in the case of the Oireachtas. Secondly, it is almost certainly the case that an Irish judge of the Superior Courts would have a closer understanding of the needs and values of the person in the street than would be so in Britain. This is not, however, the place to go into such questions as: the proper relationship between the judiciary and the other organs of the State, and whether the device of judicial review is well designed to enable the courts to fulfil their role (overdue, though such a debate would be in the Irish context.) Here we need only make the elementary points that the field of public administration involves a wide variety of rights, duties, immunities, impositions and benefits (to use legal concepts many of which have no analogues in private law.) Moreover, these differ widely from each other in terms of the levels of significance to the individuals affected. Furthermore, the interests affected and the ways in which they are affected and should be recognised, will vary enormously. Accordingly: the executive agencies; procedures; third party consultation processes; and control and appellate mechanisms should all be carefully designed and tailored to the kaleidoscope of the various possibilities. Accordingly, it is a trusim that courts are not and should not be the only mechanism for law-making or for dispute resolution, in the field of public administration. These considerations take on added force during a time of rapid change, like the present, when attempts are being made to substantially increase the levels of openness, accountability, fairness and efficiency in our system of public administration. In the past few years, the political organs have begun to wake up to their responsibility to address the difficult issues – in terms of principle and practical operation – involved in making the appropriate choice in these difficult areas. The enactment of the Public Service Management Act 1997 and the Freedom of Information Act 1997 presages significant changes in the culture of the public sector. In the state-sponsored sector, issues such as: the balance of authority between the board and the Minister; privatisation; and competition policy are beginning to receive some attention.

Other challenges lie ahead. Can the doctrine of proportionality be applied in the realm of pure administrative law, or is its utility to be confined to cases where the validity of statute law is challenged as unconstitutional? Will the courts take up the radical analysis of Keane J. in *O'Neill v. Minister for Agriculture & Food* [1997] 2 I.L.R.M. 421 and appraise non-statutory schemes superimposed on an existing statutory framework against contemporary needs? Will the courts work out a better balance between substantive requirements based on legitimate expectations and the need to allow a reasonable measure of discretion to those entrusted with discretionary powers? Will the Supreme Court re-assess aspects of *Byrne v. Ireland* [1972] I.R. 241 and *Webb v. Ireland* [1988] I.R. 353 given that much of the reasoning in these cases has been demolished by academic commentary, most recently by Costello, "The Expulsion of Prerogative Doctrine from Irish Law" (1997) 32 *Irish Jurist* 145 and that the utility of some of the former prerogatives has been demonstrated by, for instance, *Webb*. (Perhaps the best solution to this entire prerogative issue is that canvassed in the *Report of the Constitution Review Group* (Pn. 2326, 1996), namely, the introduction of a new, contemporary version of the Executive Powers (Consequential Provisions) Act 1937 which would re-cast in modern form and vest in the Government such diverse legal powers deriving from the former prerogative as the control of passports or the wardship jurisdiction.)

But even beyond these particular problems, even wider issues require to be resolved. As Murphy J. recognised in *Duff v. Minister for Agriculture & Food* [1997] 2 I.R. 22, contemporary Irish administrative law has already been heavily influenced by the reception into our law of European concepts such as legitimate expectations and proportionality. This tendency is set to increase in the future, especially if the stream of important judgments on Article 6(1) of the European Convention of Human Rights continues. European thinking on the public law/private law divide may yet help to throw light on this problem and suggestions to this effect are made in the text at pp. 771–772. Most startlingly of all, perhaps, the very foundation of administrative law – the *ultra vires* doctrine – has recently come under challenge from leading English judges and jurists. Now while it is true that many aspects of the doctrine – in tandem with the attendant specialist rules of statutory interpretation – are highly artificial, it is also the case that the entire edifice of judicial review is based on this long-established common law rule, which in this jurisdiction is reinforced by the presumption of constitutionality and the double construction rule (see, *e.g.* O'Brien *v. Bord na Móna* [1983] I.R. 256). If this elaborate edifice is deconstructed in favour of examining the *actual* intent of the Oireachtas via the reception of parliamentary debates, it will simply mean that many more items of legislation which can presently be rescued via the double construction rule will be found to be unconstitutional. In any case, with so many alternatives sources of new directions on doctrine, it will require resolution and good judgment on the part of the judiciary to maintain a predictable and coherent systems of laws.

Traditionally among lawyers in the common law world, the lion's share of whatever attention was given to administrative law was lavished upon the segment known as "judicial review of administrative action." Indeed, such figures as are available seem to show that there is considerably more judicial review litigation per capita in this jurisdiction than in Britain. The growing importance of administrative law is evidenced by the fact that in recent years significantly more than 50 per cent of the written judgments emanating from the Supreme Court are concerned with public law issues and that 1997 saw a record number of judicial review applications (just over 460 in total, although a substantial portion of this figure arises from criminal trials).

There has also been some progress in the reform of local government law, with important legislation enacted in 1991, 1994 and 1997. Further overhaul of what hitherto has been a byzantine legislative code is promised for this year to coincide with the centenary of the Local Government (Ireland) Act 1898 and the establishment of the county council system. Whether the present Government can successfully tackle the twin issues of the devolution of power and local government funding (especially given that the present Minister for Environment and Local Government has indicated his dissatisfaction with the Local Government (Financial Provisions) Act 1997) remains to be seen. In addition, the enactment of both the Public Service Management Act 1997 and the Freedom of Information Act 1997 presages significant changes in the culture of the public sector. Fourteen years have now elapsed since the appointment of the first Ombudsman. To judge by the case-load of the office and the central position which the office has quickly assumed in the polity, its establishment was a much needed reform. Finally, the enactment of an Administrative Procedures Act, with an emphasis on internal grievance procedures has been promised.

Against the background of this debate about fundamentals, the book attempts to steer a middle course, dealing with certain instruments of government, namely, Ministers, Departments and the civil service, state-sponsored bodies and local government. Although the local government chapter runs to almost 80 pages, the treatment of this subject is of necessity compressed. This is especially true of the planning section, but readers are already well catered for in this area by two excellent text-books, Scannell's *Environmental and Planning Law* (1995) and Galligan's *Irish*

Planning Law and Procedure (1997). We have also kept our account of the constitutional law background to a minimum since this is well covered by several established text-books. After the instruments of government, we describe the instruments of control, namely tribunals and inquiries (Chapter 6), licensing (Chapter 7) and the Ombudsman (Chapter 8). Chapters 9 to 12 focus on the substantive principles of judicial review of administrative action including the fundamental nature of legal powers, constitutional justice and the review of discretionary powers. The remaining chapters 13–17 – deal with procedural and subsidiary aspects of judicial review or complementary matters. Among these are: the application for judicial review itself, the divide between public law and private law and its significance; damages, legitimate expectations and the distinctive rules which apply to the State when it litigates. The present edition of this book thus contains three new chapters. Owing to the volume of material, Chapter 7 (licensing) has been split off from Chapter 6 (tribunals and inquiries). Likewise, constitutional justice has been divided into two: Chapter 11 (bias) and Chapter 12 (fair procedures and *audi alteram partem*). Finally, a new chapter (Chapter 14) has been devoted to the scope of public law.

As with previous editions, the emphasis is very much on the law and practice of the Republic of Ireland, although with some reference to the Northern Irish authorities, a task now assisted by the substantial improvements in the publication of Northern Irish Law Reports. We have endeavoured to cover developments up to the end of December 1997. As regards the readership: we have tried to cater both for the needs of practitioners and students by providing a detailed analysis of recent developments and fairly comprehensive footnote references for the former, while at the same time taking care to outline fundamental principles and to describe certain concepts whose artificiality requires some explanation. While we have striven to ensure that our analysis remains comprehensive and up-to-date, in places we have been obliged to be discriminating regarding our selection of material, so that, for example, we have not mentioned every case in which there is passing reference to *Stardust Victims' Tribunal* or *O'Keeffe v. An Bord Pleanála*. In this litigious age, it is probably necessary to add that we disclaim any liability for errors or omissions in this book, but we would be particularly grateful if any readers who notice errors or omissions would draw them to our attention.

It is a pleasure to record our thanks to the many people who have given so freely of their time and wisdom to add to, or improve, the contents of this edition of the book or who helped us by supplying copies of newly emerging judgments: Conleth Bradley, Barrister-at-Law; Rosemary Byrne, Law School, Trinity College, Dublin; Brendan Conway, Barrister-at-Law; Hilary Delany, Law School, Trinity College, Dublin; Mary Finlay S.C.; Colm Gallagher; Adrian Hardiman S.C.; Richard Haslam; David Hegarty, Barrister-at-Law; Niamh Hyland, Barrister-at-Law; Carol Leland, Barrister-at-Law; Michael McDowell S.C.; James McGuill, Solicitor; Diarmuid McGuinness S.C.; Marian Moylan, Barrister; Her Honour Judge Yvonne Murphy; Desmond O'Malley T.D.; James O'Reilly S.C.; Siobhán Phelan, Barrister-at-Law; Mark Ryan, Solicitor; Dr. Yvonne Scannell, Law School, Trinity College, Dublin; Morgan Sheehy and Gerry Whyte, Law School, Trinity College, Dublin. A special debt of gratitude is owed to Eoin O'Dell, Law School, Trinity College, Dublin who helped us extensively with the Liability in Restitution section of Chapter 15 (Damages).

Preface

We must again record our gratitude to our indexer, Julitta Clancy for her skill and professionalism. We are also grateful to Josette Cadoret who did a magnificent typesetting job on a difficult manuscript. We also thank Elizabeth Senior who gave considerable assistance with the proofs. We are indebted to all the staff at Round Hall Sweet & Maxwell, but we must particularly thank Catherine Dolan for her enthusiastic and meticulous work on the copy-editing of an enormous manuscript. Finally, we pay a special tribute to our respective wives, Karen and Deirdre for their constant encouragement and forbearance.

Gerard Hogan
David Gwynn Morgan
May 1998

TABLE OF CONTENTS

1. INTRODUCTION 1

2. SOUCES OF ADMINISTRATIVE LAW 8

3. THE DÁIL, MINISTERS, DEPARTMENTS AND CIVIL SERVANTS 58

4. STATE-SPONSORED BODIES 112

TABLE OF CASES

IRELAND

Table of Cases

Table of Cases

Table of Cases

NORTHERN IRELAND

GREAT BRITAIN

Table of Cases

l

E.U. CASES

EUROPEAN COURT OF HUMAN RIGHTS

OTHER JURISDICTIONS

Table of Cases

TABLE OF CONSTITUTIONAL PROVISIONS

Table of Consitutional Provisions

TABLE OF STATUTES

3. Acts of the United Kingdom (post-1922)

TABLE OF STATUTORY
INSTRUMENTS AND ORDERS

TABLE OF RULES OF THE SUPERIOR COURTS

TABLE OF TREATIES OF
THE EUROPEAN COMMUNITY

TABLE OF LEGISLATION OF
THE EUROPEAN COMMUNITIES

TABLE OF INTERNATIONAL TREATIES AND CONVENTIONS

TABLE OF OTHER JURISDICTIONS

CHAPTER 1

INTRODUCTION

1. Flavour of Administrative Law

Administrative law is conventionally defined as the law regulating the organisation, composition, functions and procedures of public authorities;[1] their impact on the citizen; and the restraints to which they are subject. By public authorities, we mean (to list the examples principally covered in this book): the Government in the sense, which is the one employed in Article 28 of the Constitution, of the 15 Ministers who are the central directorate of the executive; a Minister in his Department;[2] state-sponsored bodies[3] like CIÉ or RTÉ and local authorities.[4] There are other public bodies – such as the Universities; the Gardaí Síochána; or the Defence Forces – which there is no space to cover specifically here, apart from noticing that the general ideas and rules of administrative law apply to them. It ought also to be noted that there are certain private bodies which discharge public (or "quasi-public") functions, for example, the trade unions or professional associations, like the Law Society or the Medical Council. Such bodies have been characterised as "domestic governments" and it has accordingly seemed appropriate to the courts and legislature, to extend to them certain of the characteristic principles of administrative law, for example, the rules of constitutional justice.

Administrative law is clearly a public law subject, that is to say, that its focus is relations between the individual and the state, in contrast with private law (for example, the law of contract or tort), which regulates relations – mainly between private individuals. Classification of administrative law as public law raises the difficult question of the boundary and, be it said, the substantial overlap, with constitutional law. One point of distinction stems from the fact that administrative law focuses on the executive and the other two major organs (legislature and judicature) are important only so far as they impact on the executive – by contrast, constitutional law covers all three organs equally. The second point of distinction is that, generally speaking, matters of principle are fixed by constitutional law; whereas administrative law looks more to questions of detail and to matters of function more than structure. Thirdly, constitutional law includes as a major

---

[1] Of course large public companies may be as much in need of control by the law as public authorities. Companies are, in fact, controlled by company law and labour law and an interesting book remains to be written comparing these controls with those imposed by administrative law. For the present, see Chap. 14 on "The Scope of Public Law".

[2] See pp. 59–71.

[3] See Chap. 4.

[4] See Chap. 5.

1

component the law of fundamental rights – *i.e.* those legal rights which are regarded as so essential to decent, dignified life as a human being that they are established by the Constitution (augmented by judicial exegesis) and prevail over all other types of law. Yet it must be admitted that it is very often in cases involving the administrative actions of the executive that the fundamental rights have to be invoked. Thus there is a substantial, if adventitious, connection between administrative and constitutional law and at various points[5] we shall notice the fundamental rights as part of the controls upon administrative actions.

In the mid-nineteenth century, following the Industrial Revolution, and with the rise of political democracy, there was a vast increase in the activity of the executive and its intervention in the affairs of the citizen. This has taken various forms, including the regulation of land use and commercial transactions; the provision of social welfare benefits and free or subsidised health and education services; and the management of the economy by such measures as the control of prices and incomes, tax actions, subsidies, etc.[6] Since administrative law is the law regulating the administration of the executive arm of government, one might have expected such trends to be reflected in the development of administrative law as a coherent subject.

Yet the reality is that in the common law world, administrative law has only recently come to be acknowledged and studied as a unified discipline.[7] There are at least three reasons for this, the first of which is historical and is common to Ireland and Britain. The Parliamentary victory in the British Civil War in the seventeenth century led to the eradication of the central executive machinery built around the Privy Council. The organs which evolved to fill these gaps did so in a cramped, ad hoc way. It is to this historical factor that is owed such features of our system of administrative law as: the absence of the specialised administrative courts which exist on the Continent; the distorting fiction that public law is simply a special case of private law; the crab-like growth of our system of judicial review, proceeding from the baseline of the *ultra vires* doctrine[8]; the formal significance of the legislature in the control of governmental administration[9]; and the late development of professionalism in the public service. At the local level too, the institutions of government were not tailor-made for their tasks. Before the nineteenth century, the

---

[5] See, *e.g.* pp. 454–460, 503–505, 651–668.
[6] See Holdsworth, *History of English Law*, Vol. xiv, pp. 90–204.
[7] The first lectures on Administrative Law in Irish Universities were given as indicated: T.C.D. (1946, F. C. King); U.C.D. (early 1950s, P. McGilligan); U.C.G. (1975, J. M. G. Sweeney); U.C.C. (1978, D. Gwynn Morgan); Q.U.B. (1953). For recent works on Irish Administrative Law (or aspects thereof), see: Stout, *Administrative Law in Ireland* (1985); Casey, "Ireland" (written in English) in Hegen (ed.) *Gesichte der Verwaltungsrecht wissenschaft in Europa* (Frankfurt am Main, 1982); Koekkoek, "Ierland" (written in Dutch) in Prakke and Kortmann (eds.) *Het bestuursrecht van de landen der Europese Gemeenschappen* (Kluwer, 1986); Collins and O'Reilly, *Civil Proceedings and the State in Ireland* (1989); Scannell, *Environmental and Plannning Law* (1995); Hogan "Judicial Review The Law of the Republic of Ireland" in Hadfield (ed.) *Judicial Review: A Thematic Approach* (1995); Hogan, "Irland" in Schwarze (ed.) *Das Verwaltungsrecht unter europaischem Einfluss: Zur Konvergenz der mitgliedstaatlichen Verwaltungsrechtsordnungen in der Europaischen Union* (Baden-Baden, 1996); Galligan, *Planning Law and Procedure* (1997). For the administrative law of Northern Ireland Ireland, see Hadfield, "Judicial Review in Northern Ireland: A Primer" (1991) 42 N.I.L.Q. 332 and Maguire, "The Procedure for Judicial Review in Northern Ireland" in Hadfield (ed.) *op. cit.*
[8] See pp. 394–405.
[9] See p. 62.

principal institution was the amphibious justices of the peace, who also acted as local courts of law. When, as a result of the Civil War, the justices were released from the control of the Privy Council (exercised by way of the Court of the Star Chamber), they could only be called to account by the Court of King's Bench. It seemed natural simply to apply to the justices in their administrative role the same remedies as those which controlled them in their judicial duties. By another apparently natural development, the courts extended these remedies and, with them, the substantive law for the control of the justices' administrative action, so as to apply to all the other public authorities as these grew up.

The second factor was the enormous, ideological influence of the turn-of-the-century scholar, Dicey. His principal tenet was that Ministers and other state organs ought to be subject to the same law, administered by the same courts, as a private individual and that this ideal was achieved in the British system of law. Contrasted with this was the French institution of the *droit administratif* in which specialised tribunals applied law to the acts of the executive and, it was implied, gave the executive an easy ride. From such an outlook, it was a short step to the conclusion that a system of administrative law, which acknowledged the unique position of the state and systematically granted it special powers and subjected it to special controls, was anathema. It followed that to embark on a study of such elements of administrative law as there happened to be in British law was to court disaster.

The third reason why administrative law has been so slow to develop as a coherent, unified whole is that the territory which it covers is so voluminous and diverse. The subject really consists of general principles – with the substantive details being contained in such subjects as: planning law; housing and public health law; social welfare law; licensing law; and economic law. Throughout this work, we shall be examining material which could be relocated in one or other of these categories. This is a feature which distinguishes administrative law from discrete subject-blocks, like tort or criminal law, where a single book can cover more or less the whole area and where the overlap with neighbouring subjects is less significant. The result of this feature is that the most fruitful approach in explaining administrative law is to describe the leading principles and to observe their operation in certain specimen areas.

Administrative law may be regarded as made up of two components: the instruments of government and the instruments of control. The instruments of government – Ministers and Departments, state-sponsored bodies, local authorities, etc. – are, or should be, designed to enable administrators, working under the control, direct or indirect, of elected politicians, to take decisions and provide services which are in the best interests of the community. But the powers of these agencies are delineated by the law – albeit a law which allows them a great deal of latitude. The law is administered by the instruments of control: the tribunals[10]; the Ombudsman[11]; and, most important of all, the courts, enforcing a bloc of law known as judicial review.

---

[10] See Chap. 6.
[11] See Chap. 8.

2. Two Distinctions

The major difficulty inherent in administrative law is the sheer diversity of the decisions, powers, functions, etc. (these words mean more or less the same) which it comprehends. Here are some examples of typical governmental decisions; the expulsion of an undesirable alien; a local authority's decision to build a concert hall or theatre under the Local Government Act 1960; the making of a statutory instrument regulating the procedure of An Bord Pleanála; the making of a development plan by a local planning authority; a decision whether to grant planning permission in respect of a particular building; assessment of capital gains following the sale of a piece of land; award of a social welfare benefit; allocation of a corporation house. In ordering these disparate functions and in understanding the controls which administrative law imposes on them, we shall be assisted by two sets of distinctions: first, policy and administration; and secondly, legislative and individual decisions.

Policy-administration

Put briefly, administration[12] assumes that there is already in existence a principle and that all the administrator has to do is to establish the facts and circumstances and then to apply the principle. It is of the essence of good administration that the principle must be fairly clear and precise so that, in any given situation, the result should be the same, whether it is administrator A or administrator B who has taken the decision. For, in its purest form, administration requires only a knowledge of the pre-existing principle and an appreciation of the facts to which it is being applied: it is an intellectual process involving little discretion. By contrast, policy-making is largely discretionary: the policy-maker must decide, as between two alternatives, the one which he considers best in the interest of the community. He must take into account all the relevant factors and which factors are relevant is, to a considerable extent, left to him. In doing this, the policy-maker will have to draw on his own values and, in the light of this, it is no coincidence that the words policy and politics come from the same Greek root (*polis*, meaning city). For each word relates to choice in the affairs of the community and it is natural, in a democracy, that major policy questions should be taken by politicians (often on the advice of senior public servants), whether Ministers or, at local government level, elected councillors. As Mendes-France observed: "To govern is to choose." According to the democratic ideal, one elected politician is chosen in preference to another politician just because it is his policy which finds favour with the electorate.

Applying the policy-administration dichotomy to the list of governmental functions given earlier, we can say that matters such as the expulsion of an alien; building of a concert hall; making of procedural regulations; making of a development plan – are policy matters, whereas the grant of planning permission;

---

[12] Administration is one of these awkward words which takes its meaning from the word to which it is opposed, *i.e.* in this Part, to "policy". Unfortunately for clarity, it can also be used in other senses as when it is opposed to legislation or when an administrative decision is contrasted with a quasi-judicial decision (on which, see pp. 601–602).

assessment of capital gains; award of a welfare benefit; and allocation of a corporation house are acts of administration. Indeed, the planning functions afford particularly neat illustrations in that the development plan is the pre-existing standard on which the administrator bases his decision whether to grant permission for a specific development. The making of the development plan is policy and the determining of individual planning applications is administration. It must of course be admitted that such classifications over-estimates the neatness of reality; policy and administration really represent the opposite poles of a spectrum and most decisions fall at some intermediate point along the range. It would, for instance, be plainly wrong to suppose that a planning officer deciding whether to grant planning permission for a small bungalow in an area zoned as "primarily agricultural" would not have to use some of his own discretion.

Clearly the question of whether a decision is one of policy or of administration will depend in part on the wording of the statute or other instrument creating the decision. For instance, section 5(1) of the Aliens Act 1935 provides that the Minister for Justice may "if and whenever he thinks proper" expel an alien.[13] Plainly, this is a policy decision. However, the legislature might have provided that the alien could only be expelled on (say) "health grounds" or in the case of "criminal activity". Such a test would be closer to the administrative end of the scale, but would still leave considerable discretion to the Minister. The decision could have been rendered entirely administrative by providing that an alien could only be expelled if (say) he were suffering from one of a list of specified diseases or if he had been convicted of any indictable offence.

Legislative–individual decisions

The second major distinction in the field of governmental decision-making lies between legislative and individual decisions. A legislative decision affects a potentially unlimited category of persons or situations which share the specified common characteristics; whereas an individual decision is directed to, and affects only, some particular individual(s). It will be seen immediately than an Act of the Oireachtas is an example of a legislative decision. Nor is the Act the only example for the meaning of "legislation" invoked here is wider than the artificially-restricted meaning which has been imposed upon "law-making" in the context of Article 15.2.1°[14] which provides that only the Oireachtas may "make laws for the State." The definition used here is intended to comprehend any rule: for instance, a statutory instrument or by-law.

Before a legislative decision has any effect in a particular instance, an individual decision is necessary, to apply the rule to the particular situation to which it is relevant. One way in which this may be done is by the application of a law by a court.[15] But it often happens that law, especially public law, is applied not by a court but by an administrative agency and, of the list of examples given earlier, the grant of planning permission (local planning authority: county or city manager); the

---

13 For control of a discretionary (policy) decision, see Chap. 12.
14 See further, pp. 10–20.
15 Art. 34.1., see Gwynn Morgan, *The Separation of Powers in the Irish Constitution* (1997), Chap. 4.

assessment of capital gains (the Revenue Commissioners); and the award of a social welfare benefit (deciding officer in the Department of Social Welfare) are all instances of individual decisions taken by the administrative agency indicated in brackets.

We can summarise the relationship between the two sets of distinctions by saying that a legislative decision is inevitably a policy decision. On the other hand, an individual decision will usually be nearer the administrative end of the spectrum in that it is the product of the application of some (more or less) precise standard – and three examples of this were listed previously. However, in some cases, an individual decision will be the direct result of the decision maker's discretion and such individual policy decisions include, for example, the expulsion of an alien or the building of a concert hall.

Application of the two sets of distinctions

The significance of these two types of classification lies in the part they have played in influencing the design of the organs and procedures of government administration and of the controls which are exercised over this administration. Much of the remainder of the book consists of illustrations of this observation. Thus, here we can only advert to a few examples of it and direct the reader to the place where they are amplified. For example, consider the design of governmental structures at the local government level: broadly speaking, the reserved functions, which are the preserve of the elected councillors, deal with policy matters; whereas the executive functions, which are vested in the top official, the county or city manager, consist of administrative acts.[16] For historical reasons, the picture is not so clear when one examines the central government, Ministers and Departments though here, too, there is an approximate observation of the distinction.[17]

Where there are pre-existing rules, the control exercised over the decision will be necessarily stricter. In the first place, the legislature is more likely to have established a tribunal to take the decision[18] and/or to have created an appeal to a court in respect of the decision. Secondly, even where this has not been done, a court may intervene on the ground of error of law.[19] Policy decisions may, it is true, be reviewed by a court – but it is only in a very clear case that they will be struck down and at an earlier stage in the development of administrative law, courts have been heard to say that they must leave policy questions to be dealt with through the agency of ministerial responsibility to the legislature.[20] These results flow from the idea that elected persons or bodies take policy decisions, whilst courts customarily take decisions on the basis of pre-existing principles.

Reinforcing the trend noted in the previous paragraph is the fact that administrative decisions are always individual decisions. It is because individual decisions have a direct effect on individual rights that they are more stringently controlled than legislative decisions: for example certain types of decision must be taken by

---

16 See pp. 191–192.
17 See pp. 63–67.
18 See pp. 258–259, 265.
19 See pp. 430–436.
20 See p. 62.

a Minister personally rather than through his civil servants.[21] Again, where the significant procedural safeguard of constitutional justice is concerned, we find that these rules are less likely to apply to policy than to administrative decisions and usually do not apply to legislation.[22] The law of remedies also formerly observed the two distinctions we have described.[23] Finally, the Ombudsman's jurisdiction is confined to "action[s] taken in the performance of administrative functions"[24] thereby excluding legislative, though not other types of policy, decision.

---

[21] See p. 489.
[22] See pp. 602–606.
[23] See pp. 696–698.
[24] Ombudsman Act 1980, s.4(2). See further, pp. 344–348.

CHAPTER 2

SOURCES OF ADMINISTRATIVE LAW

1. Fundamental Constitutional Principles: Rule of Law

The twin concepts of the rule of law[1] and the separation of powers[2] are the most fundamental principles underlying Irish administrative law. Both the structure of our system of government and the basis of judicial review of administrative action are founded on these principles. Because of their fundamental character, a comprehensive analysis of these constitutional doctrines more properly belongs to a textbook on constitutional law. However, some of the major aspects of these principles may be sketched here and other more detailed instances of their practical impact will be mentioned throughout this book.[3]

At the heart of the rule of law there are four interrelated notions.[4] The first is the principle of legality. Every executive or administrative act which affects legal rights, interests or legitimate expectations must have legal justification. Where no such authority exists, the aggrieved party may have recourse to the courts where this decision will be invalidated. A good contemporary illustration of this principle is supplied by *Director of Public Prosecutions v. Fagan*.[5] In this case the issue was whether a member of the Garda Síochána enjoyed a right at common law or under statute to conduct random road traffic check points. A majority of the Supreme Court held that the existence of such a power was necessarily implied in a variety of statutory powers conferred by the Road Traffic Acts. The following observations of Denham J. in her dissenting judgment seem more in harmony with traditional rule of law principles:

> "A cornerstone of the rule of law is that persons in authority must be able to justify their actions, if called upon to do so, by reference to a specific rule in statute or common law. Thus, it is appropriate to look for a positive law authorising the action in question. I have found no such law in statute or common law to warrant the action of the Garda in question."[6]

---

[1] Gwynn Morgan, *Constitutional Law of Ireland* (1991) pp. 42–45; Wade and Forsyth, *Administrative Law* (1994) pp. 24–28.
[2] Gwynn Morgan, *ibid.*, pp. 36–41; Hogan and Whyte, *Kelly: The Irish Constitution* (3rd ed., 1994) pp. 37–51 and Gwynn Morgan, *The Separation of Powers in the Irish Constitution* (1997) *passim*.
[3] See pp. 10–19; 270–274; 345–348 and 394–396.
[4] There are other aspects of the rule of law, *e.g.* those which pertain to the administration of criminal justice, and which are thus are not our present concern. For instance, the prohibition of retroactive penal legislation contained in Art. 15.5 of the Constitution may be said to a feature of the rule of law.
[5] [1994] 2 I.R. 265.
[6] *Ibid.* at 288.

One way in which the rule of law is implemented in practice takes the form of the principle of *ultra vires*, which is elaborated below in Chapter 9. By this precept, not only must the administrative authority concerned show that it possesses legal authority by reference to the wording of the statute. In addition, the courts will review the exercise of discretionary power according to settled principles of reasonableness, proper motives and compliance with constitutional justice.[7]

The second principle is that everyone, including the Government and its servants, is subject to the law. This principle received graphic affirmation in cases such as: *Macauley v. Minister for Posts and Telegraphs*,[8] (where a statutory provision requiring the prior permission, or *fiat*, of the Attorney General before an action could be taken against a Minister of State was found to be unconstitutional); *Byrne v. Ireland*[9] (holding that the former Crown immunity from suit had not survived the enactment of the Constitution); and *Howard v. Commissioners of Public Works*[10] (holding that the common law rule whereby the State was presumed not to be bound by the application of statute had not survived the enactment of the Constitution).

The third aspect of the rule of law is that the legality of executive or administrative acts is to be determined by judges who are independent of the Government. The principle of judicial independence is enshrined in Article 34.1 of the Constitution,[11] and the courts have always jealously safeguarded their powers to review administrative action. Thus, legislative attempts to prevent – or even altogether to curb – review of administrative action have been viewed with disfavour by the judiciary.[12]

The final aspect of the rule of law is that the law must be public and precise: the law should be ascertainable and its operation predictable.[13] This principle underlies

---

7   See below, Chaps. 9–11.
8   [1966] I.R. 345.
9   [1972] I.R. 241.
10   [1994] 1 I.R. 101. A further aspect of this principle is that the Government may not exercise a dispensing power, *i.e.* waive or suspend the operation of statute-law. In *Hoey v. Minister for Justice* [1994] 3 I.R. 329 (a case concerning a local authority's statutory obligation to repair the court-house in Drogheda) the Minister sought to defend a mandamus application by saying that he had written to the local authority to inform it that he did not require it to provide courthouse accommodation in Drogheda since this was satisfied by the provision of suitable premises in Dundalk. Lynch J. rejected this argument, saying (at 343):
   "It is not open to the Executive by arrangements made with the local authority to alter the law by lifting obligations which statute has imposed on a local authority."
   See also *Duggan v. An Taoiseach* [1989] I.L.R.M. 710.
11   Hogan and Whyte, *Kelly, op. cit.* above, n.2, pp. 360–397. See generally, *Buckley v. Attorney General* [1950] I.R. 67; *Re Haughey* [1971] I.R. 217; and *The State (McEldowney) v. Kelleher* [1983] I.R. 289.
12   In *The State (Pine Valley Developments Ltd) v. Dublin County Council* [1984] I.R. 407 at 426 Henchy J. commented that the courts "should be reluctant to surrender their inherent right to enter on a question of the validity of what are prima facie justiciable matters", and see further, below pp. 454–460 on the issue of ouster and preclusive clauses. See also the comments of O'Higgins C.J. in *Condon v. Minister for Labour* [1981] I.R. 62 at 69:
   "A strong, healthy and concerned public opinion may, in the words of Edmund Burke, 'snuff the approach of tyranny in every tainted breeze', but effective resistance to unwarranted encroachment on constitutional guarantees and rights, depends, in the ultimate analysis on the courts. If access to the courts is denied or prevented or obstructed, then such encroachment, being unchallenged, may become habitual, and, therefore, unacceptable."
13   For criticism of excessive reliance by administrators on non-statutory rules whose existence "is known only to a handful of officials and specialists" and which are not "readily available to the public", see the comments of Costello P. in *McCann v. Minister for Education* [1997] 1 I.L.R.M. 1, discussed below at pp. 45, 46.

a number of important rules of statutory construction such as the presumption against retrospectivity[14] and the principle that taxing statutes must be strictly construed.[15] This allows the citizen to arrange his or her behaviour to conform with the law.

2. Separation of Powers and Delegated Legislation

Article 6 of the Constitution assumes that the powers of government are of three types: legislative, executive and judicial. Article 6 does not in terms prescribe a separation of powers, but the effect of other constitutional provisions – most notably, Articles 15, 28 and 34 – is to "entrench the different arms of government in varying degrees and prescribe their sovereignty in their own areas, without, however, hermetically insulating the different powers from one another in all respects".[16] As this quotation indicates, the distribution of powers, is, however, an imperfect one, and this is recognised by the very terms of the Constitution itself. The central exception, indeed, constitutes the main feature of our governmental system, namely, the fused legislature–executive and such is the strength of the party whip system, that the Oireachtas is almost completely under the control of the government of the day. It is only the judiciary which enjoys a secure position *vis-à-vis* the other branches of government.[17] This is one of the many points where the separation of powers and the rule of law coincide.

Four aspects of the separation of powers are of particular importance for administrative law. These concern: executive privilege; ouster and preclusive clauses; delegated legislation (Article 15.2.1° which vests the Oireachtas with sole and exclusive legislative power); and tribunals and whether they fall foul of Articles 34.1 and 37 (which collectively forbid the Oireachtas to vest judicial functions in bodies other than courts, save only where the functions are of a limited kind).[18]

As all but one of these matters are examined elsewhere, it remains to consider here the provisions of Article 15.2.1° and its impact on delegated legislation. While Article 15.2.1° vests the Oireachtas with exclusive power of legislation, it is nevertheless permissible for the Oireachtas to delegate power to make regulations which will give effect to the principles and policies contained in the parent Act. The question therefore is whether the parent Act has actually sanctioned the delegation of a power which goes beyond the mere giving effect to its principles and policies. The case law on this significant provision is thoroughly rehearsed elsewhere, so it suffices to refer to the leading modern authorities.[19]

---

14 *Hamilton v. Hamilton* [1982] I.R. 466; *O'H v. O'H* [1990] 2 I.R. 558; and see generally Hogan and Whyte, *Kelly, op. cit.*, above, n.2, pp. 127–131. See also Delany, "Statutory Interpretation – Can Legislation have Retrospective Effect?" (1992) 11 I.L.T. (N.S.) 133.

15 For a general exposition of this principle, see, *e.g. Inspector of Taxes v. Kiernan* [1981] I.R. 117 and *McGrath v. McDermott* [1988] I.R. 258. See also, *Attorney General v. Wilts United Dairies Ltd* (1921) 39 T.L.R. 781 (administrative body had no power to levy charges for public purposes, save where this is expressly authorised by statute).

16 See Hogan and Whyte, *Kelly, op. cit.*, above, n.2, p. 40.

17 See Hogan and Whyte, *Kelly, op. cit.* above, n.2, pp. 360–397.

18 See generally pp. 935–939 (executive privilege); pp. 454–458 (ouster clauses) and pp. 270–273 (Articles 34 and 37).

19 *Pigs Marketing Board v. Donnelly* [1939] I.R. 413. See also *National Union of Railwaymen v. Sullivan* [1947] I.R. 77; *de Búrca v. Attorney General* [1976] I.R. 38; *The State (Devine) v. Larkin* [1977]

The first modern cases were *Cityview Press Ltd v. An Comhairle Oiliúna*[20] and *Cooke v. Walsh*.[21] In the former case the provisions of the Industrial Training Act 1967 had been challenged as granting an unconstitutional delegation of legislative power. The defendants were empowered to fix the amount of a levy to be collected from industrial enterprises which was then used to train apprentices in that industry. O'Higgins C.J. observed that in this instance the Oireachtas had reserved unto itself the right to annul regulations made under the Act, and that this power of annulment was a common feature of many items of legislation. While this was a safeguard, the ultimate responsibility of ensuring that there had not been an unconstitutional delegation of power rested with the courts. The relevant test was whether the impugned legislation was more than:

> "[A] mere giving effect to principles and policies contained in the statute itself. If it be, then it is not authorised, for such would constitute a purported exercise of legislative power by an authority which is not entitled to do so under the Constitution. On the other hand, if it be within the permitted limits — if the law is laid down in the statute and details only filled in or completed by the designated Minister or subordinate body — there is no unauthorised delegation of legislative power."[22]

Judged by these standards there had not been any unconstitutional delegation of legislative power, as the court found (rather surprisingly in view of the actual provisions of the 1967 Act) that it contained clear statements of policies and objectives, and the only task left to the defendants was to calculate the size of the levy for any particular industry by reference to these principles.

In *Cooke v. Walsh*, the validity of certain ministerial regulations purportedly made pursuant to the Health Act 1970 was at issue. This Act conferred full eligibility to receive free health services on certain classes of individuals (of which the infant plaintiff was one). But another section of the Act, section 72, enabled the Minister for Health to make regulations providing for any service "being made available only to a particular class of the person" who had eligibility for that service. Ministerial regulations made pursuant to this latter provision purported to exclude persons otherwise entitled under the Act to free medical services from such entitlements where their injuries were sustained as a result of a road accident and where they were entitled to receive compensation in respect of their injuries. Read at its full width, section 72 would probably have permitted the Minister to alter the eligibility provisions contained in the Act itself. But such a construction would render section 72 invalid having regard to Article 15.2, as the Minister would have been authorised to change or alter the Act by executive decree. Accordingly, section 72 was given a more limited construction in the light of the presumption of constitutionality. While the validity of section 72 was thus saved, it rendered the impugned regulations *ultra vires*, because the section, as interpreted (which, in reality, had been radically

---

I.R. 24; *The State (Gilliland) v. Governor of Mountjoy Prison* [1987] I.R. 201; and Hogan and Whyte, *Kelly, op. cit.* above, n.2, pp. 106–112 and Gwynn Morgan, *The Separation of Powers, op. cit.* above, n.2, Chap. 11.
20 [1980] I.R. 381.
21 [1984] I.R. 71.
22 [1980] I.R. 381 at 399.

reinterpreted) did not permit the Minister to alter the eligibility requirements when making regulations thereunder.[23]

"Henry VIII clauses"[24]

Even more striking reasoning was applied by the Supreme Court in *Harvey v. Minister for Social Welfare*,[25] where the validity of section 75 of the Social Welfare Act 1952 was challenged. This section allows the Minister to adjust the payments made to a person who is in receipt of more than one benefit, pension or allowance. Regulations had been made in 1979 (Social Welfare Overlapping Benefits) (Amendment) Regulations 1979) pursuant to section 75 whereby persons potentially entitled to several such payments were confined to obtaining only one payment. However, section 7 of the Social Welfare Act 1979 provided that a widow's pension shall be payable until she remarries. Accordingly, the applicant argued that inasmuch as section 75 allowed the Minister to make regulations which overrode other statutory provisions, it amounted to an unconstitutional delegation of legislative power. The Court rejected that submission, but did so only on the basis that the 1979 Regulations were *ultra vires* inasmuch as they had purported to vary or alter the terms of section 7 of the 1979 Act. (The Court thus paralleled the reasoning in *Cooke v. Walsh.*) As far as the legislative power point was concerned, Finlay C.J. put it thus:

> "Quite clearly, for the Minister to exercise a power of regulation granted to him by these Acts so as to negative an express intention of the legislature is an unconstitutional use of the power vested in him."[26]

The striking point is that this conclusion was reached in the face of the parent section – section 75(1) of the Social Welfare Act 1952[27] – which itself explicitly stated that regulations might be made to bar the payment of two benefits (provided that these were of types specified in the section) to the same claimant, notwithstanding that the benefits were authorised in primary legislation. Thus the principle implemented by the regulations was certainly laid down in primary legislation. Accordingly, the point which emerges from *Harvey* (and also, probably, from *Cooke*) is that there are really two limbs to the case law on Article 15.2.1°. In addition to the original line of authority – that delegated legislation is unconstitutional if it goes beyond details and lays down new principle – a second strand appears to have been developed to the effect that any regulation which repeals or amends primary

---

23 One is bound to ask: what force then was left to section 72? O'Higgins C.J. thought that the provision might enable the Minister to regulate the provision of certain services provided by the Health Boards. On a different point, see now Health (Amendment) Act 1986 which reverses the decision of the Supreme Court as far as hospital charges are concerned.

24 *i.e.* a statutory provision which grants authority to make delegated legislation which may amend the parent Act or, even if this is specified, other legislation too. The derivation of the name lies in the fact that Henry VIII was regarded as the personation of executive autocracy. See also Wade and Forsyth, *op. cit.*, above n.1, pp. 863–65 and below at pp. 15–19.

25 [1990] 2 I.R. 232; [1990] I.L.R.M. 185. Similar principles were applied by Barron J. in *O'Connell v. Ireland* [1996] 1 I.L.R.M. 187. See generally, Cousins, "Overlapping Benefits: The Rise and Fall of Legislative Control" (1992) 14 D.U.L.J. 193.

26 [1990] 2 I.R. 232 at 245. See generally, *McDaid v. Sheehy* [1991] 1 I.R. 1 and Hogan, "A Note on the Imposition of Duties Act 1957" (1985) 7 D.U.L.J. (N.S.) 134.

27 Now Social Welfare (Consolidation) Act 1993, s.209 (1).

legislation is *ipso facto* unconstitutional even if (as in *Harvey*) this has been explicitly authorised in the parent section.[28]

Finally, in *Lovett v. Minister for Education*[29] Kelly J. held that paragraph 8(1) of the Secondary Teachers Superannuation (Amendment) Scheme[30] was *ultra vires* the provisions of the Teachers' Superannuation Act 1928. The Scheme had provided for the forfeiture of a retired teachers' pension following conviction and sentence to a term of imprisonment with hard labour, but Kelly J. found this provision to be *ultra vires* on *Cityview Press* grounds:

> "[The 1928 Act] had as its object the formulation and carrying out of schemes for the provision of pensions and gratuities for teachers and former teachers. It does not appear to me that it has anything to do with deterring the commission of criminal offences whether by teachers or retired teachers. If it had, one would expect to find some mention of this either in the long title or in the body of the Act. There is none."[31]

This quartet of cases — *Cityview Press, Cooke v. Walsh, Harvey*, and *Lovett* – severely limits and marks off the boundaries of delegated legislation and it is probable that the full significance of these cases has only been partially realised. Take, as an example, the several recent statutory provisions which purport to enable the relevant Minister to make regulations within a specified time period (usually three years) amending the parent Act.[32] A good recent example of this statutory formula is provided by section 5 of the Trustee Savings Bank Act 1989 which provides that:

> "If, in any respect, any difficulty arises in bringing any provision of this Act into operation or in relation to the operation of such provision, the Minister for Finance may by regulations do anything which appears to him to be necessary or expedient for removing that difficulty, for bringing that provision

---

28 For an elaboration of this analysis, see Hogan and Whyte, *Kelly, op. cit.*, above, n.2, pp. 107–108; Gwynn Morgan, *The Separation of Powers, op. cit.*, above, n.2, Chap. 11.V. The Supreme Court's decision in *Meagher v. Minister for Agriculture and Food* [1994] 1 I.R. 329 (discussed below at pp. 17–18) also tends to re-inforce this view, since the Court there accepted that, the special position of the implementation of Community law excepted, legislation which purported to enable a Minister to amend a statute by statutory instrument would be unconstitutional.

29 [1997] 1 I.L.R.M. 89.

30 S.R. & O. No. 48 of 1935.

31 [1997] 1 I.L.R.M. 89 at 97.

32 Other recent examples of this statutory formula (which are generally headed "Regulations to remove difficulties") include the Canals Act 1986, s.13, Valuation Act 1988, s.10, the Building Societies Act 1989, s.4, the Companies Act 1990, s.24, and the Local Government Act 1994, s.66. Section 6 of the Trustee Savings Bank Act 1989 is an even more remarkable provision in that it enables the Minister to make regulations amending the Act "for the purpose of assimilating the law relating to Trustee Savings Banks to the modifications of the law relating to companies, banks or building societies." Another version of this formula is contained in the Electoral Act 1992, s.164 whereby the Minister for the Environment is empowered in cases of "emergency or special difficulty" to make by order "such adaptation or modification of any statute, order or regulation" relating to election registration "subject to compliance with the principles laid down in the Electoral Acts taken as a whole". Note, however, that in *Sherwin v. Minister for Environment*, unreported, High Court, March 11, 1997 Costello P. held that the Minister could modify the terms of the 1992 Act by Ministerial order, on the basis that the Minister was simply modifying – as opposed to amending – the Act, a distinction which would appear to be incorrect in law.

into operation or for securing and facilitating its operation, and such regulations may modify any provision of this Act so far as may be necessary or expedient for carrying such provision into effect for the purposes as aforesaid but no regulations shall be made under this section in relation to any provisions of this Act after the expiration of three years commencing on the day when the relevant provision of this Act came into operation."

While the utility and convenience of this provision was defended by the Minister for Finance[33] during the second stage of the Dáil debate, it is not surprising that other deputies questioned the constitutionality of such a provision.[34] In view of the recent authorities, it is difficult to see how the Oireachtas can validly delegate the power to amend a statute by statutory instrument to a Minister, even if that power contains certain safeguards.[35] It is possible, however, that despite cases such as *Harvey*, a court might uphold the constitutionality of statutory instrument which formally effected an amendment to a statute[36] where the amendment in question came within the "principles and policies" of the legislation concerned in a situation

---

[33] The Minister said (392 *Dáil Debates*, Col. 1273):
"[This Act] is the first 'root and branch' reform of [Trustee Savings Bank Act 1863] in the history of this State. There is a strong possibility of unforeseen technical difficulties arising in giving effect to the provisions of the present Bill to enable the Minister to deal with them. There is no possibility of the provision being used to subvert the intention of the legislation and there are precedents for it."

[34] See the comments of Deputies Noonan and Taylor at 393 *Dáil Debates*, Cols. 424–428.

[35] The difficulties inherent in this area were recognised in the *Report of the Constitution Review Group* (Pn. 2632, 1996) when it commented (at p. 39) that the effect of the *Cityview Press* test may make:
". . . it difficult in many cases to use secondary legislation to fill gaps left by an Act or to deal with specific details which may not have been anticipated when the Act was passed. This problem may be of particular relevance, for example, to legislation dealing matters such as rapidly developing technology or issues of detail affecting areas in different ways."
The Group went on to recommend (at p. 40) that consideration should be given to an amendment to Art. 15.2.1°:
". . . whereby in addition to subordinate legislation which is already permissible within the limits of the *Cityview Press* test, the Oireachtas should have power to authorise by law the delegation of power to either the Government or a Minister (but no other body) to legislate, using the mechanism of a statutory instrument, in relation to the substance of the parent legislation (thereby exceeding the present limits of the *Cityview Press* test.) However, if such a change were to be made, it should be accompanied by necessary safeguards to ensure that the legislative supremacy of the Oireachtas was not thereby undermined. These safeguards would have to include, at a minimum, a requirement that any legislation pursuant to this power could not enter into law until it had been the subject of a positive resolution of both Houses of the Oireachtas."

[36] A good example is supplied by the Civil Liability (Amendment) Act 1996. By s.49 of the Civil Liability Act 1961 (as inserted by s.2(1)(a) of the 1996 Act) the maximum sum payable to dependents in respect of damages for mental distress is £20,000. Section 49(1A) of the 1961 Act (as inserted by s.2(1)(b) of the 1996 Act) provides that:
"Where the Minister for [Justice, Equality and Law Reform] is satisfied that [this] monetary amount . . . should, having regard to changes in the value of money generally in the State since the monetary amount was so specified, be varied, the Minister may by order specify an amount that the Minister considers is appropriate."
In this example the policy principle is clear: it is that the monetary amount may be varied by reference to such changes in monetary values which have taken place since the date the sum was last so amended. The Minister is nonetheless formally amending by ministerial order an item of legislation. See also the comments of Costello P. in *Sherwin v. Minister for Environment*, unreported, High Court, March 11, 1997 holding that a Minister might law fully modify the parent Act by statutory instrument if such powers were themselves conferred by the parent Act.

in which the statutory instrument only involved a change in figures by reference to some automatically applicable yardstick laid down in the parent statute e.g. the Consumer Price Index or a change in population by reference to census figures.

One other feature of Article 15.2.1° which may be mentioned here is that this sub-section in conjunction with other constitutional principles[37] prevents the statutory exclusion of judicial review of delegated legislation. In *Institute of Patent Agents v. Lockwood*[38] the House of Lords held that rules which "were to have the same effect as if they were contained in [the parent statute]" could not be examined by the courts. The Irish courts – even prior to independence – have never been willing to assent to this proposition, and *Lockwood* has been distinguished – rather unconvincingly – in a series of subsequent Irish cases.[39] However, *Lockwood* is now simply of historical interest only, as this decision and the principle which it embodies must be taken not to have survived the enactment of the Constitution. Any statutory provision which purported to confer such an immunity on delegated legislation would be the equivalent of a delegation of legislative power, and this would be contrary to Article 15.2.1° for the reasons given in *Cityview Press*.

European Communities Act 1972: The Implementation of Directives by Ministerial Order

Similar constitutional difficulties were considered to exist in the case of the European Communities Act 1972 and the European Communities (Amendment) Act 1973, but the constitutional issues raised by these statutory provisions have, to a large extent, been resolved by the decision of the Supreme Court in *Meagher v. Minister for Agriculture and Food*.[40] The 1972 Act provides, *inter alia*, that future acts adopted by the institutions of the Communities shall be binding on the State and "shall be part of the domestic law thereof under the conditions laid down in those treaties". In the case of directives issued by Community institutions, Article 189(3) of the EEC Treaty provides that: "A directive shall be binding, as to the result but shall leave to the national authorities the choice of the form and methods."

In nearly all cases, implementing measures will be necessary, in the form of domestic legislation in each Member State in order to give the directive full force

---

[37] Art. 34.3.1.° (High Court's original jurisdiction) and Art 40.3° (guarantee of fair procedures). See *Tormey v. A.G.* [1985] I.R. 283 and Pye, "The s.104 Certificate of Registration – The Impenetrable Shield No More?" (1985) 3 I.L.T. (N.S.) 213 and Hogan, "Reflections on *Tormey v. Attorney General*" (1986) 8 D.U.L.J. (N.S) 31. The entire subject of the exclusion of judicial review is examined at pp. 454–460.

[38] [1894] A.C. 347.

[39] *R. (Conyngham) v. Pharmaceutical Society of Ireland* [1894] 2 I.R. 132; *Commissioners of Public Works v. Monaghan* [1909] 2 I.R. 718; *Mackey v. Monks* [1916] 2 I.R. 200 (reversed on other grounds by the House of Lords): [1918] A.C. 59 and *Waterford Corporation v. Murphy* [1920] 2 I.R. 165. See Donaldson, *Some Comparative Aspects of Irish Law* (Duke, 1957), pp. 200–203.

[40] [1994] 1 I.R. 329. See generally, Hogan, "The Implementation of European Law in Ireland: The *Meagher* Case and the Democratic Deficit" (1994) 2 I.J.E.L. 190; Travers, "The Constitutionality of the Implementation of EC Directives into Irish Law Revisited" (1994) 88 *Gazette of the Incorporated Law Society of Ireland* 99; Whelan, "Meagher v. Minister for Agriculture and Food" (1993) 15 D.U.L.J. (N.S) 152; Murphy, "Irish Participation in European Integration: The Casual Abandonment of Sovereignty?" (1996) 31 Ir. Jur. (N.S.) 22; Hogan and Whelan, *Ireland and the European Union: Constitutional and Statutory Texts and Commentary* (1995) pp. 51–78.

and effect.[41] One of the principle methods of implementing directives in this jurisdiction is contained in section 3 of the European Communities Act 1972, which enables a Minister of State to implement such directives by statutory order. Section 3(2) states:

> "Regulations made under this section may contain such incidental, supplementary and consequential provisions as appear to the Minister to be necessary for the purposes of the regulations (including provisions repealing, amending or applying, with or without modification, other law, exclusive of this Act)."[42]

Section 4 of the 1972 Act had originally provided that such ministerial regulations required legislative confirmation, but it was later felt that this method was too cumbersome.[43] Section 4, as amended by section 1 of the European Communities (Amendment) Act 1973, provides that ministerial regulations made under the Act shall have statutory effect, *i.e.* if there is a conflict between the regulation and a Statutory Provision, the former prevails.[44]

This method of implementing directives might be thought to have been in conflict with Article 15.2, in that section 4 permits a Minister of State to make regulations which in some cases do more than give effect to the principles and policies contained in the 1972 Act. A regulation of this nature could effect a far-reaching change in the existing law. It is true that Article 29.4.5° gives constitutional cover to "measures adopted by the State necessitated by the obligations of membership of the Communities" and that the State is obliged by Article 189 of the Treaty to implement such directives. But as we have seen, Article 189 deliberately leaves the method of implementation of directives to the Member States, and does not require or prescribe that these directives be implemented by ministerial order. On this view, therefore. Article 29.4.5° cannot therefore be called in aid to justify what would otherwise be a breach of Article 15.2.1°. In this context, the views of the former Joint Committee on Secondary Legislation of the European Communities are of interest in that they drew attention to what today would be termed the "democratic deficit" and, indeed, the "information deficit" associated with the use of this procedure.[45] Of course, no such difficulties arise where the directive is implemented by an Act of the Oireachtas.

---

41   Community directives, unlike Community regulations, are not usually directly applicable, *i.e.* they do not immediately become part of the domestic law of each Member State. However, the European Court has made it clear that the implementation of E.C. directives may in certain cases be superfluous, but in such cases Member States must ensure that their nationals are aware of their rights under such a directive: Case 29/84 *Commission v. Germany* [1985] E.C.R. 166.

42   However, such regulations may not create an indictable offence: European Communities Act 1972, s.3(4).

43   In fact, one such confirming measure was enacted: see European Communities (Confirmation of Regulations) Act 1973.

44   The amended s.4 provides for an elaborate system of parliamentary scrutiny by the Joint Committee on European Affairs (formerly in the Joint Oireachtas Committee on Secondary Legislation of the European Communities) and also includes procedures whereby regulations made under the Act may be annulled by either House of the Oireachtas: see generally, Hogan and Whelan, *Ireland and the European Union: Constitutional and Statutory Texts and Commentary* (1995) pp. 178–181 and 196–197. For an account of the work of the former Joint Committee, see Robinson, "Irish Parliamentary Scrutiny of European Community Legislation" (1979) 16 C.M.L.Rev. 9.

45   In their *Twenty-Second Report* (Prl. 5141) (1975), the Committee commenting (pp. 17–18) on European Communities (Road Traffic) (Compulsory Insurance) Regulations 1975 (S.I. No. 178 of 1975) which amended the Road Traffic Act 1961, observe as follows:

These were the issues which were to come before the Supreme Court in *Meagher v. Minister for Agriculture and Food.*

The decision in Meagher v. Minister for Agriculture and Food

In this case the Minister for Agriculture and Food applied for summonses against the applicant in respect of offences arising under the terms of the European Communities (Control of Oestrogenic etc. Substances) Regulations 1988[46] and the European Communities (Control of Veterinary Medicinal Products and their Residues) Regulations 1990.[47] These summonses were served on the applicant some sixteen months after the date of the alleged offences. This prosecution would have been out of time were it not for the fact that Article 32(8) of the 1988 Regulations amend the six-month time limit provided for in section 10(4) of the Petty Sessions (Ireland) Act 1851 by allowing for such summonses to be issued within two years of the date of the commission of the offence.[48] The stage was thus set for the resolution of a major constitutional issue: could a Minister of State validly amend the substantive law by regulation in order to give effect to an E.U. directive?[49]

While Johnson J. found for the applicant (for the type of reasons indicated in our critique of the Supreme Court judgments), this decision was reversed on appeal. The Supreme Court judgments were divided into two parts: the judgment of the Court delivered by Finlay C.J. upholding the constitutionality of the 1972 Act and two separate judgments delivered by Blayney and Denham JJ. rejecting a challenge to the *vires* of the 1988 and the 1990 Regulations. In contrast to Johnson J. – who proceeded on the premise that the "necessitated obligations" test in Article 29.4.5° embraced only those measures that could fairly be said to be legal obligations deriving from Community law – the Supreme Court took a much more pragmatic view of this question:

> "The Court is satisfied that, having regard to the number of Community laws, acts done or measures adopted which either have to be facilitated in their direct

---

"The Joint Committee accepts that Ministerial Regulations made under section 3 of the European Communities Act 1972 may lawfully amend Acts of the Oireachtas or other statutes in force if such is required by the Community secondary legislation which the Regulations are to implement. However, the fact that the power exists ought not, in the Joint Committee's opinion, to mean that it is appropriate to use it in every case. Regard should be had to the relative importance of the statute to be amended and to the range of its application to determine whether the amendment should be effected by a statutory instrument or amending statute. In the case of a statute such as the Road Traffic Act 1961 which is of such importance in the everyday life of citizens the Joint Committee considers that any proposals for its amendment should be initiated by a Bill introduced in the Dail or Seanad. It recommends that when opportunity offers Regulation S.I. No. 178 of 1975 should be repealed and its terms incorporated in an amending statute."

46 S.I. No. 218 of 1988.

47 S.I. No. 171 of 1990.

48 Had such an amendment not been made the applicant could have relied on the six-months rule provided for in 1851 Act as a complete defence.

49 While the 1988 and 1990 Regulations were designed to give effect in Irish law to various E.C. Directives, it is noteworthy that none of the Directives in terms expressly *require or even provide for the the creation of criminal offences*, still less do they provide or the two-year time limit envisaged by art. 32(8) of the 1988 Regulations. Neveretheless, the evidence before the High Court demonstrated that the Minister considered that the six months time limit was inadequate having regard to the complex nature of the investigations which are required in advance of a prosecution in such cases. It was accordingly decided to extend this time period to two years: see [1994] 1 I.R. 329 at 358–359.

application to the law of the State, or have to be implemented by appropriate action into the law of the State the obligation of membership would necessitate the facilitating of these activities, in some instances, at least, and possibly in a great majority of instances, by the making of ministerial regulations rather than legislation of the Oireachtas."[50]

The essential premise of this passage is that there is no alternative to this statutory mechanism, since without it, Ireland would fall behind in its Community obligation to give effect to such directives in national law. This assumption would not seem to be correct. First, it is not, of course, in every case that the use of the 1973 Act would involve a breach of the constitutional requirements. There are numerous examples of E.C. directives (such as, for example, labelling requirements) which do not involve the amendment of earlier legislation and which are purely administrative or regulatory in nature and could therefore even under article 15.2.1° be validly transposed by way of statutory instrument, a point clearly recognised by Denham J. in her concurring judgment. Secondly, to cater for change of a more radical type, there is no constitutional objection to a procedure by which effect is given to such directives via an omnibus statute.[51] Finally, if changes to the present method of implementing directives via the 1973 Act required the Oireachtas to take an even more active legislative role, that would be no bad thing.

While it may have been true in the past to regard the Oireachtas as a law-declaring[52] rather than a law-making body[53] (*i.e.* that the Oireachtas essentially rubber-stamps Bills presented by the Government), this cannot detract from the

---

[50] *Meagher v. Minister for Agriculture and Food* [1994] 1 I.R. 329 at 352. Curtin had anticipated this view by arguing that the discretion conferred by Article 189(3) of the Treaty of Rome is not unlimited: "It must be read in conjunction with Article 5 of the EEC Treaty which obligates Member States to take all appropriate measures to give effect to Community law, an obligation clearly 'necessitated' by membership of the Community. It follows that Member States must recognise the consequences, in their internal legal order, of their adherence to the Community and, if necessary, adapt their procedures in such a way that they do not form an obstacle to the implementation, within the prescribed time limits, of their obligations within the framework of the Treaty."

[51] Thus, the Italian legislature now enacts an omnibus statute every year (the so-called *Legge La Pergola* – named after the Minister who proposed it) containing provisions "for the fulfillment of obligations stemming from Italy's membership of the European Communities": see, generally, Covassi (1996) 2 *European Public Law* 353.

[52] Note in this regard the comments in the *Report of the Constitution Review Group* (1996) p. 115, whereby the Review Group acknowledged the "utility and, indeed, the necessity for a provision such as s. 3 of the 1972 Act". It continued:
"Nevertheless, the present situation is not entirely satisfactory. The extensive use of statutory instruments to implement directives has meant that hundreds of statutory provisions, some important, have been expressly or impliedly repealed by statutory instruments, often with a minimum of publicity. The use of statutory instruments ensures speedy and effective implementation of EC law, but often at the expense of the publicity and debate which attends the processing of legislation through the Oireachtas. In this respect the operation of the 1972 Act might be said to contibute to an 'information deficit' and possibly a 'democratic deficit'."
See also the comments of Murphy, *op. cit.*, above, n.39, at p. 31:
"Reference has also been made to the regular criticism by the Joint Committee of ministerial regulations which took all sorts of liberties in the implementation of Community Directives. No account of such criticisms would appear to have been taken by those responsible for the drafting of statutory instruments. The result, in many instances, has been the implementation by way of statutory instrument, for example in the financial services sector, which emerge in confused and virtually impenetrable language from the far less rigorous process of drafting regulations."

[53] Chubb, *Cabinet Government in Ireland* (1974) p. 65.

constitutional principle that the right to legislate is the principal function of the Oireachtas. Besides, there is now increasing evidence that the Oireachtas takes its legislative role much more seriously and the last few years have witnessed a huge increase in the number of Dáil and Seanad amendments to legislation.[54]

3. Sources of Administrative Law

The sources of administrative law are various and heterogeneous, but five principal domestic sources can be identified: the Constitution, common law, primary legislation, delegated legislation and administrative circulars. In addition, there is increasing evidence that the Irish courts have been influenced by the general principles of law emerging from the jurisprudence of the Court of Justice and the European Court of Human Rights. The development at domestic administrative law level of the principles of proportionality and legitimate expectations, as well as the teleological method of statutory interpretation provides ample evidence of this latter trend.[55] It is not altogether surprising, therefore, that many modern administrative law cases raise issues drawn from more than one of these diverse sources.

A good modern example of the interaction of the various sources is provided by *O'Flynn v. Mid-Western Health Board*.[56] Section 72(1) of the Health Act 1970 allows the Minister for Health to prescribe regulations concerning the administration of schemes administered by Health Boards and regulations were duly made.[57] These regulations established the administrative structure for the medical card system (by which patients with "full" or "partial eligibility" within the meaning of the 1970 Act are entitled to free or partially free medical care). The Regulations require the making of arrangements between medical practitioners and the Health Boards including the establishment of a complaints committee. Following agreement, however, the detailed practical arrangements and the obligations of medical practitioners taking part in the scheme were set out in a ministerial circular of 1972. And, it is a requirement of participation in the scheme that each practitioner should enter into a contract[58] with a health board which incorporates the Regulations and

---

54 This is somewhat impressionistic, but members of the Oireachtas to whom the authors have spoken confirm that the committee system has brought about a situation in which individual Deputies and Senators have greater legislative influence.

55 See, *e.g.* the comments of Murphy J. in *Duff v. Minister for Agriculture* [1997] 2 I.R. 22 at 41–42; and see generally Hogan, "Irish Report" in Schwarze (ed.), *Der Verwaltungsrecht unter europäischem Einfluss* (1995), pp. 437–486.

56 [1989] I.R. 429 (High Ct.); [1991] 2 I.R. 223 (Sup. Ct.).

57 Health Services Regulations 1972, (S.I. No. 88 of 1972).

58 Thus, in *The State (O'Boyle) v. General Medical Services (Payments) Board* [1981] I.L.R.M. 14 the applicant sought to challenge Article 8(1) of the Regulations (which allows for an investigating committee to be established) as *ultra vires* the 1972 Act. Keane J. would not permit such a challenge, since he pointed out (at 15) that:

"Even if it were to be held to be *ultra vires*, this would not avail [the applicant], since as a matter of contract, irrespective of any question of statute, he has bound himself to accept the jurisdiction of the appeal committee appointed by the Minister under the terms of this Article."

See also *Grehan v. North Eastern Health Board* [1989] I.R. 422, where Costello J. granted the plaintiff doctor a declaration that the respondents were not unilaterally entitled to later the terms of her contract by issuing a new circular purporting to alter the contractual terms of doctors participating in the scheme.

the administrative schemes prescribed by the circular. In the *O'Flynn* case itself, the applicant doctors were charged with various alleged improprieties and requested further information from the chief executive officer of the respondent board. This information was not forthcoming, but the official nonetheless requested the Minister, pursuant to Article 8(1) of the applicant's contract with the Board, to convene a committee to investigate these complaints. Barr J. quashed the order establishing such committee, as he held that the official had not complied with an important pre-condition prior to invoking this Article 8(1) procedure:

> "This is a patently important step which has potentially far-reaching conse-
> quences for the doctor in question. Article 24 clearly envisages that it ought not
> to be taken until the doctor has had an opportunity to consider the complaint
> and to respond to it within a specified time limit. He cannot make a meaningful
> response if he is not as fully informed as the complaint alleged."[59]

In this passage, we see the invoking of further sources of law in that common law and constitutional principles are being brought to bear on the proper construction of the Articles in question. Since the doctors were not fully informed of the case they had to meet, Barr J. in the High Court went on to hold that the convening of the committee was invalid for want of compliance with these formal requirements. The Supreme Court, however, took a different view of the Article 8(1) procedure, holding that the chief executive officer's task was simply to filter out unsustaintable complaints against doctors. Once – as here – he had concluded that there was a serious complaint with an irreconcilable clash of views between the parties, his task was simply then to refer the complaint to the committee, so that the failure to answer the request for particulars did not invalidate the convening of the committee.[60]

An interesting example of the interaction of some of the domestic and European sources is provided by *Bhosphorus Hava Yollari Turizm Ve Tickaret Anonim Sirekti v. Minister for Transport*.[61] In this case the High Court quashed a decision of the Minister to impound, pursuant to Regulation No. 990/93 (the Serbian sanctions regulations), an aircraft which was about to leave from Dublin airport. The evidence showed that the aircraft, though owned by Yugoslav Airlines, had been leased to a Turkish airline. The lease was entirely bona fide and Murphy J. held that the Minister's action was disproportionate in the circumstances:

> "To impound an asset for the possession and enjoyment of which a wholly
> innocent party has paid a substantial sum of money simply because another
> party has a theoretical right to receive a nominal rent must be absurd . . . As
> long as the position is that no citizen of Serbia and Montenegro has any use
> or control over the aircraft in question or the opportunity to receive any income
> derived from it, then it would seem to me that the regulations have achieved

---

59 [1989] I.R. 429 at 438 (High Ct.).
60 As McCarthy J. said ([1991] 2 I.R. 223 at 239 (Sup. Ct.)):
    "Once the allegations as contained in the original complaint met with the vigorous and total
    denial that they did, it was a futile exercise to provide further information until the matter had
    been referred to the appropriate committee."
    For the a discussion of the issue of delay which arose in this case, see below p. 726.
61 [1994] 2 I.L.R.M. 551.

their purpose fully and the impounding of the aircraft would constitute a wholly unwarranted intervention in the business of Bosphorous."[62]

The European Court of Justice, however, took a different view on this question saying:

"Any measure imposing sanctions has, by definition, consequences which affect the right to property and the freedom to pursue a trade or business, thereby causing harm to persons who are in no way responsible for the situation which led to the adoption of sanctions, Moreover, the importance of the aims pursued by the regulation at issue is such as to justify negative consequences, even of a substantial nature, for some operators. As compared with an objective of general interest so fundamental to the international community, which consists in putting an end to the state of war in the region and to the massive violations of human rights and humanitarian international law in the Republic of Bosnia-Herzegovina, the impounding of the aircraft in question which is owned by an undertaking based in or operating from the Federal Republic of Yugoslavia, cannot be regarded as inappropriate or disproportionate."[63]

This interaction is also evident in the judgment of the European Court of Justice and the subsequent decision of the Supreme Court in *Duff v. Minister for Agriculture & Food*.[64] In this case the plaintiffs, who were development farmers, challenged the validity of a decision of the Minister not to allocate them milk quotas. The Court of Justice ruled that the Minister, *as a matter of Community law*, had not infringed principles of legitimate expectations. Somewhat surprisingly,[65] a majority of the Supreme Court, drawing on comments of Advocate General Cosmas,[66] appeared to hold that it could apply *national law* principles of legitimate expectations to the case at hand and concluded that the manner in which Minister had exercised his discretion infringed these national law principles.

The law of judicial review is, of course, very largely a creation of the common law in the form of rules of statutory interpretation for there is, as yet, no Irish equivalent of the United States Administrative Procedure Act 1946.[67] Accordingly, key principles – such as the scope of error of law[68] and the doctrine of reasonableness,[69]

---

[62] *Ibid.* at 559–560.
[63] Case C–84/95 *Bhosphorus Hava Yollari Turizm Ve Tickaret Anonim Sirekti v. Minister for Transport* [1996] 3 C.M.L.R. 257 at 295–296. This judgment followed an Article 177 reference by the Supreme Court.
[64] Case C–63/93 [1996] E.C.R. 569 (ECJ); [1997] 2 I.R. 22 (High Ct. and Sup. Ct.).
[65] Thus, Keane J. in a powerful dissenting judgment made the point that while it was certainly permissable to test the exercise of discretion by reference to national principles of administrative law (such as, *e.g.* reasonableness), this could not be done by reference to principles (such as legitimate expectations) which were in substance identical to those applied by the Court of Justice.
[66] The Advocate General said (at 595):
  "It is, I think useful to add that, although the above-mentioned general principles of Community Law (sc. legitimate expectations) can provide no basis for a requirement on the part of a member states to provide for the grant for special reference quantities to the [development farmers] there is nothing to prevent such a requirement from being founded *on principles of national law* which, in a appropriate case, may ensure greater protection in this respect than that awarded by the general principles applicable in the Community legal order."
[67] The enactment of an Administrative Procedures Act had been promised in the Programme for Government of the out-going Coalition Government.
[68] See below pp. 412–430.
[69] See below pp. 637–649.

legitimate expectations[70] and proportionality[71] have been formulated entirely by the judiciary. The development of these principles has, in turn, been buttressed and extended by the Constitution.[72] In addition, common law doctrines such as the rule that the State is presumed not to be bound by the application of statute,[73] state immunity[74] and executive privilege[75] have been declared to be unconstitutional and constitutional principles have been introduced to support other far-reaching judicial developments.

Primary legislation has been of lesser importance as far as the field of judicial review is concerned, as there are few statutory provisions containing principles of general application in this sphere and, indeed, the task of the administrative lawyer when confronted with primary legislation is quite often confined to engaging in a textual exegesis of the statutory language to ascertain whether administrative decisions taken pursuant to such legislation are truly *intra vires*. By contrast, in the case of what might be termed organic administrative law, *i.e.* the law relating to the structure and functions of the law relating to Government administration, Ministers and Departments, local authorities, state-sponsored bodies, etc., primary legislation has been the main source. In addition, apart from judicial review, the other institutions of control of administrative action – such as the Ombudsman,[76] tribunals and Freedom of Information Act 1997 – are also the product of statute.

Accordingly, most of the other chapters in this book are taken up with a study of statute law together with the specialised common law rules of statutory interpretation operative in the field of Government. Accordingly, the remainder of this chapter is, devoted to a consideration of the two remaining principal sources of administrative law: delegated legislation and the use of circulars and non-statutory administrative schemes.

4. Delegated Legislation

Delegated legislation is legislation which has been made by some person or body other than the Oireachtas and to whom the Oireachtas had delegated its legislative functions for strictly limited purposes. Usually, the delegate is a Minister; sometimes, it is a local authority, professional body[77] or other specialist body possessing particular expertise.[78] Delegated legislation is now an established feature of our law, it could scarcely be otherwise given the growth of the modern state. There are several practical reasons which justify the existence of delegated legislation. Parliamentary time

---

70 See below pp. 858–890.
71 See below pp. 655–663.
72 See below pp. 651–655.
73 *Howard v. Commissioners of Public Works* [1994] 1 I.R. 101.
74 *Byrne v. Ireland* [1972] I.R. 241.
75 *Murphy v. Dublin Corporation* [1972] I.R. 215.
76 See below, Chap. 8.
77 See, *e.g.* Solicitors Act 1954, s. 66 (as inserted by s. 76 of the Solicitors (Amendment) Act 1994) which provides that the Law Society may make regulations with the concurrence of the President of the High Court governing solicitors accounts.
78 *e.g.* orders made by the Joint Labour Committees under the Industrial Relations Act 1946 fixing miniumum wages for certain industries.

is scarce and the Oireachtas could not reasonably be expected to legislate for every administrative detail. It is, therefore, content to state the general principles in legislation and to allow the details to be regulated by ministerial order. There is also a need for flexibility and the law must be capable of rapid adjustment to meet changing circumstances.[79] There is, however, as we have seen in our exegesis of Article 15.2.1° in Part 2, a constitutional limit on the length to which delegated legislation may be taken.

Statutory Instruments Act 1947

The Statutory Instruments Act 1947 is designed to ensure the publication of all items of delegated legislation, thus rendering academic any doubts as to whether the Rules Publication Act 1893 applied to Ireland.[80] The term "statutory instrument" is defined by section 1(1) as meaning every "order, regulation, rule, scheme or bye-law" made in the exercise of a statutory power. However, the Act then goes on to make the quite unnecessary distinction between statutory instruments to which the Act primarily applies, and other statutory instruments to which the Act's provisions may apply. In fact, the phrase "primarily applies" is something of a misnomer, for the Act does not apply in a secondary sense to other delegated legislation. In other words, if the Act does not primarily apply to certain instruments, then they fall outside the scope of the Act. The Statutory Instrument Act 1947 "primarily applies"[81] to statutory instruments made after January 1, 1948 by either the President; Government; Minister; Minister of State; an authority having for the time being power to make rules of court; or:

---

79 See the following comments of Walsh J., in the introduction to Humphreys, *Index to Irish Statutory Instruments* (1988) (Vol. 1) at pp. xiii, xiv:
   "As the State becomes more and more involved, both directly and indirectly, in almost every aspect of our social and economic life it was inevitable that a great deal of regulations would be required. This is particularly so in a state which is as centralised as Ireland . . . Our own constitutional jurisprudence has shown that the Courts are ready to strike down any unauthorised delegation of legislative power while at the same time recognising that in the complex and frequently changing situations which confront the modern state there is a necessity for subordinate legislation."

80 In *The State (Quinlan) v. Kavanagh* [1935] I.R. 249, Kennedy C.J. had assumed that the Rules Publications Act 1893 applied to Ireland, but in *Re McGrath and Harte* [1941] I.R. 69, Sullivan C.J. pointed out that this Act had not been adapted for application in this jurisdiction. In fact, the 1893 Act was repealed by s.7 of the 1947 Act.

81 The certificate of the Attorney General to the effect that in his opinion a particular instrument is one to which the Act primarily applies is conclusive: s.2(2). Section 4(1) of the Documentary Evidence Act 1925 provides that prima facie evidence of the making of any delegated legislation by the Government, a Minister, or any statutory body, corporate or unincorporate exercising any function of government or discharging throughout the State "any public duties in relation to public administration", may be given by production of a copy of *Iris Oifigiúil* purporting to contain such regulations or the production of a copy of the instrument or regulation purporting to be published under the "superintendence or authority" of the Stationery Office. In some instances, later legislation expressly provides that the 1947 Act does not "primarily apply". Thus, s.32 of the Civil Service Regulation Act 1956 provides that orders made by the Civil Service Commissioners are orders to which the 1947 Act does not primarily apply, *i.e.* in practical terms, these orders are thereby exempted from the publication requirements of the 1947 Act.

"[A]ny person or body, whether corporate or unincorporate, exercising throughout the State any functions of government or discharging throughout the State any public duties in relation to public administration."[82]

This last category would include, for example, state-sponsored bodies and the Commissioners of Public Works, but not local authorities. The Attorney General is given power to exempt from the provisions of the Act a particular instrument of a type or class on the grounds that it is only of local or personal or temporary application or for "any other reason".[83]

The significance of the Statutory Instrument Act 1947 is as follows. Section 3(1) of the 1947 Act (as inserted by section 1 of the Statutory Instruments (Amendment) Act 1955) requires that a copy of each statutory instrument to which the 1947 Act "primarily applies" be sent to certain listed libraries[84] within 10 days of its being made; that "notice of the making thereof and of the place where copies thereof may be obtained shall be published in the *Iris Oifigiúil*" and that each instrument must also be published by the Stationery Office.[85] Section 3(2) of the 1947 Act provides that in civil cases the validity or effect or coming into operation of any statutory instrument shall not be affected by non-compliance with these publication requirements. As far as criminal cases are concerned, section 3(3) provides that where a person has been charged with the offence of contravening a provision in a statutory instrument to which the Act applies, the prosecution must prove that notice of the making of the order has been published at the date of the alleged offence unless the prosecutor can satisfy the court that reasonable steps have been taken to bring the purport of the statutory instrument to the attention of the public.[86]

---

[82] The instrument must also be one which is required by statute to be laid before both or either Houses of the Oireachtas or is of such a character as affects the public generally or any particular class or classes of the public (1947 Act, s.2(2)) and must not be a statutory instrument which is required by statute to be published in *Iris Oifigiúil* (1947 Act, s.2(1)). In some instances, legislation may impose a specific statutory duty to publish the rules, orders etc. in *Iris Oifigiúil* see, *e.g.* Roads Act, 1993, s.61(9) (notice of making of toll bye-laws); Irish Takeover Panel Act 1997, s.8(8) (notice of making of rules by Irish Takeover Panel). The effect of such provisions is that the makers of such statutory instruments are not obliged to comply with the other publication requirements of the 1947 Act, since such instruments are no longer ones to which the Act "primarily applies".

[83] Statutory Instrument Act 1947, s.2(3)(4). Notice of exemption must be published in *Iris Oifigiúil*. The compatibility of this exemption procedure with the equality guarantee contained in Art. 40.1 of the Constitution may be questioned, having regard to the decision of the Supreme Court in *East Donegal Co-Operatives Ltd v. Attorney General* [1970] I.R. 317. For a more extensive discussion of the 1947 Act, see Jackson, "Delegated Legislation in Ireland" [1962] *Public Law* 417. It is understood that Bord Telecom Éireann sought an exemption under the 1947 Act from the Attorney General in respect of statutory instruments under the Postal and Telecommunications Services Act 1983 which authorised price increases, but this was refused, presumably on the basis that such orders ought to be published.

[84] The 1947 Act, s.3(1) lists the libraries in question which include the National Library, the Law Library, the Library of the Law Society and the Libraries of the Dublin, Cork, Limerick, Waterford and Galway Chambers of Commerce, but not the Oireachtas Library.

[85] There are a number of specific statutory provisions which provide for a special exemption from these publication requirements. Thus, s.8(3) of the Roads Act 1993 provides that orders made by the Minister for the Environment under s.12 (abandonment of public roads); s.49 (approval of road schemes); s.51 (environmental impact assessment schemes); s.58 (approval of toll schemes); s.60 (revocation of toll schemes); s.61 (making of toll bye-laws); and s.73 (extinguishment of public rights of way) are all exempt from the publication requirements of s.3(1) of the 1947 Act.

[86] Statutory Instruments Act 1947, s.3(3) thus preserves the common law principles recognised in cases such as *Lim Chin Aik v. R.* [1963] A.C. 160.

This means that the common law doctrine of judicial notice may be invoked to relieve the prosecution from the burden of proving the existence of the statutory instrument, irrespective of whether it is one to which the 1947 Act primarily applies. It is true that in *The People v. Kennedy*[87] the Court of Criminal Appeal held that orders made under the Emergency Powers Act 1939 were not in the same position as a statute (*i.e.* not in the public domain), and therefore, upon a prosecution for a contravention of the order, must be proved in evidence. However, this decision was later distinguished in *The State (Taylor) v. Wicklow Circuit Judge*,[88] where it was sought to quash a conviction under the provisions of the Road Traffic Act 1933 on the grounds that the existence of a ministerial order bringing into force the relevant portions of the Act had not been formally proved in evidence. Davitt J. observed that the relevant order in *Kennedy's* case was:

> "Substantive legislation made by exercise of delegated authority; that it was continuous in its effect and that from day to day it affected personal rights and liabilities; whereas the order in question here was but momentary in its operation, bringing into force a piece of legislation enacted by the Oireachtas."[89]

By contrast the judge held in *Taylor's* case that the Circuit Court judge who had been administering the Road Traffic Act 1933 for many years was entitled to take judicial notice of the ministerial order without the need for formal proof of its making. Another qualification on the general principle of publication was laid down in *D.P.P. v. Collins*,[90] a case concerning the need to prove in evidence the existence of regulations implementing the Road Traffic (Amendment) Act 1978. Henchy J. conceded that while formal proof of the legislative provisions may be necessary where the precise ingredients of the offence are uncertain, it was otherwise where (as here):

> "[A] course of judicial conduct is so inveterate and unquestioned and of such a nature that it necessarily postulates the existence and validity of a statutory instrument. In such circumstances the court is entitled to take judicial notice of the statutory instrument."[91]

Given that in *Collins* the regulations were ones to which the 1947 Act primarily applied,[92] the court could have arrived at the same result by reference to section 3(3) of that Act. The necessity for the prosecution to prove that the order had been published could thereby have been dispensed with, as it seems clear that "reasonable steps" had been taken for the purpose of bringing the regulations to the attention of the public.

Section 10(1)(b) of the Interpretation Act 1937 permits a Minister to make regulations and orders in advance of the parent Act coming into force, where this is "necessary or expedient"[93] to enable the Act to have "full force and effect on the coming into force of the Act". (But this power does not extend to enabling the

---

[87] [1946] I.R. 517. See also *People v. Griffin* [1974] I.R. 416.

[88] [1951] I.R. 311.

[89] *Ibid.* at 319.

[90] [1981] I.L.R.M. 447. See Stevenson, (1983) 19 Ir. Jur. (N.S.) 95.

[91] *i.e.*, regulations made by a Minister of State after January 1, 1948, which were not of a purely "local or personal" application.

[92] See *The State (McColgan) v. Clifford* [1980] I.L.R.M. 75.

[93] The word "expedient" in s.10(1)(b) of the 1937 Act was defined by Morris J. in *McInerney v. Minister for Agriculture, Food and Forestry* [1995] 3 I.R. 449 as meaning "conducive to advantage in general or to a definite purpose".

regulations to come into force in advance of the Act.) It was on this basis that in *The State (McColgan) v. Clifford*[94] the Supreme Court upheld the validity of advance regulations made by the Minister for the Environment prior to the coming into force of the Road Traffic (Amendment) Act 1978. Henchy J. declared that the court could take judicial notice of the fact that the earlier legislation had broken down, and that fresh legislation was imperative. Given these circumstances, advance regulations were necessary in order to give the Act "full force and effect" once it became operational.

So far we have considered the need for publication in the particular context of criminal cases. As regards the position generally there is some English authority for the proposition that delegated legislation does not come into force until it is published.[95] However, the point appears to be dealt with, in a different sense, by section 9(2) of the Interpretation Act 1937 which provides:

> "Every instrument made wholly or partly under an Act of the Oireachtas shall, unless the contrary intention is expressed in such instrument, be deemed to be in operation as from the end of the day before the day on which such instrument is made."

Moreover, the idea that delegated legislation should have the force of law in advance of its publication would seem to be inimical to constitutional values such as legal certainty and the rule of law. In addition to the publication in most cases the parent statute will state that the statutory instrument must be "laid" before the Houses of the Oireachtas within a specified period – generally, 21 sitting days.[96] Such authorities as there are suggests that failure to comply with this "laying" requirement does not invalidate the statutory instrument.[97] However, the authorities are rather old and given that the object of the 1966 Act is to enable the Houses of the Oireachtas to examine a statutory instrument with a view to its possible annulment, it could be argued that the "laying requirement" is mandatory, and not merely directory. This view is re-inforced by *O'Neill v. Minister for Agriculture & Food*,[98] a case where the establishment of an extra-statutory scheme was condemned as *ultra vires* by the Supreme Court on a number of grounds,[99] including the fact that by establishing the scheme on this basis, the Minister had by-passed the protections contained in s. 10 of the Livestock (Artificial Insemination) Act 1947 which provided

---

[94] [1980] I.L.R.M. 75. In *McInerney v. Minister for Agriculture, Food and Forestry* [1995] 3 I.R. 449 Morris J. upheld the validity of regulations which had been made two months in advance of the coming into force of the relevant provisions of the Abbatoirs Act 1988. The Judge concluded that in the absence of the making of the statutory instrument in question one "would have had the entirely unsatisfactory position of applicants applying for licences in respect of premises without knowing the standard to which they were required to conform", although he conceded that "there was not the same degree of urgency in the present case as there as in *McColgan's* case."

[95] *Johnson v. Sargant* [1918] 1 K.B. 101. See Lanham, "Delegated Legislation and Publication" (1974) 37 M.L.R. 510.

[96] The "laying procedure" is regulated by statute: see Houses of the Oireachtas (Laying of Documents) Act 1966.

[97] *Premier Meat Packers Ltd v. Minister for Agriculture*, unreported, High Court, July 28, 1971. See also, *R. v. Sheer Metalcraft Ltd* [1951] 1 Q.B. 586. Probably on the basis of these authorities, the Attorney General's office has also advised that failure to lay does not render a statutory instrument invalid: *Report of Senate Select Committee on Statutory Instruments* (T.162) (Pr. 4685), p. 15. On mandatory/directory requirements, see below pp. 440–452.

[98] [1997] 2 I.L.R.M. 435.

[99] See pp. 329–334.

for routine powers of annulment of regulations by either House of the Oireachtas by ensuring that any such measures would be immune from parliamentary scrutiny. It is but a short step from the reasoning in this scheme to hold that the failure to lay a statutory instrument in the prescribed manner renders that instrument ineffective, since the necessary legislative scrutiny envisaged for both Houses of the Oireachtas has been thereby set at naught.

Judicial control

In the first place, as described in section 2 of this chapter, the delegation of power must not be in breach of Article 15.2.1°. In addition the courts must examine the validity of any delegated legislation according to the standard criteria of *vires* or reasonableness. As executive or administrative bodies do not possess an inherent legislative power, the validity of delegated legislation falls to be tested against the background of what is authorised by the parent statute either expressly or by necessary implication and in just the same way as any administrative action effecting only an individual change. The question of whether a statutory instrument is *ultra vires* the parent statute is essentially one of statutory interpretation. In determining the issue of *vires*, there are a number of standard presumptions which are employed by the courts. Thus, the Oireachtas is presumed not to have delegated the power to raise taxes[100]; or to oust the jurisdiction of the courts[101]; or to encroach upon the liberty of the citizen[102]; or to give retrospective effect to delegated legislation[103] or to infringe any provisions of the Constitution.[104] Subject to these presumptions, the task of the courts is to ascertain the true intent of the enabling Act, and, as Butler J. said in *Minister for Industry and Commerce v. Hales*:

> "Considerations of constitutionality apart, the judicial control of subordinate legislation operates only through the doctrine of *ultra vires* and the function of the courts can only be fulfilled by enquiry as to whether the statutory rule or order falls within the scope of the enactment from which it purports to derive its authority. This is the check placed upon arbitrary government by the executive. In a consideration of any given power, the court must not only

---

[100] *Attorney General v. Wilts United Dairies Ltd* (1921) 39 T.L.R. 781. For a discussion of whether the Oireachtas may validly delegate the power to raise taxes in view of the provisions of Arts. 17 and 22 of the Constitution, see Hogan, "A Note on the Imposition of Duties Act 1957" (1985) 7 D.U.L.J. 134 (N.S.).

[101] *Newcastle Breweries Ltd v. The King* [1920] 1 K.B. 854; *Commissioners of Customs and Excise v. Cure and Deeley Ltd* [1962] 1 Q.B. 340 and see generally, *Tormey v. Attorney General* [1985] I.R. 289.

[102] *The State (O'Flaherty) v. O'Floinn* [1954] I.R. 295; *Murphy v. P.M.P.A. Insurance Co. Ltd* [1978] I.L.R.M. 25 (presumption against interference with right to privacy); *The State (Lynch) v. Ballagh* [1986] I.R. 203.

[103] This is a general presumption of statutory interpretation: *Hamilton v. Hamilton* [1982] I.R. 466; *Doyle v. An Taoiseach* [1986] I.L.R.M. 693. But *cf. Re McGrath and Harte* [1941] I.R. 68 and *Minister for Agriculture v. O'Connell* [1942] I.R. 600. The Joint Oireachtas Committee on the Secondary Legislation of the European Communities has drawn attention to the fact that the European Communities Act 1972 does not authorise the making of delegated legislation with retrospective effect: see below pp. 40–41.

[104] There is a presumption that statutory powers (including power to make delegated legislation) granted by an Act of the Oireachtas do not authorise the donee of such powers to infringe the Constitution: *East Donegal Co-operatives Ltd v. Attorney General* [1970] I.R. 317. For recent examples of the courts' treatment of challenges to the constitutionality of statutory instruments, see *Purcell v. Attorney General* [1996] 2 I.L.R.M. 53; *Lovett v. Minister for Education* [1997] 1 I.L.R.M. 89, on which see above p. 13.

interpret the terms in which the statutory power is expressed to see that it is not given any wider power than is necessary, but must also see that the power does not exceed or interfere with or negative the provisions and intention of the enactment as a whole."[105]

There are a number of modern illustrations of this principle in cases where statutory instruments have been declared to be *ultra vires*. In the *Hales* case[106] the question at issue was whether insurance agents employed under a contract of service were "workers" for the purposes of the Holidays (Employees) Act 1961. Although the Act was expressly confined in its general application to employees and apprentices, the Minister was empowered by section 3(3) of the 1961 Act to extend its application in respect of holiday pay to any "class or description of persons" who could be deemed to be workers for the purposes of the Act. The Minister had purported by statutory instrument made under section 3(3) to so extend the Act to insurance agents, but this order was held to be *ultra vires* the parent Act by a Divisional High Court. As Henchy J. remarked:

> "It is not conceivable that the legislature, having indicated that the scope of the Act was to be limited to persons employed under a contract of service or a contract of apprenticeship, should by the use of general words in section 3(3) of the Act have given the Minister power to broaden the scope of the Act to such an extent that he could, by the making of regulations, import into work-contracts made with independent contractors a series of statutory terms as to holiday allowances, the breach of which would result in criminal liability. I cannot believe that the power to effect such radical and far-reaching changes in the law of contract was intended, or should be deemed to have been so intended, by a loosely drafted sub-section in an Act that has declared its purpose and scope to be otherwise."[107]

Other cases are more straightforward and so, for example, in *The State (Carney) v. Governor of Portlaoise Prison*,[108] rule 38(2) of the Rules for the Government of Prisons 1947[109] was held by the Supreme Court to be *ultra vires*. This sub-rule allowed for the remission of one-fourth of a sentence of penal servitude for good conduct, yet the Penal Servitude Acts 1854–1863 made no provision for such a rule. Another example in a similar context is furnished by the decision of McWilliam J. in *Incorporated Law Society of Ireland v. Minister for Justice*.[110] Here rule 2 of the

---

105 [1967] I.R. 50 at 83. In *Lovett v. Minister for Education* [1997] 1 I.L.R.M. 89 Kelly J. said (at 98) that he was not "at all sure that there is any real difference between the two tests, save that in the *Cityview Press* case, O'Higgins C.J. was also considering the constitutional authority of Parliament."
106 [1967] I.R. 50.
107 *Ibid.* at 76–77.
108 [1957] I.R. 25.
109 S.R. & O. No. 320 of 1947.
110 [1978] I.L.R.M. 112. Other examples include *The State (McLoughlin) v. Eastern Health Board* [1986] I.R. 416 (where ministerial regulations restricting the statutory right of claimants to certain fuel allowances were held to be *ultra vires*) and *American International Tobacco Co. v. Attorney General* [1990] 1 I.R. 394 (where Hamilton P. held that s.65 of the Health Act 1947 confined the Minister to declaring certain medical preparations to be "restricted articles" and that the Minister could not avail of this section to restrict the sale of non-medical articles such as tobacco sachets).

Government of Prisons Rules 1976[111] purported to allow the Minister, where he considered this necessary in the interests of the "security of the State", to restrict access of particular legal advisers to a given prison. McWilliam J. pointed out that the parent Act, the General Prisons (Ireland) Act 1877, did not enable the Minister to make rules in the interests of the security of the State and held that the Rules were accordingly *ultra vires*.

By far the greatest number of challenges have been to the *vires* of Rules of Court. The various Rules Committees for the District Court, Circuit Court and the Superior Courts have been given statutory jurisdiction to make rules concerning the "practice and procedure" of their respective courts and several cases turn on the question of whether a particular rule is properly a matter of practice and procedure.[112] In *Woolf v. Ó Griobhta*,[113] Davitt P. held that rule 85 of the District Court Rules 1948[114] was *ultra vires*. This rule had purported to confer the right, upon payment of the precribed fee, to obtain copies of depositions taken in a criminal trial upon "any person who satisfies the Clerk that he has a bona fide interest in the matter." These words were, said Davitt P., of "very wide application" and not at all confined to parties to the proceedings before the District Court. By purporting to confer such rights on persons who might be "in no way concerned with the exercise by the District Court of its jurisdiction", the Rules went beyond matters of practice and procedure and were *ultra vires*. A similar approach is evident in the judgment of the Supreme Court in *The State (Lynch) v. Ballagh*,[115] where the validity of the District Court (Criminal Procedure Act 1967) Rules 1985[116] was at issue. These Rules allowed a member of the Garda Síochána to decide to release a suspect on station bail and direct his appearance at a sitting of the District Court within 30 days. A majority of the Supreme Court held these Rules to be *ultra vires* in that they regulated the procedure to be adopted by a member of an Garda Síochána and were not concerned with the practice and procedure before the District Court.

Other cases have concerned attempted alterations – as opposed to mere necessary adaptions or modifications – of statutory requirements by the Rules Committees.[117] In *The State (O'Flaherty) v. Ó Floinn*[118] the Supreme Court held that Rule 55(4) of the District Court Rules (which had purported to enlarge the period by which a District Judge could remand a suspect in custody to 15 days) was *ultra vires* the provisions of section 21 of the Indictable Offences (Ireland) Act 1849. Ó'Dálaigh J.

---

[111] S.I. No. 30 of 1976.
[112] The power of the Superior Court Rules Committee to make Rules of Court governing "pleading, practice and procedure generally" is contained in s.36 of the Courts of Justice Act 1924, as applied by ss.14(2) and 48 of the Courts (Supplemental Provisions) Act 1961.
[113] [1953] I.R. 267.
[114] S.I. No. 431 of 1947.
[115] [1986] I.R. 203.
[116] S.I. No. 23 of 1985.
[117] Note that s.36(ix) of the Courts of Justice Act 1924 purports to confer the Committee with power to secure the "adaptation or modification of any statute that may be requisite for any of the purposes of this Act". However, it is questionable whether this power to modify or adapt an Act is one which can validly be delegated to the Rules Committee by virtue of Art. 15.2.1° of the Constitution in view of the reasoning of the Supreme Court in cases such as *Cityview Press Ltd. v. AnCO* [1980] I.R. 381.
[118] [1954] I.R. 295.

described the proposed change as "radical" and as something "more than the mere modification" of the 1849 Act. In *Thompson v. Curry*,[119] the provisions of Order 62, rule 5 of the Rules of the Superior Courts 1962 which attempted to reverse a statutory sequence prescribed by section 2 of the Summary Jurisdiction Act 1857 were found to be *ultra vires* by the Supreme Court. Walsh J. described this as an attempt to amend a condition precedent to jurisdiction and, hence, beyond the powers of the Superior Court Rules Committee. Finally, in *Rainey v. Delap*[120] the Supreme Court held rules 29 and 30 of the District Court Rules 1948 to be *ultra vires*. Section 10(1) of the Petty Sessions (Ireland) Act 1851 confers power on a District Judge to hear and determine a complaint and to issue a summons accordingly. Rules 29 and 30 purported to confer this power on a District Court clerk, but this was held by Finlay C.J. to go beyond the mere modification of an earlier statutory provision and was thus *ultra vires*.

The validity of Order 31, rule 29 of the Rules of the Superior Courts 1986[121] (which provides for the making of an order for discovery against a person who is not a party to the proceedings) has been challenged in several cases, but has been upheld on each such occasion on the ground that it does not involve any substantive change in the law. Barron J. described the change in *Holloway v. Belenos Publications Ltd.*[122] as a new rule "regulating the exercise of the inherent jurisdiction of the court"[123] a view echoed by Costello J. in *Fitzpatrick v. Independent Newspapers plc*[124] who said of the rule that it was "procedural", adding that the "Rules Committee is clearly empowered to enable the courts to make such orders."[125]

As stated already, the courts exercise control over delegated legislation in the same manner as other administrative actions and thus delegated legislation may be condemned as invalid on the ground that it is unreasonable in law[126] or disproportionate[127] or has been made in bad faith or (possibly) in breach of natural justice.[128] However, because of the legislative character of statutory instruments or other delegated legislation, it seems likely that the rules of constitutional justice will apply – if at all – only in an attenuated form.[129]

---

[119] [1970] I.R. 61.
[120] [1988] I.R. 470. Compare this reasoning with the unduly permissive approach of cases such as *Attorney General v. Bruen and Kelly* [1935] I.R. 615, where it was held that the relevant District Court Rule permitting a summons to be signed by a District Court clerk was *intra vires*, despite the express provisions of s.36 of the Illicit Distillation (Ireland) Act 1831 and s.11 of the Petty Sessions (Ireland) Act 1851 which required the summons to be signed by a Justice of the Peace (now a District Court judge).
[121] S.I. No. 15 of 1986.
[122] [1988] I.R. 494.
[123] *Ibid.* at 498.
[124] [1988] I.R. 132.
[125] *Ibid.* at 135.
[126] See, *e.g. Cassidy v. Minister for Industry & Commerce* [1978] I.R. 297; *Doyle v. An Taoiseach* [1986] I.L.R.M. 693; *McHugh v. AB Deciding Officer* [1994] 2 I.R. 139 and *Purcell v. Attorney General* [1996] 2 I.L.R.M. 53. As McCarthy J. said (at 156) in *McHugh* if a regulation "is demonstrably lacking in logic and [is] unfair it cannot be sustainable within the framework of the [statutory] scheme."
[127] *Lovett v. Minister for Education* [1997] 1 I.L.R.M. 89.
[128] *Burke v. Minister for Labour* [1968] I.R. 312; *The State (Lynch) v. Cooney* [1982] I.R. 337.
[129] *Bates v. Lord Hailsham* [1972] 1 W.L.R. 1373; *Cassidy v. Minister for Industry & Commerce* [1978] I.R. 297 See Casey, "Ministerial Orders and Review for Reasonableness" [1978] *Public Law* 130.

Procedure

One practical problem relates to the methods by which a statutory instrument may be challenged. Invalidity can generally be raised by way of defence[130] in either civil or criminal proceedings or, indeed, by way of plenary proceedings. The majority of challenges, however, arise in judicial review proceedings. It is also well established that the invalidity of a statutory instrument can be challenged by way of case stated.[131]

Where it is alleged that the statutory instrument is invalid on constitutional grounds a possible complication arises. Article 34.3.2° provides that the constitutionality of any post–1937 law can only be determined by the High Court and this has been held to mean that such issues cannot even be raised by way of case stated in the District or Circuit Courts.[132] However, as a result of the Supreme Court's decision in *Meagher v. Minister for Agriculture and Food*[133] it would appear that a statutory instrument made pursuant to a post–1937 statute is not a "law" for the purposes of Article 34.3.2°, so that it is probable that both the District Court and Circuit Court have jurisdiction to "disapply" such a statutory instrument in an appropriate case on the ground that it infringes the Constitution. It is true that both courts are the creation of statute and that there has been no express statutory devolution of such jurisdiction to such courts. However, judges of the District Court and Circuit Court are obliged by the terms of their judicial oath to uphold the Constitution,[134] so that where there is a clash between the ordinary law (in this case, a statutory instrument) and the Constitution, it would appear that the former must yield to the latter.[135]

Parent statutes and confirmation orders

One significant practical point which arises concerns the continuing validity of delegated legislation made under a parent statute when that parent statute has itself been repealed. Despite the general statutory saving clause contained in section 21(1) of the Interpretation Act 1937, it would seem that, in the event of a repeal, as might be expected, the delegated legislation will also lapse: the branch falls with the tree, unless some statute expressly provides to the contrary.[136]

If the principles of constitutional justice apply at all in this situation, they are likely to apply where (as in *Burke*), the class of persons affected is a very narrow one. Note that in *Abrahamson v. Law Society of Ireland* [1996] 2 I.L.R.M. 481 McCracken J. rejected the suggestion that the Law Society was obliged to consult with law students prior to the adoption of new regulations governing legal education. See further pp. 874–875.

130   See, *e.g. Listowel UDC v. McDonagh* [1968] I.R. 312. There may, however, be exceptions to this general rule: see pp. 797–798.

131   As happened in *Minister for Industry and Commerce v. Hales* [1967] I.R. 50.

132   *Foyle Fisheries Commission v. Gallen* [1960] Ir. Jur.Rep. 35; *Minister for Labour v. Costello* [1988] I.R. 235. See generally, Hogan and Whyte, *Kelly, op. cit.*, above, n.2, pp. 424–426.

133   [1994] 1 I.R. 329.

134   Article 34.5.1° requires that every person appointed to be a judge under the Constitution "shall make and subscribe to" such a declaration.

135   *Cf.* the analogous reasoning of Smyth J. in *Director of Public Prosecutions (Stratford) v. O'Neill*, [1998] 1 I.L.R.M. 221 (lower courts may pronounce on the validity of pre-1937 legislation).This argument cannot be taken so far as to enable judges of the District and Circuit Courts to pronounce on the constitutionality of a post–1937 statute, since this is specificially excluded by the terms of Article 34.3.2° of the Constitution itself.

136   *Watson v. Winch* [1916] 1 K.B. 688.

Moreover, inconveniently enough, this would seem to remain true even though that parent statute is repealed and replaced by another similar statute or even by a consolidation Act. There is no general doctrine of "implicit survivorship". The exception, already alluded to, is where the delegated legislation is thrown a statutory life-line. A typical example is section 302(2) of the Social Welfare (Consolidation) Act 1993 which provides:

> "All instruments and documents made or issued under the repealed enactments . . . and in force immediately before the commencement of this Act (other than the provisions of any instruments which are incorporated in this Act) shall continue in force as if made or issued under this Act."[137]

This obviously sensible device raises a novel constitutional point. As we have seen, the effect of Article 15.2.1° of the Constitution is that delegated legislation can do no more than fill in the details of principles which have been laid down by some Act of the Oireachtas. This, presumably, must mean laid down by parent legislation which is in force, but the issue is whether this has also to be the original parent legislation. It would seem, however, that this is not constitutionally required. The object of the constitutional provision is to ensure that there is no new principle of policy enunciated in delegated legislation which has not been authorised by some existing Act of the Oireachtas. There is no reason why this Act has to be the same as that which initially authorised the delegated legislation.

A further practical question has been raised by a number of recent cases. If a statutory instrument is *ultra vires*, can this order be subsequently confirmed with prospective effect by a later Act of the Oireachtas?[138] The principle behind the doctrine of *ultra vires* in this context is that an order is invalid if it exceeds the scope of the statutory powers vested in the maker of the legislation by the Oireachtas. Accordingly, it would not seem inconsistent with this principle if the Oireachtas was subsequently to confirm and validate the order in question. This is illustrated by a case concerning an order made under the Imposition of Duties Act 1957. In *Doyle v. An Taoiseach*,[139] Barrington J. held that an order made under this Act was void for unreasonableness. Section 79 of the Finance Act 1980 had purported to confirm this order (as is required under the machinery of the 1957 Act), but at the time of confirmation the Oireachtas had not realised that the order was actually invalid. Barrington J. doubted whether such a void order could be thus confirmed, but in the Supreme Court, Henchy J. appeared to suggest that an invalid order could be confirmed in this way, at least where the confirming legislation did not operate retrospectively.

---

137 A precursor of this provision was considered in *The State (Kenny) v. Minister for Social Welfare* [1986] I.R. 693 at 695 where Egan J. considered it "strange" that a statutory instrument made in 1973 should now be examined as to its *vires* in relation to the Social Welfare (Consolidation) Act 1981. However, he pointed out that the Order had been carried over by s.312(2) of the 1981 Act. For other examples of this technique, see the Irish Medicine Board Act 1995, s. 34(4) and Criminal Justice (Miscellaneous Provisions) Act 1997, s. 19(7).

138 What would be the position if the confirmatory Act purported to have retrospective effect? There appears to be no case on this point (or even a statutory example of it). While there is no general constitutional provision banning retrospectivity *per se*, it might be that the incidents or consequences of a retrospective confirmatory Act might bring into conflict with some particular constitutional provision, such as Article 15.5 or Articles 40.3.2°.

139 [1986] I.L.R.M. 693. The Supreme Court held that the confirming legislation could not operate retrospectively, since this would have had the effect of creating retroactive criminal sanctions, contrary to Art. 15.5 of the Constitution. For a case holding emphatically that confirming legislation is valid, see *McDaid v. Sheehy* [1991] 1 I.R. 1.

Categories of delegated legislation

Orders We have already seen that section 1(1) of the Statutory Instruments Act 1947 defines a statutory instrument as meaning "an order, regulation, rule, scheme or bye-law" made in the exercise of a statutory power. What is the meaning of these various terms? An order may be contrasted with regulations and rules in that it refers (or, at any rate, ought to refer) to the single exercise of an administrative power in relation to a particular person or situation.[140] Examples include commencement orders bringing statutes into force, judicial appointments and compulsory purchase orders. However, the nomenclature employed in the case of delegated legislation is not consistent and there are many examples of delegated legislation which are referred to as "orders" when, strictly speaking, they should be designated as regulations.

Regulations and Rules In contrast to orders, regulations and rules each have a definite legislative character. The term "Rules" is usually reserved for orders describing and regulating the procedure of courts[141] tribunals or other statutory bodies, whereas regulations are generally of a substantive nature.

Schemes Schemes, like orders, tend to be administrative in character, but this nomenclature is often employed where the instrument involves a system of figures or gradations, or where it prescribes the details of fees or charges. A good example is provided by section 90(2) of the Postal and Telecommunications Services Act 1983 which allows Bord Telecom to make a scheme detailing charges for its telecommunications services and the terms and conditions applicable to such charges. Thus, for example, the Telecommunications Scheme 1994[142] prescribes rules in respect of telephone charges and itemises such matters as differing costs depending on the length of the phone-call, distance between caller and receiver and so forth.

Bye-laws Bye-laws are another category of delegated legislation. As their title implies, these rules have a legislative character, but differ from regulations in that they are restricted in their ambit or field of application. Bye-laws are typically made by local authorities in respect of their own functional area, but other examples include bye-laws made by the Garda Commissioner in relation to traffic management[143] and by railway companies or airport authorities.[144] One element of what constitutes a bye-law was explained by Lord Russell in *Kruse v. Johnson*[145]:

---

140 See *Report of the Senate Select Committee on Statutory Instruments* (T.162) (Pr. 4685), p. 15.
141 See, *e.g.* Rules of the Superior Courts 1986.
142 S.I. No. 177 of 1994.
143 Thus, Road Traffic Act 1961 s. 88(1) provides that the Garda Commissioner may, with the consent of the Minister for Transport, make bye-laws "for the general regulation and control of traffic and pedestrians in public places".
144 See, *e.g.* Airport Bye-Laws 1994 (S.I. No. 425 of 1994). *Cf.* the Forestry Act 1988, s. 37(1) (Minister for Energy may at the request of Coillte Teoranta or on his own behalf "make bye-laws to regulate access to or use of any land owned, managed or used by the company"). The Law Society is given power to make bye-laws for solicitors (see Solicitors Act 1954, s.78(2), as inserted by Solicitors (Amendment) Act 1994, s.5) and the National Roads Authority is given a similar power in respect of bye-laws for tolls roads: see Roads Act 1993, s. 61) and C.I.É. may make bye-laws governing the management, control and operation of a light railway (Transport (Dublin Light Rail) Act 1996, s.24).
145 [1898] 2 Q.B. 91.

"An ordinance affecting the public, or some portion of the public, imposed by some authority clothed with statutory powers ordering something to be done or not to be done, and accompanied by some sanction or penalty for its non-compliance."[146]

This definition was approved by Walsh J. in *The State (Harrington) v. Wallace*.[147] Here the question was whether certain sheep-dipping regulations made by Cork County Council could properly be regarded as bye-laws so as to determine whether they should have been made by the councillors rather than by the county manager. Walsh J. agreed that not every administrative regulation made by a local authority could be regarded as a bye-law and where the regulation did not itself contain a sanction it could not be regarded as a bye-law. Here the regulations did contain a criminal sanction for non-observance and this fact, coupled with the local character of the regulations, was enough to make them bye-laws.[148]

While other legislation vests local authorities with power to make bye-laws in relation to specific subjects, especially in relation to environmental and public health matters,[149] a local authority's general power to make bye-laws (which is a reserved power, *i.e.* for the councillors and not the manager[150]) is now principally derived from Part VII of the Local Government Act 1994.[151] Although section 37(1) and (2) of the 1994 Act define in broad terms a local authority's power to make a bye-law, this power is nonetheless essentially confined to two types of categories: (a) the regulation or control of land, services or any other "thing whatsoever provided by or under the control or management" of the local authority; and (b) the regulation or control of "any activity or matter" or the suppression of any nuisance. Thus, the making of bye-law prohibiting the playing of certain games in a local park owned by the Council would fall within the former category, a bye-law controlling the use of dogs within its functional area would fall within the latter.

By section 37(8) of the 1994 Act the appropriate Minister may by regulation prescribe matters or classes of matters in respect of which local authorities shall not

---

146 *Ibid.* at 96.
147 [1988] I.R. 290.
148 The maxmium fine for contravention of a bye-law is £1,000 "or such lesser amount as may be specified in a bye-law . . . in respect of such contravention": Local Government Act 1994, s.40(1).
149 Examples include Public Health (Ireland) Act 1878, s.54 (empowering local authorities to make bye-laws regulating the keeping of animals so as to prevent injury to health); Local Government (Sanitary Services) Act 1948 Act, s.30 (which enables a sanitary authority to make bye-laws "regulating the use of temporary dwellings") s.41 (which deals with the power to make bye-laws in respect of public bathing) and s.42(2) (which enables a sanitary authority to make bye-laws in respect of a swimming bath or bathing place not maintained by a sanitary authority); Litter Act 1982, s.4(4) (which enables a local authority to make bye-laws requiring occupiers of land to keep free of litter "any footpath or pavement adjoining the land" or any public road); Control of Dogs Act 1986, s.17 (which enables local authorities to make bye-laws "relating to the control of dogs within its functional area"); and Casual Trading Act 1995, s.6 (giving local authorities powers to make bye-laws "in relation to the control, regulation, supervision and administration of casual trading in its functional area".)
150 Local Government Act 1994 Act, s.37(6).
151 The Municipal Corporations (Ireland) Act 1840, ss.125–127 (which enabled certain local authorities to make bye-laws for the "good rule and government of the borough" and Local Government (Ireland) Act 1898, s.16 (giving county councils similar powers) have now been repealed by Local Government Act 1994, s.4(1) and replaced by s.37 of that Act.

be entitled to make a bye-law. Of course, quite apart from this specific statutory prohibition, a bye-law cannot validate that which the general law prohibits. Conversely, a bye-law cannot render unlawful an act which the general law has made lawful.[152] This must, of course, must be read in context, for a bye-law may in certain circumstances regulate or even prohibit, conduct which, in general, is lawful.

Publication of Bye-laws and ministerial control

The special rules governing the publication of bye-laws are now contained in section 42 of the Local Government Act 1994.[153] A local authority is required to publish notice of the making of a bye-law in *Iris Oifigiúil* and also in one or more newspaper circulating in the area to which the bye-law relates. Such a notice must include "a statement of the general purpose for which the bye-law was made" and the date on which it came into force.[154] In addition to the specific controls contained in the particular statutory provisions the courts may, as with other forms of delegated legislation, invalidate bye-laws on the grounds of lack of *vires*, unreasonableness, etc.[155]

Local authorities are now required to give advance notice of the making of any bye-laws and to consider any representations made by members of the public in respect of any such proposals. By virtue of section 38(4)(1) of the Local Government Act 1994 a bye-law shall come into effect on the date specified being "not less than 30 days after its making". However, section 38(4)(2) provides that a bye-law requiring ministerial approval under section 39 shall not come into force unless such approval has been forthcoming. Finally, section 39 introduces a new method of Ministerial control of the making of bye-laws. Thus, section 39(2)(a) enables the appropriate Minister by regulations to designate any matter or class of matters to which a bye-law shall require the prior approval of the Minister. And section 37(9) provides that where "for given reasons" the "appropriate Minister" considers that a bye-law or any provision thereof is objectionable and notifies the local authority accordingly, then, if the local authority does not revoke or amend the bye-law in conformity with the notice, that Minister may do so by order with effect from a specified day. It may be noted that the appropriate Minister is so empowered by section 39 to make regulations to designate any matter or class of matters which require prior ministerial approval prior to coming into force.

---

152 *Kruse v. Johnson* [1898] 2 Q.B. 91 at 108, *per* Matthew J.
153 Section 4 of the Documentary Evidence Act 1925 had previously dealt with the publication of bye-laws in *Iris Oifigiúil*, but this section did not apply to bye-laws made by local authorities since "they were not exercising throughout the State any functions of government or discharging throughout the State any public duties in relation to public administration": see s.4(2)(d) of the 1925 Act. For the same reason the publication requirements in relation to bye-laws stipulated by the Statutory Instruments Act 1947 did not apply to local authority bye-laws.
154 Local Government Act 1994, s.39(2).
155 See, *e.g. Kruse v. Johnson* [1898] 2 Q.B. 91 (bye-law prohibiting singing within 50 yards of a dwelling-house not void for unreasonableness); *Dublin Corporation v. Irish Church Missions* [1901] 1 I.R. 387; *Enniscorthy U.D.C. v. Field* [1904] 2 I.R. 518; *Dun Laoghaire Corporation v. Brick* [1952] Ir. Jur. Rep. 37; *Limerick Corporation v. Sheridan* (1956) 90 I.L.T.R. 59; *Listowel U.D.C. v. McDonagh* [1968] I.R. 312; and see generally below, pp. 637–649.

Parliamentary control

Many hundreds of statutory instruments are promulgated each year, some of them of a very far-reaching nature. In an attempt to deal with this difficulty the Oireachtas often seeks to retain some measure of parliamentary control. The parent statute typically provides that every regulation made pursuant to that Act must be laid before each House of the Oireachtas. Either House may then pass a resolution within 21 sitting days annulling any such regulation but without prejudice to anything previously done thereunder.[156] While this procedure might be of some value in permitting the discussion of a contentious statutory instrument (though, in fact, seldom – if ever – is a resolution even proposed and one has never been passed), it ignores the reality of a government majority in both Houses of the Oireachtas, so that this method of control remains largely theoretical. One might also mention that while this annulment procedure has been described by O'Higgins C.J. as a "valuable safeguard", it cannot authorise that which is not otherwise sanctioned by Article 15.2.[157] Occasionally a statute may require that confirming legislation be passed within a particular stated period[158]; or that the draft instrument will not come into force unless confirmed by resolution of each House of the Oireachtas[159]; or provide for an appeal by any person aggrieved against the making of the instrument to the courts.[160]

Save in the case of statutory instruments made under the European Communities Act 1972, there is currently no functioning parliamentary scrutiny of delegated legislation. Indeed, even in the case of instruments made under the 1972 Act, it does not appear that the Oireachtas Committee on European Affairs has made any headway in performing such scrutiny. This is in contrast with the position which obtained between 1948 and 1983 when this function was discharged, in relation to domestic statutory instruments, by a Senate Select Committee on Statutory Instruments. This function was then vested in the Joint Oireachtas Committee on Legislation during the 1983–1987 period, but since that date the Committee has focussed exclusively on its immensely valuable task of considering the detail of primary legislation at Third Stage and has not examined statutory instruments. Since it is possible that such a Committee may be established in the future (although it is remarkable that

---

[156] On this "laying" procedure, see above pp. 26–27. Note that in *Immigration and Naturalisation Service v. Chadha*, 462 U.S. 919 (1983) a majority of the U.S. Supreme Court held that the "legislative veto" was unconstitutional. This decision was the outcome of a formal, logical application of the separation of powers: if the veto were to be classified as an executive or judicial function it would not be for Congress, alternatively, if it were a legislative function it should have been exercised by both Houses and coupled with the signature of the President, rather than by way of the resolution of one House acting alone. If *Chadha* were applied in this jurisdiction it would probably render unconstitutional the power to annul statutory instruments given to both individual Houses of the Oireachtas. Secondly, it is unlikely that *Chadha* would be followed in this jurisdiction if only because in Ireland the legislature is not just a law-making organ since, in addition, the Government is responsible to the Dáil. Secondly, this result could also be avoided if the Houses of the Oireachtas were to be characterised as being merely designated bodies to whom an administrative power (*viz.* the power of annulment) had been given.

[157] *Cityview Press Ltd v. AnCO* [1980] I.R. 380.

[158] See, *e.g.* Provisional Collection of Taxes Act 1927, s.3.

[159] See, *e.g.* Electoral Act 1963, s.6(3); Health Act 1970, s.4(5)

[160] See, *e.g.* Casual Trading Act, 1995, s.6(8) (right of appeal by a person aggrieved to the District Court against the making of bye-laws regulating casual trading); Fisheries (Consolidation) Act 1959, s.8 (appeal to the High Court).

in a recent debate on Dáil reform, this gap was not even mentioned[161]) and given that the past publications of both the Senate Committee and the Joint Oireachtas Committee are largely inaccessible to the legal community, it is proposed here to give a short account of the work of these Committees as an indicator of how this supervisory function might be discharged in the future.

Senate Select Committee on Statutory Instruments and Joint Oireachtas Committee on Legislation

Because the Joint Oireachtas Committee did not have any set criteria against which to judge statutory instruments, it is instructive to refer to the terms of reference of the former Senate Committee. This Committee was required to report to the Houses of the Oireachtas the existence of a statutory instrument on the following grounds:

"(i) that it imposes a charge on the public revenues or contains provisions requiring payments to be made to the Exchequer or any Government Department or to any local or public authority in consideration of any licence or consent, or of any services to be rendered or prescribes the amount of any such charge or payments;

(ii) that it appears to make some unusual or unexpected use of the powers conferred by the statute under which it was made;

(iii) that it purports to have retrospective effect where the parent statute confers no express authority so to provide;

(iv) that there appears to have been unjustifiable delay either in the laying of it before either House of the Oireachtas or in its publication;

(v) that for any special reason its form or purport calls for elucidation;

(vi) that its drafting appears to be defective; or

on any other ground which does not impinge on its merits or on the policy behind it;"[162]

The high constitutional significance of the first and third heads requires no under-lining. In fact, the former Senate Committee seldom had to invoke these grounds. The second ground covers a noticeably diverse collection of blemishes. For example, one instrument raised by several million pounds the maximum figure for the borrowings of a certain state agency which could be guaranteed by the Minister for Finance.[163] In another case, a statutory instrument which attempted to control the sale of commercial cream was cast so widely that it even caught a householder skimming cream off a bottle of milk with a teaspoon.[164]

---

161 469 *Dáil Debates* Cols. 1700–1755, 1893–1952 (October 9, 1996).

162 *Second Report of the Select Committee on Statutory Rules, Orders and Regulations* (1949) (T. 122), p. vii. The instrument in question was the Emergency Powers (No. 157) Order 1942 (Seventh Amendment) Order 1948 (S.I. 1948 No. 357).

163 *First Report of the Select Committee on Statutory Rules, Orders and Regulations* (1949) (T. 121), pp. xii–xviii.

164 *First Report of the Select Committee on Statutory Instruments* (1978) (Prl. 9747).

The remaining heads may be illustrated by reference to the last Report (1978–1981) of the former Senate Committee[165] which considered 333 instruments. The attention of the Senate was drawn to 36 of them. Twenty-one instruments were reported on the grounds of "unjustifiable delay" under head (iv). The criterion set by previous select committees was that a delay of more than seven days was "unjustifiable" and the delays in respect of which the Committee complained averaged 18 days and ranged from nine days to three months. The significance of these delays as the Committee observed, lies in the fact that, a member of either Dáil or Senate may put down a motion for annulment only after the instrument has been laid, yet the instrument comes into force at the date it is made and the annulment is not retrospective.

In the Senate Committee's last report (1978–81), 14 statutory instruments succumbed under the miscellaneous head (v) ("for any special reason its form or purport calls for elucidation"). The two most significant defects were: first, the lack of a brief explanatory memorandum describing the general purport of the instrument, in spite of a Department of Finance instruction to all departments that this should be provided, and, secondly, the absence of a precise citation of the parent sections of the legislation under which the instrument had been made. The point underlying this defect is the need for persons affected by the instrument to be able to check whether the instrument is *ultra vires* the enabling power contained in the parent legislation. In earlier reports, the Committee had complained that the titles of certain instruments had failed to identify the subject-matter. The Committee also condemned the practice of expressing regulations as amendments to existing regulations so that their effect could only be discovered by reference to the other regulations. Each of these defects is of importance in the context of the rule of law and is an issue on which the Committee has had to return to the attack on more than one occasion.[166]

An example of head (vi) ("drafting appears to be defective") is to be found in the 1978–1981 Report of the former Senate Committee. This concerned an order made under section 31 of the Broadcasting Authority Act 1960 which purported to ban interviews with a spokesman "for any *other or more* of the following organisations". The Committee took the view that the words which it had emphasised rendered the instrument meaningless. The Department of Posts and Telegraphs had replied that in the original instrument the emphasised phrase read "any one or more". The Committee reported to the Senate that the Department had failed in its duty to supply an accurate copy of the instrument to the House.

The inclusion of the final, unnumbered residual head ("any other ground"), as well as certain of the others, meant that the former Committee's jurisdiction was very wide and went beyond the grounds of review exercisable by a court. On the other hand, their only sanction was to report an instrument to the Houses and the annual reports were seldom debated. Nevertheless, the Committee received consistent co-operation from Departments of State and other instrument-making bodies and difficulties were often resolved in a satisfactory manner by an exchange of correspondence. However, it seems inherently unlikely that there are no excesses

---

[165] *Report of the Select Committee on Statutory Instruments* (1981).
[166] See, *e.g. Second Report of the Select Committee on Statutory Instruments* (1954) (Pr. 3864), p. 17.

or mistakes whatsoever in statutory instruments made today and it it therefore regrettable that there is no Committee (with, perhaps, even stronger teeth than its predecessors) to carry out this important task.

Joint Committee on European Affairs

At present, the only parliamentary scrutiny comes from the Joint Committee on European Affairs, which, by virtue of section 4 of the European Communities (Amendment) Act 1973 performs the statutory function of reviewing statutory instruments made pursuant to the European Communities Act 1972.[167] The Committee's brief is to examine such instruments as it "may select and to report thereon to both Houses of the Oireachtas".[168] Unfortunately, it does not appear that the present Committee performs much active work in this area and no annual reports have been published for some time.

In the past, the former Committee had drawn attention to a variety of blemishes and, in particular, has questioned the use of the 1972 Act in cases where it feels that primary legislation would have been more appropriate. Thus, for example, when considering the European Communities (Life Assurance Accounts, Statements and Valuations) Regulations 1986[169] the Committee observed that:

> "The main provisions regulating insurance companies are contained in regulations made under the European Communities Act, 1972 and so have never been considered by the Houses of the Oireachtas. In the Committee's view, this is unsatisfactory and it considers that there is a clear need for a consolidation statute in this area."[170]

The Committee had previously expressed itself in similar language with regard to the European Communities (Removal of Restrictions on Immature Spirits) Regulations 1985[171] (which had repealed two earlier Acts of the Oireachtas) where it said that:

---

[167] This statutory function was originally exerised by the Oireachtas Joint Committee on Secondary Legislation of the European Communities. (For a discussion of the work of this Committee, see Robinson, "Irish Parliamentary Scrutiny of European Community Legislation" (1979) 16 C.M.L.Rev. 9). With the establishment of the Oireachtas Joint Committee on Foreign Affairs, that function was transferred to that Committee by the European Communities (Amendment) Act 1993 s.6. Following the establishment of the Oireachtas Committee on European Affairs, the task of reviewing European secondary legislation has now been vested in that Committee by the European Communities (Amendment) Act 1995 s.1.

[168] Para. 8 of the terms of reference (see 142 *Seanad Debates*, Cols. 794–800) provides that:
"That the Joint Committee shall, in particular, consider:
(i) such programmes and guidelines prepared by the Commission of the European Communitie as a basis for possible legislative action and such drafts of regulations, directives, decisions, recommendations, and opinions of the Council of Ministers proposed by the Commission,
(ii) such acts of the institutions of those Communities,
(iii) such regulations under the European Communities Acts, 1972–1994, and
(iv) such other instruments made under statute and necessitated by the obligations of membership of those Communities as the Committee may select and shall report thereon to both Houses of the Oireachtas."

[169] S.I. No. 436 of 1986.

[170] *Report of the Fifth Joint Committee on the Secondary Legislation of the European Communities, Report No. 8* (December 14, 1988) p. 10.

[171] S.I. No. 368 of 1985.

"It is undesirable that amendments of Acts of the Oireachtas should remain indefinitely embodied in subordinate legislation. Opportunity should be taken to include such amendments in primary legislation when it presents itself."[172]

To judge by some of the published responses to the former Committee's queries about this point, it does not appear that as yet the various Departments of State share these concerns. Thus, for example, the Department of Finance responded to a query from the former Committee about the Immature Spirits Regulations 1985 by saying that regulations made under the 1972 Act have "statutory effect" and that therefore "it is not necessary to incorporate in primary legislation the amendments and repeals included in the Regulations", which rather misses the point.[173]

The retrospective operation of regulations made under the 1972 Act has also been the subject of the Committee's attention. One such example is the European Communities (Exemption from Value-Added Tax on the Permanent Importation of Certain Goods) Regulations 1985[174] which was made with retrospective effect from July 1, 1984. The Committee considered that this practice was objectionable, bearing in mind that there was ample time for the Minister for Finance to make the regulations before the time when they were needed.

"The present Joint Committee considers it objectionable that Ministers should make regulations under the 1972 Act with retrospective effect when there is no specific authority to do so. In the Joint Committee's view, the Houses of the Oireachtas should have the opportunity of considering in every case whether they are prepared to delegate power to legislate retrospectively. If it considered that such a power is essential in order to fulfil Community obligations, an amendment of the 1972 Act should be proposed in order that the Houses should have the opportunity of fully considering the matter."[175]

One might add in this context that, in the absence of express statutory authority, any attempt to give a statutory instrument retrospective effect is almost certainly *ultra vires* the 1972 Act.

In other cases, a Minister has attempted to reserve a power of exemption from the application of the particular statutory instrument in question. One such example is provided by article 4 of the European Communities (Life Assurance, Accounts, Statements and Valuations) Regulations 1986 which allows the Minister for Industry and Commerce to provide that these Regulations shall not apply to a specified undertaking. The Joint Committee could not accept that such a power was properly contemplated by the 1972 Act:

---

172 *Report of the Fifth Joint Committee on the Secondary Legislation of the European Communities, Report No. 2* (January 20, 1988) pp. 4–5. See discussion of *Meagher v. Minister for Agriculture and Food* [1994] 1 I.R. 329 at pp. 17–18.

173 Text of a letter dated February 3, 1987, from the Department of Finance to the Committee, reproduced in the Second Report of Fifth Joint Committee, p. 2. This type of "dispensing" power has previously been condemned as unconstitutional, even when contained in an Act of the Oireachtas: see *East Donegal Co-Operative Ltd v. Attorney General* [1970] I.R. 317 at 350, *per* Walsh J.

174 S.I. No. 183 of 1985.

175 *Second Report of the Fifth Committee*, p. 2.

"A power conferred on a Minister by statute to make a statutory instrument ought not, in the Joint Committee's view, to be regarded as enabling the Minister to assume a power therein to grant administratively a dispensation from an obligation to comply with it."[176]

Once again it would seem that these powers of exemption are, in fact, *ultra vires* the 1972 Act.

It is clear that the former Committee's deliberations were most interesting and their comments were invariably well-taken. Whether such observations, which have received scant publicity, carried much weight with the government departments in question seems doubtful. The evidence to date shows that many of the criticisms have not been accepted by the Departments in question. Certainly, the threat of annulment of a statutory instrument is one which carries little weight in practice.[177] Another consideration is that statutory instruments of far-reaching importance are almost regularly promulgated without any reference to the Oireachtas,[178] so that – as the former Committee has recognised – many areas of the law are regulated by delegated legislation (made under the 1972 Act) which has either substantially amended or repealed primary legislation passed by the Oireachtas. If the Joint Committee was designed to be the bulwark against the erosion of parliamentary sovereignty, then it has clearly failed in its task. If the present practice of widespread reliance upon statutory instruments is to be retained, then perhaps there is room for the strengthening of the Committee's powers. Thus, for instance, it might be provided that instruments promulgated under the 1972 Act should have legal effect unless the Joint Committee recommended by a certain date that they be confirmed by primary legislation enacted within a further date. In any event, as things stand, there is here a capital example of what the Constitution Review Group described as an "information deficit" and a "democratic deficit".[179]

5. Administrative Rules

Introduction

One of the most remarkable features of the many diverse government schemes and licensing arrangements currently in existence is the extent to which they are derived from administrative (*i.e.* non-statutory) rules and circulars.[180] Thus, our system of

---

[176] *Eight Report of the Fifth Committee*, p. 8.

[177] Indeed, one may question whether, as a matter of European Community law, it is even open to a national legislature to annul a measure which was designed to transpose a directive into national law.

[178] Although in view of the dicta of Denham J. in *Meagher v. Minister for Agriculture and Food* [1994] 1 I.R. 329, there is an increasing tendency for the Oireachtas to enact legislation to give effect to a directive by means of Act of the Oireachtas where such measures contain "policies and principles" not otherwise sanctioned by the terms of the directive.

[179] *Report of Constitution Review Group* (1996), p. 115. See further, Birkinshaw and Ashiagbor, "National Participation in Community Affairs: Democracy, the U.K. Parliament and the E.U." (1996) 33 C.M.L.Rev. 499.

[180] Somewhat surprisingly, there is not a huge amount in the literature on this topic, but see Ganz, *Quasi-Legislation: Recent Developments in Secondary Legislation* (1987); Wade and Forsyth, *Administrative*

public administration now teems with a growth of enigmatic rules (for we are not speaking here of individual executive orders) which are neither primary or subordinate legislation.[181] These instruments include: circulars (of diverse types), codes of practice, notes of guidance, 'instructions' and administrative guidelines. However, the nomenclature in this area is not of great importance since the distinction between the different instruments has never been made clear and there is little consistency. Accordingly, the term "administrative rules" is used to refer collectively to the family. The more important questions in regard to these rules is why they have been developed and what is their advantages and disadvantages (questions addressed in this section) and, secondly, what is their legal status and what (direct or indirect) effects do they have, questions examined in the succeeding sections.

Probably the easiest type of this species to justify is that which occurs where some statutory discretion has been conferred upon a public body and the body chooses to indicate the conditions on which it is going to exercise its discretion by issuing a circular. In other words, such an instrument constitutes a useful and much used means of – to use U.S. parlance – "structuring discretion" and publicising how it will be exercised.[182] A contemporary example here is supplied by the guidelines produced by the Revenue Commissioners[183] for determining whether a work in respect of which a tax exemption under section 2 of the Finance Act 1969 has been sought is, in fact, an "original and creative work" possessing "cultural or artistic merit" within the meaning of this section.

Whilst this usage is, in many ways, beneficial to the persons affected by the discretion, one difficulty here arises from the fact that the law – with its emphasis on process, rather than substance – is concerned to ensure that discretion is exercised as authorised by the legislature, rather than that discretion is limited. This difficulty will be considered in a later chapter,[184] under the heading of "fettering a discretionary power". In a succeeding section of this chapter, we shall address the question of whether the reasonableness or *vires* of a decision should be judged by reference to the terms of a relevant circular.

In a second type of instrument – often known as a code of practice – the arrangement affords a way of allowing a trade, commercial or professional group which is affected by the rule to be involved in devising its content. A good example here is

---

Law, op. cit., above, n.1 pp. 869–873; Craig, *Administrative Law* (3rd.ed.) pp. 270–273; Baldwin, *Government by Rules* (1995), Chap. 3; Baldwin and Houghton, "Circular Arguments: the Status and Legitimacy of Administrative Rules" (1986) *Public Law* 231; Hogan, "The Legal Status of Administrative Rules and Circulars" (1987) 22 Ir. Jur.(N.S.) 194; Hadfield, "The Doctrine of Legitimate Expectations" (1988) 39 N.I.L.Q. 103; and O'Reilly, "Coping with Community Legislation – A Practitioner's Reaction" (1996) 17 *Statute Law Review* 15.

[181] The term "tertiary legislation" is employed by Baldwin, "Informal Legislation" (1986) *Public Law* at p. 267.

[182] Davis, *Discretionary Justice* (1971), Chap. 4.

[183] Finance Act 1994, s.14, provides that the Arts Council and the Ministers for Arts, Culture and the Gaeltacht shall, with the consent of the Minister for Finance, draw up such guildelines. The guidelines have been produced in booklet form by the Revenue Commissioners and are issued to every applicant for such artists tax relief. Other than this they have not been published in any way. In particular, they have not been published either in *Iris Oifigiúil* or as a statutory instrument, although it is strongly arguable that such guidelines fall within the definition of a statutory instrument provided by the Statutory Instruments Act 1947, s.1(1) for which see p. 33 above.

[184] See below, Chap. 12, pp. 668–675.

provided by the "guidance notes" issued by the Pensions Board for the guidance of pensions administrators. In this genus, there is a range of possibilities with the "softest law" (for the entire area of administrative rules is sometimes known as 'soft law') occurring in the form of voluntary codes.[185] Here the thinking is that "persuasion may be preferable to compulsion".[186]

In a third type of administrative rule, such as, for example, *The Rules of the Road*, there is the advantage that non-technical language can used to explain complex legal issues to the general public.

From the perspective of public administrators, the use of circulars may have other advantages: the procedure is convenient and a statutory structure might prove to be inflexible. Parliamentary time is scarce and there may be difficulties in securing the assistance of a parliamentary draftsman to prepare the appropriate legislation or statutory instrument. Thus, one study of the method of implementing European Community legislation in the various Member States found that Irish officials did not like to have to implement directives by means of primary legislation:

> "The process of drafting a primary piece of legislation is time consuming because it requires extensive consultation with interested organisations, adequate attention from the Parliamentary Draftsman, discussion in Cabinet and parliamentary time."[187]

Although the production of delegated legislation was found to be less time-consuming than an Act of the Oireachtas, this nevertheless brought its own difficulties:

> "The drafting of statutory instruments is not a simple procedure. A proposed legal instrument makes its way slowly from the sponsoring department, to the Attorney-General's office, and finally to the Parliamentary Draftsman. This process is repeated until all interests are satisfied with the statutory instrument. Delays are generated not only by policy conflict, but also because of bureaucratic blockages in the system."[188]

Moreover, there is some evidence that some government departments issue administrative rules and circulars in preference to legislation almost as a matter of policy.[189] The main culprits in this regard appear to be the Departments of Agriculture

---

185 Some forms of non-statutory methods of consumer protection (*e.g.* the patients' charter for hospitals) may also fall within this genus.

186 Ganz, *op. cit.* above, n.180, pp. 97–98.

187 Laffan, Manning, Kelly, *"Ireland" in Making European Policies Work: The Implementation of Community Legislation in the Member States* (European Institute of Public Administration, 1986) p. 383.

188 Laffan, Manning, Kelly, *ibid.* p. 392.

189 A good example of this is provided by the Government's decision to oppose the establishment by legislation of the National Curriculum Council. The Council has advisory functions in relation to the school curriculum. The Minister for Education (Mrs. O'Rourke) gave the following reasons for refusing to place the Council on a statutory framework (374 *Dáil Debates*, Cols. 2186–2187) (November 3, 1987):

> "There is no need to enshrine advisory functions in legislation. These functions will not be enhanced in any way by putting them into a statute. An Act of the Oireachtas will not confer any greater powers for advising upon the curriculum Council. Neither will the Council's powers to

and Food, Education[190] and the Environment. It is quite remarkable, for example, that there is often no legislation underpinning various schemes administered by the Department of Agriculture.[191] One consequence of this non-statutory framework is that it is not necessary for the relevant Minister to secure parliamentary approval for a significant change in policy. One graphic illustration of this occurred in 1987 when the Minister for Education decided to reduce the pupil/teacher ratio in primary schools. This was done by means of a circular and the matter only came before the Oireachtas because the issue was raised by the opposition parties.[192] A defeat for the Government on this issue would not necessarily have resulted in the withdrawal of the circular, since the circular – unlike an ordinary Bill – does not require a majority in each House of the Oireachtas and – unlike a statutory instrument – is not subject to annulment by either House of the Oireachtas.[193]

---

advise the Minister be reduced in any way by failing to confer them by statute. Once terms of reference for a body such as a Curriculum Council are laid down in an Act of the Oireachtas, they become quite inflexible. They cannot be adjusted in any way except by [an Act] of the Oireachtas. The Curriculum Council which I intend to establish on a non-statutory basis will have more flexible terms of reference."

This statement tends to explain the Department of Education's preference for the use of non-statutory rules rather than the use of primary legislation. This informal attitude has been increasingly questioned, as witnessed by the remarks of Costello J. in *O'Callaghan v. Meath V.E.C.*, unreported, High Court, November 20, 1990 and in *McCann v. Minister for Education* [1997] 1 I.L.R.M. 1. In the former case Costello J. had said (at p. 1 of his judgment):

"It is a remarkable feature of the Irish system of education that its administration by the Department of Education is largely uncontrolled by statute or statutory instruments and that many hundreds, perhaps thousands, of rules and regulations, memoranda, circulars and decisions are issued and made by the Department and the Minister (dealing sometimes with the most important aspects of education policy) not under any statutory power but merely as administrative measures. These measures are not, of course, illegal. But they have no statutory force and the sanction which ensures compliance with them is not a legal one, but the undeclared understanding that the Department will withhold financial assistance in the event of non-compliance."

But *cf.* n.190 below.

190   Although there will be a change in the case of this Department if the Education Bill 1997 becomes law, as this will provide, for the first time, a statutory framework for the regulation of the primary and secondary school sectors.

191   Thus, prior to the European Communities (Milk Quotas) Regulations 1994 (S.I. No. 70 of 1994), virtually the entire milk quota system was administered by a series of administrative circulars: see generally O'Reilly, "Coping with Community Legislation" (1996) 17 *Statute Law Review* 15. This also meant that such circular letters and notices (*ibid.* p. 22) dealt with such matters as:

". . . reductions in quotas granted to indivdual producers in exercise of discretion conferred by Community legislation; the leasing of land and quota; the operation of a 'claw back' which is applied to leases of land; and the leasing of dairy cows by 'SLOM' or 'Mulder' producers to fulfill a SLOM quota allocation granted on a provisional basis. No formal record exists of these circulars or notices. It is difficult to imagine a less transparent system."

Not surprisingly, in *Lawlor v. Minister for Agriculture* [1990] 1 I.R. 356 Murphy J. expressed astonishment at the informal manner in which the milk quota regime was operated by the Department of Agriculture. He commented (at 366):

"I confess I would have expected to find complex administrative machinery set up by a statute to introduce and police this revolutionary regime. Virtually no such machinery exists . . . [Various administrative circulars] were put in evidence and again it would appear astonishing that such a crucial decision could be made and recorded with such simplicity and informality."

192   This was the celebrated Circular 20/87 issued by the Department of Education which sought by circular to effect a reduction in the pupil/teacher ratio in primary schools. There was a series of rather inconclusive votes in the Dáil. The Government was defeated on one of these votes, but it narrowly won on the major vote on this issue: see 375 *Dáil Debates*, Cols. 1645–1657 (November 24, 1987).

193   See pp. 36–37 above.

The disadvantages of this proliferation of such administrative rules from the point of view of a conventional constitutional system of laws scarcely needs emphasis. Despite the fact that administrative circulars may create legal rights and obligations and are subject to judicial review, their legal status defies exact classification. In a seminal article published in 1944,[194] Sir Robert Megarry described such legislation as a form of "quasi-legislation" and this seems as good as description as any of the effect in practice of such circulars. But no legal system can be content with a situation whereby public authorities and Government Departments habitually resort to circulars in an attempt to regulate legal rights.[195] The confusion resulting from the habitual use of such circulars has frequently been judicially deplored[196] and in *McCann v. Minister for Education*[197] Costello P. made the following plea for reform:

> "If administrative ministerial rules and regulations were dated; if they were identified by reference to the sub-head in the Book of Estimates to which they relate; if amendments bore the same reference and were dated by reference to the ministerial order which made them; if a register was kept of the original measure and amendments to it; if the original measure and amendments were regularly consolidated and meanwhile made available in loose leaf form to members of the public, this would be one way of obviating the danger of injustice which is inherent in the present highly informal procedures."[198]

While it is true that administrative practices would be greatly improved if these suggestions were acted on, the fact remains that the habitual use of circulars as a means of quasi-legislation is unsatisfactory. Such a practice was roundly condemned by Streatfield J. in a notable passage:

> "Whereas ordinary legislation, by passing through both Houses of Parliament or, at least, lying on the table of both Houses, is thus twice blessed, this type of so-called legislation is at least four times cursed. First, it has seen neither House of Parliament; secondly, it is unpublished and is inaccessible even to those whose valuable rights or property may be affected; thirdly, it is a jumble of provisions, legislative, administrative, or directive in character, and sometimes difficult to disentangle one from the other; and, fourthly, it is

---

[194] "Quasi-Legislation" (1944) 60 L.Q.R. 125.
[195] Sir Robert Megarry's comments (*ibid.* at p. 127) apply *a fortiori* to our modern legal system:
"A system under which the practitioner may have to search Hansard, the Stationery Office list of official publications and the weekly law papers to find out how far up-to-date text-books and the statute book itself can be relied upon as stating the effective law will commend itself to few." And as Ganz, *op. cit.*, above, n.180, sardonically observed (p. 2), the practitioner "would have to look a great deal further afield today". In *Kylemore Bakery Ltd v. Minister for Trade, Commerce and Tourism* [1986] I.L.R.M. 526 Costello J. observed (at 530) that "these non-statutory schemes have the advantage of flexibility so that they can be easily adapted to changing circumstances but . . . their informality can create considerable problems when it becomes necessary to ascertain legal relationships arise from them when a dispute in their administration occurs." See also the similar comments of O'Hanlon J. in *McKerring v. Minister for Agriculture* [1989] I.L.R.M. 82 and Murphy J. in *Lawlor v. Minister for Agriculture* [1990] 1 I.R. 356 at 366.
[196] See, *e.g. Patchett v. Leathem* (1949) 65 T.L.R. 69; *McCann v. Minister for Education* [1997] 1 I.L.R.M. 1.
[197] [1997] 1 I.L.R.M. 1.
[198] *Ibid.* at 15.

expressed not in the precise language of an Act of Parliament or an Order in Council but in the more colloquial language of correspondence, which is not always susceptible of the ordinary canons of construction."[199]

Streatfield J.'s comments are pertinent in this jurisdiction, since, as we have seen, the very inaccessibility of such circulars might well be regarded as a breach of constitutional justice. Given that the Statutory Instruments Act 1947 takes great pains to ensure that statutory instruments are published, why should a government department be permitted through the use of circulars to by-pass these requirements?[200] And while Scott L.J.'s comment[201] that such circulars were examples "of the very worst kind of bureaucracy" may be going too far, it is surely the case that the systematic use of such circulars by government departments so as to create a quasi-legislative code, which is lifted above any of the controls which apply to primary or delegated legislation, is contrary to the spirit, at least, of the Constitution in general and Article 15.2.1° in particular.

In addition the limited circulation of such circulars and their general inaccessibility may mean that the reliance on such circulars could be contrary to the guarantee of fair procedures, since it might well be thought that "any rule which is applied on the basis of an internal memorandum which is not available to the public may lack the characteristic of true law and could possibly be challenged on that ground".[202] These principles would certainly seem to have considerable relevance as far as the operation of the Tuberculosis and Brucellosis Schemes are concerned, as in *McKerring v. Minister for Agriculture*[203] O'Hanlon J. found it remarkable that the only guidance to be found regarding the grant scheme was to be found in the conditions on the back of the cattle movement permit and any changes in these conditions "were notified to the farming community by way of newspaper advertisement".[204] The issue of fair procedures arising from the restricted publication of this circular had not, however, been argued before him.

Some of these considerations were very much to the fore in *O'Neill v. Minister for Agriculture & Food*,[205] a case where the Minister had through a series of extra-statutory measures created an "exclusivity" scheme whereby for the purposes of

---

[199] *Patchett v. Leathem* (1949) 65 T.L.R. 69 at 70.

[200] On the purely legal plane the answer to this question is that since an administrative act is not made in the exercise of a statutory power, it therefore falls outside the scope of the Statutory Instruments Act 1947: see pp. 23–24.

[201] *Blackpool Corporation v. Locker* [1948] 1 K.B. 349.

[202] Byrne (1987) 22 Ir. Jur. (N.S.) 326–327. See also, the comments of Scott L.J. in *Blackpool Corporation v. Locker* [1948] 1 K.B. 349 at 361:
"The very justification for the basic maxim [that ignorance of the law is no excuse] is that the whole of our law, written or unwritten, is accessible to the public – in the sense, of course, that, at any rate, its legal advisers have access to it, at any moment, as of right."
See also the comments of Costello P. in *McCann v. Minister for Education* [1997] 1 I.L.R.M. 1, 15:
"The law should be certain and it should be readily accessible. The same applies to non-statutory administrative measures. In the case of primary and secondary education, hundreds of millions of pounds are administered by means of a large number of administrative measures whose existence is known only to a handful of officials and specialists, which are not readily available to the puplic and whose effect is uncertain and often ambiguous."

[203] [1989] I.L.R.M. 82.

[204] *Ibid.* at 83–84.

[205] [1997] 2 I.L.R.M. 435.

licences granted pursuant to the Livestock (Artificial Insemination) Act 1947 the State was divided into nine administrative regions, with one licence holder per region. This scheme was condemned as *ultra vires* by the Supreme Court on a number of grounds,[206] including the fact that by establishing the scheme on an extra-statutory basis, the Minister had by-passed the protections contained in section 10 of the 1947 Act – which provided for routine powers of annulment of regulations by either House of the Oireachtas – by ensuring that any such measures would be immune from parliamentary scrutiny. Keane J. was emphatic on this subject:

> ". . . even if the Oireachtas envisaged the adoption by the Minister of the exclusivity scheme, it is highly improbable that they intended the scheme to be established by a series of purely administrative decisions with the regulations remaining entirely silent . . . Section 10 of the 1947 Act provided that every regulation made under the Act was to be laid before each House of the Oireactas, as soon as might be after it was made, with a concomitant power for either House to pass a resultion within 21 days annulling the regulation. In addition, the adoption by the Minister of the exclusivity scheme by a series of administrative decisions ensured that it was not published in the manner required by the Statutory Instruments Act 1947. Neither the Long Title of the 1947 Act, the provisions of the measure itself, the subject matter on which it was intended to operate or the context in which it was enacted suggest in any way that it was the intention of the Oireachtas that the important safeguards shielding the power of the Minister to enact by way of delegated legislation could be circumvented. The fact that such administrative decisions may be challenged, as here, by the invocation of the judicial review procedure is not, of itself, sufficient to justify, in a case such as the present, *the departure by the Minister from the salutary practice of ensuring that a scheme in the present case is embodied in regulatory form, ensuring both legislative supervision and accessibility to the public, rather than be implemented by administrative decisions taken by the minister in private.*"[207]

If this reasoning is taken up in later cases, it might have radical implications for the validity of many administrative schemes which have been superimposed on an existing statutory framework. For example, in *Rooney v. Minister for Agriculture & Food*[208] a farmer sought to compel the Minister to implement the appropriate regulations envisaged by section 58 of the Diseases of Animals Act 1966 which, had been made, would have provided him with greater compensation for reactor animals than that provided by the existing non-statutory administrative scheme. The Supreme Court held that it had no power to compel the Minister to make regulations in the absence of any mala fides or abuse of power.[209]

In the light of *O'Neill*, aspects of the *Rooney* would surely have to be re-considered,[210] since the Minister presumably could not by-pass the legislative

---

[206] See pp. 329–334.
[207] *Ibid.* at 442 (emphasis added).
[208] [1991] 2 I.R. 539.
[209] Citing *The State (Sheehan) v. Government of Ireland* [1987] I.R. 550.
[210] And not only *Rooney*. The validity of such extra-statutory schemes which by-pass legislative safeguards has been upheld in a series of High Court decisions: see, *e.g. Grennan v. Minister for*

scrutiny envisaged for any regulations which might be made under the 1966 Act by resorting to non-statutory schemes. Put another way, any regulations which the Minister might make would have to be made under the terms of the 1966 Act and not otherwise.

The legal status of administrative rules: general principles

The major conceptual problem of the legal status of circulars and other administrative rules is, as yet, imperfectly explored. However, the following principles can be suggested.

First, circulars and the rest of their family are not law. This precept would follow from the fundamental character of the common law. And, if circulars, etc., happen to lay down fresh principles, then it could also be derived from Article 15.2.1° (on which see above in section 2 of this chapter). For, if delegated legislation which is, at least, contemplated in primary legislation cannot make law which goes beyond principles laid down in the parent Act, then the same restriction must certainly apply in the case of circulars. As a consequence, it is axiomatic that the public authority which issued such a circular may not rely on that circular as against the private citizen in order to affect or prejudice his strict legal rights nor may such a circular be relied on by one citizen against another.

Secondly, this proposition begs the question of whether a citizen may invoke a circular as against the public authority. The answer is that, although as stated, a circular may not, as a matter of strict law, alter the law, it may, and often has been, regarded as the basis of a legitimate expectation. There is nothing unique to circulars in this, as a legitimate expectation can be created in a variety of ways, ranging from an official letter to an express oral representation. The decided cases tend to show, however, that circulars are a common source of legitimate expectations.

Finally, as mentioned in the first point, although circulars do not in themselves have a legal status, they tend to have enormous impact as many will assume that they have an official legal standing. Accordingly, the courts will, exceptionally, entertain proceedings challenging the *vires* of a circular. In strict law, such a circular is of no more potency than (say) an opinion of counsel which a public authority had reason to disseminate to the public at large. However, for the sorts of reasons just mentioned, such a circular has immense practical weight and the courts properly assume the jurisdiction to declare that any statement of law contained therein is erroneous in law.

We elaborate below on the first and third of these propositions, the second being covered separately in Chapter 16.[211] It ought to be noted, too, that in the United Kingdom there has been some development (mainly at an academic level[212]) in determining the legal consequences, in terms of legal effects, of circulars and other administrative rules by drawing certain distinctions. Among these are: whether the rule or circular is (even implicitly) authorised by or contemplated in, primary or

---

Agriculture & Food, unreported, High Court, October 5, 1996 and *McCann v. Minister for Education* [1997] 1 I.L.R.M. 1.
[211] See below pp. 890–893.
[212] See further, Baldwin and Houghton, *loc. cit.*, above, n.180, pp. 245–252.

secondary legislation, so that it is not entirely lacking in legitimate means of support[213]; its terminology or whether it otherwise "looks like law"[214] (clarity, precision, justiciability, etc.); and the subject-matter and surrounding context. As yet in this jurisdiction the judiciary have not attempted to discriminate amongst the various types of administrative rules so as to assign to "soft law" different levels of "softness". Accordingly, we shall not pursue this issue of sub-categorisation any further here.

The status of codes etc. mentioned in statute law – broadcasting advertising codes

Recent years have witnessed an increasing number of statutes which expressly permit or require regulatory authorities to issue codes and guidelines, some of which have the effect of an attempt to amend the law. An example[215] here is section 4(1) of the Broadcasting Act 1990:

> "The Minister [for Communications] shall draw up and may amend, from time to time as he shall think proper, codes governing standards, practice and prohibitions in advertising, sponsorship or other forms of commercial promotion in broadcasting services and . . . every sound broadcasting contractor . . . shall comply with every such code in relation to its broadcasting services".

The responsible Minister has, in fact, promulgated such a code under the terms of this section[216] and some examples drawn from the code may be conveniently examined to illustrate its amorphous legal character. The first example concerns section 14(4) of the Radio and Television Act 1988 which imposes certain statutory limits on radio and television advertising. The word "advertising" is not defined, but section 2.3 of the Code excludes from the definition of "advertisement", as used in the 1988 Act, such matters as charity appeals given air-time free of charge and "information announcements of forthcoming concerts, recitals or performances . . . given by the National Symphony Orchestra". These exclusions are not only not warranted by any "principle or policy" contained in the existing broadcasting legislation, they contradict it by way of an indirect attempt to amend the definition of what constitutes an "advertisement".[217] A second example is provided by section 15 of the code which attempts to ban the advertising of certain alcoholic drink. It states:

---

213 Examples of this type of circular include the advertising guidelines contemplated by the Broadcasting Act 1990; the pensions guidelines issued under the Pensions Act 1990 and the artists tax exemption guildelines issued under the Finance Act 1994 outlined at p. 42.

214 Thus, many non-lawyers probably assume that the *Rules for National Schools* 1965 – which is replete with formal legal terminology – has some form of official statutory foundation.

215 Other examples include: Insurance Act 1989, s.56 (permitting Minister for Enterprise and Employment to make an order "prescribing codes of conduct" to be observed by insurance agents or insurance brokers"); Pensions Act 1990, s.10(1)(c) (as inserted by Pensions Act 1990, s.5) (authorising the Pensions Board to issue "guidelines or guidance notes on the duties and responsibilities of trustees of schemes and codes of practice on specific aspects of their responsibilities"); Finance Act 1994, s.14 (providing that the Arts Council and the Minister for Arts, Culture and the Gaeltacht, shall, with the consent of the Minister for Finance, draw up guidelines for determining whether a particular book or other work should obtain tax exemption under the Finance Act 1969 s.2); Criminal Justice Act 1994, s. 57; Irish Medicine Board Act 1995, s.34.

216 *Codes of standards, practice and prohibitions in advertising, sponsorship, and other forms of commercial promotion in broadcasting services* (1995).

217 *cf.* the comments of Lord Denning in *Laker Airways v. Department of Trade* [1977] Q.B. 643 at 699:

"The code recognises a voluntary code whereby spirit based alcoholic drinks . . . are not advertised on either radio or television. This code is framed on the assumption that this situation will continue".

Thus, drinks such as whiskey and gin may not be advertised, since this would be a breach of the code and broadcasters are clearly under a legal duty to comply with the code. As in the case of other administrative circulars, two questions arise in regard to this circular. First, is it binding at law? Secondly, what safeguards – consultation, discussion, publication, etc. – should be or have been applied to it? As regards the first question, the fact that the code is mandated by the statutory provision quoted earlier militates in favour of its being law. But the careful use of the term "voluntary" in the code itself – as well possibly as the word "code" itself in the statute – seems to counter act this. At the very least, the code is highly authoritative, if not legally binding. However – to return to the question of safeguards – while the code may have been the subject of informal consultation, this type of secondary legislation promulgated by the Minister – for this, in reality, is what the code is – does not even comply with the minimum safeguards imposed in the case of most secondary legislation, *i.e.* publication under the terms of the Statutory Instruments Acts[218] or being subject to the power of annulment by resolution of either House of the Oireachtas. Moreover, as just noted, some of these features of the code would, in any case, appear to be *ultra vires* the parent legislation. Furthermore they would seem not to comply with the "principles and policies" test contained in cases such as *Cityview Press* and *Cooke v. Walsh*.

Can administrative rules alter existing procedural or substantive law?

Leaving aside the particular category of administrative rules which are mentioned in statute law and which have been examined in the preceding section, principle and authority seem to argue that administrative rules are not law and, thus, cannot change that procedural or substantive law. Take, for example, Devitt J.'s comment in *Carberry v. Yates*[219] that a ministerial circular prescribing the teaching of Irish as a compulsory requirement of the primary curriculum was unlawful. He described

---

"The word guidance does not denote an order or command. It cannot be used so as to reverse or contradict the general objectives of the statute. It can only be used so as to explain, amplify or supplement them."

[218] One question which this raises is whether this code does in fact fall within the scope of the Statutory Instruments Act 1947. The query takes us back to the definition of a statutory instrument as "an order, regulation, rule, scheme or bye-law" made in the exercise of a statutory power. As to the second element of the test – statutory power – the 1990 Act s.4(1) states that the Minister "shall . . . draw up . . . codes". It might be said that this concerns a statutory *duty*, as opposed to a statutory power as mentioned in the 1947 Act. However, while it is generally true that the power to make a statutory instrument is usually discretionary rather than mandatory, this is by no means unexceptionable: see, *e.g.* Irish Takeover Panel Act 1997, s.8(2). In any case, the power – duty distinction does not seem a rational policy basis upon which to determine whether a rule falls within the Act.

The more difficult question is in regard to an element of the definition, namely, whether a code comes within the term "order". The answer perhaps should be in the negative if – but only if – the code is not legally binding in the way that an order is. Possibly the use of the words "voluntary code" suggest that the ban is not binding and, on this basis, does not need to be published.

[219] (1935) 69 I.L.T.R. 86.

it as a ministerial "ukase for which there is not any statutory authority".[220] The abolition of corporal punishment by circular provides a particularly good example of an attempt to change substantive law through administrative rules. This was purportedly done in 1982 by a circular emanating from the Department of Education,[221] but it is difficult to see how such a circular could have been legally effective for this purpose. There is a further point: at common law, it was permissible for a teacher and those in *loco parentis* (such as a teacher) to administer reasonable corporal punishment to a child. It seems clear that this common law right[222] can only be altered by an Act of the Oireachtas and not by circular.

Several recent High Court decisions also tend to support the view that circulars cannot change the law.[223] In *Donohue v. Dillon*,[224] Lynch J. said of a Practice Direction that as it did not have statutory force, it could not be used as an aid to the construction of the Rules of the Superior Courts 1986. In effect, Lynch J. appeared to say that these administrative notices "cannot change the law or alter it".[225]

A similar approach is evident in the judgment of Lardner J. in *Devitt v. Minister for Education*.[226] In this case the applicant had been appointed by the County Dublin Vocational Education Committee as a temporary whole-time teacher rather than as a permanent whole-time teacher. Under section 23 of the Vocational Education Act 1930, an application for a full-time position was to be made in the first instance to the Vocational Education Committee. Any appointment to that position by the Committee was in turn subject to the Minister's approval. A ministerial circular entitled Memorandum V7, issued in 1967 appeared to indicate that the Minister would abide by the Committee's decision, provided the person in question was duly qualified and there was satisfactory evidence of age, health and character. In this case, the Minister – in an apparent effort to reduce the number of permanent teaching

---

220 *Ibid.* 88. Subsequent attempts to reverse this decision through legislation failed: see Osborough, "Education in the Irish law and Constitution" (1978) 13 *Ir. Jur.* (N.S.) 145 at pp. 176–180.

221 Rule 130 of the Rules for National Schools 1965 (which provided for corporal punishment in certain circumstances) was amended by Circulars 9/82 and 7/88. The change in practice was announced in the Dáil by the Minister for Education (Professor O'Donoghue) in March 1982: see 333 *Dáil Debates*, Cols. 1430–1431. It may be, however, that teachers could lawfully be bound as a matter of contract to observe the terms of this circular and, furthermore, pupils might possibly be in a position to assert that this circular (directed as it was to the public at large) created a legitimate expectation that they should not be subjected to corporal punishment.

222 It is difficult to find judicial authority for this proposition, but this fact was conceded by the British Government in *Campbell and Cosans v. United Kingdom* (1983) 4 E.H.R.R. 293 at 297. This concession would appear to be undoubtedly correct.

223 See also *Colman (J.J.) Ltd v. Commissioners of Customs and Excise* [1968] 1 W.L.R. 1286. By contrast in *Crowley v. Ireland* [1980] I.R. 112 Kenny J. said that the use by the Minister of unqualified teachers in an industrial dispute would be a breach of the Rules for National Schools and hence an unlawful use of public funds. But this would appear to attach to the Rules a form of legal status which is not warranted, unless one takes the view that the Dáil when voting supply must be taken to have implicitly only authorised the spending of monies in the manner envisaged by the 1965 Rules.

224 [1988] I.L.R.M. 654. Yet another example is provided by *Grehan v. North Eastern Health Board* [1989] I.R. 422, where Costello J. held that the terms of the plaintiff's contract with the defendants could not be unilaterally altered by circular. Had such changes been effected by either primary or delegated legislation, then of course, this would have superseded the terms of the contract between the parties. See also to like effect the comments of Gavan Duffy J. in *Cogan v. Minister for Finance* [1941] I.R. 389 at 401.

225 See *Colman* case *ibid.* at 1291 *per* Lord Denning M.R.

226 [1989] I.L.R.M. 639.

posts created by local Vocational Education Committees – invoked her powers under section 23(2) of the 1930 Act and refused to give her consent to the appointment. It was said on behalf of the applicant that the Minister was confined to the matters (qualifications, age and health of applicant) referred to in the ministerial circular and could not invoke other matters in seeking to justify the exercise of her discretion. Lardner J. could not accept this submission:

> "No doubt in relation to the exercise of this statutory discretion the Minister may adopt general rules or procedures to guide herself or to notify other concerned persons as to the manner in which she will exercise her discretion provided that they are relevant to the exercise of her powers and are reasonable. But she is not in my view entitled by such rules or procedure to limit the scope of the discretion entrusted to her or disable herself from the full exercise of it. Nor in my judgment may such a practice be relied upon by the applicant as estopping the Minister from the full exercise of the discretion vested in her by the Act."[227]

Lardner J.'s comments necessarily imply that a circular cannot qualify or modify the terms of an Act of the Oireachtas. It is also extremely significant that Lardner J. allowed this principle to prevail in the face of the applicant's legitimate expectation that the Minister would abide by the Committee's decision. But the most graphic confirmation to date of this principle comes with the decision of Barron J. in *Browne v. An Bord Pleanála*.[228] This case concerned the manner in which the E.C. Environmental Impact Assessment Directive had been purportedly implemented by administrative circular. Barron J. referred to several decisions of the European Court of Justice which had found such methods of implementing a directive to be unlawful. Thus, in *Commission v. Belgium*,[229] the European Court held that:

> "Mere administrative practices which, by their nature, can be changed as the authorities please and which are not published widely enough cannot be regarded [as proper means of implementing a directive]".[230]

Barron J. adopted this reasoning and concluded that the Directive had not been validly implemented by circular, since this "did not have the force of law and for this reason cannot have incorporated any of the provisions of the Directive into our domestic law".[231]

---

[227] *Ibid.* at 649. Lardner J. relied on the comments of Henchy J. in *Re Greendale Properties Ltd* [1977] I.R. 256 at 264 as authority for the proposition that a public body cannot be estopped from performing a statutory duty. But *cf.* the comments of McWilliam J. in *Phelan v. Laois Vocational Education Committee*, unreported, High Court, February 28, 1977, where he acknowledged that even though a circular might not bind the Minister, it might be evidence "of improper exercise of his powers if he were to ignore his own requirements without good reason". Note also that in *O'Callaghan v. Meath V.E.C.*, unreported, High Court, November 20, 1990, Costello J. held that these Ministerial Circulars "were quite clearly not made under statutory power. They are merely administrative measures with no statutory force". The same judge made similar comments in *McCann v. Minister for Education* [1997] 1 I.L.R.M. 1.

[228] [1991] 2 I.R. 209.

[229] Case 102/79 [1980] E.C.R. 1473.

[230] *Ibid.* at 1486.

[231] *Browne v. An Bord Pleanála* [1991] 2 I.R. 209 at 220.

Judicial review of administrative circulars

It now seems clear that administrative circulars may be subject to judicial review. Given the ubiquitous nature of circulars it would be ill-advised to attempt an exhaustive classification of the circumstances in which judicial review may lie. The purpose of the present section is merely to present cases in which the issue of judicial review of circulars has been (more or less addressed) by the courts. The following three situations can be identified for the sake of description and have yielded a fair amount of case law.

(a) **Circulars stating the Law**   The first concerns circulars which, at any rate, purport not to change the law but merely to state it.[232] It not infrequently happens that government departments will issue a circular by way of guidance for the benefit of bodies such as local authorities and schools. There have also been instances where bodies such as the Competiton Authority[233] and the Medical Council[234] have issued formal notices containing what purports to be authoritative statements of the law. It would be unrealistic to pretend that such circulars have only the same status and influence de facto as counsel's opinion or a legal textbook in the same area of law and, it seems, that even this type of circular is amenable to judicial review in a suitable case.[235]

The theoretical basis for this assertion of judicial power was more fully explored by the House of Lords in *Gillick v. West Norfolk and Wisbech Health Authority*.[236] In this case, the plaintiff challenged the legality of a departmental "memorandum of guidance" issued to local health authorities giving advice in relation to the provision of contraception for children under 16. A majority of the House concluded that the provision of such advice was not unlawful. However the essential point for present purposes is that each member of the House accepted that, in particular

---

232   See, *e.g. McNamee v. Buncrana U.D.C.* [1983] I.R. 213, where the Supreme Court made reference to a circular issued by the Department of the Environment which (incorrectly, as it happened) sought to explain the duties of housing authorities in the wake of the earlier decision of the Supreme Court in *McDonald v. Feeley*, unreported, Supreme Court, July 23, 1980.

233   The Competition Authority has issued notices of this nature entitled *Employee Agreements and the Competition Act*, *Iris Oifigiúil*, September 18, 1992 and *Shopping Centre Leases*, *Iris Oifigiúil*, September 10, 1993: see Hyland, "Legal Status of Notices Issued by the Competition Authority" (1993) 11 I.L.T. 240.

234   In the wake of the (highly controversial) decision of the Supreme Court in *Attorney General v. X.* [1992] 1 I.R. 1, the Medical Council issued guidelines (now contained in *A Guide to Ethical Conduct and Behaviour and to Fitness to Practice* (4th. ed., 1994) which might be thought to contradict the tenor (at least) of the Supreme Court decision. This meant that some doctors were worried that if they "undertook terminations they would be in breach of Medical Council Guidelines, but if they refused to undertake such terminations, they might be liable legally . . ." Tomkin and Hanfin, *Irish Medical Law* (1995) p. 186. See also Bowers, "New Legal Risk for Irish Doctors on Abortion" (1993) 10 *Irish Medical News* 186. In such circumstances, it might well have been open to a doctor (or any other person with an interest) to seek judicial review of the guidelines on the ground that they attempted by directive to prevent or frustrate patients exercising such rights as were enunciated by the Supreme Court in the *X.* case.

235   See the comments of Hyland, *op. cit.*, above, n.233, at pp. 240–241:
  "It seems clear that a notice issued by the Competition Authority . . . which effectively outlines the way in which the Authority is likely to interpret an Act of the Oireachtas, in a situation where only it has the power to so interpret it, is capable of being the subject of judicial review."

236   [1986] A.C. 112.

circumstances of the case, a circular could be subject to judicial review (albeit that it could have no legal effect). Lord Bridge put the matter thus:

> "The issue by a department of government with administrative responsibility in a particular field of non-statutory guidance to subordinate authorities operating in the same field is a familiar feature of modern administration. The innumerable circulars issued over the years by successive departments responsible in the field of to town and country planning spring to mind as presenting a familiar example. The question whether the advice tendered in non-statutory guidance is good or bad, reasonable or unreasonable, cannot, as a general rule, be subject to any form of judicial review."[237]

Lord Bridge then went on to refer to *Royal College of Nursing v. Department of Health and Social Security*.[238] In these proceedings the legality of a memorandum issued by the defendants concerning certain procedures to be followed under the Abortion Act 1967 was challenged by the plaintiffs. In the event, the defendants' contentions were upheld and Lord Bridge added that, against the background of the *Royal College of Nursing* case, it would have been surprising "if the courts had declined jurisdiction".[239] He continued by saying:

> "But I think it must be recognised that the [*Royal College of Nursing*] decision (whether or not it was so intended) does effect a significant extension of the court's power of judicial review. We must now say that if a government department, in a field of administration in which it exercises responsibility, promulgates in a public document, albeit non-statutory in form, advice which is erroneous in law, then the court has jurisdiction to correct the error of law by an appropriate declaration. Such an extended jurisdiction is no doubt a salutary and indeed a necessary one in certain circumstances, as the *Royal College of Nursing* case itself well illustrates. But the occasions of a departmental non-statutory publication raising, as in that case, a clearly defined issue of law, unclouded by political, social or moral overtones, will be rare."[240]

---

[237] *Ibid.* at 192–193. *Cf.* the comments of Finlay P. in *The State (Kershaw) v. The Eastern Health Board* [1985] I.L.R.M. 235 where he said (at 239) that in so far as a ministerial circular provided guidance concerning the operation of the fuel scheme operated under the terms of the Social Welfare (Consolidation) Act 1981, it was "clearly a proper and valid administrative act". In the present case, however, social welfare appeals officers relied on the circular in the holding that the applicant was not entitled to certain social welfare benefits. Finlay P. held that this was unlawful, as the terms of such a circular could not prevent either a deciding or appeals officer from exercising their statutory powers under the 1981 Act to decide whether the applicant was entitled to the benefits claimed. For other cases where the courts took on the task of reviewing administrative decisions by reference to criteria prescribed by a circular, see *The State (Melbarien Enterprises Ltd) v. Revenue Commissioners* [1985] I.R. 706 (Commissioners took into account irrelevant consideration not permitted by non-statutory administrative scheme) and *Reidy v. Minister for Agriculture and Food*, unreported, High Court, June 9, 1989 (where the Department purported, pursuant to the terms of a ministerial circular, to impose a disciplinary penalty which was not authorised by the Civil Service Regulation Acts 1956–1958).

[238] [1981] A.C. 800.

[239] [1986] A.C. 122. This language is very reminiscent of the language used by Gavan Duffy J. almost 50 years previously in *Maunsell v. Minister for Education* [1940] I.R. 213: see p. 56 below.

[240] *Gillick* [1986] A.C. 112 at 192–193.

This is perhaps the best exposition to date of the true legal status of this type of administrative circular. While it cannot be equated with either primary or secondary legislation, such a circular can be subjected to judicial review. This reasoning was taken a step further in *R. v. Secretary of State for the Environment, ex p. Greenwich L.B.C.*[241] where judicial review was sought of a Government leaflet purporting to explain a new local government tax ("community charge"). While the application was dismissed on the merits, Woolf L.J. held that the courts could intervene if the publication in question "was manifestly inaccurate or misleading".[242] Applying this principle in an Irish context, it might mean that, in an appropriately exceptional case, judicial review could lie in respect of an explanatory memorandum to a Bill or, even, to officially sponsored government leaflets or advertisements such as are now common in the run-up to polling day in a referendum.[243]

(b) Circulars creating administrative machinery   The second type of administrative rule is where the authority purports to create some form of administrative machinery by which to adjudicate on individual rights or liabilities.[244] As examples of this category being subjected to judicial review, one could refer to the Rules for National Schools[245] or the scheme governing the Criminal Injuries Compensation Tribunal,[246] each of which has been judicially interpreted and construed on several occasions.[247]

---

241   *The Times*, May 17, 1989.
242   But *cf. R. v. Transport Secretary, ex p, Thames London Borough Council, The Times*, May 9, 1995, where Sedley J. held that patent contradictions existing in a government consultation paper were not within the purview of the courts, but were for the political process of consultation.
243   It is true that in *McKenna v. An Taoiseach (No. 1)* [1995] 2 I.R. 1 (decided in 1992) Costello J. refused to grant the plaintiff relief in respect of the *Short Guide to the Maastricht Treaty* which had been published by the Government in the run-up to the 1992 referendum on that Treaty. The plaintiff had claimed that the *Short Guide* contained expression of partisanship and advocacy "characteristic of a political and commercial advertising" and that it would mislead "an uninformed reader". Costello J. evidently considered (at 7) that the issue raised was non-justiciable:
   "It is, in my view, entirely inappropriate for the courts to adjudicate on the controversy which these differences have engendered. It is a staple of political debate for protagonists to accuse their opponents of misrepresentation of fact and even of uttering untruths. Whether the Government has been guilty of such conduct in this case, is a matter for others, not for the High Court to decide."
   However, this view would now require re-consideration in the light of the judgment of the Supreme Court in *McKenna v. An Taoiseach (No. 2)* [1995] 2 I.R. 10. The import of *McKenna (No. 2)* suggests that the courts would now assert a right of judicial review where such an official publication was – to adopt the words of Woolf L.J. in the *Greenwich case* – "manifestly inaccurate or misleading."
244   A good example is the establishment by administrative scheme of the Milk Quota Appeals Tribunal which is designed to deal with hardship cases arising from the operation of the milk super-levy system. This tribunal does not, of course, have any statutory backing and, in this respect, is similar to the Criminal Injuries Compensation Tribunal. The Milk Quota Appeal Tribunal's full terms of reference and rules of procedure do not appear ever to have been formally published, but an outline of its terms of reference was published in the advertisements in the national newspapers on May 30, 1990.
245   The cases where the Rules for the National Schools have been construed include: *Newell v. Starkie* [1917] 2 I.R. 73; *Leyden v. Attorney General* [1926] I.R. 334; *Maunsell v. Minister for Education* [1940] I.R. 213; *McEneaney v. Minister for Education* [1941] I.R. 430; *Cotter v. Aherne* [1976–1977] I.L.R.M. 248; and *Crowley v. Ireland* [1980] I.R. 102.
246   The cases where the Criminal Injuries Compensation Rules have been considered include *The State (Hayes) v. Criminal Injuries Compensation Tribunal* [1982] I.L.R.M. 210 and *The State (Creedon) v. Criminal Injuries Compensation Tribunal* [1988] I.R. 51.
247   In *White v. Glackin*, unreported, High Court, May 19, 1995 the applicant claimed that he had acquired a legitimate expectation that the procedures to be followed at a particular Garda disciplinary inquiry

(c) Circulars Structuring Discretion   The more common type of administrative rule is one referred to (at the commencement of this section) which structures and indicates how a statutory discretion is to be exercised by a public body. Thus, in a number of cases involving civil service discipline,[248] it has been assumed, albeit without consideration, that the decision of the Minister for Finance could be reviewed by reference to the terms of such a circular. Since such a circular constitutes an instruction as to how a statutory discretion should be exercised it is subject to the same disciplines – *vires*, reasonableness, etc., as an ordinary administrative action exercising a discretion. If the circular satisfies these tests, well and good. If not, then again it is in the same position as the individual administrative action and will be struck down.

In one early case, *Maunsell v. Minister for Education,*[249] Gavan Duffy J. held that the defendants had misconstrued rule 82 of the 1932 Rules for the National Schools in the course of taking an administrative decision against the plaintiff teacher and rejected the argument that he had no jurisdiction to do so because of the non-statutory nature of the Rules in question.[250] However, prior to the decision of Murphy J. in *Greene v. Minister for Agriculture*[251] the question of the courts' jurisdiction to review the legality of such administrative schemes had never received elaborate judicial consideration in this jurisdiction. Murphy J. did not appear to question his entitlement to subject such a scheme to judicial review on ordinary grounds of vires, reasonableness, etc. The plaintiffs in *Greene* succeeded in their claim that the manner in which the means test was imposed in a ministerial circular dealing with headage payments to farmers as a form of grant-aid discriminated against married couples and thus was contrary to Article 41. The important point here is that while Murphy J. said that Article 15.4.1°[252] had no relevance, as this ministerial scheme was not a "law" within the meaning of that subsection, nonetheless he could intervene to declare the offending portion of the scheme to be unconstitutional.

This type of circular also formed the background to *McCann v. Minister for Education.*[253] Here the Minister had created by circular an administrative system for the payment of incremental salaries to secondary teachers, but under this

---

would conform to those specified in a circular issued by the Garda Commissioner entitled "Notes on Disciplinary Procedures under Garda Síochána (Discipline) Regulations 1989." Costello P. did not, however, find it necessary to decide whether the terms of the circular could give rise to a legitimate expectation as he concluded that the applicant's case depended on a misconstruction of the circular in question.

248   See, *e.g. Reidy v. Minister for Agriculture*, unreported, High Court, June 9, 1989.

249   [1940] I.R. 213.

250   Moreover, in another case involving a challenge to an administrative decision taken on foot of a circular, *Mulloy v. Minister for Education* [1975] I.R. 88, the Supreme Court held that a departmental circular which discriminated against priests and members of religious orders was a discrimination on the grounds of religious belief or status, contrary to Article 44.2.4°. No question was raised in this case as to the court's jurisdiction to make such a pronouncement in view of the non-statutory (and presumably non-binding) nature of such a departmental circular.

251   [1990] 2 I.R. 17.

252   Which provides that: "The Oireachtas shall not enact any law which is in any respect repugnant to this Constitution or any provision thereof."

253   [1997] 1 I.L.R.M. 1.

administrative scheme incremental credit was given only to teachers who had been registered by the (statutory) Registration Council. Although the applicant had long standing service as a teacher, her service was only recognised for incremental purposes from 1992. It was claimed that the Minister had erred in law in refusing this application for the recognition of past incremental service on the ground that the application did not satisfy the requirements for credit spefieied by the circular. It was claimed that the Minister had, in effect, fettered her discretion by treating the rules as if they had statutory force and that she failed to evaluate the application on the merits instead of by reference to the circular. Surprisingly, perhaps, Costello P. rejected this submission:

"It seems to me a proper discharge of a Minister's responsibilities to embody a scheme for the payment of incremental salaries to secondary teachers in detailed rules which are published for all to read. It is in no way improper for those rules to make provision (a) for the teachers who will qualify for such salaries and (b) for the conditions under which the different rules of incremental salary will be paid. If this is so, then it cannot be wrong for the Minister to apply such rules when considering an application in an individual case for payment of incremental salary and in deciding whether an applicant is entitled to incremental credits for previous years service as a teacher. I think it is incorrect to regard the Minister 'as fettering her discretion' by so doing. She is not exercising a power conferred by statute which must be exercised in the manner Parliament prescribes. She is administering funds allocated to her by Parliament in accordance with rules which she or her predecessors had validly made."[254]

---

[254] The reasoning in this passage is appraised below at pp. 673–674.

CHAPTER 3

THE DÁIL, MINISTERS, DEPARTMENTS
AND CIVIL SERVANTS

The object of this chapter is to sketch the constitutional and legal framework within which the administration of central government proceeds. Part 1 deals with the part played by the Dáil and in Part 2, with the legal persona of a Minister. Thus Parts 1 and 2 deal with the forms of political and legal responsibility respectively. However, no attempt is made to deal with the Dáil's role in law-making or as the "Grand Inquest of the Nation" these being matters of constitutional law.[1] The remaining Parts cover the civil service.

1. Formal Control by the Dáil

Following the British model[2] the members of the Government (Cabinet) are formally responsible to the Dáil, though not the Senate,[3] in two ways.

(i) Collective Government responsibility

The principal form of responsibility is collective. The Constitution makes the Government collectively responsible to the Dáil. This means that, after an election, the Dáil elects a Government and also that it can remove and, without reference to the people, replace it with a new Government. However, its power to elect a replacement Government is restricted by the provision that even a Taoiseach who has been defeated in the Dáil may advise a dissolution followed by a general election and, thus far, no President has seen fit to reject such advice.[4] Moreover, all the Dáil's powers over the Government are conditioned by the basic fact of political life which is that a Government can almost always command the support of a majority of deputies, because deputies are elected principally on the basis of the party which they have pledged themselves to support in the Dáil. Such is the strength of the

---

[1] See Gwynn Morgan, *Constitutional Law of Ireland* (1990), pp. 54–87.
[2] Though at the inception of the State, some efforts were made to modify this model: on this and on the entire subject, see Kohn, *The Constitution of the Irish Free State* (1932), Pt. VI, Chap. II ; Chubb, *Cabinet Government in Ireland* (1974), *passim.*
[3] The Government is not formally responsible to the Senate in the way that it is to the Dáil. Informally, the Senate's position in regard to publicising and criticising the Government's activities and policy decisions is similar to, though less important than, that of the Dáil. For instance, the select committees constituted to review a specific area of government activity (*e.g.* the Joint Committee on Commercial State Sponsored Bodies) are invariably joint committees, but with a minority of members from the Senate. Accordingly in the limited space available the role of the Senate has not been examined.
[4] See generally, Articles 13.1; 13.2; 28.4.1°; and 28.10. The former President, Mary Robinson, however, indicated that she would be quite prepared to reject such advice in appropriate circumstances: *The Irish Times*, November 27, 1994. For a discussion of the President's powers in these circumstances, see Hogan "Legal and Constitutional Issues arising from the 1989 General Election" (1989) 24 Ir. Jur. 157.

whip-system that the legislature cannot be regarded as speaking with a voice independent of the executive and, so, it is realistic to characterise the central element in the Irish governmental system as a fused executive-legislature.

The epithet "collective" means, first, that the Government, as a collective authority, speaks with one voice and, secondly, that if the Taoiseach resigns from office (or is removed), the other members of the Government also leave office.[5] In other words, the Government stands, or falls, as a single, united entity.

(ii) Individual ministerial responsibility

A governmental decision is seldom so grave that an error in relation to it would warrant the bringing down of a Government. Thus, although from the broad constitutional perspective, collective responsibility is the more important element, it is the individual ministerial doctrine[6] which could potentially be of greater significance in checking undesirable governmental action. According to the individual ministerial doctrine, if a Minister commits certain types of error then there is an obligation on him, and on him alone, to resign. In appropriate circumstances, so the theory runs, a Minister is supposed to resign of his own accord; but if he fails to do this, he must certainly resign if a vote of no confidence in him is passed by the Dáil. The type of error which attracts this duty may be: a personal act of dishonour or indiscretion; a failure of policy; or an act of maladministration within his Department – the latter of which will be considered in greater detail in the next paragraph. Here we need note only that there have been four recent cases of ministerial resignation for what may be broadly termed 'indiscretions'.[7]

As is well known, the individual ministerial doctrine has received mainly lip-service and there have been very few resignations for breach of the doctrine since 1922.[8] In particular, there have been few if any resignations because of what might be regarded as the principal focus of administrative law, namely acts of maladministration within the Minister's department. The main reason for the failure of the doctrine is the lack of a non-partisan agency to determine conclusively when a

---

5 Arts. 28.4.2°; 28.11.1°.
6 There is no reference to this doctrine in the Constitution. However it has been accepted that the rule exists as a convention derived from the relationship of Ministers to the Dáil: see, *e.g.* 187 *Dáil Debates,* Cols. 19–59, March 7, 1961 (second stage of the Mental Treatment (Detention in Approved Institutions) Bill 1961), 256 *Dáil Debates,* Cols. 1473–1501, (November 9, 1970), Cols. 1732–1766 (November 10, 1970) (motion of no confidence in Minister for Agriculture, consequent on the Arms Trial).
7 In the first, the Minister resigned but was immediately re-appointed as a junior minister, the reason being that he had inquired whether his family business could put in a tender for a contract being awarded by a state body. In the second episode, a junior minister resigned became his political adviser had made an advance disclosure of Budget information. Thirdly, a Minister resigned because an extension to his house had been paid for by a businessman. Finally, a Minister resigned because he had received a large donation for his election campaign in circumstances which were considered to be inappropriate. See newspapers for: May 22, 1995; February 3, 1995; December 1, 1996; October 8, 1997, respectively. An earlier example involved the resignation of a Parliamentary Secretary in 1946 because of allegations of a conflict of interest between his official duties and a firm in which he had an interest: see *Report of the Tribunal appointed by the Taoiseach on November 7, 1947* (P.No. 8576).
8 It is possible, though uncommon, for an individual minister to resign, by virtue of the collective responsibility doctrine, when the Minister resigning disagrees with the rest of the Government. For the only such event in recent times see 346 *Dáil Debates,* Cols. 1822–1828 (resignation of Deputy Frank Cluskey because he believed that the terms on which the Government was taking over the assets of the former private company, Dublin Gas, were too generous).

Minister should resign and then, if necessary, to enforce this sanction: as with the collective responsibility doctrine, the Dáil is prevented from playing this part because of the strict party system. There are other reasons for the failure: the single sanction of resignation affords no gradation of sanctions to deal with the varied offences of widely varying culpability which may arise; again, resignation would not even be available as a sanction where the responsible Minister had left office before the error came to light. Moreover, a particular difficulty arises in relation to a type of error which is common in the area of administrative law, namely, abuse of power or an act of maladministration, occurring during the course of routine administration. For in any Department of State, there will be hundreds or thousands of civil servants serving under a Minister and such an error may be wholly the fault of a civil servant.[9] Where the Minister is not personally involved in the error, is it not dogmatic to expect his head to roll?[10] This situation was illustrated in 1961 in the context of the involuntary detention of mental patients. According to the relevant statute, the Minister for Health's permission had to be renewed after every six-month period of detention. The junior civil servant whose task it was to pass on the applications for the Minister's permission fell ill and failed to perform this task, with the result that almost 300 patients were illegally detained. Yet the Minister convincingly brushed aside calls for his resignation as unrealistic on the ground that an appropriate system of administration with properly qualified people, had been provided.[11]

The Government – albeit of a different political stripe – took a similar line in a more recent episode. Officials in the Department of Justice failed to relay it to a member of the Special Criminal Court that he had been 'de-listed' by the Government and, so, was no longer a member of the Court. As a result of this omission, the judge continued to exercise his functions, as a member of the Court – the most significant of which was refusing certain bail applications[12] – for some three months. The ensuing Opposition attacks on the Minister for Justice and by Government spokespersons rebuttal offered little by way of development of the principle under discussion. The Taoiseach remarked that: "Whilst Ministers in this or previous

---

[9] See 187 *Dáil Debates*, Cols. 19–59.

[10] Murray, "A Working and Changeable Instrument" (1982) 30 *Administration* 43 at 52. See also, Wheare, *Maladministration and its Remedies* (1973), Chap. 3; and Murray, "Irish Government Further Observed" (1983) 31 *Administration* 284 at 288–298.

[11] An opposition deputy (Mr Sweetman) stated:

"[The Minister] is the person whose duty it is to see and to ensure that the Department is administered properly in accordance with the directions given to it by this House from time to time . . . [I]t is the Minister who must stand over the actions of the civil servants of Parliament."

The inference he drew was that the Minister ought to resign. The Minister (Mr McEntee) refused because:

" . . . in these matters there must be some realism. It is all very well to say that constitutional justice theory requires that the Minister should accept full responsibility for everything the department does . . . Am I to accept responsibility for the fact that an officer of my Department suffers a breakdown . . . ? Is there anything I could possibly have done to ensure that this would not have occurred?"

This exchange will be found at 187 *Dáil Debates*, Cols. 19–59 (March 7, 1961).

[12] The Minister for Justice then ordered the release of the illegally detained prisoners. However, the prisoners were immediately re-arrested and re-charged upon their release and the legality of this procedure was upheld : see *Hegarty v. Governor of Limerick Prison*, unreported, Divisional High Court, February 26, 1997 and *Quinlivan v. Governor of Portlaoise Prison*, unreported, Supreme Court, November 7, 1997.

governments may not have been punished for the misdeeds of officials, in this Government, Ministers . . . have been willing to take responsibility for *personal* errors".[13] (He went on to refer to the resignations mentioned earlier.[14]) The Minister for Justice suggested[15] that there was a difference between accountability, in the sense that a Minister had to give information to the Dáil and, on the other hand, culpability, meaning that a Minister had to resign, and, that the latter only arose if a Minster, personally, had made some error. The Opposition's response was to the effect that the Minister was indeed personally responsible just because she had failed to establish a reliable system for dealing with correspondence.

The view that the existing model reflects a reality which was designed in mid-Nineteenth century Britain when departments of State were so much smaller than those of today, and is not apt for the present had long been championed by reformers.[16] It led eventually to the Public Service Management Act, 1997. Writing just a few months after the Act became law (early 1998), it is unclear how much impact the Act will make on a system whose roots go back for a century and a half. Most probably, its effect will be gradual, occurring as and when the political elite becomes accustomed to the changes. Accordingly it will be described at the end of this Part,[17] after the status quo has been analysed.

Consequences of individual ministerial doctrine

Although the ministerial responsibility doctrine is such an ineffective rule and, as noted, is presently undergoing reform and qualification, its existence (real or supposed) has had a formative influence upon the machinery for the control of Ministers and Departments in the following ways.

1. It remains the formal position that a Minister is responsible to the Dáil for all activities going on within his Department. In part, as a result of this, the Dáil attempts to shadow too wide an area of government activities and has insufficient time and attention for what should be its principal concern, namely major matters of policy. Thus, for instance, one element of ministerial responsibility to the Dáil is the Minister's duty to answer questions on behalf of his Department. A large proportion of these questions relate to the personal minutiae of constituents[18] and the discussion of these issues tends to crowd out the examination of policy issues. Again, the Dáil's supposed power and duty to police all of a Department's activities impeded the development of other, more effective means of controlling routine actions, for

---

13 47 *Dáil Debates* Col. 651 (Nov. 12, 1996) (Author's emphasis). See also Col. 563 *et. seq.* (Nov. 7, 1996) and Col. 1567 *et. seq.* (Nov. 21, 1996). See also 446 *Dáil Debates* Col 1136 (Oct. 27, 1994) and 447 *Dáil Debates* Col. 346 (Nov. 16, 1994) each of which concerned the Attorney General's responsibility for failure of his senior civil servant to process an extradition warrant promptly.

14 See above n.7, p. 59.

15 471 *Dáil Debates* Col. 669 (Nov. 12, 1996).

16 See pp. 108–109.

17 See pp. 63–66.

18 One-half of all questions to the Minister for the Environment concern individual constituents' problems. This figure is exceeded in the case of the questions for the Minister for Social Welfare: see *The Irish Times*, January 20, 1984.

instance, along the lines first proposed in the note on Administrative Law and Procedure appended to the *Devlin Report*.[19]

2. Another effect of the doctrine is to "politicise" every decision taken in a Department by converting every decision – however minor, technical or inherently non-controversial – into a potential bone of contention in a parliamentary dog-fight, which may affect the credit of the entire Government. One consequence of this was that the caution of an already-cautious civil service was increased in order to obey the supreme obligation of "protecting the Minister". Thus, for instance, files were pushed up from one level of the civil service hierarchy to another so that issues had to be resolved at a higher level than would otherwise be considered necessary. Another result is "'the representations' system [which] helps to perpetuate the misconception that everything can be 'fixed'."[20]

3. The personification of the entire activity of the Department in its Minister (politically, by the ministerial responsibility doctrine and, legally, through the Ministers and Secretaries Act 1924) left no formal position for anyone else, even senior management. The effect of this arrangement was to militate against personal responsibility and initiative on the part of civil servants.[21] One symbol of this was the practice, now fallen into disuse, of civil servants commencing routine letters with the formula, "I am directed by the Minister to . . ."

4. In the past, courts have offered it as a reason (or pretext) to justify a refusal to review some administration actions that "this is a matter for which the Minister is responsible to Parliament". This traditional and unrealistic view – which relied upon a model of Parliament which existed, only for a brief period in mid-nineteenth century Britain, before the growth of the party system and "big government" – is not part of the thinking of the contemporary Irish judiciary.[22] Nevertheless, it was an influence in shaping the doctrine of judicial review, which exists in Ireland today.[23]

---

[19] Prl. 792, App. 1. For more recent literature, see above n.239, p. 108 and n.249, p. 110.

[20] *Ibid.* at 448. This practice reached its climax in the circumstances which led to *Brennan v. Attorney General* [1995] 1 I.R. 612. Here the facts were that – to take the typical year of 1993–over 4,000 petitions were made to the Minister for Justice to use her powers, under the Criminal Justice Act 1951, to commute or remit fines; and well over half of these had been successful.

[21] See *e.g. Delivering Better Government* (May 2, 1996), p. 22 " . . . the existing structures and reporting systems encourage a risk-averse environment where taking personal responsibility is not encouraged . . . "

[22] Indeed in Ireland, this argument has been turned on its head in *Brennan v. Minister for Justice and Attorney General* [1995] 1 I.R. 612 (the facts of which are given in n.20) where Geoghegan J. stated (at 629): "There has been a long-established practice that the Minister does not answer questions in Dáil Eireann relating to individual instances of the exercise of this power. That being so, the only way that the Minister can in practice be held accountable for the proper exercise of the power is by means of judicial review in an appropriate case."

[23] See, *e.g. Liversidge v. Anderson* [1942] A.C. 206 (a case involving individual liberty). See also, the comments of Shaw L.J. in *Raymond v. Att.-Gen.* [1982] Q.B. 839 at 847 on political responsibility for decisions of the D.P.P.: "The safeguard against an unnecessary or gratuitous exercise of this power [to enter a *nolle prosequi*] is that the Director's duties are exercised under the superintendence of the Attorney-General. That officer of the Crown is, in his turn, answerable to Parliament, if it should appear that his or the Director's powers have in any case been abused." See also, Gearty, "Administrative law in the 1980s" (1987) 9 D.U.L.J. (N.S.) 21 at 39–42.

5. To set against these disadvantages, it should be said that the ministerial responsibility is necessary in order to justify the eminently practical *Carltona* doctrine[24] by which duties and powers vested in a Minister may be performed or exercised by officials in his Department. As it was put in *Carltona v. Commissioners of Works:*

> "Constitutionally the decision of such an official is, of course, the decision of the minister. The minister is responsible. It is he who must answer before Parliament for anything that his officials have done under his authority . . . The whole system of departmental organisation and administration is based on the view that ministers, being responsible to Parliament, will see that important duties are committed to experienced officials. If they do not do that, Parliament is the place where complaint must be made against them."[25]

The impact of the Public Service Management Act 1997[26]

The kernel of the Act is section 4(1) which seeks to remedy the mismatch between the responsibility and authority of the civil service by giving "the authority, responsibility and accountability" in respect of a large area of departmental[27] administration to the Secretary, who is re-titled, by section 1, the "Secretary General".[28] It is a little difficult to say what these significant[29] words – "authority, responsibility and accountability" – mean. Their meaning in relation to the Dáil is briefly considered below. One should note that it is not only the Secretary General who is to receive such responsibility: in the case of "specific elements" it may also be transferred to other officers (section 4(1)(c) and section 9).

There are five restrictions and qualifications on this transfer of authority, of which the first is the "strategy statement", upon which a good deal obviously turns. As defined in section 5 of the Act, the "strategy statement" must:

> "(a) comprise the key objectives, outputs and related strategies (including use of resources) of the Department of State or Scheduled Office concerned.
> (b) be prepared in a form and manner in accordance with any directions issued from time to time by the Government, and

---

24 See further, pp. 485–489.

25 [1943] 2 All E.R. 560 at 563. The final, rather dated, sentence in this passage is an example of the point made in para.(4) above.

26 For a surprisingly short discussion, see: 478 *Dáil Debates* Cols. 469–493: 150 *Seanad Debate*, Cols. 1260–1305; [1997–1998] I.C.L.S.A. 27.02.

27 Though note that as well as the provision, mentioned in the text, regarding Departments of State, each of the 'Scheduled Offices' (*i.e.* offices or branches of the public service listed in the Schedule or added to it, by Government order) is to have its managerial "Head" in an equivalent position to the Secretary General But this is subject, in the case of those listed in Part 1 of the Schedule, to the consent of the appropriate constitutional personage *e.g.* the Ceann Comhairle, in the case of the Oireachtas : section 2. For the sake of simplicity, the above account refers only to the Secretary General and Departments and does not refer to the possibilities concerning Scheduled Officers. Take note also of section 12 on cross-departmental arrangements.

28 The new title has been bestowed because it was deemed more appropriate to the principal official in the Department. The Minister for Finance (Deputy Quinn) related to the Senate how the term 'Secretary' had been translated by a Japanese interpreter, for the Japanese Minister for Industry and Trade as "ever-lasting typist".

29 Though *c.f.* Oscar Wilde: "Don't use big words; they mean so little."

(c) be submitted to and approved by the relevant Minister of the Government with or without amendment."

A "strategy statement" for each department must be made every three years and it must be published by being laid before each House of the Oireachtas. Progress reports on implementation must be provided annually or as specified by the Government.[30] Some (non-statutory) strategy statements have already been produced and, for instance, the statement for the Attorney General's Office runs to about 25 pages and contains a fair amount of detail.

Secondly, sections 4(1), 6 and 7 make it clear that the Government or Minister may give directions,[31] provided (in the case of the Ministers) that they are in writing, to the Secretary General as regards any of his obligations (save for those in the personnel field). Thirdly, by section 6, the Secretary General is to be 'accountable to the Minister' for all of his functions. Given the existence of the Minister's right to give directions, noted earlier, what does the word 'accountable' add to the Minister's authority. It must mean at least that the Minister can insist not only on having his questions answered; but also on being kept in touch generally with everything that is going on in his Department.

Next, section 4(1) of the Act states that it is for the Minister to "determin[e] matters of policy", a protean, although difficult term, which is discussed elsewhere,[32] (though, of course the Secretary General must still given advice on policy[33]). The final restriction is that, (despite what is said in sections 4 and 9 about the transfer of authority) by section 3, the Minister is to remain "responsible [presumably to the Dáil] for the performance of functions . . . assigned to the Department pursuant to [the Ministers and Secretaries Code]."

There may be less to the Act than meets the eye. For even under the traditional system, most of the time, Ministers leave the normal running of the Department to civil servants. And, as we have just seen, the new scheme allows Ministers ample instruments of control and authority. Moreover, to shift from the concept of authority to its obverse[34] – responsibility – even under the new régime, the Minister will usually continue to carry the can. That is the constitutional system and, as discussed below, the Act would make only a slight modification to it: politicians are known by name to the public and are, as a group, rather unpopular with it. Through the Dáil, the media – and through them, the public – have access to the doings of politicians which, especially if they are discreditable, make rather good copy.

Whilst the Act largely codifies existing practice, it does make one change (as to the significance of which, time will tell), namely to move some distance in the

---

[30] For the strategy statement, see s.5. S.5(2) provides that all strategy statements must be laid before the Oireachtas.

[31] It seems that there is distinct authority (in sections 6 and 7, for Government and ministerial directions. In relation to the former nothing is said about writing. The Explanatory Memorandum (at p.2) states that "Directions provided for in section 7 are . . . to be confidential documents."

[32] See pp. 4–5.

[33] Whether by virtue of s. 4(1)(d) or the general tradition of the *alter ego* doctrine (described at pp. 487–488), which surely survives the Act.

[34] *cf.* "Power without responsibility, the prerogative of the harlot throughout the Ages". This was Stanley Baldwin's (British Prime Minister, 1923–1924, 1924–1929 and 1935–1937) remark about the position and conduct of the press barons of his era.

direction of giving certain civil servants responsibility to match their authority. In relation to this, we need to consider the Act's impact upon relations between the Minister and/or his Department and, on the other hand, the Dáil. In respect of the Dáil, there may be a problem, at the very least during the early stages. For, as we saw earlier, the Act provides that the Minister is to remain "responsible to the Dáil". And there is no suggestion here that the Minister's responsibility is confined in any way, for example: so as to exclude responsibility for matters within the terms of the strategy statement. Yet at the same time, section 10 obligates not only the Secretary General but also any other officer to "whom . . . responsibility for the performance of functions has been assigned" to appear before an Oireachtas Committee to answer questions. This obligation is also shaped by the Committees of the Houses of the Oireachtas (Compellability, Privileges and Immunities and Immunities of Witnesses) Act 1997, section 15(1) of which precludes a civil servant from "questioning or expressing an opinion on the merits of any policy of the Government or a Minister". Despite this last restriction, there seems room here for the possibility a Minister and a civil servant might speak to the Dáil in contradictory terms. The best hope for avoiding this is that some kind of a self-denying ordinance will develop. Under it, Ministers, while speaking about strategy statement, policy, directions (in other words, the matters outlined above for which they must remain responsible) would not be asked, and not be expected to talk about, matters within the remit of the Secretary General or other civil servants. It is possible that such a Dáil rule could develop in a British "constitutional convention" way. Until such time as a convention of this type does develop, there is a danger of "bumpiness" in the operation of the new system. No doubt there will be some point-scoring in the Dáil and the undermining of the positions of the Minister and (since politicians will probably continue to regard civil servants as non-combatants) to a lesser degree, of the Secretary General A related danger is the possibility that through being publicly identified and associated with the performance of their Department, senior Civil Servants may become, in some degree "politicised".

Another likely consequence is that the new system will strengthen the authority of the Secretary General *vis-à-vis* the Minister. The reason for this is that in the event of a difference of view between the two, the Secretary General will be in a position to draw on the fact that, in regard to certain types of issue, he may have to take some outside responsibility for the policy and, therefore is entitled to some authority in respect of it. This is an inevitable price to pay for making more precise and meaningful the responsibility of senior civil servants.

Next, one should note that the Act is concerned with political and not with legal responsibility of Minister and, thus, for instance, does not affect the *Carltona* doctrine. Finally, one might ask whether the new system established by the 1997 Act is unconstitutional. This contention is based on Article 28.4.2° [35] which provides

---

[35] It seems clear that the 1997 Act does not violate Article 28.2 which provides: "The executive power of the State shall . . . be exercised by or on the authority of the Government." Leaving aside the issue of whether responsibility for any instances of that delphic term, the "executive power of the State" has been delegated, it seems clear that the Minister retains sufficient elements of control (listed in the text) to meet the requirement that it be exercised "on the authority of the Government".

There was a brief discussion of the possibility of unconstitutionality in the Senate Debate: see above, n.26.

that "the Government shall be collectively responsible [to the Dáil] for the Departments . . . administered by the members of the Government." It is eminently sensible to take this as implying, that as a member of the Government, each individual Minister is to administer his Department and to be responsible for so doing. The case in favour of unconstitutionality is solidly grounded on the divergence between the constitutional precept that the apparent Minister is "responsible" and the central provision section 4(1) of the 1997 Act, quoted above, which states that it is the Secretary General who bears "authority, responsibility and accountability" in respect of a large area of departmental administration. As against this, however, there is the cumulative effect of certain cautious features of the Act, most of which have already been noticed. In the first place, the Secretary General's autonomous authority is confined within fairly narrow bounds: apart from advising on policy, (as in the traditional system) he is confined to "managing the Department" within the terms of the strategy statement and the other controls mentioned. For the Minister retains significant controls by way of: the power of giving directions; the Secretary Generals accountability to him; and his own responsibility for policy. Most important of all is the Act's firm statement that the Minister remains responsible, the cost of which – in terms of possible contradiction – we have mentioned. Indeed many of these Ministerial control mechanisms are cast in curiously 'political' language and involve ambiguity and dual control. They do serve however (and may have been included partly for this reason) to equip the Attorney General to argue, in any constitutional action, that ultimate responsibility remains with the Minister. Furthermore, any lawyer assessing the chances of success in such an action would be influenced by the lack of precedents (Irish or foreign) in this area, coupled with the fact that, in such a peculiarly political area, a court would be inclined only to intervene in an extreme case.

2. Legal Structure of the Ministers and Departments

Before independence, the separate executive which was the great anomaly of the Act of Union which fused the British and Irish Parliaments, consisted of about 50 units described variously as "departments", "boards" or "offices". Ireland, it was said, had "as many boards as would make her coffin". The administrative units, some of which were merely the Irish branches of a mainland Department, enjoyed a variety of relationships with the Lord Lieutenant (the formal head of the executive) and the Chief Secretary (a sort of Minister for Irish Affairs who represented the Irish administration in the House of Commons).[36]

The objective of the post-independence Government was to sweep away this *disjecta membra* and to replace it with a uniform system in which the central executive power of the State flowed directly through the members of the Government, so that the Dáil could exercise control over the entire administration (for in those heady days, it was hoped that the Dail would wield substantial influence over Governments). A complementary change was made on the legal plane by the

---

[36] McDowell, *The Irish Administration* (1964); McColgan, "Partition and the Irish *Administration* 1920–1922" (1980) 28 *Administration* 147.

Ministers and Secretaries Act 1924 (a code contemplated at Article 28.12 of the Constitution) which is the chief organic law determining the framework of the executive arm of government.[37]

The 1924 Act established the (say) Minister for Justice as a statutorily-created corporation sole,[38] distinct from the temporary incumbent of the office. Linked with this development was the practice of vesting almost all central government functions[39] in a particular Minister.[40] The 1924 Act provides that "each Department and the powers, duties and functions thereof shall be assigned to and administered by the Minister"[41] but that whenever any power is vested by statute in a Minister, the administration entailed in the exercise of that power is deemed to be allocated to the Department of that Minister.[42] The result of these provisions is that the Minister is not only head of the Department; he also personifies the Department and, as corporation sole, bears responsibility in law for its every action, a responsibility which extends to branches, for example the Revenue Commissioners in the case of the Minister for Finance. At the same time, most, at least, of these actions may be performed by departmental civil servants, rather than the Minister himself (under the cover of the *Carltona* doctrine).[43]

We discussed the impact of the Public Service Management Act 1997 at the end of Part I[44] (which deals with a Minister's political responsibility to the Dáil) since the Act is most likely to make its impact in the field of political, rather than legal, responsibility (and so for instance it has no effect on the *Carltona* doctrine). In political field, an Opposition deputy might wish to argue that a Secretary General had failed to follow a direction from a Minister or a strategy statement. But it is just possible that it would suit a litigant, making a legal case against a Minister to take the same points in order to argue that the decision was invalid. His chances of success would depend upon a variety of factors including: whether some rule analogous to the "internal governance" doctrine of company law were adopted; and the exact legal status of the direction or strategy statement. This latter issue should be considered in the context of the earlier, general discussion of sources of law.[45]

---

[37] Ministers and Secretaries Act 1924, s.9.
[38] 1924 Act, s.2(1). On the Minister as corporation sole, see further, pp. 915–919.
[39] There are a few functions which, in order to mark their importance or to add lustre, are vested in the President or the Government. In addition, a very few functions are vested in designated civil servants. The principal example is the deciding officer-appeals officer in the Department of Social Welfare: see pp. 275–280. Plainly, too, the generalisation in the text does not refer to the functions vested in a state-sponsored body.
[40] Though this is subject to the overriding imperative contained in Art.28.4 of the Constitution that "The Government . . . shall be collectively responsible for the Departments of State administered by the members of the Government." See also Ministers and Secretaries Act 1924, s.5: "Nothing in this Act contained shall derogate from the collective responsibility of the [Government] as provided by the Constitution notwithstanding that members of the [Government] may be appointed individually to be Ministers, heads of particular Departments of State." It is thus open to the Government to direct a Minister as to how a decision should be taken, although the decision has been statutorily vested in a Minister.
[41] 1924 Act, s.1.
[42] Ministers and Secretaries (Amendment) Act 1939, s.6(3). See also, Art. 28.12 of the Constitution and Kiely, "Ministers and Departments" (1986) 7 *Seirbhís Phoiblí* 7. But for *delegatus non potest delegare*, and the *Carltona* doctrine see pp. 485–489.
[43] *Ibid.*
[44] See pp. 63–66.
[45] See pp. 41–57.

Here, too, we ought to emphasise that although the 1997 Act has enlarged the status and responsibility to the Dáil of the Secretary General, it has not altered the Minister's position as corporation sole with complete legal responsibility for the affairs of his Department and associated branches or offices.[46] Consequently the Minister or Ireland remains the appropriate party to litigation.

The Ministers and Secretaries Act 1924 "establish[s] the several (eleven in the original 1924 Act; 15 in 1997) Departments of State amongst which the administration and business of the public services in [the State] shall be distributed."[47] The Act also gives a generalised description of the duties of the Departments[48] which it establishes, of which the following may be taken as representative:

> "The Department of [Justice] shall comprise the administration and business generally of public services in connection with law, justice, public order and police, and all powers, duties and functions connected with the same except such powers . . . as are by law reserved to the Executive Council [now Government] and such powers . . . as are by the Constitution or by law excepted from the authority of the Executive Council or of an Executive Minister and shall include in particular the business, powers, duties and functions of the branches and officers of the public service specified in the Second Part of the Schedule to this Act [which includes the Courts, the Public Record Office and the Registry of Deeds] and of which Department the head shall be, and shall be styled, an t-Aire Dlí agus Cirt or (in English) the Minister for Justice."

Nevertheless, it is the case that almost all governmental functions are created by a specific statute. Such a statute would prevail against the job-description given in the 1924 Act, (of which that of the Minister for Justice has just been quoted as an

---

[46] S.13 of the Public Service Management Act 1997 allows the Government to confer corporate status ("declare . . . to be a corporation sole") on: the Attorney General; Comptroller and Auditor General; Director of Public Prosecutions; or the Ombudsman. But this power does not extend to branches or officers of Departments like (for example) the Revenue Commissioners.

[47] Since June 1997, the full list of Departments of State has been as follows: the Taoiseach; Foreign Affairs; Enterprise, Trade and Employment; Marine and Natural Resources; Public Enterprise; Defence; Agriculture and Food; Finance; Health and Children; Environment and Local Government; Social, Community and Family Affairs; Arts, Heritage, Gaeltacht and the Islands; Justice, Equality and Law Reform; Tourism, Sport and Recreation; and Education and Science.

[48] In this context, one ought to note the proposal put forward by the Taoiseach at the formation of the 1997 Government. This was that Mr David Andrews (and, at that time, Minster for Defence) should hold responsibility for European affairs under the Minister for Foreign Affairs and should be given the title of Minister for Defence and European Affairs. This was criticised by Opposition spokesmen on the basis that:
(i) The Ministers and Secretaries Code states that, in principle, all matters pertaining to foreign affairs should be dealt with by the Department of Foreign Affairs, which is administered by the Minister for Foreign Affairs (1924 Act, ss.1, 1(xi)).
(ii) The Constitution states, in Article 28, that the Government bears "collective responsibility". This is conventionally taken to mean that (apart from the Taoiseach), the Ministers bear equal responsibility. It was said that a position in which one Minister is publicly and officially made subservient to another would be inimical to the notion of 'cabinet government'.
In any event, on the day after the announcement, the Taoiseach 'clarified' the announcement on the basis that Mr Andrews would not have an office in the Department of Foreign Affairs, but would simply, represent Ireland (as an alternate to the Minister for Foreign Affairs) at E.U. Council Meetings or the Anglo-Irish Conference: see *The Irish Times*, June 27 and 28, 1997; 480 *Dáil Debates* Col. 66 (June 26, 1997).

example) even if it involved vesting a function in what would seem, according to that Act, to be an inappropriate Department. What then is the legal (as opposed to informational) purpose of a statutory job-description? In the first place, a Minister is a corporation sole and, as such, he has the capacity to contract, but only for the purpose of his authorised function or purposes incidental thereto. The description in the 1924 Act[49] would be significant in divining what these purposes were and, thus, in determining whether a particular contract were *ultra vires* the Minister's power. In addition the description might be helpful in fixing the scope of a civil servant's employment in the context, for instance, of a tort action against the State.[50] It might also be invoked by the Controller and Auditor General, if he were deciding whether some item fell outside an imprecisely worded vote. And in the context of the Dáil, the statutory description is an indication of the matters for which a Minister is responsible.

Where a new Department, with its ministerial head, is established, then a statute (called a Ministers and Secretaries (Amendment) Act) often has to be passed. A statute is necessary because the creation (or dissolution) of a corporation sole requires an Act of the Oireachtas. Thus the Ministers of (for example) Supplies,[51] Health,[52] Social Welfare,[53] or the Gaeltacht,[54] were not created by the Ministers and Secretaries Act 1924 and so each had to be created by its own amending statute. A statute was also passed when the office of Minister for Supplies was dissolved.[55] However, a new statute is not always necessary because of the device of "the shell of the corporation sole" which was used, for instance in 1987, in the case of the demise of the Minister for the Public Service and the constitution of the Minister for Tourism and Transport.[56] To elaborate: under the Ministers and Secretaries (Amendment) Act 1939, the Government has extensive powers, exercisable by order: to alter the name of any Department or the title of any Minister; to transfer powers between Ministers and the administration of a public service between Departments; or to allocate to any Department the administration of a public service not expressly allocated to a Department. Thus, drawing on these powers, it is possible for the Government to transpose a corporation sole originally established as the legal manifestation of one Minister and Department into the legal haven for a fresh Minister and Department. The Government is also empowered to make "such adaptations of enactments as shall appear to the Government to be consequential on anything done under [these powers]."[57]

---

49 1924 Act, s.1. For the replacement of the title 'Ministry' by 'Department', in 1924, see Fanning, *The Irish Department of Finance, 1922–1958* (1978), p. 39.
50 See pp. 915–919.
51 Ministers and Secretaries (Amendment) Act 1939.
52 Ministers and Secretaries (Amendment) Act 1946.
53 *Ibid.*
54 Ministers and Secretaries (Amendment) Act 1956.
55 Minister for Supplies (Transfer of Functions) Act 1945, s.3.
56 See: Public Service (Transfer of Departmental Administration and Ministerial Functions) Order 1987, No. 81; Public Service (Alteration of Name of Department and Title of Minister) Order 1987, No. 83. (For an explanation of this, see 2nd edition of this book at pp. 61–62.)
57 Act No. 36 of 1939, s.6(1). The words quoted in the text constitute a rare example of a "Henry VIII clause", on which see pp. 12–15. Notice also s.6(1)(e) of the 1939 Act, the neglected provision which empowers the Government, by order "to prescribe the organisation of any Department of State and for that purpose to create units of administration within such Department of State".

Recent Changes

In order to illustrate some of these themes, one can rehearse certain of the recent developments in the organisation of the structure of government business. In the first place, on the formation of the Fianna Fáil-Labour coalition in early 1993, five new Ministers and Departments were established.[58] The corporation sole of the former Minister for Industry and Commerce was re-titled the Minister for Enterprise and Employment.[59] As well as retaining the functions of Industry and Commerce, the new Minister received most of the functions of the former Minister for Labour[60] plus responsibility for Foras[61] and the country enterprise boards, thereby integrating the job promotion efforts. Next, the corporation sole of the former Minister for Labour was re-titled the Minister for Equality and Law Reform[62] and received a transfer of functions, in the civil law reform field, from the Minister for Justice.[63] Thirdly, the former Minister for Energy was re-titled the Minister for Tourism and Transport,[64] receiving tourism and foreign trade functions from the former Ministers for Tourism, Trade and Communications[65] and for Industry and Commerce,[66] respectively.

Fourthly, the former Minister for Tourism, Trade and Communications was re-titled (first the Minster for Transport, Energy and Communications,[67] and, as from 1997, Public Enterprise[68]) receiving energy functions from the former Minister for Energy[69] and thereby taking responsibility for most of the economic infrastructure and many of the commercial state-sponsored bodies. The former Minister for Energy's forestry functions were transferred to the former Minister for Agriculture and Fisheries[70] which was re-titled the Minister for Agriculture, Food and Forestry.[71] Finally, the functions of arts and culture were transferred from the Taoiseach to the

---

[58] 425 *Dáil Debates*, Cols. 618–626 (January 12, 1993). (For changes occurring on the formation of earlier governments, see pp. 61–62 of the 2nd edition of this book.)

[59] Industry and Commerce (Alteration of Name of Department and Title of Minster) Order (S.I. No.19 of 1993).

[60] Labour (Transfer of Departmental Administration and Ministerial Functions) Order (S.I. No.18 of 1993).

[61] See p. 156.

[62] Labour (Alteration of Name of Department and Title of Minster) Order (S.I. No.20 of 1993).

[63] Justice (Transfer of Departmental Administration and Ministerial Functions) Order 1993 (S.I. No. 34 of 1993).

[64] Energy (Alteration of Name of Department and Title of Minister) Order (S.I. No.16 of 1993)

[65] Tourism, Trade and Communications (Transfer of Departmental Administration and Ministerial Functions) Order (S.I. No.15 of 1993).

[66] Tourism, Trade and Communications (Transfer of Departmental Administration and Ministerial Functions) Order (S.I. No.14 of 1993).

[67] Tourism Trade and Communications (Alteration of Name of Department and Title of Minster) Order (S.I. No.17 of 1993).

[68] See Transport, Energy and Communications (Alteration of Name) Order (S.I. No.299 of 1997).

[69] Energy (Transfer of Departmental Administration and Ministerial Functions) Order (S.I. No.12 of 1993).

[70] Energy (Transfer of Departmental Administration and Ministerial Functions) Order (S.I. No.10 of 1993).

[71] Agriculture and Fisheries (Alteration of Name of Department and Title of Minister) Order (S.I. No.11 of 1993).

Minister for the Gealtacht.[72] This was a corporation sole which had been held by Mr Haughey during the period when he also held the office of Taoiseach. The Minister for the Gaeltacht was re-titled the Minister for Arts, Heritage, Gaeltacht and the Islands[73] and put in the charge of a separate incumbent. The broadcasting function was also transferred to the new Minister.[74]

On the formation of the Rainbow Coalition in late 1994, there was no restructuring of the Ministers and Departments.[75] However, on the appointment of the Fianna Fáil/Progressive Democrat Government in 1997, certain changes were effected.[76] For instance, the trade function was transferred from the former Minister for Tourism and Trade to the former Minister for Enterprise and Employment;[77] which was re-titled the Minister for Enterprise, Trade and Employment[78] The Minister for Tourism and Trade was re-titled the Minister for Tourism, Sport and Recreation.[79] The Minister for Justice received a transfer of all the functions in the field of equality and law reform (which it had lost, in 1993) when the Minister for Equality and Law Reform was set up.[80] Its name was changed to the Minister for Justice, Equality and Law Reform.[81] Not being needed for any new Minister, the corporation sole formerly utilised by the Minister for Equality and Law Reform presumably remains in some kind of legal shadow-land until it is required once more in the world of reality. The Minister for the Marine received a transfer of functions in the field of natural resources[82] and its name was changed to the Minister for the Marine and Natural Resources[83] In addition, in order to 'highlight' or 'refocus' some particular area or approach, a number of other changes of name, without transfer of functions was made.[84]

---

[72] Taoiseach (Transfer of Departmental Administration and Ministerial Functions) Order (S.I. No.21 of 1993)

[73] Gaeltacht (Alteration of Name of Department and Title of Minister) Order (S.I. No. 22 of 1993).

[74] Broadcasting (Transfer of Departmental Administration and Ministerial Functions) Order (S.I. No 13 of 1993)

[75] Vol. 447 *Dáil Debates* Cols. 1176–1182 (Dec. 15, 1994).

[76] 480 *Dáil Debates* Cols. 59–66. Appointment of Taoiseach and Nomination of Members of Governnment (June 26, 1997).

[77] Trade (Transfer of Departmental Administration and Ministerial Functions) Order (S.I. No.303 of 1997).

[78] Enterprise and Employment (Alteration of Name of Department and Title of Minister) (S.I. No.305 of 1997).

[79] Tourism and Trade (Alteration of Name of Department and Title of Minister) (S.I. No 304 of 1997).

[80] Equality and Law Reform (Transfer of Departmental Administration and Ministerial Functions) (S.I. No 297 of 1997) and Justice (Transfer) (S.I. No 34 of 1993).

[81] Justice (Alteration of Name of Department and Title of Minister) (S.I. No. 298 of 1997).

[82] Exploration and Mining (Transfer of Departmental Administration and Ministerial Functions) Order (S.I. No.314 of 1997); Forestry (Transfer) Order (S.I. No. 300 of 1997).

[83] Marine (Alteration of Name of Department and Title of Minister) Order (S.I. No. 301 of 1997). Because of the loss of forestry the Minister for Agriculture, Food and Forestry became the Minister for Agriculture and Food (Agriculture, Food and Forestry (Alteration of Name of Department and Title of Minister) Order (S.I. No.302 of 1997)

[84] For bare changes of name, see: Social Welfare (Alteration) Order (S.I. No.307 of 1997) (change of name to Social, Community and Family Affairs); Environment (Alteration of Name of Department and Title of Minister) Order (S.I. No.322 of 1997) (to Environment and Local Government); Transport, Energy and Communications (Alteration) Order (S.I. No.299 of 1997) (to Public Enterprise); Arts, Culture, Gaeltacht and Islands and the (Alteration of Name of Department and Title of Minister) Order (S.I. No.306 of 1997) (to Arts, Heritage and the Islands).

Ministers of the Government and Ministers of State

An apparent paradox arises from the fact that while Article 28.1 of the Constitution[85] fixes the maximum number of members of the Government at 15, there were (until recently) 17 Ministers. However, no difficulty arose from this apparent mis-match, because the Taoiseach, who determines which members of the Government are to be assigned as Ministers to which Department, is free to allocate more than one Department to the same member of the Government[86] (for example, the Departments of Health and Social Welfare often used to be assigned to the same Minister). At the moment as it happens, there are only 15 Ministers.[87] The Taoiseach may also appoint a member of the Government who has no responsibility for a Department, that is a Minister without portfolio.[88]

The Ministers and Secretaries Act 1924 provided for the appointment by the Executive Council of a maximum of seven "parliamentary secretaries" to act as junior Ministers.[89] In 1977, this provision was repealed and replaced by a measure allowing for the appointment of "Ministers of State" from among members of either House to a maximum figure of initially 10 and then 15 (since 1980), and 17 (since 1995).[90] The increase in the number of junior Ministers was explained in the Dáil (in 1977) on the grounds of the greater volume of government business by comparison with that in 1924.[91] The increase also had the effect of enlarging the "pay roll" vote.

In spite of this change of name, the function of these junior Ministers remains the same, that is, to assist the Minister at the head of the Department to which they are assigned by their appointment. One should write "Department or Departments" since their appointment can and sometimes does, straddle more than one Department likewise, more than one Minister of State may be assigned to the same Department.[92] A Government order[93] may be made on the request of a Minister, delegating to his

---

85 By the Irish Free State Constitution, Art.55 (as amended), there was a maximum of 12 members of the Government, though (at various times) nine, ten or eleven were actually appointed.

86 Ministers and Secretaries (Amendment) Act 1946, s.4, replacing Ministers and Secretaries Act 1924, s.3 which had significantly limited wording.

87 See, above n.47.

88 Ministers and Secretaries (Amendment) Act 1939, s.4. The device of a Minister without portfolio has only been availed of twice: once during 1939–1945 when a Minister for the Co-ordination of Defensive Measures was appointed; and, secondly, for a few months in 1977, during a period when a Minister for Economic Planning and Development was appointed before the office had been constituted by the Ministers and Secretaries (Amendment) Act 1977.

89 Ministers and Secretaries Act 1924, s.7.

90 Ministers and Secretaries (Amendment) (No. 2) Act 1977, s.1; Ministers and Secretaries (Amendment) (No. 2) Act 1980, s.2; Ministers and Secretaries (Amendment) Act 1995.

91 301 *Dáil Debates*, Cols. 59–62, November 2, 1977 (Mr Colley).

92 However one should note a further point. In recent years, when the Government has included a small party whose support in the Dáil warrants only a single seat, it has been perceived as a disadvantage that the sole Minister would have no party colleague with whom to discuss Government matters. To meet this difficulty, a party colleague (the so-called 'super junior') who is a Minister of State has been given the right to attend Government meetings (Deputy Pat Rabbitte, 1995–1997, Deputy Molloy, 1997–present). No change has been made in law to reflect this phenomenon. Nor, probably, is any necessary. After all, the Minister of State at the Department of the Taoiseach, (also known as the Chief Whip) has been attending Government meetings, as has the Attorney General for many years.

93 For example, Enterprise, Trade and Employment (Delegation of Ministerial Functions) Order (S.I. Nos. 329 and 330 of 1997) by which separate tranches of functions, dealing with, respectively, insurance and employment were delegated to the two Ministers of State at the Department of Enterprise, Trade and Employment.

Minister of State all the Minister's powers and duties under a particular Act or, more narrowly, any particular statutory power or duty.[94]

Since the functions of a Minister of State are largely the same as those formerly performed by a parliamentary secretary, the change is merely a matter of "image", the need for which has been explained on the grounds that the title "parliamentary secretary" gave people, both at home and internationally, the impression that a very junior Minister was involved. Accordingly, the new title was decreed for the position of junior Minister.[95] Probably because of its use in Britain, the title "Minister of State" was invoked. However, the same style was already in use for "members of the Government having charge of a Department of State,"[96] that is, Government Ministers. This change therefore required a new name for Government Ministers and this is now (in respect of statutes passed after 1977), provided by the title "Minister of the Government".[97]

3. Civil Service : Definitions and Context

The widest term used in this area (though not generally in the context of legislation) is the "public sector", a category which embraces not merely civil servants but all those who are employed, directly or indirectly, by some public body. In 1996, this comprised in all about 277,000 people – 21 per cent of the total number of employees in the country.

A slightly narrower term than the public sector[98] is the public service[99] – those employees whose salary and pension bill (approximately £4.8 billion or 38 per cent of the Government's total current expenditure) is paid for, directly or indirectly, out of public funds – a term which is obviously very significant in economic and financial contexts. Broadly speaking, the public service comprises the public sector less the employees of commercial state-sponsored bodies. At the centre of the public service lies the civil service manning, *inter alia,* the Departments of State. The number of civil servants increased from 28,000 in 1960 to 70,000 in 1983 just before

---

94 Ministers and Secretaries (Amendment) (No.2) Act 1977, s. 2. See also Ministers and Secretaries (Amendment) Act 1939 s.9(2)(e) (Where a function is delegated, the Minister of the Government retains concurrent power with the Minister of State.)

95 On the position generally, see 301 *Dáil Debates* Cols.59. (Nov. 2, 1977). Notice also Cols.726–727 (an interesting constitutional point relating to the right of a Minister of State to speak in the House of which he is not a member).

96 Interpretation Act 1937 (No. 38 of 1937), Schedule, Item 18; Civil Service Regulation Act 1956, s.2(1)(d).

97 Ministers and Secretaries (Amendment) (No. 2) Act 1977, s.4; 301 *Dáil Debates*, Cols. 62–63.

98 Those employed in the public sector are those made up roughly as follows: civil servants (29,000); employees of the health boards (57,000); the state-sponsored bodies (84,000); the local authorities and county committees of agriculture (27,000); security forces (25,000); and educational sector (52,000).

   In a study comparing Ireland with Sweden, Britain, Italy and U.S., Dr Murray concludes that the Irish proportion of persons working in public employment is somewhat below average and that its rate of increase in recent years was also below average and has indeed been reversed in recent years: Murray, "Public Employment Observed" (1989) 10 *Serbhís Phoblí* 32.

99 For a rare statutory example of the use of "public service", see Ministers and Secretaries (Amendment) Act 1973, ss.1, 3 and 5 (setting up the Minister for the Public Service and the Public Service Advisory Council).

the establishment of An Post and Bord Telecom Éireann.[100] In 1986, there were 35,000 civil servants and by 1996? (as a result of the restriction on recruitment and the early retirement scheme of the late 80s) the figure had fallen to 29,000.[101] The numbers and remuneration of the civil servants in each Department, formerly shown in the Book of Estimates, have appeared since 1966 in a separate publication, the *Directory of State Services*.

Civil servant

The constitutional history of the status of a civil servant in independent Ireland is authoritatively sketched in Costello P.'s judgment in *Gilheaney v. The Revenue Commissioners*.[102] This deals with : the position of civil servants transferred from the British Government in Ireland to the Provisional Government of 1921–1922; those transferred from the Provisional Government to the Irish Free State Government; the (temporary) Civil Service Regulation Act 1923; the (permanent) Civil Service Regulation Act 1924; and the (present) Civil Service Regulation Act 1956.[103] This history makes it clear, *inter alios*, that at all times civil servants were "holders of an office and not employees . . . and that their tenure was a tenure at will.[104] The significance of this distinction which was not relevant to the decision in *Gilheaney* itself is examined elsewhere.[105]

It is necessary to define the terms "civil servant" and "civil service" more precisely: for these terms are used in various statutes which provide no definition for the terms and there are also some marginal public posts whose constituent statute does not make it clear whether or not they are civil servants.[106] Most important, the term "civil servant" is used to indicate the scope of both the Civil Service Commissioners Act 1956 which regulates the selection of civil servants and the Civil Service Regulation Act 1956 (which deals with the terms and conditions of civil servants). A useful historical sketch of the terms was given by Kingsmill Moore J. in *McLoughlin v. Minister for Social Welfare* (the facts of which will be given below):

---

[100] For a point arising out of the transfer of staff to these new bodies, see *Flynn v. An Post* [1987] I.R. 68 at 75 at 80–81.

[101] This figure does not include 8,000 industrial civil servants, most of whom are craftsmen or general workers employed in the Department of Fisheries and Forestry or the Office of Public Works. The rules regarding the employment of these civil servants differ to a considerable extent from those affecting the non-industrial civil service, for instance, industrial civil servants are usually in "scheduled" positions (see p. 85, para. 1) and thus not recruited by the Civil Service Commissioners. The closest we can come to a definition of an industrial civil servant is to say that they are serving in those grades which have been designated as "workers" by the Minister for the Public Service for the purposes of the Industrial Relations Act 1946, Pt. VI (which gives the Labour Court power to investigate trade disputes). See also Industrial Relations Act 1969, s.17(1) and Public Service (Transfer of Departmental Administration and Ministerial Functions) Order (S.I. 1973 No. 294). The remaining Parts of this Chapter will deal principally with non-industrial civil servants.

[102] [1996] E.L.R. 25.

[103] *Ibid.* at 32–35.

[104] *Ibid.* at 33–35.

[105] See p. 589.

[106] Though modern statutes frequently state explicitly that the posts they create are to be civil servants, *e.g.* Law Reform Commission Act 1975, s.10(6)(*b*); Ombudsman Act 1980, s.10(2); Staff of the Houses of the Oireachtas Act 1959, s.3; Presidential Establishment Act 1938, s.6. The Ministers and Secretaries Act 1924, s.2(2) does not do this but it is clear that the positions which it contemplates meet the tests for a civil servant given in the text.

"The words 'civil service' and 'civil servant' though in frequent use on the lips of politicians and members of the general public, are not terms of legal art. The British Royal Commission on the Civil Service which reported in 1931 stated that 'there is nowhere any authoritative or exhaustive definition of the civil service.' The phrase seems to have been first used to describe the non-combatant service of the East India Company, and was well established in English political language by the middle of the nineteenth century.

Though it may be difficult to frame an exact definition, it does not seem in any way impossible to reach an approximation to the meaning of the words sufficient to meet the requirements of the present case. In Britain civil servants were servants of the Crown, that is to say, servants of the King in his politic capacity, but not all servants of the Crown were civil servants. Those who used the strong arm – military, naval and police forces – were excluded from the conception, for the service was civil, not combatant; and so also, by tradition, were judges and holders of political offices. Civil servants were paid out of monies voted by parliament and if permanent, had the benefit of the Superannuating Acts. In theory, as servants of the King, they held their positions at pleasure but in practice they were treated as holding during good behaviour . . .

The bulk of British civil servants working in Ireland, were taken into the service of Saorstat Éireann and the phrase, with the ideas attached to it, was assimilated into Irish political life. Soon it made its appearance in the Irish statute book and, after the passing of our present Constitution, in statutes of the Republic. Borderline cases have been dealt with by special legislation. Persons have been deemed to be civil servants for one purpose and deemed not to be civil servants for another. But, if we substitute 'State' for 'King' the summary which I have already given corresponds to the present conception of civil servants in Ireland.

I have no doubt that Mr. McLoughlin is a civil servant. He is a state servant engaged in administering one of the most important of State functions, that of justice: he is paid out of monies voted by the Oireachtas: the situation which he holds was dealt with by a scheduling order under section 10 of the Civil Service Regulation Act, 1924, and such an order could only be properly applicable to a post in the civil service—for its effect is to exclude a situation in the civil service from the operation of the Act."[107]

Partly in the light of this evolution, we can suggest the following guidelines in defining a civil servant. First, civil servants are paid out of moneys provided annually, through the Appropriation Act, by the Oireachtas.[108] Secondly, they serve the various organs of State created by the Constitution, including the President, the Dáil and Senate, the Attorney-General, the Comptroller and Auditor General, the Taoiseach and the other Ministers who are in charge of Departments of State. To this list must be added other offices, like the Ombudsman, which, although established

---

[107] [1958] I.R. 1 at 14–15. Quoted with approval in *Central Bank of Ireland v. Gildea* [1997] 2 I.L.R.M. 391 at 397–398, *per* Keane J.
[108] Civil Service Regulation Act 1956, s.18.

by Act of Parliament,[109] rather than by the Constitution, are plainly constitutional in nature. As might be expected from the term "servant", the actual incumbents of these offices themselves–for instance, the Ministers or the Comptroller and Auditor General or the Ombudsman are not usually[110] created civil servants and other political appointees are also excluded from the category of "civil servants". So, too, are those who help to exercise the military, police or judicial function. Although it involves an element of circularity, it should be noted that civil servants are public officials who are subject to the regime (described in subsequent Parts) which is created by the two 1956 Acts. Finally, the Civil Service Regulations Act 1956, section 20 provides that "for the purposes of this Act", the question of whether a person is a civil servant "shall be decided by the Minister [for Finance], whose decision shall be final". Kingsmill Moore J.'s analysis of the concept of a "civil servant" in *McLoughlin* was quoted with approval in *Murphy v. Minister for Social Welfare*.[111] Here the applicant had been appointed under the Industrial Relations Act 1946, as an ordinary member of the Labour Court. The main issue before the court was the question of whether the applicant was insurable under the Social Welfare (Consolidation) Act 1981. This, in turn depended on whether the applicant was "employ[ed] in the civil service of the Government or the civil service of the State" (in the language of the First Schedule to the Act). In eluciding this difficult problem, Blayney J. first quoted the passage from *McLoughlin* which is reproduced above and then went on to address the question which was before him, as follows:

"In the light of this very useful exposition of the meaning to be attached to the expressions 'civil service' and 'civil servant', the correct test to be applied in determining whether the applicant was a civil servant would appear to be whether he was a servant of the State in its politic capacity, and in my opinion he was. He was a state servant exercising an important function in the area of industrial relations; he was paid out of monies voted by the Oireachtas for the Department of Labour, and he was under the control of the Minister for Labour who could remove him from office for stated reasons: see section 10 of the Industrial Relations Act 1946. The preamble to the same Act stated that it was an 'Act to make further and better provision for promoting harmonious relations between workers and their employers and for this purpose to establish machinery for regulating rates of remuneration and conditions of employment and for the prevention and settlement of trade disputes, and to provide for certain other matters connected with the matters aforesaid.' The Labour Court was one of the instruments created to achieve the aims outlined in the preamble and to implement the terms of the Act. It was created to fulfil an important function in the area of industrial relations. As a member of that court, the applicant was executing the policy of the State and so was engaged in the service of the State."[112]

---

[109] Ombudsman Act 1980, s.2.

[110] The Director of Public Prosecutions is an exception: see Prosecution of Offences Act 1974, s.2(4).

[111] [1987] I.R. 295. See also, *Power v. Minister for Social Welfare* [1987] I.R. 307.

[112] [1987] I.R. at 305. Blayney J. buttressed his conclusion by a distinct argument which is not of such general interest, namely that s.10(6) of the Industrial Relations Act 1946 provides that the Civil Service Regulation Acts 1924 and 1926 shall not apply to members of the Labour Court. "Since

Yet the problem is surely more difficult than might appear from this passage. It is certainly true that the applicant was paid out of a departmental estimate. The second half of the passage seems to hint that industrial relations is a characteristic governmental function. But then the dirigiste state has taken to itself such a diverse collection of functions that this factor does not take the argument very far. More difficulty stems from the problematic statement, in the final sentence, that since "the applicant was executing the policy of the State [he] was engaged in the service of the State." In any case, this assertion brings us up against the major difficulty. This difficulty can be amplified by way of a statement from Kerr and Whyte's *Irish Trade Union Law* (which was written before *Murphy* was decided):

> "The members are paid out of public funds but they are not civil servants nor do they act under instruction from the Minister. In fact, when the Minister for Labour performed the official opening ceremony of the Court's new head-quarters in 1984, he expressly rejected doubts about the Court's independence and stressed that the Government in which he participated was committed to maintaining the Court's unbiased role. At the same ceremony the then Chairman of the Court stressed his determination that the Court would remain a wholly independent forum for the settlement of disputes, which would not act as an arm of government economic policy."[113]

In addition to this significant point about independence, one ought to note that while an ordinary member of the Labour Court is appointed by the Minister for Labour, before doing so, admittedly only as a matter of practice, the Minister consults trade unions. Even more significant is the fact that the Minister must appoint a person who has been nominated, not by the Civil Service Commissioners, but by a "trade union of workers [or employers]." Next, the member's term of office is fixed by the Minister but may not exceed five years. These are not normal features of a civil servant's employment. Finally, it is incomplete to state (as the passage quoted from *Murphy* does) that he may be removed by the Minister since as a matter of law, the consent of the organisation which nominated the member is also necessary. This is a far cry from the traditional notion of the will and pleasure of the Government.[114]

On what has been said so far, it might seem that the decision, in *Murphy*, is at best a marginal one, influenced by a desire to make the applicant eligible for social welfare entitlements. However, there is another point which, it is respectfully suggested, puts it beyond doubt that the applicant was not a civil servant. This argument depends on the fact that, as was stated in the passage quoted from *McLoughlin*, judges and the holders of political office are excluded from the category of civil servants.[115] Now the Labour Court is not, of course, a court of law; nor are its members judges. Rather its basic functions are the provision of conciliation and

---

these Acts applied to civil servants only, if the ordinary members of the Labour Court were not civil servants, the exclusion would not have been necessary." (p. 305) This surely is not a very strong argument: for the provisions in the 1946 Act may have been inserted *ex abundante cautela*.

113 Professional Books 1985, p. 339 (footnotes omitted).
114 For the statutory references, see Industrial Relations Act 1946, s.10(8).
115 The argument examined here was not considered in *Murphy* where Blayney J. said, in a different context, that Kingsmill Moore J. had stated in *McLoughlin* that "any service of the State which is

mediation services. However, it is suggested that the factors adduced in the paragraph quoted from Messrs. Kerr and Whyte's book mean that, so far as distance from the civil service is concerned, Labour Court members may, by analogy, be regarded as on a par with such personages as judges, politicians or the Ombudsman.

To generalise the issue: there are a number of what may be regarded as satellites of Departments which for policy reasons have always been regarded as needing some independence from the Minister. Among them are: the Revenue Commissioners; the Land Registry; the Civil Service Commission; the Local Appointments Commission.[116] These entities are usually staffed by civil servants (a matter to which we shall return in the context of the distinction between civil servants of the Government and of the State). In some cases, the heads of these entities, like the members of the Labour Court, enjoy some distinctive element in their statutory position which reflects the convention upholding their independence. If *Murphy* is to be followed faithfully, the heads of these bodies must also be classified as civil servants. It is suggested that because of the need for independence, this is an undesirable result and, in a broad sense, unconstitutional. This view certainly derives some support from the underlying tenor of the judgment in the Supreme Court in *McLoughlin* (examined below) though, as we shall see, the precise issue in that case was different from that in *Murphy*.

A further point which emerges from this discussion is that it is possible to be in the service of the State, yet not in the *civil* service of the State. This is clear from the passage quoted from Kingsmill Moore J.'s judgment in *McLoughlin*, in particular from the following:

> "not all servants of the Crown were civil servants. Those who used the strong arm – military, naval and police forces – were excluded from the conception, for the service was civil, not combatant; and so also, by tradition, were judges and holders of political office."[117]

It has also been suggested, in the previous paragraphs, that members of the Labour Court might be added to this intermediate category which may be described as employment "by the State", as opposed to "under the State" which probably means in the civil service of the Government.[118] More difficult is the question of what significance attaches to membership of this category of non-civil-servant state servants. The most that can be said is that, negatively, they are not subject to the 1956 Acts and on the positive side, the State is vicariously liable for their torts. Next, one should note that the action *per quod servitium amisit* cannot be taken by the State in respect of its "servants" (regardless of whether they are civil servants or not). This was established in *Attorney-General v. Ryan's Car Hire Ltd*[119] on the

---

not 'combatant' is entitled to be described as 'civil'" [1987] I.R. 305. As can be seen from the quotation in the text, this overlooks Kingsmill Moore J.'s reference to judges and politicians.

[116] On the Civil Service Commissioners and the Revenue Commissioners, see pp. 115–116, respectively.

[117] [1958] I.R. 14–15. See also, *Murphy v. Minister for Social Welfare* [1987] I.R. 305.

[118] See pp. 79–81.

[119] [1965] I.R. 642. This case reversed a stream of contrary authority: *Attorney General v. Dublin United Tramways Co.* [1939] I.R. 590; *Minister for Finance v. O'Brien* [1949] I.R. 91; *Attorney-General v. Coras Iompair Éireann* 90 I.L.T.R. 139.

ground that "service [to the State] is different in kind from that required or existing in the ordinary master and servant relationship."[120]

Finally, consider *Central Bank of Ireland v. Gildea*.[121] Here the net issue before the Supreme Court was whether the respondent – who had been a security guard employed by the appellant – was employed "by or under the State" within the meaning of the exemption from the Unfair Dismissals Act 1977, contained in section 2(1)(h). Finding that the respondent did not come within the exempt category, Keane J. stated:

> "[The respondent] is not a member of the staff of any of the organs of state created by the Constitution and accorded a role in the constitutional order separate and distinct from the three organs of government, legislative, executive, and judicial, such as the Attorney General. He is not a civil servant in any of the departments responsible to the individual Ministers who constitute the Government and hence is not a 'civil servant of the Government' and thus a person 'employed . . . under the state'. He is employed by a body which has been created by statute, the powers of which, however essential they may be to the functioning of the State, can be removed from them at any stage by the Oireachtas. He is thus in no different position from those employed in a vast range of what have come to be called 'semi-state bodies', the employees of which may, by specific legislative provision, be deemed to be civil servants but who, in the absence of any such provision are not to be so regarded."[122]

Civil servant of the Government or the State?

The distinction between a civil servant of the State and a civil servant of the Government was not at issue in *Murphy*, since the statutory category which was at the heart of that case embraced both types of civil servant. By contrast, this distinction was the central issue, indeed was drawn for the first time – in *McLoughlin*. The plaintiff was a temporary assistant solicitor in the Chief State Solicitor's office, which is one of the services assigned to the Attorney-General by the Ninth Part of the Schedule to the Ministers and Secretaries Act 1924. He argued that he was not to be regarded as being employed in the "civil service of the Government" and hence was not an "employed contributor" for the purposes of the Social Welfare Act 1952. The majority of the Supreme Court ignored the powerful literal argument which swayed the dissenting judge,[123] founding itself instead on the following high constitutional principle: a civil servant is a servant of the State and the State has many organs, including not only the Government, but also the President, the Oireachtas, the Comptroller and Auditor General and the Attorney-General. It is necessary for the proper functioning of each organ that it should be free and

---

120 [1965] I.R. 664.
121 [1997] 2 I.LR.M. 391.
122 *Ibid.* at 399–400.
123 The dissenting judge, Maguire C.J., relied on a narrower argument, which is peculiar to the Attorney-General (and does not extend to the President, etc.), namely, that by the 1924 Act, s.1 the administration of any public services which are not located in any of the other Departments of State is vested in the Department of the Taoiseach: see [1958] I.R. 11–12, 19–20, 23–24.

independent of any other organ of the State. Specifically, it is vital for the Attorney-General to be independent of the Government. It follows that the Attorney's staff should not be subject to the instructions of the Government or any of its Ministers and, thus, that they should be classified as civil servants of the State and not of the Government. Following this line of reasoning, the term "civil servant of the State" is now applied, by post-*McLoughlin* statutes, to the staff of other major organs of State including the President, the Oireachtas and the Ombudsman.[124] Not only the Attorney-General, but also the other organs of State listed earlier, need to be independent of the Government and its Ministers and so it seems that their staff too must be classed as being in the civil service of the State.

The logic of the derivation of the two terms is such that the term "civil service of the State" ought to include both the "civil service of the Government" and the staff working for the Attorney-General, etc.[125] In fact, common usage is to treat the two terms as if they were mutually exclusive. A further point which has emerged in a field prolific in terminological conundra is that "a civil servant of the Government" may be a misnomer since civil servants cannot be in the employment of the Government.[126] Instead it has been judicially suggested that the better term would be "persons employed . . . under the State."[127] But this suggestion has not been taken up.

The basis of the decision in *McLoughlin* was that since, in respect of some of his functions, the Attorney-General needed to be independent so, too, did his staff. If this be true of the Attorney, how much more so is it true of the judiciary? For the Attorney might himself be regarded as at least a semi-detached politician in that as one of his functions (by today his only substantial function) he is the Government's legal adviser. In addition, he leaves office with the Government. By contrast, the independence of the judiciary is a major premise of the Constitution and, indeed, is stated expressly in Article 34.5.1° of the Constitution. In the light of this, it is striking that court staff are regarded as civil servants of the Government, indeed, operate as a unit of the Department of Justice. The possibility for a conflict of interest appears obvious. It seems clear then, following the reasoning in *McLoughlin*, that court staff ought to enjoy the status of civil servants of the State. And for such a change of status to have substance, certain statutory amendments removing any say in the appointment and dismissal of court staff from the Government would have to be made.

The need, referred to in the last paragraph to mark the significance of the distinction between a civil servant of the Government and the State by some real differences in regard to the appointment and removal of the two categories of civil servant has not been taken into account in the legislation. For despite the fundamental principle enunciated by the Supreme Court in *McLoughlin* the Civil Service Commissioners Act 1956 and the Civil Service Regulation Act 1956 (which were

---

[124] Presidential Establishment Act 1938, s.6 ; Staff of the Houses of the Oireachtas Act 1959, s.3; Law Reform Commission Act 1975, s.10(6)(b) and Ombudsman Act 1980, s.10(2).

[125] *cf. Byrne v. Ireland* [1972] I.R. 241 at 286; quoted, apparently, with approval in *Gildea* [1997] 2 I.L.R.M. 391 at 398.

[126] See *Byrne* [1972] I.R. at 285–287, cited with approval by Keane J. in *Gildea* [1997] 2 I.L.R.M. 391 at 398. As to why civil servants cannot be in the employment of the Government, see pp. 917–918, including n.53.

[127] *Gildea* [1997] 2 I.L.R.M 391 at 397–398.

enacted just after *McLoughlin*), each applies a common regime to the civil service of the State and of the Government. The distinction between these two categories has thus been collapsed in that each statute is made to apply to the "civil service" which is defined in the interpretation sections to include both the civil service of the State and of the Government.[128] But this draftsman's legerdemain cannot dissolve a difference of substance which stems from the special position of independence which (in most cases) the Constitution requires the organs of State to possess.

4. Appointment and Selection

The framework of rules governing the appointment, selection, dismissal and conditions of employment of civil servants is largely statutory. However, by way of warning, in connection with the description which follows, it must be emphasised that there are also extra-statutory rules, often contained in circulars, which in practice often make a greater impact than the statute. This is related to the fact that all sections of the public sector are heavily unionised.

In the first place, it must be noted that decisions regarding the creation of new posts in the civil service, including their numbers and the grade at which they are located, are, by statute, taken by the Minister for Finance.[129] However, as mentioned in Part 7, since Administrative Budgets were established in 1991, there has been a substantial delegation of this function.

The Secretary General, is appointed by the Government on the recommendation of the Minister responsible for the Department involved.[130] Otherwise, all the civil servants in a Department are *formally* appointed by the Minister of that Department or (when the 1997 Act takes effect here[131] in the case of staff below Principal level) Secretary General. Appointment is also subject to the power of veto of the Minister for Finance[132] (which has been waived in the case of higher executive officers and posts at lower levels). But there is a distinction between appointment and selection for, as explained below, the authority of each Minister will be overridden in the many cases in which the candidate is actually selected either by the Civil Service Commissioners[133] or by the Top Level Appointments Committee.

Although all promotions are, technically, appointments, an important initial question is whether or not the post is to be "promotional" in the sense that competition for it is to be confined to existing civil servants, either in the Department

---

[128] The Acts define the terms very slightly differently: see Civil Service Commissioners Act 1956, s.3(1) and Civil Service Regulation Act 1956, s.2(1).

[129] Civil Service Regulation Act 1956, s.17(1)*(b)*; Ministers and Secretaries Act 1924, s.2(2).

[130] Ministers and Secretaries Act 1924, s.2(2).

[131] See Public Service Management Act 1997, s. 4(1)(h). But note that the Explanatory Memorandum to the Act indicated that this provision is not to come into effect until the appropriate amendments to the Civil Service Commissioners Act 1956 are enacted and this depends upon agreement with the civil service unions which (as of November, 1997) had not been reached.

[132] Ministers and Secretaries Act 1924, s.2(2).

[133] In the 1920s, soon after the establishment of the Civil Service Commissioners, a Minister refused to accept the candidate selected by the Commissioners. However, they persisted and the Minister eventually accepted their selection. So far as is known, the Commissioner's other decisions have been accepted, without demur.

in which it arises or throughout the entire civil service. This question is settled by the Minister for the Department involved, in consultation with the Minister for Finance, following negotiations with the civil service unions. Where the post is not promotional, it will usually be because the post is at a basic recruitment grade: competition for it will necessarily be open to all and selection will usually be by the Civil Service Commissioners: see below.[134]

Promotional posts

For higher posts, the competition will usually be promotional, *i.e.* confined either to the particular Department or at least to the civil service. In this case, the *modus operandi* for selection is not fixed by statute, but is determined by the Minister in whose Department the vacancy exists,[135] in consultation with his senior officials. There is an exception to this in the case of senior appointments which fall within the jurisdiction of the Top Level Appointments Committee, described in the following paragraph. However, where the exception does not apply and the *modus operandi* is determined by the Minister, he may hold a formal competition of the interview-board type, possibly operated by the Civil Service Commissioners on an agency basis; or he may observe the "seniority rule".[136] Where, unusually, the outcome of the selection process is a promotion which is not "in the customary course of promotion or transfer", as that course had been decided by the Commissioners, for instance from Engineer to Assistant Principal (crossing class barriers) the Civil Service Commissioners must be involved because the appointment is subject to the Commissioners certifying (by a process commonly known as "recertification") that the person selected is qualified as regards knowledge, ability and health for the post.[137]

Promotion via the Top Level Appointments Committee[138]

The jurisdiction of this Committee extends to posts at Assistant Secretary level or above (including non-general service grades) in all Departments, subject to the significant exceptions set out below.[139] Its main purpose was to get away from the tendency, which existed before the Committee was established in January 1984, for

---

[134] Civil Servants of the State are usually appointed by a Minister: see, *e.g.* Civil Service Regulation Act 1956, s.19; Ombudsman Act 1980, s.10(1)(*b*). But *cf.* Staff of the Houses of the Oireachtas Act 1959, s.8.

[135] Ministers and Secretaries Act 1924, s.2(2); Civil Service Commissioners Act 1956, ss.13(2), 14(2). Sometimes, even in these circumstances, the Minister for the Public Service may prefer to ask the Commissioners to hold a competition under the Civil Service Commissioners Act 1956, s.29(1)(*b*). Such competitions are often held on a service-wide basis for promotion from Executive Officer to Higher Executive Officer.

[136] For an account of a dispute arising from the Minister for the Public Service's decision to appoint a candidate who was fifteenth in order of seniority, see *The Irish Press*, November 10, 1983.

[137] Civil Service Commissioners Act 1956, ss.18–24.

[138] This section draws heavily on Murray, "The Top Level Appointments Committee" (1988) 9 *Seirbhís Phoiblí 1*, 10.

[139] Six posts at Secretary General level are excluded from the process: Department of Finance; Public Service Management and Development; Department of Finance; Taoiseach; Government; Foreign Affairs; and Chairman of the Revenue Commissioners. In addition, Assistant Secretary posts in the Departments of Foreign Affairs, including Ambassador posts at this level are not filled through TLAC.

a post to go automatically to a senior, if not the most senior, contender from within the same Department. While the new system does accommodate the possibility of open competition its main element is automatic, inter-departmental competition for the posts to which it applies. The Committee is also supposed, where this is possible, to make its decision irrespective of a candidate's background, in other words to overlook the dual structure of professional and general service streams.

The Committee consists of: the Secretary to the Government; the Secretary (Public Service Management and Development) Department of Finance (Chairman); Secretary General to the Government; two Secretary Generals of Departments and a person drawn from the private sector, each chosen by the Taoiseach after consultation with the Minister for Finance; and, in the case of the appointment of a Secretary, the outgoing incumbent. The new system is not established by statute and so it is still subject to the statutory provisions, already mentioned, by which it is the Government which appoints the Secretary of a Department and the responsible Minister who appoints to the other posts. Accordingly as a matter of law (leaving aside the possibility of the new doctrine of legitimate expectations), all that the committee may do is to make recommendations. No information has been published as to whether the Committee's recommendations have been accepted in all cases. However, it seems likely that, this has been the case.[140] Other more serious restrictions have been built into the process. Thus, the Secretary of the Department in which the vacancy exists may nominate two applicants who appear before the committee without having to be interviewed by the Civil Service Commissioners, which is a part of the process for the other candidates. Secondly, in the case of a post of Secretary, since 1987 the Committee has been required to recommend three candidates, without ranking them so that the Government may choose among them.

As regards the success of the Committee in achieving its objectives, Dr. Murray (Secretary in the Department of Finance, 1969–1976) remarks "[t]he Committee has achieved some success in promoting inter-departmental mobility at senior level, but the record is hardly outstanding, except perhaps at Secretary level."[141] (Although, notice that Dr Murray's study treats all candidates from the same Department as being within the same category. Yet this classification inevitably overlooks the occasions when, as a result of the involvement of the TLAC, the best candidate is appointed in a situation where, without TLAC, a Minister would be compelled to

---

140 Murray, *ibid.*. refers to a rumour that one recommendation involving an Assistant Secretary post was accepted only after an initial refusal.

141 *Ibid.* at 15. This conclusion is drawn from the figures for the Committee's work during the period January 1984 to mid–1987. The chart given below updates the figures in Dr Murray's article by adding in the details of later appointments by the TLAC (the figures were published in (1988) 9 *Serbhís Phoblí* 9 at 20 and (1989) 10 *Serbhís Phoblí* at 51) so bringing the figures up to the end of 1989. However the later figures appear to lead to the same conclusion as the earlier ones.

	Filled Outside Dept.	Filled Inside Dept.	Total
Secretaries and Equivalent	5	8	13
Deputy and Assistant Secretaries	13	55	68
Professional Technical Posts	3	18	21

appoint the 'favourite son' or the senior candidate.)[142] However, a report detailing the work of TLAC to late 1997 is presently being finalised and is expected to be published soon. In contrast to the earlier study, this shows a substantial amount of inter-departmental mobility.

Basic recruitment posts: selection by Civil Service Commissioners

As already stated, appointment to most basic recruitment posts is a formality since the selection for most of these posts must be made by the independent Civil Service Commissioners,[143] first set up in 1923,[144] but presently constituted under the Civil Service Commissioners Act 1956. The object of this system is to prevent jobbery and nepotism. Although the Act purports to state that the Commissioners are dismissible at "the will and pleasure of the Government,"[145] their independence has been consistently respected since the foundation of the State. They have carried their independence to the lengths of (for example) giving the Department involved the name of only the candidate placed first in the competition for a particular post and refusing to disclose whether any other candidates were regarded as qualified (something which is obviously unhelpful to the Department if it comes to bargaining over salary). According to the Act, the Commissioners are appointed by the Government, but the convention is for the Ceann Comhairle to be *ex officio* Chairman of the Commissioners and the other two members to be the Secretary to the Government and an official from the Department of Finance (usually the Director of Recruitment in the Department (an Assistant Secretary)). Their staff, who are appointed by the Minister for Finance[146] service both the Civil Service Commissioners and the Local Appointments Commission.

Subject to the exceptions to be outlined below, all civil servants must be selected by the Commissioners, and the person whom they recommend is invariably appointed.[147] Indeed, in practice the names of persons selected for appointment to

---

142 A point of interest here concerns senior posts in the administration of the courts, for instance registrars. Here the *modus operandi* seems to be that the appointing authority, under the appropriate statute is joined by members of the TLAC. In consequence, the involvement of these 'outsiders' can be offered as an 'excuse' if the senior candidate is not appointed.

143 Civil Service Commissioners Act 1956, ss.13(1) and 14(1).

144 Civil Service Regulation Act 1923; Civil Service Regulation Act 1924. See also Fanning, *The Irish Department of Finance 1922–1958* (1978), pp. 63–72. Lee, *Ireland 1912–1985*, p.107 comments: "Perhaps the major achievement of the early years, and it remains one of the most remarkable achievements in the history of the state, was the creation of a Civil Service Commission, consisting of the Ceann Comhairle (Speaker), and two civil servants, to preside over the public appointments process. The new government was naturally deluged with importunities for jobs. The scope for casualness in the appointments process was considerable. The Civil Service Commission did the state great service in setting ethical standards. Given the scope for corruption permitted by the feeble sense of public morality, the imposition of a high degree of integrity in appointments to the central administration verged on the miraculous. The same considerations did not apply to promotion within the civil service, where the criterion of seniority soon took precedence over that of merit even among men themselves originally appointed on grounds of merit. Nevertheless, this was at the time a relatively venial transgression of the code of strict personal integrity which would be rightly regarded as one of the glories of the civil service."

145 Civil Service Commissioners Act 1956, s.10(1).

146 *Ibid.* ss.13(1), 14(1).

147 The language of the statute makes this point even clearer in the case of the Local Appointments Commission: see Local Authorities (Officers and Employees) Act 1926, s.6(4) and *The State*

the basic general service grades are not even submitted to the Minister concerned.

In filling an established or an unestablished post, the Commissioners must hold a competition.[148] The competition is governed by regulations made by the Commissioners (subject to the consent of the Minister for Finance), dealing with such matters as, for example, the qualifications of candidates (*e.g.* Irish citizens only,[149] or certain specified academic qualifications).[150] The Commissioners must make their selection in accordance with the order of merit, as determined under the regulations, but only from amongst candidates whom they regard as qualified for appointment.[151]

Selection in which Commissioners not involved

There are various exceptional initial appointments[152] in which the Commissioners are not involved. In addition to the appointment of Secretaries of Departments and promotions, already described, these exceptions include the following posts.

1. Certain posts are listed in the Schedule to the Civil Service Commissioners Act, for instance, porters, messengers and cleaners.[153] The method of recruitment to such posts is left to the individual Departments.

2. The Commissioners may, on the request of "the appropriate authority" (almost always the Minister for the Department involved) and with the consent of the Minister for Finance, (assuming that he is not the appropriate authority) declare that posts of a specified grade are an "excluded position". In this case too, recruitment is done by the individual Department and is often a patronage appointment. "Excluded position" orders (which are usually only for a limited period) must be publicised by a notice in *Iris Oifigiúil* and can only be made in respect of un-established positions.[154] The Commissioners will only give their permission if the

---

(Minister for Local Government) v. Sligo Corporation (1935) 69 I.L.T.R. 72. See also, Local Appointments 1926–1972 (Anniversary Booklet), p. 11.

[148] Civil Service Commissioners Act 1956, s.13(1), 14(1).

[149] On this point, attention must now be paid to decisions like *Re Colgan* [1997] 1 C.M.L.R. 53 a decision of the Northern Ireland High Court and *E.C. Commission v. Luxembourg* (Case C–473/93) [1996] 3 C.M.L.R. 981) regarding the E.U. principle of equality of treatment and the scope of public service derogation in Article 48(4) of the E.U. Treaty. (*Colgan* also involved equality of treatment in domestic law.)

[150] *Ibid.* ss.15, 16 and 30. For an example, see *The State (Cussen) v. Brennan* [1981] I.R. 181, 305.

[151] Civil Service Commissioners Act 1956, s.17.

[152] There has been a complicated series of changes affecting female civil servants who, by virtue of the Civil Service Regulation Act 1956, s.10 had been forced to retire on marriage (though, because of s.11, they could be re-admitted if they were widowed). During the period 1973–1996, the Civil Service (Employment of Married Women) Act 1973 abolished the restriction for the future and also, extended the re-instatement scheme to include not only widows but also a woman in respect of whom it is established that she was not being supported by her husband. These women could be re-instated, subject to both the consent of the Minister for Finance and to the Commissioners certifying that an applicant was qualified as regards knowledge, ability and health: 1956 Act, s.2. The provision regarding women not being supported by their husbands was held by the Employment Appeals Tribunal to be discriminatory against married women under the Employment Equality Act 1977 (*Moran v. Revenue Commissioners* [1991] E.L.R. 187). It was repealed by the Civil Service Regulation (Amendment) Act 1996 (No.13 of 1996) on which see (1996) ICLSA Rel. 52. However by now, in any case, very few of those forced to resign, before 1973, would be young enough to apply.

[153] Civil Service Commissioners Act 1956, ss.4.6(2)(*b*) and First Sched.

[154] Civil Service Commissioners Act 1956, ss.5, 6(2)(*c*). Cf. *The State (Minister for Local Government) v. Ennis U.D.C.* [1939] I.R. 258.

appropriate authority can make a good case (*e.g.* need for speed in obtaining staff or need to recruit local staff). Special Advisers and Programme Managers, who are political advisers to a Minister were usually appointed to an unestablished, temporary post for the life of the Government, by an excluding order; now that the Public Service Management Act 1997 is in operation their position will exist by virtue of section 11 of that Act.

3. An individual may be appointed to a particular post (either established or unestablished), without the intervention of the Commissioners, if the appropriate authority with the consent of the Minister for Finance recommends the appointment and the Government decides that it would be "in the public interest".[155] Publicity must be given to such unusual appointments in the form of a notice in *Iris Oifigiúil*.[156] This exemption has been used, for instance, in the appointment of persons formerly employed by public bodies which have become defunct, such as the Hospitals Commission.

5. Dismissal and Discipline

Dismissal

Under the Civil Service Regulation Act 1956, section 5, every established[157] civil servant (a category which now catches the bulk of civil servants) "shall hold office at the will and pleasure of the Government". Note, however, that as explained below, the 1956 Act will soon have to be read subject to the significant change introduced by the Public Service Management Act 1997. Read in isolation, the 1956 Act would mean that established civil servants could be dismissed for any or no reason and that the procedure followed would be immaterial. The inspiration behind this remarkable provision is the legally insecure position of the British Crown servant.[158] This owes its origin to the exigencies of British history – frequently in the military

---

155 Civil Service Commissioners Act 1956, ss.13(3), 14(3). See *Aughey v. Ireland* [1986] I.L.R.M. 206 for discontent with possible abuses of the analogous "exceptional" system of promotion in the Garda Síochána (authorised by Garda Síochána (Promotion) Regulations 1960 (S.I. 1960 No. 203), Art. 5(2)). This provides: "Promotion of Guards who have shown special zeal and ability in the performance of their duties notwithstanding that they may not have passed class 3 promotion examinations or the Irish proficiency test").

156 Civil Service Commissioners Act 1956, s.27(1).

157 For certain purposes, the régime for the employment of civil servants distinguishes between established and unestablished positions, according to whether the position is one in respect of which a pension may be granted under the Superannuation Act 1834. Note that as regards pension rights, the Superannuation Acts of 1936, 1942, 1946, 1947 and 1954 have merely incorporated 19th–century British legislation (see Superannuation Act 1834, s.30; Superannuation Act 1859). By virtue of s.2 of the 1859 Act the decision of the Minister for Finance as to any claim for a pension "shall be final". See further Emden, *The Civil Servant in the Law and the Constitution* (1923), pp. 25–31 and App. I. There is now also a non-statutory pension scheme for unestablished civil servants.

158 For a summary of the legal position of the Crown servants in Britain and the Commonwealth, see Marshall, "The Legal Relationship between the State and its Servants in the Commonwealth" (1966) 15 I.C.L.Q. 150 and Fredman and Morris, "Civil Servants: A Contract of Employment?" [1988] P.L. 58. See also, *B.B.C. v. Johns* [1965] Ch. 32 and *Council of Civil Service Unions v. Minister for the Public Service* [1985] A.C. 385. For the wider rule that the executive cannot fetter its discretionary powers, see pp. 862–863.

and/or colonial context – which were thought to require the power of immediate dismissal of a Crown servant unhampered by any fear of legal consequences[159]; and also to the authoritarian culture which underlay the Royal Prerogative.

The power to dismiss at pleasure, bestowed by a literal reading of section 5, is probably unconstitutional on two counts.[160] First, it violates the civil servant's right to constitutional justice. Secondly, unless the provision were reinterpreted very drastically in the light of the presumption of constitutionality, it would allow dismissal on unreasonable or unconstitutional grounds, for instance, a dismissal which was motivated by religious discrimination.

In fact, the practice is such that those dismissals as do occur are almost certainly within the Constitution. For dismissals only occur on plainly justifiable grounds, often where a crime of dishonesty has either been proved before a court or, at least, is strongly suspected. And as regards procedure, the practice is to inform the civil servant why his dismissal is being contemplated and to allow him an opportunity to put his side of the case to the entire Government in written form. No doubt, as a consequence, the percentage of established civil servants who have had to be dismissed has always been unnaturally low, by comparison either with employees in the private sector or even with unestablished civil servants.

This last requirement is obviously highly impracticable. Following numerous pleas for reform, improvement has begun to come in the form of section 4(1)(h) of the Public Service Management Act 1997 which vests, in the Secretary General,[161] (or the Head, in the case of a Scheduled Office[162]) "the authority, responsibility and acccountability . . . managing all matters pertaining to appointment, performance, discipline and dismissal of staff" in his Department. There are certain restrictions upon this change. In the first place, the provision itself states that it is made subject to the existing legislation in the field and the Explanatory Memorandum (dated March, 1997) states that it will not come into effect until amendments to the [Civil Service Regulation] Act, at present being prepared by the Minister for Finance, are enacted". And (as of November, 1997) these awaited agreement with the civil service unions. Secondly, the provision is to apply only in the case of staff below the grade of Principal. Finally, while the significant formula ("appointments, performance . . . ") is intended to cover the personnel field in a comprehensive way, it omits "selection" which, as we saw in Part 4, is and remains a matter principally for the Civil Service Commissioners. Perhaps surprisingly, the 1997 Act does not alter the substance of section 5 of the 1956 Act ("will and pleasure").

The legislation controlling dismissal was given a particularly stringent interpretation in *Whelan v. Minister for Justice*[163] a case stemming from the dismissal of a probationer civil servant (a prison officer). The salient point in the case was

---

[159] *cf. Garvey v. Ireland* [1981] I.R. 75 at 95–97.
[160] See Casey, "Natural and Constitutional Justice: The Policeman's Lot Improved" (1979–1980) 2 D.U.L.J. (N.S.) 95 at 99–100. An unestablished civil servant may be removed by the appropriate authority: Civil Service Regulation Act 1956, s.6.
[161] The Explanatory Memorandum accompanying the 1997 Act, p.1 states that "these [new] responsibilities will be exercised in addition to the function which a Secretary normally exercises at present in the routine management of all staff."
[162] See above n.27, p. 63.
[163] [1991] 2 I.R. 241.

that the applicant had not been dismissed until a few weeks after the termination of his two-year probationary period. However, by the governing legislation in the case of probationers (section 7 of the 1956 Act, as amended by section 3 of the Civil Service Regulation (Amendment) Act 1958) it is "during the civil servant's probationary period" that the appropriate authority – in this case, the Minister for Justice – is required to be "satisfied that [a probationer] has failed to fulfil the conditions of probation attaching to his probationary position."[164] The only evidence before the High Court was a minute issued by the Prisons' Personnel Section of the Department of Justice, stating that the Minister for Justice had determined that the applicant had failed to fulfil the conditions of his probation in that his sick absence record was unsatisfactory (a point which was not contested). The significant finding of fact was that this communication was *dated* after the termination of the probationary period. And, according to Blayney J.: "there is no evidence that prior to that date the respondent was satisfied that the applicant had failed to fulfil the conditions of his probation."[165] If this case teaches any general lesson, it is that many judges will construe the law very strictly against the Minister or the State.

Much of the normal employment protection legislation does not apply to the public service including the civil service.[166] For instance, most civil servants are excluded from the protection of the Unfair Dismissals Acts 1977–1993[167] and the Minimum Notice and Terms of Employment Act 1973.[168] Moreover, no period of notice is stipulated in a civil servant's terms and conditions of service; in practice, however an *ex gratia* period of two or three weeks is usually allowed. Most civil servants are excluded from the scope of the Redundancy Payments Act 1967.[169] However, all categories of civil servant come within the Anti-Discrimination (Pay) Act 1974, the Employment Equality Act 1977 and the Maternity Protection of Employees Act 1981.

Discipline

The granting of the annual salary increase is usually automatic but a civil servant's conditions of employment provide that it may be withheld if the Minister of the particular Department considers it appropriate. In addition, the Civil Service Regulation Act 1956 creates a number of other disciplinary powers. The "suspending authority" – presently, the Minister for the appropriate Department; but the Secretary General when the Public service Management Act 1997 has been fully implemented[170]

---

164 *Ibid.* at 244.
165 *Ibid.* at 245. Did this mean that, as a matter of fact, the applicant's sick record became unsatisfactory only after the end of the probationary period? Such a thing appears inherently unlikely and there is nothing in the judgment to show that it was (or was not) so. If we assume that the sick record was bad during the probationary period, then it seems that the judge was focusing, rather literally, on the point in time at which the Minister actually became satisfied that the applicant had failed to fulfil the probation conditions, as opposed to the time when the failure occurred.
166 See, further, Forde, *Employment Law* (1993), pp. 288–291.
167 1977 Act, s.2(1)(*h*).
168 1973 Act, s.3(1)(*c*). *Serving the Country Better* proposed (at para. 7.2) that the law be changed to give civil servants the benefit of the Minimum Notice and Terms of Employment Act 1973 and the Unfair Dismissals Act 1977. See the comments of Keane J. in *Gildea*.
169 1967 Act, s.4(1).
170 See p. 87.

– may suspend a civil servant if, for example, "it appears to the suspending authority that the civil servant has been guilty of grave misconduct."[171] The suspension is without pay though in certain circumstances it may be reimbursed.[172] By statute, this power may be delegated and, in practice, usually is delegated to Higher Executive Officers.[173] The appropriate authority – usually the responsible Minister – is also authorised to make reductions in the pay or grading of civil servants.[174] Finally, a civil servant will not be paid his remuneration for any period of unauthorised absence.[175]

It has been assumed, justifiably we think, that the general principles of administrative (or public) law apply in the field of the employment – including the discipline (or, for that matter, dismissal – of civil servants. Four illustrations of this general precept may be offered. In the first place, each of the disciplinary powers may be conditioned by procedural rules.[176] If there are no specific procedural rules, then the general precepts of constitutional justice are usually[177] available to control the exercise of a disciplinary power. A case in point is *Ahern v. Minister for Industry and Commerce.*[178] Here the relationship between the applicant and his colleagues and superiors, in the Patents Office within the Department of Industry and Commerce, had been strained for some years. The latest episode consisted of the disclosure by the applicant of a document which he had been specifically instructed to keep confidential. At first, disciplinary proceedings against him were initiated. However, these were aborted and the matter was referred to the Chief Medical Officer in the Department. He advised that the opinion of a psychiatrist was needed and that if the applicant refused to attend the psychiatrist, it would be necessary to place him on compulsory sick leave until he was certified as fit to resume his duties. It appears that the High Court accepted the respondents' contention that authority for such suspension could be derived from Public Circular 25/78 which states that ". . . no officer who appears to require medical attention should be allowed to remain on duty." The applicant did refuse to consult a psychiatrist and, as a result, he was placed on "compulsory sick leave" until he had submitted a certificate signed by a psychiatrist, a period which, in the event, lasted for almost three months. The instruction to the applicant was in the form of a "minute" signed by the Personnel Officer, but prefaced by the conventional formula "I am directed by the Minister for Industry and Commerce . . . " It was accepted, as Blayney J. stated, that the net question was whether the court should: "quash . . . the decision of the Personnel

---

171 Civil Service Regulation Act 1956, ss.3(1), 13.
172 *Ibid.* s.14.
173 *Ibid.* s.3(2). Although where there has been a loss of money, the decision is vested in the first place in the Minister for Finance but is usually delegated to the responsible Department. For a case involving delegation, see *Flynn v. An Post* [1987] I.R. 68, 75, 80, 81, below at pp. 581–582. Another aspect covered in Flynn was the period for which the delegation was permitted.
174 *Ibid.* s.15.
175 *Ibid.* s.15(5).
176 See Department of the Public Service Circular 9/84, which governs procedures for dealing with grievance, disciplinary and promotion eligibility problems.
177 There is a possibility that constitutional justice does not apply where, because of the seriousness of the situation, immediate removal from duty is necessary. See pp. 608–609.
178 [1991] 1 I.R. 462. See also *Gallagher v. Revenue Commissioners* (No. 1) [1991] 2 I.R. 370.

Officer . . . , taken at the direction of the [Minister] . . . to place the applicant on compulsory sick leave."[179]

The respondents' first line of defence was to submit that this question was not justiciable. This was rejected by the judge, "on balance". He held that the decision was justiciable on the basis that although the applicant had been on full pay whilst he was on leave, nevertheless his right to work was affected in that he was barred from carrying out his normal work. In addition, the decision carried with it the innuendo that the applicant was unfit for work by reason of some psychotic disease.

The main argument, however, concerned the *audi alteram partem* limb of constitutional justice. Upholding the applicant's submission on this point, Blayney J. stated:

> "Reports were . . . obtained from [the applicant's superiors and colleagues] and sent to [the Chief Medical Officer]. The applicant did not see any of these reports and was unaware of their existence. The first time he had an opportunity of reading them was when he obtained discovery in the course of these proceedings. The reports were not confined to the [disclosure of the confidential document by the applicant] but dealt with the entire of the applicant's career since entering the Patents Office in 1971. The applicant had no opportunity of refuting any of the matters contained in the reports."[180]

From a general perspective, wider than the civil service, it is noteworthy that, in *Ahern*, constitutional justice was held to apply to a holding in a novel area, namely a person's health.

A second general doctrine is the *ultra vires* principle which received a straightforward, application (though not as strict as that in *Whelan*) in the case of *Reidy v. Minister for Agriculture*[181] which arose out of the punishment of a civil servant in the Department of Agriculture. In judicial review proceedings, he took a number of points, two of which are relevant here. The first concerned the withholding of his annual salary increment. The procedure governing this sanction was set out in Department of Finance Circular 9/87. However, by an oversight on the part of one of the personnel officers, the procedure set out in an earlier circular – which had been superseded by the new circular – was followed. The practical difference between the two circulars was between a decision to defer payment for a specified period, subject to review at the end of that period (as was the correct course required by the new circular) and a simple decision not to pay the increment due (as had

---

179 *Ibid.* at 467.
180 [1991] 1 I.R. 462 at 468. However, notwithstanding his finding on this point Blayney J. decided that for three reasons he would exercise his discretion not to grant the applicant an order quashing the decision to put him on compulsory sick leave. The first reason was that he was, in a significant sense, the author of his own downfall, in that he had, for some time, unreasonably refused to attend a psychiatrist. Secondly, the judge was influenced by the fact that it was only out of consideration for the applicant, and in spite of the applicant's intransigence, that the Personnel Officer had referred the matter to the Chief Medical Officer rather than continuing with the disciplinary proceedings which had, at an early stage of the episode, been initiated and then aborted. Finally, Blayney J. took the view that the order would not advantage the applicant in any way in that the presence of the decision as regards compulsory sick leave on his file would not prejudice him as regards his promotion prospects or in any other way.
181 Unreported, High Court, June 9, 1989.

actually occurred). Because of this difference, O'Hanlon J. held that the decision not to pay the increment was invalid.

The other sanction which had been applied against the applicant in *Reidy* was that he would not be allowed to compete for any promotion competitions. This was held invalid, again because there was no authority for it. O'Hanlon J. stated:

> "In the event of any dereliction of duty occurring on the part of an officer it is to be expected that the record of his service will contain particulars of any such matters which might count against him when the possibility of his promotion to a higher post is under consideration, but it appears to me that the decision taken in relation to the applicant – if upheld – would have the effect of blocking all hope of promotion for him for a fixed period of two years in a manner which seems to be incompatible with the general discretion to promote subject only to compliance with the conditions outlined in Circular No. 12/49. This penalty is one of such significance that it cannot be regarded as one capable of being imposed independently of the disciplinary powers conferred expressly by the Acts, and the further conditions of service dealt with by circulars emanating from the Department of Finance."[182]

A third general principle is the precept that a power granted for one purpose cannot be used for a different purpose. For example, it was implicit in *Reidy* that the power of transferring a civil servant may not be used to effect what is intended as a punishment. In that case, O'Hanlon J. appraised a direction that the applicant had been moved from Kilmeedy to the District Livestock Office in Limerick (a distance of about 30 miles), as follows:

> "I am satisfied that the decision to move the applicant from his previous place of employment to a new headquarters . . . was based on the bona fide belief . . . that there was a danger that the applicant was tending to relax the strict require-ments of the Beef Premium Scheme when dealing with farmers close to home with whom he would be acquainted personally, and that it would be preferable to locate him in new headquarters somewhat removed from his home area."[183]

Accordingly, the applicant's submission on this issue failed on the facts. However, the point was well made that the power of transfer could not be used as a punishment.[184]

---

182 *Ibid*. pp. 6–7. In regard to the final sentence of this passage, it may be observed that it is unfortunate that nothing further was said to elucidate what penalties, if any, were sufficiently insignificant to be imposed independently of the sources listed by the judge or what alternative sources of disciplinary penalties are acceptable – possibly, agreements worked out between the Departments and the unions representing civil servants.

183 Unreported, High Court, June 9, 1989 at p.8 of the judgment. Compare this aspect of O'Hanlon J.'s judgment with *Merricks v. Nott-Bower* [1964] 1 All E.R. 717 (where the English Court of Appeal held that the plaintiff policemen were entitled to challenge the validity of a transfer order on the ground that its real purpose was to impose disciplinary punishment) and *Re Murray's Application* [1987] 12 N.I.J.B. 1. In the latter case, Higgins J. quashed a similar transfer order on the ground that the evidence disclosed that the Chief Constable "must have been materially influenced" by the desire to impose a form of disciplinary punishment on the policemen.

184 There is a further reason why the characterisation of the power of transfer as a punishment (or not) could be significant. This is in the context of the rules of constitutional justice. As mentioned already, these rules of course apply to a punishment. But it is a more open question whether they would apply to an exclusively administrative arrangement for the well-being of the Department.

Fourthly, the *delegatus* principle has been invoked in this field, despite the *Carltona* doctrine[185] by which anything done by a civil servant is *ipso facto* regarded as having been done by the Minister. In *Reidy*, the applicant's transfer was effected under his conditions of service, which provided as follows: "An officer's head-quarters will be such as may be designated from time to time by the Head of the Department." There was no reason for O'Hanlon J. not to apply this provision literally and he did so, finding for the applicant on the following basis:

> "The decision, however, was taken by the Personnel Officer in the Department, who, at the time was a Principal Officer, and does not appear to have been ratified by the Head of the Department, as envisaged by the Conditions of Service, nor has it been shown to my satisfaction that the power to make this decision was lawfully delegated to the officer who made it."[186]

Points of elaboration may be ventured on this brief passage. It only appears to require "ratification" by the Head of Department. This is rather vague but it sounds as if not very much actual involvement of the Minister is required to make a "lawful deleg[ation]". Perhaps, this is a nod in the direction of the *Carltona* doctrine, which is otherwise conspicuously its absence from the judgment.

6. Terms and Conditions of Employment

The basic legal provision in this field is section 17 of the Civil Service Regulation Act 1956,[187] which provides as follows:

> "(1) The Minister shall be responsible for the following matters:
>   (a) the regulation and control of the Civil Service,
>   (b) the classification, re-classification, numbers and remuneration of civil servants,
>   (c) the fixing of
>   (i) the terms and conditions of service of civil servants, and
>   (ii) the conditions governing the promotion of civil servants.
>
> (2) The Minister may, for the purpose of subsection (1) of this section, make such arrangements as he thinks fit and may cancel or vary those arrangements."

It is under this provision that the Minister for Finance: fixes a civil servant's conditions of employment including such matters as pay-scale, hours of work and holidays; issues personnel circulars altering these conditions; creates new posts; or divides civil servants into classes and grades.[188]

---

[185] On which (and delegation) see pp. 481–489.
[186] *Reidy v. Minister for Agriculture*, unreported, High Court, June 9, 1989 at p. 8. See further p. 93.
[187] This section replaced the Ministers and Secretaries Act 1924, s.3(2) and the Civil Service Regulation Act 1924, s.9. On the history, see *Gilheany v. Revenue Commissioners* [1996] E.L.R. 25 at 33–35.
[188] *Inspector of Taxes v. Minister for the Public Service* [1986] I.L.R.M. 296 at 300.

A difficult question which has not yet been thoroughly or comprehensively examined by the courts is the issue of what are the sources of law governing a civil servant's conditions of employment. A convenient point of departure is the following passage from *Reidy* (the facts of which have already been given):

> "In addition, matters such as entitlement to payment of increments, the rules governing promotion within the Civil Service, and the determination of the officer's place of work from time to time, were regulated in part by the conditions of service accepted by the officer on taking up his appointment, and in part by Departmental Circulars issued from time to time, incorporating decisions made pursuant to section 17 of the Civil Service Regulation Act, 1956."[189]

It emerges from this passage that there are two main sources of law (in addition, it goes without saying, to the 1956 Act itself) governing a civil servant's employment: first, circulars incorporating decisions made under the 1956 Act; and secondly, an officer's "terms and conditions of employment", to use the normal terminology employed in the civil service, (the question of whether these conditions amount to a contract is discussed below).

Circulars

What is the legal status of such circulars? It is suggested that the admittedly ambiguous phrase, used in the passage, "circulars incorporating decisions made pursuant to the Civil Service Regulation Act, 1956" probably should not be taken so far as to mean that such a circular is a statutory instrument. One persuasive, though hardly conclusive, reason for this view is that it seems that such circulars are not intended by their maker to be statutory instruments. Such a classification would fly in the face of the customary assumption within the Government bureaucracy. Again such circulars are not explicitly authorised. Next, they are not couched in the precise legal language characteristic of a statutory instrument. In all events, a circular made section 17 is not promulgated as a statutory instrument as would be required, in the case of a statutory instrument by the Statutory Instruments Act 1947.[190]

Next, it seems likely that the holding in *Gilheaney v. The Revenue Commissioners* (analysed in the next section[191]) that there is no contract between a civil servant and the State means, necessarily, that a circular could be given legal effect as an implied term in a contract.[192]

It is suggested rather, that a circular made under section 17 would be as binding, though only as binding, as any other administrative action authorised by statute,[193]

---

[189] *Reidy v. Minister for Agriculture* at p. 3 and p. 6. On *Reidy*, see pp. 90–92.
[190] See further, pp. 23–27.
[191] [1996] E.L.R. 25. On this, see pp. 94–98.
[192] This possibility, founded on *McMahon v. Minister for Finance*, unreported, High Court, May 13, 1963, was canvassed in the 2nd edition of this book at pp. 89–90.
[193] In contrast with certain other types of circular: see, *e.g. O'Callaghan v. Department of Education*, unreported, Supreme Court, November 21, 1955, in which it was held that a circular issued by the Department of Education and not made under statute could not be invoked so as to override the

the significance of which is considered elsewhere[194] It is submitted that this view is in accord with Costello P.'s remark in *Gilheaney* that: "when a statute confers a power on a minister to grant a benefit to some person and that power is exercised it also confers a corresponding right on that person to receive a benefit."[195] (Arguably, *Reidy* (considered in Part 5) and *McMahon v. Minister for Finance*[196] (considered below) go further than this in that in each of these cases, a circular appears to have been regarded as bending even though no vested rights were involved.)

In line with the view that a circular is not fully law, Dr Forde has suggested that a Minister could not enforce a circular against a civil servant by way of court action:

> "[This] is a matter that seems never to have been considered, but since they are neither contracts nor statutory instruments, it would appear that they are not directly enforceable. Of course they can be enforced indirectly by the Minister imposing disciplinary sanctions, up to even dismissal, where their requirements are being flouted."[197]

Is there a Contract of Employment?

In Britain,[198] and elsewhere, there has been much debate as to whether a contract of employment exists between a civil servant and the State.[199] In Ireland the most recent authority to discuss the issue properly is the recent High Court case of *Gilheaney v. The Revenue Commissioners*.[200] The facts were that the applicant was an executive officer, working for the respondents, who had applied for promotion to the grade of higher executive officer. He was not, immediately successful but was placed on a panel for future promotion. Next, it was decided to fill it, by means of the transfer of an existing Higher Executive Officer (who had become redundant by virtue of the Government's decentralisation programme), as a result of which the applicant was deprived of his promotion. The applicant claimed that this decision was invalid. For the purposes of the argument analysed here,[201] it was assumed that,

---

terms of a contract between a teacher and the Department of Education, nor so as to prejudice the teacher's rights under that contract.

[194] On circulars see pp. 41–57.

[195] [1996] E.L.R. 25 at 38. The full quotation is at p. 97. This is an apt point at which to query whether s. 17(2) ("the Minister may . . . make such arrangements as he thinks fit and may cancel or vary those arrangements") would permit the changing of a circular relating to pay for conditions (and not merely the Conciliation and Arbitration Scheme, on which see pp. 104–105). The answer is probably that the word "arrangements" especially when read in the context of s.17, is wide enough to permit this. However it is unlikely (not least in view of the passage quoted in the text and at p. 97) to be given an interpretation which would permit the undoing of 'vested rights' *e.g.* it could not retrospectively affect (say) the salary for work, which had already been done.

[196] Unreported, High Court, May 13, 1963. See p. 104–105.

[197] Forde, *Employment Law* (1992), p. 311.

[198] Logan, "A Civil Servant and his Pay" (1945) 61 L.Q.R. 240. Fredman and Morris, "Civil Servants: A Contract of Employment" (1988) *Public Law* 58. and the authorities referred to at n. 1 thereof. In the U.K., the Civil Service Pay and Conditions Code, para. 14 states that civil servants do not have a contract of employment enforceable in the courts.

[199] However, see, below n.207.

[200] [1996] E.L.R. 25. Notice that *Serving the Country Better* (1985, PL. 3262), p. 63 proclaimed that civil servants would be given "contracts of employment".

[201] There were other arguments on legitimate expectation and irrationality: see *ibid.* at 39–40 and 40–41.

if there were a contract, there would be an implied term that future vacancies would be offered to candidates on the panel. Thus the issue was determined on the basis that it turned upon whether the Minister, in making the applicant's appointment, had entered into a contract with him. On this central point, Costello P. stated:

"It seems to me that this question can best be answered by applying basic principles of the law of contract by considering whether the minister when making the appointment *intended* to enter into contractual relations with the appointee. This was the way in which a similar issue was addressed in England in *R. v. Civil Service Appeal Board ex. p. Bruce* [1988] 3 All ER 686. In that case a Divisional Court was required to decide whether a civil servant's service with the Inland Revenue was given pursuant to a contract of employment enforceable in the courts or pursuant to an appointment made on the terms of a letter of appointment . . . both judges of the Divisional Court decided that the 'critical question' was whether or not there was an intention to create legal relations, namely a contract between the crown and the applicant for appointment. As the evidence did not establish such an intention existed the court concluded that no contract of employment existed. . . . When considering whether a minister intends to enter into a contract when he appoints a civil servant it is relevant to bear in mind the limits which are placed by law on the contractual terms to which he could agree. Firstly, the minister could not agree to appoint an officer for a fixed term of years because this would be prohibited by section 5 of the 1956 Act which provides that civil servants hold office at the will of the Government. Secondly, he could not enter into a legally binding agreement as to the future terms and conditions on which the civil servant would hold office because to do so would fetter the discretionary power conferred by law on the minister by section 17 of the 1956 Act to vary those terms and conditions. It is a long-established principle of administrative law that a public authority cannot by contract disable itself from exercising a discretionary power conferred on it by the legislature . . .

Furthermore, a great many of the conditions which would normally be included in a contract relating to an appointment to an office the public service (e.g. those relating to retirement, suspension, and discipline) are already regulated by the 1956 Act.

I must conclude therefore that in the absence of evidence of a clear intention to enter into the very restricted type of agreement which the law would permit him to enter into the minister in making the applicant's appointment to the civil service had no intention of entering into a contractual relationship, with him; and that the legal basis for his appointment is an administrative act made by the exercise of statutory powers."[202]

---

[202] *Ibid.* at 36–37. (Emphasis added.) At pp. 35, 38–39, another argument which is similar in principle fails for the same reason. The argument was that whatever the legal situation at the time of the applicant's appointment may have been, "later in issuing the Circular E5158 the respondents made an offer to enter into an enforceable contract with any officer who applied pursuant to its terms."

In an earlier section of his judgment, Costello J. had surveyed the legislation regulating the status throughout the period since Independence and had concluded that, even in the pre-1937 period:

> "Civil servants were not in the service of the Crown, but were in the service of the Government of Saorstát Éireann. They were not appointed by virtue of the exercise of the royal prerogative but by virtue of the exercise of statutory powers."[203]

Whilst this conclusion still leaves open (just) the possibility that there is also a contract, the thrust of the longer passage quoted earlier is to the effect that the nature of the statutory framework was such as to make it unlikely that the Minister would have intended to enter into contractual relation. Some of the commentary of Costello P. on the statutory framework might be queried. First, as to section 5 of the 1956 Act ("will and pleasure of the Government"), it has been observed, by the Privy Council that, "a power to determine a contract at will is not consistent with the existence of a contract until is so determined".[204] Secondly, it could be argued that since it this only section 17(2) – and not section 17(1) – which actually uses the word "vary", this leaves the way open for the doctrine of legitimate expectations. But Costello P. has consistently shown a preference for the traditional counter-weight to this doctrine, namely the precept against fettering a discretionary power,[205] which is referred to in the passage. Certain other judges have taken a different view on this general question. Yet, on this particular issue, it must be said that, however it is worded, the discretion contained in section 17 is a critical feature in the public service of the State and most judges would be slow to whittle it away.

Despite these queries, the aspects of the statutory framework, –itemised in the quotation above – do seem to provide a strong, if not impregnable foundation for the view that – absent special circumstances – a Minister can reasonably be taken not to have intended to make a contract.

And, as regards precedents: in *The State (Gleeson) v. Minster for Defence*,[206] the Supreme Court had characterised (admittedly very briskly) the relationship between

---

[203] [1996] E.L.R. 25 at 34.

[204] *Reilly v. R.* [1934] A.C. 176 at 179–180.

[205] See p. 862.

[206] [1976] I.R. 280. The judgment also refers to *McMahon v. Minister for Finance*, unreported, High Court, May 13, 1963 in which "[Section 17(2)] has been construed as meaning that the Minister has power to enter into contractual arrangements": *Gilheaney v. Revenue Commissioners* [1996] E.L.R. 25 at 35, *per* Costello P. But surely *McMahon* was referring not to an individual civil servant's contract; but to the Conciliation and Arbitration Scheme, on which see pp. 104–105.

See also *Inspector of Taxes Association v. Minister for the Public Service*, unreported, High Court, March 24, 1983, a case which arose out of the defendant's refusal to recognise the plaintiff's association for the purposes of the civil Service Conciliation and Arbitration Scheme. The aspect of the case which is relevant here is that the plaintiffs were confronted with the difficulty that, even assuming that the scheme was a contract, the plaintiffs were not parties to it, and, consequently, were incapable of asserting any rights which arose under it. However, Murphy J. was prepared to adopt a roundabout way to find in favour of the plaintiffs.

"In my view, the only basis on which the plaintiffs could rely upon the [Conciliation and Arbitration] scheme and the contract which constitutes it is on the basis that the members of the plaintiff association are officers or employees of the State whose terms of employment include by implication a provision that each of them shall have the benefit of the contract and scheme in accordance with its terms and provisions. Whilst the fact which would support such an inference

the State and a member of the Defence Forces as a "statutory contract".[207] This was distinguished in *Gilheaney* as "as a case dealing with an express statutory provision (absent in the 1956 Act) that privates in the army could enlist for a minimum period of three years and a maximum period of 12 years."[208]

Just because there is no contractual relationship, this is not however to say that a civil servant enjoys no rights enforceable in a court. For in a later, significant passage, Costello P. stated:

> "It seems to me that when a statute confers a power on a minister to grant a benefit to some person and that power is exercised it also confers a corresponding right on that person to receive the benefit. This means that there is a statutory right which the courts will enforce to the benefits contained in the terms and conditions of appointment of a civil servant (including, for example, those relating to remuneration) as well as to those benefits arising from the terms and conditions relating to promotion contained in administrative acts, until such time as the right is cancelled or varied by the valid exercise of a power in that behalf contained in section 17."[209]

---

was not canvassed in great detail, I would be satisfied to accept for the purposes of this judgment that the plaintiffs, as representing employees of the State, are entitled in contract to have the terms of the scheme implemented by the Minister. . . . It seems to me the high-water mark *of the contractual rights of the plaintiff association derived from its members* is to have an application made by a staff association fairly considered by the Minister and that being done his bona fide decision to grant or withhold recognition is conclusive."[Emphasis added].

This admittedly rather novel analysis depends on the assumption that there is a contract between a civil servant and the State which creates legally enforceable rights. (On appeal to the Supreme Court, ([1986] I.L.R.M 296) this preliminary point, as to the plaintiff's authority to bring the case, appears not to have been taken).

207 [1976] I.R. at 294. Exactly the same phrase is used in *Egan v. Minister for Defence*, unreported, High Court, October 24, 1988, p.10 of the judgment. At p.11 of *Egan*, Barr J. stated: "a regular officer on being commissioned for an indefinite period contracts to remain in the permanent defence forces until he reaches the retirement age . . . " See also *Glover v. BLN Ltd* [1973] I.R. 388, where it was stated (at 414) "[An office-holder] may have a contract under which he may be entitled to retain [the office] for a fixed period. But the holder of an office does not hold it under a contract : he holds it under the terms of the instrument which created it." This ruling was followed in *Murphy v. Minister for Social Welfare* [1987] I.R. 295 at 303 where one of the points at issue (in determining whether the applicant was in "insurable employment" for the purposes of the Social Welfare (Consolidation) Act 1981 was whether the applicant was "employ[ed] . . . under any contract of service." In holding that the applicant was not employed under a contract, Blayney J. stated in *Murphy* (at 303):

"The only effect of *Glover's* contract was to give him the right to retain his office for a given period. It did not in any way alter the nature of his office. So, in the present case, even if the applicant could establish some contract with the Minister, that would not in any way alter the fact that the origin of his employment was his appointment to a statutory office and not his entering into any contract of service. In the circumstances it is not necessary to go into the question of whether the applicant had any contract with the Minister. Even if he had, it would not have affected the basis of the applicant's employment which was his being appointed to any office. It could not have altered that situation into one in which the applicant held under a contract of service"

To go back to civil servants : it appears likely that a civil servant is an office-holder just because of the fact that his employment is authorised by statute ("each Minister may appoint other officers and servants to serve in the Department of which he is the head." Ministers and Secretaries Act 1924, s.2(2)). This statutory underpinning reduces the possibility of a civil servant holding his employment under a contract.

208 [1996] E.L.R. 25 at 37.
209 *Ibid.* at 38.

To summarise this passage: a civil servant can sue to enforce rights contained in his terms and conditions of employment (including, probably circulars), save in so far as these have been cancelled or varied. This proposition is , however, subject to the 'benefit' having been 'granted' by the Minister. The crux of the issue, plainly, is what is necessary for such a grant. Does it suffice if the conditions on which the entitlement to the benefit have been authoritatively announced, for example in the circular. Or is it necessary as seems to follow from the failure of the plaintiff's action in *Gilheaney* that the plaintiff should have moved some distance towards satisfying those conditions? One can presumably assume in line with the general rule of statutory interpretation that the cancellation or variation authorised by section 17 does not extend to a retrospective cancellation or variation (though the usual problems could arise as regards what exactly constitutes retrospection). Expressing the position in this way, the question is raised: is there any cash-value difference between a statutory right, thus restricted and, on the other hand, a contract which one party (the Minister) could determine at will (for *Gilheaney* denies the existence of even such a limited and anomalous contract)? The answer is that, in practice, there are probably substantial (though some of them technical) differences. One straightforward example is provided by the facts in *Gilheaney* itself. Had there been a contract – and making certain assumptions as to its terms – then the applicant would have succeeded. Again, the difference may be relevant in regard to remedies. Thus, if, for instance, the State were refusing to pay a civil servant's salary, it seems that he could claim for damages for breach of contract rather than just suing on a *quantum meruit* (which might mean a different amount of damages). Thirdly, as recent British case law shows, this question can be of significance in a number of unexpected, adventitious ways.[210] One context in which it can arise in industrial relations is the tort of inducing a breach of contract. (However, it should also be noted that a significant difference between British and Irish law is that Irish civil servants who go on strike would commit a criminal offence, although it might be considered impolitic to prosecute.[211]) Again, one or the other party, but probably the Minister/State, might wish to claim that there is a contract in order to invoke some implied term, for instance, a duty of confidentiality.

Structure of the civil service: classes and grades[212]

There are three broad (non-statutory) divisions among civil servants: the general service; the departmental; and the professional and technical classes. The general service officers perform the general duties of their department from routine clerical operations to the higher advisory or managerial work. They are subdivided into (in ascending order in the pyramid) sub-clerical, clerical, executive and administrative classes.[213] The other two broad divisions are specialists. The members of the

---

[210] Fredman and Morris, *op. cit.*, above, n.198.

[211] Offences Against the State Act 1939, s.9(2). *The Report of the Commission of Inquiry on Industrial Relations* (Pl. 114), paras. 787–789 recommended the amendment of this provision "to remove any doubt that it might apply to legitimate trade union activities in the public service."

[212] *Devlin Report*, paras. 7.3.1–7.8.5. Dooney, *The Irish Civil Service* (1976), Chap. 3 and pp. 147–152.

[213] The grades within the administrative classes are as follows: Secretary, Deputy Secretary, Assistant Secretary; Principal; Assistant Principal; Administrative Officer (A.O.); Higher Executive Officer

departmental classes are recruited with a general educational qualification, but are assigned to work peculiar to a Department in which they specialise, e.g. the Taxes Classes in the Office of the Revenue Commissioners or the Social Welfare Inspectorate in the Department of Social Welfare. In contrast, the members of the professional and technical classes specialise in work which is performed outside, as well as within, government service, for example engineers or electricians.

Within these broad groupings, there are divisions into grades. The significance of this administrative classification is that positions in the same grade share the same type of qualification, work and conditions, including a common pay scale; progress from one point on the scale to the next, at the end of each year, is usually automatic. Thus, grading affects not only pay and the other conditions of work, but also career prospects. Throughout the civil service there are about 700 different grades (some of them bygones from an earlier era)[214]: proliferation is assisted by the fact that equivalent grades in different departments usually bear different titles. The relationship between grades and classes is as follows. In the original conception, as it operated in the Irish Free State and earlier, a class meant a grouping of grades engaged on a particular type of work within which an officer would expect to make his civil service career, entering at the bottom and working up towards the top. But his final grade was normally dependent on the grade at which he entered and thus on his educational qualifications at that time. However, for the past 30 years or so, this strict concept of class has been modified so that promotion between classes is fairly common.

The question of grading was at the centre of *Inspector of Taxes Association v. Minister for the Public Service.*[215] This took the form of a claim by the plaintiff association that the Minister's refusal to recognise it for the purposes of the Conciliation and Arbitration Scheme, on the sole ground that the Inspectors of Taxes (Technical) were not a separate grade, was invalid. To appreciate this claim, it is necessary to recall that in 1960, the PAYE system of income tax collection, which had formerly been confined to the public sector, was extended to cover all employees. One consequence of this was the creation of a new post of Inspector of Taxes, holders of which were recruited from persons in the tax clerical grades. They possessed no technical qualifications; were not granted a commission by the Minister; and were designated "Clerical Inspector" as distinct from the traditional Inspector of Taxes (which then became known as "Technical Inspector"). The occasion for the case, in 1983, was that proposals were being prepared which would fundamentally alter the entire career structure open to Inspectors of Taxes. Accordingly, the plaintiff association, which had been formed in 1980 to represent only Technical Inspectors, wrote to the Minister for the Public Service requesting recognition for the purposes of the Conciliation and Arbitration scheme. The Minister rejected the plaintiff's application for recognition because it was established

---

(H.E.O.). A.O. and H.E.O. are equivalent grades; the difference is that A.O.s enter straight from university; whereas the H.E.O. is a promotional post.

214 "Fewer than 200 grades account for two-thirds of staff. At the higher levels, there are many single person grades with identical or similar pay scales. This pattern will be progressively simplified but it is recognised that this will take some time.": *Serving the Country Better*, para. 4.10.

215 Unreported, High Court, March 24, 1983; [1986] I.L.R.M. 296 (Sup.Ct.).

administrative policy (the propriety of which was not challenged) to confine recognition to only one association in respect of each grade and the constitution of the plaintiff association was confined to Technical Inspectors and excluded Clerical Inspectors from its membership.

Thus the case came down to the issue of whether the Technical Inspectors and the Clerical Inspectors constituted separate grades, even though the Minister had taken a decision not to create separate grades. According to Finlay C.J.:

> "It would be quite inconsistent with the responsibilities thus placed by [the Civil Service Regulation Act 1956, s.17] on the Minister, if his overall power to run and regulate the civil service within the terms of that section were subject to concepts of grading arising from a legal definition of what constituted a grade capable of being imposed upon him by the decision of a Court. In so far, therefore, as the plaintiff's claim in this case consisted of an assertion that a grading of Inspector of Taxes (Technical) had spontaneously occurred as a result of the development of the work of the Revenue Commissioners between 1960 and 1980 and without a decision made by the Minister under section 17, I would affirm the dismissal of that portion of the claim."[216]

However it is significant that the Chief Justice went on to hold, that the Minister's decision whether to create a new grade was, like any other administrative action, subject to judicial review. But, on the facts of the case, he found against the plaintiff:

---

[216] *Ibid.* at 300. The analogous authority to the Inspector of Taxes Association in respect of the Garda Síochána is the case of *Aughey v. Ireland* [1986] I.L.R.M. 206 (High Ct.); [1989] I.L.R.M. 87 (Sup. Ct.). The basis of this case was that the plaintiffs—who were detective officers and detective garda—believed that the existing Garda representative associations were not representing adequately their special interests as detective members of the force. However, permission to form a new association to exclusively represent detectives had been refused by the Commissioner of the Garda Síochána on the ground that to do so would contravene s.1 of the Garda Síochána Act 1977. This provision authorises the establishment of "an association or associations for all or any one or more of the ranks of the Garda Síochána below the rank of sergeant." It was held in the High Court, and appears to have been accepted in the Supreme Court (although the point does not seem to be beyond controversy) that the provision authorises the establishment of only one association for any particular rank. Given the existence at the time of the decision of representative associations, for all members of all ranks, the issue in the part of the case with which we are concerned came down to the question of whether the rank of Detective Officer or Detective Garda were separate ranks from their equivalents in the uniformed branch.

In the High Court the situation in the case of the civil service (which was examined in the *Inspector of Taxes Association* case) was distinguished on the basis that the question of what was a separate grade was a matter for an administrative decision by the (then) Minister for the Public Service whereas with the Garda Síochána the division into ranks was fixed by statutory instrument. Yet this overlooks the fact that a statutory instrument, just as much as an administrative action, may be *ultra vires* for unreasonableness.

However, in the Supreme Court, Walsh J. addressed the issue squarely in the following passage (at 90):

"It is clear from an examination of the structure of the Garda Síochána as a police force that a detective officer below the rank of Sergeant enjoys the same rank as any other member of the Garda Síochána below the rank of Sergeant. The difference in duties or operational methods does not affect the matter. There is no recognised rank of "Detective Officer" although the expression is commonly used to distinguish them from their uniformed colleagues. The same applies to those members of the detective branch or section who have the rank of Sergeant or Inspector. The Court is of opinion that the claim that a Detective Officer or a Detective Garda is an officer of a separate rank in the Garda Síochána is not established."

"It could not be said that the differences established between the work-load, responsibility, qualifications and training of Inspectors of Taxes (Technical) and Inspectors of Taxes (Non-Technical) were such that having regard to other considerations it was not open to the Minister to decide to leave both of these categories of Inspectors of Taxes in the same grade."[217]

Conciliation and Arbitration Schemes[218]

There are two negotiation systems in the public sector. About half the employees come within the Labour Court/labour relations system (to which private workers also have access). The remainder have conciliation and arbitration schemes. For notwithstanding the wide discretionary powers conferred upon the Minister for Finance by the 1956 Act, section 17, these powers are not usually exercised, to the full, in regard to conditions of service, including pay. In the first place, any increases made under the Public Service Pay Agreement (or, formerly, the National Wage Agreement) are granted automatically. Secondly, there are two distinct categories. In the case of the higher civil servants – the 200 or so Secretaries, Deputy Secretaries and Assistant Secretaries and their equivalent in the professional classes – the Minister has always accepted the recommendations of the "Review Body on Higher Remuneration in the Public Sector". This body was established in 1972, at first under the chairmanship of Mr. Liam St. John Devlin and (now in 1998) Michael Buckley, as a standing body to advise the Government on the level of pay for civil servants and local authority officers outside the scope of Conciliation and Arbitration Schemes, as well as personages such as the chief executives of state-sponsored bodies and the judiciary.

Alternatively, in the case of the great majority of the civil service, pay increases are determined (within the framework of any national wage agreement, e.g. the Programme for Competitiveness and Work of 1994) by negotiation within the framework of the Conciliation and Arbitration Schemes. Up until 1983, Principals and Assistant Principals were included among the so-called "Devlin Grades" but now they have their own Conciliation and Arbitration Scheme. This is modelled on the older – established and larger scheme which serves all non-industrial civil servants at the level of Higher Executive Officer or below.[219] This Scheme[220] comprises two parallel and similar systems. The first and most important involves a General Council which deals with problems which are not peculiar to any one

---

217 [1986] I.L.R.M. 303.
218 See Murphy and Roche, (ed.) *Irish Industrial Relations in Practice* (1997) Chap. 6 (on the Public Sector, by M.McGinley) for an excellent account. See also, the analogy drawn by O'Hanlon J. in *Association of General Practitioners v. Minister for Health* [1995] 2 I.L.R.M 481 at 490.
219 The first Scheme was established in 1950. The present Scheme established in 1955 and revised in 1976 is an appendix to Department of the Public Service Circular 6/76; for a summary of it see Dooney, *op. cit.* above, n. 213 App. 7. See also, McGinley, "Pay Negotiation in the Public Service" (1976) 24 *Administration* 76, at pp. 80–84; Massey, "A New Approach to Public Service Pay" (1986) 34 *Administration* 455; Keating, "Civil Service Negotiation Machinery–C and A or Labour Court" (1988) 9 *Seirbhís Phoiblí* 28.
220 The Scheme excludes individual cases which are dealt with according to procedures laid down in Department of Public Services Circular 9, 1984 ("Procedures for dealing with grievance, disciplinary and promotion eligibility problems.")

Department (often claims from grades which are common to more than one Department). The other system consists of Departmental Councils which deal with matters which are relevant only to a particular Department, for example, claims by Departmental classes like the building inspectors in the Department of the Environment. The official representatives on either type of council consist of no more than six (on the General Council) or four (on a Departmental Council) members nominated by the Minister for Finance (one of whom, who is at Secretary level in the case of the General Council is nominated as chairman), almost always from among his officers. On the other side are an equal number of staff representatives, drawn from the various staff associations/ unions – some 50 or so – which have been recognised by the Minister. Civil servants are heavily unionised. A total of 50 or so unions are involved and mechanisms exist, on the union side, to co-ordinate claims. On the other side, the Government lays down policy on major issues, for example, the line to be followed on general pay claims. Officials negotiate within these guidelines, keeping the Minister for Finance, or if necessary, the Government informed of progress. It is not within the competence of either type of council to make binding agreements but only to make agreed recommendations or, at the request of either side, to record disagreement.

The Scheme lists the subjects which are appropriate for discussion by the General Council, among them not only pay, allowances and hours of work but also: principles governing recruitment, discipline and promotion; suggestions by the staff for promoting efficiency in the civil service; and questions of doubt as to subjects appropriate for discussion at Departmental Council. According to one summary of the Scheme[221]:

> "It is open to either side to put forward items for inclusion in the agenda. In practice, of course, the vast majority of the items are put forward by the staff side. Whether items so put forward come within the province of the council is a matter for the chairman to decide. However, before any item is excluded, the scheme provides that the council must be given a chance of expressing its views whether it should be included or excluded."

The Civil Service Conciliation and Arbitration Scheme is the earliest of a number of such schemes, each modelled on the same pattern and covering a particular area of public sector employment, including the Garda Síochána, teachers, local authority, and health board officials. The role of the chairman of the Conciliation Council in the Garda Conciliation and Arbitration Scheme – the equivalent of the General Council in the Civil Service Scheme – came up for examination in *Garda Representative Association v. Ireland*.[222] The net issue was the chairman's refusal to place on the agenda for discussion by the Council, a proposal by the Commissioner to abolish overtime payments in respect of parading time and rostering for special duties. It was held that under the terms of the Scheme, as with the Civil Service Scheme, it was for the chairman to decide. In a passage which is of relevance also to the Civil Service Scheme, writing for the Supreme Court, Finlay C.J.:

---

[221] Dooney, *op. cit.* above, n.212 App. 7.
[222] [1989] I.R. 193 (High Ct.); [1994] 1 I.L.R.M. 81 (Sup. Ct.).

"... the scheme which was operated as between the staff and official side of the Garda Síochána ... specifically chose to provide that there should be a chairman of the council appointed from the permanent civil service, and gave under clause 17 of the agreement to that chairman the power of making a decision as to whether a topic raised was appropriate for discussion by the council or not. The scheme of conciliation and arbitration provided for in this document does not leave that question as one to be determined by the court; the parties are deemed to have agreed or accepted that it should be determined by the chairman for the time being of the council."[223]

It seems tolerably clear from this and an earlier passage[224] that the Supreme Court was here characterising the Chairman's ruling as an error (assuming for the sake of argument that it was an error) of law within jurisdiction and hence not something which a court could review.

A second argument (which was considered only by the High Court) was examined and rejected in the following passage:

"In the present case counsel for the plaintiffs have adverted to the fact that the chairman of the council is a permanent civil servant and was appointed to his office as chairman by the Minister for Justice. On the other hand there was nothing sinister or improper in that appointment. The bargain between the parties expressly provided for such an appointment to be made by the Minister. In relation to the procedure adopted I do not see how the conduct of Mr. Crowley could be challenged in any respect. He heard both parties. He considered their submissions and not only did he give his decision but he gave his reasons therefor. Insofar as judicial review concerns the manner in which a decision is made rather than the substance of the decision, it seems to me that Mr. Crowley's conduct was impeccable."[225]

To return to our account of the Civil Service Scheme (C and A Schemes): in practice, if the official side agrees with the staff side, it does so because the terms of the agreement are acceptable to the Minister. Thus, it will invariably happen that if there is an agreed recommendation to the Minister for Finance it will be accepted though in the case of a pay increase, it is often introduced "in phases". Alternatively, where the two sides disagree, the Minister's response to the report will not be favourable to the staff side. In this case, the second stage comes into play and the staff representatives have the right to refer the matter to arbitration provided that it is an "arbitrable claim". This phrase covers a narrower category than the subjects which may be discussed at the initial (Council stage). It includes for instance issues such as pay and allowances which, it is assumed, can be resolved by reference to comparable terms outside the service, but excludes matters of policy such as re-grading or productivity claims.

The Arbitration Board is a standing body with a chairman (usually a senior counsel) chosen by the Minister for Finance. In addition, each side chooses two

---

223 [1994] 1 I.L.R.M. 89. The High Court held similarly at [1989] I.R. 202–203.
224 [1994] 1 I.L.R.M. at 84, For error of law within jurisdiction, see pp. 430–436.
225 [1989] I.R. 202 (High Ct.). This point was not pursued before the Supreme Court.

members.[226] In addition, there may be one workers' member and one employers' member of the Labour Court, nominated by the Chairman of the Court, when requested for a particular claim. The Board's report, which does not have to be unanimous, is sent to the Minister.

At the third and final stage, if the Government wishes to reject or modify a recommendation from the Board, then it may only do so by securing the passage of a Dáil motion to this effect.[227]

Legal status of the Scheme

The legal status of the C and A Scheme was examined in *McMahon v. Minister for Finance*,[228] a case brought by a dissident member of the staff side. The significant part of Kenny J.'s judgment is his finding that the Scheme was legally binding (albeit as a contract rather than "a statutory scheme".[229]) After making this fundamental finding, the judge went on to hold that there were three irregularities[230] in connection with a General Council meeting and thus a declaration was granted that the meeting was invalid. As a consequence, there could be no valid report from the meeting and, since a report is an essential preliminary to arbitration, the arbitration could not proceed.

However, in appraising this case, we must bear in mind that the 1956 Act, section 17(2) (which was quoted in full *supra*) explicitly authorises the Minister to "cancel or vary those arrangements" which may be taken to mean, inter alia, that the Minister may abrogate the Scheme unilaterally. Furthermore, Article 2 of the Scheme itself states (possibly *ex abundante cautela*):

> "The existence of this scheme does not imply that the Government have surrendered or can surrender their liberty of action in the exercise of their constitutional authority and the discharge of their responsibilities in the public interest."

In contrast to *McMahon*, doubts were expressed in *Gilheaney* as to how binding the Scheme was in law. Here Costello P. remarked (*obiter*):

> ". . . in the administration of the public service there are a great many 'arrangements' entered into which may not establish contractual relations but

---

[226] Recognition will not be accorded to any association which is affiliated to any political organisation unless the affiliation subsisted prior to 1949. (This restriction is a device to include the Post Office Workers' Union. It was introduced at a time when William Norton, formerly Secretary General of the P.O.W.U., was a member of the Government).

[227] Such a motion has only been passed once, in 1953. However, a motion to this effect was passed, in 1986, under a similar Conciliation and Arbitration Scheme for teachers: see 363 *Dáil Debates*, Cols. 1839–2005. The teachers claimed that the passing of such a motion was unfair, although there is no doubt that it is part of the Scheme.

[228] Unreported, High Court, May 13, 1963.

[229] This nuance was explored at pp. 96–97.

[230] The Scheme had been violated in that (1) the chairman of the staff panel had been regarded as *ex officio* "principal staff representative" (that is, the leader of the staff representatives) on the General Council; (2) one of the staff representatives who was absent from the Council meeting had been represented by a substitute, (3) one person had been wrongfully barred from standing for election as a staff representative.

which the parties regard as binding on them in the interests of the public service and act accordingly. And there are contracts entered into which are expressly made subject to the ministerial power of unilateral variation or cancellation on the basis of an understanding, which though unenforceable is nonetheless honoured, that generally it is not in the interests of the public service that the statutory power should be exercised."[231]

It seems likely,[232] that, in this passage, the judge had in mind agreements such as the Conciliation and Arbitration Scheme, rather than the relationship between an individual civil servant and the State. It is more difficult to be definite about the substance of this passage. Perhaps it may be paraphrased as follows: despite the fact that a C and A Scheme is not binding at law (whether by contract or statute), nevertheless the Minister for Finance is under a strong conventional (extra-legal) obligation to honour the Scheme.

Bearing all this in mind, the following propositions may be tentatively suggested:

1. The Minister is free to revoke the Scheme.

2. He is also free not to use it, though in fact, for political reasons, most "conciliable" matters are negotiated through the Scheme.

3. However, once a matter has been entrusted to the machinery created by the Scheme, it must be pursued to its conclusion, following the procedure laid down in the Scheme (a point illustrated by both the *Garda Representative Association* case and the *McMahon* case) and including, if necessary, a Dáil vote.

Politics

Finally, an aspect of a civil servant's terms of employment which has wider constitutional implications may be mentioned.[233] Essentially, there is a complete embargo on political activity. There are two sets of restrictions. In the first place, in general, no civil servant, whether temporary or permanent, may be elected or sit as a member of the Dáil or Senate.[234] There is a possibility that this restriction violates the constitutional right to stand for election, bestowed by Article 16.1.1°. While this right is not absolute, it can, like other constitutional rights, only be restricted where this can be justified as being, objectively, in the public interest and where the restriction is not disproportionate.[235] This test is manifestly satisfied in

---

[231] [1996] E.L.R. 25 at 38.

[232] From the term "arrangements" (which is also used in s.17(2), quoted earlier); the phrase "the administration of the public service"; and the reference in the second sentence, to "the ministerial power of unilateral variation . . . "

[233] Note also, the Prevention of Corruption Acts 1889–1916, as adapted by the Adaptation Order No. 37 of 1928 which deals with corruption among civil servants and Department of Finance Circulars 50/1929 and 16/1936 on outside employment and conflict of interest. Section 34 of the Offences Against the State Act 1939 has been held unconstitutional in *Cox v. Ireland* [1992] 2 I.R. 503 on which see p. 655.

[234] Electoral Act 1992, s.4(1)(h) (the provision actually exempts from its scope a civil servant "who is . . . by the terms of his employment expressly permitted to be member of the Dáil."); Seanad Electoral (University Members) Act 1937, s. 16(2); Constitution, Art. 18.2.

[235] See, *e.g. Cox v. Ireland* [1992] 2 I.R. 503 at 522–523, *per* Finlay C.J.

the case of higher civil servants who are required to give impartial and independent advice to the Government and individual Ministers. However, there is a possibility that it would be unconstitutional as regards its application to lower civil servants (say telephonists or messengers) whose work is not really part of the political process.

The other restriction is contained in Department of Finance Circular 21/32 which was re-issued recently:

> "The Minister is aware that it is the view of the Civil Service itself that the action of an official who identifies himself actively or publicly with political matters is indefensible, and that such conduct is detrimental to the interests of the Service as a whole. The nature and conditions of a Civil Servant's employment should, of themselves, suggest to him that he must maintain a reserve in political matters, and not put himself forward on one side or another and, further, that he should be careful to do nothing that would give colour to any suggestion that his official actions are in any way influenced or capable of being influenced, by party motives. That is the attitude which the Minister, while not wishing in any way to interfere with or influence political views privately held, expects Civil Servants at all times to observe. Should any departures from official impartiality occur it will be followed by disciplinary action. If the Head of Department (after such consultation as he may think fit with his Minister) takes the view that the official has overstepped the bounds of propriety, he should send for him, point out to him the gravity of his fault, and obtain from him an undertaking that there will be no recurrence of similar impropriety in the future. If more severe action is called for, its severity will be related to the time and place, the standing of the official concerned, and the degree of publicity, but the Minister will look to Heads of Departments to ensure that, where punishment is deserved, it will follow.
>
> While the Minister appreciates that it would not be feasible to anticipate every occasion of the kind in question that might arise for consideration, he desires to lay down specific directions on the following points, namely,
>
> (1) An official shall not be a member of an Association or serve on a Committee having for its object the promotion of the interests of a political party or the promotion or prevention of the return of a particular candidate to the Dáil.
>
> (2) An official shall not support or oppose any particular candidate or party either by public statement or writing.
>
> (3) An official shall not make any verbal statements in public (or which are liable to be published), and shall not contribute to newspapers or other publications any letters or articles, conveying information, comment or criticism on any matter of current political interest, or which concerns the political action or position of the Government or of any member or group of members of the Oireachtas."

Again it might be queried whether in its application to the lower grades in the civil service, this circular violates the Constitution, Article 40.3.1° of which protects the right to communicate and Article 40.6 of which protects freedom of expression and the right to hold political opinions. In any case, it should be noted that since 1974, this ban has been modified, but only in its application to industrial civil servants and (subject to a proviso that officers engaged in a particular category of work may be excluded from this freedom) clerical workers.[236] Civil servants in these groups may engage in political activity, including standing for election to local authorities, but may not stand as candidates for either House of the Oireachtas.

But the central issue concerns the work of civil servants within their Departments. In order to maintain the political neutrality of the civil service, they need (at, any rate, at the higher levels) to be politically aware, but also politically neutral. This obviously involves a fairly fine line. One form which the problem takes is the question of whether civil servants should prepare material for ministerial speeches to party meetings. The conventional rule is that when civil servants are asked to provide such material, they should ensure that it is balanced and objective Another problem stems from the "private offices", *i.e.* offices within a Department, which may be staffed by as many as 20 civil servants under a Higher Executive Officer and which assist the Minister in dealing with a range of constituency and party political activities, including obtaining a health card for a constituent, sending circulars to all of a Minister's constituents; or helping to organise the Minister's local party branch.[237]

Partly because of such difficulties as these but more because Ministers wish to be advised by their own political allies, it has often been the practice, since the time of the 1973–1977 Coalition, for a Minister to bring in a 'personal' (or 'ministerial') advisor. In addition, in the Fianna Fáil-Labour Coalition of 1993–1994 and the Rainbow Coalition of 1995–1997 (but not the Fianna Fáil-Progressive Democrats Coalition of 1997) "Progamme Managers" were appointed for the Ministers. The difference between the two posts appear to be a follows. The personal advisers provide essentially political advice and act as ministerial confidantes, without performing any managerial function. By contrast the role of the programme managers was to monitor policy and legislative developments so as to try to ensure that the policy commitments contained in the 'programme for government' came to fruition (a role which was regarded as regarded as especially important in the case of Coalition Governments.[238] The status, terms and conditions of each of these two political posts are regulated by section 11 of the Public Service Management Act 1997 which uses the title "Special Advisor". This provision also fixes maximum figures for the number of special advisers. The maximum figure is two in the case of a Minister (other than the Taoiseach, Tanaiste or other party leader) or the "Minister of State" who attends Government meetings (a.k.a "super junior"); and one, in the case of other Ministers of State.

---

[236] Department of the Public Service Circular No. 22 of 1974: see statement made by the Minister for the Public Service on March 6, 1974 (reproduced by Dooney, *op. cit.*, above, n.212, App. 8). See also, Department of Finance Circulars Nos. 23/1925 and 20/1934.

[237] See Association of Higher Civil Servants, Discussion Paper on Civil Servants and Politics (April 1983). For a broader discussion, see Honohan, "The Role of the Adviser and the Evolution of the Public Service" in Hederman (ed.) *Essays in Honour of Patrick Lynch* (1988).

[238] On this area, generally, see: O'Halpin, "Partnership Programme Managers in the Reynolds/Spring Coalition", (1997) 12 *Irish Political Studies* 78 and the reference therein; Cahill, *Sunday Tribune*, December 18, 1994; Morgan, Association of Higher Civil Servants Newsletter, June 6, 1997.

7. Reform in the Civil Service

The major reform – the Public Service Management Act 1997 – has already been considered in Part I. Here we shall give a brief historial sketch of other developments in this field.

1981–1987[239]

Save for the 1973–1987 period (when it was the responsibility of the short-lived Minister for the Public Service), the personnel and organisation functions for the entire civil service have always been vested in the Minister for Finance. Because the civil service pay and pensions bill accounts for a large and increasing share of public expenditure, this function had been regarded since the foundation of the State as an intrinsic element in the control of Government expenditure. However, with the economic programming of the late 1950s, the civil service was required to play a new and more dynamic part in the economic life of the country. To assist it to adapt to this change, the Minister for Finance constituted the Public Services Organisation Review Group (*the Devlin Report*), which reported in 1969.[240] One of its major proposals was implemented fairly quickly. This was the creation of the (former) Minister for the Public Service, with a separate Department of State, freed of the shadows cast by preoccupation with the main functions of the Department of Finance and the transfer, to the new Minister, of powers over the civil service.[241] The object of this change, effected by the Ministers and Secretaries (Amendment) Act 1973,[242] was to promote a more positive attitude towards matters of organisation and personnel, as contrasted with the exclusive emphasis on cost-consciousness natural to the Department of Finance. In particular, it was hoped that the new Department would possess sufficient authority and enthusiasm to push through the other reforms proposed by the *Devlin Report*. In fact, for wider political reasons, very little happened until the mid 1980s.

The Governments of 1981–1982 and 1982–1987 were elected on a programme which included public service reform, symbolised by the fact that, between 1982 and 1986, for the first time ever, the incumbent of the office of Minister for the Public Service did not hold a second portfolio. The result was a number of specific reforms, including: the articulation of major expenditure programmes in each

---

239 Boyle and Joyce, *Making Change Work* (1988); R. Boyle, *Managing Public Sector Performance* (1989) Murray, *Civil Service Observed* (1990); Dunne, "Politics of Institutional Reform" (1989) 4 *Irish Political Studies* 1. See also n.249, p. 110.

240 Prl. 792. For comment, see Lee, *Ireland 1912–1985* (1989), pp. 547–554; Calleary, "Devlin–ten years on" (1979) 27 *Administration* 4, 395; Whelan, "Public service adaptation–its nature and requirements" (1979) 27 *Administration* 1, 96; Ó Nualláin, "Public service reform" (1978) 26 *Administration* 3, 301–302; Chapman, "The Irish public service: change or reform?" (1975) 23 Administration 2 at 138 and Dooney," 1969–1979: a decade of development?" (1980) 1 *Seirbhís Phoiblí* 2 at 29 at 32.

241 Public Service (Transfer of Departmental Administration and Ministerial Functions) Order (S.I. 1973 No. 294).

242 1973 Act, s.2. It was provided by the 1973 Act, that the Minister for the Public Service should always be the same person as the Minister for Finance. This provision was revoked by the Ministers and Secretaries Act 1980, s.7. In fact it was only during the period 1982–1987 that there was a Minister for the Public Service (Mr John Boland), who was not also Minister for any other portfolio.

Department so as to pin-point the link between costs and performance; the appointment, with effect from early 1984, of an Ombudsman to hold the office which had remained vacant since it was constituted in 1980; the establishment, in 1984, of the Top Level Appointments Committee to make recommendations for filling posts at Assistant Secretary level or above, applying the criterion of merit rather than seniority[243]; the opening up of a number of principal and assistant principal posts[244] to selection along similar lines; and the appointment of Secretaries for a maximum period of seven years. In addition: a wider and more attractive presentation of information was established, civil servants dealing with the public were required to give their names and a special unit of the Department of the Public Service (which has now been lodged in the Government Supplies Agency) undertook responsibility to "dejargonise" (sic) all Government or departmental forms. The Review Body on Higher Remuneration in the Public Sector[245] recommended that increments for Assistant Secretaries should not be virtually automatic (as formerly) but should be performance-related. This change was effected from 1989.

Finally, *Serving the Country Better: A White Paper on the Public Service* was published in 1985.[246] The major constitutional/legal change proposed by the White Paper was a modification of the ministerial responsibility doctrine somewhat along the lines eventually affected by the Public Service Management Act 1997 which is summarised in Part I.

1987–1991

The major preoccupation of the Governments in power during this period was retrenchment in public expenditure so as to reduce the public debt to a more manageable level. Partly for this reason and partly because of the lack of political interest in public service reform, the view was taken that public service reform might involve additional expenditure and, in any case, was something which could wait. Thus the Minister for – and Department of – the Public Service were abolished as an independent entity and the functions and personnel of the former Minister were restored to the Minister for Finance, as in the pre-1973 era.[247] The Public Service Advisory Council was laid to rest alongside its former sponsoring Department.

The two major reforms were Administrative Budgets and the Efficiency Audit Group.[248] As the name indicates, Administrative Budgets are concerned with such

---

[243] See further, pp. 82–84.

[244] A similar scheme had been in existence for Higher Executive Officers since 1973.

[245] Pl.5244, paras 7.22–35.

[246] Pl.3262 (Esp. 27–28). The sub-title was a misnomer since the White Paper dealt almost exclusively with the civil service. Most of these reforms are summarised in *Serving the Country Better: A White Paper on the Public Service* 1985, Pl. 3263 ("The White Paper"). For comment, see "A special issue on the White Paper" (1985) 6 *Serbhís Phoiblí* 4. The legislation to implement the new regime was drafted but never published.

[247] At the time of the transfer, there was talk of retaining some status for public service reform by rechristening the Minister for Finance as the Minister for Finance and the Public Service. But this came to nothing. In 1987, the Department of Finance became – and remains – now divided into five divisions: Finance; Public Expenditure; Budget and Planning; Personnel and Remuneration; and Organisation, Management and Training. The last two divisions are under the control of a Secretary, who was formerly at the head of the Department of Public Service.

[248] See, generally, 386 *Dáil Debates* Cols. 235–236; 395 *Dáil Debates* Col.197; 403 *Dáil Debates* Cols 1801–1804; Chubb, *The Government and Politics of Ireland* (1992, 3rd.ed), pp. 241–242.

administrative costs as: salaries, consultancy services and travelling and office expenses. One feature of the new scheme is that a commitment of funds is made on a three-yearly basis so that planning and organisation are located within a wider frame of reference and administrators are freed from obedience to the annual cycle (which as Aneurin Bevan pointed out, is more appropriate to a pastoral society dependent on the ebb and flow of the seasons than a modern polity). However Dáil approval and review will continue to be based on the present annual system[249] and no device has been established to overcome this disjointure.

The most important feature of the Administrative Budgets is that by introducing the new scheme, the Minister for Finance made an unprecedented delegation of his power to consent to expenditure. This power was delegated to the Secretary General of each Department (who, is of course, the accounting office for each Department vote). Thus there has been a delegation of authority: to expend money to an increased maximum than before; to *vire* (transfer) money between sub-heads of a vote; to create posts up to and including the level of Higher Executive Officer; and to purchase computer equipment up to a maximum figure. Concurrently with this change, there is substantial delegation of authority to line managers in each particular Department.

These changes increased the authority and, therefore, responsibility of Secretaries and line managers and, inevitably, other civil servants too. This amounts to, *inter alia*, a long overdue recognition of the decay of the individual ministerial doctrine, already considered in the context of the 1997 Act. It also removes some of the Department of Finance's minute powers of control and brings the administration of a Department of State closer to that of a large private organisation.

The Efficiency Audit Group, carried out a periodic, critical, pragmatic examination of the working of each Department. The Group has now been superseded by individual (Department of Finance) internal audit units, which carry out the same function in each Department.

1992–1997

The present wave of public sector reform[250] had a number of progenitors. Among these were: public dissatisfaction with the public economic mismanagement of the 1980s; the *zeitgeist* that the consumer was entitled to a public service which was more open, accessible and responsible; coupled with the lower age profile of the upper echelons in the civil service; the catalyst, afforded by the E.U.; and the new technology with its easier access to information. Elsewhere,[251] we shall deal with general public sector reform. Here we shall concentrate on civil service reform. This was launched, under the heading of the "Strategic Management Initiative" by the Taoiseach (Mr Albert Reynolds, who approached the business of government very much along business lines) in February 1994. It took a more definite shape, as

---

[249] For details of financial procedure, see Gwynn Morgan, *Constitutional Law of Ireland, op. cit.*, above, n.1, Chap 8.

[250] See, *e.g.* O'Halpin and Stapleton, *Administration* 38 (1991) pp. 283–302 and 303–335; Kelly, *Administration* 41 (1993) pp. 72–79; 1995 Review in *Administration* 42 (1995) 12–15; 1996 Review *Administration* 43 (1996) 17–19.

[251] See pp. 494–497.

Delivering Better Government,[252] launched two years later by Mr Reynolds' successor as Taoiseach, Mr John Bruton.

As a preliminary, one ought to notice a significant, adventitious point: whereas *Devlin* would have been largely imposed from outside the practising civil service, the well-springs of the mid 1990s reform lay largely in the upper echelons of the civil service itself. Coupled with this is the fact that, as indicated in the previous paragraph, the present initiative commands an unusual level of cross-party support. In line with this, whereas *Devlin* was predicated on a rather unrealistic dichotomy between policy and administration, the new reform is more discriminatory. In a small and politically sophisticated country, electors are accustomed to call their Ministers to account for perceived errors, regardless of whether these arise from bad policy or law or, on the other hand, its defective implementation. This is a point which, as we saw in Part 1, has been taken into account in the Public Service Management Act 1997, which is the brightest jewel in the crown of civil service reform. One ought to stress also that the change here is unlikely to be as radical as the reforms which have overtaken the British public sector,[253] Mrs Thatcher's time as Prime Minister (1979–1991) and subsequently.

In Ireland, the extent of the operational independence and authority transferred to certain civil servants, by virtue of the 1997 Act remains to be settled, over the next few years. However, apart from this Act, there are many other aspects to the "Strategic Management Initiative", designed, broadly speaking, to make the civil service more open, accessible accountable and 'consumer-citizen-friendly'. However since these will mostly be affected by administrative rather that legal change, here we shall merely suggest their flavour by giving the following list of changes which have either recently come about or are in the process of doing so. These changes include: creation of one-stop shops (*e.g.* welfare benefits, business advice); establishment of cross-departmental structures to address specific problems (*e.g.* drugs or unemployment in particular sectors); more pro-active personnel management approach; freer flow of information to the public; more accessible legislation with greater use of consolidating statutes; provision of complaints and redress mechanisms close to the point of delivery of the service; and the introduction of regulatory systems only where strictly necessary.

---

[252] This was the Second Report of the Co-Ordinating Group of Secretaries (from nine Departments) established by the Government under the "Strategic Management Initiative" (May 2, 1995) The First Report was published on March 2, 1995. See, too, the report of the 1993–1994 M.Sc. class of Assistant Secretaries, entitled "Strategic Management in the Irish Civil Service: A Review drawing on experience in New Zealand and Australia" subsequently published as (Oireachtas) *Select Committee on Finance and General Affairs consideration of SMI* (January 10 and 11, 1996).

[253] They include the following: privatisation of nationalised industries; 'contracting-out' to private business; the re-organisation and re-focusing of health and education services; Quangos and committees and other devices yoking together public, private and voluntary sectors. Most significant of all was the introduction of a hundred executive or 'Next Steps' agencies (each dealing with a discrete block of executive work and under the control of a chief executive responsible for delivering specified services within policy and resources agreed with the responsible Minister), employing (by 1993) 260,000 civil servants or 45% of the establishment. For a summary, see Morison and Livingstone, *Reshaping Public Power: Northern Ireland and the British Constitutional Crisis* (1995), Chap.2.

CHAPTER 4

STATE-SPONSORED BODIES[1]

1. Introduction

The principal objective of the Ministers and Secretaries Act 1924 was, as has been seen, to provide that all the central, executive power of the state should flow through Ministers responsible to the Dáil. However, by 1927, the first four state-sponsored bodies had been established. The functions of these four give some idea of the work of the state-sponsored sector: the Electricity Supply Board was set up to provide public financing of a huge investment project which, it was believed, could not be privately financed; the Agricultural Credit Corporation was constituted to make loans to farmers and to promote the co-operative movement; the Dairy Disposal Co. Ltd was set up to acquire, and thus prevent a foreign take-over of, Newmarket Creameries; the purpose of the Medical Registration Council – whose functions were passed on to the newly-constituted Medical Council in 1978 – was to regulate the practice of medicine in the state.

It ought to be stressed that our concern is with the structure of state bodies and their relationship with the Government, rather than their performance, which is a matter of economics and public administration. However, to exclude entirely reference to these subjects would be rather like portraying *Hamlet* as a play about a Second Grave-Digger. Thus, one should note that by 1996 there were about 120 state-sponsored bodies.[2] The total number employed in the entire sector was

---

[1] See Chubb, *The Government and Politics of Ireland* (1992), Chap. 14; Chubb, *A Source Book of Irish Government* (1981), Chap. 10; Fitzgerald, *State-Sponsored Bodies* (1963); *Industrial Policy* (Dublin:The Stationery Office, 1984); *N.E.S.C., Enterprise in the Public Sector* (Dublin: The Stationery Office); Covery and McDowell, *Privatisation: Issues of Principle and Implementation in Ireland* (1990); Zimmerman, "Irish State-Sponsored Bodies: The Fractionalization of Authority and Responsibility" (1986) 7 *Seirbhís Phoiblí*, 2, 27; O'Callaghan, "Controlling the State-Sponsored Bodies" (1983) 31 *Administration* 346; Walsh, "Commercial State-Sponsored Bodies" in *The Irish Banking Review*, Summer 1987, 27; Massey, "Privatisation: Time for a Closer Look" (1987) 8 *Seirbhís Phoiblí* 2, 2; McMahon "The Role of the State Organisation" (1987) 8 *Seirbhís Phoiblí* 2, 60; Sweeney, "Public Enterprise in Ireland: A Statistical Description and Analysis": a paper given to the Statistical and Social Enquiry Society of Ireland on February 15, 1990. The public debt crisis of the late 1980s, coupled with the backwash from the Thatcher-era in Britain, naturally attracted a good deal of writing on the present topic in the late 80s. By the 90s, the tide has ebbed. But see: Gray (ed.), *International Perspectives on the Irish Economy* (1997), Chaps. 5 and 6; Fitzgerald and McCoy (eds.), *Issues in Irish Energy Policy* (1993, E.S.R.I. Paper No. 20); FitzGerald and Johnston (eds.), *Energy Utilities and Competitiveness* (1995, E.S.R.I. Paper No. 24).

[2] For a rather out of date list of state-sponsored bodies, see 311 *Dáil Debates*, Cols. 868–886 (February 8, 1979). Notice, however, that the parliamentary question, to which this list (together with informative comments) was the answer defined "state-sponsored body" in fairly expansive terms. By contrast, the Public Expenditure Division of the Department of Finance, which operates a general overview of the entire state-sponsored body sector, requires that to qualify as a state-sponsored body: all or almost all members of the board should be appointed by a Minister; and (in the case of a non-commercial body) the bulk of the funds should emanate from the Government and the auditor should be the Comptroller and Auditor General as opposed to a private auditor. Also the Department's definition excludes advisory agencies. See also, n. 4 below.

approximately 70,000 (or 7 per cent of the total work-force, or 9 per cent of the total number of employees). The sector accounted for 10 per cent. of gross national product and consumed one-half of the state's annual investment programme. The lion's share of all these figures is taken up by the 30 or so commercial state-sponsored bodies.[3] Because of their diverse tasks, state bodies vary considerably in terms of capital, staffing, etc., ranging from a dozen staff (at the Law Reform Commission) to 11,500 employees (at Bord Telecom, in 1997).

Meaning of "state-sponsored body"

There is no general statutory definition of a state-sponsored body[4] for the reason that the term is seldom used in statute law, which almost always directs itself to a specific body as opposed to the entire sector. Yet although there is a variation from one body to another, (so that propositions in this field are inevitably generalisations) the term is useful for descriptive purposes because these bodies do raise common problems of accountability, patronage, staffing, control, organisation and legal status. Broadly speaking, the term "state-sponsored body" denotes an authority which discharges specialised, central functions sometimes of a governmental nature, yet which is set at a distance from the Government and Ministers. This last point is the central feature[5] in the concept of the state-sponsored body. For, on the one hand, these agencies exercising public functions are owned by the State and rely, in the case of non-commercial bodies, substantially on State finance; and are controlled by boards whose members are selected by the Government or a Minister. But, on the other hand, they are subject to a lesser degree of control, by the responsible Minister and the Dáil, than would apply to the activities of a Department of State.[6] As was said by the Minister when piloting the Bill to constitute the ESB through the Dáil:

---

[3] We return at pp. 128–134 to the differences between the commercial and non-commercial state bodies and to a list of commercial state bodies.

[4] But see Ministers and Secretaries (Amendment) Act 1973, s.1 (which defines the catchment area of the (former) Public Services Advisory Council as "the public service" to mean "the Civil Service of the Government and the Civil Service of the State" plus (in what may be regarded as a definition of a state body) "such bodies established by or under statute and financed wholly or partly by means of grants or loans made by a Minister of State or the issue of shares taken up by a Minister of State as may stand designated for the time being by regulations made by the Minister [for the Public Service]." No such regulations have been made. See also Ryan, "The Role of the State-Sponsored Body in the new Public Service" (1973) 21 *Administration* 387, 397. Although the N.D.C. was dissolved by the Industrial Development (Amendment) Act 1991, it should be noted that a further definition was provided by the National Development Corporation Act 1986, s.10(1) which uses the term "state-sponsored commercial enterprise" in the context of entities with which the NDC may establish joint enterprises or which it had to consult before making an investment. The term was defined by reference to a list in the Second Sched. to the Act, which enumerates all the bodies usually regarded as commercial state bodies.

[5] See for example, National Roads Authority (established by the Roads Act 1993, Part III) which co-ordinates the national roads programme. This means that it has the task of reconciling the priorities of different county or county borough councils and the Department of the Environment. Its existence, as an independent entity, is also reassuring to the European Union, a lot of whose funds it distributes.

[6] A similar definition is implicit in the following extract from a Dáil Debate on the Blood Transfusion Services Board: "The Health (Corporate Bodies) Act was intended to provide the Minister with a legally efficient means of establishing a body which would discharge a specialist executive function, under the governance of a suitably constituted board, which would be likely to discharge that function more appropriately and expertly than could be done from within the Department; and which would be the centre for expertise." 470 *Dáil Debates* Col. 433 (October 16, 1996).

"[T]here are going to be no Parliamentary questions with regard to this Board. There are going to be no complaints from a Deputy that his area is not served at such a rate as some other Deputy . . . this Board is not going to be regarded as a machine for wiping off all political obligations of this, that and the other Deputy."[7]

In addition, a state-sponsored body is usually constituted by its own distinctive statute, a point developed in Part 3 of this chapter. The staff of state bodies are usually not civil servants.[8] This particular issue arose in *Central Bank of Ireland v. Gildea*[9] where the issue was whether the respondent (who had formerly been a security guard employed by the Bank) was a person "employed by or under the State" for the purpose of exclusion from the Unfair Dismissals Act 1977. Despite the fact that the Bank is the sole currency authority in the State, the Supreme Court ruled that the respondent fell outside the exempt category. Keane J. stated that since the respondent was not a staff member of "the discrete organs of state such as the President, the Attorney General and the Auditor and Comptroller General [who] are properly regarded as civil servants 'employed by the State'", nor did the respondent fall within the second category exempted from the 1977 Act in that "he is not a civil servant in any of the departments responsible to the individual Ministers who constitute the Government and hence is not a 'civil servant of the Government' and thus a person 'employed . . . under the State'" Keane J. continued:

"[The respondent] is employed by a body which has been created by statute, the powers of which, however essential they may be to the functioning of the State, can be removed from them at any stage by the Oireachtas. He is thus in no different position from those employed in a vast range of what have come to be called 'semi-state bodies', the employees of which may, by specific legislative provision, be deemed to be civil servants but who, in the absence of any such provision, are not to be so regarded."[10]

Finally as stated already, a state-sponsored body administers a central, specialised, governmental function. Thus, local or regional bodies – such as health boards or harbour boards or local development agencies such as the Dun Laoghaire Harbour (Finance) Board established by the Dun Laoghaire Harbour Act 1994 or Temple Bar Properties Ltd[11] – are usually excluded. Again the epithet "governmental" – deliberately a rather vague term – alludes to the fact that it is conventional to exclude quasi-judicial bodies, *e.g.* tribunals like An Bord Pleanála, or the Adoption Board. Also excluded are the three traditional specialist services, of education,[12] police, and defence as well as those entities which are confined to giving advice to a Minister, for example the Heritage Council established by the Heritage Act 1995 (which has taken over the function of advising the Minister for Arts, Heritage,

---

[7] 18 *Dáil Debates*, Col.1919 (March 15, 1927).
[8] Another troublesome term, examined at pp. 74–79.
[9] [1997] 2 I.L.R.M. 391.
[10] *Ibid.* at 399–400.
[11] Temple Bar Properties Ltd is responsible for an urban renewal programme financed by £40 million of E.U. funding and blessed by fiscal advantages for investors and planning permission concessions for developers.
[12] In the case of the universities, see also the Ministers and Secretaries Act 1924, s.9(4).

Gaeltacht and the Islands, in the appropriate areas, from the National Monuments Advisory Council), the Historic Monuments Council or the Wildlife Council.[13] However bodies, like the Combat Poverty Agency or the National Social Service Board, which have a wider competence, as regards promotion and publication, are treated as non-commercial state bodies.

Commissions

There are, however, other executive[14] functions in regard to which it is desirable that a steady policy, which is not blown by the political wind, should be followed; yet which happen to be housed in an entity which cannot be regarded as a state-sponsored body. This is the explanation for the existence of the Revenue Commissioners (1923); Civil Service Commission (1924)[15] and the Local Appointments Commission (1926).[16] These bodies are not state bodies: because their staff are civil servants of the Government; because they are not constituted as independent legal entities (whether as corporations sole or companies); and because, historically, apart from the Local Appointments Commission, they were set up before the earliest state-sponsored bodies. However, what is more important is that they do enjoy the same kind of arm's length relationship with the responsible Minister. This has been achieved by vesting their functions in statutory commissioners who are free of interference in day-to-day matters, albeit largely as a result of convention. Such

---

[13] Notice also that, by s.10 of the Heritage Act 1995, the Council may veto the alteration of any heritage building (designated as such by the Minister, on the advice of the Council); but subject to the possibility of the veto being overridden by the Minister or the Government.

[14] For further similarly independent bodies consider three *sui generis* entities, whose autonomy is vital to the health of the polity: the Director of Public Prosecutions (on which see Prosecution of Offences Act 1974, s.2); the Central Statistics Office (on which see Statistics Act 1993, ss. 8–19) and the Legal Aid Board (Civil Legal Aid Act 1995, ss.3–9). In each of the first two cases, the constituent statute contains an explicit statement of independence; though in regard to the C.S.O., it is directed to the Director General and is limited to specified statistical matters. In the case of the C.S.O., the Taoiseach bears some elements of overall responsibility for the office. However the Director General is responsible for the management and control of the Office; and the National Statistics Board (of eight members: seven appointed by the Taoiseach plus the D.G.) with the agreement of Taoiseach, bears "the general function of guiding the strategic direction of the Office". The D.G. and his staff are made civil servants of the State; so too is the D.P.P. (though not his staff). There are special provisions to protect the D.P.P.'s independence at the points of appointment and removal.

In the case of the Legal Aid Board, the chief executive is a civil servant of the State and his solicitors may be designated as such, by the Minister for Justice, with the consent of the Minister for Finance. The Board is given a strong position vis-à-vis the Minister who may issue general directives as a policy but not in regard to any particular case.

In addition, a Courts Service Board and a Prisons Board were promised by the then Taoiseach John Bruton T.D. in November 1996: see further Morgan, *The Separation of Powers in the Irish Constitution* (1997), p. 214.

[15] "The fact that the Civil Service Commissioners hold office at the pleasure of the Executive Council would appear . . . unsatisfactory in view of the statutory intention that they should exercise a more or less judicial independence in certain matters . . . [we] hope that the steady development of a sound practice over a considerable number of years will eventually prove a better safeguard than might be afforded by some other system of a more logical character" (Commission of Inquiry into the Civil Service 1932–1935, Vol. 1, p. 82). This is what happened.

[16] Notice that the Irish Land Commission, established in 1881, was dissolved by the Irish Land Commission (Dissolution) Act 1992, s.4 and its remaining powers and duties transferred to the Minister for Agriculture and Food. The reason is that the former Commission's task of transferring land from landowners to tenant farmers had been effectively complete for some decades. This Act has not yet been brought into force.

commissioners usually have their own separate estimate. Since these bodies have so much in common with state-sponsored bodies it may be instructive to examine here the structure of one of them briefly.

The Revenue Commissioners were constituted in 1923 to take over the functions of tax assessment and collection formerly exercised by the British Commissioners of Inland Revenue and the British Commissioners of Customs and Excise. The three Revenue Commissioners are appointed for an indefinite term, at the pleasure of the Taoiseach, from among the existing officials of the Commissioners.[17] Finance Acts traditionally embody a provision to the effect that all taxes or duties imposed or continued by the Act "are hereby placed under the care and management of the Revenue Commissioners". It is true that the Revenue Commissioners Order of 1923 requires the Commissioners to obey any instructions which may be issued to them by the Minister for Finance. However, this provision has been substantially glossed by a convention which has frequently been enunciated by Ministers in reply to deputies' questions in the Dáil. One of its earliest formulations (in 1923) is contained in a letter sent, on the Minister's behalf, to the Commissioners' first chairman. The following is an extract from this letter:

> "[W]hile the Revenue Commissioners will be responsible directly to the Minister for Finance for the administration of the Revenue Services, the Commissioners will act independently of Ministerial control in exercising the statutory powers vested in them in regard to the liability to tax of the individual taxpayer."[18]

Plainly, a well-understood convention to this effect is helpful to Ministers and deputies in warding off importuning taxpayers. Indeed it may be that, in general and certainly in the case of the Revenue Commissioners, a commission's *de facto* independence from the executive is greater than that of a state-sponsored body.

A note on legal status

State-sponsored bodies are generally subject to the ordinary law, for example, as to torts or tax, save where they enjoy some specific statutory exemption. Yet there are a number of contexts in which they might enjoy some special position. In determining whether they do, it is necessary to consider the legal status of the body. More precisely, its degree of independence of the central executive organ, is significant. The first context stems from the international law precept, adopted in most domestic legal systems, that "foreign states" are exempt from their jurisdiction. Thus, in *Gibbons v. Údarás na Gaeltachta*,[19] the question arose before the New York courts

---

[17] Revenue Commissioners Order of 1923 made under Adaptation of Enactment's Act 1922, s.7. Read literally, the Ministers and Secretaries Act 1924, s.1(ii) ("The Department of Finance which shall comprise the collection of the revenues of [the State] . . .") coupled with the Schedule, First Part could be taken to mean that the Department of Finance had swallowed the Revenue Commissioners, but this result was not intended: see *Re Irish Insurance Association Ltd* [1955] I.R. 176 at 182–183 and Sean Reamon, *History of the Revenue Commissioners* (1981), Chap. 5.

[18] The letter is quoted in Reamon, *ibid.* pp. 56–61 where other evidence for the convention is given. On the Revenue Commissioners' independence, see also the *Beef Tribunal Report* (Pn. 1007, 1994), Chap. 9, especially p. 306.

[19] 549 F.Supp. 1094 (S.D.N.Y. 1982). An identical conclusion as to the agency's immunity was reached in *Gibson v. The Republic of Ireland* 682 F. 2d. 1022 (D.C. Cir. 1982).

in the course of an action for breach of contract and fraudulent misrepresentation allegedly arising from a joint venture agreement partially concluded in New York, as to whether Údarás, a state body, which acts as a promotional agency for the Gaeltacht, fell within the ambit of this immunity.[20] The courts rejected the agency's claim for sovereign immunity, emphasising its view of the Údarás operation as being "no different . . . from the promotional activities engaged in by a private public relations firm".

Secondly, a number of diverse statutes employ some such term as "public authority" or "public body", usually without offering any assistance by way of definition of the critical term.[21] The question could arise as to whether some particular state body is within the term. In fact, the only form in which this problem has presented itself in recent Irish law concerned the General Medical (Payments) Board (which might be classified not as a state body but as a tribunal which also discharges some routine, executive functions). In any case, the net question in *The General Medical Services (Payments) Board v. Minister for Social Welfare*[22] was whether an employee of the plaintiff board was insurable for the Social Welfare Act 1952 at the ordinary rate of contribution or at the special rate applicable to employment by a "public authority" pursuant to Article 5(1)(c) of the Social Welfare (Modification of Insurance) Regulations 1956. In short, the question for the High Court was whether the plaintiff board was a public authority. Hamilton J. commenced by observing that: ". . . it is surprising that there does not exist any general definition of what is or what is not a public authority either in statute or in court decisions."[23] Later, the judge, adopted the following definition taken from *Halsbury's Laws of England*:

"A public authority is a body, not necessarily a county council, municipal corporation or other local authority, which has public or statutory duties to perform and which performs these duties and carries out its transactions for the benefit of the public and not for private profit."[24]

The judge also summarised the function and status of the plaintiff board as follows:

"The plaintiff board is a board established by a ministerial order made in pursuance of the powers given to the Minister for Health by s.11(2) of the Health Act 1970, which Act was enacted by the legislature, *inter alia*, to provide for the establishment of bodies for the administration of the health services; it is one of the bodies established for the administration of the health services; its function is admittedly a limited one namely:

---

20 This immunity was created by s.1605 of the U.S. Foreign Sovereign Immunities Act.
21 But note that "State authority" is defined, for the purpose of the Postal and Telecommunications Services Act 1983, s.2(1) to include only Ministers of the Government, Commissioners of Public Works and the Irish Land Commission, and, for the purpose of the Statute of Limitations 1957, s.2(1), in the same way but with the addition of two other entities, the Revenue Commissioners and the Attorney-General. The State Authority (Development and Management) Act 1993, s.1 defines the term to mean a Minister of the Commissioners of Public Works in Ireland (the Land Commission now being defunct).
22 [1976–1977] I.L.R.M. 210.
23 *Ibid.* at 211. Many of the authorities opened to the judge by counsel were concerned with the interpretation of s.1 of the Public Authorities Protection Act 1893 (which is no longer law here or in England). Notice that, by the Transport Act 1950, s.10, CIÉ was made exempt from the 1893 Act.
24 *Ibid.* at 217. The quotation is from *Halsbury* (3rd ed.), Vol. 30, p. 682. This passage does not really address the difficulties with the concept of a public body.

(a) The calculations of payments to be made for the services provided by the health boards under s.58 and s.59(1) of the Health Act 1970.

(b) The verification of the accuracy and reasonableness of claims in relation to such services.

(c) The compilation of statistics and other information in relation to such services and the communications of such information to persons concerned with the operation of such services.

It cannot make a profit and its members do not receive any remuneration."[25]

The judge's conclusion that the plaintiff was, indeed, a public authority, then flowed naturally from the definition quoted earlier.

Another example of a statute employing the phrase "public body" is the Prevention of Corruption Act 1906[26] – which is still law in Ireland. By this Act, it is an offence for an employee of a "public body" to corruptly accept a gift as an inducement to show favour to persons doing business with the body. In *R. v. Manners*,[27] the House of Lords held that the North Thames Gas Board came within the definition of a "public body" for the purposes of the 1906 Act. A similar question could arise in an Irish court in a case in which the employee of a state-sponsored body was being prosecuted for the same offence.[28]

Thirdly, it may just be arguable that a state-sponsored body would be regarded as part of the State for the purposes of any former prerogative right (*e.g.* the privilege against disclosure of evidence) which may persist in independent Ireland. This argument appears unlikely to succeed however, given the historical development of the prerogative, coupled with the tenor of the reasoning in *Re Irish Employers' Mutual Insurance Association Ltd*[29] and also the Irish courts' dislike of special privileges.

Such questions, each of which may require a slightly different categorisation, have generated a certain amount of case law in Britain and elsewhere in the common law world[30] but not in Ireland. However, the criterion for the inclusion (or not) of a state body is not in doubt. As was said by Kingsmill Moore J. in regard to an analogous issue (involving, be it noted, the Commissioners of Public Works, who are less autonomous than a state-sponsored body):

---

25 [1976–1977] I.L.R.M. 215. Two subsidiary points, in the case, may be worthy of note. The first of these arose from what is anyway a rather unconvincing argument, namely that the board was set up by ministerial order rather than directly by statute. This argument was rejected by the High Court on the basis that this distinction does not cause any difference in the "fundamental nature [of the functions of the board]" (p. 217). Secondly, the functions of the plaintiff board are of "an internal administrative nature" (p. 217) in that it does not involve the making available of a general medical service to the public. However, in response to this, the Court held that the plaintiff's functions could not be considered in isolation from the duties of the health boards, which they service and which plainly are "public".

26 And see now the amendment in the Ethics in Public Office Act 1995, s.38.

27 [1978] A.C. 43.

28 Note, that the Transport Act 1950, s.10 specifically excludes the Board of CIÉ from the scope of the Public Authorities Protection Act, 1893.

29 [1955] I.R. 176. For the facts in this case, see above n.31, p. 119.

30 Foulkes, *Administrative Law* (5th ed.), pp. 12–17; Hogg, *Liability of the Crown* (1989), Chap. 8.

"The degree of direction and control which is exercised by the executive over the conduct of the work may afford an indication as to whether the Commissioners in executing the work are acting as servants of the State."[31]

European Community Law[32]

The novel concepts of European Community law have introduced a further need to categorise public authorities (embracing, *inter alia*, state-sponsored bodies) in order to resolve a number of different issues, three of which will be mentioned here. These questions are complicated by the fact that, in the interests of maintaining uniformity from Member State to Member State, they should be regarded as mixed questions of Community and national law.

The first of these questions arises from the fact that Article 48 of the EC Treaty which establishes the right to free movement of workers permits a derogation in the case of "the public service". The Court of Justice has stressed the need for a restrictive interpretation of the exemption from such a fundamental principle. Thus in several rulings, the Court has confined this exemption to posts involved in activities which are peculiar to public service, such as the armed forces, the judiciary, the diplomatic corps and local authorities, as *contra* distinguished from activities such as health-care or education, which may also be performed by the private sector.[33] What this means, in the context of state-sponsored bodies, is that commercial bodies are excluded from the exemption in that they involve industrial or commercial enterprises, whereas several of the non-commercial bodies are within the exemption because they entail distinctively public functions, such as economic regulation.

Another context in which a similar question arises is the free movement of goods. An example occurred in *R v. The Royal Pharmaceutical Society of Great Britain et al.*[34] Here the Court of Justice, notwithstanding that the respondent professional

---

[31] *Re Irish Employers' Mutual Insurance Association Ltd* [1955] I.R. 176. The facts of the case were that the Commissioners of Public Works had taken out insurance with a company which subsequently went into liquidation. The Commissioners claimed that the moneys due to them from the company should, as a matter of prerogative right, be paid in priority to the debts due to other creditors. For present purposes, the relevant question was whether assuming that this prerogative existed, the Commissioners would be characterised as sufficiently part of the State to be able to invoke it. It was held that, in general, the Commissioners were to be regarded as servants of the State. However, where the Commissioners were performing work on behalf of local authorities, then they were not acting as servants of the State. See also, *Re Maloney* [1926] I.R. 202 at 206; *Irish Land Commission v. Ruane* [1938] I.R. 148 at 152–157, 161 (Irish Land Commission characterised as a servant of the State).

A variation on the point under discussion in the text is analysed with reference to the National Treasury Management Agency in Gwynn Morgan, *The Separation of Powers in the Irish Constitution* (1997), *op. cit.*, above, n.14, Chap. 12, pp. 274–275.

There is one further point of characterisation in which state bodies are not mired: they are probably not exercising "the executive power of the State" so as to engage the separation of powers, as expressed in Article 28.2 of the Constitution.

[32] On this subject, see an excellent monograph by Deirdre Curtin, "The Province of Government: Delimiting the Direct Effect of Directives in the Common Law Context" (1990) 15 E.L. Rev. 195. see further, on the impact of Competition Law, pp. 173–182.

[33] Other examples include the question of whether a state body is a "public body or undertaking" for the purposes of public works contracts (on which, see pp. 124–128) or for Art. 90(1) of the EC Treaty, which deals with monopoly power (on which, see pp. 173–182).

[34] Joined Cases 266–267/87 [1989] E.C.R. 1295.

body could not be regarded as an organ of state so far as operational control was concerned, held that the measures which it had adopted to regulate the pharmaceutical profession could be equated with those of the state on the basis of their purpose and of the type of powers with which the respondent had been endowed.

The remaining reason for classification required by European Community law arises when an E.C. Directive has either not been implemented by a Member State after the requisite time allowed for implementation has passed or has been inaccurately translated into its national law. It has now been established that, while such Directives do not operate against a private person, they do, if they are unconditional and sufficiently precise, have direct effect against the State concerned, on the basis that the State is estopped from benefiting from the consequence of its own default.[35] This ruling immediately raises the question of the extent of "the State" and, in particular in the present context, whether it would embrace a state-sponsored body. The leading authority is *Foster v. British Gas plc.*[36] where the substantive issue here, involved Directive 76/207, the Equal Treatment Directive. The relevant issue for present purposes was whether the defendant which was, at the relevant time, a nationalised industry (as the British call their commercial state bodies) should be classified as an organ of the State. The English Court of Appeal concluded that it should not so be classified, saying that the defendant was not subject to the day-to-day control of a Minister and that its powers were original rather than delegated by a Minister or other state organ. In addition, the Court relied on the fact that the defendant could not be regarded as performing any of the classic duties of the State.[37]

The plaintiff appealed to the House of Lords, which referred the case to the European Court of Justice and this court sounded a very different note from that heard in the Court of Appeal. The kernel of the Court of Justice's judgment is the following passage:

> "[18] . . . the Court has held in a series of cases that unconditional and sufficiently precise provisions of a directive could be relied on against organisations or bodies which were subject to the authority or control of the State or had special powers beyond those which result from the normal rules applicable to relations between individuals.
>
> [19] The Court has accordingly held that provisions of a directive could be relied on against tax authorities (Case 8/81, *Becker* [1982] E.C.R. 53 and in Case C–221/88, *Fratelli Costanzo v. Comune Di Milano* [1989] E.C.R. 1839), constitutionally independent authorities responsible for the maintenance of public order and safety (Case 222/84, *Johnston v. Chief Constable of the Royal Ulster Constabulary*), and public authorities providing public health services (Case 152/84, *Marshall* [1986] E.C.R. 1651).

---

[35] Case 152/84 *Marshall v. Southampton and South-West Hampshire Area Health Authority (Teaching)* [1987] E.C.R. 723.

[36] [1988] I.C.R. 584. (C.A.); [1990] 2 C.M.L.R. 833 (ECJ).

[37] Success in regard to this factor was the basis of the plaintiff's victory in Case 222/84 *Johnston v. Chief Constable of the Royal Ulster Constabulary* [1986] E.C.R. 1651.

[20] It follows from the foregoing that a body, whatever its legal form, which has been made responsible, pursuant to a measure adopted by the State, for providing a public service under the control of the State and has for that purpose special powers beyond those which result from the normal rules applicable in relations between individuals is included in any event among the bodies against which the provisions of a directive capable of having direct effect may be relied upon."[38]

Unfortunately the last paragraph of this passage is a little inexact. In the first place, does the reference to "the control of the State" mean legal control or real, effective control and, secondly, how close must the control be? It is relevant here that Advocate General's Gerven's opinion, in this case, is much longer and better reasoned and can be used to amplify the court's judgment. The Advocate General is explicit that, generally, the "concept of a public body must be understood very broadly".[39] In particular, it extends:

"so far as 'the State' has given itself powers which place it in a position to decisively influence the conduct of persons – whatever their nature, public or private, or their sphere of activity – with regard to the subject-matter of the directive which has not been correctly implemented. It is immaterial in that regard in what manner 'the State' can influence the conduct of those persons: de jure or de facto, for example because the organ of authority has a general or specific power (or is simply able as a matter of fact) to give that person binding directions, whether or not by the exercise of rights as a shareholder, to approve its decisions in advance or suspend or annul them after the fact, to appoint or dismiss (the majority of) its directors, or to interrupt its funding wholly or in part so as to threaten its continued existence, with, however, the proviso [that] the possibility exercising influence must stem from something other than a general legislative power . . ."[40]

In addition, the passage quoted from the Court's judgment left it doubtful whether the requirements it mentioned – "a public service under the control of the State"

---

[38] [1990] 2 C.M.L.R. 833 at 856–857. An example of "special powers" in the Irish context would be Bord Telecom's and An Post's monopolies, which are examined at p. 805. When the case returned to the House of Lords, that body had little difficulty in concluding that British Gas was an emanation of the State for this purpose: [1991] 2 A.C. 93. In an Irish context, bodies with "special powers" such as Bord na Móna and An Post would almost certainly rank as "emanations of the State" for this purpose. The *Foster* definition has, however, caused its own problems. Thus, in *Doughty v. Rolls-Royce* plc [1992] 1 C.M.L.R. 1045 the English Court of Appeal held that the fact that the company had been wholly state-owned at the relevant time was not in itself sufficient, since the company did not have any special powers beyond those that result from the normal rules applicable to relations between individuals. On the other hand, in *National Union of Teachers v. Governing Body of St. Mary's Church of England Junior School* [1997] I.R.L.R. 242 a differently constituted Court of Appeal took a more expansive view of the *Foster* test, holding that a publicly funded private school was an emanation of the state for this purpose. In Schiemann L.J.'s words (at 247), the governors were "a public body charged by the state with running the school and exercising their functions with a view to securing that the school provided the national curriculum." See generally, Kvjatkovski, "What is an 'Emanation of the State'? An Educated Guess" (1997) *European Public Law* 329.

[39] [1990] 2 C.M.L.R. 833 at 850.

[40] *Ibid.* at 851.

and "[possessing] special powers beyond those which result from the normal rules" . . . must both be satisfied. The Advocate General, however, is definite, that to bring a body within the broad category of the State, it suffices if *any* of the requirements is met. Moreover, the Advocate General mentions another ground of qualification which has no counterpart in the court's judgment, namely: "bodies which pursuant to the constitutional structure of a Member-State can exercise any authority over individuals . . .".[41]

It appears likely, from the test enunciated by the Court of Justice in *Foster*, especially when read in the light of the Advocate General's opinion, that an Irish state-sponsored body (even a commercial body) would come within the category of a public body for the purpose of being bound by an EC Directive. As it happens, there are, as yet, two Irish decisions in point. Moreover the reasoning in the first case is so divergent from that in *Foster* as to be now of doubtful authority.

The case in question is *Browne v. An Bord Pleanála*[42] in which the net question was whether a grant of planning permission was invalid because the application did not comply with the provisions of Directive 85/337 in that it omitted certain requisite information from the environmental impact study. Addressing the point rather briefly, Barron J. stated: "the respondent has [no] wider powers than those of an Appellate Tribunal. In my view, the respondent can in no way be held responsible for the failure of the state to implement the directive, if failed they have."[43] In the light of *Foster*, this approach appears to be founded too squarely upon the notion that for an entity to be regarded as a public body, it should, in some sense, share responsibility for the failure in the relevant Member-State to implement the directive in national law. This approach has been rejected by the European Court, as is clear from the facts of the cases listed in paragraph 19 of the passage in Foster quoted earlier.

The next case, *Coppinger v. Waterford County Council*[44] reflects post-*Foster* developments. In this case the plaintiff had been injured by reason of a collision with a council truck which had not been fitted with rear-underrun protections. Although the plaintiff's common law negligence action failed, Geoghegan J. found that the State had been in breach of Community law in the manner in which it had implemented certain Directives[45] by not providing for such rear underrun protection.[46] Geoghegan J. had no doubt but that the council qualified as an

---

41 *Ibid.* at 850–851.
42 [1991] 2 I.R. 209. Note that in *Murphy v. An Bord Telecom* [1989] I.L.R.M. 53 one of the preliminary questions referred to the Court of Justice by the High Court involved the status of Bord Telecom for the present purpose. However, since the discrimination in question fell within Art.119 of the EC Treaty, it was not necessary to determine the applicability of the Equal Pay Directive (75/117).
43 [1991] 2 I.R. 209 at 219–226.
44 Unreported, High Court, March 22, 1996. See Travers, "The Liability of Local Authorities for Breaches of Community Directives by Member States" (1997) 22 E.L.Rev. 173.
45 Council Directive 70/221 EEC, as amended by Council Directive 79/490 EEC. The Irish implementing regulations are contained in the Road Traffic (Construction, Equipment and Use of Vehicles)(Amendment)Regulations 1985 (S.I. No. 158 of 1985).
46 Although the plaintiff was held 75% responsible for the accident, Geoghegan J. nonetheless concluded that had the State implemented the Directive in a timely fashion so that the council truck's had been fitted with such protection, the plaintiff's injuries would only have been minor ones. Geoghegan J. accordingly found the council – as an emanation of the State – 25% liable on the basis of the tort of "actionable breach of a directive." For State liability for breach of European Community law, see pp. 845–849.

"emanation of the State", since he found it "difficult to see how it could be argued that an Irish County Council does not fall within" the definition advanced in *Foster*. Unlike Barron J. in *Browne*, Geoghegan J. thus treated the county council as if it were part of the State for the purposes of holding it liable for a breach of Community law.[47]

In its own way, *Coppinger* illustrates the characterisation difficulties which are inherent in *Foster* and, by extension, in the entire horizontal/vertical effect of directives debate. Would the situation have been any different if, for example, the truck had been owned by a self-employed contractor who had been engaged by the council to perform certain tasks on its behalf?[48] In any case, if the defendant in question had not been an emanation of the State, the plaintiff's remedy would have been to sue the State in a *Francovich* action for breach of Community law.[49]

Other forms of state involvement in the economy

State-sponsored agencies are comparatively straightforward in that they are bodies which, subject to some exceptions, are under the exclusive and visible control and ownership of the State. If we range even further away from the traditional arrangement of public functions being discharged by a Department of State with a Minister at the head, we encounter manifold and subtle (even subterranean) forms of state involvement in the economy. It would be beyond our brief to do more than allude to the novel questions of control, responsibility, consistency and adequate public debate raised by arrangements like these. However, the following examples may be mentioned briefly. The first concerns the State's capacity to make contracts, a phenomenon which was sketched briefly by the then Minister for Finance in the following passage which is, if anything, of even greater relevance today:

> "Where in the past a civil service of limited size carried out the administrative functions of the state, today the range of instruments required by government for the achievement of its objectives goes well beyond the traditional concept of the organs of the State. At its extreme, this tendency has gone farthest in the United States where the phenomenon is common of the large private sector corporation almost entirely dependent on public contracts and producing almost exclusively for government. The development of bodies of this type side by side with the more familiar agencies of government has led to questioning in some countries of the traditional institutional arrangements of the performance of the executive functions of government. It has produced

---

47 Note that in *Chapelizod Residents' Association Ltd v. Dublin Corporation*, unreported, High Court, October 23, 1997 Smyth J. appeared to disagree with these views, saying that he did not consider a local authority to be an emanation of the State. This, however, was in the context of a challenge to the constitutionality of the exemption granted to local authorities from the planning process by s.4 of the Local Government (Planning and Development) Act 1963.

48 Thus, Case C–419/92 *Scholz v. Opera Univsitaria di Cagliari* [1994] E.C.R. I–505 proceeded on the "common ground" that the University in question constituted an emanation of the state. As White observes in "Equality in the Canteen" (1994) 19 E.L.Rev. 308, the question of whether other universities qualify as emanations of the state will depend on the organization and funding of the institution. See also the conflicting views of the English Court of Appeal in *Doughty v. Rolls-Royce plc* [1992] 1 C.M.L.R. 1045 and *National Union of Teachers v. Governing Body of St. Mary's School* [1997] I.R.L.R. 242.

49 *Francovich and Bonifaci v. Italy* [1991] E.C.R. I–5357: See pp. 845–849.

the concept of the 'contract state' where executive functions are performed by a range of bodies included in the broad category of 'quasi autonomous non-governmental institutions' with an emphasis on the contractual rather than the structural relationships between government and these bodies. It would be interesting to analyse the instruments through which the purposes of government are achieved in this country and to ascertain the extent, if any, to which there has been a move towards performance by contract rather than by traditional agencies . . . I don't think there has been any large scale move in this direction, but I think that the idea of a contractual relationship between government and its traditional agencies is emerging behind some of the thinking here in recent years. What is valuable about this thinking is that it concentrates attention on the problem of what government can and should do directly and what it can and should have undertaken for it by other means."[50]

Other examples of the State spreading its tentacles through the economy by means other than complete ownership include: statutory control over prices for various goods and services under the Prices Acts 1958–1972[51]; informal attempts by the Minister for the Environment to influence building society interest rates and by the Minister for Justice to encourage the Law Society of Ireland to expand the intake to its solicitors training course[52]; a complex of industrial grants and subsidies to set beside the system of taxes[53]; joint ventures between state bodies and other (often foreign) business organisations; state shareholding in private companies, either directly through the Minister for Finance or by way of a state-sponsored body, like the Industrial Development Agency (Ireland); the Prompt Payment of Accounts Act 1997 (which applied to public bodies); and the arrangement between Esat Digifone and the Gardaí, for the use of Garda Stations for the erection of tele-communications masts.[54] Another most significant example is the agreement between the "social partners" which at first took the form simply of national wage agreements but, by now, goes beyond salaries as well as spanning a number of years, the current example being the Partnership 2000 (1997–).[55]

Procedure for contracts of public bodies

Latterly, since the law in this area has become extremely complicated and now would require a monograph[56] even to outline it and its ramifications in E.U. and general administrative law. Here accordingly all that can be done is to give a flavour

---

50 Ryan, "The Role of the State Sponsored Body in the New Public Service" (1973) 21 *Administration* 387–388.
51 See, *e.g. Cassidy v. Minister for Industry* [1978] I.R. 297.
52 399 *Dáil Debates*, Col. 2311–2312 (June 13, 1990).
53 See Ussher and O'Connor, *Doing Business in Ireland*, (Matthew Bender) Chaps. 1 and 2; McMahon, *Economic Law in Ireland* (Brussels, 1977), Chap. 3 and generally.
54 *The Irish Times*, January 29, 1998.
55 Notice also that in 1925 the Abbey Theatre became the first state-subsidised theatre in the English-speaking world: Drabble, *The Oxford Companion to English Literature* (1984), p. 1.
56 Fortunately, there is a good monograph, on which the following account draws fairly heavily, namely: McCourt, *Public Buyer Guide* (published by An Bord Tráchtála in association with the Irish Institute of Purchasing and Materials Management, 1996). See also Lee, *Public Procurement* (Current E.C. Legal Developments Series, Butterworths).

of the subject. The most significant category includes those contracts which exceed specified E.U. thresholds (or those projects wholly or partly financed by E.U. institutions). Contracts in these categories are governed mainly by E.U. inspired law since this is usually more stringent than the Irish controls. By contrast, contracts for amounts falling below these amounts (and which are not financed by the E.U.) are regulated mainly by Irish law and guidelines. One has also to have in mind the distinct regime, which is applied to contracts made with commercial bodies, and which is explained below.[57]

Public bodies (other than commercial state bodies) – Irish Law

The Public Procurement Book published in 1994, by the Department of Finance, (also known as the *Green Book*) consists of two parts, of which the first sets out the Irish guidelines just mentioned and the second collects the E.U. inspired law (which is dealt with below). The rules apply to: the selection of consultants; property transactions (buying or selling, leasing or letting); purchase of goods; information technology; and planning and design contracts.[58] As regards supplies of such items as stationery or furniture, all Departments of State must order through a central body, the Government Supplies Agency (which is naturally subject to the normal régime).

According to the *Green Book* it is "a basic principle of government procurement that competitive tendering should always be used, unless exceptional circumstances apply, in which case the approval of the Government Contracts Committee (GCC)[59] must be obtained". What is "competitive tendering"? The answer is that it may take any of three forms: "open tendering" (*i.e.* anyone may tender) is not used, then either "restricted tendering" (firms on a standing list of qualified firms are invited to put in a tender); or "selective tendering" (firms are pre-qualified and then invited to tender) must be used. However, even in the case of the latter two cases, at least five firms must be invited to tender and three realistic tenders received. Notice, however, that this régime applies only in the case of contracts worth more than £20,000. Below that threshold, the public body involved is not obliged to seek a dispensation from the Committee, if it wishes to dispense with the normal competition tendering scheme; but is expected to follow whatever procedure is appropriate and proportionate to the circumstances.

Where the *Green Book* applies, the criteria to be followed in the award of a contract should be either the lowest suitable tender or the most economically advantageous tender (having regard to such matters as completion date and maintenance cost) and the criterion which is being used should be indicated by advertisement. The tender documents must be signed by the authorised officer, who is the official (at Principal Officer level or the equivalent) in each public body responsible for ensuring that the rules are followed. If they wish, unsuccessful tenderers should be given *general* reasons for the decision.

---

[57] See pp. 126–127.
[58] Further controls also apply in some of these fields for instance: "National Standard Building Elements and Design Cost Control Procedures" (3rd ed., 1993); "National Standard Control Procedures for House Construction Costs".
[59] A committee of officials from Departments and offices concerned with purchasing and construction contracts (*e.g.* Environment, Office of Public Works Agriculture and Food and Education) which is chaired by a Department of Finance official.

Various conditions must be included in the contract, for instance: in construction contracts, staff must be employed on terms which comply with approved employment agreements and should also be members of the CIF pension/sick pay scheme. Consultants should have the appropriate educational qualifications and insurance cover. In addition, any contractors must disclose a tax clearance certificate. Certain information on awards must be given to the Revenue Commissioners.

A problem here, as elsewhere,[60] is the exact legal status of *The Public Procurement Book* or the *Guidelines for State Bodies* (which is considered below). What would be the position, for instance, if a business which had failed to secure a contract, attempted to sue, on the ground that the procedure followed did not comply with the rules? Again would it be possible to seek judicial review in respect of the rules on the grounds of the unreasonableness of one of its provisions (for instance, the tax clearance requirement). In favour of some element of legal status is the existence of the Minister for Finance's statutory powers in regard to "the supervision and control of all purchases made for or on behalf of, and all supplies of commodities and goods held by any Department of State and the disposal thereof . . ."[61] but this provision is confined to "Departments of State". For the Minister for Finance's authority over the other entities, one has to go to the fact that (usually) the contracts into which they were entering will be funded by Exchequer money. The Minister's authorisation is necessary before such funds are spent[62] so that, by implication, he may have legal authority to fix conditions. But of course there are many contracts which are not funded by Exchequer money.

The position may thus change from one contract to another and may also depend upon the type of issue involved. Another way of giving some element of legal status may be to pray in aid of the doctrine of legitimate expectations.[63] However, this doctrine may not be attracted just because the *Guidelines for State Bodies* are entitled "Guidelines" and described in paragraph 1 as "recommendations".

Next, notice that it has been remarked that:

> "Although these guidelines do not have formal force of law, failure to apply them may obviously attract the displeasure of the Department of Finance. In addition, purchasers should be aware of the argument that failure to comply with the guidelines may be a breach of a representation or contractual obligation, to the effect that the purchaser will apply the proper published guidelines in consideration of the tenderer submitting his tender."[64]

One (extra-legal) way in which the rules may be enforced is through the censure of the Comptroller and Auditor General.

State-Sponsored Bodies

The position in regard to commercial and also it seems non-commercial state-sponsored bodies is more problematic. At present, their obligations are determined

---

[60] See pp. 41–57. See also Hardiman and Murphy, "Remedies in Ireland" in Tyrell and Bedford, *Public Procurement in Europe* (1997).

[61] Ministers and Secretaries Act 1924, s.1(ii).

[62] Ministers and Secretaries Act 1924, s.2(4); Exchequer and Audit Department Act 1921. For the detailed position, see Gwynn Morgan, *Constitutional Law of Ireland, op. cit.,* above, n.1, pp. 126–127.

[63] See Chap. 16.

[64] McCourt *op. cit.* above, n.56, p. 20.

by the Department of Finance's *Guidelines for State Bodies* published in 1992 (and currently – 1997 – being revised) which was based upon a *Report on Guidelines for State Bodies*. However, the *Green Book* also states that commercial state bodies should comply with the "broad principles" of the Government contracts procedures just outlined. Finally, in the wake of the controversy over the attempted sale of a CIÉ site in Cork, a task force made recommendations[65] as to improved procedures for *inter alia* procurement of goods and services and the disposal of assets, by the ten major commercial state bodies under the aegis of the Minister for Transport, Energy and Communications as it was then known. However, these recommendations which have not yet been formally adopted by the Government. With the very important exception of "utilities" – a term which is explained in the following section – the E.U. law does not apply to commercial state bodies. In other words, in this area of valuable contracts, the only controls are those derived from the 1992 *Guidelines*.

Thus, in regard to state bodies, all that will be done here is to note that the 1992 "Guidelines" are less stringent than *The Public Procurement Book*. They provide that state bodies may award "significant contracts" without competitive tendering; though only if the Board gives its express consent. And "significant" means contracts for works, equipment or goods in excess of £100,000 or contracts for professional services in excess of £25,000 from a single supplier in one year.

European Union Law: public bodies including "utilities"

At least, the status of the rules are clear here. There are a number of important E.U. Directives, which have been imported into Irish law, as statutory instruments.[66] These regulations cover all public bodies – the State, Ministers, local authorities and "other bodies governed by public law". Whilst commercial state bodies, as such, are excluded, "utilities" are included and this is a large category which covers state bodies in the fields of energy, water, telecommunications and transport – ESB, Bord Gais, Bord Telecom, Aer Rianta, CIÉ; also included are contracts in the water sector made by local authorities.

The first three of the Directives each applies above given financial thresholds, to a particular category of contract which has been entered into by a public body other than a "utility" (as defined): of purchase of goods, provision of services, or the execution of building or engineering works. by contrast, the fourth Directive[67] deals with all three categories of contracts entered into by a "utility". However, there are thresholds and (as indicated at the start of this section) it is only above the relevant threshold that a particular Directive applies. Each of the Directives conforms to a common pattern, in that it details; award procedures, including advertising; time limits controlling the tender process; how information requests from prospective tenderers must be handled; award criteria; and explanations to unsuccessful tenders. (There may be exclusions from the procedure where the basic security of the State requires it.) Contracting authorities must publish (prior to the award of any individual

---

[65] The recommendations were published on October 10, 1995
[66] S.I. No. 37 of 1992; S.I. No. 292 of 1994; S.I. No. 36 of 1992; S.I. No. 293 of 1994; and S.I. No. 173 of 1993. For further detail, see McCourt, *op. cit.*, above, n.56, Appendix III.
[67] S.I. No. 103 of 1993; S.I. No. 51 of 1995.

contract above the appropriate threshold) an individual contract notice and an individual award notice thereafter. And, at the beginning of each budgetary year, contracting authorities must (where the aggregate is to be above a specified aggregate) publish in the Official Journal of the European Community, a Periodic Indicative Notice. This must indicate, by reference to product area and CPA code, intended purchases over the following year.

As to enforcement: by virtue of the remedies Directives,[68] a special procedure is available for the speedy review of procurement decisions, by public authorities, in order to check whether there has been compliance with "community law in the field of public procurement or national rules implementing that law". In Ireland, this procedure takes the form of powers of review by which the High Court: may suspend an award procedure, by way of interim measures (though here the "public interest" has also to be taken into account); set aside unlawful decisions; remove discriminatory specifications; and award damages to persons harmed by an infringement.

The Directives just summarised apply only to contracts involving public bodies within the E.U. However, a separate but similar régime has existed (as of the completion of the Uruguay round on January 1, 1996) in the context of the GATT (General Agreement on Tariffs and Trade) which includes trade between E.U. states and the remainder of the States within the GATT (now subject to the control of the World Trade Organisation). This, too applies to all levels of Irish government departments and also to particular utilities.[69]

2. Functional Classification

Commercial state-sponsored bodies, known in other countries as "public enterprises", are under some kind of notional duty (though one which is only occasionally mentioned in legislation[70]) to make sufficient profit to cover capital expenditure and, in practice, they do receive at least a substantial portion of their revenue from the sale of their products or services. By contrast, non-commercial bodies are agencies for the disbursement of state funds, which are given to them as grants-in-aid which appear as sub-heads of their parent Department's estimates. These funds only may be released with the permission of the Minister for Finance and the responsible Minister. Stemming from this difference, the Government has a much closer control, in some cases statutory,[71] over the salaries and numbers of persons employed in the case of a non-commercial agency. For example, non-commercial state-sponsored bodies must make quarterly returns to the parent Department

---

[68] S.I. No. 38 of 1992; S.I. Nos. 5 and 309 of 1994; S.I. No. 104 of 1993 and S.I. No. 51 of 1995. The only Irish reported case to date in which the public procurement directives were judicially considered appears to be *SIAC Construction Ltd v. Mayo County Council*, unreported, High Court, June 17, 1997. In that case Laffoy J. rejected the suggestion that a judicial review challenge to an award should be determined otherwise than by reference to standard reasonableness criteria and, judged that by that standard, the award of a tender to a contractor who had not submitted the lowest tender was found on the facts not to be irrational or manifestly unreasonable.

[69] See McCourt *op. cit.* above, n.56, p. 23 and Appendix II.

[70] *e.g.* Irish Aviation Authority Act 1993, s.16; Irish Medicines Board Act 1995, s.21; but *cf.* Electricity (Supply) Act 1927, s.21(2) which states that the Board's rates etc. "should be so fixed that the revenue derived in any year . . . will be sufficient and only sufficient . . . to pay [outgoings]."

[71] *e.g.* Combat Poverty Agency Act 1986, s.13, Urban Renewal Act 1986, s.20.

supplying this information. In addition, they were subject to the one-in-three embargo on the filling of vacancies within the public service, which existed in the early and mid–1980s.

With commercial state-sponsored bodies, control is slightly less tight. There is no direct control over numbers of staff. However, as part of the policy that there should be a co-ordinated approach to pay in the entire public sector, all state-sponsored bodies are subject to central control over wages. There is a legal basis for this particular control only in certain statutes or articles of association, drafted since the late 1960s.[72]

Commercial state-sponsored bodies

Although there are only 20 or so[73] commercial bodies (just over 40 per cent. of the total), they employ approximately 65,000 people (as against nearly 5,000 in the non-commercial sector). The sector has some of the largest employers in the country, accounting for the first four of the largest employers (Bord Telecom, CIÉ, ESB and An Post) and for seven (with the addition, to the bodies already mentioned, of Aer Lingus, Bord na Móna and RTÉ) of the 17 companies which employed more than 2,000 staff. In 1996, the aggregate capital stock was £5.3 billion and the contribution to GNP. was £2 billion or 10 per cent. of total GNP. (a third of this contributed by Bord Telecom and An Post). However by the standards of other developed States,

---

[72] *Serving the Country Better* (1985, Pl. 3262), para. 8.14 proposed to extend this statutory control to all commercial bodies. The following are examples of some statutes effecting this change: Turf Development Act 1990, s.10; Roads Act 1993, s.30; National Stud (Amendment) Act 1993, s.4; Industrial Development Act 1993, Second Schedule, para. 2(4); Irish Aviation Authority Act 1993, s.39; Irish Horseracing Industry Act 1994, s.22; An Bord Bia Act 1994, s.33. For an example of Articles of Association, see Art. 70 of Bord Telecom Éireann which provides: "In determining the remuneration or allowances for expenses to be paid to any of its officers or servants or the terms or conditions subject to which any such officer or servant holds or is to hold his employment, the Directors shall have regard either to Government or nationally agreed guidelines which are for the time being extant, or to Government policy concerning remuneration and conditions of employment which is so extant, of which the Minister may notify the Company from time to time with the consent of the Minister for the Public Service." Though note that even without legal control, in 1978 the Minister for Finance instructed a state-sponsored company to cut the salary of its chief executive by 25 per cent. and this instruction was obeyed. For the chief executive salary, see pp. 154–155.

[73] The classifications are not rigorous, and each category has fuzzy edges. Some bodies which the Department of Finance deems commercial for some purposes are nonetheless excluded from the annual published assessment of the performance of the commercial state-sector (Table 6 of the Public Capital Programme) on the ground that they do not derive the entirety of the revenue from trading. There are other slight anomalies. The Department of Finance regards the following as being commercial state bodies:

"Agricultural Credit Corporation plc, Aer Lingus Group plc/Aerlinte Éireann plc, Aer Rianta, Arramara Teo., Blood Transfusion Service Board, Bord Gáis Éireann, Bord na Móna, Bord Telecom Éireann, Coillte Teo., Coras Iompair Éireann, Dublin Docklands Authority, Electricity Supply Board, Housing Finance Agency Ltd, Industrial Credit Corporation plc, Irish Aviation Authority, Irish National Petroleum Corporation Ltd, Irish National Stud Ltd, National Building Agency Ltd, National Concert Hall Company, An Post National Lottery Company, Nitrigin Éireann Teo., An Post, Irish Horseracing Authority, Temple Bar Properties, Radio Telefis Éireann, Royal Hospital Kilmainham Company, Voluntary Health Insurance Board."

Such surprising inclusions as the Blood Transfusion Service Board or the National Concert Hall Co. qualify because their income almost covers their outgoings. Notice that the British and Irish Steam Packet Company Ltd was sold to Irish Ferries and Irish Steel Ltd was sold (in May 1996) to ISPAT International.

on the criterion of fraction of GNP. contributed by state bodies, Ireland is in the middle range.[74]

The birth-rate of commercial state bodies has fluctuated, being particularly high at times of economic change. Thus most of them were established during one of the following three periods; the drive for self-sufficiency in 1932–1939; the post-Second World War recovery period; or the years of economic expansion immediately after 1958. Professor Bristow has given the following historical sketch of the growth of this sector:

> "The 1930s saw the nearest thing Ireland has experienced to the use of public enterprise in pursuit of an ideology – that is, economic self-sufficiency (which was an ideology rather than merely a development strategy in that it was the reflection of a political philosophy). The Irish Sugar Company was set up in 1933 and the decade saw the beginnings of governmental involvement in peat production (which led to the eventual establishment of Bord na Móna in 1946) and in air transport with the foundation of Aer Rianta in 1937. Import substitution continued to be important in the 1940s with the nationalisation of Irish Steel in 1947 and even after self-sufficiency had ceased to occupy a central position in development policy (Nitrigin Éireann and the British and Irish Steam Packet Company were set up as late as 1961 and 1965 respectively). A variant of it – security of supply of imports in times of international trouble – is still alive today. Not only did this idea provide the rationale for the foundation of Irish Shipping in 1941 but, in 1979, it was the stated justification for the establishment of the Irish National Petroleum Corporation (INPC) and the taking over by that company of the Whitegate refinery in 1982 . . . The Industrial Credit Company [now Corporation] was created in 1933 to remedy a lack of underwriting facilities and to provide a channel of industrial finance. Ceimici Teoranta was established in 1938 to use surplus potatoes to produce industrial alcohol (no such surplus ever materialised and this operation has always had to rely on imported molasses), and Coras Iompair Éireann was set up in its present form in 1950 because the market mechanism was in danger of eliminating the railways."[75]

The most natural question to ask is why a particular commercial enterprise is not in the private sector rather than why it is not vested in some Minister for execution by the civil service. Often, the reason why the work is not done by private enterprise is that it is not profitable. Why then does the State undertake the burden? There are a number of reasons. In the first place, the activity may form part of the infrastructure for the entire economy, frequently in sectors in which, irrespective of profit, the amount of capital required was, at the time it was set up – though possibly this is no longer the case – too great for the Irish private sector.[76] Secondly, the objective may be to develop natural resources.[77] Thirdly, the state-sponsored

---

[74] See Sweeney, "Public Enterprise in Ireland: A Statistical Description and Analysis", 3–6.

[75] Bristow, "State-Sponsored Bodies" (1982) 30 *Administration* 165 at 166.

[76] *e.g.* ESB; Aer Lingus; British and Irish Steam Packet Co. Ltd; Irish Shipping Ltd (now defunct); An Post; Bord Telecom Éireann.

[77] *e.g.* Bord na Móna; C.S.E.T.; National Stud Co. Ltd; Coillte Teo (set up by the Forestry Act 1988).

body may originate as a rescue operation designed to maintain employment after the demise of some private company.[78] Fourthly, the postal and telecommunication services were, until 1983, vested in the Department of Posts and Telegraphs. They were transferred to state-sponsored bodies in the anticipation that this change would promote a more flexible response to the challenges of the technological and commercial world.[79] The broadcasting service was also vested in the Department of Posts and Telegraphs until the establishment of Radio Éireann (which became Radio Telefís Éireann in 1966) by the Broadcasting Authority Act 1960. In this case, the major reason for the change was the need to give some measure of independence of the government of the day to such a politically-significant organ of communication. In 1990, the National Treasury Management Agency[80] was established to enable salaries to be offered to its staff which are comparable with those paid in the private sector.[81]

Thus, as a conclusion, it may be suggested that commercial state bodies have been set up as ad hoc responses to various needs and not as a device to supplant private enterprise for ideological reasons. Indeed the Directive Principles of state policy contained in Article 45.3.1° of the Constitution enjoin the state "[to] favour and, where necessary, supplement private initiative in industry and commerce." And, by way of illustration of the absence of practical zeal in regard to state bodies, one should note the lack of action over recent Governments' commitments to:

> ". . . develop a vigorous third Banking Force from within the State sector by merging the ICC Bank and ACC Bank and seeking a merger of the new entity with the Trustee Savings Banks. The new State Bank will also develop strong links with the network of An Post for money transactions and banking services."[82]

In fact, one of the reasons for the lack of action with a regard to this commitment was that it became clear (in 1996, they came close to being sold for £120 million)

---

[78] *e.g.* Irish Life Assurance Co. Ltd; Irish Steel Holdings Ltd; Coras Iompair Éireann.

[79] See Report of the Posts and Telegraph Review Group 1978–1979 (Prl. 7883) ("the Dargan Report"), which concluded, at p. 2, that "the restrictions, practices, and precedents within which [the Department of Posts and Telegraphs] functions make it an unsuitable structure for management of a business such as telecommunications"; see also Reorganisation of Postal and Telecommunication Services (Prl. 8809), Chaps. II and III. A point of interest is that when An Bord Post and An Bord Telecom were constituted it was the objective of the Postal and Telecommunications Services Act 1983 to transfer all liabilities, arising out of postal and telephone services and extant on vesting day, to the new boards. However, the relevant provisions – ss.56 and 57 of the 1983 Act – refer only to proceedings and claims brought by and against "the Minister [for Posts and Telegraphs]" leaving out of account the possibility that, as a matter of law, the appropriate person might be the State or the Minister for Finance (on which see pp. 709–713). This defect is rectified, with retrospective effect, by the Postal and Telecommunications Services (Amendment) Act 1984, ss.2–4.

[80] See below, n.94.

[81] More recently, the Irish Aviation Authority Act 1993 established the IAA to take over a substantial range of work which had previously been vested in an informally "Devlinised", unit known as the Air Navigation Services Office within the Department of Transport. The IAA (which employs 600 staff and had a turn-of £50 million) provides operational services, such as air traffic management, engineering and communications in respect of Irish airspace. It is also responsible for several licensing functions in regard to pilots, aerodromes and personnel involved in maintenance.

[82] *Fianna Fáil and Labour Programme for a Partnership Government* (1993–1997), p. 4. See too, *A Government of Renewal* (1994), p. 19.

that the Trustees Savings Bank had a substantial market value. For the legal status of this exotic bloom in the window box of state bodies had been clarified by a British case, *Ross v. Lord Advocate*[83] which involved banks established under the same Nineteenth century British code of legislation as the Irish trustee savings banks. Here the House of Lords held that the depositors did not have any proprietary rights in the bank. As a result the Trustee Savings Banks Act 1989 (which provides, for the amalgamations of savings banks and, also, for their reorganisation, by the Minister, into companies and the sale of their shares) was enacted. It seems that *Ross* (if followed here[84]) would mean that the 1989 Act would not be unconstitutional for interference with the depositors' property rights.

Non-commercial state-sponsored bodies

Non-commercial bodies are even more difficult to schematise. On one classification, they can be grouped into four types. First, there are those promotional bodies which operate as a stimulus and back-up to private enterprise.[85] Secondly, there are research and promotional bodies.[86] Thirdly, there is a large group, which provide miscellaneous services.[87] They are found frequently in the health field. Also there are such bodies as the National Lottery Company which was established to run the lottery (presumably in order to distance the enterprise from the Government) though note that the allocation of lottery proceeds is left to the Government.[88] Finally, there are bodies which regulate a particular profession or business, dealing with education and entry, maintaining proper standards and enforcing sanctions for breach of these standards. Often these bodies are at the fringe furthest away from the civil service and closest to the private sector (and indeed, on some classifications are not regarded as state bodies at all) in that some of their funds are provided by the profession or business itself; and a minority of their controlling boards are appointed by the Minister, whilst the majority are elected by members of the profession. For instance, one member of the Dental Board is nominated by the Government and three by the Medical Council, whilst the remaining five are elected by dentists. This characteristic is present outside the professions, for example[89] the Irish Horseracing Authority, established (as a successor to the Racing Board) by the Irish Horseracing Industry

---

83 [1986] 2 All E.R. 79.

84 As the Attorney General of the day advised it would be: S.D. Vol. 123, Col. 1212 (Dec., 13, 1989).

85 *e.g.* Forfas; Industrial Development Agency (Ireland); Irish Export Board (Coras Tráchtála); Bord Failte Éireann.

86 *e.g.* Irish Science and Technology Agency, Teagasc (on which see below n.207, p. 156).

87 *e.g.* Medical Bureau of Road Safety; Agency for Personal Service Overseas. Following EEC entry, agricultural marketing bodies concerned with the disposal of agricultural products surplus to commercial requirements, which were formerly state-sponsored bodies, were converted into co-operatives; see, *e.g.* An Bord Bainne Co-operative Ltd. This point is authoritatively explained at *Kerry Co-Op Creameries v. An Bord Bainne* [1990] I.L.R.M. 664 at 671.

88 National Lottery Act 1986. See too the National Cultural Institutions Act 1997 which establishes autonomous boards for the National Museum of Ireland and the National Library of Ireland.

89 See also: the Greyhound Industry Act 1958, s.9, (three out of seven members of Bord na gCon must be members of the Standing Committee of the Irish Coursing Club) ; Milk (Regulation of Supply) Act 1994, Schedule (the National Milk Agency must include representatives of distributor, retail and consumer interests). For an example of a "representative" board in a different area, see Civil Legal Aid Act 1995, s.4.

Act 1994, to develop and promote the industry, including the control of bookmakers and the allocation of race-fixtures.[90] The various groups which must be represented on the Authority include: the Irish Turf Club (which nominates two members); plus breeders; horse trainers and horse-owners. Each of these categories has a representative nominated by such persons as the Minister for Agriculture, Food and Forestry considers to be representative of them. Part of the State's response to public concern about "mad cow" disease was to add to the Board of An Bord Bia, a fourteenth member to be appointed by the Minister for Agriculture, on the nomination of organisations representing consumers.[91] A different type of shared control is represented by the Foyle Fisheries Commission where control is divided between the Governments of the Republic and the United Kingdom.[92]

Because the non-commercial state body group spans such a diverse range, it follows that the reasons why the functions they perform have not been vested in Departments of State are various. In the case of the promotional bodies, the same sort of reasons apply as in the case of the commercial state bodies, namely that their duties require "exceptional initiative and innovation",[93] qualities which are not always to be found in the civil service. Again, the civil service culture may be regarded as an inappropriate milieu for research. In regard to the final category (bodies regulating the professions etc.) its existence can be readily explained on the basis that, given the attitude of uncritical trust adopted by successive Governments towards the professions, their domestic arrangements will always be placed at arm's length from the Government. In addition, the state body form is useful in that it can accommodate the election or selection of some members of a state body's controlling agency, by persons other than the Minister.

However, many of the non-commercial state bodies – including several in the miscellaneous category – are discharging functions which could equally well have been assigned to executive branches of Departments. Why, for instance, should the National Authority for Occupational Safety and Health, (established under the Safety, Health, and Welfare at Work Act 1989 to enforce the relevant statutory provisions) be a separate state body with independent powers, when the administration of occupational injury (and all other) benefits remains vested in the Department of Social Welfare? The former Navigation Services Office (part of the Department of Tourism and Transport and is staffed by civil servants) has now become a state-sponsored body, the Irish Aviation Authority. In an area where ad hocery abounds and fashions change, this type of anomaly is common. It led the Devlin Report to propose that while the commercial state bodies should be allowed to operate with the maximum permissible freedom, the activities of non-commercial bodies and executive branches of departments dealing with similar subject-matter should be

---

90 The only matters which are excluded from the Authority's jurisdiction are the "services operated by the Racing Regulatory Board under this Act". It turns out that this formulation means that regulating the actual races themselves and other items specified in s.39 are to be the responsibility of the Irish Turf Club and the Irish National Hunt Steeplechase Committee, in relation to flat racing and national hunt racing, respectively.

91 An Bord Bia (Amendment) Act 1996, s.2.

92 See Foyle Fisheries Act 1952 and Foyle Fisheries (Northern Ireland) Act 1952.

93 Lemass, "The Organisation behind the Economic Programme" (1961) 9 *Administration* 3, 4–6.

pooled and reallocated to a common executive unit which would be subject to the control of a central Aireacht.[94] There has, however, as indicated,[95] recently been some progress in rationalisation.

3. Legal Form

A state-sponsored body must have a legal existence, which is independent not only of the Government but also of its members and staff. The reason for this is the need for it to be a continuing entity, endowed with the legal capacity to: own property, make contracts, employ servants, sue and be sued, etc. This distinct legal existence may be achieved in either of two ways. First, a state-sponsored body may be constituted as a statutory corporation (or board) by its own separate statute (or – to mention a phenomenon which is significant in a number of areas – its own statutory instrument.[96]) Such a statute typically provides that:

> "(1) As soon as may be after the passing of this Act a board to be styled and known as [*e.g.*] the Electricity Supply Board shall be established in accordance with this Act to fulfil the functions assigned to it by this Act.
> (2) The Board shall be a body corporate having perpetual succession and may sue and be sued under its said style and name."[97]

Alternatively, the state body may be cast as a statutory company, *i.e.* an ordinary company (usually registered under the Companies Acts 1963), in which almost all the shares are held by a Minister. (The exceptions are often confined to the shares, which, as a matter of general company law, are required to be held by one other person). In this case, the corporate nature of the body arises from the companies legislation and not from its own tailor-made statute, which only provides typically that "the Minister shall take steps to procure that a limited company conforming to the conditions laid down in the schedule to the Act shall be registered under the

---

[94] Gaffney, "The Central Administration" (1982) 30 *Administration* 115 at 122.

Though note, as an example of the flexibility of the state-sponsored body form, the National Treasury Management Agency (constituted by the National Treasury Management Agency Act 1990) whose principal duty is to manage the borrowing of moneys for the Exchequer. It was accepted that the main reason for the Agency was that staff, who were skilled and knowledgeable in the area of finance, were not attracted by civil service salaries. Three of the Agency's features bear emphasis. First of all, the Government was empowered to delegate, by order, to the Agency "the functions of the Minister specified in the First Schedule and any other functions of the Minister in relation to the management of the national debt or the borrowing of moneys for the Exchequer that the Minister considers appropriate and are specified in the order" (s.5(1)). However the Agency's functions are to be performed "subject to the control and general superintendence of the Minister" (s.4(3)). Moreover whilst in every other state body, the actual legal persona is a board or authority with flesh and blood incumbents, in the case of the Agency, there is no such central directorate, merely a body corporate supervised by the Minister and served by the chief executive and his staff. In short, as one might expect, given its function, the Agency enjoys next to no autonomy from the Minister.

[95] See also pp. 156–158.

[96] See Blood Transfusion Service Board (Establishment) Order (S.I. 1965 No. 78) made under Health (Corporate Bodies) Act 1961, s.3. A second parent statute authorising the establishment of state bodies by statutory instrument is the Local Government (Corporate Body) Staff Act 1971 which may be used to set up bodies which service all the local authorities in the State. And for an example of a statute which empowers the Minister for the Marine to establish several companies, each of which will manage and operate a harbour, see Harbours Act 1996, ss.7, 8 and 87.

[97] Electricity Supply Act 1927, s.2.

Companies Act."[98] Indeed as a matter of law, a special statute is unnecessary since, provided that any necessary expenditure is authorised by the Appropriation Acts, a Minister, as a corporation sole, under the Ministers and Secretaries Act, is free, like any natural person, to set up a company either by drawing up a memorandum and articles of association or by taking over all the shares in an existing company. This occurred, for instance, in 1946 when the State purchased the Irish Steel Holdings Ltd, which was in the hands of the receiver. The reason why it is usual for the creation of a state-sponsored body, even as a company, to be preceded by an enabling statute is a political one, namely to afford the Oireachtas some opportunity to discuss its objectives and structure and the sources of its investment capital. Consonant with this, the enabling statute usually contains a broad description of the functions, duties and powers of the state body in addition to the more detailed statement which is contained in the articles of association.[99] These are necessarily stated broadly (*inter alia*, so as not to be enforceable in a court).[100] For example:

> "The principal objects of [An Post] shall be stated in its memorandum of association to be –
>
> (a) to provide a national postal service within the State and between the State and places outside the State,
> (b) to meet the industrial, commercial, social and household needs of the State for comprehensive and efficient postal services and, so far as the company considers reasonably practicable, to satisfy all reasonable demands for such services throughout the State,
> (c) to provide services by which money may be remitted (whether by means of money orders, postal orders or otherwise) as the company thinks fit,
> (d) to provide counter services for the company's own and Government business and, provided that they are compatible with those services and with the other principal objects set out in this subsection, for others as the company thinks fit, and
> (e) to provide such consultancy, advisory, training and contract services inside and outside the State as the company thinks fit."[101]

It is a consequence of the *ultra vires* doctrine that state bodies may only exercise their powers, for example, to contract, in order to achieve certain types of object.[102] These objects are those specified (in the case of statutory corporations) in their constituent statute or (in the case of statutory companies) in the memorandum of association, or objects reasonably incidental thereto. Contracts to achieve purposes outside these objects would be void.

---

[98] Sugar Manufacture Act 1933, s.4 constituting Siúicre Éireann c.p.t.

[99] Deputy Cooney suggested that the Articles of Association should be laid before the Oireachtas: see, 256 *Dáil Debates*, Col. 2215 (November 17, 1971).

[100] Where one is dealing with a statutory company whose existence depends immediately upon a memorandum and articles, then it would seem that their terms would be legally enforceable, in the ordinary way.

[101] Postal and Telecommunications Services Act 1983, s.12(1). In some cases the lack of enforceability in a court is express, e.g. 1983 Act, ss.13(2), 15(2); Transport Act 1958, s.7(3); Irish Aviation Authority Act 1993, s.17(2).

[102] For some examples of the extension of these powers, see pp. 157–158.

The obvious question which arises is: on what criterion is it determined whether a state-sponsored body should be poured into the vessel of a statutory corporation rather than a statutory company? Here, as elsewhere in this area, there is no firm rule. As has been said of the variety of organisational forms for public bodies in Britain: "Like the flowers in spring, they have grown as variously and as profusely and with as little regard for conventional patterns."[103] So far as there is any guide, it is that more than two-thirds of commercial bodies are statutory companies, whereas non-commercial bodies are almost all cast as boards (or even "councils"). One significant reason for this is that it is easier to change the memorandum and articles of a company than it is to pass the necessary legislation to alter a board and such flexibility may be important to a commercial body. It was, for instance, decided to create An Post and Bord Telecom Éireann as registered companies. The reasons given by the Post and Telegraphs Review Group Report was that a company may be altered more easily and can take quicker decisions.[104] Secondly, the division of a company's assets would have been facilitated by the existence of shares and, in the first decade of the state-sponsored sector's existence, the public was usually invited – though without success – to subscribe for shares in the companies (hence the original name – "semi-state bodies"). In line with this trend, Comhlucht Siúicre Éireann which, in fact, was not to be (partially) privatised until 1991,[105] was set up in 1933 in the form of a (public) company because it was expected that it would be sold off sooner or later,[106] whereas bodies like ESB or Bord na Móna were never expected to go into private hands and so were created as statutory boards. Again, if a private company becomes the subject of a Government take-over then it will naturally remain as a company.

In principle, in the case of statutory companies, general company law applies, though it may not be well adapted to the artificial circumstances involved.[107] The position of a state-sponsored body which wears the guise of a statutory corporation is even more cloudy. It has been suggested:

> "that the general common law of corporations will govern [statutory corporations] except in so far as this is expressly or impliedly modified and that many of the judge-made principles of company law will be equally applicable to this more recent growth. But in applying common law principles recognition must be given to the consequences flowing from their dual role as commercial enterprises and public authorities . . . [In addition] the absence of shares and shareholders automatically renders large and important branches of company law totally inapplicable . . ."[108]

---

103 Street, "Quasi-Governmental Bodies Since 1918" *British Government since 1918* (Campion, ed.,) (1948).
104 Report of (Dargan) Posts and Telegraphs Review Group 1978–1979 (Prl. 7883), p. 63. (The earlier stages of the Bill were promoted by a Fianna Fáil Government, the later stages by a Coalition Government). See 343 *Dáil Debates*, Col. 1526 (June 15, 1983).
105 See pp. 162–163.
106 Indeed some shares in it – though only amounting to a single figure percentage –were in private hands and, like the Industrial Credit Corporation, it has a stock exchange quotation though there has been no dealing for some time.
107 Golding, "The Juristic Basis of the Irish State Enterprise" (1978) 13 Ir. Jur. (N.S.) 302 at pp. 310–312.
108 Gower, *Modern Company Law* (London, 1979), pp. 287–288.

This guideline means, *inter alia*, that the *ultra vires* principle, in its pristine common law form,[109] would apply to statutory corporations.

4. Control by the Minister

In most cases, the Minister who controls[110] and is ultimately responsible for a state-sponsored body is the Minister whose departmental duties fall closest to the work of the body.[111] Thus, for example, the Agricultural Credit Corporation is responsible to the Minister for Finance; the ESB and CIÉ are responsible to the Minister for Public Enterprises and the National Rehabilitation Board Ltd is responsible to the Minister for Health.

Vested in the responsible Minister (or, very occasionally, in the Government) are six statutory powers which may be used to control a state-sponsored body. After these legal powers have been described, the factors which determine the use which the Minister actually makes of his formal ascendancy will be examined.

Appointment of board members/directors

In the case of statutory corporations, members of the board are usually selected by the responsible Minister (either with the consent of or after consulting, the Minister for Finance), although in some cases they are selected by the Government.[112] The chairman is chosen usually by the responsible Minister but occasionally by the board, subject to the Minister's approval. The maximum period of the term of office is fixed by the statute and and/or the Minister is then empowered to set a term within this maximum typically three to five years. Usually, a director may be re-appointed (or disappointed) for an unlimited number of further terms. The terms and conditions of employment are usually fixed by the responsible Minister with the consent of the Minister for Finance. There will usually be four to nine directors. However, in bodies to which the Worker Participation (State Enterprises) Acts 1977 and 1988[113] apply, the size of the board has been increased to accommodate the workers' directors. Large boards are also a feature of those non-commercial bodies which

---

109 *i.e.* unaffected by the Companies Act 1963, s.8; and European Communities (Companies) Regulations 1973 (S.I. 1973 No. 163).

110 For a study of independence-control in relation to the Central Bank of Ireland (a somewhat untypical state body) in a comparative setting, by its former Governor, see Murray, "The Independence of Central Banks: An Irish Perspective" (1982) 30 *Administration* 33.

111 Note, however, that the Minister for Finance was responsible for Siúicre Éireann c.p.t. before responsibility was transferred to the Minister for Agriculture and Food by the Sugar Manufacture (Transfer of Departmental Administration and Ministerial Functions) Order (S.I. 1980 No. 55); and also had some limited statutory functions (*e.g.* appointment of directors, approval of borrowing), in relation to the now defunct Ceimicí Teo and Irish Shipping.

112 *e.g.* Roads Act 1993, s.28 (appointment by the Minister for the Environment). Though note Broadcasting Authority Act 1960, s.4 (appointment by Government); Air Companies (Amendment) Act 1993 (appointment of subsidiary company board either by Minister or with his consent, by the Chairman of the holding Company); An Bord Bia Act 1994, s.14, as amended by An Bord Bia Act 1994, s.1 (chairman and all but one of the ordinary members appointed by the Minister for Agriculture, Food and Forestry from among persons having knowledge or experience of food industry and consumer requirements; remaining member with the same qualification to be appointed on nomination of the Minister for the Marine).

113 On worker participation, see further pp. 144–145.

include the (usually elected) representatives of different interests, *e.g.* the Nursing Board or the Medical Council (29 and 25 member boards, respectively).

The position is similar for statutory companies save that their boards are usually smaller and that, in accordance with general company law, board members retire by rotation, two at each Annual General Meeting.

It often happens that a Minister will appoint one or two of his departmental civil servants as board members, a practice which has been justified as aiding smooth communication and attacked as subverting the independence of state-sponsored bodies by in effect imposing a Trojan horse upon the state body. Apart from five years in the 1950s, the Secretary of the Department of Finance has always been a "service director" of the Central Bank of Ireland. Reflecting the status of state bodies as entities pursuing their own commercial or technical purposes and co-operating smoothly with Governments of all political colours, members of boards and their employees are each barred from membership of either House of the Oireachtas.[114] As regards gender balance, statutes enacted since 1993 have fixed gender quotas for individual state bodies.[115] And during 1993–1997 state bodies (like other public bodies) were following Government decisions (of March 1993 and March 1995) subject to Government guidelines by which each gender was to have at least 40% of the membership. But the present Government (1997–) appears, to judge from recent appointments, to be allowing this policy to wither on the vine.

Dismissal

With a statutory company, the responsible Minister possesses the power of dismissal of directors, *qua* shareholder. In the case of a statutory corporation the constituent statute usually vests the power of dismissal of board members in the responsible Minister, in some cases subject to the consent of the Minister for Finance. Occasionally, the power is vested in the Government.[116] However, dismissal is an extreme step and, whatever the statutory provision may say, this is a decision which would only be taken following anxious deliberation by the entire Government.[117] Frequently, the power of removal is conditioned on such grounds as ill-health, stated misbehaviour or failure to perform duties effectively.[118] Where a state-sponsored body is a company, removal is usually not dealt with in the body's own statute, but in the articles of association which list specific grounds on which the shareholder, *i.e.* the Minister, may dismiss a director.

---

[114]   *e.g.* Electricity (Supply) Act 1927 s.3; Roads Act 1993, ss.34 and 35; Irish Horseracing Industry Act 1994, s.13; An Bord Bia Act 1994, s.31; Civil Legal Aid Act 1995, s.12; Irish Medicines Board Act 1995, s.22.

[115]   *e.g.* Broadcasting Authority (Amendment) Act 1993, s.7 (where there are seven (or eight or nine) members of the Authority, then, at least, three (or four) members, respectively, must be from each gender; Civil Legal Aid Act 1995, s.4(3) (at least five members of each gender out of a Board of thirteen); Universities Act 1997, s.15(10) (provision for gender balance to be stipulated by the Minister for Education).

[116]   *e.g.* Electricity (Supply) Act 1927, s.5(1); Transport Act 1950, s.7.

[117]   But for the resignation of Dr. Joseph Brennan from the Central Bank in 1953, see Murray, *op. cit.* above, n.110, pp. 41–42; see also Lemass, "The Role of the State-Sponsored Body in the Economy" (1958) 6 *Administration* 277 at 289.

[118]   *e.g.* Gas Act 1976, Sched. 1, Art. 4(7); Transport Act 1950, s.7.

A *cause célébre* in this field, in 1972, involved the RTÉ Authority (for whom the appointing and dismissing agency is the Government). The episode arose out of the Minister for Posts' use of his power under the Broadcasting Authority Act 1960, section 31 to issue an order which forbade RTÉ from broadcasting any matter calculated to promote the aims of "any organisation which engages in, promotes, encourages or advocates the attaining of any political objectives by violent means". The Authority protested against the vagueness of this wording and a month after the order had been made RTÉ broadcast an interview[119] with the IRA Chief of Staff. The Government gave the Authority the option of dismissing the interviewer or of all members of the Authority being removed from office and the Authority took the second option. The sequel came in the Broadcasting Authority (Amendment) Act 1976 which, first, narrowed the scope of section 31[120] and, secondly, provided some additional protection for the members of the Authority. Thenceforth, a member could only be removed by the Government from office, for stated reasons if, and only if, resolutions are passed by both Houses of the Oireachtas calling for his removal."[121]

A second instance[122] occurred, in 1983, when the Minister for the Gaeltacht dismissed three members of Údarás na Gaeltachta. Another example took place in 1995. In April, the Government elicited the resignation of the chairman of CIÉ who was then replaced by an executive-chairman. Then (in November) the Government asked for the resignation of the seven "non-worker directors": five acquiesced and the remaining two were removed (one of whom initiated legal proceedings, which resulted in an apology).[123]

Dissolution

It is uncertain whether, absent legislation, a Minister has the authority to dissolve a state-sponsored body. The constituent statute typically states, in the case of a statutory corporation, "the Electricity Supply Board . . . shall be established" or, in the case of a statutory company, "the Minister shall take steps to procure that a limited company . . . shall be registered . . .".[124] These provisions might suggest that a state body, could not be dissolved. However, as against this, section 9(1)(a) the Ministers and Secretaries Act 1924, states that: "[i]t shall be lawful for the [Government] . . . to dissolve any . . . statutory body" which category is defined widely enough to embrace a state-sponsored body.[125]

In any case, the common practice is that when state bodies are dissolved (as part of a reorganisation, for none has so far been dissolved as a matter of discipline or

---

119 This interview also led to *Re Kevin O'Kelly* (1974) 108 I.L.T.R. 97.
120 On which, see below, pp. 664, 667.
121 Broadcasting Authority (Amendment) Act 1976, s.2.
122 Notice also that in 1987, the ESB were disputing (before the Circuit Court) their liability to pay rates. The (Fianna Fáil) Government publicly threatened to remove the board unless (as happened) the rates were paid. The obligation to pay rates is now made clear by the Electricity (Supply) (Amendment) Act 1988, ss.8–10. See also, Postal and Telecommunications Services Act 1983, s.54.
123 The executive chairman, appointed in April, resigned on November 14, 1995 claiming that he had not been supported by the Board. In November, (a few weeks after her resignation) the deputy chairwoman of the outgoing Board was reappointed to the new Board: *Irish Times*, April 17 and November 15 and 30, 1995 and March 5, 1998.
124 For the references, see pp. 134–135, nn. 97 and 98.
125 See Central Bank Act 1942, s.5(b) excluding the Bank from the sweep of s.9 of the 1924 Act.

because of a policy disagreement), the change is effected by Act of the Oireachtas. The main reason for this is to afford the Houses of the Oireachtas an opportunity to debate the change.

Finance[126]

The control of finance affords the Government a range of convenient levers over most spheres of activity. In the first place, in the case of non-commercial bodies, funds are delivered in the form of grants-in-aid which can only be released with the permission of the responsible Minister and the Minister for Finance.

With commercial bodies, the position is more complicated. Investment capital may be raised by borrowing (either from the Exchequer or private sources) or, in the case of companies, by the issue of shares to a Minister, almost always to the Minister for Finance. Among the key provisions in the constituent statute of a state-sponsored body are those which fix the maximum amounts which it is empowered to raise, by borrowing or issuing shares. These limits take the form of legislation and thus their alteration provides an opportunity for the Oireachtas to review the policy and performance of the body involved. It is customary to fix the limits at such a level that if the organisation is expanding fairly rapidly, amending legislation is necessary at intervals of reasonable length.[127] As well as the Oireachtas' authorisation, the consents of the responsible Ministers and the Minister for Finance are necessary where shares are issued or money is borrowed from any source.[128]

Where loss on current expenditure is involved or pre-existing debts have to be written off, constituent statutes or amendments may provide for the making of a subsidy by the Minister for Finance.

It used to be the case that when funds were borrowed from a private source, (in some cases, by issuing stock) the Minister for Finance, after consultation with the responsible Minister, would guarantee repayment and such a guarantee constituted a charge on the central fund. Until 1984,[129] these guarantees were given very readily. However, the Minister for Finance has now announced that such guarantees will only be given for good cause and that the State will not undertake responsibility for loans which are not guaranteed. The fact that this announcement was made contemporaneously with the Government's unprecedented decision to allow Irish Shipping to go into liquidation drove home the message that the Government had changed to a more businesslike policy in relation to the commercial state-sponsored

---

[126] For the law on central Government finance, see generally, Morgan, *op. cit.* above, n. 2 pp. 112–132.

[127] See, *e.g.* ACC Bank Act 1992; ICC Bank Act 1992; Nitrigin Eireann Teo Act 1993; Gas (Amendment) Act 1993; Irish Film Board (Amendment) Act 1993.

[128] For an unusual retrospective power, in relation to borrowing see: Financial Transactions of Certain Companies and Other Bodies Act 1992 and Borrowing Powers of Certain Bodies Act 1996: each of these statutes was the product of lawyers' caution following *Hazell v. Hammersmith and Fulham L.B.C.* [1992] 2 A.C. 1 (holding that local authorities borrowing powers did not extend to interest rate swaps). The Irish Acts make it clear that any state body whose power is subject to the consent of a Minister has the power to enter into interest rate swaps (1992 Act) or finance leases (1996 Act).

[129] The occasion for the change of policy (announced by the Minister for Finance in a speech made to the Institute of Bankers on November 16, 1984) was the Irish Shipping liquidation. Irish Shipping Ltd had liabilities estimated at £114 million of which only some were state guaranteed and the (substantial) remainder went unpaid: see *Business and Finance*, November 22 and 29, 1984. See, further, 353 *Dáil Debates*, Cols. 2077–2158, December 3, 1984.

sector. Its significance is clear from the fact that in 1987, continuing Government guarantees totalled £2.7 billion (against a total capital base for the entire sector of £5.5 billion) and covered almost all long-term and some short-term loans, from banks and other private creditors.[130]

The expectation, which is sometimes expressed in the parent statute,[131] is that taking account of the need to make an adequate return on capital, a commercial body should at least break even, taking one year with another. In fact, in recent years, only two of the bodies (Irish Life and the Industrial Credit Corporation) have regularly paid any dividend. However, in the past two or three years other statutory companies, including Aer Lingus Aer Rianta, ACC Bank p.l.c. and Bord Telecom have begun to pay dividends. In addition, for most years since natural gas came on stream in 1981, Bord Gáis has remitted profits to the Exchequer.

Information

All state bodies are under duties – stated, variously, in the parent statute or articles of association – to give their Minister important information as to, for instance, profit and loss account, capital account, revenue account, etc. Frequently, the Minister has power to settle the form of annual reports and accounts and also to be given whatever specific information he requests. There is often a statutory obligation, failing which there is a practice, that the annual report and accounts should then be laid before each House of the Oireachtas.[132] In fact, it often happened in the past that these annual reports and accounts were not published until two or more years after the year to which they relate. However, in 1986 the Government established a rule of practice (which has been followed) that, save in the case of an authorised derogation, reports should be published within six months of the year to which they relate.

Shareholding

In the case of state bodies which take the legal form of companies, there is, theoretically, a further source of authority. This arises from the fact that the Minister effectively owns all the shares. Accordingly, he has the same powers to pass whatever resolution, special resolution or extraordinary resolution he wishes. Obviously, a full-blooded use of this power would subvert the whole *raison d'être* of a state body and, by a convention described in the next section, it has never been used.

5. Balance of Authority between Minister and State-Sponsored Body

Whilst many of these powers are seldom used, their very existence shapes the relationship between the state body and the responsible Minister. This naturally

---

130 These guarantees mean that it is the taxpayer rather than the creditor who bears the risk of the debt not being repaid and, accordingly, the interest rate is lower than would otherwise be the case. See Joint Oireachtas Committee on State-Sponsored Bodies: *Second Report: Irish Shipping Ltd* (1985, Pl. 3091), para. 35.

131 *e.g.* Electricity (Supply) Act 1927, s.21(2); Gas Act 1976, s.10; *cf.* Transport Act 1958, s.7(2).

132 For a particularly detailed formulation, including an obligation to make an annual report within six months of the end of the financial year, see Radiological Protection Act 1991, s.17. See also Voluntary Health Insurance (Amendment) Act 1996, s.9.

means, as we shall later in this Part, that a state body is often acutely sensitive to the wishes of the responsible Minister, even on a point in regard to which the Minister has no specific legal authority. This phenomenon has been felicitously described in the United States as "raised-eyebrow regulation". An attempt is naturally made on both sides to present a public image of harmony between the state body and the Government and of respect for the state body's independent status.[133]

The division of jurisdiction is conventionally taken to be that, in principle, "day-to-day" decisions are for the state body itself; whereas strategic and policy issues have to be resolved, if possible, by agreement between the board and the Minister, but with the Minister having the last word. Thus, for instance, whilst capital investment by ESB would involve the responsible Minister, decisions as to staff allocation or electricity load management would not.[134]

By and large it was not until the 1970s that the constituent statutes of state-sponsored bodies were drafted so as to deal explicitly with the overall relationship between the Minister and the body and to grant the responsible Minister formal power to give directions. However, the practice has now changed so that there is an explicit grant of such power. Typical of recent statutes[135] is the Postal and Telecommunications Services Act 1983. According to section 110(1) of the 1983 Act:

"The Minister [for Communications] may issue directions in writing to either company [*sc.* An Post or Bord Telecom Éireann] requiring the company:

(a) to comply with policy decisions of a general kind made by the Government concerning the development of the postal or telecommunications services . . .

(b) to do (or refrain from doing) anything which he may specify from time to time as necessary in the national interest . . .

(c) to perform such work or provide such work or provide or maintain such services for a state authority as may be specified in the direction . . ."

This statutory division of responsibilities of course, accords with the conventional division explained in the previous paragraph. Notice that the Minister threatened to issue a direction, under the provision just quoted, in 1991, as part of his campaign to pressurise An Post into modifying its plan to close 500 sub-post offices.[136]

---

133 Naturally, too, there are times when the manner on both sides becomes what has been called "Correct with a capital K". However, the sort of openly adversarial type of relationship which existed in 1995 during Deputy Michael Lowry's time as Minister for Transport, Energy and Communications (1994–1996) is unusual (See 457 *Dáil Debates*, Cols. 582–640 and 231–277 and October 1995). For the semi-public attack on the Universities Bill 1996 by the Higher Education Authority, see *Irish Times*, November 12, 1996, p. 5.

134 See 311 *Dáil Debates*, Col. 868 (February 8, 1979).

135 For other examples, see: the Housing Finance Agency Act 1981, s.6 ("The Minister [for the Environment] may . . . with the consent of the Minister for Finance, give such general directions as to policy . . ." Such directions must be laid before each House and published in Iris Oifigiúil); National Lottery Act 1986, s.29 ("Whenever the Minister [for Finance] considers it necessary to do so in the public interest, he may give a direction in writing . . . relating to the National Lottery"). See also, Gas Act 1976, s.11; Central Bank Act 1971, s.43 ; and the Programme for Economic and Social Progress (1990, Pl. 7829), para. 89.1; Radiological Protection Act 1991, s.20; Trade and Marketing Promotion Act 1991, s.7; An Bord Bia Act 1994, s.29, Roads Act 1993, s.41.

136 See *Irish Times* February 21, 1991.

Four glosses

To obtain some idea of how the Minister/state-sponsored body relationship operates in practice, one needs to add at least four glosses or exceptions to the policy-operational demarcation just outlined.

1. The Government's power of control is much greater over a non-commercial, than a commercial, body. The reasons are, first, that the commercial bodies are already subject to the discipline of the market-place (of which there is no equivalent for the non-commercial bodies which are usually little more than executive agencies) and, secondly, that the Government control over the provision of grants is even more significant where this is a state-sponsored body's only source of funds.

2. A Minister must ensure – said Sean Lemass – that a state-sponsored body is "kept in line with the overall development plans of the Government".[137] This means that the Government will sometimes use – though necessarily less so[138] than in earlier decades – its convenient hold over a large sector of industry and commerce to impose its line on economic, social or other issues. In several cases, Ministers have intervened to require a decision to be taken in order to maintain employment, even though this is not in line with commercial considerations. Take, for instance, the following Dáil question (asked at a time when B. and I. was a state body):

> "Mr. Hegarty asked the Minister for Tourism and Transport [who was then responsible for British and Irish Steampacket Co. Ltd] in view of the like-lihood of redundancies at Verolme Cork Dockyard, will he consider giving the green light to have the new B. and I. roll-on roll-off car ferry built at the yard immediately."[139]

There is no concession in this question – nor was there in the answer – to the notion that B. & I. was a separate entity from what was then the Department of Tourism and Transport, responsible for taking its own decisions along commercial lines. It is normal political practice that there should have been no such concession. Thus in the mid–1980s, the Government was grappling desperately with an economic crisis, a major element in which was massive expenditure – both on capital investment and the financing of a current deficit – by state-sponsored bodies. With the total reaction of the Government to this crisis, we shall deal later.[140] For the

---

[137] Lemass, "The Role of the State-Sponsored Body in the Economy" (1958) 6 *Administration* 278 at 288. Note the episode in which the Taoiseach informed the chairman of RTÉ that in the opinion of the Government "the best interests of the nation would not be served by sending an RTÉ team to Vietnam": 227 *Dáil Debates*, Cols. 1661–1664 (April 13, 1967) and also the remark of Mr Pat Dineen, Chief Executive of BGE that "BGE, purely from a business point of view, was most reluctant to take over the company [Dublin Gas]. We took it over because the Government wanted us to". (Business and Finance, 1987); and the report that Aer Lingus had successfully resisted Government pressure to sell certain of its hotels: *The Irish Times*, July 10, 1982, p. 1.

[138] See pp. 165–167.

[139] 307 *Dáil Debates*, Cols. 2429–2430 (June 29, 1978). See, to similar effect, 202 *Dáil Debates*, Col. 34 (April 23, 1963) (Ministerial involvement in CIÉ bus strike). For another example see, Andrews, *Man of No Property* (1982), p. 257. Note also the episode in which the Minister for Agriculture "instructed" RTÉ not to carry a report of a National Farmers Association's criticism of him, see: 227 *Dáil Debates*, Cols. 1661–1664 (April 13, 1967).

[140] See p. 156.

moment, it is only necessary to notice how faithfully the change in Government was reflected in employment by the state bodies: during the period 1980–1987, 15 of the major commercial state companies shed an average of 18 per cent. of their workforce, which thus fell from 7.2 per cent. to 6.3 per cent. of the total number of those employed in Ireland. Again, more recently, when unions were threatening strike over the introduction of new schedules by Bus Éireann, the Minister for Public Enterprise directed the company not to insist and this direction was accepted.[141]

Another substantial example of the Government using its convenient hold over the state-sponsored sector to impose a particular (social) policy concerns worker participation, which is established by the Worker Participation (State Enterprises) Acts 1977 and 1988. First of all, the 1977 Act provided for the election[142] of worker-director or board members in the case of the seven largest commercial enterprises: Electricity Supply Board; Coras Iompair Éireann, Siúicre Éireann c.p.t. (now partially privatised); Nitrigin Éireann Teo; Aer Lingus[143]; British and Irish Steam Packet Co. Ltd (now sold); and Bord na Móna. Bord Telecom Éireann and An Post were added to the ranks by the Postal and Telecommunications Act 1983.[144] The 1988 Act also bestowed worker directors/members upon a further two state bodies: Aer Rianta and the National Rehabilitation Board. The advent of worker-directors/members to a state body means that the total numbers may have to be increased. Accordingly, in order to accommodate the extra numbers, the Minister for Public Enterprise is empowered, after consultation with the Minister for Finance and the Minister responsible for the particular body, to make an order prescribing the number of directors or board members on the state bodies to which worker-directors/members may be appointed.[145] Save in one case,[146] the worker–directors/members must amount to a third of the entire number.[147] The Minister for Enterprise and Employment's powers have been utilised to provide that, with three exceptions, each of the state bodies listed earlier has 12 directors/members of whom four represent the work force.[148] It is also significant that the Minister for Enterprise and Employment, again following consultation with the Minister for Finance and the responsible Minister, may by order add fresh bodies to, or remove bodies from, the scope of the Workers' Participation Acts[149] (though this has not, so far, been done).

---

[141]　See, *The Irish Times*, July 24, 1997.

[142]　Worker Participation (State Enterprises) (General) Regulations 1988 (S.I. No. 170 of 1988) specify the general rules for elections under the 1977 and 1988 Acts. See also, The Worker Participation (State Enterprises) (Postal Voting) Regulations 1988 (S.I. No. 171 of 1988) and the Worker Participation (State Enterprises) (Preliminary Poll) Regulations 1988 (S.I. No. 172 of 1988).

[143]　See too, Air Companies (Amendment) Act 1993, s.8.

[144]　However, the relevant provisions of the 1983 Act were repealed and replaced by the 1988 Act which thus brought these two state bodies within the same legislative scheme as the original seven. But for Bord Telecom, see now Telecommunications (Miscellaneous Provisions) Act 1996, s.8, see above, n.232, p. 162.

[145]　1977 Act, s.23(1).

[146]　The exception is the National Rehabilitation Board for which the legislation specifies a maximum of one third of all board members and a minimum of two members.

[147]　1977 Act, s.23 as amended by 1988 Act, s.24 and the Second schedule to the 1977 Act. (which is inserted by 1988 Act, s.24(1)).

[148]　Worker Participation (State Enterprises) Orders (S.I. No. 186 of 1978; S.I. No. 100 of 1980; S.I. No. 149 of 1988; S.I. No. 337 of 1988). The exceptions are An Post (15 members with five representing the employees); National Rehabilitation Board (15: three) and Aer Rianta (8: two).

[149]　1977 Act, s.4(4).

Each of the orders mentioned in this paragraph is subject to the affirmative resolution of each House.[150] In addition the 1988 Act also introduced for the first time, in Irish law, the concept of worker-participation by way of sub-board arrangements[151] providing for the exchange of views between the state body and its employees. However, these arrangements have not yet been invoked and so are not detailed here.

What is significant here is the fact that it is only the state section of commercial enterprise which has been caught by any form of a development which, for numerous good and bad reasons, management and shareholders have generally viewed without exaggerated enthusiasm. Some statements have been made about extending this change to the private sector[152]; but legislation to implement it has never, so far, appeared to be a practical possibility.

3. Closely related to the impact which a state body can make on the Government's general policies is the question of party-political advantage. This is the very factor which the state-sponsored body form of organisation was designed to exclude. But, in a highly-politicised environment, this is a counsel of perfection and, as Sean Lemass remarked in 1958,[153] the main danger with state bodies is that politicians might interfere too much in their activities. The average voter may know little about the constitutional position of a state body but he knows that it is in "the public domain" and accordingly (he may think) under the Government's control. To a considerable extent, the state-sponsored sector's deeds, whether good or bad, will tend to rub off on the Government and so here is another motive for intervention, in some cases even in day-to-day activities. Thus, state bodies have sometimes delayed impending price rises often where these rises would have coincided with a general election. To take an example, given by Dr Sweeney:

> "In the 1988 Budget, the Minister of Finance, Mr. McSharry, persuaded the ESB to repay £31.4m debt outstanding instead of a planned £2m in interest and capital, and he also imposed a 5% VAT charge on electricity, stating that there 'will be no increase in consumer prices' (1988 Budget Statement). In the 1990 Budget, the Minister for Finance, Mr. Reynolds, increased the rate

---

150   1988 Act, s.24(2)(a), (b).
151   *Ibid.* s.6(2).
152   See the commentary on the 1988 Act by Tony Kerr in the *Irish Current Law Statutes Annotated* in which it is noted that the then (Labour Party) Minister for Labour insisted that the 1977 Act was the beginning of a trend which would eventually engulf the private sector. Again, when the Advisory Committee on Worker Participation (1986, Prl. 4339) was eventually appointed, its members were unanimous that: "increased employee participation was desirable but were not unanimous as to how impetus could be given to the development of participation in the private sector. The majority, including the Chairman, recommended the introduction of enabling legislation in the private sector for all organisations employing more than one hundred people (see paras. 172–188). Those members representing the Federated Union of Employers preferred a purely voluntary approach." Kerr, *op. cit.* In fact, nothing has yet come of the Committee's recommendation. It may be mentioned that, at the relevant time, the first four of the five largest employers in the country were state bodies and that of the enterprises employing over 2,000 employees, eight were state bodies and the remaining 10 were private companies.
153   Lemass, *op. cit.* above, n.137. In "The Organisation behind the Economic Programme"(1961) 9 *Administration* 3, Mr. Lemass also predicted that whenever a SSB becomes controversial, the parent Minister will exercise closer control over the body as criticisms of it reflect upon the Minister.

of VAT to 10% saying that 'I am arranging that the additional costs be absorbed by the ESB.' (They will be £18m in a full year). He also imposed 10% VAT on Telecom Éireann services stating that 'I am confident that this can be implemented without increased cost to Telecom users' (Cost of £11m in a full year) (Budget Speech 1990). He was supported by the Minister for Energy, Mr. Molloy, on the issue of the ESB increase, who, when questioned on whether the board would obey the 'suggestion' said 'the Government has made its intentions clear. The ESB is a semi-state organisation and the new policy has been defined' (*Irish Times*, 1990)."[154]

A further and possibly justifiable example of the way in which the Government is held responsible for the acts or omission of a state body occurred in the public's reaction to the plight of those persons (the so-called Hepatitis C victims) who suffered injury or death following blood transfusions provided by the Blood Services Transfusion Service Board: despite the fact that this Board is a (non-commercial) state body, the Minister for Health was held responsible.[155]

4. It emerges, from what has been said so far, that there is a potential source of conflict of interests between the Government's role *qua* owner of a state body and its parts *qua* Government or *qua* political partisan. There is a further possible source of conflict where the state body is not a monopoly[156] and here a Minister may play here a role, as a licensing authority. Thus he may be required to choose between the state body and its competitors. Two recent episodes involving RTÉ illustrate the potential for a conflict of interest arising from the different capacities in which the Government may relate to a state body. The background to each was the removal, by the Radio and Television Act 1988[157] of RTÉ's effective monopoly.

It was relevant in regard to the first episode that section 16(1) of the 1988 Act provides that: "the Minister may at the request of the Commission and after consultation with RTÉ" require the latter to provide facilities needed in connection with the independent sound broadcasting services. And the independent contractor must make such payments to RTÉ "as the Minister, after consultation with RTÉ and the Commission, directs". In 1989, there was an absence of agreement between one of the independent contractors and RTÉ as to the amount, the Minister having fixed a figure which RTÉ regarded as unfairly low.[158] In the end, a rather higher figure was agreed upon, but not before RTÉ had threatened the Minister with an application for judicial review proceedings, the first such threat ever to have been issued, by a state body, at any rate in public.

The occasion for the second episode in 1990[159] was that even after the admission of competition, all of the proceeds of the television licence fee (apart from the cost of collection) continued to go to RTÉ. This represented about £40m out of RTÉ's

---

[154] *Public Enterprise in Ireland*: Paper given to Statistical and Social Enquiry Society of Ireland on February 15, 1990, p. 30.
[155] See 469 *Dáil Debates*, Cols 1631–1675 and 1953–2001 (October 8 and 9, 1996) and newspaper reports of October 14–20, 1996.
[156] On monopolies, see further, pp. 165–169.
[157] See below pp. 283–284.
[158] See *The Irish Times*, March 20–30, 1989.
[159] See *The Irish Times*, June 29, 1990; 400 *Dáil Debates* Col. 1215–1219 (June 28, 1990).

total income of £130 million (the remainder coming mainly from advertising (£70m) and commercial enterprises (£13m)). This subvention meant, said the Government, that RTÉ's competitors were at a substantial disadvantage. Thus it was necessary, to adopt the argument and metaphor used by the proponents of change, to level the playing field. RTÉ's response was that the extra finance was necessary because of the high cost of public service broadcasting. However, the motivation imputed to the Government by the Opposition was that, in its news and current affairs programmes, RTÉ had examined the Government's performance in a thorough and impartial fashion and the Government wished to discourage this.

The Government proposed a package of four measures to improve the position of the independent broadcasters. The first of these appeared in the Broadcasting Bill 1990, though it was removed at Second Stage: it was that up to 25 per cent. (*i.e.* £10 million at 1994 figures) of the T.V. licence fee revenue should be withheld from RTÉ and apportioned among the commercial broadcasters in amounts to be determined by the Independent Radio and Television Commission. The second element was the Minister for Communication's (as he then was) proposal that RTÉ's Radio 2 FM, which is a popular music station, should become more of a cultural service and, therefore, presumably win less advertising revenue. A striking point, about this proposal is that there was never any suggestion that it should be implemented by way of legislation: it was to stand or fall on its inherent merits and the Minister's power of persuasion. The first two proposals were dropped apparently because of their unpopularity with the public. The remaining two measures, however, became law although only, as we shall see, for a brief period. The more draconian of these imposed a "cap" by which the total time for broadcasting advertisements and the maximum period to be given to advertisements in any hour were reduced by the RTÉ Authority subject to the approval of the Minister.[160] Secondly, the time allowed for broadcasting advertisements was significantly reduced.[161] Thirdly, the Authority was required not to make any more money in receipts from advertising, sponsorship or other forms of commercial promotion than its receipts from broadcasting licence fees (on pain of a corresponding reduction in its income from licence fees). However, the Broadcasting Act stipulated that the total daily advertising time is to be fixed by the Authority, subject to the approval of the Minister and thus removed the cap and restored the *status quo ante* as regards advertising.

Special statutory controls over RTÉ[162]

Broadly speaking, state-sponsored bodies are subject to the same law as other persons. In some cases there are modifications and of these, RTÉ affords the most striking examples. The best known of these controls is the Broadcasting Authority Act 1960, section 31 (as amended).[163] However, the annual order[164] made (in various

---

160 Broadcasting Act 1990, s.3(1). The effect of the change was first, that the total daily broadcasting time was not to exceed 7.5 per cent. of total daily transmission time and secondly, that the maximum hourly time was not to exceed five minutes (as compared with 10 per cent. and six minutes per hour, respectively, before the 1990 Act).
161 Broadcasting Authority Act, 1990, s.3.
162 On RTÉ generally, see, *e.g.* Hall, *The Electronic Age* (1993) Chaps. 8–22 .
163 For this provision, see below, pp. 664, 667.
164 See Morgan, "Section 31 – The Broadcasting Ban" (1990–1992) 25–27 Ir. Jur. 117.

forms) under this provision for the preceding twenty three years, lapsed in early 1994 and has not been renewed. There is, however, another analogous but broader provision which prohibits the authority from broadcasting "anything which may reasonably be regarded as being likely to promote, or incite to, crime or as tending to undermine the authority of the State".[165] On a broader front, the Authority is under a duty to broadcast news and current affairs "in an objective and impartial manner" without giving its own views (save on broadcasting policy) and to ensure that its programmes do not "unreasonably encroach on the privacy of an individual".[166] The Authority is under positive, though necessarily imprecise, duties to uphold "rightful liberty of expression" and to pay regard to the values and traditions of foreign states, particularly European Community Member States; and

> "to be responsive to the interests and concerns of the whole community, be mindful of the need for understanding and peace within the whole island of Ireland, ensure that the programmes reflect the varied elements which make up the culture of the people of the whole island of Ireland, and have special regard for the elements which distinguish that culture and in particular for the Irish language."[167]

It should be noted that even now (see previous section) the responsible Minister retains the power of fixing the amount of the broadcasting licence fee, RTÉ's major source of income.[168] The length of advertising permitted has already been explained. Advertisements on certain subjects – those directed towards any religious or political end or related to any industrial dispute – must not be accepted.[169] Next, one should notice a most striking public policy. RTÉ is statutorily obligated[170] to provide substantial amounts of money for programmes made by the independent television production sector. The specified amounts commenced in 1994 at a figure of £5m and increase, by stages, to plateau (in 1999 and subsequent years) at an amount which is: the greater of 20 per cent of television expenditure or £12.5m – (subject to annual adjustments in line with the Consumer Price Index).

There is a Broadcasting Complaints Commission to consider complaints against RTÉ, such as that any of its statutory obligations outlined in previous paragraphs have been broken, that the Authority's advertising code has been violated or that "an assertion was made in a broadcast of inaccurate facts or information in relation to an individual which constituted an attack on the dignity, honour or reputation of that individual."[171] To assist the Commission, the Authority must record and retain

---

165 Broadcasting Authority (Amendment) Act 1976, s.3. The relationship of this provision with s.3 (as amended) has not been judicially explored. In 1984, when a Noraid spokesman was banned from the airwaves by the Minister for Communications because Noraid was not on the list of proscribed organisations authorised by s.31, the Minister relied upon his power under s.3 of the 1976 Act.

166 1976 Act, s.3. The duty of impartiality does not affect the Authority's right to transmit "political party broadcasts" (a phrase which is not defined): 1960 Act, s.18(2). See, further *Madigan v. RTÉ* [1994] 2 I.L.R.M. 472; *McCann v. An Taoiseach* [1994] 2 I.R. 1.

167 1976 Act, s.13.

168 1976 Act, ss.1, 8; 1960 Act, ss.1(b), 22; Wireless Telegraphy Act 1926, s.5.

169 1960 Act, s.20. See generally, Hall and McGovern, "Regulation of the Media: Irish and European Community Dimensions" (1986) 8 D.U.L.J. 1.

170 Broadcasting Authority (Amendment) Act 1993, ss.4–6.

171 1976 Act, s.4 Broadcasting Act 1990, s.8.

for at least 180 days a copy of every broadcast. The Commission has no power to award damages or enforce any other sanction save that it may require the Authority to publish its decision on a complaint.[172] (This is done through the RTÉ Guide). Furthermore, if the Commission's findings favour the complainant, then, unless the Commission considers it inappropriate, RTÉ must broadcast the findings at a time and in a manner corresponding to those of the offending broadcast.[173]

6. Control by the Oireachtas

One of the points which emerges from a survey of the Government's controls over a state body is that the occasions on which the most effective controls are exercisable are usually points at which the Oireachtas is not involved. The Oireachtas is, of course, involved in the legislation designing a state body and any amending legislation which may be necessary, for instance to authorise an increase in share capital. But this operates spasmodically and not necessarily at the times of greatest significance not, for instance: when a new board is being appointed; when a decision whether to withdraw or to go into a certain area of activity is taken; or when a guarantee is given by the Minister for Finance to a private lender. By contrast, in the case of administration going on within a Department of State, these lacunae do not exist because the Government is responsible, to the Dáil, for all administrative acts even if these do not require a change of law. This means that such activity may be debated and Ministers may be questioned in the Dáil about them. In contrast, where any question is raised as to the activity of a state-sponsored body, it is likely to be met by the imprecise rule which excludes responsibility for day-to-day matters. And where a state body is operating in the commercial world there is obviously an additional reason for confidentiality.

Nevertheless, the performance of state-sponsored bodies is sometimes discussed in the Oireachtas. Where money is given (whether in exchange for shares or simply as a grant) or lent to commercial state bodies, this is usually done on the authority of the constituent Act or an amendment thereof, rather than during the Estimates or by way of an Appropriation Act. However, in spite of this, during the Estimates debate, deputies are permitted to discuss the performance of a state-sponsored body which comes under the wing of the Department whose vote is under examination and a Minister does sometimes take the opportunity to give an account of the past record and prospects of a state body which comes within his jurisdiction. However, the reality is, first, that many estimates go undebated for lack of time and, secondly, even where there is a debate, discussion ranges over the entire field of a Department's activities. Thus it is inappropriate as a vehicle for the kind of detailed, technical debate necessary to a state-sponsored body because such a debate would have had to be at a broad level. Again, although annual reports from each body have to be laid before each House, they have seldom, if ever, been made the occasion for a "take note" debate. The conclusion must be that debate in the Oireachtas is spasmodic and often superficial.

---

[172] 1976 Act, s.4. See also Hall and McGovern, *loc. cit.*, above, n.169.
[173] 1990 Act, s.8.

Joint Oireachtas Committees

It is of course true that it was precisely to achieve substantial exclusion of the Oireachtas that the state body form was invented. Nevertheless it was decided, especially in the light of huge expenditure of public funds by the state body sector that greater control was needed over this sector by the Government, that this process had gone too far. To meet such criticisms and following suggestions over the years that such a committee be established the Joint Oireachtas Committee on State-Sponsored Bodies was established in 1976.[174] It was anticipated, correctly, that the technique of a small select committee would create the kind of non-partisan, technical milieu which is appropriate for discussion of this area. Moreover, as a result of the Committees of the Houses of the Oireachtas (Compellability, Privileges and Immunities of Witnesses) Act 1997, *inter alia*, this Committee (amongst others) has been given power to obtain any type of evidence, it requires from any person. Disobedience to a direction from the Committee would be an offence.[175] Originally, the Committee's jurisdiction was confined to all the commercial bodies, including Údarás na Gaeltachta but excluding the National Lottery Co. and the Housing Finance Agency Ltd. Next, its title was changed to the "Joint Committee on State-Sponsored Bodies" (*i.e.* dropping the term "commercial") and its remit was extended to include Bord Fáilte, FAS, the Industrial Development agencies, the National Roads Authority and Teagasc.[176] (The reasons given,[177] originally, for the exclusion of the non-commercial bodies were, first, that with virtually all the commercial bodies, profit and loss provides an objective yard-stick for evaluating their success – which is lacking in the case of the non-commercial sector; and secondly, that the performance of non-commercial bodies could not be examined in isolation from the policy, including allocation of resources, of their parent department.) Recently the Oireachtas committee structure was changed so that most of the committees now shadow a particular Department of State. One unfortunate side effect of this is that there is no longer a single specialised committee on all of the bodies indicated earlier. This jurisdiction is now divided among a number of committees; though naturally most of them will fall within the bailiwick of the Joint Committee on Public Enterprise and Transport. Furthermore the paragraph of the Committee's terms of reference is now relatively narrow: "(i) such public affairs administered by the Department . . . as it may select, including bodies under the aegis of that Department *in respect of Government policy*."[178] The various Committees have published a large number of reports[179]; though the numbers have fallen somewhat in the 1990s.

---

174 See 293 *Dáil Debates*, Col. 1403 (November 10, 1976). It has been reconstituted in subsequent Houses (apart from the 1981–1982 Houses) up until 1997, when the new Committee described below in the text, came into effect. (The Joint Committee on Public Expenditure whose remit included both the Departments of State and the non-commercial state-sponsored bodies associated with each of them was not reconstituted after 1987.)

175 1997 Act, ss. 3 and 17. See also the Central Bank Act 1997, s.24

176 469 *Dáil Debates*, Cols. 1700–1703, October 9, 1996.

177 319 *Dáil Debates*, Cols. 169–199, (March 19, 1980) (unsuccessful motion to extend the Committee's bailiwick to the non-commercial sector).

178 135 *Seanad Debates*, Col. 798 (November 19, 1997). (Emphasis added).

179 *e.g.* An Post (1994); National Building Agency (1994); VHI (1994); ESB (1997) Pn.3829; National Stud (1979, Prl. 7869); B. & I. (1979, Prl. 8063); Min Fheir (1979, Prl. 8242); CIÉ/OIE (1979, Prl.

Comptroller and Auditor General

The question of whether the Comptroller and Auditor General should audit state-sponsored bodies is as old as state bodies themselves.[180] When the ESB was being set up in 1926 the appointment of auditors from the private sector rather than the CAG caused divisions in Dáil Éireann. In the early 1960s, a policy decision was taken that, in the case of well-established commercial state bodies, the Ministers concerned would not oppose any request from them to engage private sector auditors.[181] Subject to some exceptions a general pattern emerged over the years – the allocation of the audit of non-commercial bodies to the CAG and that of the commercial bodies to private sector auditors.[182] This was confirmed by the Comptroller and Auditor General (Amendment) Act 1993, by which the scope of the CAG's audit was extended to include all the non-commercial state bodies not already statutorily audited by him[183]; but not the commercial state bodies.[184]

The Act also makes it clear that in respect of commercial state bodies the CAG does not enjoy even the power of discretionary inspection which he has in respect of a body receiving at least half of its gross receipts from the Exchequer.[185]

8438); Ceimici Teo (1979, Prl. 8475); Aer Rianta (1979, Prl. 8582); Arramara Teo. (1980, Prl. 8686); Bord na Móna (1980, Prl. 8808); VHI (1980, Prl. 8899); ACC (1980, Prl. 8944); ICC (1980, Prl. 9261); NBA (1980, Prl. 9480); CSET (1980, Prl. 9555); Aer Lingus/Aer Linte (1980, Prl. 9584); Irish Shipping Ltd (1981, Prl. 9663); NET (1981, Prl. 9752); Foir Teo (1981, Prl. 9944); RTÉ (1981, Prl. 9945); Ostann Iompair Éireann (1984, Pl. 2); Irish Shipping Ltd (1985, Pl. 3091); Bord Gais Éireann (1985, Pl. 3638); Údarás na Gaeltachta (1986, Pl. 3747). Analysis of Financial Position of Commercial State-Sponsored Bodies (1986, Pl. 4487); Electricity Supply Board (1987, Pl. 4487); Bord Telecom Éireann (1987, Pl. 4718); Irish Life Assurance plc. (1988, Pl 5451); An Post (1988, Pl. 5731); B & I Line (1988, Pl. 5779); Irish Steel Limited (1988, Pl. 5924); Aer Lingus plc and Aer Linte Éireann plc (1989, Pl. 6554); Report on certain allegations levelled at the former Chairman of the Committee (1989, Pl. 6607); Irish National Stud Company Limited (1990, Pl. 7135); Irish National Petroleum Corporation Limited (1990, Pl. 7381); An Post – An Post National Lottery Company (1990, Pl.7382).

180 The Committee of Public Accounts *Special Report on the Future Role of the Comptroller and Auditor General and the Committee of Public Accounts* (1988, Pl. 5645) devotes a section to the question of whether the CAG should audit the state bodies. Extracts from this section, with its recurrent theme of the accountability of state bodies, were given in an Appendix to Chap. 4 of the 2nd edition of this book.

181 Four bodies took the opportunity to move to private sector auditors – Irish Life, the Air Companies (Aer Lingus and Aer Linte), Irish Shipping and Ceimici Teo. Subsequently, Irish Steel and NET also changed auditors.

182 The information in this para. comes from the Committee of Public Accounts Special Report on the future role of the CAG and the PAC (1988), Pl. 5645), para. 35. The exceptions to the general pattern described in the text were that the constituent statutes required RTE's (Broadcasting Authority Act 1960, s.25) and ESB's (Electricity (Supply) Act 1927, s.7) accounts to be audited by an Auditor appointed by the responsible Minister with the consent of the Minister for Finance (in practice, the for many years, this was CAG). In the case of RTÉ, this requirement was removed by the Broadcasting Act 1990, s.7. This provision, however, also states that, whoever does act as auditor must submit to the Minister for Communications a certified statement as to the total revenue derived by the RTÉ Authority from advertising and sponsorship.

183 Section 5.See too s. 8(1)(b) (CAG's right to inspect accounts of bodies receiving 50% or more of state funding).

184 In respect of which omission, the Minister for Finance pointed out that these bodies were already accountable to the Oireachtas, by way of the Joint Committee: 424, *Dáil Debates*, Col. 1322 (October 29, 1992).

185 Section 8(3) and Second Schedule. For an unsuccessful opposition attempt to bring commercial state bodies within the scope of this power, see 428 *Dáil Debates* Cols. 1443–1451 (March 31, 1993).

7. Board and Chief Executive

In theory, the rights, duties and identity of a state-sponsored body are concentrated in the board. The board is the body corporate, the legal personality of the body: everyone else is merely a creature, whether an officer or servant, of the board. In practice the position is radically different: the Devlin Report offered the following list of the usual duties discharged by a board:

"(a) Implement government policy; (b) Appoint top management; (c) exercise financial control; (d) stimulate development; (e) maintain liaison with the minister; (f) supervise personnel policy; (g) measure management performance."[186]

Dr Barrington was less expansive: according to him, the principal task of the board is to integrate two major influences, first, the overall policy of the responsible Minister; secondly, the stream of advice from management based on operational experience. Both these contributions are "discussed and weighed by board members of broad general experience from many walks of life. The development of policy, therefore, is a broadly participatory affair in which the board plays a central role."[187]

However even these accounts would appear to exaggerate the usual influence of the board. The central facts are that there are no statutory qualifications for membership (other than not being a deputy or senator or any specified member of an elected authority).[188] Members are often chosen as a reward for their political loyalties – so that the old gibe that appointments are the Irish equivalent of the Honours system remains substantially true. However there are exceptions: certain Ministers, or possibly Ministers making appointments in regard to certain particularly significant state bodies (*e.g.* the Central Bank), will recognise that too much is at stake for the appointments to be made of anyone other than diligent, well-qualified persons. And in other cases, individual appointees who do not, at first sight appear appropriate, turn in, for whatever reasons of patriotism or pride, first rate performances. Again certain boards have a collective reputation for vigour and intelligence. The duties of membership are usually allowed to take up only a few hours at once-monthly meetings.[189] The remuneration for a board member remains relatively small compared to the private sector and is governed by Department of Finance guidelines.[190] Civil servant

---

[186]   Devlin Report, para. 5.2.21. For the statement that appointments to boards should be based on "experience, competence and expertise, see Buckley, p. 25.

[187]   Barrington, *The Irish Administrative System* (1980), p. 59. See also Kenny, "Boards of Directors in Ireland" (1978) 26 *Administration* 107. Nowadays, the constituent statute often relegates the detail – regarding the Board's *modus operandi*; quorum, meetings, seal and even the fact that it is a corporation sole – to a Schedule: *e.g.* Roads Act 1993, Third Sched, (National Roads Authority).

[188]   Although see pp. 132–133.

[189]   In an area where anomalies are almost the norm, it would be surprising if there were no exceptions to this general pattern. And, sure enough, we find, for instance, that in the case of the ESB (the earliest of the commercial state bodies) section 2(6) of the Electricity (Supply) Act 1927 originally stated that the chairman of the Board was to be full time. However this provision was revoked by section 6 of the Electricity (Supply) (Amendment) Act 1988, as a result of which the terms and conditions of the chairman of the ESB as with other chairmen, are left to the responsible Minister acting with the consent of the Minister of Finance. At present, the chairman remains full time. In addition the chairman of CIÉ's terms and conditions provided that he be retained for "so much of your time as is necessary".

[190]   Issued in 1992, these guidelines group state companies into four categories for payment purposes.

members – and it has been recommended that each board should have a suitable senior civil servant as a member[191] – are not paid.

By contrast, a state-sponsored body's senior officials will be full-time experts who are in frequent, informal contact with the civil servants in the responsible Department. The board's effective authority is, thus curtailed from above by the Minister and Department as seen in Part 4 of this chapter but also from below, by the officials. In reality, the average board member's contribution is likely to be small and may amount merely to confirming proposals brought before it by the management. This poses a classic danger, namely that there may be a divorce between responsibility and effective power. Something of the sort materialised in the events leading up to the liquidation of Irish Shipping in 1984. One significant factor in the company's losses arose from imprudent long-term chartering agreements entered into by the company. Another source of loss was the formation (with a private shipping line) of a joint pool of shipping known as Celtic Bulk Carriers. In each case the Board was not properly informed and, thus, was not properly in control.[192]

Certain obligations of good conduct are imposed on board members in recent constituent statutes, including: a duty of confidentiality, breach of which is sometimes made an offence[193] and a duty to declare an interest.[194]

Oddly enough, the constituent statutes scarcely ever mention the chief executive and never provide a description of his functions. Nevertheless – and regardless of whether the chief executive has or has not been made a member of the board, as is

---

Directors and chairpersons of companies in Group 1 (*e.g.* Aer Lingus, ESB, An Post) receive £5,000 and £7,000, respectively per year. Of the other Groups, the figures are as follows: Group 2 (*e.g.* ACC Bank, Aer Rianta, Bord Gáis); £4,000 and £6,000; group 3 (*e.g.* Bord na gCon, Legal Aid Board, National Stud) £2,500; £4,000; Group 4 (*e.g.* Arts Council, CERT Employment Equality Agency): £2,000; £3,000.

However, the perks are left to each individual body to decide for themselves. These range from a free copy of the *RTÉ Guide* (members of RTÉ Authority) to some quite significant travel in the case of some state bodies: see *Irish Times*, October 27, 1996. For the statutory provisions, see the Broadcasting Authority Act 1960, s.5; Postal and Telecommunications Services Act 1983,s.35; Voluntary Health Insurance Act 1957, s.6(5), as amended by the Voluntary Health Insurance (Amendment) Act 1996, s.10.

191 Review Group Report, p. 25. See *Report of the Telecommunications, Energy and Communications, Task Force* (1995; Pn. 1996) p. 36: "Chairpersons and Chief Executives are of the view that senior civil servants may bring a breadth of experience to the Boards of commercial State companies, not only experience of relevant sectoral developments nationally and internationally, but also of Government and E.U. policies. Such experience may enhance a Board's capacity to carry out its role in an informed, coherent and responsible manner while maintaining its independence and flexibility. Any potential conflict of interest with a civil servant's regulatory role should be avoided." On conflict of interest see above, n.194.

192 Pl. 3091, paras. 17, 23.

193 Trade and Marketing Promotion Act 1991, s.10; Roads Act 1993, ss.38 and 39; Irish Horseracing Industry Act 1994, s.17; An Bord Bia Act 1994, s.26; Irish Medicines Board Act 1995, s.23.

194 Electricity (Supply) Act 1927, ss.10 and 11; Voluntary Health Insurance (Amendment) Act 1996, s.8; Roads Act 1993, s.40 (this provision, in respect of membership of the National Roads Authority is very elaborate, involving a register and making failure to make an appropriate entry on the Register a criminal offence.) See, similarly, Irish Medicines Board Act 1995, s.24.

See also Irish Horseracing Industry Act 1994; An Bord Bia Act 1994, s.25 (where members of Board or Authority, respectively fails to disclose an interest; Minister for Agriculture, Food and Forestry may remove him from office.) In addition, the Department of Finance's *Guidelines for State Bodies* (1992) provide that all state bodies should have written codes of conduct for board members and employees covering 'disclosure of interest' and avoidance of conflicts of interest respectively. See also Report of the Task Force (October, 1995), p. 49; and Ethics in Public Office Act 1995, Pt. VI which *inter alia* amends the Prevention of Corruption Act 1916 and the Public Bodies Corrupt Practices Act 1889.

increasingly coming to be the case – there is no doubt of his position as effectively the "managing director".[195] In respect of the older state bodies, it follows from the board's general power in appointing staff that it is the board which selects and appoints, the chief executive. It is, indeed, their principal function. However, more recent statutes explicitly vest the function in the board; but with the significant addition that it is to be exercised with the approval of the appropriate Minister.[196] However, since nothing is said in the constituent statutes about removal, as a matter of general law, this is exclusively for the board.[197]

The Government's involvement in the question of the chief executives' salaries has attracted a good deal of attention (not least among chief executives). It is worthy of note because it is symptomatic of the general tension arising from the amphibious position of state bodies. On the one hand, Feargal Quinn, who was Chairman of An Post 1984–1989, has remarked that Government restrictions on executive salaries limit the ability of commercial state bodies to recruit the best managers.[198] On the other hand, the large state bodies have an important trend-setting effect, particularly in the area of pay and conditions of employment, and it is reasonable therefore that central Government should retain overall control.

The legal position here is more clear-cut than in regard to the issue of the payment of other members of staff which was explained in Part 2 (though it is worthy of note that any decision in regard to the salary of the top person in any organisation is bound to have trickle-down effect at lower levels). "Characteristically the constitution of a state-sponsored body (whether statutory or contained in Memorandum and Articles of Association) provides that the remuneration of the chief executive shall be determined by the board with the consent of the relevant Minister."[199]

---

[195] The title used is usually "chief executive", save that certain state bodies (*e.g.* ICC and Siúicre Éireann c.p.t.) have a "managing director". *Review Body on Higher Remuneration in the Public Sector* (Report No.37, 1996 p. 25 states that "the need for an appropriate number of executive directors should be addressed: as a first step, the chief executive should be appointed to the boards." Notice that at present (1997), four in ten of the bodies under the responsibility of the Minister for Public Enterprise have the chief executive on the board.

[196] In the case of RTÉ, the Minister for Communication's (as he then was) consent is necessary for an appointment to the position of Director General. (Broadcasting Authority Act 1960, s.13(4)) an arrangement which caused tension, over an appointment, in 1985. For similar provisions, see Turf Development Act 1946, s.8(3); Combat Poverty Agency Act 1986, s.12; Industrial Development Act 1993, Second Schedule, para. 1; Irish Aviation Authority Act 1993, s.38(6); Roads Act 1993, s.29 (National Roads Authority). The chairman of the Authority may also be appointed as chief executive.

[197] Notice an unusual provision in the Roads Act 1993, which states explicitly that if a member or employee of the National Roads Authority incurs any legal obligation while discharging his duties *bona fide*, the Board will indemnify him.

[198] "State Companies and Commercial Freedom" *Management*, March, 1981. For unholy media interest in the salary and expenses paid to the chief executive of Bord na Móna, see newspapers over the period April and May, 1996.

[199] Gleeson Report on Higher Remuneration in the Public Service (1987, Pl. 5244) para. 4.9. For examples of the statutes referred to in the quotation, See: Air Companies (Amendment) Act 1976, s.6; Agricultural Credit Act 1978, s.19; Transport (Miscellaneous Provisions) Act 1979, s.7; Electricity (Supply) (Amendment) Act 1988, s.7; National Stud (Amendment) Act 1993, s.4; Industrial Development Act 1993, Second Schedule, para. 1; Irish Aviation Authority Act 1993, s.38(6); Irish Horseracing Industry Act 1994, s.21; An Bord Bia Act 1994, s.32(3). Notice that these are all amending statutes, altering the original position, which was that no ministerial consent was

As regards practice, the position hitherto has been that a non-statutory body, the Review Body on Higher Remuneration in the Public Sector has since its establishment in 1969, made recommendations as to the formula to be followed in fixing a chief executive's remuneration package and the boards have followed this (usually at the maximum point on the range) reasonably faithfully. However the most recent (Buckley) Report of the Review Body has remarked, with respect to commercial state bodies:

> "The case for a change in the existing arrangements is supported by evidence of a clear international trend to assign responsibility for determining the remuneration of chief executives of commercial state organisations to the boards of the bodies concerned. As far as we are aware, Ireland is the only remaining country in which the remuneration of chief executives of commercial state bodies falls within the remit of a review body like this."[200]

However after some delay, the Government rejected the Report's recommendation that primary responsibility should be exercised by the Boards. The Government decided that (with the exception of five commercial bodies – Telecom, AL, ICC, VHI and Bord na Móna – to which special individual arrangements apply) the decision is to be taken by the Minister for Finance submitting proposals to the Government. This power is concentrated in the Department of Finance. However (in line with Buckley) the Minister is to be guided by reference to job "size" and comparable private sector figures.[201] In the case of the non-commercial bodies, the Buckley Committee's (uncontroversial) recommendation is that the existing practice of linking the salary to a grade (Assistant Secretary) in the Civil Service should be continued.

8. Contemporary Government Policy towards the State-Sponsored Sector

It is appropriate to take the year 1987 as the base-line for this Part, since, apart from Sean Lemass' "Great Leap Forward" of the 1950s, 1987 marked the greatest sea-change in the attitude of Government towards the commercial state body sector. For, until the Fianna Fáil Government of 1987–1989 with its commitment to take hold of the public debt crisis, little attention, official or scholarly, had been devoted to these agencies. Plainly, they were constitutional novelties; yet the implications

---

required. The expression used in the statutory provision is usually "the Chief Officer however styled." For an example drawn from Articles of Association, take Art. 69 of Bord Telecom, which provides as follows:

"... officers and servants of the Company shall be paid by the Company such remuneration and allowances for expenses and shall hold office on such terms and conditions as the Directors think fit subject to in the case of its chief officer (whether that officer is described as the chief officer or otherwise), the approval of the Minister given with the consent of the Minister for the Public Service."

[200] (Buckley) Review Body on Higher Remuneration in the Public Sector (1996, Pn. 3187), chapters 2 and 3. The Report also recommends that each board should set up a remuneration subcommittee.

[201] *The Irish Times*, March 1998. Notice, also that in mid-1997, the Government vetoed a remuneration package which the ESB had wished to offer its new executive: *The Irish Times*, September 2, 1997.

which their peculiar status (neither Government nor private enterprise nor good red herring) had, both for the performance which could be expected from them and for the state policy to be adopted towards them, had been neglected. However by the late 1980s, the air was heavy with the sound of lame ducks coming home to roost. The economic performance of the state-sponsored sector in the 1980s can be illustrated by the fact that in several years major, non-financial commercial bodies made an aggregate net loss (after depreciation and the payment of interest). Secondly, the interest payments to the Exchequer as a percentage of the total government investment (by way of equity, government loans and capital grants) was very low by comparison with commercial standards.[202] (Even by 1996, the aggregate figures for all commercial bodies showed a nett loss of £100,000 against fixed assets of £5.7 billion).

One of the causes underlying the post-1987 changes was said to be "a new emphasis on financial performance, judged by the criterion of profit, with social objectives, particularly employment, being relegated."[203] A certain amount of new thinking in relation to the state-sponsored sector commenced in the late 1980s and continues.[204] In the present short survey of the contemporary debate on the role of state sponsored bodies, we shall consider some of the new thinking and developments. The matters under consideration may be listed under the following heads.

Trends in Re-Structuring

Since 1987 as a response to the need for economy in the public sector – there has been fairly extensive rationalisation for example, Bord Na gCapall and Foir Teo have been terminated by the Bord na gCapall (Dissolution) Act 1989 and the Foir Teo (Dissolution) Act 1990 and their functions transferred to the Minister for Agriculture and Food and the Industrial Credit Corporation, respectively.[205] There has also been extensive reorganisation to rationalise the ad hocery of the years. Originally, for instance, state activity in encouraging employment was divided among three agencies: AnCo (the Industrial Training Authority) a board constructed to deal with the training and employment of adults; the Youth Employment Agency, a company constituted to do similar work for young persons; and the National Manpower Service, a unit of the Department of Labour which dealt with placement and occupational guidance. The Labour Services Act 1987 dissolved AnCo; wound up the YEA and the NMS, and created FÁS,[206] to take over their functions.[207] However the administration of unemployment benefits still remains vested in the Department of Social Welfare.

---

202 Sweeney, "Public Enterprise in Ireland" 13 and 14.
203 Sweeney, *ibid.* at p. 33.
204 See recent monographs listed at n. 1. See also *Programme for National Recovery* (Pl. 5213, 1987), p. 17 and *Programme for Economic and Social Progress* (Pl. 7829, 1990), para. 83–93.
205 See also the Exported Livestock (Insurance) Act 1984 (dissolving the Exported Livestock (Insurance) Board); and the Wool Marketing Act 1984 (dissolving An Chomairle).
206 FÁS is an acronym for Foras Áiseanna Saothaoir (Institute for Labour Facilities). However, the word, Fás, also means "growth".
207 Similarly as a result of the Agricultural (Research, Training and Advice) Act, 1988, ACOT, AFT and BNCOT were wound up and their functions united in Teagasc – the Agricultural and Development Authority. In addition, by the Science and Technology Act 1987, Eolas (the National

The great objective of the 1990s, was to reduce (at least) the level of unemployment. Thus, for example, in order to give greater thrust to three areas of anticipated economic growth – forestry, horticulture, and value-added to Irish food products – Coillte Teoranta (Forestry Act 1988) and An Bord Glas (Bord Glas Act 1990) and An Bord Bia (An Bord Bia 1994) were created. Another part of the response was state action to increase the number and efficiency of small and medium sized businesses. One way in which this is being done is to multiply and transmogrify the state bodies, in the broad field of trade promotion. Thus by the Industrial Development Act 1993, the Industrial Development Authority was dissolved and replaced by the newly-constituted Forfas, the policy advisory and co-ordination board for industrial development, science and technology. The Act delegates powers to two "agencies"[208] each with its own board: Forbairt (for the promotion of indigenous industry) and the Industrial Development Agency (Ireland) and (for promoting inward investment).

In the non-commercial field, too, there has been re-structuring. Some entities have been established in a statutory form to take over from pre-cursor non-statutory bodies.[209] In other cases, there has been a re-formation of an existing statutory body to accommodate a strengthening of powers.[210] In many cases, state bodies have been set up to act as a stimulus to development, often in a particular area.[211]

According to the National Economic and Social Council,[212] some of the problems of the state bodies stemmed from the fact that the Government and responsible Departments had tended to treat them too much as a homogeneous group, notwithstanding the fact that they were set up to serve diverse purposes and to operate in different milieux. Since 1987, the Government has shown itself to be more discriminating in appraising the potential of state bodies and more innovative in the courses which it has allowed them to pursue. Thus, it has been more prepared to give the economically stronger bodies their head. Consider, for example, the Turf Development Act 1990. When Bord na Móna was first set up in 1946, its functions

---

Board for Science and Technology) and the Institute for Industrial Research and Standards were replaced by the Irish Science and Technology Agency. Again in 1987, most of the functions of An Foras Forbartha Teo (National Institute for Physical Planning) which was a town planning ministerial advisory body, were subsumed within the Department of the Environment. Likewise, the Trade and Marketing Promotion Act 1991 combines in An Bord Trachtála (the Irish Trade Board) the functions formerly carried out by Coras Trachtála (Irish Export Board) and the Irish Goods Council and the Air Navigation Services Office (which was part of the Department of Tourism and Transport) has now been replaced by the Irish Aviation Authority (established under the Irish Aviation Authority (established under the Irish Aviation Authority Act 1993).

208 In addition, structural re-organisation has been provided by the Transport (Reorganisation of Coras Iompair Éireann) Act, 1986 by which CIÉ was required to form three companies – Iarnrod Éireann (Irish Rail), Bus Éireann (Irish Buses); and Bus Atha Cliath (Dublin Buses) – as units by which the different segments of the enterprise, formerly operated by CIÉ directly, are to be run. Furthermore, the Air Companies (Amendment) Act 1993 establishes (in place of Aer Lingus plc) Aer Lingus Group plc as the holding company for two operating companies, namely Aer Lingus plc (intra-European services) and Aer Lingus Shannon plc (transatlantic services).

209 *e.g.* Radiological Protection Institute of Ireland in place of An Bord Fuinnimh Nuicleigh (Radiological Protection Act 1991); Irish Medicines Board in place of the National Drugs Advisory Board (Irish Medicines Board Act 1995).

210 *e.g.* Legal Aid Board (Civil Legal Aid Act 1995).

211 *e.g.* Dublin Docklands Development Authority Act 1997.

212 NESC, *Enterprise in the Public Sector* (Dublin, Stationery Office; 1979, Prl. 8499), p. 16. IRL 354.417 ENTE.

were restricted essentially to the extraction, production, marketing and sale of turf and turf products and all ancillary requirements necessary for this purpose. The 1990 Act extends the Board's powers into other areas in which it has, or is likely to acquire, expertise. Specifically, it is empowered to "execute engineering and building works of any kind whatsoever and research of any kind whatsoever which the Board in its discretion considers desirable".[213] Furthermore, the Board is for the first time given power to use cutaway bog for any activity unrelated to peat production for which there may be a commercial opportunity, such as tourism. However, the exercise of this power is subject to the Board giving the right of first refusal, for a 12 month period, to Coillte Teoranta (the Forestry Company).[214]

Corporate Governance

A number of factors have contributed to a concern[215] about the "corporate governance" of state-sponsored bodies. This is a vague and vogue term, which has been drawn from the private business sector and which refers to the government of a state body. Its elements include: the composition of the board; the respective responsibilities of board and management; the establishment of clear policy objectives and the regular assessment of whether these have been achieved. The factors causing concern include: the advent of competition[216]; technological change; dissatisfaction with the commercial state sector's performance; anxiety about unemployment; and the general zeitgeist in favour of public service reform. This latter factor means that issues like transparency, customer service and accountability to Government and public, loom particularly large; and in considering reform "the right balance has to be struck between the public accountability of the commercial state companies and their commercial freedom".[217]

The breadth of the term "corporate governance", is such that it embraces much of the material covered already in this chapter. Thus, for instance, such topics as; the relationships between a state body and the responsible Minister[218] or the Oireachtas[219]; board-management relations; and the selection, remuneration and role of the chief executive[220] have been considered earlier. It remains, here to consider briefly, two other, particular aspects of the subject.

The first of these which was one of the leading themes of the mid–90s was the feeling that in the commercial state sector, there was "a cosy cartel" (to use a phrase coined by the Minister for Transport, Energy and Communications, in 1995 though the theme had been around for some years earlier). In more prosaic language, this

---

[213] s.7 of the 1990 Act creating an amended s.20(1)(k) in the Turf Development Act 1946.

[214] s.7(j): as of 1988, the acreage depleted of peat was 3,770 hectares of which, however, 2,824 hectares had been transferred to the Forestry Service: 384 *Dáil Debates*, Col. 2477. (Debate on Turf Development Bill 1988) (1 hectare = 2.4 acres.)

[215] See *Report of the Task Force established to review the Controls in the Commercial State Companies* (1995; Pn. 1996), Chaps 1 and 8; *Review Body on Higher Remuneration in the Public Sector* (Pn. 3187; December 1996), Chaps 2 and 3.

[216] See pp. 173–182.

[217] Pn. 1996, p. 13.

[218] See pp. 141–149.

[219] See pp. 149–151.

[220] See pp. 152–155.

phrase evoked the idea of a conflict of interest by which some directors, and senior staff members of the state bodies, with the connivance of some politicians, abused their positions so as to assist rapacious private entrepreneurs in preying on the milk-cow of the state-sponsored sector. Yet the specific incidents[221] which, it was said amounted to "a culture" were relatively small.

In regard to these episodes, the following points should be noted. First, in each case, the Government of the day caused a formal, public investigation into the episode to be held. Secondly, with one exception, what was involved had, at most, the flavour of insider-trading rather than illegality (the exception being Greencore[222] which it should be emphasised led to the sanction of dismissal and penalties within the companies). Finally, these sins should be seen in the perspective of a closely watched group of large businesses with a total turnover of £5.3 billion (in 1995–1996). Taking these factors into account, perhaps it should be concluded that these transgressions are towards the venial end of the scale and that the type of rules, controlling tendering contracts made by state-sponsored bodies, sketched earlier, are sufficient to meet the problem.

A second and more significant focus of concern, regarding the commercial state sector, involved suspicions of over-staffing and poor productivity. One tool for improving or, at worst, monitoring this are five-year corporate plans which were introduced for most state-sponsored bodies in the late 80s. These plans (most of which are not published because of the commercial sensitivity of some of the information) are agreed between the state-sponsored body, parent Department and Department of Finance. These plans are reviewed and up-dated annually.

Control and Communication

The problem of control is, of course, peculiarly difficult in regard to state-sponsored bodies. Where there is too much control, initiative and flexibility are low and the function may as well have been vested in a Department of State in the first place. Indeed the result may be actually worse because the state body may feel itself so inhibited as not to react to commercial opportunities or difficulties, whilst the Department of State may lack the knowledge and resources to do what is not really its job. The opposite extreme is that there is too little control by the responsible

---

[221] (i) In 1990, according to widespread allegations, certain members of the management of Greencore (the successor company to Siúicre Éireann), conducted some intra-company transactions in order to generate a gain for themselves. This involved buying Odlums through a management company and then selling it on, to Greencore, at a profit. (ii) In 1990, Bord Telecom purchased a site, which it intended for use as a headquarters. The site was purchased for £9.4 million, notwithstanding that a year earlier it had been purchased for £4 million from a company in which persons associated with Bord Telecom were the shareholders. However, the site proved unsuitable because it was impossible to obtain planning permission. Episodes (i) and (ii) led to investigators being appointed under the Companies Act 1990, s.14, on which see p. 294. (iii) In 1995, Minister Lowry referred particularly to CIÉ's intended sale of a site in Cork to a private entrepreneur, without observing the proper procedure for tendering but probably not at an undervalue. (iv) In March 1995, too, it came to light that a Government Minister, whose family had a firm of quantity surveyors, remarked to Bord Gáis that he hoped that his firm would be able to tender for a contract. The Minister was demoted to the post of junior Minister (on which, see above, n.7, p. 59).

[222] See n.221, item(i).

Minister.[223] This is particularly undesirable where one is dealing with a commercial state body, enjoying a partial or complete monopoly (as is still the case in many fields). In this case, by definition there is no market-place to discipline the body and, if management is slack, it may start to free-wheel at the cost of the taxpayer and/or its customers. Considering the state body's position *vis-à-vis* its customers, it has to be said that the arrangements for state bodies include little in the way of consumer protection. It is a remarkable fact that only two state bodies – An Post and Bord Telecom – have ever been subject to surveillance by a user's council[224] and that even these provisions were dropped when these bodies were brought within the Ombudsman's remit. Only a few bodies are subject to such a control as the following and (even then, as can be seen, sub-section (2) substantially reduces the impact):

"(1) It shall be the general duty of the telecommunications company to conduct the company's affairs so as to ensure that:

(a) charges for services are kept at the minimum rates consistent with meeting approved financial targets, and

(b) revenues of the company are not less than sufficient to:

(i) meet all charges properly chargeable to revenue account (including depreciation of assets and property allocation to general reserve) taking one year with another,

(ii) generate a reasonable proportion of capital needs, and

(iii) remunerate capital and repay borrowings.

(2) Nothing in *section 14* or this section shall be construed as imposing on the company, either directly or indirectly, any form of duty or liability enforceable by proceedings before any court to which it would not otherwise be subject."[225]

---

[223] Thus, the Joint Oireachtas Committee on State-sponsored Bodies concluded that in spite of its extensive powers of surveillance, the Department of Communications was not sufficiently aware of the crisis into which Irish Shipping was sailing during the period 1979–1984: see Second Report: Irish Shipping Ltd (1985, Pl. 3091), paras. 1, 23 and 24. It has been suggested (see Sweeney, *op. cit.* above, n.1, p. 31) that the collapse could have been prevented had the monitoring been adequate. Again in 1979, Padraic O' Halpin, a former chief executive of a state body interviewed 20 chief executives and reported that "several found the absence of a definite policy on joint ventures with either foreign or home enterprises a barrier to potential development". ("The Chief Executive in State Enterprise" (Dublin: Irish Productivity Centre), p. 4 quoted in Zimmerman (1987) 8 *Seirbhís Phoiblí* 2, 2, 31.)

[224] RTÉ has a Broadcasting Complaints Commission (see pp. 148–149) but this has a different function in that its role is much wider than simply protecting the interests of the consumer, *e.g.* it must ensure impartial presentation of the material broadcast television programmes rather than protecting the viewer.

[225] Postal and Telecommunications Services Act 1983, s.15. See also, the 1983 Act, s.13 (An Post); Electricity Supply Act 1976, s.21(2). For another form of control see B. Walsh, "Commercial State-Sponsored Bodies"(1987) *The Irish Banking Review* 27 suggesting that a number of proxies for market forces should be used. Among the possibilities are:
"i. *Borrowing limits*. The total amount that a company can borrow during a year should be agreed in consultation with the relevant government department. This would replace the present practice of giving approval to borrowing as the need arises.
ii. *Investment criteria*. Proposed investments by CSSBs should be evaluated using a standard project appraisal methodology. Only projects that can meet the target rate of return equal to the cost of the funds to the Exchequer plus five per cent should be approved.

A related question concerns the need to ensure good communication and a concerted approach as between the Government and commercial state-sponsored bodies and also – though in era of competition, this has to be less important – as between different bodies.[226]

In fact, apart from individual, informal contacts, the only arrangements which currently exist for fostering relations as between state bodies are rather weak, *e.g.* Consultative Group of Chief Executives of State Organisations, composed of chief executives of mainly commercial bodies, which is an informal group serving as a forum for the discussion of common problems. There is a similar grouping in the form of the Irish section of *Centre European de L'Enterprise Publique*. Far more important are relations between the Government and each individual state body. Here two contact points with the Government are important: first the Department of Finance; and secondly the Department responsible for a particular state body. In the Department of Finance, there is the Public Expenditure Division (one of the three Divisions, each headed by a Second Secretary, a grade peculiar to the Department of Finance and which is the equivalent of a Secretary General in other Departments, into which the Department is divided). Within this Division there are a number of Principals/Assistant Principals, each of whom is responsible both for a particular departmental vote and for the state-sponsored bodies which are associated with that Department. Accordingly, there exists, in Finance, a fair concentration of expertise about the state-sponsored sector, more especially so since many of the contacts between a body and the Government involve money and since the Minister for Finance's consent (as well as that of the responsible Minister) is often required for the activities of a body. Thus the Department of Finance, at any rate used to be the de facto central office for the state-sponsored sector. However in January 1993, the Minister for Transport, Energy and Communications was brought into being as the Minister responsible for, *inter alia*, ten of the largest commercial bodies. And in mid–1997, this Minister was re-christened the Minister for Public Enterprise, in order to make the point clearer. Naturally, it is this Department which appears to have taken the lead in policy-making in relation to its own state bodies and, to an extent, by example, in regard to the others.[227] However, because of the significance of Government finance and investment in this field, the Department of Finance will always retain the ultimately predominant role, especially when it comes to major change commitments. For instance when in late 1996, a 20 per cent share in Bord Telecom (with an option to purchase a further 15 per cent after three years) was sold to a Dutch-Swedish consortium (KPN-Telia) the negotiations were conducted jointly by officials from the Department of Finance and the (then) Department of Transport, Energy and Communications.

---

iii. *Pricing policy.* The goal should be to bring the prices of the goods and services provided by CSSBs into line with the prices prevailing in other countries, especially in the EEC."

[226] "Irish State-Sponsored Bodies: The Fractionalization of Authority and Responsibility" (1986) 7 *Seirbhís Phoiblí* 2, 27, 32. As part of a survey based on interviews with 38 chairmen, chief executives and officials of state bodies, civil servants and informed observers, Professor Zimmerman appraises a number of suggested devices for improving co-ordination: information consultation and information exchange; interagency committees and agreements; a consultative body; the former National Development Corporation; the Department of the Taoiseach and "the partnership approach".

[227] See, *e.g.* the policy statements listed in n.245, p. 165; and the high profile role played by the Minister during 1994–1996 (Mr Lowry) on which see below, n.133, p. 142.

Privatisation[228]

Privatisation holds a high place on the agenda of public debate not least because it is part of the *Zeitgeist* against state involvement which, especially in the 1980s, was running so strongly in North America and Western Europe. A part of the motivation is that, as it was put by an Irish economist in 1987:

> "Technology, capital markets, the supply of entrepreneurship and attitudes towards state activity have changed dramatically since most CSSBs were established in Ireland. In the 1930s it was plausible to argue that, if the State had not undertaken radio broadcasting or sugar production or the provision of industrial credit, worthwhile employment and profit opportunities would have been missed."[229]

The writer goes on to note that, in the Irish context, the most compelling argument in favour of privatisation is that the proceeds would mean a substantial reduction in public indebtedness.[230] This line of argument is reinforced where one is considering a state body which is likely to require heavy capital investment (*e.g.* Aer Lingus – a new fleet).

The approach to privatisation has been cautious because of its unpopularity with public sector unions and formerly (for in March, 1998 there were signs of change in Labour policy) the Labour Party. It is worth noting that when An Post and Bord Telecom were created, at a time when privatisation was in the air wafting across the Irish Sea, care was taken, because of union pressure, to include in the parent statute a provision to the effect that only the then Minister for Posts and Telegraphs could own shares.[231] However, this bar was removed by the Telecommunications (Miscellaneous Provisions) Act 1996 which paved the way for the KPN/Telia (Dutch/Swedish) consortium to take an equity stake in the company and which also provided for the reduction of the employee/ directors from four to two so that the strategic partner could appoint three directors (as required by the strategic alliance agreement), to a board of twelve with the Minister still retaining a majority of seven directors.[232]

Before the 1996 Act, the two main[233] initiatives were the Insurance Act 1990 and the Sugar Act 1991[234] and the following account is largely based on these two

---

[228] See Convery and McDowell (eds.), *Privatisation: Issues of Principle and Implementation in Ireland* (1990).

[229] Walsh, *op. cit.* above, n.225 at p. 34.

[230] An estimate of the proceeds of sale of the entire enterprise (in late 1995) is as follows: ESB–£500m; Telecom Éireann–£800m; Bord Gáis–£300m; Aer Lingus–£100m.

[231] Postal and Telecommunications Act 1983, s.21. See also, 337 *Dáil Debates* Cols. 1573–1577, July 7, 1982; 101 *Senate Debates* Cols. 498 and 560 (July 5, 1983).

[232] 1996 Act, ss.8, 10. See too 469 *Dáil Debates*, Cols. 665–666 (September 26, 1996). Significantly the number of worker-directors may also be reduced so as to allow for Board membership of an employee Shareholding scheme: 1996 Act, s.8(4)–(6).

[233] Notice also the merger of NET's operating company with a Northern Ireland Irish Fertiliser subsidiary of ICI and the sale of the Joint Hospital Services Board and of Irish Ferries.

[234] Irish Life affords a good example. This state body was in fact a particularly appropriate candidate for privatisation because, as a result of its origin in a rescue operation of existing privately owned companies and its profitability, it had long been permitted an unusually high degree of autonomy. In addition to the State's natural desire to capitalise on its assets, the need for a major change in the Company was put on two grounds. The first of these was that certain foreign States, for example

measures, which are of special interest since the State took a minority holding. True to the idea that the ex-state bodies will be treated in law simply as ordinary large companies, they will be governed largely by company law. It bears noting that this is, itself, an idea which, in view of the particular nature and public perception, of some state bodies and the dominant market which they often enjoy, contains a number of policy assumptions.[235] It does, however, reflect the Anglo-Irish law's fundamental antipathy towards the establishment of specialist legal régimes to reflect varied social and/or economic circumstances. Accordingly the role of public law in regard to privatisation is limited.[236]

The changes in relation to both the Irish Life Assurance plc and Siúicre Éireann, c.p.t. were effected by way of the normal company law technique of establishing a holding company, Hold co plc and Greencore plc which, to own, respectively, a new restructured Insurance company and the existing Sugar Company. The responsible Minister was then empowered to exchange his shares in the former company for shares in the (new) holding company and also to acquire further shares in the holding company.

From the perspective of public law, the major issue in regard to privatisation remains basically the same as for state bodies, namely should the State exercise any control over the former state bodies and, if so, according to what criteria and through what technique? In the first place, in regard to the Insurance Company, the Minister for Finance has retained 34 per cent.[237] of the shares, which is sufficient to veto any special resolution and also, under the Stock Exchange Rules, to attract certain rights in the event of a predatory take-over. In the case of the Sugar Company, the figure

---

about half of the states in the United States would not permit companies owned by foreign Governments to take over native companies and this was impeding the Company's development. The other factor did not necessarily require privatisation. It was the fact that at an earlier stage in the history of the evolution of life assurance business, the Company has been virtually mutualised by virtue of the inclusion of a provision in the Company's Articles of Association that with-profits policy-holders were to have a right to 98 per cent. of the total profits. This naturally represented a substantial disincentive to any private share-holding in the Company (even though, latterly, the Company's business had evolved away from with-profits policies and towards unit-linked policies). The Articles of Association of the successor company to Irish Life allow for a more realistic dividend to be paid to share holders and thus the Company will be able to expand. However, in order to safeguard the vested rights of the with-profits policy holders, the approval of the courts in Ireland and United Kingdom was necessary and has been granted, for the transfer of business from Irish Life to the new company. On the rationales for privatisation of Irish Life see 401, *Dáil Debates*, Cols. 10–71; 238–255; 287–359; July 45, 1990; *Joint Oireachtas Committee Report* (1988, Pl. 5451).

[235] See, generally, C. Graham and T. Prosser, "Privatising Nationalised Industries: Constitutional Issues and Legal Techniques" (1987) *Modern Law Review* 16–51; C. Graham and T. Prosser, "Golden Shares: Industrial Policy by Stealth ?" (1988) *Public Law* 413.

[236] The officially used term – hallowed by usage in such documents as the Public Capital Programme – is "the sale of State assets" since "privatisation" is deemed to have disagreeable ideological overtones. The policy of successive Governments (in part because of the Labour Party's antipathy to privatisation) has been (to quote, for instance, the Programme for Renewal (the 1995 Government's programme): "the utilities will not be sold off; but this does not preclude the sale of shares in other state bodies if this be in the interest of employees, the companies themselves and the Government." This attitude has slowed the pace of privatisation and means for instance, that the Industrial Credit Corporation and the Agricultural Credit Corporation (which lend venture capital to the small–medium sized commercial and agriculture sectors respectively) have not yet been sold, despite tempting offers. However, now that Labour is no longer in government, it is likely that the Banks – and possibly also Aer Lingus and Bord Gáis – will be sold.

[237] Formerly, the Minister held 90%, with 5% being held by the staff pension fund and 5% held by private shareholders.

for shares retained is 45 per cent. The reasons for this comparatively high figure are, first, stock-exchange liquidity (lack of sufficient funds in the market to purchase more) and, secondly, industrial relations grounds (to reassure unions and other interested parties that the State will be retaining a substantial shareholding in the company and therefore a strong influence on its operations for some time to come). In addition, the Minister's influence is enhanced by the fact that in the case of the Sugar Company, the Memoranda and Articles of Association,[238] makes provision for a so-called "Golden Share". Such a share has been explained, in the British context, as follows:

> "The basis, in general, for a golden share scheme is that the share capital of the company will contain one special rights redeemable preference share of £1 held by the government or their nominee. Certain matters are then specified as being deemed to be a variation of the rights of the Special Share and therefore can only be effective with the consent in writing of the Special Shareholder ... The most common of these matters are: any amendments to the article relating to the Special Share, the article defining the restrictions on shareholding and the definitions of various terms. Also usually included are a prohibition on a voluntary winding up and on the creation of new shares, other than ordinary equity shares."[239]

In the case of the Insurance Company, the golden share was so drafted that during the five year period following the flotation of the company the Minister will be able to prevent individuals or groups gaining more than a 15 per cent. holding. Such special arrangements are not of themselves contrary to the anti-discrimination provision (Article 6 (formerly Article 7)) and the pro-competition provisions (Articles 85–94) of the Treaty of Rome. However, the Minister went further and promised to use his powers to preserve the "Irish ethos" and "local base" of Irish Life by vetoing hostile (and foreign) take-over bids[240] and this may have violated E.U. law.[241] In the case of Bord Telecom, the Minister's shareholding may not fall below a majority.[242]

A different issue concerns whether the State should attempt to exercise some degree of positive control over the ownership of the former state body to favour some group such as employees or customers of the company; the "small investor"; institutional investor, etc.[243] The usual instrument for achieving this is the way the shares are first marketed. In addition however section 2 of the Sugar Act 1991[244] goes beyond this to attempt to influence subsequent transactions:

---

[238] The possibility is specifically mentioned in s. 2(2) of the Sugar Act 1991, though not in the Insurance Act 1990.

[239] Graham and Prosser (1988) *Public Law* 413 at 414.

[240] 401 *Dáil Debates*, Col. 15, July 4, 1990.

[241] For further discussion on this possibility, see 2nd Edition of this book at pp. 153–154.

[242] Telecommunications (Miscellaneous Provisions) Act 1996, s.8(2) (a).

[243] In France where there is a lack of large institutional shareholders, the State has been afraid of the possibility of "raiders" if all the shares were divided among a large number of small holdings. Accordingly the responsible Minister is empowered to place a substantial number of shares with "hard cores" of investors from outside the financial markets. He exercises this power after receiving the opinion of the "Privatisation Commission".

[244] See too 1996 Act, s.8(3).

"(7) The Minister [for Finance], following consultation with the Minister for Agriculture and Food, may sell or dispose of shares held by him in the Holding Company on prescribed terms and conditions to such specified persons as he may prescribe.

(8) The Minister may prescribe different terms and conditions for classes of specified persons and may prescribe conditions as to consideration including conditions concerning sale or disposal for no consideration or for consideration less that the market value of the said shares at the time of their sale or disposal."

In the cases considered so far, the State retained a substantial shareholding and extensive powers of veto. However, recently, the Irish Steel Limited Act 1996,[245] (by authorising certain payments by the responsible Minister to the company) paved the way for the transfer of the entire share capital in the Company to ISPAT International. The total state-aid package was worth £50 million and this required the approval of the European Commission. This was eventually granted (following negotiations between the British and Irish Governments) on the basis of undertakings to cap the Company's production of finished steel and billets.

9. Monopolies and De-Regulation

One ought to distinguish carefully between state ownership itself; and on the other hand, a monopoly. Traditionally state bodies frequently did enjoy a "legal monopoly", as did a "natural monopoly" (which arises from economic and social realities, such as the nature and cost of the enterprise and the size of the market). About a natural monopoly little can be said, save that financial and technological developments, coupled with the increasing mobility of capital mean that they are less likely nowadays. Accordingly, the following remarks are mainly directed to legal monopolies. The coincidence between state ownership and a legal monopoly is not inevitable. One alternative would be that whilst the state body is retained, its legal monopoly is broken so that the state body is open to the competition of private enterprise.

By today, this indeed is, frequently, required by the most fundamental tenet of E.U. law: its pro-competition policy. The march of history in this field has been described – officially – as follows:

"The origins of State ownership derive from national development requirements and, in some cases, market failure. In many cases, these State companies formed what were perceived to be at the time, not only in Ireland but internationally, natural monopolies in their sectors. State ownership also carried with it the notion, implicitly or explicitly, of State sponsorship. Even for sectors such as international air travel where competition, albeit limited, was a feature, State companies were seen to be national champions to be given the best routes and most favoured treatment. This era is now, clearly, over."[246]

---

[245] See further 1996 I.C.L.S.A., on which the above account is based.
[246] Department of Transport, Energy and Communications: *Statement of Strategy*, 1997 p. 10.

Nor was a monopoly the only advantage which a state body might enjoy and which, as we shall see, [247]could violate competition law. There were other ways in which the Government might abuse its powers in order to give a state-sponsored body some unjustified immunity or some unfair advantage over trade competitors as, for instance, when £13 million of taxes owed by Ostann Éireann in respect of Great Southern Hotels was waived by the Revenue Commissioners; or when the Government promoted the Air Transport Bill 1986, which, as originally drafted, would have inflicted penalties on four operators cutting their prices below Aer Lingus rates.[248] A more complicated variation on this theme occurs where there is cross-subsidisation between commercial state bodies, usually to the advantage of one and the disadvantage of the other. For example, the ESB has, at various times, it would appear, been instructed to purchase natural gas from Bord Gáis Éireann below, and later above, the oil-related price; and to purchase peat from Bord na Móna, though, in either case, it might be possible for it to purchase cheaper raw material abroad. And N.E.T. receives gas from Bord Gáis on favourable terms.[249] It has also been said that:

> "discriminatory pricing may have reduced the surpluses of profitable State companies in order to reduce the published losses of other public enterprises. Indeed, such transfer pricing appears to be a rather common practice in the State company sector."[250]

However by today, very few of these practices (many of which would contravene E.U. law) persist. Indeed, to return to the main theme, many state-sponsored bodies now face vigorous competition in such fields as: broadcasting[251]; telecommunications[252]; health insurance[253]; freight-haulage[254]; inter-city buses[255]; and

---

[247] See pp. 173 *et seq.*

[248] The offending provision was removed, following Dáil protests: see 352 *Dáil Debates*, Cols. 853–910 (June 27, 1984). See also, Lemass, "The Role of the State-Sponsored Body in the Economy" (1958) 6 *Administration* 277 at 278.

[249] See Convery and McDowell, *op. cit.*, above, n.228 p. 148 and 154. Notice, too the comment of the Joint Committee on Commercial State-Sponsored Bodies *Report on Irish Shipping* (1985, Pl. 3091) on the fact that ESB had awarded only a half of the contract to carry coal from U.S. to Moneypoint to Irish Shipping, with the other half going to a Japanese company. The Joint Committee said that "appropriate Government guidelines should be developed which, on the one hand, would not impinge on the competitiveness of open market quotations but, on the other hand, would provide for due consideration of the Exchequer's involvement in both bodies."

[250] Massey, "Privatisation: Time for a Closer Look" (1987) 8 *Seirbhís Phoiblí*, 2. 2. In 1989 the Minister for Communications discouraged the sale, by a subsidiary of RTÉ, of Cablelink to a United States company (a potential competitor of Bord Telecom). Cablelink was sold, the following year to Bord Telecom, the Minister for Industry and Commerce having given his consent following a reference to the former Fair Trade Commission under the Mergers, Takeovers and Monopolies (Control) Acts 1978 and 1987.

[251] See pp. 283–291.

[252] See pp. 170–172.

[253] See pp. 169–170.

[254] Iarnrod Éireann is exposed to wider competition from private road hauliers by the Road Transport Act 1986, s.4: see Hogan, 1986 *Irish Current Law Statutes Annotated*. By now, it only accounts for 10% of freight traffic. There are 3,200 licensed road haulage operators, compared to 800 in 1987, when the sector was liberalised.

[255] Private operators now account for 15% of the total inter-city and rural bus market and 25% in the case of long distance services to and from Dublin. See Department of Transport Energy and Communications, *Statement of Strategy* (1997), p. 13.

international air transport.[256] Competition in electricity[257] and gas[258] can be expected to follow soon. In relation to monopolies and the other examples given earlier of advantages given to state bodies, two questions arise namely, do they violate the Constitution; and do they breach E.U. law? As to the first, the answer given, in the rather unconvincing case of *Attorney General and Minister for Posts and Telegraphs v. Paperlink Ltd*[259] is in the negative. Here, the defendants, who operated a substantial courier service, were breaching a monopoly, granted to the Department of Posts, by the precursor of section 63 of the Postal and Telecommunications Services Act 1983. They defended themselves, unsuccessfully, against the plaintiffs' claim for an injunction to restrain them, by attacking the monopoly. Their major argument was that the monopoly violated their right to earn a livelihood and carry on a business which is one of the unspecified rights bestowed by Article 40.3.1°. Costello J. accepted this argument in principle but went on to hold that the monopoly could be justified as enhancing "the common good". To support its argument as to the common good, the defendant invoked Article 45.3.1° (mentioned earlier). Costello J. held however that this Directive Principle, whilst it demonstrated a preference for public enterprise was merely a very general guideline which did not impose an onus of proof upon the State to justify the existence of a legal monopoly. The defendants second argument was that the postal monopoly did not promote "the common good" first, because it was being operated inefficiently and, secondly – a related point – because it would be possible to gain the advantages claimed for the monopoly by a system which was less restrictive of the defendants' rights. To support these claims, the defendants wished to call economists and accountants to give evidence that for instance, the Department was paying wages which were above the market rate; that the accounting system was a bad one; and that "overnight" money was not properly invested. Costello J. refused to hear such evidence because he held that to determine whether a particular postal service serves the common good was the prerogative of the legislature rather than a court.

In *Paperlink*, no mention was made of E.U. law though this would hardly be so, were the case to be re-litigated today. We shall return to the question of E.U. law after we have considered recent developments, including certain matters which may be regarded as justifying certain monopolies and other examples of discrimination in favour of state bodies.

We shall not use the word "de-regulation" here. The reason is that, despite this term's common usage else in popular parlance, the fact remains that in the Brave New World, in which many functions which were formerly the monopoly of the

---

[256] Department of Transport Energy and Communications Statement, pp. 17–19.
[257] O.J. 1992 C65/4.
[258] O.J. 1992 C65/14.
[259] [1984] I.L.R.M. 373. See also, *Nova Media Services Ltd v. Minister for Posts and Telegraphs* [1984] I.L.R.M. 161, 167; *Ulster Transport Authority v. Brown* [1953] N.I. 70; McCormack, "Monopoly Power in the High Court" (1984) 6 D.U.L.J. 152. For the suggestion that RTÉ's former *de facto* monopoly broadcasting power was unconstitutional on the ground of infringement of the constitutional right to free speech, see Kelly, "The Constitutional Position of R.T.É." (1967) 15 *Administration* 205; Kelly (1978) *Irish Broadcasting Review* 5; McRedmond (1978) *Irish Broadcasting Review* 62. For more recent developments in connection with monopolies, see pp. 173 *et seq.*

State being discharged either by private (or mixed private and State) enterprise, a good deal of regulation is necessary. This is so because of the fact that free competition does not in fact flow naturally from an absence of State involvement: all experience of business activity shows that – paradoxically – the achievement of a free market requires a certain amount of sophisticated regulation. To this problem, we shall return below.[260] For the moment, we must concentrate on the most significant of a number of heads of public policy, which is especially significant in the areas formerly occupied by State monopolies. For the functions which were the exclusive preserve of State bodies included many which were central to normal human existence, for example: energy, transport and communications. In addition, it has always been assumed, on public policy grounds that these essentials should be available at the same price, notwithstanding the fact that their production costs may vary as between different (geographical social or other) categories of consumer. Accordingly in regard to these essentials the concept of universal (or public) service obligation has long been a central tenet of state policy. This has been explained as: "the provision of a defined level of service at an affordable price throughout the country and the sharing of the cost by all consumers in a way that avoids market distortion and unfair competition."[261] In short, a substantial measure of cross-subsidisation in respect of each function, in the interest of social rather than economic grounds, was regarded as inevitable and acceptable; as was the monopoly which this drew with it.

One example of this concerns the fact that the ESB has been instructed to charge urban and rural consumers at the same rates and thus to cause one group of electricity users to subsidise another group and, also, to distort the ESB's income. In the past, the protest of state-sponsored bodies at this type of behaviour, by Ministers, had taken the form of suggesting that, in the interests of presenting a fair picture of the agency's performance, allowance should be made in its accounts – or even a grant paid – to reject the value of the social benefits.[262]

However, in the Postal and Telecommunications Services Act 1983, which granted Bord Telecom, "the exclusive privilege of offering, providing and maintaining telecommunications services . . . within the State",[263] it was – most unusually – thought appropriate to enunciate a policy justification for this privilege. Thus section 87(2) of the 1983 Act stated:

---

[260] See pp. 169–172.

[261] Department of Transport, Energy and Communications, *Statement of Strategy* (1997) p. 12.

[262] NESC Report *op. cit.* above, n.212; Bristow *op. cit.* above, n.75, p. 180. Note that the *Department of Transport, Energy and Communications Statement of Strategy* (1997), p. 13 remarked: "[The E.U. Commission] favours greater transparency in the provision of State funding for non-commercial public transport services, including mandatory public service contracts and tendering for all services in receipt of State subvention . . . The E.U. debate on the internalisation of the external costs of transport (including pollution and health costs) is only just beginning." See also, Postal and Telecommunications Services Act 1983, s.51 ("Loss-making services provided by direction of the Minister") and s.75 ("Recoupment of the postage, elections, referenda and messages to certain organs of state"). For history of these sections see Byrnes, "Profitability *vis-à-vis* the Public Interest" (1984) 31 *Administration* 372.

[263] 1983 Act, section 87(1). See also section 63(1) (exclusive privilege of An Post). Notice, though, that even before the Telecommunications (Miscellaneous Provisions) Act 1996, some thirty service providers had been licensed (under s. 111(2) of the 1983 Act) by the Minister, after consultation with the Bord Telecom, to provide services outside Bord Telecom's exclusive privilege.

"The said privilege is granted to the company –

(a) in view of its primary purpose of providing a national telecommunications service and of the general duty imposed on it by *section 15*, and

(b) in recognition of the fact that a privilege of this kind is appropriate having regard to the area and population of the State and the present state of development of telecommunications technology, and

(c) because a viable national telecommunications system involves subsidisation of some loss-making services by profit-making services."[264]

Although, as we shall see, Bord Telecom no longer enjoys a monopoly, this policy statement is significant, as a statutory affirmation of the State's commitment to its universal service obligation. With the present liberalisation, the broad issue of cross-subsidisation has come into sharp focus for private enterprise naturally prefers to go where the profit is greatest. This would necessarily mean, for instance, seeking customers where the costs are lowest (*e.g.* in most cases, east of the Dublin – Cork line) or, alternatively, if costs of supplying to a particular group are higher, charging that group a higher price. This is a consideration which can best be illustrated by way of a case-study.

The reduced importance of cross-subsidisation

Next, we consider a case-study in regard to cross-subsidisation and non-cherry-picking, which also illustrates the theme – mentioned earlier – that even liberalisation requires some form of regulation and the normal form is by way of a licensing system. Let us consider health insurance,[265] as our first example of the development from effective monopoly to regulated competition, before going on to consider, at greater length, the telecommunications area.[266] Now, before the Health Insurance Act, 1994, there was – theoretically – a conventional licensing system, with the Minister for Health as the licensing agency. But, in practice, just as, before 1988,[267] the Minister for Posts and Telegraphs had only granted a license under the Wireless Telegraphy Act, 1926 to RTÉ, so the Minister for Health exercised his power, under the Voluntary Health Insurance Act 1957, sections 23 and 24, to license only one insurer: the Voluntary Health Insurance Board, which had been established under section 3 of the Act, as a commercial state-sponsored body.

The immediate impetus to change was the Third Non-Life Directive,[268] which was designed to remove restrictions on health insurers from other E.U. Member

---

264 1983 Act, section 87(2). See also ss. 12–15 and 63(2). For another example, see case, 72/83, *Campus Oil v. Minister for Energy* [1984] E.C.R. 2727; (Requirement that all oil importers take a third of their supplies from INPC oil refinery at Whitegate upheld on the basis that the limitation on imports was justified by the "public order" exemption in Article 36 of the E.C. Treaty).

265 The brief treatment of Health Insurance Act here draws heavily on Mr Cahill's excellent annotations in the *Irish Current Law Statutes Annotated*, Rel. 49; April, 1966.

266 See pp. 170–172.

267 See p. 283.

268 92/49 EEC [1992] O.J. L228/1 at 4; Article 54 O.J. L228/23.

States, providing insurance in Ireland. The principal legislation to implement this Directive in Ireland was the Health Insurance Act 1994, as a result of which no license is required by a business which has been authorised to provide insurance in another Member State. Such a business must be automatically registered – by the Minister – provided that it complies with the provisions of the Act.[269] This proviso is, in fact, quite significant: for Preamble 24 of the Directive recognises that Member States may adopt specific legal provisions to protect the "general good". In the case of Ireland, this invitation has been taken up in the form of rules laid down in the 1994 Act, of which the main one is "community rating". This means that, in general, the health insurer must charge the same rate of premium for the same benefits, irrespective – and here is the important point – of the age, sex or health of the insured. It should be added that, during the period of the pre–1994 Act, the VHI had observed the "community rating" principle, as a non-statutory requirement.

When in 1996, the régime established by the 1994 Act was brought into effect, the first insurer other than VHI to indicate a serious interest in the Irish market was the British-based BUPA. At first, it was indicated (although no formal decision was taken at this stage) by "sources close to the Minister" that he considered that the terms of BUPA's proposed policies did not comply with the requirements of the Act, in particular "community rating". Subsequently, BUPA modified the terms of their policies and, on this basis, BUPA were registered.[270] The particular feature of the registration, which is relevant here, is that it was the Minister who was effectively put in the position of having to decide whether BUPA had complied with the necessary requirements to entitle it to register, yet the beneficiary of a decision against BUPA would have been the VHI, which is a state body. This flaw was perceived by the draftsman of the Act, who provided for a "Health Insurance Authority"[271] which would be independent of the Minister and which would, if it had been established, have taken over most of the Minister's functions, under the Act. However, no such Authority has yet been established.[272] It is probable that the existing arrangement under the 1994 Act breaches neither Irish nor E.U. law.[273] However, as a matter of principle, it seems at least desirable that there should be independent regulator, along the lines of the Health Insurance Authority.

Independent Regulator; Telecommunications

The problem of conflict of interest, in the present context, has been expressed as follows:

> "The Department currently carries out three functions in the sectors for which it is responsible – regulation, discharging the State's shareholding function

---

[269] 1994 Act, sections 5 and 14(5); and European Communities (Non-Life Insurance) Framework Regulations, 1994 of S.I. No. 359 (1994) Arts 24 and 57.

[270] See newspapers for November and December 1996.

[271] On the Authority, see s.20 and the Schedule. If and when the Minister introduces a risk equalisation scheme (under Section 12), it must be administered by the Authority. However, it may be given other or alternative functions.

[272] The Health Insurance Act 1994 (Commencement) Order 1994 (S.I. No. 191 of 1994) does not bring into effect the provision establishing the Authority. See also 444 *Dáil Debates*, Cols. 155–157 (June 21, 1994).

[273] See C–159/91 *Poucet and Pistre* [1993] E.C.R. I–637 holding that the cross subsidisation in a health insurance system was the very factor which brought it within Art.90(2) of the E.U. Treaty of Rome and thus gives an exemption from Art.90(1), on which see p. 175.

as well as policy development. It is clearly unsatisfactory to continue to carry out these three functions in the one Department when the possibility exists of companies from the private sector entering those markets which up to now have been characterised for the most part by State owned monopolies. Ownership interests should not dictate or be perceived to dictate how a sector is regulated and to that extent it is essential that the regulatory function be separated clearly and transparently from the shareholder function . . . it is fundamental that the development of policy and legislation remain with the Minister. However, it is possible for the Minister to relinquish one or both of the other two functions, (*i.e.* regulatory and shareholder roles). One option would be to privatise the State companies and for both regulation and policy development to remain under the direct control of the Government . . . the other option is for regulation to be independent of the Minister. Under this option, it is important that any regulatory authority be properly funded and staffed; that it be independent, and be seen to be independent, of Government in its decisions and rulings and that it take account of Government policy for the sector. However, it must also, as a public institution, be accountable in a meaningful way to the Oireachtas. The Government's role would be to decide on the regulatory structure and sectoral policy. Regulatory authorities would be responsible for making decisions within the legal framework and policy established by Government."[274]

Thus it seems to have been accepted , at any rate in principle, that the licensing function should be vested in an agency which is independent of the Government. The principle has been implemented in the area of telecommunications in the form of the Telecommunications (Miscellaneous Provisions) Act, 1996. And, as we shall see, the model established by the Act is likely to be followed in the future.[275] In the first place the Act establishes the office of Director of Telecommunications Regulation. The Director is declared to be "independent in the exercise of his or her functions." The Director is to be a position in the Civil Service (though it is not indicated whether this is in the Civil Service of the State or the Government.[276] The incumbent is to be appointed by the Minister for Public Enterprise, with the consent of the Minister for Finance, for a term of up to six years, with eligibility for re-appointment. He can be removed, by the Minister only for ill health or stated misbehaviour and, in either case, a statement of the reasons must be laid before each House. The costs incurred by the Director in the discharge of his functions under the Act are to be met from a levy imposed on providers of telecommunications services.[277] As regards the Director's functions, these will include the issuing and enforcement of licences: for telecommunications service providers; and for the use

---

[274] Statement of Strategy: Department of Transport Energy and Communications (1997) pp. 10–11. For the E.U. impetus behind this change, see Directive 95/62, O.J. 1995 L321/16; Directive 95/51 O.J. 1995 L256/49.

[275] 469 *Dáil Debate* Col. 662. (Deputy Lowry). Notice, too: "This separation is also a feature of the telecommunications development in most of our E.U. partners and requirement of pending E.U. legislation" (*Ibid.*)

[276] See pp. 79–81.

[277] 1996 Act, ss. 2–3 and First and Second Schedules.

of the radio frequency spectrum, including the use of the spectrum for broadcasting, and cable television infrastructure.[278]

In addition, the Act deals with the regulation of telecommunications services. However, this regulation only applies where either: there is no competition in the market for the supply of those services, or the provider of the service holds a dominant position in that market.[279] Can one assume that the phrases "market" or "dominant position" mean the same as in the Competition Act 1991–96 and/or E.U. law so that, the circumstances of the market are such that it is outside the scope of the Act, it is also outside their scope? The other question is whether if the market is subject to the scope of the Act and the price cap régime, described in the next paragraph, this in some way gives it cover against general or specified E.U. law or the Competition Acts 1991 to 1996.

The price cap order will specify the annual permitted price change, by reference to the following formula: the annual percentage change in the Consumer Price Index less an adjustment factor specified by the Director.[280] The order will be defined by reference to a "basket of telecommunications", so that the service provider is allowed some flexibility to adjust tariffs for individual services within the basket.[281] The way in which the Director and the Minister will inter-relate in the implementation of this control has been explained as follows:

> "This function will be transferred to the director along with the Minister's other regulatory functions. However, to allow companies a stable environment in which to implement business plans, any price cap order which is in force at the time of the transfer will not be subject to review by the director until two years after it is made and then only at the request of the Minister. The director may modify the order on the basis of that review. Five years after the price cap order has been made by the Minister, the director may review and modify the order on his or her own initiative."[282]

The then Government announced in 1996[283] that it intended, in the near future, to establish a multi-sector regulator covering energy and communications (into which the telecommunications regulator will be subsumed.) if this plan materialises, in contrast to the British regime (Oftel; Ofgas, etc.), there will be a single authority watching over utilities in a number of fields. Thus, the expertise will be derived from a number of sectors and the regulator will be able to establish and implement broadly common standards. In addition, the personality factor will be reduced. Each of these considerations will be especially valuable in a small State.

Most state bodies are exempted from the Mergers, Take-overs and Monopolies (Control) Act 1978.[284]

---

[278] 1996 Act, ss. 3–4.
[279] *Ibid*. s.7(3).
[280] *Ibid*. s.7(1).
[281] *Ibid*. s.7(2).
[282] *Statement of Strategy*, 1997, p. 12.
[283] 469 *Dáil Debates*, Col. 669 (Deputy Lowry).
[284] Though in the case of Bord Telecom Éireann and An Post, this dispensation was removed by s.3 and the Second Schedule of the Restrictive Practices (Amendment) Act 1987.

10. The Impact of Competition Law

In addition to particular Directives, the effect of some of which have just been mentioned, the general pro-competition precepts contained in Articles 37 and 90 apply in a modified form to state bodies. After considering this central theme, we must consider the threshold issue of whether a state body is an undertaking for the purposes of competition law, and finally the overlap between competition law and judicial review of an administrative action. However, as a preliminary, we ought to notice that the material treated here comes close to that covered in the E.U. section of Chapter 7 on Licensing. There is, however, a distinction. This distinction is not exactly that here we are dealing with state-sponsored bodies since in fact: Article 37 speaks of "State monopoly"; whereas Article 90 refers to ". . . undertakings to which Member States grants special or exclusive rights." Rather our concern here is with the impact of the E.U. pro-competition policy upon public bodies and/or purposes which are claimed to be public in character, as this impact is mediated by way of the special régime established by Articles 37 and 90. By contrast, the focus of the E.U. section of Chapter 7 is whether a licence may be used to limit the numbers of persons engaged in a business or other occupation, regardless of whether this is to a private person, as in *Carrigaline Community Television v. Minister for Communications*[285] or a state-sponsored or other public body, as in *O'Neill v. Minister for Agriculture.*[286]

Articles 37 and 90 of the Treaty of Rome

The joint effect of Articles 37 and 90[287] of the Treaty is to permit Member States to maintain public undertakings with special or exclusive rights while at the same time ensuring that any such special regime does not effect unfair discrimination against persons or goods on the grounds of nationality[288] or otherwise effect a breach of the competition rules. Article 37(1) is concerned with State monopolies enjoying exclusive rights in the procurement and distribution of goods and provides that:

> "Member States shall progressively adjust any State monopolies of a commercial character so as to ensure that when the transitional period has ended no discrimination regarding the conditions under which goods are procured and marketed exists between nationals of Member States. The provisions of this Article shall apply to any body through which a Member State, in law or in fact, either directly or indirectly supervises, determines or appreciably influences imports or exports between Member States. These provisions shall likewise apply to monopolies delegated by the State to others."

To fall within the ambit of Article 37, it is necessary that the monopoly body, first, has, as its object, trade in commercial goods capable of being the subject-matter of

---

285 [1997] 1 I.L.R.M. 241, see pp. 331–336.
286 [1997] 2 I.L.R.M. 435, see pp. 330–336.
287 See generally in relation to Arts. 37 and 90, Wyatt and Dashwood, *The Substantive Law of the EEC* (1993, 3rd edition), Chaps. 8 and 19; Bellamy and Child, *Common Market Law of Competition* (1987), Chap. 13; McMahon and Murphy, *European Community Law in Ireland* (1989), Chap. 21.
288 Art.90(1) forbids discrimination contrary to Art.6, which in turn prohibits discrimination based on nationality.

competition and trade between Member States and, secondly, plays an effective part in such trade.[289] There have been no Irish cases involving Article 37, but since the German, French and Swedish alcohol[290] monopolies and the French potash fertiliser monopoly[291] have all been held to be within the scope of Article 37, it would seem that commercial state bodies such as Bord na Móna, Bord Gáis Éireann and Nitrigin Éireann Teo. would all come within its scope. Likewise, if the Deutsche Bundespost[292] can be held to come within the scope of Article 37 insofar as its monopoly in cordless telephones is concerned, the same might well be true of the special rights conferred on Bord Telecom Éireann by section 87(1) of the Postal and Telecommunications Services Act 1983.

Article 37(1) does not require the entire abolition of State commercial monopolies, but rather that they should be adjusted in such a way as to ensure that no discrimination regarding the conditions under which goods are procured and marketed exists between nationals of Member States.[293] As a result, a national monopoly may not enjoy exclusive importation rights and exporters from other Member States must retain the right to sell their product directly in the Member State.[294] In addition, the rules regulating the state monopoly may not have a discriminatory effect in practice on imported products.[295] The purpose of Article 37 was thus summarised by the Court of Justice in *Re Franzen*, a case concerning the validity of the Swedish state alcohol monopoly system:

> "39. The purpose of Article 37 of the Treaty is to reconcile the possibility for Member States to maintain certain monopolies of a commercial character as instruments for the pursuit of public interest aims with the requirements of the establishment and functioning of the common market. It aims at the elimination of obstacles to the free movement of goods, save, however, for restrictions on trade which are inherent in the existence of the monopolies in question.
>
> 40. Thus, Article 37 requires that the organization and operation of the monopoly be arranged so as to exclude any discrimination between nationals

---

[289] Case 6/64, *Costa v. ENEL* [1964] E.C.R. 585; Case 91/78, *Hansen v. Hauptzollamt Flensburg* [1979] E.C.R. 935. Art.37 only applies to trade in goods and has no application to services: Case 30/87, *Bodson v. Pompes Funebres* [1988] E.C.R. 2479; Joined Cases C–46/90 and C–93/90, *Lagauche and Evrard* [1993] E.C.R. I–5267 and *Gemeente Almelo v. Energiebedrijf IJsselmij NV* [1994] E.C.R. I–1477. In *Almelo* the Court of Justice said (at para. 29) that Article 37 applies to situations "in which the national authorities are in a position to control, direct or appreciably influence trade between Member States through a body established for that purpose or a delegated monopoly."

[290] See, *e.g.* Case 91/75, *Hauptzollamt Göttingen v. Miritz* [1976] E.C.R. 217; Case 120/78, *Rewe Zentral AG v. Bundesmonopolverwaltung für Branntwein* ("Cassis de Dijon") [1979] E.C.R. 649; Case 91/78, *Hansen v. Hauptzollamt Flensburg* [1979] E.C.R. 935 and *Re Franzen*, unreported, Court of Justice, October 23, 1997.

[291] See *Fourteenth Report on Competition Policy* (1985), para. 288.

[292] See the approach taken by the EC Commission in their decision, *Re Cordless Telephones in Germany* [1985] 2 C.M.L.R. 397.

[293] Case 59/75, *Pubblico Ministero v. Manghera* [1976] E.C.R. 91; Case 91/78, *Hansen v. Hauptzollamt Flensburg* [1979] E.C.R. 935; Case C–347/88, *Commission v. Greece* [1990] E.C.R. I–4747; Case C–38793, *Banchero* [1995] E.C.R. I–4663 and *Re Franzen*, unreported, Court of Justice, October 23, 1997.

[294] Case 78/92, *Commission v. Italy* [1983] E.C.R. 1955; Case C–387/93, *Banchero* [1995] E.C.R. I–4663 and *Re Franzen*, unreported, Court of Justice, October 23, 1997.

[295] Case 90/82, *Commission v. France* [1983] E.C.R. 2011.

of Member States as regards conditions of supply and outlets, so that trade in goods from other Member States is not put at a disadvantage, in law or in fact, in relation to that in domestic goods and that competition between the economies of Member States is not distorted . . ."

In this case the Court found that the monopoly system did not in fact disadvantage imported products. While its sales network was "imperfect", the number of outlets were not so restricted "to the point of compromising consumers' protection of supplies of domestic or imported alcoholic beverages", so that the retail monopoly met these conditions. However, conditions which required the monopoly to import supplies only from traders holding production licences were found to be contrary to Article 30, as the conditions under which such licences were granted were highly restrictive and imposed additional and disproportionate costs on importers.

Article 90(1): General Principles

There is some overlap between Article 37 and Article 90. Article 90 seems to be a complementary provision designed to ensure that public undertakings may not engage in discriminatory conduct or otherwise infringe the competition rules. Article 90(1) provides:

> "In the case of public undertakings and undertakings to which Member States grant special or exclusive rights, Member States shall neither enact nor maintain in force any measure contrary to the rules contained in this Treaty, in particular to those rules provided for in Article 7 and Articles 85 to 94."

Article 90(1) is directed towards Members State and it applies to any measure[296] by which public undertakings and undertakings performing economic activities have been given "special or exclusive rights".[297] Examples of such special or exclusive rights including the granting of regional monopoly funeral concessions[298]; the granting of an exclusive television re-transmission service[299] and the granting of regional monopoly licences for the artificial insemination of cattle.[300] It will be seen from the language of Article 90(1) (". . . public undertakings and undertakings . . .") that the grantees of the special or exclusive rights need not be state bodies (however defined) and this is borne out by the case law.[301] Indeed, it would appear from the language of the opening sentence of Article 90(1) that this provision applies to all public undertakings, even if they have not been granted special or exclusive rights.

---

[296] In Case C–18/88, *GB-Inno-BM SA* [1991] E.C.R. I–5941 the Court of Justice held that Article 90(1) precluded Member States from maintaining in force any "laws, regulations or administrative measures" which were contrary to the Treaty. In *O'Neill v. Minister for Agriculture & Food*, unreported, High Court, July 5, 1995, Budd J. held that a long-standing administrative practice constituted a "measure" for the purposes of Article 90(1). (Note that it was not necessary for the Supreme Court to address the Article 90(1) issue on appeal: see [1997] 2 I.L.R.M. 435).

[297] Case C–18/88, *GB-Inno-BM SA* [1991] E.C.R. I–5941.

[298] Case 30/87, *Bodson v. Pombes Funebres des Régions Libérées* [1988] E.C.R. 2479.

[299] Case C–260/89, *E.R.T.* [1991] E.C.R. I–1979.

[300] Case C–323/93, *Societe Civille Agricole du Centre de la Crespelle v. Cooperative d'Elevage et d'Insemination Artificielle du Departement de la Mayenne* [1994] E.C.R. I–5077; *O'Neill v. Minister for Agriculture and Food*, unreported, High Court, July 5, 1995.

[301] Thus, in *Bodson* the holder of the privilege was a private undertakers' firm. Likewise, in both *Crespelle* and *O'Neill* the majority of the holders of exclusive regional artificial insemination licences were agricultural co-operatives.

Article 90(1) cannot be read in isolation from the other Treaty provisions, as a Member State can only be found to have infringed this provision if the infringement of the other Treaty provisions (particularly the non-discrimination on grounds of nationality rule contained in Article 6 and the competition rules in Articles 85 and 86) "is the direct consequence of the national law" or administrative practice.[302] Thus, for example, it is possible for a Article 90 undertaking *independently* to abuse its dominant position, contrary to Article 86. In such circumstances, the injured victim has the right to sue the undertaking for a breach of Article 86, but it would appear that the Member State would not in this example be liable for a breach of Article 90(1). After some confusing formulations by the Court of Justice in 1991, this principle was finally made clear in *Societe Civille Agricole du Centre de la Crespelle v. Cooperative d'Elevage et d'Insemination Artificielle du Departement de la Mayenne.*[303]

In the 1991 the Court of Justice ruled that a Member State is in breach of Article 90 if the undertaking in question, merely by exercising the exclusive rights granted to it cannot avoid abusing its dominant position[304] or when such rights are liable to create a situation in which that undertaking is induced to commit such abuses.[305] As the Court said in *GB-Inno-BM*:

> "Member States must not, by laws, regulations or administrative measures, put . . . undertakings to which they grant special or exclusive rights in a position which the said undertakings could not themselves attain by their own conduct without infringing Article 86."[306]

This formulation was inherently unsatisfactory, since, for example, in the case of state monopolies it followed almost *ex hypothesi* that this would never have attained that monopoly position were it not for the grant of the exclusive right in the first place. The other formulae were equally ambiguous, since they did not define "what factors make it possible to distinguish *a situation necessarily leading to an abuse* from a situation which on the other hand does not have that effect."[307] This was clarified in *Crespelle*, where the contention was that the French régime establishing regional artificial insemination monopolies had induced the undertakings concerned to abuse their dominant position by charging excessive prices. This claim was rejected, since any abuse was not a direct consequence of the national law:

> "It should be noted in this regard that the law merely allows insemination centres to require breeders who request the centres to provide them with semen from other production centres to pay the additional costs entailed by that choice. Although it leaves to the insemination centres the task of calculating those costs, such a provision does not lead the centres to charge disproportionate costs and thereby abuse their dominant position."[308]

---

[302] Case C–323/93, *Societe Civille Agricole du Centre de la Crespelle v. Cooperative d'Elevage et d'Insemination Artificielle du Departement de la Mayenne* [1994] E.C.R. I–5077 at 5105.
[303] *Ibid.* For a very useful analysis of contemporary Article 90 issues, see Edward and Hoskins, "Article 90: Deregulation and EC Law" (1995) 32 C.M.L.Rev. 157.
[304] *Höfner v. Macrotron* [1991] E.C.R. I–1979.
[305] Case C–260/89 *ERT* [1991] E.C.R. I–1979.
[306] Case C–18/88 *GB-Inno-BM SA* [1991] E.C.R. I–5941at 5980.
[307] Case C–320/91, *Re Corbeau* [1993] E.C.R. I–2533, *per* Advocate-General Tesauro at para. 11 of his opinion (emphasis in the original).
[308] [1994] E.C.R. I–5077 at 5103

Member States have been found to breach Article 90(1) where the privileged undertakings have infringed the competition rules (particularly Article 86): by not catering adequately for market needs and those of consumers[309]; by the granting of special (or exclusive) rights where this is likely to lead to the undertaking favouring its own products[310]; by the extension by the State of a monopoly without any obvious justification[311]; by State measures which confer on Article 90 bodies an "obvious advantage over its competitors" in a given market.[312]

The Article 90(2) defence

Article 90(2) provides that:

> "Undertakings entrusted with the operation of services of general economic interest or having the character of a revenue-producing monopoly shall be subject to the rules contained in this Treaty, in particular to the rules on competition, in so far as the application of such rules does not obstruct the performance, in law or in fact, of the particular tasks assigned to them. The development of trade must not be affected to such an extent as would be contrary to the interests of the Community."

As Article 90(2) constitutes a derogation from the competition rules, the onus is on the undertaking concerned to demonstrate that it can avail of this exception.[313] It is not sufficient for the undertaking concerned to show that it has been entrusted with the task of performing a service which is of "general economic interest" or "having the character of a revenue-producing monopoly". In addition, it must also be shown that the application of the Treaty's competition rules obstructs the performance of the particular tasks assigned to the monopolies and that the interests of the Community are not affected.[314]

The phrase "general economic interest" has been narrowly defined. Thus, in the *Porto di Genoa* case the performance of dock works was held not to be such a

---

[309] Case C–320/91, *Re Corbeau* [1993] E.C.R. I–2533 (offering "certain additional services which the traditional postal service did not offer, such as collection from the sender, greater speed or reliability of distribution"); Case C–41/90 *Höfner v. Macrotron* [1991] ECR I–1979 ("A Member State creates a situation [contrary to Art.86(b)] in which the provision of a service is limited when the undertaking to which it grants an exclusive right extending to executive recruitment activities is manifestly not in a position to satisfy the demand prevailing on the market for activities of that kind . . ."). Cf. the judgment of Budd J. in *O'Neill v. Minister for Agriculture and Food*, unreported, High Court, July 5, 1995 where a "failed market" argument based on *Hofner v. Macrotron* failed on the facts. The applicant had succeeded in obtaining just over 2% of the national market and Budd J. said that in cases of this kind the proportion and quantity of the actual market share obtained was of vital importance.

[310] Case C–260/89, *ERT* [1991] E.C.R. I–2925 at 2962 (infringement of Article 90(1) in conjunction with Article 86 where an undertaking has been granted special or exclusive rights in circumstances "where those rights are liable to create a situation in which that undertaking is led to infringe Article 86 by virtue of a discriminatory broadcasting policy which favours its own programmes."); Case C–242/95, GT-*Link AS v. De Danske Statsbaner* [1997] 5 C.M.L.R. 601 (breach of Art.90(1) read in conjunction with Art.86(c) where a port authority levied port duties pursuant to statutory authority in circumstances where it exempts its own ferry services from the payment of such duties as the application of dissimilar conditions to equivalent services).

[311] *Re Corbeau, ibid.*, para. 44 of the judgment.

[312] Case C–18/88, *GB-Inno-BM SA* [1991] E.C.R. I–5941.

[313] *Merci Convenzionali Porto di Genoa* [1991] ECR I–5889 at 5980.

[314] *Hofner v. Macrotron* [1991] E.C.R. I–1979 at 2017.

function[315] and in *Höfner v. Macrotron* the Court of Justice arrived at a similar conclusion in respect of employment agencies. Likewise, in *GB-Inno-BM SA*[316] the Court of Justice stressed that:

> "The exclusion or the restriction of competition on the market in telephone equipment cannot be regarded as justified by a task of a public service of general economic interest within the meaning of Article 90(2) . . . The production and sale of terminals, and in particular of telephones, is an activity that should be open to any undertaking. In order to ensure that the equipment meets the essential requirement of . . . the safety of users . . . and the protection of public telecommunications networks against damage of any kind, it is sufficient to lay down specifications which the said equipment must meet and to establish a procedure for type-approval to check whether those specifications are met."[317]

As Advocate-General Van Gerven observed in the *Port di Genoa* case, Article 90(2) only covers certain limited categories of "activities of direct benefit to the public" such as the provision of: telecommunications or television services[318]; of electricity supplies[319]; postal service[320]; or facilities for ensuring the navigability of an important waterway.[321]

Finally, even undertakings performing activities of general economic interest can rely on the Article 90(2) derogation "only if they succeed in showing before the national court the exact nature of the needs of general economic interest in question and their impact on the conduct of the undertakings concerned."[322] Thus in the *Gemeente Almelo* case the Court of Justice appeared to suggest that the nature of the obligations imposed on an electricity undertaking (the obligation to supply uninterrupted supply, coupled with universal service obligations) might justify a derogation from the competition rules:

> "Restrictions on competition from other economic operators must be allowed insofar as they are necessary in order to enable the undertaking entrusted with such a task of general interest to perform it. In that regard, it is necessary to take into consideration the economic conditions in which the undertaking operates, in particular the costs which it has to bear and the legislation, particularly the environment, to which it is subject. It is for the national court to consider whether an exclusive purchasing clause prohibiting local distributors from importing electricity is necessary in order to enable the regional distributor to performs its task of general interest."[323]

---

[315] See also Case C–242/95, *GT-Link AS v. De Danske Statsbaner* [1997] 5 C.M.L.R. 601 (operation of a commercial port does not constitute the operation of a service of general economic interest).

[316] Case C–18/88 [1991] E.C.R. I–5941 at 5980.

[317] *Ibid.*, at 5980.

[318] See, *e.g.* Case 41/83, *Italy v. Commission* [1985] E.C.R. 873; Case 155/73, *Saachi* [1974] E.C.R. 429 and Case C–18/88, *GB-Inno-BM SA* [1991] E.C.R . I–5941 at 5979.

[319] Case C–393/92, *Gemeente Almelo v. Energiebedrijf Ijseelmij* [1994] E.C.R. I–1477.

[320] Case C–320/91, *Re Corbeau* [1993] E.C.R. I–2533.

[321] Case 10/71, *Ministère Public of Luxembourg v. Hein née Muller* [1971] E.C.R. 723.

[322] *Merci Convenzionali Porto di Genoa* [1991] E.C.R. I–5889 at 5920, *per* Van Gerven A.G.

[323] See also C–320/91, *Re Corbeau* [1993] E.C.R. I–2533 (need for cross-subsidisation of postal service in order to fulfill universal service obligations might justify derogation from the competition rules.)

In sum, therefore, in order to rely on Article 90(2), the Member State must show that the restrictions on competition are necessary for the effective discharge of the service of general economic interest.

Are state bodies "undertakings" for competition law purposes?

In regard to this vital preliminary issue, as a general rule it may be said that commercial state bodies constitute "undertakings" for the purposes of E.U. or Irish competition law. On the other hand, Ministers, regulatory bodies and other similar authorities generally fall outside the scope of competition law since they do not rank as "undertakings" for this purpose. The dividing line is not always easy to draw, a point illustrated by a series of recent authorities.

In *Deane v. VHI (No. 1)*[324] the Supreme Court ruled that the VHI was an "undertaking" for the purposes of the 1991 Act. Although it was statutorily enjoined from making a profit, this did not mean that it was not "engaged for gain" within the meaning of the 1991 Act. In the second case, *SAT Fluggesellschaft GmbH v. Eurocontrol*,[325] a German airline challenged, as contrary to Article 86, the amount of route charges fixed by Eurocontrol. This latter body is an international Organisation which is responsible for European air safety and its administrative costs are discharged by the payment of fees ("route charges") by airlines depending on the length etc. of the route flown by each airline. The Court of Justice rejected the argument that Eurocontrol was an "undertaking" for this purpose, saying that:

> "Taken as a whole, Eurocontrol's activities, by their nature, their aim and the rules to which they are subject, are connected with the exercise of powers relating to the control and supervision of air space which are typically those of a public authority. They are not of an economic nature justifying the operation of the Treaty rules of competitions."[326]

It seems implicit in the judgment of the Court of Justice that Eurocontrol was not an "undertaking" for competition law purposes, precisely because it enjoyed special powers, autonomy and authority going beyond that which is normally bestowed by contract.[327]

This analysis may prove to be instructive in borderline cases. Thus, in *Carrigaline Co. Ltd v. Minister for Transport*[328] Keane J. held that the Minister who had charged an administrative fee in the course of granting a communications licence was not an "undertaking" for the purposes of the Competition Act 1991:

---

[324] [1992] 2 I.R. 319.
[325] [1995] 3 C.M.L.R. 208.
[326] *Ibid.* at 225.
[327] *cf.* the judgment of Denham J. in *Geoghegan v. Institute of Chartered Accountants in Ireland* [1995] 3 I.R. 86 on the question of whether the Institute was amenable to judicial review (see p. 768). For while the standing of the institute of Chartered Accountants might have rested formally on contract, in reality it was seeking to exercise quasi-governmental powers. The powers of suspension, disqualification etc. are not really appropriate to contractual relationships and this, coupled with the monopolistic status of this and similar bodies, suggests that these bodies should have been held to be amenable to judicial review.
[328] [1997] 1 I.L.R.M. 241.

".... if the Minister in granting licences for transmission is engaged in no more than a regulatory or administrative function, then the fact that he imposes a charge for the granting of the licence does not of itself mean that he is 'engaged for gain' ... If no such charges were levied, the taxpayers would have to fund out of their own pockets the necessary regulatory and administrative scheme as a result of which the successful applicants for licences can expect to make profits. It is a misuse of language to describe the imposition of charges of this nature as the provision of a service in return for payment and the licensing authority as being in any meaningful sense 'engaged for gain'."[329]

This passage recognises that just because the Minister was invested with special statutory powers, he ought not to be described as an "undertaking" for competition law purposes, i.e. considerations of Article 90 aside. It follows that any remedy for abuse of power would lie within the provenance of judicial review. This approach is also evident in the judgment of the Court of Justice in *Diego Cali v. Servizi Ecologici Porto Di*,[330] where the issue was whether a private company which had been entrusted by the Port of Genoa with the discharge of its anti-pollution surveillance was an "undertaking" within the meaning of Article 86. These activities were financed by tariffs imposed on vessels using the oil terminal in the port and these tariffs were approved by the public authorities. For this purpose the Court distinguished between situations where the State acted in the exercise of official authority and the situation where it carried on economic activities of an industrial or commercial nature by offering goods or services on the market. In the present case, the Court concluded that the activities was a task in the public interest "which formed part of the essential functions of the State as regards protection of the environment." It continued by saying that such surveillance:

".... was connected by its nature, its aim and the rules to which it was subject with the exercise of powers relating to the protection of the environmental which were typically those of a public authority. The system was not of an economic or commercial nature and therefore the Treaty rules on competition did not apply to it."

But other cases may not be so easy, especially where one is concerned with the actions of utilities enjoying special, statutorily conferred powers with either de facto or de jure monopoly status which straddle both public law and private law. If, for example, Aer Rianta were improperly to withdraw a landing "slot" from an airline without good reason, should this be classified as an abuse of a dominant position (as it certainly could be, as an unreasonable exercise of discretionary power)?[331] This brings us directly to issues of abuse of dominant position in competition law and unreasonableness in judicial review.

---

[329] *Ibid.* at 290. See also *Greally v. Minister for Education* [1995] 3 I.R. 481.
[330] Case C–343/95 [1997] E.C.R. I–1547.
[331] *cf.* the reasoning of Keane J. in *Deane v. Voluntary Health Insurance Board (No. 2)*, unreported, High Court, April 22, 1993 and that of Kelly J. in *Zockoll Group plc v. Telecom Éireann*, unreported, High Court, November 28, 1997.

Abuse of dominant position and unreasonableness in judicial review

A number of Irish cases illustrate the mutual cross-over of these concepts and the manner in which they interact. In *Deane v. VHI (No.2)*,[332] the issue was whether VHI could unilaterally pull out of negotiations with a customer with which it had a difficult and unprofitable relationship. What is interesting is that Keane J. held that this action was unreasonable in law, but did not amount to a breach of abuse of a dominant position. On the former question the judge said:

> "The actions of the VHI . . . might have been unexceptionable in legal terms in the case of a private commercial firm vigorously protecting its own interests. They were not, however, a fair and reasonable use of the powers entrusted expressly and by implication to the VHI by the Oireachtas for the common good . . ."

But dealing with the abuse of dominant position point, Keane J. rejected the argument that just because the plaintiffs' hospital suffered loss as health service providers by reason of the VHI's actions, that this constituted an abuse of a dominant position:

> "The plaintiffs' claim is in essence that the activities of the VHI constituted an abuse of their dominant position in the health insurance market because they damaged in an indirect manner the plaintiffs in their capacity as providers of health care. If that contention were correct in law, it follow that the action of the VHI in requiring the plaintiffs to accept a 15% reduction in their cash limit in 1989 was also an abuse of that position . . . I have, however, already indicated my view that the VHI were entitled as a matter of law to take that action, if they had come to the conclusion that it was necessary in order to protect their reserves and prevent an unacceptable large rise in the level of premiums.
>
> Mr. McDowell's [expert witness for the plaintiff] description of the VHI's actions in this context as those of a 'discriminating monopsonist' is doubtless accurate from an economist's perspective, but that is the role which they have been assigned by the Oireachtas."

This reasoning is, with respect, not the easiest to follow, but it seems to amount to saying that the normal concepts of abuse of a dominant position were *pro tanto* modified having regard to the statutory context in which the VHI were required to operate. Likewise, in *Zockoll Group Ltd v. Telecom Éireann*[333] while Kelly J. doubted whether the rules of natural justice applied to the withdrawal of a telephone number, he nonetheless held that the withdrawal of the number amounted to an unreasonable exercise of statutory power by the defendant company. In many ways, commercial state bodies seem to suffer the worst of both worlds, since both *Deane* and *Zockoll* illustrate that – uniquely – they are simultaneously bound both by the principles of both administrative law and competition law.

Donovan v. Electricity Supply Board[334] is a case on the other side of the line. Here the plaintiffs challenged the admission rules of a trade association which was

---

[332] Unreported, High Court, April 22, 1993.
[333] Unreported, High Court, November 28, 1997.
[334] [1994] 2 I.R. 305.

effectively controlled by ESB. Costello J. held that in one respect the ESB had abused its dominant position:

> ". . . the combination of factors . . . namely, the imprecision of the criteria for enrolment, the lack of objective standards for registration, the arbitrary power to refuse enrolment not required for the objects for which the register was formed imposed unjustifiable restrictions on enrolment on the register. These resulted in a restriction on competition in the electrical contracting trade because non-registered contractors had been placed at a competitive disadvantage . . ."[335]

What is interesting about this reasoning in both cases is that in effect the language of reasonableness and abuse of a dominant position have been transposed. The unilateral withdrawal of services seems like an abuse of a dominant position, yet it was classified by Keane J. in *Deane* and by Kelly J. in *Zockoll* as a species of unreasonableness, even though the latter judge doubted whether the commercial activities of Telecom were governed by public law. On the other hand, the operation of arbitrary admission criteria etc. under the auspices of a public body seems apposite for judicial review, yet in *Donovan* such was characterised by Costello J. as an abuse of a dominant position.

It seems apparent from these judgments that while there is a definite inter-action between principles of competition law and administrative law, yet this interaction remains rather inchoate and fitful. At one level, this inter-action should not surprise us, since one of the objects common to both competition law and administrative law is to protect the private citizen against an abuse of power. And, of course, we have been speaking about an inter-action between the two different bodies of law. Given their essentially different roles and functions, there is no question of some form of merger between competition law and administrative law principles. But given the growing importance of the dirigiste and regulatory State, it is a fair assumption that this interaction will develop further with potentially significant implications for commercial state bodies.

---

[335] *Ibid.* at 324.

CHAPTER 5

ASPECTS OF LOCAL GOVERNMENT LAW

1. Historical Introduction and Modern Developments

Pre-1922 Developments

It has been stated that the "basic structure of [Irish] local government has remained that enacted by the British parliament in 1898."[1] In that year the Local Government (Ireland) Act 1898 was passed, and this legislation effected a major reorganisation of the system of local government which had operated prior to that date. Until 1898 the functions of local government had been discharged by a range of diverse and often single-function bodies, of which only the most important can be mentioned. First, the construction, repair and maintenance of roads and bridges lay in the hands of the grand jury, who also had a supervisory function in relation to other public works.[2] The grand jury was appointed by the assize judge, who was required to approve the grand jury's "presentments", *i.e.* expenditure proposals. The grand jury raised revenue by means of taxes on local landowners, and these taxes were known as the "grand jury cess". The corrupt[3] and undemocratic nature of this system led to reform, which was to come when the grand juries were relieved of their local government functions by the Local Government (Ireland) Act 1898.

Secondly, the poor law and sanitary services were administered, in most parts of the country, by boards of guardians. In Ireland, the poor law union was an area 10 miles in radius around each of the 130 market towns,[4] and the guardians were elected by the poor-law ratepayers. Local ratepayers also sat, *ex officio*, on the board of guardians. Because the guardians – unlike the grand juries – were permanent bodies holding regular meetings, their functions were extended by legislation throughout the nineteenth century.[5] By 1840 there were also 68 borough corporations to certain of which the powers of grand juries had been transferred. Ten of these (Dublin, Cork, Belfast, Limerick, Waterford, Londonderry, Sligo, Kilkenny, Drogheda,

---

[1] Alexander, "Local Government in Ireland" (1979) 27 *Administration* 3 at 7. What follows is necessarily a brief and very selective account of the principal features of local government law. Readers who desire a fuller treatment of this complicated subject are referred to Keane, *The Law of Local Government in the Republic of Ireland* (1982); Street, *The Law of Local Government* (1955) and Roche, *Local Government in Ireland* (1982). See also, Chubb, *The Government and Politics of Ireland* (1991), Chap. 15.

[2] The grand jury system, which had originated in the Grand Jury Act 1634 had been reorganised by the Grand Jury (Ireland) Act 1836.

[3] See generally, Roche, *op. cit.* above, n.1, pp. 29–43.

[4] See Alexander, *op. cit.* above, n.1, p. 6. The numbers were increased to 163 after the Famine.

[5] See, *e.g.* Births and Deaths Registration Act 1863 which required the compilation of mortality statistics by local authorities.

and Clonmel) were retained as municipal boroughs by section 12 of the Municipal Corporations (Ireland) Act 1840. Borough status was later granted to Wexford (by petition, 1845); Dún Laoghaire (by petition, 1930) and Galway (by private Act of the Oireachtas, 1937). Further reform came with the passage of the Local Government Act 1871, which gave a centralised body – the Local Government Board – control over the activities of local boards. By the end of the nineteenth century the local guardians enjoyed wide powers and "were loaded with the administration of public and personal health services and the provision of housing that went far beyond the relief of destitution".[6] Side by side with the boards of guardians system, town commissioners were elected in the towns which had adopted the Towns Improvement (Ireland) Act 1854 or which had been appointed under the Lighting of Towns (Ireland) Act 1828 or other local Acts.[7] The town commissioners had functions in relation to lighting, draining, paving, water supplies, land acquisition, railways, and in some cases, policing.

Major reform of this system was not to come until the Local Government (Ireland) Act 1898. This Act set up a two-tier system of local government, organised along county lines.[8] Each county was to have a county council, apart from Tipperary which is divided into North and South Riding.[9] The Local Government (Dublin) Act 1993 provided for the dissolution of the existing Dublin County Council and Dún Laoghaire Corporation and their replacement by the creation of three new counties: Fingal; South Dublin and Dún Laoghaire-Rathdown.

Returning to the 1898 Act: Dublin, Cork, Belfast, Waterford, Londonderry and Sligo were made county boroughs in which the Corporations were to have the functions of a county council, together with those functions which as borough councils they had previously enjoyed. In addition, Galway was established as a county borough by section 5 of the Local Government (Re-organisation) Act 1985.[10] Each county was divided into local districts, with an urban or rural district council. In rural areas, the public health functions of the boards of guardians were transferred to the rural district councils. The power to levy the poor law rates was assigned to the county councils, but the boards of guardians were still responsible for the administration of the poor law system, including the provision of medical relief. Finally, and perhaps most importantly, the franchise was extended to all adult male ratepayers.[11] This extension of the franchise not only ensured that local government was to be more representative in nature, but also created a form of local politics in

---

6   Chubb, *op.cit*. above, n.1, p. 268.
7   Some towns had elected representatives by virtue of local Acts: see Vanston's *Law of Municipal Towns*, pp. 6 and 358.
8   See generally, Roche, *op. cit*. above, n.1, pp. 32–36.
9   For the reasons as to why Tipperary was divided into North and South Ridings, see App. IX to Roche, *op. cit*. above, n.1.
10 For commentary, see Hogan, (1985) I.C.L.S.A. 7–01.
11 The Local Government Act 1994, s.5 provides that all Irish citizens and all other persons "ordinarily resident in the State" who have reached 18 years and who are not otherwise disqualified by law shall be eligible "for election or co-option to and membership of a local authority." This provision complements s.23 of the 1994 Act and s.10 of the Electoral Act, 1992 which provide in similar terms for the right to vote at local elections.
    Article 8b of the Treaty of Rome (as inserted by the Maastricht Treaty) provides in relevant part that:

Ireland which, in the following 20 years or so, was to be the backbone of the nationalist struggle for Irish independence.

Post-1922 developments

The first major piece of local government legislation following the establishment of the Irish Free State in 1922 was the Local Government (Temporary Provisions) Act 1923. This was enacted at a time when the country was split between pro- and anti-Treaty factions. Against this background, it seemed natural to the Government of the day to promote a policy of taking greater control over local authorities. For example, the Minister for Local Government's power to "dissolve and transfer functions to any body or persons or person he shall think fit" which had hitherto applied only to boards of guardians was extended to all local authorities.[12] And, indeed, this power was to be frequently availed of in the next few years.[13] Secondly: "Sinn Féin policy on local government, from which much of the reform thinking of this time derives, was aimed at clearing away most, if not all, of the undergrowth of small local bodies at sub-county level."[14]

Accordingly, boards of guardians (outside Dublin) were abolished by the 1923 Act, replacing them with boards of health, which were statutory committees of county councils.[15] Health and sanitary functions were discharged by the boards of health until these were abolished in 1940 and their functions became the direct responsibility of the county councils.[16] Eventually, by the Health Act 1970, the health functions (but not the sanitary functions) were transferred to eight regional health boards. In the same vein of thinning out the undergrowth of small bodies,

---

"Every citizen of the Union residing in a member State of which he is not a national shall have the right to vote and stand as a candidate at municipal elections in the Member State in which he resides, under the same conditions as nationals of that State."
The right of other Community nationals to vote at local elections has never been as problematic in Ireland as it has been other jurisdictions, such as France. This may reflect an element of national tolerance, but probably also reflects the fact that Ireland has a relatively low percentage of non-nationals residing in this State in comparison with other jurisdictions. On the effect of Article 8(b), see generally, O'Keeffe, "Union Citizenship" in O'Keeffe and Twomey, *Legal Issues of the Maastricht Treaty* (London, 1994) at 94–98 and Oliver, "Electoral Rights under Article 8B of the Treaty of Rome" (1996) 33 C.M.L.Rev. 473.

At all events, the non-citizens who are resident in the State were first given the right to vote at local elections by s.1 of the Local Elections Act, 1972. This section has now been replaced by the combined provisions of s.10 of the Electoral Act, 1992 and s. 23 of the 1994 Act. The right of non-nationals resident in the State to stand as candidates in local elections is now recognised for the first time by s.5 of the 1994 Act. However, Article 8b acknowledges that restrictions can be placed on the eligibility of potential candidates, provided these conditions apply equally to citizens and non-nationals. Section 6 imposes certain disqualifications (e.g., persons serving a prison sentence for longer than six months), but these disqualifications apply equally to nationals and non-nationals alike. It may be noted that these provisions apply to all resident non-nationals and not simply to citizens of other Community countries.

12   1923 Act, s.12. Similar provisions are now contained in the Local Government Acts 1941–46, save that under this later legislation the Minister for the Environment is not entitled to direct the removal of the elected representatives but only to dissolve the Council.
13   In 1923 five authorities were dissolved. The corresponding figures for 1924 and 1925 were 13 and five respectively.
14   Roche, *op. cit.*, above, n.1, p. 52.
15   1923 Act, ss. 3–7 and Local Government Act 1923, ss. 9 and 10.
16   County Management Act 1940, s.36.

the Local Government Act 1925 abolished rural district councils and their functions were assigned to the appropriate county council.[17]

The Local Government (Officers and Employees) Acts 1926–1983 provide that most major local authority officers cannot be appointed save on the recommendation of the Local Appointments Commissioners.[18] This process of selection by an independent body was a desirable reform, and guards against the political and other forms of patronage which are an all-too-common feature of Irish life. Another major step in the same direction was the introduction of the management system by the County Management Act 1940.[19] This constitutes the most far-reaching change in the local government system since the passing of the Local Government (Ireland) Act 1898, and is described below.

The Health Act 1970 represented the next major change in the local government system. This legislation established eight regional health boards composed of representatives of local authorities, the medical and other professions and ministerial nominees. The Act removed the administration of the health services from the local authorities, a stark reminder of the stringent control of local authorities by centralised government. 1971 saw the publication of a White Paper[20] on local government reorganisation and this was the first comprehensive review of local government since 1922. The White Paper proposed the abolition of the *ultra vires* rule; new legislation on the modernisation of the constitution, membership and procedure of local authorities; new accounting and auditing procedures; and the concentration of central government controls on "key points" only, while at the same time allowing local authorities "the greatest possible discretion in the exercise of their powers".

These proposals initially went unimplemented and the trend of centralisation continued with the Local Government (Financial Provisions) Act 1978 which effectively abolished domestic rates. The difficulties faced by local authorities were rendered even more acute by the Supreme Court's decision in *Brennan v. Attorney-General*[21] – which held that the method of collecting rates on agricultural land was unconstitutional – and made urgent reform of the local government system imperative.[22]

The critical financial position of local authorities was alleviated to an extent by the passage of the Local Government (Financial Provisions) (No. 2) Act 1983[23]

---

[17] Local Government Act 1925, s.3.

[18] There are some exceptions to this general rule, including the posts of part-time professional staff, nurses, midwives and technical posts. For the equivalent system in respect of the civil service, see pp. 85–86.

[19] The management system had earlier been imposed by a series of separate Acts on Cork, Dublin, Limerick and Waterford county boroughs. See Roche, *op. cit.* above, n.1, pp. 100–104. For the background to the development of the management system see Chubb, *op. cit.* above, n.1, pp. 275–278 and O'Halpin, "The origins of city and county management" in *City and County Management 1929–1990: A Retrospective* (Dublin, 1991) at pp. 1–21.

[20] *Local Government Reorganisation: Proposals for the reorganisation of the existing structure of local government and for modifications and improvements in the operation of the system* (Dublin, 1971).

[21] [1984] I.L.R.M. 355.

[22] The Supreme Court observed that the anomalous method of valuing agricultural land contained in the Valuation (Ireland) Act 1852 was used as the basis for assessing rates, then the method of collecting such rates (s.11 of the Local Government Act 1946) infringed the plaintiff's property rights as guaranteed by Art. 40.3, and was unconstitutional.

[23] See O'Hagan, McBride, Sanfey, "Local Government Finance: The Irish Experience" [1985] B.T.R. 235.

which substantially extended the power of the local authority to charge for certain essential services (*e.g.* water supply and refuse collection) but this was recognised as a (highly controversial) stop-gap measure and one which was not intended to be a substitute for a radical overhaul of the entire local government system. Some significant reforms were effected by the Local Government Act 1991 (which abolished the *ultra vires* rule) and the Local Government Act 1994 (which re-cast and modernised much pre-1922 legislation in relation to such matters as the making of bye-laws). Finally, the Local Government (Financial Provisions) Act 1997 abolished services charges and rate support grants, but local authorities were instead given a lucrative source of independent revenue by the assignment of the proceeds of motor tax revenue.[24] To several of these features we must return later in this chapter.[25]

2. The Management System

The essence of the management system is that certain functions (known as "reserved functions") may be exercised by the elected members, while all other functions ("executive functions") are discharged by a salaried officer, known as "the City Manager" or "the County Manager," as the case may be. However, the elected members are entitled to give the Manager binding directions as to the manner in which certain executive functions shall be discharged.[26] Draft estimates of expenditure must be prepared by either the Estimates Committee of the council or, if, as is far more usual, there is no such committee, by the Manager.[27] In either case, the estimates must then be adopted at a full meeting of the council at which "the Manager shall be present."[28] The Manager's status *vis-à-vis* the local authority is further enhanced by the provisions regarding his appointment and renewal. Selection is by the Local Appointments Commissioners,[29] who, as a matter of law, may recommend either one or two persons for the post. However, by an inveterate practice, the Commissioners recommend only one person who is then automatically appointed by the particular local authority. In addition, a Manager can only be removed from office with the sanction of the Minister for the Environment[30] and following the passage of a resolution, of which at least seven days' notice has been given, by a two-thirds' majority of the councillors. No Manager has as yet been removed. However, a few

---

24 The Minister for the Environment (Mr. B. Howlin T.D.) estimated that in 1996 the motor tax revenue exceeded the combined income from domestic water and services charges and rate support grant by IR£12 million: 478 *Dáil Debates* Col. 1016 (April 30, 1997). Theses changes had been foreshadowed in the White Paper *Better Local Government: A Programme for Change* (1996) Chap. 5.

25 See pp. 203–206; 249–252.

26 City and County Management (Amendment) Act 1955, ss. 2, 3 and 4. See pp. 193–199.

27 1955 Act, s.7.

28 *Ibid.* s.10(1).

29 Local Authorities (Officers and Employees) Act 1926, s.6; City and County Management (Amendment) Act 1955, s.6.

30 *Local Government Reorganisation: Proposals for the reorganisation of the existing structure of local government and for modifications and improvements in the operation of the system* (Dublin, 1971). Whereas formely Managers held office until retirement, Managers appointed after 1991 hold office for a period of seven years: see Local Government Act 1991, s.47(1) and Local Government (Tenure of Office) Order, 1991 (S.I. No. 128 of 1991), Article 4(1).

have been suspended, a process which requires a resolution of the same type as for a removal, but no ministerial consent.[31] Given the need for consistency between a county council and any lower authority within its area, it is most important that a County Manager is *ex officio* made Manager for every elective body within the county.[32]

Distinction between Reserved and Executive Functions

Most of the reserved functions of local authorities are set out in the Second Schedule to the County Management Act 1940. Subsequent legislation has increased their number.[33] In addition, section 16(3) of that Act provides that the Minister for the Environment may by order direct that certain functions or powers should also be reserved functions in addition to those scheduled to the 1940 Act. This power overlaps with that in s.41(2) of the Local Government Act 1991 which enables the Minister by order to declare that "a specified function or specified functions of local authorities shall be performed by resolution of the members of the authorities."[34] Section 17 of the 1940 Act states that every power, function or duty of a local authority or elected body which is not declared to be a reserved function shall be an "executive function" of such council or body and exercisable by the Manager.[35]

Thus in the case of a reserved function, the relevant provisions will expressly state that the power in question is to be a reserved function. Section 19(7) of the Local Government (Planning and Development) Act 1963 provides, for example, that: "The making of a development plan or any variations thereof shall be a reserved function."[36]

---

[31] 1940 Act, s.7.

[32] County Management Act 1940, s. 7.

[33] See, *e.g.* Housing Act 1988, s.11(6)(making of scheme of priority for letting of houses to be a reserved function); Roads Act 1993, s.11(2) (declaration of roads to be a reserved function) Casual Trading Act 1995, s.8(7) (extinguishment of local authority market to be a reserved function); Local Government (Financial Provisions) Act 1997, s.9(8) (local variation of car tax rates to be a reserved function).

[34] *e.g.* County Management (Reserved Functions) Order 1985 (S.I. 1985 No. 341) (making of domestic service charges under ss.2 and 8 of the Local Government (Financial Provisions) (No. 2) Act 1983; Local Government Act 1991 (Reserved Functions) Order 1993 (S.I. 1993 No. 37) (making of a contribution under s.40 of the Local Government (Sanitary Services) Act 1948; making of arrangements under s.96(1) of the Road Traffic Act 1961; the making of a request to the Minister to extend the period during which a planning authority may comply with the requirements of s.20(1) of the Local Government (Planning and Development) Act 1963); entry into an agreement under s.7 of the Local Authorities (Traffic Wardens) Act 1975; the making of a contribution under s.29 of the Local Government (Water Pollution) Act 1977; the making of a plan under Article 4 of the European Communities (Waste) Regulations 1979; the making of a scheme under s.279(5) of the Social Welfare (Consolidation) Act, 1993; entry into arrangements under ss.15(2), 15(3) and 15(4) of the Control of Dogs Act 1986 (other than the provision of services of staff); the making of a decision to provide a public abattoir under s.19(1) of the Abbattoirs Act 1988 and the consideration of a request to make a boundary change under s.30(3) of the Local Government Act 1991.

[35] See, to similar import, s.19(1) of the 1940 Act:
"Every act or thing done or decision taken by a county manager for the council or an elective body which, if done or taken by such council or an elective body would be required by law (other than this Act) to be done or taken by resolution of such council or elective body, shall be done or taken by such county manager by an order in writing signed by him."

[36] In some cases, however, this is not expressly stated and an example is provided by s. 13(1) of the Gaming and Lotteries Act 1956: "A local authority may by resolution adopt this Part in respect of

An executive function must be performed by the Manager by way of a signed order in writing.[37] A register must be kept of all such orders made by him for inspection by the elected representatives at a council meeting.

It is of practical importance that the Manager has extensive powers of delegation to an assistant County Manager, or to a County Manager or to a county secretary, town clerk or other "approved officer".[38] Within this category come specified senior administrative officers, who are the equivalent at local government level of the grade of principal in central government.

A curious and amusing example of the legal relationship between the Manager and the elected members is provided by *Waterford Corporation v. O'Toole*.[39] The defendant was interested in the life and works of the composer William Vincent Wallace[40] and he sought to erect on his own hotel premises two stone plaques commemorating the composer which had come into the possession of the Corporation. The City Manager agreed to the defendant's proposal that he should take possession of the plaques for this purpose. This decision was subject to ratification by the council, but Mr. O'Toole was given to understand that this would be a mere formality. In fact, the City Council refused to give their consent to this

---

the whole or a specified part of its administrative area and by resolution rescind such resolution." In the absence of an express statement to the contrary, it might be thought, on the one hand, that the effect of s. 17(1) of the County Management Act 1940 was that this function was to be an executive function.

On the other hand, the very wording of s. 13 of the 1956 Act (which refers to a "resolution" and the policy nature of the decision in question would all seem to imply that the function should be regarded as being a reserved function. The matter is probably put beyond doubt by the Schedule to the 1940 Act which provides that the following shall be among the matters to be regarded as reserved functions:

"The making or revoking an order or the passing or rescinding a resolution by virtue of which an enactment is brought into operation in or is made to apply to the functional area or a part of the functional area of the council of a county or of an elective body."

Moreover, the powers of local authorities under s. 13 of the 1956 Act have to date been regarded as reserved functions exercisable by the elected members and this does not appear to have attracted any judicial comment. See, *e.g. The State (Divito) v. Arklow U.D.C.* [1986] I.L.R.M. 123; *Re Camillo's Application* [1988] I.R. 104. Note that Keane, *op. cit.* above, n.1, p. 27 characterises this function as being a reserved function. On the other hand, in *Ferris v. Dublin County Council*, unreported, Supreme Court, November 7, 1990, Finlay C.J. rejected the argument that the reserved nature of a local authority function might arise by implication. He said (at p. 4 of the judgment): "The existence of a reserved function within the code of local authority law with which I am concerned, must be expressly provided and cannot be implied in the manner in which it was submitted in this case."

37 1940 Act, s.19. Moreover, the courts will not go behind a Manager's signed order "to supply any want or deficiency in it by evidence of the process of discussion or agreement between officers of the authority which led to the making of the order": *Athlone U.D.C. v. Gavin* [1985] I.R. 434 at 443, *per* Finlay C.J. In practice, signed orders are usually only made in the case of major matters or issues which may lead to litigation. Another way of characterising the practice is to say that signed orders are only made where, in the pre-manager era, a council resolution would have been required.

38 s.13(5) of the County Management Act 1940 permits the City Manager to delegate his executive powers to an Assistant Manager: *Cassels v. Dublin Corporation* [1963] I.R. 193. S. 17(9)(a) of the City and County Management (Amendment) Act 1955 allows the Manager to revoke that delegation, in which case, he resumes the power to discharge the statutory function in question: *Dublin Corporation v. McDonnell*, unreported, High Court, July 3, 1968.

39 Unreported, High Court, November 9, 1973.

40 William Vincent Wallace was born in Waterford in 1812 and died in France in 1865 after an eventful and colourful career. No less a figure than Wagner was compared favourably with Wallace by many local enthusiasts, but, alas, *Die Walküre* has proved more durable than *Maritana* and, in terms of international reputation, the Waterford Light Opera Festival cannot as yet compete with Bayreuth.

arrangement and the Corporation subsequently sought the return of the plaques which, by this time, had been embedded in concrete. The question arose as to whether the City Manager had power to make these arrangements with the defendant. Finlay J. held that such ratification was not required:

"[A]s a matter of law, the disposal or, more properly, the erection and display of these plaques on any particular premises was not a reserved function and that it was within the power of the City Manager to have made any arrangement he liked with Mr. O'Toole in regard to the plaques without obtaining the ratification or approval of the City Council."

However, Finlay J. further found, on the facts, that as Mr. O'Toole was aware that the City Manager had not intended to transfer the plaques without such consent and, in the absence of such consent, a condition of Mr. O'Toole's bailment failed, with the result that he committed a detinue of the goods.[41]

Section 17 of the 1940 Act appears to have received judicial consideration in only one other case: *The State (Harrington) v. Wallace.*[42] The Second Schedule to the 1940 Act provides, inter alia, that the "making, amending or revoking of a bye-law" shall be a reserved function. Cork County Council promulgated certain sheep-dipping regulations and the question arose as to whether these regulations were a bye-law within the meaning of the 1940 Act. Walsh J. accepted that if they were not, then they would be invalid in that the making of such regulations would not have been a reserved function within the meaning of the Act and that such powers could only have been exercised by the County Manager. However, Walsh J. decided, without much discussion, that, on their true construction, the regulations were, in fact, bye-laws.[43] This case illustrates what, in any event, are unexceptionable propositions, namely, that it is unlawful for the City or County Manager to exercise reserved functions and, conversely, that subject to one important statutory exception presently to be considered, the elected representatives may not usurp the executive functions of the Manager.

Moreover, it may be tentatively suggested that the elected members may not delegate their reserved powers to the Manager. This point is illustrated by *Grange Developments Ltd v. Dublin County Council (No. 2)*,[44] where the terms of the Dublin City development plan (the making of which is a reserved function) purported to invest the City Manager with a power to grant undertakings to grant planning permissions where this was considered by him to be expedient so as to avoid a claim for compensation under the Local Government (Planning and Development) Act 1963. Both Murphy J. and the Supreme Court considered that the effect of this

---

[41] The Corporation was awarded £1 nominal damages for detinue and Finlay J. refused on discretionary grounds to order the return of the plaques, since the cost and likely damage of removing the plaques from the concrete structure in which they were now embedded would be out of all proportion to their intrinsic value.

[42] [1988] I.R. 290.

[43] Walsh J. thought (*ibid.* 294) that it "would be hard to improve on" the definition of a bye-law given by *Kruse v. Johnson* [1898] 2 Q.B. 91 at 96: "An ordinance affecting the public, or some portion of the public, imposed by some authority clothed with statutory powers ordering something to be done or not to be done, and accompanied by some sanction or penalty for its non-observance."

[44] [1986] I.R. 246.

clause was to attempt to give the Manager power to rewrite the terms of the development plan as and when it seemed convenient to do so and that this represented an illegal delegation of powers. As Murphy J. said:

> "As the making of a development plan and any variation of such plan is a reserved function by virtue of s.19(7) of the 1963 Act, it seems to me that the wide-ranging powers conferred on the executive authority by the 1983 development plan is an illegal and invalid intrusion on that power."[45]

It should be noted that the exercise of a reserved function by the elected members does not, in general, involve any special procedures and a simple majority of members at a quorate meeting will suffice. One should note that one of the exceptions to this generalisation concerns the making or amendment of a development plan and, accordingly,[46] the *Grange Developments* ratio might be distinguished in a case involving a different area. The tentative proposition at the commencement of this paragraph (which is founded on the passage just quoted) may be too broadly stated. As Finlay C.J. said in *P. & F. Sharpe Ltd v. Dublin City & County Manager*[47]:

> "A reserved function can be carried out by a local authority by any lawful method of procedure which is contained in the rules of its proceedings and does not require any specific majority or number of persons voting in favour of it. [It may also] be carried out by a local authority without the necessity for any specific notice of its intention so to do to be given to the county manager or to anyone else."[48]

There is no comprehensive method of characterising the functions which the legislature has chosen to make reserved rather than executive; nevertheless, it is generally true to say that the latter are of an administrative nature. Reserved functions tend to deal with political and policy-making matters, or involve quasi-legislative or financial powers. Section 13 of the Local Government (Financial Provisions) Act 1978 provides a good example of this distinction. The section provides that "the making of a rate" (*i.e.* the individual assessment of a multitude of rateable properties) shall not be a reserved function, but section 13(2) stipulates that this shall not be taken to affect the local authorities' power to strike a rate in the pound.[49] Accordingly, the power of the elected local representatives to levy finance is not affected,[50] but the execution of that policy decision – essentially an administrative

---

[45] *Ibid.* at 312.

[46] See pp. 234–236.

[47] [1989] I.R. 701.

[48] *Ibid.* at 716.

[49] This power is contained in s.10(4) of the City and County Management (Amendment) Act 1955. Section 4 of the 1955 Act requires that the notice of the resolution must specify a day not later than seven days after the receipt of the notice by the Manager for the holding of the meeting at which the resolution is to be considered. This is to be contrasted with the ordinary procedures to be followed in the case of reserved functions: *P. and F. Sharpe Ltd v. Dublin City and County Manager* [1989] I.R. 701, *per* Finlay C.J.

[50] However, from a practical point of view, the abolition of domestic rates diminished the power of the elected representatives. Prior to the coming into force of the Local Government (Financial Provisions) Act 1997, local authorities were increasingly dependent on central government as a source of revenue. By virtue of s. 9(2) and s. 9(7) of the 1997 Act, local authorities may raise the rate of car tax payabale by up to 6% above the standard rate. This decision is, of course, a reserved function: see s. 9(8).

function – is assigned to the Manager. Naturally, too, dignified and representational functions, such as conferring civic honours,[51] entering into "twinning arrangements" with other towns and areas,[52] electing a member of the council to represent it on a harbour authority or nominating a Presidential candidate are also reserved functions.[53]

As mentioned, an executive function must be performed by the Manager by way of a signed order in writing.[54] Although there does not appear to be any authority directly in point, first principles would seem to require that the Manager must identify the legal source of his powers on the face of the order, at least where the order is such as to affect individual rights or liberties. Should the Manager fail to identify the correct legal basis of his powers in the order, then the order will fall as *ultra vires*. This happened in *Lyons v. Kilkenny Corporation*,[55] where the services charged imposed by the County Manager incorrectly referred to the Casual Trading Act 1980, instead of the Local Government (Financial Provisions) (No. 2) Act 1983. In this respect, it may also be significant that in *Dublin Corporation v. Ashley*[56] the Supreme Court was prepared to condemn as invalid a managerial order that was "uncertain and ambiguous" and which failed clearly "to comply with the limits of the statutory power of Dublin Corporation as a sanitary authority".[57] These observations of Finlay C.J. might be taken to suggest that a managerial order must show jurisdiction on its face.

As a matter of practicality, an inflexible operation of the "separation of powers" between the elected members and the Manager would plainly be unworkable. Although under this demarcation of functions the Manager is theoretically consigned to a purely administrative role, in practice, the council will rely on the Manager's expertise for advice and guidance, and the Manager's "contribution to the development of local policy is considerable".[58]

If anything, this last formulation understates the point, since the Manager can after all draw on the advice of his staff, who are full-time experts. As to the balance of authority between the Manager and councillors: on the one hand, a Manager has the right to attend council meetings and it is his duty to advise the council, generally and particularly, in regard to the exercise of his functions.[59] In the other direction,

---

[51] Local Government Act 1991, s. 48(2).

[52] *Ibid*. s. 49(2).

[53] Local Government (Remission of Rates) Act 1940, Second Schedule, Ref. Nos. 16 and 17 respectively.

[54] County Management Act 1940, s.19(1). Thus, in *Relihan v. Kerry County Council*, Supreme Court, May 14, 1970, Ó Dálaigh C.J. held that as local authority appointment were placed (by s.16 of the 1940 Act) in the hands of the County Manager, he can only act by order under s.19(1). In the absence, therefore, of a signed order under s.19(1), the plaintiff could not have been appointed as the holder of a permanent office with the authority. In *Kildare County Council v. Goode*, High Court, June 13, 1997, Morris J. allowed the applicant Council to tender formal proof of the making of a managerial order by producing it in Court. However, Morris J. admitted that in this respect he was influenced by the fact that the application was under s.27 of the Local Government (Planning and Development) Act 1976 and that in such cases, the court "acting in its capacity as guardian and supervisor of matters relating to planning, has a duty to receive all relevant evidence."

[55] Unreported, High Court, February 14, 1987.

[56] [1986] I.R. 781.

[57] *Ibid*. at 787.

[58] *Report of the Public Services Organisation Review Group ("the Devlin Report")* (1969, Prl. 792), para. 25.2.12.

[59] 1940 Act, ss. 30 and 31.

consider the City and County Management (Amendment) Act 1955 which was passed after a series of Departmental circulars designed to enhance the status of the councillors *vis-à-vis* the Manager had been ignored by many Managers. This Act, as we shall see, strengthened the position of the councillors, but in recent times, its key provisions – sections 2, 3 and 4 – have been rather reduced by judicial decisions.

To elaborate on the councillors' powers: in the first place, the councillors' right to information has been improved. In relation to either any, or every, performance of a specified executive function (other than staffing), the councillors may by resolution direct that before the Manager exercises that function, he must inform them of the manner in which he proposes to perform that function.[60] Again, even without a resolution, the Manager must inform the councillors before any works are undertaken or expenditure for work is committed.[61] This question arose in *O'Reilly v. O'Sullivan*[62] where the Dún Laoghaire-Rathdown County Manager took action to develop a particular site as a temporary halting site for travellers without informing the councillors. Keane J., however, noted that this right was abridged in cases of emergency[63] (such as had arisen in the present case) and the following passage graphically demonstates the extent to which fundamental democratic principles have been abridged at local level:

> "[Counsel for the applicant] has urged that the section should not be construed so as to enable the Manager to frustrate what he described as the democratic right of the elected members to be informed and (where appropriate) to direct that particular works should not be carried out. That submission, however, overlooks the fact that the Oireachtas, since the enactment of the County Management Act 1940 has maintained in place a system of local government under which the members of the elected members are heavily circumscribed. Since the Constitution at no point requires the assignment to elected local authorities of any of the powers of central government, it follows that the extent of any of the powers vested in such bodies remains at all times a matter for the Oireachtas. If the legislature were of the view that the effective use of the powers given to housing authorities by the 1988 Act might be inhibited by political considerations . . . and that the rights and privileges of the elected members under s.2 of the 1955 Act should be correspondingly abridged, that was a matter for them."[64]

---

[60] 1955 Act, s.2.

[61] *Ibid*. s.2(7).

[62] Unreported, Supreme Court, February 26, 1997.

[63] S.2(9) of the 1955 Act provides that nothing in this section shall prevent the Manager "from dealing forthwith with any situation which he considers is an emergency calling for immediate action without regard to those provisions." Section 27 of the Housing Act 1988 provides that an "emergency situation" for the purpose of section 2(9) of the 1955 Act shall be deemed to exist where, in the opinion of the Manager, the works concerned "are urgent and necessary (having regard to personal health, public health and safety considerations) in order to provide a reasonable standard of accommodation for any person . . . " In *O'Reilly v. O'Sullivan* Keane J. defined an "emergency" in s.2(9) as "a set of circumstances which had arisen suddenly and unexpectedly and which required, in the terms of the section, 'immediate action.'" He noted, however, that s.2(9) of the 1955 Act has been given an "artificial and extended meaning" by s.27 of the 1988 Act.

[64] However, the Court quashed the Manager's order since there was no evidence that the travellers who had been offered accommodation were "homeless persons" within the meaning of s.2 of the Housing Act.

Thirdly, section 3 of the 1955 Act provides that the elected representatives may direct that the works be not proceeded with, save where such works are works "which the local authority are required by or under statute or by order of a Court to undertake."[65] In addition, section 27 of the County Management Act 1940 provides that:

> "Every County Manager shall whenever requested by the Council of his County or by an elective body for which he is the Manager or by the Chairman of such Council or of any such body to do so, afford to such Council, Body or Chairman (as the case may require) all such information as may be in the possession or procurement of such County Manager in regard to any act, matter, or thing appertaining to or concerning any business or transaction of such Council or body (as the case may be) which is mentioned in such request."

In *Cullen v. Wicklow County Manager*[66] McCracken J. held that the word "information" in the section was not confined to written matters but has a "very wide and general meaning." This meant that the Chairman of the County Council was entitled pursuant to this section to have access to all documents pertaining to litigation involving the Council in respect of an alleged contravention of the relevant development plan.

Section 4 of the 1955 Act

Most important of all, section 4 of the City and County Management (Amendment) Act 1955 enables the elected members to give the Manager directions as to how certain of his executive functions shall be performed.[67] Section 4(1) of the 1955 Act provides:

---

[65] In *East Wicklow Conservation Community Ltd v. Wicklow County Council* [1997] 2 I.L.R.M. 72 the respondents had treated as a nullity a s.3 direction requiring them not to build a waste disposal site at a particular place. The question arose as to whether these were works which the authority was required to do by or under statute. The Supreme Court held that these works came within the exception to s.3, even though it was clear that the authority was under no *specific* statutory obligation to perform the works at that *particular site*. In a judgment whose conclusion is by no means self-evident, Blayney J. held that since by virtue of s.55 of the Public Health (Ireland) Act 1878 an authority is required to provide "fit buildings or places for the deposit of any matters collected by them", the proposed works were ones which the local authority were bound to carry out. This may be true, but it still does not meet the applicant's fundamental objection that as the authority was under no obligation to build the waste site at that particular place, the works did not fall within the statutory duty exception to s.3. Thus, *East Wicklow* provides another example of the fundamental lack of democratic accountability at local level and to that extent this decision may be regarded as being at odds with one of the stated objectives of the 1955 Act.

[66] [1996] 3 I.R. 474.

[67] Of course, in addition to formal s.4 motions, councillors sometimes pass ordinary resolutions which concern executive functions. These motions do not bind the manager and simply amount to "formal recommendations . . . as to the performance by him of any particular executive function": *Browne v. Dundalk UDC* [1993] 2 I.R. 512 at 520, *per* Barr J. The judge continued:
> "The local government statutes do not specifically provide for such recommendations by formal resolution of the elected body, but in my view the power to make them is implicitly derived from the general nature and purpose of such bodies. A council resolution directed to its chief executive which is not an exercise of a reserved function or of a power derived from section 4 is not binding on him. He is free to act on it or not as he thinks fit."

"[A] local authority may by resolution require any particular act, matter or thing specifically mentioned in the resolution and which the local authority or the Manager can lawfully do or effect to be done or effected in performance of the executive functions of the local authority."

The power of the local authority to pass such a resolution is, however, subject to a number of important qualifications. Special notice must be given[68] compliance with which is specially stringent in the planning field, a point to which we shall return below.[69] Significantly, a resolution of this nature can only require the performance of an executive function in a lawful manner, and it is clear that a resolution which required the Manager to act in an unreasonable or arbitrary manner, or in a manner contrary to the requirements of constitutional justice, would be *ultra vires*.[70] Furthermore, section 4(9)(a) states that a resolution may not "apply or extend" to:

"[T]he performance of any function or duty of a local authority generally [or] to every case or occasion of the performance of any such function or to a number or class of such cases or occasions so extended as to be substantially or in effect every case or occasion on which any such function is performed in that area."[71]

The purpose of this subsection is to ensure that the Manager is not stripped of an entire executive function by means of a general resolution. So, for example, while a section 4 resolution may validly direct that a particular planning permission should be granted, it may not require that all applications of that type should be acceded to. In addition, it would seem that this procedure cannot be used to compel the Manager not to do any particular act, matter or thing, *i.e.* it can only be used to direct the Manager to take some positive step.[72]

These questions might have – but ultimately did not – arise in the aftermath of the long-running *Grange Developments* case. On March 14, 1989, Murphy J. granted leave to the developers to enforce an arbitrator's award for £1.9 million under the Arbitration Acts 1954. Following a decision by the Supreme Court not to put a stay on the payment of the award, Dublin County Council were faced with the prospect of an immediate payment of this sum.[73] Following a special meeting of the County Council, it was suggested that the councillors were about to order the Manager not to pay over the sum of money. Although this was later denied[74] and the matter does not appear to have been finally judicially decided, it is arguable (as mentioned in the previous paragraph) that a section 4 motion could not have been used for this negative purpose. Section 4 expressly refers to any "act, matter or thing" which the

---

68 Section 4 of the 1955 Act requires that notice of the resolution must specify a day not later than seven days after the receipt of the notice by the Manager for the holding of the meeting at which the resolution is to be considered.

69 See pp. 196–197.

70 See, *e.g. McDonald v. Feeley*, unreported, Supreme Court, July 23, 1980; *P. & F. Sharpe Ltd v. Dublin City and County Manager* [1989] I.R. 701; *Child v. Wicklow County Council* [1995] 2 I.R. 447.

71 In addition, such resolutions do not extend to the exercise or performance of the Manager's executive functions in relation to the control, remuneration, etc., of the council's officers or servants.

72 See Keane, *op. cit.* above, n.1, pp. 35–36.

73 *The Irish Times*, March 22, 1989.

74 The County Manager handed over the sums in question to the receiver appointed by the High Court, *The Irish Times*, March 23, 1989.

local authority or Manager "can lawfully do" but, significantly, omits any reference to a negative act or deed. And, as section 4 represents an exception to the separation of powers between the Manager and the elected members, it is to be expected that – like all statutory exceptions – it will be strictly construed. On the other hand, in *P. J. Sharpe Ltd v. Dublin City Manager*, Finlay C.J. said in passing that section 4 applied to the whole range of "executive functions, namely, those associated with the granting or refusing of planning permissions."[75]

There is a stronger reason why the councillors could not have lawfully instructed the Manager not to pay the arbitrator's award in the *Grange Developments* case. Section 4 refers to any act which the local authority or the Manager can "lawfully do." Thus, the mechanism of a section 4 motion cannot be used to achieve an unlawful object and the Manager may decline to obey a section 4 resolution where it is clear that the resolution would require the performance of an illegal act.[76] In addition, section 16 provides that if the proposed resolution would involve an illegal payment, or would likely result in a deficiency or loss of the authority's funds, then the names of the persons voting for such a proposal must be recorded, and those voting in favour of the resolution are liable to be surcharged. Of course, as O'Hanlon J. pointed out in *P. & F. Sharpe Ltd v. Dublin Corporation*,[77] the mere fact that a local authority receives certain legal advice does not decide the issue "beyond yea or nay." A local authority may elect to ignore the advice tendered, but they clearly do so at their own risk: "They may be vindicated by a later decision of the courts confirming the validity of what was done, or they may face a finding that their action was unlawful and have to pay the penalty for such unlawfulness".[78] However, if the councillors do reject expert advice, they "must have some basis for refusing to accept that advice" such as "an opinion from another expert or a reasoned judgment as to why the advice of expert officials is incorrect", as otherwise there is a real risk that they will be deemed to have acted unreasonably in law.[79]

Section 4 in the planning context

Most section 4 resolutions arise in the context of the granting of planning permission and section 26(3)(c) of the Local Government (Planning and Development) Act

---

[75] [1989] I.R. 701 at 714.
[76] Where the case involves an "obvious and patent illegality, the Manager would be not only entitled, but in duty bound, to refuse to comply with the directions given to him by the Council": *P. and F. Sharpe Ltd v. Dublin City Manager* [1989] I.R. 701, *per* O'Hanlon J. This view has been consistently followed in other cases: see, *e.g.*, *Griffin v. Galway City and County Manager*, unreported, High Court, October 31, 1990; *Flanagan v. Galway City and County Manager* [1990] 2 I.R. 66; *Kenny Homes & Co. Ltd v. Galway City and County Manager* [1995] 1 I.R. 178; *Child v. Wicklow County Council* [1995] 2 I.R. 447. Furthermore, a s.4 motion cannot be used to compel the manager to breach an otherwise valid contract: *Browne v. Dundalk UDC* [1993] 2 I.R. 512.

In the *Child* case, Costello P. said (at 452) that if a County Manager "decides that a s.4 resolution is *ultra vires* there is . . . authority to the effect that he is entitled to ignore it without applying to the court to have it quashed". But for a suggestion (in a different context) that the decision-maker might be obliged to apply to the High Court to have the decision quashed, see the (inconclusive) discussion in the judgment of Geoghegan J. in *Hegarty v. Governor of Limerick Prison*, unreported, Divisional High Court, February 26, 1997 discussed at pp. 464–465.
[77] [1989] I.R. 701.
[78] *Ibid.*
[79] *Child v. Wicklow County Council* [1995] 2 I.R. 447 at 452.

1963 prescribes a special procedure where the City Manager is of opinion that the granting of such permission pursuant to a section 4 resolution would materially contravene the provisions of either the development plan or a special amenity order. In such a case the Manager must ensure that the provisions of section 26(3)(a) of the 1963 Act are complied with, which include, *inter alia*, the publication of a newspaper notice indicating the intention of the authority to grant the permission,[80] the invitation of submissions from members of the public within 21 days of the publication of such newspaper notice and, finally, the passage of a resolution by the local authority. In addition in the case of any s.4 motions touching on planning issues, by virtue of amendments effected by s. 44 of the Local Government Act 1991, the required notice in relation to the resolution must be signed by not less than three-quarters of the total number of the members elected for the electoral area or areas concerned. It is further necessary that three-quarters of the total number of members of the local authority vote in favour.[81]

The general scope of the powers conferred by section 4 was considered by the Supreme Court in the important case of *P. & F. Sharpe Ltd v. Dublin City and County Manager*.[82] In this case the applicants had obtained planning permission to erect a large housing development in the vicinity of a dual carriage-way. The applicants then sought permission for access to the dual carriage-way from the housing estate. Despite the fact that there were several reports before the City Council strongly recommending against acceding to this request for road safety reasons, a section 4 motion requiring the City Manager to grant the permission in the terms sought was carried. The City Manager, however, refused to comply with the resolution on the ground that he considered that it was *ultra vires* and mandamus proceedings were then commenced by the applicants.

The main focus[83] of the court's decision concerned the application of the principles of fair procedures and the reasonable exercise of a quasi-judicial function could be applied in the case of a section 4 resolution of this nature. It was clear that the granting of planning permission involved the exercise of quasi-judicial powers and that a planning authority was required to act reasonably and exclude all irrelevant considerations. In the context of a section 4 resolution this did not mean that the Manager was required to exercise a discretion independently of the members, but rather that:

---

80 For a case raising evidential issues concerning proof of whether the appropriate newspaper notices were circulated in the context of a resolution rescinding the application of Pt. III of the Gaming and Lotteries Act 1956, see *Re Murphy's Application* [1987] I.R. 667.

81 Local Government Act 1991, s.44(1)(b). The Barrington Committee *Local Government Reorganisation and Reform* (Pn. 7918, 1991) had recommended (at para. 48) that the s.4 procedure should have no application whatever to planning decisions because of the existence of an independent appeal tribunal and because in accordance with the "general reserved/executive framework, decisions on individual cases should rest with the executive."

82 [1989] I.R. 701.

83 The court had rejected the respondents' contention that the scope of section 4 did not extend to planning matters by reason of the express provision made for a number of reserved functions, by the terms of the Local Government (Planning and Development) Act 1963. Such a ruling would have blurred the distinction between the two types of functions and such a construction of the relevant statutory provisions would have been unacceptable having regard to the unambiguous terms of section 17 of the 1940 Act.

"[T]he obligation to act in a judicial [sc. quasi-judicial] manner is by virtue of the service of notice of intention to propose a resolution under section 4 of the 1955 Act transferred from the County Manager to the elected members. They must act in a judicial manner before reaching any conclusion on the resolution. If, however, having done so they resolve to give a direction to the County Manager, I have no doubt but that the proper construction of section 4 is that he carries that out as part of his statutory duty as a mere executive duty and is not entitled, provided the resolution is valid and lawful, to exercise any separate or independent discretion as to whether or not he will obey it. If, of course, the elected members do not resolve to operate section 4 of the 1955 Act, the County Manager's duty to act in a judicial manner in considering the application for permission revives."[84]

Here the uncontradicted evidence pointed to the fact that the access road would have involved a material contravention of the development plan. At a minimum – and in line with the special statutory procedures envisaged by section 26(3)(c) of the Local Government (Planning and Development) Act 1963 – fair procedures and the general requirement that the elected members discharge their functions in planning matters in a quasi-judicial manner meant that "specific public notice of their intention to consider this resolution" should have been given. Accordingly, the section 4 resolution was a nullity in law. It followed that if the elected members still wished to put down such a resolution in relation to the access road, they would be required to serve a fresh notice on the Manager. The Manager would then be required to implement the special statutory procedure under section 26(3) of the 1963 Act and, once that was done, it would be open to the elected members "to consider this application anew, having served the appropriate notices and having heard and considered all matters concerning it."[85]

These principles were applied in a series of subsequent decisions. In *Flanagan v. Galway County Council*,[86] where the elected representatives had directed the County Manager by way of section 4 resolution to grant the applicant the planning permission sought by him. The evidence showed that the Council had been heavily influenced by the personal circumstances of the applicant and it had been stated on the applicant's behalf by the proposer of the motion that he would otherwise be obliged to emigrate and to close his business, with consequential loss of several jobs in the area. Blayney J., however, decided that the elected members were confined to a consideration of the proper planning and development of their own functional area and that matters such as the personal circumstances of the developer or the provision of employment were irrelevant. Accordingly, the section 4 resolution was invalid because such irrelevant considerations had been taken into account by

---

[84] *Ibid.* at 718.

[85] *Ibid.*

[86] [1990] 2 I.R. 66. See also, *Griffin v. Galway City and County Manager*, unreported, High Court, October 31, 1990, a case with similar facts, where Blayney J. held that a s.4 motion was invalid as it failed to have regard to the fact that the proposed grant of planning permission would breach the development plan and that the councillors proposing the motion had failed to disregard irrelevant considerations.

the elected members[87] and mandamus would not therefore issue to compel the County Manager to implement it. A similar approach is evident in the judgment of Costello P. in *Child v. Wicklow County Council*[88], where the councillors had disregarded the advice tendered by expert official and had by section 4 resolution directed the Manager to grant a particular planning permission. Costello P. explained that the elected members were not bound by the advice tendered by the county engineer:

> "The elected members could decide not to take that advice but I think that there must be some basis for refusing to accept it. The elected members are not entitled just to ignore what the County Council's expert official have said would be the effect of the section 4 resolution, which seems to me to have been the position in this case. If the advice of the County Council's expert official indicates that a proposed development would be contrary to the proper planning and development of the area, the elected members must have some basis for a refusing to accept that advice; perhaps an opinion from another expert or a reasoned judgment as to why the advice of the expert officials is incorrect. Neither existed in this case."[89]

Costello P. therefore concluded that the Council had acted unreasonably "in not accepting the advice which was given to them."

The practical effect of these decisions – which display almost universal judicial unease at the use of section 4 in this context – together with the changes effected by the Local Government Act 1991 has led to a significant decrease in the use of section 4 motions in planning matters.

3. The Doctrine of *Ultra Vires*

The traditional ultra vires *rules as applied to statutory corporations*

Corporations could be created at common law by virtue of the royal prerogative, but even prior to 1922, the tendency was very much to favour the creation of corporations

---

[87] *cf.* Lynch J.'s unwillingness to presume that the councillors had been similarly improperly influenced by representations from the public in the making of a development plan: see *Malahide Community Ltd v. Fingal County Council*, unreported, Supreme Court, May 14, 1997

[88] [1995] 2 I.R. 447.

[89] *Ibid.* at 452. See also *Kenny Homes & Co. Ltd v. Galway City and County Manager* [1995] 1 I.R. 178 (where a s.4 resolution directing the Manager to grant permission was held to be invalid as it was drafted in a manner which precluded the councillors from considering, in the manner envisaged by s.26 of the Local Government (Planning and Development) Act 1963, whether conditions should attach to the grant of permission). Note that, while Blayney J. accepted in that case that *Sharpe* was authority for the view that a planning permission could be granted by means of a s.4 resolution, he was nonetheless of opinion that s.4 was "much more suited to executive functions which do not have to be exercised in a judicial manner." ([1995] 2 I.L.R.M. at 597). But *cf.* the comments of Lynch J. in *Malahide Community Council Ltd v. Fingal County Council*, unreported, Supreme Court, May 14, 1997 in the (admittedly different) context of the making of a development plan:

> "The evidence of what was mainly debated [at relevant Council meetings] does not establish the reasons motivating each Councillor in casting his/her vote. With their local knowledge added to the 8,462 representations which they had received it was not open to the High Court to assume [that they did not have regard to appropriate planning considerations.]"

by statute. Nowadays, the number of corporations in existence which have been created otherwise than by statute is insignificant. However, the theoretical difference as to the scope of their powers and the important limitation upon those of a statutory corporation, created by the *ultra vires* doctrine, is as follows:

> "A corporation [incorporated by royal charter] stands on a different footing from a statutory corporation, the difference being that the latter species of corporation can only do such acts as are authorised directly or indirectly by the statute creating it; whereas the former can, speaking generally, do anything that an ordinary individual can do."[90]

Borough corporations were originally created by royal charter but their status as statutory corporations was recognised and confirmed by section 12 of the Municipal Corporations (Ireland) Act 1840. County councils and urban district councils were designated as statutory corporations by Article 13(1) of the Local Government (Application of Enactments) Order 1898 and section 65 of the Local Government Act 1955 is to the same effect as far as Town Commissioners are concerned. Accordingly, prior to the enactment of the Local Government Act 1991, the doctrine of *ultra vires* applied quite rigidly in the case of all local authorities, since by now, they all have the status of statutory corporations. This meant that enabling legislation has tended in the past to be very specific and even after the relaxation of the *ultra vires* rules the parliamentary draftsman has remained cautious. Thus, section 56 of the Local Government Act 1941 invests local authorities with the power to decorate their functional area "on the occasion of public rejoicing" and section 113 of the Housing Act 1966 permits a housing authority to award prizes to householders for the tidy maintenance of houses and gardens. And even though the *ultra vires* rule was relaxed by section 6 of the Local Government Act 1991(considered below), sections 46, 48 and 49 of the same Act display the traditional caution of the draftsman. Section 48 allows local authorities to bestow civic honours; section 49 permits a local authority to enter into a "twinning" arrangement with other areas, while section 46 permits local authorities to incur:

> "reasonable expenditure for and in connection with the provision of receptions and entertainment for, and the making of presentations –
>
> (a) to distinguished persons, and
>
> (b) in connection with the holding of special events relevant to its functions."

Naturally, the *ultra vires* rule assumes particular importance in the area of compulsory acquisition and the principal statutory provision – section 11 of Local Government (Ireland) Act 1898 (as inserted by s.11 of the Local Government (No. 2) Act 1960) is comprehensive in its scope.[91]

---

[90] *Att.-Gen. v. Leeds Corporation* [1929] 2 Ch. 291 at 295, *per* Luxmoore J. For modern applications of the express or necessarily implied authorisation principles, see the judgment of Costello J. in *Howard v. Commissioners of Public Works* [1994] 1 I.R. 101; Lardner J. in *Huntsgrove Developments Ltd v. Meath C.C.* [1994] 2 I.L.R.M. 36; and that of the Supreme Court in *Keane v. An Bord Pleanála and Commissioners of Irish Lights* [1997] 1 I.R. 184.

[91] This section could "hardly be more comprehensive in its terms": *Leinster Importing Co. Ltd v. Dublin County Council* [1984] I.L.R.M. 605 at 607, *per* McWilliam J.

The consequence of the *ultra vires* rule and this cautious approach to drafting was that a local authority might find itself without power to do something which one might reasonably expect it to be able to do. This difficulty might arise not because there was any reason why it should not have such a power but simply because this had not previously been anticipated. This restriction tended to induce a sense of caution on the part of local authority officialdom who might think in the absence of express statutory authorisation that discretion was the better part of valour and prefer not to take the risk. The Barrington Committee had recommended reform of the rule, adding that such a change would

" . . . give local authorities a new freedom to take action in areas where they are at present excluded at present by lack of legislative authority. It is entirely in accord with the view of local authorities as development agencies and of their status as democratically elected bodies."[92]

The incidental powers doctrine

Even before the relaxation of the *ultra vires* rule, express statutory authorisation was not necessary, for it was – and still is – enough if the powers in question may be necessarily inferred from the terms of the enabling statute: "Whatever may be fairly regarded as incidental to, or consequential upon, those things which the legislature has authorised, ought not (unless expressly prohibited) to be held by judicial construction to be *ultra vires*."[93]

Many of the reported cases turn on the question of whether the actions of the local authority may be said to be reasonably incidental to the powers expressly conferred, and a number of miscellaneous examples may now be given.[94] For instance, in *Hendron v. Dublin Corporation*[95] it was held that the Housing (Miscellaneous Provisions) Act 1931, the law which then governed compulsory acquisition for housing purposes, simply conferred on the local authority the right

---

[92] At p. 45. *The Devlin Report* recommended in 1969 (para. 25.3.8) that local authorities should have a general competence to act for the good of the community. This view which is endorsed at para. 25.3.8 of the *Devlin Report* states:
"The current application of the doctrine of *ultra vires*, together with the specific terms in which local government statutes tend to be drawn, encourage rigid control over local authority activities by the Department and deter local authority initiative. In a number of other countries, local authorities operate successfully within a general competence to act for the good of the community. Similar powers could be extended to local authorities, subject to such specific limitations as were considered necessary."

[93] *Att.-Gen. v. Great Eastern Ry. Co.* (1880) 5 App.Cas. 473 at 478, *per* Lord Selborne L.C.

[94] It is hard to improve on the comments of Lord MacNaghten in *Attorney General v. Mersey Rly. Co.* [1907] A.C. 415, 417, a case where it was held that the running of buses was not reasonably incidental to the business of a railway company:
"Is the business of omnibus proprietors . . . reasonably incidental to their powers as authorized by their special Act? The principle to be applied is perfectly clear. The difficulty is all in the application. Hundreds of cases may be suggested where the thing is done comes very near the line and may fairly be open to a difference of opinion . . . If [the defendants] wish to extend their undertaking beyond the limits authorised by their charter, the proper course is to apply to Parliament for further powers . . . [A] matter of this kind is better left to Parliament. There everybody who has a right to be heard will be listended to and there the interests of the public will be protected."

[95] [1943] I.R. 566

to acquire land compulsorily where such land was required immediately for housing purposes; no such power of compulsory acquisition existed where the land was to be used for future housing purposes, or where (as in the instant case) the authority had yet to reach a final decision on the matter. Many other "incidental powers" cases have arisen in the context of planning law, as conditions may be imposed by the planning authority where they are necessary "for the proper planning and development" of the area. In *Dublin Corporation v. Raso*[96] the defendant had obtained planning permission for use of premises as a "fish and chips" shop on condition that the premises were not used for this purpose between the hours of 11 p.m. and 8 a.m. Finlay P. held that this condition was *intra vires* as it was up to the planning authority to impose conditions of this kind with a view to: "[C]utting down nuisance, noise and the frequenting or gathering of people which would disturb the residential aspect of a neighbourhood. Such an object and condition is clearly within the planning code."

A stricter attitude is taken in cases where property rights might be affected. Thus, in *The State (F.P.H. Properties S.A.) v. An Bord Pleanála*[97] the Supreme Court held that certain conditions requiring the restoration of Furry Park House, a house of considerable architectural significance (which was owned by the applicant) were invalid. The applicants had sought and obtained planning permission for the building of luxury apartments in the grounds of Furry Park House on condition that the house (which was not within the scope of the application) was so restored, but McCarthy J. could not accept that such conditions regulated the "development or use" of the lands in respect of which planning permission was sought, namely, the grounds of Furry Park House. Finally, in the rather unusual case of *Huntsgrove Development Ltd v. Meath C.C.*[98] Lardner J. held that it was *intra vires* the powers of a local authority – even in the absence of a specific statutory authority – to accept a gift of moneys which were used for the purpose of enabling it to perform a statutory function, namely, the review of a development plan.[99]

Another good example is provided by *Re Cook's Application*[100] which concerned the legality of certain actions taken by the Unionist majority of Belfast City Council in opposition to the Anglo-Irish Agreement if 1985. The applicants – who were Alliance Party councillors – challenged the *vires* of resolutions which had been passed by the Council delegating its functions to the Town Clerk and affixing a banner – bearing the legend "Belfast says No" – to the City Hall. These resolutions had been passed as part of the Council's campaign against the Anglo-Irish Agreement, but this campaign, it was submitted, did not constitute a local government function and, consequently, these functions were *ultra vires*. Both Hutton J. and the Northern Irish Court of Appeal held, in the first instance, that the *ultra vires* doctrine applies, not only to the exercise of powers and the expenditure of monies by a council, but

---

[96] [1976–1977] I.L.R.M. 139.
[97] [1987] I.R. 698. See also *Maher v. An Bord Pleanála* [1993] 1 I.R. 439 (depreciation of property a proper matter for the planning authority to take into account); *Keane v. An Bord Pleanála* [1997] 1 I.L.R.M. 508 (planning authority entitled to have regard to beneficial effects of development, even if those benefits occur largely outside of its functional area).
[98] [1994] 2 I.L.R.M. 36.
[99] *Ibid.* at 54. The bias issue in this case is dealt with at pp. 527–528.
[100] [1986] N.I. 242.

also to a council resolution.[101] However, it was held these acts were *intra vires* the Council because the workings of the Agreement could affect functions – such as transport, parks and recreation – which are either the functions of, or are incidental to, the functions of Belfast City Council.[102] In *Hazell v. Hammersmith and Fulham Council*[103] the House of Lords held that, where, as in this case, there had been no attempt by a local authority's financial officers to match the Council's debts and investments, the authority had by, entering into sophisticated transactions on the spot and capital markets, simply engaged in speculative trading and this was held not to be incidental to the defendant's borrowing powers, having regard, in particular, to the statutory context in which such powers operated.[104]

Relaxation of the ultra vires rule

The Local Government Act 1991 significantly reduces the rigours of the *ultra vires* rule. It does so in two ways. In the first place section 8(1) deals with the objective for the action. It shifts the focus from any specific statute (or powers incidental thereto) which will usually be concerned with a relatively narrow objective and places it, instead, on the wider concept of what can advantageously be performed by the authority. Section 8(1) is as follows:

> "A local authority may do anything which is ancillary, supplemental or incidental to or consequential on or necessary to give full effect to or is conducive to the performance of, a function conferred on it by this or any other enactment or which can advantageously be performed by the authority in conjunction with the performance of such a function."[105]

Despite the comprehensiveness of this statutory language,[106] this provision should not be taken as having removed all restrictions on local authorities. This is not only inherent in the statutory formulation just quoted, but is, in any event, made clear by section 8(2):

---

101 *Ibid.* at 252.
102 *Ibid.* at 254, 276. But the Council was held to have acted *ultra vires* in other respects: see p. 637.
103 [1992] 1 A.C. 1.
104 As Lord Templeman stressed (at 31): ". . . a local authority is not a trading or currency or commercial operator with no limit on the method or extent of its borrowings or with powers to speculate." It may be noted that in the wake of this decision the Oireachtas enacted two statutes, Financial Transactions of Certain Companies and Other Bodies Act 1992 and the Borrowing Powers of Certain Bodies Act 1996 designed to confirm the power – subject to ministerial control – of statutory bodies to engage in interest rate swaps and other (now-standard) debt management practices. Thus, s.2(2) of the 1992 Act vests the Minister for Finance with regulatory powers to prevent essentially speculative transactions under the guise of hedging. It should be stressed that *neither* Act applies to local authorities. This exclusion was justified by the then Minister for Finance (Mr B. Ahern) in the case of the 1992 Act on the grounds that the amount of local authority debt was relatively small and that local authorities did not engage in swaps: 424 *Dáil Debates*, Col. 420.
105 Section 35 of the Local Government Act 1994 clarifies the extent of section 8(1) by providing that it extends to "anything which is related to the general administration or operation of the authority" and that the reference to a function of the authority shall be construed as referring "to all such functions as may be at any material time stand conferred on the local authority by or under any enactment (including that Act and this Act) . . . "
106 Section 8(1) is "framed in extraordinarily broad and general terms": *Huntsgrove Developments Ltd v. Meath C.C.* [1994] 2 I.L.R.M. 36 at 53, *per* Lardner J. In that case, Lardner J. held that s.8(1)

"A local authority shall not by virtue of this Part perform any function –

(a) which it is prohibited from enjoying or performing by this or any other enactment, or

(b) without being subject to or complying with any conditions or restrictions to which, by virtue of this or any other enactment, the performance of the function is subject."

In summary, therefore, the effect of sections 6 and 8 of 1991 Act is, broadly speaking, that local authorities have a general competence to do things which are conducive to their statutory powers and functions, save that in doing so they may not contravene an express statutory prohibition or statutory condition.

Whereas section 8(1) deals with the objective of a local authority act, the other relevant provision – section 6(1) is directed to widening the character of the permissible acts. Section 6(1) provides that:

"(a) A local authority may, subject to the provisions of this section, take such measures, engage in such activities or do such things in accordance with law (including the incurring of expenditure) as it considers necessary or desirable to promote the interests of the local community.

(b) For the purposes of this section a measure, activity or thing shall be deemed to promote the interests of the local community if it promotes, directly or indirectly, the social, economic, environmental, recreational, cultural, community or general development of the functional area (or any part thereof) of the local authority or of the local community (or any group consisting of members thereof)."

Section 6(2) provides that, without prejudice to the generality of sub-section 1 and for the purposes of giving effect to that sub-section, a local authority may:

"(a) (i) carry out and maintain works of any kind,
   (ii) provide, maintain, perserve or restore land, structures of any kind or facilities,
   (iii) fit out, furnish or equip any building, structure or facility for particular purposes,
   (iv) provide utilities, equipment or materials for particular purposes,
   (v) provide any service or other thing or engage in any activity that, in the opinion of the authority is likely to benefit the community;

(b) provide assistance in money or in kind, upon and subject to such terms and conditions as the authority considers appropriate, to persons engaging in any activity that, in the opinion of the authority, benefits the local community;

(c) provide assistance in money or in kind (including the provision of prizes and other incentives) upon and subject to such terms and conditions as

---

would have in itself provided statutory authority for the receipt of a gift "provided it was done genuinely to enable them to carry out one of their statutory functions", but for the fact that the gift in question had been donated a short while before the coming into force of the 1991 Act. Note, however, the comments of Lord Templeman in *Hazell v. Hammersmith and Fulham LBC* [1992] 2 A.C. 1, in respect of the corresponding English legislation: ". . . a power is not incidental merely because it is convenient, desirable or profitable."

the authority considers appropriate in respect of the organisation or promotion of, competitions, seminars, exhibitions, displays, festivals or other events, or organise or promote such events;

(d) enter into such contracts and other arrangements as the authority considers necessary and expedient."

The ultra vires *rules, section 7 of the Local Government Act 1991 and the need for rational use of local authority resources*

Section 7 of the 1991 Act is an entirely novel – and potentially highly important – provision which deserves to be set out in full:

"(1) Subject to *subsection (2)*, a local authority, in performing the functions conferred on it by or under any other enactment, shall have regard to —

(a) the resources, wherever originating, that are available or likely to be available to it for the purpose of such performance and the need to secure the most beneficial, effective and efficient use of such resources,

(b) the need to maintain adequately those services provided by it which it considers to be essential and, in so far as practicable, to ensure a reasonable balance is achieved, taking account of all relevant factors, between its functional programmes,

(c) the need for co-operation with, and the co-ordination of its activities with those of, other local authorities and public authorities, the performance of whose functions affect or may affect the performance of those of the authority so as to ensure efficiency and economy in the performance of its functions,

(d) the need for consultation with local authorities and public authorities in appropriate cases,

(e) policies and objectives of the Government or any Minister of the Government in so far as they may affect or relate to its functions.[107]

(2) A local authority shall perform those functions which it is required by law to perform and this section shall not be construed as affecting any such requirement.

(3) Every enactment relating to a function of a local authority shall be construed and have effect subject to the provisions of this section."

This section has the potential to impact on several aspects of the *ultra vires* rule. First, it provides a statutory context by reference to which the reasonableness of any local authority action or inaction may be judged. Thus, to take a particularly strong example, the effective abdication of local authority functions – as happened in *Re Cook* (outlined earlier) – is plainly unreasonable in law in this particular statutory context,[108] since any such authority would be failing to have proper regard to section

---

[107] A roughly analogous duty to keep itself informed of Government policies had already been imposed on An Bord Pleanála by s.5 of the Local Government (Planning and Development) Act 1976.

[108] Although, of course, the protests which gave rise to the litigation in *Re Cook* were perfectly reasonable and legitimate forms of protest by elected members of Belfast City Council.

7(1)(b). Likewise, an authority which engaged in extravagant spending on entertainment[109] or which hazarded the Council's finances by excessive spending on a risky or speculative project[110] might well be said to be acting unreasonably in law by reference to section 7(1)(a).[111] Of course, a local authority which acted in defiance of Government policy and objectives would be acting *ultra vires* section 7(1)(e).[112]

Secondly, section 7(1) might yet have considerable relevance for cases such as *Ward v. McMaster*[113] where a local authority has been sued in respect of the alleged negligent exercise of a statutory function. It may be that, for example, where the authority elects (assuming, of course, that it has a discretion in the matter) for policy reasons not to undertake a particular task (*e.g.* the inspection of a newly constructed house) that it can rely on section 7(1) to justify its stance on the ground that it needs to conserve its resources in order that it may provide other, more essential services. An argument of this kind was very much visible in the slightly different context of the provision of certain services by a health board in *McC v. Eastern Health Board*.[114] In this case, a dramatic and sudden rise in the number of prospective adopters of Chinese infants, coupled with a shortage of suitably trained personnel, meant that the length of time required for a statutory assessment[115] was now more than a year and half. The Supreme Court held that in the circumstances there had been no breach of a statutory duty to carry out the duty "as soon as practicable" and there is here at least a hint in the judgment of Keane J. that a statutory body is not obliged to divert resources in order to deal with sudden and unexpected demands.

Finally, the language of section 7(2) indicates that section 7(1) cannot be prayed in aid to justify an authority from failing to perform its statutory duty,[116] even if section 7(1) can assist in providing a backdrop from which it may be determined whether the body in question has, in fact, breached such a duty.

In addition, even though the local authority may have the legal capacity to do certain acts, its decision may well be flawed by some procedural irregularity or abuse of discretionary power. These general principles of administrative law which apply to all public bodies are explained elsewhere. Thus, a local authority may not abdicate, surrender or contract out of its statutory powers and it must exercise its discretionary powers in good faith[117] and in a reasonable manner.[118]

---

109 As in *R. (Bridgeman) v. Drury* [1894] 2 I.R. 489
110 *cf.* the comments of Lord Templeman in *Hazell v. Hammersmith and Fulham LBC* [1992] 1 A.C. 1 quoted above, n. 106.
111 Or, to put it another way, an authority which did not have regard to the need for efficiency and the effective use of resources would be acting *ultra vires* s.7(1)(a).
112 As in *Glencar Explorations plc v. Mayo C.C.* [1993] 2 I.R. 237 (mining ban included in development plan in defiance of stated Government policy). See also *Keane v. An Bord Pleanála* [1997] 1 I.L.R.M. 508 (planning authority entitled to give planning permission for the construction of large international radio mast when this project represented Government policy and was the subject of an international agreement which had been ratified by the Dáil in accordance with Art. 29.5.2° of the Constitution).
113 [1988] I.R. 337, discussed at pp. 837–841.
114 [1996] 2 I.R. 296.
115 Required by s.8(1) of the Adoption Act 1991 to be conducted "as soon as practicable."
116 *Brady v. Cavan C.C.* [1997] 1 I.L.R.M. 390 at 399, *per* Carroll J.
117 *The State (O'Mahony) v. South Cork Board of Health* (1941) Ir. Jur.Rep. 79; *Limerick Corporation v. Sheridan* (1956) 90 I.L.T.R. 59 and *The State (Divito) v. Arklow U.D.C.* [1986] I.L.R.M. 123.
118 *Limerick Corporation v. Sheridan* (1956) 90 I.L.T.R. 59; *P. and F. Sharpe Ltd v. Dublin County Council* [1989] I.R. 701.

Financial charges and ultra vires

An even stricter attitude is taken towards the question of *ultra vires* where the authority's action involves the imposition of financial charges. If a local authority is vested with a discretionary power, by virtue of the (rebuttable) presumption against the imposition of taxes, charges, etc., it may not lawfully impose a charge as a condition of exercising that power unless this is clearly authorised by statute.[119] While the Local Government (Financial Provisions) (No. 2) Act 1983 sought to provide a comprehensive, contemporary legal basis for such charges, there have been quite a number of decided cases in which such service charges have been found to be *ultra vires* as a result of such a strict construction.[120]

4. The Audit System

A local authority owes a fiduciary duty to its ratepayers,[121] and it seems that a ratepayer may take appropriate action to restrain proposed expenditure which is *ultra vires* the local authority.[122] But the audit system which operates *ex post facto* to expose financial irregularities and surcharges those responsible[123] is an even more effective means of ensuring that local authority finances are strictly controlled.[124] An auditor, known as the local government auditor (usually a fee-earning accountant retained for a few weeks in the financial year), is appointed each year by the Minister for the Environment[125] and the Minister may also decide to hold an extraordinary audit.[126]

The Auditor's jurisdiction

What is the auditor's jurisdiction? His duty is to examine "having regard to the principles and practice of local government audit . . . such accounts as are necessary for the purpose of discharging the duties and functions of the auditor under this Act."[127]

Section 12 of the 1871 Act entitles the auditor to raise a surcharge in respect of payments which are "contrary to law, or which he deems unfounded." The phrase

---

119 *City Brick and Terra Cotta Ltd v. Belfast Corporation* [1958] N.I. 44; *Commissioners of Customs and Excise v. Cure and Deeley Ltd* [1962] 1 Q.B. 340; *McCarthy & Stone (Development) Ltd v. Richmond upon Thames London BC* [1992] 2 A.C. 48 and *The State (Finglas Industrial Estates Ltd) v. Dublin County Council*, unreported, Supreme Court, February 17, 1983.

120 See pp. 227–230.

121 *Prescott v. Birmingham Corporation* [1955] Ch. 210; *Bromley L.B.C. v. Greater London Council* [1983] 1 A.C. 789.

122 *R. (Bridgeman) v. Drury* [1894] 2 I.R. 489; *Arsenal F.C. v. Ende* [1977] A.C. 1. But see *Weir v. Fermanagh County Council* [1913] 1 I.R. 193.

123 County Management Act 1940, s.10.

124 But see the comments of the *Devlin Report* (at para. 25.3.10): "The practice of surcharge should be abolished. Surcharges are rarely upheld on appeal and adequate alternative sanctions exist with which to discipline inefficient local authority officers." On the other hand, however seldom used, (and it will be noticed that many of the authorities cited here are of a venerable age) the existence of the surcharge power is long-established and well known among councillors and officials and will sometimes be a factor of some weight in their calculations.

125 Local Government Act 1941, s.68.

126 Local Government (Ireland) Act 1902, s.21. For an instance of where an extraordinary audit was held to be warranted, see *Asher v. Environment Secretary* [1974] Ch. 208.

127 Local Government (Ireland) Act 1871, s.12 (as amended by the Local Government Act 1994, s.4(2) and Second Schedule).

"contrary to law" clearly deals with *ultra vires* payments,[128] but the phrase "one which he deems unfounded" has given rise to some difficulty. Is the phrase "unfounded" simply a synonym for *ultra vires*, or does it extend to expenditure on the part of the local authority which in the circumstances is "unnecessary and extravagant?" The weight of authority now supports the latter construction, and indeed, the matter can now be regarded as settled. However, some doubts had been created by the observations of Palles C.B. in *R. (Duckett) v. Calvert*[129] to the effect that while the auditor might surcharge councillors for a breach of trust, this must be established in substantive proceedings. In other words, it was only where a court had ruled that the payments were unnecessary and extravagant that the auditor could surcharge on the grounds that such expenditure had been "unfounded." The other pre-independence authorities disputed this view, and it was stated that the auditor was entitled to surcharge not only in the case of *ultra vires* expenditure, but also where the authority had entered into contracts which imposed an unnecessary burden on the ratepayers.

Not surprisingly, given the unsatisfactory nature of these authorities, Davitt P. in *The State (Raftis) v. Leonard*[130] felt he was justified in taking a fresh approach to the interpretation of the section and, in effect, returning to the pre-*Calvert* law. In his view, the purpose of the section was to prevent the ratepayer "from being burdened with expenses for which there was no proper justification." Accordingly, the auditor was entitled to surcharge, not only in respect of *ultra vires* payments, but also payments which are *intra vires*, and which are, in the opinion of the auditor, unfounded, and the judge instanced a payment under an enforceable contract which was wholly unnecessary as an example of expenditure of the latter variety. He conceded that the court might be bound to follow *Calvert* as an authority for the proposition that the payment of a judgment debt cannot be deemed by the auditor to be unfounded,[131] but he did not think that the principle of that case should be further extended.

Section 20 of the Local Government (Ireland) Act 1902 also enables the auditor to impose a charge on any member or officer of a local authority in respect of "any deficiency or loss incurred by his negligence or misconduct." It is now clear that the negligence referred to in the section is the ordinary standard of negligence applied in civil cases and that this need not involve "any element of moral culpability or gross negligence."[132]

---

[128]   *R. (Bridgeman) v. Drury* [1894] 2 I.R. 489; *R. (Ferguson) v. Moore O'Ferrall* [1903] 2 I.R. 141.
[129]   [1898] 2 I.R. 511. Palles C.B. adhered to this view in *R. (King-Kerr) v. Newell* [1903] 2 I.R. 355. A Divisional Court had earlier reached the contrary conclusion in *R. (Inglis) v. Drury* [1898] 2 I.R. 528; and this was affirmed in *R. (Kennedy) v. Browne* [1907] 2 I.R. 505. For a survey, see H.A. Street, *The Law Relating to Local Government* (1955), pp. 1259–1260. See also, *Hazell v. Hammersmith and Fulham D.C.* [1990] 2 W.L.R. 17 at 46–48, *per* Woolf L.J.
[130]   [1960] I.R. 381.
[131]   In *Calvert*, a Divisional Court quashed a surcharge which had been imposed in respect of a street lighting contract. Judgment had been entered against the Council, and although the Court's reasoning was not unanimous, all were agreed that payment of a sum due on a judgment could not be regarded as unnecessary or unfounded.
[132]   *Downey v. O'Brien* [1994] 2 I.L.R.M. 130 at 136, *per* Costello J. In this case it had been alleged that the chairman of harbour commissioners had negligently sold the commissioner's shares in a joint venture company at undervalue. Costello J. said (at 136) that under s.20 of the 1902 Act the

Recent reforms have extended the auditor's remit to include value for money audits. An administrative unit known as the Local Government (Value for Money) Unit has now been established within the Department of the Environment.[133] The unit consists of a number of Departmental officials and local government auditors[134] and the Minister for the Environment may request them to carry out

". . . a study of systems, practices and procedures (including systems, practices and procedures employed outside the State), being a study which they consider will enable them to make recommendations . . . with respect to measures that could be taken to —

(a) secure the provision by local authorities of services in a more economical, efficient and effective manner,

(b) improve the manner in which the local authorities are managed."[135]

Section 15 of the 1997 Act empowers local government auditors to engage in a value for money audit[136]:

"(1) A local government auditor may, in the course of an audit of the accounts of a local authority or at any other time, carry out such examinations as he or she considers appropriate for the purpose of ascertaining —

(a) whether and to what extent the resources of the local authority —
  (i) have been used, and
  (ii) if acquired or disposed of by the local authority, have been so acquired or disposed of,
  effectively and economically, and

(b) whether any such disposal has been effected upon the most favourable terms reasonably obtainable."

By virtue of section 12 of the Local Government (Ireland) Act 1871 a person aggrieved by an auditor's decision has two distinct remedies. First, he may apply to the High Court for an order of statutory certiorari. The High Court's jurisdiction

---

auditor was "required to consider whether the chairman . . . owed a duty of care to the harbour commissioners,the nature of that duty (if it existed), whether it was breached and whether the commissioners thereby suffered loss." See Keane, *op. cit.* above, n.1, pp. 313–314 and *Pentecost v. London District Auditor* [1951] 2 K.B. 759. Note, however, the comments of Carswell J. in *Re Baird* [1989] N.I. 56 at 70 that the standard of proof in surcharge cases should be "high because of the gravity of the accusation and its consequences". See also *Lloyd v. McMahon* [1987] A.C. 56. Perhaps the apparent conflict between *Downey* and *Baird* can be resolved by saying that the onus should be higher where the accusation of impropriety was especially grave. *Cf.* the similar approach to the onus of proof advocated by O'Flaherty J. in the context of statutory disciplinary tribunals in *O'Laoire v. Medical Council*, unreported, Supreme Court, July 27, 1997.

133 Local Government (Financial Provisions) Act 1997, s.14(2). In fact, the unit has been operating since 1993, but s.14 establishes it on a statutory footing: see the comments of the Minister for Environment (Mr. B. Howlin TD) 478 *Dáil Debates* Col. 1021 (April 30, 1997).

134 s.14(3).

135 s.14(4)

136 But there is nothing in the Act linking up these new powers with the auditors long-established sanction surcharge. It seems doubtful therefore, whether he could surcharge anyone who had breached an obligation imposed in the 1997 Act.

in such cases is – in contrast to ordinary certiorari applications – plenary in nature, and is not confined to issues of law, but can also deal wth issues of fact.[137]

If the person aggrieved adopts this first alternative and the surcharge is confirmed by the High Court, then he may apply to the Minister by way of administrative appeal, who is empowered to remit the surcharge "if [he] is of opinion that the circumstances of the case make it fair and equitable that this should be done." The second alternative is that the person aggrieved may apply directly to the Minister to inquire into and to decide upon the lawfulness of the reasons stated by the auditor.[138]

Originally, the councillors were the persons who in law authorised expenditure. And it is the person who authorises an illegal payment who may be surcharged and consequently, formerly, it was the councillors who were surcharged. However, as a result of the establishment of the management system, it is the Manager who authorises the payment and he would have been surcharged had there been no adjustment of the law. Because of the nature of reserved functions, their exercise does not generally lead directly to expenditure, or, at any rate, the expenditure of significant sums. However, it is possible for the elected representatives to take over an executive function via a section 4 motion.[139] Accordingly, section 16 of the City and County Management (Amendment) Act 1955 provides that councillors who vote in favour of a section 4 resolution involving the making of an illegal payment are liable to be surcharged instead of the Manager.[140]

Although in some respects a local government auditor may be compared to a company auditor, his functions are altogether more onerous. Although not bound by any statutory rules of procedure, he must act in an independent manner[141] and he is obliged to give all interested parties a fair hearing, and to give them an opportunity to show why they should not be surcharged.[142] The auditor is entitled to take evidence on oath, and he can also compel the attendance of any person at

---

[137] *R. (King-Kerr) v. Newell* [1903] 2 I.R. 335; *R. (Ferguson) v. Moore O'Ferrall* [1903] 2 I.R. 141; *Walsh v. Minister for Local Government* [1929] I.R. 377 (Murnaghan J. (*dubitante*)); *The State (Raftis) v. Leonard* [1960] I.R. 381. An appeal also lies (by virtue of s.12) to the Minister for the Environment against the making of a surcharge. In *Downey v. O'Brien* [1994] 2 I.L.R.M. 130 Costello J. having referred to the judgments in the *Raftis* case, said (at 135):

"... it is clear (a) that these certiorari proceedings [under s.12 of the 1871 Act] are not an appeal by way of re-hearing but (b) unlike ordinary certiorari proceedings the court may come to a different conclusion on the evidence which was before the auditor and is not confined merely to considering whether there was evidence to support his findings of fact."

[138] Local Government Act 1946, s.68(8).

[139] Local Government (Ireland) Act 1871, s.12.

[140] The City Manager is obliged to inform the members that if they vote in favour of such a resolution that they will be surcharged; and the names of those voting in favour of the resolution are recorded in the minutes: City and County Management (Amendment) Act 1955, s.16(1).

[141] *R. (Local Government Board) v. McLoughlin* [1917] 2 I.R. 174; *The State (Deane & Walsh) v. Moran* (1954) 88 I.L.T.R. 37.

[142] *The State (Dowling) v. Leonard* [1960] I.R. 421; *R. (Butler) v. Browne* [1909] 2 I.R. 333; *R. (Kennedy) v. Browne* [1907] 2 I.R. 505. *Cf.* the comments of Costello J. in *Downey v. O'Brien* [1994] 2 I.L.R.M. 130, 150 where he rejected the suggestion that the surcharge should be quashed on the ground that the auditor had failed to comply with the rules of natural justice:

"[The auditor] took considerable care to inform all the commissioners . . . of his grave concerns at what had happened, that he explained in considerable detail, what, in effect, were the complaints of wrong-doing he was advancing and that he warned each . . . that the possibility of the imposition of a charge could arise. He gave to each an opportunity to answer the complaints and I fail to see how there was any unfairness in the procedures which he adopted."

an extraordinary audit and issue the equivalent of a *subpoena duces tecum* to that person.[143] Nevertheless, the auditor cannot be compelled to turn the audit into a judicial inquiry. In *The State (Deane and Walsh) v. Moran*[144] the applicants objected to the auditor's allowance of certain expenditure on what they claimed were private roads. They contended that the only way in which the matter could have been satisfactorily resolved was if a sworn inquiry had been conducted, with legal representation and an opportunity to cross-examine witnesses. Davitt P. rejected this suggestion. He agreed that the auditor was obliged to act fairly and to give the parties concerned a fair opportunity of making their case, but he stressed that an audit:

> "[W]as primarily and essentially an examination of accounts which was usually conducted by a person whose qualifications were those of an auditor and accountant and not those of a judge. A close examination of the enactments left the impression that it was never intended that such an audit could be turned into something essentially different such as a sworn inquiry or a judicial trial at the mere wish of some interested person, no matter how well intentioned."[145]

5. The Rating System

The annual expenditure for the local government system, in 1996, was £2 billion and its staff totalled 30,000. Until relatively recently the rating system was the principal source of revenue for local authority expenditure. With the passage of the Local Government (Financial Provisions) Act 1978 rates on domestic dwellings were relieved and local authorities came to rely heavily on grants in aid from the Exchequer for financial support. The technique by which this was achieved was that the authority was required "to make an allowance to the [ratepayer] and, accordingly, the rate so made shall be abated."[146] In this way, domestic rates were kept in being, in some conceptual sense, although no domestic rates were actually paid. The reason for this indirect approach was, presumably, because of the use of rateable valuations, in other areas of the law, for instance the status of a ratepayer was formerly important in establishing *locus standi*[147] and the rateable value of a hereditament is significant in determining whether a leaseholder can buy out his freehold under Part II of the Landlord and Tenant (Ground Rents) (No. 2) Act 1978.

However, the Minister for the Environment was obliged to compensate each local authority, at first, by making "a grant equal to the aggregate of the allowances made by the authority." This would have necessarily imposed some pressure on the Central Exchequer because, in general, it is the councillors who fixed the rate in the pound and, hence, it might seem, the amount which the Minister would have to pay.

---

143 Local Government Act 1941, s.68.
144 (1954) 88 I.L.T.R. 37.
145 *Ibid*. at 43.
146 Local Government (Financial Provisions) Act 1978, s.3.
147 The 1978 Act makes express provision for this, as s.17 provides: "A person shall not be regarded as not being a ratepayer within the meaning, or for the purposes, of any enactment by reason only of the making to him of an allowance under this Act."

This in turn would have tended to encourage local authorities to spend freely since they were in large measure absolved (with the exception of business rates which are fixed at the same rate as domestic rates) from the obligation to answer to their local electorates for large rate bills. To meet this possible danger, section 10 of the Local Government (Financial Provisions) Act 1978 empowered the Minister, with the consent of the Minister for Finance, to issue directions to rating authorities fixing limits upon their expenditure estimates and/or the rate in the pound. During the 1978–1983 period the Minister fixed the rate in the pound via the mechanism of circulars specifying the maximum permissible percentage increase at a percentage invariably less than the rate of inflation. Then, by section 9 of the Local Government (Financial Provisions) (No. 2) Act 1983, the Minister's obligation to compensate local authorities for the rates foregone was substantially modified. The compensation (originally called the rate relief grant and then the "rate support grant") no longer equalled the amounts notionally refunded; rather, it was required not to exceed that figure. This obligation was further modified by section 46(1) of the Local Government Act 1994 which substitutes the following bleak subsection for section 9(1) of the 1978 Act.[148] "The Minister shall in relation to a local financial year out of moneys provided by the Oireachtas make a grant to a rating authority."

It will be seen that the new version of section 9 was even further removed from the notion of compensation consequent upon the removal of domestic rates. Naturally, in view of these changes, since 1983 it has not been necessary for the Minister to use the other controls.[149] Eventually, section 9 of the 1978 Act, in whatever form, was terminated by the Local Government (Financial Provisions) Act 1997, sections 3 and 18, which assign motor tax revenue to local authorities.

A second severe – and, perhaps, fatal – blow to the viability of the present rating system came with the decision of the Supreme Court in *Brennan v. Attorney General*[150] where it held that the system of collecting rates on agricultural land was unconstitutional. The Court observed that the method of collecting rates contained in section 11 of the Local Government Act 1941 was based on the anomalous Griffiths poor law valuation of agricultural land in 1852 and that the use of such an outdated system combined with the absence of any effective review mechanism constituted, in the circumstances, an unjust attack on the plaintiff's property rights. However, the anomalies do not exist to the same extent in the case of non-agricultural land, not least now because of the possibility of an appeal to the new

---

[148] As inserted by s.9 of the Local Government (Financial Provisions) (No.2) Act, 1983.

[149] Note, however, that by virtue of s.10A of the City and County Management (Amendment) Act 1955 (as inserted by s.44 of the Local Government Act 1994) if the Minister is of opinion that any estimate of expenses is "insufficient to defray the expenses to be incurred by the authority in that financial year" in:

"(a) maintaining at a reasonable standard the public service for the maintenance of which the local authority is responsible, and

(b) paying to any other body any sums which the local authority are bound to supply to that body, the Minister may by notification in writing require the local authority, by resolution to revoke or to amend, whether by addition, omission or variation, the estimate of expenses, including a rate in the pound and any charges determined in accordance with such estimate of expenses."

The local authority is bound to comply with this requirement and the members of the authority may be removed for failure to comply with the requirement: see s.10A(2) of the 1955 Act.

[150] [1984] I.L.R.M. 355.

Valuation Tribunal, established by the Valuation Act 1988. The net result is that the only type of rates remaining are those on business premises.

Business Rates

As regards these business rates, as far as urban houses and buildings are concerned, the valuation was originally based upon "an estimate of the net annual value thereof."[151] These valuations are also based on the Griffiths valuation survey, and they bear scant relation to present letting values. However, unlike the position which formerly existed in relation to agricultural land, the valuations can be revised in various ways. First, there is the possibility of a general revision.[152] Secondly, each clerk of a local authority may send to the Commissioner of Valuation a list of specific items of property for revision.[153] But by far the most important method of revision or creating new valuations is that provided for by section 3 of the Valuation Act 1988.[154] Section 3(1) states that:

> "An owner or any occupier of property, the rating authority or an officer of the Commissioner of Valuation may apply at any time for a revision of the valuation of any property entered in the Valuation Lists or for the inclusion of any property not so entered."[155]

Section 3(2) of the 1988 Act contemplates that such applications shall be made in the first instance to the rating authority who, in turn, will forward them on a monthly basis to the Commissioner of Valuation. The Commissioner is then obliged to determine the application within six months after receiving the application or "as soon as may be thereafter." The owner and occupier of the property may then appeal on an informal basis (known as a "first appeal")[156] against the decision of the Commisioner under sections 19, 20 and 31 of the Valuation (Ireland) Act 1852. The

---

151 But *cf.* the comments contained in the White Paper, *Local Finance and Taxation* (1972, Prl. 2745), para. 51.2: "The defects in the system have given rise to inequities which have become more pronounced with the passage of time and have been aggravated by the constant and substantial increases in rate poundages." See de Buitléir, *Problems of Irish Local Finance* (Dublin, 1974), pp. 9–16.

152 Valuation (Ireland) Act 1852, s.11.

153 Under s.34 of the Valuation (Ireland) Act 1852, a County Council may apply to the Minister for the Environment for a general revision of lands in the county, but no such valuation has ever been carried out. By virtue of s.65 of the Local Government (Ireland) Act 1898 the Corporations of the cities of Dublin, Cork, Limerick and Waterford may apply for a general revision of 14 years. Dublin City was revalued in 1908–1915 and Waterford in 1924–1926. See de Buitléir, *op. cit.* above, n. 148, pp. 11–12.

154 See Ó Caoimh (1988) I.C.L.S.A. 2–01.

155 It would, perhaps, have been preferable had the 1988 Act abolished the other methods of obtaining a valuation revision. For example, section 3(1) would seem to have overtaken the second method just referred to (sending by local authority clerk a list of specific items of property for revision) but section 4 of the Valuation (Ireland) Act 1854 which provided for this procedure has not been formally repealed. It is true that section 3(7) appears to contemplate some form of implied repeal of older statutory procedures in that it declares that this section shall have effect "notwithstanding" anything to the contrary in the Valuation Acts, but this formula seems awkward and much less desirable than that of express repeal.

156 The operation of this informal "first appeal" system has been described by O'Connor as follows: see "Rating Valuation in Ireland – The Appeal System" (1993) 87 G.I.L.S.I. 317:

> "At this first appeal stage there is no formal hearing. The Commissioner appoints a valuer other than the person who made the original valuation to inspect and report on the property. In arriving

Commissioner then directs that a valuer who has not previously been employed in making the original valuation to inspect the hereditament and investigate the complaint and report to him. This method of appeal has been described in the following terms: "The 'first appeal' is normally informal and usually involves a fresh survey of the property in question by a valuer, referred to as the 'appeal valuer,' who reports on his findings to the Commissioner of Valuation."[157]

There is a further possibility of appeal in that the owner/occupier may appeal within a further 28 days to the Valuation Tribunal and the notice of appeal must contain particulars of the valuation and a "statement of the specific grounds of appeal." Section 3(5)(c) provides that the Tribunal shall then:

> "[T]ransmit a copy of every notice received by it to the Commissioner of Valuation (who shall be respondent in and entitled to be heard and adduce evidence at the hearing of, the appeal concerned), to the rating authority or authorities concerned and to any other person appearing to the Tribunal to be directly affected by the determination and any such person shall be entitled to be heard and to adduce evidence at the hearing of the appeal."[158]

A further appeal lies by section 5 on a point of law by way of case stated[159] to the High Court which has extensive powers "to reverse, affirm or amend the determination in respect of which the case has been stated." The High Court has also power to "remit the matter to the Tribunal with the opinion of the Court thereon, or make such other order in relation to the matter as the Court thinks fit." However, a party wishing to appeal by way of case stated is required by section 5(1) "immediately after the determination of an appeal by the Tribunal" to "declare his dissatisfaction to the Tribunal."[160] In *Siuicre Éireann CPT v. Commissioner of Valuation*[161] McCarthy J. said that he "wholly agreed" with this conclusion and that "it would

---

at his decision the Commissioner considers submissions from the appellant, the report of the 'appeal valuer', other studies on economic trends, market conditions or regional developments and the relevant case-law. About 90% of the appeals are finalised at this stage and at minimum expense to the appellant apart from [a small] appeal fee."

[157] Ó Caoimh, *op. cit.*, above, n.151, 2–05.

[158] The Tribunal's procedures are regulated by the Valuation Act 1988 (Appeal) Rules 1988 (S.I. No. of 1988).

[159] Dissatisfaction with the termination of the appeal must be expressed "immediately after the determination" of any appeal by the Tribunal: s.5(1). This provision appears to be modelled on s.428(1) of the Income Tax Act 1967 (now Taxes Consolidation Act 1997, s. 941). In *The State (Multi-Print Labels Ltd) v. Neylon* [1984] I.L.R.M. 545 Finlay P. held that the similar provisions of s.428(1) of the 1967 Act were not mandatory and, moreover, should not be given "the extraordinarily strict meaning which would involve an expression of dissatisfaction at the conclusion of the actual hearing."

[160] Section 5 is modelled on sections 22 and 23 of the 1852 Act (which allowed an appeal from the Commissioner to the Circuit Court) and section 10 and 11 of the Valuation (Ireland) Act 1860 (which permitted a further appeal by way of case stated to the High Court). These provisions of the 1852 and 1860 Acts could have – and should have – been repealed without any loss by the Valuation Act 1988, but these old statutory procedures remain and may still be used as an alternative to the new appeal procedures under section 5 of the 1988 Act. Nevertheless, the old procedures provide a guide as to how the High Court's powers under section 5 will be interpreted. Thus, in *Pfizer Chemical Corporation v. Commissioner of Valuation (No.2)* unreported, High Court, May 9, 1989. Costello J. said, of the power to reverse, confirm or amend conferred on the High Court by section 11 of the 1860 Act, that it "could not have been wider" and that it clearly extended to the power "to amend an error in the valuation lists." This reasoning will presumably apply, *mutatis mutandis*, to appeals under section 5 of the 1988 Act.

[161] [1992] I.L.R.M. 682 at 688.

be absurd if a court empowered to review the validity of the Commissioner's assessment were unable to make it good."

It is also essential as far as section 5 appeals are concerned, that the case stated should set out the facts as found by the Valuation Tribunal. This point was made by Blayney J. in *Mitchelstown Co-operative Agricultural Society Ltd v. Commissioner of Valuation*[162] which was the first appeal under the 1988 Act. Here the Tribunal had simply annexed the entire transcript of the evidence to the case stated, but there was no "clear statement of the facts" as found by the Tribunal. Blayney J. ruled that this was not an acceptable form of case stated:

> "There must be a finding of fact based on evidence. There is no finding in the case. Furthermore, it is the case that the facts must be found and stated. This Court should not be required to go outside the case stated to some other document in order to discover them."[163]

Apart from the appellate procedures provided for by the 1988 Act and the older statutory appeal mechanisms, an appeal also lies against the "making of the rate" (i.e., the fixing of the actual amount to be paid by the occupier of a hereditament which is simply the product of the rateable value and the rate in the pound)[164] and thus it is open to the Commissioner of Valuation to hold that any persons have been wrongly included or excluded from the rate, or that the rate itself is illegal. A rate may also be quashed on certiorari,[165] but a ratepayer who fails to avail of the statutory procedures to correct the determination of the Commissioner, will be later estopped from doing so.[166] A local authority is empowered to amend the rates "so as to make them conform with the enactments relating thereto."[167]

Method of valuation

The principal method of valuing units of property (upon which the assessment of rates is then based) is now contained in the Valuation Acts 1852–1988, but – in a manner characteristic of the needless intricacies[168] of the rating code – this cannot be fully understood without reference to the provisions of section 64 of the Poor Relief (Ireland) Act 1838. This section provided for a uniform method of valuation

---

162 [1989] I.R. 210.
163 *Ibid.* at 212.
164 Poor Relief (Ireland) Act 1838, ss.106–112, as amended by Valuation (Ireland) Act 1852, s.28 and ss.22, 23, 29 and 30 of the Poor Relief (Ireland) Act 1849.
165 *R. (McEvoy) v. Dublin Corporation* (1878) 2 L.R. Ir. 371.
166 *Whaley v. Great Northern Ry. Co.* [1913] 2 I.R. 142; *Stevenson v. Orr* [1916] 2 I.R. 619. But this estoppel does not apply to entries which are *ultra vires: Dublin Corporation v. Dublin Cemeteries Committee,* unreported, Supreme Court, November 12, 1975.
167 Local Government Act 1941, s.60. This power means that a local authority can, *inter alia*, rectify the register of ratepayers in order to correct misdescriptions and omissions and alter changes in occupation of rateable property.
168 Thus, Costello J. could comment in *Pfizer Chemical Corporation v. Commissioner of Valuation (No. 2)*, unreported, High Court, May 9, 1989 (at p. 19 of the judgment): "The rating and valuation code is a confusing mosaic of partly repealed and imperfectly drafted Victorian statutes encrusted with a century and a half's judicial decisions. It should long ago have been repealed and modernised." These views were approved by Egan J. in *Denis Coakley & Co. Ltd v. Commissioner of Valuation* [1996] 1 I.L.R.M. 90 who also observed that many of the judicial decisions in question are inconsistent with each other.

of rateable hereditaments (known as the "hypothetical rent" basis) and stated that every rate shall be:

> "[A] poundage rate made upon the estimate of the net annual value of the several hereditaments rated thereunto; that is to say, of the rent at which one year with another the same might in their actual state be reasonably expected to let from year to year, the probable average cost of the repairs, insurance and other expenses, if any, necessary to maintain the hereditaments in their actual state, and all rates, taxes and public charges, if any being paid by the tenant."

Section 11 of the Valuation (Ireland) Act 1852 effected changes in the method of assessing the rates for certain types of rateable hereditaments. Henceforth land was to be valued having regard to the "net annual value thereof" with reference to the average price of certain types of agricultural produce.[169] The reference to "land" in section 11 of the 1852 Act was held by the Supreme Court in *Roadstone Ltd v. Commissioner of Valuation*[170] to refer only to land that had preserved its original pastoral or agricultural nature. Land used for business, commercial or manufacturing purposes was not valued on the agricultural price basis of section 11 of the 1852 Act, but was instead valued by reference to the hypothetical rent basis of section 64 of the 1838 Act. "Houses and buildings" were to be valued on the same "hypothetical rent" basis as heretofore, save that now section 11 required that every tenement or rateable hereditament must be separately valued. This has been held to mean that: "[T]he characteristic of a tenement to be separately valued, is a tenement, all of which is under the occupation of the same occupier, under the same immediate lessor, under one contract of tenancy."[171] Thus, in *Coal Distributors Ltd v. Commissioner of Valuation*[172] Blayney J. held that the Commissioner was wrong in not valuing separately two separate lots of property held under different titles by the same occupier.

How is the hypothetical rent to be arrived at? A good recent example of where this issue was considered is provided by the judgment of Barron J. in *Rosses Point Hotel Co. Ltd v. Commissioner of Valuation*.[173] Here the plaintiff company ran a

---

[169] While the net annual value remains the statutory method of calculation, in practice, certain "rules of thumb" are employed to arrive at this figure. As O'Connor, *op. cit.* above, n. 156, has explained (at 317): "The net annual value is derived mainly from the annual rent but other methods are sometimes used either as a cross-check on rental figures or as a substitute when rental information is not readily available. Examples are (a) the contractors' basis which estimates the capital cost of providing a premises allowing for depreciation and obsolescence and (b) the profits method which assesses its profit earning capacity. The theory is that those figures determine the rent which a hypothetical tenant would offer the tenant for the premises in its present state. In the absence of a revaluation the net annual value is then reduced by a specified factor to maintain relativities with the rateable values of similar properties. The factor in use in the Greater Dublin area is 0.63% which is based on pilot studies of relationships between current rents and rateable valuations in selected areas in Dublin as at November 1988. For example, if the net annual value calculated on a current rent is £50,000, the rateable valuation is £50,000 x 0.63/100 = £315."

[170] [1961] I.R. 239.

[171] *Switzer & Co. v. Commissioner of Valuation* [1902] 2 I.R. 275 at 281, *per* Palles CB. See also *R & H Hall Plc v. Commissioner for Valuation*, unreported, High Court, November 16, 1994. In *Nixon v. Commissioner of Valuation* [1980] I.R. 340 at 345 Henchy J. said that the idea that "if a rated occupier erects a new building on the tenement it becomes a separate rateable tenement is unsupported by statute or practice."

[172] [1989] I.R. 472.

[173] [1987] I.L.R.M. 512.

hotel which was initially successful, but then encountered financial problems due to the then unfavourable economic and financial climate. The Circuit Court held that these factors could not be relied upon in order to reduce the valuation of the hotel property where the intrinsic value of the hotel property remained the same, but Barron J. held that this ruling was incorrect in law:

> "Profit earning ability is the basic element in determining the net annual value. It is based not on actual profits but on what the prospective tenant would anticipate would be his profits. Again, it is not the termination or curtailment of the business or an identifiable part of the business which will justify a reduction in the valuation. It is the effect which such cesser or curtailment will have on the prospective tenant which is material."[174]

On the other hand the courts will have regard to the variety of different uses to which the property may be put in that in determining the hypothetical tenant envisaged by the section "one must look to all possible tenants."[175] Thus, in *Waterford Crystal Ltd v. Commissioner of Valuation*[176] Costello P. held that the Valuation Tribunal erred in law in making allowances in the course of determining the hypothetical rent for the obsolescent character of certain parts of the appellant's plant. That approach would have been correct had the plant been a specialised one and not capable of any other use. However, since the Tribunal had made a specific finding that this part of the plant was not a specialised plant "and that the buildings . . . are conventional in construction and are capable of use other than for the manufacture of crystal", it followed that the Tribunal had erred in law as it "only took into account as a hypothetical tenant a crystal manufacturer" and thereby "failed to have regard to the existence in addition of other hypothetical tenants who would use the entire premises . . . for other manufacturing purposes".[177]

Because of the difficulties which obtained prior to the passage of the Valuation Act 1988 of ensuring that the majority of valuations were up to date, a practice had evolved from about 1947 of fixing the valuation at about one-third of the net rental value and of giving revised valuations broadly in line with the general run of figures for similar properties in the areas involved. This practice had no statutory foundation and was held to be illegal, on at least two occasions[178] by the High Court. In response, section 5(1) of the Valuation Act 1986 now provides that the amount of a valuation may be reduced by such amount as is necessary to ensure, in so far as it is reasonably practicable, that:

> "[T]he amount of the valuation bears the same relationship to the valuations of other tenements and rateable hereditaments as the net annual value of the

---

[174] *Ibid.* at 515–516.
[175] *R v. School Board for London* 17 Q.B.D. 738 at 740, *per* Lord Esher M.R.
[176] Unreported, High Court, December 10, 1996.
[177] See also *Iarnród Éireann v. Commissioner of Valuation*, unreported, High Court, November 27, 1992 where Barron J. said the concourse at a passenger terminal was rateable on a hypothetical rent basis, adding that: "If, as a matter of fact, there is a hypothetical tenant who would be prepared to pay rent for such premises, then the hereditament must be valued appropriately. Otherwise, it would have a nil valuation."
[178] *Scholfield v. Commissioner of Valuation*, unreported, High Court, July 24, 1972; *Munster & Leinster Bank Ltd v. Commissioner of Valuation* [1979] I.L.R.M. 246.

tenement bears to the net annual values of the other tenements or rateable hereditaments."

By way of a further exception to section 11 of the 1852 Act, a special regime for the valuation of "public utility undertakings" (including those belonging to the Electricity Supply Board, Bord Telecom Éireann, Bord Gáis Éireann and piped television networks) on a global basis was established by section 4 of the Valuation Act 1988. Section 4 allows the Minister for the Environment to order that certain types of public utility undertakings shall henceforth be valued on a global valuation basis. The net annual value of such property is deemed to be 5 per cent of the effective capital value of the undertaking.

Rateable hereditaments

Section 61 of the Poor Relief (Ireland) Act 1838 Act provides that rates are to be levied on the "occupier"[179] of "rateable hereditaments."[180] The property must be beneficially occupied[181] and property in the occupation of the general public will, accordingly, be held not to be rateable. The word "occupier" has, however, been given a special extended meaning by virtue of sections 14 and 23 of the Local Government Act 1946 and the term now includes the owner of the building where

---

[179] Defined by s.124 of the 1838 Act as including "every person in the immediate use or enjoyment of any hereditaments rateable under this Act, whether corporeal or incorporeal . . . " In *Dublin County Council v. Westlink Toll Bridge Ltd* [1996] 1 I.R. 487 at 497 O'Flaherty J. said that the rateability attached to "the occupier of the hereditament rather than the beneficiary of the profit or use derived from the hereditament." See also *Dublin Corporation v. Dublin Cemetries Committee*, unreported, Supreme Court, November 12, 1975.

[180] Where the property (be it corporeal or incorporeal) is "annexed or physically complementary to rateable property" it is also regarded as rateable: see *Dublin Corporation v. Dublin Port and Docks Board* [1978] I.R. 241 at 266, *per* Henchy J. In that case certain transit sheds were held to be "islands in a sea of unrateability", distinct and separate from any rateable hereditament and, hence, not rateable. This distinction is valid so far as it goes, but there seems to be no reason why the sheds should not have been rateable in their own right as separate hereditaments. For further criticism of this case, see Keane, *op.cit.* above, n.1, pp. 287–288. In *Dublin County Council v. Westlink Toll Bridge Ltd* [1994] 1 I.R. 77 at 83–84 (affirmed by the Supreme Court, [1996] 1 I.R. 487) Geoghegan J. rejected the argument that tolls and toll offices should not be regarded as rateable on the ground that they were merely ancillary to a non-rateable hereditament, namely, a public road:
"[T]he tolls are in the nature of a very specific property right vested for thirty years in the defendant and should properly be regarded as a separately privately occupied incorporeal hereditament. The corporeal hereditament in the form of toll offices, store and car parks are also in my view *prima facie* rateable as being ancilliary to the tolls rather than to the public road."

[181] This does not mean that the occupier must derive a pecuniary profit therefrom. In *Sinnott v. Neale* (1948) Ir. Jur. Rep. 10 the owner of an uninhabited island which was used solely as a bird sanctuary was held to be in rateable occupation.

[182] The test as regards occupancy is the *de facto* position, and, accordingly, mere licensees or even trespassers may be liable for rates if they have the unrestricted use and enjoyment of the hereditament: see *Carroll v. Mayo County Council* [1967] I.R. 364. However, in *Aer Rianta CPT v. Commissioner of Valuation*, unreported, Supreme Court, November 6, 1996 Murphy J. held that a oil company which had entered into an agreement with the Minister for Transport to manage a fuel depot at Shannon Airport as his agents were simply providing a "service function" for the depot, so that in these special circumstances they were not thus in rateable occupation. Note also the comments of Geoghegan J. in the High Court *Dublin County Council v. Westlink Toll Bridge Ltd* [1994] 1 I.R. 77 at 83 to the effect that the defendants were in "paramount ocupation" of the rateable hereditament (a toll-bridge) and not merely as an agent for the local authority "as would be so, for instance. in the case of a caretaker."

it is unoccupied.[182] These sections also provide for rebates where the building is unoccupied because of the execution of repairs, alterations or additions[183] or where the owner is bona fide unable to find a tenant at a reasonable rent. The occupation of the hereditament must be permanent and not merely transitory in nature.[184] Property which is in occupation of the general public is not rateable.[185]

Section 12 of the Valuation (Ireland) Act 1852 set out a list of the character of hereditaments which were to be rateable for the purposes of the Act:

> "[A]ll lands, buildings, and opened mines; all commons and rights of commons to be had, received or taken out of any land; all rights of fishery; all canals, navigations and rights of navigation; and rights of way and other rights or easements over land and the tolls levied in respect of such rights and easements, and all other tolls."

In essence, to qualify as a rateable hereditament under this section, the right in question must be one which is in the nature of a right or easement over land. This emerges from *Telecom Éireann v. Commissioner of Valuation*[186] where the installation of telephone apparatus in a shopping centre was held not to constitute a rateable hereditament. As Barrington J. explained, the right in question was really in the nature of a "licence to place pieces of personal property on another man's land" but did not create "any right or easement over land of the kind contemplated by the 1838 Act."[187]

Section 14 of the 1852 Act provided that no hereditament was liable to be rated in respect of any increase in value arising from "any drainage, reclamation or embankment from the sea or any lake or river" or any "erection of farm, outhouse or office buildings or any permanent agricultural improvement."[188] A further important

---

183 This includes the demolition of the premises: see *Carlisle Trust Ltd v. Commissioner of Valuation* [1965] I.R. 456.

184 Keane, *op. cit.* above, n.1, pp. 283–286. In *Telecom Éireann v. Commissioner for Valuation* [1994] 1 I.R. 66 O'Hanlon J. said (at 71) that the "essential ingredients of rateable occupation" were that it must be:

> "(1) Exclusive, in the sense that the person using the hereditament can prevent any other person from using it in the same way;
> (2) Of value or benefit to the occupier, but not necessarily of financial benefit;
> (3) Not for too transient a period."

While O'Hanlon J.'s conclusion in respect of the particular facts was reversed on appeal by the Supreme Court [1998] 1 I.L.R.M. 64, the principles he enunciated remain nonetheless valid. In *Dublin County Council v. Westlink Toll Bridge Ltd* [1994] 1 I.R. 77 Geoghegan J. applied similar principles when he held that an agreement where the builders of a public bridge and toll road received the benefit of the tolls for thirty years meant that the defendants were in rateable occupation of the tolls and the ancilliary buildings. See also *Iarnrod Éireann v. Commissioner of Valuation*, unreported, High Court, November 27, 1992 (Iarnrod Eireann held to be rateable occupier of passenger terminal by reference to the above three criteria).

185 *Lambeth Overseers v. London County Council* [1897] A.C. 625 at 629 *per* Lord Halsbury L.C., quoted with approval by O'Keeffe P. in *Dublin Corporation v. Port and Docks Board* [1978] I.R. 241 at 258.

186 [1998] 1 I.L.R.M. 64.

187 But it may be argued that the right to install equipment of this kind could at least in some circumstances amount to some form of proprietorial rights, as opposed to being classified as being a mere licence.

188 See *Nixon v. Commissioner of Valuation* [1980] I.R. 340 (poultry houses rank as "farm buildings"); *Commissioner of Valuation v. International Mushrooms Ltd* [1994] 3 I.R. 472 (building in an industrial estate used for the production of mushroom spawn was not a farm building for this purpose, since the legislative object had been to ensure agricultural lands which had been improved by the carrying out of the specified works should not attract an increased valuation as a result).

rating exemption was provided by section 7 of the Annual Revision of Rateable Property (Ireland) (Amendment) Act 1860 which provides that in making the valuation of any "manufactory" or building erected or used for such purpose, the Commissioner shall not take into account the value of any "machinery" therein, save only such as shall have been erected and used for the purpose of motive power. This exemption had received generous judicial interpretation in a series of cases in the last two decades and this judicial trend is, perhaps, best exemplified by the judgment of the Supreme Court in *Beamish and Crawford Ltd v. Commissioner of Valuation.*[189] Here the question was whether certain fermentation and conditioning tanks used by the appellants in the brewing process constituted "machinery" within the meaning of section 7 of the 1860 Act and, hence, exempt from rating liability. O'Higgins C.J. answered in the affirmative, saying that the word "machine" within the meaning of section 7:

> "[C]onnotes apparatus by means of which force is applied, modified or used by mechanical means for a specific purpose, whether such apparatus is moving or fixed, and that in determining whether the apparatus so qualifies as a machine or machinery the components should not be regarded separately or piecemeal but as integral parts of the process in which they are used."[190]

This reasoning was followed in a series of cases and had the effect of greatly extending the scope of section 7 beyond that which had previously been thought to be the case. Thus, in *Pfizer Chemical Corporation v. Commissioner of Valuation (No.1)*[191] Costello J. held that "thickener tanks" (which were part of the manufacturing process by which dolomite rock was converted into magnesium) were "machinery" and Barrington J. held in *Mitchelstown Co-operative Agricultural Society Ltd v. Commissioner of Valuation*[192] that a grain bin used for the conversion of barley into malting barley was "machinery" and was not a "building" for the purposes of the Valuation Acts. A similar view was taken by the Supreme Court in *Siúicre Éireann Cpt v. Commissioner of Valuation*[193] where McCarthy J. held that heavy fuel tanks used for the process of manufacture in the plant were "machinery."

The general thrust of the Valuation Act 1986 was to restore the status quo which existed prior to this series of decisions.[194] Sections 2 and 3 of the 1986 Act stipulate

---

[189] [1980] I.L.R.M. 149.

[190] *Ibid.* at 151. See also *Denis Coakley & Co. Ltd v Commissioner of Valuation*, unreported, Supreme Court, November 7, 1995 (bins forming the grain silos required agitation as part of the manufacturing process and, *per* Egan J., "ought justly be described as 'machinery' for the purposes of ss. 10 and 11 of the 1860 Act.")

[191] Unreported, High Court, July 31, 1984.

[192] [1989] I.R. 210.

[193] [1992] I.L.R.M. 682.

[194] As Keane J. observed in *Commissioner of Valuation v. International Mushrooms Ltd* [1994] 3 I.R. 472 at 480:

> " . . . the object of the Oireachtas in enacting ss. 2 and 3 of the Act of 1986 was not to afford an exemption to 'buildings' which had hitherto been rateable hereditaments. It was to extend the categories of fixed property deemed to be rateable hereditaments so as to include the five categories set out at the reference numbers in the schedule."

Earlier in his judgment, Keane J. had instanced the fact that reference No. 1 in the schedule referred to "constructions", thus extending the category of rateable hereditaments to structures which were not "buildings" in the special sense in which that provision of the s.12 of the 1852 Act had been interpreted in *Cement Ltd v. Commissioner of Valuation* [1960] I.R. 283.

that certain categories of fixed property are to be deemed to be rateable hereditaments.[195] The Schedule referred to in these provisions is as follows:

"1. All constructions affixed to lands or tenements, other than buildings referred to in section 14 of this Act.

2. All lands developed for any purpose other than agriculture, horticulture, forestry or sport, irrespective of whether the land is surfaced, and including any constructions affixed thereto which pertain to the development.

3. All cables, pipelines and conduits (whether undergound, on the surface or overhead) and including all pylons, supports and other constructions which pertain to them.

4. All fixed moorings, piers and docks.

5. Plant falling within any of the categories of plant specified in the Schedule to the Annual Revision of Rateable Property (Ireland) Amendment Act, 1860 (inserted by the *Valuation Act 1986*)."

But even these apparently straightforward provisions have given rise to potential difficulties. Thus, in *Commissioner of Valuation v. International Mushrooms Ltd*,[196] the respondent used premises in an industrial estate for the production of mushroom spawn, from which mushrooms were ultimately cultivated elsewhere. Keane J. held that as the buildings in question came within the definition of "buildings" under section12 of the 1852 Act,[197] the Valuation Tribunal did not have to look any further and, in particular, did not have to consider the schedule specified in section 3 of the 1986 Act, with its exemption for agricultural and horticultural constructions. In other words, if a hereditament satisfies the confined definition of "buildings" laid down in *Cement Ltd v. Commissioner of Valuation*,[198] *it is rateable on that basis*. It is only where a hereditment does not so qualify as a "building", but is properly regarded as a "construction" for the purposes of the 1986 Act that the section 3 schedule will come into play. Thus, a tennis club housing indoor tennis courts would be rateable as a 'building" under section 12 of the 1852 Act. On the other hand, an all-weather outdoor tennis court would not be so regarded as a "building" for this purpose. It would, however, qualify as a "construction" within the meaning of reference No.2 to section 3 of the 1986 Act's schedule which could claim the benefit of the exemption for sport contained therein.

A similar problem was identified by the Supreme Court in *Trustees of Kinsale Yacht Club Ltd v. Commissioner of Valuation*.[199] Here Finlay C.J. held that a yachting marina was rateable as a "fixed mooring" in reference No. 4 to section 3. Despite

---

[195] Section 3(2) purports to give the Minister for Finance power to vary or amend the schedule, but the constitutionality of this is doubtful having regard to the jurisprudence on Article 15.2.1° (see pp. 12–15). It would be also open to the objection that it allowed the executive to determine what (in effect) is a form of tax liability by ministerial order: see Horgan and Whyte, *Kelly, The Irish Constitution* (1994, 3rd ed.), pp. 173–175.

[196] [1994] 3 I.R. 472.

[197] Despite the fact that the buildings were used for agricultural purposes, they did not benefit from the exemption for farm buildings within the meaning of s.14 of the 1852 Act, as (at 478) the buildings in question "could not be regarded as buildings on a farm which are used in connection with farming operations."

[198] [1960] I.R. 283.

[199] [1994] 1 I.L.R.M. 457.

the fact that the mooring was developed for sporting purposes, it did not qualify under reference No. 2, since this did not constitute a development of lands. However, Finlay C.J. also accepted that there was an "apparent inconsistency" between Nos.1 and 2 in the Schedule and hinted that if constructions attached to lands which prima facie fell within No. 1 were nonethless capable of being exempted under No. 2, the Court would lean against rateability where this would constitute "an unfair creation of a fresh imposition of liability by the use of oblique or slack language."[200]

The new section 7 of the 1860 Act (as inserted by section 7(1) of the 1986 Act) now provides as follows:

> "(a) In making the valuation of any mill or manufactory or any building used or erected for any such purpose, the Commissioner of Valuation shall in each case value the water or other motive power thereof, but shall not take into account the value of any machinery therein, save only such as shall be erected and used for production of motive power.
>
> (b) For the purposes of this subsection, machinery erected and used for the production of motive power includes electrical power connections."

The 1986 Act also took the opportunity to include certain categories of fixed property within the scope of the valuation code. Section 7(2) refers to certain items of fixed property contained in a schedule to the Act (such as car-parks, furnaces,[201] ovens and reservoirs) so as to ensure that they are to be valued and are rateable. The schedule also seeks to re-define the rateability of certain industrial plant by providing as follows:

> "All constructions affixed to the premises comprising a mill, manufactory or building (whether on or below the ground) and used for the containment of a substance or for the transmission of a substance or electric current, including any such constructions which are designed or used primarily for storage or containment (whether or not the purpose of such containment is to allow a natural or a chemical process to take place), but excluding any such constructions which are designed or used primarily to induce a process of change in the substance contained or transmitted."[202]

The effect of these statutory changes is to permit the Commissioner of Valuation to continue to value most kinds of industrial plant as if it were not "machinery" for the purposes of section 7 of the 1860 Act, some earlier judicial decisions to the contrary notwithstanding.

---

[200] *Ibid.* at 463, applying the principles identified by Henchy J. in *Inspector of Taxes v. Kiernan* [1981] I.R. 117.

[201] Provided, of course, that the ovens are genuinely fixed plant within the meaning of s.1(2)(a) of the 1986 Act so that they were "so attached or secured to or integrated with the premises . . . as to be of a permanent or semi-permanent nature." In *PWA International Ltd . v. Commissioner of Valuation*, unreported, High Court, July 26, 1996 Carroll J. held that there was evidence on which the Valuation Tribunal could properly conclude that ovens "bolted to the floor for stability", but capable of being relocated, were not fixed plant for this purpose.

[202] Where industrial tanks, etc., are prima facie rateable as "plant" the onus of proof is on the ratepayer to establish that it comes within the exclusion clause ("designed or used primarily to induce a process of change in the substance contained"): *Caribmolasses Ltd v. Commissioner of Valuation* [1994] 3 I.R. 189 at 196, *per* Blayney J.

Exemptions for charitable or public purposes

Hereditaments, which would otherwise be rateable, are exempt if they are used for charitable or public purposes. However, the subject of rating exemption "is one of considerable difficulty and obscurity, even by the standards of our law of local government"[203] and much of the difficulty has been caused by the diverging views as to what is the appropriate statutory basis for the exemption. Apart from certain specific statutory exceptions in favour of domestic dwellings[204] and secondary schools and community halls,[205] the principal statutory basis is contained in the proviso to the Poor Relief (Ireland) Act 1838 which exempts buildings used "exclusively for religious worship, or for the education of the poor, cemeteries, burial grounds and hospitals or other buildings used exclusively for charitable or public purposes." It might have been supposed that this proviso would have been overtaken by section 2 of the Valuation (Ireland) Act 1854 which required the Commissioner of Valuation to distinguish for valuation purposes: "[A]ll hereditaments and tenements, or portions of same, of a public nature, or used for charitable purposes, or for the purposes of science, literature and the fine arts." However, in *Londonderry Union v. Londonderry Bridge Commissioners*[206] the Court of Exchequer Chamber held that the 1854 Act was not designed "to create new, or abolish old, rating obligations" but only "to provide a machinery for valuing standards according to the standards provided by the existing legislation."[207] Accordingly, the court held that the words of section 2 of the 1854 Act must be read subject to the words of the proviso to section 63 of the 1838 Act. This rather strained construction was confirmed by the Irish Court of Appeal in *O'Neill v. Commissioner of Valuation*[208] and the matter was put beyond all doubt by the Supreme Court decision in *McGahan & Ryan v. Commissioner of Valuation*[209] where Murnaghan J. said of the *Londonderry Union* case that:

> "[I]t involves that the exemption from the poor rate is to be ascertained, not from the language of [section 2 of the 1854 Act], but from the rating provisions of the Poor Relief (Ireland) Act 1838, section 63 with its proviso. We do not

---

203 Keane, *op. cit.* above, n.1, p. 289.
204 "Domestic hereditaments" are exempted by virtue of s.1 of the Local Government (Financial Provisions) Act 1978 and are defined as: "Any hereditament which consists wholly or partly or premises used as a dwelling and which is not a mixed hereditament." It is significant that there is no requirement that the dwelling must be occupied by the owner or his family and so holidays homes let out during the summer period still qualify for the exemption: *Kerry County Council v. Kerins* [1996] 3 I.R. 493. Dwellings do not cease to be such by reason solely of the fact that they are used as lodgings, but premises registered as hotels, guesthouses etc. cannot avail of the exemption by reason of their exclusion from the definition of "lodgings" in s. 1(1) of the 1978 Act.
205 Certain relief is provided in the case of secondary schools and community halls by s.2 of the Local Government (Financial Provisions) Act 1978. There are a number of local and private Acts which provide either full or partial relief for certain notable important buildings, e.g. Local Government (Dublin) Act 1930 (which gives exemptions in respect of, *inter alia*, the King's Inns, Corn Exchange and the College of Surgeons). The exemption for Trinity College, Dublin only applies to buildings occupied as of the date of the passage of the 1930 Act: *Dublin Corporation v. Trinity College, Dublin* [1985] I.L.R.M. 283.
206 (1868) I.R. 2 C.L. 577.
207 *Ibid.* at 586, *per* O'Hagan J.
208 [1914] 2 I.R. 447.
209 [1934] I.R. 736.

think that the decision can now be departed from. It explains how section 63 has been considered as the guiding section governing rateability and has never been treated as repealed. In subsequent legislation the basis of the poor rate has been adopted widely for rating purposes outside the scope of the original Poor Relief Act 1838 and it would, in our opinion, bring about results not intended by the Legislature, if the exemption were now to be sought, not in the proviso to section 63 of the Poor Relief Act 1838, but in the Valuation Act 1854."[210]

This view was, however, rejected by the House of Lords in *Governors of Campbell College, Belfast v. Commissioner of Valuation for Northern Ireland*[211] who took the view that the statutory basis for the exemption was to be found in section 2 of the 1854 Act. Lord Radcliffe described the *Londonderry Bridge* and *O'Neill* cases as "unsatisfactory" and as involving "an incoherent rule of construction," saying that there was no justification for limiting the ambit of the exemption conferred by the words "of a public nature, or used for charitable purposes" in section 2 of the 1854 Act as being coterminous with the exemptions set out in the proviso to section 63 of the 1838 Act.

Yet in its latest pronouncement on this issue, *Governors of Wesley College v. Commissioner of Valuation*,[212] the Supreme Court reaffirmed that the statutory basis for the exemption is the proviso to section 63 of the 1838 Act. In view of the fact that counsel for Wesley College had initially suggested that the decision of the House of Lords in the *Campbell College* case should be followed,[213] it is surprising that the Supreme Court did not reply to the criticisms of the *Londonderry Bridge* and *O'Neill* cases which had been voiced in the *Campbell College* case. Of course, even if the reasoning in the *Campbell College* is to be preferred – and there is much to be said for this particular point of view – it may be that the earlier Irish decisions have become so embedded in the fabric of our law that they can only be reversed by legislation.[214] We must now consider the main heads of exemption under section 63 of the 1838 Act.

"Charitable purposes"

It has been held that the term "charitable" in the proviso to section 63 does not extend to any charitable purpose which is not mentioned explicitly in the list of purposes contained in the provision therein.[215] Accordingly, it was thought up to

---

210 *Ibid.* at 752.
211 [1964] N.I. 107.
212 [1984] I.L.R.M. 117.
213 *Ibid.* at 119, *per* Henchy J.
214 Thus, Murnaghan J. remarked in *Kerry County Council v. Commissioner of Valuation* [1934] I.R. 527 at 538:
> "I am of opinion that it is futile at this lapse of time to seek to interpret the [*Londonderry Bridge* case] in a sense different to that in which it has so long been understood in this country, and that if any change in the law is to be made it should be sought from the Legislature."
And in *Dublin County Council v. Westlink Toll Bridge Ltd* [1994] 1 I.R. 77 Geoghegan J. acknowledged (at 84) that while the decision might be "controversial", he thought that "it would not be proper for the High Court to query it." Likewise, Keane, *op. cit.*, above, n.1, p. 293 considers that, given that this decision is of such long standing, the Supreme Court, even if "unhappy" about this line of authority, might "apply the maxim *communis error, facit jus.*"
215 *Barrington's Hospital v. Commissioner of Valuation* [1957] I.R. 299.

quite recently that buildings used for educational purposes must be confined to the education of the poor.[216] But in its most recent pronouncement on this vexed question, *Governors of Wesley College v. Commissioner for Valuation*,[217] the Supreme Court has struck a slightly different note. In that case an exemption had been claimed on behalf of a private fee-paying school which was geared towards making a profit. It was this fact, rather than that the education provided was not exclusively for the benefit of the poor (whereas the provision speaks of "the education of the poor"), which meant that the plaintiffs could not obtain the benefit of the exemption. The *Wesley College* decision may well extend the grounds for exemption, for the test now appears to be whether the buildings are used exclusively for charitable or public purposes (*i.e.* in the sense of no private gain), and a building is not precluded from being considered charitable simply because is benefits are not confined to the poor.

The decision in *Wesley College* may well have other implications in this area, for in *Maynooth College v. Commissioners for Valuation*,[218] it was held that a Catholic seminary was a rateable hereditament. The building was not "exclusively dedicated to religious worship" (to use the language of the proviso to section 63 of the 1838 Act), and as the word "charitable" excluded any charitable purpose expressly mentioned earlier in the proviso, the seminary could not be said to be used for charitable purposes merely because it was for the advancement of religion.[219] In the light of the *Wesley College* decision, it may be that an institution of this nature could now claim to be charitable if it were non-profit-making in nature, and would otherwise be regarded as charitable for tax purposes.[220]

Infirmaries, hospitals or other buildings used exclusively for charitable purposes

The same difficulties do not arise in the case of the final ground of exemption in favour of "infirmaries, hospitals or other buildings used exclusively for charitable purposes" because such charitable purposes have not already been expressly mentioned in the proviso. Thus, in *Barrington's Hospital v. Commissioner for Valuation*,[221] a public voluntary hospital was held to be charitable in its purpose, despite the fact that some of its patients were fee-paying, as these fees were not used for private profit. It may well be argued that in the *Wesley College* decision the Supreme Court effectively applied this test to all charitable or public institutions,

---

216 *O'Neill v. Commissioner of Valuation* [1914] 2 I.R. 447; *McGahan and Ryan v. Commissioner of Valuation* [1934] I.R. 736.
217 [1984] I.L.R.M. 117. Neither *O'Neill* nor *McGahan and Ryan* is referred to in the judgment of Henchy J. for the Court.
218 [1958] I.R. 189.
219 Even though the building would be regarded as charitable for ordinary tax purposes under the test laid down by the House of Lords in *Income Tax Special Purposes Commissioners v. Pemsel* [1891] A.C. 531. See also *Brendan v. Commissioner of Valuation* [1969] I.R. 202.
220 Though note that in *St. Macartan's Diocesan Trust v. Commissioner of Valuation* [1990] 1 I.R. 508, it was conceded before Gannon J. (at 512) that "the question of charitable purpose [did] not arise because the use of the hereditaments, although being for [non-profit making] education, [was] not for the education of the poor."
221 [1957] I.R. 299. See also *Dublin Corporation v. Dublin Cemetries Committee*, unreported, Supreme Court, November 12, 1975.

despite the fact that in the case of educational and religious institutions the scope for exemption would appear to have been severely limited by the terms of the proviso.

"Public purposes"

This head of exemption has also been considered in a series of decisions commencing with *Londonderry Union v. Londonderry Bridge Commissioners*,[222] where the issue was whether the tolls received by the defendants from the operation of a bridge were exempt from rating. The Court of Exchequer Chamber held that as the basis of exemption from rating was to be found in the proviso to section 63 of the 1838 Act, this question turned on the meaning of "public purposes" in the 1838 Act. The bridge in question was open for use by all members of the public subject to payment of a toll and were being run on a non-profit making basis.[223] Hence, it was held that the tolls themselves were exempt from rating on the public purposes ground. This decision has been distinguished in a number of cases,[224] but has otherwise retained its authority. Indeed, by an application of this principle, Belfast[225] and Sligo[226] harbours, technical schools,[227] the quays of the port of Dublin,[228] and the constituent colleges of the National University of Ireland[229] all succeeded in securing rating exemption. The rationale of the *Mayor of Limerick* decision was confirmed by the Supreme Court in *Kerry County Council v. Commissioner of Valuation*,[230] where it was held that premises occupied by Kerry County Council did not qualify for an exemption. Murnaghan J. agreed that this was a case where a "limited and defined class of the public" (in this case, the ratepayers of Kerry) has an interest in the property in question, but, on the authority of the *Londonderry Bridge* case, this did not of itself suffice to enable an exemption to be claimed.

This question was reexamined by Gannon J. in *St. Macartan's Diocesan Trust v. Commissioner of Valuation*.[231] In this case an agricultural college was established in the 1940s and organised along denominational lines. Some time later the college began to receive considerable financial support from the State and it became non-

---

[222] (1868) I.R. 2 C.L. 577.

[223] In *Dublin County Council v. Westlink Toll Bridge Ltd* [1996] 1 I.R. 487 O'Flaherty J. emphasised that the *Londonderry Bridge* case had turned on the fact that the tolls in that case were used exclusively for the maintenance and upkeep of the bridge. In the *Westlink* case the bridge had been built under statutory authority, but as the operating company derived a direct profit from the tolls and "did not seek altruistically [to] benefit . . . the public without expectation of profit", the *Londonderry Bridge* rationale could not apply.

[224] See, *e.g. Mayor of Limerick v. Commissioner of Valuation* (1872) I.R. 6 C.L. 420 (where it was held that a gas works operated by Limerick Corporation was carried on for the benefit of a limited class of ratepayers in a defined locality and, hence, was not exempt) and *Dublin County Council v. Westlink Toll Bridge Ltd* [1994] 1 I.R. 77 (contrary to the decision in the *Londonderry Bridge* where O'Hagan J. had been "primarily influenced by the non-commercial role of the commissioners and the exclusive public purposes to which the tolls were to be applied", the tolls in the present case had been primarily applied for the benefit of a private enterprise so that the "public purposes" exemption did not apply.)

[225] *Belfast Harbour Commissioners v. Commissioner of Valuation* [1897] 2 I.R. 512.

[226] *Sligo Harbour Commissioners v. Commissioner of Valuation* [1899] 2 I.R. 214.

[227] *Pembroke U.D.C. v. Commissioner of Valuation* [1904] 2 I.R. 429.

[228] *Dublin Corporation v. Ports & Dock Board* [1978] I.R. 241 at 266, *per* Henchy J.

[229] *Governing Body of University College, Cork v. Commissioner of Valuation* [1912] 2 I.R. 328.

[230] [1934] I.R. 527.

[231] [1990] 1 I.R. 508.

denominational in character. It was also non profit-making, although students were required to pay relatively sizeable fees. Gannon J. concluded, although not without some regret, that the college could not be regarded as being used for "public purposes" within the meaning of the 1838 Act:

> "The educational establishment comprised of these hereditaments was originally founded for the benefit of a limited section of the public. It was later adapted and adopted by the State for wider public service. That educational establishment has never been taken over by the State, although it has been staffed and maintained with the aid of money provided by the State. Nevertheless, the vicarious State involvement in the use by the occupiers of the hereditament could not reasonably qualify them as 'dedicated to or used for public purposes' as these words of the proviso of section 63 of the 1838 Act have been interpreted."[232]

Interestingly enough, it was conceded that, since the educational establishment was not dedicated exclusively for the use of the poor, it could not avail itself of the charitable exemption. As we have seen, given that the college was operated on a non-profit-making basis, this concession would seem questionable in view of the reasoning of Henchy J. in the *Wesley College* case.

Service charges

By 1983 the financial state of so many local authorities had become so parlous following the effective abolition of rates on domestic dwellings and agricultural land that it was considered desirable that they should have the power to impose charges in respect of a diverse number of services provided by them. The Local Government (Financial Provisions) (No. 2) Act 1983[233] was designed to this end. By extending the power of local authorities to impose such charges, even though such power was not contained in the substantive statute authorising the specific statute, it was intended to restore some measure of fiscal autonomy to local government. However, the charges have proved to be controversial, and this legislation was never really regarded as an adequate substitute for some proper form of local taxation. Originally, the making of service charges was an executive function for the Manager (something which was itself unusual given the usual distinction between the Manager and the councillors and suggests that it was anticipated that service charges would be unpopular with the people whom the councillors represented). However, by virtue of the County Management (Reserved Functions)

---

[232] *Ibid.* at 513.
[233] Historically, an inequitable division prevailed as between the urban and rural dwellers. S.65A of the Public Health (Ireland) Act 1878 (as inserted by s.7 of the Local Government (Sanitary Services) Act 1962) provided for the payment of water charges by (essentially) rural consumers. This obligation was later extended to all consumers by s.8 of the Local Government (Financial Provisions)(No.2) Act 1983, although the decision whether to levy such charges rested with the local authority. By virtue of the Local Government (Delimitation of Water Supply Disconnection Powers) Act 1995, the right of local authorities to withdraw supply in respect of defaulting consumers was itself terminated (unless a court order was obtained).

Order 1985,[234] the making of domestic service charges was made a matter for the elected representatives.

Section 2 is the key section of the 1983 Act:

> "(1) Subject to *section 4* of this Act, any existing enactment which requires or enables a local authority to provide a service but which, apart from this subsection, does not empower the authority to charge for the provision of the service shall be deemed so to empower that authority.
>
> (2) *Subsection 1* of this section shall have effect as regards an enactment notwithstanding the inclusion in the enactment of a provision which either precludes a local authority from charging for the provision of a service or requires that a service be provided by such authority free of charge.
>
> (3) Subject to *section 4* of this Act, notwithstanding any provision in any existing enactment whereby there is specified —
>
> > (a) the amount of the charge which may be made by a local authority in respect of a service which the authority is required or enabled to provide, or
> >
> > (b) an amount which a charge described in *paragraph (a)* of this subsection is not to exceed,
>
> the local authority may make a charge which exceeds the amount so specified, and any charge made by virtue of this subsection shall for all purposes be deemed to have been duly made under this enactment.

Section 3 provides that the amount of such charges shall be such that as "the authority considers appropriate" and further states that the charge shall:

> "be payable and recoverable from the person for whom the charge is provided, or, where the service is provided in respect of premises –
>
> (a) in case the premises are not owned by a local authority and comprise more than one dwelling, the owner of the premises, and
>
> (b) in any other case, the occupier of the premises,
>
> and different such charges may be made by an authority in respect of persons, premises or services of different classes or descriptions."

Ministerial control is provided for under section 4. The Minister for the Environment is empowered to exclude certain classes of services from the scope of section 2 charges, but no such order appears to have been made to date. However, section 5 empowers a local authority via the Manager (since this is an executive function) to waive "all or portion of a charge" if it is satisfied that "it is appropriate to do so on the ground of personal hardship", a power which has been extensively used to exempt, for example, the old and the unemployed.

The validity of the imposition of service charges has been challenged in a series of cases, all of which illustrate the principle that as the 1983 Act is, in effect, a taxing statute, it must be strictly construed. *Athlone U.D.C. v. Gavin*[235] concerned the

---

[234] S.I. No. 341 of 1985.
[235] [1985] I.R. 434.

validity of a charge of £60 levied on every domestic dwelling for water, refuse and sewage services for a particular year. Finlay C.J. held that the charge was invalid in that section 2(1) of the 1983 Act conferred a power to make a charge for a single service and could not, said Finlay C.J., be construed "as enabling a local authority to fix a single charge for a number of services."[236]

Finally, section 8 amends the provisions of section 65A of the Public Health (Ireland) Act 1878 and allows for the imposition of water charges. These are made payable on an instalment basis and the strict construction approach was continued in *Dublin Corporation v. Ashley*.[237] Here the local authority had sought to impose water charges payable on demand and not on instalment, as contemplated by these statutory provisions. Finlay C.J. said that the word "instalment" when applied to payment meant "part of the payment and could not be construed as the entire of it." Accordingly, the County Manager had acted *ultra vires* in seeking to provide for the fixing of a charge "payable in one single amount."

The word "service" is given a broad definition by section 1 as meaning:

"any service, facility, licence, permit, certificate, approval or thing which a local authority may render, supply, grant or issue or otherwise provide in the performance or exercise of any of its functions, powers or duties to any person or in respect of any premises and includes the processing of an application for such a licence, permit, certificate or approval."

However, even this definition has been narrowly construed. In *Ballybay Meat Exports Ltd v. Monaghan County Council*[238] the applicants had attempted to connect their drains with the respondent's sewers, but the respondents claimed to be entitled to impose service charges in respect of this connection. Gannon J. held that an owner or occupier of premises enjoyed a right to cause his drains to empty into a sewer without charge was a public right conferred by section 23 of the Public Health (Ireland) Act 1878. Accordingly, this right was not "merely an individual service provided by the sanitary authority to such owner or occupier" and the charges were to that extent *ultra vires*. This decision might have far-reaching consequences for local authorities in that it means that their power to impose service charges is not as broad as had been imagined.

Moreover, a local authority may not seek to collect service charges where the service has not been availed of. This emerges from another judgment of Gannon J. on this issue, *Louth County Council v. Matthews*,[239] where the defendant had refused to pay service charges for refuse collection when he had not availed of the collection service. Gannon J. said that he could not accept the submission that:

"[T]he word 'service' when used in sections 2 and 3 should be interpreted as being provided for a person without regard to whether or not it was provided to that person. The wording of section 3 which empowers the plaintiff to

---

236   *Ibid.* at 442. See also, *O'Donnell v. Dun Laoghaire Corporation (No. 1)* [1991] I.L.R.M. 301 (where orders which failed to specify the dates on which instalment payments were to be made were held to be invalid).
237   [1986] I.R. 781.
238   [1990] I.L.R.M. 864.
239   Unreported, High Court, April 14, 1989.

prescribe appropriate different charges for different classes of persons, when coupled with section 5 in relation to giving relief in cases of hardship seems to me more consistent with creating a contractual relationship."

In consequence, since the defendant had not actually used the service, he should not be charged for it. On the other hand, a local authority is entitled to impose a charge for statutory registration, at least where the applicant derives some personal benefit therefrom.[240]

Finally, it should be noted that where a local authority has already imposed a charge in virtue of another statutory enactment, it may not proceed to impose a further charge under the terms of the 1983 Act. This occurred in *Lyons v. Kilkenny Corporation*[241] where the holders of casual trading permits under the Casual Trading Act 1980 had previously paid a charge in respect of the granting of such a permit. The Corporation then sought to levy an additional sum from them by way of a service charge under the 1983 Act, but Barron J. ruled that this was *ultra vires*. The permit holders were entitled to park their vehicles at designated areas for trading purposes and "have, in effect, paid for the right to do so, but are now being compelled to pay a further sum."

Water charges have always been especially unpopular and, as a result of the Local Government (Financial Provisions) Act 1997, s.12(2), the right to impose water charges in respect of any domestic dwellings have now been terminated. Charges for refuse and for commercial water and sewerage services remain. The rate support grant (by which the Department of the Environment assisted poorer local authorities) is also terminated. But in place of these two sources of income, section 3 of the 1997 Act assigns motor tax revenue (which is regarded as a buoyant source of revenue) to local authorities.

6. Conduct of Meetings

As a matter of general principle and subject to certain express and implied legal restraints, local authorities are free to conduct their business in whatever manner they see fit. By section 30(1) of the Local Government Act 1994, the Minister for the Environment is empowered to make regulations with respect to "meetings and procedures or to any matter arising in connection therewith or related thereto" but to date, no such regulations have been made. However, section 62(1) of the Local Government Act 1955 permits local authorities to adopt their own standing orders:

> "A local authority may make standing orders for the regulation of their procedures, other than proceedings, the regulation of which is provided for by, or under statute (including this Act), and may amend or revoke such standing orders."

---

[240] *O'Leary v. Cork C.C.* [1994] 1 I.R. 59 at 61, *per* O'Hanlon J. In this case, the charge was the registration as a dairyman under the terms of the Milk and Dairies Act 1935. It seems difficult to align the reasoning in this case with that of Gannon J. in *Ballybay Meats.*

[241] Unreported, High Court, February 14, 1987.

Most local authorities have adopted standing orders which are occasionally revised from time to time. Notice though, that as the proviso to section 62(1) makes clear, the special procedures provided for by statutory provisions such as section 4 of the City and County Management (Amendment) Act 1940 cannot be defeated by the operation of a local authority's standing orders.

Section 41 of the Local Government Act 1941 specifies that the method by which votes at such meetings shall be decided is by a simple majority of those present. Save where the chairman is not a member of the local authority, the chairman has "a second or casting vote" in the case of a tied vote. It should be noted that section 41 of the 1941 Act does not apply to subsequent enactments prescribing special voting procedures, section 4 of the 1955 Act (which requires, inter alia, that the number of members of the local authority voting in favour of the resolution must exceed one-third of the total members of the authority) being a notable case in point. The matter of an equality of votes is dealt with by sections 62 and 63 of the Local Government Act 1946.

The procedure to be followed at meetings to consider the estimates of annual expenditure and the striking of a rate is regulated by section 10(1) of the City and County Management (Amendment) Act 1955:

> "An estimate of expenses shall be considered by the local authority at a meeting of the local authority at which the manager shall be present and which shall be held during the prescribed period and of which not less than seven days' notice shall have been given to every person who is a member of the local authority when such notice is given."[242]

7. Specimen Functions

Over the centuries, local authorities gathered accretions of diverse statutory functions and powers of varying importance. This may be illustrated by listing the programme groups in which they are categorised by the Public Bodies (Amendment) Order 1975 for estimates of expenditure purposes: housing and building; road transportation and safety; water supply and sewerage; environmental protection; recreation and amenity; miscellaneous services; agriculture, education, services, health and welfare; and development incentives and controls. To take some particular examples: local authorities have responsibility for such matters as the maintenance and improvement of local roads[243]; the protection of the environment[244]; litter[245]; waste management[246]; fire services[247]; vocational education[248]; the licensing of gaming

---

[242] See also Public Bodies (Amendment) Order 1992 (S.I. No. 327 of 1992).
[243] Roads Act 1993, Part II.
[244] Local Government (Water Pollution) Acts, 1977–1990. See generally, Scannell, *Environmental and Planning Law* (1995), pp. 312–399.
[245] Litter Pollution Act 1997, Part III.
[246] Waste Management Act 1996, Parts, III, IV and V.
[247] Fire Services Act, 1981, Part II.
[248] Roche, *op. cit.*, above, n.1, pp. 273–275. Local authorities have also responsibility for higher education grants: see Local Authorities (Higher Education Grants) Acts, 1968–1992.

and amusement halls[249]; the maintenance of a register of all multi-storey buildings in its functional area[250]; casual trading[251]; the compilation of electoral registers[252] and miscellaneous functions relating to the administration of justice, such as the appointment of coroners[253] and the provision of courthouses.[254] Later in this part, we shall briefly examine three specimen functions – planning control; housing and certain functions under the Gaming and Lotteries Act 1956. Before this, however, two preliminary points must be made. In recent years the Oireachtas has sought, on the one hand, to add to the responsibilities of local authorities[255]; while at the same time in other areas it has been decided that some of their functions should be given to other, nationally-based bodies.[256]

A question of some complexity is the demarcation line in respect of responsibility for each function as between any lower tier authority (non-county borough; urban district council or town commissioners) and the county council. This is a difficult matter depending as it does on transfers from grand juries and an intricate analysis of "the tortuous labyrinth of an unexplored administrative code."[257] However, as a generalisation, it may be said that, leaving aside town commissioners, each type of authority bears responsibility in law for each type of function within its own functional area. Where the more important functions are concerned, the major exception to this is that the maintenance and construction of all county roads shall be the responsibility of the county councils, even if the roads run through an urban district council.[258] But besides this exception, there are a number of cases, where because of the inadequate size and resources of the lower-tier authority the formal position created by the legislation would be thoroughly impracticable. To circumvent this difficulty, the Local Government Act 1955 provides that the power of one authority may be exercised on its behalf by another authority.[259] This device has been frequently used to enable a county council to exercise many of the functions of the lower-tier authorities, for instance, urban roads and aspects of water supply.

---

[249] See below at pp. 247–248.
[250] Local Government (Multi-Storey) Buildings Act 1988, s.2(1).
[251] Casual Trading Act 1995.
[252] Electoral Acts, 1992–1996.
[253] Coroners Act 1962, s. 8.
[254] Courthouses (Provision and Maintenance) Act 1935, s. 3.
[255] See, *e.g.* Local Government Act 1991, s.52 (giving power to Minister for the Environment to remove certain controls in earlier enactments which required ministerial control and consent) and the Local Government Act 1991 (Removal of Controls) Regulations 1993 (S.I. No. 172 of 1993); Local Government (Financial Provisions) Act 1997, s.9 (power to raise revenue by raising levels of motor taxation with certain prescribed limits).
[256] The transfer of responsibilities for integrated pollution licences to the Environmental Protection Agency by the Environmental Protection Agency Act 1992 and for national roads to the National Roads Authority by the Roads Act 1993 are good examples of the latter phenomenon.
[257] *Devanney v. Dublin Board of Assistance* (1949) 83 I.L.T.R. 113, *per* Gavan Duffy J.
[258] By virtue of the Roads Act 1993, Part III, the National Roads Authority now has responsibility for primary roads.
[259] s.59.

(i) Planning control[260]

Although the potential for planning control has been in existence in Ireland since 1934,[261] it was not until the coming into force of the Local Government (Planning and Development) Act 1963 that a comprehensive scheme of planning control or licensing[262] was established. Local authorities were designated by this Act as planning authorities for their functional area,[263] and were now obliged to produce, and regularly to update, a development plan. Furthermore, enforcement powers and the power to restrain unauthorised developments were greatly increased.

But even this legislation proved to be defective in a number of important respects. An appeal lay to the Minister for Local Government, who in practice was susceptible to local political pressures[264] and who often granted permissions which materially contravened the development plan.[265] Moreover, the enforcement powers while frequently utilised, proved cumbersome in dealing with the growing problem of unauthorised developments. The Local Government (Planning and Development) Act 1976 sought to deal with these problems. It transferred the Minister's appellate functions to an independent body, known as An Bord Pleanála. In addition, the enforcement controls were strengthened, and the Act envisaged a greater role for third-party objectors. Further detailed changes were made both to the planning process and to An Bord Pleanála by legislation enacted in 1982, 1983,[266] 1992[267] and 1993,[268] the frequency of which statutes indicates the legal, commercial and political sensitivity of this area, as does the plethora of case law.

---

[260] See generally, Walsh, *Planning and Development Law*, (2nd ed.);O'Donnell ed. O'Sullivan and Sheppard, *Irish Planning Law and Practice* (Dublin, 1996) ; Scannell, "Planning Control: Twenty Years On" (1982) 4 D.U.L.J. 41 (Part 1); (1983) 5 D.U.L.J. 225 (Part 2); Scannell, *Environmental and Planning Law* (1995) and Galligan, *Irish Planning Law and Procedure* (1997).

[261] Town and Regional Planning Act 1934; Town and Regional Planning Act (Amendment) Act 1939. For an account of this legislation (which was repealed in its entirety in 1963) see Miley and King, *Town and Regional Planning in Ireland* (1951).

[262] For licensing in general, see Chap. 7.

[263] Local Government (Planning and Development) Act 1963 ("the 1963 Act") s.2(2). An exception arises in the case of town commissioners, who, although they are local authorities, are not designated as planning authorities. These functions are discharged in the case of a town with commissioners by the county council of the county in which the town is situated.

[264] This was held to be *ultra vires* by the Supreme Court in *The State (Pine Valley Developments Ltd) v. Dublin County Council* [1984] I.R. 407. This decision was reversed by the Local Government (Planning and Development) Act 1982, s.6. An Bord Pleanála is expressly vested with a jurisdiction to depart from the terms of the development plan: Local Government (Planning and Development) Act 1976, s.14(8).

[265] *cf.* the comments of Henchy J. in *The State (Pine Valley Developments Ltd) v. Dublin County Council* [1984] I.R. 407 at 425 and see pp. 258–259.

[266] The Local Government (Planning and Development) Act 1983 sets out the procedure governing the appointment of the chairman and members of An Bord Pleanála. This Act represents yet another legislative attempt to augment the impartiality of the Board and to reduce political interference with its operations. For a fuller account of this legislation, see Walsh, *op. cit.*, above, n. 260, pp. 79–83; Stevenson, "Planning Appeals in the Republic of Ireland" (1985) 7 *Urban Law and Policy* 170, and see pp. 258–259.

[267] The Local Government (Planning and Development) Act 1992 effected a number of miscellaneous changes, including important provisions governing An Bord Pleanála's procedures, the method of challenging the validity of planning decisions (see pp. 794–797) and inserting a new version of the s.27 planning injunction powers (see pp. 240–242).

[268] The Local Government (Planning and Development) Act 1993 was enacted in the wake of the Supreme Court's decision in *Howard v. Commissioners of Public Works* [1994] 1 I.R. 101 and subjects State authorities to the ordinary planning process.

While undoubtedly the most important function of a planning authority – the granting or refusing a planning permission – is an executive function, which is vested in the City or County Manager, nevertheless the elected representatives do have an important say in the planning process. It is the task of the local councillors to make a development plan,[269] and they may also revoke or modify a planning permission.[270] In addition, the councillors may declare any particular area to be one of special amenity.[271]

The development plan A development plan drawn up by a local authority must follow certain objectives.[272] A local authority is required to keep a draft of the development plan on public display for at least three months, and to take into consideration any objections or representations made with regard to the draft plan.[273] The authority is entitled to make non-material alterations to the draft plan without going through the statutory notification and exhibition procedure again.[274] At the same time, the authority is not required "to include in the development plan every possible knock on benefit or detriment which may be hoped for or feared."[275]

Subject to one important qualification, the planning authority is, first, bound by the terms of the development plan and, secondly, is not entitled to grant a permission which materially contravenes the terms of the development plan. The development plan was described by McCarthy J. as

". . . an environmental contract between the planning authority, the Council and the community, embodying a promise by the Council that it will regulate private development in a manner consistent with the objectives stated in the plan, and, further the Council itself shall not effect any development which contravenes the plan materially."[276]

This is a matter which was considered by O'Hanlon J. in *O'Leary v. Dublin County Council*[277] where the issue was whether the respondents were entitled to

---

[269] s. 19(7) of the 1963 Act. While the making of the development plan is, of course, subject to judicial review, the courts "must be very slow to interfere with the democratic decision of any local; elected representatives entrusted with making such decisions by the legislature": *Malahide Community Council Ltd v. Fingal County Council*, unreported, Supreme Court, May 14, 1997, *per* Lynch J.

[270] s.30 of the 1963 Act.

[271] s.42 of the 1963 Act, as amended by s.40 of the 1976 Act.

[272] s.19(2)(a) of the 1963 Act. In the case of urban areas, a local authority is required to have regard to the following objectives: (a) indicating the zoning of particular areas for particular purposes; (b) improving road safety by the provision of parking places or road improvements; (c) the development and renewal of obsolete areas; (d) the preservation, improvement and extension of amenities. In rural areas, the objectives include (c) and (d), but also the improvement and extension of water and sewage supplies. The objectives must be positive in nature, so that a development plan which purports to include a blanket ban on all mining development is *ultra vires: Glencar Explorations plc v. Mayo C.C.* [1993] 2 I.R. 237.

[273] Local Government (Planning and Development) Act 1963, s.21A(2). For the application of the principles of fair procedures to the making of a development plan, see *Finn v. Bray U.D.C.* [1969] I.R. 169.

[274] However, if the amendment constitutes a material contravention, the authority is required to satisfy the publication requirements and failure to do so will invalidate any purported amendment: *Keogh v. Galway Corporation (No.2)* [1995] 3 I.R. 466.

[275] *Malahide Community Council Ltd v. Fingal County Council*, unreported, Supreme Court, May 14, 1997, *per* Lynch J.

[276] *Attorney General (McGarry) v. Sligo Corporation* [1991] 1 I.R. 99 at 113.

[277] [1988] I.R. 150. See generally, Simons, "Travellers: Planning Issues" (1997) 4 I.P.E.L.J. 8 and "Unauthorised Travellers' Halting Sites" (1997) I.P.E.L.J. 53.

provide a halting site for members of the travelling community in an area of high amenity which had been designated as such in the relevant development plan. O'Hanlon J. accepted that this proposal constituted a material contravention of the development plan, observing that the "praiseworthy motives of the County Council" were not sufficient to absolve them from compliance with the planning law. He added that:

> "I think that the requirements of the planning law have to be applied with the same stringency against the local authority, in this case, as would be the case if the proposal came from a private developer."[278]

A similar approach is manifest in a series of decisions, of which the following may be taken as representative. In *Grange Developments Ltd v. Dublin County Council,*[279] the local authority was not itself the putative developer; but had given a private developer an undertaking to grant planning permission in respect of an unspecified number of industrial buildings and hotels. The grant of an undertaking to give planning permission for one type of development as a sort of consolation prize, when an application for permission for a different development has been refused is authorised by section 57 of the Local Government (Planning and Development) Act 1963. In *Grange* this undertaking was apparently granted in an effort to avoid a large compensation claim by the developer, who had been refused planning permission to develop some 500 residential houses. The Supreme Court held that the undertaking was invalid on the ground that, *inter alia*, it involved the planning authority violating the terms of its own development plan. The lands in question were zoned for agricultural use and, as Finlay C.J. observed, "the erection of industrial buildings or structures for recreational purposes would have been inconsistent with that zoning."[280] In *P. & F. Sharpe Ltd v. Dublin County Council,*[281] the Supreme Court held that the planning authority would have acted *ultra vires* were it to grant a particular planning permission in respect of a road access to a dual carriage-way. The evidence showed that such permission would have involved "a significant and very important road hazard." Yet road safety was a major feature of the planning authority's development plan and, hence, the granting of such permission would have involved a material contravention of its own development plan.[282] And in *Roughan v. Clare County Council*[283] Barron J. granted an injunction restraining the Council from developing a halting site for travellers in circumstances where such a site had not been provided for by the development plan. Stressing that the question of whether the development plan had been materially contravened was a matter of law,[284] Barron J. laid down the following test:

---

[278] *Ibid.* at 154.

[279] [1986] I.R. 246.

[280] *Ibid.* at 255.

[281] [1989] I.R. 701.

[282] Something which planning authorities are expressly forbidden from doing: see 1963 Act s.39(1). See also *Calor Teo v. Sligo County Council* [1991] 2 I.R. 267 (default permission claimed would have been *ultra vires* the development plan so that the grant a permission of this kind was outside the competence of the planning authority to grant).

[283] Unreported, High Court, December 18, 1996.

[284] See *Tennyson v. Dun Laoghaire Corporation* [1991] 2 I.R. 527 and *Healy v. Dublin C.C.*, unreported, High Court, April 28, 1993.

"What is material depends upon the grounds upon which the proposed development is being, or might reasonably be expected to be opposed by local interests. If there are no real or substantial grounds in the context of planning law for opposing the development, then it is unlikely to be a material contravention . . . "

Barron J. also rejected the argument that the Council was not required to enumerate all its development objectives in the plan, as were it otherwise, the local consultative procedures prescribed by the 1963 Act prior to the making of the plan could thereby be set at naught.

Even though a local authority is absolutely bound by the terms of its own development plan, the elected members are entitled to grant a permission which effects a material contravention of the plan following the passing of a special resolution to that effect.[285] The Manager can also be required to grant planning permission if directed by a valid resolution under section 4 of the City and County Management (Amendment) Act 1955, where the proposed development would not materially contravene the development plan.

Planning conditions The planning authority is entitled by virtue of section 26(1) of the 1963 Act to attach conditions to a grant of permission, but all such conditions imposed must be in furtherance of the proper planning and development. Section 26(2) states that, without prejudice to the generality of section 26(1), the conditions attached may include "any and all" of a list of specified conditions.[286] The planning authority is required to give reasons in respect of each condition imposed.[287] While the authority may provide by condition that certain matters (typically matters such as contributions and detailed technical matters) are to be agreed subsequently between the developer and the authority, principles of legal certainty[288] require that

---

[285] In addition, An Bord Pleanála is entitled to grant a permission which materially contravenes the terms of the development plan: Local Government (Planning and Development) Act, 1976, s.14(8).

[286] Among the conditions specifically authorised are: conditions requiring the carrying out of works (including the provision of car parks) which the authority consider are required for the purposes of the development authorised by the permission; conditions abating noise or vibration levels; and conditions requiring contributions in respect of local authority expenditure. See generally, Scannell, *op. cit.* above, n.260, pp. 200–206.

[287] Local Government (Planning and Development) Act 1963, s.26(8), as inserted by Local Government (Planning and Development) Act 1976, s.39(9). The object of this provision is to enable the applicant to obtain "such information as may be necessary and appropriate for him firstly to consider whether he has got a reasonable chance of succeeding in appealing against the decision of the planning authority and, secondly, to enable him to arm himself for the hearing of such appeal": *The State (Sweeney) v. Minister for the Environment* [1979] I.L.R.M. 35 at 37, *per* Finlay P. In *O'Donoghue v. An Bord Pleanála* [1991] I.L.R.M. 750 Murphy J. said (at 757):
"It is clear that the reason given by the [Board] must be sufficient first to enable the courts to review it and, secondly, to satisfy the persons having recourse to the tribunal that it has directed its mind adequately to the issue before it. It has never been suggested that an administrative body is bound to provide a discursive judgment as a result of its deliberations, but on the other hand the need for providing the grounds of the decision . . . could not be satisfied by recourse to an uninformative, if technically correct, formula. For example, it could hardly be regarded as acceptable for the [Board] to reverse a decision of a planning authority stating only that 'they considered the application to accord with the proper planning and development of the area of the authority.'"

[288] The conditions must not be so vague as would effectively frustrate a third party's right of appeal. Thus, as Blayney J. said in *Boland v. An Bord Pleanála* [1996] 3 I.R. 435 at 472, that conditions

---

the authority must nonetheless "lay down criteria by which the developer and the planning authority can reach agreement."[289]

The discretionary power to attach conditions is, of course, governed by ordinary principles of administrative law. The conditions imposed must fairly and reasonably relate to the proposed development, and the reasons given in support of the condition must be capable of justifying the imposition of the condition.[290] Not only that, but the courts will quash the decision to attach conditions – even where the conditions are valid on their face – where it has been shown that the decision has been actuated by improper motives, or that the planning authority has rejected legitimate considerations, or has introduced irrelevant considerations, or has otherwise manifested unreasonableness in arriving at its decision[291] or if the conditions are void for uncertainty.[292] In addition, the courts may quash a condition which disproportionately interferes with private rights of the developer.[293] The question of constitutional justice is considered elsewhere.[294]

Default permission An applicant may also obtain planning permission in default, for section 26(4) of the 1963 Act provides that where an application has been made to a planning authority in accordance with the regulations for the time being in force;[295]

---

which were expressed to be subject to the agreement of the developer and the planning authority must be such, that having regard to "very detailed instructions set out in the conditions", no member of the public "could reasonably have objected to them" and so the Board in imposing conditions in this form could not thus be said to be "interfering with or prejudicing any right of the public."

289 *Boland v. An Bord Pleanála* [1996] 3 I.R. 435 at 467, *per* Hamilton C.J. In both *Boland* and *McNamara v. An Bord Pleanála* [1996] 2 I.L.R.M. 339 conditions of this kind were upheld on the ground that in each case they left matters of technical detail to be agreed, subject to criteria specified in the condition itself. This approach was foreshadowed by the judgment of Murphy J. in *Houlihan v. An Bord Pleanála*, unreported, High Court, October 4, 1993 where on the facts one of the conditions concerning effluent discharge was held to be *ultra vires* as delegating too wide a discretion to the planning authority. See further, on this issue p. 483.

290 *Killiney and Ballybrack Residents Assoc. Ltd v. Minister for Local Government (No. 2)* [1978] I.L.R.M. 78.

291 *The State (Fitzgerald) v. An Bord Pleanála* [1985] I.L.R.M. 117; *P. and F. Sharpe Ltd v. Dublin County Council* [1989] I.R. 701; *Flanagan v. Galway County Council* [1990] 2 I.R. 66; *Kenny Homes & Co. Ltd v. Galway City and County Manager* [1995] 1 I.R.178.

292 In *Irish Asphalt Ltd v. An Bord Pleanála*, unreported, High Court, July 28, 1995, Costello P. adopted the language of Lord Denning in *Fawcett Properties Ltd v. Buckinghamshire C.C.* [1961] A.C. 636 where the latter said that a planning condition would only be condemned as being void for uncertainty "if it can be given no meaning or no sensible or ascertainable meaning and not merely because it is ambiguous or leads to absurd results." In *Irish Asphalt* it was argued that a condition which specified that certain vibration limits were to be measured by its proximity to the nearest building was void as the developer could never know with certainty what level of vibration was permitted during the life of the permission. Costello P. rejected this argument, saying that it was a complaint about the burden imposed by the condition, but this did not affect its validity.

293 *McDonagh & Sons Ltd v. Galway Corporation* [1995] 1 I.R. 191 (where Finlay C.J. hinted that conditions imposed pursuant to s.26(2)(f) of the 1963 Act which were in excess of the immediate needs of the development and in respect of which the developer "could neither derive a profit from his ownership or occupation of them, nor impose responsibility for their maintenance upon a local authority and therefore obtain a contribution for them" might be *ultra vires*). In addition, a planning authority cannot, through the imposition of conditions, seek to interfere with vested rights by oblique means: *The State (O'Hara and McGuinness) v. An Bord Pleanála*, unreported, High Court, May 8, 1986.

294 See, especially Chap. 11.

295 The following are the regulations currently in force: Local Government (Planning and Development) Regulations 1994, S.I. No. 86 of 1994; Local Government (Planning and Development) Regulations

then if notice of the decision has not been given to the applicant within the appropriate period (which is generally two months),[296] a decision by the planning authority to grant permission shall be regarded as having been granted on the last day of the period. It is of some practical significance that if the planning authority acting bona fide requires the developer to provide further information, time starts to run again from the date when the information was provided.[297] The purpose of these default provisions may be said to be to compel the planning authority to direct its mind to the planning application and to adjudicate upon such application within the appropriate period.

It is now clear that even a decision which, is *ultra vires* (and thus liable to be set aside as a nullity), is still a "decision" for the purposes of section 26(4), and thus the applicant cannot claim that "no decision" has been given in such a case and that he is consequently entitled to permission in default.[298] Moreover, a default permission cannot arise where this would result in the obtaining of a permission which would contravene the terms of the development plan or would be otherwise *ultra vires*.[299]

An Bord Pleanála   Any person may appeal against the decision of the planning authority to An Bord Pleanála.[300] The Board is required to act judicially and there have been several cases where decisions have been quashed either because the Board breached the rules of constitutional justice, or because it was held to have abused

---

1995 S.I. No. 69 of 1995 (amending principal regulations regarding exempted development); Local Government (Planning and Development) (No.2) Regulations, 1995 (S.I. No. 75 of 1995)(making available for public inspection documents relating to planning appeals); Local Government (Planning and Development) Regulations 1997 (S.I. No. 78 of 1997) (mobile phone antennae attached to radio masts generally constitute exempted development); Local Government (Planning and Development) (No.2) Regulations 1997 (S.I. No. 121 of 1997) (circulation of draft development plans to Dublin Transport Initiative and relevant health boards). For an example of a case where the applicant was held to have failed to comply with these regulations, (and was, thus, disentitled to default permission) see *Crodaun Homes Ltd v. Kildare C.C.* [1983] I.L.R.M. 1. But see *Mulloy and Walsh v. Dublin C.C.* [1990] 1 I.R. 90 (where Blayney J. held that the non-compliance with the Regulations could be ignored as *de minimis* so that the plaintiffs were held to be entitled to a default permission). Default permission does not arise where the authority declines to rule on a lapsed application: *Murray v. Wicklow County Council* [1996] 2 I.L.R.M. 411.

296   Although the time period is extended where the local authority makes a bona fide request for further information: see s.26(4)(b) of the 1963 Act or if the applicant consents or if the Environmental Impact Assessment Regulations are involved. The "appropriate period" may be extended on more than one occasion: *Flynn & O'Flaherty Properties Ltd v. Dublin Corporation* [1997] 2 I.R. 560.

297   *The State (Conlon Construction Co. Ltd) v. Cork C.C.*, unreported, High Court, July 31, 1975; *The State (NCE Ltd) v. Dublin C.C.* [1979] I.L.R.M. 249; *O'Connor's Downtown Properties Ltd v. Nenagh UDC* [1993] 1 I.R. 1.

298   *The State (Abenglen Properties Ltd) v. Dublin Corporation* [1984] I.R. 381.

299   *Calor Teo v. Sligo County Council* [1991] 2 I.R. 267 (no default permission as proposed development would have constituted a fire hazard in contravention of the terms of the development plan).

300   The right of appeal is now contained in s.26(5) and (5A) of the Local Government (Planning and Development) Act 1963 (as inserted by s.3 of the Local Government (Planning and Development) Act 1992). The right of appeal now lasts one month, but s.4(1) of the 1992 Act requires that the appellant state in full in writing the various grounds of appeal and the "reasons, considerations and arguments on which they are based", thus reversing the Supreme Court's decision in *The State (Elm Developments Ltd) v. An Bord Pleanála* [1981] I.L.R.M. 108. To emphasise the point, s.4(2)(a) provides that an appeal "which does not comply with the requirements of [s.4(1)] shall be invalid." For case-law illustrating the mandatory character of these statutory requirements: see *McCann v. An Bord Pleanála* [1997] 1 I.L.R.M. 1; *Graves v. An Bord Pleanála* [1997] 2 I.R. 132.

its power,[301] where it acted on irrelevant considerations, topics which are considered elsewhere.

The procedures governing planning appeals are now contained in sections 7–10 of the Local Government (Planning and Development) Act 1992. Section 7 prescribes the procedures to be followed in respect of submissions and observations by other parties; section 8 deals with submissions and observations by persons other than parties[302]; section 9 enables the Board to request submissions or observations. Next, section 10(1) deals with the power of the Board to require the submission of documents

> "Where the Board is of opinion that any document, particulars or other information is or are necessary for the purpose of enabling it to determine an appeal, the Board may serve on any party, or on any person who has made submission or observations to the Board in relation to the appeal, a notice under this section
>
> (a) requiring that person ... to submit to the Board such document, particulars or other information (which document, particulars or other information shall be specified in the notice) and,
>
> (b) stating that, in default of compliance with the requirements of the notice, the Board will, after the expiration of the period so specified and without further notice to the person, pursuant to section 11 dismiss or otherwise determine the appeal."

These procedures also recognise the need for speedy decision-making and administrative finality. Thus, section 2 imposes a duty on the Board "to ensure that appeals ... are disposed of as expeditiously as may be" and normally within four months.[303] Exceptionally, however, this period may be extended where it would not be "possible or appropriate" to determine any given appeal: in such circumstances, the Board must cause a written notice to that effect to be sent to the parties.[304] Again, section 7(4) provides that:

> "Without prejudice to section 9, a party shall not be entitled to elaborate in writing upon any submissions or observations made in accordance with subsection (2) or make further submissions or observations in writing in relation to the appeal and any such elaboration, submissions or observations that it or are received by the Board shall not be considered by it."[305]

---

[301] For the special judicial review procedure prescribed in planning cases, see pp. 794–797.

[302] Thus curing the striking anomaly disclosed in *The State (Haverty) v. An Bord Pleanála* [1987] I.R. 485 whereby, under the previous regime prescribed by the (now repealed) s.18 of the Local Government (Planning and Development) Act 1983, third party objectors had no right to make submissions in respect of appeals to the Board.

[303] Local Government (Planning and Development) Act 1992, s.2(2). By s.2(1) the Board is placed under a duty to ensure that appeals and other matters are disposed of "as expeditiously as may be" and "to take all such steps as are open to it to ensure that, in so far as practicable, there are no avoidable delays at any stage in the determination of appeals and other matters."

[304] Local Government (Planning and Development) Act 1992, s.2(3). Such notice is required to inform the parties of the reasons for the delay and must "specify the date before which the Board intends that the appeal or other matter shall be determined."

[305] s.9 deals with the Board's powers to request further submissions or observations. S.8(4) contains a provision analogous to s.7(4) in the case of submissions made by persons other than parties to the appeal.

The Board is also entitled "in its absolute discretion" to dismiss an appeal where "having considered the grounds of appeal, the Board is of opinion that the appeal is vexatious, frivolous or without substance or foundation."[306] It may also declare appeals and applications to have been withdrawn.[307] The Board is alone entitled to determine whether development has taken place, and, if so, whether it is exempted development[308] for the purpose of the planning code. The Board is also entitled to refer any point of law to the High Court for determination.[309]

As a general rule, a party aggrieved by a planning decision should first exhaust his appellate remedies by appealing to An Bord Pleanála. However, where the applicant wishes to impugn the *vires* of a planning decision, it may be that he may now apply directly to the High Court for judicial review of that decision at least in certain circumstances.[310]

Enforcement   The planning code may be enforced in a number of ways, namely: criminal sanctions, enforcement or warning notices or by the granting of injunctive relief. By virtue of section 24 of the 1963 Act a person who carries out any development in respect of which permission is required without or in contravention of such permission is guilty of an offence. The prosecution may proceed summarily or by way of an indictment.[311] On the other hand, the planning authority may choose to take the less drastic step of issuing an enforcement notice or a warning notice, if of the opinion that a development is being carried out in an unauthorised manner, or contrary to the requirements of conditions attached to the permission. The enforcement notice[312] must specify the nature of the unauthorised development, or the development constituting non-compliance with a condition, and require the developer to take such steps as are necessary to restore the land to its original condition. Alternatively, a warning notice may be issued by a planning authority where it appears that the land is being, or is likely to be, developed in an unauthorised manner,[313] or where unauthorised use is being made of the land, or where any structural or natural feature of the land, the preservation of which is required by a condition subject to which a permission for the development of any land was granted, may be removed or damaged. Disobedience to the enforcement or warning notice is an offence.

The section 27 planning injunction   The planning injunction is undoubtedly the most effective method of ensuring compliance with the planning code. Section 27(1)

---

306 Local Government (Planning and Development) Act 1992, s.14
307 Local Government (Planning and Development) Act 1992, s.16(1).
308 1976 Act, s. 14(2).
309 1976 Act, s. 42.
310 See, *e.g. P & F Sharpe Ltd v. Dublin City and County Manager* [1989] I.R. 701; *Tennyson v. Dun Laoghaire Corporation* [1991] 2 I.R. 527. But there may well be cases where the real issue concerns planning merits and where the courts will defer to An Bord Pleanála (if an appeal is pending), even if the judicial review of the planning authority's initial decision also raises issues of law: *Healy v. Dublin County Council*, unreported, High Court, April 28, 1993. See, further, pp. 734–739.
311 s.24 of the 1963 Act, as inserted by s.8 of the Local Government (Planning and Development) Act 1982. The maximum penalty is now a fine not exceeding IR£1m. plus two years' imprisonment, together with a maximum of IR£10,000 fine per day in respect of each continuing offence.
312 Local Government (Planning and Development) Act 1963, ss. 31, 32 and 35. See generally, Galligan, *op. cit.* above, n.260, pp. 297–305 and *Dublin C.C. v. Hill* [1994] 1 I.R. 86.
313 Local Government (Planning and Development) Act 1976, s.26.

of the 1976 Act (as inserted by s.19(4)(g) of the 1992 Act)[314] authorises the High Court and Circuit Court to restrain unauthorised development or use of land and to ensure "so far as practicable" that the land "is restored to its condition prior to the commencement of the development or unauthorised use."

Section 27(1) expressly provides that an applicant need not satisfy ordinary *locus standi* requirements:

"We are all, as users and enjoyers of the environment in which we live, given a standing to go to the Court and to seek an order compelling those who have been given a development permission to carry out the development in accordance with the terms of that permission. And the Court is given a discretion sufficiently wide to make whatever order is necessary to achieve that objective."[315]

An applicant for section 27 has thus no obligation to show that he or she has suffered any damage beyond that which all citizens suffer once the planning legislation has been breached and public amenities thereby impaired.[316]

Although the section 27 procedure was a highly successful innovatory feature of the 1976 Act, the rather lax language of the original section 27(2) gave rise to certain anomalies.[317] The new section 27

". . . brings coherence to the planning injunction remedy . . . Under the new section 27, the court can issue a planning injunction even where a development for which the required permission obtained is not being worked on. Moreover, the anomaly whereby a person carrying out development without permission was in a better position than a person who obtained a permission but was not carrying out the development in accordance [therewith] is now reformed."[318]

The new section 27(2) is thus comprehensive in its terms and provides that:

"Where any development authorised by a permission granted under Part IV of the Principal Act has been commenced, but has not been, or is not being, carried out in conformity with the permission because of non-compliance with the requirements of the condition attached to the permission or for any other reason, the High Court or Circuit Court may . . . by order require any person to do or not to do, or to cease to do, as the case may be, anything the Court considers necessary and specifies in the order to ensure that the development is carried out in conformity with the permission."

The effectiveness of the section 27 remedy has been strengthened by a series of decisions in which it has been said that it would require "exceptional circumstances" for the court to refrain from exercising its powers under this section.[319] However,

---

[314] See generally, Scannell, *op. cit.* above, n.260, pp. 254–257 and Galligan, *op. cit.* above, n.260, pp. 276–297 and McGrath, "Planning Injunctions under Section 27" (1996) 18 D.U.L.J. 1.

[315] *Morris v. Garvey* [1983] I.R. 319 at 323, *per* Henchy J.

[316] *Avenue Properties Ltd v. Farrell Homes Ltd* [1982] I.L.R.M. 21. A competitor has sufficient standing to seek s.27 relief: *Robinson v. Chariot Inns Ltd* [1986] I.L.R.M. 621.

[317] See, *e.g. Dublin County Council v. Kirby* [1985] I.L.R.M. 325; *Loughnane v. Hogan* [1987] I.R. 322.

[318] Cooney, (1992) I.C.L.S.A. at 14–01 and 14–21–22.

[319] *Morris v. Garvey* [1983] I.R. 319; *Stafford and Bates v. Roadstone Ltd* [1980] I.L.R.M. 1.

there have been a fair number of cases which have managed to squeeze themselves within this category.[320] A discordant note was, furthermore, struck by the Supreme Court's decision in *Mahon v. Irish Rugby Football Union*[321] in which Denham J. (emphasising the wording of s.27(2) – "has been commenced") held that the section 27 remedy was not available to restrain an anticipatory breach of the planning laws. This decision will almost certainly require fresh legislation and a further amendment of section 27. It is scarcely consistent with the fundamental objective of the planning laws that they could be flouted by, *e.g.* the illegal demolition of a listed building and that the courts should have no power in an appropriate case pursuant to section 27 to restrain such an anticipatory breach.

(ii) Housing

Numerous pieces of legislation dating from the mid-nineteenth century have sought to deal with the problem of poor and overcrowded housing, and to provide suitable accommodation for persons of modest means. The principal legislation on this topic is now contained in the Housing Act 1966, although this reforming and consolidating Act has been amended on a number of occasions, most notably by the Housing (Miscellaneous Provisions) Act 1979, the Housing Act 1988, the Housing (Miscellaneous Provisions) Act 1992 and the Housing (Miscellaneous Provisions) Act 1997.[322]

Local authorities are vested with the powers of a housing authority for their functional area. Section 8 of the Housing Act 1988[323] now requires housing authorities to prepare an estimate of existing and prospective housing requirements at any time that appears to them expedient or as they may be directed to do by the Minister for the Environment. In making such assessment, the housing authority are required to have regard, *inter alia*, to information:

> "[I]n relation to the housing conditions in the area, including the number of houses which are in any respect unfit or unsuitable for human habitation, are over-crowded,[324] are shared involuntarily or are expected (through obsole-

---

[320]   The "exceptional circumstances" referred to by Henchy J. in *Morris* include: genuine mistake (*Dublin County Council v. Sellwood Quarries Ltd* [1981] I.L.R.M. 23; *Dublin Corporation v. McGowan* [1993] 1 I.R. 405); persistent acquiescence (*Dublin Corporation v. Mulligan,* unreported, High Court, May 6, 1980); lack of good faith (*O'Connor v. Frank Harrington Ltd*, unreported, High Court, May 28, 1987); where the breach is technical and *de minimis* (*Leech v. Reilly*, unreported, High Court, April 26, 1983) and gross or disproportionate hardship (*Dublin C.C. v. Sellwood Quarries Ltd* [1981] I.L.R.M. 23; *Avenue Properties Ltd v. Farrell Homes Ltd* [1982] I.L.R.M. 21; *White v. McInerney Construction Ltd* [1995] 1 I.L.R.M. 374) See generally, Scannell, "Planning Control–Twenty Years On II" (1983) 5 D.U.L.J. 225 at pp. 241–247 and Scannell, *op. cit.*, above, n.244, pp. 254–257 and Galligan, *op. cit.* above, n.260, pp. 284–290. In *White* the Supreme Court approved the words of Barrington J. in *Avenue Properties* to the effect that in s.27 proceedings the courts should, to some extent at least, be influenced "by the factors which would influence a court of equity in deciding to grant or withhold an injunction." This, to some extent, dilutes the necessity to demonstrate the "exceptional circumstances" referred to by Henchy J. in *Morris v. Garvey.*

[321]   Unreported, Supreme Court, August 1, 1997.

[322]   See Keane, *op. cit.* above, n.1, pp. 128–147; Roche, *op. cit.*, above, n.1, pp. 220–243.

[323]   See generally, Maher, "Grafting the Homeless on to the Housing Code" (1989) 24 *Ir. Jur.* 182.

[324]   By virtue of s.63 of the Housing Act 1966, a house is deemed to be overcrowded when the number of persons ordinarily sleeping in the house and the number of rooms therein either: (1) are such that any two of those persons, being persons of 10 years of age or more of opposite sexes and not being

scence, demolition or conversion to other uses) to be lost to the supply of housing over the period to which the estimate relates."

A related provision, section 9 requires a housing authority to make an assessment, on at least a three-yearly basis, of the need for provision by the authority:

". . . of adequate and suitable housing accommodation for persons —

(a) whom the authority have reason to believe, require, or are likely to require, accommodation from the authority, and

(b) who, in the opinion of the authority, are in need of such accommodation and are unable to provide from their own resources."

Section 9(2) provides that, without prejudice to the generality of section 9(1), a housing authority is enjoined to have regard, *inter alia*, to the housing needs of the homeless; travellers; persons living in sub-standard or overcrowded accommodation; young persons leaving institutional care or without family accommodation; persons in need of accommodation for medical or compassionate reasons; the elderly or those who are disabled or handicapped. Section 11 (which replaces the previous section 60 of the Housing Act 1966) requires the housing authority to draw up a scheme of priorities for the letting of dwellings to persons in need of accommodation and who have insufficient means to provide for their own accommodation. Section 11(2)(a) permits the authority to reserve a particular number or proportion of dwellings for "persons of such category or categories" as it may determine.

The purpose and effect of section 60 of the Housing Act 1966 (which corresponded to the present section 11 of the 1988 Act) was examined by the Supreme Court in *McDonald v. Feeley*.[325] In this case, itinerants residing within the County Council's functional area had trespassed on lands belonging to the Council. The Council members resolved, pursuant to section 4 of the City and County Management (Amendment) Act 1955 that the County Manager should take action to evict the itinerants. Initially, no alternative accommodation had been offered to the itinerants. The Supreme Court noted that a County Manager could only be required to perform a lawful act by lawful means. The Court hinted that action of this nature would not have been lawful had not alternative accommodation been offered at the eleventh hour by the County Council because the housing authority would have acted without having regard to the housing needs of persons resident within their functional area.

As far as the specific housing needs of the travelling community are concerned, section 13 of the Housing Act 1988 now provides that:

"A housing authority may provide, improve, manage and control sites for caravans used by [members of the travelling community] and may carry out any works incidental to such provision, improvement, management or control, including the provision of such services for such sites."

In *University of Limerick v. Ryan*[326] Barron J. agreed that section 13 was permissive, but said that the authority's discretion was one "which must in appropriate circum-

---

persons living together as man and wife must sleep in the same room, or (2) are such that the free air space in any room used as a sleeping apartment for any person is less than 400 cubic feet.

[325] Unreported, Supreme Court, July 23,1980.

[326] Unreported, High Court, February 21, 1991.

stances be exercised." He added that, by virtue of section 13, "a housing authority cannot meet its statutory obligations by offering only a conventional dwelling to travellers." And in *Co.Meath VEC v. Joyce*[327] Flood J. added that a housing authority had a duty to perform its statutory functions "in a rational and reasonable manner" and to provide accommodation for homeless, including travellers. The duty, while not an absolute one, is that housing authorities are required to provide travellers with halting sites of the same general standard as local authority housing: *Mongan v. South Dublin County Council.*[328] Here Barron J. held that a traveller family were entitled to refuse to be accommodated upon the grounds that the services there were inadequate, but were not entitled to refuse on other grounds, such as, for example, that they were required to share the site with others.

In some respects, the Housing Act 1988 represents a dilution of the obligations formerly imposed by the Housing Act 1966. For example, section 55 of the 1966 Act obliged the local authority to draw up a building programme, but this section is now expressly repealed by section 30 of the 1988 Act. This repeal was justified[329] on the basis that as the cost of local authority building programmes were increasingly met by central government funds, the importance of the building programme had accordingly diminished to the point of redundancy. On the other hand, some statutory obligations contained in the 1966 Act have been strengthened and added to by the 1988 Act. Section 56(1) of the 1966 Act provides that a housing authority:

"... may erect, acquire, purchase, convert or reconstruct, lease or otherwise provide dwellings (including houses, flats, maisonettes and hostels) and such dwellings may be temporary or permanent."

Section 13(2) of the 1988 Act now extends these powers of housing authorities to include the management and control sites for caravans used by members of the travelling community.

Defective buildings and the Housing Acts Lettings made by a housing authority under the provisions of the Housing Acts are subject to an implied warranty that the premises are fit for human habitation. This was decided by the Supreme Court in *Siney v. Dublin Corporation,*[330] where two months after the plaintiffs moved into a flat provided by the defendants under the Housing Act 1966 water appeared under the floor covering of the bedroom of the flat and a fungus spread over the walls. Eventually the plaintiff and his family were compelled to leave the flat and they were housed elsewhere by the Corporation. O'Higgins C.J. held that the plaintiff was entitled to damages for breach of an implied warranty contained in the lease:

---

[327] [1994] 2 I.L.R.M. 210. See also *Ward v. South Dublin C.C.* [1996] 3 I.R. 195 and *O'Reilly v. O'Sullivan,* unreported, Supreme Court, February 26, 1997.

[328] Unreported, High Court, July 31, 1995.

[329] See the comments of the Minister for the Environment (Mr. Padraic Flynn T.D.) at *Seanad Debates,* Vol. 120, col. 2171.

[330] [1980] I.R. 400. For an excellent account of this case, see Kerr and Clarke, "Council Housing, Implied terms and Negligence – A Critique of *Siney v. Dublin Corporation*" (1980) 15 Ir. Jur. 32. See also, *Coleman v. Dundalk U.D.C.,* unreported, Supreme Court, July 17, 1985. For a general discussion of this case insofar as it impacts on the law of negligence, see pp. 835–836.

"[This] was a letting made by the defendant corporation of a dwelling provided under its building programme and let by it in accordance with its scheme of priority for, inter alia, the ending of overcrowding and the elimination of houses unfit in any respect for human habitation . . . It seems to me that to not imply such a condition or warranty would be to assume that the defendant corporation was entitled to disregard, and was disregarding, the responsibilities cast upon it by the very Act which authorised the building and letting of the accommodation in question."[331]

This entire question was further explored by Blayney J. in *Burke v. Dublin Corporation*,[332] where the defendants had installed a defective heating system (which had caused asthma and other bronchial conditions) into a number of houses let by them under the Housing Act 1966. The defendants argued that the house was not unfit for human habitation within the meaning of section 66(2) of the Housing Act 1966:

"The housing authority in considering whether a house is unfit for human habitation shall have regard to the extent (if any) to which the house is deficient as respects each of the matters set out in the Second Schedule to the Act."

The matters expressly referred to in the Second Schedule did not include heating systems, but Blayney J. could not accept that the standards in the Second Schedule by reference to which the fitness for human habitation was to be determined were exclusive. In his view, the houses were not fit for human habitation at the time of the letting by reason of the defects in the heating system:

"Suppose at the time of the letting it was known that there was a risk that the use of the heating [system] might cause one of the tenants to develop asthma, would the house have been let to the [plaintiff]? I have no doubt but that it would not. The defendants would have taken the view that it was unfit for letting in the condition in which it was, and would have substituted some other form of heating [system]."[333]

Blayney J. then went on to hold that the claim of another plaintiff who had actually purchased the dwelling that had been originally let to her under the Housing Act 1966 by the authority should, likewise, be upheld.[334] These results might be thought to be a far-reaching extension of the duties of a housing authority under the Housing Act 1966, but, of course, the *Burke* decision does not mean that the authority will have a potential liability in perpetuity, as it were. In the first place, the essential element of this part of Blayney J.'s judgment is that a local authority is responsible

---

[331] *Ibid.* at 410. In *Howard v. Dublin Corporation* [1996] 2 I.R. 235, another defective heating case, Lavan J. held that the duty identified in *Burke* extends to loans made by a housing authority pursuant to s.40 of the Housing Act 1966, but that the duty in such cases is often "tenuous", so that there was no continuing warranty (unlike in the case of a tenant) that the heating system installed by independent contractors with the assistance of the loan would be fit for human habitation: see further at p. 842.

[332] [1990] 1 I.R. 18

[333] *Ibid.* at 27. The reasoning of Blayney J. was expressly approved on appeal by the Supreme Court: [1991] 1 I.R. 341.

[334] *Ibid.* at 29.

for any breach of implied warranties existing at the time of the sale of the premises to a tenant-purchaser, but not for any defects that subsequently arise. Secondly, it is unclear whether the obligation would run on to successors in title of the original tenant-purchaser.

As far as private accommodation is concerned, a local authority is entitled to send the equivalent of what in the planning process are called warning notices where it is satisfied that a particular house is overcrowded or is unfit for human habitation. Section 65 of the 1966 Act entitles the authority to serve a notice on the owner of the premises requiring him to desist from causing or permitting the overcrowding. Failure to comply with such a notice is an offence.[335] In the case of unfit houses, the authority may serve a notice on the owner of such premises requiring him within 28 days to carry out specified works. If the house is unfit for human habitation, but is not capable of being rendered habitable at a reasonable expense, then the owner must be afforded the opportunity of carrying out such specified works, or using the house in a particular manner. If this is not possible, the authority may make a closing order (which prohibits the use of the house or any part thereof for any purpose specified by the housing authority) or a demolition order. A person aggrieved by a closing order or a demolition order may generally appeal to the Circuit Court.[336]

Most important of all, the Minister for the Environment and Local Government has now made regulations, by which a private landlord of a rented house must provide accommodation to a specified standard, must provide a rent book and must publish details of the letting in a register kept by a local authority. Failure to perform any of these obligations constitutes an offence.[337]

1992 and 1997 Acts: major provisions The Housing (Miscellaneous Provisions) Act 1992 seeks to improve the position of local authority tenants and to counteract the effects of social segregation in housing. Housing authorities are thus entitled to carry out works on sub-standard private accommodation[338]; and to make contributions to approved voluntary housing bodies.[339] While section 10 enables a housing authority to remove temporary dwellings which are unlawfully placed on a public place within five miles of a serviced housing site, but such an order may only lawfully be served if the site in question is suitable for accommodation of the persons on whom the notice is served.[340] Section 20 of the 1988 Act is amended by section 28 of this Act so as to require local authorities to draw up a policy statement "to counteract undue segregation in housing between people of different social backgrounds."

By virtue of the Housing (Miscellaneous Provisions) Act 1997 a housing authority is empowered to take action against persons believed to be engaged in "anti-social

---

[335] s.65(4) of the 1966 Act, as amended by Housing (Miscellaneous Provisions) Act 1992, s.33(1), provides that the maximum penalty which may be imposed is IR£1,000 and one month's imprisonment.

[336] ss. 72 and 73 of the 1966 Act.

[337] Housing (Miscellaneous Provisions) Act 1992, ss. 17–22, 34.

[338] s.5.

[339] s.6.

[340] *Ward v. South Dublin C.C.* [1996] 3 I.R. 195. In this case Laffoy J. held on the facts that the site in question was not suitable for the accommodation of further temporary dwellings by reason of its physical condition and the inadequacy of services on the site in question.

behaviour".[341] Thus, a local authority tenant is entitled to apply to the District Court for an excluding order against any such person[342] and the authority may similarly apply if they consider that there is a risk that an existing tenant may be deterred from so applying and that if they consider that such an application is in the interests of good estate management.[343] The authority is also empowered to refuse to sell or let local authority dwellings to a person whom it considers "is or has been engaged in anti-social behaviour."[344]

Demolition of habitable houses   Following the repeal of the Housing Act 1969,[345] the demolition of habitable houses is now dealt with by the Local Government (Planning and Development) Regulations 1994[346] and Class 45(a) of the Second Schedule of the 1994 Regulations provides that the demolition of a habitable house is not regarded as an exempted development and consequently planning permission is required.

(iii) Functions under the Gaming and Lotteries Act 1956

Part III of the Gaming and Lotteries Act 1956 confers important functions on local authorities in that such authorities can by resolution determine whether they wish to permit the operation of gaming at amusement halls and funfairs within their functional area. Unless the local authority has resolved that the provisions of Part III shall be so applied within their functional area, the operation of gaming at amusement halls or funfairs is unlawful.

Once such a resolution is in force, then the District Court has jurisdiction to grant a certificate authorising the issue of a gaming licence,[347] to which conditions may be attached. The District Court is required to have regard to various statutory criteria, including the character of the applicant or the persons exercising control and management; the number of gaming licences already in the vicinity; the suitability of the premises and the class of persons likely to have resort to it.[348] The Revenue Commissioners are then obliged to grant a gaming licence on payment of the appropriate excise duty.[349] However, a certificate of this kind has been held to be an annual certificate of limited duration and it is not in the nature of a permanent property right which attaches to the premises. This was decided by Johnson J. in

---

[341]   Defined by s.1(1) as including a person engaged in the supply or manufacture of illegal drugs and also:
  "any behaviour which causes or is likely to cause any significant or persistent danger, injury, damage, loss or fear to any person living, working or otherwise lawfully in or in the vicinity of a house provided by a housing authority under the *Housing Acts 1966 to 1997*, or a housing estate in which the house is situate and, without prejudice to the foregoing, includes violence, threats, intimidation, coercion, harassment or serious obstruction of any person."

[342]   s.3(1).

[343]   s.3(2) and 3(3).

[344]   s.14.

[345]   The Act required permission from a housing authority for the demolition of a habitable house, or the use "otherwise than for human habitation" of any habitable house. The Act lapsed on December 31, 1984.

[346]   S.I. No. 86 of 1994.

[347]   On licensing systems, generally, see Chap. 7.

[348]   s.17.

[349]   s.19.

Dublin Corporation v. O'Hanrahan,[350] where he held that a certificate granted by the District Court must be renewed annually and that a "certificate can be refused in respect of a premises which was previously certified."[351]

The vast majority of local authorities did exercise their powers under Part III of the Acts, but increased social concern as to the perceived evils associated with such gaming halls led to many local authorities exercising their powers under section 13 to rescind such resolutions, at least in part.[352] This in turn has given rise to litigation,[353] but the courts have displayed a marked disinclination to interfere with the exercise of such discretion by local authorities.

A good example is supplied by *The State (Divito) v. Arklow U.D.C.*[354] Here the local authority, anticipating an application by the applicant to the District Court for a gaming licence, rescinded an earlier resolution which had applied Part III of the 1956 Act to the entirety of their functional area. The authority then readopted Part III for part of their functional area, but excluded a stretch of the street where the applicant's premises were situated. This resolution was assailed on a number of grounds and among them was the argument that the local authority was motivated by bias. Henchy J. said:

> "I have no doubt that in the eyes of the applicant, the council's resolutions appear as a personalised obstruction of his efforts to convert his premises into a licensed amusement hall. However, looking at the situation objectively, I cannot hold that he has shown that the council were actuated, wholly or primarily by personal considerations [T]here is ample evidence to lend support to the council's claim that, in removing the application of Part III of the Act from a stretch of Upper Main St. which contains the applicant's premises, they were motivated by considerations such as the undesirability of having an amusement arcade in the vicinity of five schools, the adequacy for the town of Arklow of the four existing amusement arcades, and the declared wishes of the local community."[355]

Accordingly, therefore, a resolution to rescind or vary the extent of a previous resolution under Part III of the 1956 Act will be upheld where it is based on objective considerations. Once such a resolution has been passed, then it is clear that the District Court has no further jurisdiction to grant certificates under the terms of Part III of the 1956 Act and that any gaming on premises within the area specified by the rescinding resolution becomes unlawful.[356]

---

[350] [1988] I.R. 121.
[351] *Ibid.* at 124.
[352] For the background to the recission of the Part III resolution by Dublin Corporation, see *Re Murphy's Application* [1987] I.R. 667.
[353] See, *e.g. Re Camillo's Application* [1988] I.R. 104.
[354] [1986] I.L.R.M. 123.
[355] *Ibid.* at 126.
[356] *Re Camillo's Application* [1988] I.R. 104.

8. Central Government Controls

The powers of the elected representatives have not only been eroded from below by the management system, but also reduced from above by the ascendency of the Minister for the Environment.[357] For local authorities are subject to extensive and diverse controls exercised by the Minister for the Environment, of which there is one at almost every aspect of a local authority's structure and functions. Local authorities, for instance, enjoy a general power to borrow money, but subject to the control of the Minister.[358] In practice, most local authorities borrow from either the Local Loan Fund[359] (which is under the control of the Minister for Finance) or (for short term loans) from the banks. Dealing with the former, more important source, Roche states:

> "In applying for sanction, the local authority submits details of the proposed work. The Minister has professional and technical staff who examine the proposals. If there is no technical objection and the Minister is satisfied that the project is one for which borrowing should be permitted, that the authority has power to borrow for this purpose and the ability to repay, sanction is given. By this the Minister does not assume any responsibility for the plans or schemes put forward. If the loan is sought from the Local Loans Fund, the Minister will recommend the issue from the Fund."[360]

It is significant that, as a result of the Local Loan Fund (Amendment) Act 1987, section 1 by which the Minister is empowered to waive the whole or part of any local loan "if it seems to him desirable so to do", all major local authority capital projects are now funded by way of capital grants, thereby eliminating the circular transfers of the local loan funds. However, this does not affect the power of control explained in the passage just quoted.

In more specific matters, the Minister for the Environment enjoys a power of consent or veto,[361] for example, with regard to the making of bye-laws.[362] Some statutes

---

[357] For a particular power of delegation by the Minister for the Environment and Local Government "to a named officer", see local Government Act 1994, s. 61(1).

[358] Local Government (No. 2) Act 1960, s.4.

[359] Constituted by the Local Loan Funds Acts 1935–1987. The maximum aggregate amount which can be advanced by the Fund is increased every few years. By the Local Loan Funds (Amendment) Act 1986, it was fixed at IR£4.5 billion.

[360] Roche, *op. cit.* above, n.1, p. 182.

[361] See, *e.g.* s.26(1) of the Local Government Act 1941 which provides that the consent of the Minister for Environment is necessary before an officer of any local authority may lawfully be removed from his post: see *O'Mahony v. Arklow U.D.C.* [1965] I.R. 710. However, it may be noted that s.52(1) of the Local Government Act 1991 enables the Minister for the Environment to make an order removing certain statutory controls (requiring, *e.g.* the Minister's consent before certain functions can be performed) from earlier enactments and one such order has been made: Local Government Act 1991 (Removal of Controls) Regulations 1993 (S.I. No. 172 of 1993).

[362] The powers here are very extensive. Section 37(8) of the Local Government Act 1994 enables the appropriate Minister to make regulation specifying the matters or classes of matters in respect of which a local authority shall not make bye-laws. Section 37(9) provides that where "for given reasons" the "appropriate Minister" considers that a bye-law or any provision thereof is objectionable and notifies the local authority accordingly, then, if the local authority does not revoke or amend the bye-law in conformity with the notice, that Minister may do so by order, with effect from a specified day. Section 39(2)(a) enables the appropriate Minister by regulations to designate any matter or class of matters for which a bye-law shall require the prior approval of the Minister. In

even give the Minister power to make regulations for local authorities, as, for example, in planning matters.[363] Even when this is not the formal legal position, substantially the same result is achieved (in terms of uniformity throughout the country and Ministerial ascendancy) by the Department of the Environment issuing circulars containing model bye-laws or other regulations which most local authorities are pleased to adopt. In certain cases (such as a dispute as to whether a local authority dwelling which is being sold to a former tenant has been put into "good structural condition,")[364] an individual may appeal to the Minister against a decision of the local authority. In other cases, the Minister's power of command is given specific statutory foundation. For example, section 15 of the Public Health (Ireland) Act 1896 provides:

> "Where complaint is made to the [Minister for the Environment] that a sanitary authority has made default in providing their district with sufficient sewers. [the Minister], if satisfied, after due inquiry that the authority has been guilty of the alleged default shall make an order limiting a time for the performance of their duty in the matter of such complaint. If such duty is not performed by the time limited in the order, such order may be enforced by mandamus or [the Minister] may appoint some person to perform such duty."

Modern examples may be found in diverse statutory provisions. The consent of the Minister is required before any officer of any local authority is lawfully removed from his post.[365] Section 15(1) of the Roads Act 1993 provides that a road authority must comply with any direction in relation to "the maintenance or construction of public roads"[366] which is given by the Minister. The Minister may also give directions specifying the maximum amount which local authorities may expend on entertainment and receptions.[367]

The Minister is even entitled to penetrate to the very heart of local democracy by removing the elected members on any number of specific grounds:

(i) where he is satisfied following a local inquiry that the authority is not effectively performing its duties;

(ii) where the local authority refuses to obey any court order,

---

the case of bye-laws requiring such approval, s.39(3) requires the local authority to submit a copy of the bye-law to the appropriate Minister, together with copies of any submissions received by the authority and any comments which it may have on them. The Minister is thus enabled either to approve or to amend the bye-law or, if necessary, to refuse to approve the bye-law. See also Local Government Act 1994 (Bye-Laws) Regulations 1995 (S.I. No. 360 of 1995). See, further, p. 35.

[363] Local Government (Planning and Development) Act 1963, s.10; Local Government (Water Pollution) Act 1977, ss.26, 27 and 30.

[364] Housing Act 1966, s.106(1).

[365] Local Government Act 1941, s. 26(1). See *O'Mahony v. Arklow UDC* [1965] I.R. 710.

[366] For further examples of this type of power, see Housing Act 1966, s.111; Local Government (Financial Provisions) Act 1978, s.15.

[367] Local Government Act 1991, s. 46(3). For a modified version of such type of powers, see, e.g., Litter Pollution Act 1997, s.29 whereby the Minister for the Environment is entitled to issue policy guidelines regarding the effective operation of the Act and to which the local authorities are required to have regard, in performing their statutory functions and in the making of a litter management plan, under s.10 of that Act. See also Roads Act 1993, s.15(3)(ministerial power to issue policy guidelines to which road authorities must have regard).

(iii) where the authority refuses to permit its accounts to be duly audited;

(iv) where the number of members is not sufficient to permit a quorum to be formed for meetings[368]

(v) where the authority refuses to strike an adequate rate,[369]

(vi) where the authority refuses or wilfully neglects to comply with an express requirement which is imposed upon them by any enactment or order,[370]

(vii) where the local authority adopts estimates that are, in the Minister's opinion, insufficient to maintain public services at a reasonable level.[371]

It should be noted that ground (vi) would authorise the Minister to dismiss the elected members if, for example, they refused to comply with his directive that the rate struck in the pound should not exceed a specific amount. These powers were employed in 1969 to dismiss the members of Dublin Corporation where the Council had deliberately struck a rate less than the full amount required to meet the demand for health services.[372] Where the elected members are dismissed, the Minister may appoint one or more persons to act as commissioners for the local authority.[373] The commissioner discharges the reserved functions of the elected members in the interim period pending the next elections.[374]

Naturally, the very existence of these powers presupposes that they will be exercised on an informed basis. Accordingly, the Minister may require a local authority: "to make to him any return or report or furnish him with any information in relation to their functions which he may consider necessary or desirable."[375] Moreover, the Minister may even cause a local inquiry to be held for the purpose or any of his powers or duties.[376]

Secondly, by section 2(4) of the Local Elections Act 1972 the Minister has the power to order that local elections be postponed, although this power is made subject to confirmation by Dáil and Seanad resolutions. This power has been exercised surprisingly often[377] and the All-Party Oireachtas Committee on the Constitution in its *First Progess Report* recommended[378] that in order to enhance the "democratic value" of local democracy that the Constitution should be amended to provide that "elections to local authorities shall be held at least once every five years."

---

[368] Grounds (i)–(iv) are contained in the Local Government Act 1941, s.44.

[369] Local Government Act 1946, s.30(4).

[370] Local Government Act 1941, s.44 as inserted by s.64 of the Local Government Act 1946.

[371] City and County Management (Amendment) Act 1955, s.10A (as inserted by the Loval Government Act 1994, s.44).

[372] Roche, *op. cit.* above, n.1, p. 123. The members of Naas UDC were dismissed in similar circumstances in 1985; see *The Irish Times*, August 3, 1985.

[373] Local Government Act 1941, s.48.

[374] Local Government Act 1941, s.49.

[375] *Ibid.* s.84.

[376] *Ibid.* s.83.

[377] In May 1973 the then Minister for Local Government stated that the order postponing the local elections from 1973 to 1974 was the fifteenth such postponement since 1919: see *Dáil Debates* Vol. 265, col. 1050 (May 15, 1973). Since then local elections have been postponed in both 1984, 1990, 1994 and 1997. The Minister for Local Government (Mr N. Dempsey T.D.) has announced that the next local government elections will be held in 1999: *The Irish Times*, December 13, 1997.

[378] Pn. 3795 (April 1997) at pp. 70–71. The present Minister has stated that a referendum to give effect to this recommendation will be held at the first opportunity: *The Irish Times*, December 13, 1997.

In reality, of course, even without particular legal warrant, a Minister or Departmental civil servant's suggestion will carry enormous weight because of the relationship of ascendancy and subservience within which it is made. It is true that in recent years the trend of legislation since the Local Government Act 1991 has been to confer more powers (including reserved functions) on local authorities. But this development simply mirrors the increased legislative output of the Oireachtas and the functions conferred are often highly specific duties in relation to traditional functions of local authorities, such as roads, planning and waste management. The exception here is, of course, the Local Government (Financial Provisions) Act 1997 which genuinely restores a large measure of local autonomy by enabling local authorities to raise local finance by altering the rates of car tax. In addition, section 9(1)(a) of the 1991 Act allows the Government to transfer by order

> "a function of a Minister for the Government (other than a function that is required by the Constitution to be performed by a Minister of the Government) that, in the opinion of the Government, could be performed effectively by local authorities of a specified class or classes and is a function relating to the provision of a public service in the functional area of local authorities ... "

No such order has been made to date.

9. Prospects for Local Government Reform

The entire question of local government reform was considered by the Constitution Review Group in the context of whether local government should enjoy constitutional protection.[379] While the Group recommended, in principle, some form of recognition, it was far more guarded about detailed and specific provisions because, *inter alia*,

> ". . . any constitutional clause with teeth could give rise to new separation of powers issues between government and regions (a fruitful source of litigation in countries such as the USA and Germany). It could also lead to the invalidation of a whole range of central government controls (examples might include controls to secure the soundness of local finances, control of bye-laws etc.) and might require the insertion of a specific equalisation clause similar to Article 107 of the German Constitition allowing the redistribution of local government incomes (rates, service charges etc.) to poorer local authority areas."[380]

The All-Party Oireachtas Committee on the Constitution in its *First Progress Report*[381] found the the Review Group's arguments against specific recognition "telling" and concluded that while there ought to be general constitutional recognition, given the present state of flux in the relationship between central and

---

[379] *Report of Constitution Review Group* (1996, Pn. 2632) at pp. 428–431.

[380] *Ibid.* at 430. It may be noted that following the decision to allot car taxation receipts to local authorities in lieu of rate support grants it was found necessary to set up an equalisation fund to ensure equality of treatment for poorer counties: Local Government (Financial Provisions) Act 1997, ss. 4–7.

[381] Pn. 3795 (April 1997).

local government "it would be ill-advised to set down specific provisions in the Constitution."[382] Some of these issues were canvassed in the Department of the Environment's White Paper, *Better Local Government: A Programme for Change* in 1996. Further codification and modernisation of the local government law was promised.[383]

On the crucial issue of democratic accountability of local government, the White Paper recognised defects in the present arrangements[384] but merely proposed the establishment of strategic policy committees which would enable sub-committees of the full Council to work in partnership with the Manager in order to "identify particular policy areas for special consideration, arrange for their in-depth examination and report on necessary changes to the full Council."[385] Whether this would in practice effect a fundamental change in the existing councillor/Manager relationship remains to be seen.

Unless fundamental change does come about, it would be difficult to gainsay the observation of one commentator to the effect that "local authorities are little more than executive agencies,"[386] nor, indeed, the more figurative comments of Dr. Barrington:

> "Local government is like any other historical ruin: something that we are perhaps reluctant to see removed wholly, but which we are prepared to see moulder away."[387]

---

[382] *Ibid.* at 70. The Committee therefore recommended the insertion of the following new clause in the Constitiution:
  "1. Local authorities shall be empowered to carry out the functions which the Oireachtas may from time to time devolve upon them by law.
  2. Elections to local authorities shall be held every five years."

[383] Para. 7.22–7.23 noted that:
  "A good start has also been made towards updating the general local government law with the Local Government Acts of 1991 and 1994. However, the fundamental legislative basis for existing county/city and sub-county authorities is outdated and scattered over various nineteenth century and other enactments. It is unduly complex and fragmented, often with different provisions applying to the different classes of local authorities – a classification system which itself is archaic and of little relevance to the public. Comprehensive legislation will be [enacted in 1998] to provide in a convenient format a statutory basis for our local government system . . ."

[384] Para 2.18 states that:
  "While the law envisages councillors exercising the policy-making role, the current dynamics of local government organisation make it difficult for councillors to fulfill that function, other than by the formal adoption of statutory policy documents prepared by management."

[385] Para. 2.19. Broadly similar recommendations to those contained in *A Programme for Change* may be found in the two reports of the Devolution Commission, an expert review body established by the Government to consider the future of local government: *Devolution Commission, Interim Report* (June 1996) and *Devolution Commission, Second Report* (April, 1997)

[386] Walker, *Local Government Finance in Ireland* (E.R.S.I., 1962), p. 4.

[387] Barrington, *The Irish Administrative System* (Dublin, 1988), p. 40.

CHAPTER 6

TRIBUNALS AND INQUIRIES[1]

1. Introduction

One may begin an explanation of the nature of tribunals by listing a few examples (most of which are considered below). In the fields of taxation and compulsory acquisition, there are: Appeal Commissioners[2]; the Valuation Tribunal[3]; Employment Appeals Tribunal; the Mining Board[4]; and arbitrators appointed by the Land Values Reference Committee under various statutes to fix compensation for land compulsorily acquired.[5] Tribunals which resolve disputes arising from the running of the welfare state include the appeals officers in the Department of Social Welfare,[6] and the General Medical Services Payments Board.[7] In related fields there are the Criminal Injuries Compensation Tribunal[8] and the Legal Aid Board.[9] Several tribunals have been set up to operate various types of control and regulation in the public interest, often by way of a licensing system. These include the Censorship of Films Board[10]; the Censorship of Publications Board[11]; An Bord Pleanála[12]; the Registrar of Friendly Societies[13] and the Independent Radio and Television Commission[14]; and the Bookmakers Appeal Committee.[15] A number of tribunals exist to discipline

---

[1] See generally, Stout, *Administrative Law in Ireland* (1985), Chaps. 7–9 and App. 1; Grogan, "Administrative Tribunals" in King (ed.) *Public Administration in Ireland III* (1954), p. 32; Donaldson, *Some Comparative Aspects of Irish Law* (1957), pp. 192–198 and Grogan, *Administrative Tribunals in the Public Service* (1961).

[2] Taxes Consolidation Act, 1997, s.850 and Part 40.

[3] Valuation Act 1988, s.2.

[4] Minerals Development Act 1940, s.33.

[5] Acquisition of Land (Assessment of Compensation) Act 1919, as amended by Acquisition of Land (Reference Committee) Act 1925.

[6] See further, pp. 275–282.

[7] See p. 557.

[8] *Scheme of Compensation for Personal Injuries Criminally Inflicted* (1974) (Prl. 3658). See Osborough, "The Work of the Criminal Injuries Compensation Tribunal" (1978) 13 Ir. Jur. (N.S.) 320.

[9] Civil Legal Act 1995, s.3. *Scheme of Legal Aid and Advice* (1979, Prl. 8534), pp. 7–11. For an analysis of the state of affairs prior to the establishment of the Board on a statutory footing, see Whyte, "And Justice for Some" (1984) 6 D.U.L.J. (N.S.) 88.

[10] Censorship of Films Act 1923, s.1. See also, Video Recordings Act 1989, s.10.

[11] Censorship of Publications Act 1946, s.2. Nowadays, the Censorship Board is rarely used.

[12] Local Government (Planning and Development) Act 1976, ss.3–13 and Schedule to the Act. See Stevenson, "Planning Appeals in the Republic of Ireland" (1985) 7 *Urban Law and Policy* 170.

[13] For an account of the miscellaneous work of the Registrar, see Kerr and Whyte, *Irish Trade Union Law* (1985), pp. 41–48.

[14] Radio and Television Act 1988.

[15] This Committee is chaired by a judge or practising barrister or solicitor of at least seven years' standing and it hears appeals from the Irish Horseracing Authority in relation to course betting permits and course-betting representative permits: see Irish Horseracing Industry Act 1994, Pt. VI.

employees in the public service, for instance in the police and defence forces and in the prison service.[16]

As can be seen, the majority of the tribunals operate in the field of public law, assisting in the dirigiste and welfare aspects of the State's responsibilities. However, when creating a statutory innovation in the private law area, the Oireachtas sometimes chooses to vest responsibility for implementing the scheme in a tribunal, rather than a court. Examples include An Bord Uchtála[17]; the Labour Court[18]; the Employment Appeals Tribunal[19]; the Rent Tribunal[20]; the Pensions Tribunal[21] the Controller of Patents, Designs and Trade Marks[22]; or to take a recent and specifically designed example, the Irish Takeover Panel.[23]

A further anomaly is that, while most tribunals have been established by statute, in some cases – for instance, the Criminal Injuries Compensation Tribunal, Motor Insurance Bureau and the Stardust Compensation Scheme – they are established merely by administrative scheme. The extra-statutory character of these tribunals does not, however, preclude judicial review of their decisions. This question was raised in *The State (Hayes) v. Criminal Injuries Compensation Tribunal*,[24] which followed the English case of *R. v. Criminal Injuries Compensation Board, ex p. Lain*.[25] In *Hayes,* Finlay P. said that the High Court would review a decision of the tribunal in appropriate cases, such as where the principles of constitutional justice had been violated, or where the scheme of compensation had been misinterpreted.

We ought to mention here a sub-group which are sometimes called (in a further example of the vague terminology endemic in this field) "domestic tribunals". Any profession, trade union, organisation or even club may have rules for dealing, itself, with the discipline of its own members. Quite often, in the interest of fairness, a domestic tribunal will be set up to apply these disciplinary rules so as to determine whether the member is guilty of some transgression and, if so, what his punishment should be. In some cases the rules will be statutory in origin. Examples are those relating to the legal, medical and dental[26] professions. In other cases, notably trade

---

16 See, *e.g.* the disciplinary mechanism established by the Garda Síochána (Discipline) Regulations 1989 (S.I. No. 94 of 1989) and the Garda Síochána (Complaints) Act 1986; for the latter see the 2nd edition of this book, pp. 230–231.

17 Adoption Act 1952, s.8.

18 Industrial Relations Act 1946, Pt. II. See Mortished, "The Industrial Relations Act 1946" in King (ed.) *Public Administration in Ireland II* (Dublin, 1949).

19 Redundancy Payments Act 1967, s.39, as amended by s.1 of the Unfair Dismissals Act 1977. The Employment Appeals Tribunal has replaced the former Redundancy Payments Tribunals which had been established under the 1967 Act. For an account of the work of this tribunal, see Redmond, *Dismissal Law in the Republic of Ireland* (1982), pp. 120–128.

20 Housing (Private Rented Dwellings) (Amendment) Act 1983, ss.2–4. For an account of the procedure before the Rent Tribunal, see de Blacam, *The Control of Private Rented Dwellings* (1984), pp. 55–62.

21 Pensions Act 1990, Pt. II.

22 Patents Act 1992, s.6.

23 The Irish Takeover Panel Act 1997 includes many state of the art features of administrative agency for example the panel is constituted as a company (section 3); it makes some of its own substantive rules (like an U.S. administrative agency (section 8); it may act on its own initiative or at the request of a party to a takeover (section 10).

24 [1982] I.L.R.M. 210. See further at p. 771.

25 [1967] 2 Q.B. 864.

26 See, respectively, Solicitors (Amendment) Act 1960, Pt. II (as amended by the Solicitors (Amendment) Act 1994; Medical Practitioners Act 1978, Pt. V; Dentists Act 1985, Pt. II.

unions[27] but also sports associations, like the G.A.A., they will derive their authority ultimately from the agreement of their members. In either category and especially where the tribunal is constituted by statute, the tribunal will probably be subject to judicial control and at least some of the principles of substantive public law will apply.[28] The rationale for this intervention is doubtless that while these bodies may not be formally or completely "public" in nature, they make such a crucial impact on their members and on the rest of the community that their affairs warrant the attention of the court. In *Abbott v. Sullivan*[29] Denning L.J. said of trade union committees:

> "These bodies, which exercise a monopoly in an important sphere of human activity, with the power of depriving a man of his livelihood, must act in accordance with the elementary rules of justice. They must not condemn a man without giving him an opportunity to be heard in his own defence: and any agreement or practice to the contrary would be invalid."[30]

Although Denning L.J. was in dissent, it is these views which represent the modern law.[31] However, notwithstanding this principle, in practice, a court will sometimes resile from interfering in certain cases with the internal affairs of a tribunal whose authority derives from contract. Thus, in *McGrath and O'Ruairc v. Trustees of Maynooth College*[32] Henchy J. observed that a civil court was not the ideal forum in which to decide what was a "grave delinquency against clerical obligations" within the meaning of the college's own internal statutes. The court could only reject the conclusion of a domestic tribunal when it was one "that could not reasonably have been come to in the circumstances", or where the decisions had been arrived at in breach of natural justice or other internal procedure prerequisites.

As with Cleopatra, so with tribunals: "Age cannot wither them nor custom stale their infinite variety". This lack of uniformity extends even to the nomenclature. Not only do the names of tribunals differ – board, commission, tribunal, officer, registrar, controller, referee, umpire – but different authorities use different titles for the entire species. Thus one finds tribunals described as: administrative tribunals; special tribunals; statutory tribunals, or even, quasi-judicial tribunals. Modern usage is adopted here, we simply use the term "tribunals".

Before going further, we ought to mention the commonly-accepted definition of the term "tribunal". It is a body, independent of the Government or any other entity but at the same time not a court, which takes decisions affecting individual rights, according to some fairly precise (and usually legal) guidelines and by following a

---

27 See Kerr and Whyte, *Irish Trade Union Law* (1985), pp. 100–102.
28 See, *e.g. O'Donoghue v. Veterinary Council* [1975] I.R. 398 and *Re M., a Doctor* [1984] I.R. 479 (review of statutory tribunals) and *McGrath and O'Ruairc v. Trustees of Maynooth College* [1979] I.L.R.M. 166; *Connolly v. McConnell* [1983] I.R. 172, *Bane v. Garda Representative Association* [1997] 2 I.R. 449. See further, p. 767.
29 [1952] 1 K.B. 189.
30 *Ibid.* at 198.
31 See, *e.g. Edwards v. SOGAT* [1971] Ch. 354; *Enderby Town F.C. v. Football Association* [1971] Ch. 591; *N.E.E.T.U. v. McConnell* (1983) 2 J.I.S.L.L. 97 and *Connolly v. McConnell* [1983] I.R. 172.
32 [1979] I.L.R.M. 166.

regular and fairly formal procedure.[33] This is an explanation on whose elements we shall enlarge in Part 3 of this chapter.

Such a definition leads straightaway to the question: why does it matter whether or not a body is classified as a tribunal? It should be made clear, first of all, that the term tribunal (just like "state-sponsored body") is not a statutory category from membership of which certain definite legal consequences flow. Rather it is a term popularised by academic lawyers as an organising principle for books, lectures, etc. and as a basis for comparisons. Secondly, and more importantly, a court exercising the power of judicial review over a public body may be more likely to insist on rigorous standards of constitutional justice, reasonableness, etc., if it takes the view that the body before it possesses the attributes of a tribunal. However, the question of whether or not the body is stamped with either the name "tribunal" (or one of its commonly used synonyms) will be of secondary importance, in guiding a court to such a decision.

It ought to be stated, parenthetically, that naturally in a large number of judicial review cases, the body whose decision is under review is indeed a tribunal. However, in general, such cases will be considered together with similar cases involving other bodies, in the appropriate chapter on judicial review, and not here.

2. Why a Tribunal?

Not only is uniformity lacking from tribunal to tribunal, there is also a lack of consistency as to whether a tribunal should be created at all. If one leaves aside local authorities, state-sponsored bodies and other specialist institutions, it may be said that an individual decision may be vested in any one of three different types of body: a Minister and his Department, a court, or a tribunal. Let us now review these options.

---

[33] For instance, the Data Protection Commissioner, established by the Data Protection Act 1988, s.9 and 2nd Sched., and examined in Clarke, *Data Protection Law in Ireland* (1988) Chap. 8, does not warrant the designation "tribunal". In regard to this point of classification, first, it is not significant that he has functions (in regard, for example, to promoting codes of practice (s.13); or prosecuting for offences under the Act (s.30)) – in addition to those in respect of which he might be thought to be acting as a tribunal. (See p. 262). This consideration is more than outweighed by the fact that by his constitution, and indeed by express declaration, he is made "independent in the performance of his functions". The most important of the functions in the performance of which he might be thought to act as a tribunal is the issuing of an enforcement notice (s.10). This is issued where the Commissioner is of the opinion that a data controller (one who controls the contents of personal data) is contravening a provision of the Act, which is not itself designated as directly attracting criminal liability. An example would be an individual's right of access to data about himself or his right of rectification or erasure (ss.4–6). If the data controller fails to comply with an enforcement notice, he commits a criminal offence. Thus the Commissioner does make a substantial impact on individual rights. However this impact means that a criminal prosecution is necessary before a data controller suffers any sanction. Moreover on turning to examine procedure, it seems even less likely that the Commissioner can be regarded as a tribunal. For the salient and connected facts are that, first, there is a full right of appeal to the Circuit Court against the issue of an enforcement notice and, secondly, the 2nd Schedule to the Act contains none of the procedural formalities which are normally laid down for a tribunal (although the Commissioner does in fact permit informal representations to be made). Accordingly the Commissioner must be regarded as probably falling outside that nebulous category, the "tribunal".

Tribunal or Minister?

It would certainly make for consistency if the following demarcation line for functions between a Minister and a tribunal were consistently observed by the Oireachtas: matters should be allocated to a tribunal where they require a decision to be taken independently of the executive by the determination of facts according to a fairly formalised procedure, and the application to the facts of a fairly precise set of rules. In short, a tribunal would take all quasi-judicial decisions. This would leave to the Minister and his Department decisions containing a high policy content, which are not susceptible to regulation by a code of law.[34]

In fact, this division of functions as between a tribunal and a Minister fails as an adequate description of reality at two points. First, by no means all of the decisions of a type suitable for resolution by a tribunal are actually vested in a tribunal. Dealing with the question of allocation of functions in Britain, the Council of Tribunals remarked frankly:

> "[T]he choice is influenced by the interplay of various factors – the nature of decision, accidents of history, departmental preferences and political considerations – rather than by the application of a set of coherent principles."[35]

This is at least as true in Ireland as it is in Britain. Occasionally, functions which one would expect to be located in a tribunal are, for historical or other reasons, vested in a court, or, more often, in a Minister. The lack of correlation between a particular type of decision and a particular forum can be illustrated by the fact that, as it happens, in regard to three important functions, a decision is taken in the first instance by a body which is part of the executive arm of government; thence an appeal may be taken to a tribunal, with a further right of appeal from the tribunal (in the first two of the examples to be given, on a point of law only) to the High Court. One can see this pattern in the areas of planning, social welfare and tax law. Moreover, the transfer of planning appeals from the Minister for Local Government to An Bord Pleanála in 1977 does not appear to have radically altered the decisions emerging from the planning appeals process.[36]

As compared with a Minister, tribunals possess various advantages. The first of these was adverted to by Henchy J. in *The State (Pine Valley Developments Ltd) v. Dublin County Council*[37] Speaking in the context of an "aberrant" and *ultra vires* grant of outline planning permission by the Minister for Local Government, Henchy J. said that the Minister had:

> "[I]gnored the rights of the respondent planning authority and of those who were entitled to get notices and to be heard before such a material contravention could take place. It is no wonder that Parliament, in its wisdom, by the [Local Government (Planning and Development) Act 1976] transferred

---

[34] This allocation of functions would be in line with the proposals contained in the Devlin Report: see Prl. 792, App. 1.

[35] *The Functions of the Council on Tribunals* (1980) (Cmd. 7805), para. 1.7.

[36] But for the advantages of An Bord Pleanála over the Minister for Local Government, see Stevenson, "Planning Appeals in the Republic of Ireland" (1985) 7 *Journal of Urban Law and Policy* 170.

[37] [1984] I.R. 407.

to an independent appeal board the appellate power which had been vested by the [Local Government (Planning and Development) Act 1963] in an individual who might be influenced in his decisions by political pressures or other extraneous or unworthy considerations."[38]

Secondly, a tribunal is less affected by changes of government than a Minister and Department would be and thus there may be some gain in consistency, a quality very desirable in an area in which the policy-content is usually low. Finally, the amorphous quality of a Department of State with its various activities and interests may mean that an individual would be more confident that his arguments had been fully taken into account by a tribunal.[39] In short, tribunals are regarded as more likely to be fair and to provide greater safeguards for the individual than would be the case with a Minister. It follows that a tribunal is more often created where the area of government administration involved requires interference with valuable private property rights.

There is a qualification to the principle that decisions for which guidelines are provided are vested in tribunals. This principle is largely correct for "court-substitute tribunals" but not for "policy-orientated tribunals".[40] For the purpose of a policy-orientated tribunal is to allow policy, in a narrow field, to be worked out case by case by a specialist body, free of day-to-day interference by party politics and party politicians. One example of a tribunal of this type is administered by An Bord Pleanála.[41] The Labour Court, which is vested, *inter alia*, with the function of making "recommendation[s] setting forth its opinion on the merits of the [trade] dispute and the terms on which it should be settled"[42] provides another example of a "policy-orientated tribunal" at work. In truth, though, many tribunals possess elements of each category of tribunal.

Tribunal or court?

The other general perspective, from which to survey tribunals, is by a comparison with the courts. Since most Irish tribunals are of the court-substitute type, could their functions not simply have been vested in a court of the appropriate level?[43]

---

38 *Ibid.* at 425.
39 Thus, the establishment of an independent Refugee Applications Commissioner to determine asylum applications and a similar independent Refugee Appeal Board to hear appeals from decisions of the Commissioner (see Refugee Act 1996, ss. 6 and 15) was probably prompted by concerns that the former system whereby all such application were determined by the Minister for Justice lacked "transparency" and was generally unsatisfactory.
40 Farmer, *Tribunals and Government* (1984), Chap. 8.
41 Note that s.7 of the Local Government (Planning and Development) Act 1976 allows the Minister for the Environment to issue general policy directives to local authorities. This power has been exercised twice: see Local Government (Planning and Development) General Policy Directive 1982 (S.I. No. 264 of 1982) (large scale shopping developments) and Local Government (Planning and Development) General Policy Directive 1988 (S.I. No. 317 of 1988) (air quality standards). A similar power may be found in the Environmental Protection Agency Act 1992, s.79(1).
42 Industrial Relations Act 1946, s.68(1), as inserted by s.19 of the Industrial Relations Act 1969. See Von Prondzynski and McCarthy, *Employment Law* (1989): "This new criterion was intended to reflect a belief, current in the [Labour] Court itself, that it should approach its task in a wholly pragmatic and flexible way."
43 Indeed, because tribunals are so similar to courts, the question has arisen in Britain as to whether they are to be treated as courts for particular purposes such as contempt of court (*Attorney General*

The short answer is that the growth of tribunals is largely due to the failure of the legal system to respond in a flexible manner to new challenges. Indeed, the creation of one of the first modern tribunals – the court of referees system, established under the National Insurance Act 1911 to hear national insurance claims – occurred because of the dissatisfaction with the handling of workmen's compensation cases by the County Court.[44]

It is usually agreed that, by comparison with courts, tribunals carry certain practical advantages. In the first place, the procedure before a tribunal is simpler and more flexible than that of a court. Although a tribunal may not adopt procedures which are unfair or which imperil a just result, it is nonetheless master of its own procedures, and enjoys a considerable discretion as to whether to depart from the strict rules of evidence or permit legal representation or cross-examination of witnesses.[45] These features, together with the frequent absence of an adversarial framework,[46] the fact that the proceedings are often held in private,[47] and the less formal atmosphere of a tribunal combine to make an appearance before a tribunal a less daunting experience than the "day in court". Often, especially to people from a humbler background, the very image of a court – with its criminal connotations – is unwelcome. For example, the Housing (Private Rented Dwellings) Act 1982 – which provides for a new system of rent assessment following the invalidation of the former Rent Restrictions Act 1960[48] – originally vested this jurisdiction in the District Court. This jurisdiction was subsequently transferred to a Rent Tribunal by the Housing (Private Rented Dwellings) (Amendment) Act 1983 because of the concern aroused among the tenants by the prospect of the courtroom.[49]

A further example of a tribunal being substituted for a court occurred recently in the field of rating valuation. Until the Valuation Act 1988, an appeal lay from a determination of the Commissioner of Valuation to the Circuit Court. As a result of the Act, an appeal now lies to the Valuation Tribunal, which it establishes. From the tribunal there is an appeal on a point of law (just as, before, there was an appeal from the Circuit Court) to the High Court and thence to the Supreme Court.[50]

Secondly, many tribunals possess a particular expertise. This would be true, for example, in the case of bodies such as An Bord Pleanála, the Appeal Commissioners for Income Tax and the Employment Appeals Tribunal. The courts take cognisance of this fact, for they are sometimes reluctant to interfere with the workings of specialist tribunals.[51]

---

v. British Broadcasting Corporation [1981] A.C. 303) and immunity from defamation proceedings for witnesses (*Trapp v. Mackie* [1979] 1 W.L.R. 377). See further, pp. 302–303.

44 Abel Smith and Stevens, *Lawyers and the Courts*, (1967) pp. 111–118.

45 See the comments of *Report of the Public Services Organisation Review Group* ("the Devlin Report") (1969, Prl. 792), App. I, pp. 448–449, on this aspect of tribunals.

46 For tribunal procedure, see pp. 266–269.

47 Contrast Art. 34.1 which requires that the administration of justice by courts shall be in public, save in "such limited and special cases as may be prescribed by law".

48 *Blake v. Attorney General* [1982] I.R. 117. For an account of this decision, and the flurry of legislative activity which followed in its wake, see McCormack, "Blake-Madigan and its Aftermath" (1983) 5 D.U.L.J. (N.S.) 205.

49 See generally, 344 *Dáil Debates* Cols. 2514–2544 (July 7, 1983).

50 See generally, Valuation Act 1988, ss.2 and 5 and First Sched. See further, pp. 183–185.

51 See *O'Keeffe v. An Bord Pleanála* [1993] 1 I.R. 39; *Brandon Books Ltd v. RTÉ* [1993] I.L.R.M. 806; *Madigan v. RTÉ* [1994] 2 I.L.R.M. 472; *ACT Shipping Ltd v. Minister for Marine* [1995] 3 I.R. 406

Thirdly, tribunals are quicker and cheaper for all the parties concerned. Their simpler procedure means that it is usually unnecessary for a lawyer to appear.[52] Fourthly, it will often be appropriate for the legislature to constitute an agency which is not only a tribunal but also possesses a number of regulatory, promotional or advisory functions, along the lines of United States "administrative agencies" which are often vested with diverse non-judicial functions. A leading example is the Labour Court, which combines general arbitration functions in the field of industrial relations with quasi-judicial (or, indeed, possibly judicial) functions under the Redundancy Payments Act 1967 and the Anti-Discrimination (Pay) Act 1974. Fifthly, it is sometimes appropriate that a public body be devised which, in its structures and functions, mingles the characteristics of a tribunal with those of other constructs covered very tangentially in the chapter on state-sponsored bodies.[53] Thus in some of its roles, it may exercise statutory powers which have a direct impact on an individuals legal rights (usually property rights); whilst it may also bear duties and powers, in such areas as information-collection and dissemination; policy-making or advising on policy, which make it akin to a commercial state-sponsored body. Such an amalgam is perhaps more familiar in the U.S. scheme of government where it goes under the generic title of an "administrative agency". But the breed is spreading to Ireland. One example is the Environmental Protection Agency established by the Environmental Protection Agency Act 1992, Part II. This is responsible for a significant number of licensing, regulating, and controlling functions in the environmental field, many of them transferred from local authorities. In respect of these functions, the Agency is generally subject, like a straightforward tribunal, to the rules of constitutional justice, such as reasonableness. Thus, for example, it has been remarked in respect of Integrated Pollution Control licences that: "the procedures governing the EPA's determination of a licence application or review when there are objections to the proposed determination are substantially similar to the procedures governing planning appeals [before An Bord Pleanála].[54] However, in addition, the Agency must: monitor environmental quality and disseminate information; provide support and advisory services to local and public authorities; liaise with the European Environmental Agency; and carry out such other functions as the Minister for the Environment assigns or transfers to it.[55]

---

and *Radio Limerick Ltd v. IRTC* [1997] I.L.R.M. 1 and *Henry Denny and Co. (Irl.) Ltd v. Minister for Social Welfare*, unreported, Supreme Court, December 1, 1997.

[52] *cf. Employment Appeals Tribunal Sixteenth Annual Report* (1983, Pl. 2733): "While the procedures of the Tribunal were intended to be informal, speedy and inexpensive, the increasing involvement by the legal profession, particularly in claims under the Unfair Dismissals Act 1977, has tended to make the hearings more formal, prolonged and costly, with an over-emphasis on legal procedures and technicalities" (p. 4). According to the 1983 Report, 19.7 per cent. of employees and 23.9 per cent. of employers opted for legal representation. In the Twenty Fifth Annual Report (1992, P.L. 9986) the equivalent figures were employees: 18 per cent were represented by lawyers and 22 per cent by trade unions; employers: 19 per cent were represented by lawyers and 3 per cent by trade unions. (However the figures for employers are an under-estimate because more than one claim may be taken against the same employer.)

[53] See p. 114.

[54] For this quotation and generally, see Scannell, *Environmental and Planning Law in Ireland* (1995), Chap. 14.

[55] 1992 Act, s.52.

Another example is the Pensions Board constituted by Part II of the Pensions Act 1990. The Board is not only a tribunal, it also bears the functions of: devising guidelines on the duties of the trustees of pensions schemes; encouraging the provision of training schemes for them; advising the Minister for Social Welfare; and monitoring the operation of the Act and pensions developments generally.[56] Concomitant with its responsibilities, the Board is also an example of a "balanced" (or representative) tribunal[57] in that 10 of its 12 ordinary members must be nominated by bodies representing variously: employees, employers, occupational pension schemes, accountants, lawyers or actuaries.[58] However, notwithstanding its many other functions just listed, the Board also acts as a tribunal. For one of the techniques employed in the Act is that certain fairly detailed standards are fixed, either by the Act or regulations made under it, in regard to such matters as: the preservation of benefits; adequate funding; the disclosure of information to interested parties; and equal treatment of men and women.[59] The Act then provides that where there is any conflict between any of these standards and the rules of a pension scheme, it is the statutory standards which prevail. The duty of determining whether there is any conflict is vested in the Board.

Where a court, rather than a tribunal, was involved in such a combination of roles it was successfully argued, elsewhere in the common law world, that the arrangement contravened the equivalent of Article 34.1[60] and, in Ireland, such an arrangement would certainly be regarded as undesirable and unconventional.

Finally, tribunals tend to take a less rigid attitude to questions of statutory interpretation and to precedent. Indeed, it is possible that a tribunal which adhered rigidly to a doctrine of precedent, as far as its own decisions are concerned, would run foul of the rule against inflexible policies.[61] However, in the interest of consistency, tribunals do follow precedent to some extent and, indeed, this trend is likely to accelerate given that section 16 of the Freedom of Information Act 1997 requires the publication of decisions likely to be of precedential value.[62] In particular, where points of law are concerned, tribunals must apply the law, employing the standard principles of statutory interpretation and following the decisions of the High Court and Supreme Court. This point was made emphatically by McCarthy J. in *McGrath v. McDermott*,[63] where the Supreme Court was considering a decision of the Appeal Commissioners. This decision had purported to adopt the doctrine of "fiscal nullity" (a British principle by which financial transactions, which had no purpose other

---

[56] Pensions Act 1990, s.10.
[57] For this phrase, see pp. 274–275.
[58] 1990 Act, First Sched., para. 8.
[59] See especially, ss.26, 38, 53, 58 and 75 of the Act.
[60] Legislation which vested a court with non-judicial arbitral functions in the area of industrial relations was held to be contrary to s.71 of the Commonwealth Constitution in *Attorney General of Australia v. R. and the Boilermakers' Society of Australia* [1957] A.C. 288. Keane J. appeared to endorse this view in *Re Neilan* [1990] 2 I.R. 267.
[61] *Merchandise Transport Ltd v. British Transport Commission* [1962] 2 Q.B. 173, 197; *R. v. Greater Birmingham Appeal Tribunal, ex p. Simper* [1974] Q.B. 543 (tribunal cannot consider itself bound by its own "rules of thumb"). For this rule, see pp. 668–675.
[62] See further pp. 495–496. Decisions of important tribunals such as the Employment Appeals Tribunal, the Valuation Tribunal and the Competition Authority are already published on a systematic basis.
[63] [1988] I.R. 258 at 278.

than the avoidance of tax and which did not involve a real loss, should be disregarded). The Commissioners had either ignored or had been unaware of the relevant decisions of the Supreme Court.

As against these advantages, the wisdom of allocating certain judicial functions to tribunals rather than courts has been questioned by Walsh J. Writing in the context of the work of An Bord Uchtála the judge opined, extra–judicially, that:

> "[C]ertain aspects of family law are of such fundamental importance, such as those cases which can alter the legal status of a person, that they should be decided in the High Court. . . . This prompts one to question the wisdom or desirability of permitting the legal adoptions to take effect without judicial intervention or confirmation. . . . [The powers of An Bord Uchtála] are limited. It cannot decide questions concerning the validity of the marriage of couples who seek to adopt. Yet if adoption is approved for a couple whose marriage is not a valid subsisting marriage in the eyes of the law of the State the resulting invalidity of the adoption may not be discovered until it is too late to avoid . . . the inevitable legal consequences."[64]

Webster J. indicated another range of difficulties, in considering prison disciplinary tribunals in *R. v. Home Secretary, ex p. Tarrant*.[65] He listed a number of considerations which the prison authorities should take into account before deciding whether to permit the prisoner to be legally represented. These factors included: the seriousness and gravity of the charge; whether any points of law are likely to arise; the capacity of a particular prisoner to present his own case; the need for reasonable speed in making the adjudication; and the need for fairness as between prisoners, and as between prisoners and prison officers. If the result of those guidelines would be that serious disciplinary offences were more frequently referred to the criminal courts, then Webster J. did not regard such a result "as a matter of regret"[66] and it seems fair to infer that he considered that prison tribunals were inherently unsuited to the task of adjudication in cases involving serious disciplinary charges.

Excursus: *Impact of court proceedings on related matters before a tribunal*

The majority of this book is concerned with the law relating to an application for judicial review and hence with the intervention which a court may make in the proceedings of a tribunal or other public body. However, this brief excursus is devoted to the impact of a court in a narrower sense. It is concerned with the situation in which the outcome of substantive court proceedings, (as opposed to a judicial review), may be thought to have an impact upon related or parallel proceedings

---

64 In foreword to Binchy, *A Casebook on Irish Family Law* (1984), p. vii.
65 [1985] Q.B. 251.
66 *Ibid.* at 287. Similar sentiments were also expressed by Carswell J. in *Re Morrison's Application* [1991] N.I. 70. In the course of quashing a disciplinary finding where he found that the adjudicating prison governor had misdirected himself as to meaning of the concept of possession, Carswell J. observed (at 76) that:
> "one can readily sympathise with governors holding adjudications in which difficult legal concepts such as possession have to be dealt with. They have not had the benefit of legal training, and have to exercise fairness and common sense in their disposition of cases."

before a tribunal.[67] The commonest example of this situation occurs where it is alleged that some person has committed an act which may be both a crime and a disciplinary offence against the rule of his employer or disciplinary body. The consequences may be both a criminal prosecution before a court and disciplinary proceedings before a disciplinary tribunal. In principle, one should not affect the other. In the present context, neither conviction nor acquittal before the court should mean that the same result must follow before a disciplinary tribunal. Moreover to continue with the disciplinary proceedings (it was held in a case in which there had been extensive criminal and civil litigation) is not "so unfair and oppressive as to constitute harrassment of the applicant and an abuse of his constitutional right to fair procedures".[68]

However, it is inherent in the nature of the situation that there are intersections and the law must take account of these. In the first place, the outcome of the disciplinary proceedings might have an influence on the court and, hence, constitute contempt of court or, at any rate, render the trial unfair. In order to avoid this, the criminal proceedings will usually go first and, if a delay[69] in disciplinary proceedings occurs because of this, then the person being disciplined cannot be heard to complain, on that account. Secondly, despite the general principle enunciated in the previous paragraph, in the particular circumstances of *McGrath v. Commissioner of Garda Síochána*,[70] it has been held that the logical consequence of an acquittal could be such that it was not open to the disciplinary authority to investigate the same (or similar) charge arising on the same facts. The facts were that the applicant-garda had been found not guilty by the Circuit Court, on charges of embezzlement of money. Subsequently, a disciplinary inquiry was initiated against the applicant based on two types of wrong-doing. The first of these related to the appearance of the applicant in a public court. The Court held (in light of the applicant's acquittal) that this could not of itself constitute a breach of discipline. The other charge depended on allegations of "corrupt or improper practice" arising out of the acts of which the accused had earlier been acquitted. The Supreme Court ruled that the disciplinary hearing could proceed on an allegation in which the wording "improper practice" (which was itself a disciplinary offence) was substituted in place of the original charge of "corrupt or improper practice". The reason for this was that for the member of the Garda to be tried again on identical "charges" to those on which he had been acquitted by a jury would be a form of unfair and oppressive procedure.[71]

3. Common Features

We must now elaborate on the remarks, made above in Part 1 of this chapter, about the types of feature which distinguish a tribunal.

---

[67] The reverse situation occurs where some element in proceedings before a court are vested in some agency other than a court, for instance a tribunal. Then Art. 34.1 would be violated. See Morgan, *The Separation of Powers in the Irish Constitution* (1997) Chapter 8.III.

[68] *McGrath v. Garda Síochána* [1993] I.L.R.M. 38 at 42. Contrast *The State (Murray) v. McRann* [1979] I.R. 133, 135 (albeit in a slightly different context). But see also *Mooney v. An Post* unreported, Supreme Court, March 20, 1997.

[69] See pp. 580–584.

[70] [1991] I.R. 69. See too, *McCarthy v. Commissioner of Garda Síochána* [1993] 1 I.R. 489 at 497.

[71] [1991] I.R. at 73–74. See also [1989] I.R. 241 (High Ct.).

Rule bound

As far as one can generalise about tribunals it can be said that they take decisions in regard to which the range of options is sufficiently narrow and predictable for it to be crystallised in the form of a reasonably precise set of rules or at least a specific catalogue of factors. This is in contrast with the wide discretionary power which, for instance, permits a Minister to exercise a particular power if he deems it "necessary in the public interest".[72] Yet on the other hand, law administered by a tribunal is more likely than law administered by a court to include a range of factors which tends to create a discretion and so to be expressed in terms of standards as opposed to rules.[73] It is, however, a discretion which must be exercised reasonably, objectively and judicially. In other words, in this respect, as in others, tribunals occupy an intermediate position between Ministers and courts. To take some examples: first, An Bord Uchtála must not make an adoption order unless it is satisfied "that the applicant is of good moral character, has sufficient means to support the child, and is a suitable person to have parental rights and duties in respect of the child".[74] Again, the Rent Tribunal is required to fix the rent in respect of formerly rent-controlled tenancies by having regard to the:

> "nature, character and location of the dwelling, the other terms of the tenancy; the means of the landlord and the tenant; the date of purchase of the dwelling by the landlord and the amount paid by him therefor; the length of the tenant's occupancy of the dwelling and the number and ages of the tenant's family residing in the dwelling."[75]

Even where the wording of the statutory test administered by the tribunal is vague, the effect of the open, formal procedure, together with an accumulation of informal precedents, will have the effect of restricting its discretion. This is especially so when the tribunal maintains a public register of its decisions, as does the Employment Appeal Tribunal. However, it must be said that often a tribunal does not publish its decision, much less its reasons.[76] For example, the reports submitted by the planning inspector – who chairs an oral inquiry – to An Bord Pleanála are not published at all. This effectively means that no system of precedent is established whereby the members of the public can assess the likelihood of a successful appeal.[77]

---

72 For controls on discretionary powers, see Chap. 12.
73 But this is not always the case: see, *e.g.* Succession Act 1965, s.117 (which allows the court to make provision for the child out of a deceased parent's estate where it is of opinion "that the testator has failed to make proper provision for the child in accordance with its means").
74 Adoption Act 1952, s.13(1).
75 Housing (Private Rented Dwellings) Act 1982, s.13(2). However, these criteria are not in the nature of an "automatic check list, they are only to be considered when they are relevant": *Quirke v. Folio Homes Ltd* [1989] I.L.R.M. 496 at 499, *per* McCarthy J.
76 Though note that in the case of many tribunals, once the Freedom of Information Act 1997, s. 18 comes into effect, the person affected will have to be given reasons: see pp. 574–580.
77 Clark, "Social Welfare Insurance Appeals" (1978) 13 Ir. Jur. (N.S.) 265 at p. 282 makes the same point about the non-publication of decisions of social welfare appeals officers' decisions: "If decisions are at present poorly recorded, this will hinder even the most primitive and informal system of *stare decisis*. Appeals officers may then run the risk of operating within an appeals system in which uniformity of decision making is singularly absent". This will also change when s.16 of the Freedom of Information Act 1997 takes effect on April 21, 1998.

Appeals

Since decisions taken by tribunals are, first, bound by fairly precise rules and, secondly, involve questions of individual rights, it might be predicted on the basis of earlier discussion[78] that a statutory appeal would be created from a tribunal to a court. In fact, provision is generally made for an appeal to the High Court but this is usually confined to points of law.[79] In some cases an appeal will lie to a specialised appellate tribunal. For instance, a party aggrieved by a prohibition order made by the Censorship of Publications Board – nowadays, a comparatively rare event – may appeal *de novo* to the Censorship of Publications Appeal Board.[80] A further example is provided by the Seanad Electoral (Panel Members) Act 1947, whereby an appeal lies to a Judicial Referee from a decision of the returning officer on the eligibility of a candidate for a particular electoral panel.[81] If no appeal is created then, naturally, none will be available. By contrast there is no need for judicial review to be explicitly provided for since the High Court always retains an inherent right of review.[83] Very occasionally a statutory attempt will be made to declare that a tribunal's decision is final and thus to render it (probably unconstitutionally[82]) proof against judicial review. However, there is a view that the applicant must, in general, exhaust all other rights of appeal before he can seek judicial review of a tribunal's decision.[84]

Procedure

Procedure is laid down, in the first instance, by the constituent statute, and is generally supplemented by procedural regulations made pursuant to statutory instrument or contained in the Schedule to the constituent statute[85] or both. These provisions typically deal with matters such as the following: how many members constitute a quorum and a majority; the circumstances in which an oral hearing is required;

---

[78] See p. 6.

[79] See, *e.g.* Adoption Act 1952, s.20(1); Local Government (Planning and Development) Act 1976, s.42(a); Housing (Private Rented Dwellings) (Amendment) Act 1983, ss.12 and 13; Farm Tax Act 1985, s.8(4); Valuation Act 1988, s.5; Social Welfare (Consolidation) Act 1993, s.271. In the case of the Appeals Commissioners for Income Tax, the tax-payer may appeal *de novo* to the Circuit Court. Either party may ask for a case stated on a point of law from the decisions of the Appeal Commissioners or the Circuit Court: Taxes Consolidation Act 1997, s.840. However, for an unrestricted appeal from the Controller of Patents, Designs and Trade Marks, see the Trade Marks Act 1996, s.79. For the difficult distinction between law and fact, see *Rahill v. Brady* [1971] I.R. 69 and pp. 478–480.

[80] Censorship of Publications Act 1946, ss.2 and 3.

[81] ss.36–38 of the 1947 Act. In *Ormonde and Dolan v. MacGabhann*, unreported, High Court, July 9, 1969, Pringle J. held that the plaintiffs were entitled to by-pass this judicial referee procedure in order to seek a declaration from the High Court that they had the proper and appropriate qualifications for nomination on the Labour Panel.

[82] For an attempt to declare the decision of a tribunal (appeals officer) final, see *Kingham v. Minister for Social Welfare*, unreported, High Court, November 25, 1985 at p. 281.

[83] *Tormey v. Attorney General* [1985] I.R. 289.

[84] *The State (Abenglen Properties Ltd) v. Dublin Corporation* [1984] I.R. 381; *Creedon v. Dublin Corporation* [1984] I.R. 427. The alternative views are canvassed at pp. 734–739.

[85] For modern examples, see: Farm Tax Act 1985, Schedule; Valuation Act 1988, Schedule. Notice an unusual feature of the Valuation Tribunal, namely that, by para. 3 of the Schedule to the 1988 Act, the tribunal is required to issue a written judgment.

whether the tribunal has the power to subpoena witnesses and to administer oaths; whether the witness commits an offence if he gives false evidence; and whether the witness enjoys the same privileges as a witness before a court. The provisions may also specify: whether certain types of hearings are to be in public or in private[86]; whether the tribunal may sit in divisions; and whether it may delegate its powers to a smaller group of members. These issues aside, the tribunal is generally authorised to regulate its own procedure.[87]

In the case of a few modern tribunals, the constituent statute states that "[a] witness . . . before a tribunal shall be entitled to the same privileges and immunities as a witness before a court".[88] This, be it noted, is a rather restricted protection in that it only covers actions against witnesses in respect of evidence given by them. However, even in the case of statements not within this limited protection or, alternatively, where the tribunal enjoys no statutory protection whatsoever, it is clear that proceedings before a tribunal attract qualified privilege on the ground that the performance of a public duty is involved.[89] The more difficult question is whether common law absolute privilege would apply, in the same way as if the tribunal were a court. As yet, there appears to be no Irish authority on this point (though given the national predilection for defamation proceedings, this seems unlikely to last). In a Scottish authority, *Trapp v. Mackie*,[90] the House of Lords held that, provided that the body in question was one "recognised by law", there was no single element which would be conclusive to show that – adopting the conventionally-accepted test[91] – it had attributes sufficiently similar to those of a court to create absolute privilege. Lord Diplock then went on to list certain characteristics of the body in question – which was inquiring into the dismissal of a teacher – which cumulatively were more than enough to justify the granting of absolute privilege.[92]

---

86 For a rare statutory reference to this aspect, see the Irish Takeover Panel Act 1997, s.11(2) and s.14(2).
87 See, *e.g.* Adoption Act 1952, First Sched.; Social Welfare (Appeals) Regulations 1990 (S.I. No. 344 of 1990), (appeals officers); Local Government (Planning and Development) Regulations 1994 (S.I. No. 86 of 1994), Art. 74(5). In *The State (Casey) v. Labour Court* (1984) 3 J.I.S.L.L. 135 at 138, O'Hanlon J. observed that the Labour Court was given a discretion by s.21 of the Industrial Relations Act 1946 to regulate its own procedures in relation to the taking of evidence on oath. Accordingly, neither the parties nor the High Court could dictate to the Labour Court the manner in which it conducts its own procedures "once it exercises its powers in accordance with the statute from which it derives its authority to act". See also the following *obiter dictum* of Costello P. regarding the Hepatitis-C Compensation Tribunal in *Ryan v. The Compensation Tribunal* [1997] 1 I.L.R.M. 194 at 204: "Evidence can be given in writing by means of medical reports, or vive voce. Witnesses are not sworn. They are not subject to cross-examination. The Tribunal is, in my opinion, free to accept or reject any evidence adduced before it and is free to conclude that the evidence or some of it is exaggerated." For a similar – somewhat *laissez-faire* – attitude to tribunal procedures, see *Keane v. An Bord Pleanála*, unreported, High Court, June 20, 1995 (no breach of fair procedures where a planning inspector stopped cross-examination of witnesses).
88 Garda Siochána (Complaints) Act 1986, Second Sched., para. 6.; Valuation Act 1988, First Sched., para. 6; Committees of the Houses of the Oireachtas (Compellibility, Privileges and Immunities of Witnesses) Act 1997, s.11.
89 *Royal Aquarium Society v. Parkinson* [1892] 1 Q.B. 431 at 443, 454.
90 [1979] 1 W.L.R. 377.
91 *Royal Aquarium Society v. Parkinson* [1892] 1 Q.B. 431, at 448, 452.
92 With particular reference to the Labour Court, Kerr and Whyte, *Irish Trade Union Law* (1985), p. 356 state:
   "The Labour Court is recognised by law. The Court is empowered to summon witnesses before it, to examine witnesses on oath and require any such witnesses to produce documents. The

But irrespective of what the constituent statute may say or what administrative practice may develop, a tribunal is always subject to constitutional justice in its more stringent form and, so, it is the courts which have the last word on such questions as whether an oral hearing should have been held.[93] The impact of constitutional justice is demonstrated by a British parallel: out of the three examples cited by Professor Wade[94] of amendments to draft procedural regulations secured by the British Council on Tribunals, all three changes (disclosure to both sides of information given to the tribunal; a right to representation; and the duty imposed on persons discharging quasi-judicial functions to give reasons for their decisions) have been effected in Ireland through the courts.[95]

Accusatorial v. Inquisitorial style

There are two other factors which it might be expected would draw many tribunals towards the inquisitorial model. First, as regards subject-matter, the accusatorial model is appropriate in ordinary civil proceedings where the court is usually deciding a *lis inter partes* involving two identifiable private parties, each with diametrically opposing interests. By contrast there is often only one individual interest at a hearing before a tribunal, as, *e.g.* in an application for a grant or a licence. On the other side, there is or may be that nebulous thing, the "public" or "community" interest, which may, according to the circumstances, consist of divergent interests, some of which may even pull in the same direction as the individual interest.

There is, secondly, a practical factor militating in favour of the inquisitorial system, namely, that the accusatorial system works best when the two adversaries are equally experienced and informed. This requirement will often not be met in the case of tribunals where the private individuals involved are usually not legally represented.

However, despite these natural features, a form of adversarial system has been imposed by the law. First, the rules of constitutional justice – which are imposed by judges with the court system, no doubt, in mind, as a role–model, apply to hearings before tribunals. Secondly, in certain tribunals it has been thought necessary to establish a *legitimus contradictor* and this tends to give a hearing an adversarial

---

investigation can be held in public and witnesses can be cross-examined. The relative informality of procedure does not outweigh those factors, and the authors would submit that the general principle expressed by Lopes L.J. [in *Royal Aquarium Society*] should be extended to [give absolute privilege to] Labour Court investigations but not to conciliation proceedings with an Industrial Relations Officer."

93 "Tribunals exercising quasi-judicial functions are frequently allowed to act informally – to receive unsworn evidence, to act on hearsay, to depart from the rules of evidence, to ignore courtroom procedures and the like – but they may not act in such a way as to imperil a fair hearing or a fair result," *per* Henchy J. in *Kiely v. Minister for Social Welfare* [1977] I.R. 267 at 281. See generally at pp. 556–560.

94 *Administrative Law* (1994), pp. 931–945.

95 *Geraghty v. Minister for Local Government* [1976] I.R. 153; *Nolan v. Irish Land Commission* [1981] I.R. 23; *The State (Williams) v. Army Pensions Board* [1983] I.R. 308; (disclosure of information); *McGrath & O'Ruairc v. Trustees of Maynooth College* [1979] I.L.R.M. 166; *Flanagan v. University College Dublin* [1988] I.R. 724; *Gallagher v. Revenue Commissioners (No.2)* [1995] 1 I.R. 55 (legal representation); *The State (Creedon) v. Criminal Injuries Compensation Board* [1988] I.R. 51 and *International Fishing Ltd v. Minister for Marine* [1989] I.R. 149 (duty to give reasons). For these points, see Chap. 11.

flavour. Thus, the responsible Inspector of Taxes appears in front of the Appeal Commissioners to argue in support of his earlier decision.

Independence[96]

Tribunals exercising public law powers are required to strike an even balance between the individual on the one hand and the administrative authorities who represent the public interest on the other: they should be guided only by the law and their own non-partisan discretion. At times, queries have been raised – either in regard to tribunals as a whole or in regard to specified tribunals – as to whether they measure up to these standards. In the first place, tribunals lack the tradition, status and institutional arrangements necessary to promote independence which the courts have long enjoyed. Moreover, the fact that all the cases before a particular tribunal often involve the same administrative agency may breed a certain cosiness.

Particular doubt has arisen about the independence of the deciding officer/appeals officer system for determining social welfare claims because it is manned by serving civil servants operating within a Department of State.[97] Deciding officers are selected by the Minister for Social Welfare at executive or staff officer level and they hold this position at the pleasure of the Minister. Deciding officers appear to regard themselves as subject to departmental directions and policy considerations, although it seems likely that it was the intention of the Oireachtas to give the deciding officer a similar status to that of the appeals officer. After some years as a deciding officer a civil servant will generally return to service within the Department. Later he may be appointed, usually at assistant principal grade, as an appeals officer by the Minister and again holds his position at pleasure.[98]

Suspicion of the appeals officer's independence – and, by implication, that of the deciding officer – had been fuelled by decisions such as *McLoughlin v. Minister for Social Welfare.*[99] In this case the question arose as to whether the plaintiff was

---

[96]   *cf.* Patents Act 1992, s.6(3): "The Patents Office shall be under the control of the Controller [of Patents, Designs and Trade Marks] who shall be independent in the discharge of the functions conferred on him by this Act or any other enactment."

[97]   Though for some recent improvements, see pp. 279–280.

[98]   See generally: Social Welfare (Consolidation) Act, 1993, ss. 246 and 251; and Clark, "Social Welfare Insurance Appeals" (1978) 13 *Ir. Jur.* (N.S.) 165. Notice also the Ombudsman's comment (as late as his 1993 Report, p. 64) in relation to the Appeals Officer (*not* of the Department of Social Welfare but of a health board though the point is the same):

   "The experience of the appellant in this case and several others which have been brought to my attention would appear to substantiate many of the general criticisms of the SWA [Supplementary Welfare Allowance] appeal system. It would appear that in his original decisions the Appeals Officer was heavily influenced by prevailing health board policy in relation to such cases. It would appear that the appeal procedure did not enable the appellant to make the best possible case. The question of an oral appeal hearing did not arise. It would appear that the opinion of the SCWO [Superintendent Community Welfare Officer] weighed very heavily with the Appeals Officer. On the other hand, the appellant did not really know the nature of the case against him and, indeed, was not informed that the SCWO had substituted another reason in place of the original reason for refusing the application. In this particular case the appellant was able to present his case in writing but only when he had been made fully aware of the nature of the case against him. Finally, there was by any standard an unreasonable delay in this case.

   Given the very significant role played by SWA in overall income maintenance arrangements, I have serious concerns as to the fairness and adequacy of the existing SWA appeal procedures."
   See, to similar effect, 1993 Report, p. 61.

[99]   [1958] I.R. 1. See further, on this case, pp. 75, 80.

employed "in the civil service of the Government" for social insurance purposes. The appeals officer considered that he was bound to adhere to the terms of a minute from the Minister for Finance which, in effect, directed the officer to find that the plaintiff was so employed. This decision was reversed by the Supreme Court, with O'Daly J. stating that the appeals officer had abdicated his duty to act in an impartial and independent fashion:

> "The Appeals Officer said that he was bound to adhere to a direction, purporting to have been given to him by the Minister for Finance, an observation which disclosed not a concern for the niceties of the probative value, but the belief that a public servant in his position had no option but to act on the direction of a Minister of State. Such a belief on his part was an abdication by him from his duty as an Appeals Officer. That duty is laid upon him by the Oireachtas and he is required to perform it as between the parties that appear before him freely and fairly as becomes anyone who is called upon to decide on matters of right or obligation."[100]

Further recognition of the anomalous position of the social welfare appeals system is provided by the fact that decisions of both the deciding officer and the appeals officer have been placed within the scope of the Ombudsman's jurisdiction.[101]

Constitution: Articles 34.1 and 37

Doubts about the independence of the tribunals were probably part of the inspiration for the constitutional rule, Article 34.1, which provides that (subject to certain exceptions) "justice shall be administered in courts established by law by judges . . ." and not by tribunals. Article 37 provides the exception to the pure milk of the separation of powers principle in that it permits the Oireachtas to vest "limited functions and powers of a judicial nature in matters other than criminal matters" in a body which is not a court. The wording of Article 34.1 and Article 37 includes three highly problematic concepts: (1) the distinction between judicial and non-judicial powers; (2) what is a "limited" judicial function; and (3) what is a "criminal matter". These are matters of constitutional definition which are discussed in constitutional law books.[102] It is not intended to attempt to cover the same ground here but merely to outline some of the leading cases in order to alert the reader to the issues. One should note, though that even if Article 34.1 did, at one time, pose a constitutional threat to certain tribunals, recent developments suggest that this danger has substantially reduced.

In the first place, it must be emphasised that there are several tribunals which are plainly out of danger because they do not administer justice. An example is An Bord Pleanála: it has been held[103] that this tribunal is not administering justice when it grants (or withholds) planning permission because such a large measure of policy

---

100 *Ibid.* at 27.
101 Ombudsman Act 1980, s.5(1)(a)(iii).
102 See: Hogan and Whyte, *Kelly, The Irish Constitution* (3rd ed., 1994), pp. 330–346 and 560–569; Casey, *Constitutional Law in Ireland* (1987), pp. 200–212; Forde, *Constitutional Law of Ireland* (1987), pp. 152–160 and Morgan, *The Separation of Powers in the Irish Constitution* (1997), Chap. 5.
103 *Central Dublin Development Association v. Attorney General* (1975) 109 I.L.T.R. 69 at 93–96 (*per* Kenny J.).

discretion is involved; and, secondly, (to take another of the Board's powers), that although the function of determining what is "development" or "exempted development" constitutes an administration of justice, it falls within the Article 37 exception.

The high-water mark of the tide in favour of using Article 34.1 to strike down a tribunal was *Re Solicitors'Act, 1954*,[104] in which the power of the Disciplinary Committee of the Incorporated Law Society to strike off solicitors who had been found guilty of serious disciplinary offences was held to be an administration of justice. Moreover the Supreme Court also held that even if there were a full appeal, by way of rehearing from the Disciplinary Committee's decision to the High Court, this appeal would not restore constitutionality to the Committee's decision.

In order to avoid the difficulties disclosed by the *Re Solicitors Act, 1954* decision, certain crucial features were included when the medical disciplinary system was restructured in the Medical Practitioners Act 1978. First, the Medical Council does not have the power to strike off a doctor, although it does have the significant power and duty of making an elaborate inquiry as a result of which it may decide that the doctor should be struck off. If it does so decide, then the doctor has the right to apply within 21 days to the High Court, which may either cancel or confirm the decision. Finally, the Council bears the onus of proving before the court, in the usual way, any contested facts.

The disciplinary system constituted by the 1978 Act was upheld, in *Re M*.[105] by Finlay P. (as he then was) in the High Court. The *Re Solicitors'Act, 1954* decision was distinguished in *Re M*. on the basis that one criterion for an "administration of justice" is that it must be "final and conclusive", as opposed to recommendatory. Since the Medical Council's decision was not blessed with the quality of conclusiveness it was held that the Council was not "administering justice". In a related case, *M. v. Medical Council*,[106] it was accepted that, in the situation in which the professional body makes the necessary recommendation and the practitioner does not object, the legislation meant that the court must accept the professional body's decision unless it sees good reason to do otherwise. On this basis, it was found to be constitutional. These authorities appear to represent a legislative development of the law as enunciated in the *Solicitors Act* decision. It is now possible, if the correct formula be used – that is, "confirmation" by the High Court rather than appeal – to allow some involvement by the relevant professional body. Nevertheless,

---

[104] [1960] I.R. 239. See also, the remarkable comments of McKenzie J. in *Government of Canada v. E.A.T.* [1992] 2 I.R. 484, 488.

[105] [1984] I.R. 479.

[106] [1984] I.R. 485. Designed according to the same specification and to meet the same constitutional imperative – satisfying Article 34.1 of the Constitution – as the medical disciplinary system is the nurses' disciplinary system constituted by the Nurses Act 1985. This system came up for constitutional scrutiny before the Supreme Court in *Kerrigan v. An Bord Altranais* [1990] 2 I.R. 396. Following the statutory procedure, allegations against the plaintiff had been heard by the Fitness to Practice Committee of the Board in an oral inquiry which lasted for 12 sittings. The Committee's report, finding that the plaintiff was guilty of professional misconduct, was submitted to the Board which gave the plaintiff an opportunity to be heard and then decided that her name should be erased from the Register of Nurses. Nevertheless the Supreme Court held (at 403) that before the High Court could confirm this decision, the High Court must hold a full oral hearing (at any rate where, as in the instant case, there were disputed questions of fact).

it must be said, as a criticism of the influence of the Separation of Powers in this area that it does seem desirable that the relevant factual points and professional standards should be allowed to be settled – as they are in most cases in the United States (another jurisdiction in which the Constitution imposes a strong form of the separation of powers) – by experienced members of the profession, who are appointed or elected to represent the entire profession. For there seems little danger in Ireland, where the independence of the professions is a fundamental tenet, that a disciplinary tribunal would be less independent of the executive branch than are the courts.

However the judicial tide appears to have turned away from the *Solicitors*-style rigorous application of Article 34.1, though the precise extent of the change, which occurred in *Keady v. Garda Commissioner*,[107] is not yet clear. *Keady* concerned the question of whether the Garda Disciplinary Tribunal that is, a public service employment tribunal – was administering justice. Accordingly, what was said about tribunals for disciplining professionals or other self-employed persons was, strictly speaking, *obiter*. Nevertheless, the theme which emerges most strongly from each of the two written judgments, is a concern to confine the *Re Solicitors'* line of authority strictly to solicitors, on the basis that "historically the act of striking solicitors off the roll was reserved to judges."[108] It seems likely, therefore, that, as a result of *Keady* and certain other developments,[109] tribunals are now less vulnerable to an attack based on Article 34.1; though, in each case, the particular features of the tribunal involved are very significant.

In addition, in a number of cases, the courts have been prepared to uphold the constitutionality of a tribunal on the basis that it fell within Article 37.1 (quoted above) in that the function being exercised was "limited". This argument was, however, tried unsuccessfully, in *Re Solicitors Act, 1954*, where the appellants had actually been struck off the roll of solicitors. Finding that the powers thus exercised were not limited, Kingsmill Moore J. observed: "If the exercise of the assigned powers and functions is calculated ordinarily to affect in the most profound and far-reaching way the lives, liberties, fortunes and reputations of those against whom they are exercised, they cannot properly be described as 'limited'."[110]

However, a slightly more flexible approach may be discerned in the judgment of McMahon J. in *Madden v. Ireland*.[111] At issue in this case was the power of the Land Commission's lay commissioners and appeal tribunal to fix the price of land in cases of compulsory acquisition. McMahon J. first accepted that this was not merely the exercise of an administrative function, but involved the administration of justice, as there was no room "for policy concepts, and what is being decided is solely a question of legal right". But the judge went on to hold that this was a power of a limited nature and he adverted to the role which Article 37 had obviously been intended to play:

> "Experience has shown that modern government cannot be carried on without many regulatory bodies and those bodies cannot function effectively under a

---

[107] [1992] 2 I.R. 197.
[108] *Ibid.* at 210–211. See also McCarthy J. at 205.
[109] See Morgan, *The Separation of Powers in the Irish Constitution, op. cit.* above n. 102 at p. (viii).
[110] [1960] I.R. 239 at 263.
[111] Unreported, High Court, May 22, 1980.

rigid separation of powers. Article 37 had no counterpart in the Constitution of Saorstát Éireann and in my view introduction of it to the Constitution is to be attributed to a realisation of the needs of modern Government. The ascertainment of the market value of a holding of lands by an administrative body with special experience appears to me to be the kind of limited judicial power contemplated by Article 37."[112]

Finally, it should be noted that because of doubts which had been cast on the constitutionality of An Bord Uchtála, Article 37 was extended, by constitutional amendment, specifically in order to safeguard adoption orders against the possibility of a challenge grounded on Article 34.1.[113]

Article 6.1 of the European Convention

The same theme – that of independence of tribunals – emerges from Article 6.1 of the European Convention of Human Rights which states: "In the determination of his civil rights and obligations or any criminal charge against him, everyone is entitled to a . . . hearing . . . by an independent and impartial tribunal." Recently, the phrase "civil rights and obligations" has been given a surprisingly expansive definition.[114] Earlier jurisprudence had established that the word "civil" connoted the distinction between private and public law,[115] with civil rights being rights in private law. Latterly, it has been commented that the Court has now reached the following conclusion:

> ". . . Article 6 regulates many more kinds of disputes between the individual and the state than that [phrase] might suggest. Thus cases concerning public control of land, the licensing or other regulation of commercial or professional activities, compensation for illegal public acts and social security and assistance rights now fall within the bounds of the right to a fair trial."[116]

Assuming that one is considering a situation in which Article 6.1 does apply, the next question is: what exactly does the provision require. In many ways, it is more flexible than Article 34.1. In the first place, the Article is satisfied where the hearing is heard before an independent tribunal: there is no need for a court, *strictu senso* to be involved. Secondly, consider a situation in which a decision has been taken by the executive or some other body, which is plainly not a court or tribunal; yet there is a recourse, from the decision of the executive to a court or independent tribunal. While here, too, the law is in a state of flux so that one cannot be definite, it seems probable that Article 6.1 is satisfied, provided that the court or tribunal has "full appellate jurisdiction". Thus, for example, in *Oerlemans v. The Netherlands*[117] the applicant's land had been designated by government order as a protected natural

---

[112] *Ibid.* p. 9 of the judgment.
[113] Art. 37.2 was enacted by the Sixth Amendment of the Constitution Act 1979 to quieten doubts raised by the Supreme Court's decision in *M. v. An Bord Uchtála* [1977] I.R. 287.
[114] On this subject see generally, Harris, O'Boyle and Warbrick, *Law on the European Convention on Human Rights* (1995), pp. 174–196 and 230–234.
[115] *Ibid.*
[116] *Ibid.* at p. 184.
[117] (1993) 15 E.H.R.R. 561.

site, with the consequence that his farming activities were restricted. However, the applicant's case before the European Court of Human Rights failed by virtue of the fact that he was able to bring proceedings before the civil courts for a full review of the lawfulness of the (unfavourable) administrative decision. Given that Irish law often does provide for an appeal from a decision taken by the executive to an independent tribunal or court, (*e.g.* An Bord Pleanála) then this is obviously a significant relaxation. On the other hand, equally significant is the fact that it has been held, in an English case,[118] that the availability of judicial review of a decision of the executive did not suffice to satisfy Article 6.1 on the ground that judicial review affords too limited a form of control. Article 6.1 thus throws a sharp focus on the question of, first, whether a tribunal is provided in regard to a wide category of individual decisions of a public nature, and, secondly, on whether the tribunal is sufficiently independent. As regards this last point, the European Court had hitherto set a fairly modest standard. For instance, as to the requirement that tribunal members be protected from removal during their term of office, it suffices if this is 'recognised in fact'.[119] Indeed, in one of the few cases on this point, it was held by the European Court of Human Rights that the Special Criminal Court satisfied this standard.[120] Yet, even here there are signs of change. Thus, in *Findlay v. United Kingdom*[121] the European Court held that the British court martial system violated Article 6(1). As the prosecuting officer appointed the members of the court and given that they generally fell within his chain of command, concerns about the independence and impartiality of the tribunal were objectively justified.

Appointment and removal of members of tribunal

The type of institutional arrangements designed to create independent pedestals for judges are largely absent in the case of tribunals. Thus, in the case of a typical tribunal, the chairman and other members will be selected by the Minister. The term of office is usually fixed at a maximum of three to five years. Members are generally eligible for reappointment.[122] However, in certain other cases, the appointment is intended as a full-time career post.[123]

Frequently, no statutory qualifications are laid down for appointment, but in some exceptional cases the chairman must be a lawyer.[124] The two ordinary members of the Mining Board[125] must be property arbitrators, and it is assumed that some members of the Rent Tribunal[126] must have knowledge or experience of the valuation of property. Further examples occur in the case of "balanced" or representative tribunals. For instance, in the case of the Labour Court[127] and the Employment

---

[118] *W. v. United Kingdom* (1987) 9 E.H.R.R. 121.
[119] *Campbell and Fell v. United Kingdom* (1985) 7 E.H.R.R. 165.
[120] *Eccles, McPhilips and McShane v. Ireland* Application No. 12839/87 (1988) 59 *D and R* 212.
[121] (1997) 24 E.H.R.R. 221.
[122] See, *e.g.* Minerals Development Act 1940, s.33; Adoption Act 1952, s.8 and First Sched. (Art. 2); Housing (Private Rented Dwellings) (Amendment) Act 1983, ss.2 and 3; Local Government (Planning and Development) Act 1983, ss.5 and 7; Pensions Act 1990, First Sched.
[123] See, *e.g.* Controller of Patents, Designs and Trade Marks: see Patents Act 1992, s.97.
[124] See, *e.g.*, Refugee Act, s.15, Second Schedule, (Chairperson of the Refugee Appeal Board must be a practising solicitor or barrister of at least 10 years standing).
[125] Minerals Development Act 1979, s.41.
[126] Housing (Private Rented Dwellings) Regulations 1983 (S.I. No. 222 of 1983), Art. 6(6).
[127] Industrial Relations Act 1969, s.2.

Appeals Tribunal,[128] the employers and employees are represented equally. By convention one of the Appeals Commissioners is chosen from among the senior officials of the Revenue Commissioners while the other is a member of the Bar. The most sophisticated attempt in this direction involves An Bord Pleanála. Section 7 of the Local Government (Planning and Development) Act 1983 allows the Minister for the Environment to prescribe certain organisations[129] which are variously representative of particular interest groups. These groups are: professions or occupations relating to physical planning; organisations concerned with protection and preservation of the environment; business groups including those representing the construction industry; and community groups. The Minister is then required to choose one member of the Board from among the names nominated by each category of organisation. The fifth ordinary member is chosen from among the Minister for the Environment's own civil servants.[130]

Removal of members of tribunals is generally a matter for the responsible Minister. The power to remove members is generally confined to specific grounds, such as ill-health, stated misbehaviour or where the removal appears to the Minister to be necessary for the effective performance of the Board's functions.[131] In fact, dismissals are rare, and the most spectacular dismissals in recent times – those of the members of An Bord Pleanála in 1983 – were brought about directly by an Act of the Oireachtas.[132]

4. The Social Welfare Appeals System[133]

A study of the detailed substantive operation of a tribunal would extend beyond the bounds of administrative law and into the particular substantive law field in which the tribunal was operating. However, in order to give some flavour of the operation of tribunals, we give, in this and the following Part, brief case-studies of two of the most important tribunals, focusing on structure rather than substance.

In 1995, one and a half million claims (worth an aggregate of £4 billion which is 35% of current government expenditure or 12% of GNP) are made on the Minister for Social Welfare[134] in respect of such social welfare payments as: disability benefit; unemployment benefit and assistance; occupational injuries benefit and old-age

---

128 Redundancy Payments Act 1967, s.39(4).
129 The list of prescribed organisations is to be found in Local Government (Planning and Development) Regulations 1994 (S.I. No. 86 of 1994), Part XI.
130 s.7(2)(e) of the 1983 Act. Appointment of the Chairman of An Bord Pleanála is by way of a similar, if not quite identical, process: see s.5 of the Act.
131 See, *e.g.* Mineral Developments Act 1940, s.33(3) (Mining Board); Adoption Act 1952, s.3(1) (An Bord Uchtála); Local Government (Planning and Development) Act 1983, ss.4 and 7 (An Bord Pleanála); though see also, Pensions Act 1990, First Sched., para. 5.
132 Local Government (Planning and Development) Act 1983, s.10. See further, p. 504.
133 The principal statutory provisions and regulations include the following: Social Welfare (Consolidation) Act 1993, Pt. VII and the Social Welfare (Appeals) Regulations 1990 (S.I. No. 344 of 1990). This statutory instrument is continued in force by s.302(2) of the 1993 Act. See generally, Clark, *Annotated Guide to Social Welfare Law* (ICLSA Reprint, 1995); Clark, "Social Welfare Insurance Appeals" (1978) 13 Ir. Jur. (N.S.) 265; Whyte and Cousins, "Reforming the Social Welfare Appeals System" (1989) 7 I.L.T. (N.S.) 198 and Ward, "Financial Consequences of Marital Breakdown" (1990), pp. 20–22 and Cousins, *The Irish Social Welfare System* (1995).
134 Cousins, *ibid.*, p. 9.

pensions. The statutory basis for these vast administrative schemes is now consolidated in the Social Welfare (Consolidation) Act 1993, under which entitlement to payment turns on the interpretation of such phrases as "capable of work [and] available for work" (unemployment benefit)[135]; "accident arising out of and in the course of employment" (occupational injury benefits)[136]; or whether a claimant has submitted to the necessary medical examinations (maternity benefit).[137]

For some purposes, there is or used to be a dichotomy between, on the one hand, social insurance schemes (where the benefits are in part financed out of contributions already made by the claimant) and, on the other hand, social assistance allowances (in respect of which no direct contributions have been paid). However this dichotomy only has a slight impact on the system by which the schemes are administered for the administration of social insurance schemes and most social assistance schemes each fall within the jurisdiction of the deciding officer, from whom an appeal lies to the appeals officer.[138] Each of these officers are designated officers in the Department of Social Welfare.[139]

Deciding Officer

In practice most applicants will, first, be advised by junior Department of Social Welfare officials as to their entitlement to the benefit which has been claimed. If the advice is in the negative, then the applicant can insist that a deciding officer adjudicate upon the claim. This officer may make various inquiries (*e.g.* to former employers of the applicant) but there is no oral hearing and, in general, no attempt is made to observe the rules of constitutional justice. It is clear, then, that the present practices are defective, at least where the effect of the decision of the deciding officer is to terminate payments to persons already in receipt of social welfare benefits or assistance. This emerges from the judgments of Barron J. in *The State (Hoolahan)*

---

135 Social Welfare (Consolidation) Act 1993, s.42(4).
136 1993 Act, ss.49 and 53.
137 *Ibid.* s.40.
138 There are a number of other schemes which are administered by the Health Boards and which therefore fall outside these particular appeal procedures. These include: supplementary welfare allowances (Social Welfare (Consolidation) Act 1993, ss.170–191, 266–269.); infectious diseases maintenance allowance (Health Act 1947, s.41); domiciliary care allowances (Health Act 1970, s.61); and disabled person's maintenance allowance (Health Act 1970, s.69). For the summary appeal procedures operated by the Health Boards in the case of supplementary welfare allowances, see Ward, *op. cit.* above, n.133 at 23. There does not appear to be any appeal mechanism available in the case of the other allowances operated by the Health Boards, although the more formal and expensive remedy of judicial review is always available in respect of decisions of Health Boards in relation to such allowances: see, *e.g. H. v. Eastern Health Board* [1988] I.R. 747. The payment of unemployment benefit or unemployment assistance to employees on strike is now a matter for the Social Welfare Tribunal: see Social Welfare (Consolidation) Act 1993, ss.274–276 and Social Welfare (Social Welfare Tribunal) Regulations 1982 (S.I. 1982 No. 309). See generally, Clark, *Social Welfare (Consolidation) Act 1993*, pp.27, 303–310; Kerr and Whyte, *Irish Trade Union Law* (1985), pp. 371–376; Clark, "Towards the 'Just' Strike? Social Welfare Payments for Persons Affected by a Trade Dispute in the Republic of Ireland" (1985) 48 M.L.R. 569. The effect of the change is to build in a tribunal between the two existing appellate tiers, viz. the appeals officer and the High Court, in respect of the question whether a person is disqualified from receiving unemployment benefit or assistance, by virtue of stoppage of work or a trade dispute.
139 The deciding officer has a seldom-used power to refrain from deciding the case himself, but to seek the assistance of an appeals officer: Social Welfare (Consolidation) Act 1993; s.250(3).

v. Minister for Social Welfare[140] and of O'Hanlon J. in *Thompson v. Minister for Social Welfare*.[141] In *Hoolahan*, the applicant was alleged to have fraudulently obtained social welfare benefits, but since the decision to disqualify her from benefit was based on facts which had not been brought to her attention, Barron J. held that the decision could not stand. He added that the claimant:

"Should know fully the extent of the case being made against her and that no decision should be made until she has been given proper opportunity to deal fully with a case."[142]

In *Thompson v. Minister for Social Welfare*, the deciding officer ruled that the applicant should be disqualified from receiving unemployment benefit for a six-week period because of the latter's refusal to participate in a career advice programme. O'Hanlon J. held that, in such circumstances, before a deciding officer terminates the payments of an applicant who has been in receipt of unemployment assistance for some time:

"he should inform the person concerned that the position is being reviewed by him; the grounds upon which he is considering disallowing further payment; and the person concerned should be given an opportunity to answer the case made against him."[143]

Because of the failure of the deciding officer to satisfy these requirements, "however informally", his decision had to be set aside for non-compliance with constitutional justice. It is as yet too early to say whether this decision will presage a significant change in the procedures actually adopted by deciding officers. It is also noteworthy that in *Corcoran v. Minister for Social Welfare*,[144] the High Court was prepared to consider a challenge (albeit an unsuccessful one) based on substantive "unreasonableness" against the termination by a deciding officer of the plaintiff's unemployment assistance.

Appeals Officer

An appeal[145] against a refusal is supposed to be filed with the Chief Appeals Officer within 21 days, although, in practice, this time limit is not strictly adhered to, since the Minister has a discretion to admit late claims. The appeal is initiated by a "notice of appeal" (which states the relevant facts and arguments on which the applicant

---

[140] Unreported, High Court, July 23, 1986.
[141] [1989] I.R. 618.
[142] *Ibid.* at 621
[143] *Ibid.* However, on receiving the news of the decision, the applicant sought and obtained an interview with the deciding officer. The officer explained why he proposed to review the applicant's entitlement and made inquiries of the applicant as to why he had refused to attend a training course. O'Hanlon J. held that, at this point, the deciding officer had sufficiently complied with fair procedures, so that the disqualification decision, which took effect later, was not invalid.
[144] [1991] 2 I.R. 175 at 180, *per* Murphy J.("If [the deciding officer] drew [from the motor car which the applicant owned] the inference that the applicant had a more substantial income . . . which would result in the applicant exceeding the . . . permitted figure, that such a decision could not be described as unreasonable . . .").
[145] Below is a table detailing the number of appeals (of all types) against decisions of deciding officers 1991–1995 (Pn. 46323)

proposes to rely) and accompanied by any documentary evidence.[146] If a replying statement is filed, it will generally be confined to a summary of the original basis of the decision under appeal and the applicant will generally be permitted to have access to this document. The appeals officer hears the case *de novo*.[147]

The appeals officer is given a broad discretion to decide whether to grant an oral hearing save that the Minister has power to direct that a particular case shall be heard orally, where he considers that this is warranted in the circumstances.[148] In fact, oral hearings are held in a substantial number of appeals.[149] Each appeals officer decides an average of about 1,000 cases each year, and many oral hearings are disposed of in less than 15 minutes.

The decision as to whether to grant legal representation is at the discretion of the appeals officer.[150] In practice, legal representation is not very common[151] but, where it is permitted, solicitors and counsel are awarded costs in accordance with the scale rate.[152] While constitutional justice does not require legal representation in all cases, the failure on the part of the appeals officer to permit representation in an appropriate case would probably amount to an unreasonable exercise of his discretion.[153]

Type of Appeal	On hand at start of year	Received during year	Decided by Appeals Officers	Reconsidered on facts, by Deciding Officer	Withdrawn	On Hand at end of year
1991	5,135	19,314	12,673	‡	3,489	8,287
1992	8,287	17,610	13,254	‡	5,590	7,053
1993	7,053	18,285	14,115	‡	5,906	5,317
1994	5,317	13,504	10,358	2,946	1,667	3,850
1995	3,850	12,353	8,048	2,729	1,310	4,116

‡ For the years 1991–1993, this category is not broken down but is included in the numbers decided by Appeals Officers.

146 Social Welfare (Appeals) Regulations 1990 (S.I. No. 344 of 1990), Art. 8.
147 1993 Act, s.257(3).
148 Social Welfare (Appeals) Regulations 1990 (S.I. No. 344 of 1990) Art. 12; now: 1993 Act, s.270. In *Kiely v. Minister for Social Welfare* (No. 2) [1977] I.R. 267 at 278, Henchy J. stated that if there were "[U]nresolved conflicts in the documentary evidence, as to any matter essential to a ruling of the claim, the intention of these Regulations is that those conflicts shall be resolved by an oral hearing." See also *Galvin v. Chief Appeals Officer* [1997] 3 I.R. 240 where Costello P. held that the respondent had breached fair procedures in not holding an oral inquiry to resolve conflicts of fact regarding the payment of insurance contributions. But this approach tends to overlook the fact that in practice "[m]ost, if not all, of the documentary evidence will be adduced by the deciding officer who may fail to set out clearly the appellant's view of the appeal": Clark, "Social Welfare Insurance Appeals" (1978) 13 Ir. Jur. (N.S.) 265 at p. 274.
149 Some recent figures are: 50 per cent (1995); 46 per cent (1994); 36 per cent (1993).
150 Social Welfare (Appeals) Regulations 1990 (S.I. No. 344 of 1990), Art. 14.
151 According to Ward, above, n.128 at p. 58, only 12 per cent. of claimants in an admittedly small sample had legal representation before an appeals officer.
152 Social Welfare Act, 1996, s.34. For an unidentified High Court case on legal costs, see Social Welfare Appeals Office Annual Report for 1995 (Pn 7783), p. 19.
153 *R. v. Home Secretary, ex p. Tarrant* [1985] Q.B. 251; *Flanagan v. University College, Dublin* [1988] I.R 724; *Gallagher v. Revenue Commissioners (No. 2)* [1995] 1 I.R. 55. But *cf.* the comments to the contrary of Murphy J. in *Corcoran v. Minister for Social Welfare* [1991] 2 I.R. 175 at 183.

The appeals officer has power to subpoena witnesses and to take evidence on oath.[154] Where a person required to attend or to produce documents fails to comply with such a request, the appeals officer may, on serving notice to such a person, apply to the District Court for an order requiring attendance or production of documents, as the case may be. Written evidence may also be admitted if the appeals officer thinks it "just and proper" to do so; however, this evidence ceases to have effect if "oral evidence of probative value is adduced which controverts the written statement so admitted".[155] However, one commentator has described the appeal proceedings as being more in the nature "of an interview of the claimant by the appeals officer, rather than the tribunal hearing which it should be".[156] The decision of the appeals officer is then sent to the Minister for Social Welfare. The applicant will then receive a memorandum of the Minister's decision. In the case of unsuccessful appeals, reasons must be given.[157] (The memorandum is in standard form, and, in the case of unsuccessful appeals, sets forth a list of alternative reasons for the decision. The reasons which are inapplicable are deleted). The fact that appeals officers' decisions are not published means that there is no system of *stare decisis*, and this in turn leads to the operation of an appeals system "in which uniformity of decision-making is singularly absent".[158]

The Chief Appeals Officer is empowered to appoint an assessor to sit with an appeals officer in an appropriate case. [159] For example, two assessors – one drawn from an employees' panel and the other from an employers' panel – sit on unemployment benefit appeals. The role of the assessors is to assist the appeals officer with their knowledge of prevailing local employment conditions. This information is relevant in considering, for example, whether an applicant is making himself available for work. The role of the medical assessors under the analogous Social Welfare (Occupational Injuries) Act 1966 was examined by the Supreme Court in *Kiely v. Minister for Social Welfare*.[160] In the view of Henchy J. (which appears to have adopted the procedure in a court of law, as a role model) the regulations envisaged that the medical assessors' role should be a strictly limited one. The assessors should not take any active part in the proceedings: their task was simply to give information on medical matters when requested to do so by the appeals officer.

Given the "Departmental" character of the appeals system, it may be questioned whether the procedures adopted violate constitutional justice, in that institutional bias may be involved.[161] For the system is administered by civil servants working

---

154 Social Welfare (Consolidation) Act 1993, ss.258–259.
155 *Kiely v. Minister for Social Welfare* [1977] I.R. 267 at 279, *per* Henchy J. See Social Welfare (Appeals) Regulations 1990 (S.I. No. 344 of 1990), Art. 17(3) which gives a discretion to the appeals officer to admit evidence in writing on a prima facie basis.
156 Ward, *op. cit.* above, n.128 at p. 21.
157 S.I. No.344 of 1990, art.18.
158 Clark, above, n.128 at p. 382. This will change with the advent of the Freedom of Information Act 1997, s.16 (see p. 496).
159 Social Welfare (Consolidation) Act 1993, s.255.The Social Welfare (Consolidation) Act, 1981, s.298(12)(c) stated that the parties may waive the absence of an assessor. There is no equivalent of this provision in the 1993 Act, yet Clarke, p. 294 remarks: "in practice appeals are heard without an assessor if the appellant waives the need for the assessor . . ."; Social Welfare (Appeals) Regulations 1990 (S.I. No. 344 of 1990), Art. 13.
160 [1977] I.R. 267. See Clark, *op. cit.* above, n.128 at pp. 278–279.
161 Though on institutional bias, see *O'Brien v. Bord na Móna* [1983] I.R. 265 and see pp. 518–520.

in the Department of Social Welfare whose independence is not guaranteed by law and who, perhaps, are unduly influenced by Departmental policy considerations.[162] It is true that some attempt was made by the Social Welfare Act 1990 to ameliorate this perceived lack of independence. Thus, the appeal now formally lies to the Chief Appeals Officer, instead of the Minister for Social Welfare. Moreover, it is the Chief Appeals Officer (instead of the Minister) who is entrusted with such diverse functions as assigning the appeals to other appeals officers; determining whether assessors should sit with an appeals officer in a particular case and referring questions of law to the High Court. A further innovation is that the Chief Appeals Officer is obliged to produce an annual report on the working of the appeals officers, which report must be laid before both Houses of the Oireachtas.[163]

While these reforms go beyond the merely superficial, their significance may be overstated. The basic lack of even-handedness, already identified, remains and it is only when the social welfare appeals system is remodelled along the lines of the An Bord Pleanála or the Valuation Tribunal that the independence of this system will be beyond question.

Review of deciding officer's or appeals officer's decisions

In the first place, a deciding officer may review an earlier decision of a deciding officer or even an appeals officer if there is new evidence, or if the earlier decision was based on a mistake on a point of law or fact, or if there has been a change in circumstances. It is also open to an appeals officer to review the earlier decision of an appeals officer, though on slightly narrower grounds than in the case of a deciding officer. By virtue of these provisions, a deciding officer (or, where appropriate, an appeals officer) is entitled not only to increase but even to reduce or disallow payments, save that the latter order will not have retrospective effect, except in the case of fraud.[164]

Secondly, section 271 of the Social Welfare (Consolidation) Act 1993 creates an appeal on a point of law[165] from a decision of an appeals officer to the High Court. However, read literally, the scope of this appeal would seem to be extraordinarily

---

[162] Clark, "Towards a 'Just' Strike? Social Welfare Payments for Persons Affected by a Trade Dispute in the Republic of Ireland" (1985) 48 M.L.R. 659 comments as follows (at 666): "Appeals officers provide an efficient method of internal administrative review but, given the status of the appeals officer – at the time of such appointment such a person is, and remains, employed within the Department of Social Welfare and holds office 'during the pleasure of the Minister' – it is unrealistic to regard this form of adjudication as an independent appeals mechanism." See further, pp. 269–270.

[163] On the Chief Appeals Officer and the powers outlined in the text, see 1993 Act, ss. 251–263; S.I. No. 344 of 1990, Part II.

[164] 1993 Act, ss. 248–249, 262–264. See, also, *Lundy v. Minister for Social Welfare* [1993] 3 I.R. 406.

[165] The Chief Appeals Officer is entitled to refer "any question" arising from a decision of the appeals officer to the High Court (*i.e.* this reference is not confined to points of law), provided that the question does not fall within section 265: 1993 Act, s.253. A further welcome recent innovation is that where the Chief Appeals Officer certifies that the ordinary appeal procedures "are inadequate to secure the effective processing of such appeal", the appeal is then transferred to the Circuit Court which may affirm the decision or substitute the decision of the deciding officer in accordance with this Act and upon the same evidence as would otherwise be available to the Appeals Officer": Social Welfare (Consolidation) Act 1993, s.253A(1) (as inserted by the Social Welfare Act 1997, s.34). By virtue of s.253A(3), no appeal lies from the decision of the Circuit Court "on an appeal under this section", a provision which must be of doubtful constitutionality having regard to Article 34.3.4° of the Constitution.

narrow in that a question arising "in relation to a claim for benefit" would be excluded, and the decision of the appeals officer rendered "final and conclusive".[166] As Lynch J. observed in *Kingham v. Minister for Social Welfare*,[167] such a literal interpretation would have the effect of excluding appeals in:

> "the vast majority of questions that might arise under the provisions of the 1981 Act, leaving only a minority of cases where persons claim not to be within the Act and therefore not liable to pay contributions under the Act nor entitled to benefits thereunder."

Indeed, section 265 of the 1993 Act goes even further and purports to exclude from judicial review (the formula "final and conclusive" is used) virtually all decisions of an appeals officer. It is significant that the scope of the decisions so excluded is defined to be coterminous with the extent of the decisions from which no appeal is allowed. In sum, apart from the negligible area conjectured in the passage quoted from *Kingham*, there would be neither appeal nor review. The demarcation line identified in *Kingham*, would appear to be based on the rather quaint view that there should be an appeal in all cases where the citizen was required to make payments to the State, but not where the appellant was a mere recipient of the State's largesse. In *Kingham's* case, Lynch J. reacted against such a construction of (the earlier equivalent of) section 271, saying that the matter excluded should be construed narrowly so as not to oust the jurisdiction of the High Court "save where such ouster is clear". The apparent effect of *Kingham* is that an appeal now lies to the High Court by virtue of section 271 of the 1993 Act in respect of all decisions of an appeals officer, the provisions of section 265 notwithstanding.[168]

In *The State (Power) v. Moran*[169] Gannon J. ruled that an absence of probative evidence to support a decision of an appeals officer was not an error affecting jurisdiction, and the decision could not be impeached in certiorari proceedings. This restrictive interpretation of the scope of jurisdictional error is out of line with some of the modern authorities.[170] However, in the subsequent decision of *Foley v. Moulton*[171] the same judge was at pains to stress that, in *Foley*, the appeals officer had based his decision on "evidence which was reasonably capable of supporting the determination he made"[172] which, perhaps, may be said to raise the inference that Gannon J. would have quashed the decision had it not been so based. *Murphy v. Minister for Social Welfare*[173] provides some further evidence that the courts are

---

166   s.271 refers the reader on to s.265. As it happens, s.247(2)(a) is the principal provision to which s.265 applies, and s.247(2)(a) refers to a question arising "in relation to a claim for benefit". The "final and conclusive" clause contained in s.265 could not, however, bar judicial review by the High Court: see pp. 454–456.

167   Unreported, High Court, November 25, 1985. This case concerned identical provisions of the earlier Social Welfare (Consolidation) Act 1981.

168   Note that in *Foley v. Moulton* [1989] I.L.R.M. 169 the respondents accepted that an appeal could lie to the High Court under ss.298–300 of the 1981 Act on all questions of law.

169   [1976–1977] I.L.R.M. 20.

170   See pp. 420–426. But *cf. Galvin v. Chief Appeals Officer* [1997] 3 I.R. 240 where Costello P. held that incorrect inferences, which had not been based on evidence, constituted errors within jurisdiction and could not be quashed in judicial review proceedings.

171   [1989] I.L.R.M. 169.

172   *Ibid.* at 176.

173   [1987] I.R. 295.

now more willing to scrutinise decisions of deciding and appeals officers in judicial review application, for here Blayney J. had little hesitation in quashing a decision of an appeals officer who had answered "the wrong question" and, thereby erred in law. Similarly, as far as challenges to the validity of social welfare legislation on constitutional[174] and European Community law[175] grounds are concerned judicial caution has not been much in evidence. However, pulling in the other direction is the fact that the courts[176] have sometimes been unwilling to interfere with the decisions of specialists such as appeals officers,[177] especially if this means interfering with a long-standing interpretation of the relevant regulations.[178] This was certainly the approach taken in *Henry Denny & Sons (Ireland) Ltd v. Minister for Social Welfare.*[179] In this appeal under section 271 of the 1993 Act, the Supreme Court upheld an appeals officer's conclusion that a supermarket demonstrator was actually employed by the appellant. The appeals officer's findings of fact could not be disturbed "unless they were incapable of being supported by the facts or were based on an erroneous view of the law." Hamilton C.J. added that the courts:

> "should be slow to interfere with the decisions of expert administrative tribunals. When conclusions are based upon an identifiable error of law or an unsustainable finding of fact by a tribunal such conclusions must be corrected. Otherwise, it should be recognised that [where] tribunals which have been given statutory tasks to perform and [who] exercise their functions (as is now usually the case) with a high degree of expertise and provide coherent and balanced judgments on the evidence and arguments heard by them, it should not be necessary for the Courts to review their decisions by way of appeal or judicial review."

---

[174] See, *e.g. H. v. Eastern Health Board* [1988] I.R. 747 and *Hyland v. Minister for Social Welfare* [1988] I.R. 624.

[175] See, *e.g. McDermott and Cotter v. Minister for Social Welfare* [1987] I.L.R.M. 324.

[176] Note the manner in which Gannon J. refused to disturb a finding by an appeals officer in *Foley v. Moulton* [1989] I.L.R.M. 169 to the effect that the claimant was co-habitating with a man and was thus disqualified from receiving a widow's pension by virtue of s.92(3) of the Social Welfare (Consolidation) Act 1993.

[177] "Where a real error of law is shown then this court will interfere, but it would in my opinion be wrong to set up this Court as in effect a court of appeal of fact from decisions of these specialised tribunals", *per* May J. in *R. v. National Insurance Commissioner, ex p. Michael* [1976] I.C.R. 90 at 94 (D.C.), *affirmed* [1977] 1 W.L.R. 109 (C.A.). See also, *R. v. Industrial Injuries Commissioner, ex p. Amalgamated Engineering Union* [1966] 2 Q.B. 31; *R. v. Preston Supplementary Benefits Appeal Tribunal, ex p. Moore* [1975] 1 W.L.R. 624. Traces of this approach may also be found in the judgment of Keane J. in *Radio Limerick v. IRTC* [1997] 2 I.L.R.M. 1 and that of Geoghegan J. in *Murphy v. IRTC* [1997] 2 I.L.R.M. 435.

[178] *R. v. National Insurance Commissioner, ex p. Stratton* [1979] Q.B. 361 at 369 (Lord Denning). Of course, statutory interpretation is in the last analysis an objective matter for judicial determination: *Shannon Regional Fisheries Board v. An Bord Pleanála* [1994] 3 I.R. 449; *Lambert v. An tÁrd Chláraitheoir* [1995] 2 I.R. 372.

[179] Unreported, Supreme Court, December 1, 1997.

5. Independent Radio and Television Commission[180]

The need for some form of regulation of broadcasting – which was early recognised as an even more potent form of mass communication than that provided by the printing press – led to the passing of the Wireless Telegraphy Act 1926. Employing the standard licensing technique (more fully explored in Part 8 of this chapter) sections 3 and 5 of the 1926 Act made the possession of "wireless telegraphy apparatus" (as now defined in section 2(1) of the Broadcasting and Wireless Telegraphy Act 1988) a criminal offence unless it was authorised by a licence granted by the then Minister for Posts and Telegraphs.

In fact the first systematic Irish broadcasting service began, as "2RN" on New Year's Night, 1926. The unit providing this service was to remain a section within the Department of Posts and Telegraphs until 1960. Some gestures were made in the direction of its unusual nature and the need for some independence: the unit was placed under the control of a Director of Broadcasting and in 1953, he was fortified by the establishment of a non-statutory *Comhairle* of five persons, given temporary civil service appointments, who were to be responsible to the Minister for the general control and supervision of the service.[181]

The Broadcasting Authority Act 1960 at last established broadcasting on a footing independent of the Government[182] by constituting the Radio Éireann (from 1966, Radio Telefís Éireann) Authority as a state-sponsored body. Some modifications to RTÉ were effected by amending statutes, enacted in 1976 and 1990. Other aspects of RTÉ, including its relations with the Government and the Order formally made under section 31 of the Broadcasting Authority Act 1960 (as amended) are covered elsewhere in this book.[183]

For present purposes, what is significant is that until the new settlement (in the late 1980s, described below) the licence to broadcast was granted only to the official services provided first by the Department and thereafter by RTÉ (notwithstanding unsuccessful applications by some pirate pop stations). This *de facto* monopoly was threatened by the pirate broadcasters at first, in the 1960s, from a maritime base, but by the 1980s, within the jurisdiction. Because of the popularity of the pirate stations with the electorate, especially its younger members, official action to counteract the pirate stations was sluggish and ineffectual. The policy followed by successive Ministers for Communication was to take legal action against unlicensed stations only if they were causing interference to authorised users of wireless telegraphy apparatus.[184] The suggestion was made[185] that the Minister's apparent policy of

---

180 See generally, Hall, *The Electronic Age: Telecommunications in Ireland* (1993); Hall and McGovern, "Broadcasting and Wireless Telegraphy Act 1988 and Radio and Television Act 1988" (1988) *Irish Current Law Statutes Annotated*; Hall and McGovern, "Regulation of the Media" (1986) 8 D.U.L.J. (N.S.) 1.
181 O'Broin, *Just Like Yesterday*, pp. 167–180.
182 For the first decade or so, this independence was rather faltering: see Kelly "The Constitutional Position of RTÉ" (1967) 15 *Administration* 205; O'Broin, "The dismissal of the Irish Broadcasting Authority" *E.B.U. Review*, March 1973, p. 24 and September, 1975, p. 39.
183 See pp. 147–149 and 663–664 and 667.
184 120 *Senate Debates*, Col. 787, June 21, 1988 (Mr. R. Burke, Minister for Communications).
185 Kelly, "Are Our Broadcasting Structures Out of Date?" *Irish Broadcasting Review*, Summer 1978, p. 5. *A contra*: McRedmond, "Irish Radio Controversy" *Irish Broadcasting Review*, Autumn 1978, p. 62.

confining broadcasting to the official services amounted to an unjustified inhibition on other would-be broadcasters' freedom of expression (under Article 40.6.1°) and also to a violation of their right to earn a livelihood (under Article 40.3.1°). These points seem to have been raised but not settled in *Nova Media Ltd v. Minister for Post and Telegraphs*.[186] Article 10.1 of the European Convention on Human Rights[187] might also be relevant, as would E.C. competition law. In addition, as explained, a failure properly to exercise a discretion – in this case, in regard to the grant of a licence – may be invalid.

Eventually, falteringly,[188] the legislature confronted the problem of providing a legal framework within which to exercise such control over private broadcasting as was considered necessary. The final settlement retained the requirement already mentioned of a licence to broadcast, under the 1926 Act (albeit that the Broadcasting and Wireless Telegraphy Act 1988 established enhanced penalties for unlicensed broadcasting: see below). The major innovation was the constitution of a *de luxe* tribunal, the Independent Radio and Television Commission, by the Radio and Television Act 1988. It is this Commission which bears the responsibility of allocating the franchises to private broadcasters and thereafter policing them. The Schedule to the Radio and Television Act 1988 provides that:

> "A person shall not be appointed to be a member of the Commission unless he has had experience of, or shown capacity in, media or commercial affairs, radio communications engineering, trade union affairs, administration or social, cultural, educational or community activities."

The "independent" broadcasting franchises embrace: a national radio service; and 20-odd regional radio services plus a television service (which has not yet come into operation[189] and 11 pilot community or community of interest radio stations. However, the RTÉ services remain under the control of the RTÉ Authority, unaffected, so far as the law is concerned, by the new régime.[190]

Licences and contracts

One particular point of interest in this regulatory system concerns the demarcation of control functions between the Commission and the Minister for Arts, Heritage the Gaeltacht and the Islands (formerly Communications and before that, Posts and Telegraphs). Broadly speaking the Minister controls the technological matter of

---

186 [1984] I.L.R.M. 161 at 167. See also, *Cooke v. Minister for Communications, Irish Times Law Report*, February 20, 1989.

187 See, *e.g. Autronic AG v. Switzerland* (1990) 12 E.H.R.R. 485 (ban on reception of foreign satellite television by satellite dish "not necessary in a democratic society" and, hence, contrary to Art. 10(1)). But see *Groppera Radio AG v. Switzerland* (1990) 12 E.H.R.R. 321 (legislation banning foreign retransmissions justifiable where necessary to give effect to international broadcasting rules.)

188 There were a number of attempts to legislate before the 1988 Acts were passed. The history of these other measures is recorded in Hall and McGovern, *Radio and Television Act 1988, op.cit.*, above, n.180 (at n.179).

189 In the *TV3 case* (on which see pp. 541–542) in 1993, the Supreme Court decided that the Windmill consortium (TV3) was entitled to continue contract negotiations with IRTC to operate this. But, as of the beginning of 1998, there was still no independent television service in operation.

190 See, however, Government Green and White Papers on Broadcasting (fn. 1540 April 27, 1995 and 1996 respectively).

broadcasting frequency management, whilst the Commission is concerned with the broadcasters and the material broadcast. The reasons given by the Minister as to why the frequency management could not be transferred to the Commission so that both functions would be united in the same body were two-fold. In the first place, broadcasting frequencies are but one element of the radio frequency spectrum which also has to accommodate aeronautical, mobile or emergency communications and it is necessary for all elements on the spectrum to be vested in the same authority.[191] Secondly, the entire radio-communications area is governed by international treaties for which the Government is responsible.

It is the Commission which appears to have the determining voice. How the dual control is co-ordinated is as follows. First, as we shall see, the key organising concept is the "contract". The provisions in the Act regarding sound broadcasting contracts and the television programme service contract are similar save that the latter do not contemplate that the contractor itself will have to establish a transmitter.[192] Accordingly in this account we shall concentrate on sound broadcasting. The provision in respect of sound contracts is as follows:

"The Commission shall enter into contracts (in this Act referred to as 'sound broadcasting contracts') with persons (in this Act referred to as 'sound broadcasting contractors') under which the sound broadcasting contractors have, subject to the provisions of this Act, the right and duty to establish, maintain and operate sound broadcasting contract and to provide, as the sound broadcasting contract may specify, a sound broadcasting service."[193]

On the other hand, it is for the Minister to decide whether to issue a licence and to specify the transmitter and area of the country to which it relates and also the frequency on which it is to operate and "such [other] terms and conditions as [he] sees fit to attach to the licence."[194] The Minister may also vary any term or condition of a licence on any of a number of specified grounds, including the fact that "it appears to him to be necessary so to do in the interests of good radio frequency management."[195]

The yoke between the contract and the licence is constructed in this way: the Commission cannot authorise a broadcasting contractor to operate a transmitter and provide a broadcasting service pursuant to a sound broadcasting contract "unless and until the Minister has issued . . . to the Commission a licence in respect of the . . . transmitter to which the contract relates."'[196] However when the licence has been issued by the Minister, provided its terms and conditions have been complied with, then the

---

191 120 *Senate Debates*, Col. 781. "In the vast majority of countries in the world this function is vested in central Government. The only practical alternative would be the American model of vesting responsibility for managing the whole of the spectrum in one body – the Federal Communications Commission in their case. To achieve that here one would effectively have to convert the Department of Communications into a semi-State body."

192 It is contemplated that it should share RTÉ's facilities.

193 Radio and Television Act 1988, ss.4(2)(a), 18(1).

194 *Ibid.* s.4(5).

195 *Ibid.* s.7(2).

196 *Ibid.* s.4(3).

197 *Ibid.* s.4(5). Notice also that, by ss.4(6) and 14(5), every licence and contract is open to inspection by the public.

contract automatically conveys the benefits of the licence to the contractor.[197] (And, incidentally, any transmitter established under the licence shall also be deemed to be licensed for the purposes of the Wireless Telegraphy Act 1926.[198])

However, the licence is made to be valid for the same period as the contract: if the contract is terminated or suspended, then so too is the licence.[199] And, equally, any breach of a condition of the licence is to be treated as if it were a breach of a term of the contract.[200] In short, since the licence is, in the ways mentioned, tied to the contract, it is the Commission which, by its control over the contract, determines who has the contract-licence and for how long.

Allocating the contract

Section 17 of the Radio and Television Act 1988 lays it down that there may be only a single television programme service. However as far as sound broadcasting services are concerned, the first step is for the number and catchment area of such services to be determined. A fair degree of formality is required in regard to this process. According to section 5:

> "(1) In order to secure the orderly development of sound broadcasting services and, having regard to the availability of radio frequencies for sound broadcasting, to allow for the establishment of a diversity of services in an area catering for a wide range of tastes including those of minority interests, the Commission shall as soon as may be after it has been established and may thereafter from time to time by notice published in at least one national newspaper, invite expressions of interest in the securing of contracts for sound broadcasting services under this Act. Such expressions of interest shall indicate in general terms the type of service that would be provided and shall not be regarded as an application for a sound broadcasting contract
>
> (2) The Commission shall make a report of its findings under *subsection* (1) to the Minister who, having considered the report and after consultation with the Commission, shall specify the area (which area may consist of the whole or any part of the State) in relation to which applications for a sound broadcasting contract are to be invited and the Commission shall comply with such direction.
>
> (3) The Minister, having regard to the report furnished by the Commission under *subsection* (2) and having regard to the availability of radio frequencies for sound broadcasting, may limit the number of areas which he may specify under that subsection."[201]

After this information-gathering exercise has been completed, the contracts must be allocated by the Commission. First of all, the Commission invites applications

---

[198]   *Ibid.* s.4(5).
[199]   *Ibid.* s.4(4).
[200]   *Ibid.* s.4(5).
[201]   There is an exemption from ss.5, 6 and 9(1)(c) in the case of temporary or institutional sound broadcasting: s.8(4).

for a contract (whether television or sound) by advertisement published in at least one national newspaper and, where the catchment area of the contract is restricted to one part of the country, in one local newspaper circulating in that area.[202] The Commission specifies the procedure which is to be followed in its adjudication on the applications. At its initial award of contracts, in 1989–1990 (in the case of sound broadcasting) and 1990 (in the case of television), it issued detailed specifications as to the types of information which each applicant should supply. These included: the applicant and his experience and management team; an advertising market analysis together with revenue targets; the types of programmes envisaged; production facilities; and the financial structure. Thereafter oral hearings were held at which the applicants could be cross-examined on their submissions.

The criteria on which the Commission is to draw, in awarding contracts, are specified in section 6(2) of the Radio and Television Act, as follows:

"In the consideration of applications received by it and in determining the most suitable applicant to be awarded a sound broadcasting contract, the Commission shall have regard to: –

(a) the character of the applicant or, if the applicant is a body corporate, the character of the body and its directors, manager, secretary or other similar officer and its members and the persons entitled to the beneficial ownership of its shares;

(b) the adequacy of the expertise and experience and of the financial resources that will be available to each applicant and the extent to which the application accords with good economic principles;

(c) the quality, range and type of the programmes proposed to be provided by each applicant or, if there is only one applicant, by that applicant;

. . .

(h) the desirability of allowing any person, or group of persons, to have control of, or substantial interests in, an undue amount of the communications media in the area specified in the notice under section 5(5);

(i) the extent to which the service proposed—

   (i) serves recognisably local communities and is supported by the various interests in the Community,

   or

   (ii) serves communities of interest, and

(j) any other matters which the Commission considers to be necessary to secure the orderly development of sound broadcasting services."

Neither the Minister, nor anyone else, has the authority to issue any directions. Thus, it is for the Commission to decide on the successful applicant with the only assistance coming from the guidelines in the Act. Inevitably, this entails both policy decisions (for example whether to prefer drama to documentaries) and factual decisions (whether an applicant is likely to obtain the finance he anticipates). Since the Commission has such a wide policy discretion, it would be inappropriate for

---

[202]   *Ibid.* s.5(5), (7).

any appeal to exist[203] and none has been created. An application for judicial review of a decision to award to a particular applicant (probably brought by a disappointed applicant) remains a possibility.[204] However save in an extreme case, success would seem unlikely, for each of the factors listed in the passage quoted involves what is very much a matter of opinion, again the trade off between them constitutes a further point of discretion, as does paragraph (j).

Contractors' duties

The sources of a contractor's duties are to be found in the Radio and Television Act, itself, and in the individual contracts. By the Act; all news and current affairs must be presented in an objective and impartial manner and without any expression of the broadcasters' own views[205] and nothing must be broadcast which offends against good taste or decency[206] and the Commission is required to draw up a code governing standards and practices in relation to such matters and obedience to any direction (and none is now in force) made under section 31 of the Broadcasting Authority Act 1960 as amended.[207] The total times for advertising may not exceed 15 per cent. of the daily broadcasting time or 16 $2/3$ per cent. in any particular hour.[208] The contractor must comply with a code governing standards and practices in advertising to be drawn up by the Commission.[209] A contractor must give "due and adequate consideration to any complaint made by a member of the public" and records of such complaints are to be kept and made available to the Commission, on request.[210] However, the Minister has not yet exercised his statutory power to make regulations giving jurisdiction to the Broadcasting Complaints Commission so that, in contrast to RTÉ, the contractor is left in the position (absent any intervention by the IRTC) of policing itself. A most significant provision – by virtue of its inherent importance and its cost to the contractor – is section 9(1)(c) which requires, in the case of sound broadcasting only, that a minimum of:

---

[203] See p. 8.

[204] See *Maigueside Communications Ltd v. I.R.T.C.*, unreported, Supreme Court, June 10, 1997 (interlocutory application in judicial review challenge to decision of IRTC to award a radio franchise); *Maigueside Communications Ltd. v. I.R.T.C.*, unreported, High Court, July 18, 1997 (I.R.T.C. under no obligation to give reasons for its decision to award the licence to another consortium and not to short-list the applicants).

[205] *Ibid.* s.9(1)(a), (b). *Cf.* 120 *Senate Debates*, Col. 790 ("There was some concern that such a provision could run counter to the 'freedom of expression' provisions of Article 40 of the Constitution but it is considered that the risk is small").

[206] *Ibid.* s.9(1)(d). Further by section 10(3) the 1988 Act, no advertisement may relate to an industrial dispute or be directed towards a political or religious end (on this latter prohibition, see *Murphy v. IRTC* [1997] 2 I.L.R.M. 435).

[207] *Ibid.* s.9(3) In addition, the private broadcasters are subject to the requirements already imposed on RTÉ, namely avoidance of material which might promote crime. When, in January, 1994, the section 31 Order was not renewed, the IRTC issued guidelines (presumably under s.9(3)), to ensure that independent stations would operate in "a balanced manner." 1994 IRTC Review.

[208] *Ibid.* s.9(1)(c). This is deliberately fixed at a higher level than for RTÉ because private broadcasters enjoy no equivalent of the licence fee income: 120 *Senate Debates*, Col. 791 (Mr Burke).

[209] *Ibid.* s.10.

[210] *Ibid.* s.11.

"(i) not less than 20 per cent. of the broadcasting time
and

(ii) if the sound broadcasting service is provided for more than 12 hours in any one day, two hours of broadcasting time between 07.00 hours and 19.00 hours, is devoted to the broadcasting of news and current affairs programmes; provided a derogation from this provision is not authorised by the Commission under *section 15*".[211]

Other significant matters are dealt with in the contract: section 14 provides as follows:

"(1) Every sound broadcasting contract may contain such terms and conditions as the Commission thinks appropriate and specifies in the contract.

(2) Without prejudice to the generality of subsection (1), the Commission may specify in a sound broadcasting contract all or any of the following terms or conditions:

(a) the period during which the contract shall continue in force;

(b) whether the contract may be renewed and, if so, the manner in which, the terms of which, and the period for which, the contract may be so renewed;

(c) a condition prohibiting the assignment of the contract or of any interest therein;

(d) if the sound broadcasting contractor be a company, a condition prohibiting any alteration in the Memorandum or Articles of Association of the company or in so much of that Memorandum or of those Articles as may be specified or prohibiting any material change in the ownership of the company;

(e) a condition requiring the sound broadcasting contractor to provide the quality, range and type of programmes which he proposed to offer in his application for the award of the contract."

The first generation of sound broadcasting contracts were made in 1989–1990, for seven years. Accordingly, the second set of contracts (which are fairly uniform) were granted in 1996–1997 (though this time, there was a right of renewal). In addition to the information required by section 14(1)(d)(above), the Contractor must state the extent to which the Contractor is a "Media Operator" as defined in the contract. The Contractor must pay the IRTC 3 per cent of "Relevant Revenue" (as defined) so that the IRTC is more or less paid for, by the independent broadcasters. As regards the programmes, these must be in accord with the Programme Statement made by the Contractor as well as the codes issued by the Minister (as regards, for instance, technical or advertising standards) or the Commission (as to, for instance, standards of programme content). The programmes must be, to quote a specimen

---

[211] There is a statutory exemption from s.9(1)(c) in the case of temporary or institutional sound broadcasting: s.8(3). Concern has been expressed, informally, by the Commission, as to whether certain contractors are honouring the obligation that 20 per cent of their programme content should be news.

contract, "in the opinion of the Commission . . . of high general standard [and] of a high quality transmission [and] contain a specified proportion of material of Irish origin and performance and contain a specified proportion of Programmes in the Irish language."[212]

Revocations

A most significant question is: what happens if any of these conditions is broken. The central provision here is section 14(4)(a) of the Act which states:

"(4) Every broadcasting contract shall –

  (a) provide that the Commission may, at its discretion, suspend or terminate the contract –
    (i) if any false or misleading information was given to the Commission by or on behalf of the sound broadcasting contractor prior to the making of the contract,
    (ii) if the sound broadcasting contractor has, in the opinion of the Commission, committed serious or repeated breaches of his obligations under the broadcasting . . . contract or under this Act."

However, the following tentative comments may be offered. In the first place, in the precarious state of many stations at the moment, a suspension (unless it were for a negligible period) would have the same effect as a termination. In substance, then there is only a single sanction in the Act. However, the contracts remedy this gap by providing that if "the Contractor has, in the reasonable opinion of the Commission, committed a serious breach or reported breaches of its obligations under this contract or the Act, limit the total daily times during which the Contractor may broadcast advertisements . . ." As of early 1997, the only contract to have been revoked is that of Radio Limerick which was withdrawn because of seventeen breaches, a withdrawal which led to the case of *Radio Limerick One Ltd. v. I.R.T.C.*[213] These included: a failure to provide the required proportion of news and current affairs, failure to supply the Commission with tapes of programmes broadcast (as required by the Act and contract); and exceeding the permitted advertising time by presenting "outside broadcasts which took the form of programmes containing details of the products and prices of the businesses concerned".[214]

Whilst it is surprising that no procedural safeguards are provided for in the Act, this gap is remedied in the contract. For example, in the *Radio Limerick case*, there was a Notice of Termination which enumerated the breaches and advised that the Commission would consider any written representation. In fact, representations both oral and written representations were received and considered before the Notice was implemented.

---

[212] In August, 1994, the Commission fixed 30 per cent as a proper proportion and defined Irish music as material recorded, performed or composed by Irish artists: 1994 IRTC Review.

[213] [1997] 2 I.L.R.M. 1.

[214] *Ibid.*

As noted already (1) a contract is made co-extensive with the accompanying licence; and (2) broadcasting without a licence is a criminal offence. It follows that if a contract is terminated, the licence falls with it and any further broadcasting would be a criminal offence just as much as if no licence had ever been granted.

As will be explained in Part 7.1 of this Chapter, the courts have often been unwilling to impose meaningful sanctions on those convicted of regulatory offences. Accordingly the draftsman of the Broadcasting and Wireless Telegraphy Act 1988 has displayed some ingenuity in devising strategies which will adequately discourage unlicensed broadcasting. In the first place, the maximum punishments for unlicensed broadcasting is increased from a maximum fine of £10[215] to a maximum of £800 and/or three months imprisonment, on summary conviction.[216] On conviction on indictment, the maximum punishments are £20,000 and/or two years imprisonment.[217] The same sanctions apply to a number of novel offences whose broad thrust is to discourage persons whose assistance is vital to a working broadcasting service. Thus it is now an offence for anyone to provide accommodation, equipment or programme material for unlicensed broadcasts, or to advertise by means of, or take part in, such broadcasts.[218] It is also an offence (though only punishable, on summary conviction, by a fine of up to £1,000) for anyone to allow their telephone service or electricity supply to be used to promote, further or facilitate a business engaged in making illegal broadcasts.[219] The Act also enables the Minister to serve a *prohibition notice* on either Bord Telecom Éireann or the Electricity Supply Board requiring them not to provide telephone or electricity services, respectively, to premises in which illegal broadcasts are made.[220]

6. Compensation Tribunals

There have been at least two[221] ad-hoc, compensation tribunals set up to meet the exigencies of high-profile mass tragedies. The first arose out of a fire in the Stardust discotheque which claimed the lives of forty-eight young people and injured many others. It was considered that because of the inherent uncertainties of the legal

---

[215] Wireless Telegraphy Act 1926, s.3(3).
[216] Broadcasting and Wireless Telegraphy Act 1988, s.12(1).
[217] *Ibid.* s.18.
[218] *Ibid.* ss.3–6.
[219] *Ibid.* s.7.
[220] *Ibid.* s.6.
[221] For a third, earlier model, take note of the Expert Medical Group on Whooping Cough Vaccine. This extra-statutory entity was established by the Minister for Health on November 16, 1977. The Group (which comprised doctors) had the following terms of reference:
"To examine persons who it is claimed have been permanently damaged by whooping cough vaccination, review the medical information available in relation to them and indicate whether in their opinion, the damage is attributable to the vaccination."
Of the 93 cases which presented themselves to the Group, the Group found that there was a reasonable probability that the vaccine was responsible for damage in 16 of the cases. An offer of an *ex gratia* payment of £10,000 was made in each case where the Expert Medical Group had found in favour of the children on the understanding that it did not involve the acceptance of any liability on the part of the State or any public authority in respect of the child's disability. Thirteen families accepted the offer of the *ex gratia* payment.

process and its delays, it would be better that these claims should be adjudicated by a tribunal. In addition, such was the public feeling that a policy decision was taken so that the State should make available compensation for the injured and the families of the deceased. In order to do this in an orderly, informal and expeditious way, a tribunal – the Stardust Victims' Compensation Tribunal – was set up. This Tribunal was composed of three members and the Chairman was a judge. In the other case – that of up to 1,600 people who had been infected with Hepatitis C from blood supplied by a non-commercial state sponsored body, the Blood Transfusion Services Board, it is very likely that a negligence action would have lain. However, in order to avoid the trauma and delay of (possibly unsuccessful) court proceedings, the Hepatitis C Compensation Tribunal was set up.[222] It comprised five members and was chaired by a retired judge, Egan J. and the members sat in chambers of three. At first, this Tribunal, like the Stardust Tribunal, was non-statutory. However, following a political campaign, it was reconstituted under the Hepatitis C Compensation Tribunal Act 1997. Claimants who had had their claim determined by the non-statutory Tribunal were free to apply, on certain grounds (*e.g.* to claim an award for aggravated or exemplary damages) to the statutory tribunal. [223]

In the case of each of these Tribunals, negligence did not have to be established so that the Tribunal was mainly concerned with *quantum*. In determining this, the general civil law of damages was to be applied, save that no exemplary or aggravated damages were payable. The claimant was given an option as to whether to accept the Tribunal's award. If he did so, then he was precluded from initiating or continuing court action (though there was nothing to prevent a plaintiff who had failed before a court from making a claim before a Tribunal).[224] The Stardust Scheme purported to withdraw a final decision of the Tribunal from judicial review. However, there may have been doubts about the constitutionality of this provision. In any case it was omitted from the Hepatitis C Tribunals.

---

[222] See generally, *Scheme of Compensation for Personal Injuries suffered at the Stardust, Artane on the 14th February 1981* laid before each House on 22nd October 1985; *Scheme to compensate certain persons who have contracted Hepatitis C from the use of human immunoglobulin-Anti-D, whole blood or other blood products*, laid before each House on December 15, 1995. (See also the Health Act 1996 which provides for free medical services for Hepatitis C victims.) See also *Report of the Stardust Victims' Compensation Tribunal* Pl. 7831, 1987. The Minister responsible for setting up each tribunal was the same person, Deputy Michael Noonan. For the debate as to whether the Hepatitis C Tribunal should be statutorily grounded, see 459 *Dáil Debates* Cols. 1263–1302 (December 12, 1995); 479 *Dáil Debates* Cols. 274–297 (May 13, 1997). One element in this controversy concerned whether a non-statutory tribunal may be judicially reviewed, on which, see p. 255. In fact the tribunal has been subject to judicial review on at least one occasion: see *Ryan v. Compensation Tribunal* [1997] 1 I.L.R.M. 194. Another issue was the Minister's view that the tribunal could not be statutory since it was empowered to make provisional awards and payments by instalments: ". . . if we had to extend [sic] a statutory tribunal that can make provisional awards and payments by instalments it would apply to every case of compensation that goes through the courts, whether as a result of a motor accident."(469 *Dáil Debates* Col. 1290).

[223] 1997 Act, s.6. Art. 34.3.1° provides that the High Court shall have "full original jurisdiction in and power to determine all matters and questions . . .". On this provision, see p. 455.

[224] 1997 Act, s.5(7) that one of the leading authorities: *The State (Keegan) v. The Stardust Victims Tribunal* [1986] I.R. 642 did in fact involve a tribunal and that counsel for the Tribunal conceded (at 646) that if the Tribunal acted in excess of jurisdiction or contrary to the rules of "natural justice", then its order could be reviewed.

As to procedure, the emphasis in each Tribunal was on informality. The non-statutory Hepatitis C Tribunal Report states: "Witnesses appearing before the Tribunal were not sworn, written medical reports were accepted as well as oral testimony of doctors and there was no cross-examination of the persons appearing either the claimant or witnesses on his behalf. We accepted both hearsay and opinion evidence."[225] Each of these Tribunals sat in private.

Given the tragic circumstances, the Stardust Tribunal appears to have been a success: it received 953 applications, sat for forty-nine days and made awards totalling £10.5 million (almost all below £30,000) to 820 applicants. £1.1 million was spent on legal and administrative costs.

However, the circumstances of the Hepatitis C Tribunal were slightly different. It was perceived that an agency of the State had been guilty of serious wrongdoing. Here some 1,600 claimant-victims were involved.[226] Over-simplifying a complicated forensic enterprise, one can say that in some cases, the type of error was such that the claimant was in a position probably to be able to establish negligence; in other cases, the claimant was not. Claimants in this latter category – the majority processed their claims through the Tribunal, where the sums awarded ranged from £15,000 to a few hundred thousand pounds. However, where there was negligence – and indeed, sometimes it was felt, culpability – it was natural that many of the victims would have preferred their day in court and also the possibility of exemplary damages to the decent obscurity of a tribunal sitting in private (more especially since a failure in the court did not preclude a later claim before the Tribunal). The first of the High Court proceedings – that of Mrs McCole – was settled (on the plaintiff's terms) in late September, 1996, a few hours before her death. Due to the media coverage of Mrs McCole's case and the public sympathy for victims, the Tribunal of Inquiry, chaired by former Chief Justice Finlay was set up[227] and the report of this Inquiry led to the passage of the 1997 Act constituting the statutory tribunal. The main difference between the two forms of tribunal was that the statutory tribunal was empowered to award aggravated or exemplary damages.[228]

7. Statutory Inquiries

There are, generally speaking, two types of statutory inquiry. The first type of inquiry (and the one which is more frequent and less well known) is the "standard device for giving a fair hearing to objectors before the final decision is made on some question of government policy affecting citizens' rights or interests."[229]

---

[225] Pl. 7831, pp. 6–7. See also Hepatitis C Compensation Scheme, para. 6(g)–(m) and the 1997 Act, s.3.

[226] According to provisional figures, before the non-statutory Tribunal the average award and legal costs, in the first 140 cases were £110,000 and £11,000 respectively.

[227] On which see p. 296. Take note that a claimant who received an offer of an award from the Tribunal was given the advantage, by the Minister for Health, of not having to decide whether to accept it until after the report of the Inquiry (see p. 307) had been published.

[228] 1997 Act, s.5. The statutory tribunal could also subpoena witnessses: s.3(10).

[229] Wade, *Administrative Law* (1994), p. 964. The historical roots of this type of inquiry go back to enclosures of land in the early Nineteenth Century.

This type of inquiry (hereinafter "decision inquiry") is statutorily required before the taking of certain categories of decision including: the siting of a new burial ground[230]; the removal or suspension of persons holding office under the Vocational Education Acts[231]; the removal of members of a health board[232] local authority for failure to perform their duties[233]; the making of a compulsory purchase order by a local authority[234]; the determination of certain planning appeals[235] and whether to proceed with major construction projects.[236]

The second type of inquiry (hereinafter "post mortem inquiry") is, one which is given the task of investigating the causes of accidents, natural disasters or other matters of general public concern. The terms of reference of this type of inquiry – which usually involves fact-finding as to the causes of, (say), a shipping collision and recommendations as to improvements for the future – will usually be "at large", simply because the conclusions of the inquiry cannot be anticipated in advance. The most dignified and high-powered example of this latter type of inquiry is one which is constituted under the Tribunals of Inquiry (Evidence) Acts 1921–1998. However, there is also specialised legislation regulating accidents involving railways,[237] shipping[238] or aeroplanes.[239] In addition, the Companies Act 1990, s.14(1) empowers the Minister for Enterprise, Trade and Employment to appoint an inspector to investigate a company for the purpose of determining the identity of "the true persons", who are financially interested in it or who are able to shape its policy. Sometimes, an episode (for example, involving a possible conflict of interest), which engages the wider public interest, will also happen to come within the scope of this provision. Investigations of this type occurred in the case of Greencore and Bord Telecom.[240]

Each type of statutory inquiry may be regarded as having many of the characteristics of a tribunal: for the procedures adopted before an inquiry and a tribunal are similar in that each of them approximates to that of a court. However, there are

---

[230] Public Health (Ireland) Act 1878, s.163.

[231] Vocational Education Act 1930, s.27(2).

[232] Health Act 1970, s.12(1)(a).

[233] Local Government Act 1941, s.44. See also, Harbours Act 1946, s.164 (local inquiry into performance by harbour authority of their "powers, duties and functions" and other related matters).

[234] See, *e.g.* Housing Act 1966, s.76 and Third Sched. (Compulsory Purchase Order) Procedure.

[235] Local Government (Planning and Development) Act 1963, s.82 and Local Government (Planning and Development) Regulations 1994 (S.I. 1994 No. 86).

[236] See, *e.g.* Transport (Dublin Light Rail) Act 1996, s.8.

[237] Regulation of Railways Act 1871, s.9. For a recent example of an inquiry held under the terms of this section, see *Report of the Investigation into the Accident on the CIÉ Railway at Buttevant, Co. Cork on 1 August, 1980* (Prl. 9698, 1981).

[238] Merchant Shipping Act 1894, s.465. This section was invoked by the Minister for the Marine to set up an inquiry chaired by a District Judge with nautical assessors charged with an investigation into the deaths of four lifeboat officers off Ballycotton, Co. Cork: see *The Irish Times*, September 24, 1990. For a case arising from this tragedy, see *Haussman v. Minister for the Marine* [1991] I.L.R.M. 382.

[239] Air Navigation and Transport Act 1936, s.60 and Air Navigation (Notification and Investigation of Accidents and Incidents) Regulations 1997 (S.I. 1997 No. 205). For an example of an inquiry held pursuant to these provisions, see *Accident to Reims Cessna F.182 Q in the Blackstairs Mountains, Co. Wexford on 7 September, 1983* (Department of Communications, 1984).

[240] The several cases arising out of the investigation are reported at [1993] 3 I.R. 1–151. For the Companies Act 1990, s.14, see Courtney, *The Law of Private Companies*, (1994) pp. 807–821

three differences between a tribunal and an inquiry. First, the latter's conclusions do not bind the Minister or other responsible decision-making authority,[241] though in practice it would be rare for the Minister to depart from the conclusions of at any rate, the first type of inquiry. Secondly, an inquiry is set up *ad hoc* for each episode examined; whereas a tribunal enjoys a continuous existence. Finally whilst a tribunal is a decision-making body, an inquiry may be regarded as an instrument of participation in government.

As regards the procedure adopted at a statutory inquiry of either type, much will be left to the chairman of the inquiry, but he must act subject to the procedural requirements imposed by the particular statute and the overriding requirements of constitutional justice. Normally, statutory inquiries take the form of public hearings where the witnesses give evidence under oath and are subject to cross-examination by the opposing parties.[242]

Statutory provision has been made for the appointment of assessors to assist in certain types of inquiries.[243] The purpose of an assessor is generally to assist in the evaluation of complex scientific and technical evidence.[244]

The Beef Tribunal and its aftermath

There have been several occasions recently when public disquiet at some official or big business ineptitude or bad practice have been such that some form of inquiry has been necessary. Accordingly because of their interest and importance, it is proposed to give a general sketch of the Rolls-Royce of "post-mortem" inquiries – in terms of public interest. We refer to those which are set up under the Tribunals of Inquiry legislation. An inquiry of this type is set up, by a Minister following the passage of identical resolutions by each House to the effect: "that it is expedient that a tribunal be established for inquiry into the following matter of urgent public importance."[245] By inveterate convention, though not law, such an inquiry is always

---

[241] It is of interest to notice the reasons given by the *Martin Report on Certain Aspects of Criminal Procedure* (March, 1990) which recommended that persons who have been convicted of criminal offences and who have exhausted the normal appeals procedures should have their convictions re-examined not by a court but by a statutory inquiry. Those reasons were: (i) a departure from the rules of evidence might be necessary for a full investigation; but a departure from these rules by a court would be undesirable (p. 11); (ii) because of the wide-ranging nature of the inquiry, the inquisitorial mode of procedure is to be preferred to the accusatorial method, which is characteristic of a court (p. 12); (iii) before someone who had already unsuccessfully exercised his option of appealing to the Supreme Court could litigate any further within the court system a constitutional amendment would be necessary because the Supreme Court is the final court of appeal (Art. 34.4.1°) (p. 11). Not mentioned as reasons but possibly relevant, all the same, are: (i) the court system's possible reluctance to confess that it had committed an injustice; (ii) the fact that court decisions are characteristically conclusive and not (as proposed in the Report) merely an expression of opinion as to whether doubt existed as to the propriety of the conviction, with the status of a recommendation as to whether the Government should advise the President to grant a pardon. The reason for the Committee's proposal on this point was its view that for an inquiry to go further than an expression of opinion would possibly amount to "a trespass into the judicial domain" (p. 16).

[242] See, *e.g.* Local Government Act 1941, s.86.

[243] Regulation of Railways Act 1871, s.7(i); Air Navigation (Investigation of Accidents) Regulations 1957 (S.I. No. 19 of 1957), Art. 7(2); Tribunal of Inquiry (Evidence) (Amendment) Act 1979, s.2.

[244] Assessors were appointed in two Tribunals: *Whiddy Island and Stardust*. See p. 296, n.246.

[245] Tribunals of Inquiry (Evidence) Act 1921, s.1(1). Notice the legislation, Tribunals of Inquiry (Evidence) (Amendment) Bill 1998, which would, if it becomes law, permit the amending of terms of reference.

chaired by a (serving or retired) judge of one of the superior courts. It would almost be possible to write a history of modern Ireland, centering upon the subject matter of these inquiries.[246] Thus: the inquiry dealing with allegations against the Minister for Local Government would portray the advent of planning control and its various consequences; the *Kerry Babies Tribunal* would portray the troubled changes in sexual mores of the 1980s and the *Beef Tribunal* (to use its colloquial name) and the *McCracken Tribunal* inquiring into alleged payments by Dunnes Stores would represent many of the seamier sides of public life and big business including: the link between businesses and political parties; inadequate implementation of regulations by public authorities; tax evasion and the significance of E.U. grants. Slackness in certain public bodies with tragic consequences would be represented by the *B.T.S.B. Tribunal*.[247] As of late 1997, two Tribunals were sitting, one dealing with the personal finances of two named politicians following on from the *McCracken Tribunal* and the second inquiring into the planning history of an area of land in County Dublin.[248]

The *Beef Tribunal* was set up to investigate various alleged abuses and malpractices in the beef industry.[249] It was one of the central events in Irish public life during the three years, for which it sat (1991–1994). It was brought before the High Court and Supreme Court, by way of judicial review, on a number of occasions. Only two of these need be mentioned here.[250] In the first case, *Goodman International v. Hamilton (No. 1)*[251] it was held that since the inquiry was simply to make "a finding of fact, in effect, in *vacuo*."[252] and report thereon to the Oireachtas

---

[246] Tribunals of Inquiry have been appointed to investigate very diverse matters: (i) allegations against politicians (*Report of the Tribunal appointed by the Taoiseach* on November 7, 1947 (P. No. 8576) (sale of Locke's distillery); *Report of the Tribunal appointed by the Taoiseach on 4 July 1975* (Prl. 4745) (allegations against Minister for Local Government)); (ii) Garda practices (*Coghlan shooting inquiry: Tribunal Report* (1928) J.34; *Death of Liam O'Mahony: Report of the Tribunal appointed by the Minister* (1967, Pr. 9790); *Report of the Tribunal of Inquiry: The "Kerry Babies" case* (1985, Pl. 3514); and (iii) natural disasters (*Report of the Tribunal of Inquiry: Disaster at Whiddy Island, Bantry, Co. Cork* (1980, Pl. 8911); *Report of the Tribunal of Inquiry: Fire at the Stardust, Artane, Dublin* (Pl. 853). Other Tribunals of Inquiry appointed since 1922 concerned: *Great Southern Railway Stock* (Prl. 6792, 1943) (allegations of improper dealings in shares); an investigation into the making of an RTÉ programme on moneylending: *Report of the Tribunal* appointed by the Taoiseach on 22 December, 1969 (Prl. 1363); *Report of the Tribunal of Inquiry into the Beef Processing Industry 1994* (Prl. 1007) (allegations of favouritism and malpractice in the beef industry; though this also involved elements of category (i) above; Report of the *Tribunal of Inquiry (Dunnes Payments)* (Prl. 4199); *Report of the Tribunal of Inquiry into the Blood Transfusion Service Board* (Pn. 3695). See generally, Hillyard, "The Use of Judges to Chair Social Inquiries" (1971) 6 Ir. Jur. 93.

[247] For detailed references, see previous footnote.

[248] 480, *Dáil Debates* cols. 827–874 (September 11, 1997); 481, *Dáil Debates* col 49–102 (October 7, 1997) respectively.

[249] Pn. 1007, 1994. According to its terms of reference, the Tribunal was to: "inquire into the following definite matters of urgent public importance:
    (i) allegations regarding illegal activities, fraud and malpractice in and in connection with the beef processing industry made or referred to:–
    (a) in Dáil Éireann, and
    (b) on a television programme transmitted by ITV on 13 May 1991 . . ."

[250] The others are: *Attorney General v. Hamilton (No. 2)* [1993] 3 I.R. 227 and *Goodman International v. Hamilton (No. 2)* [1993] 3 I.R. 307 (each concerned with parliamentary privilege of deputies called as witnesses); *Boyhan v. Hamilton* [1993] 1 I.R. 210 (on which see pp. 299–300; *Kiberd v. Hamilton* [1992] 2 I.R. 257 (on which see p. 303).

[251] [1992] 2 I.R. 542.

[252] *Ibid.* at 590 (Finlay C.J.) *Cf.* "The function of the Tribunal was to carry out a simple fact-finding operation" (Pn. 1007, p.33).

296

consequently it was not "administering justice". Accordingly, Article 34.1[253] (which requires the "administration of justice" to be vested in a court) was not engaged. Secondly, however, in *Attorney General v. Hamilton (No. 1)* the Attorney General successfully challenged the Tribunal's right to question a former Government Minister about whether a particular decision had been taken at a Government meeting. This Supreme Court ruling was grounded, in part, on Article 28 (collective Government responsibility, from which the need for absolute confidentiality was deduced by the Court). However, what is relevant here is the other plank on which the decision rested. This is the precept that, whilst by virtue of Article 34.1, it is for a court to weigh up competing heads of the public interest (justice *versus* confidentiality) in respect of admitting evidence in a case before it; there is nothing in the Constitution (or elsewhere) giving this power to a tribunal of inquiry. Recently[254] it was reported that an action was being taken against the legality and constitutionality of the *Moriarty Tribunal* by one of the named politicians on the ground, *inter alia*, that its inquiries into his personal finances and those of his family would amount to interference with the constitutional right to privacy.

Probably the most lasting reaction to the *Beef Tribunal* was the public and media disquiet at its cost (estimated at a total of £20 million for the legal representation and other expenses of all parties; but often unreliably estimated as more). This disquiet was intensified by a widespread feeling that no tangible advantages, (*e.g.* sanctions or improvements for the future) had emerged from this elaborate exercise, which involved 475 witnesses, yielding 452 books of transcripts, giving evidence over 226 days.[255] For present purposes, the significant consequence of these judgments was a great reluctance on the part of politicians to set up any more "formal inquiries" of this sort. Yet circumstances arose, which seemed both objectively and in the view of the media and the public, to cry out for some form of independent investigation. It is instructive to consider the various alternatives to formal inquiries, which were experimented with in three *causes célèbres* in the immediate aftermath of the *Beef Tribunal*. This will be done in the Appendix to this Chapter. However here we can anticipate this material and say that the conclusion from these experiments was that none was wholly successful and (as of early 1998) the tide of political and media opinion appears to be running cautiously in favour of Tribunals of Inquiry. Before proceeding, one ought to list the four sets of issues which can arise in regard to any category of inquiry, formal or otherwise. First, is it to be clothed with the power to subpoena witnesses? In other words, is refusal by a witness, whether to appear, to answer questions or to produce relevant documents to be made a criminal offence? Secondly, an analogous question is does the inquiry have the power to administer the oath so that telling a lie is also an offence. Thirdly, is a witness granted privilege against defamation action and other less likely consequences (*e.g.* breach of confidentiality or offences under the Official Secrets

---

[253] On Article 34.1 see pp. 270–273.
[254] See *The Irish Times,* December 20 and 22, 1997.
[255] For an unofficial account of the *Beef Tribunal's* work, see F. O'Toole, *Meanwhile Back at the Ranch.*

Act 1963) which may flow from what he says, in evidence? There is a connection between this issue and the earlier two, for it has always been accepted that it would be unfair to oblige a witness to answer questions truthfully and then to leave him exposed to the risk of defamation action if he does so.[256] The final issue is the extent to which constitutional justice (in one form or any other) applies to anyone (not just a witness) whose reputation may be affected by the inquiry.

Accusatorial v. Inquisitorial procedure

Traditionally, it was thought that the principles of constitutional justice should not apply in the case of persons conducting preliminary statutory inquiries (*e.g.* such as where the report of an inspector requires confirmation by the decision-making authority). However, this argument has been rejected by the Irish courts. In *The State (Shannon Atlantic Fisheries Ltd.) v. McPolin*[257] an inspector had been appointed to investigate the causes of the wrecking of the applicant's fishing vessel. The inspector took depositions from members of the ship's crew, but he did not interview the owners of the vessel or give them an opportunity of refuting the allegations against them. The inspector's findings of fact impugned the good name and reputation of the ship owners and Finlay P. ruled that the inspector's report should be quashed for breach of the *audi alteram partem* rule. Finlay P. continued:

> "The fact that it is not the investigating officer but the Minister for Transport and Power who must decide, having regard to the content of the report, whether any further action should be taken by him in relation to prosecutions under the Act seems to me not to affect the true decision-making role of the person carrying out the preliminary inquiry."[258]

In the case of a Tribunal of Inquiry it has been accepted that the inquiry "is a body – unusual in our legal system – an inquisitorial Tribunal. It has not an adversary format".[259] Despite this, lest the Tribunal itself be obliged to "descend into the forensic arena"[260] it is provided with solicitor and counsel to the Tribunal. It is their duty:

> "to enable the Tribunal to undertake investigations, to have investigations carried out on its behalf, to obtain statements from witnesses, to arrange the attendance of witnesses in due order, to prepare and serve Book of Documents and statements of witnesses on all "interested parties", to present the evidence and examine the witnesses."[261]

---

[256] Gwynn Morgan, *Constitutional Law of Ireland* (1990), pp. 161–162 and 241. This association between privilege and subpoena does not necessarily operate in reverse. In the case of Select Committee on Legislation and Security of Dáil Éireann (Privilege and Immunity) Act, 1994, privilege was bestowed on witnesses. However, (for political reasons) no subpoena was given: on this Act, see Gallagher (1994) *Irish Current Law Statutes Annotated* 32–02.

[257] [1976] I.R. 93. The inquiry was held pursuant to s.465 of the Merchant Shipping Act 1894.

[258] [1976] I.R. 93 at 98.

[259] *Boyhan v. The Beef Tribunal* [1993] 1 I.R.210 at 222, *per* Denham J.

[260] *Kiely v. Minister for Social Welfare (No.2)* [1977] I.R. 267 at 283, *per* Henchy J.

[261] Pr. 1007, p.3. Why is the function no longer performed, as it was traditionally, by the Attorney General? The answer given in the *Whiddy Island Report* (Prl. 8911), pp. 6–7 (the first Tribunal of

In short, counsel for the Tribunal is thought to be necessary to satisfy the first rule of constitutional justice (*nemo iudex*). In addition, in order to meet the requirement of the second rule of constitutional justice (*audi alteram partem*), the Tribunal "ha[s] power to authorise the representation before them to any person appearing to them to be interested to be by counsel or solicitor or otherwise, or to refuse to allow such representation."[262] [*sic*] One should also note that in the case of the Hepatitis C Tribunal, there was (in addition to lawyers for the Tribunal, the State and other parties) a legal team representing the public interest.[263]

In the case of the *Beef Tribunal*, it was found necessary to use the discretion, quoted in the preceding paragraph, fairly widely to allow parties (listed in Appendix 3 to the Report) to be represented. Four sets of persons or bodies were allowed full representation, namely: the Tribunal itself, the Attorney General and all State authorities, Goodman International and its subsidiary companies and Mr Larry Goodman as were the politicians who made the principal allegations giving rise to the Tribunal. More than 70 other persons or bodies were allowed "limited representation" (the distinction between "limited" and "full" representation is explained below)

The test for being accorded a right of representation adopted by the Tribunal was whether a person's "reputation could be affected by the findings of the Tribunal."[264] Yet this seems a very different and a lower standard from that implied in *Re Haughey* (which was invoked to sustain it though no reference was made to this divergence). The *Re Haughey* test, quoted earlier, is whether the person claiming representation is analogous to that of a party in legal proceedings. Moreover, the allegations in the *Haughey case* were very grave. One of the few bodies to seek unsuccessfully to be granted representation were members of the United Farmers Association, who in *Boyhan v. Beef Tribunal*[265] sought judicial review of this refusal to be granted full representation (they were allowed only limited representation). Rejecting their claim, Denham J. stated:

> "As there are no allegations against the plaintiffs who are not a party in that sense, the principles set out therein would not appear to apply to the plaintiffs. In fact, the Tribunal will have no function in treating the plaintiffs in any way other than as witnesses. This was also the decision in *K. Security Ltd. and*

Inquiry not to use the Attorney General) is: "The Attorney General suggested that this practice should not be adhered to and that, instead, he would assign solicitor and counsel to the Tribunal . . . A tribunal . . . is not a court of law hearing evidence adduced by opposing parties, its function is to conduct an inquiry. In the present instance, it would have been very difficult for it adequately to carry out its statutory functions if it had not been able to consider, with its own solicitor and counsel, what evidence should be obtained, and direct what steps should be taken in search of the cause of the disaster. A further reason for adopting this procedure arose from the fact that the role of the public authorities could come under the scrutiny of the Tribunal and it was obviously not desirable that the Attorney General – who would represent the government departments involved and the Garda authorities – should at the same time be responsible for the presentation of evidence to the Tribunal."

(There seems to be some confusion in *Boyhan* [1993] 1 I.R. 210 at 216 as to whether the Attorney General or counsel for the Tribunal represents the public interest and also whether the Attorney General represents the public interest or State authority.)

[262] Tribunals of Inquiry (Evidence) Act 1921, s.2(b).
[263] 470 *Dáil Debates* Cols. 519–520, 553 (October 17, 1996).
[264] Prl. 1007, para. 36. Para 38 has a slightly modified formulation.
[265] [1993] 1 I.R. 210. However, see now the *Kirrane v. The Hon. Mr Justice Finlay*, a case in which it was held that for a doctor to be criticised in the Hepatitis C Tribunal, without having been adequately represented, was a breach of constitutional justice: *The Irish Times*, March 4, 1998, p. 3.

William Kavanagh v. Ireland and the Attorney General (Unreported, High Court, Gannon J., 15th July 1977). At page 13 of the transcript Gannon J. said:

> 'But the Tribunal had no function nor authority to deal with the plaintiff or his activities in any way other than in his capacity as a witness before them. In my opinion neither the good name, reputation, business connection or property rights nor any other personal rights of the plaintiff were ever interfered with or exposed to unjust attack or injustice of any kind in the proceedings before the Tribunal nor did they require vindication or defence during the course of the proceedings of the Inquiry.'"[266]

Here it is worth underlining that the quotation from the *K Security case* implicitly rejects the notion that the good name of a witness could be impugned by virtue of his "activities . . . in his capacity as a witness".

As regards the manner in which oral testimony was given at the *Beef Tribunal*:

> "The Tribunal adopted the procedure which had been followed in recent Inquiries of a similar nature, such as the Whiddy Island, Stardust and Kerry Babies Inquiries, which was that:
>
> (i) All witnesses were called by the Tribunal's counsel and first examined by him;
> (ii) They were then available for cross-examination by Counsel or Solicitor for the parties to whom the right of representation had been granted and who had a legitimate interest in the evidence of the witness in the appropriate order;
> (iii) If necessary, they were then cross-examined by Counsel to the Tribunal."[267]

The difference between those accorded "full and limited" representation is that the latter only enjoyed these rights in respect of the issues in which they had been specified to have a legitimate interest; whereas the former had these rights in respect of all areas touched by the investigation.

One should notice too that the *Beef Tribunal* eschewed hearsay, having regard only to "properly admitted evidence which had been where necessary subjected to cross-examination."[268] Yet "tribunals" (in the sense of the word used in earlier parts of this Chapter)[269] some of them determining more severe threats to individual rights, have not been barred from acting on the basis of hearsay.

---

266 *Ibid.* at 222. It is notable that the only inherent interference which Denham J. seemed to acknowledge as giving a right to representation is "allegations against the plaintiff's [character]". By contrast, in *K*: "good name, reputation, business connection or property rights . . ." were all regarded as appropriate for this purpose. However, the reason for this apparent discrepancy is that in *Boyhan* (as is often though not inevitably the case), it was good name which was concerned. Take note also that at 218, Denham J. refers to an unsuccessful unreported High Court decision (further details were not given) against granting representation to certain persons before the Whiddy Island Tribunal.
In December 1996, Transfusion Positive, Irish Kidney Association and certain haemophiliacs sought judicial review of a refusal to allow them representation before the BTSB Tribunal. Their claim was settled out of court on the basis that they were granted a substantial measure of rights of representation.

267 Pr. 1007, p.8.

268 Pr. 1007, p. 9, para. 33. See also para. 34 ("the Tribunal . . . has sifted through rumour but relies only on evidence, properly admitted for its findings.").

269 In *Goodman International Ltd v. Hamilton (No. 2)* [1991] 3 I.R. 307 at 317, Geoghegan J. held that the Beef Tribunal adequately complied with fair procedures where it did "not permit hearsay evidence to impugn [a] good name".

In assessing the procedure adopted by the *Beef Tribunal*, it is instructive to consider the contrasting approach adopted in the (British) non-statutory *Scott Inquiry*[270] into illegal export of arms to Iraq.[271] Here all witnesses were called and examined either by the Tribunal itself or (mainly) by counsel for the Tribunal.[272] In other words, none of the witnesses or anyone else were represented (as occurred in the *Beef Tribunal*). This feature was criticised[273] on the ground that such persons were not permitted to defend themselves against damage to their reputations arising out of either evidence given at the Inquiry or some comment in the ensuing Report. In effect defending himself against this line of attack, Sir Richard Scott stated:

> "In summary, as a general rule, fairness at an Inquiry certainly enquires that witnesses be given adequate advance notice of the matters in respect of which questions will be asked. It requires that adverse and damaging allegations (if they are relevant but not otherwise) should be drawn to the attention of the object of the allegations so that he or she can, if desired, respond to them. It requires that proposed criticisms be drawn to the attention of the object of the criticism so that he or she can, if desired, make representations in response. It requires that legal assistance be available to those involved, both at the stage of giving evidence and at the stage of responding to criticism. Fairness does not, in my opinion, require that adversarial procedures such as the right to cross-examine other witnesses, the right to have an examination-in-chief or a re-examination conducted orally by a party's lawyer or the right for a party to participate, over and above the extent mentioned, in oral hearings, should always be incorporated into the procedure at inquisitorial Inquiries. The golden rule in my opinion, is that there should be procedural flexibility with procedures to achieve fairness tailored to suit the circumstances of each Inquiry."[274]

Perhaps, it is most important in practice, as the final sentence of this quotation indicates, that the circumstances of each inquiry be taken into account in determining what is an appropriate procedure.[275] Many inquiries, such as the *Scott Inquiry* itself,

---

[270] See Scott, "Procedures at Inquiries" (1995) 111 L.Q.R. 596. In this lecture Scott *inter alia* critiques (at 605) the "cardinal principles of procedure laid down in the (Salmon) *Report of the Royal Commission on Tribunals of Inquiry* (Cmnd. 3121 1966)". These six principles which (to simplify) are rather stronger on classic natural justice than was the *Scott Inquiry*, are quoted with approval at Pr. 1001, p.4. See Howe (1996) *Public Law* 445 for an entirely different viewpoint. See too, Craig at 306–307.

[271] Oddly enough, this was the same country the export of beef (with massive government-funded export credit guarantee) to which was at the centre of many of the allegations investigated by the *Beef Tribunal*.

[272] In the *Scott Inquiry*, every witness received a document setting out the initial questions to which answers were sought together with the background evidence that gave rise to the questions (the latter running in the case of some witnesses to one hundred pages). Again six witnesses who attended oral hearings (as opposed to giving written evidence) read out statements before replying. Finally, each witness who attended an oral hearing was sent a transcript of the proceedings, and invited both to correct the transcript where necessary and to provide supplementary answers if she/he so wished.

[273] See, *e.g.* Howe, "Procedures at the Scott Inquiry" (1996) *Public Law* 445 (Lord Howe is a Queen's Counsel and as a former Foreign Secretary, one of the Ministers whose conduct was being examined in the Inquiry) as regards the questions of Counsel for the Inquiry.

[274] *op. cit.*, above, n. 270 at 615–616.

[275] See, *e.g. Re Pergamon Press Ltd.* [1971] 1 Ch. 388 at 400, 403 and 407.

are of a diffuse character, with myriad considerations to be taken into account. However, by contrast, where there is a single issue inquiry in which opposing sides can be readily identified, it may well be the case that opposing sides can be readily identified and in this situation, that the procedures followed in adversarial litigation, such as the right to cross-examine opposing witnesses, ought to be applied. In appraising the *Beef Tribunal* (or Irish Inquiries generally) the great question is which category is involved. If we consider the *Beef Tribunal's* background (for the reason that its actual terms of reference were rather diffuse), it seems clear that its *fons et origo* was to examine the performance of Goodman International. In view of this, it seems to be well in line, even with the Scott precepts, that Goodman International should have had a plenitude of representation. However the query which Scott (and more importantly the universal difference between litigation and an inquiry) raises, is whether it is necessary for all of the persons represented before the *Beef Tribunal*, *e.g.* Dáil Deputies and trade rivals of Goodman International to have been granted representation (even limited representation). To put it briefly: could not their interest in the matter – the vigorous prosecutions of the accusations against Goodman International – have been left in the competent hands of counsel for the inquiry. Is there not a qualitative difference between the substantive and substantial allegations made against Goodman International business reputation and, on the other hand, the question of whether Deputies were guilty of making unfounded allegations? (Incidently, said deputies have been jocularly referred to as "alligators".)

As to the question of whether an inquiry must sit in public, in the case of a Tribunal of Inquiry under the 1921 Act, section 2(a) requires a public sitting unless a closed session is "in the opinion of the tribunal . . . in the public interest expedient for reasons connected with the subject matter of the inquiry or the nature of the evidence to be given." It seems unlikely that (as a matter of fairness to a person whose good name was adversely affected by certain evidence) a tribunal could be required to sit in private (*Goodman International v. Hamilton*[276]).

Attendance of witnesses: subpoena

Section 4 of the Tribunals of Inquiry (Evidence) (Amendment) Act 1979[277] provides that the Tribunal "may make such orders as it considers necessary for the purposes

---

[276] [1992] 2 I.R. 542 at 565 and 605 (Costello and McCarthy JJ. disavowing a suggestion to this effect made by McLoughlin J. in *Re Haughey* [1971] I.R. 217 at 268. Yet the *Moriarty Tribunal's* terms of reference "required it to carry out investigation . . . including where appropriate conducting its proceedings in private in order to determine whether sufficient evidence exists . . . to warrant proceeding to a full public inquiry." (480, *Dáil Debates* Cols. 827 *et seq.* (September 11, 1997)) And in fact, despite the requirement in another part of the terms of reference that the Tribunal's powers be exercised only "to the extent that it may do so consistent with the (legislation)", private investigations were made. This was reported (*The Irish Times* December 20 and 22, 1997) to be one of the arguments to be relied upon, by Mr C.J. Haughey, in his case against the Tribunal, despite the fact that part of the reason for the private investigation was to minimize the danger to Mr Haughey's reputation. It may be that one of the lines of defence available to the Tribunal would be that conformity with the Constitution and its protection of reputation required the Tribunal of Inquiry (Evidence) Act 1921 to be interpreted in this sense. This would entail some kind of a presumption of constitutionality argument.

[277] In the case of inquiries held at the instance of the Minister for the Environment (whether under the provisions of section 83 of the Local Government Act 1941 or any other Act), the inspector

of its functions," and it is invested with all such "powers, rights and privileges of the High Court" in that regard.[278] On the basis of this provision, the chairman of the *Beef Tribunal* summoned two journalists (who had published articles allegedly based on statements made to the Tribunal by prospective witnesses who had not yet given evidence) to appear before the Tribunal to answer questions. Before the High Court,[279] the journalists argued unsuccessfully that there were no grounds to support the view that the Tribunal could be hampered in performing its functions by their acts and hence that the order was *ultra vires*. However, the Court held that the Tribunal would clearly be hampered if the witnesses were dissuaded from coming forward because of such an episode.

Immunity from defamation

There is no general statutory provision which provides that statements made during the course of a statutory inquiry are privileged. However, although the issue is not free from doubt, it would seem that the common law rule that statements during the course of judicial proceedings are absolutely privileged extends to statutory inquiries which follow a quasi-judicial procedure.[280] In addition, as just stated, a tribunal of inquiry, established under the 1921–1979 legislation, is invested, in respect of its orders, with the powers, rights and privileges of the High Court and its witnesses with the immunities and privileges of those appearing before the High Court.[281] Thus, for instance, it would seem that statements made during the course of proceedings before the tribunal are absolutely privileged.

Costs

In the case of Tribunals of Inquiry, the relevant legislation[282] provides:

> "Where a Tribunal, . . . is of the opinion that, having regard to the findings of the tribunal and all other relevant matters, there are sufficient reasons

---

conducting the inquiry enjoys a statutory power to subpoena witnesses and to take evidence on oath. (L.G.A. 1941, s.86). Similar provisions exist in respect of other statutory inquiries. See, *e.g.* Regulation of Railways Act 1871, s.7(3); Air Navigation and Transport Act 1936, s.60.

[278] See also Tribunals of Inquiry (Evidence) (Amendment) Act 1997.

[279] *Kiberd v. Hamilton* [1992] 2 I.R. 257. Subsequently the journalists declined to answer the questions put to them (which would have involved revealing their sources) Hamilton P. directed that the papers be sent to the D.P.P. See Casey, *Constitutional Law of Ireland*, (2nd ed., 1992) p. 468. Notice, too, that the *McCracken Tribunal* sent relevant documents regarding Mr Haughey allegedly misleading the Tribunal as to whether he received bank drafts personally from Mr Dunne, to the D.P.P.: Pn. 4199, Chap. 10. As of December 1997, no prosecution had been taken.

[280] McMahon and Binchy, *The Irish Law of Torts* (2nd ed.), p. 646. See also, *Trapp v. Mackie* [1979] 1 W.L.R. 377. For a justification in a constitutional context of the absolute nature of this immunity in civil proceedings, see *Cooney v. Bank of Ireland* [1996] 1 I.R. 157.

[281] Tribunals of Inquiry (Evidence)(Amendment) Act 1979, s.4; Tribunals of Inquiry (Evidence) Act, 1921, s.1(3). See, too, Tribunals of Inquiry (Evidence) (Amendment) Act, 1997. In addition by virtue of s.5 of the 1979 Act, statements made during the course of a hearing before a Tribunal of Inquiry are inadmissible in all subsequent criminal prosecutions (with the exception of perjury). A perjury prosecution was commenced after the publication of the Report of the Tribunal into the Whiddy Island; the charge was dismissed (*Goodman International v. Hamilton* [1992] 2 I.R. 542 at 605).

[282] Tribunals of Inquiry (Evidence) (Amendment) Act 1979, s.6(1). Costs may be awarded against a local authority or other body in the case of inquiries held at the instance of the Minister for the Environment under the provisions of section 83 of the Local Government Act 1941 or any other Act: Local Government Act 1941, s.83(2). (See, too, Public Health (Ireland) Act, 1878, s.210.) The

rendering it equitable to do so, the tribunal . . . may by order direct that the whole or part of the costs of any person appearing before the tribunal by counsel or solicitor, as taxed by a Taxing Master of the High Court, shall be paid to the person by any other person named in the order."[283]

As mentioned already, one of the major aspects of the *Beef Tribunal* was the huge cost. The Chairman of the *Beef Tribunal* made orders directing the Minister for Finance to pay the legal and other costs of (with one small exception) all the parties represented at the Tribunal. Two statements of principle were offered to justify this result. First:

"the Tribunal has in the course of its introductory chapter to this Report referred to a statement of Lord Justice Salmon made in the course of the *Report of the Royal Commission on Tribunals of Inquiry* (1966) that a person who is involved in an inquiry should normally have his legal expenses met out of public funds and the statement of the late Mr Justice McCarthy, concurred with by the Chief Justice, in the case of *Goodman International and Laurence Goodman v. The Tribunal* that 'ordinarily, any party permitted be represented at the inquiry should have their costs paid out of public funds.'

The tribunal is satisfied that in exercise of its discretion to award the whole or part of the costs of any party appearing before the Tribunal, it cannot have regard to any of its findings on the matters being inquired into by it but is only entitled to consider 'conduct of or on behalf of that party at, during or in connection with the inquiry' that unless such conduct so warrants, a party, permitted to be represented at the inquiry should have their costs paid out of public funds."[284]

Minister may certify that the local authority or other body should make a contribution towards the costs and expenses reasonably incurred by any person (other than the local authority or other body) in relation to the inquiry.

[283] The Tribunals of Inquiry (Evidence) (Amendment) Act 1997, now empowers the Tribunal to award costs to itself against any person where the Tribunal had incurred costs because of the non-cooperation of that person before it and, secondly, gives the Tribunal power to order, of its own motion, costs to be paid to persons before it by any other person. The gap in the existing law had become evident when the Chairman of the *McCracken Tribunal* ruled, on October 28, 1997, that he had no power to order a person to pay the cost of the Tribunal's expenses. See 484, *Dáil Debates* Cols. 861–888 (December 10, 1997).

[284] *Report of the Tribunal of Inquiry into the Beef Processing Industry* (Pn. 1007) p. 719. As regards the quotation given in the second paragraph of the extract, "conduct . . . in connection with . . . the inquiry", one should note that this was the ground of the sole refusal to allow the costs of a person represented (see pp. 719–720 of the report). The unattributed reference, in the second paragraph, to "conduct of or on behalf of that party . . ." Secondly, although unattributed the quotation is in fact from *Goodman International v. Hamilton (No. 1)* [1992] 2 I.R. 542 at 605. The full passage reads: ". . . Section 6: the liability to pay costs cannot depend upon the findings of the Tribunal as to the subject matter of the inquiry. When the inquiry is in respect of a single disaster, then, ordinarily, any party permitted to be represented at the inquiry should have their costs paid out of public funds. The whole or part of those costs may be disallowed by the Tribunal because of the conduct of or on behalf of that party at, during or in connection with the inquiry. The expression "the findings of the tribunal" should be read as the findings as to the conduct of the parties at the tribunal. In all other cases the allowance of costs at public expense lies within the discretion of the Tribunal, or where appropriate, it's chairman."

It may be observed: (i) this passage is very much *obiter dictum* and by way of scene-setting and it has no analogue whatsoever in the other judgments in *Goodman*; (ii) there is no attempt to square it with the reference in section 6, which is not quoted, to "the findings of the tribunal"; (iii) there

The second statement of principle made by the Beef Tribunal reads as follows:

"Having regard to the nature, extent and length of the inquiry it would be inequitable to require that persons, necessarily appearing at or before the Tribunal should be required to pay their own costs of such appearances and as the Houses of the Oireachtas had considered it expedient to establish the Tribunal, the Tribunal considers it equitable that the Minister for Finance should pay, out of monies provided by the Oireachtas the costs of the persons named in Appendix 3."[285]

We shall appraise these principles after we have considered the way in which costs were dealt with in the *Whiddy Inquiry*. In regard to the present point, there was a good deal in common between the two inquiries – in that each involved an investigation into the conduct of big business, whose conduct was found to be far from blameless. Despite this, there was no reference to the *Whiddy Inquiry* in the *Beef Tribunal*. The *Whiddy Inquiry* was set up to investigate a fire in an oil tanker and storage depot. The fire claimed the lives of a number of people. In this inquiry, applications for an award of costs (whether against the Minister for Finance or the oil companies) were made by seven persons or bodies, who had been represented, but were granted only in the case of one (private) party, who was not in a financial position to discharge his own costs.

In approaching the question of costs, the Chairman of the *Whiddy Inquiry*, Costello J. (as he then was), observed that "there can be no hard and fast rules as to how a Tribunal's discretion to award costs should be exercised."[286] He continued by rejecting, (in line with the decision which he reached, which was summarised in the previous paragraph) the proposition "that *prima facie* the costs of all public inquiries should be borne by the State"[287] – the view which appears to have more or less been adopted, in the *Beef Tribunal*. And, of course, the outcome of the costs applications, already noted was in accord with this rejection.

One of the propositions on which Hamilton P. (as he then was) relied in the *Beef Tribunal*, was that in determining whether to award costs, a Tribunal "cannot have regard to any of its findings on the matters being "inquired into by it" (as it was put in the first of the two passages just quoted). There was also the notion, which emerges from the second passage quoted that, since it was the Houses of the Oireachtas which willed the end, the State should be responsible for paying the bill for the means. In fact, the antithesis, as it were to this thesis, might be to say that if a party is shown to have been responsible for the event which caused the setting up of the inquiry, then it might well be said that he ought to be responsible for the costs of each of the other parties to the inquiry. In fact, the synthesis reached in the *Whiddy Tribunal* inquiry was that the party found guilty of misconduct should pay its own costs but not those of the State: for "[the Attorney General's expenses] are incurred

---

is no justification or explanation for the distinction implicit in the second and final sentence in the passage ("when the inquiry is in respect of a single disaster . . ."). This most significant distinction was not mentioned in the *Beef Tribunal* Report.

285 Report, p.720.
286 *Report of the Disaster at Whiddy Island* (Pr. 8911) p. 345.
287 *Ibid.* at p. 346.

for a public purpose and generally speaking, it would appear that they should properly be paid out of public funds."[288]

There is another point: in other contexts,[289] it has been held that while constitutional justice means a right to legal representation it does not mean that the State must pay the costs of same. Why should there be a difference in the present context? But the most significant point of all is the plain words of the 1979 Act, quoted earlier: "... having regard to the findings of the Tribunal ..." There is no (constitutional or other) reason to overlook these plain words.

Take finally a case in which there was no statutory authority to award costs to, or against, any person appearing before the inquiry. In *Condon v. C.I.É.*[290] Barrington J. ruled that a statutory inquiry constituted under the provisions of section 7 of the Railway Regulation Act 1871 did not have power to award costs. However, the plaintiff was an employee of CIÉ and he claimed that he had been "singled out" as the person principally responsible for a serious train crash at Buttevant Station, Co. Cork, in 1980. Since his good name and his livelihood were at stake, the plaintiff engaged a solicitor and counsel to represent him at the inquiry. It was argued that if the inquiry had no jurisdiction to award him costs, a constitutional duty was imposed on the State by the terms of Article 40.3 to defray the cost of such representation. Barrington J. rejected this argument, saying that while the guarantee of fair procedures contained in Article 40.3 required that the plaintiff be allowed to defend himself, "it was quite another thing to say that the State must pay the costs of his defence."[291] However, as CIÉ had been negligent and responsible for the accident, Barrington J. found (1) that it was almost unthinkable that the Minister for Transport would not establish a statutory inquiry into the disaster and (2) that the plaintiff, as a person immediately involved in the events leading up to the disaster, would naturally seek to be legally represented before the inquiry. The judge concluded that as the plaintiff "was placed in the position of needing such representation as a consequence of the negligence of CIÉ," this was a reasonably foreseeable consequence of such negligence, and so he was entitled to recover the reasonable costs of being legally represented. (Presumably, this rather forced reasoning owes something to the fact that the CIÉ is a public body.)

---

[288] *Ibid.*

[289] See p. 562.

[290] Unreported, High Court, November 22, 1984. For the background to this case, see *Report of the Investigation into the Accident on the CIÉ Railway at Buttevant, Co. Cork on August 1, 1980* (1981, Pr. 9698).

[291] Barrington J. followed the earlier decision of *K. Security Ltd. v. Ireland*, unreported, High Court, July 15, 1977 in this regard. In *K. Security*, Gannon J. held that the State was not under any constitutional duty to discharge the costs of the plaintiff company which had been legally represented at a tribunal of inquiry. (This was before the enactment of the Tribunal of Inquiry (Evidence) (Amendment) Act 1979, s.5 of which makes provision for the payment of the parties' costs by the State or other party appearing before the tribunal).

THE INVESTIGATIONS OF THREE
CAUSES CÉLÈBRES

1. The Non-Statutory Hepatitis C Tribunal

Up to 1,600 people were infected with hepatitis C from blood supplied by the Blood Transfusion Board.[292] Initially a non-statutory inquiry[293] was established to ascertain the relevant facts. However, because it lacked the subpoena power, it failed to do so. The result was a build-up of pressure, not least from the victims of these tragic errors, in favour of a Tribunal of Inquiry. This was resisted by the Minister for Health on the stated ground that the negligence action being brought by one of the victims against the State, in the High Court would result in the truth emerging.[294] However, the action was compromised and the plaintiff died a few hours later, a tragedy which increased the pressure on the Minister who then agreed to the setting up of the Tribunal (chaired by the former Chief Justice Finlay).[295]

2. Dáil Inquiry into the Fall of the Fianna Fáil-Labour Government

The Fianna Fáil-Labour Coalition Government led by Albert Reynolds fell when the Labour Party withdrew in November 1994. The circumstances of the fall[296] of

---

[292] For discussion of the Hepatitis C Tribunals see pp. 292, 296.

[293] *Report of the Expert Group on the Blood Transfusion Service Board* (Pn. 1538, 1995) chaired by Ms Hederman O'Brien, dated January 1995 and published by the Government (which was not under an obligation to do so) in April, 1995.

[294] 470 *Dáil Debates*, Col. 431 (October 16, 1996) (and for the susequent fortnight).

[295] Because of the popular indignation at the huge legal costs engendered by the *Beef Tribunal*, elaborate methods were devised to restrict the length of this Tribunal. Its terms of reference (470 *Dáil Debates* 517, October 17, 1996; *The Irish Times*, October 9, 1996) included the following:
"... And that the tribunal be asked to report on an interim basis not later than the 20th day of any oral hearings to the Minister for Health on the following matters.
The number of parties then represented before the tribunal.
The progress which has been made in the hearings and the work of the tribunal.
The likely duration (so far as that may be capable of being estimated at that point in time) of the tribunal proceedings.
Any other matters which the tribunal believes should be drawn to the attention of the Minister at that stage (including any matters relating to the terms of reference)
And that the Minister for Health should inform the person selected to conduct the inquiry that it is the desire of the House that the inquiry be completed in as economical a manner as possible and at the earliest date consistent with a fair examination of the matters referred to it."
However, no indication was given as to any sanction which might follow if the inquiry were conducted unsatisfactorily as regards these matters. Probably, therefore, judicial review would not be available and the only sanction would be "public opinion". Is reliance on this improper if it amounts to an attempt to "overawe" the inquiry? On this Tribunal, see also 474 *Dáil Debates*, Cols. 122 ff (29 January, 1997); Vol. 476, cols. 1449 ff (25 March 1997).

[296] The proximate causes of the fall were the Fianna Fáil Ministers' insistence on appointing the then Attorney General Mr Harry Whelehan as President of the High Court; and the delay within the

this Government were so surprising and controversial that they were thought to call for an inquiry. By Dáil Resolutions,[297] the Dáil Committee on Legislation and Security was charged with the duty of investigation. One of the main reasons why this forum was chosen was a desire to avoid the lavish legal representation thought to be endemic in an inquiry under the Tribunals of Inquiry (Evidence) legislation. However, constitutional justice is ubiquitous. And one of the seminal authorities in the field is, in fact, *Re Haughey*[298] in which the Supreme Court had held that the duty to observe fair procedures could arise despite the fact that the investigating agency was the Dáil Public Accounts Committee and its report of an inquiry would not have apportioned liability nor imposed penalties. In *Haughey*, the plaintiff had sought leave to cross-examine witnesses appearing before the Dáil Committee of Public Accounts, and to have counsel appear on his behalf. Ó Dálaigh C.J. held that Haughey was more than a mere witness. The true analogy in terms of High Court procedure is not that of a witness but that of a party before the Committee – he was in effect a party. His conduct and reputation were the very subject-matter of the investigation. In that situation he had the same rights as those guaranteed by Article 38.1 to accused persons facing trial, and basic fairness of procedures demanded that he be afforded the right to cross-examine (by counsel, if he wished), to call rebutting evidence and to make closing submissions. Without those rights, no person in the plaintiff's position could hope to defend his good name.

According to the sub-committee's legal adviser, *Re Haughey* also applied to the instant proceedings,[299] so that the sub-committee's proceedings fell short of the necessary standard of fair procedure in several respects.[300] Accordingly:

Attorney General's office in processing a warrant for extradition to Northern Ireland. For accounts, see Casey, *The Irish Law Officers* (1996) pp. 186–229 and Apps. 5–7; Duignan, *One Spin on the Merry-go-Round* (1995).

[297] 447 *Dáil Debates* Cols. 695, 848 and 1174 (December 6, 8 and 15, 1994). The Report is entitled, awkwardly, *Report of the sub-committee of the Select Committee on Legislation and Security* (Pn. 1478, 1995). The advice from the sub-committee's legal adviser, G. Durcan S.C., is in Appendices 6 and 7. The sub-committee's position was strengthened by the grant of privileges to its witnesses by section 2 of the Select Committee on Legislation and Security of Dáil Eireann (Privilege and Immunity) Act 1994.

[298] [1971] I.R. 217. See also, *Mahon v. Air New Zealand Ltd.* [1984] A.C. 808.

[299] On this view, Report of the sub-committee . . . (Pn. 1478), above n.300, (Appendices 6 and 7) 32–04 quoting Deputy O'Donnell, 470 *Dáil Debates* Col. 1069. The 1994 Act itself stated warningly though non-commitally: "The Committee shall take all steps which in the opinion of the Committee are necessary to protect and vindicate the good name, character and other constitutional rights of witnesses and other persons".

[300] "1. The sub-Committee has not had the benefit of hearing sworn evidence in regard to any factual matters which may be in controversy.

2. The sub-Committee has not been in a position to give advance notice to other witnesses of the nature of the evidence which is to be given by a particular witness.

3. At the moment it would appear likely that the only cross examination of witnesses which will take place is by members of the Committee rather than by legal representatives of other witnesses who might be in a position to more fully put the case being made by those other witnesses.

4. Many of the members of the sub-Committeee are members of political organisations who would be perceived as having a considerable interest in how some of the actual disputes between the witnesses are resolved . . .

5. The system of substitution of members as operated by the sub-Committee means that certain members of the sub-Committee are not present on particular days and therefore do not have an opportunity to hear witnesses on that day giving evidence and assess the demeanour of the witness while doing so.

".. . the more that the sub-Committee on its Report reaches factual conclusions of express opinions which are likely to affect the good name of witnesses or indeed other persons, the more will the courts expect the sub-Committee to act . . . in accordance with the rules of constitutional . . . justice."[301]

Thus, the advice continued and – was accepted – the only way to avoid judicial review of the Report by someone whose reputation might be affected was for the report "to confine itself to reporting the evidence which it has received, to the Dáil, rather than reaching any conclusion or expressing opinions in regard to such evidence."[302]

As a statement of the modern Irish law, it would be hard to gainsay this analysis.

However, the following broad comments on the law might be made. First, it is a central tenet of the Constitution (Article 28.2) that the Government is responsible to the Dáil (partisan body though that may be). It might have been thought, in the light of this, that the Committee ought to have been regarded as one (possible) way in which the Dáil fulfilled its over-riding constitutional obligation to investigate the circumstances surrounding the collapse of a Government. Moreover, classically, it is for the Dáil to determine its own procedure.[303] And in respect, it might be argued that the issues before the Committee were distinguishable from the circumstances disclosed in *Re Haughey,* where ministerial behaviour was not directly impugned. From another perspective, however, it might be said that the Committee was seeking to portray itself as having the authority and impartiality of a neutral tribunal and, accordingly, it should be subject to the full rigours of normal procedural requirements. The simple answer to this is that it is debatable whether the public would perceive a group of politicians – many of them opposition politicians – as being impartial in the first place. The final comment which might be made is that the procedure followed by the Committee – especially its abstention from reaching any conclusion – is eloquent testimony to the value set on individual rights in the procedural field.

---

6. When asking questions of a witness some members of the Committee have clearly expressed their own view as to particular factual matter in respect of which the witness is being asked the question. I believe that a careful analysis of the transcript of the meetings of the sub-Committee would disclose a picture which gives the appearance at least that a number of members of the sub-Committee had formed pre-judgements . . .

7. I have noted that the matters which have been discussed at the private sessions of the sub-Committeee have become public knowledge within a very short period. I believe that such disclosure of private information . . . is again indicative of a failure to adopt a quasi-judicial attitude and to abide by fair and impartial procedures.

8. The evidence which has been given to the sub-Committee has included a great deal of hearsay and of comment in regard to the events which occurred. I believe that a Court might well view the acceptance of such evidence, at least to the extent which it has been allowed by the sub-Committee, as being inconsistent with the adoption of suitable procedures and that such evidence would not constitute a proper basis on which to found adverse findings affecting a person's good name." (App. 6, pp. 958–959.)

The following brief comments may be made: (i) it might be contended that item 6 fails sufficiently to take into account the notion that different types of decision require varying standards as regards the *nemo iudex* precept and pre-judgment of issues. (see pp. 529–534); (ii) as to item 8, hearsay is not *ipso facto* a violation of constitutional justice (see pp. 558–559). However, see, in broad agreement with the legal adviser's view, those of the Attorney General summarised at 447 *Dáil Debates,* Col. 851 (December 8, 1994).

301 Pn. 1478, p.957.
302 *Ibid.* p. 960.
303 *cf. O'Malley v. An Ceann Comhairle* [1997] 1 I.R. 428.

3. Dunnes Stores Tribunal

In late 1996,[304] it was disclosed that during the course of intra-family litigation in regard to Dunnes Stores, a Price Waterhouse Report had been drawn up, which showed that about 1,500 donations (running to £1.1 million in one case) had been made to diverse persons, some of whom were involved in public life. Now the list included the names of several persons not involved in public life whose privacy and reputation, it was considered by the Government had to be respected. Thus, irrespective of how the main investigation was to be effected, it was assumed that there had to be private proceedings by which some responsible person sifted out the names of these private parties from the Report. Accordingly, a retired Circuit Court judge, Judge Gerard Buchanan was given the task of extracting – to quote the terms of the extra-statutory investigation process designed by the Government – "the details of payments made to or transactions entered into by elected representatives, holders of public office and members of public service." In addition, persons possibly within this category were allowed "an opportunity to explain and clarify the basis of the payments or transactions", such explanations being reported to the Committees. This presumably is a device to try to minimise the danger of a defamation action. Certainly for this sort of procedure to be observed at this preliminary stage goes beyond what would normally be required by the *audi alteram partem* stage. The remaining names on the list were then forwarded to the Committees on Procedure and Privileges of each House, each of which constituted a joint public sub-Committee to investigate the circumstances of the donations, similar to the sub-Committee on the fall of the Reynolds Government.

This procedure was criticised by the Opposition[305] on a number of bases. First, the sub-Committee lacked the subpoena power. In contrast to the Reynolds sub-Committee, the witnesses were not all current members of the Dáil or civil servants and consequently this was a serious defect. In addition, it meant that the evidence relating to the Price Waterhouse Report could not be called before the sub-Committee, which was thereby deprived of a vital element of the background. Finally, the sub-Committee had no real investigative machinery. Furthermore, the former judge enjoyed no legal investigatory powers.

Conclusion

As a general comment on these episodes, we may say that the net result of the forum selected in case 2 and, initially, in case 3 was that the conduct was being investigated

---

[304] This *modus operandi* was set out in an agreement between the Government and Dunnes Stores of December 9, 1996. The following account is taken , save where the contrary is indicated from: 472 *Dáil Debates* Cols.1181–1211 and 1478–1510 (December 10 and 11, 1996) and the newspapers for November 30–December 13, 1996. Deputy De Rossa raised the spectre of a tribunal of inquiry with more than 1,500 persons represented. The suggestion was made notably by Deputy Mary Harney that a suitable mechanism for investigation which would force disclosure of the Report would be under the Companies Act 1990, ss.8, 14 and 19. However, the difficulty with this is that, in such investigations, the main focus would be the shareholders or directors or those "who are . . . financially interested", rather than persons who may have received money.

[305] 472 *Dáil Debates Cols.* 1181–1210 and 1478–1510 (December 10 and 11, 1996).

by other (allied or opposing) politicians. This of course was just the type of arrangement, which had been discredited by the House of Commons Select Committee (with its Liberal majority) investigation into the Marconi scandal involving Liberal Ministers in 1912.[306] This led to the Tribunals of Inquiry (Evidence) Act 1921 with its unspoken but unbroken assumption that the public respect, enjoyed by the judiciary should be drawn upon to engender confidence in the impartiality of the inquiry. Given that the last virtue which politicians would claim, in an era of strict party discipline, is impartiality it may seem unnatural to foist such a duty on them. The most that can be said in its favour is that each of the above three episodes was peculiarly "political" in flavour.[307]

---

[306] The committee was set up to investigate allegations arising from the ownership by two Government Ministers of shares in the Marconi Company, which had benefited from large official contracts. Punch's cartoon on the episode had the chairman of the Committee remarking to the Ministers: "You leave the Committee, boys, without a stain on your character, apart from the whitewash."

[307] Indeed, in the case of the investigation of the Dunnes Stores episode, there was an Electoral Bill dealing with the public funding of electoral campaigns which was pending before the Dáil, at the same time. Incidentally, note also Deputy Noonan's observation à propos the *Beef Tribunal:* "what was dealt with there was what is proper for this House–the question of political accountability (469 *Dáil Debates* Col. 1664 (October 8, 1996). But it would seem that this last phrase is more apt for the three inquiries just discussed in the text.

CHAPTER 7

GENERAL PRINCIPLES OF LICENSING

1. Introduction

Licensing[1] is one of the most common techniques by which the dirigiste State regulates activities which are potentially harmful to its citizens. Such unlicensed activity is made a criminal offence (which will be tried in the usual way) by specific legislation. However, the legislation also provides, implicitly, that the activity in question is lawful so long as it is carried out within the terms of the licence issued by some official or quasi-official authority.

How does the Oireachtas decide which activities ought to be licensed? Broadly speaking (as will be seen from the examples given below), they involve acts which are not in themselves harmful in the same way as ordinary crimes (such as murder or larceny). Indeed, they are activities which, if carried out in the appropriate circumstances by a suitably qualified person, will usually be beneficial (or, at any rate, neutral) to the community. On the other hand, if performed by the wrong person or in the wrong circumstances (such as medical treatment carried out by an unqualified practitioner), they may be positively harmful. A further contrast with traditional crimes is that licensing is preventative rather than curative. A licensing régime is not content to wait until a vendor of land has his money misappropriated by an auctioneer or estate agent. Rather, it seeks to strike at an earlier point in time by prosecuting unlicensed auctioneers and by seeking to ensure that only auctioneers of good character are granted a licence.[2]

---

[1] The meaning explained in this paragraph describes the use of the term "licence" as used in public administration. As used in private law, the term also means permission but with the implication that the remedy for performing the action without permission is merely a civil wrong and not an offence.

    Note that, in general, a licence involves permission to take some positive action or, more usually, series of actions (whether trading, practising a profession or possessing a potentially harmful object). By contrast, there may be a direction to *refrain* from doing some act or series of acts. Examples of this include the making of a prohibition order under the Censorship of Publications Acts 1929–1967 or the making of an order by the Central Bank under s.21 of the Central Bank Act 1971 (as inserted by s.38 of the Central Bank Act 1989) directing that the holder of a banking licence shall not carry on banking business. However, very little turns on this point of characterisation. For "the directing power", (to borrow U.S. parlance), see Stout, *Administrative Law in Ireland* (1985), pp. 373–419.

    In some administrative regulatory systems, the onus is placed upon the private individual to "declare" or "certify" that what he is doing is not potentially injurious. For example, under ss.2, 3 and 12 of the Local Government (Multi-Storey Buildings) Act 1988, if a local authority serves notice on the owner of a building with five or more storeys, the owner must submit to the local authority a certificate signed by a "competent person" (a chartered engineer, etc.) certifying, *inter alia* that the building is constructed in accord with the appropriate codes of practice and standards. Failure to submit a certificate, or the submission of a false certificate, is an offence.

[2] See Auctioneering and House Agents Acts 1947–1973.

Each area of licensing has its own specific statutory régime so that the resolution of any particular practical point will usually depend upon the specific context and, often, upon an issue of statutory interpretation.[3] Rich examples of this may be found in the voluminous law relating to the substance of planning permission[4] or liquor licensing.[5] More recently established licensing systems deal with private broad-casting licences (or franchises)[6]; or casual trading licences.[7] Despite their diversity, each of these is located at an economic, political or social pressure point and is likely to be involved in substantial controversy and litigation. The observation regarding the particularity of much of licensing law ought to be emphasised by way of a Government health warning, since this Part does not advert to particular details, but merely attempts to delineate such administrative law principles as are common to the field of licensing.

We may commence by considering, first, the stage at which a licence is granted or withheld and, secondly, the enforcement stage.

(i) Licensing stage: grant and revocation[8]

Consonant with the haphazard design of our system of government administration, the task of licensing (which usually includes the powers to grant and to revoke) may be vested in any one of at least six different types of agency. In the first place, this

---

[3] e.g. *Re Application of Pies Ltd* [1994] 3 I.R. 179 (meaning of "in the immediate vicinity" in the context of transfer of a liquor licence); *Lovett v. Grogan* [1995] 3 I.R. 132 (whether, in order for a person to operate an occasional road passenger service, so as to require a licence, under the Road Transport Act 1932, ss.2, 7 and 12, that person has to own the bus involved); *O'Rourke v. Grittar* [1995] 1 I.R. 541 (exchange of one type of licence for another); *Slevin v. Shannon Regional Fisheries Board* [1995] 1 I.R. 460 (fishing licences).

[4] See pp. 233–242.

[5] Licencing Acts 1833–1995. See further, Cassidy, *The Licensing Acts 1833–1995* (1996); Woods, *Guide to the Intoxicating Liquor Acts* (1974) and *Supplement* (1977); Woods, *District Court Guide* (1977), Vol. 1, Pt. XI.

[6] See, *e.g.* pp. 331–332 and pp. 672–673.

[7] The Casual Trading Act 1995 is an example of another way of using licences, for it involves a kind of double-jointed control system by which control in respect of different factors is imposed at different points. For instance, under the 1995 Act, a person selling goods in a public place must in the first place have a casual trading licence which is granted (or not) by a local authority by reference to the personal qualities of the applicant. A local authority may also designate an area as a "casual trading area". If it does so (though not otherwise), then a casual trader must hold not only a licence but also a casual trading permit, which latter control enables the local authority to specify the place which the trader may occupy on specified days: see further 1995 Act ss.2–4; *Shanley v. Galway Corporation* [1995] 1 I.R. 396.

[8] A case arising from the revocation of a licence is *Sheehan v. District Judge Reilly* [1992] 1 I.R. 368. On one level this case involves a not uncommon set of facts in the licensing area; yet, at another level, engages a fairly technical legal issue. The applicant had been granted a public music and singing licence (under the Public Dance Halls Act 1935) by the respondent. However, because of the numerous objections to the grant of the licence – the gist of which was that the premises created a public nuisance in the neighbourhood – a condition (which was the central point in the case) had been imposed on the licence, namely that the objectors had liberty to re-enter the proceedings on 48 hours notice. Five days after the grant of the licence and on the hearing of what was in effect their further objection, the licence was revoked.

A critical point in the case is that as a matter of statute, namely, s. 51(9) of the Public Health (Amendment) Act 1890, the power of revocation was predicated upon the holder of the licence becoming liable to a penalty as therein provided. Since the terms of the licence contained no condition the breach of which would have given the respondent jurisdiction to revoke the licence or even re-hear the case, the applicant's claim for judicial review was successful. Barron J. stated:

function may be vested in a court, generally the District Court, but occasionally the Circuit Court, and examples here include: selling intoxicating liquor[9]; running dance halls[10]; and auctioneering.[11] Secondly, control over a number of activities is vested in the local authorities. These activities are generally in the environmental or public health field and include: land use[12]; discharge of effluent[13]; waste collection[14]; air pollution,[15] and running a caravan park[16] or abattoir.[17] Sometimes, however, local authorities are given licensing functions in matters of social concern to the community and the powers given to local authorities in respect of gaming halls under Part III of the Gaming and Lotteries Act 1956 provide the best example in this context.[18] Thirdly, the licensing functions may be allocated to the relevant Minister, as, for example, in the case of: road passenger licences[19]; livestock marts[20]; bull-breeding[21]; tour-operators[22]; the operation of licensed health insurance schemes[23] and insurance services.[24] Fourthly, in some cases, the allocation of licences has been considered sufficiently important to warrant the vesting of these functions in an autonomous agency which also bears functions other than licensing but in the same substantive field. Thus, the Central Bank is the ultimate regulatory authority in respect of banking licences,[25] building societies,[26] investment business firms and investment product intermediaries,[27] trustee savings[28] and *bureaux de change*[29] while the Director of

---

"The reality seems to be that the respondent was not fully satisfied that the applicant was entitled to either licence. For this reason, he inserted the condition in each order giving liberty to re-enter. In the event, he became satisfied that his original doubts were justified and revoked the licences. I think that having granted the licences, the respondent was *functus officio*. The matter could only have come before him again upon a prosecution as provided for in the respective Acts which, if successful, would have given him jurisdiction to revoke the licences."

[9]   Licensing Acts 1833–1995.
[10] Public Dance-Halls Acts 1935–1997.
[11] Auctioneering and House Agents Acts 1947–1973.
[12] Local Government (Planning and Development) Act 1963, s.26. See further, pp. 233–242.
[13] Local Government (Water Pollution) Act 1977, s.4(1)(b).
[14] Waste Management Act 1996, ss.33 and 34.
[15] Air Pollution Act 1987, Pt. III.
[16] Local Government (Sanitary Services) Act 1948, s.34(4).
[17] Abattoirs Act 1988, s.9.
[18] See also Casual Trading Act 1995, s.6 (local authorities given extension powers to control casual trading); Control of Horses Act 1996, Part II (which enables a local authority to adapt bye-laws strictly controlling the keeping of horses where "it is satisfied that horses in that area should be licensed having regard to the need to control the keeping of horses, the need to prevent nuisance, annoyance or injury to persons or damage to property by horses and such other matters as it considers relevant.").
[19] Road Transport Act 1932, ss.8–12.
[20] Livestock Marts Act 1967, s.3.
[21] Control of Bulls for Breeding Act 1985, s.3.
[22] Transport (Tour Operators and Travel Agents) Act 1982, s.6.
[23] Voluntary Health Insurance Act 1957, s.22.
[24] European Communities (Non-Life Insurance) Regulations 1976 (S.I. 1976 No. 115); European Communities (Life Assurance) Regulations 1984 (S.I. 1984 No. 57).
[25] Central Bank Acts 1971–1997.
[26] Building Societies Act 1989, ss.17 and 119 and Pt IV.
[27] Investment Intermediaries Act 1995, s.4 and Pts II, III and IV. This function is shared to some extent with the Minister for Enterprise and Employment.
[28] Trustee Savings Banks Act 1989, s.10. For another example, see Bord Fáilte's registration of tourist accommodation under the Tourist Traffic Acts 1939–1995.
[29] Central Bank Act 1997, Pt V.

Consumer Affairs is now given regulatory responsibility for consumer credit (including hire purchase, moneylending and housing lending).[30] Alternatively, an independent tribunal may be established to deal with licensing matters. Thus, An Bord Pleanála deals with all planning appeals[31] and the Independent Radio and Television Commission distributes broadcasting franchises.[32] But even here practice is inconsistent. There is no independent tribunal dealing with licensing matters in the agricultural area, with the unsatisfactory result that it is the Minister for Agriculture who retains full legal responsibility for licensing in such diverse areas as milk quotas, bovine artificial insemination and the rural environmental protection scheme. There is, in fact, a body known as the Milk Quota Appeal Tribunal, but this nomenclature is misleading, since this Tribunal "is no more than an advisory body to advise the Minister on certain comparatively minor matters concerning milk quotas".[33] The case for an independent agricultural tribunal which would establish its own transparent procedures and a body of written decisions, with an appropriate right of appeal, seems compelling.

Fifthly, licences to practise professions (such as law,[34] medicine,[35] veterinary science,[36] nursing[37] or dentistry[38]) are issued by the respective professional body. Finally, licences which have a security or policing dimension (such as firearms,[39] bookmaking[40] and house-to-house and street collections[41]) are handled by the Gardaí. There are also licensing systems which fall outside any of these six categories, such as, for example, a licence to drive a taxi (which is dispensed by the Garda carriage office under the auspices of the Garda Commissioner)[42] or a supply certificate in respect of video recordings (which is granted by the Official Censor).[43]

The power to grant licences is invariably accompanied by powers to attach conditions or even to revoke the licence when prescribed violations of its terms are established. Revocation is regarded as an interference with the right to earn a livelihood.[44] Accordingly, powers to revoke, in the absolute discretion of the

---

[30] Consumer Credit Act 1995, s.4, Pts II–XIII.
[31] Local Government (Planning and Development) Act 1976, s.26. See pp. 238–240.
[32] Radio and Television Act 1988, ss.6 and 7 and pp. 283–291.
[33] O'Reilly, "Legal and Administrative Aspects of the Operation of the European Milk Quota Regulations in Ireland" in Findlater (ed.), *Milk Quotas in Ireland* (1996), pp. 80–81. O'Reilly continues by observing:
> "If by tribunal is meant an independent body established on a statutory basis with power to make binding decisions, this description is a misnomer . . . [The Tribunal] has no statutory powers, functions or duties nor can it make any binding determination or ruling in any dispute between the two conflicting dairy producers. That would be a matter that would have to be resolved by the courts."
[34] Solicitors Acts 1954–1994 (Law Society of Ireland).
[35] Medical Practitioners Act 1978 (Medical Council).
[36] Veterinary Surgeons Act 1931 (Veterinary Council).
[37] Nurses Act 1985 (An Comhairle Altranais).
[38] Dentists Act 1985 (Dental Council).
[39] Firearms Acts 1925–1990.
[40] Betting Act 1931, s.6.
[41] Street and House to House Collections Act 1962, ss.5, 6, 9–11.
[42] Road Traffic (Public Service Vehicles) Regulations 1963 (S.I. No. 191 of 1963), Art. 20.
[43] Video Recordings Act 1989, s.3(1).
[44] But as for whether a licence may be regarded as a form of property right enjoying constitutional protection, see pp. 324–327. For the statutory procedure to be followed in a revocation under the Livestock Marts Act 1967, see ss.3 and 6 of the Act.

315

licensing authority, while once common,[45] are rarely, if ever, conferred today. Moreover, the governing legislation will invariably provide for some form of appeal against an adverse decision of the licensing authority. Sometimes the right of appeal will lie to another administrative agency,[46] but more often it will lie to the District Court[47], the Circuit Court[48] or even to the High Court.[49] In *Cashman v. Clifford*[50] Barron J. rejected the argument that, when hearing such appeals from licensing authorities, the courts were merely discharging administrative functions and were not thereby administering justice, under Article 34.1 of the Constitution.[51] Here the applicant had challenged the validity of section 13 of the Betting Act 1931 which had established an appeal to the District Court against a decision of the Garda Superintendent refusing a licence, but had also provided by section 13(5) that only the Garda Síochána and the Revenue Commissioners and "no other person" were entitled to be heard on the appeal. Barron J. held that the exclusion of other potential objectors (such as the applicant, who was already a bookmaker in the area) represented an unconstitutional interference with the administration of justice. In the result, section 13(5) was found to be invalid.

In any event, in addition to any form of (administrative or judicial) appeal, the revocation of a licence is subject to a fairly stringent application of the principles of judicial review of administrative action, including not only substantive checks as to, for instance, reasonableness, but also the rules of constitutional justice. The same is true, although to a lesser extent, of the refusal of a renewal (which amounts, in principle, to the granting of a fresh licence) or even possibly the refusal of an initial grant.[52] These matters are dealt with in later chapters.[53]

---

45 See, *e.g.* Road Transport Act 1932, s.17(3) ("The Minister may at any time on his own motion and at his absolute discretion revoke an occasional passenger licence"); Voluntary Health Insurance Act 1957, s.22(1) ("The Minister may, in his absolute discretion, revoke a health insurance licence."). The latter subsection has, in any event, been repealed: see Health Insurance Act 1994, s.5.

46 See, *e.g.* Local Government (Planning and Development) Act 1976, s.14; Air Pollution Act 1987, s.34; Local Government (Water Pollution) Act 1977, s.20 (as inserted by s.15 of the Local Government (Water Pollution) (Amendment) Act 1990) (appeal lies in all cases to An Bord Pleanála); Video Recordings Act 1989, s.10 (appeal to Censorship of Films Appeals Board); Irish Horseracing Industry Act 1994, Pt V (appeals to Bookmakers Appeal Committee in respect of course-betting permits).

47 See, *e.g.* Betting Act 1931, s.13; Street and House to House Collections Act 1962, s.13; Health (Nursing Homes) Act 1990, s.5.

48 Consumer Credit Act 1995, s.93(13) (appeal to the Circuit Court against decision of Director of Consumer Affairs to refuse to grant moneylender's licence).

49 See, *e.g.* Central Bank Act 1971, s.21(3) (as inserted by s.38 of the Central Bank Act 1989) (right of appeal to the High Court by holder of banking licence against order of Central Bank suspending carrying on of banking business); Transport (Tour Operators and Travel Agents) Act 1982, s.9(3) (appeal to the High Court against refusal or revocation of tour operator's licence by Minister). For an unsuccessful appeal against a revocation under the 1982 Act (the revocation being based on breach of a condition of a licence), see *Balkan Tours Ltd v. Minister for Communications* [1988] I.L.R.M. 101.

50 [1989] I.R. 122.

51 Barron J. followed the earlier decision of the Supreme Court in *The State (McEldowney) v. Kelleher* [1983] I.R. 289, where that court had declared a section of the Street and House to House Collections Act 1962 (which had in effect purported to allow a Garda Superintendent to direct a District Judge to dismiss certain types of appeals against the Superintendent's refusal to grant a collecting licence) to be unconstitutional. However, in neither authority was the precise point mentioned in the text – whether Art. 34.1 of the Constitution applied where a court is exercising a regulatory function – really addressed.

52 *East Donegal Co-Operative v. Attorney General* [1970] I.R. 317 at 344–347 *(obiter)*. *A contra*: de Smith, Woolf and Jowell *Judicial Review of Administrative Action* (1995) p. 412: "Applicants are in a different position from those whose existing licences are . . . not renewed."

53 See, *e.g. East Donegal Co-Operative v. Attorney General* [1970] I.R. 317; *TV3 v. IRTC* [1994] 2 I.R. 439 (on which see p. 594) *Madden v. Minister for the Marine* [1997] 1 I.L.R.M. 136; *International*

Because of the variety of different cases to which any licensing system will have to apply, the need for flexibility is particularly great. This need for flexibility is accommodated by empowering the licensing agency to grant a licence not only absolutely but also subject to specified conditions. In practice, licences are seldom, if ever, granted free of conditions.

(ii) Enforcement stage

In principle, there is less to say with regard to enforcement. As a general rule, the governing statute will provide for criminal offences triable summarily before the District Court or, on indictment, before the Circuit Court. In addition, the licensing agency will be given a special prosecuting role in summary prosecutions.[54] However, in practice, presumably because there is no readily identifiable victim, the punishments imposed tend to be small if not altogether derisory.[55] They rarely have a deterrent effect and may, indeed, be regarded as simply additional "overheads" of running the unlawful activity.

Recent legislation tends to rely more heavily on civil remedies in aid of enforcement. Thus the licensing agency or some other person with *locus standi* is entitled to seek an injunction against the unlicensed operator. The best-known injunctions of this type are in the field of planning control, where such a remedy is specifically made available by section 27 of the Local Government (Planning and Development) Act 1976.[56] It is a cardinal legal principle that, in general, an injunction may be sought by or on behalf of the Attorney-General, to enforce a statutory obligation, even without explicit authorisation.[57] In this case, however, it

---

Fishing Ltd v. Minister for the Marine (No. 2) [1991] 2 I.R. 93 on which see pp.545–547; *Shanley v. Galway Corporation* [1995] 1 I.R. 396; *Slevin v. Shannon Regional Fisheries Board* [1995] 1 I.R. 460.

    In regard to a public body's obligation, as part of the law of judicial review, not "to take irrelevant factors into account", a particular example which may arise in the present context is that factors relevant to one licence (*e.g.* planning permission) may not be taken into account in deciding whether to issue a different type of licence (*e.g.* a slaughter house licence): see *Doupe v. Limerick Corporation* [1981] I.L.R.M. 456 at 462.

54 But not in prosecutions on indictment. In fact, the function of prosecuting on indictment in respect of all offences (apart from the few, responsibility for which remains with the Attorney General) is vested in the Director of Public Prosecutions: Prosecution of Offences Act 1974, s.3(1); Criminal Justice (Administration) Act 1924, s.9. This is not required by Art. 30, or any other Article, of the Constitution. However, there appears to be a policy that the independent and specifically-established office of the D.P.P. should bear responsibility for all prosecutions on indictment.

55 See, e.g. the comments of Costello J. in *Attorney General v. Paperlink Ltd* [1984] I.L.R.M. 373 at 392 and those of O'Hanlon J. in *Parsons v. Kavanagh* [1990] I.L.R.M. 560 at 567 (where he referred to the unchanged monetary penalties provided by the Road Transport Acts 1932–1933 and with "the fall in the value of money in the meantime, they appear to me at the present time to be somewhat derisory as against possible breaches of the Acts.")

56 As inserted by Local Government (Planning and Development) Act 1992, s. 19(4)(g). As to this, see pp. 240–242. For further examples of a "statutory injunction", see Local Government (Water Pollution) Act 1977, s.11; Waste Management Act 1996, s.57; Central Bank Act 1997, s.74.

57 "Whenever Parliament has enacted a law and given a particular remedy for breach of it, such remedy being in an inferior court, nevertheless, the High Court always has a reserve power to enforce the law so enacted by way of an injunction or other suitable remedy. The High Court has jurisdiction to ensure obedience to the law whenever it is just and convenient to do so," *per* Lord Denning in *Attorney General v. Chaudry* [1971] 1 W.L.R. 1614 at 1624. This statement was quoted with approval by Costello J. in *Attorney General v. Paperlink Ltd* [1984] I.L.R.M. 373. See also, *Attorney General (O'Duffy) v. Appleton* [1907] 1 I.R. 252; *O'Connor v. Williams* [1996] 2 I.L.R.M. 382 and *MMDS Television v. South East Deflector Association Ltd*, unreported, High Court, April 8, 1997.

is a vexed question as to whether a competitor has any remedy against an unlicensed rival in the absence of statutory provisions conferring such a right of objection. Certainly, a competitor has sufficient standing to seek judicial review of the decision actually to grant a licence to the rival where he alleges that the requisite statutory formalities have not been complied with.[58] But what if the situation is the more common one in which there is no licence (or perhaps the licence has been struck down) and yet the business is trading: where the Attorney General does not take action, can a private individual seek an injunction to restrain the activities of an unlicensed rival? The traditional English authorities[59] were to the effect that a licensed operator did not have standing to complain about the activities of an unlicensed rival.

However, in *Parsons v. Kavanagh*,[60] confirmed in *Lovett v. Grogan*[61] (authorities which are reviewed later[62]), it was held that these common law principles must yield, in this jurisdiction, to the constitutional right to earn a livelihood as a result of which a competitor may take such a case. There seems to be no reason in principle not to apply these constitutional authorities to a situation in which the rival trader seeks damages rather than an injunction.[63]

A further type of enforcement procedure may be provided by statute in the form of a "concretising" directive (often called a "notice"). With this technique, the licensing authority must give the offender precise instructions as to how the law (including any conditions attached to a licence) has been broken and what must be done to put matters right. Where such a notice is invoked, if and when its terms have been defied for a specified time period, then an offence is committed.[64]

Finally, the lack of a licence, where one is required, may have various consequences in private law. These consequences may amount to an indirect sanction against the failure to obtain a licence. A well-known example is the principle that a contract in respect of the unlicensed activity may not be enforceable.[65]

Having considered both the licensing and enforcement stages, we may now proceed to identify some more detailed characteristics of licensing legislation.

---

[58] *Irish Permanent Building Society v. Caldwell (No. 2)* [1981] I.L.R.M. 242.

[59] *RCA Corporation v. Pollard* [1983] Ch. 135 at 153. But see, *a contra: Re Island Records* [1978] 3 All E.R. 824 and *Rickless v. United Artists* [1987] 1 All E.R. 679.

[60] [1990] I.L.R.M. 561. Moreover, in *Robinson v. Chariot Inns Ltd* [1986] I.L.R.M. 621 it was held that a competitor has sufficient standing to seek an injunction pursuant to s.27 of the Local Government (Planning and Development) Act 1976 restraining the unauthorised use by a business rival of his property.

[61] [1995] 3 I.R. 132. See also *O'Connor v. Williams* [1996] 2 I.L.R.M. 382 and *MMDS Televisions Ltd v. South East Deflector Association Ltd*, unreported, High Court, April 8, 1997.

[62] See pp. 761–762.

[63] See pp. 819–827.

[64] Again an example is provided by the planning legislation: see enforcement notice and warning notices described at p. 240. For enforcement notices in the context of the Data Protection Act 1988, see p. 257, n.33.

[65] See Cheshire and Fifoot, *Law of Contract* (11th ed.), pp.334–341; *Re Moneylenders Act 1933 and Lynne, Applicants v. Attorney General* 74 I.L.T.R. 96.

2. Characteristics of Licences

(i) A licence is generally personal to the grantee and is not assignable

As a general rule, a licence is personal to the holder, since it was only granted on proof of the applicant's suitability of character, skill, qualifications, etc. This is so even if it is not explicitly stated in the statute (as it is, for example in section 13(1) of the Abattoirs Act 1988 which provides that: "(t)he holder of an abattoir licence shall not transfer the licence to any other person . . .").

Despite the fact that this principle of non-assignability is clear, there are occasional exceptions and indeed the law actually authorises trading in taxi-plates[66] and it appears that taxi-plates are currently being freely traded as if they were commodities. There is, however, a second category of cases where the grant of the licence does not depend on the personal suitability or qualifications of the applicant but instead attaches to the land, business, etc., involved.[67] As we shall see, in this sort of case, the licence or permission may not be severed and sold independently. A grant of planning permission is an example in point, for section 29(5) of the Local Government (Planning and Development) Act 1963 provides that:

> "Where permission to develop land or for the retention of a structure is granted . . . then, except as may otherwise be provided by the permission, the grant of permission *shall enure for the benefit of the land* or structure and of all persons for the time being interested therein . . ."(emphasis added)

The planning permission attaches to the land (which will invariably make the land more valuable) and any subsequent purchaser will take the lands with the benefit of that permission.[68] Indeed, such is the effect of section 29(5) that a planning permission has been judicially described as an "appendage to the title of the property".[69]

There is a third category of cases which combines elements of the first two by requiring both the existence of a licence attaching to the premises and the suitability of the applicant to hold the licence in question. This is the case with the Licensing Acts 1833–1995, which require attestation both as to the suitability of the licensed premises and the applicant before a licence is granted. Again, in the case of applicants seeking a special restaurant licence under Part II of the Intoxicating Liquor Act 1988 (which entitles restaurants to serve intoxicating liquor for consumption by patrons of the restaurant with their meals), even higher standards are required. The applicant must first establish the suitability of the restaurant to the satisfaction of Bord Fáilte: section 8(2) requires that the restaurant must, *inter*

---

66 See below, n.98.
67 Such as registered bulls under s.3(1) of the Control of Bulls for Breeding Act 1985.
68 See, *e.g. Pine Valley Developments Ltd v. Minister for the Environment* [1987] I.R. 23 where the plaintiffs purchased lands with the benefit of development permission for £550,000. The planning permission was ultimately found to be invalid and the plaintiffs sued the Minister for the Environment and Ireland for damages, since the market value of the lands without the permission was far less. However, the action failed for other reasons: see pp. 814–815 and 823–824.
69 *Readymix (Éire) Ltd v. Dublin County Council*, unreported, Supreme Court, July 31, 1974, per Henchy J. at p. 4 of the judgment. The same judge made similar observations in *Pine Valley Developments Ltd v. Minister for the Environment* [1987] I.R. 23 at 42.

alia, be "well equipped, well furnished and provide comfortable seating in the dining area and waiting area" and must also provide "a high standard of catering" and "maintain a high standard of hygiene". Secondly, the applicant must also establish his own personal suitability, since by section 8(1), the Circuit Court may refuse to grant a licence on the grounds of "character, misconduct or unfitness of the applicant" or of the "unfitness or inconvenience of the premises".

As mentioned, where the licence attaches to the land, it cannot be sold independently from the land. This is illustrated by a series of decisions on the Licensing Acts 1833–1995, of which two recent cases may serve as examples. In *Re Sherry-Brennan*[70] a bankrupt publican was the owner of licensed premises in respect of which a judgment mortgage and other charges had been registered in the Land Registry. The premises were sold. However, the Official Assignee claimed to be entitled to retain the notional value of the licence (as reflected in the enhanced purchase price) for the benefit of the unsecured creditors, basing himself on the argument that the licence (as distinct from the premises itself) was not captured by the judgment mortgage and the other charges. Hamilton J. rejected this submission, stating that:

> "As a licence cannot be regarded as a property capable of separation from the licensed premises, I am satisfied that the licence is subject to the same charges and incumbrances as the property and hold that it is incapable of passing to the Official Assignee in priority to incumbrances registered against the property to which it is attached."[71]

And in *Macklin v. Graecen & Co.*,[72] a specific performance action, the Supreme Court held that a purported sale of a seven-day publican's licence, in isolation from the premises, was void and inoperative. Griffin J. said:

> "For almost 100 years it has been accepted that a licence to sell intoxicating liquor is inalienable and must be attached to the premises. The law on the matter has been stated succinctly by O'Connor's, *Irish Justice of the Peace* as follows: – "The doctor cannot sell his degree, because it is attached to himself; on the other hand, the holder of a licence cannot sell the licence to any other person, unless such other person also buys the premises. The licence *per se* is inalienable. It must always, so long as it exists at all, remain attached to the premises."[73]

---

[70] [1979] I.L.R.M. 113.
[71] *Ibid.* at 117. Hamilton J.'s reasoning was affirmed on appeal by the Supreme Court.
[72] [1983] I.R. 61.
[73] *Ibid.* at 66. The quotation was from O'Connor's *Irish Justice of the Peace* (1915), Vol. 2, p. 368. See also, *Brennan v. Dorney* (1887) 21 L.R.Ir. 353. In some cases, however, the legislation may explicitly permit the transfer of the licence to another authorised person (see, *e.g.* Pawnbroking Act 1964, s.9(1) (as inserted by the Consumer Credit Act 1995, s.153) (transfer of pawnbroking licence subject to consent of Director of Consumer Affairs); Environmental Protection Agency Act 1992, s.91 (transfer of integrated pollution licence permitted provided notice given to the Environmental Protection Agency). However, where the licensing régime involves a trade or business, the governing statute will usually permit other persons (such as close relatives or personal representatives) to carry on the business of the licence-holder on a temporary basis in circumstances such as illness, incapacity, death, etc. So the Abattoirs Act 1988, s.13(2) provides that:

This principle of non-assignability is reflected in the latest licensing system involving land, namely, milk reference quantities or quotas. As a general rule, it may be said that a milk quota is land-based[74] and that it attaches to the land. Article 7 of Council Regulation 857/84, as inserted by Article 4 of Council Regulation 590/85, provides that:

> "Where a [farm] holding is sold, leased or transferred by inheritance, all or part of the corresponding reference quantity shall be transferred to the purchaser, tenant or heir."

While Article 7 states the general rule there are some limited exceptions which permit the sale, or leasing, of milk quotas separately from the land itself.

(ii) A licence will generally only be granted for a limited duration

Since it is of the essence of licensing statutes that they are intended to provide and maintain essential standards regulating the conduct of trade, business or activity in the public interest, it follows that, in the absence of an express statutory provision to the contrary, a licence will generally be deemed to have been granted for a limited duration. Moreover, simply because the licensing authority has seen fit to grant a licence in the past, it does not follow that the licensee will be taken to have a right to engage in the regulated activity in perpetuity.

Some statutes take care to state explicitly that the licence granted is not of indefinite duration. Thus section 3(5) of the Radio and Television Act 1988 provides that a sound broadcasting licence:

> "shall be valid only for such period of time as a sound broadcasting contract between the [Independent Radio and Television] Commission is extant."[75]

But what of the situation where the licensing provisions are not explicit on this point? This was considered in *Dublin Corporation v. Judge O'Hanrahan*,[76] where a gaming licence had been granted by the respondent, in face of a statutory resolution passed by the applicants rescinding the licensing provisions of the Gaming and Lotteries Act 1956. The notice party sought to justify the decision on the basis that, once a gaming licence had been granted, it attached to the property in perpetuity and that the effect of the rescission resolution was simply to prevent the grant of new licences. Johnson J. agreed that there was nothing in the 1956 Act which expressly declared that the certificate in question was an annual certificate, but said that it was implicit in the statutory framework that a licence subsisted from year to

---

"Where the holder of an abattoir licence dies, the licence shall continue in full force and effect for the benefit of the licence holder's personal representative, or, as the case may be, his spouse or any other member of his family, for the period of four months, or for the period then unexpired of the term of the licence, whichever is the longer, after the death of the licence holder and shall then expire."

74 *Lawlor v. Minister for Agriculture* [1990] 1 I.R. 356. See Geoghegan, "The Superlevy, Sales, Lease and Clawbacks" and Laffoy, "Milk Quotas as Security for Loans" in Robinson (ed.), *Milk Quotas: Law and Practice* (Irish Centre for European Law, 1989), pp. 21 and 27 respectively.

75 See also, *e.g.* Casual Trading Act 1995, s.4(8) (casual trading licence to last for a maximum of 12 months, unless previously revoked).

76 [1988] I.R. 121. This view was confirmed by Griffin J. in *Re Camillo's Application* [1988] I.R. 104.

year. Consequently the notice party's annual licence had lapsed and, because of the resolution, they were unable to apply for a new one. It would seem, therefore, that where the parent Act is not explicit on the question, the duration of the licence must be deduced from the surrounding statutory background.

(iii) Registration

It is noteworthy, that although the use of different nomenclature is not, of itself, decisive[77] where the Oireachtas uses the word "registration" (as opposed to "licence"), it generally intends that the entry on the register should be effected automatically (subject always to a power of amendment or revocation or erasure) and, often, should be indefinite. In this sense, registration is an act of recording which is required of persons carrying out certain types of activity, by some scheme of public administration, and which may be permitted as a matter of right, provided that certain (often formal) conditions are satisfied.[78]

The object of registration is often to facilitate monitoring and the legislation generally provides that the register is open to the public for inspection without a fee.[79] The expression, "registration", is usually employed by the legislation governing the professions and connotes an indefinite permission to practise the profession in question. One such example is provided by section 27(2) of the Medical Practitioners Act 1978 which provides that eligible persons:

> "shall . . . on making application in the form and manner determined by the [Medical] Council and on payment of the appropriate fee, be registered in the register."

This, of course, is without prejudice to a possible refusal to register the applicant on the grounds of unfitness to practise. Nevertheless, subject to these disciplinary provisions, an entry in the register is intended to be of indefinite duration and, indeed, provision is made for the practitioner to apply to have his name removed from the register; and also for the Registrar to erase the name of a practitioner in the case of death. Similar provisions are contained in the Veterinary Surgeons Act 1931 and

---

[77] However, the term "registration" may also be used as a synonym for licensing: see s.10(3) and (4) of the Building Societies Act 1989; s.17(2) and (3) of the Data Protection Act 1988; and s.4 of the Health (Nursing Homes) Act 1990 and Part III of the Tourist Traffic Act 1939, as amended by the Tourist Traffic Act 1995.

[78] See, *e.g.* Registration of Potato Growers and Potato Packers Act 1984; Control of Bulls for Breeding Act 1985, and Control of Dogs Act 1980–1986. In exceptional cases, the onus of compiling the register is put on the public authority rather than the person registered: see, for example, Local Government (Multi-Storey Buildings) Act 1988, s.2(1).

[79] For some diverse examples, see, *e.g.* Solicitors Act 1954, s.9(2) (as inserted by Solicitors (Amendment) Act 1994, s.65, roll of solicitors "available for public inspection during office hours without payment"); Local Government (Planning and Development) Act 1963, s.8 (register of planning permission); Local Government (Water Pollution) Act 1977, s.9 (register of licences granted); Video Recordings Act 1989, s.14 (register of certificated video works); and Electoral Act 1992, Second Schedule, Art.14(1) (electoral register); Casual Trading Act 1995, s.13 (register of casual trading licences). Occasionally, an inspection fee is prescribed, see, *e.g.* s.7(2) of the Insurance Act 1989 (which provides that the fee for inspection of the register under section 21 of the Insurance Act 1936 is not to exceed £10, unless the Minister for Enterprise and Employment and the Minister for Finance otherwise direct); Control of Horses Act 1996, s.11(2).

the 1978 Act, itself, has served as a model for other regulatory legislation, such as the Nurses Act 1985 and the Dentists Act 1978.

The scheme of the Solicitors Acts 1954–1994 is somewhat different in that each solicitor already on the "roll of solicitors" (the equivalent of registration) must apply annually for a practising certificate.[80] Although section 61 of the 1994 Act empowers the Law Society to refuse to renew the practising certificate for what are essentially disciplinary reasons, nevertheless the entry on the roll (again subject to the disciplinary provisions of the legislation concerning refusals) lasts indefinitely and the necessity to obtain annually a practising certificate is little more than a revenue-raising mechanism for the Society.

(iv) *The refusal or revocation of a licence must be in the public interest and not a punishment*

The refusal or revocation of a licence will generally only be justified where this is established as being itself directly in the public interest and not a punitive measure. A good example of the application of this principle may be found in *Re Crowley*,[81] where the applicant solicitor had been refused a practising certificate by the Law Society. It appeared that the applicant had engaged in "touting" for business on one occasion in the past and this was relied on by the Society as justification for the refusal of the certificate. Kingsmill Moore J. held that, save in cases where the solicitor is actually being charged with a disciplinary offence, the refusal or withdrawal of a certificate could only be justified where this was in the public interest. The judge went on to admit that there might be circumstances where the public interest required that a solicitor should be restrained from practising; but he added that: "[s]uch action is only justified as a necessary precaution against the likelihood of future misdoing reasonably to be inferred from past conduct."[82]

Again, in *Ingle v. O'Brien*[83] Pringle J. held that simply because the applicant taxi-driver was convicted in the District Court of carriage offences did not entitle the licensing authorities, *ipso facto*, to revoke the applicant's licence.

In other cases, the licensing legislation itself will stipulate the circumstances in which the licence will automatically lapse. Thus, section 28(1) of the Intoxicating Liquor Act 1927 provides that upon the recording of a third licensing conviction on a licence, the licence is thereby automatically forfeited. Sections 2 and 3(3) of the Licensing (Combating Drug Abuse) Act 1997 are in similar terms – even if more drastic in their effect. They provide that:

---

[80] Solicitors Act 1954, s.48, as inserted by Solicitors (Amendment) Act 1994, s.55(2).

[81] [1964] I.R. 106. See also, *Balkan Tours Ltd v. Minister for Communications* [1988] I.L.R.M. 101.

[82] *Ibid.* at 129. This approach also finds support in the judgment of Walsh J. for the Supreme Court, in a different context, in *Conroy v. Attorney General* [1965] I.R. 411 where it was held that the disqualification of a driver for drunk driving, coupled with the loss of a driving licence, was not, as such, a punishment. As Walsh J. explained (at 441):

> "One must not lose sight, however, of the real nature of the disqualification order which is that it is essentially a finding of unfitness of the person concerned to hold a driving licence."

[83] (1975) 109 I.L.T.R. 7.

"Any person who has been convicted of a drug trafficking offence shall be disqualified for ever from holding any intoxicating liquor licence, any public dancing licence or any public music and singing licence . . ."[84]

(v) The terms of the licence must be construed by reference to objective standards

Since a licence is a public document, the governing legislation often provides that the licence is open to public inspection or, even, that the terms of the licence must be publicly displayed.[85] A corollary of this is that the terms of the licence must be objectively construed and any private arrangements or understandings as between the licensing authority and the licence holder are not admissible. This is illustrated by *Readymix (Eire) Ltd v. Dublin County Council*,[86] where it was argued that the planning permission granted by the local authority should be construed as having merely the meaning or effect given to it by the planning officials and agreed to by the developer. The Supreme Court rejected that submission, with Henchy J. observing:

> "The Act does not in terms make the register the conclusive or exclusive evidence record of the nature and extent of a permission, but the scheme of the Act indicates that anybody who acts on the basis of the correctness of the particulars in the register is entitled to do so. Where the permission recorded in the register is self-contained, it will not be permissible to go outside it in construing it. But where the permission incorporates other documents, it is the combined effect of the permission and such documents which must be looked at in determining the proper scope of the permission . . . Since the permission notified to an applicant and entered in the register is a public document, it must be construed objectively as such, and not in the light of subjective considerations special to the applicant or those responsible for the grant of permission."[87]

In sum, a licence is a self-contained public document and must be construed as such.

3. Licences as Property Rights and Changes in Licensing Régimes

In some contexts and by some judges, licences have been regarded as property rights or, at least, rights to earn a livelihood.[88] Consequently, protection by way of licensing

---

[84] See also s.17(3) of the 1997 Act.
[85] See, *e.g.* Medical Practitioners Act 1978, s.26(4) ("Every person whose name is entered in the register shall cause [his] certificate to be displayed at the place where he conducts the practice of medicine at all times during which his registration continues and at no other time."); Casual Trading Act 1995, s.5(1) (obligation on licensee to display casual trading licence).
[86] Unreported, Supreme Court, July 31, 1974.
[87] *Ibid.* at p. 4 of the judgment. See also, *Jack Barrett Builders Ltd v. Dublin County Council*, unreported, Supreme Court, July 28, 1983; *McD Management Services Ltd v. Kildare County Council* [1995] 2 I.L.R.M. 532 and *McMahon v. Dublin Corporation* [1997] 1 I.L.R.M. 227 and Galligan, *Irish Planning Law and Procedure* (1997), pp. 224–229.
[88] See, *e.g. East Donegal Co-operatives Ltd v. Attorney General* [1970] I.R. 317 and *Moran v. Attorney General* [1976] I.R. 400 and see p. 594.

has been provided from the arbitrary refusal or revocation of that right. Thus the applicant is entitled to a fair hearing before his application is refused or revoked,[89] he is entitled to reasons if the licence is refused[90] and, indeed, he may have acquired a legitimate expectation that the licence will be renewed.

On the other hand, a licence has been regarded as, in the words of Carroll J. in *The State (Pheasantry Ltd) v. Donnelly*,[91] merely "a privilege granted by statute and regulated for the public good".[92] The reason why this distinction matters is that the right of the Oireachtas to regulate in the public interest area is said to be greater in the case of privileges, than in that of property rights. In the *Pheasantry* case, the applicants challenged the constitutionality of section 28 of the Intoxicating Liquor Act 1927 whereby the licence attaching to licensed premises is forfeited when three convictions are duly recorded and indorsed on the licence. Carroll J. agreed that the property rights protected by Article 40.3 included the licence in conjunction with the premises, but she could not agree that the forfeiture provisions were, thereby, unconstitutional:

> "The licence is a privilege granted by statute and regulated for the public good. It is, *ab initio*, subject to various conditions, one of which is the inherent possibility of automatic forfeiture under section 28. If the conditions necessary for statutory forfeiture are fulfilled, this is brought about through the licensee's own default. There is no constitutional right to a liquor licence or a renewal thereof. There are only such rights as are given by statute subject to limitations and conditions prescribed by statute."[93]

This line of thought has attracted a judicial consensus in a number of cases[94] in the licensing field.

The logical consequence of this line of judicial reasoning is that the Oireachtas could constitutionally terminate a particular licensing system where this was established to be in the public interest and prohibit the previously licensed activity without payment of any compensation to the existing licence holders, even though such licensees might have invested heavily in that particular licensed business. It was probably a consequence of this, that when Dublin Corporation rescinded the operation of Part III of the Gaming and Lotteries Act 1956 in 1986 (thus effectively closing all existing gaming halls), the former licence holders refrained from making any claim for compensation.

A related issue arose in *Hempenstall v. Minister for the Environment*[95] when the Minister made regulations which had the effect of removing a moratorium (which the Minister had imposed earlier) on the granting of new taxi licences. These regulations, it was claimed by the applicants, who were licensed taxi owners, constituted

---

[89] *International Fishing Vessel Ltd v. Minister for Marine* [1989] I.R. 149.
[90] *The State (Pheasantry Ltd) v. District Justice Donnelly* [1982] I.L.R.M. 512.
[91] *Ibid.* at 516.
[92] *Ibid.*
[93] *Ibid.*
[94] See *Hand v. Dublin Corporation* [1989] I.R. 26; *Permanent Motorists Protection Society Ltd v. Attorney-General* [1983] I.R. 339; *Cafolla v. Attorney-General* [1985] I.R. 486.
[95] [1993] I.L.R.M. 318. On licensing and the constitutional right to a livelihood see, *Shanley v. Galway Corporation* [1995] 1 I.R. 396 at 404–406.

an unjust attack on their property rights in that it diminished the capital value of the "taxi-plates" (a phrase explained below). Even on the assumption that the factual basis was correct, the claim failed. It was accepted, in the first place, that the applicants' taxi licences were constitutionally protected property rights. However, Costello J. (as he then was) held that there had been no unjust attack. Costello J. stated:

> "Property rights arising in licences created by law (enacted or delegated) are subject to the conditions created by law and to an implied condition that the law may change those conditions
>
> . . .
>
> a change in the law which has the effect of reducing property values cannot in itself amount to an infringement of constitutionally protected property rights. There are many instances in which legal changes may adversely affect property values (for example, new zoning regulations in the planning code and new legislation relating to the issue of intoxicating liquor licences) and such changes cannot be impugned as being constitutionally invalid unless some invalidity can be shown to exist apart from the resulting property value diminution. In this case no such invalidity can be shown. The object of the exercise of the ministerial regulatory power is to benefit users of small public service vehicles. It has not been shown or even suggested that the minister acted otherwise than in accordance with his statutory powers. Once he did so then it cannot be said that he has 'attacked' the applicants' property rights thereby because a diminution in the value may have resulted."[96]

Another field in which the constitutional nature of licences might be significant is that of the allocation of licences. In most fields of licensing, the situation as it operates on the ground is that provided an existing licence-holder's conduct does not go seriously awry, then – whatever the legal theory about a fresh licence having to be granted – "his licence" will be renewed, more or less automatically. And from the perspective of a new-comer wishing to break into the field, unless new licences are being issued, the only way to do so will be to purchase the property which is

---

[96] *Ibid.* at 324–325. This approach may also be found in the jurisprudence of the Court of Justice. It is true that Advocate General Jacobs once famously observed of milk quotas (Case 5/88, *Wachauf v. Bundesamt für Ernahärung* [1991] 1 C.M.L.R. 343 at 342) that:

> "[The argument has been advanced] that a quota is nothing more than an instrument of market management and cannot be considered as a kind of intangible asset in which property rights can arise . . . While this might correspond to the intention of the Community legislation, it does not reflect economic reality . . . In a market which is effectively ossified by the introduction of quotas, such a 'licence' is bound to acquire an economic value."

However, the Court of Justice has consistently rejected the "milk quota as property right" argument, most notably in the Irish development farmers case, Case C–63/91 *Duff v. Minister for Agriculture* [1996] E.C.R. I–535. Here the Court rejected the argument that, even in a case with strong facts (see pp. 843–844), the failure to allot an extra quota infringed fundamental principles of law, such as respect for property rights and legitimate expectations, saying (at para. 30):

> "[The milk quota] rules, which meet the general aim of correcting surpluses existing on the market for milk, do not affect the actual substance of the right to property and the freedom to pursue a trade or profession. Even though they authorise the national authorities to exercise their discretion in such a way that producers who have adopted development plans may ultimately be prevented from increasing their production, they nevertheless enable those producers to continue to produce milk at the level of their production in 1983."

necessary for the occupation, which will often bring with it, as part of the transaction, the necessary licence. A well-known example is the purchase of a public-house which will usually carry with it the necessary licence and the reasonable assumption that, at the end of the year, it will be renewed in favour of the purchaser. Again trading in taxi-plates is actually authorised by law:

> "provided only that the Commissioner is satisfied that he would grant a licence to the new owner if an application for the grant of a licence under Article 6 [which lays down conditions for the grant of a licence *ab initio*] were made to him at that time by the new owner."[97]

This is a far cry from a world in which licences were awarded on a competitive basis, without reference to whether an applicant already had an established business or was a newcomer; but simply by reference to the criterion of which applicant would give a better or more economic service to the public. Against this background, three types of query arise:

(i) Could an existing licence-holder complain if his licence were not renewed but instead re-allocated to a newcomer on the basis of superior merit?

Here one feels instinctively that an Irish judge would find some way of giving an affirmative answer to such a novel question. In fact there may be a legitimate route by which to reach this result. In the first place, one should appreciate that the argument in favour of there being a freedom to effect such a change is afforded a secure foothold in the opening sentence in the passage from *Hempenstall*, quoted above. ("Property rights arising in licences . . . are subject to the conditions created by law . . .") Does it not follow (it might be argued) that if a licence is limited in duration to one year, that no property right enures after this year has expired? The countervailing and, it is submitted, stronger argument is as follows. There may be doubt (in view of the one year limit of the licence) as to whether there is here a classic legitimate expectation[98] that the licence should be renewed, in the absence of some positive misconduct by the licence-holder. Nevertheless such is the necessary investment by a licence-holder in (some or all of the following): premises; staff; experience; qualifications, etc., that one would expect that some expectation or property right would be discerned.[99]

In addition, despite what was said earlier, the licence-holder might well be able in these extreme circumstances to rely upon the constitutional property right. (In

---

97 Road Traffic (Public Service Vehicles) (Licensing) Regulations (S.I. No. 292 of 1978). In 1997 the Minister for Enterprise and Employment referred the question of whether the number of taxi-plates ought to be increased to the Competition Authority.

98 It is notable that in *Hempenstall* the figure of £44,000 for the market value of taxi licences in Dublin was quoted, without any observation being made to the fact this figure pre-supposed that the purchaser could expect that the licence would, in effect, last for several years and then be sold on. One had the feeling that this observation went without saying, as it does in popular discourse.

99 The uncertainty and unsatisfactory nature of the law in this area is paralleled elsewhere, *e.g.* if I have an annual contract with an insurance company, can the insurance company refuse to re-new it, perhaps because they wish to deny me the no-claims bonus?

contrast with the situation in *Hempenstall*, the interference by the licensing authority would not be with the surrounding circumstances, which affected the value of the right; but rather would amount to a direct interference with the right to carry on the activity.)

(ii) Ought the number of licences to be increased if the public interest requires it?

This is obviously a contention which an applicant who wished to break into a particular line of business might wish to advance. In *Hempenstall*, it was held that it was open to the licensing agency to increase the number of taxi-plates. But does the law go further and actually require this to be done in an appropriate case? In principle there seems to be no reason why the usual controls, by way of judicial review, should not be applied to the determination of the number of licences as they do to other functions. These would require the agency fixing numbers to take into account relevant factors, including the interests of: existing licence-holders; would-be licence holders; consumers and (perhaps in an appropriate case) environmentalists. The various interests would have to be balanced against each other reasonably. The public interest in competition would have to be given due weight. All this might militate in favour of an increase, in appropriate circumstances. However one should sound a note of caution: this function is very much at the policy end of the policy-administration spectrum, depending as it does on a complex of social, commercial, economic, political, etc., factors. Accordingly, it is only in an extreme case that a judge would be prepared to intervene in this field.

(iii) Can the number of licences be restricted if the public interest requires it?

In the first place, one should distinguish the unusual cases where the governing legislation explicitly allows the licensing authority to impose a restriction on the number of licences to be granted – as does, for instance, section 6(1) of the Radio and Television Act 1988.[100] A further striking example is provided by Article 5(1) of the Health (Community Pharmacy Contractor Agreement) Regulations 1996[101] which provides that no new community pharmacy contractor agreement may be made unless the chief executive of the relevant health board is of the opinion, *inter alia*, that:

> "there is a definite public health need for the supply of community pharmacy services in the particular catchment area to which the application relates."

An elaborate definition of the phrase "definite public health need" is given by Article 2(1) by reference to existing pharmacy outlets so as to ensure, *inter alia*, that the new application:

---

[100] At least as this provision was interpreted by Murphy J. in *Dublin and County Broadcasting Ltd v. Independent Radio and Television Commission*, unreported, High Court, May 12, 1989. See, to similar effect, Intoxicating Liquor Act 1960, s.14 *Re Matter of Thank God it's Friday Ltd* [1990] I.L.R.M. 228.

[101] S.I. No. 152 of 1996.

"will not have an adverse impact on the viability of [an] existing community in their respective catchment areas to the extent that it will affect the quality of pharmacy services being provided by them."

Given that as a matter of practical necessity most pharmacies could not easily operate without the benefit of such a health board contract,[102] the effect of these Regulations is to introduce what amounts to quantative regulatory restrictions via a licensing scheme on the number of new pharmacies which may be opened.

However, apart from such exceptional cases, it might be expected that, following the general precepts just mentioned in the context of increasing licences – reasonableness, taking relevant factors into account etc. – there might be a valid restriction on the number of licences granted in appropriate cases. As we shall see, Budd J. took this view in the High Court in *O'Neill v. Minister for Agriculture & Food*,[103] but the Supreme Court disagreed. The tenor of other decisions[104] – such as, e.g., the judgments of Keane and Murphy JJ. in *O'Neill* – has been that statutory licensing schemes should not be used to restrict numbers, but only to control qualification or quality standards.

In the first of these cases, *East Donegal Co-operative Livestock Mart Ltd v. Attorney General*,[105] the plaintiffs attacked the licensing provisions of the Livestock Marts Act 1967 on the ground, *inter alia*, that they would enable the Minister to use his discretion to limit the number of marts in operation. This submission was rejected by Walsh J., who said that the object of the Act was directed to:

"The proper conduct of the business concerned, the standard of hygiene and veterinary standards in relation to such places and to provision of adequate and suitable accommodation and facilities for such auctions . . . Nowhere in the Act is there anything to indicate that one of the purposes of the Act is to limit or otherwise regulate the number of auction marts as distinct from regulating the way in which business is conducted in auction marts. In the absence of any such indication in the Act, the Minister is not authorised by the Act to limit the number of businesses . . ."[106]

In *Re Application of Power Supermarkets Ltd*,[107] the Supreme Court addressed the question of whether the Circuit Court could take the economic consequences to other publicans in the area into account in deciding whether or not to grant an off-licence to a major supermarket chain. Walsh J. said that this was an irrelevant factor in the exercise of the judge's discretion:

"The object of the [Intoxicating Liquor Acts] was to safeguard the public interest by preventing a proliferation of licensed premises and not to shelter

---

[102] The contracts in question are contracts with the health boards for the supply of medicines and reimbursements in respect of medicines supplied under the general medical card system.

[103] Unreported, High Court, July 5, 1995; [1997] 2 I.L.R.M. 435 (Sup.Ct).

[104] There seems to be some uncertainty on this point in England: see Wade and Forsyth, *Administrative Law*, pp. 362–363.

[105] [1970] I.R. 317.

[106] *Ibid.* at 342–343.

[107] [1988] I.R. 206.

existing publicans from competition. To decide that a licence ought not to be granted because the competition it would offer to existing licences would be economically disadvantageous to the holders of those licences is not a ground which is contemplated by the code and therefore is not one which can be said to be an exercise of judicial discretion."[108]

It is notable that, in contrast to *East Donegal*, while rejecting the argument founded on the economic consequences to other publicans, Walsh J. did accept (in the context of the Intoxicating Liquor Acts) the possibility of a restriction upon the number of licences provided that it was in "the public interest".[109] In short, this was a rather different view from that given in *East Donegal*, albeit one either expressly or necessarily contemplated by such legislation.

It might have been thought that, in certain circumstances, there could be a causative link between preventing excessive competition and maintaining adequate standards so that the use of licensing to prevent competition might be regarded as acceptable on the ground that it tended to maintain standards. This appears to have been the line of thought adopted by Budd J. in *O'Neill v. Minister for Agriculture*.[110] The ostensible issue in the case was the Minister's refusal to grant the applicant a licence (under the Livestock (Artificial Insemination) Act 1947 and regulations made thereunder) to run a course to train personnel in the artificial insemination of cattle. However, as Budd J. remarked:

". . . the reality behind the case was a challenge to the present system of state-authorised regional monopolies in that the State has authorised the granting of the exclusive right to provide an A.I. field service in each region to one of eight or nine regional monopolists . . . [It is argued by the applicant that] Departmental policy, which places geographical and quantitative restrictions on the number of licences granted [is] firstly, contrary to Irish law and, secondly, contrary to EC competition law."[111]

---

[108] *Ibid.* at 210–211.
[109] In *Re Connellan's Application*, unreported, High Court, October 19, 1973 an objection was raised to the grant of a declaration that the applicant's premises was fit to be licensed under s.15 of the Intoxicating Liquor Act 1960. The objectors intended to build a community centre immediately adjacent to the applicant's premises and the centre would only be economically viable if it had the sole right to sell intoxicating liquor in that area. However, Finlay J. said that this consideration was not one which could properly be taken into account by the Circuit Court:
"No matter how much I might, as a matter of social policy, favour the provision of a community centre and favour a situation in which it could from a monopoly sale of intoxicating liquor in its own area fund itself in an economic and profitable way, I do not consider that the licensing code gives me a discretion to implement that view." (At p. 7 of the judgment).
The judge went on to observe that as the objects of the Licensing Acts were to restrict the proliferation of public houses and to increase standards generally, it was in these respects essentially "a negative or restrictive code" and could not properly be construed as "a positive weapon of social policy". Thus, one should remark that here the facts were more extreme than in *East Donegal* in that the social policy which the licensing agency sought to serve was not even the efficient operation of licensed premises (a policy which might be contemplated in the 1960 Act), but rather an altogether extraneous policy.
[110] Unreported, High Court, Budd J., July 5, 1995.
[111] At p. 12 of the judgment.

Irish Law

As regards Irish law (the principles of EC Competition law will be considered later.),[112] Budd J. recounted the *East Donegal* and *MacGabhann*[113] cases from each of which he was to diverge. All he said by way of distinguishing these authorities was to refer to "the need for a close scrutiny of the content and actual wording of the statute and regulations under analysis."[114] He could perhaps have added that his judgment was the first Irish case in which the present point had received elaborate analysis. In any event, Budd J. concluded:

> "After careful scrutiny it seems to me that the evolution of the regime of exclusive contiguous areas of operation divided up between the licensees was done with the agreement of the farming community through the involvement of the co-ops owned by the farmers and was a reasonable way of achieving the Minister's objectives of ensuring a quality A.I. service throughout the land, supported by progeny testing and the keeping of appropriate records. Section 7(2) of the 1947 Act empowered the Minister to attach conditions as he thinks fit to a licence. The conditions attached with regard to a defined operative area are *intra vires* the Minister."[115]

It is instructive to compare *O'Neill* with another roughly contemporaneous High Court case, *Carrigaline Community Television Broadcasting Company Ltd v. The Minister for Transport, Energy and Communications*[116] (neither case being referred to in the other). Whilst the outcomes of the two cases were different, it may be that they can be distinguished. In *Carrigaline*, too, the licensing agency had refused the plaintiff a licence on the broad ground of protecting the quality of the service provided by existing licence-holders. Specifically, in *Carrigaline*, the Minister was pursuing a policy of refusing licences (under the Wireless Telegraphy Act 1926, section 5, providing for a licence to keep wireless telegraphy apparatus) to those, like the plaintiff, who were transmitting their signals in the VHF waveband because (the Minister claimed) to do so would risk overcrowding that waveband. Instead, the Minister was confining licences to persons who owned a Microwave Multipoint Distribution System (MMDS). Plainly there are two inter-related points here. As to the first, the Court held – apparently as a finding of fact – that "the evidence establishes overwhelmingly that the provision of four national programmes services

---

[112] See pp. 334–336.

[113] *MacGabhann v. The Incorporated Law Society of Ireland* [1989] I.L.R.M. 854 on which see p. 640.

[114] At p. 27. This was the main ground on which *MacGabhann* was distinguished. See, to like effect on *East Donegal*, p. 25.

[115] At p. 90. It is also significant for future cases that Budd J. referred with approval to a letter written to the applicant, on behalf of the Minister (at p. 70 of the judgment):
"... the Department does not consider that the operation of AI field services on the lines envisaged in your proposal would be in the interests of the quality of the national AI service. Such enterprises could be reasonably expected to target the more lucrative sections of the market whereas, under the present system, AI organisations are required to service all herdowners in their operational areas on a year-round basis whether they are small breeders or breeders in remote areas (*e.g.* islands) which would be considered uneconomic to service in a free-for-all market."

[116] [1997] 1 I.L.R.M. 241.

in the VHF band does not represent the optimum use of that band". And as to the second point, which is the ground on which the case may be compared with *O'Neill*, Keane J. stated:

> ". . . the Minister was undoubtedly entitled to adopt the policy of protecting and encouraging the development of the cable [MMDS] infrastructure which had been recommended by the Downes Committee. There was, however, no evidence whatever that the existence of the plaintiff's rebroadcasting system had affected to even the slightest degree the economic viability of the cable system operated in Cork City by Cork Communications for the past thirteen years. There was no evidence that the signals transmitted by the plaintiffs were received to any significant extent in Cork city and the evidence was that they discouraged any attempt to transmit them to that area.
>
> . . . there was also no evidence whatever to justify the suggestion that the granting of the MMDS licences on a basis which would exclude any other form of retransmission would encourage the extension of the cable system to other towns and villages thereby facilitating, as it was claimed, the establishment of the 'information highway'."[117]

The significant point is that here, as Budd J. had held in *O'Neill* (and in contrast to *East Donegal*) it was accepted by Keane J. that a policy of protecting one category of licence-holder (at the expense of another) could be pursued provided (it is probably legitimate to assume) that the selection of the favoured group depended upon some factor related to the public interest.

However, the Supreme Court in *O'Neill* took a significantly different line from that of the High Court in *O'Neill* or *Carrigaline*. The applicant succeeded and the High Court was reversed, on a number of points, of which the one of relevance here was expressed as being whether the Minister, in granting licences was entitled to "adopt a particular policy". In answering this question in *O'Neill*, Keane J. commenced by quoting the following from his own judgment in the High Court in *Carrigaline*:

> "It is clear that, in the case of at least some licensing regimes, questions of policy cannot play any part. This would be the case, for example, with television reception licences and driving licences, provided that in the latter case, certain conditions of eligibility are met. At the other extreme, questions of policy must obviously affect the granting or refusal of planning permission and indeed in that area the authority is obliged by statute to adopt a specific set of policy objectives in the form of a development plan.
>
> The licensing regime established under the 1926 Act as amended by subsequent legislation belongs to an intermediate category. In the case of this and similar licensing regimes, the adoption by the licensing authority of a policy could have the advantage of ensuring some degree of consistency in the operation of the regime, thus making less likely decisions that might be categorised as capricious or arbitrary. But it is also clear that inflexible

---

[117]   *Ibid.* at 297.

adherence to such a policy may result in a countervailing injustice. The case law in both this jurisdiction and the United Kingdom illustrates the difficulties involved in balancing these competing values."[118]

Unfortunately this passage does not directly address the question of whether the licensing may, as a general matter, adopt a particular policy, for instance, as regards limiting the number of licences. In the first place, to refer to the first paragraph of the quotation, probably the reason why the licensing régimes differ from others is their statutory language and their context. Secondly, the burden of the second paragraph is the well-known precept against fettering a discretionary power by a policy rule.[119] However, later on in the judgment in *O'Neill*, Keane J. quoted the Department of Agriculture's policy justification for the adoption of the exclusivity scheme:

"to ensure a comprehensive quality service . . . to all farmers; also veterinary controls in respect of animal welfare, health and good conception rates and the provision of high genetic merit semen . . . to all breeders with large and small herds. The regional monopoly system [is] . . . a mechanism to ensure that all farmers would have access to an available service."[120]

Keane J.'s comment on this was:

"There is no indication in the 1947 Act that these undoubtedly laudable objectives constituted the underlying policy of the Act, with two qualifications. The evidence in the High Court established, and common sense would have in any event suggested that it was the case, that the major reason for introducing statutory controls over AI in 1947 was because of the desirability of controlling disease and improving the general quality of the national herd. The system of control spelled out is negative rather than positive: the practice of AI may only be carried on where a licence is granted. There is nothing in the Act to suggest that the Oireachtas intended that, for the reasons given in the passage from the High Court judgment already cited, the Minister should divide the country into a number of regions, in respect of which only one licence was to be granted."[121]

---

[118] [1997] 1 I.L.R.M. 241 at 284. In *Carrigaline* itself, in addressing the general question posed in the passage, Keane J. stated (at 286):

"In the present case, the minister, while under a duty to consider all applications for licences made to him in a fair and impartial manner, was also entitled, and indeed obliged to have regard to what might be described as certain policy considerations. First, he was obliged to have regard to the principles of good frequency management . . . Secondly, he was bound to ensure that the objectives enshrined in other legislation, including the reception on a national basis of the two existing RTÉ programme services and of the contemplated TV3 and Telefís Na Gaeilge programme services, were not frustrated by the exercise of his licensing functions. Thirdly, he was obliged to have regard to the obligations of the State under international conventions . . .".

[119] See pp. 668–675.
[120] [1997] 2 I.L.R.M. 435 at 441.
[121] [1997] 2 I.L.R.M. 435 at 441–442. Notice that Keane J. later remarked:

"The evidence in the High Court established overwhelmingly that some scheme of this nature was essential if the practice of artificial insemination was to be both controlled and facilitated in the interests of an industry of paramount importance in the Irish economy. This court is solely concerned, however, with the legality of the scheme."

The other judge to give a written judgment, Murphy J., said something similar, fortifying it with a reference to "the manner in which [the licensing scheme] affects the property or other constitutional rights of the citizens" and a substantial nod in the direction of Article 15.2.1º.[122]

The only general inference to be drawn from this divergent case law is, perhaps, that the courts will be slow to infer from the general words in a statute a licensing system which can be used to control numbers or, at any rate, an exclusive régime (which was in issue in both *O'Neill* and *Carrigaline*). It may be significant that in *O'Neill* Murphy J. condemned the scheme as *ultra vires* on the basis that it was "so radical in qualifying limited number of persons and disqualifying all others who may be equally competent from engaging in business." This passage carries the hint that had the facts been otherwise, so that the Minister had abandoned the exclusivity scheme, but had nonetheless had regard to the adequacy of demand for artificial insemination service by imposing a variable quota a different outcome might just have been possible, especially if a clear nexus between the quota of licences granted and the quality of service could have been demonstrated. This was certainly the view of Carroll J. in *Navan Tanker Services Ltd v. Meath County Council*[123] where she held that a local authority could have regarded to the adequacy of demand and impose a quota on the number of vehicle testers applying for a statutory licence. This decision was delivered after Budd J.'s judgment in the High Court, but prior to the Supreme Court's judgment in *O'Neill* and its authority would now have to be viewed with some reserve. It is true that the scheme in *Navan Tanker Services* was more flexible and less radical than that actually operated in *O'Neill* – in that it was not rigidly exclusive and the quota appeared to be kept under constant review – so that the decisions are not necessarily incompatible with each other. The fact remains, however, that a strong *leitmotif* running through the Supreme Court judgment in *O'Neill* is that should the Oireachtas wish to interfere with the citizen's right to earn a livelihood by limiting numbers by means of quantative restrictions on the number of licences to be granted, express legislative authority is required. A further important practical point is that often such schemes as that which were held invalid by the Supreme Court in *O'Neill* or by Keane J. in *Carrigaline* may, when they were first put in place have met this test; yet because of changed circumstances no longer do so at the time when their legality is later challenged.

E.U. Law

Finally, one should note that, in *O'Neill*, one of the grounds on which the applicant assailed the exclusive A.I. licensing system was E.U. competition law (the first occasion on which such a point has been taken in regard to an Irish licensing system). Budd J. summarised the position as follows:

> "The nub of the challenge is to both the geographical area condition imposed in the licence and the restriction to one licence per area. There is no allegation that the 1947 Act or the 1948 Regulations [Livestock (Artificial Insemination)

---

122 [1997] 2 I.L.R.M. 435 at 447–450. On Art. 15.2.1º see pp. 10–15.
123 Unreported, High Court, December 19, 1996.

Regulations 1948] are contrary to the E.C. Treaty and so the Act and regulations are unscathed. The real attack is on the administrative practice of delimiting an area exclusively for the operations of one A.I. licensee as being contrary to Articles 86 and 90(1). It is conceded that the existing A.I. licence stations are undertakings to which Ireland has granted exclusive rights within the meaning of Article 90 and that the administrative practice of imposing geographical restrictives and one licence per area are measures within the meaning of Article 90(1). It is accepted that the A.I. licensees are undertakings in a dominant position in a substantial part of the common market (as in *Crespelle*) and that the granting of exclusivity may affect trade between Member States. The market in this case is the A.I. field service element of the A.I. business. Applying the principle in *Crespelle* (which concerned as it happened, the French A.I. régime and in which the claimant also failed) the creation by the State of regional monopolies is not contrary to Articles 86 and 90(1): the applicant to succeed must also prove that in exercising the exclusive rights the A.I. licensees cannot avoid abusing their dominant position (see paragraphs 18 and 20 of *Crespelle*). It may be helpful if I pose the questions:

1. Are the alleged abuses of their dominant position by the A.I. licensees the direct consequence of the present administrative practice?

2. Are the existing A.I. stations, in merely exercising the exclusive right granted to them, unable to avoid abusing their dominant position?

The applicant has contended that, firstly, the A.I. stations were not catering for certain market needs and thus were limiting production, markets or technical development to the prejudice of consumers and secondly, that the A.I. stations were not using semen of the best genetic merit or the best technology."[124]

On the points of fact indicated at the end of this passage, Budd J. found against the applicant. More broadly, it emerges from the passage quoted that arrangements such as that under attack in *O'Neill* do not necessarily violate E.U. law. Because the Supreme Court held, as we have seen for the applicant in *O'Neill*, on other grounds, the Court did not consider the E.U. point and the High Court judgment remains the governing authority in this jurisdiction.

In *Carrigaline*, there was also an argument grounded on E.U. law. Here, too, the defendant was able to find shelter under Article 90(1) of the Treaty, with Keane J. holding:

"It was argued on behalf of the plaintiffs that the Minister could not rely on this ruling or the subsequent ruling of the court to the same effect in ERT

---

[124] Unreported, High Court, July 5, 1995, pp. 101–102. The reference in this passage to *Crespelle*, is to Case C–323/93, *Société Civile Agricole du Centre d'Insemination de la Crespelle v. Cooperative d'Élevage et d'Insemination Artificielle du Departement de la Mayenne* [1994] E.C.R. I–5077. It is, of course, merely coincidence that *Crespelle* too, concerned regional artificial insemination monopolies. In this case (considered in more detail at pp. 176–177), the Court of Justice found that this exclusive scheme was not necessarily incompatible with E.U. law.

because the Minister's action in granting the licence to a commercial body on an exclusive basis could not be regarded as an action taken in the public interest for considerations of a non-economic nature.

This is, in my view, a wholly unsustainable argument. Whether the Minister was right or wrong in the view he took that the granting of the MMDS licenses on an exclusive basis was the best method of ensuring the widespread reception of multi-channel television and the protection and development of the cable infrastructure, it was unarguably a decision taken in what he saw as the public interest in ensuring that as many people as possible had access to the widest range of television broadcasting and that the cable infrastructure was protected and developed."[125]

---

[125]   At p. 193.

CHAPTER 8

THE OMBUDSMAN

1. Introduction

The task of the Ombudsman is to secure redress when a person suffers harm or loss, through some act of governmental maladministration.[1] The mistakes of large, hierarchical organisations are hard to correct, especially when they have been endorsed by senior management. It might be expected that the courts would undertake this task. In fact, as we shall see in Parts 1 and 2 of Chapter 9 the structure of our law on the judicial review of administrative action is – perhaps inevitably – so designed as to exclude from its scope many cases of injustice arising from maladministration. Moreover, the High Court – and usually it is only the High Court which has jurisdiction – is a relatively expensive and inaccessible place. The result is that relatively few instances of maladministration surface as court cases. Traditionally, public representatives have seen it as their principal duty to use their moral authority, behind the scenes, to remedy the grievances of individual constituents against governmental services, a fact reflected in the title of Basil Chubb's classic study of public representatives, "Going about persecuting civil servants"[2] as well as in the very high number of representatives per head of population. There are, indeed, far more deputies per person in Ireland than in any other E.U. Member

---

[1] This chapter draws to a very limited degree on Gwynn Morgan, "The Ombudsman Act" (1982) 17 Ir. Jur. (N.S.) 105. See also, J.F. Zimmerman, "The Office of Ombudsman in Ireland" (1989) 27 *Administration* 258; F.C. White, "The Irish Ombudsman" (unpublished LL.M. thesis available for consultation in U.C.C. Library). For the flavour and personality of the Ombudsman, see Clothier (former British Parliamentary Commissioner for Administration) (1986) *Public Law* 204.

References to "Reports" are to the Ombudsman's Annual Report for the year indicated.

[2] "Going about Persecuting Civil Servants: The Role of the Irish Parliamentary Representative" (1963) 11 *Political Studies* 272. *Cf.* the views of the Minister for Finance reported in the *Irish Times*, November 12, 1966 (and quoted by Kelly, "Administrative Discretion and the Courts" (1966) 1 Ir. Jur. (N.S.) 209 at p. 211):

"There is hardly anyone without a direct personal link with someone, be he Minister, T.D., clergyman, county or borough councillor, who will interest himself in helping a citizen to have a grievance examined and, if possible, remedied. My own experience is that members of the Dáil are extremely assiduous and persistent in taking up individual cases and raising them by way of that truly democratic device, the parliamentary question. The basic reason therefore why we do not need an Ombudsman is that we already have so many unofficial but nevertheless effective ones."

Professor Kelly went on to comment on this passage as follows:

"In the large perspective of European social and legal history this utterance is a fascinating testimony to the survival in 20th century Ireland of the primitive system of clientship and patronage. This phenomenon was, in the distant past, a sure sign of a society where a weak man had no hope of justice without the aid of a strong one, and its general replacement in civilised countries by a regular, strong and impartial process of law is a major social milestone. It is disheartening to find this primitive doctrine being not alone practised, but also blandly preached from the topmost minaret of the Irish administrative structure.

State, apart from Greece. Yet this is not a desirable approach, either from the viewpoint of the effective and economic settlement of grievances or from the wider perspective of the health of the body politic. Finally, there are, it is true, tribunals to oversee government administration; but these only exist in a few areas.

The gaps and defects in these traditional institutions for remedying grievances suffered at the hands of officialdom mean that there remains a need for the sort of comprehensive, flexible, informal, free service which is offered by the Ombudsman. This need has been acknowledged outside Ireland too and there are now about 100 Ombudsmen in existence in States and provinces throughout the world. Further testimony to the fact that the Ombudsman principle is an idea whose time has come is provided by the way in Ireland[3] (as elsewhere) this constitutional species has multiplied and spread to fresh fields of activity. For example, in the wake of the Maastricht Treaty, Article 8[d] of the Treaty of Rome now provides for a European Ombudsman to supervise the E.U. institutions.[4]

The idea of an Irish Ombudsman was first suggested, authoritatively, as part of the package of reforms proposed by the *Devlin Report*.[5] Later, a debate was held in the Dáil,[6] which resulted in the constitution of an All-Party Informal Committee on Administrative Justice. This committee produced a report (the All-Party Report) in 1977, favouring the introduction of an Ombudsman.[7] Eventually, goaded by a

---

All this would be unimportant if, in fact, the Minister's preferred system of controls were effective (as was claimed). But it is not, and in the nature of things cannot be. It is very probable that some ignorant poor old man, denied some modest grant or pension because of his own failure to make his position clear, will get redress without question if a deputy or parish priest writes a letter for him. But what machinery can these informal patrons invoke to extract from an unwilling Minister the real history behind a planning application?"

[3] The Central Bank Act 1989, s.94(1) provides for the establishment of an Ombudsman for the major credit institutions. Goaded by this threat of a statutory Ombudsman, the banks and building societies have set up a voluntary complaints investigation scheme : *Irish Times*, June 14, 1990. Such a proposal was initially part of the Solicitors (Amendment) Bill 1991, but was dropped before the Solicitors Act 1994 became law. And on September 2, 1992, insurance companies appointed a (non-statutory) Insurance Ombudsman. Notice also that: University College, Cork is the only university in Europe, apart from the University of Helsinki, to have a Student Ombudsman (appointed in 1987). In the case of the legal profession, s.18.42 of the Fair Trade Commission Report, *Report of Study into Restrictive Practices in the Legal Profession* (1990), recommends the establishment of a Legal Ombudsman's Office. In 1989, the Progressive Democrats proposed a Private Member's Bill to establish a Health Ombudsman to investigate improper or wasteful decisions of public hospitals or health board administrators: see 390 *Dáil Debates* Col. 1901, May 23, 1989. See, to similar effect, *The Irish Times*, May 14, 1992. Deputy Austin Currie, then Minister of State with responsibility for children at the Department of Health, made a proposal for an Ombudsman for children which has also borne no fruit: *The Irish Times*, December 23, 1996.

[4] See Hogan and Whelan, *Ireland and the European Union, Constitutional and Statutory Texts* (1995), pp. 273–274 and 386–389; 1995 Report, p. 8; 1996 Report, p. 10.

[5] *Report of Public Services Organisation Review Group 1966–1969* (Prl. 792), App. I, pp. 447–458. The Devlin Committee's working paper on Administrative Law and Procedure proposed a "Commissioner for Administrative Justice", whose secondary role would be to act as an Ombudsman. His primary task would have been to watch over the extensive system of tribunals required by Devlin's chief proposal, which was to remove routine executive functions from control by Ministers and the Dáil, and vest them in executive units overseen by the tribunals.

[6] The motion was: "That Dáil Eireann favours the appointment of an Ombudsman." See 280 *Dáil Debates,* Cols. 1199–1206, 1257–1284, May 6 and 7, 1975.

[7] The Committee held 10 meetings in 1976 and 1977. It received three submissions including one (dated October 29, 1976) from a well-qualified group convened by the Institute of Public Administration and chaired by Mr. Justice Hamilton.

Private Member's Bill put forward by the Opposition in 1979,[8] the Government published its own Bill, which was modelled fairly closely on the All-Party Report. This Bill became law, as the Ombudsman Act 1980, following an unusually constructive debate in the Oireachtas. However, the first incumbent of the office, who was appointed following consultation with the principal opposition party (something not repeated on subsequent occasions), did not take up office until January 3, 1984.[9] He was Mr Michael Mills (formerly a political correspondent with *The Irish Press*), who retired at the statutory age of 67 and was succeeded, on November 1, 1994, by the present incumbent, Mr Kevin Murphy (formerly a senior civil servant at the head of the public service management and development in the Department of Finance[10]).

As we shall see throughout this chapter, the Ombudsman has established itself rapidly as a significant element on the Irish constitutional scene.[11] One of the ways in which this success has been demonstrated lies in the (actual or proposed) vesting in the office of a number of additional supervisory roles. We have considered elsewhere the office's monitoring and regulating functions in connection with the Freedom of Information Act 1997[12] and the (proposed) Administrative Procedures legislation. In addition, the Ombudsman is a member of the Public Offices Commission, established by the Ethics in Public Office Act 1995, and of the Constituency Commission, established by the Electoral Act 1997. The most important example, however, arises under the Access to Information on the Environment Regulations 1993[13] which came into effect in May 1993. These provide for the release of information on the environment held by a number of public bodies – the most important being local authorities. A typical example is refusal to release data on the quality of drinking water. So far the complaints have fallen into three major categories: delays, excessive charges for the information, or simply refusal to provide it.[14] As in many other

---

8 Bill No. 20 of 1979.

9 Following resolutions passed in the Dáil (October 25, 1983) and Senate (November 2, 1984). His warrant of appointment is dated November 8, 1983. The 1980 Act was brought into force as from July 7, 1983; Ombudsman Act 1980 (Commencement Day) Order 1983 (S.I. No. 424 of 1983). See further, 345 *Dáil Debates* Col. 605 (October 25, 1983).

10 For debate of Mr Murphy's appointment, see 443, *Dáil Debates*, col 959–986 (June 1, 1994) and 140 *Dáil Debates*, Cols 1401–1435 (June 15, 1994).

11 In addition to the examples given in the text, note that in 1995, 1996 and 1997, the Ombudsman was one of the three office-holders (the others being the Clerks of the Dáil and the Senate) vested with (non-statutory) responsibility for organising the preparation of a non-partisan information leaflet for the public, in advance of the referenda to amend the Constitution, in respect of divorce, bail and cabinet confidentiality (respectively). This arrangement is now likely to be put on a statutory basis: Referendum Bill 1998.

12 See p. 494.

13 S.I. No. 133 of 1993, made under the Environmental Protection Agency Act, 1992, ss.6 and 110 to give effect to E.C. Directive 90/313 O.J. L158/56 (June 7, 1990), p. 56. See further 1993 Report, pp. 47–48; 1994 Report, pp. 6, 26–30 and 45–50.

14 According to the 1994 Report, p. 26:
   "In 1993, my Office received only five such complaints. In 1994, I received forty two. Of the 27 complaints which had been finalised by the end of 1994, seven (26%) were resolved in favour of the complainant, with a further 11 (41% of complainants) being provided with assistance of some form or another and nine (33%) were either discontinued or not upheld. Twenty complaints were carried forward to 1995."
   By comparison, only 168 requests for information were made during the year from May 1993 to May 1994.

countries, the Ombudsman will be nominated by the Government as the Information Commissioner under the Freedom of Information Act 1997.[15]

Constitutional setting

The Ombudsman must be, and be seen to be, independent of the Government or any other body or person. Thus he has been provided with a similar, though not identical, institutional pedestal to that occupied by the higher judiciary. The Ombudsman Act 1980 contains a declaration that: "[t]he Ombudsman shall be independent in the performance of his functions",[16] and it has been authoritatively stated[17] that the office should be put on a constitutional basis. He or she is to be appointed by the President, acting on a recommendation contained in a resolution passed by both Houses. No qualifications are laid down for the incumbent save that he or she must be no more than 61 years of age (at the time of first appointment), and must retire at the age of 67.[18] He or she cannot be a public representative, or a member of the Reserve Defence Force, or hold any other paid office or employment apart from that of Ombudsman. The Ombudsman may only be removed from office "for stated misbehaviour, incapacity or bankruptcy", and then only on resolutions passed by each House of the Oireachtas. The term of office is six years and a holder is eligible for a second or subsequent term. The Ombudsman is to be paid the same salary and expenses as a High Court judge.[19]

Finally, the Ombudsman derives some limited support for his independence from the fact that his civil servants are to be civil servants of the State,[20] and that he has his own separate vote in the Estimates.

The Ombudsman has not yet encountered a high profile case (along the lines of the British *Sachsenhausen* or *Barlow Clowes* cases[21]) which has drawn him into very public conflict with the bodies which he oversees. Nevertheless, it is eloquent of the significance of the new office that during the first six years of its existence,

---

[15] 1996 Report, p. 9.

[16] On independence in general, see 1996 Report, p. 11 ("Protection of the term 'Ombudsman'"). For allegations concerning pressure brought to bear by insurance companies on the first Insurance Ombudsman (Pauline Marrinan-Quinn), see press coverage (Feb. 8, 1998).

[17] *Report of the Constitution Review Group* (Pn. 2632, 1996) pp. 425–428. A majority of the All-Party Oireachtas Committee (Pn. 3795, 1997) p. 81 agreed.

[18] The Ombudsman Act 1980, s.2(3), (7). Yet the Government offered, as the reason for its hesitancy in appointing Mr Mills for a second term (see further p. 342) the fact that Mr Mills would be 67 in 1994, part of the way through his second term, although the statutory restriction is directed at the incumbent's age at the time of his appointment for his first term. This justification was coupled with the claim that s.2(3) and (7) was lacking in clarity: 394 *Dáil Debates* Cols. 1675 and 1816, December 14 and 15, 1989. An interesting point of speculation concerns the position which would have arisen had there been a gap of even a few days between the end of Mr Mill's first appointment and his re-appointment. Could it then have been argued that he would not have been eligible on the basis of section 2(7) which states: "A person shall be not more than 61 years of age upon first being appointed . . .". For it might have been contended that the policy underlying the concession in the words "upon *first* being appointed" (which might have been something upon which the Government was relying) is such that they would only have been relied upon to benefit a person who was actually an incumbent at the time of re-appointment; rather than someone who came in from outside.

[19] *Ibid.* ss.10(2), ss.2, 3. For the Ombudsman's Superannuation Scheme, made under s.3(2), see S.I. 1987 No. 70.

[20] See p. 379.

[21] See Gregory and Drewry (1991) *Public Law* 192, 408.

two episodes occurred which could plausibly be regarded as attempts to undermine its independence. The first of these concerned the need for adequate staffing. For one of the main factors governing the Ombudsman's efficacy and public image is the provision of sufficient staff to investigate complaints adequately and promptly. The size and grading of the Ombudsman's staff is determined by the Minister for Finance.[22] Following the extension of his remit in 1985,[23] the work of the Ombudsman's Office was divided into four units (dealing with complaints against, respectively: the civil service, local authorities, health boards, and Bord Telecom and An Post). Each unit consisted of one Senior Investigator (the equivalent of a Principal in the civil service) assisted by four Investigators (at Assistant Principal level). At the apex was the Director of the Office (at Assistant Secretary level). Now, in April 1987, the incoming Fianna Fáil Government's budget, reducing the Ombudsman's vote by £100,000, or 13 per cent. of the previous year's figure, necessitated a reduction in staff of four investigators. In July, it was announced that the vote for 1988 would show a further reduction of £125,000 and consequently a further loss of staff. The Minister for Finance also refused to allow the replacement of the Director and one senior investigator, upon the resignation of the existing incumbents.

These reductions were explained by reference to the crisis in public expenditure and to cuts elsewhere in the public service. But it was noticeable that the cuts in other sections of the public service did not amputate nearly a half of the establishment. A fact which made the cuts particularly damaging was that, at the time the cuts were made (though, in the event, there was to be a reduction in complaints to the Ombudsman in 1988 and 1989), the number of complaints for 1985–1987 had exceeded 5,000, each year; and that by the end of 1987, there was already a back-log of 2,000 or the equivalent of eight months' work. The staff reductions attracted a good deal of protest in the media and the Dáil and Senate.[24] The Ombudsman himself took to informing complainants that there was likely to be considerable delay in dealing with their complaints, and in November he made a special report on the matter – the only special report to issue so far – to the Houses of the Oireachtas. This report[25] commences: "It is necessary under the provisions of the Ombudsman Act to report that the Office of Ombudsman is unable, due to staff cutbacks, to fulfil the functions assigned to it by the Oireachtas."

In response, in mid-1988, the Department of Finance carried out a review of the Ombudsman's staffing needs. The recommendations of this review led to the Ombudsman being able to take on three investigators and to replace the senior investigator who had resigned. In addition, some staff were loaned to the office until the back-log of complaints – running at 2,000 cases at the end of 1988 – had been reduced to manageable proportions.

---

22 Ombudsman Act 1980 s.10(1)(a). The Minister for the Public Service is the "appropriate authority" for the purpose of the Civil Service Regulation Act 1956 but almost all his powers as such have been delegated to the Ombudsman: 1980 Act, s.10(4); 1985 Report, Chap. 10.

23 See, pp. 343–344.

24 See *Irish Times*, January 4, 1988, February 11, 1988, June 4 and 7 1988, May 13, 1988; *Sunday Independent*, June 12, 1988, ("The Ombudsman and Hypocrisy"); *Cork Examiner*, November 6, 1988 ("Watchdog with no Teeth"); 380 *Dáil Debates* Col. 1423, May 12, 1988.

25 Published as an Appendix to his 1987 Report (Pl. 5258). For special reports, see p. 379.

The second occasion when political controversy surrounded the office was in late 1989, upon the making of an appointment of the office-holder for the second term.[26] Although the Charter-Ombudsman, Mr Michael Mills, had, in the privately-held and publicly-expressed views of politicians of all parties, done a good job, there were circumstances which led the Opposition to claim, plausibly enough, that the Government intended to have someone else appointed. In fact, under pressure from the minority party in the Government and at the very last moment, the Government did propose a motion recommending that the President reappoint Mr Mills. What is certain is that, in contrast to the appointment for the first term of office, there was on this occasion no consultation with the opposition parties as to who should be proposed.

2. Jurisdiction

The restrictions upon the type of complaint which the Ombudsman is empowered[27] to scrutinise may be examined under five heads. First, the public bodies whose actions may be investigated must be one of those specified. Secondly, the action must have "adversely affected" some person. Thirdly, the complainant must have a sufficient interest in the matter. Fourthly, the action must have been taken in the performance of administrative functions. Finally, the action must be affected by one of the defects specified. These questions will now be examined.

Public bodies within field of investigation[28]

The bodies against whom a complaint may be heard have always included all the Departments of State, but not the Government itself, or any of the public bodies listed in the Second Schedule.[29] Since April 1, 1985, the Ombudsman's bailiwick has been extended to include: Bord Telecom Éireann; An Post; local authorities (excluding the "reserved functions" exercised by elected representatives) health boards excluding "[p]ersons when acting on behalf of health boards and (in the opinion of the Ombudsman) solely in the exercise of clinical judgment in connection

---

26 See 394 *Dáil Debates* Cols. 1668–1676 and 1806–1820, December 14 and 15, 1989; *Sunday Tribune*, December 17, 1989. See also above, n.18.

27 Even where all five conditions are satisfied, the Ombudsman still has a discretion whether to exercise his jurisdiction: see 1980 Act, s.4(2) and (8) and Foulkes, "The Discretionary Provisions of the Parliamentary Commissioner Act 1967" (1971) 43 M.L.R. 377, 391–393.

28 It bears mentioning (in part because of the comparative references made throughout this chapter) that in the United Kingdom, the Ombudsman has proved to be a very fertile genus and the field of investigation which, in Ireland, is vested in a single office is divided among a number of entities: the Parliamentary Commissioner for Administration; the English (and Welsh) Commissions for Local Administration; the Scottish Commissioner for Local Administration; (separate) Health Commissioners for England, Wales and Scotland; the Northern Ireland Parliamentary Commissioner; and the Northern Ireland Commissioner for Complaints. The last two offices have been held, since 1973, by the same person. References to "the Ombudsman" in the British context should be understood as referring to the entire flock, save where the context directs otherwise.

29 Ombudsman Act 1980, s.4(2), (4) and Sched. 1 and 2. See also, Ombudsman Act 1980, (First Schedule) (Amendment) Order 1984 (S.I. No. 332 of 1984); Ombudsman Act 1980 (First Schedule) (Amendment) Order 1985 (S.I. No. 66 of 1985). For a complaint involving a Government decision, see 1988 Report (Pl. 5991), p. 71.

with the diagnosis of illness or the care or treatment of a patient, whether formed by the person taking the action or by any other person."[30]

This qualification is mentioned only once in the annual reports of the Ombudsman. The complaint concerned a Disabled Person's Maintenance Allowance which had been refused one year, but granted in the following year, although the complainant insisted that her medical condition had not deteriorated in the interim. The complainant passed the preliminary examination. However, at the investigation, it became clear that the decision depended solely upon the exercise of clinical judgment. Accordingly, the Ombudsman proceeded no further with the investigation.[31]

The Government may extend (or restrict) the Ombudsman's jurisdiction by making an order amending the First Schedule to the 1980 Act. Such an order is unusual in that it requires the approval of each House.[32] Since 1987, an Ombudsman (Amendment) Bill has been gestating. The most significant feature of this would extend the Ombudsman's remit to cover, *inter alia*, non-commercial state bodies and voluntary hospitals.[33]

"Adversely affected"

It must appear to the Ombudsman that the action has or may have "adversely affected" some person. This wide phrase is not defined and, as far as the Reports show, the concept has only been invoked once. This was in a case in which he came close to finding that a health board ought to have paid the costs of the complainant's treatment at the Mayo Clinic but then concluded:

> "[t]he financial costs had been met from a fund created by public subscription so no adverse financial effects were suffered by the complainant's family. In the circumstances, it was not open to me under the Ombudsman's Act to make a finding or recommendation on the question of finance."[34]

The same factor was the basis of the Ombudsman's defeat in *R. v. Local Commissioner, ex p. Eastleigh B.C.*,[35] a case which arose from the Ombudsman's finding that a local authority had failed to properly inspect a sewer. However, the Ombudsman had also observed that he could not affirm categorically that even a proper inspection would have revealed this particular defect. There was a division between the majority and the dissenting judge as to the interpretation of this observation. However, the English Court of Appeal was unanimous that if (as the majority thought) the

---

30 Ombudsman Act 1980, (First Schedule) (Amendment) Order 1984 (S.I. No. 332 of 1984); 356 *Dáil Debates* Cols. 852 *et seq.*, February 27, 1985. Before April 1985, Bord Telecom Éireann, the local authorities and health boards agreed to co-operate with the Ombudsman, though they were not formally within his jurisdiction.

31 1990 Report, pp. 53–54. There have been other cases on clinical judgment, but usually these are weeded out early on, on the grounds of no jurisdiction, and hence are not reported. It seems likely that the clinical judgment exemption will be removed in the case of the British Ombudsmen.

32 Ombudsman Act 1980, s.4(10), as amended by Ombudsman (Amendment) Act 1984, s.1. See 356 *Dáil Debates* Cols. 1300 *et seq.*, November 7, 1984.

33 1995 Report, p. 4; 1996 Report, p. 9. The 1996 Report indicates impatience and suggests that if the Bill is not published without delay, then the extension of remit should be effected by statutory instrument (as just explained).

34 1987 Report, p. 54.

35 [1988] Q.B. 855; M. Jones (1988) *Public Law* 608.

Ombudsman meant: "I cannot say whether the failure to inspect led to the expenditure, but as the council was at fault it would be fair that it should contribute to the cost of remedial measures", then the Ombudsman had exceeded his powers. The reason was that it could not be said that the complainant householder had been "adversely affected" as a result of the council's maladministration.

Complainant

The All-Party Committee had realistically recommended that there should be no requirement that a complaint should be made by the victim himself.[36] However, the Ombudsman Act 1980 provides that if, as in almost all cases, the investigation is initiated by way of complaint (rather than by the Ombudsman of his own motion) the complainant must have, in the Ombudsman's opinion, "a sufficient interest in the matter".[37] Nevertheless, it seems that the Ombudsman has taken the view that the provision enables him to entertain complaints submitted by, for instance, social workers[38] and professional advisers[39] (only approximately 5 per cent of complaints travel via public representatives[40]). In addition, neither the person affected nor the complainant may be a Department or other body specified in the First or Second Schedule.[41] Indeed, the chief purposes of the Second Schedule which consists of a list of several public bodies, including state-sponsored bodies, is to extend the category of public authorities which may not make a complaint. The thinking behind this is to remove the possibility that the Ombudsman might be used as a forum for internecine warfare by public bodies (as has happened in Britain).

"Taken in the performance of administrative functions"

The requirement that the "action" be "taken in the performance of administrative functions"[42] is designed to exclude judicial or legislative decisions. Since, as already mentioned, the only bodies against whom the Ombudsman can hear complaints are Departments or other executive agencies, this requirement has been inserted largely *ex abundanti cautela*, but not entirely so. It does at least have the effect of excluding

---

[36] Section VIII: "since a significant proportion of those affected by administrative action may lack the skills or confidence to approach the Ombudsman themselves, they may feel more secure if the matters can be taken up on their behalf." See 1984 Report, p. 54 (where a social worker made a report on behalf of a deserted wife).

[37] Ombudsman Act 1980, ss. 4(2)(a), 4(3), 9.

[38] In his 1992 Report, at p. 2, the Ombudsman refers to development in the co-operation between his office, the National Social Service Board and the Citizens Advice Bureau.

[39] Indeed, in at least one complaint, it has been recommended that the public body pay the complainant's legal costs: 1991 Report, p. 105.

[40] The 1992 Report states as follws at p. 2:
"Many public representatives appear to be hesitant about bringing their constituents' complaints to my office . . it is almost always the same nucleus of Deputies, Senators and local Councillors who continually send in complaints."
See further 1993 Report, p. 110 and 1990 Report, p. 3–4. Where the complaint is received via a public representative (mainly from a small "hard-core" of deputies), the Ombudsman's practice is to keep him in touch with developments, *e.g.* by copying him in on correspondence.

[41] 1980 Act, s.4(2)(a), 3(a), (9). See also, Ombudsman Act 1980 (Second Schedule) (Amendment) Order 1985 (S.I. 1985 No. 69) extending this Schedule.

[42] For definitions of "action" (to include, *inter alia*, failure to act) and "functions" see Ombudsman Act 1980, s.1.

actions taken by the executive which are incidental to the judicial function, *e.g.* the involvement of the Department of Justice in extradition proceedings, or a Department deciding whether to prosecute for breach of some specialist legislation for which it is responsible. However, it is very clear that "quasi-judicial" decisions – broadly, those which have a high law content and which directly affect a single individual – are regarded as falling within the Ombudsman's jurisdiction, for instance, decisions in regard to housing grants or welfare benefits. As regards policy issues, notwithstanding the statutory restriction to "administrative functions", the Ombudsman has been prepared to appraise what might be called, at least, low-level policy questions.[43] And he has also been prepared to intervene in commercial or business dealings, for example, telephone billing.[44] In an interesting comparison, the Ombudsman has remarked that:

> "the consumers of faulty goods and services are entitled to refunds or other protection. In my view, the consumers of public services should in principle be treated no differently to private sector consumers. They have a right to expect that, if they pay a charge for a service, the service will be of good quality and fit for the purpose intended. The legislation enabling local authorities to supply water for domestic purposes and to charge for water for domestic purposes envisages that a domestic water supply will not just be fit for drinking but that it will also be suitable for washing and sanitation."[45]

"The bad rule"

A more difficult question arises where the adverse consequences of an administrative action can be traced back, not to any error by the administrator, but to the content of a statute, statutory instrument or extra-legal rule (contained in, for example, a circular), which determined the way the administrative decision had to be taken. If it is the rule which is the source of, say, unfairness, has the Ombudsman jurisdiction? In the first place, where the maladministration is dictated by an Act of the Oireachtas or a common law rule, the Ombudsman has no authority to deal with the case: all he can do is to state his opinion that the law is in need of reform and this will presumably be of some weight with a Government deciding whether to bring forward amending legislation. Indeed, large parts of the Ombudsman's Annual Reports are taken up with criticisms of various laws.[46]

The position is similar in regard to statutory instruments and administrative circulars since these are legislation or quasi-legislation,[47] rather than administration. However, as with other sources of law, while he cannot intervene in the instant case,[48]

---

43 See further, pp. 351–357.
44 There are many, many examples, for instance: 1992 Report, pp. 133–134; 1993 Report pp. 117–118; 1994 Report, p. 41. See also 1993, pp. 110 (discounts given to business users of local authority dumps); 1990 Report, p. 289 (compensation for damages to a parcel carried by An Post, even though the terms of the insurance excluded liability in the circumstances).
45 1994 Report, p. 68.
46 For examples, see, pp. 391–393.
47 As to the classification of statutory instruments and circulars, see above, Parts 4 and 5 of Chap. 2.
48 See, *e.g.* 1988 Report, p. 27. For the British position on the doctrinal problem of the bad rule, see Gregory (1982) *Public Law* 49 at 68–70.

the Ombudsman feels free to comment on "the bad rule." Naturally, his pressure for change is more likely to bear fruit quickly than in cases where primary legislation would be required. One example of this arose from his criticisms of the procedure for the revision of rateable valuations by the Commissioners of Valuation.[49] The complaint which was made was that the date for the publication of revised rating valuation lists was December 1, so that, given the Christmas holiday period, the statutory period of 28 days within which an appeal to the Circuit Court had to be lodged was substantially reduced. The Minister for Finance acceded amicably (without challenge to the Ombudsman's authority, which was thus not tested) to the request to change the date for publication of lists from December 1 to November 1 although this change necessitated a statutory instrument.

The Ombudsman has also succeeded in getting Departments to issue or to amend circulars.[50] The second defect in the rateable valuations revision system, described in the last paragraph, concerned the function (which is vested in local authorities) of informing a person that the valuation of his premises has been increased so that he can decide whether he wishes to appeal. Certain local authorities did not inform the persons affected directly but simply placed a notice in a newspaper. The Ombudsman could not address himself directly to the local authorities concerned because this case occurred before local authorities were brought within his terms of reference. Instead, the Department of the Environment issued a circular suggesting to local authorities that they should notify ratepayers affected, personally by letter.

A significant discussion of the important question of the bad rule arose in the course of a recent investigation into the refusal, by the Department of Social Welfare, to pay arrears of pensions to persons who were later than the specified period (six months) in applying for their pension.[51] This withholding was said, by the Department, to flow inevitably from the relevant statutory instrument. Dealing with this preliminary aspect of the complaint, the Ombudsman stated:

> "I was conscious, however, that the investigation would inevitably have to deal with the manner in which the relevant time limits for claims, and the accompanying disqualification for pension arrears, have been set by successive Ministers by regulation. Section 4(2) of the Ombudsman Act, 1980 refers to actions 'taken in the performance of administrative functions' and I am advised that I would be precluded from enquiring into legislative actions. A legislative action is the making of a law; it is not the application of that law to individual cases or categories of cases. A question I may be faced with, therefore, is: may I criticise in an investigation report the particular provisions of statutory regulations? I certainly may if I consider the regulations are *ultra vires* the primary legislation because in such an event the decisions in individual cases would be 'taken without proper authority'. But what if the decisions in individual cases were fully in accordance with the provisions of the statutory regulations and did not involve the unreasonable use or withholding of

---

49 1984 Report, pp. 41–42. See also, 1986 Report, p. 19; 1989 Report, p. 23.
50 For examples, see 1984 Report, pp. 46–48; 1985 Report, pp. 27–28.
51 *Report of Investigation of Complaints against the Department of Social Welfare regarding Arrears of Contributory Pensions* (March 14, 1997). Hereafter "Report of March 14, 1997".

Ministerial discretion? Here the position is more complex but I am satisfied that I may criticise the particular provisions of a statutory regulation if they result in decisions in individual cases which are 'contrary to fair or sound administration'. By this I mean that, in their application, they have an adverse effect which I consider to be unfair and unreasonable."[52]

As a preliminary comment, one ought to advert to the fact that in the instant case (as indicated in the last two sentences of this quotation), the Ombudsman does not find it necessary "to take a position" on this question (though he has certainly thrown down a significant marker for the future). The reason why this statement was – as it were – *obiter dicta* was that the Minister had a long-established, though rarely-exercised, "extra-statutory" discretion on the basis of "equity"[53] to pay arrears, in respect of a period before the six months permitted by the statutory instrument, The legal basis of a non-statutory discretion may be doubtful, given that the expenditure of public moneys requires substantive (*i.e.* apart from the Estimates and Appropriation Act) statutory authority. Notwithstanding, this rather legalistic point (which is not even mentioned in the Report), the Ombudsman avoided the need to take a position on the issue under discussion here ("the bad rule"), by recommending that the Department assist the complainants, on the basis that their situations fell within "the equity".

To return to the main channel of the discussion: the way that the British PCA has adopted to blunt the edge of the investigation of the "bad rule" precept is that he will ask the body which has made the bad rule to review it, if, as would be unlikely, they fail to do so, then that would be regarded as a case of "constructive maladministration". However, if they do so and confirm the rule, then the Ombudsman can do no more.[54] However the Irish Ombudsman now appears to go beyond the position in Britain and to advocate that delegated legislation does "not constitute law" in the strict sense of the term. Accordingly, if delegated legislation is substantively unfair it is open to the Ombudsman to review it. In Appendix 2 of the Report, where the issue is discussed most fully, three reasons are given for this view.

The first of these is Professor Wade's robust attitude which is represented by many quotations from his book,[55] to the effect that to draw a distinction between a bad rule and a bad decision is to make a distinction without difference. But surely (leaving marginal cases aside) there *is* a relevant difference, namely that a rule is more likely to involve large-scale policy and this is just what the Ombudsman of his nature should leave to the judgment of public bodies. The second major plank on which the view, in the Appendix, rests is Article 15.2.1° of the Irish Constitution which states that "the sole and exclusive power of making laws for the State" is

---

52 Report of March 14, 1997, pp.11–12.
53 Social Welfare (Consolidated Payments Provisions) Regulations 1994, Arts. 100–107.
54 See Gregory (1982) *Public Law* 49 at 70.
55 In the Ombudsman's Report, references are to Wade *Administrative Law* (5th ed.) pp. 83 and 733. (For the current edition, see Wade and Forsyth *Administrative Law* (7th ed.), p. 91 and 859). But notice that Wade qualifies its remark by the following formula: "statutory instruments . . . should fall within the Commissioner's field, *at least as regards their effect and the action taken to review them*" (Our emphasis). See, further, Gregory (1982) *Public Law* at 70; Marshall (1973) *Public Law* 32, 41–44.

vested in the Oireachtas. As is well known, in order to circumvent this provision, a well-established line of cases has held that delegated legislation does not constitute "law", provided that it does not introduce a novel principle not to be found in the parent statute. But it is, in our opinion, incorrect to say that just because an instrument is not "law" in the rather specialised sense of that term which has been developed by the judges for the artificial purpose of reconciling delegated legislation with Article 15.2.1° therefore it is "not law" in all other contexts too and, accordingly, must be within the Ombudman's remit. Thirdly, it is an object of scandal and concern that since 1987 (when no Joint Oireachtas Committee on Legislation was re-established) there has been no committee of the legislative to review the substance (or anything else) of delegated legislation.[56] The Ombudsman may be able to get it established as a convention that since there is no adequate forum for reviewing delegated legislation he should be able to remedy that deficiency (just as he is moving into other areas, such as environmental information; referendum campaigns; and supervision of the Administrative Procedure Bill). Such a convention would go some distance to circumvent the argument that he may not concern himself with the substance of delegated legislation.

Types of defect

The British Parliamentary Commissioner Act 1967 relies heavily on a term, which it does not define "maladministration". In contrast, the Irish legislation does not use this term,[57] yet provides what might be regarded as a definition of it: for section 4(2)(b) of the 1980 Act gives a list of defects which may attract the Ombudsman's attention. The Ombudsman may investigate any action where it appears to the Ombudsman:

> "(b) that the action was or may have been—
>
> (i)   taken without proper authority,
> (ii) taken on irrelevant grounds,
> (iii) the result of negligence or carelessness,
> (iv) based on erroneous or incomplete information,
> (v)   improperly discriminatory,
> (vi) based on an undesirable administrative practice, or
> (vii) otherwise contrary to fair or sound administration."

In view of the vagueness of some of these categories; the discretion in their application which is vested in the Ombudsman; and the informal attitude adopted by the Ombudsman (whose Reports, it is worth noting, do not usually identify individual statutory heads but refer, instead, to such notions as "fairness"), there seems to be little point in a comprehensive scrutiny of each type of defect. However, the following tentative observations may be made. In the first place, as might be expected, there is a substantial overlap between some of the items in the statutory catalogue and the grounds on which a court would exercise its power of judicial

---

[56] See p. 41.
[57] Though for a rare use of this term in the Reports, see 1993 Report, p. 115.

review of an administrative action.[58] Thus, head (v) "improperly discriminatory" is similar to Article 40.1[59] of the Constitution which would be available to a court reviewing an administrative action. Again, heads (i) ("taken without proper authority") and (ii) ("taken on irrelevant grounds") establish grounds which would also be available in a court reviewing an administrative action. Take, for instance, a complaint arising from the health boards' refusal to pay Disabled Persons' Maintenance Allowance to persons attending secondary school because this meant that they were not available for employment. The Ombudsman upheld the complaint because the statute created an entitlement to payment provided that three factors – which related to the applicant's age, means and level of disability – were satisfied. In conventional legal parlance, the health boards had taken irrelevant considerations into account.[60] However, the remaining heads create wider powers than their judicial equivalents. Thus, in head (iii) ("the result of negligence or carelessness"), since negligence is mentioned, "carelessness" must mean something in addition to negligence. It may be that the "duty of care" or "remoteness of damage" elements do not have to be established or, at least, not to the same standard as for negligence. In any case, given the under-developed state of the law on public authority torts,[61] it is useful to have a flexible alternative to negligence *stricto sensu*. And head (iv) ("based on erroneous or incomplete information") is clearly wider than the embryonic and limited "no-evidence" rule in the field of judicial review of administrative acts.[62] Likewise, as we shall see, head (vii) ("otherwise contrary to fair or sound administration") goes beyond constitutional justice.

The Ombudsman has now[63] now laid down a "checklist . . . [as a] guide to standards of best practice by public officials". Basing himself on the theme that "citizens are entitled to be dealt with properly, fairly and impartially", he goes on to offer the following elaboration:

"Dealing 'properly' with people means dealing with them –

- promptly, and without undue delay;
- correctly, in accordance with the law or other rules governing their entitlements;
- sensitively, by having regard to their age, to their capacity to understand often complex rules, to any disability thay may have and to their feelings, privacy and convenience;

---

58 The question of this overlap is discussed further, pp. 309–313.
59 "All citizens shall, as human persons, be held equal before the law. This shall not be held to mean that the State shall not in its enactments have due regard to differences of capacity, physical and moral, and of social function."
60 1985 Report, p. 32. For taking into account irrelevant considerations see pp. 631–635 and for a close parallel in the context of judicial review, to the facts in the text, see *The State (Keller) v. Galway County Council* [1958] I.R. 142.
61 See pp. 655–668.
62 On which see de Smith, Woolf and Jowell, *Judicial Review of Administrative Action* (5th ed., 1995). pp. 126–141.
63 1996 Report, p. 5. An earlier version (under the title "Principles of Good Administration") was published at p. 4 of the 1994 Report (the first Report to be issued by the present incumbent, Mr Murphy) and 1995 report, p. 10. The Guide to standards of best practice, in addition to being included in the 1996 Report, is printed as a separate leaflet, which is available from the Office.

- helpfully, by simplifying procedures, forms and information on entitlements and services, maintaining proper record cards, and providing clear and precise details on time or conditions which might result in disqualification;
- responsibly, by not adopting an adversarial approach as a matter of course where there may be a fear of litigation.

Dealing 'fairly' with people means –

- treating people in similar circumstances in like manner;
- accepting that rules and regulations, while important in ensuring fairness, should not be applied so rigidly or inflexibly as to create inequity;
- avoiding penalties which are out of proportion to what is necessary to ensure compliance with the rules;
- being prepared to review rules and procedures and change them if necessary;
- giving adequate notice before changing rules in a way which adversely affects a person's entitlements;
- having an internal review system so that adverse decisions can be looked at again and reviewed by someone not involved in the first decision;
- informing people how they can appeal, co-operating fully in any such appeal and being open to proposals for redress.

Finally, dealing 'impartially' with people means –

- making decisions based on what is relevant in the rules and law and ignoring what is irrelevant;
- avoiding bias because of a person's colour, sex, marital status, ethnic origin, culture, language, religion, sexual orientation, attitude, reputation or because of who they are or who they know;
- ensuring, where a service is based on a scheme of priorities, that the scheme is open and transparent;
- being careful that one's prejudices are not factors in a decision"

As can be seen, most of these guidelines draw on existing law or practice. Some items are a (slight) re-formulation of the statutory catalogue, quoted earlier (*e.g.* "treating people in similar circumstances in like manner" or "based on what is relevant [not] irrelevant"). Or they involve principles already developed or used, by the Ombudsman (*e.g.* promptness, proportionality, flexibility, openness, informing citizens of their rights, no bias). The closest we come to a novelty is the requirement not to "adopt an adversarial approach as a matter of course". In summary, there appears to be nothing which goes beyond the statutory catalogue as augmented by the internationally understood precepts of the Ombudsman and the general principles of Irish Adminstrative Law. Consequently, there seems scant chance that anyone would succeed in persuading a court that the Guide was *ultra vires* the powers of the Ombudsman.

The usefulness of such a proclamation is partly exhortatory (to public bodies) and partly that it gives some guidance regarding the Ombudsman's recommendations and encourages consistency .(It seems probable that when the Administrative

Procedure legislation[64] comes into operation, the Ombudsman will operate – so far as he is left with a discretion under the legislation and the particular Charter involved – the same type of standard as in his jurisdiction under the Ombudsman Act.) As regards consistency in the Ombudsman's decisions, one should note that occasionally, in his Reports, there are explicit references to previous decisions.[65] Reference back to previous decisions is also facilitated by the establishment (in 1986)[66] of a computerised system of digests of previous decisions.

A substantial portion of Annual Reports are not marshalled under the headings provided by the Guide.[67] However this categorisation is not followed here since we are adopting broader themes suggested by general Administrative Law. The Annual Reports disclose that the Ombudsman has been prepared to intervene on such broad bases as consistency, equity and flexibility, as, for instance, in cases: where the Department of Agriculture refused to deal with an accountant as a professional representative of a farmer on the ground that it was departmental policy only to deal with solicitors[68]; where a local authority's method for valuing a house for a Housing Finance Agency loan was based only on site cost plus building cost per square metre, with the result that small houses in urban areas were undervalued[69]; where welfare payments had been made as from the date of certification of eligibility by the health board rather than the date of application[70]; where a widow's pension had been very substantially reduced in view of her "means" which were taken to include a judgment debt, which she had, in practice, very little hope of enforcing[71]; or where there was an absolute entitlement under the Urban Fuel Scheme which operates in 17 urban districts, whereas the National Fuel Scheme, which applied elsewhere, was discretionary.[72]

Fairness, merits and policy

We are, in this section, drawing no distinction, since the Ombudsman does not do so, between two types of decision: on the one hand, policy decisions which potentially affect a large number of cases and, on the other hand, the exercise of a discretion which of its nature can only affect a single situation.

As we shall see, it is clear, from his annual reports, that the Ombudsman is more prepared than a court would be to review questions of merits or judgment.[73]

---

64 See p. 494.

65 1988 Report, pp. 86 and 78. ("This case extended the principle I outlined in my Annual Report of 1987 relating to the giving of incorrect information by a public body.")

66 1986 Report, p. 29. See, now, also Freedom of Information Act 1997, ss.15 and First Sched. (publication of information). Another aid to consistency is provided by communication with the Ombudsman offices of other states, mainly by way of the International Ombudsman Conference and the International Ombudsman Institute. Some members of the international community gave the Ombudsman advice when the Irish Ombudsman was first established: 1984 Report, p. 27.

67 An exception is "improperly discriminatory" which was used in a case in which a local authority required certain disabled persons applying for housing transfers to sign an undertaking which was not required of able-bodied applicants: 1992 Report, pp. 53–54.

68 1985 Report, p. 65.

69 *Ibid.* p. 53.

70 *Ibid.* pp. 31, 52.

71 1989 Report, see pp. 73–74; see also, 1986 Report, p. 48.

72 1985 Report, p. 33.

73 Notice that in England, it has been said that "maladministration is concerned with the manner in which decisions are reached and implemented and [has] nothing to do with the nature, quality or

Intertwined with this is the fact, noted in the preceding Part, that he is prepared to appraise questions which reach beyond administration to low-level policy. He has been prepared – to quote a characteristic phrase used by the first incumbent in various public talks – "to push the boat out".

Matters like fairness, merits and policy are so closely related that it seems best to consider examples of them together. The first illustration arose from the fact that under the rubric of "fairness", the Ombudsman was prepared to intervene when a mother complained that the Department of Education bus route for taking children to school was so drawn that her five-year-old child had to walk one and a half miles to the bus, whilst certain older children were being picked up much closer to their homes. The Ombudsman put forward a proposal which, without extra overall cost, enabled the bus to collect the five-year-old closer to his home whilst requiring some older children to walk somewhat further. The Department of Social Welfare accepted his proposal.[74]

The Ombudsman also condemned as a case of "Catch 22" a situation in which the Department of Social Welfare had refused to allow a complainant to register retrospectively as unemployed in respect of the five-week period during which the Department was hearing his appeal (ultimately rejected) concerning the termination of his disability benefit. The complainant was naturally unwilling to register prospectively as unemployed during this period for to do so would be to imply that he was capable of work and thus, possibly, to jeopardise his appeal on the disability benefit claim. The net result was that he had been unable to claim either benefit in respect of this period.[75]

Further examples include recommendations: that a health board allow the complainant access to the medical records of his infant son[76]; that a health board permit a relation of the mother (other than her husband) to be present at the birth of her child[77]; and that the Department of Foreign Affairs allow a joint passport to be issued for a one-year period only at a fee of £3 to an elderly couple (the one-year passport being a concession which had formerly been confined to individuals)[78];

---

reasonableness of the decision itself": *R v. Local Commissioner, ex p. Eastleigh B.C.* [1988] Q.B. 855, 863, *per* Lord Donaldson. See also *R. v. Local Commissioner, ex p. Bradford MCC* [1979] Q.B. 287, 311, 314, 318 and *R. v. Local Commissioner, ex p. Croydon LBC* [1989] 1 All E.R. 1033 at 1043. It should be noted, though, that the British legislation bans the Ombudsman from investigating the "merits" of a decision taken without maladministration: Local Government Act 1974, s.34(3); Parliamentary Commissioner for Administration Act 1967, s.12(3). Also that the British Ombudsmen do not always adhere to this precept.

[74] 1984 Report, p. 37. For other school transport complaints which are a fairly regular source of complaint, see: 1990 Report, pp. 74–75; 1992 Report, pp. 94–95; 1993 Report, p 90; 1994 Report, pp. 17–19.

[75] *Ibid.* p. 33. Another example of "Catch 22" arose when a local authority refused to allow a Disabled Persons Grant in respect of a downstairs bathroom for the use of the disabled mother of the complainant. The complainant had been given an informal indication from the local authority staff that his mother was eligible. In reliance on this, he had gone ahead and completed the work before and in anticipation of formal approval. Accordingly the grant was refused on the basis that at the relevant time there was a downstairs bathroom in the house: see 1994 Report, pp. 62–63.

[76] 1986 Report, p. 65.

[77] 1987 Report, p. 91.

[78] 1986 Report, p. 50. The Ombudsman's occasional concern not to trench too far on policy matters is shown by his approach here: "I asked the Department if, at the time of initiating the concession it was *their clear intention* to exclude holders of a joint passport from availing of the concession. The

that anomalies in the rent scheme for local authority dwellings be removed because they seemed to allow for the payment of two different levels of rent in respect of the same household income.[79] The next example to be mentioned concerns the situation of a local authority tenant who has purchased his house and then (possibly because his family has grown up) wishes to be rehoused again as a local authority tenant in a smaller house. In some cases, the complainant was required to surrender the original house, for which he has paid, to the local authority with no compensation. The Ombudsman recommended a re-examination "with a view to ensuring that the system operates on a basis that is consistent and fair to all concerned."[80]

Another complaint which succeeded arose out of the refusal of a disabled person's grant, which is granted at the discretion of the County Manager. The grant was sought to help with the installation of a stair-lift in the home of the complainants who were an elderly couple. The reason given for refusal was that the complainants were over seventy years of age and, at a time of scarce financial resources, funds should have been retained to cater for younger physically handicapped persons. The Ombudsman noted that grants had been awarded to persons over seventy (although it was not said whether this was done at the same time as the refusal of the complainants' application); but also that the Department of the Environment took the view that the right to decide on entitlement in individual cases, lay with the local authority. The Ombudsman then stated: "I found that in the implementation of a national scheme for the physically disabled, the exclusion of persons over 70 years of age was contrary to fair and sound administration and it amounted to discrimination against older citizens."[81]

In another case, the Ombudsman was prepared to review a local authority's failure to initiate legal proceedings. This arose from the fact that a person was generating a great deal of noise and disturbance manufacturing aluminium windows in his house. The local authority admitted to the Ombudsman that it "could and should have taken action under housing legislation". Because of its failure to do so, neighbours were compelled to take action at law. Accordingly the Ombudsman approved the payment of £3,000 by the local authority to cover the costs of the action and for damage caused to the neighbours' boundary fence.[82]

As we shall see in the context of judicial review of administrative action, a more sharply focussed version of fairness may be characterised as "proportionality"[83] and this option has, in the 1995 Report been identified as "a principle of good administration". It was illustrated in the following way:

"Public bodies still tend to administer their schemes and programmes in a rigid manner, even minor breaches of a scheme [*e.g.* delay]or minor failures to meet

---

Department considered the matter and decided that it would be the Minister's wish to interpret the rule in the most favourable way for those entitled to the concession." (Emphasis added).

[79] 1994 Report, pp. 39–40.
[80] 1987 Report, p. 30. For another unfairness case, see 1995 Report, p. 28.
[81] 1990 Report, p. 47. Notice the unusual use of the precise wording of one of the grounds from the statutory catalogue of defects, quoted above, p. 348.
[82] 1992 Report, pp. 26–27.
[83] See, pp. 655–663.

qualifying conditions tends to attract the same penalties as major ones. In short the principle of proportionality has not yet been given sufficient recognition."[84]

Another precept which has been identified by the Ombudsman and applied, as a principle of good administration, is the avoidance of "unfair discrimination".[85]

In one complaint, the Department of Education had refusal to grant an award under the non-statutory[86] Vocational Education Committee Scholarship Scheme. The complainant did not fulfil the formal criteria for eligibility (two honours in the Leaving Certificate or the equivalent outside the State.) He had however completed a *third level* course in the United Kingdom. Furthermore – and here is the point which the Ombudsman regarded as critical – in other cases, exceptions had been made to the Scholarship Scheme.

Many policy differences, of course, come down in the end to money. The Ombudsman has naturally been prepared to accept this as a factor justifying a public authority's action. For example, in one case concerning allegedly inadequate refuse collection arrangements, he found that "the Council's justification for those arrangements was reasonable in light of their financial constraints and I consider that it outweighed the inconvenience experienced by the complainant as a result of these arrangements."[87]

Other complaints have been found to fall on the other side of the line. Take, for instance, a case which involved a refusal or, at any rate, delay (the facts were rather uncertain) in the provision of health board eye operations. The complainant had had the operation done privately and then sought to recover the costs from the health board. It was said by way of unsuccessful defence, that to pay these monies would be "to open the floodgates for all kinds of situations where patients opted for private treatment rather than wait for the public health services." The Ombudsman was unimpressed:

> "[I]n deciding to reject Mr A's application for financial assistance, the Health Board was influenced mainly by considerations of precedent: that the background to the case had not been properly examined and that due consideration had not been given to the merits and particular circumstances of the case."[88]

---

[84] 1995 Report, p. 14.
[85] *Ibid.* at pp. 12–13.
[86] 1992 Report, p. 26. See too, 1996 Report, p. 20.
[87] 1989 Report, p. 91. See also: 1987 Report, p. 32 and 1992 Report, p. 35–36. Note also the 1990 Report at p. 83 which states as follows:

"As the holder of a medical card, the complainant was legally entitled to free dental services, including the provision of dentures, under specific provisions of the Health Act, 1970.

Normally, I would expect a Health Board or other authority within my remit to adhere to the provisions of the law. I considered, however, that the issue in this case was primarily a funding problem. The Health Board was quite willing to make dentures available to medical card holders if the necessary funds were provided. I could not, in these circumstances, establish that there was maladministration on the part of the Health Board.

I feel, however, that attention should be drawn to the plight of people like the complainant, obliged to live in discomfort and, perhaps, distress due to the curtailment of a service which remains on the statute books as a legal entitlement of those concerned."
[88] 1991 Report, pp. 70–71.

In appropriate cases, the Ombudsman has been prepared to recommend the payment of substantial sums of money, for example, in the case of; orthodontic treatment[89]; and the education of a deaf child[90]; and under the Treatment Abroad Scheme.[91]

The Ombudsman has accepted the need for a fairly administered queue in appropriate circumstances:

> "I could not pursue other cases because the medical records available to me indicated that the health boards concerned were not unreasonable in putting the patients on a waiting list with other children requiring similar treatment, at a time when sufficient financial resources were not available to the boards to enable them to provide early treatment."[92]

However a complaint flowing from the failure to maintain a water supply was upheld when its source lay in a dispute between two local authorities as to which of them was responsible for the scheme.[93] The position would appear to be slightly different from that in the United Kingdom: take, for example, *R. v. Local Commissioner, ex p. Eastleigh B.C.*,[94] a case arising from a British Ombudsman's investigation of a local authority's inspection of the construction of a sewer. It was common cause among the judges of the Court of Appeal that the decision to inspect at only the four most important – rather than at all – of the stages of the construction was a matter of policy and, so, outside the Ombudsman's jurisdiction, (leaving the Ombudsman only to examine the execution of the inspections). One of the three judges, Taylor L.J., however, went further and held that even the question of whether an inspection required a "gradient test" to be made of every drain and sewer was also a matter of policy. It seems likely from his treatment of the complaints mentioned earlier, in this Part, that the Irish Ombudsman would, like his British cousin, have thought that he did have jurisdiction to appraise these "policy issues".

On a moderate view of the Ombudsman's jurisdiction it would seem implicit in both the nature of the Ombudsman's role and the list of deficiencies quoted earlier, that the Ombudsman only has authority to intervene where there is some specific defect in the process or reasoning leading up to the decision, rather than simply where he differs from the result. In short, he must not usurp the position of the body in which the decision in question has been vested. In one case where the Ombudsman was following this trend, he rejected a complaint against the Revenue Commissioners. The facts were that the Commissioners had refused to grant a cartographer a tax

---

89   1989 Report, pp. 50–59. It is striking that this Report quotes from the Health Board's response to the Ombudsman that:

> "[it] may well be that the policy itself is open to criticism or even to legal challenge but that, of itself, does not imply that it is necessarily a matter where change is incumbent on the Board as a result of the Ombudsman's observations."

The Ombudsman's Report, however, makes no comment on this contention.

90   1989 Report, p. 43.
91   1989 Report, p. 64; see also 1987 Report, p. 53.
92   1987 Report, p. 28; see also 1989 Report, p. 60.
93   1996 Report, p. 31.
94   [1988] Q.B. 855. The division between the majority and the dissentient judge was not primarily about the demarcation line between policy and administration but rather about whether, as a matter of fact, the Ombudsman had crossed the line.
95   1984 Report, p .46. See also 1985 Report, p. 30.

exemption under the Finance Act 1969 for producing work which is "original and creative" and displays "cultural and artistic merit". The complainant claimed that the Revenue commissioners had taken no account of evidence of his work's artistic merit. The Ombudsman's view was that:

> "Having studied and consulted on the case at length I came to the conclusion that no fault could be found with the efforts of the Revenue Commissioners to arrive at a decision in a fair and reasonable way. I might not agree with the decision but I have no authority to set up an alternative source of assessment to challenge the advice given to the Commissioners."[95]

At the same time, it has to be said that there have been cases in which the Ombudsman has upheld a complaint merely because he took a different view as to the appreciation of the facts from the public body, for example as to whether the complainant was "available for work", in the context of a claim for unemployment benefit.[96] Or: "I decided, based on the evidence available, that the level of [telephone] usage being billed to this man was most improbable . . ."[97] In such cases, the Ombudsman has come close to acting as an appeal court.

In another category of complaint, there is a triangular situation in that as well as the public body and the complainant, a further private person, with divergent interests from those of the complainant is involved. For example, in one case a dispute had arisen as to whether planning permission should be allowed for an access between two housing estates so as to shorten the children's journey to school, even though this access would disturb the privacy of the complainant who lived in one of the estates. The Ombudsman concluded that whatever decision was reached was bound to be unacceptable to one of the parties and that the local authority had "acted reasonably and with common sense." Accordingly, he did not recommend any change.[98]

"Anomaly, inequity"

Occasionally the Ombudsman will use the terms "anomalous" or "inequitable". Examples include complaints that the free electricity allowance for old age pensioners does not apply in the case of night rate electricity[99]; that social welfare law discriminates against handicapped persons living in residential care (*e.g.* as to free travel) as compared to their counterparts living at home; or the application of a more stringent means test, for higher education grants, in respect of students who defer entry to third level education to a year later than that in which they take their leaving certificate.[100]

A particular example of this arises where a complaint involves two public bodies, which take divergent attitudes to the same concept. For example:

---

[96] 1986 Report, p. 49; 1988 Report, p. 80 (whether complainant was sharing the house with another person, in the context of rent assessment for a local authority house).

[97] 1994 Report, p. 41.

[98] 1985 Report, p. 54. For another "triangular" case in which the Ombudsman recommended no change, see 1993 Report, pp. 107–108. In that case, a local authority had erected a bollard to bar cyclists; however, this had the effect of facilitating burglary to the complainant's house.

[99] 1992 Report, p. 26. See , too, 1996 Report, p. 20.

[100] 1991 Report, p. 21.

"I had reservations, however, about the fairness of the decision in this case given that the Revenue Commissioners were levying income tax and PRSI on the basis that the family was 'ordinarily resident' here. The Department of Social Welfare, on the other hand, was refusing child benefit on the basis that the family was not 'ordinarily resident' here."[101]

Often the decisions in issue involve a wide administrative scheme or circular made by a public body (frequently the Department of Social Welfare or a local authority) in the exercise of a statutory discretion. Plainly, this is an area in which the Ombudsman feels that he should tread warily: on the one hand, there may be an injustice affecting not only the complainant but also several others; on the other hand, what amounts to an anomaly requires a decision whether a differentiating factor is significant. In other words, it really involves a policy question. The resolution of these divergent factors is often couched in this form "Arising from my discussions with the Department, I understand that they are reviewing the entire question."[102]

New facts

In a surprising number of cases, investigation – some of it very resourceful and imaginative – by a member of the Ombudsman's staff has led to the discovery of new facts or information, or cast a fresh light on the existing information, and this has led to a change of heart in the responsible authority.[103] For example, in one case, the Department of Social Welfare had decided that the complainant was not available for employment except as an actor and that this constituted "unreasonable limitations on his availability for work" which was a statutory ground for terminating his unemployment benefit. The Ombudsman suggested various new factors to the appeals officer – including the fact that the complainant has previously worked as a car-park attendant and that this showed that he was willing to take any kind of work. Acting on the Ombudsman's suggestion, the appeals officer reversed the original decision.[104] In another case, the Department of Health had refused to grant financial assistance in respect of medical treatment which he had received in London on the ground that the treatment had been available in Ireland, free of charge. The Ombudsman was able to establish that at the relevant time the treatment had not been available. The Department reversed its decision and also reviewed its administrative arrangements for obtaining the relevant information (requirement of hospital consultant's certificate).[105] In another instructive case, the information given

---

101 1992 Report, p. 30. See also 1991 Report, pp. 41–42; 1995 Report, pp. 23–24.
102 1992 Report, p. 27.
103 In one set of cases, a fund of money overlooked by the public authority, was discovered. It had been set aside in the care of the Public Trustee, for the future maintenance of embankments (1994 Report, pp. 23–24.) See, also, 1996 Report, pp, 15–16, 31 and 32.
104 1984 Report, pp. 49–50; 1992 Report, pp. 15–17. In one occupational injuries benefit decision, the Ombudsman discovered that a widow's late husband had been exposed to one of the prescribed diseases in his second last employment. Consequently she was entitled to occupational injuries benefit which had been refused by an Appeals Officer, who had considered only her husband's most recent employment. See also 1992 Report, pp. 102–103, 106 and 107.
105 1985 Report, p. 47. See further, 1990 Report, p. 47.

by an applicant for unemployment benefit, as a result of which his claim had been refused, was wrong – it had been supplied by the applicant only because he had misunderstood the form.[106] In yet another case, involving an application for a contributory widow's pension, it was discovered that the complainant had paid the appropriate number of social insurance contributions, but they had been paid under her maiden name (something which the Department had not checked, although they had the complainant's maiden name). The complainant was awarded £13,000 back-payment plus £6,000 for loss of purchasing power.[107]

"Negligence or carelessness"

Another category of case included the "administrative bungling"[108] by which a wedding dress and two bridesmaid's dresses, which had been sent by registered post, were mislaid – though eventually recovered – a few days before the wedding. Following the intervention of the Ombudsman, An Post made an *ex gratia* payment of £80 to compensate for expenses (travelling and phone calls) incurred in searching for the dresses.

A further set of cases involved the Land Registry's practice of returning original deeds in letters which have been registered at the lowest registered post fee so that the maximum compensation payable is £20, although the value of the loss would often be a great deal higher. In two complaints of this type,[109] the Ombudsman was informed that "*ex gratia* payments [are made] in appropriate circumstances after each case has been examined on its merits."

Procedure

As might be expected, a great number of complaints to the Ombudsman fall into a category which might broadly be called "procedure". Procedural defects naturally include breaches of constitutional justice.[110] One element of this to which the Ombudsman has recently contributed[111] concerns the duty to give reasons.[112] In one

---

106 1988 Report, p. 55.
107 *Ibid.* p. 63. See also 1985 Report, pp. 56–57. See also 1993 Report, pp. 112–113.
108 1984 Report, pp. 39–40. See further, p. 386.
109 1987 Report, 26–27. See also 1992 Report, pp. 66–69 (incompetent plumbing in water supply to complainant's house) and pp. 134–135; (Bord Telecom cutting away part of a tree to make way for telephone poles); 1993 Report, pp. 91–92 (passport application mislaid by the Department of Foreign Affairs).
110 *e.g.* "I was concerned that the Appeals Officer had finalised his review of the case on the basis of a very detailed report from the SCWO (Superintendent Community Welfare Officer) which appeared to contain much new argument and which had not apparently, been put to the appellant": 1993 Report, p. 63.

   Another complaint arose when Disability Benefit was suspended by the Department of Social Welfare because the complainant had failed to attend an examination by a medical referee. The point on which the Ombudsman focused was that: "Had the Department advised in time that it did not regard his request as reasonable then he would have clearly understood that failure to attend would have resulted in suspension." 1991 Report, p. 95. See, to similar effect: *Thompson v. Minister for Social Welfare* [1989] I.R. 618. See also 1993 Report pp. 85–88 (in a claim under the Suckler Cow Scheme, a farmer was not informed that the Department of Agriculture doubted that the animal was a suckler). See also 1989 Report, p. 48.
111 1997 Report, p. 25. The case is not put as plainly as this in the report. See also 1995 Report, p. 18.
112 On the duty to give reasons, as developed in the courts see pp. 570–573.

case, the complainant had, in 1981–1992, failed in a claim for Deserted Wife's Benefit before the deciding officer on the ground that she had not obtained maintenance from her husband. However, she had failed before the appeals officer, on the distinct ground that she had not proven constructive desertion. The complainant had not been made aware of this difference. In 1997 the Ombudsman recommended that the appeals officer's decision of 1982 ought to be reviewed and that she be awarded £24,000 in arrears. The Department of Social Welfare's preliminary line of defence had been that of the complainant's delay. However this failed on the basis that the complainant had not been informed that it was on the contructive desertion point that she had lost her appeal in 1982. A serious case which went beyond procedure to a question of substantive *vires*, occurred when a local authority attempted to take some land, without paying for it or serving the appropriate notice under the Roads Act 1993. The Ombudsman ordered the payment of compensation.[113]

The Ombudusman will also provide a remedy where there has been a breach of particular regulations. An example of this which has come up on a number of occasions concerns the closure of pedestrian rights of way in residential areas in violation of the statutory procedure[114] which requires advertising in the press (or, where there is an objection, an oral hearing). There is one notable feature of these cases, (which is entirely incidental to the question of procedure). There is a strong public sentiment both for and against closure. By contrast, in most other Ombudsman cases, (at least, at first sight) the line-up is straightforward, *i.e.* complainant *v.* public body.

As to this novel feature the Ombudsman has, so far, merely observed: "[a]dherence to the established procedures would allow both sides to air their views on closure proposals and would be in accordance with the principles of fair and sound administration."[115]

Other instances of bad procedure are: delay[116]; (which is rather common) and bureaucratic bad manners which at worst, shade into "the insolence of office". In another area, the Ombudsman has required full written communication:

> "I felt that it was not satisfactory that the Health Board should rely entirely on verbal communications in a matter of such importance. I felt that the Board should, at least, communicate with parents in writing where a child's dental condition is to be monitored and assessed, and that parents should be given some explanation in writing of what is involved in the assessment procedure. I also felt that it should be clearly conveyed to parents that referral and ongoing review did not carry any assurance of treatment."[117]

Speaking generally in 1984 about the performance of the Revenue Commissioners, the Ombudsman made the following observation:

---

[113] 1996 Report, p. 14.
[114] Under the Local Government (Planning and Development) Act 1963, as amended.
[115] 1991 Report, p. 37.
[116] In 1984, 10 per cent. of all complaints to the Ombudsman involved delay. (See Chap. 7 of Report). By s.1(1) of the 1980 Act, his jurisdiction includes "failure to act".
[117] 1992 Report, p. 112.

"Coping with the harsh economic realities of the Eighties is a traumatic experience, particularly for widows and pensioners. Both are extremely vulnerable and dependent. When sharp cryptic demands for payments are issued from the computer system no account is taken of the age or circumstances of the recipient. The elderly are easily frightened and upset by authoritative demands for payment. It may be that such categories are difficult to identify but some thought should be given as to how the problem might be overcome in order to avoid unnecessary distress to the weak and elderly in our community."[118]

A concrete case which is relevant in the present context involved an American citizen (there is, of course, no requirement that a complainant should be Irish) who arrived at Dublin Airport, on holiday with his golf clubs. Because he attempted to carry the clubs through the green channel, a customs officer decided that he was trying to smuggle them into the country and accordingly that they were liable to forfeiture. As a compromise, they were returned to the complainant on payment of £100 (import tax plus penalty). The Ombudsman recommended that, because there was a reasonable doubt about the complainant's intentions, the penalty should be refunded and that, if he subsequently removed the clubs from the country, the taxes should also be refunded. The Ombudsman also disapproved of two procedural features of the Customs authorities' treatment of the visitor: first, he had not been given a receipt for his golf clubs until he had asked for one; secondly, the customs officers had seized and opened a private letter explaining this action on the ground that it might contain evidence. The Ombudsman's judgment was that there was insufficient justification for opening the letter and, further, that the (non-statutory) instructions governing the opening of such letters, issued by the Revenue Commissioners, had not been followed. The Ombudsman recommended that the instructions for opening personal letters be conveyed clearly to all customs staff.

Ranging rather more widely, we find a number of cases in which the Ombudsman – although "accepting that [in the absence of an Act of the Oireachtas] the Department has to devise its own administrative procedures"[119] – has in effect suggested that a public body ought to overlook breaches of administrative rules or practices by the complainant where such breaches do not affect the spirit of the particular legislation or scheme. The most common example of this is where the complainant has been refused some grant or other advantage on the ground that he has missed a dead-line.[120] In a second type of case, the complainant succeeded on the basis that: ". . . another article of the same Regulation provides that the Minister

---

[118] 1984 Report, p. 18. See also, 1987 Report, p. 25 and 1992 Report, p. 48 (on the proper procedure for removing a child from foster parents). Note also the 1990 Report, p. 86 ("I considered it was a most undesirable administrative practice, to ask any person, but particularly a recently bereaved widow, to sign a contract for accounts which had never issued")

[119] 1992 Report, p. 108. This statement was actually made in a wider context.

[120] 1991 Report, p. 84 ("I was of the opinion that the company had acted within the spirit of the Scheme's conditions. I drew the attention of the Department of Labour to the conflicting information in their documentation on the Scheme and the fact that payment had been made in respect of two of the three other recruits to the company even though their Eligibility Certificate deadlines had not been met") See also 1990 Report, pp. 93–94, 1994 Report, pp. 20, 32–33, 45 and 60. *A contra* 1992 Report, p. 118.

has the discretion to accept an application even where it has not been made in the prescribed manner."[121] In another case, the complaint was upheld since "there was sufficient alternative evidence to satisfy the requirement of the House Improvement Grant [so that] it did not seem reasonable to refuse payment" on the ground that a "completion card" had not been submitted by the complainant.[122] Finally, in one complaint, a farmer had been refused a grant under the Special Beef Premium Scheme because he had not had his cattle's identity cards notched before he sold them. In spite of this breach of the requirement specified by the Department of Agriculture, the Ombudsman went so far as to uphold the complaint on the ground that the farmer was not aware of this requirement because he said that he had not seen the Department's advertisements.

Rather remarkably, there is nothing explicit in the Ombudsman's "Guide to Standards . . . " regarding "openness and transparency", though this concept is plainly implicit in the general formula "dealing properly". In any case, the concept of openness was to the fore, though not mentioned explicitly, in a recent claim upheld by the Ombudsman.[123] This arose out of the failure of the Department of Health to show, to the parents of autistic children, a report of a visit paid by the Department's advisor, to a U.S. treatment centre attended by the children.

Finally, the Ombudsman has recently highlighted a group of cases that the level of service to the public through the Irish language is inadequate.[124]

Information about rights

The Ombudsman has treated it as axiomatic that when the complainant has been given incorrect advice – whether as to the facts or law or administrative practice – that he or she should be given a remedy.[125] A typical example arose out of the refusal by the Department of Agriculture and Food to pay the complainant farmer a grant in respect of a piggery. The Ombudsman stated:

> "In all the circumstances of this case and taking into account especially the advice given to the complainant by ACOT and the misleading information given to him in the out-of-date form, I found that the decision of the Department of Agriculture and Food to refuse to pay the complainant the grants was *contrary to fair and sound administration*."[126]

This approach has also been followed in a case where the advice was correct when given, although circumstances later changed, thus rendering the advice bad.[127] Moreover, the Ombudsman has stated: "As a general point, I consider that where entitlements are concerned, the onus is on public bodies to send a reminder to people who have not replied to the original notification".[128]

---

121 1992 Report, p. 104.
122 1991 Report, p. 78. See, similarly, 1990 Report, p. 77.
123 1996 Report, p. 30.
124 1996 Report, p. 22.
125 1991 Report, p. 12B.
126 1990 Report, pp. 35–42 (Italics supplied. Note, again, the unusual use of the precise words of the statutory heads of maladministration.) This approach was followed even in a case in which the information was correct when given but subsequently revised: 1993 Report, pp. 54–55.
127 1993 Report, pp. 54–55.
128 Report of Investigation of Claims (1997) p. 55.

Another related form of maladministration has been found to exist where a public authority fails to supply information sought by the complainant. In one complicated case, in which the Ombudsman had to hold an investigation, he ruled that:

> "A person owning a dwelling house in need of essential repairs, which lies along the route of a local authority development plan is entitled to basic information from the authority to enable him to protect his rights. In this instance, the basic information which the complainant was entitled to know and to have it stated to him in writing in response to his letter of July 31, 1986 was that if he proceeded with necessary repair work on his house, regard would be had to that expenditure if the Local Authority found it necessary to purchase the property either by agreement or arbitration."[129]

Eventually, the Ombudsman concluded that (to summarise):

(i) the complainant was not in a position to renovate his house because of losing the opportunity to avail of grants;
(ii) the house was consequently uninhabitable and devalued as an asset, and
(iii) he had consequently incurred a liability for rent which he would not otherwise have had as an owner-occupier.

The complainant accepted the local authority's offer to make an *ex gratia* payment of £3,000.[130]

One finds in the Reports, as general comments upon the performance of public bodies, strictures against: the use of "language which, although technically accurate, is not capable of being understood by members of the public"[131]; Bord Telecom's predilection for "standard replies produced by word processor [which] do not respond to the specific point made by the complainant"[132]; and Disabled Persons Maintenance Allowance regulations which "are unsatisfactory in their lack of clarity".[133] Furthermore,

---

[129] 1992 Report, p. 80. See also 1994 Report, pp. 16–17, 19–20.

[130] Again, the Ombudsman has censured the Departments of State involved for their failure, over a period of five years, to reply to letters from a public servant, inquiring what her pension rights would be. (1985 Report, p. 63) Another problem stemmed from section 37 of the Road Traffic Act 1961, under which a person can apply for the removal of a driving licence endorsement after he has had a clean licence for a continuous period of five years, *i.e.* if a new licence is necessary, there must be no gap between the two licences. The Department of the Environment agreed to the Ombudsman's suggestion that the explanatory leaflet provided by the Department should be amended to make it clear that, if a person in this situation has to obtain a new licence, he should ensure that the two licences are absolutely continuous. (1985 Report, p. 28)

Notice, likewise, the following strong statement in 1993 Report, p. 35, in respect of a different area of administration:

"[T]here are basic deficiencies in the information available about the existence and operation of the Treatment Abroad Scheme. This lack of information is evident not only among patients and members of their families, who might need to avail of the scheme but also, unfortunately, among medical and administrative personnel in the health boards. I am concerned also that the operation of the scheme is not sufficiently transparent, that practices differ between health boards and that staff, including medical staff, are not sufficiently familiar with schemes in order to advise or direct the patients at the appropriate time to the relevant administrative scheme."

[131] 1986 Report, p.15.

[132] *Ibid.* p. 23.

[133] 1988 Report, p. 25.

"I would urge public bodies to appreciate that the general public do not have the same level of familiarity with schemes and services as the staff of the bodies themselves. . . If some action is required on the part of the recipient, this should be stated very clearly. If a prescribed format or application form exists for particular schemes or services, it should be included within the correspondence."[134]

A particular instance of the failure to supply information concerns the need to notify a person, with whom there is a dispute, about the availability of grievance procedures. In dealing with one complaint, the Ombudsman referred to,

"the lack of information about complaint procedures in Telecom Éireann. The current telephone directory provides very little information to the subscriber who wishes to dispute an account. Attention is drawn to the freephone facility for querying bills but no information is given on procedures which Telecom Eireann use to check such queries."[135]

Most significant of all in a number of complaints the Ombudsman appears to have gone further and drawn upon a broad, though unspecified principle, that the State is under a positive duty to supply the citizen with relevant information about his rights, whether this involves legal advice or facts about his own personal situation.[136]

---

[134] 1994 Report, p. 37.
[135] 1990 Report, p. 58. See, too, Civil Service Executive Union Annual Report 1985–1986, App. 2, paras. 4.6 and 4.7. ("If an application [for a housing grant] is refused and the citizen disputes the refusal on certain grounds, the Department of the Environment will arrange for the matter to be investigated again by an officer of higher rank than the officer who carried out the first investigation. However, the citizen is not told that such a facility exists. Again, in instances such as this, the necessity for intervention by the Ombudsman's office would be reduced if the appeals system were formalised and the public made aware of their rights.")
[136] See, for example, 1990 Report, pp. 42–44; 1995 Report, p. 23. In the 1992 Report, pp. 30–31, the ombudsman stated:
   "The common thread in all of these cases is an absence of information and a general lack of clarity regarding the health boards' obligations in respect of such long-stay patients. In the case of some of the boards concerned, it would appear that the situation is made worse by the shortage of long-stay beds and by the resultant need to place patients in private nursing homes. It would appear that patients and their families are not being informed of the statutory obligation on the health board in relation to such cases and, accordingly, do not have accurate information regarding the financial implications of this situation."
   See also, 1992 Report, pp. 44 and 71 (Council failed to inform planning applicants that they could apply for a refund in respect of their fees) and pp. 47 and 64 ("Health Boards have a duty, where they are professionally involved in the management of allowances for the handicapped to impart information about specific allowances to the parents."); 1991 Report, p. 102 ("I suggested to the Department that in order to avoid situations like the one experienced by the complainant, they might consider elaborating on the form relating to the requirements for re-registration of a vehicle."); 1990 Report, p. 82 ("Parents whose children are in receipt of Domiciliary Care Allowance up to a limit of 16 years of age should be informed that payment is about to end and that it is necessary to [apply] for D. P. M. A. [as a successor grant]"); 1997 Report, p. 22 ("Dealing 'fairly' with people means . . . giving adequate notice before changing rules in a way which adversely affects a person's entitlement"). For a slight twist on the basic principle, see *Report of Investigation of Complaint*, (1997) p. 56: "the relevant provision is sufficiently flexible to allow the Department to accept a claim for one payment as having been made on account of another payment." For a case involving a failure of internal communication between two sections of a health board, see 1994 Report, p. 38.
   In Britain, advice case have represented 20 per cent of all the investigations published by the PCA in his selected case reports: Mowbray, "A Right to Official Advice" (1986) *Public Law* 68 at 69.

At a specific level, there have been a number of cases in which welfare agencies have been censored for failing to mention to the complainant benefits or allowances which might have applied to him.[137] In such circumstances, the agency has granted the benefit or allowance with retrospective effect. In addition, as a result of the Ombudsman's prompting, the Department of Social Welfare now gives to farmers details of its assessment of their means where this assessment has led to a reduction in their social welfare payments.[138]

All in all, the Ombudsman shows no sympathy whatsoever with the well-established legal principle (which was actually put to him unavailingly on one occasion, by the Department of Social Welfare,[139]) that "ignorance of the law is no defence."[140] This outlook is likely to have even more significant consequences in the future because of the Ombudsman's wider role as overseer under the administrative procedure legislation.[141]

3. Exemptions from Jurisdiction

Even within the subject area thus staked out, six categories of case are exempted from the Ombudsman's jurisdiction.

1. The Ombudsman is excluded where there is a right of appeal in respect of the decision to a court.[142] It is striking that, in contrast with the position in Britain, there is no provision preventing a potential complainant from going to the Ombudsman merely because he could have instituted legal proceedings (for example, judicial review of an administrative action) in a court in respect of the complaint.[143] However, the Ombudsman is, naturally, prevented from hearing a case where the person aggrieved has actually initiated "civil legal proceedings".[144] Even then, the Ombudsman will not be excluded if "the proceedings have been dismissed for failure to disclose a cause of action or a complaint justiciable by that court".[145] This limitation upon the matters over which the Ombudsman has no jurisdiction evidently arises because (as noted above), the grounds on which complaints may be made to

---

[137] 1985 Report, p. 23.

[138] 1987 Report, p. 68; 1988 Report, p. 65; 1989 Report, p. 73.

[139] 1987 Report, p. 68.

[140] Indeed the Ombudsman has remarked:

"The experience of my office over 12 years has been that the vast majority of . . . late claimants say that they were poorly informed about their social insurance rights . . . Despite genuine advances in the Department's information services over the past decade and despite the efforts of the Citizen's Information Centres and the National Social Service Board . . . many people are ill-informed . . . The Department has been taking the line that . . . ultimately ignorance of the law is not an unacceptable excuse for having failed to claim in time. I feel that, in the context of social insurance, this is not a reasonable position to adopt." *Report of Investigations of Complaints 1997*, pp. 62–63.

[141] On the forthcoming administrative procedure legislation, see p. 494.

[142] s.5(1)(a)(ii). But though a person is entitled to apply to the High Court for habeas corpus, he may still refer his grievance to the Ombudsman: see Gwynn Morgan, *op. cit.* above, n.1, p. 110.

[143] Compare pp. 734–739.

[144] s.5(1)(a)(ii). "Civil legal proceedings" is probably (if only from its context) intended to include both civil actions and applications for judicial review.

[145] *Ibid.*

the Ombudsman are wider than those which apply to a court, and it is thought to be harsh to prevent a case going to the Ombudsman on the basis that the case has been before a court, if the grounds of complaint anyway fall outside the court's jurisdiction. Pursuing a similar line of reasoning, it might be asked whether a complainant ought to lose his chance of going to the Ombudsman if his court case had failed because it was out of time, or because he had adopted the wrong procedure, or for any other reason unrelated to the merits. If the provision is read strictly, such a person would not be within the Ombudsman's jurisdiction. There is, however, an equitable proviso which permits the investigation of actions "if it appears to the Ombudsman that special circumstances make it proper to do so"[146] even though those actions would otherwise be excluded (under either this, or the next, exemption). This proviso would probably enable the Ombudsman to investigate in a case in which the court had turned the complainant away for some reason other than the merits of his claim.

2. The Ombudsman has no jurisdiction over a decision from which an appeal lies to "a person other than a Department of State or other person specified in Part I of the First Schedule", irrespective of whether any appeal has actually been taken.[147] The effect of the phrase quoted is that, following the recommendation of the All-Party Report,[148] the Ombudsman retains jurisdiction over decisions if the appeal lies to a Minister or civil servant[149] in a Department. Thus subject to the local remedies rule (see exemption 5 below), the Ombudsman has jurisdiction[150] over claims for social welfare benefit which are heard by deciding officers in the Department of Social Welfare or appeals from deciding officers, which are heard by appeals officers (again within the Department).[151] By contrast, on the other side of the line, the exclusion of cases where there is an appeal to someone other than a Department means, for instance, that the Ombudsman is excluded from planning cases (either at the initial or appeal stage) because of the appeal to An Bord Pleanála. Similarly, he may not review decisions of the Revenue Commissioners where there is an appeal to the Appeals Commissioners. Nevertheless the Ombudsman has investigated a large number of complaints against the Revenue Commissioners in respect of other matters, for instance: delay in sending out tax rebates or statements of allowance; excessive zeal in investigating suspected evasion. He has also investigated complaints against the Customs and Excise area, at a time where there was no appeal in respect of the area. Likewise, it has been assumed that the Ombudsman is not shut out in the case of procedural or other incidental matters in

---

[146] Proviso to s.5(1).
[147] s.5(1)(a)(ii), (iii).
[148] All Party Report, s.VII, para. 12.
[149] See s.1(2).
[150] Although note 1992 Report, p. 106:
"I was advised that an oral hearing of her appeal was to be held shortly. I therefore explained to the complainant that it would not be appropriate for me to intervene in her case until her appeal had been finalised but that she could contact me again if she was not satisfied with the outcome of the appeal."
[151] Notice that s.5(1)(a)(iii) is fortified by s.1(1) which defines "action" to include "decision" and section 1(2) which defines Department of State "to include not only a Minster but also his officers", *i.e.* civil servants. See also, s.5(2).

relation to planning. Examples include a local planning authority's failure to inform applicants on how to apply for a refund,[152] and failure to inform complainants of a local authority decision so that they were not in time to appeal to Bord Pleanála.[153]

3. The Ombudsman does not have jurisdiction over actions relating to "national security or military activity or (in the opinion of the Ombudsman) arrangements regarding participation in organisations of states or governments"; "the administration of the law relating to aliens or naturalisation"; the exercise of the power of pardon and the administration of prisons or other similar institutions.[154] In addition, the Ombudsman is forbidden to investigate recruitment or appointment to any of the bodies listed in the First Schedule[155] or any matter relating to the terms or conditions upon which a person holds any office or employment in any of the bodies listed in the First or Second Schedule.[156] However, there is no ban on investigating the dismissal of a servant or officer nor (as there is in Britain) the making or terms of a commercial contract between a department and a private person.

4. A Minister of the Government may prevent or restrain the Ombudsman from investigating any action of that Minister's Department (or of a person "whose business and functions are comprised" in that Department) simply by making a written request to that effect, setting out in full the reasons for the request.[157] The justification for this provision, offered by the Minister of State at the Department of the Public Service piloting the Bill through the Dáil, is the need to exclude from the Ombudsman's jurisdiction points of judgment for which a Minister should be answerable only to the Dáil.[158] The safeguard, which is designed to prevent Ministers from drawing too freely on this blank cheque, is publicity: not only must the communication to the Ombudsman be in writing, but it must be passed on by the Ombudsman to the complainant and must also be recorded in the Reports which the Ombudsman has to lay before the Oireachtas.[159] This device has not yet been used.

5. The Ombudsman has a jurisdiction not to hear a complaint if he considers that it is "trivial or vexatious"; that the complainant has not exhausted his local remedies; or that the subject-matter of the complaint has been, is being, or will be, sufficiently investigated in another investigation by the Ombudsman.[160]

6. The complaint must be made within 12 months of the time of the action or – and this could be a significant extension – the time when the complainant became aware of the complaint, whichever is the later. However, an exception to this rule may be

---

152 1992 Report, pp. 69–72.
153 1991 Report, p. 39.
154 s.5(1)(b), (e)(i), (ii) and (iii).
155 s.5(1)(c).
156 s.5(1)(d)(i). (In 1984 and 1985, 13 per cent. and 3 per cent., respectively, of all complaints made to the Ombudsman had to be excluded on the grounds that they involved civil service personnel matters. Thereafter this figure was diminished.)
157 s.5(3).
158 321 *Dáil Debates*, Cols. 867–869 (May 28, 1980). See too All Party Report, ss.II, VII.
159 ss.5 (3), 6 (7).
160 s.4 (5), (6).

allowed where "it appears to the Ombudsman that special circumstances make it proper to do so".[161]

4. Procedure

An investigation (which must be "conducted otherwise than in public")[162] may be initiated either by way of complaint or by the Ombudsman acting of his own motion if it appears to him that an investigation would be warranted.[163] No formality is necessary: even a simple phone call will suffice.[164] In some cases, the Ombudsman has criticised a public body for its delay in responding to a complaint, which he has put to it.[165]

Preliminary examination

First, the Ombudsman carries out a preliminary examination[166] at which a number of complaints are weeded out, for instance, because they involve social welfare claims by persons who clearly have not paid sufficient contributions; or because they seek to inveigle the Ombudsman to intervene in the merits of income tax disputes which are the preserve of the Appeals Commissioners.[167] Where the Ombudsman decides not to proceed with a complaint, then he must write to the complainant stating his reasons.[168]

The 1980 Act, section 8(3) provides that: "[s]ubject to the provisions of this Act, the procedure for conducting an investigation shall be such as the Ombudsman considers appropriate." And, indeed drawing on this freedom, more than 99 per cent of the Ombudsman's cases are settled at the first stage, which the Act contemplates

---

[161] s.5 (1), proviso. In addition the action must not have taken place before the commencement of the Act(s.5(1)(g)). The Act was brought into force on July 7, 1983, by statutory order, made under s.12(2). S.5(2) provides that notwithstanding the time limits in the text, the Ombudsman may "investigate insurability and entitlement to benefit under the Social Welfare Acts 1952 to 1979" (now the Social Welfare (Consolidation) Act 1993: see 1993 Act, s. 3(9)). Even apart from specific provision the Ombudsman observes a general "continuing effect" doctrine by which he is prepared to investigate circumstances or facts occurring before the time limit, if these are relevant to decisions taken after the time limits.

[162] s.8(1). This phrase may have been used in preference to "in private" so as to indicate that the Ombudsman retains a power to allow selected persons to be acquainted with the investigation.

[163] s.4(3)(b).

[164] In *R. v. Local Commissioner for Public Administration, ex p. Bradford MCC* [1979] Q.B. 287, 313 the argument that a complaint must specify the particular maladministration which led to the injustice to the complainant was rejected by a majority of the Court of Appeal.

[165] "It is not reasonable that the Department should delay taking a decision to seek legal advice for some seven months after receiving a detailed anylsis from this office. A further six months elapsed before the advice was received by the Department and one month later it responded to this office.": 1997 Report, p. 28. See also pp. 19 and 30 of the Report.

[166] s. 4(2). See also, s.4(5).

[167] *cf.* Civil Service Executive Union Report for 1985–1986, App. 2, para. 3.3, complaining that provided a matter falls within his jurisdiction, "the Ombudsman's enquiries are becoming akin to representations by public representatives – *i.e.* almost all cases taken up without discrimination."

[168] s.6(1).

would be merely a preliminary examination.[169] In the 1984 Report, this device was characterised as a "Review Procedure"[170] and explained as follows:

"I have adopted a system of seeking to find a solution to many cases by way of a request to the Department involved for a review. Requests for a review are normally made in the context of our having conducted fairly detailed preliminary examination and having reached certain tentative conclusions as to the outcome. At the stage where I have established in my mind the nature of the likely recommendation, I sometimes ask the Department concerned if they would like to respond favourably along certain lines.

The purpose of a review of this kind, which is widely used by Ombudsmen throughout the world, is to enable a Department to look again at a particular case in the light of new evidence or fresh argument. A review enables a Department to alter an earlier decision on its own initiative rather than to await a formal recommendation from the Ombudsman's Office when the opportunity will have been lost to act independently."

The Ombudsman has made formal agreements[171] as to procedure with the Departments of State, local authorities and health boards. These provide, in the first place, that a particular official – at the levels indicated – should act as a contact point with the Ombudsman: Principal (Department of State); County Secretary (Local Authority); Programme Manager (Health Board). On first receiving a complaint (assuming that it is not outside jurisdiction or manifestly unsustainable) the Ombudsman contacts, usually by letter but sometimes by phone, the appropriate official, who is supposed to ensure that a reply is furnished within one month. There may also be further exchanges. The matter may be concluded by the Ombudsman accepting that there has been no maladministration or that for some other reason there is no ground for the complaint. Alternatively, the public body complained against may accept from the Ombudsman what is, strictly speaking, at this stage merely a suggestion as to how the maladministration may be remedied. A further way in which a complaint may be resolved at this stage is through the Ombudsman writing to the head of the public body explaining that he is concluding the preliminary examination and suggesting that the public body review its performance along specified lines.

Formal investigation

Almost all complaints are concluded at the preliminary examination stage. However, a small number – of the order of a dozen each year – go on to what the 1980 Act calls simply an "investigation", though it is usually referred to, in the Ombudsman's

---

[169] The proposed Ombudsman (Amendment) Bill (see, p. 343, n.33) would modify the legislation to bring it closer to the practice.

[170] Pl. 2909, pp. 9–10. See also 1986 Report, p. 13, 1985 Report, p. 19. Related points of difference between the two procedures are that, following an investigation (in contrast to a preliminary inquiry), the Ombudsman must notify, in writing, the head of the body concerned of its results and, also, may publish a report.

[171] See DPS Circular 30/83.

annual reports, as a "formal investigation".[172] Such investigations (a sample of which are reported in their own special part of the annual reports) are expensive for the Ombudsman's office and, accordingly, he prefers to reserve them for complaints which are particularly serious, (usually because there are a number of similar complaints.[173] First of all, the Ombudsman writes, to the head of the organisation under scrutiny, a letter which must include an explanation of the complaint and a statement that the Ombudsman has completed a preliminary examination, has decided to proceed and is now commencing an investigation. The head of the organisation then replies giving his view of the matter. Next, the Ombudsman sends out two persons – usually an investigator and a senior investigator – to check documents, interview each person, etc. When an interview has been put in the form in which it is going to be used, it is checked with the interviewee, who may, at this point, for instance, suggest that something be omitted because it would cause him embarrassment, which suggestion would be taken seriously by the Ombudsman. When the first draft of a report has been prepared, with no recommendations at this stage, it is sent to the head of the organisation for his comments. It is only after these have been considered that the Ombudsman completes his report and adds on a recommendation.[174]

As already mentioned, the statutory statement that the Ombudsman can choose his own procedure is qualified by the *caveat* "[s]ubject to the provisions of this Act." The principal provisions referred to consist of a formulation of the *audi alteram partem* rule: the public must have an opportunity to comment upon both the complaint and any adverse finding or criticism by the Ombudsman.[175] These statutory obligations are, we believe, satisfied, by the procedure which is described in the previous paragraph.

Information

The Act gives the Ombudsman virtually full access to all relevant files for the purposes of a preliminary investigation or an examination. Considering the extent to which public authorities record information, it is one of the Ombudsman's most potent weapons that he may require any person who, in his opinion, possesses relevant information, or a relevant document or "thing", either to send the information, document or thing to the Ombudsman or, where appropriate, to attend before the Ombudsman to furnish the information, document or thing[176]: "The issue of my

---

172 For the most detailed of these, see *Report of Investigation of Complaints against the Department of Social Welfare*, especially so far as the Ombudsman's procedure is concerned, pp. 7–8, 36 and Appendix I.

173 1980 Act, s.6(2), (7). See also: 1988 Report, pp. 11–12; 1990 Report, pp. 3–4; 1993 Report, pp. 3–4.

174 The Ombudsman's wide discretion in regard to procedure would allow him to hold oral hearings (s.8(3), (4)) but not a single hearing has yet (1996) been held. A former British Commissioner was reluctant to hold oral hearings: "because they are alien to the ombudsman tradition which seeks to solve disputes between citizens and state with the least degree of confrontation or formality. People in general do not want confrontation or to appear in anything resembling a court." Clothier (1984) L.S. Gaz. 3108 at 3110. It seems probable that the Irish Ombudsman feels the same.

175 1980 Act, ss.8(2), 6(6). This right probably extends to any public servant whose behaviour is criticised because he or she would probably be included in the word "person" in s.6(6). However, in practice, the Ombudsman avoids allocating responsibility to individual officials. See also, s.6(2), (4).

176 Section 7(1)(a). Failure to comply is not made an offence by the Act (whatever the common law

access to medical records has long since been clarified and I regularly obtain files with clinical details from the health boards and the Department of Health."[177]

There are only two curbs on the Ombudsman's access to information. The first is that the Ombudsman may not ask for information or a document which "relates to decisions and proceedings of the Government or of any of its committees".[178] And, for the purposes of determining whether information or a document does fall within this category, a certificate given by the Secretary to the Government is to be conclusive.[179] The second exception is only partial: it does not prevent information or a document from being given to the Ombudsman, but only from being disclosed by the Ombudsman to anyone else, even those involved in the complaint. It applies where any Minister of the Government has given notice, in writing, to the Ombudsman, that the disclosure of any document or information or class thereof would in his opinion and for the reasons stated in the notice, "be prejudicial to the public interest".[180] As of 1996, neither restriction has been invoked.

Sanctions

If, as a result of the investigation, it does appear to the Ombudsman that the action had an adverse affect and that, otherwise too, it fell within his jurisdiction, then the Ombudsman may choose between three specified types of recommendation to the Department which took the decision, namely, that the action be reconsidered; that the reasons for it be given to the Ombudsman; or, finally, that measures or specified measures be taken to remedy, mitigate or alter the adverse effect of the action.[181] In some cases, there might have to be further sets of responses and recommendations in the dialogue.[182] The only matters which the Ombudsman is required by his parent

---

position). It is assumed that public servants would not wish to jeopardise their careers by a refusal to comply. The basic principle that the Ombudsman may call for whatever evidence is relevant is buttressed by other rules: witnesses are entitled to the same privileges as High Court witnesses (s.7(1)) though in contrast to certain other Ombudsmen, he has no authority to administer an oath; a witness' evidence may not be used against him in criminal proceedings (s.7(6)); expenses of witnesses or complainant may be paid (s.7(5)); the Official Secrets Act 1963 is suspended in respect of examinations or investigations (s.7(4)); executive privilege is restricted to the rules stated in the next paragraph of the text (s.7(4)); the same protection created for a court by the contempt of court rules is extended to the Ombudsman, though no power is given to commit for contempt (s.7(3)); and information obtained by the Ombudsman can be disclosed only for the purpose of the Act or for proceedings under the Official Secrets Act and not for any other proceedings (s.9(1)).

[177] 1997 Report, p. 19.
[178] s.7(1)(b). This is the first statutory acknowledgment of the existence of Government committees.
[179] *Ibid.* Contrast the position before a court, described at pp. 935–952.
[180] S. 9(2)(a)(c). See also, s. 9(2)(b).
[181] S. 6(3).
[182] See, *e.g.* 1991 Report, p. 57:
"In the light of my recommendation the Department offered to make a payment of £4,500 to the complainant. I indicated that I found this offer unreasonable because the complainant had already suffered a substantial penalty through being deprived of the use of the money over the previous 5 years. It seemed to me that the Department were then seeking to impose a double penalty on the complainant by fining him a sum of £662 for the delay in submitting his claim and a further sum of about £200 because of the reduction in the value of the money in the previous 5 years. The Department subsequently agreed to pay the full amount of £5,162."
Another example is to be found in the 1991 Report, p. 72:
"I recommended that the Health Board pay £1,500 to (Mr A) to meet the expenditure by him of £1,368 on operations to his eyes in 1987 and 1988 and as compensation for the declining

statute, to communicate to the complainant – and all he does transmit – are "the result of the investigation, the recommendation (if any) made by [the Ombudsman] and the response (if any) made to it by the Department of State or other person to whom it was given".[183] In addition, he will usually give a fairly brief indication of his reasons, thereby fulfilling the general duty to give reasons,[184] imposed as a matter or constitutional justice or the Freedom of Information Act 1997.

Apart from the three specified types of recommendation which have just been itemised, no further guidance is given, by the Act, as to the type of remedies to be granted. A very great deal is thus left to the discretion of the Ombudsman in consultation with the public body under investigation. Moreover, with one exception, described below, the Annual Reports do not yet offer much in the way of clarification in this field. In at least one case, an apology was forthcoming (where the Motor Registration Office claimed that the complainant had been given too much change).[185] However, in the overwhelming majority of cases, the remedy is the payment of money and the calculation of the amount is, in principle, straightforward: for example, it is the amount of the grant or benefit which the complainant was wrongfully denied or the amount by which his telephone bill was too high (though the precise assessment of this may require some give and take). The Ombudsman is not, of course, concerned with whether the public authority is legally obliged to pay the money. His objective is simply to achieve "a reasonable outcome",[186] an inevitably inexact phrase which was used to explain the acceptance of a local authority's offer to pay a round figure of £1,000 to cover any possible defects in building work which a council engineer had certified as completed for the purpose of a grant.

Potentially, the Ombudsman could be confronted with the entire gamut of problems[187] regarding consequential loss, pecuniary loss, etc., which arise in the law of tort.[188] What would happen, to take just one hypothetical example, in a situation in which a complainant had set up a business on the basis of (wrong) advice

---

value of that money since 1987. The Health Board's initial response to this recommendation was that it was unwilling to implement it. Following an exchange of correspondence, the Health Board modified its position to one where it was prepared to implement my recommendation in part, viz. it was prepared to pay Mr A the costs incurred in the first operation only. I did not accept this offer. Following further discussion, involving the Department of Health, the Health Board agreed to implement my recommendation in full and paid Mr A an amount of £1,500."

[183] S. 6(4)

[184] See pp. 570–577 and the Freedom of Information Act 1997, Pt. II and First Sched.

[185] 1988 Report, pp. 78–79. See, too, 1997 Report, p. 17.

[186] 1989 Report, p. 13.

[187] In the 1991 Report, p. 105, the Ombudsman recommended that Bord Telecom pay £62 to discharge the legal costs which the complainant had incurred when he went to a solicitor because his telephone had been cut off.

[188] In the 1994 Report, p. 43, a complaint is reported which arose out of a delay in cashing a Savings Certificate, which meant that the complainant had lost an opportunity to avail of favourable interest in re-investing the proceeds:

"I could not recommend that the complainant be compensated for a potential loss of opportunity of re-investing elsewhere. After examining all the factors involved, I recommended that An Post should increase the amount of the *ex gratia* payment which had already been made, by £100. An Post agreed with this and made the additional payment."

But for a case in which compensation was ordered for consequential loss, see 1992 Annual Report, p. 80.

from a public servant that he was entitled to a grant? The grant is refused, and the business crashes. Is the complainant awarded: merely the value of the grant; the amount of his loss of capital money; and/or compensation for potential loss of profits?[189] Again, in a distinct situation – in which there is minor, non-material damage, yet no objectively determinable figure for compensation is available – the Ombudsman has sometimes decided that £100 would compensate for "the stress and inconvenience".[190]

Third Parties

It is axiomatic that the Ombudsman's authority is confined to remedies against public bodies; he may not interfere with the legal rights of third parties. This considerably limits the Ombudsman's powers. For example, the Ombudsman could not have a decision to grant planning permission rescinded where the local authority had denied the complainant-objectors their statutory rights of appeal to An Bord Pleanála (An offer for payment of compensation by the local authority had already been made and declined).[191]

Given that the Ombudsman is often concerned with the allocation of scarce resources, one could easily envisage a situation in which giving a remedy to the complainant would involve retrospectively demoting the claims of some other, innocent person. What if, for instance, the Ombudsman recommended that the complainant's claim to a local authority letting be promoted (inevitably, above those of other claimants)? Surprisingly, this type of difficulty has not quite arisen (since the case just mentioned above involved actual statutory rights).[192] However, the following tri-angular situation has occurred: Several complaints have been made against Bord Telecom because burglar alarm systems attached to telephone lines had developed faults and, as a result and unknown to the subscriber, the automatic dialling system made a number of calls to a central monitoring station. The outcome was that a number of local calls were registered on the subscribers' meters. Their telephone bills increased, in one case to £1,200. The Ombudsman concluded that since there was no fault in the Telecom equipment, he could not recommend that Telecom should rebate the charges. One of the complainants subsequently sued the supplier of the alarm system and the action was settled out of court.[193]

---

[189] In the U.K., the following comment has been offered on the Ombudsman's approach to one complaint: "the Commissioner is seeking to distinguish between financial losses directly attributable to the defective advice and those flowing from other sources. But this process of allocation is far from precise and the PCA has considerable leeway in making his calculations": Mowbray, "A Right of Official Advice" (1986) *Public Law* 68 at 82.

[190] 1994 Report, p. 22. The quotation is from a case in which a local authority had mistakenly allocated the complainant's grave space to another person, but had given the complainant an alternative space. For other accounts of awards of £100, see 1991 Report, p. 39 and 1994 Report, p. 43. Note, however, 1992 Report, pp. 128–129, in which £500 was awarded when Bord Telecom had continued to bill the complainant for phone numbers she had cancelled. This amount appears to have been awarded because of the trauma suffered by the complainant before the necessary rebates and corrections were made.

[191] 1994 Report, p. 51. The complainants were said to be taking advice as to whether to initiate legal proceedings.

[192] Although for a near miss see 1994 Report, p. 64.

[193] 1993 Report, p. 69. See likewise, 1992 Report, p. 27.

Interest on the money not paid

One particular situation which has frequently arisen is where the Ombudsman orders the payment of money which should have been paid, say, several years earlier.[194] In these cases the Ombudsman may wish to include an amount (which may or may not be called "interest") to compensate for late payment. His ability to do this was at first opposed by the Department of Finance and the Government, their opposition being put on the basis of the principle that in making such a recommendation, the Ombudsman was trespassing in the field of policy; yet, surely, assuming that there has been an action involving maladministration, if payment in respect of it has been delayed, then the necessity for compensation for late payment flows fairly automatically from the Ombudsman's obligation to "remedy the adverse affect [*sic*] of the action."[195] In any case, in 1986, following a threat by the Ombudsman to make what would have been his first special report to the Oireachtas, a decision of the Government led to an agreement between the Ombudsman and the Department of Finance, providing for the payment of compensation in Social Welfare cases. (The Department of Finance also agreed that this precedent would be followed in cases in which payments by other Departments were excessively delayed.) By this agreement, the Department of Finance, whose sanction (either direct or delegated) is necessary for all departmental expenditure, delegated sanction to the Department of Social Welfare to pay compensation based on the movement of the Consumer Price Index, where a payment is made more than two years late.[196]

Late claim for arrears by applicant

A distinct, though similar, situation arises where the failure is on the applicant's part in that his or her claim for payment by a public body is made late. The issue of a public body's refusal to make a payment because a person, who is otherwise fully entitled, applies late has arisen in a number of complaints throughout the period since the origin of the Ombudsman office in 1984. It was recently the subject of the Ombudsman's only substantive Report.[197] The complaints (which were typical of 59 other cases contemporaneously before the Ombudsman) concerned the Department of Social Welfare's refusal to pay arrears to persons who had been late in applying for a pension. (One should emphasise that this is a different situation from that in which interest is claimed on arrears, though somewhat similar issues are involved.[198]) The Ombudsman has summarised his reasons for recommending in the complainants' favour as follows:

> "(1) that the general approach of the Department to late claims, especially where there is good cause for the delay, reflects a failure to mitigate the effects of rigid

---

194 1986 Report, pp. 16, 36 and 67. See also: 1984 Report, p. 42; 1985 Report, p. 8.
195 s.6(3)(b).
196 For this agreement, see 1986 Report, pp. 16, 36: "The Department of Finance have also supported my suggestion that there should be statutory provision for such payments as soon as practicable and they have asked the Department of Social Welfare to consider bringing forward statutory provisions to formalise the new arrangements."
197 *Report of Investigation of Complaints against the Department of Social Welfare regarding Arrears of Contributory Pensions*, (March 14, 1997). On this, Report see further pp. 346–347.
198 See above.

adherence to the strict terms of the Regulation where that produces manifestly inequitable and unfair treatment; (2) that there has been a failure, by the Department, over time, to take action to ameliorate the consequences of the application of the Regulation and (3) that the application of the Regulation, in individual cases, does not comply with basic fairness or reasonableness nor does it satisfy the requirements of the principle of proportionality."[199]

Special Report

If the response to any recommendation is not "satisfactory", the Ombudsman's ultimate and only sanction is to make a "special report" on the case to the Houses of the Oireachtas.[200] This term is always used by the Ombudsman in the sense of a report which is separate from the annual report and which is laid before the Houses of the Oireachtas immediately after the public body's unsatisfactory response, thereby attracting greater publicity than a report which is merely included as part of the annual report. The Ombudsman has stated:

> "Battles of the early years are mainly a memory now but from time to time major difficulties are still encountered because some public bodies cannot accept that they have been guilty of maladministration. Eventually, and only after detailed correspondence and contacts, they are faced with the possibility of a special report being made to the Oireachtas unless they are prepared to respond reasonably to the Ombudsman's recommendation. This provision in the Ombudsman's Act is also a very powerful weapon which has been given to the Office of the Ombudsman. I am very glad that, over the past ten years, despite my being compelled on a number of occasions to inform public bodies and public servants of the possibility of my using this power, I have never had occasion to use it."[201]

As of mid-1997, there had only been a single special report dealing with a substantive issue, as contradistinguished from the report dealing with staffing cutbacks. This was the report on arrears of the contributory pensions. Here the special report was justified by the Director of the Ombudsman's Office on the basis:

---

[199] Note that this summary is taken not from the Special Report itself but from the Annual Report for 1997, p. 21. Notice, too, that mainly on foot of the Ombudsman's Special Report, the period in respect of which arrears may be made if a claim is late has been extended from six to twelve months and has also been made part of primary legislation (Social Welfare Act, 1997, s.32).

[200] S.6(5), (7). The Ombudsman's functions under s.6(5), (7) (together with those in the personnel field) are the only ones which he is not empowered to delegate to his officers: s.10(3).

[201] 1993 Report, p. 2. See, to similar effect, 1986 Report, p. 5; 1989 Report, p. 11. As mentioned, at p. 341, a special report was made on the cuts in the Ombudsman's staff: see 1987 Report, p. 119. Notice, too, that in 1993 Report, p. 10, the Ombudsman remarked that he had been "preparing to submit a special report" in regard to compensation for late payment for social welfare benefits, but the issue was then resolved. (This is the only one of the cases alluded to in the final sentence of the passage quoted in the text to be actually identified in the reports.) The present (second) Ombudsman, Mr Murphy, has remarked: "I will also issue individual reports on cases I consider to be of particular importance." (1994 Report, p. 7)

"of [both] the instrinsic interest of the issues raised and . . . the Ombudsman's commitment to increasing public awareness of the nature of the work undertaken by his Office."[202]

5. Legal Control of the Ombudsman

In view of the expansionist policy adopted by the Ombudsman, it is worth stating that, like any other public authority, he is subject to the law. His jurisdiction and procedure are governed by public law. This means that he is subject to the 1980 Act; the Constitution (including constitutional justice); as well as various general principles, such as the doctrine of reasonableness in the exercise of his various discretions.[203]

As regards the procedure by which these controls might be mobilised, it would be open to (say) a Department of State which wanted to stop the Ombudsman from investigating their activities, to move the High Court, by way of an application for judicial review seeking an order restraining such an investigation.[204] (In fact, even the threat of legal action has not yet been made by a public body). A second possibility is an action brought against the Ombudsman by a private individual whose complaint he had rejected. (In practice, this is unlikely, not least because if such a person were prepared for High Court litigation, then in almost all cases, it would be possible – and tactically better – to go directly against the erring public body; though, on one occasion, a disappointed complainant threatened legal proceedings.)

In the opposite direction, some body or person might refuse to co-operate with the Ombudsman. If a public body fails to heed the Ombudsman's recommendation, the Ombudsman should be able to invoke the sanctions of publicity, presumably through a special report. However, it would not be open to him to enforce the recommendation by way of a court order.[205] Contrast, the wording of the Act in a different context. Section 7(1)(a) provides: "The Ombudsman may . . . require any person . . . to furnish [any] information document or thing . . . and the person shall comply with the requirements." Thus here the Ombudsman could have recourse to an application for judicial review against the recalcitrant Minister or other public body.[206]

---

202 This quotation is from the official covering letter sent out with *Report of Investigation of Complaints against the Department of Social Welfare* (1997).

203 For example, by s.4(2) of the 1980 Act, he has a discretion as to whether to investigate an action at all.

204 For some English cases in which the public body took the Ombudsman to court, see *Re Fletcher's Application* [1970] 2 All E.R. 527 ; *R v. LCA ex p. Eastleigh* [1988] Q.B. 855 and cases described in Foulkes, *Administrative Law* (8th ed., 1995), pp. 553–555. For a case in which it was the complainant who took proceedings see *R v. PCA ex p. Dyer* [1994] 1 All E.R. 375 (held that the PCA was subject to the courts' jurisdiction. See to similar effect, *R. v. Parliamentary Commissioner for Standards ex p. Fayed* [1998] 1 All E.R. 93.

205 S. 6(5) discussed at p. 379.

206 The sanction envisaged by the Ombudsman in his Annual Report for 1989, p. 4 would be premature: "It might have been expected that it would not be necessary to draw [any public servants'] attention to the risk of contempt proceedings for their failure to respond adequately or in good time to this Office." But surely however, for extra-legal reasons (for example career prospects) a public servant

In any case, whether proceedings were taken against, or by, the Ombudsman, it is realistic to suppose that any private individual, or, *a fortiori*, any public body, which was opposing the Ombudsman would have an uphill battle. In the first place, the Ombudsman is popular with the public and the courts are not insensible of the feelings of the public. In addition, a court would be influenced by the reversal of its own normal role in a public law case. Ordinarily, its task is to consider whether to control a public body in the interest of an individual. In a case in which it had to decide whether to restrain the Ombudsman from controlling a public body in the interest of an individual, the scales would probably be weighted in favour of the Ombudsman.[207]

However, the Ombudsman is naturally bound to take a challenge to his jurisdiction seriously. Sometimes, legal advice has to be taken. There is no provision for a lawyer as a member of the Ombudsman's staff [208] and it would be inappropriate for him to go to the Attorney General who would usually be advising the public body against whose action the Ombudsman wished to investigate. Accordingly, he takes legal advice from private practitioners (around 20 times a year).

In fact, so far, in all of the complaints in which legal obstacles have been raised,[209] the matter has been resolved – eventually – by agreement. With a few exceptions, this resolution has always been in favour of permitting the investigation to continue. Some of the challenges, most of which occurred in the first year of the Ombudsman's existence, arose from the novelty of the new office – an unwelcome novelty in some quarters – and plainly had little substance behind them. For instance, in spite of the fact that the 1980 Act is clearly to the contrary, an unsuccessful challenge was mounted by the Department of Social Welfare to the Ombudsman's authority to investigate the decisions of appeals officers.[210] More substantial was the argument of the Department of Posts and Telegraphs when it claimed that the Ombudsman was not competent to investigate telephone accounts in respect of the period after December 1983, when the telephone service was transferred to Bord Telecom Éireann and before April, 1985, when the necessary regulation was made.[211] Eventually the Bord permitted investigation, for this period, on an *ex gratia* basis.

However, the Ombudsman's progress was halted by a legal argument in a case[212] in which the complainant had been selected as a lecturer by a voluntary education committee. However his appointment had not been sanctioned by the Department of Education because he did not have the normal qualifications (although the

---

would be most unlikely to defy the Ombudsman. However, it also bears relation to this passage that a coercive order, issued as a conclusion to judicial proceedings, would have had to be defied before contempt proceedings became a possibility.

[207] *cf.* the comments of Lord Donaldson M.R. in *Eastleigh* [1988] Q.B. 855: "judicial review of an Ombudsman's report, bearing in mind the nature of his office and duties and the qualifications of those who hold that office, is inherently unlikely to succeed" (at 867). And: "An ombudsman's report is neither a statute nor a judgment. It is a report to the council and to the ratepayers of the area. It has to be written in everyday language and convey a message. This report has been subjected to a microscopic and somewhat legalistic analysis which it was not intended to undergo." (at p. 866).

[208] Though for some years one of his investigators happened to be qualified as a solicitor.

[209] See 1984 Report, pp. 11–12; 1986 Report, p. 38.

[210] Section 5(1)(a)(iii) as read with ss.1(2) and 2. See further, p. 365.

[211] See pp. 342–343.

[212] 1984 Report, pp. 11–12, 1985 Report, pp. 45–46.

complainant did have what might be regarded as equivalent, or even superior, qualifications). The successful[213] legal ground of objection taken by the Department concerned the general prohibition against examining complaints about recruitment or appointment."[214] This prohibition is contained in section 5(1)(c) of the Act, which refers to "recruitment or appointment to any office or employment in a Department of State or by any other person specified in the First Schedule to this Act." Now Vocational Education Committees are neither Departments of State nor within the First Schedule so that, as far as this provision is concerned, the Ombudsman would have had jurisdiction. However, the Department of Education invoked two other subsections which persuaded the Ombudsman that he did not have jurisdiction. The first of these is section 4(4) by which "the Ombudsman shall not investigate an action taken by or on behalf of a person specified in the Second Schedule to this Act" which Schedule includes vocational educational committees. The other provision, section 1(3)(b), extends this provision. Its effect, in the present context, is that references to a vocational educational committee are taken to include the Department of Education as far as functions performed by the Department in relation to the VEC is concerned. In sum, the exclusion of the VEC also covers the Department acting in relation to the VEC.

Another way in which legal proceedings may become relevant is where there is a possibility that the same issue may become the subject of both court proceedings and a complaint to the Ombudsman. This is a situation which has received less attention, here or elsewhere, than might have been expected. To take the first, easiest case, if litigation has commenced or is reasonably anticipated, then the Ombudsman should – and does[215] – withdraw from the field. To do otherwise might be a contempt.

However, to go to a situation at the other extreme, the Ombudsman has stated:

> "I find that, when there is conflict between a public body and a client which
> may involve a claim for compensation or possible legal action, the public
> body may tend, as a matter of course, to adopt an adversarial approach. Little
> consideration is given to the merits of the case, the public body puts up its
> defences and the client is left with no option but to take the matter to court
> or, if appropriate, to my Office. I acknowledge that a public body has a duty
> to defend its own interests and those of the taxpayer but a primary duty as a
> public body is to ensure that it responds to its clients in a proper, fair and
> impartial manner. This means that it is required to consider fully the merits
> of any case and not to force clients unnecessarily to resort to the courts or to
> my Office to achieve their rights."[216]

---

[213] An unsuccessful objection was grounded on the fact that the action complained against had occurred before the Ombudsman Act commenced, thus contravening the requirement described in paragraph 6 of Part 3 above. However, as the Department eventually accepted, this argument failed on the facts, in that the complainant, upon learning of his rejection, had appealed. Hence, it happened that a final decision on his case was not reached until a date which was within the Ombudsman's jurisdiction.

[214] 1985 Report, p. 45.

[215] See, *e.g.* 1996 Report, p. 24: "I had to withdraw from my examination of two of the [three] cases because the schools in question sought leave to apply for judicial review [of the Department of Education's refusal to recognise them as Gaelscoileanna]".

[216] 1996 Report, p. 17. The precept of not adopting an adversarial stance is mentioned explicitly in the "Principles of Good Administraion" on which see pp. 349–350.

The type of conduct which the Ombudsman seems to be condemning here is where a public body refuses to entertain a complaint on the ground that if a person is aggrieved, then he or she should bring the matter before a court. Not only is this attitude disingenuous, it also overlooks the fact that conduct which is legal may still amount to maladministration. The passage quoted (including the last few words about the complainant not being forced "to resort . . . to my Office") fits in with the Ombudsman's policy[217] of championing internal complaints procedures. In one of the cases, which the Ombudsman gives as an example of this type, the complainant's house had been damaged by flooding caused, he claimed, by the neglect of Galway County Council.[218] The local authority's response was that since it had successfully defended, before the courts, claims for compensation of a similar nature to those before the Ombudsman, it would not pay compensation. Our comment is that, if correct, there might be something to be said for the local authority's attitude: after all, why should one land-owner be compensated, when others had been told, by the court, that they had no entitlement.[219] However as a matter of fact in this particular case, the local authority had not successfully defended all compensation claims. Consequently, the Ombudsman's view was that here the authority had been too quick to rely upon the court judgment as a justification and consequently had not really considered the complaint at all.[220] In this area, one practical difficulty, of course, is that there will be many situations where a public body has not been officially informed that legal action is being taken; yet it suspects that this is so. And it fears that an Ombudsman's investigation is really a Trojan horse which is being invoked to fuel the complainants' position in court action, as by gathering information or by securing an admission. The Ombudsman's attitude to a public body refusing to cooperate with him, because of a suspicion of this sort is (it seems probable from the passage quoted) that it may be justifiable, but it must be reasonably grounded.

Finally, what is the position where a complainant goes first to the Ombudsman, and subsequently has recourse to a court? If he is unsuccessful before the Ombudsman, there appears to be nothing, in principle, against his going to a court. (*Quaere*: whether the delay caused by the reference to the Ombudsman would count against the litigant?) By contrast, what is the position if he were successful (whether partially or completely) before the Ombudsman? Presumably, if compensation had been paid by the public body then this would go to reduce the value of his loss, for the purpose of assessing damages before a court. And, if the case took the form of an application for judicial review, then possibly the recourse to the Ombudsman would be a ground on which the court would exercise its discretion against granting a remedy. But there does not seem to be any doctrine (analagous to waiver) which could be invoked to stop the litigant in his tracks.

---

[217] See p. 392.

[218] It was in the 1995 Report (p. 3) that the Ombudsman first took to disclosing the identity of local authorities and health boards, save where doing so could identify the complainant. (This was Mr Murphy's first full year of tenure).

[219] For a more elaborate discussion, see pp. 386–388.

[220] 1996 Report, p.19.

6. Appraisal

It is worth emphasising some of the new institution's more novel features. In the first place, section 6(5) of the Act states that if ". . . the measures taken . . . in response to a recommendation . . . are not satisfactory, [the Ombudsman] may, if he so thinks fit, cause a special report on the case" to be laid before each House. Especially because of the use of the word "recommendation" (which is also used elsewhere in this Act), this provision appears to contemplate that if the Ombudsman's recommendation is not accepted he will not be able to elicit any support from a court. In this sense (as in others which we shall see in this Part), it is instinctive to characterise the Ombudsman as a form of "alternative dispute resolution" in the public law field. Nevertheless he is not on a par with a deputy or local councillor making "representations." This is something which, in the light of the attitude of certain public representatives and public servants, the Ombudsman has considered it necessary to point out clearly in his Annual Report on several occasions.[221] It should be stressed, though, that the advent of the Ombudsman has been deliberately designed to effect as little change as possible in existing constitutional relationships: there has, for instance, been no alteration in the relationship between the individual public servant, the State and a member of the public affected by an official action. The 1980 Act contains no provision making the State or a public servant liable where there was no liability before 1980. The major conceptual innovation introduced by the Act is to provide a remedy against the public body in the case of maladministration, even if this falls short of a breach of law. The emphasis is on compensation and not punishment. It is true that section 6(6) of the Act explicitly

---

[221] For the attitude of certain politicians and officials, see: 1985 Report, p. 20; 1986 Report, pp. 3, 5 and 38; 1989 Report, p. 4; 1993 Report, pp. 2, 4 and 1994 Report, p. 66. On this subject, 1985 Report, p. 16 states:

"[S]ome County Managers saw my role as making representations. Arising from this they considered that locally elected public representations might see my involvement as interfering with their traditional role and, indeed, some Managers felt that I was merely duplicating this role. My staff at all times stressed that this Office was not involved in making representations. The Ombudsman has been charged by the Oireachtas with the statutory function of investigating complaints."

And in 1996 Report, p. 19, the Ombudsman's hackles were raised at the statement from a Department, that the Department's legal advisor had referred the Ombudsman's request for access to medical records to the Department's legal advisor "for adjudication" [*sic*].

Notice also the following statement by Lord Eastleigh in *Eastleigh* ([1988] Q.B. 555 at 867), in which the Court of Appeal correctly rejected an extraordinary statement of the High Court (which appeared to suggest that the Ombudsman enjoyed only moral or political authority): "Next there is the suggestion [of the High Court] that the council should issue a statement disputing the right of the Ombudsman to make his findings and that this would provide the council with an adequate remedy. Such an action would wholly undermine the system of Ombudsman's reports and would, in effect, provide for an appeal to the media against his findings. The parliamentary intention was that reports by ombudsmen would be loyally accepted by the local authorities concerned."

Finally, consider the attitude of the medical profession. Regarding medical records, a matter which arises in the context of investigations into health boards, 1985 Report, p. 15 states:

"The Director of my Office met with the Irish Medical Council and also with the Irish Medical Organisation to discuss this matter. Both bodies recognised my unconditional right to all records, medical and otherwise. Notwithstanding this, I was happy to assure them that I would request medical records only when I considered it absolutely necessary and that, . . . I had the permission of complainants . . .". See also Taxes Consolidation Act 1997, s.1093.

grants a right to constitutional justice to a "person" (which word, we consider, includes a public servant as well as a public body) against whom the Ombudsman is considering making an adverse "finding or criticism a statement, recommendation or report." Nevertheless, the legislation is not designed to pillory or even identify the "guilty" public servant, assuming (as will often not be the case) that there is a single culprit. And, in practice, the Ombudsman's attitude has manifestly been based upon the assumption that disciplining the responsible public servant is not his function and that any straying in such a direction would mean a risk of losing the co-operation of the public service upon which he depends.[222] On the political, as opposed to the legal, plane, it is of course true that the entry of the Ombudsman upon the constitutional scene means a dilution of the pure milk of the individual ministerial responsibility doctrine, which holds that a Minister is responsible to the Dáil and only to the Dáil, for the performance of his Department. However, this doctrine has always been a rather broken-backed one.[223]

There is no doubting the potency of the Ombudsman. To quote from an Annual Report:

> "Many of the complaints to the Office had previously been made through the normal channels by local representatives, Dáil Deputies and members of the Seanad. Despite the best efforts of politicians of all parties and strong representation to various sections of officialdom, the complaints remained unresolved – simply because the politicians did not have access to the relevant documentation.

> With the passing of the Ombudsman Act 1980, politicians provided this authority to the Ombudsman and for the first time in the history of the State, the files of Government Departments and public bodies subject to remit were open to scrutiny by an independent office. The result was that many complaints which had gone unresolved for a long time were found to be justified and were settled in favour of the complainant."[224]

Ombudsman compared with the courts

Professor Bradley has written about the British Ombudsman[225]: "I am in no doubt that the Ombudsman's methods enable him to get closer to reconstructing the administrative history of a citizen's case than does High Court procedure". The reasons for this assessment apply in Ireland too. These reasons include the facts that the Ombudsman follows an inquisitorial, flexible and private process of inquiry with unrestricted access to departmental files; that this usually occurs in a non-confrontational milieu; and that the investigators are almost all themselves former public servants.[226] Finally, the system for devising a remedy – the inter-play of

---

[222] It follows that we respectfully disagree with the suggestion contained in the 1986 Report, pp. 3–4, that the establishment of the Ombudsman has altered the corporation sole system by which it is the Minister and not (save to a limited extent) the civil servant actually involved, who is legally responsible for what is done by the civil servant.

[223] See pp. 61–62.

[224] 1989 Report, p. 30.

[225] "Role of Ombudsman in Relation to Citizens' Rights" (1980) C.L.J. 304, 322.

[226] See, for example, 1992 Report, p. 1.

recommendation from the Ombudsman and response from the public body – is more likely to yield a result satisfactory to all parties than would the polarised concepts administered in a court. Indeed, the Ombudsman has a very conciliatory manner. For example:

"I sought the views of the Department on the circumstances of this case. Initially, they were not well disposed toward the case but they agreed to consider it if the local authority processed the application in the normal way and submitted a full report on the matter to them. The local authority did this and I am glad to report that the Department paid the £5,000 grant to the complainants."[227]

Only seldom has the goad of a special report to be made explicit.

The Ombudsman himself has drawn no comparisons with the courts of law, but it seems probable that in many ways, besides the one just mentioned, he is superior to the courts. In the first place, his examination of a case involves no costs to the victim of maladministration, even where the complaint is unsuccessful. The complaint can be initiated informally, if the complainant is involved thereafter, this is usually done in the most unalarming way, often by an investigation interviewing the complainant at home.

The *persona* of the Ombudsman is very different from that of a court. While it should be emphasised that the Ombudsman entertains complaints from businesses (including companies) and indeed, such complaints loom particularly large in his Reports because of their complexity, he plainly sees himself as the tribune of the people. The Irish version of the Ombudsman is "Fear a Phobal" (literally, "the man of the People") although the translation used in the Act is simply "Ombudsman".[228]

In some cases, especially social welfare cases, the Ombudsman operates almost as a well-informed and resourceful advocate for the complainant.[229] In one case, for instance, a complainant had sought pension arrears, something which was prohibited by legislation. However, the Ombudsman was able to find a way of securing a refund for her on the following indirect basis:

"It was my view that the woman's error in not claiming the pension to which she was entitled could, by extension, constitute her having paid PRSI

"Examining files is a long and painstaking process; but it is a task for which the staff of my Office are specially prepared. The key leading to a solution may sometimes be found only after files have been examined several times. If there is a flaw in a case, however, it is unlikely to escape the attention of a number of examiners.

One case was recently brought to the Office which had remained unresolved over a period of six years. In this time, social workers, a doctor, a priest, a solicitor and public representatives had become involved, without success. When it was brought to the attention of my Office, and the files were examined, it emerged that one crucial piece of evidence had been overlooked throughout the period. When this evidence was pinpointed, the case was quickly resolved."

[227] 1988 Report, p. 78. See also, for example, 1986 Report, p. 50.

[228] *cf.* the concerns expressed in *Constitution Review Group Report*, p. 425: "The word 'Ombudsman' is not intended to have a gender connotation . . . [However] some members of the Review Group take the view that there could be a misunderstanding on this point and would prefer a gender-neutral term."

[229] In the 1993 Report, p. 54, the Ombudsman opined that "the loss of any social welfare payment for as much as six days can be significant."

contributions in error. I received legal advice which supported this view. I asked the Department to reconsider its decision."[230]

More generally, the Ombudsman has made the following observation:

"The law in this area can be quite complex and there is a particular problem in keeping track of the range of secondary legislation (statutory instruments) which continues to have application, over a period of decades in some cases. Because of the complexity and inaccessibility of some of this legislation, it is not surprising that complainants are frequently not in a position to articulate a reasoned legal argument in support of their complaints. In relation to social welfare complaints, much of our work involves establishing the relevant legislation and forming an opinion as to whether it has been correctly applied in the particular case."[231]

The office of Ombudsman has been deliberately designed and utilised to promote maximum usage. He projects a high public profile, with substantial media publicity. A particular feature of his *modus operandi* is regional visits.[232] He publishes attractively presented reports,[233] with catchy headlines, within six months of the year to which they relate. It happens that in the great majority of cases which are described in the reports, some advantage is achieved for the complainant (although this is not true of overall complaints to the Ombudsman, as can be seen below). This no doubt helps to attract other complainants. He leans towards whichever

---

[230] 1992 Report, pp.14–15. See also 1992 Report, pp. 109–110; 1994 Report, p. 61.

[231] 1994 Report, p. 31.

[232] Such a visit consists of one or more investigators, heralded by a local advertising campaign, setting up a temporary office in either the Southern Capital or some provincial centre. Indeed during the period 1985–1986, a visit was made to each of the counties in the country. In addition to heightening the general public's awareness of the Ombudsman, this brought in a substantial number of complaints: about 1,000 (1985); 700 (1986), 500 (first half of 1987), 300 (1989). (Visits were suspended during the second half of 1987 and 1988 because of the staff cut-backs). The Ombudsman is of the opinion that fewer of these complaints would have reached him, were it not for the regional visits: "there are many instances where the presentation of a complaint in writing or on the telephone is just not possible; in such instances the only option available to the individual is to call to my Office and have the matter discussed and examined by my staff. Individuals living outside the Dublin area are at a disadvantage. Regional visits represent an attempt to redress the balance." (1989 Report, p. 13). See also 1986 Report, p. 28; 1987 Report, p. 9, 1988 Report, p. 7. 1992 Report, pp. 2, 5, 8, 9. Notice also the following extract from 1991 Report, p. 3:
"Two areas which showed a significant increase in the volume of complaints were the health boards and local authorities. The reason for this may be the increased level of awareness of the availability of my Office to deal with complaints against these bodies as a result of the publicity in connection with visits of my staff to local areas."
See also 1992 Report, p. 2 on increased level of co-operation between the Ombudsman's office, the National Service Board and the Citizens' Information Centres. *Cf.* 1992 Report, p. 9: "In the course of 1992 the Office participated in the RDS Spring Show, the Dublin Active Age Week, the Cork Adult Education Exhibition and the Ideal Homes Exhibition (Dublin)."

[233] As of 1995, the Reports are available on the internet and computer diskette. The 1989 Report, p. 71 states: "The cases chosen for this part of my report are mainly cases where I have been successful in having decisions of public servants reversed. I must emphasise that they are not meant to give an unbalanced view of the efficiency or effectiveness of any one organisation. They have been selected purely because they highlight interesting issues and they can be presented fairly and accurately in summary form." The Reports are naturally aimed at a fairly diverse audience, including: the public bodies who are under the Ombudsman's surveillance, potential complainants, the news media and commentators. Reports could be improved if their accounts of cases were less factual and more contextual and analytic – so as to give greater guidance.

method of interpretation, whether literal or ultra-liberal, will be most favourable to the complainant (although, in this, he is not all that different from the approach adopted by some judges). An example of this stemmed from a local authority's refusal to permit an elderly tenant to purchase his corporation house. The justification advanced by the County Manager was that because of the financial cutbacks, all applications from elderly persons were refused in order to keep up the store of dwellings available for letting. From an administrative non-legal perspective this might seem a reasonable approach. However, applying a classic administrative law approach,[234] the Ombudsman ruled:

> "My investigation established that the Local Authority had not sought the sanction of the Minister for the Environment to the exclusion of all dwellings, occupied by elderly persons living alone, from the terms of the Scheme. I concluded that neither this decision nor its consequences had been fully or properly considered. While I appreciated the Manager's concerns in regard to his primary duty to meet general housing needs, I had to balance this view against the complainant's rights under the scheme. I concluded that the Local Authority's decision was arbitrary and taken without proper authority and that it was contrary to the terms of the 1989 Tenant Purchase Scheme."[235]

Yet, in contrast, as we shall see later,[236] there have been many other cases in which the Ombudsman has been prepared to overlook the fact that the public body has the legalities on its side and to grant a remedy for what he regards as maladministration.

Maladministration and the law

There is another ground on which the Ombudsman and the courts may be compared and that is in relation to their subject-matter. These, in fact, have a great deal in common. For, as will be demonstrated in succeeding paragraphs, to assert that the Ombudsman and the courts are involved in different types of regulation in that the Ombudsman is concerned with "maladministration" whereas the courts deal with judicial review or causes of action is merely playing with words.[237] Indeed, so far from its being the Ombudsman's business "to operate beyond the frontier where the law stops"[238] (*e.g.* rudeness or delay), a substantial number of the complaints for which he has provided a remedy could have come before a court. In part, this is because during the past decade or so, the rising tide of public law has engulfed the island of "maladministration". This can be demonstrated by reference to: legitimate expectations[239]; the liability of public authorities[240]; the *audi alteram*

---

234 On which see pp. 677–678.
235 1992 Report, p. 77.
236 See pp. 386–388.
237 See further Craig, *Administrative Law* (3rd. ed.), pp. 139–141; Crawford (1985) *Public Law* 246 at 262.
238 A phrase used by Professor Wade in the 1967 and 1971 editions of *Administrative Law* but not in later editions.
239 See 1985 Report, pp. 55; 1987 Report, pp. 13, 17, 75, 80, 81, 88 and 96; 1988 Report, pp. 39, 70, 78; 1989 Report, pp. 82 and 86.
240 See 1989 Report, p. 93 – recipient of a grant complained that renovations which a council engineer

partem rule[241] taking irrelevant factors into account[242]; failing to implement the ruling in a High Court case[243]; and the duty to give reasons for decisions[244] – each of which has been the subject of both Ombudsman and court decisions. In some cases, it is only in terminology that there is a difference from a court. Take, for instance, the following complaint involving what a court would style "abuse of power". The complainant, who had purchased his house from the local authority, wished to alter the ownership of the house by adding his wife as joint owner. This transaction required the local authority's consent which was being withheld because the complainant had not paid his local service charges for a number of years. The complainant's solicitor referred the matter to the Ombudsman who found "that while the housing legislation gave local authorities power to refuse to grant a consent in certain specific circumstances, refusal to pay service charges was not an appropriate reason for such refusal."[245]

Moreover, a remarkably large proportion – as many as 20–30 per cent of the cases summarised in the Annual Reports (although these are not typical of the entire case-load) – require the Ombudsman to take a view on actual legal issues. This often involves the interpretation of legislative or administrative schemes which have scarcely been considered by the courts.[246] Let us list some examples: the Higher Education Grant Scheme (as to whether certain moneys should be treated as capital or income or whether a step-parent's means were to be counted as the means of a "guardian")[247]; the 1988 Tenant Purchase Scheme[248] or a local authority's letting priority scheme[249]; the deduction "from my examination of the relevant legislation" that a Disabled Persons Maintenance Allowance is payable as from the date of application and not the date of award[250]; the proper assessment of spouses income for the purpose of Disabled Persons Maintenance Allowance[251]; the question of whether revenue Commissioners, in raising interest charges on late payments of VAT, should have taken into account interest on VAT, which had already been paid[252]; exemption from stamp duty on the basis that the complainant had purchased a newly-completed house rather than, as the Revenue Commissioners, had decided

---

certified, for the purposes of the grant, to have been completed, were unsatisfactory. ("Council decided, while not accepting any liability in the case, to pay £1,000 to cover any possible defects in the work"). See also, p. 372.

[241] See 1989 Report, p. 41.
[242] 1996 Report, p. 27.
[243] *Ibid.* p. 14–15.
[244] See, 1988 Report, p. 88, 1985 Report, p. 23 and 1997 Report, p. 27.
[245] 1989 Report, p. 89. See also 1988 Report, p. 25.
[246] For examples of especially rough and ready legal analysis by the Ombudsman see 1992 report, pp. 72 and 119–120.
[247] 1987 Report, p. 71; 1989 Report, p. 85; 1985 Report, p. 28, respectively. On interpretation of this Scheme, see also: 1991 Report, p. 58–62; 1992 Report, pp. 93–94; 1994 Report, p. 23.
[248] 1992 Report, pp. 75–77.
[249] 1993 Report, pp. 37–39.
[250] 1985 Report, p. 31. On the Disabled Persons' Grant Scheme, see 1990 Report, pp. 45–52.
[251] 1992 Report, pp. 39–42. On this point, the Ombudsman waited for the decision in *H. v. Eastern Health Board* [1988] I.R. 747. For another issue in regard to DPMA, see 1993 Report, pp. 100–101. On Carers' Allowance, see 1993 Report, pp. 26–27.
[252] 1994 Report, p. 71. For a somewhat similar case, involving witholding tax, see 1994 Report, p. 24.

a partially developed site[253]; unlawful impounding of cattle in a County Pound[254]; and the provision of facilities for home births.[255]

A most basic and broad legal precept on which the Ombudsman has drawn in a number of cases is the *ultra vires* doctrine[256] *i.e.* the notion that, in many situations, there must be specific statutory authorisation before a public authority can perform an action; levy a charge; take into account a particular consideration, etc. For example, the Ombudsman has made recommendations on the basis, in a case about senior citizens in long-stay institutions, that "there would appear to be no statutory ground for a means-testing system which includes the income of the family as well as that of the patient."[257] He has also stated that there is no statutory basis to charge either for a non-domestic water supply[258] or fees to a tenant purchase for the release of his title documents by a local authority's law agent.[259] The Ombudsman has also ruled that: "The Health Board view that [the complainant] was not keen to attend training appears to have been a factor in the decision to refuse DPMA. However, this is not a consideration provided for in DPMA law."[260] A related type of error can arise from a public body's commitment to some administrative scheme or memorandum, notwithstanding the fact that – as the Ombudsman discovers when he reads the legislation – there is a discord between the scheme and the legislation. One such case arose out of the Revenue Commissioners' refusal of an application for tax relief. The Ombudsman stated:

> "From my examination it appeared that the question as to whether or not the institution was on the list of 'approved nursing homes' was not relevant. The institution was in fact a residential centre for chemical dependency treatment. The question to be decided [under the Finance Act 1967, s.12] appeared to be whether or not the institution could be regarded as a hospital for the purposes of the relief."[261]

There are other, general legal concepts which the Ombudsman has invoked. One of these is *proportionalité*[262] which was mentioned in the context of the fact that

---

253 1990 Report, pp. 76–77.
254 1993 Report, pp. 38–39. See, too, 1993 Report, pp. 83–84 (improper procedures operated by the Registrar of Companies in striking a company off the Register); 1997 Report, p. 28 (house, improvement grant under the Housing (Gaeltacht Act, 1929); 1997 Report, p. 33 (Interpretation of nursing home subvention regulations).
255 1997 Report, p. 28.
256 See pp. 394–398.
257 1992 Report, p. 34. See also: 1992 Report, pp.14, 39, 42; 1991 Report, pp. 72–73.
258 1993 Report, pp. 65–68.
259 1993 Report, pp. 103–104.
260 1992 Report, p. 114. For a court case on a similar point, see *State (Keller) v. Galway County Council* [1958] I.R. 142. See, too, 1994 Report, p. 36.
261 1993 Report, p. 49. For discussion of this sort of point, by a court, see pp. 631–632.
262 1993 Report, p. 59: "I find it hard to accept that the penalty imposed should, in many cases, be so severe. It would appear that the penalty being imposed in this kind of case is totally out of proportion to whatever 'fault' may have occurred. The principle of proportionality is a feature of European Union law and one which may well evolve as a feature of our public law. The present arrangements would appear to be out of step with this principle."

pension entitlements based on social insurance contributions could be lost simply by virtue of a failure to apply in time.[263]

Furthermore, the Ombudsman does not seem concerned to observe any border line between public and private law. Complaints which refer to actions by public bodies which sound in the private law field have been investigated (probably correctly) without the issue of whether there is a boundary shutting off such matters from the Ombudsman even being raised. Some examples of this have just been given (in Part 2) under the earlier heading of "negligence or carelessness". One further instance arose when Bord Telecom quoted a price for a replacement telephone to the complainant, but then charged more than the quoted price.[264] Another example concerned the interpretation of a term of an agreement for (non-compulsory) transfer of land to a local authority (by which the local authority was obliged to build a restraining wall).[265] In a third example, rather surprisingly, An Post was encouraged to waive an excess of £100 for compensation for lost international soccer tickets sent through the post. There was a stipulation in the contract, providing for this excess. This had been brought to the attention of the consignor; though not the consignee. On this basis, An Post waived the excess.[266] In other instances, there have been complaints about such private law points as: trespass to land (damage to a garden wall done by the Department of Posts)[267]; whether the complainant had been given too much change[268]; negligent conveyancing by a local authority[269]; and trespass to goods involving the unlawful seizure of a van by the Revenue Commissioners.[270]

The striking point here is that although the Ombudsman's jurisdiction centres upon the concept of "maladministration", he is in effect giving a remedy where he decides[271] that some act of a public agency is unlawful. Whilst he has no direct mandate to do this, it is perhaps acceptable (at any rate, in most cases) on the assumption that if an act is unlawful, it also *ipso facto* amounts to maladministration. Next, what if an act is lawful: can it still constitute maladministration? The answer – implicitly and correctly – given by the Ombudsman is in the affirmative. For, as

---

[263] For another example, see 1990 Report, pp. 64–66. Here women whose husbands had deserted them to go to Britain, obtained a divorce there and subsequently died. These women had been refused a widow's pension by the Department of Social Welfare, on the basis that they were not married at the time of their husband's death and, thus, were not widows. The Department had been assuming – incorrectly – that *all* divorces obtained in Britain were valid in Ireland; or, at least that to rule on the validity of a divorce was a matter not for it, but for the courts. The Ombudsman suggested that this was wrong and, as a result, the Department requested the Attorney General for advice who, in effect, upheld the Ombudsman. As a result, the appeals officer of the Department now rules on the validity of the divorce obtained in each case.

[264] 1992 Report, p. 124.

[265] 1992 Report, pp. 116–117.

[266] 1992 Report, p. 121. See also 1992 Report, p. 135 and 1993 Report, p. 112.

[267] 1987 Report, pp. 94–95, see also 1989 Report, p. 90.

[268] 1988 Report, p. 78. (The complainant claimed that it was implied that he had been given too much change and had "owned up.").

[269] 1988 Report, p. 80.

[270] 1989 Report, pp. 34–38.

[271] It is not suggested that the Ombudsman is "administering justice" so as to attract Article 34.1 because he is missing many of the necessary characteristics *e.g.* his decision is recommendatory and not binding. See Gwynn Morgan, *The Separation of Powers*, Chap. 4. However, if the Ombudsman got the law wrong, he would be subject to judical review.

Mr Yardley – a former Professor of Public Law – who is now chairman of the English Commission for Local Administration has stated:

> "We take the view, sir, that we are not dealing primarily with legality as opposed to illegality; we are dealing with, in a public sense in a public area, morality as opposed to immorality; reasonableness as opposed to unreasonableness."[272]

The only situations in which this might cause difficulty would be those in which the formal law-making agencies (Oireachtas or courts) have deliberately addressed an issue and decided to grant an immunity from liability to a public body. If in such a case, the Ombudsman persists in granting compensation is he not, in a sense, usurping their authority? The answer to this contention might well be that such an immunity was only intended to apply in a court and not in a complaint to the Ombudsman in respect of which he had found there to be maladministration. To the supplementary question why then make a difference between the court and the Ombudsman, thus permitting a complainant to secure a remedy from the Ombudsman which would be barred to him, in a court: the (not entirely convincing) answer might be that a greater sum is usually at stake before a court.

Let us take some examples, commencing with those statutory immunities from tort action of which section 64(1) of the Postal and Telecommunications Act 1983 is an instance. This provision gives An Post immunity from all liability in respect of any loss suffered in the use of a postal service. One complaint to the Ombudsman concerned a wedding dress which had been misplaced – though subsequently found – in the post.[273] The Ombudsman took the matter up as a case of "administrative bungling" and secured the payment of £80 to the bride to compensate her for expenses incurred in looking for the dress in Dublin. However, the significant point here is that no mention whatever was made of any difficulty arising from the fact that the legislature had exercised its prerogative to determine (for policy reasons,

---

Notice that in regard to a pending court case at 1988 Report, p. 26, the Ombudsman remarked: ("I have refrained from making a recommendation in the case for the moment as there is a case before the Supreme Court involving similar circumstances and the same issues. In view of this I accept that the Health Boards should await the final judicial decision before deciding on the case I investigated"). See too 1992 Report, p. 40 where the Ombudsman (in a series of complaints on the assessment of income for DPMA purposes where the applicant's spouse has income either from employment or a social welfare payment) anticipated the High Court's decision in *Healy v. Eastern Health Board* [1988] I.R. 747. 1992 Report, p. 121. See also p. 135 and 1993 Report, p. 112.

272 Select Committee on P. C. A. H. C. 448 (1985–1986), Minutes of Evidence, p. 10, quoted by Crawford, *op. cit.* Though *cf., R. v. Local Commissioner, ex p. Croydon L.B.C.* [1989] 1 All. E.R 1033 at 1045 which dealt to some extent with this point, Woolf L.J. stated:

"Issues whether an administrative tribunal has properly understood the relevant law and the legal obligations which it is under when conducting an inquiry are more appropriate for resolution by the High Court than by a commissioner, however eminent."

However, the judge went on actually to resolve the case on the following rather strange basis (at 1045f): "The problem in this case is that the commissioner apparently never appreciated that there was a conflict between his jurisdiction and that of the court. In my view he should have done so at least before he concluded his investigation and then he should have exercised his discretion whether to discontinue his investigation. However, as he indicates that if he had considered the question of discretion he would undoubtedly have decided to proceed, I would not be prepared to grant relief solely on this basis."

273 1984 Report, p. 39; see also 1987 Report, p. 26.

387

arising from the operation of the postal service) that a person who suffers loss through negligence in the postal service cannot recover against An Post. It may be that this result could be justified on the basis that the payment was made "strictly on an *ex gratia* basis"; the amount was trivial; in the practical world, there is less to this conceptual law than meets the eye; and, anyway, as Ralph Waldo Emerson said: "Everyone loves a lover."

Let us turn to a second series of examples. This is a series of a dozen or so cases[274] which can be put under the broad heading of legitimate expectations and misleading advice, shading off into a failure to supply relevant information. One such case[275] concerned the Department of Agriculture's refusal to pay the complainant-farmer, who had carried out certain farm development work, the full rate of a grant under the Farm Modernisation Scheme. The reason for this refusal was a change which had been made to the Scheme after the complainant's application had been approved. Following the Ombudsman's intervention, the Department agreed to pay the grant in full. However, in a minority of cases, the Ombudsman has probably gone further than would a court. One case concerned the loss of a letter carrying £100.00, which had been registered at the minimum fee of 95p for which the maximum compensation payable was £20. The critical point was that there was no notice on display to indicate the conditions regarding the sending of money by post. This omission meant, the Ombudsman found, that An Post should compensate the complainant for the entire amount lost.[276] Yet, in these circumstances, a court would have been most unlikely to have inferred a misrepresentation or estoppel from silence.[277]

The final example, which admittedly is from Britain arises out of the Minister for Trade and Industry's failure properly to use his supervisory power over a firm of financial brokers (Barlow Clowes) with the result that persons who had invested with these brokers were fraudulently deprived of an aggregate amount of £30 million. The British P.C.A recommended that the British Government reimburse this money to the investors and the Government – after some grumbling – did so.[278] Contrast this episode with the Privy Council case of *Yuen Kun Yeu v. Attorney General of Hong Kong*.[279] Here, in comparable circumstances to those in the Barlow Clowes complaint, the court held that a public regulatory agency owed no duty of care in negligence, to the victims of a fraud. Notwithstanding the huge sum of money, no one suggested that the Minister for Trade could have defended itself against the intervention of the Ombudsman by seeking a Declaration from a court that he was not responsible in law.

Numbers of complaints[280]

As can be seen, in terms of sheer volume of complaints there is no doubt that the office has been a success. In each year, the sum of complaints against the

---

274 For more detail, see pp. 361–364.
275 1987 Report, pp. 79–80.
276 1987 Report, p. 96.
277 See also 1988 Report, pp. 77–78.
278 See (1994) *Public Law* 192 and 408.
279 [1989] A.C. 53. See also *McMahon v. Ireland* [1988] I.L.R.M. 610.
280 See 1984 Report, Chaps. 5 and 12; 1985 Report, Chaps. 3 and 12; 1986 Report, Chaps. 2 and 10;

Complaints within jurisdiction received in recent years

	1991	1992	1993	1994	1995	1996
Departments of State	1,165	1,301	1,237	1,240	1,076	1,228
Telecom Éireann	726	486	331	298	261	272
Local Authorities	356	430	459	582	497	569
Health Boards	295	369	332	302	345	411
An Post	61	51	60	75	71	56
Total	2,603	2,637	2,419	2,497	2,250	2,536

Departments of State account for nearly 50 per cent of the total, the remainder coming from: local authorities, closely followed by the health boards, with An Post and then Telecom Éireann[281] a long distance behind. Out of the complaints against the Departments of about State, about two-thirds are against the Department of Social Welfare[282] (throughout the 1990s, 700–800) and the next largest number is against the Revenue Commissioners.

At the outset, the annual figures for 1985–1987 (about 4,700 plus) were exceptionally high by international standards.[283] The Ombudsman has suggested that the

---

1987 Report, Chaps. 2 and 7; 1988 Report, Chaps. 2 and 6; 1989 Report, Chaps. 5 and 9; 1993 Report, p. 5 and Chap 6; 1994 Report, pp. 10 and pp. 74–84; 1995 Report, pp.9, 32–36; 1996 Report, pp. 6, 35–39. One unexpected feature of the figures is that for the early years the number of complaints against Telecom Éireann (almost all in respect of telephone bills) were so high, and indeed, in 1987–1989 they slightly exceeded the total number of complaints against all the Departments of State. However, there was a fall from a high of 2,022 in 1987 to 298 in 1994, in part due to the introduction of itemised billing and other technical and administrative improvements.

[281] See, for example, 1993 Report, pp. 115–120; 1994 Report, pp. 40–42.A typical complaint out of a large group which presents few features of wider interest is the following: "A subscriber complained about the charges on an account in respect of a period in which he alleged the telephone had been locked away. He complained that the usage recorded could not be consistent with a private telephone. Telecom Éireann said that increased usage was first recorded on the line immediately following the conversion of the telephone from manual to automatic working. They also claimed that the telephone was used for business purposes. In the course of my examination of the case, I confirmed that the telephone was, in fact, used for business purposes. In the circumstances, I found no reason to make a recommendation in the complainant's favour." As can be seen from this example, until Bord Telecom Éireann introduced an itemised billing system, there was no incontrovertible method of establishing how many phone calls have been made. However, in 1985, the Board agreed on methods to streamline their investigation of complaints and, by 1991, an itemised billing had been introduced in several areas of the country.

Members of the Dáil Public Accounts Committee have suggested that any public body (and especially Bord Telecom Éireann since so many of the complaints were against it, against whom the Ombudsman makes an adverse finding, should pay a levy towards the cost of the Ombudsman's office: *The Irish Times*, July 8, 1988. For other complaints, see 1992 Report pp. 85–87 and 124–135; 1990 Report, p. 84

[282] See 1988 Report, p. 4.

[283] The Irish complaints emanate from a population of 3.5 million. Compare this with recent figures for Denmark (1,650 complaints from a population of 5.1 million); Sweden (3,374; 8.4 million); New Zealand (1,906; 3.1 million); and Finland (2,027; 4.9 million): comparative figures from 1986 Report, p. 8.

reduction in numbers of complaints for 1988–1989 to a figure of about 3,000, was connected with the limited programme of regional visits and the recent long delays – each of which arose because of the staff reductions of 1987 and 1988. From 1988 onward, the number of complaints has been running at about 2,500. Complaints falling outside jurisdiction have fluctuated. In 1984 there were, *inter alia*, about 300 complaints from civil servants regarding personnel matters, a field which had been carefully excluded from the Ombudsman's jurisdiction. Thereafter, complaints falling outside jurisdiction declined until they were running at 6 per cent in 1989. However, they subsequently increased to over 20 per cent in 1994–1996. The Ombudsman commented: "This perhaps points to the need for simplification of the terms in my remit. I intend to address the question of public awareness through a publicity campaign. I also hope to ensure that my remit is made clearer by seeking amendments to the Ombudsman Act, 1980." Possibly, another factor explaining the change in these figures may be improvement in the performance of the public service.

The most important statistic, perhaps, is the following: of the cases determined in 1990–1996, an average of 18 per cent were resolved in favour of the complainant. However, a further 27 per cent were "assisted" (a term explained below) in one way or another.[284] The category of "complainants assisted" covers cases in which, for instance, a complainant is told that he is not eligible for the benefit claimed but he may be eligible for another benefit – for example a benefit administered by a health board, when a Social Welfare benefit was claimed. Another example would be those cases in which no maladministration is found so that the complainant is obliged to pay his telephone bill; nevertheless circumstances are such that payment by instalments is arranged. Often the assistance takes the form of "information provided" and such cases are almost as significant as those complaints resolved in the complainant's favour. They confirm one of the Ombudsman's major themes – the point, discussed earlier, that the public service should supply citizens with better quality information. As regards the majority of complainants, who are unsuccessful, these have at least the consolation of knowing that their grievance has received a thorough investigation by an independent agency[285] – the poor man's equivalent of the Day in Court. In addition, such investigations enhance confidence in the public service by giving it an independent imprimatur. Finally, it should be remarked that in the light of these figures – no change whatsoever in more than 60 per cent of the complaints – the Annual Reports may be misleading because they concern, almost exclusively, cases in which the complainant was successful.[286]

---

[284] The breakdown of the figures given in the text for 1990–1996; is as follows: 1990: 14% and 25%; 1991; 18% and 31%; 1992: 16% and 38%; 1993 21% and 27% and 1994: 18% and 25%; 1995: 18% and 25%; 1996: 18% and 22%. The equivalent average figures for the 1984–1988 period are 23% and 27% respectively.

[285] *e.g.* "When I have pointed out to pensioners the difference between the 'maximum' and 'minimum' rates and how it is arrived at, they have generally been satisfied that they have not been unfairly treated." (1991 Report, p. 24.)

[286] *cf.* Seneviratue, *Ombudsmen in the Public Sector* (1994) p. 16: "There is a danger that complainants, and the public at large, may have expectations of ombudsmen which are too high. Any publicity about the institution must guard against raising expectations that are unrealistic."

General Improvement in Administrative Practice

As well as his duty in respect of individual grievances, the Ombudsman has a second role, namely to act as a critic and catalyst to encourage general improvement in administrative practices.[287] As he has remarked: "I will always highlight . . . systemic weakness as, once corrected, they can lead to long term improvements in service across a range of public bodies.[288] (Possibly, there is a correlation between a vigorous discharge of this second function and a lack of a nice concern for the policy-administration border which, if punctiliously observed, would cramp an Ombudsman's style). The Irish Ombudsman (like his New Zealand colleague, but in contrast to the British P.C.A.[289]) has been alert to the potential of his office to act in this role. His 1989 Report[290] summarises some 16 legislative or policy changes which have come about, partly or entirely, as a result of recommendations of the Ombudsman. For example: Social Welfare legislation has been amended to reduce discrimination against husbands and widowers; the Department of Social Welfare has agreed to change its practice to admit claims for unemployment from those on holiday outside the state[291]; the Domicile and Recognition of Foreign Divorces Act 1986 uprooted the law of dependent domicile, ("the last barbarous relic of a woman's servitude"[292]) by which a woman whose husband had deserted her, gone abroad and obtained a divorce was deemed also to be domiciled abroad, with the consequence that the divorce was recognised and, thus, the wife might lose a welfare benefit. A spectacular example of a change of law arising because of an Ombudsman recommendation is section 32 of the Social Welfare Act 1997, which extends the maximum arrears period from six to twelve months. Again, the Revenue Commissioners have promised to review the law dealing with the payment of interest where too much tax is levied, which, at the moment, varies depending on the type of tax which happens to be involved.[293] An Post agreed to reintroduce the facility of paying a television and radio licence by instalments; and Bord Telecom agreed to alter their billing system so that the issue of a first account to new subscribers should occur within six months in contrast to the long delay (up to 18 months in one case) which had occurred in the past. More radically, Bord Telecom established the post of a

---

287 See, *e.g.* 1994 Report, pp. 1–5.

288 1996 Report, p. 16.

289 See Harlow, "Ombudsman in Search of a Role" (1978) 41 M.L.R. 446.

290 Chap. 2 and pp. 23 and 28. See, too, 1993 Report, pp. 9–16 (Mr Mills' swan song) reviewing some of the legislative and administrative changes which had been brought forward because of his efforts. Most of these changes were in regard to social welfare benefits or allowances. See, too, 1992 Report, pp. 21, 26–28, 35, 51–52. In the context of environmental information, see 1994 Report, pp. 23–30.

291 In at least one of the complaints of this type, the case was exacerbated by the fact that the holiday was in Northern Ireland. The Ombudsman commented, in his 1987 Report, p. 21: "It would seem reasonable in view of our often expressed attitude towards Northern Ireland that a person visiting Northern Ireland should not be regarded as 'absent from the State' for the purposes of social welfare payments."

292 *Gray v. Formosa* [1963] P. 259 at 267 (*per* Lord Denning); 1984 Report, p. 13; 1985 Report, p. 46. Note that this rule was held to be unconstitutional (quite independently of its legislative abrogation) by Barr J. in *C.M. v. T.M.* [1988] I.L.R.M. 456 and by the Supreme Court in *W v. W* [1993] 2 I.R. 476 on the ground that it infringed Art. 40.1 of the Constitution.

293 1996 Report, pp. 19–20. The Ombudsman referred to *O'Rourke v. The Revenue Commissioners* [1996] 2 I.R. 1 and to the principle of unjust enrichment described at pp. 850–857.

294 1994 Report, p. 42; 1995 Report, p. 30. See also 1977 Report, p. 33.

specific Premium Rate Service Regulator (because of the high rates charged for premium rate services) the appointment being organised by the Director of Consumer Affairs.[294]

However, not all of these suggestions have borne fruit. In 1994, for instance, the Ombudsman scrutinised the practice in relation to a range of additional benefits (including free telephone rental, television licence, and over 80's allowance) for the elderly, sick or disabled who are in receipt of long-term payments. These additional benefits are paid on a "passport" system by which entitlement depends upon being already in receipt of one of a number of qualifying payments, *e.g.* Contributory Old Age Pension. While this is convenient, the Ombudsman received a number of complaints which "suggest that it would be more equitable if the additional benefits were based on some separate objective indicator of need . . . but [the Department of Social Welfare's] response does not indicate that they intend to revise the eligibility criteria for the free schemes in a way which would meet the equity argument raised by our complainants."[295] Recently, the Ombudsman has made a strong statement about the inadequacy of the parliamentary scrutiny of statutory instruments[296] and called for a language Act to improve the quality of service in the Irish language.[297]

In addition, the Ombudsman has encouraged public bodies to develop and publicise their own internal complaints procedure.[298] It will be noted that, as with the individual cases, many of these changes will be of most benefit to the poorer sections of the community. This is appropriate since other, better-off groups are often well equipped to make their own representations felt by the administrative machine, for example accountants' organisations lobbying the Revenue Commissioners for extra-statutory concessions or farmers' groups negotiating with the Department of Agriculture in regard to grants.

In his role as general progess-chaser, the Ombudsman can counter a frequent failure of communication at the interface at which the citizen meets his Government. Thus the Ombudsman has described his duty as "giving the citizen a role in

---

[295] 1994 Report, pp. 36–37. See also 1993 Report, pp. 53–54 (time gap between award of old age pension and withdrawal of unemployment payment); pp. 55–56 (inflated assessment of property in the social welfare means test); p. 60 (lack of services for autistic children); 1992 Report, p. 55 (to introduce something like the U.K. "blight notice" system, requiring a local authority to buy property when it is impossible to obtain market value for a property because it may be compulsorily acquired by the local authority at a later date; pp. 56–57 (to provide for a formal consultation when a street is made one way). 1991 Report, pp. 33–34 (leave from employment for adoptive mothers); 38 (appeal system for Disabled Persons' Maintenance Allowance or Domiciliary Care Allowance); 40–42 (anomalies relating to separated persons); 1993 Report, pp. 78–79 (recommendations, accepted by Bord Telecom to improve its treatment of disputed accounts); 1990 Reports, pp. 15–18 (anomalies in social welfare benefits).

[296] Report of Investigation of Complaints (1997), pp.6, 60 and Appendix 2. See also pp. 346–347.

[297] 1997 Report, pp. 21–22.

[298] 1985 Report, p. 30; 1987 Report, p. 34. 1996 Report, p. 24. See also 1994 Report, p. 42 (noted in the previous paragraph of the text) appointment of a Premium Rate Service Regulator: this appointment is to be organised by the Director of Consumer Affairs."

[299] See, *e.g.* 94 *Senate Debates*, Col. 1593, July 2, 1980. For debates on 1984 Annual Report, see 364 *Dáil Debates*, Cols. 483 *et seq.*, February 26, 1986; 109 *Senate Debates*, Cols. 478 *et seq.* October 17 and November 7, 1985. For debate on 1997 Report, see 480 Dáil Debates, Col. 1475 (Oct. 12, 1997) 481 Dáil Debates, Col. 289 (Oct. 8, 1997); 482 Dáil Debates 891 (Nov. 6, 1997).

government administration".[299]

As regards the Ombudsman's formal integration with the organs of the State, there is, as mentioned already, no equivalent of the House of Commons Select Committee on the P.C.A. However, the Ombudsman has reasonably sound links with the central organs of the polity. His annual reports are occasionally debated, usually it must be said in the Senate (for two or so hours) where more time is available than in the Dáil. In addition, his performance occasionally comes to the attention of Oireachtas committees. His Director of the Office (the principal civil servant) is the accounting officer for his estimate and, as such, usually appears before the Public Accounts Committee. His activities are so diverse that he or a member of his staff may appear before other specialised committees.[300]

It may be that the Ombudsman's most significant service will, in the long term, be to stimulate improvements which raise the level of public administration (quicker decisions; more flexibility; better explanations; good manners) and so reduce the amount of clientelism embedded in the Irish political system.

---

[300] *e.g.*, the Ombudsman appeared before the Committee on Security and Legislation (Nov. 29, 1995) to talk about the then forthcoming Freedom of Information Bill.

CHAPTER 9

FUNDAMENTAL PRINCIPLES OF
JUDICAL REVIEW

1. The Doctrine of *Ultra Vires*

General Principles

The following elementary points should be made. First, public bodies are often endowed by statute with the legal power to perform certain acts which is not given to ordinary private persons. Examples include the power to make regulations, issue licences and to make grants. As will be seen presently, the *ultra vires* doctrine requires that in exercising those powers, the public body may not go beyond the limits (*vires*) fixed by the empowering statute. In addition, however, to these specific and special powers, public bodies will usually also enjoy what are sometimes (for shorthand) described as "common law powers" in that these powers are not bestowed by statute and are common to public bodies and ordinary citizens. These powers include, for example, the power to make contracts, hold land, sue and be sued and borrow or spend money.[1]

The extent to which a public body enjoys such "common law" powers depends ultimately on the legislation which constitutes the public body. As was said in an English case on the question of whether a statutory corporation was empowered to borrow money:

> "What you have to do is to find out what this statutory creature is and what it is meant to do; and to find out what this statutory creature is you must look at the statute only, because there and there alone, is found the definition of this new creature."[2]

At a more helpful level one can say that this issue will depend upon the statute constituting the public body and, also, upon whether, given the statutory structure and objectives, it seems that the power claimed is an "incidental power".[3] A good deal will depend on whether the public body is constituted as a corporation sole. Thus, section 2(1) of the Ministers and Secretaries Act 1924 was intended to bestow a good deal of legal personality upon the Ministers which it established:

---

[1] For a helpful discussion, see Halsbury's Laws of England (4th ed), Vol. 9, para. 1333ff. For some of these points in the context of local government, see pp. 199–203.
[2] *Baroness Wenlock v. River Dee Company* (1887) 36 Ch. D. 674 at 685, *per* Bowen L.J.
[3] See pp. 402–405.

"Each of the Ministers . . . shall be a corporation sole . . . and may sue and . . . be sued . . . and may acquire, hold and dispose of land for the purposes of the functions, powers or duties of the Department of State of which he is head."

The last few words of this provision draw attention to a most salient feature of this area. It is that the public body or corporation sole will usually only be empowered to perform a legal action – for example, making a contract – so far as this is necessary to its statutory objectives or reasonably incidental thereto. Thus, in *Howard v. Commissioners of Public Works*,[4] a case in which it was held that the defendants were not empowered to build a visitors' centre, Costello J. remarked:

> "Can it be said that a power to *build* a public amenity in the form of a visitors' centre is *incidental* to any of the powers conferred on the Commissioners by any of the Public Works Acts to which I have been referred or any of the special Acts conferring specific powers? I do not think so. Nor can any such power be said to be *consequential* on any of the relevant statutory powers which have been conferred on the Commissioners. Nor can a power to *manage* a visitors' centre be said to be incidental or consequential upon any of the relevant statutory provisions."[5]

These issues are examined more fully below.[6]

Judicial review of administrative action is founded on the doctrine of *ultra vires*.[7] Although the High Court possesses an inherent jurisdiction to supervise the activities of inferior courts[8] tribunals and other public authorities and the *ultra vires* doctrine means that this power of review may only be exercised in circumstances where the

---

[4] [1994] 1 I.R. 101.

[5] *Ibid*. at 113.

[6] See pp. 402–406.

[7] In the United Kingdom the modern utility of the *ultra vires* doctrine has been questioned both by leading judges (see, *e.g.* Woolf, "Droit Public – English Style" (1995) *Public Law* 57; Laws, "Law and Democracy" (1995) *Public Law* 72) and academics (Craig, *Administrative Law* (1994, 3rd ed.), at pp. 12 *et seq.*) Thus speaking of modern developments in administrative laws, Laws opines (at 79):

> "They are, categorically, judicial creations. They owe neither their existence nor their acceptance to the will of the legislature. They have nothing to do with the intention of Parliament, save as a fig–leaf to cover their true origins. We do not need the fig–leaf any more."

This view has proved to be controversial and has provoked a substantial response: see, *e.g.* Forsyth, "Of Fig Leaves and Fairy Tales: the *Ultra Vires* Doctrine, the Sovereignty of Parliament and Judicial Review" (1996) *Camb. L.J.* 122; Wade, "Habeas Corpus and Judicial Review" (1997) 113 L.Q.R. 55. Apart from the facts that the *ultra vires* doctrine provides the entire foundation stone for judicial review and that in any democracy it is not unreasonable to assume that the legislature intended that statutory powers will be exercised in a manner consistent with the rule of law and fundamental freedoms, in this jurisdiction there is the further consideration that the "double construction rule" requires the courts (if necessary) to impute an artificial intention to the Oireachtas in order to save the constitutionality of a law conferring discretionary powers. In other words, save where the Oireachtas makes its (unconstitutional) intentions perfectly plain on the face of the statute, the courts will assume that the powers in question are to be exercised in a manner which is consistent with fundamental principles and constitutional rights. This question is further discussed in the context of discretionary powers below at pp. 635–640.

[8] The inferior courts are the District Court, the Circuit Court and the Special Criminal Court. The High Court, Court of Criminal Appeal and the Supreme Court are all superior courts of record and are not subject to judicial review: see *People (D.P.P.) v. Quilligan (No. 2)* [1989] I.R. 46 at 57, *per* Henchy J. and *Blackhall v. Grehan* [1995] 3 I.R. 205. See also *Re Weir and Higgins's Application* [1988] N.I. 338.

inferior body has exceeded its jurisdiction. The High Court, when exercising its powers of judicial review, is not concerned with the merits, but rather with the legality of the decision under review. In short, a finding of *ultra vires* is a prerequisite to judicial intervention by means of judicial review. To this there is one recognised exception: the court may quash a decision, otherwise within jurisdiction, which is flawed by the presence of an error "on the face of the record", *i.e.* where an error of law is patent.[9] The power to quash for error of law on the record is an historical anomaly which is now probably too well established to be disregarded. Where a decision exhibited a patent error of law, this irregularity is regarded "as an affront to the law which cannot be overlooked" and more "than judicial flesh and blood could resist."[10]

A decision which is vitiated by jurisdictional error is void, and will, save in exceptional cases, be declared to be void *ab initio* in the appropriate proceedings. Nevertheless such a decision – unless flagrantly illegal – remains valid for all purposes unless and until it is set aside by the courts.[11] The public law remedies are discretionary in nature, and a quashing order will only be granted to a proper plaintiff with the requisite *locus standi* who can persuade the court to exercise its discretion in his favour.[12]

No comprehensive account can be given of what errors will destroy the jurisdiction of a lower court or tribunal, thus rendering its decisions liable to be quashed. It is clear that an error committed in the course of an adjudication may go to jurisdiction,[13] but that said, the leading authorities do not disclose a governing principle which facilitates the classification of errors as "jurisdictional" as opposed to being within jurisdiction and consequently – unless they appear on the face of the record – immune from correction upon an application for judicial review.[14] In truth, the common law doctrine of *ultra vires* is based on the artifice of statutory

---

9   See pp. 430–436.
10 Wade and Forsyth, *Administrative Law* (7th ed., 1994) at 360.
11 *The State (Llewellyn) v. Ua Donnchadha* [1973] I.R. 151; *Re Comhaltas Ceolteoirí Éireann*, unreported, High Court, December 5, 1977; *Campus Oil v. Minister for Industry and Energy* [1983] I.R. 88; *The State (Abenglen Properties Ltd) v. Dublin Corporation* [1984] I.R. 381; *Hoffman–La Roche v. Trade Secretary* [1975] A.C. 295 and *C.W. Shipping Co. Ltd v. Limerick Harbour Commrs.* [1989] I.L.R.M. 416. But *cf.* the comments of Lord Denning in *R. v. Paddington Valuation Officer, ex p. Peachy Properties Ltd* [1966] 1 Q.B. 380, those of Lord Diplock in *Dunlop v. Woolahra M.C.* [1982] A.C. 158 and Walsh J. in *Mahon v. Shelley* [1990] 1 I.R. 36 at 41. By way of exception to this general rule, the courts appear prepared to allow county managers to treat certain decisions of councillors as invalid without actually seeking to have these decisions quashed in judicial review proceedings: see pp. 196–199. See also the inconclusive discussion of the interim status of an (admittedly invalid) order made by an irregularly constituted Special Criminal Court in *Hegarty v. Governor of Limerick Prison*, unreported, High Court, February 26, 1997. On this difficult subject, see pp. 463–465.
12 See pp. 739–755.
13 *The State (Holland) v. Kennedy* [1977] I.R. 193; *Sweeney v. Brophy* [1993] 2 I.R. 202; *Greene v. Governor of Mountjoy Prison* [1995] 3 I.R. 541; *Killeen v. Director of Public Prosecutions* [1998] 1 I.L.R.M. 1.
14 See generally pp. 430–434. A "routine mishap" does not affect jurisdiction (see, *e.g.*, *Maher v. O'Donnell* [1995] 3 I.R. 530 at 540, *per* Laffoy J.), but there is a spectrum and the characterisation of errors as between routine mishaps and more serious errors affecting jurisdiction tends to be inherently subjective. However, the courts seem particularly reluctant to interfere where it is contended that there was an insufficiency of evidence to justify a conclusion drawn by an inferior court: see, *e.g.*, *Roche v. Martin* [1993] I.L.R.M. 651; *Truloc Ltd v. McMenamin* [1994] 1 I.L.R.M. 151; *Stokes v. O'Donnell* [1996] 2 I.L.R.M. 538; *Lennon v. Clifford* [1996] 2 I.R. 590. The intractability and complexity of these issues is considered further below at pp. 417–428.

interpretation. The courts presume that the Oireachtas did not intend that the donee of a statutory power should exercise that power in an unfair or arbitrary fashion. Thus, the courts will intervene not only to restrain administrative action which contravenes some express statutory provision, but also where some implied condition of the Act – for instance, adherence to the rules of constitutional justice, or the doctrine of reasonableness – has been infringed. The common law principles of judicial review of administrative action are thus based upon this edifice of parliamentary intent and statutory interpretation.

In recent times, Irish courts have elevated these common law doctrines onto the constitutional plane. Legislation authorising administrative action which was arbitrary, unfair, or contrary to principles of fair procedures would plainly be unconstitutional.[15] The presumption of constitutionality requires that a constitutional interpretation be given to the impugned statutory provisions if this is at all possible. The presumption extends to proceedings, procedures, discretions and adjudications which are permitted, provided for or prescribed by an Act of the Oireachtas and, it means that, in these contexts, a statutory provision is entitled to the presumption:

> "That what is required, is allowed to be done, for the purpose of its imple-
> mentation, will take place without breaching any of the requirements, express
> or implied of the Constitution. If [the donee of the statutory power] exercised
> his discretion or his powers capriciously, partially or in a manifestly unfair
> manner it would be assumed that this could not have been contemplated or
> intended by the Oireachtas and his action would be restrained and corrected
> by the Courts."[16]

The courts have used this principle to hold that the exercise of administrative discretion in an improper fashion,[17] or in a manner contrary to constitutional justice[18] is *ultra vires* the principal Act, while at the same time upholding the constitutionality of the parent legislation.

The modern tendency has been to increase the range of errors which affect the jurisdiction of administrative bodies and lower courts, almost to the point where all errors of law are assumed to destroy that jurisdiction.[19] But this tendency – which

---

[15] See, *e.g. Loftus v. Attorney General* [1979] I.R. 221; *O'Brien v. Bord na Móna* [1983] I.R. 265.

[16] *Loftus v. Attorney General* [1979] I.R. 221at 238 at 241, *per* O'Higgins C.J.

[17] See, *e.g. Irish Family Planning Association Ltd v. Ryan* [1979] I.R. 295; *O'Callaghan v. Ireland* [1994] 1 I.R. 555.

[18] *O'Brien v. Bord na Móna* [1983] I.R. 255; *Barry v. Medical Council*, unreported, High Court, February 11, 1997.

[19] In *Radio Limerick One Ltd v. Independent Radio & Television Commission* [1997] 2 I.L.R.M. 1 at 19 Keane J. said that it was "self-evident" that "if the exercise of the statutory discretion is grounded on an erroneous view of the law, it should not normally be allowed to stand". This is the position in the United Kingdom where the distinction between errors of law going to jurisdiction and those which do not has effectively been abolished: *Anisminic Ltd v. Foreign Compensation Commission* [1969] 2 A.C. 147; *R v. Hull University, ex p. Page* [1993] A.C. 682. See also the comments of Costello P. in *Ryan v. Compensation Tribunal* [1997] 1 I.L.R.M. 194 at 207 and those of Keane J. in *Killeen v. Director of Public Prosecutions* [1998] 1 I.L.R.M. 1. In the latter case Keane J. quoted from the speech of Lord Reid in *Anisminic* with approval, adding that "it *may* be that an error of law committed by a tribunal acting within its jurisdiction is not capable of being set aside on certiorari: *The State (Davidson) v. Farrell* [1960] I.R. 438" (emphasis added). The underlined words suggest, perhaps, that the Supreme Court is paving the way for the full endorsement of *Anisminic* and *Page*, thereby in the process overruling cases such as *Davidson*.

is doubtless prompted by a judicial desire to protect the citizen against legally unjustifiable administrative actions – is often at odds with the legislative policy of allocating tasks to a specialised public body.[20]

In view of this tension, and given the inherent difficulty in distinguishing satisfactorily between matters bearing on the merits and those relating to *vires* (or jurisdiction), the entire doctrine of jurisdictional review has become increasingly artificial and complex. It may be useful, therefore, to separate out by way of introduction the seven heads of judicial review. Four of these heads – (a), (d), (f) and (g) – will be examined in some detail later in this Part. The other three heads will only be mentioned in this Part since two – (b) and (c) – of them will be dealt with more extensively elsewhere in this book and the third – (e) – falls more properly into the field of constitutional law. (There is one other ground of judicial review – error on the face of the record – which is not dealt with here because it is not based on jurisdiction or *ultra vires*: see Part 4.)

(a) Correct authority.

The power may only be exercised by the administrative authority in whom it was vested by the Oireachtas. One aspect of this is the *delegatus non potest delegare* principle: a power may only be delegated to a body or person other than that designated by the Oireachtas if this is authorised, expressly or by implication, by the legislation in question. Another aspect is that the authority must be properly appointed, properly constituted and, where relevant, properly qualified.[21] Two good examples of this are supplied by *Thompson v. Minister for Social Welfare*[22] (where O'Hanlon J. quashed a decision of a social welfare appeals officer, as that officer had not sat with the two assessors required by section 298(12) of the Social Welfare (Consolidation) Act 1981 and the appellant had not consented to this course of action) and *Hegarty v. Governor of Limerick Prison*[23] (where Geoghegan J. held that orders made by an irregularly constituted Special Criminal Court were invalid).

(b) Discretionary powers.

The courts assume (unless the contrary is clearly established) that the fact that the Oireachtas did not intend to confer a discretionary power on public authorities does

---

[20] *R. v. Preston Supplementary Benefits Appeal Tribunal, ex p. Shine* [1975] 1 W.L.R. 624; *R. v. National Insurance Commissioner, ex p. Stratton* [1979] Q.B. 361. This attitude is also apparent in a series of Irish decisions: see, *e.g.*, *Irish Permanent Building Society v. Caldwell* [1981] I.L.R.M. 242; *The State (Casey) v. Labour Court* (1984) 3 J.I.S.L.L. 135; *The State (Abenglen Properties Ltd) v. Dublin Corporation* [1984] I.R. 381; *Harte v. Labour Court* [1996] 2 I.R. 170; *Radio Limerick One Ltd v. Independent Radio and Television Commission* [1997] 2 I.L.R.M. 1 and *Henry Denny and Co. (Ire.) Ltd v. Minister for Social Welfare*, unreported, December 1, 1997. A determination by an administrative tribunal or personage on a pure issue of law "need not be treated with the same deference as the determination of a specialised tribunal on an issue of fact": *Lambert v. An tArd Chláraitheoir* [1995] 2 I.R. 372 at 384, *per* Kinlen J.

[21] *The State (Walshe) v. Murphy* [1981] I.R. 275; *Shelley v. Mahon* [1990] 1 I.R. 36 (convictions imposed by improperly qualified District Judge quashed); As far as the *delegatus* rule is concerned, see pp. 481–485.

[22] [1989] I.R. 618.

[23] Unreported, Divisional High Court, February 26, 1997. A Circuit Court judge had continued to sit on the Special Criminal Court following his "de-listing" from that Court, because officials had never informed him that the Government had made the appropriate order under s.39 of the Offences against the State Act 1939.

not mean that the public authority may act in an unreasonable or arbitrary fashion.[24] Consequently discretionary powers must be exercised reasonably and bona fide, relevant considerations taken into account and irrelevant considerations ignored. These matters are considered elsewhere.[25]

(c) Constitutional justice

The rule against bias is dealt with in Chapter 10 and the principle of *audi alteram partem* in Chapter 11.

(d) Other formal and procedural requirements.

Where an administrative authority violates the principles of natural justice or constitutional justice, its decision will generally be quashed on the application of an aggrieved party. The position in the case of disregard of other procedural and formal requirements is not as clear-cut. In some cases procedural requirements have been found to be directory only, so that breach does not lead to the nullification of the administrative or judicial decision under challenge, especially if the breach is a purely technical one or one which has not caused any interested party to be prejudiced as a result.[26] These matters are considered elsewhere.[27]

(e) Unconstitutionality.

Any administrative authority which acts in an unconstitutional fashion[28] or pursuant to a law which is adjudged to be unconstitutional will thereby exceed jurisdiction.[29]

(f) Conditions precedent to jurisdiction

An administrative authority can only exercise its powers over subject-matter which falls within the description, as to law, facts and circumstances, specified in the authority's field of competence. In other words, some errors made by an administrative authority affect its jurisdiction, where that jurisdiction depends upon a condition.[30] Even though the error is one on a point of fact, where its existence must be established before the authority has power to act. Where the facts in question are truly collateral or pre-conditions to jurisdiction, their existence can and will be reviewed in judicial review proceedings. Moreover it is no answer for the deciding

---

24 *East Donegal Co-operatives Ltd v. Attorney General* [1970] I.R. 317; *Loftus v. Attorney General* [1979] I.R. 221.
25 See pp. 631–635.
26 The governing principles are set out in the judgment of Henchy J. in *Monaghan UDC v. Alf-A-Bet Promotions Ltd* [1980] I.L.R.M. 64.
27 See pp. 440–452.
28 See the comments of Henchy J. in *The State (Holland) v. Kennedy* [1977] I.R. 193 at 201 and *The State (Byrne) v. Frawley* [1978] I.R. 326, 345 and those of Walsh J. in *Shelley v. Mahon* [1990] 1 I.R. 36 at 45. In *Coughlan v. Patwell* [1993] 1 I.R. 31 a District Judge was held to have exceeded jurisdiction when he refused to entertain an argument that particular evidence should be excluded for breach of constitutional rights.
29 Examples include *M v. An Bord Uchtála* [1975] I.R. 81; *Cox v. Ireland* [1992] 2 I.R. 503 and *Lovett v. Minister for Education* [1997] 1 I.L.R.M. 89.
30 Sometimes described as "jurisdictional fact" (*Anisminic Ltd v. Foreign Compensation Commission* [1969] 2 A.C. 147, or "precedent fact" (*R v. Home Secretary, ex p. Khawaja* [1984] A.C. 74).

body to plead that its conclusion as to whether it had jurisdiction is a reasonable one, albeit incorrect.[31] On the other hand, if the deciding authority correctly satisfies the statutory pre-conditions as to jurisdiction, its subsequent conclusions on mixed questions of law and fact will not lightly be disturbed, especially if the body in question is a specialist one.[32] These matters are examined in greater detail below.[33] In some circumstances the availability of an adequate appellate remedy may prompt a court to hold that the error of fact complained of did not affect jurisdiction.[34] In general, however, the difficulty is that there is no *a priori* method whereby the critical question of whether certain facts should be treated as jurisdictional may be determined. The formulation is that the facts necessary to give jurisdiction must be preliminary to, or collateral to, the merits of, the issue.[35] But even this formula gives rise to its own difficulties, as is well illustrated by a series of conflicting Irish decisions in licensing matters.[36]

(g) Within the power conferred by statute.

The administrative decision must fall within the substantive power conferred – whether expressly or by implication – by the statute. Before going on to discuss this precept, we must notice the gloss introduced by the Constitution: in some cases the validity of actions taken without express statutory authority will be upheld on the ground that such actions were necessary to vindicate the personal rights of the citizen as required by Article 40.3.1°. The most remarkable instance of this free-standing jurisdiction is supplied by *DG v. Eastern Health Board*,[37] where a majority of the Supreme Court upheld a High Court order committing a seriously disturbed – but innocent – juvenile to a penal institution for a short period in the absence of any alternative secure accommodation. Hamilton C.J. held that, in the very special circumstances of the case, the detention was justifiable – even in the absence of any statutory authority for this course of action – as necessary to vindicate the child's welfare.[38]

---

[31] *Shannon Regional Fisheries Board v. An Bord Pleanála* [1994] 3 I.R. 449 at 456, *per* Barr J.; *Lambert v. An tÁrd Chláraitheoir* [1995] 2 I.R. 372 at 384, *per* Kinlen J.; *Radio Limerick One Ltd v. Independent Radio and Television Commission* [1997] 2 I.L.R.M. 1. This complex matter is considered further below at pp. 422–426.

[32] *Shannon Regional Fisheries Board v. An Bord Pleanála* [1994] 3 I.R. 449 at 456, *per* Barr J.; *Radio Limerick One Ltd v. Independent Radio and Television Commission* [1997] 2 I.L.R.M. 1 and *Harte v. Labour Court* [1996] 2 I.R. 171.

[33] At pp. 422–426.

[34] Thus, in *Harte v. Labour Court* [1996] 2 I.R. 171 Keane J. held that determinations by the Labour Court on the appropriate comparators for equal pay purposes was not jurisdictional in this sense, partly because (at 178):

"The Oireachtas has vested in the Labour Court the power to decide not merely questions of fact, but also mixed questions of fact and law such as came before them in the present case. It also afforded a remedy to a party dissatisfied with their decision on a question of law in the form of an appeal to this Court."

[35] *R. v. Fulham Rent Tribunal, ex p. Zerek* [1951] 2 K.B. 1 at 6, *per* Lord Goddard; *Re Doherty's Application* [1988] N.I. 14 at 28–29, *per* Kelly L.J.

[36] See *The State (Attorney General) v. Durcan* [1964] I.R. 279; *Re Riordan* [1981] I.L.R.M. 2; *The State (Reddy) v. Johnston*, unreported, High Court, July 31, 1980 and *Re Doherty's Application* [1988] N.I. 14. See also, the series of the "orchard" cases which plagued the Irish courts in the early part of this century culminating in *R. (Greenaway) v. Armagh JJ.* [1924] 2 I.R. 55.

[37] Unreported, Supreme Court, July 16, 1997.

[38] The Court expressly reasoned that on these facts the court's constitutional duty to protect the child's welfare took precedence over his constitutional right to liberty.

This exceptional jurisdiction aside, adminstrative action taken without either express or implied statutory authority will be found to be *ultra vires*. There are numerous instances where an express statutory restriction has been violated by the administrative body in question and, save in cases where the requirement has been found to be merely directory,[39] the decision will invariably be set aside in such circumstances. Most of the cases in this area turn on questions of particular statutory interpretation, nevertheless the following heterogeneous modern examples may be cited for the purpose of illustrating the far-flung operation of the principle.

In *Meade v. Cork County Council*[40] the Minister for Local Government made an order pursuant to section 98(5) of the Housing Act 1966 approving the sale of the applicant's cottage subject to payment of an amount to the respondents in redemption of an annuity under the 1966 Act. In fact, this subsection did not authorise the repayment of an annuity and Griffin J. held that in purporting to make such a condition, the Minister had failed to comply with the express requirements of the 1966 Act. Another clear example is provided by *Reidy v. Minister for Agriculture and Food*[41] where, as a disciplinary measure, the applicant civil servant was not allowed to compete for any civil service post for a two-year period. O'Hanlon J. set aside this decision, saying that there was no authority in either the Civil Service Regulation Acts 1956–1958, or the regulations made thereunder, for a disciplinary penalty of this kind. The third example is *Devitt v. Minister for Education.*[42] Section 23(2) of the Vocational Education Act 1930 requires the Minister to approve of any appointment submitted to her by a vocational education committee. Here a committee submitted the applicant's name for approval to a whole-time permanent post, but the Minister instead approved her appointment to a whole-time temporary post. Lardner J. quashed this decision, since the Act merely enabled the Minister to approve or disapprove of the appointment submitted to her: it did not enable her to approve the appointment of a candidate to a different type of post. Next, in *Phillips v. Medical Council*[43] Carroll J. ruled that the Council had acted *ultra vires* in requiring the parties to a disciplinary inquiry to make mutual discovery of documents. Section 45(6) of the Medical Practitioners Act 1978 simply enabled that body to make production orders in respect of documents, a power which did not extend to the making of discovery orders. In *Bowes v. Devally*[44] the applicant was convicted in the District Court of possession of a controlled drug. The District Judge ordered, pursuant to s. 30(1) of the Misuse of Drugs Act 1977, that a sum of money which had been found nearby which had traces of the drug should be forfeited. By virtue of this sub-section, the court by which a person was convicted of the offence "may order anything shown to the satisfaction of the court to relate to the offence to be forfeited . . ." Geoghegan J. quashed the forfeiture as having been made without jurisdiction, since even if the respondent had drawn the inference that the money "was intended to be used to acquire more drugs, it had no relevance to the actual offence for which the applicant was convicted". In *Keogh v. Galway*

[39] See pp. 440–452.
[40] Unreported, Supreme Court, July 31, 1974.
[41] Unreported, High Court, June 9, 1989.
[42] [1989] I.L.R.M. 696.
[43] [1991] 2 I.R. 115.
[44] [1995] 1 I.R. 315.

Corporation[45] Carney J. quashed a purported amendment to a development plan: the amendments were material ones and the respondents had failed to comply with their statutory duty[46] to publish in Iris Oifigiúil and in one newspaper circulating in the area. In *Greene v. McLoughlin*[47] the Supreme Court held that a coroner had acted *ultra vires* in leaving to the jury the question of whether a deceased's mind was disturbed at the time of the incident leading to death, since this suggested that the jury was being invited to consider whether the deceased "could be relieved from criminal liability which would otherwise have attached to him".[48] Finally, in *Smeltzer v. Fingal County Council*[49] Costello P. held that the Council had acted *ultra vires* in purporting to develop certain lands in respect of which there existed a public right of way without having complied with the statutory consultation procedures prescribed by section 73 of the Roads Act 1993. It is also part of the precept that a public body cannot be damnified for failing to go beyond its statutory powers. A recent illustration of this self-evident proposition is *Keogh v. Garda Commissioner*[50] where in an action brought by a trainee garda, it was held that the power conferred by s.13 of the Garda Síochána Act 1977 did not empower the Minister for Justice to extend the category of persons who could be represented by the Garda Representative Association to include trainees.

2. The *Ultra Vires* Doctrine and Particular Rules of Statutory Interpretation

Incidental powers: General Principles

However, in many of the reported cases, the real issue is whether the impugned administrative action is reasonably incidental to the express power and thus falls within the implied powers envisaged by statute. The general rule remains that stated by Lord Selborne in *Attorney General v. Great Eastern Ry. Co.*:

> "Whatever may fairly be regarded as incidental to or consequential upon, those things which the legislature has authorised, ought not (unless expressly prohibited) to be held by judicial construction, to be *ultra vires*."[51]

Specific Examples

Thus, in *Dublin Corporation v. Raso*[52] it was held that the local authority was entitled to impose restrictions on the opening hours of a "fish and chips" shop under

---

45 [1995] 3 I.R. 457.
46 As imposed by the Local Government (Planning and Development) Act 1963, s.21A(2).
47 Unreported, Supreme Court, January 25, 1995.
48 This was contrary to the Coroners Act 1962, s.30:
   "Questions of civil or criminal liability shall not be considered or investigated at an inquest and accordingly every inquest shall be confined to ascertaining the identity of the person in relation to whose death the inquest is being held and, how, when and where the death occurred."
49 [1998] 1 I.L.R.M. 24.
50 Unreported, High Court, November 6, 1997.
51 (1880) 5 App. Cas. 483. See also *In re the Worth Library* [1995] 2 I.R. 301 (health board's express power "to acquire any estate or interest in land" extends to an implied power to become the custodian of a library).
52 [1976–1977] I.L.R.M. 139.

its powers under the Planning Acts because conditions restricting the amount of noise and preserving the residential character of the neighbourhood were reasonably incidental to the authority's powers to impose conditions for the "proper planning and development" of the area in question. Another example is provided by *Minister for Transport and Power v. Trans World Airlines Inc.,*[53] where the question arose as to whether the Minister was entitled to prescribe landing charges for Shannon Airport. In the High Court, O'Keefe P. found against the Minister on the ground that while the Air Navigation and Transport Act 1936 gave the Minister power to establish and operate an airport, it did not expressly authorise him to prescribe charges of this kind. The Supreme Court took a different view, with Walsh J. holding that the power to prescribe fees was impliedly authorised by the 1936 Act:

> "I agree that the Minister is not essentially a trading corporation, but when a statutory provision expressly gives him a right to establish and maintain an airport this power carries with it the inherent right to determine the conditions under which the aircraft will be permitted to use the airport and that would include the charges which may be made for the same."[54]

In *Deane v. Voluntary Health Insurance Board*[55] Keane J. held that a statutory corporation which was under a duty to set its insurance premiums at a level which ensured that it remained solvent enjoyed an implied power to take such steps as were necessary to confine the level of their insurance exposure. A further good example is supplied by *An Blascaod Mór Teo. v. Commissioners of Public Works,*[56] where the issue arose as to whether the Minister for the Gaeltacht had power to make regulations governing aspects of the compulsory acquisition procedure contained in An Blascaod Mór National Historic Park Act 1989. Through what appears to have been sheer oversight the 1989 Act made no express provision for the kind of regulations which were actually made, although curiously other sections of the Act expressly permitted the making of other types of regulations. While Kelly J. agreed that on an application of the *expressio unius, exclusio alterius* rule this must be a "strong indicator that it did not wish to confer power on the Minister to make regulations other than those expressly specified" and that this presumption was re-inforced since the fact that the legislation granted powers of compulsory acquisition, he nonetheless concluded that he could imply the power in question. Noting that the issue was nothing more than a "straightforward question of statutory interpretation" which had as its object "the ascertainment of the intention of the Oireachtas", the structure of the Act was such that Kelly J. considered it would be

---

53 Unreported, Supreme Court, March 6, 1974.
54 *Ibid.* p. 11 of the judgment of Walsh J. But for cases on the other side of the line, see, *e.g. Waterford Corporation v. Murphy* [1920] 2 I.R. 165; *Irish Benefit Building Society v. Registrar of Friendly Societies* [1981] I.L.R.M. 73 (Registrar given statutory power to ensure the "orderly and proper regulation of building society business"; held, this power relates only to matters of honesty, legality, administration and propriety and does not cover matters of business judgment such as the interest rate paid to shareholders); *McMeel v. Minister for Health* [1985] I.L.R.M. 616 (ministerial power to give directions concerning "arrangements for providing services" in hospitals contemplates positive action and not the discontinuance of hospital services).
55 Unreported, High Court, April 22, 1993. This point was not dealt with by the Supreme Court on appeal in judgments delivered on July 28, 1994.
56 Unreported, High Court, December 19, 1996.

"perverse to conclude that the Oireachtas did not intend to confer a power on the Minister to make [these] regulations."

An Blascaod Mór illustrates a further, related point, namely, that the "reasonably incidental" principle is often supplemented by the principle of effectiveness: *ut res magis valeat, quam pereat.* Thus, as in that case, the courts will seek to avoid a construction of a statutory provision which renders it largely ineffectual. This principle was applied in *McGlinchey v. Governor of Portlaoise Prison*[57] in order to uphold the validity of the Government order establishing the Special Criminal Court. Part V of the Offences against the State Act 1939 contains detailed requirements prescribing the composition, jurisdiction and procedure of the Special Criminal Court but it does not actually specify by whom the members of the court are to be appointed. While Lynch J. acknowledged that the relevant statutory provisions could have been more "felicitously drafted", he invoked the principle of effectiveness in order to uphold the validity of the order:

> "I have no doubt at all but that a necessary inference arises that the Government is given power to establish the first Special Criminal Court following the making of the [Government's] proclamation, having regard to the mandatory terms of section 38(1) [of the 1939 Act] that such court should be established."[58]

It will be seen, therefore, that often the *ultra vires* principle is not applied with unnecessary strictness and the courts will only intervene where the administrative action cannot fairly be said to be reasonably incidental to the statutory provisions.

Limits to the scope of the implied powers doctrine

There are, of course, definite limits to the scope of the implied powers doctrine. Thus, in *Howard v. Commissioners of Public Works*[59] Costello J. held that the Commissioners had no implied power to build a visitors' centre at certain areas of natural beauty, as these powers were not either incidental to or consequential upon the certain specific statutory powers to construct public works such as roads, bridges and the maintenance of public monuments.[60] These general principles were also applied by the Supreme Court in *Keane v. An Bord Pleanála and Commissioners*

---

[57] [1988] I.R. 671.
[58] *Ibid.* at 681.
[59] [1994] 1 I.R. 101.
[60] The Oireachtas acted speedily on foot of this decision and such a general power was conferred by the State Authorities (Development and Management) Act 1993. S.1(a) provides that a state authority shall have power "to carry out, or procure the carrying out of, development" and s.1(d) provides that it shall have the power "to supply goods and to provide services, whether upon payment or free of charge." Interestingly, s.2(2) provides that:
> "A State authority shall have, and be deemed always to have had, all such incidental, supplemental, ancillary and consequential powers as, in the the opinion of the authority, are necessary or expedient for the purposes of the exercise by it of the powers aforesaid."

The Oireachtas acted speedily on foot of this decision and such a general power was conferred by the State Authorities (Development and Management) Act 1993. S.1(a) provides that a state authority shall have power "to carry out, or procure the carrying out of, development" and s.1(d) provides that it shall have the power "to supply goods and to provide services, whether upon payment or free of charge." Interestingly, s.2(2) provides that: There is here a subtle shift in the implied powers doctrine: the scope of the implied power turns on the opinion of the authority itself. See also Commissioners of Public Works (Powers and Functions) Act 1996 which provides the Commissioners with express powers to acquire and dispose of lands etc, and to provide assistance to flood victims (including compensation and the provision of temporary accommodation).
[61] [1997] 1 I.R. 184.

of Irish Lights[61] where the issue was whether the Commissioners had power to construct a new form of long range beacon. While the *vires* issue essentially turned on the meaning of the word "beacon" in s.634 of the Merchant Shipping Act 1894, several members of the Court re-affirmed the incidental powers rules. As Hamilton C.J. observed:

> "The powers of the Commissioners, being a body created by statute, are limited by the statute which created it and extended no further than is expressly stated therein or is necessarily and properly required for carrying into effect the purposes of incorporation or may fairly be regarded as incidental to or consequential upon those things which the Legislature has authorised."[62]

Hamilton C.J. also quoted the following passage from *Halsbury* with approval: "What the statute does not expressly or impliedly authorise is to be taken to be prohibited."[63] A majority of the Court concluded, in the words of the Chief Justice, that the proposed navigational system could not be regarded as a beacon in this sense. Furthermore, this navigational system covered an area far beyond the responsibility of the Commissioners.[64]

In addition, pulling in the opposite direction to the "reasonably incidental" principle are certain specialised rules of statutory interpretation such as the presumption against unnecessary interference with vested or property rights; the strict construction of penal statutes and the need for express language in the case of taxing or revenue-raising statutes. These rules are in part but specialised examples of a more general principle of statutory interpretation: the presumption against unclear changes in the law. However, it will be convenient if the case law is considered under these separate headings.

Presumption against interference with common law or vested rights

The presumption that the Oireachtas does not intend to interfere with common law or other vested rights means that clear statutory language is called for where it is sought to interfere with such rights. This presumption is often applicable in the case of regulatory or licensing statutes. Thus, in *Limerick Corporation v. Sheridan*[65] Davitt P. set aside an order of the local authority made under the Local Government (Sanitary Services) Act 1948 which had the effect of prohibiting all temporary dwellings within their functional area. This order involved "such gratuitous interference with the common law rights of those affected" that it could not be justified by the mere general words of the 1948 Act and, in the absence of such clear

---

[62] *Ibid.* at 212.
[63] *Ibid.* quoting *Halsbury* (4th ed.) Vol. 9, para. 133.
[64] By virtue of s.634 of the Merchant Shipping Act 1894, the Commissioners powers only extended "throughout Ireland and the adjacent seas and islands." This decision has now been comprehensively reversed by new legislation: Merchant Shipping (Commissioners of Irish Lights) Act 1997. Section 3(1) now gives the Commissioners extensive powers to construct and maintain radio navigation systems; s.3(2) provides that the Commissioners shall be deemed to have "such incidental, supplemental, ancillary and consequential powers as, in the opinion of the Commissioners, are necessary or expedient for the purpose of the exercise by them of the powers aforesaid." and s.4 gives the Commissioners extensive powers to co-operate with other national and international agencies in relation to the provision or operation of radio navigation systems.
[65] (1956) 90 I.L.T.R. 59.

statutory language, the order was condemned as *ultra vires*. Another example is provided by *C.W. Shipping Ltd v. Limerick Harbour Commissioners*,[66] where the respondents sought to prevent the applicant tug owner from operating in the Shannon estuary without a licence. Section 53 of the Harbours Act 1946 gave the respondents licensing powers in respect of "lighters, ferry-boats or other small boats." O'Hanlon J. held tugs were not of the same genus as lighters or ferry-boats, so that the licensing requirements did not apply in the applicant's case. He further observed that the 1946 Act must be strictly construed bearing in mind the fact that the "ordinary common law rights to use the waters of the harbour as a highway are being curtailed."[67] This approach clearly emerges from the judgment of Murphy J. in *O'Neill v. Minister for Agriculture*,[68] a case where an exclusive licensing scheme operated by the Minister was found to be *ultra vires* the Livestock (Artificial Insemination) Act 1947, in part because the Act did not provide express authority for so confining this otherwise perfectly lawful activity:

> "The scheme manifestly affects the right of citizens to work in an industry for which they may be qualified and the rights of potential customers to avail of such potential services. It is not that there is any reason to doubt that the scheme ultimately devised by the Minister was desirable, and may well have operated in the national interest, it is simply that such a scheme is so radical in qualifying limited number of persons and disqualifying all others who may be equally competent from engaging in business. . . . I would be unwilling to accept that in using general words the Oireachtas contemplated such a far reaching intrusion on the rights of citizens."[69]

Presumption against unclear changes in the law

A related presumption is that the courts will lean against any interpretation of a statutory provision which would have the effect of reversing settled law or legal principles or unless the language used is plain and unmistakeable. Thus, in *Minister for Industry & Commerce v. Hales*[70] Henchy J. held that regulations which sought to give the word "workers" an extended meaning so as to cover insurance agents working under contracts of service were *ultra vires*. The Oireachtas could not be presumed to have intended by means of a "loosely drafted sub-section" to effect "such radical and far-reaching changes in the law of contract." In some cases, even where plain language has apparently been used, the courts will, following a restrictive interpretation of the statutory language, deem certain actions to be *ultra vires*. Another example of this judicial attitude is supplied by the judgment of Finlay C.J. in *McDonagh & Sons Ltd v. Galway Corporation*.[71] In this case a

---

66 [1989] I.L.R.M. 416.
67 *Ibid.* at 426.
68 [1997] 2 I.L.R.M. 435. This important case is discussed further at pp. 46–47 and pp. 330–336.
69 In the light of this statement, the decision of Carroll J. in *Navan Tanker Services Ltd v. Meath County Council*, unreported, High Court, December 19, 1996 to the effect that a local authority could have regard to the adequacy of demand and impose a quota on the number of vehicle testers applying for a statutory licence would have to be viewed with some reserve.
70 [1967] I.R. 50.
71 [1995] 1 I.R. 191.

planning authority had, as a condition of granting planning permission for a hotel complex, required the developer to build a multi-storey car park. These conditions were in excess of the developers needs[72] and the developer sought a declaration to the effect that he was entitled to receive a contribution from the local authority by virtue of section 26(7) of the Local Government (Planning and Development) Act 1963 which provides that where such conditions are imposed "a contribution towards such of the relevant roads, open spaces, car parks, sewers, watermains or drains as are constructed shall be made by the local authority who will be responsible for their maintenance . . ." The Supreme Court could not accept, however, this bare statutory language could have the interpretation for which the applicant contended and impose an obligation on a local authority to maintain such excess works.[73]

There are, of course, limits to the principle, a point well illustrated by *Farrell v. Attorney General*,[74] a case where the Attorney had directed a new inquest following complaints by the deceased's widow about the first inquest. Although the wording of section 24(1) of the Coroners Act 1962[75] appeared expressly to permit the Attorney to direct a new inquest, in the High Court Smyth J. held that the subsection must be given a more restricted meaning, as the Oireachtas could not have intended "a situation of having two or more inquests with verdicts which could either be duplicitous or varying" concerning the identity of the deceased or the manner of his death. The Supreme Court, however, disagreed with this analysis, with Keane J. stating that as "on any view" of the section, it "envisaged a major change in the law", the presumption against oblique or unclear changes in the law was simply inapplicable.

Presumption against unnecessary interference with property rights

A particularly strong case of the presumption against interference with vested rights is the case of interference with property or other proprietary rights. This traditional common law presumption was placed in a constitutional perspective by Budd J. in *Dunraven Estates Ltd v. Commissioners of Public Works*,[76] where speaking in the context of the validity of an arterial drainage scheme under the Arterial Drainage Act 1945 which the Commissioners proposed to carry out on the plaintiff's lands, he said:

---

[72] Such conditions are, however, expressly authorised by s.26(2)(f) of the Local Government (Planning and Development) Act 1963 which provides that a planning authority may include conditions "for requiring roads, open spaces, car parks, sewers, watermains or drains in excess of the immediate needs of the proposed development. . . ."

[73] Finlay C.J. described such as a result as "inconceivable", adding ([1995] 1 I.R. at 201) that:
"In the instant case it would seem to be most unlikely that five storeys of a car park situated exclusively on the property of a developer and under his undoubted control and ownership would in respect of maintenance become the responsibility of the local authority, merely by the inclusion of the words 'who will be responsible for its maintenance' in the sub-section."

[74] Unreported, High Court, January 30, 1997; unreported, Supreme Court, November 21, 1997.

[75] Which provides in relevant part:
"Where the Attorney General has reason to believe that a person has died in circumstances which in his opinion make the holding of an inquest advisable he may direct any coroner . . . to hold an inquest into the death of that person, and that coroner shall proceed to hold an inquest in accordance with the provisions of this Act . . . whether or not he or any other coroner has viewed the body, made any inquiry, held any inquest in relation to or done any other act in connection with the death."

[76] [1974] I.R. 113.

"In the course of elucidating the interpretation of these sections, one has to bear in mind the constitutional position of the plaintiffs with regard to their lands, fisheries and other proprietary rights. There can be little doubt that an Act such as this, aimed at the improvement of large areas of land, is one for the benefit of the community, but the delimitation of property rights which is constitutionally permissible must be made with regard, as far as possible, to the property rights of citizens. The relevant articles of the Constitution do not, to take an extreme example, entitle the State to despoil a person of his property by taking a great deal more of it than is necessary for purposes connected with the common good. The Act of 1945 should be construed on the basis that it was not the intention of the legislature to deprive the plaintiffs of their property or interfere with it save and in so far as that was necessary for the common good and was in accordance with the Constitution."[77]

In the light of this rule of construction, Budd J. went to hold that section 6 of the Act (which required the Commissioners to provide the owner of the lands with full details of the proposed works so that he could make observations on these proposals) was mandatory and must be fully complied with as:

"An owner must be in a position to know precisely what is proposed to be done to his property, be it land or fisheries or any other proprietary rights, and what precise interference is intended before he is in a position to make observations of any worth."[78]

Since the Commissioners had not provided sufficient details of their proposals, the impugned decision was held to be *ultra vires*.

This principle of strict construction was also applied by the Supreme Court in *Hussey v. Irish Land Commission*,[79] where the Commission was held to have acted *ultra vires* in acquiring land which was not required for immediate resale. The Land Acts authorised the Commission to acquire lands for the purposes of resale and it was argued that this empowered the Commission to create a stockpile of acquired lands, from which resales might take place from time to time. Henchy J. rejected this argument, saying that compulsory purchase legislation must be strictly construed. In the absence of express statutory language, the Commission's power of compulsory acquisition could not be construed as authorising them to build up a land bank.[80]

---

[77] *Ibid.* at 132. This passage represents a perfect statement of the proportionality principle as it applies to interference with property rights, but before that term or concept ever came into vogue. But *cf. Crosbie v. Custom House Dock Development Authority* [1996] 2 I.R. 531, a case where, by reason of the threatened exercise of the Authority statutory powers of compulsory purchase, the plaintiff agreed to sell certain property. The lands were to be used for a planned national sports centre, but when this project was later abandoned, the Authority refused to re-convey the property to the plaintiff. Costello P. rejected the argument that this constituted a disproportionate interference with the plaintiff's property rights, but it may be noted that, in a case with strikingly similar facts, the German Constitutional Court took a different view: B Verf. GE 38, 175 (1974). In that case the Court held that when expropriation has taken place but the specific public purpose could not be achieved for other reasons the expropriated property has to be given back to the former owner.

[78] *Ibid.* at 134.

[79] Unreported, Supreme Court, December 13, 1984.

[80] For a similar approach, see *Meaney v. Cashel U.D.C.* [1937] I.R. 56; *Hendron v. Dublin Corporation* [1943] I.R. 566. But *cf. Crosbie v. Custom House Docks Authority* [1996] 2 I.R. 531 where, on the

The context and background to the legislation is often relevant and these factors, together with the presumption, will often help to determine the exact scope of the regulatory legislation. An example of this is afforded by *U.S. Tobacco International Ltd v. Minister for Health*,[81] where the Minister had declared certain forms of tobacco products to be restricted articles for the purposes of section 66 of the Health Act 1947. This section enabled the Minister to restrict the sale of "substances" involving the "risk of serious injury to health or body." This section might, at first sight, be thought to justify the restriction in question. However, Hamilton P. first drew attention to the fact that section 66 was contained in Part VI of the Act, which was stated to deal with "provisions in relation to medical and toilet preparations and certain other articles." Furthermore, section 66(3) allowed the Minister to grant a licence to a registered medical practitioner to deal in such restricted products. Hamilton P. considered that as the object of Part VI was to allow the Minister to restrict the sale and distribution of medicinal, toilet and other similar preparations which, if unrestricted and not under the control of a medical practitioner might cause injury to members of the public, the Minister could not rely on the section to restrict the sale of substances which were not of the same genus as medicinal and toilet preparations. The Minister could not rely on the general words of section 66 to restrict the sale of such tobacco products, as clear statutory authorisation for such a banning order would be required.

The need for express language in the case of taxing or revenue-raising statutes
One of the more deeply rooted presumptions of the common law is that taxes or charges may not be levied by the State or public authorities in the absence of express words, for as Atkin L.J. explained in *Attorney General v. Wilts United Dairies Ltd*[82]:

> "The circumstances would be remarkable indeed which would induce the courts to believe that the Legislature had sacrificed all the well-known checks and precautions, and, not in express words, but merely by implication, has entrusted a Minister with undefined and unlimited powers of imposing charges upon the subject for purposes connected with his department."[83]

In this jurisdiction, this presumption is probably given express constitutional underpinning by the Money Bill provisions of Articles 21 and 22 of the Constitution, which ensure that general taxation or charges may not be levied save by means of an Act of the Oireachtas. The effect of this presumption is that even statutes authorising local taxation or charges must be couched in express language. A good

---

facts, it might be argued that in effect the Authority had exercised its statutory powers (or the threat of the exercise of such powers) in order to "landbank" once its original plans for the land had fallen through.

[81]   [1990] 1 I.R. 394.

[82]   (1921) 37 T.L.R. 781 at 884 (affirmed by the House of Lords (1922) 91 L.J.K.B. 897). See also *Liverpool Corporation v. Maiden (Arthur) Ltd* [1938] 4 All E.R. 200. *R v. Richmond-upon-Thames, ex p. McCarthy & Stone (Developments) Ltd* [1992] 2 A.C. 48.

[83]   *Ibid.* This judgment was cited with approval by Murphy J. in *O'Neill v. Minister for Agriculture* [1997] 2 I.L.R.M. 435 at 450 as illustrating the wider proposition that even in jurisdictions "where the separation of powers is not governed by the requirements of a written constitution a presumption appears to arise that in delegating legislation Parliament did not intend to confer radical powers of a legislative nature" – a proposition which, Murphy J. considered, applied *a fortiori* to this jurisdiction.

example of the use of express language is section 26(2)(h) of the Local Government (Planning and Development) Act 1963 which provides expressly that planning authorities may impose the following conditions upon a grant of planning permission:

> "Conditions for requiring contribution (either in one sum or by instalments) towards any expenditure (including expenditure on the acquisition of land) that is proposed to be incurred by any local authority in respect of works (including the provision of open spaces) facilitating the proposed developments [subject to stipulations providing for repayment in the event that the works in question are not completed within a specified period]."

The need for strict compliance with these statutory requirements is illustrated by *Bord na Móna v. An Bord Pleanála*,[84] where the plaintiffs had been granted planning permission for a factory subject to a condition that they should pay a contribution towards the cost of the reconstruction of certain roads. This contribution was to be paid immediately over a three-year period but there was no period specified in the condition within which the works were to be carried out. Keane J. held these conditions to be *ultra vires* on two grounds. First, they frustrated the statutory right of the grantee of the permission, which was to wait for five years before implementing the permission. Secondly, the authority had not complied exactly with the terms of section 26(2)(h) of the 1963 Act, since they had not specified a time by which the works were to be completed. This was a significant omission, since:

> "It clearly would not be open to a planning authority to impose a condition requiring a contribution towards the cost of works which would facilitate a development, but expressly excluding any right on the part of the applicant to a refund of contributions in the event of the works not being done."[85]

But, in response to a third argument, Keane J. refused to condemn the condition on the ground that the proposed contribution would amount to the total cost of the relevant works, saying that this of itself was not objectionable. In view of the fact that a revenue-raising provision such as section 26 must be strictly construed, this conclusion seems questionable. The word "contribution" implies financial assistance towards the cost of local authority works, but would not seem to encompass payment of the full cost of these works.

The operation of this presumption can also be seen in the context of the cases arising under the Local Government (Financial Provisions) (No. 2) Act 1983, which authorises local authorities to charge for certain services provided by them. This legislation has been strictly construed by the courts and service charges have been held invalid where there is no clear statutory authorisation for the charge in question.[86] These cases are considered elsewhere.[87]

---

[84] [1985] I.R. 205.

[85] *Ibid.* at 210. See Scannell, "Invalid Planning Conditions" (1986) 8 D.U.L.J. (N.S.) 96.

[86] See, *e.g. Athlone U.D.C. v. Gavin* [1985] I.R. 434; *Louth County Council v. Mathews*, unreported, High Court, April 14, 1989; *Ballybay Meat Exports Ltd v. Monaghan County Council* [1990] I.L.R.M. 864. See also *Kinsale Yacht Club v. Commissioner of Valuation* [1994] 1 I.L.R.M. 457 (occupier of hereditament not to be rated where the rating statue seeks to impose a liability "by the use of oblique or slack language").

[87] See pp. 227–230.

Strict construction of penal statutes

At common law there is a particularly strong presumption in favour of a statutory construction which protects individual liberty. This common law presumption must now, of course, be read in the light of constitutional provisions protecting such fundamental rights and which elevate the status of such rights to a somewhat higher legal plane. A modern restatement of this presumption (in which the notion of constitutionally-protected personal rights appears to be implicit) is to be found in the judgment of Henchy J. in *Director of Public Prosecutions v. Gaffney*[88] where, speaking in the context of a statutory power of arrest, he said:

> "The right to arrest without a warrant given by section 49(6) of the Road Traffic Act 1961 [is a] substantial invasion of the personal rights enjoyed before the enactment of those provisions and there should not be attributed to Parliament an intention that such personal rights were to be curtailed further than the extent expressed in the statute."[89]

This principle is not confined to administrative decisions with implications for personal liberty. Thus, in *HMIL Ltd v. Minister for Agriculture and Food*[90] Barr J. ruled that an attempt by the Minister to impose administrative fines for alleged infractions of E.U. agricultural regulations was *ultra vires* in the absence of express legislative authority for this course of action.[91] The principle is likewise reflected in decisions involving taxing and rating statutes whereby the courts will not permit the imposition of a tax or other fiscal measure through the use of slack or oblique language.[92]

And yet it might be thought that this principle has not been consistently applied by the Supreme Court in recent years. In the first such case, *Director of Public Prosecutions (Stratford) v. Fagan*,[93] a majority of the Supreme Court held that members of the Gardaí enjoyed a common law power to stop motor vehicles for the purpose of detecting drink driving offences. This conclusion was reached despite the fact that the Oireachtas had hitherto refrained from conferring such a power on the Gardaí and in this respect the dissent of Denham J. – where she maintained that such a far-reaching powers of quasi-arrest should either be enshrined in statute or

---

[88] [1987] I.R. 177.

[89] *Ibid.* at 181. See also *Director of Public Prosecutions v. Bracken* [1994] 2 I.R. 523.

[90] Unreported, High Court, February 8, 1996.

[91] Barr J. was characteristically trenchant in his comments:
> "The Minister's implied authority to devise and operate a system of financial corrections . . . does not include the imposition of penalties for which there is no legislative authority in the relevant regulations. The Minister's function is limited to administration and he has no legislative power. Penalties of a quasi-criminal nature which the Minister has sought to impose on Hibernia ex post facto and for which there is no legislative authority must be struck down as unlawful . . . . Even if the penalties were not quasi-criminal in nature, the requirement of legal certainty demands that such provisions must be firmly based in law at the time of the transgression which gives rise to the penalty."

[92] See, *e.g. Inspector of Taxes v. Kiernan* [1981] I.R. and *Kinsale Yacht Club v. Commissioner of Valuation* [1994] 1 I.L.R.M. 457 (where Finlay C.J. held that the occupier of an hereditament was not to be rated where the rating statue sought to impose a liability "by the use of oblique or slack language".)

[93] [1994] 3 I.R. 265.

must be found in some well-established common law power – seems distinctly preferable. In the second case, *DG v. Eastern Health Board*,[94] a majority of the Supreme Court accepted – although, it must be said, with evident reluctance – that the High Court was correct in ordering the short-term detention of an unruly (although wholly innocent) juvenile in a penal institution in circumstances where no other secure accommodation was available. While all members of the Court accepted that this constituted an interference with the applicant's constitutional right to liberty, a majority felt that this order was necessary in the special and acute circumstances of the case in order to effectuate the court's constitutional duty to protect his welfare.

3. Jurisdictional Review

Seven types of jurisdictional error have already been listed in Part 1. However, as mentioned, it is not every error of law committed by an administrative body or lower court which will affect the jurisdiction of that body so as to invalidate the resulting decision. The question of which errors are jurisdictional is an intractable one and is intrinsically linked to questions of statutory interpretation and judicial policy. While the various theories of jurisdictional error provide some guide to the extent of review, the matter is nonetheless not one of abstract logic, but, at root, judicial policy, for it depends upon what degree of supervision the courts wish to exercise over decisions of administrative bodies and of lower courts. There have been several judicial suggestions that the courts will be reluctant to interfere with decisions of specialist tribunals or decisions taken pursuant to expert advice,[95] and, as far as the lower courts are concerned, there is some evidence that with the advent in 1924 of District and Circuit Courts staffed by professional judges, the High Court has been more reluctant to interfere with decisions of the lower courts. As Davitt P. said in *The State (Attorney General) v. Durcan*[96]:

> "Since 1924 the superior courts in this country [have been] more reluctant to interfere on certiorari with the decisions of the District Court and the Circuit Court than was the King's Bench Division to correct the legal errors of the justices at Petty and Quarter Sessions. It is possible that that tribunal was on occasions inclined to act as if it were hearing appeals from the justices. It has, of course, to be remembered that, generally speaking, the justices possessed no legal qualifications or training; that, in licensing matters particularly, canvassing was a distinct possibility; and that in such matters there was no appeal from their decisions at Quarter Sessions."[97]

Nevertheless, this judicial policy must bear in mind that it is important that tribunals and lower courts do not wrongfully usurp jurisdiction and that errors of law must not go uncorrected. While not stating so openly, the courts have by and

---

[94] Unreported, Supreme Court, July 16, 1997.
[95] See, *e.g., O'Keeffe v. An Bord Pleanála* [1993] 1 I.R. 39; *ACT Shipping Ltd v. Minister for the Marine* [1995] 3 I.R. 437.
[96] [1964] I.R. 279.
[97] *Ibid.* at 288–289. See also the comments of Gannon J. in *Clune v. Director of Public Prosecutions* [1981] I.L.R.M. 17, 20.

large sought to strike what they regard as the proper balance as between these competing considerations rather than seeking to decide the issues which arise by exclusive reference to any set formula or theory of jurisdictional review. The question of whether the decision of the tribunal or lower court goes to jurisdiction or not, can arise in regard to a decision about law (mainly points of statutory interpretation), fact or "mixed questions of fact and law". As it happens, these cases have arisen in the area of law, and, accordingly, it is proposed to deal mainly with these cases in the next sections of this Part and to leave until the final two sections the position regarding decisions about facts (or "mixed questions of fact and law.")

Something must be said at this stage about the evolution of various theories of jurisdiction.

The pure jurisdiction doctrine

This theory held sway from the first half of the nineteenth century until relatively recently.[98] The crucial feature of this theory is that jurisdiction is determined at the "commencement, and not at the conclusion of, the inquiry."[99] If an administrative authority or lower court has "subject-matter" or "original" jurisdiction, it does not lose such jurisdiction even if there is no evidence to support its findings of fact.[100]

This was decided by a very strong Divisional Court in *R. (Martin) v. Mahoney,*[101] where it was held that a conviction under section 1 of the Betting House Act 1853 which was (admittedly) based on insufficient evidence could not be quashed on certiorari, since the absence of sufficient evidence did not affect the jurisdiction of the convicting magistrate; as Lord O'Brien L.C.J. remarked:

> "To grant certiorari merely on the ground of want of jurisdiction, because there was no evidence to warrant a conviction, confounds want of jurisdiction with error in the exercise of it. The contention that mere want of evidence to authorize a conviction creates a cesser of jurisdiction, involves the unwarrantable proposition that a magistrate has jurisdiction only to go right; and that, though he had jurisdiction to enter upon an inquiry, mere miscarriage in drawing an unwarrantable conclusion from the evidence, such as it was, makes the magistrate act without and in excess of jurisdiction."[102]

The wealth of erudition displayed in the judgments of Lord O'Brien, Palles C.B. and Gibson J., coupled with the reputation of these judges, seems to have almost hypnotised successive generations of judges, since the authority of the reasoning

---

98 For an historical account of these developments, see Rubinstein, *Jurisdiction* (Oxford, 1965), Chap. 4; Jaffe and Henderson, "Judicial Review and the Rule of Law: Historical Origins" (1956) 72 L.Q.R. 345 and Jaffe, "Constitutional and Jurisdictional Fact" (1957) 70 Harv.L.Rev. 953 and de Smith, Woolf and Jowell *Judicial Review of Administrative Action* (5th ed.), pp. 225–228.

99 *R. v. Bolton* (1841) 1 Q.B. 66, 74, *per* Lord Denman C.J.

100 *R. (Martin) v. Mahoney* [1910] 2 I.R. 695. Such was the influence of the "original jurisdiction" theory that in *McDonald v. Bord na gCon (No. 3)*, unreported, High Court, January 13, 1966, Kenny J. held that the defendants had acted invalidly in breaching the *audi alteram partem* rule, but since they had original jurisdiction in the matter, they did not thereby exceed jurisdiction.

101 [1910] 2 I.R. 695.

102 *Ibid.* at 707.

in this case remained unquestioned until very recently.[103] Indeed, the emphasis on the original jurisdiction theory in *Mahoney's* case appears to have been so influential that even today many judges are reluctant to classify an error made in the course of exercising jurisdiction (such as misconstruing a statutory provision or admitting inadmissible evidence) as one which destroys that jurisdiction.

There are numerous Irish cases in which this doctrine has been followed and the following representative example from the mid-1950s illustrates how narrow as a result the scope of review was to become for a substantial period. In *The State (Batchelor & Co.) v. O'Floinn*[104] the applicants sought to quash a search warrant issued under section 12 of the Merchandise Marks Act 1887. It was said that there was insufficient evidence before the respondent District Judge to justify the warrant. But O'Daly J. for the Supreme Court disposed of this argument by stating that it was well settled that providing the error did not appear on the face of the record, questions as to the sufficiency of evidence amounted to errors within jurisdiction. The District Judge clearly had jurisdiction to make an order under the Act, and he did not lose jurisdiction by making an error of this nature. In the view of O'Daly J., questions as to the sufficiency of evidence were the very matters committed to the jurisdiction of the District Judge. The result of this and other similar decisions was that the scope of review was rather narrow, and this could often lead to injustice, particularly in criminal cases.[105]

"Conditions precedent to jurisdiction"

One method of escaping the confines of this doctrine was to classify certain findings of fact as "collateral" or as "conditions precedent to jurisdiction."[106] Administrative authorities do not possess an inherent jurisdiction; their jurisdiction depends upon facts which must have an objective existence before the authority has power to act. Hence, any decision of the authority as to the boundaries of its jurisdiction could not be conclusive, as otherwise it would usurp power never conferred on it by the Oireachtas. If, for example, the Circuit Court has jurisdiction to hear ejectment cases where the rateable valuation of the premises does not exceed £60, that court cannot acquire jurisdiction by reason of an erroneous conclusion as to the rateable valuation of the premises.[107] In other words, an administrative authority cannot give itself a jurisdiction which it cannot have, and the High Court will enforce the *ultra vires*

---

103 In Northern Ireland, *Mahoney* is regarded as "the accepted authority on certiorari": *R . v. Belfast Recorder, ex p. McNally* [1992] N.I. 217 at 229, *per* Lord Lowry L.C.J.

104 [1958] I.R. 155. See also, *R. (Limerick Corporation) v. Local Government Board* [1922] 2 I.R. 76; *R. (Dillon) v. Minister for Local Government* [1927] I.R. 474 and *McDonald v. Bord na gCon (No. 3)*, unreported, High Court, January 13, 1966.

105 See, *e.g. The State (Lee-Kiddier) v. Dunleavy*, unreported, High Court, August 17, 1976 where McWilliam J. held that the question of whether there was sufficient evidence to support a conviction was not reviewable in certiorari proceedings, absent error on the face of the record. Contrast this with the observations of Kenny J. in *The State (Holland) v. Kennedy* [1977] I.R. 193 where he doubted whether the rule in *Mahoney* was compatible with Art. 38.1 of the Constitution which prescribes trial "in due course of law."

106 Thus, in *The State (O'Neill) v. Shannon* [1931] I.R. 691 it was held that the principle of *Martin's* case only applied to decisions arrived at on the merits and was not relevant in the case of preliminary objections to jurisdiction.

107 *The State (Attorney General) v. Durcan* [1964] I.R. 279; *Harrington v. Judge Murphy* [1989] I.R. 207.

doctrine by insisting on the objective existence of certain facts upon which some jurisdiction depends.

The difficulty with this, of course, is that there does not appear to be any clear-cut method of determining which legal points or facts are "jurisdictional," and which are not.[108] In *The State (Davidson) v. Farrell*[109] Kingsmill Moore J. sought to answer this question by referring to the jurisdiction conferred – whether expressly or by necessary intendment – by statute on the authority concerned. In this case the applicant, a tenant in a controlled dwelling, sought to quash decisions of the District and Circuit Courts awarding her landlord certain sums as allowances in respect of the repair of the premises. She claimed that these decisions were flawed by juris-dictional error as a result of the misconstruction of the phrase "premises", as defined by the Rent Restrictions Act 1946. A majority of the Supreme Court concluded, following an examination of the 1946 Act, that the Oireachtas had intended to vest the District Court with jurisdiction to determine the basic rent and allowances. It was not a precondition to jurisdiction that the word "premises" be correctly construed, and as Kingsmill Moore J. explained:

> "The [District] Court may make an error in law in interpreting the word 'premises,' or an error in fact in determining that money has been expended when it has not, but these are errors within the jurisdiction conferred."[110]

Another example of this approach from this period is to be found in *The State (Attorney General) v. McGivern*[111]; a case where the Court refused to quash the granting of an exemption under section 5 of the Intoxicating Liquor Act 1927. The applicant had contended that dances at the local hotel could not constitute a "special occasion" within the meaning of the section. O'Daly J., having engaged in a rigorous examination of the statutory context, rejected the argument that this determination of what was a "special occasion" was a condition precedent to jurisdiction. The following passage contains one of the very few useful expositions of what constitutes a collateral fact or condition precedent to jurisdiction:

> "There is nothing in the structure of the sub-section to indicate that the Oireachtas is subtracting from the substantive jurisdiction of the [District Judge] the determination of what is a special occasion and placing it upon the pre-existing absolutes to jurisdiction. Moreover, the very nature of the subject matter is one of the strongest indications to the contrary. Matters collateral to jurisdiction are usually distinguished by their clear-cut and identifiable character, arising from the terms used or the appended definition. The words "special occasion" or "special event" have the very opposite character; they

---

108 See, *e.g.* the division of judicial opinion in the "orchard" cases: *R. (De Vesci) v. Queen's Co. JJ.* [1908] 2 I.R. 365; *R. (D'Arcy) v. Carlow JJ.* [1916] 2 I.R. 313 and *R. (Greenaway) v. Armagh JJ.* [1924] 2 I.R. 55.

109 [1960] I.R. 438. See also *The State (Davidson) v. Farrell* [1964] I.R. 279 for a useful judicial discussion of this question.

110 [1960] I.R. 438, 455. But if the District Judge had asked himself the wrong question in seeking to determine either of these issues, it seems probable that this case would now be decided differently: *Killeen v. Director of Public Prosecutions* [1998] 1 I.L.R.M. 1.

111 Unreported, Supreme Court, July 25, 1961.

range over a wide variety of circumstances, their very imprecision is of itself a mark that their meaning is being committed to the Justice as part of his substantive jurisdiction."

Some examples may now be given of where tribunals and inferior courts were held to have exceeded jurisdiction by reason of non-compliance with an essential precursor to jurisdiction. In *The State (Ferris) v. Employment Appeals Tribunal*[112] the respondent body declined to rule on the merits of an unfair dismissal case. The tribunal had erroneously concluded that wrongful dismissal proceedings arising out of the case were pending in the High Court, and that, as a result, it was precluded by section 15(3) of the Unfair Dismissals Act 1977 from ruling on the case. The tribunal's decision was quashed by the Supreme Court, for, as Henchy J. pointed out, the initiation of "a claim [for wrongful dismissal] as an objective fact must be proved before the Tribunal can exercise the jurisdiction given to it by section 15(3)." Since, in point of fact, no such common law claim for damages had been initiated, that order was invalid as being in excess of jurisdiction.

Kennedy v. Hearne[113] is another instance of a case in which certain facts were treated as jurisdictional. Here, through an administrative error, the Revenue Commissioners caused an enforcement notice in respect of unpaid income tax to be sent to the sheriff under section 485 of the Income Tax Act 1967 (now section 942 Taxes Consolidation Act 1997). The Supreme Court held that such a notice was invalid, as the powers contained in that section could only be validly activated upon condition that there was an actual default in the payment of a levied tax. As Finlay C.J. explained:

> "The section must be construed as vesting in the Revenue Commissioners the power to issue a notice to the sheriff only in cases where an actual default of a levied tax has occurred. Where, as happened in this case, they issued such a notice where that default had not continued up to the time that the notice was issued, what they did was a nullity."[114]

It is easy to understand why the Supreme Court should hold that an actual default in the payment of tax was a condition precedent to the operation of a section with such potentially far-reaching consequences. Yet in other cases the courts have refrained from classifying even matters touching on constitutional rights as pre-conditions to jurisdiction.[115]

The basic difficulty is that the concept of "collateral fact" is a malleable one – virtually any fact may be classified as "collateral" to jurisdiction. Moreover, this issue is not solely one of statutory interpretation. The essential legal policy behind the *ultra vires* doctrine is that it is vital that administrative authorities respect the

---

[112] (1985) 4 J.I.S.S.L. 100. See also, *M. v. An Bord Uchtála* [1977] I.R. 287, where the existence of a valid consent to adoption by the natural mother was held by the Supreme Court to be a condition precedent to jurisdiction of the Board to make a valid adoption order.

[113] [1988] I.R. 481. See also *Greene v. Governor of Mountjoy Prison* [1995] 3 I.R. 541.

[114] *Ibid.* at 491. See also, *e.g. O'Connor v. Giblin*, unreported, Supreme Court, December 19, 1994.

[115] See, *e.g. Irish Times Ltd v. Ireland* [1997] 2 I.L.R.M. 541 where Morris J. held that he could only interfere with a Circuit Court judge's decision to hold a case in camera where there this decision was unreasonable in law. There was no concession here to the principle that Art. 34.1 of the Constitution prescribed a mandatory rule, compliance with which was a pre-condition to jurisdiction.

principle of legality and have due regard to constitutional precepts of fairness. For these reasons the courts have recently tended to turn away from this theory of jurisdiction in order to increase the scope of review.

The modern doctrine of jurisdictional error

We have now reached the furthest extreme from the "pure theory of jurisdiction" for the modern trend is to treat all errors of law committed by lower courts or administrative tribunals as jurisdictional in character. There have also been suggestions that the courts may invervene to quash findings based on inadequate evidence.[116] But the law in this area is far from settled. Contradictory opinions have been expressed by eminent judges and the Supreme Court has yet to give a fully authoritative and comprehensive exposition on the subject of jurisdictional error. Earlier authorities such as *Farrell's* case have never been formally overruled, and are still on occasion relied on as good law.[117] Moreover, it is not clear whether traditional doctrine can safely be relied on where the errors in question involve infringements of constitutional rules or principles.

The leading modern Irish authority is *The State (Holland) v. Kennedy*.[118] The Children Act 1908 forbids the imposition of a prison sentence on a young person between the ages of 15 and 17 unless it is shown that he is of such an "unruly character" that he cannot be detained in an approved place of detention. In this case the defendant had been convicted of a particularly serious assault. He was certified as of unruly character by the respondent District Judge, and she sentenced him to a period of imprisonment.

The Supreme Court held that the bare facts of this assault, unrelated to any previous evidence of a behavioural pattern, could not justify a conclusion that this young person would not be amenable to detention in a suitable institute. Turning to the question of whether an error of this nature was reviewable on certiorari, Henchy J. observed:

> "Having considered the authorities, I am satisfied that this error was not within jurisdiction. [I]t does not necessarily follow that a court or tribunal which commences a hearing within jurisdiction will be treated as continuing to act within jurisdiction. For any number of reasons it may exceed jurisdiction and thereby make its decisions liable to be quashed on certiorari. For instance, it may fall into an unconstitutionality, or it may breach the requirements of natural justice, or it may fail to stay within the bounds of the jurisdiction conferred on it by statute. It is an error of the latter kind that prevents the impugned order in this case from being held to have been made within jurisdiction. It was necessarily the statutory intention that a legally supportable certificate to that effect is to be a condition precedent to the exercise of jurisdiction to impose a sentence of imprisonment. Otherwise the sentencing limitation could be nullified by disregarding what the law regards as essential

---

[116] See below at pp. 426–428.

[117] *The State (Lee-Kiddier) v. Dunleavy*, unreported, High Court, August 17, 1976; *The State (Cole) v. Labour Court* (1984) 3 J.I.S.S.L. 128. But *cf.* the comments of Keane J. in *Killeen v. Director of Public Prosecutions* [1998] 1 I.L.R.M. 1 for a hint that *Farrell's* case might no longer represent good law.

[118] [1977] I.R. 193.

for the making of the certificate. In the present case, the certificate, having been made without evidence, was as devoid of legal validity as if it had been made in disregard of uncontroverted evidence showing that the young person was not what he had been certified to be."[119]

An order of certiorari quashing the conviction and sentence was granted.

The precise significance of *Holland* was difficult to assess. The above passage contains some reasoning reminiscent of the collateral fact approach.[120] However, the judgment of Henchy J. suggests that errors of law committed by a lower court or tribunal in the course of a hearing will be deemed – almost as of course – to go to jurisdiction. Yet other passages in the judgments of Henchy and Kenny JJ. give the impression that the existence of a legally supportable certificate was a collateral fact – a condition precedent to jurisdiction which the District Judge had failed to satisfy. If the latter interpretation had proved to be correct, *Holland* would have represented no more than an application of principles approved in earlier decisions such as *The State (Davidson) v. Farrell*, and the case could hardly have been said to have broken new ground. On the whole, however, *Holland* is regarded as having made the same breakthrough in this jurisdiction as *Anisminic Ltd v. Foreign Compensation Commission*.[121]

While this case law appeared to presage the abolition of the time-honoured distinction between errors which go to jurisdiction and those which do not, nothing of the kind immediately happened. The old distinctions retained an exiguous vitality and the courts veered from one direction to another without ever once reproaching themselves for their lack of consistency in this matter.

This point is well illustrated by the Supreme Court's next pronouncement on this topic. In *The State (Abenglen Properties Ltd) v. Dublin Corporation*[122] the Supreme

---

119 *Ibid.* at 201.
120 As Henchy J. said (at 201):
   "It was necessarily the statutory intention that a legally supportable certificate to that effect is to be a condition precedent to the exercise of the jurisdiction to impose a sentence of imprisonment."
   See, *e.g. Greene v. Governor of Mountjoy Prison* [1995] 3 I.R. 541 a case with facts identical to *Holland*, where the certificate under the Children Act 1908 was regarded as a condition precedent to the District Court's jurisdiction to send a young person to prison.
121 [1969] 2 A.C. 147. See, e.g. the comments of Keane J. in *Harte v. Labour Court* [1996] 1 I.R. and *Killeen v. Director of Public Prosecutions* [1998] 1 I.L.R.M. 1. and *Farrell v. Attorney General*, unreported, Supreme Court, November 21, 1997. In the latter case Keane J. observed that a coroner's verdict could only be quashed where:
   "there was fraud by the coroner, or an error by him going to jurisdiction, or where an error of law appeared on the face of the record. Today, however, the jurisdiction to review judicially the proceedings in a coroner's court is significantly wider and will extend to the circumstances identified by the House of Lords in *Anisminic Ltd v. Foreign Compensation Commission* and by this Court in *The State (Holland) v. Kennedy*. Even where there is no error as to jurisdiction, no fraud on the part of the coroner and no error on the face of the record, there may have been some frailty in the course of the proceedings, such as an error in law or a want of natural justice and fair procedures, which would entitle the High Court to set aside the verdict in whole or in part."
   For other examples of where "asking the wrong question" was held to be jurisdictional, see *The State (Cork County Council) v. Fawsitt*, unreported, March 13, 1981; *The State (Cork County Council) v. Fawsitt (No. 2)*, unreported, Supreme Court, July 28, 1993; *The State (McMahon) v. Minister for Education*, unreported, High Court, December 21, 1985 and *Killeen v. Director of Public Prosecutions* [1998] 1 I.L.R.M. 1.
122 [1984] I.R. 381. Hederman J. joined in the judgment of Henchy J. The other three members of the Court reserved their position on this question.

Court refused to quash a planning permission where the developer claimed that the respondents had acted *ultra vires* in attaching restrictive conditions to the grant of permission, and that the entire permission rested on an erroneous identification of the relevant development plan. Henchy J. replied by stating:

> "The alleged errors arose in the course of identifying and construing the Dublin City Development Plan. There is no doubt but that on a true reading of the relevant Acts and Regulations, the Corporation had jurisdiction to identify and construe the relevant Dublin City Development Plan in its relation to Abenglen's application. If, therefore, they erred in either respect, they erred within jurisdiction, and any error they may have made does not appear on the face of the record."[123]

In these circumstances certiorari would only lie if the respondents had disregarded the principles of natural justice, and the alleged error of law was one within jurisdiction. Henchy J.'s reasoning is similar to that employed by the former Supreme Court in *The State (Davidson) v. Farrell*: if a court or tribunal has "subject-matter" jurisdiction then it does not lose that jurisdiction by erring in the course of its adjudication, unless that error relates to a collateral fact, or where the rules of natural justice have been breached. It is, of course, almost impossible to align Henchy J.'s dicta in *Abenglen Properties* with his earlier judgment in *Holland*.[124] The reasoning of the court may also have been coloured by judicial perceptions as to the motives of the applicants in seeking this relief.

Barrington J. employed a more sophisticated and rather novel approach to this question in *Irish Permanent Building Society v. Caldwell*.[125] In this case the Registrar of Building Societies had misconstrued the relevant sections of the Building Societies Act 1976 when he came to register the Irish Life Building Society, and Barrington J. was satisfied that the Registrar had "asked himself the wrong question", and had erred in law in registering the Society's rules under the 1976 Act. But the judge did not think that the case turned on that point:

> "The real issue in the present case is whether, because of the Registrar's mistake of law, the incorporation of the building society is a nullity. It seems to me that the answer to this question is not to be found in abstract questions

---

123 [1984] I.R. 381 at 399–400. This passage has served to resuscitate the distinction in this jurisdiction between errors of law affecting jurisdiction and those which do not. See, *e.g.* the judgment of Blayney J. in *The State (Keegan) v. Stardust Compensation Tribunal* [1986] I.R. 642 at 650 where this passage of Henchy J. was quoted with approval.

124 *cf.* the earlier judgment of Henchy J. in *The State (Costello) v. Bofin* [1980] I.L.R.M. 223 where a coroner's decision to adjourn an inquest *sine die* was quashed. The Supreme Court ruled that the Coroner's Act 1962 did not allow for indefinite adjournments of this kind. As a result of this mere error of statutory construction, it was held that the coroner thereby exceeded his jurisdiction. The court appeared to assume that a mere error of construction automatically destroyed the coroner's jurisdiction. This line of reasoning seems quite at odds with *Abenglen Properties*, unless it is suggested that *Costello* involved "asking the wrong question" in a matter touching on jurisdiction permitting the coroner to adjourn for a definite period of time whereas *Abenglen Properties* concerned a decision on a mixed question of law and fact (*i.e.* the interpretation of the development plan). But this elaborate and – it might be thought – artificial rationalisation does not appear in the judgments.

125 [1981] I.L.R.M. 242.

of law, but in ascertaining the intentions of the legislature in this particular statute."[126]

Barrington J. pointed out that the scheme of the Act was such that had the Registrar failed to reach a decision within the prescribed time, the Society would have been entitled to have been incorporated under the Acts, the defect in its rules notwithstanding. Furthermore, it was no longer required that the Registrar should be a person with legal qualification. He concluded that it would have been surprising:

> "[I]f the incorporation of a society could be invalidated by an honest mistake such as was made by the Registrar in the present case. If the law were otherwise people might in good faith deal with a society for many years only to find that because of some defect in the rules the society did not exist as a corporate body. To hold that the society was not validly incorporated would clearly cause great damage to many innocent people, and I cannot accept that the Oireachtas intended that such a catastrophic result should ensue."[127]

While there is much merit in this approach, it might have been better for the sake of judicial consistency had Barrington J. acknowledged that "asking the wrong question" destroyed the Registrar's jurisdiction, but that the drastic relief sought – the nullification of the incorporation of the Society – should have been withheld as a matter of discretion on the ground that it would have prejudiced innocent third party investors.

Recent developments: 1982–1997

The decisions which we have just been discussed all date from a period in the early 1980s when this area of the law was in a constant state of flux, both here and in England. This pervasive judicial inconsistency[128] and the lack of clear general principles governing the question of jurisdictional error has not really abated. Indeed, this lack of consistency has been so prevalent that one suspects that the courts are prepared to characterise an error of law as being jurisdictional (or not) depending on whether this leads to conclusions already reached.[129]

As in all difficult legal questions, the matter is often one of degree. Thus, in *Sweeney v. Judge Brophy*[130] the Supreme Court appeared to suggest that the legal

---

[126] *Ibid.* at 268.

[127] *Ibid.* at 269–270.

[128] Contrast, for example, *Attorney General v. Sheedy* [1990] 1 I.R. 70 in which it was assumed by the Supreme Court that the error would be reviewed as jurisdictional (without even a discussion to the contrary) with *The State (Daly) v. Ruane* [1988] I.L.R.M. 117, where a very restrictive approach to the scope of review was taken by O'Hanlon J. in the High Court.

[129] See, *e.g. Re Riordan* [1981] I.L.R.M. 2; *Killeen v. Director of Public Prosecutions*, unreported, High Court, May 18, 1994 (reversed by the Supreme Court [1998] 1 I.L.R.M. 1). In both cases, a finding of invalidity was perceived as being potentially unjust to private parties affected thereby, so the court in each case conveniently classified the error as one not affecting jurisdiction. This approach is also clearly evident in the judgment of Barrington J. in *Irish Permanent Building Society v. Caldwell* [1981] I.L.R.M. 242.

[130] [1993] 2 I.R. 202. The distinction drawn here had been anticipated in the decision of Lynch J. In *Gill v. Connellan* [1987] I.R. 541 the applicant sought to quash a conviction in the District Court in circumstances where the respondent had wrongly prevented the applicant's solicitor from persisting with a certain line of cross-examination. Lynch J. considered that this error went to jurisdiction and

error in question must be decisive and that "routine mishaps" would not give rise to jurisdictional error. In this case a District Judge with original jurisdiction to try an assault case committed a number of "fundamental irregularities" in the course of convicting the applicant. Hederman J. considered that such errors destroyed the jurisdiction of the District Judge:

> ". . . *certiorari* is an appropriate remedy to quash not only a conviction bad on its face or where a court or tribunal acts without or in excess of jurisdiction but also where it acts apparently within jurisdiction but where the proceedings are so fundamentally flawed as to deprive an accused of a trial in due course of law. I take this opportunity of emphasising that *certiorari* is not appropriate to a routine mishap which may befall any trial; the correct remedy in that circumstance is by way of appeal. However, if there be a breach of fundamental tenets of constitutional justice in the hearing or a failure to hear the evidence in the case the trial can properly be categorised as one which has not been held in due course of law . . ."[131]

After a series of decisions with contrasting – and not always reconcilable – reasoning, the judgment of Keane J. in *Killeen v. Director of Public Prosecutions*[132] strongly suggest a rationalisation of the authorities along the lines of *Anisminic* and *Holland*, but even here uncertainties abound. In this case a District Judge discharged the

---

duly quashed the conviction. By contrast, however, in *O'Broin v. Ruane* [1989] I.R. 214 at 217 where cross-examination of a witness was incorrectly disallowed by a District Judge, Lynch J. refused to set aside the conviction, saying that the error was within jurisdiction:

"It is part of his function as the presiding justice to decide what evidence is admissible and to decide what sort of examination-in-chief and cross-examination may be pursued. Unless the error was so gross as to oust jurisdiction, which can be so in exceptional circumstances, the error would not justify the making of an order of certiorari."

[131] *Ibid*. at 211. These principles have been applied in a number of subsequent decisions: see, *e.g. Duff v. Mangan* [1994] 1 I.L.R.M. 94 (where Denham J. held that a District Judge exceeded his jurisdiction in refusing to examine the applicant's submission that summonses issued under the Road Traffic Act 1961 were invalid); *Grennan v. Kirby* [1994] 2 I.L.R.M. 199 (where Murphy J. quashed a conviction where the District Judge insisted on proceeding with the hearing of a prosecution, despite the fact that both prosecution and defence had agreed that the matter be adjourned to enable the defence to obtain the services of counsel); *Dineen v. District Judge Delap* [1994] 2 I.R. 228 (where Morris J. held that the manner in which the judge appeared to assist the prosecution was "improper" so that the "unsatisfactory" conviction could not stand); *McNally v. Martin* [1995] 1 I.L.R.M. 350 (where the Supreme Court ruled that while the District Judge had erred in law in a manner affecting jurisdiction in refusing to allow the defence to raise a legal argument , she had "behaved impeccably" in relation to a separate charge, so that the second conviction was not tainted by the error in the first case); *Byrne v. McDonnell* [1996] 1 I.L.R.M. 543 (wrongful refusal to grant adjournment affected jurisdiction in criminal prosecution); *Maher v. Judge O'Donnell* [1995] 3 I.R. 530 (where Laffoy J. held that the non-attendance of a witness at a District Court prosecution whom an accused expected to attend but whose attendance he did not arrange for was the type of "routine mishap" which did not affect the jurisdiction of the District Judge); *Farrelly v Devally*, unreported, High Court, July 19, 1996 (any irregularity in method of arrest of suspect did not deprive High Court of jurisdiction).

[132] [1998] 1 I.L.R.M. 1. *Cf. Harte v. Labour Court* [1996] 2 I.R. 171 where the applicant claimed that the respondent had exceeded jurisdiction by, *inter alia*, taking into account the existence of male comparators in an equal pay case taken by certain female part-time workers. Keane J.'s judgment rather curiously points in two directions. He first suggested, citing *R. (Martin) v. Mahoney* with approval, that any error of law would be within jurisdiction. Keane J. then (at 176–177) indicated regard must be had to "the development of judicial review in recent decades", including the "milestone" decisions of *Anisminic and Holland* ". . . that are cases in which an error of law may be of such a nature, although apparently committed within jurisdiction, as to render the entire proceedings a nullity. In such cases, the decision in *R. (Martin) v. Mahoney* is not applicable."

applicants and, erroneously, refused to order their return for trial[133] on the ground that the arrest warrant was defective. Keane J. first observed that:

> "It may be that an error of law committed by a tribunal acting within its jurisdiction is not capable of being set aside on certiorari: see *The State (Davidson) v. Farrell.* It is otherwise where the error of law has its consequence the making of an order which the tribunal had no jurisdiction to make ... *The State (Holland) v. Kennedy* ..."[134]

Having referred with approval to the speech of Lord Reid in *Anisminic* and the judgment of Henchy J. in *Holland,* Keane J. summarised the net question thus:

> "If the District Judge in the present case discharged the applicants because he considered he was precluded from sending them forward for trial by reason of the defect in the warrant, was that an error of law which it was within his jurisdiction to make? I am satisfied that it was not. If the District Judge was of that view, it follows that he failed to determine the precise question assigned for decision to the District Court, i.e., as to whether, on the materials before the court, there was a sufficient case to put the applicants on trial. If that was his decision, it constituted an error of law which rendered his order a nullity in accordance with the legal principles already set out."[135]

The effect of this decision is to restore some order and consistency to judicial views on the scope of jurisdictional error. It is clear that decisions such as *The State (Daly) v. Ruane*[136] which advocate a restrictive approach to the scope of jurisdictional review cannot now stand in the light of this decision.

Mixed questions of fact and law

The tangled issue of the type of error which attracts the supervisory jurisdiction of the High Court has just been considered, first with reference mainly to errors of law and, thereafter, more briefly with regard to errors of fact. It remains in this section to consider the even more difficult marshland which runs between the two extremities. Although this unwelcoming terrain has not yet been fully judicially recognised, it is worth making some preliminary comments since the case law is likely to increase in the future. We may start with the following helpful account:

> "Perplexing problems may, however, arise in analysing the nature of the process by which a tribunal determines whether a factual situation falls within or without the limits of a category or standard prescribed by a statute or other legal instrument. Every finding by a tribunal postulates a process of abstraction and inference, which may be conditioned solely by the adjudicator's practical

---

133 Keane J. acknowledged that this had the same status in law as an acquittal.
134 [1988] 1 I.L.R.M. 1 at 8.
135 *Ibid.* at 10.
136 [1988] I.L.R.M. 117. For a suggestion that the courts' power of review in Article 40.4.2° proceedings is even broader than in judicial review proceedings, see *Russell v. Fanning* [1988] I.R. 505. This seems questionable, since the extent of the courts' power of review should not turn on the form of the proceedings or on the (fortuitous) fact that the applicant happens to be in custody.

experience and knowledge of affairs, or partly or wholly by his knowledge of legal principle. He hears evidence and, by satisfying himself as to its reliability, finds what were the "true" facts; it may then be necessary for him to draw a series of interferences from these primary findings in order to determine what were the material facts on which he has to base his decision; in order to draw certain of these inferences correctly he may need to apply his knowledge of legal rules. At what point does an inference drawn from facts become an inference of law? Is the application of a statutory norm to the material facts always to be classified as the determination of a question of law? And where in this spectrum lie questions of policy".[137]

Fairly typical examples of what the first sentence of the passage calls "a category or standard prescribed by a statute . . ." include the issue of "domicile" (which was at the heart of *Lambert v. An tArd Chláratheoir*[138] or "sow" (in *Shannon Regional Fisheries Board v. An Bord Pleanála*[139] each of which will be analysed below. With these examples in mind and drawing in part on the above pretext, we can say that the characteristic decision in this area may require the decision maker to follow up to four stages of reasoning. First, a primary finding of fact will be required. Secondly, inferences will be drawn from these facts so as to reach a result at an appropriate level of abstraction for the statutory category. Thirdly, he must compare the result of this second stage with the statutory category. Fourthly, it will sometimes be necessary to interpret the statutory category in the light of these facts. (In practice, some of these stages will be conflated or taken out of sequence so that it will not be clear at which stage the error lies). In any case, we can say that stages one and four involve fact and law, respectively. Stages two and three – where the decision maker is appraising and characterising the facts in the light of his understanding of the statutory category – is the difficult area marked "mixed law and fact". As regards the issue of whether errors in this area can be received by the High Court, very little can be said since the matter has yet to be fully confronted by the Irish courts. All that one can do is note, the English view (which is also mainly based on principle rather than authority) that the closer the error is to the "law" end of the sequence the more likely is a Court to review it.[140]

Before, finally, turning to the Irish case law, we may make the general observation that a particular difficulty in regard to this case law is that in a number of cases in which this problem has arisen, it has been identified – or, it might be thought, misidentified – as a case of the control of discretionary power by reference to the conventional standards of reasonableness, rationality etc.[141] There is, however, an important difference. In the present case the administrative body is generally concerned with evaluating the facts in the light of an interpretation of the law. The High Court, in reviewing an administrative agency's decision of this type is in a

---

137   de Smith, Woolf, Jowell, *op. cit.*, above, n.98, p. 297. This extract is taken from a first-rate analysis of a knotty area.

138   [1995] 2 I.R. 372.

139   [1994] 3 I.R. 449.

140   de Smith, Woolf, Jowell, *op. cit.*, above, n.98, pp. 284–286.

141   *cf.* in particular the judgment of Keane J. in *Radio Limerick One v. Independent Radio and Television Commission* [1997] 2 I.L.R.M. 1 and see p. 424, n.144.

different position and should apply different rules from a case in which the administrative agency is exercising a discretionary power.

This analysis, broadly speaking, appears to have underpinned *Lambert v. An tÁrd Chláraitheoir*.[142] In this case the applicant sought to compel the Registrar-General to grant him a licence enabling him to re-marry. Permission was refused on the ground that the foreign divorce would not have been recognised here and this in turn raised the question of whether the parties to the first marriage had been domiciled in England at the relevant time. Kinlen J. first rejected the argument that the Registrar-General's conclusion on the issue of domicile could only be assailed on irrationality grounds:

> "This case is not concerned with a situation where an administrative tribunal has been afforded a discretion in an administrative manner . . . "

The judge continued:

> "The present case turns on the determination of [the] legal issue of domicile . . . It is clear that the determination of a person's domicile involves consideration of a legal issue; the Registrar-General cannot enjoy any discretion in the determination of this matter. The determination of the Registrar-General of an issue of law need not be treated with the same deference as the determination of a specialised tribunal on an issue of fact . . ."[143]

As Kinlen J. was satisfied that the relevant party was domiciled abroad, the Registrar-General's conclusion was thereby set aside. It is worth emphasising that in *Lambert* the facts were not at issue; the Registrar-General appears to have misdirected himself in law and the incorrect inferences were drawn from the primary facts. It is thus a matter of applying the law to the facts and it appears that the courts will intervene by classifying a wrong inference of this kind as jurisdictional error.[144]

---

[142]   [1995] 2 I.R. 372.

[143]   *Ibid.* at 384.

[144]   But *cf. Harte v. Labour Court* [1996] 2 I.R. 171 for a suggestion that determinations of mixed questions of law and fact were not amenable to review on grounds of jurisdictional error. The wider problem was also in view in a case involving the meaning of the word "advertising" in section 10 of the Radio and Television Act 1988: *Radio Limerick One Ltd v. Independent Radio and Television Commission* [1997] 2 I.L.R.M. 1. Here the applicant company had its broadcast licence terminated by reason, *inter alia*, of the fact that it had breached the advertising minutage limitations contained in section 10(4) of the Act. The breaches consisted of outside broadcasts in local shops "containing details of the products and prices" and the businesses were selected "on the basis of the extent to which they had contributed to the station's advertising revenues over a given period." The substantive issue was whether this amounted to "advertising". While Keane J. stated (at 24) that it would seem:
"... self-evident that, if the exercise of the statutory discretion is grounded on an erroneous view of the law, it should not normally be allowed to stand. . . . [I]f the only ground on which the Commission terminated the applicant's contract was the carrying of the outside broadcasts and it was wrong in law in treating . . . those broadcasts as advertisements within the meaning of the Act, it is difficult to how its decision could be described as 'reasonable' either in the *Wednesbury* sense or on the application of the criteria proposed by Henchy J. in *The State (Keegan) v. Stardust Victims' Tribunal.*"
(Keane J. thus seemed to be applying the rules for a control of a discretionary power as the Supreme Court entirely agreed with the "common sense" interpretation of the word "advertising" which had been adopted by the Commission, Keane J. was not required to examine the circumstances in which the courts would review a determination of mixed law and fact for jurisdictional error.)

Barr J. had earlier noted the difference between error of law and abuse of discretionary authority in *Shannon Regional Fisheries Board v. An Bord Pleanála*[145] when rejecting the submission that the Board's interpretation of the word "sow" was reviewable only on rationality grounds.[146] However, the next passage suggests that the court would review the application of the law to the facts on rationality criteria only, provided that the authority started from the correct legal premise:

> ". . . this does not imply that a competent body, such as a local planning authority, is not entitled to determine whether, for example, a certain aspect of a proposed development conforms to a statutory requirement. In such a case, where the statutory obligation is clear, the issue is whether the development conforms to it. That is a matter which is peculiarly within the competence of the planning authority and the court ought not to interfere unless there is no reasonable basis on which the decision of the authority might be upheld."[147]

This approach has also been adopted by the House of Lords. Thus, in *R v. Monopolies and Mergers Commission, ex p. South Yorkshire Transport Co.*[148] the question was whether the Commission had correctly concluded that a proposed merger involved "a substantial part of the United Kingdom." Lord Mustill agreed that while the Commission must correctly direct itself in law on the jurisdictional question (*i.e.*, did the merger involve a substantial part of the United Kingdom):

> ". . . the criterion so established may itself be so imprecise that different decision-makers, each acting rationally, might reach differing conclusions when applying it to the facts of a given case. In such a case the court is entitled to substitute its own opinion for that of the person to whom the decision has been entrusted only if the decision is so aberrant that it cannot be classed as rational."[149]

---

[145] [1994] 3 I.R. 449.

[146] He said (at 456) that it had been argued that it was not for the court:
> ". . . to arrive at its own definition of 'sow' within the meaning of this regulation as this is a matter solely within the competence of the planning authority [and] that the court ought not to interfere unless it concludes that the definition adopted by them is wholly irrational . . . I reject this proposition. Statutory interpretation is solely a matter for the courts and no other body has authority to usurp the power of the court in performing that function."

[147] *Ibid.* 456. There is a clear hint of this approach in another case involving the meaning of "advertisement": *Murphy v. Independent Radio and Television Commission* [1997] 2 I.L.R.M. 467. In this case the applicant wished to transmit an advertisement which would have invited the listener to examine the historical facts about Christ and the Resurrection and to attend a meeting where a religious broadcast would have been transmitted. The Commission refused to sanction the transmission on the ground that it would have infringed section 10(3) of the Radio and Television Act 1988 which provides that:
> "No advertisement shall be broadcast which is directed towards any religious or political end or which has relation to an industrial dispute."
Geoghegan J. concluded that the advertisement infringed the sub-section or "at the very least that the [Commission] was entitled to take the view that it did", thereby again suggesting that providing the Commission's initial interpretation of the statutory provision was correct in law, its application of the law to the facts (*i.e.* whether the broadcast was an advertisement) could only be challenged on rationality grounds. However, this approach has not always been evenly adopted: see the discussion of *Lennon v. Clifford* [1996] 2 I.R. 590, below at pp. 427–428. See also *Irish Times Ltd v. Ireland* [1997] 2 I.L.R.M. 541. (High Court could review balancing exercise made in respect of competing constitutional rights only on rationality grounds)(*semble*).

[148] [1993] 1 W.L.R. 23.

[149] *Ibid.*

Of course, it may be expected that the courts will be slow to interfere on rationality grounds with a conclusion on a mixed question of law and fact which has been arrived at by a properly directed specialist tribunal.[150]

"No evidence" and "insufficient evidence"

Jurisdictional review is principally based on errors of law, rather than on errors of fact, so that the absence or insufficiency of evidence is not a ground of review. Indeed, it has been frequently stated in judicial review proceedings that the High Court does not act "as a court of appeal from other tribunals."[151] However, in some circumstances the absence of evidence or the insufficiency of evidence may be grounds for judicial review.[152] But once again difficulties and inconsistencies abound.

In the first place, if the court's jurisdiction is dependent on the existence of a collateral fact, there must be sufficient evidence on which the court can conclude that its jurisdictional requirements have been satisfied. This may be illustrated by *The State (Holland) v. Kennedy*[153] itself. In that case the District Court's jurisdiction to sentence a young person to prison was contingent on evidence that the accused was "depraved." Henchy J. concluded that the District Judge erred in law in a manner going to jurisdiction when she wrongly concluded that this statutory requirement was satisfied by one single aberrational incident. In other words, there was no or insufficient evidence to enable the District Court to conclude that this jurisdictional requirement had been satisfied. Secondly, discretionary powers must be exercised in a manner in which is capable of being factually justified,[154] so that an administratative determination for which there is no adequate evidence can be set aside on irrationality grounds.[155]

The general rule, however, is that matters of evidence are not reviewable by way of certiorari.[156] This is illustrated by a series of contemporary decisions. In *The*

---

[150] This is at least implicit in Barr J.'s judgment in *Shannon Regional Fisheries* and seems to follow from *O'Keeffe v. An Bord Pleanála* [1993] 1 I.R. 39. This is also the approach of the English courts: see, *e.g.* the *South Yorkshire* case; *R v. National Insurance Commissioner, ex p. Michael* [1977] 1 W.L.R. 109; *R. v. Preston Supplementary Benefits Appeal Tribunal, ex p. Moore* [1975] 1 W.L.R. 624.

[151] *Lennon v. Clifford* [1992] 1 I.R. 382 at 386, *per* O'Hanlon J. This statement was expressly approved by the Supreme Court on appeal: [1996] 2 I.R. 590 at 593, *per* Murphy J. Similar comments may be found in, *e.g. Chief Constable of the North Wales Police v. Evans* [1982] 1 W.L.R. 1155 at 1173, *per* Lord Brightman (a frequently quoted passage); *Truloc Ltd v. McMenamin* [1994] 1 I.L.R.M. 151; *Garda Representative Body v. Ireland* [1994] 1 I.L.R.M. 81 at 88, *per* Finlay C.J.

[152] *Kiely v. Minister for Social Welfare* [1971] I.R. 21; *The State (Holland) v. Kennedy* [1977] I.R. 193; *The State (Cork C.C.) v. Fawsitt (No. 2)*, Supreme Court, July 28, 1983; *The State (Casey) v. Labour Court* (1984) 3 J.I.S.S.L. 135; *M. v. M.* [1979] I.L.R.M. 160; *The State (Burke) v. Garvey* [1979] I.L.R.M. 232; and *The State (McKeown) v. Scully* [1986] I.L.R.M. 133. The wrongful admission of evidence may also be a ground for intervention by way of judicial review: *The State (Keeney) v. O'Malley* [1985] I.L.R.M. 31. A strong recent authority is *Galvin v. Minister for Social Welfare*, [1997] 3 I.R. 240 (where Costello P. held that incorrect inferences which were not based on evidence constituted errors within jurisdiction and could not be quashed on review).

[153] [1977] I.R. 193. See also *Greene v. Governor of Mountjoy Prison* [1995] 3 I.R. 541.

[154] See, *e.g. The State (Lynch) v. Cooney* [1982] I.R. 337; *The State (Daly) v. Minister for Agriculture* [1987] I.R. 615 ; *Kiberd v. Hamilton* [1992] 2 I.R. 257.

[155] See, *e.g. The State (Creedon) v. Criminal Injuries Compensation Tribunal* [1988] I.R. 51.

[156] The *locus classicus* is *R. (Martin) v. Mahony* [1910] 2 I.R. 695 This view is, however, also borne out by modern authorities: *The State (Power) v. Moran* [1976–1977] I.L.R.M. 20 (decision based on evidence of little probative value not reviewable by certiorari); *The State (Shinkaruk) v. Carroll*, unreported, High Court, December 15, 1976 (wrongful exclusion of evidence not reviewable by

State (Keegan) v. Stardust Compensation Tribunal[157] the applicant sought to have a decision of the tribunal quashed on the ground that insufficient regard had been paid to the medical reports concerning his case. Blayney J. referred with approval to passages from *R. (Martin) v. Mahoney*[158] and the judgment of Henchy J. in *Abenglen Properties* and held that:

> "The [applicant's] case is that the Tribunal ought to have decided on the basis of medical reports that [he] was entitled to an award. But even if the Tribunal was wrong, it did not mean that it exceeded its jurisdiction. What it did was to make an error within its jurisdiction."[159]

The Supreme Court did not deal with this issue on appeal, save to confirm (in contrast to Blayney J.) that had the tribunal acted unreasonably in law, it would have thereby affected its jurisdiction. Likewise, in *Roche v. Martin*[160] where the applicant sought to quash a conviction for copyright infringement on the ground that no evidence had been tendered by any copyright owner that they owned the copyright in the video tape and that insufficient evidence had been given regarding the applicant's *mens rea* in respect of the offence. While Murphy J. hinted that he might have quashed the conviction if there was demonstrably no evidence regarding a jurisdictional pre-condition (in this instance, copyright ownership),[161] in regard to the contention that there was insufficient evidence on the *mens rea* charge:

> "It seems to me that it is virtually impossible to make such a case on an appeal by way of certiorari. In different appellate procedures insufficiency of evidence may be a ground for reversing a decision of a court of first instance but insufficiency of evidence – save in the most extreme case – does not deprive the District Judge of jurisdiction to reach a decision on the matter before him."[162]

This passage was expressly approved by the Supreme Court in *Lennon v. Clifford*,[163] a case where the the applicant had been convicted of failing to make the appropriate tax returns on the prescribed form. The applicant claimed that as there was no evidence that any such form had been prescribed, the conviction should

---

certiorari); *Memorex World Trade Corporation v. Employment Appeals Tribunal* [1990] 2 I.R. 184 (certiorari will not be granted on the basis "that there was want of evidence to support a finding").
[157] [1986] I.R. 642.
[158] [1910] 2 I.R. 695.
[159] [1986] I.R. 642 at 648.
[160] [1993] I.L.R.M. 651.
[161] Murphy J. concluded (at 655) that having regard to the evidence as a whole there was
> "evidence in relation to the vital links in the chain of guilt and that the District Judge did not overlook the necessary proofs or otherwise deprive herself of jurisdiction in the matter."
[162] [1993] I.L.R.M. 651 at 656. See also *Truloc Ltd v. McMenamin* [1994] 1 I.L.R.M. 151 (not the function of the High Court in judicial review proceedings to assess whether the "evidence was sufficient to support the conviction which has been entered against a defendant"); *Stokes v. O'Donnell* [1996] 2 I.L.R.M. 538 and *Harte v. Labour Court* [1996] 2 I.R. 171 (semble). In *The State (Holland) v. Kennedy* [1977] I.R. 193 Kenny J. reserved the question of whether the "no evidence" rule enunciated in *R (Martin) v. Mahony* was as applied to criminal convictions compatible with the guarantee of right to trial in due course of law. Kenny J. is probably correct in hinting that such a rule would be unconstitutional, but having regard, *inter alia*, to the lack of stenographic facilities for courts of summary jurisdiction, the High Court would presumably only interfere with convictions on this basis in the rarest and clearest of cases.
[163] [1996] 2 I.R. 590, affirming the decision of O'Hanlon J. [1992] 1 I.R. 382 (High Ct.).

accordingly be quashed. Murphy J. noted that this word – "prescribed" – was capable of several possible interpretations, but it was not his function to determine this meaning in judicial review proceedings:

> "the different possible interpretations underscore the fact that it is the function of the trial judge to evaluate the evidence before him."[164]

This latter conclusion – while understandable in the context of the courts' disinclination not to review the merits on "no evidence" grounds – seems too narrow. For despite the use of the word "fact" what was really at stake here was a question of pure statutory interpretation (*i.e.* the meaning of "prescribed") and such a question should surely not fall outside the review process.

Recent English developments

The modern trend in English administrative law has been expressly to collapse the distinction between errors of law affecting jurisdiction and those which do not. This has been clear since the majority decision of the House of Lords in 1969 in *Anisminic Ltd v. Foreign Compensation Commission,*[165] where it was held that the taking into account of an irrelevant consideration was sufficient to destroy jurisdiction. After some initial hesitancy, it was gradually recognised that the pre-1969 authorities on jurisdictional error had been superseded. This was made clear by Lord Diplock in two major cases, *Re Racal Communications Ltd*[166] and *O'Reilly v. Mackman.*[167] In the former case, he explained that:

> "The break-through made by *Anisminic* was that, as respects administrative tribunals and authorities, the old distinction between errors of law that went to jurisdiction and errors of law that did not, was for practical purposes abolished. Any error of law that could be shown to have been made by them in the course of reaching their decision on matters of fact or of administrative policy would result in their having asked themselves the wrong question with the result that the decision they reached would be a nullity."[168]

He went on to state that whereas there was a presumption that Parliament did not intend to confer administrative authorities with the power to determine their own jurisdiction, inferior courts might still have authority to make errors of law within jurisdiction.[169] While in *O'Reilly v. Mackman,* Lord Diplock included lower courts along with administrative tribunals as bodies to which the old distinction would no longer apply, in *R. v. Hull University, ex p. Page*[170] the House of Lords subsequently

---

[164] *Ibid.* at 594.
[165] [1969] 2 A.C. 147.
[166] [1981] A.C. 374.
[167] [1983] 2 A.C. 237.
[168] *Ibid.*at 278.
[169] This presumption is a rebuttable one. Thus, in *R. v. Registrar of Companies, ex p. Central Bank of India* [1986] Q.B. 1114 it was held that an error of law made by the Registrar in registering certain securities for the purposes of the Companies Acts was not reviewable in certiorari proceedings. The need for certainty in commercial transactions meant Parliament must have intended that the Registrar could err in law and still remain within jurisdiction.
[170] [1993] A.C. 682.

adopted Lord Diplock's earlier views. It is now clear that, as a matter of English law at any rate, the distinction between errors of law affecting jurisdiction and those which do not has, for all practical purposes, been abolished as far as *administrative authorities are concerned*.[171] However, it seems from *Page* that the old distinction may have some residual vitality in the case of inferior courts. The present law is, however, sufficiently complex and uncertain enough without introducing a further – and, it might be thought, unnecessary – distinction of this kind.

Conclusions

No clear picture emerges from a consideration of the modern Irish cases, save that there is a trend towards treating all decisive errors of law as jurisdictional. Part of the problem is that many of the Irish judges formerly used the word "jurisdiction" in the narrow sense of "original jurisdiction" and were disinclined to accept the argument that this jurisdiction might have been lost by reason of a serious error of law. And while it has been long accepted by the Supreme Court since *The State (Holland) v. Kennedy*[172] that a tribunal may lose its jurisdiction by reason of legal error, with the possible exception of Keane J.'s authoritative judgment in *Killeen v. Director of Public Prosecutions*,[173] there has, as yet, been no elaborate judicial statement of principle on this difficult issue as has occurred in England in cases such as *Anisminic* and *Page*. Indeed, one of the other major judicial pronouncements – that of Henchy J. in *The State (Abenglen Properties Ltd) v. Dublin Corporation* – based as it was on incorrect analysis of the post-*Anisminic* English authorities, only served to revive the old distinction and gave inconsistent signals as to the scope of jurisdictional review. While Keane J.'s judgment in *Killeen* goes a long way in this direction, a fully comprehensive review of these issues is clearly required.

Some indications of possible future developments in this area of the law are provided by *Tormey v. Attorney-General*.[174] In this case, speaking of a situation in which exclusive jurisdiction has been committed to a lower court or administrative authority exercising judicial powers under cover of Article 37, Henchy J. observed that the High Court's full jurisdiction under Article 34.3.1° might be invoked so as to ensure that "the hearing and determination *will be in accordance with law*" (authors' italics). The context of this observation was an explanation that even though the High Court did not have original jurisdiction, yet, nevertheless, it retained a complete supervisory control over lower courts and tribunals. Accordingly, this remark can be taken to mean that the High Court's power of review must be broad enough to allow it to quash at least for major errors of law committed by a lower court or administrative authority exercising exclusive jurisdiction. It may also be that the High Court may review decisions of lower courts or administrative authorities which have been based on insufficient evidence. Similar results might well be achieved through an extension of the constitutional principles of fair procedures

---

171 This was acknowledged by Costello P. in *Ryan v. Compensation Tribunal* [1997] 1 I.L.R.M. 194 at 206, but he reserved the position as to whether Irish law had developed this far.
172 [1977] I.R. 193.
173 [1998] 1 I.L.R.M. 1.
174 [1985] I.R. 289 at 296–297.

and the right of access to the courts.[175] In any event, despite some recent inconsistent signals, our courts will probably find the trend towards increasing the scope of jurisdictional review to be well nigh irresistible.

4. Error on the Face of the Record

The jurisdiction to review for error on the face of the record is an anomalous one since the power to review is not based on jurisdiction or *ultra vires*.[176] Nevertheless, this power of review enables the High Court to quash a decision, otherwise within jurisdiction, if that decision contains an error of law,[177] provided that error appears on the face of the record.[178]

What is the record? Denning L.J. has provided us with a comprehensive answer:

> "[T]he record must contain at least the document which initiates the pro-
> ceedings; the pleadings, if any; and the adjudication; but not the evidence,
> nor the reasons, unless the tribunal chooses to incorporate them. If the tribunal
> does state the reasons, and the reasons are wrong in law, certiorari lies to
> quash the decision."[179]

To this it may be objected that a court or tribunal could avoid review for error on the face of the record by the High Court by the simple expedient of refusing to make a judgment part of the final order or refusing to give any reason for a decision at all. But it is clear that English law, at any rate, has now progressed to the point

---

[175] For example, it could be argued that the constitutional guarantee of fair procedure requires that a decision be based on adequate, probative evidence, and Henchy J. has already argued along these lines in *M. v. M.* [1979] I.L.R.M. 160 and there are hints of this in *The State (Daly) v. Minister for Agriculture* [1987] I.R. 165.

[176] This anomaly has sometimes led judges to hold that error on the face of the record must be a form of jurisdictional error: see the comments of Palles C.B. in *R. (Martin) v. Mahoney* [1910] 2 I.R. 695 at 721. By the turn of the century the jurisdiction to quash for error of law on the face of the record had fallen into decline, and in England, the very existence of this jurisdiction was denied by the Court of Appeal in *Racecourse Betting Control Board v. Secretary of State for Air* [1944] Ch. 114. This jurisdiction was revived following the decision of the Court of Appeal in *R. v. Northumberland Compensation Appeal Tribunal, ex p. Shaw* [1952] 1 K.B. 338. These decisions "came as a surprise to the Bench and Bar in Ireland, both North and South, since the weapon [of quashing for error on the face of the record] had never become rusty, but in this country continued to be wielded vigorously throughout the period in question" *R v. Belfast Recorder, ex p. Kelly* [1992] N.I. 217 at 229, *per* Lowry L.C.J.

[177] But this jurisdiction does not extend to errors of fact: see, *per* Carroll J. in *The State (C.I.É.) v. An Bord Pleanála*, unreported,High Court, February 12, 1984.

[178] Thus, in *R. v. Knightsbridge Crown Court, ex p. International Sporting Club Ltd* [1982] Q.B. 304 a Divisional Court was evenly divided as to whether a particular error of law went to jurisdiction, but held that, as they were agreed the error of law appeared on the record, the decision could be quashed.

[179] *R. v. Northumberland Appeal Compensation Tribunal, ex p. Shaw* [1952] 1 K.B. 338 at 352. In *Ryan v. Compensation Tribunal* [1997] 1 I.L.R.M. 194 at 200 Costello P. approved this passage as a correct statement of the extent of the record in civil cases. In a powerfully written article, "Documentary Error as a Ground of Judicial Review in Irish Law" (1993–5) 28–30 *Irish Jurist* 145 at p. 150 K. Costello has disputed the historical basis for Denning L.J.'s conclusion:
> "On inspection, however, it does not, in fact, appear that historical materials do sustain Denning L.J.'s conclusion. On the contrary, it appears that the practice on the Crown-side was quite rigid and consistent in refusing to regard such material as part of the record, and, that for the greater part, the record was no more than the order alone."

whereby the reasons given orally for a decision are now regarded as forming part of the record, which is, when thus augmented, known as a "speaking order."[180] Moreover, the English courts have strongly hinted that they have jurisdiction, at least in appropriate cases, to call for reasons to be given for the decision by the tribunal or lower court,[181] so that if these reasons exhibit an error of law, the resulting decision may be quashed as appearing on the "face" of the record, irrespective of whether that error would otherwise affect jurisdiction.

This judicial expansion of what constitutes the record is probably due to two reasons. First, the supporting documentation (pleadings, transcripts, written reasons for decisions, etc.) is generally now more elaborate than was the case in the early part of this century when the jurisdiction to review for error on the record had fallen into decline. In addition, the facilities for recording spoken judgments is also nowadays far superior.[182] Secondly, the courts are nowadays loath to allow a decision containing an error of law to survive review and will tend to classify such error as either going to jurisdiction or appearing on the face of the record.

More recent authority in Northern Ireland has shown that the courts have expanded the concept of record if this is necessary to do justice. Thus, in *Re Stevenson's Application*[183] (where certiorari was sought to quash the grant of a bookmaker's licence), Carswell J. held that he could look at the affidavit filed by

---

180 See, *e.g. R. v. Chertsey JJ., ex p. Franks* [1961] 2 Q.B. 152; *R v. Supplementary Benefits Commission, ex p. Singer* [1973] 1 W.L.R. 713; *R v. Kinghtsbridge Crown Court, ex p. International Sporting Club Ltd* [1982] Q.B. 304. Costello, *loc.cit.* (at 150) has advanced the following compelling argument against this development:

> "The doctrine of error on the face of the record depends, by definition, on errors which have been recorded. To dispense with this requirement, and permit the introduction of unrecorded material, as these cases do, is to cease to rely on the doctrine at all and to rely on something quite different: the principle that proof, however, presented, of an error of law impairs jurisdiction. The approach adopted in those authorities is historically unprecedented and contradicts the principle underlying the doctrine."

This view finds support in the judgment of Lowry L.C.J. in *R v. Belfast Recorder, ex p. McNally* [1992] N.I. 217 at 236:

> ". . . I do not think that the judgment of a court, whether it is delivered in writing or is spoken and later transcribed and authenticated by the author, is part of the record. So to hold would abolish the hitherto generally recognised rule that a decision of a court made within its jurisdiction cannot without more be quashed for error of law, since every decision of a court is inevitably embodied in a written or oral judgment. I have to recognise that in taking this view I have refused to go as far as Griffiths L.J. did in *R v. Knightsbridge Crown Court* [1982] Q.B. 304. There must, however, be many cases in which, in the absence of any other 'record' such as a court order, the written decision of a tribunal must be regarded as 'the record' for the purposes of judicial review . . . [As there may be many cases] in which the written decision of the tribunal is the only place where the determination can be found [this] means that the written decision must be the record."

Earlier the Northern Irish Court of Appeal had taken a broader view of the concept of the "record" (in which the *Knightsbridge* judgment had been expressly followed) in *Re Doherty* [1988] N.I. 14, a case to which Lowry L.C.J. did not refer.

181 "The Court has always had power to order an inferior tribunal to complete the record", per Denning L.J. in *R. v. Medical Appeal Tribunal, ex p. Gilmore* [1957] 1 Q.B. 574 at 582–583. See also, *R. v. Knightsbridge Crown Court, ex p. International Sporting Club Ltd* [1982] Q.B. 304. This view is also implicit in the Supreme Court's judgment in *The State (Creedon) v. Criminal Injuries Compensation Tribunal* [1988] I.R. 51.

182 See the comments of Griffiths L.J. in *R. v. Knightsbridge Crown Court, ex p. International Sporting Club Ltd* [1982] Q.B. 304. However, the presence of a stenographer in the District Court is a rare occurence.

183 [1984] N.I. 373.

the notice party in order to supplement the record, saying that the notice party "must be taken" to have consented to the affidavit being used for this purpose.[184] Similar reasoning was applied by the Northern Irish Court of Appeal in *Re Weir and Higgins' Application*[185] where it was held that an affidavit by the respondent Taxing Master setting out the reasons for his decision formed part of the record. Lowry L.C.J. said that the court inclined to the view that:

> "When the lower deciding authority of its own motion files an affidavit setting out its reasons, it will be taken to have made it part of the record by incorporating therein the reasons for its decision. We would not be dissuaded from this opinion by the objection that the affidavit was not in being at the time when the order to be challenged was made, since this could frequently be said with regard to a speaking order."[186]

In line with traditional teaching, in this jurisdiction, the former Supreme Court has affirmed the traditional rule that an administrative body may not file an affidavit "for the purpose of adding to, explaining or contradicting their written orders."[187] Again, where the respondents or notice party objects, it has been held that the court may not look at the applicant's affidavit in order to supplement the record, at least where the affidavit contains documentary material not otherwise before the court.[188]

In criminal cases, the record has been held to include the warrant, the formal records and the transcript of the trial.[189] In some cases, the scope of the record has been restricted by statute. The Summary Jurisdiction Act 1848 originally restricted the scope of the record for the purposes of summary convictions[190] and when the District Court was made a court of record by the Courts Act 1971, section 14[191] provided that the record in cases of summary jurisdiction before that court, was confined to the

---

[184] *Ibid.* at 386.

[185] [1988] N.I. 338.

[186] *Ibid.* at 358. *Cf.* the comments of the same judge in *R v. Belfast Recorder, ex p. McNally* [1992] N.I. 217 at 236:
"... affidavits cannot be used to supplement the record. I think, however, that there is probably an exception when, as in this case, an affidavit is adduced on behalf of the court whose adjudication is challenged. In such a case the court (or tribunal) may be said to have 'completed the record' and, as a speaking order provided by the court can constitute material on which the superior court can adjudicate, it seems logical to regard as part of the record material which the court itself has provided in another way."

[187] *The State (Crowley) v. Irish Land Commission* [1951] I.R. 250 at 264, *per* O'Byrne J. This rule has been described as contrary to "modern common sense administration": *The State (Power) v. Jones* [1942] I.R. 68 at 74, *per* Gavan Duffy J. It is questionable whether a modern Supreme Court would take such a restrictive view and might prefer the pragmatic approach of the Northern Irish courts. For an extremely helpful discussion of these questions, see Costello, "The Burden of Proof on Judicial Review" (1993) 15 D.U.L.J. 134.

[188] *R v. Agricultural Lands Tribunal, ex p. Bracey* [1960] 2 All E.R. 518.

[189] *Re Tracey*, unreported, Supreme Court, December 21, 1963.

[190] This had the effect of limiting the opportunities of challenging summary convictions on the ground of error on the face of the record and, indeed, the 1848 Act was designed to counteract the then prevailing tendency to quash convictions exhibiting purely formal defects. As Lord Sumner explained in *R. v. Nat Bell Liquors Ltd* [1922] 2 A.C. 128 at 159:
"The effect of [the 1848 Act] was not to make that which had been error, error no longer, but to remove all opportunity for detection. The face of the record 'spoke' no longer: it was the inscrutable face of the sphinx."

[191] As inserted by the Criminal Justice (Miscellaneous Provisions) Act 1997, s.20(b)

formal court order signed by the District Judge. This means that external documentary material cannot be availed of in order to impeach an order of the District Court in such a case. Thus, in *Friel v. McMenamin*[192] the applicant sought to rely on the note of the respondent District Judge in order to challenge the conviction. Barron J. held that the respondent was under no obligation to supply the note, adding that section 14 of the 1971 Act would not allow "the note to be used to go behind the order."

There seems to be scant modern authority in this jurisdiction where there appears to be some confusion as to the scope of review for error of law on the face of the record, but it does not appear to be quite as broad as that suggested by the recent English and the majority of the Northern Irish authorities. Yet again, however, the authorities are not easily reconcilable. In *Walsh v. Minister for Local Government*,[193] the former Supreme Court agreed that if the Minister had set out his reasons in arriving at a decision, these reasons would form part of the record, thus rendering the impugned decision liable to be quashed if the Minister had erred in law. In this case the applicant sought to quash a surcharge imposed by the local government auditor. The auditor's certificate was said to contain an error of law. The applicant exercised his statutory right of appeal to the respondent Minister, who issued a sealed order upholding the auditor's decision. The ministerial order mentioned – but did not set out – the reasons give by the auditor. Murnaghan J. observed:

> "We do not see how this [ministerial] order can in any sense be said to be a speaking order, stating the views of the Minister upon some point of law, so as to make an erroneous view of the law apparent on the record."[194]

The court went on to hold that the Minister's order had not incorporated the reasons of the auditor so as to make these reasons the view of the law taken by the Minister and thus appear "on the face of the record." It seems improbable that such a narrow approach would be taken by the modern Supreme Court.

In *The State (Attorney General) v. Binchy*,[195] the former Supreme Court implied that the record in a criminal trial on indictment was confined to the formal record of the trial (*i.e.* only the official court documents, the verdict and record of conviction, if any). Yet, some three years later, the Supreme Court held in *Re Tynan*[196] that the record in such a case included the court orders and the transcript (thus rendering a conviction liable to be quashed if, for example, the judge erred in law in his summing-up). More recently, in *The State (Abenglen Properties Ltd) v. Dublin Corporation*,[197] Henchy J. adopted a more restrictive attitude to this question. The judge implied that the record in planning cases is confined to the formal decision of the local authority or An Bord Pleanála, *i.e.* whether or not to grant planning permission.[198] This view seems incorrect and is certainly at odds with the classic re-statement of the law by Denning L.J. in *Shaw*. Finally, in one of the few recent

---

[192] [1990] I.L.R.M. 761.
[193] [1929] I.R. 377.
[194] *Ibid.* at 404.
[195] [1964] I.R. 395.
[196] Unreported, Supreme Court, December 20, 1963.
[197] [1984] I.R. 381.
[198] The judge appears to have overlooked the provisions of s.26(8) of the Local Government (Planning and Development) Act 1963 which provides that the conditions attached to the grant of a planning

Irish cases on this point where an administrative order was quashed for error on the face of the record, *Bannon v. Employment Appeals Tribunal*[199] an error of law appearing in the Tribunal's decision was held to have appeared on the record and it was accordingly quashed.

It should be noted that traditionally certiorari was the only remedy which could correct an error of law on the face of the record.[200] The combined effect of Order 84, Rules 18 and 19 of the Rules of the Superior Courts 1986 is to rob this procedural anomaly of any practical signficance.[201]

The necessity for official orders, etc., to demonstrate jurisdiction on their face

There is a common law requirement that court orders, official documents and statutory instruments should show jurisdiction on their face but it is less clear whether it applies to other administrative decisions.[202] The rationale for this requirement has been variously justified as demonstrating that the court or the maker of secondary legislation has directed its mind to the appropriate statutory conditions of jurisdiction[203] and that it enables the applicant to seek a judicial review on the ground of jurisdictional error or error of law on the face of the record.[204] This rule has been somewhat erratically applied,[205] but orders affecting fundamental rights

---

permission, together with the reasons given for the imposition of such conditions, form part of the record. See further, Hogan, "Remoulding Certiorari" (1982) 17 *Irish Jurist* 32 at pp. 37–39. *Cf.* the more convincing analysis offered by the Northern Irish Court of Appeal in *Re Doherty's Application* [1988] N.I. 14 at 31, where Kelly L.J. held that the plans and specifications contained in a licensing application constituted part of the "record", as the documents were essential documentary proofs and were referred to in the magistrates' court's order, adding that it was clear that:

"... if the decision or order challenged refers to or contains extracts of other documents, all of these documents will be taken to be incorporated in the record."

[199] [1993] 1 I.R. 500.

[200] *Punton v. Ministry for Pensions (No. 2)* [1964] 1 W.L.R. 226. But *cf. King v. Attorney General* [1981] I.R. 233, where a declaration was granted invalidating a conviction for error on the face of the record. The conviction had failed to show jurisdiction on its face, and this is a well-recognised ground for quashing for error of law on the face of the record: see, *e.g. The State (Carr) v. Youghal D.J.* [1945] I.R. 43; *The State (Leahy) v. Cork D.J.* [1945] I.R. 426 and *The State (Browne) v. Feran* [1967] I.R. 147 and p. 435.

[201] See pp. 701–702.

[202] "Every order of a justice must not only be one within his jurisdiction, but must show on its face the facts which brought the matter within [his] jurisdiction": *R. (Boylan) v. Londonderry JJ.* [1912] 2 I.R. 347 at 379, *per* Palles C.B. See the most helpful article of Costello, "Error on the Face of the Record in Irish Law" (1993–1995) *Irish Jurist* 148.

[203] In *The State (Roche) v. Delap* [1980] I.R. 170 at 173 Henchy J. said of a District Court order committing a juvenile offender to an adult detention centre should recite his age:

"thus indicating the basis of the sentence and the fact that the court has addressed its mind to the conditions necessary for the exercise of statutory jurisdiction."

[204] See Costello, *op.cit.* above, n.202, at pp. 168–9.

[205] In *The State (Burke) v. Lennon* [1940] I.R. 136 Gavan Duffy J. ordered the applicant's release from a detention where the internment warrant did not contain a recital referring to the Government's order bringing into force the internment provisions of Part IV of the Offences against the State Act 1939. In *Re McGrath and Harte* [1941] I.R. 68 a few months later Gavan Duffy J. dismissed the argument that the orders bringing the accused before a military court should contain similar recitals as to the manner in which the statutory pre-conditions to jurisdiction had been satisfied. As Costello has laconically observed (*loc.cit.*, 166) the omission "of the same recital which invalidated Burke's internment was not sufficient to save McGrath and Harte from the death penalty."

such as deportation orders,[206] search warrants,[207] extradition orders[208] and compulsory purchase orders[209] have all been set aside for failure to show jurisdiction.

A conviction imposed by an inferior court "in respect of an offence created by statute must show that the matters do constitute a criminal offence by referring to the statute which makes them such or at least to the fact that there is such a statute."[210] The extent to which the recitals must contain details of the offence, etc., may vary. Thus, in *Re Tynan*[211] Walsh J. held that since there was no "quantitative limitation" of the Circuit Court's jurisdiction in respect of offences under the Larceny Act, there was no need to recite details of the offence as once the warrant discloses "an offence in respect of which the Circuit Court has unlimited jurisdiction, there is a presumption of a legal conviction to found the warrant."[212] Where, however, a fine exceeds the statutory maximum for the first offence (where, *e.g.* the statute allows for a higher fine in respect of a second or subsequent offence) this fact ought to be recited on the face of the order.[213] A District Court conviction should also recite relevant statutory pre-conditions to jurisdiction,[214] as well as any relevant amendments to a statutory offence and failure to do so renders the conviction bad on its face and liable to be quashed.[215] Finally, there have been instances where relief has been refused on what amounts to a discretionary basis where no prejudice has been caused by the irregularity. *Walsh v. Governor of Limerick Prison*[216] may be classified as an example of this trend. Here Laffoy J. refused to order the applicant's release from custody where the order of the Special Criminal Court did not show jurisdiction on its face. The judge did not actually decide the question of whether the order must show jurisdiction, adding that:

---

206   *Kajli v. Minister for Justice*, unreported High Court, August 21, 1992
207   *Director of Public Prosecutions v. Dunne* [1994] 2 I.R. 537.
208   *The State (Holmes) v. Furlong* [1967] I.R. 210; *The State (Furlong) v. Kelly* [1967] I.R. 210.
209   *Movie News Ltd v. Galway C.C.*, unreported, High Court, March 30, 1973 (although note Henchy J.'s reservation of this question on appeal before the Supreme Court, July 15, 1977).
210   *The State (Cunningham) v. O'Floinn* [1960] I.R. 198 at 201 (Davitt P.) and approved by O'Daly J. (at 216–217); *The State (Gleeson) v. Connellan* [1988] I.R. 559 at 562, *per* Griffin J.
211   [1969] I.R. 269.
212   *Ibid.* at 280–1, *per* Walsh J. The judge had earlier explained that in these circumstances it was
    "quite immaterial to the legality of the detention by the Governor that he should be informed
    that the [larceny] conviction was in respect of a cow, rather than a horse or a sheep . . . ."
  Likewise, once the court has a jurisdiction to hear an assault charge and the fact of the charge is shown on the face of the order, "jurisdiction to bind to the peace is thereby shown on the face of the order" without any necessity for a recital "as to the facts upon which the judge was relying in the same way as an order for conviction or dismissal does not need a recital of the facts which justify such order": *Clarke v. Judge Hogan* [1995] 1 I.R. 310 at 312, *per* Barron J. See also *R. (Mulholland) v. Monaghan JJ.* [1914] 2 I.R. 156.
213   *The State (Gleeson) v. Connellan* [1988] I.R. 559 at 563, *per* Griffin J. See also *Tangney v. District Justice for Co. Kerry* [1928] I.R. 358 (failure to recite forfeiture order in the conviction rendered it bad on its face); *The State (Carr) v. District Justice for Youghal* [1945] I.R. 43 (failure to recite identity of party to whom fine is paid renders conviction order bad on its face). *The State (Leahy) v. District Justice for Cork* [1945] I.R. 426 (similar principle).
214   *The State (Browne) v. Feran* [1967] I.R. 147 (failure to recite that the accused consented to summary trial having being informed of his right to trial by jury rendered conviction bad on its face.)
215   *King v. Attorney General* [1981] I.R. 233 at 261, *per* Henchy J.
216   Unreported High Court, July 31, 1996. But *cf. The State (O'Duffy) v. Bennett* [1935] I.R. 70 (orders of the former Constitution (Special Powers) Tribunal must show jurisdiction on their face); *The State (Hughes) v. Lennon* [1935] I.R. 128 (similar principle).

". . . insofar as the warrant or order of the Special Criminal Court is defective for the failure to disclose jurisdiction *ex facie*, in my view, this does not amount to 'such a default of fundamental requirements that the detention may be said to be wanting in due process of law.'"

5. Power or Duty?

"Shall" can sometimes mean "may"

The use of permissive language (such as "may" or "it shall be lawful") generally imports a discretionary power which is enabling or permissive, whereas mandatory language (such as "shall" or "must") usually implies the existence of a statutory duty. The fact, however, that there are exceptions to the latter precept is illustrated by the leading authority in the common law world, *Julius v. Lord Bishop of Oxford*.[217] In this case, the relevant statutory provisions provided that "it shall be lawful" for a bishop to convene a commission of inquiry in case of alleged misconduct by a clergyman, either on the application of a complainant or of his own motion. The bishop refused to act on a complaint and the issue arose as to whether this refusal was lawful. The House of Lords concluded that this power was enabling only, since it was evident not only from the wording but also from the background and context of the statute that the bishop might use his own discretion and disallow complaints that were insubstantial or frivolous. Otherwise clergymen might be subjected to unjustified and vexatious complaints.

Similar reasoning has been employed in a variety of recent Irish cases. Thus, in *Duffy v. Dublin Corporation*[218] the question arose as to whether section 80 of the Dublin Improvement Act 1849 (which provided that "it shall be lawful" for the Corporation "to build and improve" a cattle market) was obligatory or simply created a power. Henchy J. referred with approval to *Julius v. Bishop of Oxford* and held that, when viewed in the context of the statute as a whole, these words were simply enabling. Express statutory language would have been required had it been intended to impose on the Corporation "a perpetual obligation to maintain and improve a market place, regardless of the costs to the ratepayers or the absence of public demand or its unsuitability."[219] In *Stafford v. Roadstone Ltd*[220] Barrington J. rejected the argument that, where an unauthorised use was made out, the words "the High Court *may* prohibit the continuance of the development or unauthorised use" (emphasis added) (contained in section 27 of the Local Government (Planning and Development) Act 1963) obliged the court to grant an order. The Oireachtas presumably intended that this new jurisdiction would be exercised on principles similar to those governing injunctions and it could not have been intended that:

---

[217] (1880) L.R. 5 App.Cas. 214.
[218] [1974] I.R. 33.
[219] *Ibid.* at 44.
[220] [1980] I.L.R.M. 1.

"The High Court should have no discretion but to issue an injunction where the plaintiff has no interest in the lands in question and the breach of the planning law has been innocent or technical."[221]

This question was also considered by the Supreme Court in *The State (Sheehan) v. Government of Ireland*,[222] where the construction of section 60(7) of the Civil Liability Act 1961 was at issue. Section 60(1) abolished the common law rule whereby a highway authority was not liable for acts of non-feasance, but section 60(7) was in the following terms:

"This section shall come into operation on such day, not earlier than the 1st day of April 1967 as may be fixed therefor by order made by the Government."

As no order had been made by 1986, the question arose as to whether the Government could be compelled by mandamus to make such an order. This in turn raised the issue of whether the words used were obligatory or permissive only. Henchy J. thought that the latter construction was the correct one:

"The uses of 'shall' and 'may,' both in the subsection and the section as a whole, point to the conclusion that the radical law-reform embodied in the section was intended not to come into effect before the 1st April 1967, and thereafter only on such day as may be fixed by an order made by the Government. Not, be it noted, on such day as shall be fixed by the Government. Limiting words such as 'as soon as may be' or 'as soon as convenient,' which are to be found in comparable statutory provisions, are markedly absent."[223]

However, the passage quoted from *Sheehan* does not satisfactorily come to terms with the distinct, but related, issue, which commonly arises in this area, namely, that even permissive language conferring a discretion does not absolve the donee of that power from the obligation to exercise that discretion reasonably.

Anheuser Busch Inc. v. Controller of Patents, Design and Trade Marks[224] and *Elwyn (Cottons) Ltd v. Master of the High Court*[225] are two contemporary examples

---

[221] *Ibid.* See also, *Bradley v. Meath County Council* [1991] I.L.R.M. 179 where Costello J. held that it was clear from the interchange of the words "may" and "shall" in s.52 of the Public Health (Ireland) Act 1878 that a statutory duty to collect refuse only arose where the sanitary authority had been required to do so by ministerial order. In *Jennings Truck Centre (Tullamore) Ltd v. Offaly County Council*, unreported, High Court, June 14, 1990 Murphy J. held that regulations providing that a local authority "may" appoint applicants who fulfilled certain requirements for the position of vehicle tester did not impose an enforceable regulation upon them to do so. The regulations in question conferred a supervisory role upon the authority, which discretion was not exhausted by satisfying the specified criteria. See also *Navan Tanker Services Ltd v. Meath County Council*, December 13, 1996 (similar principle involving later vehicle testing regulations).

[222] [1987] I.R. 550. See Hogan, "Judicial Review of an Executive Discretion" (1987) 9 D.U.L.J. 91.

[223] *Ibid.* at 561.

[224] [1987] I.R. 329. See also *Point Exhibition Co. Ltd v. Revenue Commissioners* [1993] 2 I.R. 551 (applicant successfully demonstrated that it was "legally entitled" to a licence under s.7 of the Excise Act 1835 and mandamus was granted accordingly).

[225] [1989] I.R. 14. In contrast, Costello J. found in *Bradley v. Meath County Council* [1991] I.L.R.M. 179 that the provisions of ss. 52 and 54 of the Public Health (Ireland) Act 1878 simply empowered a sanitary authority to take steps for the removal of household waste and they could not therefore be coerced by mandamus to perform certain acts in respect of which they were under no statutory duty to perform.

of cases where such an unambiguous statutory duty was found to exist despite the absence of obligatory language in the governing statute. In the former case, Barron J. granted an order of mandamus compelling the Controller to state his reasons for his failure to remove a particular trade mark on the grounds of non-use. Barron J. considered that section 56 of the Trade Marks Act 1963 enabled the High Court to direct the Controller to furnish such reasons so as to enable the applicants to appeal against his decision and granted an order of mandamus accordingly. In *Elwyn Cottons*, O'Hanlon J. held that section 11(3) of the Jurisdiction of Courts and Enforcement of Judgments (European Communities) Act 1988 did oblige the respondent Master to grant protective measures in favour of the applicant for an enforcement order of a foreign judgment once such an enforcement order had been made. Accordingly, O'Hanlon J. granted an order of mandamus direct to the respondent to grant such protective measures. By contrast, in *The State (Finglas Industrial Estates Ltd) v. Dublin C.C.*,[226] the Supreme Court held that mandamus would not lie to compel the respondents to accept a contribution towards the construction of sewerage facilities in the absence of such a statutory duty.[227]

"May" can sometimes mean "shall"

But while the use of permissive language will generally be held to mean that the statute merely confers an enabling power, there exists an important exception to this general rule in cases where a statutory body is given a discretionary power coupled with a duty to exercise this power in a particular way in prescribed circumstances. In other words, there are cases in which, when applied to action of an administrative character, "may" means, in effect, "must." In short, the result is the converse of the *Julius* case because the context is again allowed to prevail over the express words. For example, in *Bakht v. Medical Council*[228] Griffin J. rejected the submission that section 27(2) of the Medical Practitioners Act 1978 conferred a discretion and held that the subsection imposed a statutory duty on the Council to make such rules. The subsection provided for the registration of certain categories of doctors who had passed such examinations "as are specified in rules made by the Council." Likewise, in *R. (Local Government Board) v. Guardians of the Letterkenny Union*,[229] it was held that the provisions of section 10 of the Vaccination (Amendment) Ireland Act 1879 were mandatory. This section provided that the guardians of any union "may direct proceedings" to be instituted for the "purpose of enforcing obedience" to the Vaccination Acts. The Letterkenny Union, apparently deferring to local opinion, had taken no action against some 290 defaulting parents, claiming that in doing so, they were exercising bona fide a discretion conferred by the Act. Cherry L.C.J. said:

---

[226] Unreported, Supreme Court, February 17, 1983. Similarly, mandamus will not lie to compel the Government to ratify an international treaty where there is no legal or constitutional obligation on it to do so: see *Hutchinson v. Minister for Justice* [1993] 3 I.R. 567 or where a previous legal obligation has since been repealed: *Donegal Fuel & Supply Co. Ltd v. Londonderry Harbour Commissioners* [1994] 1 I.R. 24. Nor will mandamus be granted to compel a local authority to abide by an invalid resolution: *Kenny Homes & Co. Ltd v. Galway City and County Manager* [1995] 1 I.R. 178.

[227] See also *The State (Sheehan) v. Government of Ireland* [1987] I.R. 550. See further, p. 437.

[228] [1990] 1 I.R. 515.

[229] [1916] 2 I.R. 18.

"It is settled law that provisions in a statute merely of a permissive character may impose a duty [and] it has been held that where a statute directs anything to be done which is for the public good, words of permission may be construed as mandatory in their operation."[230]

The background to the Act, coupled with the provision for the expense of the proceedings to be paid out of the rates, indicated that the legislature intended that a duty should be imposed "upon the guardians of enforcing the provisions of the Acts in all proper cases."

This principle has been applied by the Supreme Court in a series of cases. Thus, in *Dolan v. Neligan*,[231] Walsh J. held that the words "hereby authorised" in section 25 of the Customs Consolidation Act 1876 were mandatory. The Revenue Commissioners were empowered by this provision to repay overpaid customs duties and it had to be assumed:

"That a statutory power authorising the repayment or the return of over-payments of customs duties authorises that repayment for the sake of justice or for the good of the person for whose benefit the provision exists. Upon the [statutory] conditions [as to overpayment in error] being fulfilled, the person who has paid the duties is entitled to call for the repayment of the over-payments. In my view, the statute is not to be construed as merely conferring a discretion to return the overpayments when those other conditions have been satisfied."[232]

Likewise, in *Re Dunne's Application*,[233] Walsh J. held that the phrase in section 19(2) of the Intoxicating Liquor Act 1960 that the District Court "may order" the extinguishment of a seven-day publican's licence where certain statutory criteria were fulfilled was mandatory. The section was conferred for the benefit of persons holding hotel licences, who could, via the operation of the extinguishment procedure, have their existing licences converted to full licences. This fact, coupled with the absence of notice to potential objectors and the general informality of the procedure, led to the conclusion that, upon "the giving of the required proofs in the particular case," there was no discretion to refuse the order sought.

The converse principle may also be true, in that there are occasions in which the apparently mandatory language of the statute will nonetheless be held to connote a discretion, at least in cases touching on constitutional rights. An example here is *McMahon v. Leahy*[234] where the Supreme Court held that, despite the mandatory language of the Extradition Act 1965, the court retained a discretion to refuse extradition where this would infringe the accused's constitutional rights. Henchy J. said that a contrary construction would be tantamount to saying that the court's function was:

"mechanical, discretionless and without regard to the fact that its order would have an unconstitutional impact on the person sought to be extradited."[235]

---

230 *Ibid.* at 24–25.
231 [1967] I.R. 247.
232 *Ibid.* at 275, *per* Walsh J.
233 [1968] I.R. 105. See also *The State (McGuinness) v. Maguire* [1967] I.R. 348.
234 [1984] I.R. 525.
235 *Ibid.* at 541.

Interpretation Act 1937, section 15

It remains to note the provisions of the Interpretation Act, 1937, section 15:

> "(1) Every power conferred by an Act of the Oireachtas or by an instrument made wholly or partly under any such Act may, unless the contrary intention appears in such Act or instrument, be exercised from time to time as occasion requires.
>
> (2) Every power conferred by an Act of the Oireachtas or by an instrument made wholly or partly under any such Act on the holder of an office as such shall, unless the contrary intention appears in such Act or instrument, be deemed to be conferred upon him and accordingly be exercised by the holder for the time being of such office.[236]
>
> (3) Every power by an Act of the Oireachtas to make regulations, rules or bye-laws shall, unless the contrary intention appears in such Act, be construed as including a power, exercisable in the like manner and subject to the like consent and conditions (if any) to revoke or amend any regulations, rules or bye-laws made under such powers and (where requisite) to make other regulations, rules or bye-laws in lieu of those so revoked."[237]

These provisions emphasise that, unless the statutory context suggests to the contrary, statutory powers must be exercised as the occasion requires. Thus, in *R v. Ealing MBC, ex p. McBain*[238] the English Court of Appeal held that a housing authority had erred in law in refusing to entertain a second application for housing assistance from an applicant who had earlier unreasonably refused an offer of housing. However, as the applicant's conditions had materially changed in the meantime, Neill L.J., relying on the corresponding provisions of the English Interpretation Act 1978, held that the new circumstances required the duty to be performed again, so that in the light of these changed circumstances, the authority was bound to reconsider the matter afresh.

6. Formal and Procedural Requirements

As we have seen, nearly every question pertaining to jurisdiction turns on a question of statutory interpretation. This is especially true in the case of the disregard of procedural and formal requirements laid down by statute. When the Oireachtas

---

[236] Section 16 of the 1937 Act contains corresponding provisions in relation to ss. 15(1) and (2) as far as the construction and performance of statutory duties are concerned.

[237] In *Minister for Agriculture v. Gallagher* [1941] I.R. 278 Martin Maguire J. said that the Minister's power to issue certificates under s.19 of the Slaughter of Cattle and Sheep Act 1934 detailing the amount of a levy due was "spent once the certificates had been properly issued" under the section. The judge added (at 283):

> "If the Legislature had intended to confer upon the Minister power to revoke certificates and to issue new ones, this sub-section ought to have been worded in a different way."

Judgment was not reserved and the judge's attention does not appear to have been drawn to the provisions of ss. 15 and 16 of the Interpretation Act 1937.

[238] [1985] 1 W.L.R. 1351.

stipulates that certain formal and procedural requirements must be observed before an administrative decision is arrived at, it rarely states what consequences follow non-compliance with these statutory requirements. Of course, to this general observation there are exceptions: section 5 of the Adoption Act 1976, for example, states that an adoption order shall not be declared invalid solely on the ground that certain statutory prerequisites have not been complied with; section 17(1)(a) of the Local Government (Planning and Development) Act 1992 provides that an appeal received by the Board after the expiration of the appropriate period shall be invalid as not having been made in time[239] and section 15 of the Irish Takeover Panel Act 1997 provides that the failure to comply with certain scheduled principles, rules and directions contained in that Act will not necessarily lead to the invalidation of any given transaction. Nevertheless, it is true to say that the courts are for the most part left to their own devices as far as the consequences of non-compliance with procedural requirements is concerned. Whether a statutory provision which on the face appears to be obligatory is to be regarded as truly mandatory or is merely to be regarded as directory in nature depends on the statutory intent and whether compliance with the provision can fairly be said to be essential to the general object intended to be secured by the Act.[240] The relevant test has been stated in the following terms:

> "If the requirement which has not been observed may fairly be said to be an integral and indispensable part of the statutory intendment, the courts will hold it to be truly mandatory, and will not excuse a departure from it. But if, on the other hand, what is apparently a requirement is in essence merely a direction which is not of the substance of the aim and scheme of the statute, non-compliance may be excused."[241]

But even in the case of directory provisions, the courts will not readily sanction a radical departure from what the legislature has ordained. Thus, even provisions which are directory as to precise compliance are generally mandatory as to substantial compliance.[242] On the other hand, courts are rarely impressed by defects of form, and will often excuse an irregularity where the "requirements of justice and the substance of the procedure have been observed."[243] Thus, in *Veterinary*

---

239 In *McCann v. An Bord Pleanála* [1997] 1 I.L.R.M. 134 (a case where, through an oversight, the appeal was received a day late) Lavan J. held that the language of section 17(1)(a)("shall be invalid") reflected clearly the "statutory intendment" and that, accordingly, the statutory requirements were mandatory and non-compliance with them could not be excused (in this case, at least) on a "de minimis" basis. See also *Graves v. An Bord Pleanála* [1997] 2 I.R. 205 considered below at pp. 451–452.

240 *Monaghan U.D.C. v. Alf-A-Bet Promotions Ltd* [1980] I.L.R.M. 64; *The State (Elm Developments Ltd) v. An Bord Pleanála* [1981] I.L.R.M. 108.

241 *The State (Elm Developments Ltd) v. An Bord Pleanála* [1981] I.L.R.M. 108 at 110, *per* Henchy J. For a dubious application of similar principles, see *Re Philip Clarke* [1950] I.R. 235. In *Connolly v. Sweeney* [1988] I.L.R.M. 483 McCarthy J. said (at 488) that he "would be slow to accept the underlying principle [in *Elm Developments*] in criminal cases."

242 *The State (Doyle) v. Carr* [1970] I.R. 87.

243 *O'Mahony v. Arklow U.D.C.* [1965] I.R. 710 at 735 (Lavery J.). See also, *The State (Toft) v. Galway Corporation* [1981] I.L.R.M. 439; *The State (Elm Developments Ltd) v. An Bord Pleanála* [1981] I.L.R.M. 108; *The State (Coveney) v. Special Criminal Court* [1982] I.L.R.M. 284; *McGlinchey v. Governor of Portlaoise Prison* [1988] I.R. 671 at 695 (Lynch J.); *Rhatigan v. Textiles Y Confecciones Europeas S.A.* [1990] 1 I.R. 126; *Schwestermann v. An Bord Pleanála* [1994] 3 I.R. 457 and *Blessington & District Community Council Ltd v. Wicklow County Council* [1997] 1 I.L.R.M. 519.

Council v. Corr[244] the appellants had requested a case-stated from a decision of the Circuit Court. The relevant statutory provisions required that the case-stated be served on the respondents "at or before the time" that the case-stated was transmitted to the High Court. On the day that the case-stated was lodged in the High Court, a representative of the appellant's solicitors was delayed in court and found that the respondents' offices had closed. The case-stated was, however, delivered the following day. While the Supreme Court accepted that these statutory requirements were mandatory, Maguire C.J. held that, on these facts, there was sufficient compliance with the terms of the section.[245]

In addition, in view of the fact that in nearly all cases the remedy sought will lie in the discretion of the court, there is increasing evidence that the crucial factor is probably whether the irregularity will cause real prejudice. If the party aggrieved cannot show that he has been "wrong-footed or damnified" or that the "spirit and purpose" of the statutory provisions have not been breached, then relief may be withheld on discretionary grounds.[246] There is a further point. In the decided cases so far the outcomes appear always to have been either a finding of invalidity or no sanction whatsoever. Theoretically, there are other possibilities. But, in practice, no case appears to have arisen in which the applicant has been able to show even some loss, yet the court has characterised the situation as involving a directory provision. The possibility exists that, in future, the courts may become more alive to the possibility of damages as a sanction, and, accordingly, may less frequently reach a finding of invalidity.

There are, however, no universal rules which can be used to determine whether a statutory provision is mandatory or directory – each will turn on the proper construction of the legislation in question, and the citation of authorities is not always especially helpful. Difficult issues of principle have been thrown up by cases such as *O'Mahony v. Arklow U.D.C.*[247] where the plaintiff, who was town clerk of Arklow, was suspended for certain irregularities in the performance of his duties. He was subsequently removed from office with the consent of the Minister for Local

---

[244] [1953] I.R. 12. There is an interesting analysis of this case in *Hughes v. Viner* [1985] 3 All E.R. 40.

[245] See also *Attorney General v. Wallace*, unreported, High Court, June 18, 1996 where it was held that there had been adequate compliance with a statutory provision contained in the Fisheries (Consolidation) Act 1959, s.234(1) which required a sea fisheries protection officer to bring the owner of a detained boat before a District Judge ("as soon as may be" where the owner had been brought before the Court on the following day. No judge was available on the day that the owner had been detained as all the judges were present at an annual meeting. Geoghegan J. said:

> "The State took all reasonable steps to have the matter heard as soon as practicable. The obligation of the State does not go beyond that."

But *cf.* the approach of Kelly J. in *Graves v. An Bord Pleanála* [1997] 2 I.R. 205, discussed below at pp. 451–452.

[246] *The State (Elm Developments Ltd) v. An Bord Pleanála* [1981] I.L.R.M. 108; *The State (Coveney) v. Special Criminal Court* [1982] I.L.R.M. 284. But *cf. R v. Governor of Crumlin Road Prison, ex p. Jordan* [1992] N.I. 148 where Carswell J. quashed the imposition of a prison disciplinary punishment for failure to hold the hearing within specified mandatory time limits. The judge added (at 158):

> "[The prisoner] did not, however, bring about the breach of the rule by any act or request on his part, nor was he guilty of any culpable act, delay or acquiescence which should make the court ready to deprive him of a remedy. No issue arises of pointlessness of making an order of certiorari ... [The] fact that there was no prejudice to the applicant is an insufficient reason to exercise my discretion against him. . . ."

[247] [1965] I.R. 710.

Government pursuant to section 26 of the Local Government Act 1941. That application provided that a written application to the Minister for his consent for such dismissal was necessary. No such letter was sent, though the Minister was generally kept informed of the situation and was aware of the dissatisfaction of the council with the plaintiff's performance as town clerk. Although the misconduct of the plaintiff was admitted to be such as would have justified dismissal, the validity of his dismissal was put at issue by the plaintiff.

The dismissal was upheld by a majority of the Supreme Court. Lavery J. was of the opinion that as the Minister was fully aware of the situation, and as the plaintiff was given every opportunity to explain his conduct, the irregularities complained of were "defects of form and not of substance." He did not think that the court should:

"[P]arse and construe rules of procedure in a narrow and unreal way, looking for some flaw in procedure to invalidate a transaction where the requirements of justice and the substance of procedure have been observed."[248]

Kingsmill Moore J. in dissent considered that as the procedural requirements of the Act had not been adhered to, this represented a fundamental procedural defect which invalidated the dismissal. This approach seems unduly narrow and rigid; the majority view that the dismissal should not be invalidated as there was substantial compliance with the statutory requirements seems preferable, given that the plaintiff was allowed every opportunity to prepare his case – which was the very object of this procedural safeguard.

Director of Public Prosecutions v. Dunne[249] is a case falling on the other side of the line. Here a peace commissioner issued a search warrant under the Misue of Drugs Act 1977 to enable Gardaì to search a private residence. The warrant was in standard form, but an essential recital[250] was ommitted in error. Carney J. held that the warrant was invalid, since if a specific constitutional right – in this case, the inviolability of the dwelling as protected by Article 40.5 – were to be set aside "by a printed form" it was essential that "the form should be in clear, complete, accurate and unambiguous terms."[251]

The conventional distinction between mandatory and directory provisions has, perhaps, been somewhat blurred, however, by three Supreme Court decisions even though the traditional language is employed in all cases. In *Monaghan U.D.C. v. Alf-A-Bet Promotions Ltd*[252] the respondent developer sought planning permission which would enable him to convert a drapery store into a betting office and an amusement arcade. The relevant regulations required the developer to publish a notice in a newspaper stating the "nature and extent of the development." The

---

[248]   *Ibid.* at 735.

[249]   [1994] 2 I.R. 537.

[250]   Namely, that as required by s. 26 of the Misuse of Drugs Act 1984 the District Judge was satisfied on oath that there were reasonable grounds for suspecting that controlled drugs were "on any premises."

[251]   Contrast this with the same judge's rather trenchant rejection of the argument that a place of safety order was invalid because it misdescribed a date of birth as one "not . . . to be taken seriously by this or any other court": *Herron v. District Judge of Mallow District Court*, unreported, High Court, June 12, 1992. Likewise, in *Madden v. Minister for Marine* [1993] 1 I.R. 567 Johnson J. was quite unimpressed with the argument that a fisheries licence was invalid as being bad on its face because it gave the incorrect number for a particular statutory instrument.

[252]   [1980] I.L.R.M. 64.

developer's notice referred only to "alterations and improvements." The Supreme Court held that the notice did not convey the nature and extent of the proposed development. Inclusion, in the notice, of information as to the nature and extent of the proposed development was vital to the statutory scheme for the grant of planning permission because it was the way of publicising the development. The misleading notice that was published was held not to comply with a mandatory provision, and such non-compliance was held to be fatal to the developer's case. In view of the fact that planning permission could radically affect the rights and amenities of others, and substantially benefit or enrich the grantee of the permission, Henchy J. considered that the courts should not countenance deviation from that which had been deemed obligatory by the Oireachtas save on an application of the *de minimis* rule:

> "What the legislature has prescribed ... in such circumstances as necessary should be treated as nothing short of necessary and deviation from the requirements must, before it can be overlooked, be shown, by the person seeking to have it excused, to be so trivial or so technical, or so peripheral, or otherwise so insubstantial that on the principle that it is the spirit rather than the letter of the law that matters, the prescribed obligation has been substantially, and therefore adequately, complied with."[253]

This matter was further considered by the Supreme Court in *The State (Elm Developments Ltd) v. An Bord Pleanála.*[254] A developer sought and obtained a grant of planning permission from a local authority. An appeal was lodged by local residents against the grant of such permission. The developer claimed that failure by the residents to state the grounds of appeal in writing at the actual time of filing a notice of appeal rendered such appeal a nullity in law. The court concluded that the requirement that the grounds of appeal be stated contemporaneously with the notice of appeal was directory rather than mandatory in nature. The purpose of the regulations was informative in nature: the Board was quite entitled to listen to points other than those mentioned in the grounds of appeal. Furthermore, in the instant case grounds of appeal had been furnished to the satisfaction of the Board within a few weeks of the appeal, and Henchy J. concluded that the developer could not say that he had been in any way "wrong-footed or damnified" or that the "spirit or purpose" of the Planning Acts and regulations had been breached. In addition, perhaps the fact that the courts are traditionally less zealous in classifying statutory provisions as mandatory where they have been ignored by a private individual rather than by a public body was also an (unarticulated) factor in this decision (as possibly also occurred in *Alf-A-Bet*). The last point prompts the observation that where it is

---

[253] [1980] I.L.R.M. 64 at 69. In *McDonagh & Sons Ltd v. Galway Corporation* [1995] 1 I.R. 191 the applicant company was wrongly misdescribed on a planning application as the owner, whereas an associated company was, in fact, the true owner. Finlay C.J. (at 202) did not consider that this misdescription affected the validity of the application as it was one:

> "which was not intentional, which did not have the effect of misleading anyone and could not possibly have been in any way to the disadvantage either of the planning authority or of the public who would have the right to object."

For further applications of the *Alf-A-Bet* principles, see *Schwestermann v. An Bord Pleanála* [1994] 3 I.R. 437; *Littondale Ltd v. Wicklow C.C.* [1996] 1 I.L.R.M. 519; *An Blascaod Mór Teo. v. Commissioners of Public Works*, unreported, High Court, December 16, 1996.

[254] [1981] I.L.R.M. 64.

a public body which has fallen down on a failure to observe the requisite statutory procedure, a court is much more likely to require strict compliance: the basis of this tendency is the notion that where the State gives itself (through the Oireachtas) powers which often infringe citizens' rights, it is appropriate that it should be kept to strict adherence to the terms of any conditions attached to the power. By contrast, however the applicant succeeded in his alternative argument in *Elm Developments*. The statutory provisions which required that an appeal to the Board be accompanied by a deposit and be in writing were mandatory:

> "The requirement that the appeal be in writing is so obviously basic to the institution of the appeal that it must be considered to be mandatory. So also must the requirement that the written appeal state the subject-matter of the appeal, for the absence of such identification could lead to administrative confusion. The lodgment of a deposit with the appeal (perhaps not necessarily physically or contemporaneously with the appeal) would also seem to be an essential part of the statutory scheme, so as to discourage frivolous, delaying or otherwise worthless appeals."[255]

The third case is *Rhatigan v. Textiles Y Confecciones Europeas S.A.*[256] The plaintiff challenged the validity of an order made by the Master of the High Court providing for the enforcement of contested English judgments under the terms of the Jurisdiction of Courts and Enforcement of Judgments (European Communities) Act 1988. It was claimed that as the Master's order did not state that the judgments in question were judgments of a Contracting State which was a party to the Convention, it was to that extent invalid. Griffin J. stated that in so far as there was any such requirement, this was governed by national law:

> "The Court must therefore ascertain where the balance of justice lies as between the parties – in other words, it must determine whether the interests of justice require that the plaintiff should be permitted to rely on the breach of the procedural requirements of the Master's order or whether Textiles should be permitted to enforce the order notwithstanding such breach."[257]

On this question, Griffin J. held that the "interests of justice overwhelmingly require that this conflict should be resolved in favour of Textiles." The plaintiff had contested these judgments in the English courts and he could not "have been under the slightest misapprehension" as to the origin of the foreign judgments which were the subject of the enforcement order.

These cases – *Alf-A-Bet*, *Elm Developments* and *Rhatigan* – tend to blur the conventional and traditional distinction between mandatory and directory provisions. The purpose of the conventional mandatory/directory distinction was to ensure that one party could not rely on a minor or technical breach of prescribed statutory requirements in order to invalidate an administrative decision. In practice, this conventional distinction has proved difficult to draw and, increasingly, the courts

---

[255] [1981] I.L.R.M. 108.
[256] [1990] 1 I.R. 126.
[257] *Ibid.* at 136.

seek to examine all the circumstances of the case in order to ascertain whether the disregard of procedural requirements in that particular context has caused real prejudice. If an applicant cannot show that he has been "wrong footed or damnified" by a breach of the prescribed procedure, then either the provisions in question will be classified as directory (so that, in fact, the decision-maker did not act *ultra vires*) or the courts will admit that there was an inadvertent excess of jurisdiction, but will refuse relief on discretionary grounds, since this breach did not prejudice the applicant.[258]

Moreover, the courts seem more prepared to excuse non-compliance on the part of a private litigant than is the case with public bodies. Having stated what appears to be the emerging general principles, it will be convenient if we now consider particular categories.

Legislation promoting fair procedures

Where legislation requires that an administrative or judicial body must follow a set or prescribed procedure before arriving at its decision, non-compliance will usually be fatal to the validity of an order, where the prescribed procedure is designed to ensure compliance with the requirements of a fair hearing. Thus, in *Ahern v. Kerry County Council*,[259] a councillor complained that the local authority had not complied with section 10(1) of the City and County Management (Amendment) Act 1955 in considering the estimates of expenditure for the following year. Section 10(1) requires the authority to consider all estimates of expenditure and Blayney J. held that it was not sufficient compliance for the councillors simply to consider some of the estimates. It followed that the resolution adopting the estimates was invalid, as Blayney J. said: "Once a statute prescribes what is to be done at a meeting . . . what is prescribed must be observed . . . if the resolution that was passed . . . is to be valid."[260] This was buttressed by the fact that section 10(4) expressly contemplated that the local authority might amend the estimates. As Blayney J. said: "It would be impossible to conceive that the local authority could amend the estimate . . . without considering it."[261]

It will be noted that strict compliance with procedural requirements will be insisted on, even – and this is an important point – where those requirements go further than what is required by constitutional justice (as was the case here).[262] A

---

[258] See, *e.g. McNamara v. An Bord Pleanála* [1996] 2 I.L.R.M. 339 where Barr J. said that even if a planning application advertisement had been defective, he would have declined on discretionary grounds to quash the planning permission which had subsequently been granted. There had been a very full oral hearing before a planning inspector and Barr J. was not aware of any who contended that they had been "misled by the advertisement" or who were "inhibited from making his or her case at the appeal on that account." This conclusion is unexceptionable on the facts of this case, as there had been a very full oral hearing with lots of attendant publicity, etc. However, *McNamara* should not be viewed as authority for the proposition that the performance of a statutory requirement imposed for the benefit of the general public could be excused simply because nobody has come forward who claims to have been misled by reason of the breach of the procedural requirement in question: *cf.* the approach of Barrington J. in *Dublin C.C. v. Marren* and p. 451.

[259] [1988] I.L.R.M. 392.

[260] *Ibid.* at 396.

[261] *Ibid.* at 397.

[262] Interestingly, the applicant had also complained that what transpired was also a breach of constitutional justice. But while Blayney J. accepted that the statutory formalities had not been complied

strict view will be taken where the formal procedures are designed to protect fundamental interests such as property rights. Thus, in *Dunraven Estates Ltd v. Commissioners of Public Works*,[263] the Supreme Court held that the defendants were obliged to tender full particulars of their proposed arterial drainage works on the plaintiff's lands, as was required by sections 5 and 6 of the Arterial Drainage Act 1945. As Budd J. observed, the object of these sections was to enable an owner of land "to know precisely what is proposed to be done to his property." If he was not made aware of the proposals, he would not be in a position to make "observations of any worth"[264] on these proposals and his statutory right to do so would be defeated. The Supreme Court accordingly concluded that these provisions were mandatory and must be strictly complied with. Likewise, in *McNeill v. Garda Commissioner*[265] the Supreme Court held that the requirements of Article 8 of the Garda Síochána (Discipline) Regulations 1989 (which states that alleged breaches of disciplinary be investigated as "soon as practicable") were mandatory. The regulations clearly intended, said Hamilton C.J., that such alleged infractions "be dealt with expeditiously and as a matter of urgency." In the light of the lengthy delays that had attended the holding of the disciplinary inquiry, the Court accordingly prohibited the holding of such inquiry.

The converse proposition is also true: if the formal requirements do not affect individual rights and are simply prescribed for the convenience of the authorities and for good administration generally, then they are likely to be classified as directory only. Thus, Finlay P. held in *Cahill v. Governor of Mountjoy Prison*,[266] a case in which this relaxation happened to benefit a public body, that prisoners cannot complain of breaches of the Prison Rules requiring the authorities to furnish Bibles in cells or have a serving medical officer appointed, where these breaches do not in any way imperil his welfare or breach his constitutional rights. In a similar fashion, a Divisional High Court held in *McGlinchey v. Governor of Portlaoise Prison*[267] that the provisions of the Special Criminal Court Rules 1975 giving the court power to determine when and where to sit, etc., were administrative only and did not confer enforceable legal rights on persons coming before that court. *Thompson v. Minister for Social Welfare*[268] is on the other side of the line. Here a social welfare appeals officer sat without the assessors required by section 298(12) of the Social Welfare (Consolidation) Act 1981. This failure to comply with an imperative statutory requirement was sufficient to warrant the quashing of the appeals officer's decision.

---

with, he rejected the suggestion that there had also been a breach of constitutional justice, saying that as the applicant was actually present at the meeting, "it would be difficult to say" that the resolution was passed in breach of constitutional justice. But *cf. Farrell v. South Eastern Health Board* [1991] 2 I.R. 291 at 296 where Barron J. held that actions of the majority of the Board in stifling the applicant from expressing his views at a contentious meeting amounted to a denial of fair procedures, as he "did not get the reasonable opportunity to which he was entitled as a member of the Board to express his views on the motion before the Board."

263 [1974] I.R. 113.
264 *Ibid.* at 134.
265 [1997] 1 I.R. 469.
266 [1980] I.L.R.M. 191.
267 [1988] I.R. 671.
268 [1989] I.R. 618.

Time limits

A large proportion of the cases raising non-compliance with formal requirements occur in the context of time limits. No universal principles can be stated as to the consequences of non-compliance with such time limits, but four guiding principles in relation to time limits were stated as being relevant by Lord Lowry L.C.J. in *Dolan v. O'Hara*.[269] It will be convenient if we examine the case law in the light of these four principles.

> "1. A time limit is likely to be imperative where no power to extend time is given and where no provision is made for what is to happen if the time limit is exceeded."

An example of this principle was given by Henchy J. in *The State (Elm Developments Ltd) v. An Bord Pleanála*[270] where commenting on the 21-day appeal period for appeals prescribed by section 26(5) of the Local Government (Planning and Development) Act 1963, he said:

> "The decision of a planning authority to grant a development permission will become final if an appeal is not lodged within the time fixed by the Act. Since an extension of time is not provided for, the requirement as to time is mandatory, so that a departure from it cannot be excused."[271]

Of course, these are but working principles which, as might be expected, will not cater for every case and will sometimes have to bow to other principles in this series. Thus, in *Irish Refining plc v. Commissioner of Valuation*,[272] the Supreme Court held that a six-month time limit prescribed by section 10 of the Annual Revision of Rateable Property (Ireland) (Amendment) Act 1860 was merely directory, despite the absence of any power to extend the time limit, since a contrary conclusion might produce an injustice. This case is distinguishable from *Elm Developments*: unlike the planning context, where third party rights are vitally concerned, the Irish Refining case did not potentially involve third party rights.

> "2. Requirements in statutes which give jurisdiction are usually imperative."

This principle was illustrated in *Dolan v. O'Hara*[273] itself, where an obligation on the appellant to transmit a case-stated within a 14-day period was held to be mandatory by the Northern Ireland Court of Appeal. Both Lord Lowry L.C.J. and Jones L.J. observed that, as the section itself conferred jurisdiction and as there was no provision for an extension of time, only impossibility could excuse non-compliance with this mandatory provision. This principle has also been applied to other statutory provisions, such as section 26(5) of the Local Government (Planning and Development) Act 1963[274] and section 8 of the Unfair Dismissals Act 1977.[275]

---

269 [1974] N.I. 125.
270 [1981] I.L.R.M. 108.
271 *Ibid.* at 111. See also *McCann v. An Bord Pleanála* [1997] 1 I.L.R.M. 134.
272 [1990] 1 I.R. 568.
273 [1974] N.I. 125.
274 *The State (Elm Developments Ltd) v. An Bord Pleanála* [1981] I.L.R.M. 108; *McCann v. An Bord Pleanála* [1997] 1 I.L.R.M. 314.
275 *The State (I.B.M. Ltd) v. Employment Appeals Tribunal* [1984] I.L.R.M. 31.

"3. Where the act is to be done by a third party for the benefit of a person who will be damnified by non-compliance, the requirement is more likely to be directory."

This principle is well illustrated by several cases raising the issue of the six-month limit for the signature of a case-stated by a District Judge prescribed by rule 17 of the District Court Rules 1955. In *Prendergast v. Porter*,[276] the District Judge had failed to sign the case-stated within this period and the party opposing the case-stated claimed as a result that the appeal was not maintainable. Davitt P. rejected this argument, saying that the time limit was intended simply:

> "to provide a period after which the [Judge] could clearly be said to have neglected or refused to perform his duty. It never could have been the intention to deprive a party of his right of appeal by way of case-stated."[277]

In *McMahon v. McClafferty*[278] Costello J. took a similar view, saying that Rule 55 was not mandatory and he held that a District Judge could sign the case-stated after the six-month limit. Another example is afforded by the judgment of the Supreme Court in *Irish Refining plc v. Commissioner of Valuation*,[279] where the Circuit Court judge had not signed the case-stated within the 21-day period prescribed by section 10 of the Annual Revision of Rateable Property (Ireland) (Amendment) Act 1860. Finlay C.J. held that the provision was directory only, since any contrary interpretation would mean that the person applying for the case-stated:

> "Would be entirely at the mercy of the judge concerned and that, for practical purposes, it would be impossible for him, under a number of different hypothetical circumstances, such as the absence from the country on vacation or illness of the judge, to prosecute his appeal by way of case-stated. Such a manifestly unfair or unjust procedure should not, in my view, be assumed to have been the real intention of the legislature."[280]

> "4. Impossibility may excuse non-compliance even where the requirement is imperative."

Clearly the courts will not readily countenance arguments such as impossibility or *force majeure* in the face of imperative statutory provisions, so it is hardly surprising that there are few authorities on this point. However, it does seem that this principle may apply where it has proved impossible to effect service on the other side within the requisite period or where every effort has been made to comply with the statutory provisions. In *Veterinary Council v. Corr*,[281] for example, the appellants attempted to serve a case-stated on the respondents on the last day permitted by the legislation, but found that the offices had closed. This was held by the Supreme Court to be a

---

276   [1961] I.R. 440.
277   *Ibid.* at 441–442.
278   [1989] I.R. 68.
279   [1990] 1 I.R. 568.
280   *Ibid.* at 577.
281   [1953] I.R. 12. See also *Attorney General v. Wallace*, unreported, High Court, June 18, 1996 (non-availability of District Judge excused non-compliance with obligation to bring the applicant before the court as soon as practicable).

sufficient compliance with the (mandatory) statutory requirements. On the other hand, in *McCann v. An Bord Pleanála*[282] (a case where, through a misunderstanding, a planning appeal was received a day late) Lavan J. distinguished *Corr* as inapplicable on the ground that in that case "it was possible to achieve compliance which was substantial but nonetheless incomplete."[283]

Where non-compliance might affect third-party rights or the rights of the public

Where the non-compliance might affect third-party rights or the rights of the general public, then the provisions will generally be regarded as mandatory and the courts will be even more reluctant to excuse anything less than full and precise compliance with the statutory requirements. This is especially true of statutory requirements contained in planning, licensing and other regulatory legislation designed to protect the participation or other rights of third parties and the general public.

In *Monaghan U.D.C. v. Alf-A-Bet Promotions Ltd*[284] the plaintiffs (who claimed to have secured planning permission by default under section 26(4) of the Local Government (Planning and Development) Act 1963) had failed – whether by inadvertence or otherwise – to state the true nature of the proposed development in their advertisement in the local newspapers, as required by Article 14 of the Local Government (Planning and Development) Regulations 1977.[285] The Supreme Court held that the application was invalid, as the plaintiffs had not sufficiently complied with a mandatory provision. As Henchy J. observed:

> "One of the primary purposes of the notification [in the newspaper] is defeated if the notice does not, at least in fair and general terms, state the nature and extent of the proposed development. Whether the unilluminating words used in this case ("alterations and reconstructions") were chosen deliberately for their vagueness or casually through inattention to the stated requirements of the regulations, they were so wanting in compliance with the spirit and purpose of the Act and the regulations, that the published notice, and therefore the application, must be deemed to have been nullified. Such powers as have been given to planning authorities, tribunals or the courts to operate or review the operation of the planning laws should be exercised in such a way that the statutory intent in its essence will not be defeated, intentionally or unintentionally, by omissions, ambiguities, misstatements or other defaults in the purported compliance with the prescribed procedures."[286]

---

[282] [1997] 1 I.L.R.M. 134.

[283] For an even stricter approach, see also *Graves v. An Bord Pleanála* [1997] 2 I.R. 405 discussed below at pp. 451–452.

[284] [1980] I.L.R.M. 64. See Cooney (1982) 17 *Irish Jurist* 346 and Scannell, "Planning Control: Twenty Years On" (1982) 4 D.U.L.J. (N.S.) 41. See also, *Dunne Ltd v. Dublin C.C.* [1974] I.R. 45; *McCabe v. Harding Investments Ltd* [1984] I.L.R.M. 105 and *The State (Multi-Print Labels Ltd) v. Employment Appeals Tribunal* [1984] I.L.R.M. 545.

[285] See now Articles 18–23 of the Local Government (Planning and Development) Regulations 1994 (S.I. No. 86 of 1994).

[286] [1980] I.L.R.M. 64 at 69. See also *The State (Toft) v. Galway Corporation* [1981] I.L.R.M. 439 (no certiorari to quash planning permission granted to a company which had been innocently misdescribed in the planning application); *Schwestermann v. An Bord Pleanála* [1994] 3 I.R. 437; *Littondale Ltd v. Wicklow County Council* [1997] 1 I.L.R.M. 519 (similar principles).

The courts' insistence on strict compliance with mandatory provisions where the interests of the public might be affected is also illustrated by *Dublin County Council v. Marren.*[287] The issue in this case was whether an applicant for planning permission had complied adequately with the relevant regulations which require the submission of such plans, drawings and other particulars as are necessary "to identify the land and to describe the work or structure to which the application relates." The applicant had previously applied unsuccessfully for planning permission in respect of certain premises. He made a fresh application some years later, but on this occasion he omitted to include details of plans and drawings. The reasons for this omission were, however, contained in the application itself, where he stated that the house plans were to be the same as in the previous application. While Barrington J. took the view that the planning officials were not in any way incommoded or prejudiced by this failure to comply precisely with the terms of the regulations, he observed that this was not simply a matter of *inter partes*. If it had been, he would have ruled that there had been substantial compliance and that any non-compliance was covered by the *de minimis* principle. But it was not simply an *inter partes* matter, as the relevant regulations contemplated that the application, together with the plans, drawings, etc., would be made available to the public. As it was possible that a member of the public might have been misled or incommoded by the failure to include the relevant drawings and plans, Barrington J. ruled that there had not been adequate compliance with the regulations.[288]

An even stricter approach may be taken where the Oireachtas has "prescribed very carefully the procedure which has to be followed" in any particular case: *Graves v. An Bord Pleanála.*[289] In this case, a Cork-based firm of solicitors sought to appeal on behalf of their client against a decision of a planning authority and the final day for receipt of the appeal fell on a Monday. Their agent duly lodged the appropriate papers with a security guard (who was not, however, an employee of the Board) over the previous weekend at a time when the Board's offices were closed. While the Board

---

[287] [1985] I.L.R.M. 593. See also, *R. (Byrne) v. Dublin JJ.* [1904] 2 I.R. 190 (21–day notice in Licensing Acts held to be mandatory, as otherwise "there might be frequent disputes as to whether the notice was given within a reasonable time or not", thus prejudicing the interests of the members of the public who might otherwise wish to lodge an objection in licensing matters).

[288] For an example of a purely *inter partes* matter in this context, see *The State (I.B.M. (Ireland) Ltd) v. Employment Appeals Tribunal* [1984] I.L.R.M. 31. The stance adopted in *Alf-A-Bet* and *Marren* may be contrasted with that of Lavan J. in *Cunningham v. An Bord Pleanála*, unreported, High Court, May 3, 1990. In that case a planning notice had failed to recite that the proposal involved the demolition of habitable houses, an omission which Lavan J. considered did not satisfy Henchy J.'s *Alf-A-Bet* test of being "trivial, technical, peripheral or insubstantial." However, this did not determine the matter, as Lavan J. found that (i) the planning authorities were not misled by any omission and (ii) the objectors had led the developers to believe "that they [the developers] had dealt with or defeated all of the objections which were likely to be put in their path." Of course, the objection remains that other potential members of the public might have been misled by such omission, but would it have been fair to grant judicial review to an applicant in such circumstances? In this regard, see *Dooley v. Galway County Council*, unreported, High Court, February 4, 1992 where Denham J. held that a planning application did not adequately comply with the requirements of the planning regulations where only the name of the townland to describe the location of the proposed development had been used:

"when there are 18 townlands of the same name in the country [and the application] does not give ready and reasonable identifiable notice to the public of the location of the land."

[289] [1997] 2 I.R. 205.

duly received the documents on the Monday, Kelly J. accepted that as the appeal had not been left "with an employee of the Board at the offices of the Board during office hours" as required by s.4(5)(b) of the Local Government (Planning and Development) Act 1992, it was invalid. The sub-section had very carefully prescribed the procedures to be followed in order to make a valid appeal and:

> "To permit of a departure from that procedure would not merely run counter to the statutory procedure but would, in my view, introduce an element of uncertainty into a procedure which must be construed strictly and rigidly so as to ensure certainty and the protection of third party rights."

While Kelly J. is correct regarding the necessity for legal certainty and the protection of the third party, yet it must be queried whether these objectives would have been compromised were *Graves* to have been decided differently. At all events, *Graves* must be regarded as a special case, turning on the provisions of a particular – and, it might be thought, an unnecessarily rigid – statutory regime.

On the other hand, as is evidenced by another decision of the same judge, the requirements as to compliance are not always interpreted with particular strictness, even in planning cases. In *Blessington & District Community Council Ltd v. Wicklow County Council*[290] the applicants sought leave to challenge the validity of the grant of planning permission on the grounds, *inter alia*, that the grantee had described itself as "Aosog Centres" instead of "Aosog Centres Limited." Kelly J. did not regard that lacuna as fatal to the grant of permission, saying that it was difficult to see how any member of the public might have been prejudiced thereby and that it was so "insubstantial and technical as not to warrant" judicial intervention. A further issue concerned the mis-description of the current user of the premises as being that of an outdoor youth centre. While the applicants had never received planning permission for this user, the premises had been thus used for more than ten years and could no longer be the subject of enforcement proceedings. While Kelly J. accepted that the user remained unauthorised, he was again satisfied that the misdescription did not affect the validity of the planning application:

> ". . . if the original use were mentioned in the advertisement, it ran the risk of being misleading because it would not be a fair or accurate reflection of the de facto situation which had obtained for in excess of ten years . . . I think that there was a greater risk of the public being misled if the advertisement had made mention of the original authorised use [so that the criticism of the misdescription is] excessively technical."[291]

7. Waiver and Consent

The fundamental rule is that waiver and consent cannot confer jurisdiction. However, as shall be seen, the exceptions are as prevalent as the holes in Gruyère cheese. In any case, the rule – since it is grounded on the fundamental public policy that a

---

[290] [1997] 1 I.R. 273.
[291] *Ibid.* at 282.

jurisdiction laid down by statute for the good of the community and cannot be altered – applies, irrespective of whether the waiver emanates from the public body or the private individual affected. The precept as it applies in cases where the waiver comes from the public body will be further considered in the context of legitimate expectations in a later chapter.[292] In the present chapter, the issue is how the principle with its many exceptions applies where the waiver emanates from the private individual affected. The doctrines of waiver, acquiescence and estoppel by conduct represent in varying degrees the idea that a plaintiff cannot approbate and reprobate. It has been stated that it would be inconsistent with the due administration of justice if a plaintiff "were allowed to reserve unto himself the right to argue later a point touching on the validity of a decision," should that decision prove adverse to his interests.[293]

The traditional rule has been put in the following terms by Lord Reid:

> "[I]t is a fundamental principle that no consent can confer on a court or tribunal with limited statutory jurisdiction any power to act beyond that jurisdiction, or can estop the consenting party from subsequently maintaining that such court or tribunal lacks jurisdiction."[294]

Irish courts have been reluctant, however, to commit themselves unequivocally to such a position.[295] Nevertheless in the leading case, *Corrigan v. Irish Land Commission*,[296] Henchy J. acknowledged that a totally new jurisdiction[297] could not be created by means of an estoppel. The crucial test was whether the court or tribunal had initiated jurisdiction to enter upon the inquiry. For once such jurisdiction was present, any errors committed in the course of the inquiry could be waived. In *Corrigan*, itself, it was clear that the Appeals Tribunal of the Land Commission plainly had jurisdiction to hear the plaintiff's appeal. The question was whether two particular lay commissioners were debarred from exercising that jurisdiction by reason of their prior dealing with the case. Henchy J. found that that point could be, and indeed had been, waived by the plaintiff when he accepted the tribunal as he found it composed on the day of the hearing.

---

292 See p. 861.
293 *Corrigan v. Irish Land Commission* [1977] I.R. 317 at 325, *per* Henchy J. But see *The State (Gallagher, Shatter & Co.) v. de Valera* [1986] I.L.R.M. 3 where a solicitor's firm permitted a taxation of costs to proceed while maintaining an objection as to the Taxing Master's jurisdiction. The Supreme Court, *per* McCarthy J., held that there had been no waiver of jurisdictional objection:
> "[I]t does not appear to me that justice is served by determining a case of this kind against a solicitor because, whilst maintaining his objection, he thought it more practicable to allow the taxation to proceed, in the hope that the result would, in any event, be satisfactory. When, far from being short of satisfactory, it held him guilty of making a gross overcharge, in my view he is not to be defeated by a plea of waiver"
([1986] I.L.R.M. at 9).
294 *Essex Incorporated Church Union v. Essex C.C.* [1963] A.C. 808. See also, *The State (Byrne) v. Frawley* [1978] I.R. 326 at 342, *per* O'Higgins C.J.
295 *The State (Byrne) v. Frawley* [1978] I.R. 326; *Corrigan v. Irish Land Commission* [1977] I.R. 317 and *The State (Cronin) v. Circuit Judge for the Western Circuit* [1937] I.R. 34.
296 [1977] I.R. 317. See also, unreported, *Re Creighton's Estate*, High Court, March 5, 1982; *The State (Grahame) v. Racing Board*, unreported, High Court, November 22, 1983.
297 The word "jurisdiction" is used by Henchy J. in the restrictive sense of "jurisdiction to enter upon an inquiry." Contrast this with his judgment in *The State (Holland) v. Kennedy* [1977] I.R. 193 where the judge stated that a tribunal which had jurisdiction at the start of an inquiry could lose that jurisdiction for any number of reasons.

In other cases, waiver and estoppel have been regarded as a bar to discretionary relief. In *R. (Kildare C.C.) v. Commissioner for Valuation*[298] the applicants sought to quash a revised valuation order made on appeal by a County Court. The applicants had allowed the appeal to proceed on the basis that there was jurisdiction in the County Court to revise the valuation: it was only when the decision of the Court did not prove as favourable to their interests as they had expected that they sought to question the jurisdiction of the tribunal. The former Irish Court of Appeal agreed that the adjudication of the County Court was *ultra vires*, but held nevertheless that the applicants were precluded by their conduct from obtaining the relief sought. A similar conclusion was reached in *The State (Byrne) v. Frawley*[299] where the Supreme Court held that the applicant by his conduct had approbated a jury selected in an unconstitutional fashion. He could not now be heard to say that the jury lacked competence to try him.[300]

It is sometimes difficult to know whether given behaviour actually constitutes a waiver. A litigant will generally be deemed to have waived objections based on the composition of a tribunal[301] or the procedure adopted if the jurisdictional question is not raised at the appropriate time in the proceedings. Persons who attend court hearings are deemed to have waived any possible irregularities which might exist.[302] In one case,[303] the applicant attended petty sessions and participated in the case to the extent of asking for an adjournment on a number of occasions. It was decided that he was deemed to have waived any possible irregularity, and that he had estopped himself by his conduct from obtaining certiorari. The Supreme Court ruled to like effect in *Re Tynan*,[304] where the applicant had sought an order of prohibition restraining the District Court from dealing with an allegedly irregular summons. In the opinion of Walsh J. the conduct of the applicant in appearing at the District Court, his giving of evidence, and his failure to raise prompt objection were all consistent with the inference that he had waived the point.

8. Statutory Restriction of Judicial Review

Full ouster clauses

The courts have never looked favourably on legislative attempts to curb the High Court's supervisory jurisdiction over decisions of lower courts and administrative

---

[298] [1901] 2 I.R. 215. See also, *The State (McKay) v. Cork Circuit Judge* [1937] I.R. 650; *The State (Cronin) v. Circuit Judge for Western Circuit* [1937] I.R. 34; *R. (Dorris) v. Ministry of Health* [1954] N.I. 79.

[299] [1978] I.R. 326. See also, *Whelan v. R.* [1921] 1 I.R. 310. For cases where the plea of waiver was disallowed, see *The State (Redmond) v. Wexford Corporation* [1946] I.R. 409; *The State (Cole) v. Labour Court* (1984) 3 J.I.S.L.L. 128; *The State (Gallagher, Shatter & Co.) v. de Valera* [1986] I.L.R.M. 3 and *Browne v. An Bord Pleanála* [1991] 2 I.R. 209

[300] But *cf.* the comments of Moriarty J. in *Meagher v. Judge O'Leary* [1998] 1 I.L.R.M. 211 that "if a penal statutory provision that is applicable to particular facts is found repugnant to the Constitution, the consequences *inter partes* must not be negatived by reason of how those parties have conducted themselves procedurally."

[301] *Corrigan v. Irish Land Commission* [1977] I.R. 317.

[302] *Whelan v. R.* [1921] 1 I.R. 310; *The State (Grahame) v. Racing Board*, unreported, High Court, November 22, 1983.

[303] *R. (Sherlock) v. Cork JJ.* (1909) 42 I.L.T.R. 247.

[304] [1969] I.R. 1. See also, *Moore v. Gamgee* (1890) 25 Q.B.D. 244.

bodies.[305] Even at common law, both the High Court[306] and the Supreme Court[307] when confronted with widely-drafted statutory[308] ouster clauses have affirmed on many occasions that such clauses will not protect a decision which is *ultra vires*. However, it does seem that an ouster clause will have the limited effect of preventing the High Court from granting certiorari where the alleged defect is a non-jurisdictional error of law only.[309]

More fundamentally, the constitutionality of legislative attempts to oust the High Court's power of review must be doubtful in light of the decision of the Supreme Court in *Tormey v. Attorney-General*.[310] In that case Henchy J. observed that while Article 34.3.1°, when read in conjunction with Article 34.3.4° and Article 37,[311] permitted the Oireachtas to vest lower courts or administrative tribunals with exclusive jurisdiction in respect of certain justiciable controversies, but where this had been done:

> "[The] full jurisdiction [of the High Court] is there to be invoked – in proceedings such as habeas corpus, certiorari, prohibition, quo warranto, injunction or declaratory action – so as to ensure that the hearing and determination will be in accordance with law. Save to the extent required by the terms of the Constitution itself, no justiciable matter may be excluded from the range of the original jurisdiction of the High Court."[312]

This is a clear indication that legislative ouster clauses are unconstitutional, at least where the lower court or tribunal has been vested with exclusive jurisdiction to determine particular justiciable controversies.[313]

---

305 "[T]he courts should be reluctant to surrender their inherent right to enter on a question of what are prima facie justiciable matters", *per* Henchy J. in *The State (Pine Valley Developments Ltd) v. Dublin County Council* [1984] I.R. 417 at 426. And see the strict manner in which the Supreme Court has construed such clauses in cases such as *Pine Valley*; *The State (Finglas Industrial Estates Ltd) v. Dublin County Council*, February 17, 1983 and *KSK Enterprises Ltd v. An Bord Pleanála* [1994] 2 I.R. 128. The courts have declined to apply such clauses retrospectively, as to do so would unconstitutionally infringe on vested rights: see *Child v. Wicklow County Council* [1995] 2 I.R. 447.

306 *The State (O'Duffy) v. Bennett* [1935] I.R. 70; *The State (Hughes) v. Lennon* [1935] I.R. 128; *Murren v. Brennan* [1942] I.R. 466 and *The State (Horgan) v. Exported Livestock Board Ltd* [1943] I.R. 581. See also, *R. (Conyngham) v. Pharmaceutical Society of Ireland* [1899] 2 I.R. 132; *Commissioners of Public Works v. Monaghan* [1909] 2 I.R. 718; *R. (Sinnott) v. Wexford Corporation* [1910] 2 I.R. 403 and *Waterford Corporation v. Murphy* [1920] 2 I.R. 165.

307 *The State (McCarthy) v. O'Donnell* [1945] I.R. 126; *Brannigan v. Keady* [1959] I.R. 283 (semble). This was also the attitude of the House of Lords: see *Anisminic Ltd v. Foreign Compensation Commission* [1969] 2 A.C. 147. But a different attitude prevails in the case of clauses imposing brief limitation periods: *R. v. Environment Secretary, ex p. Ostler* [1977] Q.B. 122; *Inver Resources Ltd v. Limerick Corporation* [1988] I.L.R.M. 47.

308 This reasoning applies *a fortiori* to non-statutory ouster clauses. In *Casey v. Minister for Agriculture*, unreported, High Court, February 6, 1987, McCarthy J. held that a provision of the (non-statutory) Bovine Brucellosis Eradication Scheme which had stipulated that the Minister's decision was "final" meant "final" only in the administrative sense: it could not exclude the supervisory jurisdiction of the High Court.

309 *R. v. Medical Appeal Tribunal, ex p. Gilmore* [1957] 1 Q.B. 574. But in *Gilmore* it was decided that the court may still intervene to quash for error of law on the face of the record even where the tribunal's decision is expressed to be "final."

310 [1985] I.R. 289.

311 Art. 34.3.1° vests the High Court with "full original jurisdiction" in respect of all matters and questions "whether of fact or law, civil or criminal." Art. 34.3.4° goes on to permit the Oireachtas to establish courts of "local and limited jurisdiction" and Art. 37 enables tribunals to exercise judicial functions of a limited nature in non-criminal matters.

312 [1985] I.R. 289 at 296–297.

313 See also, *Re Loftus Bryan's Estate* [1942] I.R. 185 and *O'Doherty v. Att.-Gen.* [1941] I.R. 569.

Partial ouster clauses: brief limitation periods

Legislative provisions which, instead of attempting to effect a complete ouster of the High Court's supervisory jurisdiction, purport to impose brief limitation periods on the right to seek judicial review may stand on a different footing. While there is a definite (and prudent) trend away from complete ouster clauses on the part of the parliamentary draftsman, recent legislation has seen the enactment of some important partial ouster clauses. Partial ouster clauses (which generally take the form of very short limitation periods) may be defended – at least, in some cases – on the ground that, in the case of certain types of administrative decisions, there is an overwhelming need for a swift determination and finality.[314]

The most important clause of this kind is section 82(3A) of the Local Government (Planning and Development) Act 1963,[315] which provides for a two-month time limit in any case where it is sought to challenge a decision of a planning authority or An Bord Pleanála. Any such application must be brought by way of judicial review[316] on notice to the planning authority or An Bord Pleanála (as the case may be), the developer and other interested parties. The two-month time period is absolute, but proof that "a notice of motion grounded as is provided in 0.84 has been filed in the High Court and it has been served on all the mandatory parties provided for in the sub-section" constitutes adequate compliance with the requirements of the sub-section.[317]

The question arises as to the constitutionality of this provision, especially where there is no judicial discretion to cater for "hard cases", such as where the applicant had no means of knowing of the facts giving rise to the application for judicial review until the time period had elapsed. In *Brady v. Donegal County Council*[318] Costello J. found this provision to be unconstitutional at any rate in its present unqualified form while his decision was set aside by the Supreme Court on factual grounds[319] (and not on the merits), his reasoning casts considerable doubt on the validity of this subsection (and, indeed, by implication, other unqualified time bars of this kind). In this case, it appeared that the advertisement placed by the applicant

---

[314] As Finlay C.J. said in *KSK Enterprises Ltd v. An Bord Pleanála* [1994] 2 I.R. 128 at 135:
    "... it is clear that the intention of the legislature was greatly to confine the opportunity of persons to impugn by way of judicial review decisions made by the planning authorities and, in particular, one must assume that it was intended that a person who has obtained a planning permission should at a very short interval after the date of such decision in the absence of a judicial review be entirely legally protected against subsequent challenge to the decision that was made and therefore presumably left in a position to act with safety upon the basis of that decision."
    See also to like effect the comments of Costello J. in *Brady v. Donegal County Council* [1989] I.L.R.M. 282 at 289 and Kelly J. in *Ní Éilí v. Environmental Protection Agency* [1997] 2 I.L.R.M. 458 at 464 (in the latter case concerning the analogous (but not identical) two-month limitation period prescribed by s.85(8) of the Environmental Protection Agency Act 1992).
[315] As inserted by Local Government (Planning and Development) Act 1992, s.19(3).
[316] Section 82(3A). See further at pp. 794–797.
[317] *KSK Enterprises Ltd v. An Bord Pleanála* [1994] 2 I.R. 128 at 137, *per* Finlay C.J.
[318] [1989] I.L.R.M. 282.
[319] Costello J. had not reached a final determination as to whether the planning notice itself was invalid. The Supreme Court pointed out, however, that if the facts were such that it was valid, then the applicants' challenge to the validity of the permission would fall *in limine* and there would be no need for the courts to pronounce on the constitutionality of s.82(3A) of the 1963 Act. The finding of unconstitutionality was therefore vacated and the matter remitted back to the High Court. The case appears to have proceeded no further.

for planning permission had not been published in a newspaper circulating in the area, as required by Article 14 of the 1977 Planning Regulations. Some neighbours sought to quash this permission, but found that they were a few days out of time to challenge its validity. On the basis of these assumed facts, Costello J. concluded that the subsection was unconstitutional. It is noteworthy that this conclusion was grounded not on Article 34.3.1° or Article 34.1 but rather on the notion that the sub-section amounted to an impermissible invasion of the neighbours' property rights, contrary to Article 40.3.2° (which could have a narrowing effect on the scope of the authority as a precedent):

> "If the plaintiff's ignorance of his own rights during the short limitation period is caused by the defendant's own wrong-doing and the law still imposes an absolute bar unaccompanied by any judicial discretion to raise it, there must be very compelling reasons indeed to justify such a rigorous limitation on the exercise of a constitutionally protected right. The public interest in the establishment at an early date of certainty in the development decisions of planning authoritiescould well justify the imposition of stringent time limits for the institution of court proceedings. Certainly the public interest would not be quite as well served by a law with the suggested saver as by the present law, but the loss of the public interest by the proposed modification would be slight while the gain in the protection of the plaintiff's constitutionally protected rights would be very considerable. I conclude, therefore, that the present serious restriction on the exercise of the plaintiff's constitutional rights imposed by the two-month limitation period cannot reasonably be justified."[320]

This reasoning would also seem to apply *a fortiori* to cases of permission obtained in bad faith or, even, perhaps, where the requirements of the 1994 Regulations were manifestly disregarded.[321]

The unqualified nature of the two month rule prescribed by the 1963 Act may be contrasted with the even shorter time period of seven days prescribed by s.13(3)(a) of the Irish Takeover Panel Act 1997 in the case of challenges (which must be brought by way of judicial review) to decisions or rulings of the Takeover Panel. This very short time period is understandable given the need for certainty and finality of decisions in takeovers and mergers, but its rigour is tempered by the provisions of section 13(5) which enables the High Court to extend time if it is satisfied that the following conditions are satisfied:

---

[320] [1989] I.L.R.M. 282 at 288–289. Perhaps some of the force of this reasoning has been diluted by the subsequent decisions in *Hegarty v. O'Loughran* [1990] 1 I.R. 148 and *Tuohy v. Courtney* [1994] 3 I.R. 1. In the former case the Supreme Court inclined to the view that a similarly unqualified three-year time limit for personal injuries prescribed by s.11(2)(b) of the Statute of Limitations 1957 was not unconstitutional and in the latter case actually upheld the constitutionality of the six-year time limit for non-personal injuries contained in s.11(2)(a) of the 1957 Act.

[321] Note that at present the language of s.82(3A) is such as it would appear to bar even challenges resting on bad faith or other serious flaws in the decision-making process: see, *e.g. Inver Resources Ltd v. Limerick Corporation* [1988] I.L.R.M. 47. Here a planning permission had been granted to a non-existent company, but Barron J. held that this absence of jurisdiction could not now be questioned by reason of the fact that the application for judicial review was made outside the (original pre-1992 version of the) two-month period. While the applicant company was non-existent, the application for permission had been in reality made on behalf of its principal shareholder and Barron J. was satisfied that the application "had substance or reality."

"(a) the failure by the applicant for the extension to make such an application for leave within the period aforesaid was not due to any neglect or default of that person or any person acting on his or her behalf, and

(b) the extension of the period aforesaid would not result in an injustice being done to any other person concerned in this matter and for this purpose the Court shall have regard to –

(i) where appropriate, the length of time that has elapsed since any takeover or other relevant transaction to which the rule, derogation, waiver, ruling or direction the subject of the intended application for leave, relates, or any step of a substantial nature in the effecting of such a takeover or other relevant transaction, has been completed,

(ii) the nature of the relief that could ultimately be granted to the applicant for an extension on an application for judicial review. . . ."

While rigid time limits have their attractiveness especially in circumstances where certainty is almost everything, the existence of a discretionary jurisdiction to extend time within certain narrow confines seems, on the whole, preferable. Certainly, the balance struck between access to the court and legal certainty by the 1997 Takeover Panel Act seems more in harmony with the approach of Costello J. in *Brady* than the rigid cut off period now prescribed by the 1963 Act (as amended by the 1992 Act).

Conclusive evidence provisions: indirect exclusion of judicial review[322]

These constitutional developments not only call into question the validity of "no certiorari" clauses, but also the many other statutory provisions which seek to exclude or restrict judicial review, indirectly, by providing that an administrative decision shall be "conclusive evidence" of the existence of certain facts or of the status of specified legal entities. Some important, miscellaneous examples of this legislative device include: section 2(1) of the Trade Union Act 1913[323] (which provides that the certificate of the Registrar of Friendly Societies is conclusive evidence of the status of a trade union); section 19(4) of the Offences Against the State Act 1939[324] (which provides that a Government suppression order under section 18 of that Act shall be conclusive evidence of the fact that the suppressed organisation is unlawful); section 104 of the Companies Act 1963[325] (which provides that the Registrar of Companies' certificate that a particular charge has complied with the registration requirements of Part IV of the 1963 Act shall be conclusive evidence of this fact); and, finally, section 31(1) of the Registration of Title Act 1964[326] (which states that the register shall be "conclusive evidence" of title, subject to the right of the Circuit or High Court to order rectification of the register on the grounds of actual fraud or mistake).

---

[322] For an excellent analysis of this topic, see Pye, "The Section 104 Certificate of Registration – An Impenetrable Shield No More?" (1985) 3 I.L.T. 213. See also, Hogan, "Reflections on the Supreme Court's decision in *Tormey v. Attorney-General*" (1986) 8 D.U.L.J. 31.

[323] See Kerr and Whyte, *Irish Trade Union Law* (1985), pp. 42–48 where the constitutionality of this and other similar conclusive evidence clauses is discussed.

[324] See Hogan and Walker, *Political Violence and the Law in Ireland* (1989) at pp. 245–248.

[325] Ussher, *Company Law in Ireland* (1986), pp. 467–471.

[326] Wylie, *Irish Land Law* (3rd ed., 1997).

It is true that in *Lombard & Ulster Banking Ltd v. Amurec Ltd*[327] a charge had been registered some 17 months after its actual creation. While the charge had been left undated at the date of its creation, a much later date was inserted shortly before it was submitted for registration to the Companies Office. Hamilton J. held that the validity of this charge could not now be challenged by a liquidator, as this was prohibited by the conclusive evidence provisions of section 104. The judge drew attention to the importance – from a commercial point of view – of the finality of the register, a factor which also weighed heavily with the English Court of Appeal in *R. v. Registrar of Companies, ex p. Central Bank of India*,[328] where the equivalent clause in the English Companies Act was held to preclude judicial review.

There would seem, however, to be a real risk that such "conclusive evidence" will be held either to be unconstitutional or otherwise ineffective, at least in certain types of cases. In *Maher v. Attorney-General*[329] the Supreme Court held that a "conclusive evidence" clause contained in the Road Traffic Act 1968 was unconstitutional, as it attempted to oust the jurisdiction of the courts to determine an essential ingredient (alcohol levels) of a criminal prosecution. Similar thinking prevailed with the European Court of Justice in *Johnston v. Chief Constable of the Royal Ulster Constabulary*,[330] where a "conclusive evidence" certificate issued by the Chief Constable pursuant to the provisions of Article 53(2) of the Sex Discrimination (Northern Ireland) Order 1976 purported to establish that the conditions for derogating from the equal treatment directive had been satisfied. The court held that such a clause was contrary to the "principle of effective judicial control," which itself "reflects a general principle of law which underlies the constitutional traditions common to the member states" and was therefore ineffective. All of this would seem to point to one of two conclusions. Either the "conclusive evidence" does not preclude judicial review, or, should it do so, it is unconstitutional as inconsistent with the High Court's full original jurisdiction under Article 34.3.1°.

The only judgment directly on this issue, however, points in the other direction. In *Sloan v. Special Criminal Court*[331] the applicant challenged the validity of section 19(4) of the Offences against the State Act 1939, in so far as it provided that a suppression order made by the Government shall be "conclusive evidence" of the suppressed organisation's illegality. Costello J. could not accept this submission, saying that:

> "If an order is made under section 19(4), then the justiciable dispute is whether an accused is a member of an illegal organisation and not whether the organisation itself is illegal."[332]

It may be thought, however, that this analysis is incomplete and does not cater for the case where the accused admits membership of the suppressed organisation, but

---

[327] (1978) 112 I.L.T.R. 1.
[328] [1986] Q.B. 1114.
[329] [1973] I.R. 140. Though admittedly in this case the decision depended upon the particular circumstances that a court was involved (since the main part of the case concerned a criminal trial) and, hence, Art. 34.1 and the separation of powers were engaged.
[330] Case 222/84, [1986] E.C.R. 1651.
[331] [1993] 3 I.R. 528.
[332] *Ibid.* at 532.

says that, by virtue of the changed circumstances of the organisation, it should no longer be regarded as illegal. The effect of the "conclusive evidence" provision of section 19(4) is that the accused is not permitted to raise this argument, yet (were it not for this purported statutory ouster) the justiciable controversy would be whether the organisation had, in fact, illegal objectives. Accordingly, it is difficult to see how this type of statutory provision (assuming it precludes judicial review) would survive constitutional challenge either on the ground that it infringes the High Court's full original jurisdiction as conferred by Article 34.3.1° (as this provision was interpreted in *Tormey v. Ireland*)[333] or that (following *Maher*) it constitutes an impermissible invasion of the judicial domain, which is protected by Article 34.1. Despite the remarks of Costello J. in *Sloan*, it remains to be seen, therefore, whether this form of "conclusive evidence" provision will survive future challenges.

9. Invalidity

General principles

As a general rule – which is subject to major exceptions – *ultra vires* decisions are null and void and have no legal consequences. The one important Irish case where there was an extended discussion of the nature of invalidity, *Murphy v. Attorney General*, [334] arose in the special context of constitutional law, but a majority of the Supreme Court had little difficulty in holding that legislation (and, by implication, *ultra vires* administrative acts) found to be unconstitutional must be deemed to be void *ab initio*. Henchy J. described this principle as one which was "inherent in the nature of such limited powers."[335] Another graphic example of the application of this principle is provided by *Shelley v. Mahon*,[336] where the Supreme Court held that a criminal conviction imposed by a person who was not a duly appointed District Judge was void and had been arrived at in breach of the applicant's constitutional rights. In this case, the irregularity had occurred because of an oversight as to the respondent's date of birth. (The Courts Act (No. 2) 1988[337] had been passed with a view to curing this flaw retrospectively, although the Supreme Court found it was ineffective for this purpose.) As a result, thousands of judicial decisions were liable to be set aside. Indeed, in a subsequent case, *Glavin v. Governor of the Training Unit, Mountjoy Prison*,[338] a conviction in the Circuit Court for robbery was quashed some four years later, since the return for trial to the Circuit Court had been made by Mr. Mahon at a time when he was not a qualified District Judge. Finally, in *Mallon v. Minister for Agriculture & Food*[339] the Supreme Court was required to examine the legal status of an (unconstitutional) purported amendment of 1988

---

[333] [1985] I.R. 289.
[334] [1982] I.R. 241.
[335] *Ibid.* at 309–310.
[336] [1990] 1 I.R. 36.
[337] See Hogan, (1988) I.C.L.S.A. 34–01.
[338] [1991] 2 I.R. 241.
[339] [1996] 1 I.R. 517.

regulations by subsequent regulations in 1990. The 1988 regulations provided for a one years' maximum prison sentence for certain offences, but the 1990 amendments purported to increase this period to two years. This amendment was held to be unconstitutional (as it provided for the summary trial of a non-minor offence contrary to Article 38.2), but, crucially, the Supreme Court held it to be invalid *ab initio* , so that it "never had the force of law and was ineffective to amend" the earlier 1988 Regulations,[340] with the result that the charges based on the 1988 Regulations could proceed as if they had not been amended by the (void) 1990 Regulations.[341]

The cases described so far have concerned laws which have been held to be unconstitutional. The conventional view is that a similar principle and exceptions (considered below) apply to both this situation and the case of an administrative action (or, for that matter, delegated legislation) held to be *ultra vires* a statute. This assumption is borne out by the sequel to *Gilmer v. Incorporated Law Society of Ireland*,[342] when the Education Committee of the Incorporated Law Society was found to have unwittingly acted *ultra vires* in raising the compensation standard for candidates attempting professional examinations. It was subsequently reported that the Society had reopened the cases of other similarly placed candidates and admitted them to its professional course.[343] The assumption mentioned earlier seems to be reasonable since the considerations behind both principles and exceptions are the same. And, indeed, the language employed in Henchy J.'s judgment in *Murphy* (*e.g.* the use of the word "invalidity") would seem apt to cover both types of case. Accordingly, it seems appropriate to treat the constitutional authorities as if they also applied, *mutatis mutandis*, to ordinary cases of *ultra vires*.

Exceptions and qualifications: "came the dawn"

However, cases such as *Shelley* and *Glavin* would appear to represent the high-water mark of the classic doctrine of invalidity, as the rule that *ultra vires* decisions are a nullity is itself subject to considerable qualification. As Costello J. remarked pregnantly in *O'Keeffe v. An Bord Pleanála*:[344]

> "It is usual to say that an ultra vires decision is void and a nullity. But it is clear that it is wrong to conclude that such decisions are completely devoid of legal consequences."[345]

This perceptive analysis is borne out by the fact that, with the possible exception of a flagrantly invalid decision, invalidity can only be established in legal proceedings.[346] If the court sets aside the impugned decision this will have retrospective effect, but

---

340   *Ibid.* at 528, *per* Hamilton C.J.
341   For the application of the doctrine of severance in this case, see above at p. 473.
342   [1989] I.L.R.M. 590.
343   *The Irish Times*, May 14, 1988.
344   [1993] 1 I.R. 39.
345   *Ibid.* at 49. This meant that an appeal could be taken from an *ultra vires* administrative decision, which even though ultimately adjudged to be void, was not legally non-existent. See also *Stringer v. Minister for Housing* [1970] 1 W.L.R. 1281; *Calvin v. Carr* [1980] A.C. 574 (similar principles).
346   *Smith v. East Elloe R.D.C.* [1956] A.C. 736; *The State (Abenglen Properties Ltd) v. Dublin Corporation* [1984] I.R. 381; *C.W. Shipping Ltd v. Limerick Harbour Commissioners* [1989] I.L.R.M. 416; *McDonnell v. Ireland*, unreported, Supreme Court, July 23, 1997 (O'Flaherty J.). In *C.W. Shipping*, O'Hanlon J., speaking in the context of an allegedly invalid planning decision, said (at 426) that it

until this is done the decision will enjoy a presumption of validity and the decision will be regarded as binding.[347] Moreover until this has occurred, it cannot be confidently anticipated that it will necessarily occur for even where invalidity has been established in the appropriate, subsequent proceedings, the court may refuse to grant relief on public policy or discretionary grounds.[348] Again, there are sometimes statutory provisions which govern the consequences of invalidation,[349] or which prescribe a limitation period which serves to preclude judicial review once that time limit has expired.[350] Another possibility is that the statutory context may be such that, as Costello J. said in *O'Keeffe*, the court must "give legal efficacy to an ultra vires decision if the construction of the statute so requires."[351] In short, invalidity is a relative concept and the courts have refrained from pushing that concept to extremes.[352]

Perhaps it is because the Irish courts have, in general, taken such a pragmatic approach that the void/voidable controversy which has plagued English administrative law has not given rise to the same difficulties in this jurisdiction.[353] *Irish Permanent*

---

was "unrealistic" to suggest that the developer should rely on legal advice as to its invalidity and proceed "to expend money in the belief that the courts will later uphold his view of the law, rather than that taken by the planning authority." As to whether orders of an irregularly constituted Special Criminal Court was flagrantly invalid in this sense, see the (inconclusive) discussion of Geoghegan J. in *Hegarty v. Governor of Limerick Prison*, unreported, High Court, February 26, 1997.

347 *Hoffman-La Roche & Co. v. Secretary for Trade and Industry* [1975] A.C. 295; *Abenglen Properties, supra; Campus Oil v. Minister for Industry and Energy (No. 2)* [1983] I.R. 88 at 107 (O'Higgins C.J.), and, in the special context of constitutional law, *The State (Llewellyn) v. UaDonnachada* [1973] I.R. 151; *Pesca Valentia Ltd v. Minister for Fisheries* [1985] I.R. 193.

348 See, *e.g. The State (Cussen) v. Brennan* [1981] I.R. 181; *Murphy v. Att.-Gen.* [1982] I.R. 341.

349 See, *e.g.* Adoption Act 1976, s.6 (no child to be removed from custody of its adoptive parents solely on the grounds that the adoption order was invalid); Irish Takeover Panel Act 1997, s.15 (take-over which has not been conducted in accordance with the 1997 Act is not to be regarded as necessarily thereby invalid.)

350 Housing Act 1966, s.78(2) (three-week time limit in respect of challenges to validity of a compulsory purchase order); Local Government (Planning and Development) Act 1963, s.82(3A) (two-month time limit in respect of challenges to the validity of a planning permission); Environmental Protection Agency Act 1992, s.85(8)(two month time limit) and Irish Takeover Panel Act 1997, s. 13(3)(seven-day period for challenge to decisions of the Irish Takeover Panel, but with power to extend time under strict parameters: see s.13(5)). *Cf.* the comments of Egan J. in *Foras Áiseanna Saothair v. Minister for Social Welfare*, Supreme Court, May 23, 1995:

"Although [*ultra vires*] acts are clearly void *ab initio* and destitute of legal effect, it may happen in practice that the validity of the void act may become immune from challenge. Such a situation is to be found, for example, under the Local Government (Planning and Development) Act 1992. Under this Act, strict time limits are laid down for the questioning of the validity of planning decisions. It is conceivable that an otherwise void decision might not be challenged within the appropriate time limit. Thus, the act, although void, must be accepted as valid."

351 [1993] 1 I.R. 39 at 50. Thus, Costello J. held that even if the planning authority's decision was void and a nullity, this did not mean that An Bord Pleanála had no jurisdiction to entertain an appeal against this decision.

352 Take, for instance, the converse case to *Glavin v. Governor of Mountjoy Training Training Unit* [1991] 2 I.R. 421. This is *McCarthy v. Garda Commissioner* [1993] 1 I.R. 489 in which Flood J. refused to treat as invalid the acquittal of the applicant on charges of fraudulent conversion, despite the fact that his return for trial by the former District Judge Mahon was void, so that, strictly speaking, the trial court had no jurisdiction. Flood J. (at 498) was trenchant in his rejection of this argument:

"It seems to me that to rip the certificate of innocence from the hands of the applicant and metaphorically to shred it and declare it a total nullity and to claim that it never in fact existed, all by reason of a clerical error made in 1977 as to the age of a District Justice, would be wholly inequitable."

353 See, *e.g. D.P.P. v. Head* [1959] A.C. 83; *R. v. Paddington Valuation Officer, ex p. Peachey Property Corporation Ltd* [1966] 1 Q.B. 380; *Hoffman-La Roche & Co. v. Secretary of State for Trade and*

Building Society v. Caldwell[354] provides an interesting example of this pragmatic judicial attitude. Here Barrington J. refused to accept that the incorporation of a building society could be nullified by reason of an error on the part of the Registrar of Building Societies in construing the relevant legislation. Such a result would be "catastrophic," and the judge could not believe that the Oireachtas intended that "an honest mistake" could have such drastic consequences.[355]

It remains to elaborate on certain of these propositions. Take, first, the proposition that, save in the case of a flagrantly invalid decision, an administrative act enjoys a presumption of validity and will have legal consequences until it is set aside. This fact has been recognised either expressly or by implication by recent Irish decisions. For example, in *Re Comhaltas Ceolteoirí Éireann*,[356] the applicants sought renewal of a certificate under the Registration of Clubs (Ireland) Act 1904. Local residents objected to the renewal before the District Court, claiming, inter alia, that the club was being operated in breach of the planning laws, since the planning permission granted by the local authority was invalid. The District Judge stated a case as to whether he could hear evidence concerning the validity of this planning permission, but Finlay P. said that, as a general rule, this could not be done:

> "A planning authority is a public authority with a decision-making capacity acting in accordance with statutory powers and duties. In my view, there is a rebuttable presumption that its acts are valid. A challenge to the validity of the acts of a planning authority can only be made by review on certiorari or by a substantive action seeking a declaration of invalidity [in the High Court]. To either form of proceeding, the planning authority is an essential party and it would be contrary to natural justice for a court to be called upon to adjudicate on the validity of the acts of the planning authority in a case to which they were not a party. There is no method by which the planning authority can be made a party to this application for renewal."[357]

To this general rule there was but one exception. Finlay P. suggested that if it appeared to the District Judge that the document purporting to be a planning permission did not emanate from the authority or was not "executed or signed by the planning authority," then he was bound to inquire further. *Comhaltas Ceolteoirí Eireann* is a good example of how this general rule operates in practice and illustrates

---

Industry [1975] A.C. 295; *R. v. Environment Secretary, ex p. Ostler* [1977] Q.B. 122. But the English courts no longer view nullity as an absolute concept: *Calvin v. Carr* [1980] A.C. 574 and *London & Clydeside Estates Ltd v. Aberdeen D.C.* [1980] 1 W.L.R. 182. See generally, Cane, "A Fresh Look at Punton's Case" (1980) 43 M.L.R. 264.

354 [1981] I.L.R.M. 242. See also *Re Riordan* [1981] I.L.R.M. 2 for a similar approach.

355 [1981] I.L.R.M. 242.

356 Unreported, High Court, December 5, 1977. See also, the comments of O'Higgins C.J. in *Campus Oil Ltd v. Minister for Industry and Commerce* [1983] I.R. 88 at 107:
   "The order which is challenged was under the provisions of an Act of the Oireachtas. It is, therefore, valid and is to be regarded as a part of the law of the land, unless and until its invalidity is established."

357 See also the comments of O'Flaherty J. in *McSorley v. Governor of Mountjoy Prison* [1997] 2 I.L.R.M. 315 at 319 to the effect that fair procedures generally requires that the trial judge be given an opportunity to be heard before a conviction is quashed, so that most applications of this kind should proceed by way of judicial review as opposed to Article 40.4.2°.

how decisions bearing "no brand of invalidity" or flagrant illegality on their face must be regarded as valid until they are set aside by either the High Court or Supreme Court. *The State (Abenglen Properties Ltd) v. Dublin Corporation*[358] provides another example of this type of reasoning. Here Henchy J. said of an allegedly invalid planning permission, which was good on its face, that it remained a "decision" for the purposes of the Planning Acts until it was set aside in the appropriate proceedings.

Similar thinking was employed by Costello J. in *O'Keeffe v. An Bord Pleanála*,[359] where he held that, at least in the context of the special statutory features of the Planning Acts, one could appeal an *ultra vires* decision of the planning authority to An Bord Pleanála. The judge drew attention to the special features of the Planning Acts, such as section 26 of the Local Government (Planning and Development) Act 1963, whereby An Bord Pleanála is required to determine the matter *de novo* and the Board's decision has the legal effect of annulling the decision of the planning authority. He concluded that it followed that the statute should be construed as meaning that:

> "No defect in the proceedings before the planning authority should have any bearing, or impose legal constraints, on the proceedings before the Board. The Board had no jurisdiction to consider the validity from a legal point of view of the [planning authority's] decision and it seems to be contrary to the proper construction of the section now to hold that the Board lacked jurisdiction to entertain the appeal because the decision was ultra vires. There is no logical inconsistency in this conclusion for it would mean that as a matter of law (a) the County Manager's order did not confer permission to develop, but (b) did enable the appeal machinery to be brought into operation – a result which seems to me to be a reasonable construction of the statute and to produce a sensible result."[360]

This question was also plainly visible in *Hegarty v. Governor of Limerick Prison*,[361] where the issue arose as to whether the Minister for Justice was correct in directing the release of certain remand prisoners, once it transpired that the Special Criminal Court which had made the orders for their detention had been irregularly constituted.[362] It was argued that there was no necessity for the Minister to apply to the High Court for such an order of release since

> "the relevant commital warrant . . . was not just a bad order made by a lawfully constituted court, but was an order which was bad because it was made by an unlawfully constituted Court."

---

[358] [1984] I.R. 381.

[359] [1993] 1 I.R. 39. See also *Stringer v. Minister for Housing* [1970] 1 W.L.R. 1281.

[360] *Ibid.* 52–53. This point was not pursued on appeal before the Supreme Court. Although that Court reversed Costello J. on the merits of the application, this does not take from the point which he sought to make.

[361] Unreported, High Court, February 26, 1997.

[362] One of the judges of that Court had sat following his removal from the Special Criminal Court by order of the Government because the judge in question had not been informed of the Government's decision.

Geoghegan J. did not find it necessary to resolve this issue – as it could not have affected the legality of the prisoner's re-arrest and consequent detention – but he agreed that "the legal position was by no means clear and that there are legitimate arguments both ways." Yet the order of the Special Criminal Court bore no "brand of invalidity" on its face. If the Minister were free, as it were, to disregard the Court's order, where would this stop?[363] Could, for example, an ordinary member of the Gardaí have similarly disregarded such an order and released a prisoner of his own volition? Or could, for example, the prisoner have fought his way free, using whatever force was necessary on the basis that he had been falsely detained? Such questions have only to be asked to demonstrate that in this area the law must take account of reality.

The very fact that the courts have found themselves obliged in appropriate cases to grant interlocutory relief to a person affected by the consequences of an administrative decision pending a challenge to its legality is significant and indicates that in this interim period there may be legal consequences of the fact that a decision which may ultimately prove to be *ultra vires*. Thus, in *Pesca Valentia Ltd v. Minister for Fisheries*,[364] Finlay C.J. said that the courts had power, in an appropriate case, to grant an interlocutory injunction restraining the implementation of administrative action which derived its authority from statutory provisions "which might eventually be held to be invalid having regard to the provisions of the Constitution." From this it may be inferred that the court recognised that administrative action which is not patently illegal will be presumed to be valid and if there is no such interim order, the administrative action will have legal consequences during this period for the individual, pending a decision as to its invalidity.[365]

However, if an administrative act which is not flagrantly invalid enjoys a presumption of validity and has the force of law until quashed, how is it possible to assert, once that presumption has been displaced, and the decision quashed as *ultra vires*, that it was a legal nullity? Cane has provided a convincing answer to this apparent paradox by suggesting that *ultra vires* decisions, although void, are not nullities which never had any legal existence or force. In his view, when administrative decisions are invalidated by the courts, this invalidation has retrospective effect:

---

[363] *cf.* the comments of O'Flaherty J. in *McDonnell v. Ireland*, Supreme Court, July 23, 1997, below, n. 365.

[364] [1985] I.R. 193. See also *Hoffmann-La Roche v. Department of Trade* [1975] A.C. 295 and, in the special context of European Community law, *R. v. Transport Secretary, ex p. Factortame Ltd* [1990] E.C.R. I-2433.

[365] In *O'Keeffe v. An Bord Pleanála* [1993] 1 I.R. 39 at 50 Costello J. appeared to hint that he agreed with this proposition but said that he could decide the issue which arose in that case by reference to a construction of the relevant provisions of the Planning Acts without having to deal with this larger issue. *Cf.* the comments of O'Flaherty J. in *McDonnell v. Ireland*, Supreme Court, July 23, 1997:
"The correct rule must be that laws should be observed until they are struck down as unconstitutional . . . Members of society are given no discretion to disobey such law on the ground that it might later transpire that the law is invalid having regard to the Constitution . . . The consequences of striking down legislation can only crystallise in respect of the immediate litigation which gave rise to the declaration of invalidity. This is what occurred in the *Murphy* case. . . ."
Would O'Flaherty J.'s comments have been any different if the law in question had borne the "brand of invalidity" on its face by *e.g.* forbidding certain types of religious practice? Perhaps this is a question of degree, but there may be some (admittedly quite extreme) circumstances in which the citizen might be justified in ignoring a flagrantly unconstitutional law.

"[o]n this view acts done in pursuance of ultra vires decision would be treated as lawful until made unlawful by the quashing of the decision which supported them."

Consequences of invalidity

One of the most difficult problems facing the courts is how to deal with the *de facto* consequences of *ultra vires* administrative action. The most obvious and, perhaps, most logical solution is to pronounce that all that was previously done under an unconstitutional statute or invalid decision is *ultra vires* and without legal effects. Yet the courts have understandably displayed a reluctance retroactively to interfere where this would cause manifest injustice, prejudice acquired rights or cause administrative chaos. The substantive element of *Murphy v. Attorney General* was that it was unconstitutional to tax a married couple by a more unfavourable tax code than that which was applied to two single co-habiting persons as this amounted to a violation of Article 41. The aspect of the case which is relevant here concerns the primary rule of redress which was stated in the following terms by Henchy J. in *Murphy v. Attorney General*:

"Once it has been judicially established that a statutory provision [or administrative decision] is invalid, the condemned provision [or decision] will normally provide no legal justification for any acts done or left undone, or for transactions undertaken in pursuance of it; and the person damnified by the operation of the invalid provision will normally be accorded by the Courts all permitted and necessary redress."[366]

But this "primary rule" was subject to exceptions, especially where public policy factors or the need to avoid injustice to third parties justified the courts refusing to set aside the consequences of invalid administrative decisions.[367] Thus, in *Murphy* itself, redress was limited to the small number of married couples who had instituted proceedings to challenge the operation of the Income Tax Act 1967. Even though these statutory provisions were held to have been unconstitutional *ab initio*, the vast majority of married couples were unable to recover moneys collected in this unconstitutional fashion. Henchy J. explained that the courts had only a limited power to undo what had been done:

"[T]he law has to recognise that there may be transcendent considerations which make such a course [of legal redress] undesirable, impractical or impossible. Over the centuries the law has come to recognise that factors such as prescription, waiver, estoppel, laches, a statute of limitations, res judicata, or other matters (most of which may be grouped under the heading of public policy) may debar a person from obtaining redress in the courts for injury

---

[366] [1982] I.R. 241 at 313.

[367] In Professor Corbin's phrase (quoted by Goodhart, (1971) *Law Quarterly Review* at 202):
"*Fiat justitia, ruat coelum* is a phrase impressive mainly because of its being in Latin and not understandable. When the skies begin to fall, Justice removes the blindfold from her eyes and tilts the scales."

which would be justiciable and redressible if such considerations had not intervened."[368]

The sequel to this aspect of *Murphy* was section 21 of the Finance Act 1980, which sought to impose the same burden of taxation on married couples, who had not already paid, for the tax years immediately prior to the date of the *Murphy* decision. The justification for this section was that persons who had been assessed for this unconstitutional tax but who, for some reason, had not paid it prior to the *Murphy* decision, should now be treated in the same way as those who had already paid. This provision was, however, found to be unconstitutional in *Muckley v. Ireland* which followed the substantive part of *Murphy*[369] Barrington J. observed that Article 40 obliges the State to defend and vindicate the personal rights of the citizen as far as it was practicable to do so and, in the *Murphy* case:

> "It was found to be impractical to vindicate the personal rights of the married couples who paid an invalid tax because directing the State to refund taxes unconstitutionally collected would have caused financial and administrative chaos."[370]

But, on the other hand, the same public policy justifications stemming from the need to avoid administrative chaos were not present in the case of the married couples in *Muckley*, in respect of whom the taxes were merely assessed, but never collected: "There is no impracticability in defending the citizen against exactions which the State has no authority to impose." This reasoning was subsequently confirmed by the Supreme Court and *Muckley* would seem to exemplify Henchy J.'s "primary rule" of redress in *Murphy*.[371]

Yet not long after this decision, there were several judicial indications that it would require the most exceptional of circumstances before the courts would give retroactive effect to an earlier decision.[372] In *Connors v. Delap*,[373] the applicant sought to quash a conviction imposed *in absentia* on the ground that the summons was defective in the light of the subsequently-announced decision of the Supreme Court in *The State (Clarke) v. Roche.*[374] Lynch J. admitted that, in view of the decision in *Clarke*, the summons was defective, but refused, on discretionary grounds, to quash the conviction. He invoked the principles in *Murphy* as justification:

---

[368] *Ibid.* at 314.
[369] [1985] I.R. 472.
[370] *Ibid.* at 482. But *cf.* the decision of the European Court of Human Rights in *National Provincial Building Society v. United Kingdom* (1998) 25 E.H.R.R. 127 which upheld the validity of retrospective legislation which precluded other building societies from claiming restitution in the wake of the *Woolwich* litigation (see p. 857). The Court concluded that the United Kingdom was justified in so acting, partly by reason of the massive sums of tax revenue which might otherwise have been lost had such retrospective legislation not been enacted.
[371] See p. 466.
[372] It should be noted, however, by way of distinction, that in none of the decisions to be discussed was the significant feature of *Muckley* – legislation which sought positively to do what had been condemned – present. Nor was this feature present in the situations considered below (at pp. 470–473) under the heading of "Validating Statutes", since these statutes provided defences for the public body concerned, as opposed to a line of attack.
[373] [1989] I.L.R.M. 93.
[374] [1986] I.R. 619.

"The Supreme Court made it clear that other citizens were not entitled in the light of [the] decision [in *Murphy*] to reopen past accounts. It seems to me that what the applicant seeks to do in this case is analogous to reopening past accounts. He seeks to rely on the subsequent Supreme Court judgments in the case of *The State (Clarke) v. Roche* already referred to, purely as a means of avoiding a liability which he [had already] chosen not to contest."[375]

Barr J. adopted this reasoning and, indeed, elaborated upon it, in *White v. Hussey,*[376] a case whose facts were on all fours with *Connors*. He refused to apply the *Clarke* decision retroactively, saying:

"It seems to me that if the Supreme Court intended that its finding as to the invalidity of the erstwhile practice under which complaints were received and summonses issued by District Court clerks or Peace Commissioners was to be regarded as having retrospective effect then that conclusion would have been specifically stated in that judgment."[377]

This reasoning seems dubious. First, the fact that the Supreme Court in *Clarke* was silent as to the retrospective effect of its judgment would not seem to be a relevant factor, given that that Court had already stated in *Murphy* that the essential issue in such cases is whether discretionary relief should, in the light of the circumstances of the later case, now be granted. Secondly, all of the members of the Court in *Murphy* rejected the argument that the retrospective consequences should depend on some arbitrary cut-off date decided by the courts, and Henchy J. spoke of the:

"Arbitrariness and inequality, in breach of Article 40.1, that would result in a citizen's constitutional rights depending on the fortuity of when a court's decision would be pronounced."[378]

Finally, both Lynch J. and Barr J. appeared to regard certiorari as a purely discretionary remedy, whereas the true rule appears to be that certiorari lies *ex debito justitiae* in a criminal case such as this.[379]

A further instance of a judicial attempt to restrict the retroactive consequences of an earlier judgment – albeit in the very special context of European Community law – comes with the decision of Hamilton P. in *Cotter v. Minister for Social Welfare (No. 2)*.[380] Following the decision of the European Court of Justice in *McDermott and Cotter v. Minister for Social Welfare (No. 1)*[381] in 1987 which held that the EC

---

[375] [1989] I.L.R.M. 93 at 97–98.
[376] [1989] I.L.R.M.109.
[377] *Ibid.* at 112.
[378] [1982] I.R. 241 at 311. Moreover, the Supreme Court has also accepted that its rulings do have retroactive effect, save that, due to acquiescence, effluxion of time and other factors it may not always be possible to grant relief: see *The State (Byrne) v. Frawley* [1978] I.R. 326 and *McDonnell v. Ireland*, Supreme Court, July 23, 1997. Exceptionally, however, there may be cases where legislation which was not unconstitutional when it was enacted has *become* unconstitutional by reason of changing circumstances, such as inflation, population movements, *etc.*: see, *e.g.* *McMenamin v. Ireland* [1997] 2 I.L.R.M. 177.
[379] See pp. 717–719 and Collins, "Ex Debito Justitiae?" (1988) 10 D.U.L.J. 130.
[380] [1990] 2 C.M.L.R. 141. See generally, Whyte, *Sex Equality, Community Rights and Irish Social Welfare Law* (1988).
[381] Case 265/85 [1987] I.L.R.M. 324.

equality directive 79/7/EEC had had direct effect in Irish law since December 1984, the applicant sought declarations to the effect that she was entitled to be paid certain social welfare benefits between the months of December 1984 and March 1985. In other words, she sought to have the decision of the European Court applied retrospectively to the circumstances of her case. Any such ruling would probably have had very large financial consequences, since thousands of other women were in a similar position, many with pending claims. In the light of these public policy considerations, Hamilton P. refused to grant her such relief, and relying on the principles of *Murphy*, observed that the "equity of the case" was against her. This reasoning also seems dubious. First, the European Court[382] has now ruled that the issue of the retrospective effect of its own decisions is a matter for itself, and, that, in the absence of any express pronouncement to that effect contained in the original judgment, the judgment will have retrospective effect. Secondly, the reasoning in *Murphy* was premised, at least, in part, on the fact that the State had no advance knowledge of the unconstitutionality and altered its position accordingly. This factor was not present here, where the State had plenty of advance warning of the impact and legal consequences of the equality directive.

But the more recent cases have seen a swing away from this trend in favour, once again, of regarding nullification as the more general consequence of a finding of invalidity. This proposition has already been illustrated by the references, at the start of this Part,[383] to the facts in *Shelley v. Mahon*[384] and *Glavin v. Governor of the Training Unit, Mountjoy Prison*.[385] Perhaps, as with so many difficult public law questions, this issue does not readily admit of any tidy and logically satisfying answer and these issues will fall to be adjudicated on a case by case basis. The alternative is to provide for a constitutional amendment which will give the courts express power:

> ". . . where justice, equity or, exceptionally, the common good so requires to afford such relief as they consider necessary and appropriate in respect of any detriment arising from acts done in reliance in good faith on an invalid law."[386]

---

382 Case 309/85 *Barra v. Belgium* [1988] 2 C.M.L.R. 409. Note that in *Carberry v. Minister for Social Welfare* [1990] 1 C.M.L.R. 29. Barron J. refused to follow the lead given by Hamilton P. in *Cotter* on the ground that it was clear from the subsequent decision in *Barra* that only the European Court itself had jurisdiction to pronounce on the retroactive effect of its rulings.

The European Court itself has emphasised that it will require exceptional circumstances before the Court will countenance the non-retroactive application of a ruling: see Case 43/75, *Defrenne v. SABENA (No. 2)* [1976] E.C.R. 455; Case 42/86, *Blaizot v. University of Liege* [1988] E.C.R. 379; Case C–262/88, *Barber v. Guardian Royal Exchange Assurance Group* [1990] E.C.R. I–1889; Cases C–38/90 and 151/90, *R. v. Lomas* [1992] E.C.R. I–1781; Case C–163/90, *Legros* [1992] E.C.R. I–4625. Generally the Court will only permit non-retroactivity where not to do so would be to interfere with third-party vested rights or where to undo past transactions would cause chaos or where, as was said in *Lomas*, such a limitation is necessary in the "interests of overriding considerations of legal certainty involving all the interests at stake in the case concerned.". It was precisely for these reasons that the Court in *Defrenne* (equal pay); *Blaizot* (differential fees for university education) and *Barber* (discriminatory occupational pension schemes) refused to apply its ruling retroactively. See generally, Hyland, "Temporal limitation of the effect of judgments of the Court of Justice" (1995) 4 *Irish Journal of European Law* 208.

383 See pp. 460–461.
384 [1990] 1 I.R. 36.
385 [1991] 2 I.R. 421.
386 *Report of the Constitution Review Group* (Pn. 2632, 1996) at p. 168. The Report also recognised that the risks that giving such an express constitutional jurisdiction "might lead to a weakening of

Validating statutes

One of the ways in which the Oireachtas has sought to counteract the potential disruption to the legal system is by enacting validating statutes which seek to confer retrospective validity on invalid administrative decisions. Provided the Oireachtas did not enact retroactive penal sanctions, contrary to Article 15.5, it had been thought up to relatively recently that there were no constitutional restrictions on the power of the Oireachtas to enact such validating legislation. Indeed, the Military Service Pensions (Amendment) Act 1945 affords a good example of this laissez-faire attitude. In *The State (O'Shea) v. Minister for Defence*[387] the applicant had obtained in the High Court an order of certiorari quashing a decision of the referee appointed under the Military Service Pensions Act 1934. It was accepted by Davitt J. that the referee had adopted an incorrect procedure in the light of a then recent Supreme Court decision in *The State (McCarthy) v. O'Donnell*.[388] The 1945 Act, however, allowed the Minister to appeal to the Supreme Court against the High Court's order and, furthermore, purported retrospectively to validate the procedure which had actually been adopted by the referee in the applicant's case. When the case came before the Supreme Court, that court simply applied the new Act to the applicant's case and allowed the Minister's appeal. The reasoning of Maguire C.J. appears entirely oblivious to the separation of powers considerations that would almost certainly nowadays render legislation of this kind unconstitutional.[389]

In the more recent legislation of this kind, a more sophisticated approach may be discerned on the part of the Oireachtas. Following a decision of the Supreme Court in *Garvey v. Ireland*[390] to the effect that the dismissal of a previous Garda Commissioner was invalid, the Oireachtas sought via section 1(1) of the Garda Siochana Act 1979 to validate the acts of his successor (who had been improperly appointed to replace Mr. Garvey following that latter's invalid dismissal). Section 1(2), however, contained a new form of saving clause of a kind that was later to become standard:

---

the protection intended by Article 15.4" (which provides for a prohibition on the enactment of unconstitutional legislation) and inhibit the courts from "developing their jurisdiction to prevent any damaging consequences for society of a declaration of invalidity."

[387] [1947] I.R. 49.

[388] [1945] I.R. 126.

[389] Contrast against *O'Shea* the famous authority of *Buckley v. Attorney General* [1950] I.R. 67 where the statute at the centre of the case – the Sinn Féin Funds Act 1947 – bore the same sort of flaws as the Military Service Pensions (Amendment) Act 1945. Yet although *Buckley* was decided in the same era as *O'Shea*, the 1947 Act was found to be unconstitutional. Another less dramatic example in that no court action was involved is the Mental Treatment (Detention in Approved Institutions) Act 1961 (on another aspect of which, see pp. 59–60). This Act validated the detention of certain inmates in mental institutions where, by reason of a clerical oversight, the statutory procedures prescribed by the Mental Treatment Act 1945 had not been followed. Section 1(iii) of the Act provided, however, that:

"No damages shall be recoverable by or on behalf of that person in respect merely of his detention during the same period ending on the passing of this Act."

A provision of this kind, which purported to deprive potential plaintiffs of their right to sue for false imprisonment, would clearly nowadays be regarded as highly suspect and open to constitutional attack on the ground that the State by its laws had failed to vindicate such a plaintiff's constitutional rights.

[390] [1981] I.R. 75.

"If, because of any validation expressed to be effected by subsection 1that subsection would, but for this subsection, conflict with a constitutional right of any person, the validation shall be subject to such limitation as is necessary to secure that it does not so conflict, but shall otherwise be of full force and effect."[391]

A similar clause was contained in section 6(2) of the Local Government (Planning and Development) Act 1982, where the Oireachtas sought to confirm the validity of certain planning permissions in the wake of the Supreme Court's decision in *The State (Pine Valley Developments Ltd) v. Dublin County Council*.[392] However, the saving clause contained in section 6(2) naturally[393] had the consequence that the applicants in the original proceedings, Pine Valley Developments Ltd, could not claim the benefit of this validating legislation, since this would clash with the constitutional rights of Dublin County Council, who had succeeded in establishing that such permission was invalid.

The interpretation of such clauses, in a much wider context than that presented by *Pine Valley*, was considered by the Supreme Court in *Shelley v. Mahon*[394] where the applicant succeeded in having his conviction quashed on the ground that the respondent who purported to convict him was not a duly qualified judge at the time. Walsh J. (joined by Hederman J.) did not think that the saving clause contained in section 1(3) of the Courts (No. 2) Act 1988 had any relevance, since in his view the conviction was a nullity and an "unconstitutional procedure cannot subsequently be declared by the Oireachtas" to be valid. The other majority judges, Griffin and McCarthy JJ., took the view that the purported validation would have taken effect, save that any such validation would have conflicted with the constitutional right of the applicant to trial in due course of law, as guaranteed by Article 38.1.[395] Accordingly, in their view, this validation became inoperative and the conviction was thus invalid. On the radical view adopted by Walsh and Hederman JJ., the effect of *Shelley* would appear to be that the power of the Oireachtas retrospectively to confer validity on what were originally invalid administrative or judicial decisions

---

[391] Note that in *McHugh v. Garda Commissioner* [1986] I.R. 228 the Supreme Court accepted (although without any reference to the terms of the Garda Síochána Act 1979) that an order made by the then Commissioner of the Garda Sochana directing the holding of a sworn inquiry into the plaintiff's conduct as a member of the Gardai was invalid, since the appointment of the then Commissioner to replace the former Commissioner, Mr. Garvey, was itself invalid.

[392] [1984] I.R. 407. On which see, Morgan, *The Separation of Powers in the Irish Constitution* (1997) at pp. 143–145.

[393] The planning permission obtained by *Pine Valley* had been declared invalid in 1982: *The State (Pine Valley Developments Ltd) v. Dublin County Council* [1984] I.R. 407. In the subsequent damages action (*Pine Valley Developments Ltd v. Minister for Environment* [1987] I.R. 23), the Supreme Court pointed out that had the 1982 Act purported to reverse the effects of that decision as between the parties to the original action it would have been unconstitutional as an improper invasion of the judicial domain: see *Buckley v. Att.-Gen.* [1950] I.R. 67. When, however, the matter came before the European Court of Human Rights that Court held that the failure to extend the benefit of the validating statute to the applicant constituted a violation of Article 14 (non-discrimination) taken in conjunction with Article 1 of the first Protocol (property rights) of the European Convention of Human Rights: *Pine Valley Developments Ltd v. Ireland* (1992) 14 E.H.R.R. 319.

[394] [1990] 1 I.R. 36.

[395] In *McCarthy v. Garda Commissioner* [1993] 1 I.R. 489 Flood J. relied on this sub-section to validate a defective return of trial which ultimately resulted in the acquittal of the applicant.

is very limited, since any such validation is likely to conflict with some other constitutional rights. To take obvious examples, the retrospective legislation could not validate an act which had violated the rules of Constitutional Justice, or the right to property, equality or personal liberty. On the other view taken by Griffin and McCarthy JJ. (and, it may be legitimate to add, by the dissenting judge, Costello J.), *Shelley* may come to be seen as a special case, turning on the applicant's right to trial in due course of law. On either view, it appears that the Oireachtas has a much freer hand where it seeks to validate an ordinary *ultra* vires act where that original invalidity does not stem from constitutional grounds.

As noted already, there are other statutory provisions which attempt to regulate the consequences of invalidity. A good example is provided by s.7(3) of the Criminal Justice Act 1984 which states that:

> "A failure on the part of any member of the Garda Siochana to observe any provision of the [Criminal Justice Act, 1984 (Treatment of Persons in Custody in Garda Siochana Stations) Regulations][396] shall not of itself render that person liable to any criminal or civil proceedings or of itself affect the lawfulness of the custody of the detained person or the admissibility in evidence of any statement made by him."

In *Director of Public Prosecutions v. Spratt*[397] the complaint was that as there was no evidence that the arresting Gardaí had complied with the requirements of Articles 8 and 9 of the Regulations (which impose a duty on the "member in charge" to inform the accused of his right to seek a solicitor and, if a solicitor has been sought, to notify that solicitor of the request), this had affected the legality of the accused's detention. O'Hanlon J. referred to the words of s. 7(3) and said:

> "The phrase 'of itself' is obviously an important one in the construction of statutory provisions, and I interpret the sub-section as meaning that non-observance of the regulations is not to bring about automatically the exclusion from evidence of all that was done and said while the accused person was in custody. It appears to be left to the court of trial to adjudicate in every case as to the impact the non-compliance with the regulations should have on the case for the prosecution."[398]

These principles have been subsequently applied in other cases, each of which demonstrate the need to establish that any breach of the regulations prejudiced the suspect. In *People (Director of Public Prosecutions) v. O'Shea*[399] the issue was whether the appointment of a particular Garda as the "member in charge" of a particular station was defective. Blayney J. ruled that in the absence of the suspect "receiving any unfair treatment or being in any way prejudiced", s.7(3) operated to cure any such defect. Kelly J. adopted a similar approach in *Director of Public*

---

[396] S.I. No. 119 of 1987.
[397] [1995] 1 I.R. 585.
[398] *Ibid.* at 591. O'Hanlon J. remitted the case to the District Court judge (who had earlier stated a case for the High Court), but it seems fair to observe that the judgment contains a strong hint that any non-compliance with the regulations in the instant case did not affect the lawfulness of the detention.
[399] [1996] 1 I.R. 556.

Prosecutions (Lenihan) v. McGuire[400] where substantially the same point was at issue, adding that "it is only where there is a causal connection between the breach and the prejudice that the . . . court could conclude that it would be legitimate to consider dismissing the charge." While the result of these cases would probably have been the same even, if s.7(3) did not exist, nevertheless, the subsection probably provides the courts with some vestigial extra authority to deal with the consequences of any invalidity.[401]

10. Severance

General principles

In some cases, the condemned legislation or administrative decision may only be partially invalid. The question arises as to whether it is open to the court to excise offending sections of the Act, order or decision leaving the remainder valid. The classic statement of the courts' attitude to the question of severance is to be found in the judgment of Fitzgerald C.J. in *Maher v. Attorney General,*[402] where speaking in the context of an unconstitutional statute, he said that, if, following the deletion of an unconstitutional portion of a statute:

> "The remainder may be held to stand independently and legally operable as representing the will of the legislature [then effect will be given to it]. But if what remains is so inextricably bound up with the part held invalid that the remainder cannot survive independently, or if the remainder would not represent the legislative intent, the remaining part will not be severed and given constitutional validity. If, therefore, the Court were to sever part of a statutory provision as unconstitutional and seek to give validity to what is left so as to produce an effect at variance with legislative policy, the Court would be invading a domain exclusive to the legislature and thus exceeding the Court's competency."[403]

While these principles were enunciated in the context of an unconstitutional statute, it would seem that they are of general application.[404]

---

[400] [1996] 3 I.R. 586.

[401] See also Irish Takeover Panel Act 1997, s.15 (breach of Acts' rules and scheduled principles does not of itself entitle an aggrieved person to a decision setting aside any takeover or merger).

[402] [1973] I.R. 140.

[403] *Ibid.* at 147–148. This is an example of what the House of Lords was later to describe in *D.P.P. v. Hutchinson* [1990] 2 A.C. 783 as the test "substantial severability" as opposed to "textual severability". In *Hutchinson* a majority held that the former test was the appropriate one , since it rested on presumed parliamentary intent as opposed to whether the remaining words made grammatical sense. Lord Bridge added (at 811) that where the severance could only be effected by modifying the text, this should only be done "when the court is satisfied that it is effecting no change in the substantial purpose and effect of the impugned provision." For an example of what amounts to the *de facto* application of this principle, see *Desmond v. Glackin (No.2)* [1993] 3 I.R. 67.

[404] See the elaborate discussion of this point in *Desmond v. Glackin* [1993] 3 I.R. 67 and *Mallon v. Minister for Agriculture and Food* [1996] 1 I.R. 517.

Administrative decisions

Like principles have been applied in a series of administrative cases. In *Cassidy v. Minister for Industry and Commerce*[405] the Supreme Court severed the application of an invalid maximum prices order for alcoholic drink by limiting its application by means of "horizontal severance"[406] to public bars, but excluding lounge bars. In *The State (Sheehan) v. McMahon*[407] a member of the Garda Síochána challenged the validity of certain disciplinary penalties imposed on him. The Supreme Court found that the Appeal Board acted *ultra vires* in declining to hear his appeal. But as the first tier of the procedure laid down by the regulations had been correctly observed, it did not follow that the error of the Appeal Board in thinking that they had no jurisdiction should be held to invalidate what had gone before. The court accordingly remitted the matter to the Appeal Board who could then hear the appeal. Similarly, in *The State (McKeown) v. Scully*[408] that part of the record which recorded a verdict of suicide was quashed as *ultra vires*, leaving untouched the other aspects of the verdict. Finally, in *Glencar Expolorations plc v. Mayo County Council*[409] Blayney J. quashed such portion only of a development plan as contained a ban on mining. No injustice would be done by simply removing the ban and leaving the rest of the plan intact. The ban was not contained in the plan as originally drafted and the Council was perfectly free to review the terms of the development plan at any time.[410]

This question has also assumed relevance in planning cases where an invalid condition had been attached to the grant of a planning permission. In these cases, the court will quash the entire permission if what remains when shorn of the invalid condition is such that the planning authority would not have been willing to grant it in the first instance. As Keane J. observed in *Bord na Móna v. Galway County Council*[411]:

> "[W]here the condition relates to planning considerations and is an essential feature of the permission granted, it would seem wrong that the permission should be treated as still effective, although shorn of an essential planning condition."[412]

---

[405] [1978] I.R. 297.
[406] This was defined by Henchy J. (at 313) as severing the order
 "in the range of [its] application, so that [it] may be preserved and implemented in so far as they are *intra vires* and ruled inoperable only in so far as their application would run into the area of ultra vires."
 See also *Ulster Transport Authority v. James Brown & Sons Ltd* [1953] N.I. 79; *Belfast Corporation v. O.D. Cars Ltd* [1960] A.C. 490 and *Burke v. Minister for Labour* [1979] I.R. 354.
[407] [1976–1977] I.L.R.M. 305.
[408] [1986] I.L.R.M. 133. See also, *The State (Moloney) v. Minister for Industry and Commerce* [1954] I.R. 253 (severance of ministerial order). But severance is not possible in the case of a criminal conviction: *The State (Kiernan) v. deBurca* [1963] I.R. 348; *Bowes v. Judge Devally* [1995] 1 I.R. 315.
[409] [1993] 2 I.R. 237.
[410] Local Government (Planning and Development) Act 1963, s.20(1).
[411] [1985] I.R. 205. See also, to like effect, *Killiney & Ballybrack Development Assoc. v. Minister for Local Government (No. 2)*, unreported, High Court, April 1, 1977 and, generally, *Potato Marketing Board v. Merricks* [1958] 2 Q.B. 316; *Kent C.C. v. Kingsway Investments (Kent) Ltd* [1971] A.C. 72; *Dunkley v. Evans* [1981] 1 W.L.R. 1522; *Thames Water Authority v. Elmbridge B.C.* [1983] Q.B. 570; *R. v. Transport Secretary, ex p. G.L.C.* [1985] 3 All E.R. 300; *R. v. North Hertfordshire D.C., ex p. Cobbold* [1985] 3 All E.R. 486; *D.P.P. v. Hutchinson* [1990] 2 A.C. 783.
[412] *Ibid.* at 211.

In the *Bord na Móna* case, a condition requiring the contribution of a large sum of money towards the cost of restructuring a public road was held to be invalid. Keane J. was of the opinion that severance was not possible, and that the entire permission must fall. The offending condition could not be regarded as inessential or peripheral to the grant of the permission, and it would have been unjust to the defendants to enforce a permission stripped of such a vital condition. A similar attitude is to be found in the judgment of the Supreme Court in *The State (F.P.H. Properties S.A.) v. An Bord Pleanála.*[413] Here the applicants were granted planning permission to develop a house of significant historical and architectural interest, subject to conditions that the house be restored. McCarthy J. found that these conditions were invalid, but could the rest of the permission be upheld by means of severance? McCarthy J. did not think so, saying the permission could not stand "with the conditions severed from them," as to do otherwise "would be to rewrite the permission."

Delegated legislation and administrative circulars

Many of the cases on this topic have arisen in the special context of delegated legislation. In *Pigs and Bacon Commission v. McCarren & Co.*[414] the plaintiffs were empowered by the Pigs and Bacon Acts 1935–1941 to fix the rate of an appropriate levy which pig producers were required to pay, save that the prior consent of the Minister for Agriculture was required for this purpose. Following reference by the High Court under Article 177 of the Treaty of Rome, the European Court of Justice held that, inasmuch as the statutory scheme permitted the Commission to pay export bonuses and to engage in direct selling activities outside the State, it was contrary to Community law. The Supreme Court rejected the argument that, in response to this reasoning, it was open to the Court to declare a rate of levy which would have been appropriate to finance those purposes; yet which would not offend against Community law. O'Higgins C.J. pointed out that the rate fixed:

> "[Could] not be broken up, and the portion attributable to lawful purposes salvaged by severance. To do this would involve the Court, and not the plaintiff Commission in declaring a rate of levy. This, however, is not what the legislature authorises or permits, nor would a rate so declared [be compatible with the statutory scheme]."[415]

In that case it was impossible to effect a severance, with the result that the impugned orders were condemned as wholly *ultra vires*. This issue was also considered by the Supreme Court in *The State (McLoughlin) v. Eastern Health Board,*[416] where regulations which sought to exclude certain persons who drew supplementary welfare benefits from obtaining fuel allowances were held to be *ultra vires*. Finlay C.J. relied on the principles enunciated in *Maher* to hold that severance was not possible, since this would be to expose the exchequer to substantial, unanticipated claims. In

---

[413] [1987] I.R. 698.
[414] [1981] I.R. 451.
[415] *Ibid.* at 469.
[416] [1986] I.R. 416.

his concurring judgment, McCarthy J., however, appeared to attach significance to the provisions of Article 15.4.2° of the Constitution, which provides that:

> "Every law enacted by the Oireachtas which is in any respect repugnant to this Constitution or to any provision thereof, shall, but to the extent only of such repugnancy, be invalid."

McCarthy J. observed that Article 15.4.2° did not apply to statutory instruments, at least where the defect was said to be merely *ultra vires*, as opposed to a defect arising from constitutional grounds. Where the statutory instrument was found to be *ultra vires* on non-constitutional grounds, there was "no constitutional provision to enable it to be restored [or] cleansed of the defect." He then continued:

> "I greatly doubt if any statutory instrument can remain valid when any material portion of it has been condemned: I cannot identify any legal principle of construction to support judicial resuscitation of truncated subordinate legislation."[417]

In so far as McCarthy J. is suggesting that the courts cannot sever the good from the bad in the case of delegated legislation held to be *ultra vires*, at common law this would seem to be incorrect. As Finlay C.J. recognised for the majority in *McLoughlin*, the test enunciated in *Maher* is one of general application and can be applied to the severance of statutory instruments in cases of plain *ultra vires*. Moreover, the same technique is followed in British courts which are without the aid and comfort of any equivalent of Article 15.4.2°. Nevertheless, there are some indications that McCarthy J.'s suggestions have taken root, for in *Howard v. Minister for Agriculture*,[418] Murphy J., following the *McLoughlin* principles, held that the entirety of the Bovine Tuberculosis (Attestation of the State and General Provisions) Order 1978 must fail, even though only a single (and rather inessential) feature of the order was actually found to be *ultra vires*.

The question of whether the severance principles can be applied to a partially invalid administrative circular was considered for the first time in *Greene v. Minister for Agriculture*.[419] In this case, the circular sought to implement an EC directive providing for headage payments to farmers. However, the circular also imposed an off-farm income limit which was found by Murphy J. to be unconstitutional on the ground that this condition discriminated against married couples, contrary to Article 41 of the Constitution. Murphy J. considered that he could apply the standard severance principles to this case, even though, of course, the circular was not a "law" within the meaning of Article 15.4.2° and could not benefit from the restorative features of that

---

[417] *Ibid.* at 426. See also *Bloomer v. Incorporated Law Society of Ireland* [1995] 3 I.R. 14 where Laffoy J. held that a statutory instrument conferring exemptions from exams on law students graduating from law schools in the Republic of Ireland was invalid on the ground that it contravened Article 6 of the Treaty of Rome. Although the effect of the declaration of invalidity was to prejudice the rights of persons not before the court (by taking away the exemptions of students who had graduated in the Republic), Laffoy J. tersely rejected the submission that she should "level up" by extending the exemption to law students graduating in Northern Ireland in the manner suggested by the Supreme Court in the case of a common law rule in *McKinley v. Minister for Defence* [1992] 2 I.R. 333.

[418] [1990] 2 I.R. 260.

[419] [1990] 2 I.R. 17.

provision. Nevertheless, the judge did not think that severance was possible since, just as in *McLoughlin*, the presence of the off-farm income limit served to restrict the numbers of farmers who could avail of the scheme:

> "[T]he operation of the ministerial schemes without excluding therefrom the married couples who exceeded the income limits for the time being would be to operate a very different scheme from that which had been intended by the Minister. . . . "[420]

11. Appeals from Administrative Decisions

In some contexts the Oireachtas provides for a statutory right of appeal from a decision of an administrative body. The right of appeal is usually confined to an appeal on a point of law, although this need not necessarily be the case.[421] The appeal will generally lie to the High Court.[422] If, however, a right of appeal to the lower courts is granted by statute, the decision of the lower court on appeal may itself be quashed upon an application to the High Court for judicial review.[423]

The nature and scope of the court's jurisdiction on an appeal is in all cases a matter of statutory construction. Nevertheless, it would be surprising if the Oireachtas, having created a right of appeal, did not intend to vest the High Court with powers in addition to, and distinct from, the inherent powers of judicial review which it enjoys at common law. As Costello J. explained in *Dunne v. Minister for Fisheries*:[424]

> "[It does not follow] that in every case the Court's jurisdiction on a statutory appeal is the same; in every case the statute itself must be construed. In construing a statute it does not seem to me helpful to apply by analogy the rules of judicial review, since, by granting a statutory appeal, the legislature must have intended that the Court would have powers in addition to those already enjoyed at common law."[425]

From a conceptual point of view, an appeal must be contrasted with judicial review. This means that when the High Court exercises such an appellate jurisdiction it has, generally speaking, the power to alter or vary an administrative decision. In judicial review proceedings, these options are restricted. Traditionally, the court was faced with the stark question: to quash (save where the order is severable) or not to quash.

---

[420] *Ibid.* at 27.
[421] For example, some administrative bodies have power to state a case for the High Court: see Adoption Act 1952, s.20 (An Bord Uchtala); Local Government (Planning and Development) Act 1976, s.42 (An Bord Pleanála).
[422] See, *e.g.* Competition Act 1991, s.9(1) ("person aggrieved" may appeal to the High Court against the grant of licence or certificate granted by the Competition Authority). The right of appeal does not always lie to the High Court: see, *e.g.* Taxes Consolidation Act 1997, Pt 40 (appeal on a point of law to the Circuit Court); Casual Trading Act 1995, s.6(8)(appeal to District Court against the making of casual trading bye-laws).
[423] See, *e.g. The State (McEldowney) v. Kelliher* [1983] I.R. 289.
[424] [1984] I.R. 230.
[425] *Ibid.* at 237.

Since 1986 however there has been the possibility of an award of damages.[426] Moreover, even when an appeal is allowed, this will only have a prospective effect and will not call into question the legality of earlier administrative decisions in respect of the period between the actual decision and the appeal. There is finally the distinction between "legality" which is all that can be examined on review and "merits" which are the proper province of an appeal. This has already been explained[427] and, with it, the fact that in practice there may not be a great deal of difference between the reach of the High Court's jurisdiction to hear appeals where these appeals are confined by statute to an appeal on a point of law and, on the other hand, its supervisory jurisdiction over administrative bodies and the lower courts now that the reach of jurisdictional error has been so greatly expanded.[428] In addition, one would be hard pressed to draw a satisfactory distinction between the scope of appellate review for errors of law and that of certiorari to quash for errors of law on the face of the record. But other important differences remain. In the first place, the remedies available on an application for judicial review are discretionary in nature.[429] Secondly, the High Court's power of judicial review is an inherent jurisdiction derived from Article 34.3.1°, and it is doubtful whether this supervisory jurisdiction may be removed by statute.[430] In contrast, any appellate jurisdiction is entirely the creation of statute and there are no constitutional impediments to the abolition of such a jurisdiction. Finally, a finding of invalidity has effect *erga omnes*. In other words, there may be a large category of persons who, being similarly affected by the impugned legislation or administrative act, will be permitted to rely on this finding of invalidity.[431] In contrast, because of the nature of the circumstances in which an appeal has been created, a decision of the High Court on appeal is a ruling in an *inter partes* matter between the appellant and the administrative body concerned and such a decision will not necessarily have general significance.

A good example of an appeal on a point of law is provided by Part 40 of the Taxes Consolidation Act 1997 which allows such an appeal from the Appeal Commissioners to the High Court. The effect of the precursor to these provisions was extensively discussed in *Mara v. Hummingbird Ltd*[432] The Appeal Commissioners had found as a fact that Hummingbird's purchase and sale of development property was for investment purposes, and, accordingly, could not be regarded as a sale "in the course of trade."

---

[426] See Chap. 15.
[427] See p. 477.
[428] See pp. 417–422.
[429] See pp. 717–739.
[430] *Tormey v. Attorney General* [1985] I.R. 289 and see further at pp. 454–458.
[431] For a more extended discussion of the difference between appeal on the merits and judicial review, see Hogan, "Remoulding Certiorari" (1982) 17 *Irish Jurist* 32 at pp. 48–54.
[432] [1982] I.L.R.M. 421. Kenny J., delivering the Supreme Court judgment, referred with approval to the speech of Lord Radcliffe in *Edwards v. Bairstow* [1956] A.C. 14. See also, *Rahill v. Brady* [1971] I.R. 69. The test enunciated in *Hummingbird* has been followed in a series of subsequent decisions. See, *e.g. O'hArgain v. Beechpark Estates Ltd* [1979] I.L.R.M. 57; *Re McElligott* [1985] I.L.R.M. 210; *MacCarthaigh v. D.* [1985] I.R. 73 and *Brosnan v. Mutual Enterprises Ltd* [1998] 1 I.L.R.M. 312. For an application of these principles in the non-revenue context, see *Brewster v. Burke and the Minister for Labour* (1985) 4 J.I.S.L.L. 98.

In the Supreme Court, Kenny J. drew a distinction analagous to that discussed earlier[433] under the rubric of "mixed questions of fact and law" between findings of primary fact, and the inferences to be drawn from those facts. Findings of primary fact – in this case, for example, Hummingbird's intentions when purchasing the premises – should not be disturbed "unless there was no evidence whatever to support them." In the case of inferences of conclusions based on these primary facts, a different approach was called for. If these conclusions were based on the interpretation of documents, the court should reverse them, for it was in as good a position as the Appeal Commissioners to determine the meaning of these documents. The court should only reverse other conclusions based on primary facts if these conclusions are ones which could not reasonably have been drawn, or which are based on a mistaken view of the law. Kenny J. urged a cautious approach, noting that the Appeal Commissioners will often have evidence:

> "[S]ome of which supports the conclusion that the transaction under investigation was an adventure in the nature of trade and he will have some which points to the opposite conclusion. These are essentially matters of degree and his conclusions should not be disturbed (even if the court does not agree with them, for we are not retrying the case) unless they are such that a reasonable commissioner could not draw them, or they are based on a mistaken view of the law."[434]

The effect of this test is to allow effective control over unreasonable decisions, or decisions based on "no evidence" or a mistaken view of the law, while at the same time allowing the administrative authority a tolerable margin of error. While the extent of the court's appellate jurisdiction is always a matter of statutory construction, the principle enunciated in *Hummingbird* can be readily adopted for other administrative appeals "on a point of law", *e.g.* under section 271 of the Social Welfare (Consolidation) Act 1993. This occurred in *Henry Denny & Sons (Ireland) Ltd v. Minister for Social Welfare*[435] where Keane J. applied *Mara v. Hummingbird* principles in holding that an appeals officer was correct in concluding that a supermarket demonstrator was actually employed by the appellant. The appeals officer's findings of fact could not be disturbed "unless they were incapable of being supported by the facts or were based on an erroneous view of the law." In this case, the appeals officer was found to have correctly directed himself in law and his application of the legal principles to the facts could not be disturbed. Hamilton C.J. added that the courts:

> "should be slow to interfere with the decisions of expert administrative tribunals. When conclusions are based upon an identifiable error of law or an unsustainable finding of fact by a tribunal such conclusions must be corrected. Otherwise, it should be recognised that [where] tribunals which have been given statutory tasks to perform and [who] exercise their functions (as is now usually the case) with a high degree of expertise and provide coherent and balanced judgments on the evidence and arguments heard by them, it should not be necessary for the Courts to review their decisions by way of appeal or judicial review."

---

[433] See pp. 422–426. For recent application of these principles, see *Ó Cúlacháin v. McMullan Brothers Ltd.* [1995] 2 I.L.R.M. 498 and *Proes v. Revenue Commissioners* [1998] 1 I.L.R.M. 333.

[434] [1982] I.L.R.M. 241 at 426.

[435] Unreported, Supreme Court, December 1, 1997.

There are, however, statutory provisions which serve to confer even broader powers on the courts than simply an appeal on a "point of law." A typical example is section 11 of the Fisheries (Consolidation) Act 1959 which provides that, on appeal by a "person aggrieved," the High Court may "confirm or annul" a byelaw made by the Minister for Fisheries. In *Dunne v. Minister for Fisheries*[436] Costello J. held that this section empowered the court to rule on the merits of the appeal and rejected the submission that the court could only interfere where it was established that the Minister had erred in law. The judge contrasted this section with other statutory appeal procedures, which restricted the appeal to an appeal on a point of law. When it transpired on the evidence given before him that the byelaw made by the Minister revoking certain restrictions on drift-net fishing in County Kerry ran counter to the "overwhelming scientific evidence," Costello J. concluded that the order should be annulled.

Another interesting example of the application of the court's appellate role is provided by *Balkan Tours Ltd v. Minister for Communications*.[437] Section 3 of the Transport (Tour Operators and Travel Agents) Act 1982 gives the Minister power to revoke a tour agent's licence. This power had been exercised by the Minister in the present case, since there had been a history of a "careless, unbusinesslike approach" on the part of the applicants as far as the observance of their trading licences was concerned. One of the more serious breaches of these conditions lay in the fact that the applicants had apparently circulated their travel brochures to the public without ensuring that the correct tour operator's licence had been reproduced in the brochures. Since no satisfactory explanation had been forthcoming, Lynch J. concluded that the Minister had been correct "to revoke the licences at the time and in the circumstances when he did so." However, further evidence had come to light at the hearing before Lynch J. showing that this error had been principally the fault of the applicants' printers, who had "acted on their own initiative and without any instructions." This evidence had not been before the Minister and Lynch J. concluded that the effect of section 3 was that:

> "The High Court is to ascertain all the relevant facts of the case, whether they were before the Minister or not and to give effect to them."[438]

The judge accordingly relied on this evidence to decide the appeal on the merits and he decided to allow the appeal on terms.

A slightly different form of appellate procedure is to be found in section 54(7) of the Fisheries Act 1980, which provides that "any person who is aggrieved" by the making of a ministerial order designating an area as one in which it shall be lawful to engage in aquaculture, "may appeal to the High Court against the order" within a 28-day period. This section was invoked in *Courtney v. Minister for the Marine*,[439] where local residents opposed on environmental grounds the making of such an order in respect of Smerwick Harbour, Co. Kerry. While O'Hanlon J. acknowledged that the court should be slow to interfere with a ministerial opinion,

---

[436] [1984] I.R. 230.
[437] [1988] I.L.R.M. 101.
[438] *Ibid.* at 107.
[439] [1989] I.L.R.M. 605.

he took the view that the appeal envisaged by the section enabled the High Court to review the merits of the decision:

> "The court should be slow to interfere with a ministerial decision in a matter of this kind where a question of industrial development and a conflict with local interests is involved. However, the Act requires the High Court, once an appeal is taken, as permitted by the provisions of section 54, to assess again whether a designation should be made in regard to a particular locality or stretch of sea and to review the ministerial order which has already been made."[440]

O'Hanlon J. did proceed to set aside the order, but chiefly because he was not satisfied that the Minister had been fully informed on all the potential environmental aspects of the project at the time he made his decision.

12. *Delegatus Non Potest Delegare*

The general principle here is that a power must be exercised by the authority (*delegatus*) in which it has been vested by the legislature. It cannot be transferred (*delegare*) to any other person or body. A straightforward example is *O'Neill v. Beaumont Hospital Board*.[441] In this case, a certificate, stating that the plaintiff's services were unsatisfactory with the consequence that he could not be confirmed in his post as a hospital consultant, was declared by Murphy J. to be invalid. The reason for this decision was that the certificate had been issued by the chief executive officer of the hospital rather than by the (part-time) Board in which the statutory instrument constituting the hospital had vested this function.

In principle, the maxim may apply to all types of decision whether quasi-judicial, legislative, administrative or policy (discretionary) (which is why the subject is treated in this general chapter and not in the chapter on the control of discretionary powers). However, the nature of the decision is undoubtedly one of the factors conditioning whether the rule applied in any particular situation.[442] The principle is at its strictest in the case of court proceedings.[443] It is fairly stringently applied in the case of legislative, quasi-judicial or wide discretionary powers. However, the

---

440 *Ibid.* at 611. See also *Guiry v. Minister for the Marine*, unreported, High Court, July 17, 1997.

441 [1990] I.L.R.M. 419. (This point was not taken in the Supreme Court). For unsuccessful delegatus arguments, see *Flynn v. An Post* [1987] I.R. 68, 75, 80–81; *Heneghan v. Western Regional Fisheries Board* [1986] I.L.R.M. 225 at 228.

442 De Smith, Woolf and Jowell, *Judicial Review of Administrative Action* (5th ed., 1995), pp. 364–368.

443 In regard to courts, the decision of the Supreme Court in *The State (Clarke) v. Roche* [1986] I.R. 619 is relevant. This case is best known for a far-reaching *obiter dictum* (which is quoted below) in connection with Article 34.1 and the administration of justice. However, the major point in the case was the *delegatus* principle. The case centred on the procedure for the issuing of a District Court summons. Under the relevant legislation (Petty Sessions (Ireland) Act 1851, ss.10, 11) a complaint could be made to, *inter alia*, a District Court clerk, who thereupon issued a summons. The point which was taken by counsel for the applicant was that there was no proof that the issue of a summons against the applicants had been made by the District Court clerk personally as opposed to some person under his general supervision and that, accordingly, the *delegatus* principle had been violated.

courts may allow some latitude in the case of routine administrative matters.[444] The essential point is that the maxim is merely a rule of statutory construction, rather than a rule of law and, in predicting its operation it has been said that:

> "Whether a person other than that named in the empowering statute is empowered to act will be dependent upon the entire statutory context, taking into account the nature of the subject matter, the degree of control retained by the person delegating and the types of person or body to whom the power is delegated."[445]

But even with the tolerance which the attitudes, correctly summarised in this passage evince, the *delegatus* principle has immense and often unwelcome implications in an era of mass government which is, executed in practice largely by anonymous public servants, rather than the chieftains in whom the function has been formally vested. The principle is, indeed, as might be guessed from its formulation, a survival from Roman law and fairly substantial exceptions to it have been developed in an attempt to reconcile it with modern conditions. The first of these applies only to the special, though common, case of the relationship between ministers and civil servants: it is covered in Part 13 of this chapter. Secondly, a Government order may be made on the request of a government minister, delegating to his Minister of State all the minister's powers and duties under a particular Act or, more narrowly, any particular statutory power.[446] Thirdly, at local government level, a county (or city)

The success of this submission depended, in part, on a point which was accepted as beyond controversy by the Supreme Court, namely, that in the case of a judicial, in contrast to an administrative, act, no delegation would be possible. It thus became relevant to ascertain whether "the activity of a District Court in deciding to issue a summons is not the carrying out of a judicial act but is rather the carrying out of an administrative or ministerial act" (at 640). Finlay C.J. concluded that the act was a judicial one for the purpose of non-delegation.

This would have been sufficient to determine the matter in the applicant's favour. However, having reached this finding, Finlay C.J. then went on to make what, it is submitted is a separate point, namely the speculation referred to earlier regarding Article 34.1. Finlay C.J. stated (at 64):

"No argument in this case was submitted to the Court with regard to the consequences from the point of view of constitutional validity of a conclusion that the powers given to the Peace Commissioner and District Court clerk to receive a complaint and issue a summons constituted the carrying out of a judicial act in a criminal matter. I, therefore, express no view upon it, but would refer to the query raised by Walsh J. in his judgment in *The State (Lynch) v. Ballagh* [1986] I.R. 203 as to the constitutional validity of giving to a Peace Commissioner powers to grant bail."

It is suggested that this query, which was taken up and answered in the affirmative in subsequent High Court decisions was based on an identification of a "judicial act" for the purpose of the *delegatus* principle with an administration of justice in Article 34.1. It is submitted that this identification is erroneous in view of the wide scope of the *delegatus* principle and the purpose of Article 34.1. which is different from that of the *delegatus* principle. See also, *Rainey v. Delap* [1988] I.R. 470.

[444] *The State (Keller) v. Galway County Council* [1958] I.R. 142 at 148 (chief medical officer can delegate physical examination of applicant for a grant, but not duty of forming the necessary opinion as to whether the applicant was substantially handicapped). See also, *Bridge v. R.* [1953] 1 D.L.R. 305; *Hookings v. Director of Civil Aviation* [1957] N.Z.L.R. 929. In the case of routine tasks performed by servants of a public authority, foreign courts have sometimes achieved this result by characterising the situation as involving the creation of an agency and so evading the *delegatus* principle: see de Smith, Woolf and Jowell, *op. cit.*, above, n.442, pp. 361–364.

[445] Craig, *Administrative Law* (3rd ed., 1994), p. 386. See further, Willis, (1943) 21 Can. B.R at p. 257.

[446] Ministers and Secretaries (Amendment) Act 1977, s.2; Criminal Justice Act 1951, s.23A(1)(as inserted by s.17(b) of the Criminal Justice (Miscellaneous Provisions) Act 1997). See, *e.g.* Public Service (Delegation of Ministerial Functions) Order (S.I. 1978 No. 117). See also, *Geraghty v. Minister for Local Government* [1976] I.R. 153 at 154, 160.

manager is empowered to delegate any of his functions to an assistant county (or city) manager, county secretary, town clerk, or officer approved by the Minister for the Environment, as an approved officer for the purposes of the delegation.[447]

Within the areas in which they operate, these exceptions are fairly far reaching (though the second and third categories are, of course, qualified by the terms of the order implementing them). The second and third exceptions are also, of course, examples of the *delegatus* principle being forced to bow before a statutory provision. There are numerous other statutory restrictions of the principle,[448] one of which is a formula which is often included in the constituent statutes of public bodies:

> "[the Agency] may perform any of its stated functions through or by any of its officers and servants duly authorised by [the Agency] in that behalf."[449]

A further example concerns An Bord Pleanála which would be substantially affected by the *delegatus* principle since it exercises quasi-judicial functions over significant property rights, were it not for the following statutory dispensation:

> "(a) Subject to paragraphs (b) and (c) of this subsection, the Board may perform or exercise any of its functions through or by any member of the Board or other person who, in either case, has been duly authorised by the Board in that behalf.
>
> (b) Paragraph (a) of this subsection shall be construed as enabling a member of the Board finally to determine a particular case if, and only if, the case to which an authorisation under that paragraph relates has been considered at a meeting of the Board prior to the giving of the authorisation.
>
> (c) Paragraph (a) of this subsection shall not be construed as enabling the Board to authorise a person who is not a member of the Board finally to determine any particular case with which the Board is concerned."[450]

However, such statutory dispensations are usually fairly specific and narrow so that, in certain areas of public administration, it may happen that there is a gap in the statutory patchwork, at which the delegatus principle will operate to strike down an administrative action for no better reason than legislative oversight.

Finally, three incidental points may be made, the first two of which involve merely the operation of the general principles of administrative law in association

---

447 County Management Act 1940, s.13; City and County Management (Amendment) Act 1955, s.17; *Cassels v. Dublin Corporation* [1963] I.R. 193.

448 See, *e.g.* Extradition (Amendment) Act 1987, s.5(1) (delegation of A.G.'s functions to D.P.P. in case of the former's "illness or absence"); Irish Takeover Panel Act 1997, s.6(2)(Panel may delegate functions to executive if it "reasonably considers it is appropriate to do so having regard to its duties generally under this Act, perform any of its functions regarding the carrying out by the directors of their duties in so far as they relate to the functions of the Panel.")

449 Thus the Censorship of Films (Amendment) Act 1992 provides in s. 2 for the appointment of assistant film censors

"to perform or to perform to such extent as the Official Censor may, subject to any decisions that may be given to him by the Minister [for Justice] determine, the functions . . . of the Official Censor." See also Statistics Act 1993, s.15.

450 Local Government (Planning and Development) Act 1983, s. 18. The special situation where An Bord Pleanála delegates matters of detail in planning permissions to be agreed with local planning authorities is dealt with elsewhere at p. 237 and see *Boland v. An Bord Pleanála* [1996] 3 I.R. 435.

with an act of delegation.[451] In the first place, there is the possibility of a waiver being deemed to authorise a delegation. For example, in *Flanagan v. University College, Dublin*[452] a University committee of discipline, in which the duty of disciplining students had been vested, took action solely on the recommendation of an independent expert from another institution from whom it had commissioned a report on an alleged case of plagiarism. This amounted, Barron J. held, to an improper delegation of its function by the committee of discipline. What is striking is that Barron J. appeared to suggest that if the student had given her "informed consent"[453] to the committee's total reliance on the opinion of the independent expert, then the delegation would have been proper. This appears to be the first suggestion that the *delegatus* principle may be waived. In its favour is the fact that, in an appropriate case, it appears to meet the justice of the situation. As against this, however, it may be argued that the *delegatus* principle is supposed to be a bulwark of good public administration having wider implications than its effects upon any particular individual.[454]

Secondly, where there is a statutory authority to delegate, then it will usually happen that this power will be discretionary. As such, like any substantive or, for that matter, procedural, discretionary power, it is subject to the general controls upon the exercise of discretionary powers, *e.g.* the requirement of reasonableness. An illustration of this occurred in the Northern Irish case of *Re Curran and McCann's Application*.[455] Here the Craigavon Borough Council had exercised its power, under section 18(d) of the Local Government Act (Northern Ireland) 1972, to appoint a committee consisting of all the council members, apart from the two Sinn Féin councillors: and then delegated almost all the functions of the Council to that committee. The object of this device was to exclude the Sinn Féin councillors from the work of the Council. However, Hutton J. held that the legislative intendment of the delegation provision was to promote the better management and regulation of the Council's business. Accordingly, in reliance on the general principle that a power given for one purpose cannot be exercised for another, Hutton J. struck down the resolution effecting the delegation since the purpose behind the resolution was not to further the better management of business.

The third point worth noting is that while the general question of the appropriate body to take an administrative action has usually arisen in the particular form of the correctness of a transfer of the power to take the action, it is perfectly possible that variations on this theme may occur. For example, in *McGabhann v. Incorporated Law Society of Ireland*[456] a query was raised by Blayney J. (though he did not determine the issue, since it had not been argued by the parties) as to the particular entity in which the power had been vested in the first place. It was clear from the relevant legislation that the Society's Educational Committee was to lay down the standard of proficiency to be achieved in the qualifying examination before a

---

[451] For delegation coupled with the *audi alteram partem* rule, see pp. 565–566.
[452] [1988] I.R. 724.
[453] *Ibid.* at 732.
[454] For analogous arguments in the context of whether the infractions of the rule against bias could be waived, see pp. 536–537.
[455] [1985] N.I. 26.
[456] [1989] I.L.R.M. 854.

candidate could gain entry to the Society's training course; but unclear as to whether it was for the committee or the examiners to decide whether the student had actually passed. On the one hand, the regulations stated that: "the committee shall also consider and adjudicate upon the report of the examiners", but gave no authority to delegate. On the other hand, according to Blayney J.:

> "the question might arise as to whether the committee, having appointed examiners, as it is given power to do under the regulations [just quoted], can reserve to itself what may necessarily be a function of the examiners, namely the decision as to whether a candidate has passed or not."[457]

13. The *Carltona* Principle: The Delegation of Ministerial Powers to Civil Servants

It would plainly be an impossible state of affairs if the law required a minister, even with the assistance of his minister for state, to keep in personal contact with each of the hundreds of decisions taken in his department each day. In most cases, the *delegatus* doctrine can be side-stepped by regarding each civil servant as the alter ego of the minister at the head of the department. This is a principle which is known as the "*Carltona* doctrine."[458] The principle that the powers vested in a minister may be exercised, without any express act of delegation, by responsible officials on his behalf is according to an English authority "a common law constitutional power",[459] but one which is capable of being negatived or confined by express statutory provisions or by clearly necessary implication." (The doctrine is buttressed,

---

[457] *Ibid.* at 865.
[458] *Carltona Ltd v. Commissioners of Works* [1943] 2 All E.R. 560. In that case, private property had been requisitioned under defence regulations by an official purporting to act on behalf of the responsible minister, Lord Greene M.R. rejected (at 563) the argument that the requisition was invalid on this ground:
> "In the administration of government in this country, the functions which are given to Ministers . . . are functions so multifarious that no Minister could ever personally attend to them. To take the example of the present case, no doubt that there have been thousands of requisitions in this country by individual ministeries. It cannot be supposed that this regulation meant that, in each case, the Minister in person should direct his mind to the matter. The duties imposed upon Ministers and the powers given to Ministers are normally exercised under the authority of the Ministers by responsible officials of the department. Public business could not be carried on if that were not the case."

See also, *Point of Ayr Collieries Ltd v. Lloyd-George* [1943] 2 All E.R. 546; *R. v. Skinner* [1968] 2 Q.B. 700; *Re Golden Chemical Products Ltd* [1976] Ch. 300, 310; and *McKernan v. Governor of H.M. Prison* [1983] N.I. 83; *R. v. Secretary of State for the Home Department, ex p. Oladehinde* [1991] 1 A.C. 254. In Britain, there is a narrow exception to the *Carltona* doctrine in that in cases involving personal liberty, the responsible minister must truly bring his mind to bear on the issue: Wade, *op. cit.* pp. 368; de Smith, Woolf and Jowell, *op. cit.*, above, n.442, pp. 369–373. In *Olahinde* the House of Lords appeared to accept that a deportation decision must be taken by the responsible Minister if her or she was available. But *cf.* the comments of Hutton J. in *McKernan v. Governor of H.M. Prison* [1983] N.I. 83; the approach of both Laffoy J. in *McM. v. Manager of Trinity House* [1995] 1 I.R. 595 and that of the Supreme Court in *Tang v. Minister for Justice* [1996] 2 I.L.R.M. 46.
[459] *R v. Secretary of State for the Home Department, ex p. Olahinde* [1991] 1 A.C. 254 at 282, *per* Lord Donaldson M.R. This statement of principle was expressly approved by Hamilton C.J. in *Devanney v. Minister for Justice* [1998] 1 I.L.R.M. 81. See also De Smith, Woolf and Jowell, *op. cit.*, above, n.442, p. 372.

in form anyway, by the notion that the minister bears political responsibility to the Dàil and legal responsibility, under the Ministers and Secretaries Act 1924, for all actions going on within his Department.)

The extent to which the *Carltona* doctrine formed part of Irish law had been the subject of some uncertainty prior to the decision of the Supreme Court in *Tang v. Minister for Justice*[460] and *Devaney v. District Judge Shields*.[461] One of these cases is *Geraghty v. Minister for Local Government (No. 2)*[462] which arose out of a planning appeal heard by the Minister (in the period before the creation of An Bord Pleanála). An oral inquiry was held by an inspector who was an official in the Department of Local Government. He made a report on the hearing, recommending that the appeal be rejected for reasons which he stated. This report was channelled through the routes normally followed by internal departmental documents and, as it went, gathered accretions of suggestions, comments and additional information from various civil servants. These included information which had been gained in another appeal from the same locality and suggested alternative reasons which might be given for rejecting the appeal. Eventually, the file reached the Parliamentary Secretary to whom the Minister's powers had been (properly) delegated and he rejected the appeal. The Supreme Court was unanimous that the *audi alteram partem* rule had been broken in that the plaintiff had no opportunity to know about or comment upon the additional material added to the report after the oral inquiry. The second issue – which is the relevant one here – arose from the fact that the inspector and other civil servants had given their views and that the Parliamentary Secretary appeared to have been influenced by them. Did this violate the *delegatus non potest delegare* principle? Upon this issue, differing views were expressed (although these differences were of no significance to the actual decision). Walsh J. (with whom Budd J. concurred) said that a Minister could not regard himself as bound even by the findings of fact made by an inspector holding an oral inquiry. Gannon J. (with whom Griffin J. agreed) and Henchy J. each disagreed with this and stated that the inspector could make (non-binding) recommendations as to the outcome which the Minister could take into account. In addition, they said that the Minister, as a layperson, could obtain expert advice on technical (*e.g.* legal or planning) matters from his departmental civil servants or elsewhere.[463]

These differences are of considerable practical significance for upon their resolution turns the question of how much scope is to be allowed to a civil servant and how much time and attention a Minister must actually give to a case himself. The second practical question is what range of decisions would attract the rule, followed by Walsh J., that it is the Minister himself who must decide. It seems probable from the nature of the facts in *Geraghty (No. 2)* that, at its highest, the rule would be confined to what are loosely called "quasi-judicial" decisions.[464]

The policies underlying the two approaches are demonstrated in the following quotations. In *Murphy*, Walsh J. stated:

---

[460] [1996] 2 I.L.R.M. 46.
[461] [1998] 1 I.L.R.M. 81.
[462] [1976] I.R. 153. See also *Murphy v. Dublin Corporation* [1972] I.R. 215.
[463] *Ibid.* at 171 (Walsh J.); 174–175 (Henchy J.) and 181–182 (Gannon J.).
[464] This was the view of Laffoy J. in *McM. v. Manager of Trinity House* [1995] 1 I.R. 595 where *Murphy* and *Geraghty* were distinguished. In this case the Minister for Education had made an order under

"[The Minister] is *persona designata* in that the holder of the office of the Minister for Local Government is the person designated for that function. If the Oireachtas had so enacted, the Act could just as easily have assigned the functions to the chairman of Coras Iompair Eireann or to the chairman of the Electricity Supply Board."[465]

By contrast, Lord Diplock said in *Bushell v. Secretary of State for the Environment*[466]:

"To treat the Minister in his decision-making capacity as someone separate and distinct from the department of government of which he is the political head and for whose actions he alone in constitutional theory is accountable to Parliament is to ignore not only practical realities but Parliament's intention. Ministers come and go; departments, though their names may change from time to time, remain. Discretion in making administrative decisions is conferred on a Minister not as an individual but as the holder of an office in which he will have available to him in arriving at his decision the collective knowledge, experience and expertise of all those who serve the Crown in the department of which, for the time being, he is the political head. The collective knowledge, technical as well as factual, of the civil servants in the department and their collective expertise are to be treated as the Minister's own knowledge, his own expertise. It is they who in reality will have prepared the draft scheme for his approval; it is they who in the first instance will consider the objections to the scheme and the report of the inspector by whom any local inquiry has been held and it is they who will give to the Minister the benefits of their combined experience, technical knowledge and expert opinion on all matters raised in the objections and the report. This is an integral part of the decision-making process itself; it is not to be equiparated with the Minister receiving evidence himself, expert opinion or advice from sources outside the department after the local inquiry has been closed."[467]

More recent Irish case law appears to have come down in favour of what is submitted is the common sensical view expressed in this passage.[468] In *Gallagher*

---

s.69(2)(c) of the Children Act 1908 transferring a young offender to a reformatory school on the ground that he was exercising a malign influence over other children in an industrial school and the question arose as to whether she was required to take the decision personally. Laffoy J. held that the *Carltona* principle applied. Unlike the functions of the Minister for Local Government under the Housing Act 1966 which were at issue in *Murphy*, the Minister for Education was here "performing an administrative or executive function, not a quasi-judicial function."

465 *Ibid.* at 238. This passage was quoted with approval by O'Higgins J. in the High Court in *Geraghty*: see [1976] I.R. 160–161. See to similar effect, Walsh J. in *Geraghty (No. 2)* [1976] I.R. 189.

466 [1981] A.C. 75.

467 *Ibid.* at 95. See also, *McKernan v. Governor of H.M. Prison* [1983] N.I. 83, a case where an order authorising the solitary confinement of a prisoner was signed by a Minister of State. The relevant prison regulations required that the order be signed by either a member of the prison board of visitors, or the Secretary of State for Northern Ireland. Hutton J. (and affirmed by the Court of Appeal) rejected the argument that this was a matter which was peculiarly committed to the Secretary of State, saying that it was most unlikely that Parliament intended that a member of the board of visitors could sign an authority under the regulations, but that a Minister of State could not.

468 *Ibid.* at 95. *Cf.* the comments of Laffoy J. in *McM. v. Manager of Trinity House* [1995] 1 I.R. 595 to the effect that the *Carltona* principles applied to the exercise of ministerial powers "for the practical and sensible reasons" adumbrated in the judgment of Lord Greene M.R. in that case. Likewise, in

v. Corrigan,[469] which concerned the disciplining of a prison officer, the facts were that the investigation of the applicant's transgression had all been done by a Higher Executive Officer in the Department of Justice; but no question whatsoever was taken as to whether the Minister could regard himself as bound by the official's views on the facts. A similar point of omission could be made in regard to *Pok Sun Shum v. Ireland*[470] which, it may be noted, was a deportation case, *i.e.* it concerned a peculiarly significant and delicate area of personal rights in which the Minister's involvement as an exception to the normal rule been required even in the United Kingdom.[471]

This line of authority has been recently confirmed by the Supreme Court in another deportation case, *Tang v. Minister for Justice.*[472] In this case, a senior official refused to grant Hong Kong immigrants who breached the terms of their entry conditions permission to reside in the State. The official had responsibility for the immigration and citizenship section in the Department of Justice and acted in the name of the Minister when making the decision: the Minister was not, however, consulted about the decision. The Supreme Court was not impressed by the argument that this decision ought to have been made by the Minister personally. Hamilton C.J. explicitly endorsed the *Carltona* doctrine and added:

> "Having regard to the *extensive powers* conferred by the Minister by the Aliens Act 1935 and the regulations made thereunder, *it cannot be supposed that it was the intention of the legislature that the Minister personally should exercise these powers*. The duties imposed upon the Minister and the powers given to the Minister can be artificial and are normally exercised under the authority of the Minister by responsible officials of the Minister's Department."[473]

Tang was further reinforced by the Supreme Court's decision in *Devanney v. Minister for Justice.*[474] Here the issue was whether the Minister was personally obliged to consider the appointment of each District Court clerk having regard to the provisions of s.46(2) of the Court Officers Act 1926.[475] In the High Court McCracken J. held that the purported appointment of a District Court clerk by a civil servant was invalid, as the *Carltona* principle had no application to such appointments. The clerks had important statutory responsibilities and held office at the will of the Minister and there were relatively few such appointments In these circumstances, it was – in contrast to the situation in *Tang* – "perfectly practical" for the Minister personally to appoint such clerks. This decision was reversed on appeal by the

---

Devanney v. District Judge Shields [1998] 1 I.L.R.M. 81 McCracken J. described (at 90, 92) the principles as "based on common sense", but stressed that the *Carltona* case "originated in rather peculiar wartime circumstances and in a case where the relevant decision was one of thousands of similar decisions which it would have been impractical for . . . the Minister . . . to make personally."

[469] Unreported, High Court, February 1, 1988. See pp. 551–552.
[470] [1986] I.L.R.M. 593.
[471] de Smith, Woolf and Jowell, op. cit., above, n.442, p. 370.
[472] [1996] 2 I.L.R.M. 46.
[473] *Ibid.* at 60–61. (emphasis supplied). The executive power/*persona designata* question was not addressed in this case.
[474] [1998] 1 I.L.R.M. 81.
[475] Which provides in relevant part that "every District Court clerk shall be appointed by the Minister and shall . . . hold office at the will of and may be removed by the Minister."

Supreme Court which unanimously affirmed the general applicability of the *Carltona* principle. Hamilton C.J. stressed the comparative importance of such an appointment compared to the decision in *Tang*:

"The appointment of a District Court clerk is, no doubt, an important matter. But it is not more more important than many of the decisions which fall to be made by civil servants, in the name of the Minister, under the Aliens Act 1935. Yet the Aliens Act 1935 was expressly approved by this Court in the *Tang* case as being a correct application of the *Carltona* principle. Logically, therefore, it seems to me that the Court must regard what happened in this case as being also a correct application of the *Carltona* principle."

Denham J. also stressed the general applicability of the *Carltona* doctrine, while conceding that "there are exceptions in matters of significant importance where the Minister is expected to make the decision personally." Keane J. emphasised the particular fact that the Minister's role in the purely formal task of appointing the candidate who had been selected by the Civil Service Commission, so that it must be presumed that the Oireachtas did not intend that he must personally make each appointment.

It would seem, therefore, that while the *Carltona* principle is one of general application (certainly as far as the exercise of routine bureaucratic powers is concerned), its scope depends in the last analysis on statutory interpretation. *Tang* is explicable on the basis that the Minister could not be expected to decide every immigration case personally, but there could well be other types of cases where the statutory context is such that it was clear that the Oireachtas must have intended that the decision would be personal to the Minister.[476] While the earlier decisions in *Murphy* and *Geraghty* were not addressed in the judgments in *Tang* and *Devanney*, the approach of Walsh J. has been effectively disavowed as far as the generality of civil service decisions are concerned.[477] It has, however, a residual application to those cases where having regard, *inter alia*, to the importance of the decision and the presumed statutory intent, it is clear that the Minister's own personal decision is called for.

14. Acting Under Dictation by Another Body

In the field next to the delegation of a decision by an authorised body to another body is a case in which the authorised body does, in form, take the decision, but in substance is merely rubber-stamping an instruction from another body.[478] A

---

[476] As McCracken J. said in *Devanney v. District Judge Shields* [1998] 1 I.L.R.M. 81 at 92 the *Carltona* principle "arose out of practical necessity" and therefore "must be considered in relation to specific ministerial functions both in the light of the practicality of the Minister personally exercising those functions and in the light of the importance of each individual decision."

[477] Thus in *Director of Public Prosecutions v. O'Rourke*, unreported, High Court, July 25, 1983 Finlay P. held that the assigning of a District Court clerk to a specific District Court area was not a matter which required the personal decision of the Minister. In *Devanney*, McCracken J. said that *O'Rourke* concerned "a purely administrative matter and one to which the *Carltona* principle clearly applies."

[478] The two classes plainly overlap. For instance, *Geraghty v. Minister for Local Government* [1976] I.R. 300 could have been classified under the present heading, but, as against this, it is usual for the "dictation" to emanate from an internal source. As it happened, the "advice" in *Geraghty* was from civil servants to their Minister. In any event, nothing turns on the distinction.

straightforward example of this occurred in *McLoughlin v. Minister for Social Welfare*.[479] Here the substantive point which has already been discussed was whether the appellant solicitor, employed in the Chief State Solicitor's Office, was to be classified as being in the employment of the State or of the civil service of the Government. The context in which this issue arose was that the appellant had claimed that he was not employed in the civil service of the State and accordingly was not an employed contributor for the purpose of making payments under the Social Welfare Act 1952. In deciding against the appellant, the appeals officer in the Department of Social Welfare said that he had received a minute from the Minister for Finance directing that the appellant was in the employment of the civil service of the Government and that he believed that he was bound to adhere to the Minister's direction.[480] That belief was characterised by O'Daly J. (as he then was) in the Supreme Court as:

> "[A]n abdication by him from his duty as an appeals officer. That duty is laid upon him by the Oireachtas and he is required to perform it as between the parties that appear before him fairly and freely as becomes anyone who is called upon to decide on matters of right and obligation."[481]

The principle thus robustly laid down in *McLoughlin* was followed in *The State (Rajan) v. Minister for Industry and Commerce*.[482] This case arose out of "directives" issued by the Controller of Patents, Designs and Trade Marks to members of his professional staff which were designed to reduce the arrears of applications in the Patent Office. These directives stated, *inter alia*, that if exactly the same patent application had already been accepted in another European Patent Office then that specification should be accepted in Ireland without any further checks as to matters such as "patentability" and "novelty", which the Act requires to be tested. The crucial point here is that the duty to make such checks was vested not in the Controller but in members of his staff known as "examiners." For section 11(1) of the Patents Act 1964 stated:

> "When the complete specification has been filed in respect of an application for a patent, the application shall be referred by the Controller to an examiner for examination."

In the light of this, Barron J. held that the Controller's instruction was invalid. First, he found that there is a statutory obligation to examine all applications for both

---

479 [1958] I.R. 1. Another aspect of the case is discussed at pp. 74–81 See also, *H. Lavender & Co. Ltd v. Minister of Housing* [1975] 1 W.L.R. 1231.

480 See also, *The State (Meade) v. Cork C.C.*, unreported, High Court, May 27, 1971 (local authority wrongly considering themselves bound by ministerial circular).

481 *Ibid.* at 12. The phrase "natural justice" is also used by O'Daly J., but it is submitted that the more appropriate analysis is that adopted in the text. *The State (Kershaw) v. Eastern Health Board* [1985] I.L.R.M. 235 would also appear at first sight to engage the principle against acting under dictation. But Finlay P. made it plain (at 239) that such was not the case:

> "The Minister has, of course, in addition a general administrative function with regard to the administration of the scheme for supplementary benefits which he himself has prescribed in the Regulations of 1977 [the Social Welfare (Supplementary Welfare Allowances) Regulations 1977]. In so far, therefore, as the circulars issued on his behalf on June 22, 1983, form advice and guidance to health boards carrying out the National Fuel Scheme it is clearly a proper and valid administrative act."

482 [1988] I.L.R.M. 231.

patentability and novelty, irrespective of anything done abroad. Secondly, Barron J. states that it was "erroneous" for the Controller to believe:

> "that he has a general power of control over the Examiners even extending to telling them the extent of the investigation of applications which they are to perform. The examination is a statutory function and there is nothing in the relevant statutory powers giving him such a right either as persona designata or as head of the Patent Office."[483]

The point was strengthened by the fact that the 1964 Act in effect provided for an appeal from the examiner to the Controller, so making it even less appropriate for an examiner to be subject to instructions from the Controller.

The following points of comparison may be made: *Rajan* involved a more extreme situation case than *McLoughlin*. For in *Rajan* what was involved was interference with a statutory obligation imposed upon another person, as opposed to a discretion, as in *McLoughlin*. Thus, in *Rajan*, there was purported interference with a mandate from the legislature. Next, in both *McLoughlin* and *Rajan*, there was little doubt that an instruction had been given; rather the live issue before the court was whether (as the applicant successfully submitted, in each case) the person receiving the instruction was independent, and not under the control, of the person giving it.[484] By contrast, in a third case, *The State (McCormack) v. Curran*,[485] what was mainly in contention was whether an instruction had been given, bearing in mind that the Director of Public Prosecutions and the Garda Síochána have a constitutional position, which makes them independent of each other.[486]

---

[483] *Ibid.* at 240.

[484] This principle is occasionally enshrined in legislation. Thus, while the Irish Takeover Panel consists of directors nominated by individual members (such as, *e.g.* the Irish Stock Exchange), s.6(3) of the Irish Takeover Panel Act 1997 provides that:

> "The members of the Panel shall not at any meeting of the members of the Panel or by any other means instruct the directors of the Panel regarding the carrying out by the directors of their duties in so far as they relate to the functions of the Panel."

[485] [1987] I.L.R.M. 225.

[486] The facts of the case were rather unusual. The central provision in the case was Article 2 of the Third Schedule to the Northern Irish Criminal Law Jurisdiction Act 1975. This provides that where a person is accused before a Northern Irish Court of an extra-territorial offence – that is, one committed in the Republic – then, provided that a warrant for his arrest for the same offence has been issued in the Republic, the accused may not opt for trial in Northern Ireland. In the present case, the applicant was awaiting trial before the Belfast Crown Court but had intimated that he wished to be tried in the Republic. However, in the Republic, no warrant had been sought in respect of the applicant. Accordingly, in the instant proceedings, he sought an order against the respondent that they seek a warrant for his arrest. The particular point of relevance, here, concerned the interaction between the Chief Superintendent and the D.P.P. The applicant alleged that the D.P.P. had issued a direction to the Chief Superintendent not to apply for a warrant for the applicant's arrest. The Supreme Court found that the applicant's case failed on the facts as there was no evidence to show such an instruction. However, the analysis of the relationship between the D.P.P. and the Garda Síochána is of interest. Walsh J. stated, in the first place, that on the authority of the Supreme Court in *The State (Collins) v. Ruane* [1984] I.R. 39 "all members of the Garda Siochana in the exercise of their duties are completely independent of the D.P.P. as he is completely independent of them." In consequence, if there had been any direction from the D.P.P., it "would be devoid of legal effect." The applicant's second point was that there had been consultations at which the D.P.P. had intimated to the Chief Superintendent that if he went ahead in procuring a warrant, the D.P.P. would not put down an indictment. However, according to Finlay C.J., such intimation would be "perfectly reasonable and proper, since it is the D.P.P.'s function to decide whether to prosecute".

Search warrant cases

This issue has also arisen in a series of cases dealing with search warrants, where, typically, applicants seeking to quash the warrants allege that the District Judge or Peace Commissioner has simply signed the warrant at the say-so of the requesting Garda officer, without having carefully examined the nature of the order sought. A good example of this is supplied by *People (Director of Public Prosecutions) v. Kenny*,[487] where McCarthy J. observed:

> "There was no evidence that the Peace Commissioner inquired into the basis of the Garda's suspicion. On the contrary, on the evidence adduced at the trial the only conclusion is that the Peace Commissioner . . . acted purely on the say-so of [the Gardai]. In doing so, he failed to exercise any judicial discretion: he failed to carry out his function under the section and, accordingly, the warrant is invalid."[488]

It follows that the District Judge or Peace Commissioner must be personally satisfied that there is, for example, reasonable ground for suspicion before granting the warrant and is not entitled to rely on the mere assertion or even sworn averment of the person applying for the warrant (such as a member of the Gardaí or the Customs and Excise) that he or she had reasonable grounds for such suspicion.[489]

In these circumstances, as Walsh J. stated, the Chief Superintendent "could not reasonably be expected to undertake proceedings which he might have had good reason to believe would be abortive."

[487] [1990] 2 I.R. 110.

[488] *Ibid.* at 117. See also *Rederei Kennermerland N.V. v. Attorney General* [1989] I.L.R.M. 821 (identical principle). Thus, for example, in *R . v. Southwark Crown Court, ex p. Sorsky-Defries* [1996] Crim. L.R. 195 McConnell L.J. quashed the warrant authorising a search of accountant's premises on suspicion of alleged money laundering, saying:
> "It is plain that such an intrusion upon the liberty of the subject could not be allowed to go through on the nod. Unfortunately, the plain impression given by what happened with regard to this application was that the Judge approached it on the basis that he could rely on what [the police] had sworn to and [had] not applied his own mind to being satisfied as to the various matters upon which it was necessary for him to be satisfied."

[489] See, *e.g. Byrne v. Grey* [1988] I.R. 31; *Rederei Kennermerland N.V. v. Attorney General* [1989] I.L.R.M. 821; *People (Director of Public Prosecutions) v. Kenny* [1990] 2 I.R. 110; *R . v. Southwark Crown Court, ex p. Sorsky-Defries* [1996] Crim. L.R. 195; *Hanahoe v. District Judge Hussey*, unreported, High Court, November 14, 1997.

CHAPTER 10

CONSTITUTIONAL JUSTICE I

Constitutional justice is an aspect of procedural law and procedural law looms especially large in the field of administrative law. The reason for this importance is that administrative law is directed to public authorities. One of the cardinal features distinguishing public authorities from private persons – so the theory runs – is that public authorities are taken to be non-partisan and open to persuasion provided that all the relevant facts and arguments are placed before them. With a fair procedure, the relevant matters are more likely to emerge and to be properly weighed by the decision-maker. Accordingly there is a causative link between proper procedure and the quality of the decision. In short, "[t]he whole theory of 'natural justice' is that ministers, though free to decide as they like, will in practice decide properly and responsibly once the facts have been fairly laid before them."[1] By today, the justifications offered for constitutional justice have gone beyond the "instrumental end" of accuracy. To some extent, procedural rectitude has been regarded as compensation for the latitude which the courts have traditionally allowed to the merits of an administrative action. There are other reasons, too, for the importance of procedure and we shall return to this basic question in Part 5 of the next chapter.

Next, take a fundamental point, namely whether it is appropriate for the courts to have moulded the procedure to be followed by public administrators so closely to their own form of procedure. (The truth of the observation contained in the last sentence may be tested against the case law, to be described in the course of this and the following chapter.) This question has also been raised in the context of English law where it has been remarked:

"What is of immediate importance is the realisation, often lost sight of when discussing procedure, that adjudication is but one form of decision-making. As has been evident, our procedural rules are sown in an adjudicator framework. . . . [T]here has been little thought directed to the broader question of whether adjudication is the correct decision-making process on which to be fashioning procedures. The vital point, brought out forcefully by Fuller, is that just as adjudication is distinguished by the form of participation that it confers so are other types of decision-making, and just as the nature of adjudication shapes the procedures relevant to its decisional form, so do other species of decision-making. Nine categories are listed by Fuller: mediation; property; voting; custom; law officially declared; adjudication; contract; managerial direction; and resort to chance. In each of these instances the relationship between the type of decision-making, and the procedural rules which are

---

[1] Wade, "Quasi-Judicial and its Background" (1949) 10 Camb.L.J. 216 at 217.

attendant thereon, can be presented in the following manner. The procedural rules will be *generated* by, and *will* protect the integrity of, the type of decision-making which is in issue. . . . What relevance has all of this? The answer, at least in outline, is simple. There may well be situations when the procedures modelled on adjudication are not the most effective or appropriate."[2]

Fascinating though this topic is, we shall pursue it no further here since there is no sign that any Irish judge has questioned the view that what is good for a court is (in a somewhat modified way) good for a public administrator.

1. Procedural Rights other than Constitutional Justice

It should be emphasised that the over-arching concept of constitutional justice does not comprehend the whole of the procedural law in the field of public administration. For, in addition, in the first place each decision may have its own particular procedural rules.[3] Some examples of such rules have already been given in – Chapter 9 (under the heading of "Formal and Procedural Provisions")[4] and in Part 7 of Chapter 5 (dealing with planning law[5]). Here we shall deal with two other important sources of such rules.

New Legislation

Earlier,[6] we referred to a package of public service reform measures, at various stages of development. Here may be the most convenient point at which to mention those elements in the package which relate to good procedure. The first item is the proposed Administrative Procedure Bill, which has not yet been published, although it has been the subject of official discussion[7] for a few years. This will set out a number of principles of good administration to which public bodies will be expected to adhere. These will include: the fixing of minimum response times; the provision of adequate information; and the establishment of appeal or other grievance mechanisms. It is expected that the Ombudsman will play a significant role in ensuring that each public body devises arrangements which satisfy these principles and also that it observes them in practice.

The second item is the Freedom of Information Act 1997 which (save in the case of local authorities and health boards) will come into effect on April 10, 1998.[8] Its

---

[2] Craig, *Administrative Law* (3rd. ed., 1994), pp. 302–303. The reference to Fuller is to his seminal article "The Forms and Limits of Adjudication" 92 Harv.L.Rev. 353 at 364.

[3] See Lord Diplock's well-known restatement in *C.C.S.U. v. Minister for Civil Service* [1985] 1 A.C. 374 at 411:

> "I have described the third head as 'procedural impropriety' rather than failure to observe basic rules of natural justice or failure to act with procedural fairness towards the person who will be affected by the decision. This is because susceptibility to judicial review under this head covers also failure by an administrative tribunal to observe procedural rules that are expressly laid down in the legislative instrument by which its jurisdiction is conferred, even where such failure does not involve any denial of natural justice."

[4] See pp. 440–452.
[5] See pp. 238–239.
[6] See p. 110.
[7] *e.g. 1995 Ombudsman Report*, p. 14; *1996 Ombudsman Report*, p. 9.
[8] S.1(2), (3) states that, save for local authorities and health boards, the Act shall come into operation one year after its passing. In these exceptional cases, it is to come into operation on such day no later

main purpose, which is to provide individuals with a legal right of access to information, mainly about themselves, held by public bodies, falls outside the scope of this work. However, three of its subsidiary provisions are relevant here, since they set down proper procedures, which must be followed by "public bodies". Before turning to these provisions the key term "public body" must be explained. This is defined widely in section 2 and the First Schedule, to embrace not only the Departments of State but also: An Bord Pleanála; the Land Registry; the Environmental Protection Agency; the Pensions Board; the Revenue Commissioners and fifty-odd other agencies; as well as the local authorities and health boards. In addition, the Schedule provides that the Minister for Finance (with the consent of such other Minister as he considers appropriate) may make regulations which will bring several other categories of public or quasi-public bodies (including the Garda Síochána, the Law Society of Ireland plus all state-sponsored bodies) into the scope of the Act. There are few exceptions. Among them, probably[9] are records held by a court or tribunal of inquiry or "by the Attorney General or the Director of Public Prosecutions . . . (other than a record concerning the general administration of either of those offices)".

The first of the three obligations mentioned is defined as follows, in section 15(1):

"A public body shall cause to be prepared and published and to be made available . . . a reference book containing:

(a) a general description of its structure and organisation, functions, powers and duties, any services it provides for the public and the procedures by which any such services may be availed of by the public,

. . .

(c) a general description of the matters referred to in paragraphs (a) and (b) of *section 16(1)* [see below]

. . .

(e) the names and designations of the members of the staff of the body responsible for carrying out the arrangements aforesaid

. . .

(g) appropriate information concerning:

   (i) any rights of review or appeal in respect of decisions made by the body (including rights of review and appeal under this Act), and

   (ii) the procedure governing the exercise of those rights and any time limits governing such exercise,

(h) any other information that the head of the body considers relevant for the purpose of facilitating the exercise of the right of access, and

(i) information in relation to such other matters (if any) as may be prescribed [by the Minister for Finance]."

---

than eighteen months after the date of its passing (April 10, 1997) as may be fixed by the Minister for Finance with the consent of the Minister for Environment (local authorities) or the Minister for Health (health boards). See too, ss.15(2), 16(2). See generally, Meehan "The Freedom of Information Act in Context" (1997) 12 I.L.T. 231.

9   The doubt indicated in the text arises because the provision – s.46 – which (probably) creates the exceptions regarding the A.G. and the D.P.P., refers to "records". It might be inferred from this that it is only in respect of access to records on a person that (say) the D.P.P. is exempted from the Act. In short, the other obligations in the Act, *e.g.* an obligation to give reasons (on which see pp. 574–578) as to why a person was not prosecuted, would apply to the D.P.P. This could be a significant point.

In relation to this provision, one should notice the following points. First, the phrase "the rights of review or appeal", referred to in section 15(1)(g)(i) include, but are not restricted to, rights under the 1997 Act itself. Secondly, in preparing "the reference book", referred to at the start of the extract, the public body must have regard to "the fact that the purpose of the book is to assist members of the public . . .".[10] Thirdly, the Minister for Finance must ensure that public bodies take appropriate measures to train staff and make arrangements to ensure compliance with the Act.[11]

The second obligation is contained in section 16(1), which provides:

> "A public body shall cause to be prepared and published and to be made available in accordance with *subsection* (5)
>
> *(a)* the rules, procedures, practices, guidelines and interpretations used by the body, and an index of any precedents kept by the body, for the purposes of decisions, determinations or recommendations, under or for the purposes of any enactment or scheme administered by the body with respect to rights, privileges, benefits, obligations, penalties or other sanctions to which members of the public are or may be entitled or subject under the enactment or scheme, and
>
> *(b)* appropriate information in relation to the manner or intended manner of administration of any such enactment or scheme."[12]

Plainly, in respect of the category of "decisions, determinations . . . " to which it applies this is a far reaching provision. Notice though that certain consequences of failure to follow the provision are stated in such a way as to suggest that breach of the obligation will not always lead to any form of compensation or other remedy for the person affected. For even if there has been a breach, the person affected must show: that he was not aware of the "rule, procedure . . . "; and that but for such non-publication he or she would have been aware of it. In addition, the public body must be unable to show that "reasonable steps [as an alternative to publication] were taken by it to bring the rule or requirement to the notice of those affected." Where these conditions are satisfied, then the consequence is rather unspectacular: "the public body concerned shall, if and in so far as it is practicable to do so, ensure that the person is not subjected to any procedure (not being a penalty imposed by a court upon conviction of an offence)."[13]

Probably a court order could be obtained to enforce obedience with this provision. However, plainly, a good deal remains to be worked out in regard to both the practical operation and the consequences of breach of sections 15(1) and 16(1).

The third significant element of the 1997 Act (contained in section 18) establishes "a right to reasons", which is considered below.[14]

---

[10] s.15(3).
[11] s.15(5).
[12] See also s.15(d)(iii).
[13] All quotations in this paragraph are from s.16(4)(3).
[14] See pp. 574–578.

'Charters'

A number of public bodies, (among them, the Departments of Health and Agriculture, the Revenue Commissioners, Bord Telecom, ESB) have now published "Customer Charters" or "Charters of Right". Whilst these lack the coherent, ideological edge of their British counterparts,[15] they are certainly intended to improve the quality of public services and to make them more responsive to their users. Thus they deal with such matters as: prompt service; non-discrimination; openness and accessibility; courtesy; privacy; and a right to complain. These "Charters" are usually published with a fanfare of trumpets (copy to each consumer, etc.). The fact that a charter sets a standard to which a public body has committed itself, means that it may be judged fairly according to that standard, by citizens, politicians and media and pilloried where it falls short of the standard promised. From the legal point of view, the interesting conceptual question is whether these charters have legal effect. Given their variety, generalisation poses difficulties. However, it can be said that they certainly do not have direct legal effect partly because of their generally imprecise language and mostly because they fall into the fuzzy category of "soft law".[16] One way in which these gnomic creatures could have an indirect effect is in fixing the factors by which, on a judicial review application, a public body could be held to have behaved unreasonably or overlooked a relevant consideration (for example – in the case of the Revenue Commissioners' Charter of Rights – confidentiality, compliance costs or a presumption that the taxpayer would be honest). Sometimes, the Charters restate what is already a legal right, for example, privacy in the case of "A Charter of Rights for Hospital Patients" of 1992.

Again, the doctrine of legitimate expectations, in one of its forms,[17] may require public bodies to honour their declarations of policy, regarding (say) standards of service. Obviously, a good deal depends upon whether it was reasonable for the consumer to have relied upon the commitment in the Charter (for instance, because of its precision). In this context, an example may be the Bord Telecom Customer Charter (of May 22, 1996) which states that if it fails to connect a new customer within 15 working days, it will allow a credit of £20.00. This might be regarded indeed as going beyond an expectation and as amounting to a representation. Apart from the law, failure to honour a Charter commitment could amount to mal-administration, which would attract censure under the Ombudsman Act 1980. It may be possible, too, that a Charter would be given an indirect effect, by breathing more precision into the Administrative Procedure legislation, referred to earlier.

Procedure of a deliberative body

One example of this is the City and County Management (Amendment Act 1955, section 10(1), which came up for discussion in *Ahern v. Kerry County Council*.[18] This case concerned the internal proceedings of a local authority. The provision

---

15 For the British position, see: Drewry, [1993] P.L. 248; Barron and Scott (1992) 55 M.L.R. 526; Wade and Forsyth, *Administrative Law* (7th ed., 1994), pp. 106–107; Craig, *op. cit.*, above, n. 2, p. 93.

16 See pp. 42–57.

17 See, *e.g. Fakih v. Minister for Justice* [1993] 2 I.R. 406 at p. 868.

18 [1988] I.L.R.M. 392.

states that "an estimate of expenses shall be considered by the local authority at a meeting . . .". In *Ahern*, Blayney J. was required to consider whether the procedures adopted at an estimates meeting complied with the section. At the meeting, the chairman had confined discussion to the first group of estimates, with the remaining groups being immediately put to the vote together with no further discussion and the rate being thereby struck. Blayney J. held that an argument founded on breach of constitutional justice failed (though only on the facts) on the curious basis that the applicant-councillor had been present and had had the chance to speak (though, necessarily only in respect of the first group). However, the judge also ruled that the procedure did not comply with section 10(1) of the 1955 Act (since "it would at least be necessary that each programme group should come up for discussion.[19]

A case which was grounded on a wider basis than *Ahern* in that it turned not on a specific statute, but it seems (though nothing precise is stated in the judgment) on the judge's understanding of free speech and democratic process in a deliberative body is *Farrell v. South Eastern Health Board*,[20] a case which may have some potential for growth. The case grew out of a long-running controversy concerning the location of the acute general hospital for South Tipperary, support being divided between Clonmel and Cashel. The applicant complained of two aspects[21] of the way the dispute was treated both at and before a meeting of the respondent health board. First, he had been allowed by the chairman to put his views before the meeting but he was eventually allowed only two minutes in which to do so. Secondly, he had been frustrated in collecting information regarding fire safety standards at Clonmel Hospital. He eventually compiled the report and placed it before the members of the Board. Barron J. stated: "The function of the Board is an administrative one and the members vote in accordance with their views as to the appropriate course which the Board should follow. As such, there is no place for the principles of [constitutional] justice."[22] However, the judge went on to find for the applicant and to make a declaration that the Board's resolution should be set aside. The central passage in the judgment is as follows:[23]

> "[The applicant] was entitled to a reasonable opportunity to express his views on the motion and to put before the Board evidence in support of those views. It was a matter for the chairman to place reasonable fetters on the exercise of that right. Did the first applicant get that opportunity? Unfortunately, the essential facts in this case are blurred by the unnecessary confrontation which occurred. Meetings such as the one with which we are dealing can become very heated. Clashes occur between individuals or factions holding divergent views. One side or the other may resort to varying lawful tactics to ensure that their side wins the vote. But what must not occur is the stifling or

---

[19] *Ibid.* at 397.

[20] [1991] 2 I.R. 291. Conceivably, *Association of General Practitioners v. Ministers for Health* [1995] 1 I.R. 382 at 388–392 could also be regarded as a case of this type. However, it was not so analysed by O'Hanlon J. in the High Court.

[21] A further point in *Farrell* was that no details of the cost of the scheme were put before the meeting for the purpose of the resolution, as required by standing order 4.2.

[22] [1991] 2 I.R. 291 at 295.

[23] *Ibid.* at 291 at 295–296.

attempted stifling of any member or group of members. By this I mean preventing unfairly that members from expressing his, her or their views."

In *Doyle v. Croke*[24] the plaintiffs were members of the I.T.G.W.U. and former employees of a company which had gone into liquidation. A strike committee had been set up mainly to negotiate redundancy payments greater than the statutory minimum on behalf of the employees all of whom were members of the defendant-union. The strike committee organised a picket against the employer's premises.

Two resolutions were passed at meetings of union members. The first, in June, laid it down that workers who thenceforth did not perform satisfactory picket duty would not be represented by the strike committee in pursuance of redundancy payments or permitted to participate in any lump sum which might be obtained from the employer. However, Costello J. found that, for whatever practical reason of difficulty in keeping count of who in fact had completed the requisite six-hour picket shift, compliance with the resolution's terms was not required when it came to compiling the list of those entitled to share in the settlement of the union's claim. The second meeting was held in November. Prior to the meeting, the strike committee had drawn up the list mentioned of 150 employees (out of a total of 270 involved) among whom it was proposed to divide the settlement of £380,000. And it was submitted by the defendants that the resolution passed at the November meeting could be relied upon both as impliedly validating the June resolution (the defects of which, as regard notice, are mentioned below) and also as approving the list, not-withstanding the fact that it was not compiled in accord with the June Resolution. The 83 plaintiffs in the case were among the employees who were not to share in the settlement moneys. In the first place, Costello J. found that the plaintiffs had not been given adequate notice in respect of either resolution. As regards the November meeting, only those 150 members of the union who were on the list were notified that the meeting was to be held. Other members learnt of the meeting and attended but were informed that they would not be permitted to vote at it.

Thus the central question was whether "the right to fair procedures" (the phrase, constitutional justice not being used in the case though it seems that no significance was attached to this) extended to resolutions passed at trade union meetings. Costello J. grounded his decision that it did so apply upon three bases. The first was Article 40.6.1° iii (the constitutional rights of association). The second was Lord Denning M.R.'s well-known observation in *Breen v. A.E.U.*[25] that: "even though the rules of a union might provide committees with wide discretionary powers . . . the contract between the members would be construed as containing an implied term that the discretion would be exercised fairly." Thirdly, Costello J. invoked the generalised guarantee to the citizen of basic fairness of procedures established in *Re Haughey*.[26]

One should add, though, that in contrast to *Ahern or Farrell*, it would be possible to give *Doyle* a narrower or wider operation. Take, as an example, the decision of a trade union resolution authorising a strike in which the complainant was not

---

24 Unreported, High Court, May 6, 1988. See to similar effect, *Rodgers v. ITGWU* [1978] I.L.R.M. 51.
25 [1971] 2 Q.B. 175 at 190.
26 [1971] I.R. 217 at 264. See p. 557.

himself involved. The full-blooded application of the *ratio* – which was based on the idea of democratic processes in a trade union might well lead to the idea that *audi alteram partem* should apply. As against this, on the facts of *Doyle*, the plaintiff's own significant material interests were peculiarly engaged in the resolutions passed at the meeting. Indeed in *Doyle*, the resolution might be regarded as constituting, with its application, a single transaction which substantially disadvantaged the plaintiffs. It is very significant that Costello J. was careful to restrict the scope of his *ratio* to what was necessary to "protect individual members against procedures which might be unfair to them" or to "decision[s] materially affecting the members' rights."[27]

2. Constitutional Justice and Natural Justice

Natural justice

The best way of explaining constitutional justice is to begin with natural justice, which consists of two fundamental procedural rules, namely: that the decision-maker must not be biased; and, secondly, that anyone who may be adversely affected by a decision should not be condemned unheard; rather he should have the best possible chance to put his side of the case.

The title, in particular the epithet "natural," has attracted a certain amount of attention. According to Costello J. in *Nolan v. Irish Land Commission*:

"... [T]he adjective 'natural' before justice was not used to describe justice by reference to man in a state of nature or in primitive society. Rather it has been employed as part of a phrase which developed from a philosophical view of man's nature as that of a being endowed with reason and capable of ascertaining objective moral values. As pointed out by de Smith, *Judicial Review of Administrative Action* [now 5th Ed. at p. 378]: 'The term expresses the close relationship between the common law and moral principles and it has an impressive ancestry.'"[28]

The universality of natural justice can also be illustrated by the inclusion of the two principles of natural justice in the European Convention of Human Rights, Article 6(1) of which provides that: "In the determination of his civil rights and obligations or of any criminal charges against him, everyone is entitled to a fair and public *hearing* within a reasonable time by an *independent and impartial* tribunal established by law."[29] Similarly, O'Higgins C.J. has remarked:

---

[27] *Doyle*, at pp. 13 and 16 of the unreported judgment.

[28] [1981] I.R. 23 at 34. Costello J. was countering criticism of the term contained in *Green v. Blake* [1948] I.R. 242. See also the lyrical passage of Gavan Duffy J. in *Maunsell v. Minister for Education* [1940] I.R. 213 at 234 : "... elementary justice ... The principle cannot be more tersely expressed than in the lines of Seneca: '*Quicunque aliquid statuerit, parte inaudita altera, Aequum licet statuerit, haud aequus fuerit.*'". Dr Cronin of the U.C.C. Classics Department translates Seneca as follows: "Whoever has made a decision, the second party not having been heard, although he has decided justly, will not have been just."

[29] Author's emphasis. See *Campbell v. United Kingdom* (1985) 7 E.H.H.R. 165 (guarantee of Art. 6(1) extends to adjudications of Prison Boards, at least in serious disciplinary cases) and *Findlay v. United Kingdom*, (1997) 24 E.H.R.R. 221 (court-martials). See also pp. 562–563.

"The application of [the principles of natural justice] to the different situations which competing interests in society create has never been capable of precise definition. For that reason they have been criticised and even rejected by those who believe precise definition to be the *sine qua non* of true law. They came to be recognised, however, at a time when society was emerging from the rule of might and force and when men looked for the protection of their rights in the oral sphere of justice and fairness. Natural justice, imprecise though the term may be, was something which came to be regarded as each man's protection against the arbitrary use of power."[30]

Constitutional Justice ". . . more than the two well-established principles . . ."

In 1965, natural justice in Ireland was reincarnated as constitutional justice. In what was obviously intended to be a seminal *obiter dictum*, Walsh J. stated: "In the context of the Constitution, natural justice might be more appropriately termed constitutional justice and must be understood to import more than the two well-established principles that no man shall be judge in his own cause, and *audi alteram partem*".[31] *Audi alteram partem* means "hear the other side". This will be dealt with in detail in Chapter 11.

There has been rather uneven progress in divining what these additional factors comprise and the courts have sometimes appeared reluctant explicitly to draw upon this reservoir (possibly because of the width of natural justice (*simpliciter*)). It seems, however, that the constitutional right to fair procedures embraces not only the "two great central principles" of *nemo iudex in causa sua* and *audi alteram partem*,[32] but also includes a range of (as yet) imprecise procedural guarantees which are designed to avoid the unfair treatment of accused persons, litigants and persons appearing before administrative tribunals. One example appeared in *M v. M*[33] where Henchy J. stated that a judge (in a nullity case, where collusion was suspected) was not entitled to disregard the "corroborated and unquestioned evidence of witnesses", since to do so was not in accordance with the proper administration of justice[34] in that it was not on probative evidence. Other possibilities (some of which are elaborated later on in this or the following chapter) – which to a greater or (often) lesser extent have been accepted by the courts – include the following: a requirement that tribunals should generally sit in public[35]; the right to a reasonably prompt decision[36];

---

30 *Garvey v. Ireland* [1981] I.R. 75 at 91.
31 *per* Walsh J. in *McDonald v. Bord na gCon* [1965] I.R. 217 at 242. For a discussion of the significance of these remarks, see Casey, "Natural and Constitutional Justice – The Policeman's Lot Improved" (1979–1980) 2 D.U.L.J. (N.S.) 95 and Hogan, "Natural and Constitutional Justice: *Adieu* to *Laissez-Faire*" (1984) 19 Ir. Jur. (N.S.) 309. For the analagous European Convention, umbrella doctrine of the "fair . . . hearing", which has an open-ended residual quality, see Harris, O'Boyle and Warbrick, *Law of the European Convention on Human Rights* (1995), pp. 202, 208–210.
32 *Mooney v. An Post* [1994] E.L.R. 103 at 116, *per* Keane J.
33 [1979] I.L.R.M. 160.
34 *Ibid.* at 162. See also: *R. v. Deputy Industrial Injuries Commissioner, ex parte Moore* [1965] 1 Q.B. 456; *Mahon v. Air New Zealand Ltd* [1985] A.C. 808. But *cf. The State (Power) v. Moran* [1976–1977] I.L.R.M. 20 and *The State (Shinkaruk) v. Carroll*, unreported, High Court, December 15, 1976.
35 *Barry v. Medical Council*, unreported, High Court, February 11, 1997. (Obviously Art. 34.1 of the Constitution does not apply in this context since it is directed exclusively to the courts).
36 See, *e.g., Bosphorus Hava Yollari Turism ve Tickaret Anonim Sirketi v. Minister for Transport (No.2)*,

the right to reasons for a decision[37]; the right to some form of administrative appeal against a decision[38]; the right to free legal aid for certain types of administrative decisions[39] and the right that, in a criminal trial, the accused should be able to confront his accusers.[40] However, the courts have emphatically declined[41] to take up the suggestion that the burden of proving facts which, if established, would lead to a loss of livelihood, should be beyond reasonable doubt.

The judgment of Costello P. in *McCormack v. Garda Síochána Complaints Board*[42] provides an example of how the courts may approach this issue. In this case the applicant claimed that the failure by the Board to give reasons for its decision not to take further steps in respect of a particular complaint violated his right to fair procedures. Costello P. explained:

"In theory our courts would be free to extend the common law principles of natural justice as they are judge-made rules, but it would seem preferable that the existence, scope and nature of the duty to provide reasons for an administrative decision should be considered in the light of the constitutional requirement relating to what the courts have termed 'constitutional justice', rather than as an extension of the common law rules of natural justice.

. . . Constitutional justice imposes a constitutional duty on a decision making authority to apply fair procedures in the exercise of its statutory powers and functions. If it can be shown that that duty includes in a particular case a duty to give reasons for its decision then a failure to fulfil this duty may justify the court in quashing the decision as being *ultra vires* . . .

Where a claim is made that a breach of a constitutional duty to apply fair procedures has occurred by a failure to state reasons for an administrative decision the court will be required to consider (a) the nature of the statutory function which the decision maker is carrying out (b) the statutory framework in which it is to be found and (c) the possible detriment that the complainant may suffer arising from the failure to state reasons."[43]

It would seem from this unusual passage that constitutional justice is a more policy-led and flexible concept than natural justice. At common law, a breach of natural

---

unreported, High Court, January 22, 1996; *McNeill v. Garda Commissioner* [1997] 1 I.R. 469 and *Re Gallagher's Application (No.2)* [1996] 3 I.R. 15. See pp. 580–585.

[37] See, *e.g. The State (Creedon) v. Criminal Compensation Tribunal* [1988] I.R. 51; *Gavin v. Criminal Injuries Compensation Tribunal* [1997] 1 I.R. 132 and *McCormack v. Garda Síochána Complaints Board* [1997] 2 I.L.R.M. 321. See further at pp. 569–580.

[38] *Carroll v. Minister for Agriculture & Food* [1991] 1 I.R. 230 at 235, *per* Blayney J. (although the absence of a right of appeal against test findings by veterinary surgeons was held to be justified in the circumstances).

[39] *Kirwan v. Minister for Justice* [1994] 1 I.L.R.M. 333. But *cf. Corcoran v. Minister for Social Welfare* [1991] 2 I.R. 175.

[40] *White v. Ireland*, unreported, High Court, December 21, 1993 and *Donnelly v. Ireland*, unreported, High Court, December 3, 1996.

[41] See now *Grant v. Garda Síochána Complaints Board*, unreported, High Court, June 12, 1996; *Georgopoulos v. Beaumont Hospital Board*, unreported, Supreme Court, June 4, 1997 and the comments of O'Flaherty J. in *O'Laoire v. Medical Council*, unreported, Supreme Court, July 25, 1997.

[42] [1997] 2 I.L.R.M. 321.

[43] *ibid.* at 331–332.

justice was not in itself tortious.[44] It now seems probable that an infringement of the constitutional right to fair procedures may sound in damages and such awards have been in fact made by the courts on this express basis.[45] This is a point which is elaborated in a later chapter.[46]

It may be better to confine constitutional justice to procedural safeguards, and not, as is sometimes done, to apply the term so widely that it encompasses substantive rights, lest it become too imprecise a concept.[47]

Foundation in the Constitution

There is another point of contrast between constitutional and natural justice, namely that natural justice remains a mere common law (and therefore rebuttable) presumption to be applied, in appropriate contexts, in the interpretation of statutes. By contrast, constitutional justice is judicially regarded as implicit in the Constitution (Article 40.3).[48] The reasoning seems to be that words like "respect" and "protect . . . from unjust attack" in Article 40.3 refer not only to substantive protection but also mean that even where substantive interference is permitted, it must be accompanied by a fair procedure. This difference in the sources of constitutional and natural justice is important. A British statute can, if it uses clear enough words, exclude the rules of natural justice because of the absence of a written constitution.[49] By contrast, an Irish statute attempting to exclude the rules of constitutional justice in a situation where they would be appropriate would be unconstitutional. A straightforward and (in that a nineteenth-century statute was involved) not untypical example of a statute being overridden by the principles of constitutional justice occurred in *Jaggers Restaurant Ltd v. Ahearne*.[50] The case arose out of a Circuit

---

44 *Dunlop v. Woollahra M.C.* [1982] A.C. 158.

45 See, *e.g. Healy v. Minister for Defence*, unreported, High Court, July 7,1994; *McAuley v. Garda Commissioner* [1996] 3 I.R. 208 at 232.

46 See p. 821.

47 In *The State (Gleeson) v. Minister for Defence* [1976] I.R. 280 at 295, Henchy J. defined constitutional justice very widely to include a number of constitutional guarantees some of which are peculiar to criminal courts (e.g. the right to jury trial) and some of which are substantive (*e.g.* that unconstitutional laws should not be applied). He then commented:

> "Because of the wide scope of such constitutional guarantees . . . a plea of denial of constitutional justice lacks the concreteness and particularity necessary to identify and bring into focus the precise constitutional issue which is being raised."

However, this view of constitutional justice has largely fallen into disfavour: see Hogan, "Natural and Constitutional Justice: Adieu to Laissez-Faire" (1984) 19 Ir. Jur. (N.S.) 309.

48 *Re Haughey* [1971] I.R. 217; *Glover v. B.L.N. Ltd* [1973] I.R. 388. *Kiely v. Minister for Social Welfare (No. 2)* [1977] I.R. 267; *Garvey v. Ireland* [1981] I.R. 75; *Ryan v. V.I.P. Taxi Co-operative Ltd* (High Court, *ex tempore*) *Irish Times Law Report*, April 10, 1989; *Halal Meat Packers v. E.A.T.* [1990] I.L.R.M. 293 at 307–309.

49 See, *e.g. O'Brien v. Bord na Móna* [1983] I.R. 255 at 270–271 where Keane J. held that an enactment which created a situation where the decision-maker was a judge in his own cause would conflict with the constitutional guarantee of fair procedures, unless a different form of procedure was not practicable. By contrast in *Bushell v. Environment Secretary* [1981] A.C. 75 it was held that the fact that the Minister was the person to consider objections to a provisional motorway route, which he himself had prepared was beyond challenge because *it had been clearly established by statute*. Keane J. commenting on *Bushell's* case, said ([1983] I.R. 270) that it was "a reasonable inference" that the difference between the different approaches in the two jurisdictions was to be explained "by the absence in England of a written constitution containing express guarantees of fundamental rights and fair procedures in the protection of those rights." See also, *S. v. S.* [1983] I.R. 68.

50 [1988] I.R. 308. See, also *O'Cleirigh v. Minister for Agriculture* [1996] 2 I.L.R.M. 12.

Court order declaring that a liquor licence should be granted (under section 14 of the Intoxicating Liquor Act 1960) for a premises substituted for a demolished licensed premises. According to section 4 of the Licencing (Ireland) Act 1833 (which was the relevant provision regarding procedure) the only persons who could object to such a declaration were inhabitants of the civil parish in which the premises proposed to be licensed are situated. The Supreme Court unanimously refused to accept this restriction.[51]

The same point may also be illustrated by speculative reference to section 10 of the Local Government (Planning and Development) Act 1983. This Act abolished the original Bord Pleanála (replacing it with a differently constituted Board) and also in effect, dismissed the members of the original Board from office (section 10(1) states that they shall "cease to be . . . members"). These members then brought an action against Ireland which was settled out of court. Had the case proceeded to hearing, one of the plaintiffs strongest arguments would have been that their dismissal from office without being granted a hearing violated the *audi alteram partem* rule.[52]

Moreover, even where no such clear-cut question has been involved, the Irish judges have given constitutional/natural justice a keener cutting edge than have their British counterparts. They have been prepared not only to strike down decisions for breach of constitutional justice but also, on the positive side, to suggest improvements in procedure which would meet the requirements of constitutional justice. For example, in *Nolan v. Irish Land Commission*,[53] the Supreme Court upholding the High Court, granted an injunction restraining the hearing of objections by the Land Commission to the compulsory acquisition of the plaintiff's land unless discovery and inspection of the Commission's documents were allowed. Costello J. in the High Court gave an explanation as to how the procedure should operate in this novel setting and this advice was approved in the Supreme Court. The same trend was manifest in the following extract, which has frequently been adopted in later cases, from Walsh J.'s judgment in *East Donegal Co-Operative Ltd v. Attorney-General*:

> "The presumption of constitutionality carries with it not only the presumption
> that the constitutional construction is the one intended by the Oireachtas but

---

51 Likewise in *Madden v. Minister for Marine* [1997] 1 I.L.R.M. 136 at 146, Blayney J. refused to interpret s.15 of the Fisheries (Amendment) Act 1959 as meaning that the Minister could grant a licence without "any worthwhile enquiry" being held since this would expose the section to the risk of being found unconstitutional.

52 For another example, see *The State (Haverty) v. An Bord Pleanála* [1987] I.R. 485 (where Murphy J. held that even on the assumption that the planning legislation did not require an objector to a planning application to be heard on an appeal by an unsuccessful applicant for permission, yet this was required by the constitutional requirement of fair procedures). An even more far-reaching use of constitutional justice might be adopted to repair what it is suggested is a major deficiency in our planning legislation, namely the (former) inadequate provisions for notifying interested parties, such as neighbours, regarding a planning application (on which, see pp. 546–548). If a neighbour does not learn of an application in time to object, may he not argue that the rules of constitutional justice require that he be genuinely (and not notionally) alerted to a decision which affects his own property rights. This is not exactly what was said, in the High Court by Costello J., in *Brady v. Donegal County Council* [1989] I.L.R.M. 282 examined at pp. 456–457 but this case would provide some support for such a submission.

53 [1981] I.R. 23 (*Cf. Philips v. Medical Council* [1992] I.L.R.M 469 at 478). For other examples, see *M. v. The Medical Council* [1984] I.R. 485; *O'Donoghue v. Veterinary Council* [1975] I.R. 398.

also that the Oireachtas intended that proceedings, procedures, discretions and adjudications which are permitted, provided for, or prescribed by an Act of the Oireachtas are to be conducted in accordance with the principles of constitutional justice."[54]

Walsh J. went on to hold that constitutional justice would apply to an application to the Minister for Agriculture for a mart licence, under the Livestock Marts Act 1967, even though the wording of the Act would seem on the *expressio unius exclusio altero* principle of statutory interpretation, to militate against this result.

A number of cases involving court procedure further illustrate the potency of constitutional justice. The first is *S. v. S.*,[55] in which the High Court, in the name of "constitutional entitlement to fair procedures," uprooted the long-established common law rule in *Russell v. Russell*.[56] This rule, whose policy was to maintain the unity of the family, excluded any evidence from a wife which would tend to prove that a child born to her during wedlock was not the child of her husband. Again, in *O'Domhnaill v. Merrick*[57] the Supreme Court held, in effect, that notwithstanding the existence of the Statute of Limitations fixing precise time limits, the court retained, in addition, an inherent constitutionally derived power to stay proceedings, where the passage of time could be taken to work an injustice.[58]

Finally, in *Director of Public Prosecutions v. Doyle*[59] the Supreme Court drew on these constitutional principles in order to significantly augment the rights of accused persons facing complex indictable charges at District Court level. Although the book of evidence provisions of the Criminal Procedure Act 1967 do not apply to such trials, Denham J. ruled that as the District Court was obliged to abide by fair procedures, this meant that in some circumstances an accused would be entitled to advance sight of the witness statements and other documents of importance to the prosecution's case. In her view, the requirements of "constitutional concepts of justice and fair procedures" meant that "a person accused of an indictable offence which is being tried summarily" had a right in certain circumstances to see in advance the "statements on which the prosecution will rest its case."[60]

---

54 [1970] I.R. 317 at 341. For a similar approach, see, *e.g. Hogan v. Minister for Justice* [1976–1977] I.L.R.M. 184; *Loftus v. Attorney General* [1979] I.R. 221; *O'Brien v. Bord na Móna* [1983] I.R. 255; *McCann v. Racing Board* [1983] I.L.R.M. 67; *McKeen v. Meath County Council* [1997] 1 I.R. 192; *Mishra v. Minister for Justice* [1996] 1 I.R. 189. The passage has been quoted with approval on several occasions, in, *e.g. TV3 v. IRTC* [1994] 2 I.R. 439 at 455, *per* Egan J. In *McKeen* Barron J. held that District Court must abide by fair procedures in deciding whether to exercise statutory powers permitting a local authority to enter upon private lands
55 [1983] I.R. 68.
56 [1924] A.C. 687.
57 [1984] I.R. 151.
58 See, *e.g. Toal v. Duignan (No.1)* [1991] I.L.R.M. 135; *Toal v. Duignan (No.2)* [1991] I.L.R.M. 140; *Tuohy v. Courtney* [1994] 3 I.R. 1 at 48, *per* Finlay C.J. and *Primor plc v. Stokes Kennedy Crowley* [1996] 2 I.R. 459 at 475, *per* Hamilton C.J.
59 [1994] 2 I.R. 286.
60 *Ibid.* at 300. She added (at 302) that the factors which a District Judge might take into account in deciding whether constitutional justice required the production of documents included:
"(a) the seriousness of the charge;
(b) the importance of the statements or documents;
(c) the fact that the accused has already been adequately informed of the nature and substance of the accusation;
For the relationship between constitutional justice and the executive privilege agains disclosure, see pp. 948–949.

Constitutional justice has been grounded in Article 40.3 of the Constitution which confers rights explicitly on "citizen[s]". Nevertheless it has been held by Barrington J. in *The State (McFadden) v. The Governor of Mountjoy Prison* (No. 1),[61] (a case arising out of extradition proceedings) that the duty to observe "basic fairness of procedures" applies even where aliens are involved. The reason according to Barrington J. is that:

> ". . . [W]hen the Constitution prescribes basic fairness of procedures in the administration of the law, it does so not only because citizens have rights, but also because the courts in the administration of justice are expected to observe certain forms of due process enshrined in the Constitution. Once the courts have seisin of a dispute, it is difficult to see how the standards they should apply in investigating it should, in fairness, be any different in the case of an alien than those to be applied in the case of a citizen."[62]

Whilst there may be some variation in degree from one judge to another,[63] there is no doubting the significance which the Irish judiciary has assigned to constitutional justice. Take, for instance, the tone of the following passage:

> "A court must wonder if in fact there is a true concern on the part of the applicant that he should be afforded fair procedures or alternatively if he is merely using his entitlement to fair procedures as an obstacle to his having to face up to his responsibilities.
>
> Having considered the position I have come to the conclusion and I have never heard an argument to the contrary, that a citizen's constitutional rights to fair procedures cannot be altered or diminished merely by his attitude or reasons for ensuring that these rights are afforded to him. The rights cannot be taken away from him merely because his conduct is alleged to be un-meritorious. His rights remain inviolate no matter what his motive may be for invoking the rights."[64]

Constitutional Justice in Court Procedure[65]

Whilst it is true that most constitutional justice cases emanate from the executive branch of government, it is an aspect of the rules' universality that they can apply,

---

(d) the likelihood that there is no risk of injustice in failing to furnish the statement or documents in issue to the accused."

For the obligation of a coroner to adapt procedures to ensure that an inquest is conducted in accordance with constitutional justice, see *The State (McKeown) v. Scully* [1986] I.L.R.M. 133. For another strong application of constitutional justice in the context of a Coroner's Court which had failed to investigate the matter before it properly, see *Davitt v. Minister for Justice*, unreported, High Court, February 8, 1989. See further at pp. 422–426.

61 [1981] I.L.R.M. 113.

62 *Ibid.* at 122.

63 See, *e.g. Rajah v. Royal College of Surgeons* [1994] 1 I.R. 384 and *Corcoran v. Minister for Social Welfare* [1991] 2 I.R. 175.

64 *Gallagher v. Revenue Commissioners* (No. 2) [1995] 1 I.R. 55 at 63, *per* Morris J. See also Part 3 of Chapter 12.

65 For the operation of constitutional justice in arbitration, see Forde, *Arbitration Law and Procedure* (1994), p. 118.

in appropriate circumstances, to each of the three arms of government: legislature; judicature; or executive. The rules regulate decisions affecting individuals directly and these are just the sort of decisions which are usually not taken by the Oireachtas. However, in appropriate circumstances constitutional justice has been extended even to the Oireachtas, as was demonstrated in the multi-faceted case of *Re Haughey*.[66] The aspect of the case which is relevant here is that it applied the *audi alteram partem* rule to an investigation by a committee of the legislature (specifically, the Dáil Public Accounts Committee).

At the opposite pole from the legislative function is the judicial function, which deals almost exclusively with individual decisions. But here procedure is regulated by a minute specialised code of procedural and evidential law. For example, at the pre-trial stage in the Superior Courts, provision is made by the Rules of the Superior Courts, as to pleadings, interrogatories, discovery etc. in order to ensure that litigants have an adequate opportunity to meet their opponent's case.[67] Fair procedure in the courts is underpinned by such specialised constitutional provisions as Articles 38.1, 34.1, as well as 40.3.[68] This law is inspired by the same policy which underlies constitutional justice.[69] However, it is not usual to classify procedural law or the

---

[66] [1971] I.R. 217 at 263–264. Another episode involving a House of the Oireachtas occurred in 1991. The Senate Committee on Procedure and Privileges recommended to the House that Senator Norris be disciplined by being suspended from the service of the Senate for one week (T. 279 (Pl. 7181), March 14, 1990) and this recommendation was adopted (124 *Seanad Debates*, Cols. 772–804, March 15, 1990). The basis of Senator Norris' offence was an allegation he had made against the Cathaoirleach. Notwithstanding this, it was the Cathaoirleach who, in line with the usual practice, chaired both the Committee and the Senate, at the relevant times. In addition, the Committee refused the Senator's request that he be allowed legal representation, to call witnesses, etc. Senator Norris was then granted leave by the High Court to apply for a judicial review of his disciplining by the Senate on the ground of violation of both the first and second rules of constitutional justice. As a result of the order made by the High Court, Senator Norris was reinstated and eventually his action was withdrawn before it had received a substantive hearing: see, especially, 124 *Seanad Debates*, Cols. 1039–1145; Vol. 125, Cols. 381–385, May 25, 1990.

[67] Thus, in *Cooney v. Browne* [1984] I.R. 185 at 191 Henchy J. said that the rules governing the delivery of particulars were essentially designed to ensure a fair hearing:

> "'The object of particulars is to enable the party asking for them to know what case he has to meet, and so save unnecessary expense, and avoid allowing parties to be taken by surprise: *Spedding v. Fitzpatrick* (1888) 38 Ch.D. 410, 413. Thus, where the pleading is so general or so imprecise that the other side cannot know what case he will have to meet at the trial, he should be entitled to such particulars, as will inform him of the range of evidence . . . which he will have to deal with at the trial."

While Henchy J.'s comments were in the context of delivery of particulars, they could just as easily be applied, *mutatis mutandis*, to the whole panoply of High Court procedures, such as discovery, interrogatories, etc. See also *Balkanbank v. Taher*, unreported, Supreme Court, January 19, 1995 where Hamilton C.J. held that the trial judge had breached fair procedures by allowing a very belated radical amendment of the plaintiff's statement of claim at the close of the hearing. Fair procedures in this context required that "a party to an action be given notice of the nature of the claim and an adequate opportunity of defending all aspects of such claim." The Chief Justice continued: "The obligation to ensure that fair procedures are followed in the conduct of all proceedings before the courts and elsewhere is of such constitutional importance that the failure to do so in this case entitles the appellants to succeed in this ground of appeal".

[68] Art. 38.1 provides that "No person shall be tried on any criminal charge save in due course of law." Art. 34.1 states that "Justice shall be administered in courts established by law. . . ."

[69] See for example *Staunton v. Toyota* [1996] 1 I.L.R.M 171 at 177–178. F was a third party in an action brought by the plaintiff, who was an accident victim, against the first and second defendants. The Supreme Court held that F had a version of events which should have been put before the trial judge and that the failure to allow this amounted to a denial of justice to F. See, too *Clarke v. District Judge*

law of evidence as part of constitutional justice. Nevertheless, constitutional or natural justice has, very occasionally been invoked *eo nomine*, to augment procedural law. Some examples have been mentioned already.[70] Another example is *N. v. K.*[71] in which Henchy J. suggested that constitutional justice may require separate representation for children in appropriate cases where their welfare is at stake. The same argument could be made in favour of representation rights for the victim in rape cases, in the not uncommon circumstances that the accused is claiming that she consented, thereby impugning her reputation. In addition, it is likely that in suitable cases, constitutional justice could be used as a device with which to extirpate some of the less justifiable results of the rule excluding hearsay evidence or other exclusionary rules or to make good the omission of the Rules of Court which provide no system of discovery of documents before the District Court.[72] Such examples draw attention to the connection which exists between the principles of constitutional justice and the right of access to the courts, a continuum which was acknowledged in the following passage from *S. v. S.* (the facts of which are given above):

> "The combined effect of Articles 34.1, 38.1 and 40.3 [of the Constitution] appears to me to guarantee (*inter alia*) something equivalent to the concept of 'due process' under the American Constitution in relation to causes and controversies litigated before the Court. . . . Just as the parties have a right of access to the courts when this is necessary to defend or vindicate life, person, good name or property rights, so they have a *constitutional right to fair procedures* when they get to court. . . . Because the rule in *Russell v. Russell* ran counter to [the] paramount public policy [of ascertaining truth and doing justice] and was calculated to defeat the due and proper administration of justice, I would hold that it ceased to have legal effect in the State after the enactment of the Constitution in 1937."[73]

Hogan [1995] 1 I.R. 310 at 312–314. (District Judge should have indicated that he was thinking of binding over to keep the peace, a person called before the court as a witness.) For another, hypothetical example, take the case of the law students and graduates discussed below, n.74.

[70] See pp. 505–506. See also, *The State (Buchan) v. Coyne* [1936] I.R. 485; *The State (Killian) v. Minister for Justice* [1954] I.R. 207; *The State (Walshe) v. Murphy* [1981] I.R. 275; *The State (O'Regan) v. Plunkett* [1984] I.L.R.M. 347; *Director of Public Prosecutions v. Doyle* [1994] 2 I.R. 306.

[71] [1985] I.R. 733 at 749.

[72] See *Nolan v. Irish Land Commission* [1981] I.R. 23; *Director of Public Prosecutions v. Doyle* [1994] 2 I.R. 286.

[73] [1983] I.R. 75 at 80, *per* O'Hanlon J.
The issue of the impact of constitutional justice upon court procedure might also seem to have arisen when, immediately following the enactment of the Companies (Amendment) Act 1990, the Goodman Group Plc applied *ex parte* to the High Court for the appointment of an examiner to the Group. The order was duly made by Hamilton P. (*The Irish Times*, August 30, 1990). Because the order was made *ex parte* the creditors of Goodman Group were precluded from taking steps to realise their securities as against the Group, as, for example, seeking to have the company put into liquidation. The question of whether this *ex parte* procedure constituted a breach of the creditors' right to fair procedures was much discussed but not addressed in the judgment.
However the following comments may be of interest : It seems clear that the *ex parte* order of Hamilton P. appointing the Examiner was not simply a procedural interlocutory order such as that in *Butler v. Ruane* (see below in the text). In *Butler*, the Supreme Court had held that the High Court was entitled to make an *ex parte* order allowing a respondent in judicial review proceedings further time to file affidavits and notice of opposition. An order appointing an examiner to a company is, in

The general rule would appear to be that where a court makes a final order which affects the rights of interested parties, fair procedure means that both sides must be heard. Thus, to take but one example from many,[74] in *The State (O'Sullivan) v. Buckley*,[75] the Supreme Court quashed an order of a District Judge where he had purported to grant, *ex parte*, an enlargement of time to allow an appeal to be taken to the Circuit Court. The Court added that, save for purely procedural orders (of which this was not one), persons discharging judicial functions must hear both sides before proceeding to make a final order.

The courts will (or, at least, should) never make *final* orders *ex parte*, in cases affecting legal rights or interests.[76] So well established is this principle that it is not easy to find authorities for it. *The State (Rogers) v. Galvin*[77] does, however, afford such authority. Here Hamilton J. (as he then was) had made an order *ex parte* releasing the applicant from custody. This Order was set aside by the Supreme Court. The provisions of Article 40.4.2° requiring the respondents to be given an opportunity to justify the detention in writing were, said Henchy J., mandatory because they were: "A constitutional recognition of the rule of natural justice is expressed in the maxim *audi alteram partem*. It guards against the risk that on an *ex parte* application an unjustified release from custody may be made."[78] The judge went on to doubt whether Order 84, rule 9 (which purported to allow the making of such orders) was actually *intra vires* the Superior Court Rules Committee and, in consequence this Rule was deleted from the Rules of the Superior Courts when the

---

fact, a *final* order, albeit one of a definite duration. Moreover, there is no question but that the order trenches upon and affects many valuable rights of creditors since s.5(2) of the Companies (Amendment) Act 1990 prevents a winding-up and execution against the company's property during the currency of the protection period. In these circumstances, constitutional justice would seem to require that the creditors be given a say as to whether an Examiner should be appointed. If they are heard, they may be able to persuade the court to refuse the petition or to agree to some other course of action. But even irrespective of whether the result might have been otherwise, the failure to afford the creditors a hearing in the *Goodman* case would appear to have constituted, a "major breach of the constitutional guarantee of fair procedures." While, of course, speed was of the essence in the *Goodman* case, this, of itself, cannot justify the making of a *final* order appointing an examiner *ex parte*, no more than urgency could justify the granting of a *final* (or even interlocutory) injunction on an *ex parte* basis. Fair procedures would seem to require, therefore, that the intitial appointment of an examiner is on an *interim* basis (as in *Re Heffernan Kearns Ltd, The Irish Times*, October 13, 1990). During this interim period, the interests of the company seeking protection would be adequately cared for, since by virtue of s.5(1) of the 1990 Act, court protection commences from the date of the presentation of the petition. For further comment on this detailed point see, too *Re R Ltd* [1989] I.R. 126 at 133.

74 For one of many examples to be found in the Rules of Superior Courts 1986, take Order 84, rule 22(2) by which : "The notice of motion or summons [in a judicial review application] must be served on all persons directly affected . . .". It is possible that there was a breach of this rule in *Bloomer v. Law Society of Ireland* [1995] 3 I.R. 14, the decision in which vitally affected interests of persons (whether law graduates of, or law students at, law schools in the Republic) who had not been notified of the fact. It might however be argued that, on the facts of this rather surprising case, it was not known until the time of judgment that the law graduates from the Republic and students were going to be "directly affected" by the outcome of the case.

75 (1967) 101 I.L.T.R. 152. See also the comments of Hamilton C.J. in *Balkanbank v. Taher*, unreported, Supreme Court, January 19, 1995: see pp. 39–40.

76 Though in *Butler v. Ruane* [1989] I.L.R.M. 159, the Supreme Court sanctioned the making *ex parte* of certain purely procedural orders, such as giving the respondents additional time to file affidavits in judicial review matters.

77 [1983] I.R. 249. For another example, see *Re Zwann's Application* [1981] I.R. 395 at 404.

78 [1983] I.R. 249 at 253.

new Rules were promulgated in 1986. Again in *The State (D) v. Groarke*,[79] natural justice was applied to court proceedings even at the pre-trial stage.

Nomenclature

At least two, and possibly three, different judicial attitudes to the relationship between constitutional and natural justice have emerged. The first takes the view that constitutional justice only applies where a possible breach of some constitutionally-protected interest, for example, a property right, is involved, whereas natural justice continues to exist to protect other, rights or privileges created by statute, common law or contract.[80] A further refinement on this attitude has it that whilst constitutional and natural justice should be distinguished as just indicated, even natural justice should be read in the light of the Constitution, thereby giving rise to the dual concepts of constitutional justice and constitutionalised natural justice.[81] The other, simpler view is that constitutional justice has succeeded and subsumed natural justice. As McCarthy J. observed: "In my view the two principles of natural justice as they pre-existed the Constitution are now part of the human rights guaranteed by the Constitution."[82]

Both constitutional and natural justice are elastic and vague concepts and the differences between them contemplated in the seminal passage from *McDonald*, quoted above, have not developed significantly. Indeed in a number of cases, the phrase "constitutional and/or natural justice" has been used indiscriminately.[83] Other judgments have betrayed impatience with the rather precious difference between the two concepts.[84] Accordingly, it may be that a split-level procedural system only creates complication without adding anything to the stock of legal ideas or rules. Thus we shall normally speak only of constitutional justice. In addition, we shall take it that such variants as "basic fairness of procedures"[85] are synonymous with constitutional

---

[79] [1990] I.L.R.M. 130. For other aspects of this case, see p. 587. The case arose from the exercise by a District Judge, who suspected that a child was being abused, of his power (under the Children's Act 1908) to issue a warrant for the removal of the child to a place of safety, pending the child's being brought before a court for committal to the care of a relative. *Groarke* was considered in *Southern Health Board v. CH* [1996] 2 I.L.R.M. 142 at 150.

[80] *The State (Gleeson) v. Minister for Defence* [1976] I.R. 280; *Kiely v. Minister for Social Welfare* [1977] I.R. 287; *The State (Donnelly) v. Minister for Defence*, unreported, High Court, October 8, 1979; *Ní Bheoláin v. Dublin V.E.C.*, unreported, High Court, January 28, 1983.

[81] See *Gleeson, Kiely and Nolan v. Irish Land Commission* [1981] I.R. 23.

[82] *The State (Furey) v. Minister for Defence* [1988] I.L.R.M. 89 at 99. This was the approach taken in *Garvey v. Ireland* [1981] I.R. 75 and *The State (Williams) v. Army Pensions Board* [1983] I.R. 308.

[83] e.g. *The State (Boyle) v. General Medical Services (Payment) Board* [1981] I.L.R.M. 14; *O'Brien v. Bord na Móna* [1983] I.R. 255.

[84] See, *e.g.* the comments of Costello J. in *Doupe v. Limerick Corporation* [1981] I.L.R.M. 456 at 463 and *McHugh v. Garda Commissioner* [1985] I.L.R.M. 606. See also the same judge's well worked out observations in the analogous context of constitutional torts in *W. v. Ireland* [1997] 2 I.R. 241.

"The courts are required by the Constitution to apply the law and the causes of actions it confers and when these adequately protect guaranteed rights they are not called upon, in order to discharge their constitutional duties, to establish a new cause of action. Indeed, it would be contrary to their constitutional function to do so."

But *cf. McCormack v. Garda Síochána Complaints Board* [1997] 2 I.L.R.M. 321 at 333 where Costello P. expressly justified a requirement that administrators given reason by reference to constitutional justice as opposed to extending "the common law rules of natural justice."

[85] This was the language used by the Supreme Court in *Re Haughey* [1971] I.R. 217. In *S. v. S.* [1983] I.R. 68 at 80 O'Hanlon J. spoke of "a constitutional entitlement to fair procedures." See also, *Gunn*

justice. Again, to the extent that ideas peculiar to court procedure, such as "due process" go beyond constitutional justice we shall not be concerned with them in a book whose primary focus is government administration, rather than court procedure. One should note, finally that the British have a somewhat analogous terminological-substantive dilema centering on the issue of the relationship between "fairness" and natural justice.[86]

3. *Nemo Iudex in Causa Sua*[87]

Sources of bias

The principle that no person shall be a judge in his own cause is fundamental[88] and well established not only in public administration but in the procedure of courts. Indeed, as we shall see, three of the most recent cases in the present Part centre upon members of the judiciary. Bias may be conscious or unconscious and does not necessarily mean "a corrupt state of mind".[89] This is one of the features which distinguishes bias from *mala fides*, though admittedly there is a great deal of overlap between the two concepts. Perhaps the volume of case law on the *nemo iudex in causa sua* rule is inevitable in a small country with a far-reaching bureaucratic state apparatus, though as an opening generalisation that a smaller proportion of these have been successful than in any other major section of administrative law. Possible sources of bias are infinitely varied and the following list is certainly not exhaustive.[90] Moreover, the list is only intended for descriptive purposes since, with the possible exception of the first category, no legal consequences turn on the particular pigeon-hole to which a case is allocated:

(a) **Material interest** The most obvious source of bias is financial (or material) interest of which *The People (Attorney-General) v. Singer*[91] is a straightforward example. In this case, the Court of Criminal Appeal ordered a re-trial on a fraud charge because the foreman of the jury had been an investor in the company which

---

v. National College of Art and Design [1990] 2 I.R. 168, 179–181, *per* Walsh J; *O'Neill v. Beaumont Hospital Board* [1990] I.L.R.M. 419 at 437, *per* Finlay C.J.; *McCormack v. Garda Síochána Complaints Board* [1997] 2 I.L.R.M. 321 at 333, *per* Costello P. and *Barry v. Medical Council*, unreported, High Court, February 11, 1997.

86 See Craig, *op.cit.*, above, n.2, pp. 289–292.

87 For the right to an "independent and impartial tribunal" under Art.6.1 of the European Convention, see Harris, O'Boyle and Warbrick, *op. cit.*, above, n.31, pp. 230–239.

88 To impute bias against a judge may amount to a contempt of court: *Attorney General v. Connolly* [1947] I.R. 213; *The State (D.P.P.) v. Walsh* [1981] I.R. 412; *R. v. Editor of New Statesman, ex p. D.P.P.* (1928) 44 T.L.R. 301. See Walker, "Scandalising in the Eighties" (1985) 101 L.Q.R. 359.

89 *R. (de Vesci) v. Queen's Co. JJ.* [1908] 2 I.R. 285. For *mala fides*, see pp. 628–631.

90 According to one classification: "there are two types of bias, one based on pecuniary interest and the other described as 'a challenge to the favour', being a bias deriving from a special relationship or kindred causes": *O'Neill v. Irish Hereford Breed Society Ltd* [1992] 1 I.R. 431 at 447, *per* Murphy J. See also the same judge's comments in *Chestvale v. Glackin* [1993] 3 I.R. 35.

91 [1975] I.R. 408. (decided in 1963). In some cases, there is a statutory disqualification in cases of personal interest: see, *e.g.* s. 856(1), Pt. 37 of the Taxes Consolidation Act 1997 (special commissioner for income tax disqualified from adjudicating on his own personal tax liability). For examples of disclosure of interest provisions, see Environmental Protection Agency Act, 1992, ss. 37, 38; Ethics in Office Act 1995, ss.5–7. See also p. 153, n.194 (on state sponsored bodies).

was the vehicle for the alleged fraud and was thus one of the victims. Interest was also found to have been present in *Connolly v. McConnell*,[92] a case arising out of the dismissal of a general secretary of a trade union on the authority of the executive council of the union. This dismissal was found to be void, as some of the members of the union's executive council had financial or other interests in the outcome of the disciplinary hearing. For example, one of the charges involved the defendant's disobedience to an order of the plaintiff trade union to pay a recoupment of expenses to a person who was actually a member of the executive council.

Again, in *Doyle v. Croke*[93] an employer, whose company was drifting towards liquidation, paid £360,000 in settlement of an official strike. The strike committee decided that this fund was to be divided equally among the former employees, who had adequately performed picket duty. As a result, the committee drew up a list of 150 persons (out of a work-force of about 270) who were to participate in the distribution of these monies. However, in a case brought by 83 of the disappointed employees, the procedure was held to be invalid because, *inter alia*, according to Costello J.:

> "All the members of the strike committee were former employees of Irish Meat Producers Limited and as such had a financial interest in the settlement and, accordingly, a financial interest in the actual number of persons who would participate in it. It has not been suggested that they in fact allowed this interest to influence the decisions in which they were involved but the test to be applied is an objective one and a reasonable person could conclude that there was a risk that an even-handed decision might not be taken by a committee all of whose members had a financial interest in its outcome."[94]

An unsuccessful claim occurred in the case of *Dublin and County Broadcasting Ltd v. Independent Radio and Television Commission*[95] which arose out of the allocation of contracts to provide sound broadcasting services, under the new broadcasting régime created by the Radio and Television Act 1988. To discharge the duty of selecting contractors, the Act constitutes the Independent Radio and Television Commission, which is chaired by a former Supreme Court judge, Mr Justice Henchy. In early 1989, the Commission awarded two contracts to broadcast in the Dublin City and County area. In the present action, which was brought by the only serious contender among the unsuccessful applicants, the plaintiff's major argument was that the Commission's decision in regard to the contract was void because Mr O'Donovan, one of the ordinary members of the Commission, was biased, by virtue of both his pecuniary and his non-pecuniary interest in one of the successful companies, Radio 2000 Limited. The question of the non-pecuniary interest will be covered below.

---

[92] [1983] I.R. 172. Interest was found not to exist on the facts in *The State (Divito) v. Arklow U.D.C.* [1986] I.L.R.M. 123, where the respondent's refusal of a gaming licence to the applicant company was under challenge. Henchy J. found that there were no "financial or other connections" between the council and a rival company such as "would be likely to deflect the council from fairness or even-handedness in their dealings with the applicant – or such as would be likely to lead a reasonable person to think that the Council would thus act."

[93] Unreported, High Court, May 6, 1988.

[94] *Ibid.* pp. 19–20.

[95] Unreported, High Court, May 12, 1989.

Before coming to the matter of Mr O'Donovan's pecuniary interest, it is worth noting that, the High Court treated two general points as being beyond dispute. First, Murphy J. noted that, under the Act, the Commission must have seven to 10 members; yet he stated that if even one of the members were affected by bias, this would invalidate the Commission's decision.[96] Secondly, he accepted the conventional wisdom that pecuniary bias is a uniquely heinous departure from the rules of constitutional justice. It seems reasonable to infer from this that it is to be judged by a more austere standard.

Mr O'Donovan's interest stemmed from the fact that he had been involved with E-Sat Television Ltd The pecuniary aspect of Mr O'Donovan's alleged involvement lay in the fact that he had owned some £30,000 worth of shares in E-Sat which owned 70 per cent of the shares in Radio 2000 Ltd However, about a year before the contract was awarded, he had sought to transfer these shares. In fact, as a matter of strict law concerning the assignment of shares, Murphy J. accepted that, unknown to Mr O'Donovan, he had retained some residual legal (but not beneficial or equitable) rights in the shares. However, Murphy J.'s crucial finding on the facts was that:

> "Mr. O'Donovan had sought to divest himself of his shares in E-Sat, and he bona fide believed he had successfully done so. I would also accept that the vast majority of people would believe that such was the case and he could not as a matter of law or honour resile from the action he had taken and he has shown no indication of any intention to do so. . . . [And although] as a matter of law, Mr. O'Donovan does have certain rights, . . . I could see a serious challenge being mounted if he were at this stage to seek to exercise those rights."[97]

Given these facts, the plaintiff's argument failed on the ground that "[the pecuniary loss or gain] must be a real possibility, and one which is known to the person exercising the judicial function, if it is to invalidate his decision."[98] Murphy J. was also probably influenced, in regard to both alleged sources of bias, by the fact that Mr O'Donovan had made a frank and unforced admission of his interest.[99]

---

[96] On this type of numbers point, see too *Connolly v. McConnell* [1983] I.R. 172.

[97] At pp. 16–17 of judgment.

[98] At pp. 15–16 of judgment.

[99] For example, Mr O'Donovan wrote two letters on the difficulty of his position to the Chairman of the Commission, each of which is quoted in the judgment at pp. 6, 7. The letter of January 3, 1989, reads as follows:

> "Dear Chairman,
> I have a problem and I need your wisdom. Having read the four applications for the National Radio franchise I formed the following conclusions. The application for Nova International could not be treated seriously. That left three applicants, two are of a very high standard and herein lies my problem. Century has Oliver Barry and James Stafford. Now Oliver Barry is an old friend of mine, an ex-RTE Authority member under my Chairmanship. Radio 2000's Chairman is Denis O'Brien and he is Chief Executive in E-Sat, and at one stage was engaged to my daugher. I am quite happy to give you an honest professional opinion on all the applications, but I do believe I am in a no-win situation provided either of these two win the franchise. How do you think I should approach this in the interest of the Commission, myself and the applicants."

At p. 8 Murphy J. states (for the reason indicated in the text):

> "The decision of the Chairman [Henchy J.] was that he took the view that Mr. O'Donovan's assistance should not be dispensed with and he wasn't disqualified and should not be debarred from the consideration of and implementation of the decisions." [*sic*]

(b) Personal attitudes, relationships, beliefs. Bias may arise from the decision-maker's personal attitudes, relationships, or beliefs in the case. In a number of clear cases personal hostility has been found to be present. For example, in *R. (Donoghue) v. Cork County JJ.*[100] a conviction imposed by a magistrate who had remarked shortly after the case that he "would not leave any member of the [accused's] family in the district" was quashed on this ground. Similarly, in *R. (Kingston) v. Cork County JJ.*[101] an evicted farmer brought charges of assault against the purchaser of the farm. The charges arose out of a boycott which had been imposed on the purchaser by the United Irish League. The purchaser was convicted of assault by a magistrates' bench of four, including two members of the League, who had attended the meeting where the decision to impose the boycott had been taken. The High Court had little difficulty in quashing the conviction.

A case of what, the Supreme Court held, may have appeared to an "unprejudiced onlooker" as personal involvement occurred in *The State (Hegarty) v. Winters.*[102] Here an arbitrator appointed under the Acquisition of Land (Assessment of Compensation) Act 1919 was assessing the amount of compensation to be awarded to the applicant land owner for damage done to his land by a county council. The arbitrator went to inspect the land himself and was accompanied by the county council engineer with nobody to represent the applicant. The court quashed the arbitrator's award.

On the other side of the line from *Hegarty* was *Dublin and County Broadcasting Ltd* (already mentioned) Here it was claimed unsuccessfully that the Independent Radio and Television Commission's decision was vitiated, first by O's pecuniary interest (an argument examined above) and, secondly, by O's non-pecuniary interest. The High Court's treatment of this second issue is of even wider significance than its claim under the first head of this case, in that it is so likely to recur. The reason is that the claim arose out of the inevitable difficulty in discovering, in a relatively small state like Ireland, a respected figure within a particular specialised field who yet has no links with any of the parties to the issue which he is obliged to decide. In the case of the Commission, section 1(5) of the Schedule to its constituent statute, the Radio and Television Act 1988 provides that no one may be appointed as a member "unless he has experience of or has shown a capacity in media or commission affairs, radio communications, engineering, trade union affairs, administration or social, cultural, educational or communications activities."

In view of this statutory requirement, it is not so surprising that one of the members, from the world of radio communications, should have had a connection with one of the applicants. Indeed, in O's case, he himself said in evidence that, out

---

[100] [1910] 2 I.R. 271. For a case where judicial conduct was thought to "reasonably give rise in the mind of an unprejudiced observer to the suspicion that justice was not being done", see *Dineen v. Delap* [1994] 2 I.R. 228 at 234, *per* Morris J. See too, *McDonough v. Minister for Defence* [1991] I.L.R.M. 115 at 120, *per* Lavan J."the Commanding Officer's decision to delegate Captain Holmes to conduct the interview [was unreasonable] having regard to the applicant's complaints against that Officer."

[101] [1910] 2 I.R. 658. See also, *R. (Harrington) v. Clare JJ.* [1918] 2 I.R. 116. For cases on the other side of the line, see *R. (Findlater) v. Dublin JJ.* [1904] 2 I.R. 75 and *R. (Tavener) v. Tyrone JJ.* [1909] 2 I.R. 763. For other examples occurring during the course of the famous *Sinn Féin Funds case*, see Hogan (1997) *The Bar Review* 375 at 379.

[102] [1956] I.R. 320. For a more extreme example than *Hegarty*, see *The State (Horgan) v. Exported Livestock Insurance Board* [1943] I.R. 600.

of 13 applications to the Commission, he knew the promoters of 12 of them. However, the ground on which the plaintiff's case rested was O's former involvement with E-Sat, which owned 70 per cent. of the shares in one of the successful applicants for a radio service contract. O had been promoter of E-Sat and until about six months before the Commission had awarded the contract to the company, he had been its chairman and a director. He resigned at that time because of a serious disagreement with his promoter and effective partner, who was also the chief executive of Radio 2000 Ltd and at one time engaged to his daughter. Nevertheless, the judge decisively rejected the plaintiff's case on the following brief ground:

> "It seems to me that in the nature of the functions he was discharging that there was no real likelihood of bias and that no right-minded man would have thought so. . . . Mr. O'Donovan was in a position to bring an independent mind to bear on the problems which the Commission was called on to address."[103]

An instance of personal reputation or professional pride, as a source of bias, could just possibly arise out of the arrangements for compensation payable in the case of an error in the Land Registry. It is the Registrar himself who must adjudicate upon a claim for compensation arising out of loss to a land-owner caused by error, misstatement, misdescription, etc., of officials of the Registry or even the Registrar himself. Although it is the Minister for Finance who actually pays the compensation, it has been judicially remarked ". . . it seems very desirable that the adjudicator should be chosen from outside the Land Registry."[104]

---

[103] Unreported, High Court, May 12, 1988 at p. 18. This issue has arisen in other jurisdictions in relation to jury trials and lay assessors. In *R v. Gough* [1993] 1 A.C. 646 the House of Lords upheld the accused's conviction for robbery. His defence had been, *inter alia*, that his brother had been responsible for the robbery, but it emerged immediately after the trial that his brother's immediate neighbour had been sitting on the jury. Lord Goff applied the test of whether there was been a "real danger" of bias and concluded on these facts that there was not such a danger. The judgment of the European Court of Human Rights in *Pullar v. United Kingdom* (1996) 22 E.H.R.R. 391 is to similar effect. In this case the accused had been convicted of corrupt practices, although it later emerged that one member of the jury had been employed by the firm in which a key prosecution witness was a partner. The Court (at 405) stated that:
> "The principle of impartiality is an important element in support of the confidence which the courts must inspire in a democratic society, However, it does not necessarily follow from the fact that a member of the tribunal has some personal knowledge of one of the witnesses in a case that he will be prejudiced in favour of that person's testimony. In each individual case it must be decided whether the familiarity in question is of such a nature and degree as to indicate a lack of impartiality on the part of the tribunal."
Here the juror had not worked on the project which had given rise to the allegations of corruption and, accordingly, the Court concluded that no breach of Art.6(l) had been established. It also stressed the safeguards attending jury trial: the selection of the jurors at random, the directions given to jurors by the trial judge and the juror's oath to try the case impartially.
On the other hand, in *Landborger v. Sweden* (1989) 12 E.H.R.R. 416 the Court concluded that a Swedish housing and tenancy court had failed to comply with the requirements of Art.6(l) in that two lay assessors who had taken part in the proceedings had been nominated by and had close links with two associations which both had interests contrary to those of a party to the proceedings. Likewise in *Holm v. Sweden* (1994) 18 E.H.R.R. 79 the Court concluded that there had been a breach of Article 6(l) where a majority of the members of a libel jury had been active members of a political party whose publishing house had been – unsuccessfully – sued for libel by a political opponent. The Court concluded that the "independence and impartiality" of the trial court "were open to doubt" and that that applicant's "fears in this respect were objectively justified."

[104] *Application of Sean Leonard*, unreported, High Court, D'Arcy J., June 30, 1981; unreported, Supreme

McMahon J. gave an instance of bias arising from the decision-maker's personal observation in *The State (Fagan) v. Governor of Mountjoy Prison*.[105] Here the validity of certain disciplinary punishments imposed by a deputy prison governor were under challenge:

> "If . . . the Deputy Governor had witnessed some of the events to which the charges related I could understand an objection to his sitting in judgment since it would be difficult for the prisoner to deal with and to be heard in relation to the impression of the facts which may have been formed by the Deputy Governor as distinct from the evidence given by prison officers at the inquiry."

However, McMahon J. ruled that this claim failed on its facts.

Another obvious instance of bias would be party political advantage in the context of a Minister (usually the Minister for Environment) taking decisions in regard to elections. The point was made obliquely but successfully in *Dillon v. Minister for Posts and Telegraphs*[106] in which the plaintiff was a Dáil candidate yet the Minister would not allow him to circulate his election brochure free of charge to the voters on the ground that some of the material which it contained did not relate to the election. Henchy J. said:

> ". . . [T]he expression 'matter relating to the election only' should be liberally construed. This is particularly so when, as in this case, the person seeking to block the free postal circulation of the plaintiff's election brochure is a member of the Dáil and whose party leader is seeking re-election to the Dáil in the same constituency as the plaintiff has chosen to contest."

The idea that a pre-determined belief or outlook might give rise to a reasonable suspicion[107] of bias, was successfully invoked in *Dublin Well-Woman Centre Ltd v. Ireland*.[108] In this case the plaintiff applied in the High Court to have an earlier injunction (restraining them from providing information about abortion services abroad) lifted in the light of the enactment of the 14th Amendment of the Constitution Act, 1994.[109] When the action came on for hearing before Carroll J. in the High Court, counsel for the Society of Unborn Children (Ire.) Ltd (a notice party to the action) applied to her to discharge herself from the hearing of the action. The ground was that in her capacity as Chairwoman of the Commission for the Status of Women (an official body) she had with other members of the Commission made a written submission to the government regarding the availability of abortion information.

Court, December 15, 1982; McAllister, *Registration of Title* (Incorporated Council of Law Reporting for Ireland, Dublin, 1973), p. 302. See also, Fitzgerald, *Land Registry Practice* (1989), p. 248. See now to like effect, *O'Cleirigh v. Minister for Agriculture* [1996] 2 I.L.R.M. 12 at 15, *per* Barron J.

[105] Unreported, High Court, March 6, 1978.

[106] Unreported, Supreme Court, June 3, 1981. The type of point discussed in the text does not appear to have been canvassed in *The State (Lynch) v. Cooney* [1982] I.R. 337.

[107] On reasonable suspicion, see pp. 532–534.

[108] [1995] 1 I.L.R.M. 408. For a striking case involving a family relationship between a Circuit Court judge and counsel in which bias was successfully claimed, see *O'Reilly v. Judge Cassidy* [1995] I.L.R.M. 306 at 309–311, 319. But see *McNally v. District Judge Martin* [1995] 1 I.L.R.M. 350.

[109] This provides that nothing in Art. 40.3.3° (the "pro-life" provision) shall limit "freedom to obtain or make available, in the State, subject to such conditions as may be prescribed by law, information relating to services lawfully available in another State."

When Carroll J. refused, the notice party appealed successfully to the Supreme Court. Writing on behalf of the Supreme Court, Denham J. observed that:[110]

". . . where many reasonable people in our community hold strong opinions, it is of particular importance that neither party should have any reasonable reason to apprehend bias in the courts of justice. Further, once the question of a possible perception of bias has been raised reasonably on the grounds of pre-existing non-judicial position and actions, it would be contrary to constitutional justice to proceed with a trial."

It is necessary, at this point, briefly to recall the category of material interest in order to examine a situation which straddles two categories; namely: material interest and personal association. It is most likely to be suggested in the area of domestic tribunals in which the decision-maker and the person affected by the decision are each members of the same profession, trade or industry and, consequently, the alleged wrong-doing of the person affected may have some effect on the financial interest or possibly reputation of the decision-maker. Take, for the sake of discussion (since the question seems not to have been considered in any other case), the following discursive passage from the judgement of Kingsmill Moore J. in *In Re Solicitors Act*, 1954:

"It is true that in a hearing before the Committee a solicitor will not have the protections he would receive in a Court of justice. Complainant, tribunal and the person who conducts the complaint are inextricably interconnected. Moreover the circumstances are such as to make it difficult for the tribunal to be impartial. In many cases the person against whom a complaint is made will be a solicitor with whom members of the tribunal have had professional dealings which may have predisposed them in his favour or against him. All of the members are liable to contribute yearly to a compensation fund established under the Act to relieve or mitigate losses sustained in consequence of dishonesty of solicitors and the amount of contribution may be increased if found necessary (ss. 69, 70) so that there might be a tendency to bear hardly on a solicitor charged with dishonesty. Although the character and standing of the members are such that they can be expected to resist and rise superior to any influences which might affect their impartiality, and it is not suggested that they do not so do, the tribunal is not constituted in a manner best calculated to provide the security against bias and partiality which a Court of justice affords. In the opinion of the Court these considerations, though advanced by the appellants, are not in point. If the Committee is not administering justice, the Constitution imposes no restrictions on the composition of the body."[111]

As is attested, by numerous cases,[112] the final, concluding sentence seems to be incorrect and also probably the result of a preoccupation with the main theme of

---

110 [1995] 1 I.L.R.M. at 423.
111 [1960] I.R. 239 at 272. See also, *McCann v. The Racing Board* [1983] I.L.R.M. 67 at 75 and *Dublin and County Broadcasting Ltd v. IRTC*, unreported High Court, May 12, 1989 at pp. 14–15, and inconclusively, *Geoghegan v. Institute of Chartered Accountants in Ireland* [1995] 3 I.R. 86 at 99–100.
112 See, e.g. *O'Donoghue v. Veterinary Council* [1975] I.R. 398. See also n.142, p. 525.

this well-known case (which was about Article 34.1 of the Constitution and the administration of justice being vested in the courts). Secondly, it is odd that the point was not raised in the passage that the powerful pull of professional brotherhood may make the domestic government unduly favourable to the member of the fraternity who is said to have fallen by the way-side. The adage, "dog doesn't eat dog", after all, commands a considerable following. The reasonable outsider might well regard this as a far more powerful influence than the possibilities canvassed in the passage just quoted. In addition, the passage refers to the compensation fund but does not consider the argument that a finding of unprofessional conduct would facilitate a claim against the fund and, so, might be thought to bias members of the Disciplinary Committee against such a finding. It must also be said that there is certainly no authority to suggest that the law on bias is sufficiently accommodating to balance two sources of bias against each other, and so cancel out, interests pulling in opposite directions. Such a random approach would fly in the face of the principle in this area. The other and more important point is the doctrine of necessity, described below, which is a major qualifying factor: for the Solicitors Act, 1954 requires the Disciplinary Committee to be composed exclusively of practising solicitors. Accordingly the doctrine would be an answer to any claim of bias. At the same time, the possible source of bias under discussion might indicate that no solicitor from the same part of the country or (if relevant) the same speciality as the accused should be included on the Committee.

(c) **Loyalty to the institution.** It might be contended that the servants of an institution might be regarded as being, *ipso facto*, so committed to the objectives or to the interests of that institution, that they might be incapable of holding the balance fairly between these objectives and other interests. This argument, which anyway makes the assumption that the objectives of what is, after all, a public body are partisan, has been rejected save in a situation in which the public body has acted "capriciously" in the following passage:

> "It would be manifestly impossible for [public bodies] to discharge their particular responsibilities in an efficient and sensible manner if every such decision could be successfully challenged by a litigant on the ground that the official who made it was actuated by a conscientious desire to advance the authority's interests rather than a spirit of judicial detachment. . . . [A] decision is not vitiated simply because the official who made it can be said to have a natural bias in favour of advancing the interest of the authority whose interest he is there to serve; but if, in addition, he exercises an administrative discretion 'capriciously, partially or in a manifestly unfair manner' his action would be restrained and corrected by the Courts."[113]

---

[113] *O'Brien v. Bord na Móna* [1983] I.R. 255 at 269, quoting O'Higgins C.J. in *Loftus v. Attorney General* [1979] I.R. 229. The present point was not mentioned in the Supreme Court in *O'Brien*. See also, *Collins v. County Cork V.E.C.*, unreported, High Court, May 26, 1982. *The State (McEldowney) v. Kelleher* [1983] I.R. 289. See Hogan, "Judicial Independence and Mandatory Orders" (1983) 5 D.U.L.J. 114. In *McEldowney* Costello J. was reversed by the Supreme Court, but nothing was said on this point. *Cf.* the comments of Keane J. in *The State (Comer) v. Minister of Justice*, unreported, High Court, December 19, 1980 where he said that the principle of *nemo iudex* "could not be literally applied" to an adjudication by the prison authorities as to whether a prison officer was guilty of neglect of his duties. Keane J. is probably suggesting here that some allowance must be made for a degree of institutional bias which may tend to creep into this assessment by the authorities.

Another unsuccessful submission of this type occurred in *Flynn v. Director of Public Prosecutions*.[114] However, in *Ó'Cléirígh v. Minister for Agriculture*[115] *O'Brien* was distinguished (the reasons for which are given below) and the plaintiff succeeded. This case concerned the assessment of the determination of the amount of compensation payable to a lay commissioner on the dissolution of the Irish Land Commission. According to the relevant statute (Irish Land Commission (Dissolution) Act 1992, section 9), "The Minister [for Agriculture], with the concurrence of the Minister for Finance, may . . . provide such compensation to . . . a lay commissioner ceasing to hold office . . . as the Minister considers reasonable." Holding the statutory provision unconstitutional, Barron J. stated:

> "The section can, however be impugned upon two other grounds. The need for the concurrence of the Minister for Finance involves budgetary considerations, something which has no place in a judicial determination. Further, since it is a judicial determination, justice must not only be done, but must be seen to be done. In such circumstances, the party paying cannot at the same time be the party determining the amount of the payment. To do so would be to make him a judge in his own cause."[116]

This potentially far-reaching conclusion is worthy of rather more exploration and substantiation than it received in the passage (or here). Its predicate is that the assessment of compensation is "a judicial determination". (Probably since there is no mention of Article 34.1 or the Separation of Powers, in general, we are justified in translating this into a "quasi-judicial determination".) In any case, on what basis is it said to be "judicial or quasi-judicial"? Probably, because as held earlier in the judgment, the plaintiff's constitutional (property) rights were involved. This was

---

114 [1986] I.L.R.M. 290. Here the plaintiff-postman had been suspended by An Post for various offences committed at work. He first brought successful proceedings against An Post seeking, *inter alia*, a declaration that his suspension was *ultra vires* (on which see pp. 394–398). Next, he was prosecuted on indictment in respect of the offences. The plaintiff's case, in respect of this prosecution, was grounded on the fact that the D.P.P. had appointed An Post's solicitor, S., to act in the prosecution of the plaintiff. This, the plaintiff argued, violated his right to a fair trial (the argument, in this case, being put on the basis of Article 38.1) in view of S's commitment to his employer and the action which the plaintiff was bringing against it. The Supreme Court rejected this argument on the ground that: "[t]here are no conceivable grounds for supposing that Mr. S, a responsible solicitor against whom no allegation of mala fides is made, would act in some improper manner so as unjustly to prosecute the plaintiff." (at 295). Yet, in later proceedings, arising out of the same episode, *Flynn v. An Post* [1987] I.R. 68: McCarthy J. who had sat on the bench in the instant case, remarked (at 84): "In my view, [the present] case shows that [the D.P.P.'s retention of An Post's solicitor] though legally proper, may, in practice, be unwise." One of the specific factors inspiring this remark is probably identified in the passage quoted in the text on p. 582.

In this context, see also environmental legislation in which encouragement is given to prosecute for an offence, by a provision that, on the application of the prosecuting authority, any fine must be paid to the prosecutor: Local Government (Water Pollution) (Amendment) Act 1990, s.26; Environmental Protection Agency Act 1992, s.10.

115 [1996] 2 I.L.R.M. 12; *Davitt v. Minister for Justice*, unreported, High Court, Barron J., February 8, 1989. In *Davitt*, Barron J. stated (at pp. 7–8): "The coroner acted on all the relevant evidence available to him. *But he had the power to summon witnesses, but did not exercise it.* I am sure that he was influenced by the fact that the Gardaí appeared to be satisfied and the fact that the next of kin did not attend. To him, it must have appeared to have been routine. The reality of the matter is that there was never an inquiry by someone with an open mind." (Emphasis in original judgment.)

116 *Ibid.* at 15.

an element which was relied upon, by the judge, in holding that the statutory provision should be glossed to mean that the Minister's assessment must be objectively reasonable. (However one should note that in the case distinguished by the judge – *O'Brien* – what was at issue was the plaintiff's right to own farmland which interfered with a compulsory purchase order; in other words, the constitutional right to property was engaged in *O'Brien* too.). There is, of course, difficulty regarding the meaning of "quasi-judicial", a term which is now used only fitfully. However, it would probably mean more than a requirement of objective reasonableness. It is perhaps best to eliminate talk of "judicial" or "quasi-judicial" and (overlooking *O'Brien*) characterise *O'Cleirigh* as a case in which since a constitutional right was involved, a very high standard of constitutional justice was required. More simply, though less rationally, *O'Cleirigh* might be confined narrowly to its own facts, in particular the fact that a Minister rather than any other type of personage, was the decision-maker. In any case, it should be said that it is clear from the authorities cited in footnotes earlier in this section,[117] that the weight of authority is in favour of *O'Brien*.

(d) Prior involvement and pre-judgment of the issues. This source will often be interwoven with: "(c) Loyalty to the institution" above, (since prior involvement will often arise because some institution is so structured that the same person is concerned at two stages of the decision-making process); or even with "(b) Personal attitudes, relationships, beliefs".[118]

As a matter of principle, it seems objectionable that a decision-maker exercising quasi-judicial functions should sit with an appellate body to hear an appeal against his own decision.[119] Statutory recognition of this is to be found in section 24 of the

---

117 See above, footnotes 113–114.
118 An example of this may be the hypothetical case mentioned by McMahon J. in *The State (Fagan) v. Governor of Mountjoy Prison*, unreported, High Court, March 6, 1978: see p. 516. Confusion is worse confounded by the fact that, in certain circumstances, there may be pre-judgment because the decision is regarded as having been more or less taken by some other body, *e.g.* a sub-committee as in *Clancy v. IRFU* [1995] 1 I.L.R.M. 189, 199–200. It is difficult to know whether to classify this flaw under the present rubric or under that of failure to exercise a discretion, by virtue of delegation or acting under the dictation of another body. For a case in which it was held that Art. 6.1 of the E.C.H.R. was contravened, see *Procola v. Luxembourg* (1996) 22 E.H.R.R. 193 (The Judicial Committee of the Conseil d'État heard a judicial review of regulations, even though four of the five members of the Committee had earlier taken part in the drawing up of the Conseil d'État's advisory opinion on the lawfulness of the proposed regulations.) For a discussion of the Supreme Court's advisory jurisdiction under Article 26, in the present context, see Gwynn Morgan, *The Separation of Powers in the Irish Constitution*, (1996), p. 216. Prior involvement may also constitute a breach of Art.6(l) depending "on the scope and nature of the measures taken by a judge before his trial": *Saraiva de Carvalho v. Portugal* (1994) 18 E.H.R.R. 534 at 547. In that case it was held that there was no breach where the trial judge had previously ordered that there was a prima facie case against the accused, but where the issues which the judge had to settle "when taking this decision are consequently not the same as those which are decisive for his final judgment." On the other hand, it is impermissible for a judge who rejected bail for an accused on the ground that there had been "a particularly confirmed suspicion" that the accused was guilty to try the subsequent criminal charges: *Hauschildt v. Denmark* (1990) 12 E.H.R.R. 266. Likewise, a judge may not previously have been a member of the prosecution team (*Huber v. Switzerland* (1990), Series A., No. 249-A) or have previously acted as investigating magistrate in respect of the charges against an accused (*De Cubber v. Belgium* (1985) 7 E.H.R.R. 236).
119 For a rather strange example of this, see Irish Horseracing Industry Act 1994, s.45, as commented on at I.C.L.S.A. Rel. 18–28.

Courts of Justice Act 1924 which prohibits the judge who heard a case from sitting as a member of the court of appeal when the case at which he presided is being considered.[120] Contrast this with section 14 of the Charities Act 1961 which provides that any judicial members of the Commissioners for Charitable Bequests and Donations are not to be disqualified, on that account from hearing charity cases.

Usually, where this category of the *nemo iudex* principle is engaged the involvement arises from the fact that some institution is so structured that the same person is involved at two stages of the same serpentine bureaucratic process. An example is *Heneghan v. Western Regional Fisheries Board*[121] in which the dismissal of a fisheries inspector was set aside because the prime mover in the dismissal process had acted as "witness, prosecutor, judge, jury and appeal court."[122] A slightly less extreme case is *Flanagan v. University College Dublin*,[123] a university disciplinary case. Before the three-member committee of discipline, the Registrar of the University acted as prosecutor. The accused student and her two representatives were then asked to retire. The committee, the Registrar and his principal assistant remained. When the student and her representatives returned, they were informed that the alleged plagiarism would be sent to an independent expert to assess, a course to which she agreed. The choice of an independent assessor was left to the Registrar as was both the consultation with the relevant Professors who assisted in this choice and the correspondence with the assessor. The applicant was not involved in the selection process. All this was stigmatised as bias by Barron J. in the High Court. Again in *R. (Snaith) v. Ulster Polytechnic*,[124] the applicant's dismissal was quashed as the members of the committee who had taken the initial decision to dismiss sat with the Governors of the College when the appeal was heard.

On the other side of the line was *Philips v. Medical Council*[125] which arose out of an inquiry under the Medical Practitioners Act 1978 into alleged professional misconduct. Here Carroll J. ruled that "the Registrar [of the Medical Council] acted very fairly throughout". For example, "he did not provide copies of the allegations against [the doctor involved] to [the expert consultant] prior to making his report in order that he could maintain an open mind". Furthermore, "the registrar is under no obligation to furnish the Fitness to Practice Committee with a copy of [the] report before the actual hearing. His duty is to present the evidence in the context of the inquiry."[126]

---

120 In *Wallace v. John Daly & Co. Ltd* [1949] I.R. 352, Black J., who was a member of the Supreme Court, sat as a judge of the High Court on circuit and then stated a case for the opinion of the Supreme Court. Black J. proceeded to sit on the Supreme Court to hear the case-stated he had himself stated. He formed the third member of a majority of three to two.

121 [1986] I.L.R.M. 225 (upheld in the Supreme Court). See also *O'Neill v. Irish Hereford Breed Society Ltd* [1992] 1 I.R. 431 at 452.

122 [1986] I.L.R.M.225 at 229. See also *O'Donovan v. Veterinary Council* [1975] I.R. 398 and *Bane v. Garda Representative Association* [1997] 2 I.R. 449 in each of which the charges against the applicant were actually instigated by the decision-maker.

123 [1988] I.R. 724. On *Flanagan*, see also, pp. 543–544.

124 [1981] N.I. 28. See also, *Cooper v. Wilson* [1937] 2 K.B. 309; *R. v. Kent Police Authority, ex p. Godden* [1971] 2 Q.B. 662; *R. v. Barnsley M.B.C., ex p. Hook* [1976] 1 W.L.R. 1052.

125 [1992] I.L.R.M. 469.

126 *Ibid.* at 475.

Drawing on a distinction between administrative and quasi-judicial functions,[127] it has been said that in the case of the former, the responsible body is entitled to reach a provisional or tentative conclusion in respect of the matter. It has been held that it will generally suffice if such a tribunal approaches its task with an open mind, and a "will to reach an honest conclusion after hearing what was urged on either side." This statement was made in *McGrath and O'Ruairc v. Trustees of Maynooth College*,[128] a case which, it may be thought, goes to the very limits of tolerance for a tribunal's procedure. The facts were that two university lecturers had been removed from office by the trustees of the seminary at which they taught. The plaintiffs had questioned certain aspects of Church teaching. Thus the trustees were bound to have "firm views" on this question, and might very well "have had strong views." Nevertheless, it seems to have been held that even if there were a marked disagreement as to religious belief between the trustees and the plaintiffs, coupled with an element of pre-judgment, this would not have precluded the trustees from giving a fair hearing. Moreover, as the plaintiffs had elected, rather oddly, not to attend the hearing by the trustees, hence, the Supreme Court refused to listen to any complaints concerning the impartiality of the trustees. The outcome was different in *The State (McGeough) v. Louth County Council*[129] where the applicant complained of a county manager's refusal to give his consent to the sale of a labourer's cottage. This consent was required by the Labourer's Act 1936. It was clear that the county manager disapproved of the sale of such cottages; indeed the refusal of the present application was the twelfth consecutive refusal. The manager's refusal was struck down on the grounds, of *inter alia*, bias. It may be possible to reconcile *McGeough* with *McGrath and O'Ruairc* on the grounds that first, the county manager had gone beyond the stage of holding "firm views" to the point of no longer having an "open mind." Secondly, the plaintiffs in *McGrath and O'Ruairc* had submitted to this contractual jurisdiction, whereas in *McGeough* the county manager had been invested with statutory powers which he was bound to exercise fairly.

In line with what has just been said, it might have been anticipated that a very high standard of impartiality and detachment would be required of a judge. A particular example of this precept – which may be regarded as being an instance of the rule against pre-judgment or may be so fundamental as to have acquired separate existence of its own – is regarded as the corner-stone of the *accusatorial* trial structure (especially a criminal trial). It is that the judge must not take an active part but must remain above the forensic contest rather like a tennis umpire monitoring the play. This axiom was recently illustrated in *Magee v. O'Dea*.[130] This was an

---

127 On which see pp. 601–602.
128 [1979] I.L.R.M. 166. All the quotations in the text are drawn from Griffin J.'s judgment. See also, *R. (Campbell College) v. Department of Education* [1982] N.I.125; *Re Wislang* [1984] N.I. 69; *Murtagh v. St Emer's National School* [1991] I.L.R.M. 549 at 552 (Barron J.).
129 (1973) 107 I.L.T.R. 13. On the question of a closed mind, see *Franklin v. Minister for Town and Country Planning* [1948] A.C. 87.
130 [1994] 1 I.R. 500. *Cf.* the judgment of Barr J. in *Aziz v. Midland Health Board* [1995] E.L.R. 48, a case where the applicant medical registrar was dismissed for disobeying an instruction given to him by a particular consultant. The decision to dismiss lay with the health board's chief executive officer pursuant to the provisions of the Health (Removal of Officers and Servants) Regulations 1971 (S.I. No. 110 of 1971), but it was contended that the officer in question had infringed fair procedures by

extradition application. At the conclusion of the evidence, the presiding District Judge was not satisfied as to the question of identity. Accordingly he returned to court and recalled, of his own motion, a witness as to the identity of the plaintiff. He did this, without informing either the plaintiff's solicitor (who, in fairness to the District Judge, it should be noted, had only been engaged within minutes before the matter came to court) or the state solicitor as to what he intended to do. Holding the order of the District Court invalid, Flood J. stated:

"... our system of justice is an adversarial system. The State presents its case and as this is a quasi-criminal matter it should establish the necessary proofs beyond reasonable doubt. I accept that a judge has a right to recall, or in fact call, on his own motion, a witness. All the authorities would suggest that this is a practice which should be sparingly used, and in particular, sparingly used in criminal matters, where the onus of proof is a strict onus of proof, as otherwise it may appear that he is descending into the arena and becoming partisan."[131]

What is perhaps more surprising is that the same notion – the idea of the accusatorial trial – was drawn upon in the context of a hearing in the Supreme Court case of *Kiely v. Minister for Social Welfare (No. 2)*[132] which involved an appeals officer in the Department of Social Welfare. (Strangely similar language, had been used in the *Kiely* to that in the *Magee* judgment although there was no reference to *Kiely* in *Magee*). The particular feature of *Kiely* which is relevant here[133] concerned the behaviour of the medical assessor who had sat with the appeals officer and had asked questions (of a medical nature) of the applicant's expert medical witness. Henchy J. stated:

"It ill becomes an assessor who is an affiliate of the quasi-judicial officer, to descend into the forensic arena ... the taint of partiality will necessarily follow if [the appeals officer or assessor] intervenes to such an extent as to appear to be presenting or conducting the case against the claimant."[134]

---

having a conversation with the consultant in the absence of the applicant. Barr J. acknowledged that in adopting this course of action the officer "ran a serious risk of invalidating the proceedings", but concluded that (at 61):

"Although the CEO ought not to have had any communication with [the consultant] other than orally in the presence of the applicant, I accept [his evidence] that his conversations ... did not add materially to his knowledge of the facts of the case and did not impinge on his conclusions thereon.... There is insufficient evidence to cast doubt on the fairness of the decision ... to dismiss the applicant ... [T]he foregoing defect in the procedure, which in other circumstances might have been fatal to the validity of the proceedings, did not give rise to a reasonable possibility that injustice might have been done to the applicant."

In this case Barr J.'s understandable unease at even the appearance of pre-judgment appears to have been tempered by the special facts of the case, including his acceptance that the conversation did not substantially impact on the officer's decision making and his earlier observation (at 56) that while the Health Board was obliged to abide by fair procedures, a non-judicial body "such as a ... health board has no obligation to apply formal court procedures in the investigation and determination of disciplinary charges brought against an employee or officer holder."

131 [1994] I.R. 500 at 507.
132 [1977] I.R. 267.
133 For other features, see pp. 554.
134 [1977] I.R. at 283. *A contra* Keane J. in *Rajah v. The Royal College of Surgeons* [1994] 1 I.R. 384 at 394.

There is a problem which commonly confronts the legal adviser to a public body in the wake of successful judicial review proceedings. The problem is that fresh proceedings may be and often will be brought. Yet in most cases, the statutory design will be such that this set of proceedings will have to be brought in the same forum which has already heard and decided the initial proceedings. The obvious danger of prejudice arising from prior involvement and pre-judgment can be substantially reduced, if it can be arranged that the personnel of the forum is different from that of the initial hearing.[135] But circumstances may be such that this is not possible. In this situation, further proceedings may or may not be lawful. A case in which this difficulty was discussed (though necessarily only *obiter*) is *O'Shea v. Commissioner of An Garda Síochána*.[136] This case, which arose out of disciplinary proceedings, resulted in the applicant obtaining an order of certiorari, to quash (on the ground of breach of *audi alteram partem*) the Notice of Proposal to dismiss the applicant, issued by the respondent. Carroll J. held that this Notice merely asserted that the respondent believed there to be the equivalent of a strong prima facie case to answer: the respondent had not "expressed himself by the notice to be 'beyond doubt'".[137] Thus, and this is the significant point, the matter could be remitted to the respondent for reconsideration by the respondent himself. This problem was also in view in *McAuley v. Garda Commissioner*[138] a case where a trainee Garda had his contract terminated in a manner which clearly violated the guarantee of fair procedures. In the High Court Barr J. restrained the Garda authorities from conducting a fresh inquiry, since he considered that the risk of prejudice flowing from the "furnishing of prejudicial extraneous matter" to the Commissioner was too great. The Supreme Court reversed this particular finding, with Hamilton C.J. observing that such an order would have the effect of:

> " . . . depriving the Commissioner of the power to and responsibility of terminating the training of the applicant if after an inquiry or investigation conducted in accordance with fair procedures he formed the opinion that the applicant was unsuitable for continued employment as a trainee by reason of misconduct. . . . It cannot be assumed that such an inquiry would not be conducted in accordance with fair procedures. If it were, the decision made on foot thereof would be subject to judicial review."[139]

It seems probable that these two decisions were, to some extent, inspired by the doctrine of necessity.[140] A further aspect of *McAuley* is that the Supreme Court evidently considered that on the facts of that case the risk of prejudice was not so

---

135 *e.g.* in the *Kiely* saga (see pp. 521, 554), Mrs Kiely's three appeals were each heard by different appeals officers in order to avoid the danger contemplated in the text. See *Kiely v. Minister for Social Welfare (No. 2)* [1977] I.R. 267 at 270 at 276 and *Doyle v. Kildare County Council* [1995] 2 I.R. 424 at 432. But note *Fawsitt (No.2)*, which was heard by the same Circuit Court judge as *Fawsitt*: see p. 418, n.121. The details are in the 2nd Edition of this book at pp. 346–347.

136 [1994] 2 I.R. 408.

137 *Ibid.* at 413.

138 [1996] 3 I.R. 208.

139 *Ibid.* at 232.

140 *cf.* the somewhat similar pragmatic attitude taken in *O'Neill v. Beaumont Hospital Board* [1990] I.L.R.M. 419. See also *Hughes v. Garda Commissioner*, unreported, High Court, July 23, 1996 (appointment of investigating officer under Garda Síochána (Discipline) Regulations 1989 by a

manifest as would inevitably jeopardise the fairness of any fresh hearing.[141] Had the facts been otherwise, perhaps different considerations would have prevailed.

Standards of bias

In the first place, in articulating, the standard, the majority[142] of the judges have steadily taken a view which entails distinguishing between judicial or quasi-judicial and, on the other hand, administrative functions and applying a less strict form of

---

Chief Superintendent who was also the complainant was held by McCracken J. to be "quite undesirable", but did not of itself invalidate the inquiry).

[141] cf. D v. Director of Public Prosecutions [1994] 2 I.R. 465 and Nolan v. Director of Public Prosecutions [1994] 3 I.R. 626 where the Supreme Court held that an accused seeking to restrain the holding of a criminal trial on the ground of lack of fair procedures must establish in the words of Blayney J. in Nolan (at 632) "that there is a real risk that by reason of those circumstances he could not obtain a fair trial." While recognising that, in the words of Barrington J. in Mooney v. An Post, unreported, Supreme Court, March 20, 1997, "to attempt to introduce the procedures of a criminal trial into an essentially civil proceeding only serves to create confusion", it may be, nonetheless that the test enunciated in D. and Nolan is applicable by analogy to the question of whether the risk of prejudice, which may be caused by a second hearing is sufficiently great. See also the comments of O'Sullivan J. in the subsequent judicial review arising from this case: McAuley v. Chief Superintendent Keating, unreported, High Court, July 8, 1997, which is discussed at pp. 531–532.

[142] The best known exception is the extremely stringent standard set by Kenny J. in O'Donoghue v. Veterinary Council [1975] I.R. 398 which took the form of an appeal by a veterinary surgeon to the High Court from a finding by the Veterinary Council that he had been guilty of unprofessional conduct. The first stage in the procedure for the investigation of alleged misconduct was an assessment by the Standing and Penal Cases Committee of the Council. Next, the Council convened a special committee of inquiry to investigate the allegations and it reached the unanimous opinion that the appellant was guilty. Finally, the Council considered the transcript of the evidence before the special committee and decided that the facts proved by the special committee had been proved to their satisfaction. The alleged misconduct consisted of duplicating blood tests for brucellosis and the real victim was the person paying for the tests, namely the Minister for Agriculture. However, the Attorney General had advised the Minister not to act as complainant himself because some members of the Council were veterinarians employed in his Department. In these circumstances N, a member of the council agreed to allow his name to be used as complainant. He took no part in the case against the petitioner: the solicitors who nominally acted for N were in fact instructed by the registrar of the Council and he had not been a member of the special committee which had investigated the allegation. However, N was one of the 13 members of the Council present when the Council met and confirmed the special committee's decision and fixed the petitioner's punishment. In these circumstances, although the judge characterised N as a "nominal complainant" (the real complainant being the Minister) he held that the nemo iudex rule was violated and the Council's decision must be cancelled.

The obvious question which this decision suggests is how a claim of bias against the Veterinary Council can be avoided when a complaint to the Council emanates from the Minster for Agriculture. The answer given by Kenny J. at the end of his judgment (at p. 407) is that:

". . . those who are in the full-time employment of the State and are working in the Department of Agriculture and Fisheries should not go forward for election to the Council. Similarly, the person nominated by the Minister to the Council should not be an official of his but should be a veterinary surgeon in private practice."

The outcome in O'Donoghue could be explained on the basis that the Veterinary Council was trying the appellant for a disciplinary offence and was, thus, following the authority of Re Solicitors Act 1954 administering justice, or, at least, discharging a quasi-judicial function. Such an analysis would bring O'Donoghue into line with the judicial/administrative functions dichotomy adopted in the O'Brien-Collins line of authority, outlined in the following paragraphs, and thus reconcile O'Donoghue with the view adopted by the majority of judges. However, considering the tenor of the judgment in O'Donoghue – the emphasis laid on the need for justice to be seen to be done – coupled with Kenny J.'s dissent in Corrigan (below), it is more realistic to regard O'Donoghue as representing a minority view, namely that a very rigorous standard of nemo iudex should be adopted.

the rule against bias in the case of administrative functions. This point is illustrated by the leading case of *O'Brien v. Bord na Móna*.[143] The plaintiff challenged the compulsory acquisition of a large portion of his farm. In the system of compulsory acquisition created by the Turf Development Act 1946, both the drawing up of a provisional list of land to be acquired and the hearing of objections to the inclusion of land on that list is vested in the defendant. It was argued that the fact that the Board had drawn up the provisional list meant that it might be thought of as prejudiced at the second stage of the hearing, in that it would be predisposed to uphold its own earlier decision. Following a review of the provisions of the Act, the Supreme Court concluded that the Board's functions were administrative in nature as they entailed the "balancing of the desirability of the production of turf on the one hand, and the interest of an individual owner of land on the other. . . ." Accordingly, whilst the Board could not act from "an indirect or improper motive or without due fairness of procedure," yet a less stringent standard was required than in the case of persons or bodies exercising judicial functions.

A similar distinction has been drawn by Murphy J. in *Collins v. County Cork Vocational Education Committee*.[144] The central point of the case was the plaintiff's claim that the resolution of the defendant body suspending him from his duties as headmaster of a vocational school was void. It was said that the Committee was biased because of the prior involvement by some members of the Committee in the case, and the existence of a conflict of interest. Murphy J. found it necessary to distinguish between: "[t]he application of the rules of natural justice where it is sought to set up an independent tribunal and other cases in which a particular function is by the terms of a statute, order or agreement conferred on a designated body." The judge observed that were the position otherwise, then "the supervision and administration of any organisation involving a number of office holders would be quite impossible."

A point which is explicit in the quotations from *Collins*, and which clearly must also have been a factor in *O'Brien*, is that, given the respective statutory structure of the VEC and Bord na Móna some appearance of possible bias was inevitable. It is reasonable to assume that one of the policies underlying these two decisions was the doctrine of necessity[145] which states that, in general, the no bias rule will not be permitted to destroy the only tribunal with authority to decide an issue.[146]

---

143 [1983] I.R. 255. See Coffey, "Procedural Curbs on powers of Compulsory Acquisition" (1984) 6 D.U.L.J. 152.
144 Unreported, High Court, May 26, 1982. This decision was affirmed by the Supreme Court on March 18, 1983, but this point was not dealt with. For another authority along the same lines, see *McCann v. Racing Board* [1983] I.L.R.M. 67; *O'Neill v. Beaumont Hospital Board* [1990] I.L.R.M. 419 at 437; and *Radio Limerick v. IRTC* [1997] 2 I.L.R.M. 1 at 25–56, *per* Keane J.
145 On this point, see further, pp. 534–536.
146 It is possible to distinguish this line of authority from *Re Grogan's Application* [1988] 8 N.I.J.B. 88. Here the applicant was a prisoner and his main submission was that disciplinary proceedings against him violated the first rule of natural justice in that the Governor had retired with the Board of Visitors when it considered its decision. Carswell J. found, as a fact, that the Governor did not take any part in the decision-making process and only remained with the Board for a few seconds in order to answer one question put to him by the Board. Nevertheless, Carswell J. quashed the adjudication of the Board. The outcome in *Grogan* can be distinguished from *Collins* and *O'Brien* on the ground that *Grogan* involved what Murphy J. in the passage quoted from *Collins*, called "an

It is less easy to justify a series of cases involving the Land Commission. The procedure before the Commission is in two stages and in each of these cases, a commissioner who initially certified that the lands were suitable for acquisition had sat as a member of the tribunal which, at the later stage, decided whether to confirm the initial decision. (There are four Commissioners, two only of whom are involved at each stage so that, in most circumstances, it is unnecessary for the same Commissioner to be involved at both stages). In the first of these cases, *Corrigan v. Irish Land Commission*[147] a majority of the Supreme Court, with Kenny J. dissenting, ruled that an appellant, who with full knowledge of the facts had made no objection to the membership of an Appeal Tribunal (composed of the same two lay Commissioners, who had had earlier certified provisionally that his land was required for the relief of congestion) was estopped by his conduct from raising the issue of bias.[148]

Corrigan may be justified on the particular ground of waiver (examined below). However it seems, from the tenor of the judgment in this and, other cases mentioned in the footnotes, that they were intended to lay down a broader rule, namely, that the no bias principle is not broken when a Land Commissioner is involved at the two stages, even though there are no extenuating circumstances. This line of cases involving the Land Commission is surprising and is certainly out of step with other authority which has been exemplified.

It is appropriate, next, to outline two recent cases in which it was held that the alleged bias occurred too early in the exercise of the function. The first case is *Huntsgrove Developments Ltd v. Meath County Council*[149] in which the facts were as follows. In May, 1989, the respondent local authority had adopted a development plan. Six months later, Ladgrove Stores – who were competitors of the applicant – had approached the respondent for pre-planning discussions with regard to a proposed shopping-centre. The respondent's reaction was that, although it was agreeable in principle to the proposed development, the lands proposed for its site were not appropriately zoned. The local authority added that financial constraints prevented them from undertaking the in-depth survey and analysis in regard to the future development of the area which would be necessary for a review of the plan. Thus encouraged, Ladgrove gave the respondents £20,000 as a contribution towards the cost of conducting the preliminary surveys and the preparation of a proposed draft revision of the 1989 plan. The review was then initiated and in February 1992, a revised draft plan was put on public display. A few weeks later, the applicant sought judicial review, with a claim of bias, by virtue of the payment, being its strongest ground.

Lardner J. emphasised, in the first place, that a decision to initiate a review of an existing development plan is merely the first step in a statutorily-prescribed process which includes the collection of data; an opportunity for interested members

---

independent tribunal [as contrasted with] *a designated body*." Or, as the same point was put in *Grogan* (at 90) "the courts have insisted on a high standard of purity on the issue of possible bias of tribunals hearing such matters as charges of disciplinary offences."

[147] [1977] I.R. 317.

[148] See to similar effect, *The State (Curran) v. Irish Land Commission*, unreported, High Court, June 12, 1978 and *Re Creighton's Estate*, unreported, High Court, March 5, 1982.

[149] [1994] 2 I.L.R.M. 36.

of the public to make representations; and, finally, adoption of the plan, possibly with amendments, by the planning authority. The kernel of Lardner J.'s judgment is contained in the following passage:

> "[The planning authority's consideration] whether to prepare a draft revision . . . involves a decision whether in the light of perceived needs, present and future, the development objectives and purposes formulated and the provisions made to achieve them in the existing plan ought to be revised . . . In my view, decisions on these matters may properly be regarded as the choice and formulation of a policy . . . What is challenged in this judicial review is a decision which does not even go as far as that. . . . The decision whether at any time to initiate and conduct preliminary surveys and the collection of data and the subsequent decision to propose a draft revision plan for consideration are essentially administrative decisions, largely concerned with matters of public policy for the area."[150]

Thus a fairly sharp distinction was drawn between the initial administrative steps, which was all that was involved here and, on the other hand, the later stages, including, for example adoption of the plan by the local authority. It might have been thought that this distinction would have been open to objection on the basis that the reasonable man might consider that if a local authority had jumped the initial hurdle hand-in-hand with a developer, the local authority might feel itself to be committed to that developer even at the later and conclusive stage of the decision. However, the judge's response to this line of argument was that in the case of an administrative act,[151] an applicant must establish "a real likelihood of actual bias",[152] the suspicion of the reasonable man being *nil ad rem*.

The second case is *Chestvale Properties Ltd v. Glackin*.[153] The background to this application for judicial review was that the Minister for Industry and Commerce had used his powers under Part II of the Companies Act, 1990, to appoint the respondent as an inspector to investigate the affairs of the applicant company because of its possible involvement in the acquisition of certain lands by Bord Telecom. The argument depended upon the facts that the inspector was a partner in a firm of solicitors which had acted professionally both for a partner of *D* (*D* was the beneficial owner of the shares in the applicant company) and also for certain companies in which *D* had an interest – though not for the applicant company itself.[154]

Murphy J. stated that: *D* was not himself the client; the respondent was not the partner who had dealt with the case and the transaction was not substantial – and

---

150 *Ibid*. at 47–48. This passage should probably not be read as necessarily suggesting that policy decisions, in contrast with individual decisions, do not attract the rules of constitutional justice: on this point, see pp. 604–606.

151 *Ibid*. at 50. Lardner J. summarised, approvingly, the ratio in *O'Brien v. Bord na Móna* in this way: "where an administrative act is concerned, beyond the obligation to act fairly 'and in that sense judicially' the requirement of constitutional justice and natural justice, *nemo iudex in causa sua*, did not apply."

152 [1994] 2 I.L.R.M. at 51.

153 [1993] 3 I.R. 35.

154 And in view of the fact that any injustice which existed did so *vis à vis* D himself, it was held as an alternate *ratio* that the applicant company had no *locus standi* to complain.

concluded that the relationship was "tenuous".[155] Nevertheless Murphy J. gave it as his opinion that[156]: "the respondent would be necessarily disqualified from exercising a quasi-judicial function in any matter in which [D] was involved." However, significantly, the judge then went on to hold that the applicant's claim failed because at the time of the court application, the inspector's investigation had not reached the stage at which it could be regarded as judicial or quasi-judicial in nature.[157] The Court was naturally pressed, by the applicants, with such authorities as *The State (Shannon Atlantic Fisheries Ltd) v. McPolin*.[158] Such cases were distinguished on the basis that in the instant case, the Inspector's inquiry had reached "only a very preliminary and exploratory stage."[159] Murphy J. appears to have been influenced (and this is a rather unusual phenomenon, in view of the fact that Irish law is more pro-individual and anti-public body than English law) by an English case of *Pergamon* in which Buckley L.J. stated:[160] "Until an inspector has reached a stage at which he thinks that he will, or, at least, may have to report adversely on a director or officer, it will be premature for him to decide what, if anything, he should do to give the director or officer a fair chance of explaining the matter."

Formulation of the test for bias

The recent statements of the law which have been extracted from *O'Brien, Collins, Dublin Well Woman, Hunstgrove* and *Chestvale* (and other cases mentioned in footnotes) rest a heavy weight upon two sets of distinctions, each of which appears to be unsatisfactory, in principle, and vague in practical operation.

(a) Take, first the administrative – quasi-judicial boundary (invoked in the first three cases on the above list): this is a line which it is extremely difficult to draw in practice, and no Irish case has yet attempted to set out a framework of rules by which to define this boundary.[161] In English law, where the distinction was in vogue for some decades, it has now largely been abandoned as unworkable.[162] An

---

155 *Ibid.* at 52. It is noteworthy that at no point does the judgment consider whether the previous contact would have been likely to predispose the inspector for or against *D*. It seems likely (to judge by the tenor of the judgment and the silence on this point) that the assumption was made that, if a sufficiently substantial contact had been made, this might have led to bias against *D* and he had to be allowed the benefit of the doubt.
Notice, secondly, that Murphy J. also remarks (at p. 92): "Presumably it could occur that the association or connection would be so direct or so close that an inspector could not continue with the inquiry and would feel compelled to resign."

156 *Ibid.* at 48.

157 In this case, as in others the nomenclature shifts as between "judicial" and "quasi-judicial". (See [1993] 3 I.R. at 48, 49 and 51). This is especially unfortunate in view of the frequent use of "judicial" in the context of Arts. 34.1 and 37.1.

158 [1976] I.R. 93. In *McPolin*, the facts concerned a statutory investigation by an inspector into a marine accident, following which the inspector had reported to the Minister, without affording the owners an opportunity to be heard, (expressing the view that the owners had been guilty of criminal offences in permitting the vessel to sail). Notwithstanding that it was a preliminary inquiry and that the final decision rested with the Minister, Finlay P. concluded that the inspector was exercising a quasi-judicial role (see esp. p. 98).

159 [1993] 3 I.R. at 51.

160 *Re Pergamon Press Ltd* [1971] Ch. 388 at 407.

161 See pp. 601–602. The same distinction used also to be applied, equally unsatisfactorily in the field of remedies: see pp. 697–698.

162 Wade and Forsyth, *op. cit.*, above, n. 15, pp. 502–514; Craig *op. cit.*, above, n. 2, pp. 283–288.

alternative boundary to the administrative quasi-judicial line was used in *Huntsgrove* and *Chestvale*, namely whether the alleged bias occurs at a premature stage of the exercise of a function. However this too is open to criticism: if there is bias at an earlier stage, is there not a risk that it might, as it were, seep through to contaminate a later stage of the proceedings? (It bears noting that each of the cases cited as precedents in *Chestvale*[163] in fact involved the second, rather than the first, rule of constitutional justice[164]; yet no notice was taken of this difference in *Chestvale*.)

(b) Two formulations of the test vie with each other in the common law world. The more stringent test is whether there is a "real likelihood" of bias. The alternative test is whether there is a reasonable suspicion of bias. It was said (in the first three cases on the list given above) that the first test was appropriate in the case of a quasi-judicial function and the second test for an administrative function. And, in *Huntsgrove* it was said that the first test would apply even at a premature stage of the function. The second – reasonable suspicion – test is inspired by a desire on the part of its judicial adherents to maintain public confidence in the administration of justice (a consideration usually expressed as: "justice should not only be done, but should manifestly and undoubtedly be seen to be done"[165]). (Recently, in Ireland an equivalent distinction has been drawn in terms of on the one hand, "actual" or "subjective" bias *i.e.* relating to the actual state of mind of the deciding officer and, on the other hand, "objective" bias, *i.e.* 'whether a person in the position of the appellant in this case, being a reasonable person, should apprehend that his chance of a fair and independent hearing . . . does not by reason of the previous non-judicial position, statements and actions of the . . . judge on issues which are at the retrial of this case."[166])

The cases listed in (a) have indicated that the real likelihood test is to be preferred where the function is administrative in character. Other recent authorities have preferred this test, without even going into the issue of the character of the function in question. Among these are: *O'Neill v. Beaumont Hospital Board*,[167] *Dublin Well*

---

[163] *McPolin; Pergamon; Haughey.*

[164] On which see Part 3 of Chap. 11.

[165] See *R. v. Sussex JJ., ex p. McCarthy* [1924] 1 K.B. 256 at 259 (Lord Hewart C.J.). Although first articulated in *McCarthy* "it is probably a concept as old as the common law itself and it is in perfect harmony with our constitutional situation": *O'Reilly v. Cassidy* [1995] I.L.R.M. 306 at 310 (O'Flaherty J.). See also *Dublin Well Woman Centre Ltd v. Ireland* [1995] 1 I.L.R.M. 408 at 418–419 (Denham J.) and *Radio Limerick v. IRTC* [1997] 2 I.L.R.M. 1 at 25, *per* Keane J.:
  "It would unquestionably have been difficult for an inference [of bias] *not* to have been drawn had Ms. Brophy [a member of the IRTC] participated in the discussions concerning the 'blacking' of the news item supplied by her or even if she had attended the relevant meeting at which it was discussed. It would have been irresistible if she had participated in, or even perhaps attended at, the meeting at which the decision to terminate the [applicant's] contract was taken [by the IRTC]. The unchallenged evidence before the High Court was that she had absented herself from the two meetings when the 'blacking' of her report was discussed and from the meeting at which the decision was taken to terminate the applicant's contract . . ."

[166] *Dublin Well Woman Centre Ltd v. Ireland* [1995] I.L.R.M. at 418 and 420, *per* Denham J. Another way of formulating what is probably the same distinction is to distinguish "between bias which may have been an operative factor in reaching the decision in question and the existence of circumstances which might give rise to a suspicion of bias."(*O'Neill v. Irish Hereford Breed Society Ltd* [1992] 1 I.R. 431 at 447, *per* Murphy J.).

[167] [1990] I.L.R.M. 419 at 438.

Woman Centre v. Ireland;[168] *Bane v. The GRA*[169] and *McAuley v. Chief Superintendent Keating.*[170] The latter two cases, in which different outcomes were reached – justifiably, on the facts, it is submitted – afford instructive examples. *Bane* originated "in the sorry and, some might think, unseemly, saga of bitterness and dissent which has afflicted the representation of rank and file members of the police force." In an earlier judicial review proceedings, two of the applicants in the instant proceedings had been applicants and had sought to no avail, an order restraining the Garda Representative Association from conducting a ballot of its members. The sequel to these earlier proceedings was the disciplining by the GRA, of *inter alia*, the applicants in the present case. Accordingly, the applicants claimed that the disciplinary proceedings were flawed by virtue of bias. Accepting this contention, Kelly J. stated:

> "It clear that the test which has to be applied is an objective one. I must therefore ask myself whether a reasonable man would, in the circumstances outlined here, have a reasonable fear that the applicants would not have a fair and independent hearing of the issues which arose. In my view a reasonable man would have such a fear . . .
>
> In the present case the Committee which decided the fate of the applicants had present on it a number of the respondents who had been called as witnesses for the GRA in the earlier High Court proceedings and who had given evidence which clearly controverted that given by the applicants. Yet it was those very persons who were called upon to adjudicate on charges levelled against the applicants to the effect that they gave false or misleading evidence to the High Court in those proceedings."[171]

In *McAuley*, too, there had been earlier proceedings. The circumstances, however, were that the applicant had successfully challenged disciplinary proceedings on procedural grounds. The instant application for judicial review arose out of the fresh disciplinary proceedings. The applicant claimed that the respondent who was the superintendent holding the inquiry had pre-judged the issue by virtue of such statements as the following which was made in a letter replying to the applicant's solicitors:

> "I have decided that Student Garda McAuley has committed a breach of discipline in respect of the facts as set out in the relevant investigation file. I now propose to put these breaches to Student Garda McAuley on the 3rd December, 1996 and afford him an opportunity to reply to them or to examine the witnesses."

O'Sullivan J. rejected this contention. Distinguishing *O'Neill* and *Dublin Well Woman Centre* (where "the utterances which gave rise to the successful challenges . . . were articulate and reasoned"), he stated:

> "I must apply the objective test as described in the above authorities to a determination as to whether in all circumstances the first respondent is culpable

---

168 [1995] I.L.R.M. 408.
169 [1997] 2 I.R. 449.
170 Unreported, High Court, July 8, 1997.
171 [1997] 2 I.R. 449 at 472.

of prejudgment bias. In my view he is not. I think a reasonable man, appraised of all the circumstances which I have set out in this judgment, might well come to the conclusion that the first respondent had expressed himself in an infelicitous fashion, or that a legal adviser would have insisted on rephrasing the utterances relied on. I also think, however, that the same reasonable man would be obliged to take note of the careful if not elaborate preparations conducted by or at the direction of the first respondent in advance of the oral hearing, his manifest and repeatedly stated concern to comply with the requirements of the relevant code and indeed his explicit statement to the applicant . . . that he proposed to hold an oral enquiry before coming to a final decision."[172]

Reasonable suspicion and real likelihood

Yet if one looks at the two tests (identified in (b) above) – reasonable suspicion and real likelihood – closely, it is hard to classify separately the factors which should be considered under each head. For, in the first place, a reasonable person would only suspect bias where there is a real likelihood of such occurring; and, secondly, it is inherent in the nature of bias that it cannot be perceived but has to be inferred from the circumstances – in other words, a reasonable suspicion is the major factor by which the existence of a real likelihood of bias is determined. Accordingly the difference between the two is at most one of emphasis with the reasonable suspicion test being largely concerned with outward appearances, whereas the real likelihood version focuses on the court's own view of the realities of the situation. In *Dublin & County Broadcasting Ltd*, Murphy J. stated:

"Certainly it does seem to me the question of bias must be determined on the basis of what a right-minded person would think of the likelihood, of the real likelihood of prejudice, and not on the basis of a suspicion which might dwell in the mind of a person who is ill-informed and did not seek to direct his mind properly to the facts. . . . [But] I entirely accept it would be irrelevant and immaterial if in a case such as the present it was established as a matter of fact that bias was non-operative, or that the particular person accused of the bias was out-voted or whatever. If it is shown that there are on the facts circumstances which would lead a right-minded person to conclude that there was a real likelihood of bias, this would be sufficient to invalidate the proceedings of the Tribunal."[173]

A significant practical question is how well-informed the "reasonable man" must be taken to be. On the one hand, according to the passage, he must not be "ill informed." But, on the other hand, it seems that there are certain "matters of fact" (such as that the bias was non-operative) which he must be taken not to know. Where

---

[172] Quotations from pp. 9 and 22 of the unreported judgment.

[173] *Dublin and County Broadcasting v. IRTC*, unreported, High Court, May 12, 1989 at p. 13 of the judgment. Compare Murphy J.'s judgment in *O'Neill v. Irish Hereford Breed Society Ltd* [1992] 1 I.R. 431 at 449–451. In *Huntgrove*, Lardner J. stated ([1994] 2 I.L.R.M. at 51) tantalisingly: "A further submission of some length was devoted to the scope of knowledge which should be attributed to the reasonable man who considered the facts of the present case." Unfortunately nothing further was said on this point.

is the line to be drawn? In England, there is authority for the proposition that it is not necessary to formulate the test in terms of the reasonable man: the reason is that the court personifies the reasonable man; and also because the court has to ascertain the relevant circumstances, which might not be available to an ordinary observer; yet which – and here is the significant point – whether known to the public generally or not, were in evidence on the hearing of the application for review.[174] However, the passage quoted earlier from the *Dublin Well Woman Centre* case speaks sensibly enough of "a person in the position of the appellant" which suggests that it is only facts which should have been known to the applicant, which may be taken into account. Notice though that, in *Dublin & County Broadcasting Ltd*, Murphy J. was influenced by the circumstance that the person allegedly affected by bias had sought to transfer his share, several months before the relevant time. This private transaction was accepted as crucial, yet there was no attempt to consider whether the "reasonable man" would have known of it.

In the past, there have been cases[175] in which the courts appear to have employed the "reasonable suspicion" test when they wished to set a high standard of impartiality and to strike down the decision before them, and the "real likelihood" formulation when they wished to reach the opposite result. Such an approach is obviously undesirable, for its unpredictability and arbitrariness. But the new teaching appears equally unsatisfactory. What is needed is a re-formulation of the no-bias test which is sufficiently comprehensive and flexible to take into account all relevant factors including: the nature of the decision and the body taking it as well as the seriousness of the actual bias and the appearance thereof.

It may be said, by way of final observation, that in the area of bias, as evidenced in such cases as *Dublin & County Broadcasting*, the Land Commission cases,

---

[174] *R. v. Gough* [1993] 2 W.L.R. 883 at 904–905, varying *R. v. West Yorkshire Coroner ex p. Smith, The Times*, November 6, 1982; *R. v. Liverpool City Justices ex p. Topping* [1983] All E.R. 490 at 491. See Craig, *Administrative Law, op. cit.* above, n.2, p. 332.

[175] One such case may have been *The State (Hegarty) v. Winters* [1956] I.R. 320. For the facts of this case, see p. 514. In the High Court, Davitt P. upheld the arbitrator's award, saying that mere suspicion of bias was not enough. However, the award was quashed by the Supreme Court because the actions of the arbitrator in the words of Maguire C.J. might have given rise to the suspicion that justice was not being done. Another example is provided by Kenny J.'s judgment in *O'Donoghue* [1975] I.R. at 405–407, though there is some reference to the other test at 405. (For other examples of the reasonable man test leading to a finding of bias, see *Killiney & Ballybrack Residents Assoc. v. Minister for Local Government (No. 1)* (1978) 112 I.L.T.R. 9 and *The State (Cole) v. Labour Court* (1984) 2 J.I.S.L.L. 128, *Doyle v. Croke* and *O'Neill v. Beaumont Hospital Board* [1990] I.L.R.M. 419 at 438.) and Kenny J. (dissenting) in *Corrigan v. Irish Land Commission* where he employed the test of reasonable suspicion, but, in contrast, one of the majority judges, Griffin J., spoke of the need to establish a real likelihood of bias. It is likely that the outcome of a case would(or should) depend less on which formula is used and more on such factors as the type of tribunal or administrative agency involved; the nature of the decision and the source of bias.

Take note that some Irish cases have been decided without reference to either test: see, *e.g. The State (Curran) v. Irish Land Commission*, unreported, High Court, June 12, 1978; *Collins v. County Cork V.E.C.*, unreported, High Court, May 26, 1982; *O'Brien v. Bord na Móna*, [1983] I.R. 255 (Sup. Ct.). In *The State (Divito) v. Arklow U.D.C.* [1986] I.L.R.M. 123, Henchy J. cited both tests without differentiating between them. The pre-independence cases had all plumped solidly for the "real likelihood" test: *R. (Ellis) v. Dublin JJ.* [1894] 2 I.R. 527; *R. (Findlater) v. Tyrone JJ.* [1909] 2 I.R. 763; *R. (Kingston) v. Cork JJ.* [1910] 2 I.R. 658; *R. (de Vesci) v. Queen's Co. JJ.* [1908] 2 I.R. 285; *R. (Donoghue) v. Cork JJ.* [1910] 2 I.R. 272. However, there is some support for the suspicion test in *R. (Giant's Causeway Tram Co.) v. Antrim JJ.* [1895] 2 I.R. 603. See Sweeney, "Lord O'Brien's Doctrine of Bias" (1972) 7 Ir. Jur. (N.S.) 17.

Chestvale and *Huntsgrove*, most Irish judges have proved uncharacteristically charitable towards the difficulties of public authorities. In relatively few of the cases cited in this Part has the applicant succeeded.

Rule of necessity

Throughout the common law world, the no bias rule gives way to necessity in that the disqualification of the adjudicator will not readily be permitted to destroy the only tribunal with power to decide. Consider, for example, *O'Byrne v. Minister for Finance*[176] in which the High Court and Supreme Court were obliged to pass judgment on the constitutionality of legislation rendering them (and their judicial brethren) liable to income tax on their salaries. In the High Court, Dixon J. had proceeded with the case only because there was no other tribunal to which, under the law, recourse could be had on a matter of this kind.[177]

A more typical example is afforded by *O'Neill v. Beaumont Hospital Board*.[178] In this case, as a result of a finding of bias, the Supreme Court granted an injunction restraining the Chairman and two other members of the Hospital Board from taking part in any meeting which would consider whether to retain the plaintiff as a consultant.[179] The Court declined, however, to grant an injunction in the terms sought by

---

[176] [1959] I.R. 1 where the doctrine was "applied if not expressly invoked". In *Collins v. County Cork V.E.C.*, unreported, High Court, May 26, 1982, Murphy J. said that it was the "clear constitutional duty" of the Supreme Court to decide the *O'Byrne* case, "notwithstanding the interest which the members of the Court had in the outcome." See also, Hogan and Whyte *Kelly, The Irish Constitution*, (3rd ed., 1994), p. 354 for an explanation of the composition of the Supreme Court in *The State (Killian) v. Minister for Justice* [1954] I.R. 207. *O'Byrne* was followed in *O'Neill v. Irish Hereford Breed Society Ltd.* [1992] 1 I.R. 431 at 449 and, in less acute circumstances, in *Flynn v. Allen*, unreported, High Court, May 2, 1988. In *Flynn*, noting that the defendants in the action were Benchers of Kings Inn, Lynch J. stated (at p. 3):

"I am, of course, as is every other High Court Judge and Judge of the Supreme Court, a Bencher of the King's Inns and I am conscious of the fact that in one sense I myself could be said to be a defendant in these matters. Be that as it may, the matter has to come to be decided by some Judge of the High Court and it has come before me and I must not shirk my duty of dealing with it.
. . .
I have been referred to the decisions of the High Court and the Supreme Court in the case of *O'Byrne v. Minister for Finance and the Attorney General* [1959] I.R. 1 [and] of course the difficulty that arises here arose there. The necessity for proceeding notwithstanding that unfortunate difficulty was emphasised and I accept that that is so and that I should and must deal with the matter."

Likewise in *District Judge McMenamin v. Ireland* [1996] 3 I.R. 100, the Supreme Court adjudicated on the constitutionality of judicial pension arrangements. O'Flaherty J. alluded (at 143) to the doctrine of necessity in this way:

"I appreciate we do well when dealing with judicial colleagues to preserve a certain Caesarean detachment: *what touches us ourselves should be last serv'd.* (Shakespeare: Julius Caesar, Act III, Sc. 1) Nonetheless, judges of the District Court are entitled to the same measure of justice as anyone else in the land who appears in this Court: no more and no less . . ."

[177] Another example occurred in *Attorney General (Humphreys) v. Governors of Erasmus Smith's Schools* [1910] 1 I.R. 325 a relator action involving a charitable trust administered by the defendants. Cherry L.J. commenced his judgment in the Irish Court of Appeal with the following apologia (at 332):

"I am in a rather difficult position in adjudicating upon this case, in as much as I was Attorney-General when the writ was fiated. I would have preferred not to have been a member of the Court which had to decide this appeal, but as all the Judges of the Court except Lord Justice Holmes and myself are Governors of the Schools, a Court could not otherwise have been formed."

See also, *Dimes v. Grand Junction Canal Co.* (1852) 3 H.L.C. 759; *Tolputt (N.) & Co. Ltd v. Mole* [1911] 1 K.B. 836.

[178] [1990] I.L.R.M. 419.
[179] Followed, on this point, in *O'Neill v. Irish Hereford Breed Society Ltd* [1992] 1 I.R. 431 at 448–449, *per* Murphy J.

the plaintiff, which would have restrained any meeting of the Board. The first reason for this was that the other members of the Board had not committed themselves to a fixed position in advance of the meeting in the same way as had the Chairman and the two members who were enjoined. The other reason was the doctrine of necessity, whose application in the instant case was explained by Finlay C.J. as follows:

"It is not a dominant doctrine, it could never defeat a real fear and a real reasonable fear of bias or injustice but it is a consideration in relation to the question of the entire Board being prohibited, for if that were to be done there can be no other machinery by which something which is of great importance both to the Board of the Hospital and to the plaintiff and I might add, to the public who will attend the Hospital, namely the continuance or noncontinuance of the plaintiff's services in the hospital, can be determined in accordance with the terms of the probationary agreement."[180]

O'Neill turned in part on the fact that the Board was a statutory body with members who were required to be capable of independent judgment. But different considerations must of necessity apply to most employee disciplinary matters, so that the room for the application of the *nemo iudex* rule is even further attenuated. This was recognised by both Keane J. and the Supreme Court in *Mooney v. An Post*,[181] a case concerning the dismissal of a postman for alleged misconduct, when the former remarked that:

". . . the *nemo iudex* requirements cannot be literally applied to every employer confronted with a decision as to whether or not he should dismiss a particular employee. If it were, an employer could never dismiss an employee, since he would always be an interested party in the decision by a particular employee."[182]

In the Supreme Court[183] Barrington J. endorsed these sentiments adding that there was no mechanism providing for the independent adjudication of the allegations against the plaintiff:

"[An Post] were not in a position to set up an independent tribunal with power to subpoena witnesses even had they wished to do so. At the same time they had received serious complaints from members of the public touching the integrity of the postal services. An Post could not reasonably ignore these complaints."

Clearly the necessity requirement will be strictly applied. In particular, it plainly depends, in substantial measure upon the content of the relevant statute. Take for instance *The State (Curran) v. Irish Land Commission*[184] (already described) in which Doyle J. opined, *obiter*, that the argument of necessity could not have excused

---

[180] *Ibid.* at 440. Followed in *O'Neill v. Irish Hereford Breed Society Ltd* [1992] 1 I.R. 431 at 451.
[181] [1994] E.L.R. 103.
[182] *Ibid.* at 116.
[183] Unreported, Supreme Court, March 20, 1997.
[184] Unreported, High Court, June 12, 1978. See also, *R (Snaith) v. Ulster Polytechnic* [1981] N.I. 28. The dismissal procedure laid down in the University statutes required, first, that the initial decision should be taken by a sub-committee of 11 Governors and secondly, that on appeal, this decision must be upheld by a two-thirds majority of the Governors of whom there were 42 in all. This arrangement plainly breached the "no bias" rule. Given the numbers of Governors involved at each level, it would have been very difficult if not impossible to work this system without some overlap of personnel. However, Hutton J. ruled that the necessity doctrine did not apply because the difficulty

the respondents in certain circumstances, *e.g.* ill-health – for the reason that the Land Act 1950 allowed for the appointment of a temporary replacement where a lay commissioner is temporarily disabled from fulfilling his function on account of illness, absence "or other sufficient reason".

The rule of necessity is probably compatible with constitutional justice. For, as has been seen, constitutional justice is grounded in Article 40.3 the rights contained in which are not absolute but qualified by such phrases as "far as practicable" and "as best it may." And, as Murphy J. observed in *Collins v. County Cork Vocational Education Committee*, the courts cannot conjure up a new tribunal to take the place of a tribunal which has been held unconstitutional. Thus in some cases chaos would result if the *nemo iudex* rule were applied at its full width. On the other hand even, in England, the rule of necessity may not operate to enable an adjudicator to sit where actual bias can be shown and as indicated in the passage just quoted from *O'Neill*, this qualification certainly applies in Ireland.[185]

Waiver

The right to object to a breach of the *nemo iudex* principle may be waived by a party with full knowledge of the facts which entitle him to raise a complaint.[186] The rule has been stated to be as follows:

> "[W]here a decision is challenged on the grounds of bias in the tribunal which gave it, [the] Court will not interfere where it appears that the fact or suspicion of bias was present to the mind of the challenging party at the hearing before the tribunal, and the point as to bias or suspected bias was not made by or on his behalf at the hearing by the tribunal."[187]

Exceptions to the rule exist where the complainant is so taken by surprise that he forgets to make an objection or where the court deems it proper to interfere because of the scandalous state of affairs involved.[188]

Bias is a particularly heinous defect (more so than failure to give a hearing) which may lead to a general erosion of confidence in public or judicial administration. In addition, bias or the possibility of bias, is a matter peculiarly within the knowledge of the deciding authority, giving rise in other contexts, to a duty to declare an interest.[189] Moreover, it is a particularly embarrassing matter to have to raise in front of the person whom it is alleged is partial. Such factors underlay the dissenting

---

arose "from the scheme for termination of appointments which the Governors themselves had provided [in the statutes]" rather than from some externally-imposed instrument.)

[185] See de Smith, Woolf and Jowell, *Judicial Review of Administration Action* (5th ed. 1995), pp. 544–545.

[186] *Corrigan v. Irish Land Commission* [1977] I.R. 317 distinguished in *O'Neill v. Irish Hereford Breed Society Ltd* [1992] 1 I.R. at 455 on the ground that the plaintiff did not have knowledge of all the relevant circumstances. *The State (Cole) v. Labour Court* (1984) 3 J.I.S.L.L. 128.

[187] *R. (Harrington) v. Clare JJ.* [1918] 2 I.R. 116, *per* Sir James Campbell C.J.. See also, *Corrigan's* case, above, and *The State (Grahame) v. Racing Board*, unreported, High Court, November 22, 1983. See, too, Finlay C.J. in *O'Reilly v. Judge Cassidy* [1995] 1 I.LR.M. 306, 309: "If no objection is taken to any relationship between an advocate and a judge there could be no conceivable impropriety in the judge continuing to hear the case." (See, further, above at pp. 00).

[188] *R. (Giants Causeway Tram Co.) v. Antrim JJ.* [1895] 2 I.R. 603; *R. (Poe) v. Clare JJ.* (1906) 40 I.L.T.R. 121; *R. (Harrington) v. Clare JJ.* [1918] 2 I.R. 116.

[189] *R. (Malone) v. Tyrone JJ.* 3 N.I.J.R. 77; *The State (Cole) v. Labour Court* (1984) 3 J.I.S.L.L. 128 (semble).

judgment of Kenny J. in *Corrigan v. Irish Land Commission*. In his view, the no bias rule is founded on public policy – the desire to maintain respect for the administration of justice – and thus it is not competent for the parties to waive this rule. Nevertheless the prevailing consensus seems to be in favour, for practical reasons, of a wide concept of waiver in the context of bias. As Henchy J. remarked in *Corrigan v. Irish Land Commission*:

> "It would obviously be inconsistent with the due administration of justice if a litigant were to be allowed to conceal a complaint of that nature in the hope that the tribunal will decide in his favour, while reserving to himself the right, if the tribunal gives an adverse decision, to raise the complaint of disqualification."[190]

In the case law considered so far, waiver occurs because of some action (or inaction) of the plaintiff at the time of the dispute. A distinct category of waiver exists where in the case of, for example, a trade union or other so-called voluntary association, the plaintiff is regarded as having consented to the defect of which he wishes to complain, simply by virtue of having joined the union or association, in the first place. This may be a rather far-reaching and unrealistic notion, but it was never-theless adopted by Lardner J. in *I.D.A.T.U. v. Carroll*[191] (the facts of which are described below) in the situation, it is true, not of a trade union and a member, but in the different situation of the I.C.T.U. and a member union. In *Carroll*, Lardner J. stated in an *ex tempore* judgment[192]:

> "In the present case, the court is concerned with Congress, an association of trade unions and its members who are trade unions who have negotiated and freely accepted its rules. There is nothing in the evidence before me to suggest that there was any inequality between the plaintiff union and Congress at the time this constitution was adopted. Having regard to the fact that the clause complained of is part of the Constitution of Congress, which was freely accepted by the plaintiff, I am not satisfied by [plaintiff's] counsel's submission that this clause is contrary to natural justice."

Withdrawal of suspect members

One obvious way of avoiding trouble, which may be available where the decision has yet to be taken and where the deciding body has a number of members, is for the suspect members not to sit, as was suggested by *I.D.A.T.U. v. Carroll*. Here the General Secretary of the plaintiff union had made a number of derogatory references to other trade unions. Accordingly the plaintiff had been informed that, would be required to show cause before the Irish Congress of Trade Unions who were, in effect, the defendants as to why it should not be suspended from Congress. The plaintiff's response was to seek an injunction to restrain the defendant from passing

---

190 [1977] I.R. 326. *Corrigan* was naturally distinguished in *Bane v. The Garda Representative Association* [1997] 2 I.R. 449 where the applicants protested by going as far as actually to decline to appear at the hearing. See also the following bald statement: "If no objection is taken to any relationship between an advocate and a judge there could be no conceivable impropriety in the judge continuing to hear the case." (*O'Reilly v. Cassidy* [1995] 1 I.L.R.M. 306 at 309, *per* Finlay C.J.)

191 [1988] I.L.R.M. 713.

192 *Ibid.* at 719.

or considering any sanction upon the plaintiff. One of the plaintiff's submissions was grounded on bias in that, in Lardner J.'s summary of the argument:

> "The Irish Transport and General Workers Union and the Federated Workers Union of Ireland who were each members of I.C.T.U. cater to some extent for the same category of workers as are catered for by the plaintiff union. A conflict of interests was suggested here. It was suggested that these unions might secure an advantage in this situation and if any of their representatives sat on the executive council, that would be in breach of the rules of natural justice."[193]

The salient point here is that one of the reasons why Lardner J. rejected this argument was that:

> ". . . the executive council consists of [27 members] . . . Seven is a quorum. When this matter was raised, counsel on behalf of the defendants undertook that no member of the executive council who had any direct interest in the matter of the kind mentioned by Mr. Donnelly, the plaintiff's president, would sit or take part in the deliberations of the executive council dealing with this matter."[194]

Again in *O'Neill* mentioned earlier[195] the outcome was the grant of an injunction but one which prevented only the chairman and two other members of the Board from taking part in a meeting to consider the plaintiff's fate.

These issues were also to the fore in *Radio Limerick One Ltd v. Independent Radio and Television Commission.*[196] Here the applicant had its broadcasting licence terminated following breaches of the Radio and Television Act 1988 which consisted of the "blacking" of a broadcast involving a former employee of the station who had become a member of the Commission. Although she had absented herself at the meetings concerning the "blacking" allegations, she had been present at other meetings when matters affecting the applicant were discussed, (albeit without taking part in the discussion). Keane J. said that in the circumstances:

> ". . . unless one can identify some other step which it was open to the commission to take with a view further to guaranteeing the impartial consideration by the commission of the matter, it would follow inevitably that the applicant's claim that the commission's decision should be set aside on the ground of objective bias would mean that the commission was effectively precluded from discharging its statutory function of considering breaches of contract alleged against the applicant. . . ."[197]

As the applicant could not point to any of these "steps [being] open" and, moreover the Commission had no power to restrain the former employee-member from sitting as a member, it followed that the allegation of objective bias had not been established.

---

193 *Ibid.* at 718.
194 *Ibid.* at 718–719. See also *Bane v. The Garda Representative Association* [1997] 2 I.R. 449 where the applicant succeeded in part, because the committee of the respondent could have been constituted by persons other than those who had given evidence in the earlier proceedings, and so the necessity doctrine, see pp. 534–537.
195 See pp. 534–535.
196 [1997] 2 I.L.R.M. 1.
197 *Ibid.* at 25.

CHAPTER 11

CONSTITUTIONAL JUSTICE II

1. Introduction

It is trite law that tribunals and administrative agencies are not required to follow the same strict rules of evidence and procedure as a court of law,[1] provided that the procedures actually adopted are not in themselves unfair.[2] As Henchy J. said in a much-quoted passage in *Kiely v. Minister for Social Welfare (No.2)*:[3]

> "Tribunals exercising quasi-judicial functions are frequently allowed to act informally – to receive unsworn evidence, to act on hearsay, to depart from the rules of evidence, to ignore courtroom procedures, and the like – but they may not act in such a way as to imperil a fair hearing or a fair result."[4]

As might be expected from the inexact, pragmatic nature of constitutional justice, the standard is plastic, varying with the circumstances, for "domestic and adminis-

---

[1] *McElroy v. Mortished*, unreported, High Court, June 17, 1949; *Fitzpatrick v. Wymes* [1976] I.R. 301; *The State (Boyle) v. General Medical Services Board* [1981] I.L.R.M. 14; *Re McNally's Application* [1985] N.I. 17. The courts have also deprecated attempts to import principles of criminal procedure into civil disciplinary proceedings: *O'Laoire v. Medical Council*, unreported, Supreme Court, July 23, 1997. Further, as Keane J. said in that case in the High Court (unreported, January 27, 1995), a notice of inquiry convening a statutory disciplinary inquiry was not to be construed as if it were an indictment in a criminal case.

[2] *Kiely v. Minister for Social Welfare (No.2)* [1977] I.R. 276; *R v. Hull Prison Visitors, ex p. St. Germain (No.2)* [1979] 1 W.L.R. 1401; *Flanagan v. University College, Dublin* [1988] I.R. 724; *Gallagher v. Revenue Commissioners (No.2)* [1995] 1 I.R. 55.

[3] [1977] I.R. 276.

[4] *Ibid.* at 281. A well reasoned example of this principle may be found in *Vogel v. Cheevers*, unreported, High Court, April 30, 1996. This case arose when the plaintiff sought an injunction restraining the defendant from conducting a disciplinary inquiry without affording him an opportunity to hear, and test by cross-examination, the evidence of the complainant who was mentally handicapped and who alleged that she had been sexually abused. Shanley J. rejected the claim, saying that:
"... in considering the question of the admissibility of hearsay evidence one must look at all the facts and the rights and, indeed, the interests of all the parties must, as far as it is practicable to do so, be safeguarded. In the present case, I am satisfied that the requirements of natural justice do not dictate that the complainant be produced to be examined and cross-examined [before] the proposed tribunal. I have evidence before me that this may seriously damage her mental health and I have to balance this evidence against any risk that injustice would be done to the plaintiff. The requirements of natural justice must depend on the circumstances of each case and the nature of each particular inquiry. In the present case, injustice to the plaintiff (taking into account the complainant's psychiatric condition) can, in my opinion, be avoided by directing that a further validation exercise be performed by a psychologist or a psychiatrist nominated by the plaintiff's legal representatives...".
Likewise, while hearsay evidence is admissible in wardship proceedings, the "procedures to be adopted in the light of the admission of hearsay evidence should protect the right to fair procedures of persons likely to be affected by the evidence": *Southern Health Board v. CH* [1996] 1 I.R. 219 at 229, *per* Costello P. On the other hand, in most ordinary court proceedings insofar as "crucial evidence ... is tendered on a hearsay basis ... natural justice requires [counsel] to be provided with an opportunity to cross-examine and challenge [this evidence] *via voce*: *MM. v. DD.*, unreported, High Court, December 10, 1996, *per* Moriarty J.

trative tribunals take many forms and determine many different kinds of issues and no hard and fast rules can be laid down. . . ."[5] At one end of the scale, Costello J. has stated:

> "The courts must not interfere officiously in the affairs of private associations such as trade unions and must only do so in clear cases to prevent or remedy some manifest injustice. And when considering what procedures can properly be regarded as fair it must consider procedures which would be appropriate to the type of organisation or association which is to adopt them and the nature and scope of the decision to which they relate."[6]

Keane J. echoed these views in *Mooney v. An Post*[7] when he remarked that:

> ". . . the concept [of natural justice] is necessarily an imprecise one and what its application requires may differ significantly from case to case. The two great central principles – *audi alteram partem* and *nemo iudex in causa sua* – cannot be applied in a uniform fashion to every set of facts. To take the obvious example, the *nemo iudex* requirements cannot be literally applied to every employer confronted with a decision as to whether or not he should dismiss a particular employee. If it were, an employer could never dismiss an employee, since he would always be an interested party in the decision by a particular employee."[8]

And, at the other end of the scale, in *Flanagan v. University College Dublin*[9] in which a disciplinary committee was adjudicating on a charge of plagiarism, Barron J. set a particularly stringent standard:

---

[5] *Russell v. Duke of Norfolk* [1949] 1 All E.R. 109 at 118, *per* Tuker L.J.quoted with approval by Henchy J. in *Kiely v. Minister for Social Welfare* [1977] I.R. 267. In *International Vessels Ltd v. Minister for Marine (No.2)* [1991] 2 I.R. 92 at 102, this extract was again quoted with approval. Immediately afterwards, McCarthy J. went on to make the following observation:
> "Neither natural justice nor constitutional justice requires perfect or the best possible justice, it requires reasonable fairness in all of the circumstances; often it is a matter of impression as to whether or not there was unfairness."
The same extract was approved in *Gallagher v. Revenue Commissioners* [1995] 1 I.L.R.M. 241 at 259; *Tang v. Minister for Justice* [1996] 2 I.L.R.M. 46 at 61; *McAuley v. Garda Commissioner (No. 1)*, [1996] 3 I.R. 208 (Hamilton C.J. in each case). See, to similar effect the passage in the text, *Kealy v. Garda Commissioner* [1992] 2 I.R. 197 at 213, *per* O'Flaherty J. See too, *Georgopoulus v. Beaumont Hospital Board*, unreported, Supreme Court, June 4, 1997 at pp. 11–16; *O'Laoire v. Medical Council*, unreported, High Court, January 27, 1995 holding that "a broad untechnical procedure" (as opposed to the stricter standard required in a criminal trial) would suffice.

[6] *Doyle v. Croke*, unreported, High Court, May 6, 1988. See, to like effect: *The State (Keegan) v. The Stardust Victims Compensation Tribunal* [1986] I.R. 642; *McGowan v. Wren* [1988] I.L.R.M. 744; *Ryan v. VIP Taxi Co-operatives Ltd* unreported, High Court, January 20, 1989, (reported in *The Irish Times*, Law Report, April 10, 1989). See also the comments of Murphy J. in *Grant v. Garda Síochána Complaints Board*, unreported, High Court, June 12, 1996 ("no justification for importing practice and procedure of the High Court or the common law principles governing the conduct of the courts into proceedings under the Garda Síochána (Complaints) Act 1986").

[7] [1994] E.L.R. 103.

[8] *Ibid.* at 116. These comments were referred to with approval by Barrington J. on appeal: unreported, Supreme Court, March 20, 1997.

[9] [1988] I.R. 724.

". . . [P]rocedures which might afford a sufficient protection to a person concerned in one case, and so be acceptable, might not be acceptable in a more serious case . . . Matters to be considered are the form in which the complaint should be made, the time to be allowed to the person concerned to prepare a defence and the nature of the hearing at which the defence may be presented. In addition depending on the gravity of the matter the person concerned may be entitled to be represented and may also be entitled to be informed of their rights. Clearly, matters of a criminal nature must be treated more seriously than matters of a civil nature but ultimately the criterion must be the consequences to the person concerned of an adverse verdict."[10]

The *audi alteram partem* rule embraces two types of obligation (although there is a substantial overlap and nothing turns on the distinction). First, the person to be affected by the decision must have notice of it, that is, he must be alerted to it and be given details. Secondly, he must be allowed appropriate facilities to make the best possible case in reply. Let us now go on to consider particular aspects of the *audi alteram partem* rule *seriatim*.

2. Person Affected Must Have Notice

As a preliminary point, one might ask: of what exactly must the person be given notice? In response to this question the following typology may be offered (although as above these are overlapping categories and nothing turns on the distinction: they are mentioned merely for the purpose of analysis):

  (i) a notification that a decision adverse to the person affected is in contemplation;

  (ii) the grounds upon which the action is to be taken;

  (iii) all information relevant to the issue, including details of the case against and (probably) in favour of the person affected;

  (iv) the possible consequences of the decision–sanctions, etc.

The recent case of *TV3 v. Independent Radio and Television Commission*[11] affords a rather graphic example of the first and also probably the last of the categories just enumerated. The background to this case was that in 1989, the respondent Commission had announced that it had decided to award the national television franchise to the applicant, "subject to the negotiation of a satisfactory broadcasting contract between the Commission and TV3." Subsequently, problems arose in the negotiations of the contract, partly because of changes in the broadcasting advertising environment, which affected the applicants' finance. Eventually, the applicants agreed to provide a complete list of its investors and the amounts to be invested, by August 31, 1991. The applicants did not supply this information. Instead they wrote

---

10 *Ibid.* at 730–731, quoted with approval in *Beirne v. Commissioner of An Garda Síochána* [1992] I.L.R.M. 699 at 707, Flood J. and by Hamilton C.J. in *Gallagher v. Revenue Commissioner (No. 2)* [1995] 1 I.R. 55 at 80. See, to like effect, *McDonough v. Minister for Defence* [1991] 2 I.R. 33 at 40.

11 [1994] 2 I.R. 439. For a case in which notice of each of these elements was given, see *Downey v. O'Brien* [1994] 2 I.L.R.M. 130 at 150.

to the respondents saying that they would be unable to supply these details pending the outcome of the review of the broadcasting legislation,[12] then being undertaken by the Minister for Communications. In October, 1991, the respondent wrote abruptly to the applicants informing them that "the conditional grant of the franchise ... is withdrawn." The applicants' case succeeded (in both the High and Supreme Courts) on the basis that: "there should have been a clear warning that the franchise would be withdrawn if the information required by the Commission was not furnished on the promised day."[13]

Contrast with *TV3*, the decision of Morris J. in *Greaney v. Dublin Corporation*[14] in which it was held that the local authority was not required – if the application was not in order – to contact an applicant for a fire safety certificate, but could simply go ahead and refuse the application. It is hard to reconcile *Greaney* with *TV3*. Possibly this could be done on the basis that in *TV3*, as the Court held, the applicants had a type of property right in the contract, whereas *Greaney* was an "applicant" case and secondly, the applicant should have been aware that failure to supply the necessary details would lead to rejection. It should be added too that *Greaney* was argued on the basis that the applicant had a legitimate expectation that it would be contacted and this failed on the facts; no constitutional justice *simpliciter* argument appears to have been made.

Ryan v. V.I.P. Co-operative Society Ltd,[15] which arose out of the suspension of a taxi-driver by his co-operative for allegedly abusing some passengers, is a helpful authority on the question of what information ought to be given to the person affected. These passengers, who it was said had been verbally abused, had not been present at the hearing. In holding the suspension to be invalid, Lardner J. identified certain procedural deficiencies. He had:

> "... full sympathy with the objectives of the society which were to maintain a high standard of quality of service to their customers. But despite the fact that they were a small co-operative, they had to observe certain minimal obligations in relation to the conduct of disciplinary hearings ... [T]he applicant was entitled to be furnished with the names and addresses of the complainants. He was entitled to specific details of the complaints. The society should have sent someone to interview the complainants and to have secured a detailed testimony of the allegations made against the applicant. The applicant was also entitled to be told all relevant matters which might have assisted him properly to prepare his defence. Finally, the applicant was entitled to be given details of any other reasons which may have been taken into account by the committee in reaching their decision."

---

12 See pp. 146–147.
13 *Ibid.* at 463, *per* Egan J. Notice that no argument founded upon the substantive issue of the Commission's withdrawal from the contract was made: see [1994] 2 I.R. at 456.
14 [1994] 3 I.R. 384 at 392–393.
15 Unreported, High Court, January 10, 1989. See also *The State (Gleeson) v. Minister for Defence* [1976] I.R. 280. *Gleeson* was followed by Hamilton J. in *Hogan v. Minister for Justice*, [1976–1977] I.L.R.M. 184 and *The State (Furey) v. Minister for Defence* [1988] I.L.R.M. 89. See to similar effect *Gleeson, O'Shea v. Commissioner of Garda Síochána* [1994] 2 I.R. 408. *Gleeson*, was however, distinguished in *The State (Duffy) v. Minister for Defence* [1979] I.L.R.M. 65 and *The State (Donnelly) v. Minister for Defence*, unreported, High Court, October 8, 1979.

In another disciplinary case, *Beirne v. Commissioner of An Garda Síochána*,[16] the applicant had been dismissed following misbehaviour in the bus after a student garda outing. The main point on which he succeeded was that he had been given no information whatsoever regarding the witness statements, which had been collected from the other students on the outing.[17]

The second point on which the applicant succeeded in *Beirne*, was that a range of penalties was available for his offence and it may have seemed to him that it was the more lenient end of the scale of penalties which was under consideration. The point was given most emphasis in the High Court where Flood J. stated:

"... there is a degree of ambivalence in the reaction of Inspector Murray in that almost in the one breath, of saying that he takes a serious view of the matter in relation to the applicant's future presence in the college ... he accepts an offer from the applicant to publicly apologise to his fellow student and to the class in general. A great sound of fury accompanied no concrete statement of intended action and more important no suggestion that the apology would be of no avail."[18]

A public authority's duty to give notice is not confined to details of the case against him. In *Flanagan v. University College, Dublin*, for example, Barron J. having made the point that the applicant was entitled to legal representation, continued: "... she should have been informed, in sufficient time to enable her to prepare her defence, of such right and of any other rights given to her by the rules governing the procedure of the disciplinary tribunal."[19] Although this was only a brief unconsidered part of *Flanagan*, it could, if developed, become a significant part of the law. In parenthesis, one could add that *Flanagan* appears to be one more example[20] of a case which arose because the staff of certain tribunals or administrative agencies have not taken on board recent developments in the field of judicial review of administrative actions.[21] Between them and the courts, there is almost what might be called a culture clash.[22]

---

16 [1992] I.L.R.M. 699(High Ct.), [1993] I.L.R.M. 1 (Sup. Ct.). The main point in *Beirne*–whether the issue was amenable to judicial review–is covered at pp. 781–782.

17 The judgments do not need to be, and are not, specific as to whether the applicant should have been shown the statements or whether it would have sufficed if their authors had been identified and their gist given to him: [1992] I.L.R.M. 699 at 708; [1993] I.L.R.M. at 10 at 13.

18 [1992] I.L.R.M. 699 at 707–708. The Supreme Court took a similar view on appeal: [1993] I.L.R.M. 1 at 9, *per* Finlay C.J.

19 [1988] I.R. 724 at 731. See also, *Cooney v. An Post*, unreported, High Court, April 6, 1990, p. 28. *McSorley v. Governor of Mountjoy Prison* [1996] 2 I.L.R.M. 331 at 338 (failure of a judge proposing to impose a custodial sentence to advise an unrepresented accused of his constitutional right to legal aid renders conviction void). But an accused in garda custody has no constitutional right to be informed of a right to a lawyer: *D.P.P. v. Spratt* [1995] 2 I.L.R.M. 117 at 123.

20 For another striking example, see *The State (Williams) v. Army Pensions Board* [1983] I.R. 308 which is analysed in the 2nd edition of this book at pp. 445–446. See also, *Maunsell v. Minister for Education* [1940] I.R. 213; *The State (Hussey) v. Irish Land Commission* [1983] I.R. 23 at 36. In the criminal field, see *D.P.P. v. Doyle* [1994] 2 I.R. 286 at 296–302 and *Maher v. O'Donnell* [1996] 2 I.L.R.M. 321 at 326–327 (considering the right of an accused to statements in advance of a trial).

21 *cf. Flanagan v. University College Dublin* [1988] I.R. 724 at 732, *per* Barron J.: "The failure to apply proper procedures arises, as the Registrar accepted, because this committee has always sat in his experience to deal with cases where guilt, if not admitted, cannot reasonably be denied. This is aggravated by the absence of any published college regulations under which the committee purported to act."

22 An attempt to mitigate this clash, in the British context, has been made by the publication of a pamphlet, designed for the lay-civil servant and entitled "The Judge Over your Shoulder. Judicial Review of Administrative Decisions": see (1987) *Public Law* 485.

One could say that the information not given in *Flanagan* was specific to the applicant's case. What would be the position if the information were of a general nature, albeit relevant. It has been held that there is an entitlement to be given information not only as to facts, but also as to any policy or principles in the light of which the case is to be decided so as to have "the opportunity of conforming with or contesting such a principle or policy."[23]

It is hard to know how to classify *Frenchurch Properties v. Wexford County Council.*[24] But it seems probable that it fits into the present area. Here the applicant-developer had been allowed to meet and make representations to the local planning authority; yet the local authority had not drawn the vital consideration to the applicant's attention. The particular facts centred upon the Local Government (Planning and Development) Act 1982, section 4(1), by which a planning authority shall extend the period of operation of a planning permission, provided that, *inter alia*, "substantial works" had already been executed prior to the permission's expiry. The substantive question turned on the application of the phrase quoted, in particular whether it included the manufacture of floor slabs and steel works (whose measurements restricted their use to that particular development) albeit that they had not been incorporated in the building. The Court held – overruling the local planning authority – that in these circumstances the test was satisfied. However the important point, for present purposes, was procedural and stemmed from the fact that at the meeting the planning authority failed to draw to the applicant's attention its view that the floor slabs and steel works would not be taken into account in determining the application for extension of time. Lynch J. stated:

> "A planning authority is not obliged to enter into a dialogue with an applicant or to indicate in advance to an applicant the planning authority's thinking or views before deciding on the application. Nor is the planning authority bound to conduct any sort of adversarial hearing of an application before deciding the matter. In the ordinary course of events the planning authority will receive an application; consider it; and decide on it without giving any advance reasons. If the planning authority refuses the application it must give its reasons for such refusal at that stage but not earlier.
>
> If a bona fide applicant reasonably and not vexatiously or capriciously requests to make submissions to the planning authority, he should be given an opportunity to do so. Then if there is a point on which the planning authority knows that the applicant relies to a significant extent and which the planning authority (unknown to the applicant) thinks is invalid, the planning authority should draw the applicant's attention to this point to give the applicant an opportunity of trying to persuade the planning authority that he is right and they are wrong. This does not mean any obligation to conduct any sort of formal hearing or debate; simply an indication that such and such a point on which the applicant appears to rely to a significant extent seems to the

---

23 *The State (McGeough) v. Louth County Council* (1973) 107 I.L.T.R. 13 at 28, *per* O'Daly J. See also, *Mahon v. Air New Zealand* [1984] A.C. 808. However, these authorities may be contradicted by *Corcoran v. Minister for Social Welfare* [1991] 2 I.R. 175 at 184, *per* Murphy J.
24 [1992] 2 I.R. 268.

planning authority to be invalid and what has the applicant got to say about that?"[25]

Three points in this passage may be emphasised. First, there is the unusual (albeit limited) application of constitutional justice, at the local planning authority stage. Secondly, it seems (from the start of the second paragraph) that it is up to the applicant to ask to be granted a hearing. Thirdly, the line of thought, towards the end of the passage echoes *Doupe*[26] in that there too, the court held if an applicant had been given a chance yet failed to take advantage of it, he has nothing of which to complain.

Misleading Statements

Analogous to and even worse than a failure to give notice of relevant information is a situation in which the public body misleads the person affected. In the two decided cases[27] on this theme (in neither of which was there any mention of legitimate expectations or estoppel) a misleading impression had been given as to the state of the public body's mind as to how the case was going. In the earlier case, *Kiely v. Minister for Social Welfare*,[28] K succeeded on the ground (which was put on the basis of constitutional justice) that the appeals officer, at an oral hearing in respect of a death benefit claim, had given K the impression that her claim was likely to succeed. In consequence, K's solicitor did not persist with his request for an adjournment to enable him to call a medical witness who would have fortified K's case. In the other case, *Madden v. Minister for the Marine*[29] one of the minor grounds for the applicant's success was that: "that the Minister appears to have taken his decision in respect of the foreshore licence and had taken it at a time when he was still representing as appears from his letter of 18 May to the objectors that he was considering the objections in this matter . . . "[30] Nothing further was said by way of justification or explanation in either case.

By way of comment, it may be said that for a public body to mislead is a serious matter – indeed it is conventionally regarded as more heinous than to fail to disclose relevant information. Nevertheless, one would expect that before a misleading statement or act were to attract legal consequences, it should be shown that it had been acted upon to the detriment of the applicant.[31] However it is true that this

---

25 *Ibid.* at 284–285. See also *Mishra v. Minister for Justice* [1996] 1 I.R. 189 at 206, *per* Kelly J. An applicant for citizenship was turned down because of a general assumption that he would later emigrate, despite his solemn declaration to the contrary. Kelly J. said that if the applicant were to be turned down on this basis, "fundamental fairness" required "he be given an opportunity to clarify his position." *Frenchurch Properties* was distinguished by Laffoy J. in *Littondale Ltd v. Wicklow County Council* [1996] 2 I.L.R.M. 519 at 537 on the basis that "it must have been patently obvious to the applicant [developer] having regard to the decision of the respondent on foot of the application for an extension in 1987 that this was the issue it had to address in its submission to the respondents."

26 *Doupe v. Limerick Corporation* [1981] I.L.R.M. 456 on which see pp. 550–551.

27 However, it is also possible that *Frenchurch* should be squeezed in, under this rubric.

28 [1971] I.R. 21.

29 [1993] I.L.R.M. 436.

30 *Ibid.* at 448–449.

31 *cf.* The comments of Murphy J. in *Corcoran v. Minister for Social Welfare* [1991] 2 I.R. at 184: "the applicant could not in any event succeed in this argument and certainly a discretionary order would

requirement appears not to have been insisted upon in the (substantive) area of legitimate expectations.[32]

Objectors' Rights

Next, let us consider the proposition that where a public body is exercising its authority, *e.g.* in the grant of a licence, fair procedures must be afforded not only to the applicant who would benefit if the licence were granted; but also to the objector who would suffer thereby. Surprisingly, this came up for consideration as a *ratio*, only recently. This was the case of *Madden* – already mentioned briefly – which arose out of the grant of licences to V, to construct fish farming facilities in Ballyvaughan Bay in Co. Clare. The significant feature of the case was that the licence had been granted pursuant to section 15 of the Fisheries (Consolidation) Act 1959 rather than section 54 of the Fisheries Act 1980. The latter avenue requires notice to be given and permits public inquiry and recourse to the High Court; whereas the former lacks each of these features. It was argued for the Minister that he was free to utilise either provision. However, the High Court (Johnson J.) and on appeal, the Supreme Court[33] held against this contention in part, it is true, on a point of statutory interpretation; but also to a greater degree, on the general doctrine of constitutional justice (and presumably, though this was not mentioned in the judgment, the presumption of constitutionality). In consequence of this doctrine, it was held that the objectors "had an absolute right to see and deal with the case being made for the applicant [for the licence] and this is particularly so when the minister decided not to have a public inquiry."[34] Later in his judgment, Johnson J. also referred to the fact that : "the Minister appears to have taken his decision . . . without having made available to the applicants the information upon which he had based his decision".[35]

Plainly *Madden* was correct on the facts. However, one may query the limits of the doctrine which it has brought to the surface. In the first place, whilst it may sometimes happen that an objector will have the same legal and/or moral interest as an applicant – or, even, in rare cases, a greater interest – the contrary will usually be the case: for an applicant for a licence will necessarily usually have sufficient legal interest to carry out the activity authorised by the licence, whereas the interest of an objector will vary. To take an example, an objector to an application for planning permission may be the owner of the house next door to the site of the proposed development; or the tenant of the next door house; or merely a concerned passer-by. The question which arises is whether each of these different levels of objectors should have a right to the same quantum of constitutional justice as the applicant, who will usually own the land to be developed. This line of comment

---

not be made in his favour unless he could establish that he was in fact misled by the information furnished by him."

[32] See pp. 897–898.

[33] *Madden v. Minister for the Marine* [1997] 1 I.L.R.M. 136 at 146.

[34] [1993] I.L.R.M. 436 at 447–448.

[35] *Ibid.* at 448–449. *Madden* was followed on this point and more generally, in a similar case under the Fisheries (Consolidation) Act 1959, namely: *Mulcahy v. Minister for the Marine*, unreported, High Court, November 4, 1994.

advanced here leads ultimately to the question: at what point does the objector's interest become so insubstantial that s/he is not entitled to be heard.[36] It is perhaps an indication of some element of hedging of bets that the judgment uses such vague and circumlocutious formulations as "an obligation to act fairly and judicially in accordance with the fair principles of constitutional justice."[37]

Secondly, as a matter of administrative practicability, it is always easier for a public body to grant constitutional justice to an applicant because it is inherent in the process of (say) granting a licence that the public body will be in contact with the applicant. Thus, even in a situation where constitutional justice is not built in, by way of statutory system, it may be fairly convenient to afford it to an applicant. This is less true of an objector. Some features of this practical problems may become apparent in the next decade or so, in the field of planning. This will probably not happen at the Bord Pleanála stage since here opportunities for objectors are specified in the legislation. However if the development towards some element of constitutional justice at the local authority stage continues,[38] then the argument is likely to be heard that there should be a parallel development for objectors. And this may prove difficult to implement. For example, we know that frequently negotiations go on between developers and planners *after* the advert has appeared at the site and hence at a time when it would be hard to inform potential objectors about them.[39]

Some of these considerations might have been thought to arise, albeit from the reverse perspective, in regard to *Maher v. An Bord Pleanála*.[40] For here it was the objector to a grant of planning permission who was directly involved and the landowner (who was also the applicant before the High Court) who would have been – on the particular point involved – in effect, the objector. The landowner complained that he had been shut out from constitutional justice. What had happened was that a residents' association had successfully appealed to the respondent against the grant of permission to the applicant. In the instant proceedings, the applicant was counter-attacking on the basis that the residents' association's appeal had been accepted, notwithstanding that the payment of appeal fees had been somewhat unconventional (a neighbour had sent a blank cheque to the respondent, who had then filled in the amount incorrectly). The applicant submitted that he should have been given the opportunity of making representations on this point to the respondent. All Blayney J. said, on rejecting this submission was that: ". . . in my opinion the validity or otherwise of the two appeals at that stage was a matter which concerned the respondent [An Bord Pleanála] and the Residents' Association solely."[41] Thus, nothing was said about either of the two lines of thought, mentioned in the earlier

---

36 For this question, in the particular statutory context of the Tribunal of Inquiry, see *Boyhan v. Beef Tribunal* [1993] 1 I.R. 210 discussed at pp. 299–300. The query in the text is similar to the question of *locus standi*. The reason is that an applicant will usually have *locus standi* before a court regarding an *audi alteram partem* point, if, but only if, he had a right to be heard. Thus, the substantive hearing argument and the *locus standi* argument are usually effectively the same. For this reason, very few of the cases labelled *locus standi* involve *audi alteram partem*.
37 *Ibid.* at 447
38 On which developments, see pp. 544–545.
39 See p. 566.
40 [1993] 1 I.R. 439.
41 *Ibid.* at 447.

comment, namely the applicant's entitlement to be heard; or the practicability of enabling this to be done. However, the result of the case may suggest that the High Court felt that here an appalling vista was being opened up.

Orders bringing the applicant within the scope of controlling legislation

An even wider vista is opened up, when one considers the situation arising when a public body, acting under legislation of a public regulation or public betterment character, makes an order which potentially applies to the property or business of *inter alios* the applicant, even though it may have no direct or immediate effect. To take the most obvious and significant example of this type of control – land-use planning – if land is being re-zoned,[42] for the purposes of planning permission, from (say) industrial to agricultural use, would the general advert in a local-circulating newspaper suffice, as notice to a person whose land is affected? Thus the question is whether the applicant is entitled to actual notice. One fundamental line of defence which might be available to the public body is that such an order is so large in both its scope and its socio-economic and public policy characteristics, as to be legislative or policy[43] in character and thus immune from the rules of constitutional justice. However this argument was not advanced in the only (rather brief) judgment in this field : *MacPharthaláin v. Commissioners of Public Works*.[44] In this case the applicant-land-owner succeeded because the respondent had not given him notice of an intention to consider designating his land as an area of international scientific interest, under E.U. legislation, such designation carrying adverse consequences for the land-owner.

The case of *Keogh v. Galway Corporation*[45] is also worth mentioning. A development plan provided, as a specific objective, for halting sites for travellers at four named locations. When the respondent corporation decided to develop a halting site on lands at a different location, the neighbours successfully challenged this development. Their argument was put on the basis that it is central to the scheme of the planning legislation that a citizen be given notice of a development which might affect him and also be afforded the opportunity of stating his case. In response, the High Court (Carney J.) held that the respondent could not develop the halting site in the location proposed without engaging in the statutory consultation process. However, Carney J. qualified his ratio by the statement: "I express no view as to the situation which would have prevailed had the development plan been silent as

---

42 For this procedure see pp. 234–235.
43 See pp. 602–606.
44 [1992] 1 I.R. 111 at 118. Notice that in *MacPharthaláin*, no reference was made to *Wilkinson v. Dublin County Council* [1991] I.L.R.M. 605 at 611 in which the applicant's case, on which see p. 633n failed. However it is suggested that *Wilkinson* could have been distinguished on the ground that it held that there was no need for a local authority to consult as to what it did with its own property. *McPharthaláin* was appealed to the Supreme Court ([1994] 3 I.R. 353 at 359) where, the present point was not seriously disputed by the respondent.
45 [1995] 1 I.L.R.M. 142. See also a later episode in the same proceedings: *Keogh v. Galway Corporation (No. 2)* [1995] 2 I.L.R.M. 312 at 317–318. Here the applicants had been misinformed as to detail of the material change to the development plan, in respect of which they had the right to make submissions: so held by Morris J.

to hard stands or halting sites."[46] In the light of this possible qualification, it may be that this case could be construed narrowly by putting it on the same basis as the cases[47] dealing with a misleading statement by a public body.

Keogh seems to be grounded upon the planning code and especially the content of the particular development plan (the specific reference to the location of the halting sites) : no attempt was made to invoke constitutional justice in order to argue that a notice in a locally-circulating newspaper would not suffice to alert a person who might be affected in a substantial way, to what was going to happen. However it is still a decision of potentially wide significance in that it could apply where a local authority was going ahead with any sort of development, for example a high-way or a slaughter-house. And, to judge from the silence in *Keogh*, on this point, a person relying on the decision would not have to adduce any special interest or standing.

Mixed Motives

What if a deciding agency is motivated by a number of reasons about only some of which the applicant has been appraised or given an opportunity to be heard? This situation materialised in *International Fishing Vessels v. Minister for Marine (No. 2)*[48] where the respondent had set forth, in a letter, a number of grounds for refusing to grant the applicant's request for a renewal of his sea-fishing licence. But there were other grounds of which the applicant had not been notified. McCarthy J. held:

> ". . . I am satisfied that if the Minister intends to take into consideration a variety of different factors in making his decision, he must notify the person or body seeking the renewal of a sea-fishing licence of each of the matters; if he fails to notify the applicant of a matter which, on its own, causes him to make his decision, then his decision must be quashed. If, however, there are valid reasons for his decision based upon matters of which he has notified the applicants and given them ample opportunity to make representations, the fact that there are other reasons of which he had not given them notice, does not, in my view, invalidate his decisions."[49]

Although this passage is a little ambiguous, it seems tolerably clear that even if some grounds are not notified, this does not invalidate the decisions unless these grounds were not the predominant ones. Thus the law on the procedural plane is as we shall see, roughly equivalent to that on mixed motives in the substantive field of the control of discretionary powers.[50]

Person affected "well-knew"

It will often happen that the person affected will have a pretty fair idea of the case against them, although they have not actually been explicitly informed about it by the public body. The law accommodates this feature of common experience by the

---

[46] *Ibid*. at 148.
[47] See pp. 545–546.
[48] [1991] 2 I.R. 92. See also below pp. 570–576 on reasons.
[49] *Ibid*. at 103. Each of the other two judges agreed with McCarthy J.
[50] See pp. 626–628.

notion that the plaintiff "well knew" of the particular aspect of the case against him about which he claimed he should have had explicit notice. This pregnant phrase was used by Blayney J. in *Gallagher v. The Revenue Commissioners (No. 1)*,[51] which arose out of the suspension of a Customs and Excise officer. Accepting that "natural justice" required that the person suspended be informed as to the grounds why he had been suspended, Blayney J. made an exception because the circumstances were such that the plaintiff "well knew why he had been suspended."[52] Another example is *Doupe v. Limerick Corporation*[53] in which the plaintiff had been refused a licence to operate an abattoir by the defendant local authority. Rejecting one of the plaintiff's arguments, Costello J. stated:

> "But there is no doubt that he was told the substance of the case against his application and it seems to me that he had ample opportunity before any final decision was reached to approach the council with an expert view, if one could be obtained, which challenged the conclusion that in the interests of public health weekly killings should be limited as the Chief Medical Officer required. But he did not avail of this opportunity, and he maintained his refusal to accept the recommended limitation. There was, of course, no formal 'hearing' of his application – but none was needed. He was, albeit informally, given notice

---

51 [1991] 2 I.R. 370. The same judge was alert to this possibility in *TV3 v. Independent Radio and Television Commission* [1994] 2 I.R. 455 where Blayney J. stated: " It was submitted on behalf of the Commission that the 31st August, 1991 was the deadline . . . and that Mr Morris should have known that if the required information was not submitted in time that was the end of the negotiations. I accept Mr Morris' evidence that he was unaware of this . . ."

52 [1991] 2 I.R. 370 at 374. Blayney J. added, following *Flynn v. An Post* [1987] I.R. 68, that (at 374–375): "in my opinion the only explanation for the failure of the plaintiff's solicitors to insist on being furnished with the details they had sought is that the plaintiff *well knew* why he had been suspended. And the reason he knew was because he had been interviewed on two occasions about the matters which are the subject of the charges now being brought against him . . . At the end of the first interview, in the course of which the plaintiff had been questioned for a whole day about 41 files, it was put to him by Mr. Darcy that he had fictionalised reports, grossly understated the value of vehicles seized and issued receipts in the names of people he had not dealt with, and in the second interview he was shown statements of persons who figured in his reports which statements were at variance with what he had stated in his reports. I am satisfied that when the plaintiff was suspended he must have known that it was because of the matters in respect of which he had been interviewed. He could not have come to any other conclusion." (Emphasis added)
See also *Lang v. Government of Ireland* [1993] E.L.R. 234 at 245, *per* O'Hanlon J. ("the applicant was well aware for some years before his dismissal of the matters which were causing concern to his superiors" and was "given every opportunity").

53 [1981] I.L.R.M. 456. See also, *The State (Curtin) v. Minister for Health* [1953] I.R. 93 at 99; *The State (Murphy) v. Kielt* [1984] I.R. 458; *Doran v. Commissioner of Garda Síochána* [1994] 1 I.L.R.M 303 at 311 ("well aware in general terms") And in *Ní Bheoláin v. City of Dublin V.E.C.* unreported, High Court, January 28, 1983, pp. 36–37, Carroll J. stated:
"If it can fairly be said that the person suspended knew or ought to have known that the act or conduct which led to the suspension could, in all the circumstances, have that result (either because of prior warnings or because the act *per se* was blatantly provocative) then in my opinion there is no breach of constitutional guarantees, as, for example, in the *Collins case* where the plaintiff blatantly refused to carry out his duty.
In my opinion the plaintiff was being ingenuous when she said in her letter of the December 17, 1976, (say) to discipline that she failed to see what was required of her. It must have been or should have been obvious to her that her conduct in refusing to communicate verbally with [her Head of Department] and her general attitude to him was at the root of the problem."

of the advice the council had obtained and he was afforded an adequate opportunity to answer the objection raised."[54]

By contrast certain cases have set a rather high standard of explicitness and formality in regard to the warning which the public authority must give to the person affected. An example is *Gallagher v. Corrigan*[55] which centred on the need to give notice of the likely consequences. The case which arose out of the purported disciplining of four prison officers – the applicants in the case – following on the escape of a prisoner from St. Patrick's Institution. Blayney J. (as it happened, the same judge who had decided *Gallagher v. The Revenue Commissioners (No. 1)* (above)) posed the following question:

"Was [the *audi alteram partem* rule] complied with? . . . It was submitted . . . that the reports of Chief Officer O'Sullivan, dated the 1st November 1986, which were furnished to the applicants, endorsed by the Deputy Governor 'for explanation please' constituted charges of negligence. In my opinion they did not. They were not addressed to the applicants. They were addressed to the Deputy Governor. The only part that was addressed to the applicants was the endorsement of the Deputy Governor 'for explanation please.' The purpose was clearly to obtain from each of the applicants, and from the other six officers who were also asked for an explanation, information which when pieced together would enable the Deputy Governor to come to a conclusion as to how the escape occurred. It was part of the investigation he was carrying out . . . The applicants may have had reason to believe that if they did not give a satisfactory explanation of how they had performed their duties on the day of the escape, they might be charged with negligence, but *they had no reason to believe that such a charge had been preferred against them*."[56]

---

[54] [1981] I.L.R.M. 456 at 464. See also *O'Laoire v. Medical Council*, unreported, High Court, January 27, 1995, where it was also accepted that the litigant "must have known". Here it was alleged that the appellant had declined for improper motives to treat certain patients. It was claimed that he had had no advance notice that the Council intended to adduce evidence of improper motive, as this had not been formally set out in the notices convening the Fitness to Practice Committee Inquiry. Keane J. agreed that the appellant was entitled:

"to adequate notice of the allegations made against him so as to enable him to conduct his defence and to meet them with whatever legal assistance was appropriate and with the production of whatever evidence was considered necessary. That is one of the basic requirements of natural justice or fair procedures in a case such as this. Provided that they are met, I do not think it is appropriate to treat the notices of the inquiry as if they were in the same category as summonses or indictments in a criminal prosecution."

The judge noted that in *Georgopulous v. Medical Council*, unreported, High Court, March 3, 1992 Carroll J. had held that the procedure envisaged by the Medical Practitioners Act 1978 was one which was "broad" and "untechnical", so that the Committee was entitled to have regard not merely to the complaint of misconduct as originally formulated, but also to the manner in which it had been subsequently elaborated in a further letter to the Committee's Registrar.

Keane J. then continued:

"Adopting a similar approach in this case, I am satisfied that the allegations as formulated in the notices . . . put Mr. O'Laoire and his advisers clearly on notice of the case they would have to meet and that, having regard to the nature of the allegations in both inquiries, it must have been obvious to them that questions of motive and intention would inevitably arise."

[55] Unreported, High Court, February 1, 1988.

[56] *Ibid.* at pp. 13–14 of the judgment.(Emphasis added.)

The length to which the last sentence goes is clear when one bears in mind the content of the reports which each applicant had received. One of these reports (that of the first applicant) may be quoted to illustrate their suggestively damning character: "1. Anthony Gallagher, I am to report that on Friday the 31st October 1986 officer A. Gallagher was on duty in the visiting box. At approx. 4.15 p.m. on the termination of inmate Kenneth Noonan's visit this inmate was allowed to leave the visiting box and escape via the main gate."[57] In face of this, it might be assumed, by a lay-person of average intelligence who had some explanation of his conduct to offer that it would be prudent to offer it. However, Blayney J. rejected such a common sensical approach[58] and required something more akin to a formal charge.[59]

One might remark by way of criticism, that there is only a very fine line of distinction between this line of law and the doctrine of waiver which whould have afforded a defence for the respondent; yet which was not mentioned in the judgment.

Information obtained outside the hearing

One form of denial of *audi alteram partem* occurs when although some type of hearing (whether oral or written) has been allowed, the decision-maker relies upon information or argument, which has been obtained outside that hearing and not disclosed to the party adversely affected by it. Some illustrations of this fairly common situation will be given before the merits are briefly examined. The first illustration occurred in *Killiney and Ballybrack v. Minister for Local Government (No. 1)*[60] which arose from a planning appeal in which one of the factual issues was whether

---

57 *Ibid.* at pp. 2–3 of the judgment.
58 Moreover, the paragraph of the judgment (quoted above) dealing with the need for a charge is immediately succeeded by the following (at p. 14 of the judgment):
  "Even if they had reason to construe the reports in this way, the Deputy Governor was still at fault in failing at any time to inform them of the nature of the evidence against them, and in failing to give them an opportunity to speak and adduce evidence on their behalf. All that happened after they had supplied the explanations sought in the reports was that they received some further queries. At no time were they informed of the nature of the evidence against them or given an opportunity of making their defence."
  This passage extends the obligation imposed by the previous passage in that it states that as well as informing the person affected, the public body must positively offer him an opportunity to make his defence: he is not expected to take the initiative by seeking out the decision-maker and proffering his side of the story.
59 The applicant also succeeded, in rather similar circumstances, in *Quirke v. Bord Luthchleas na hÉireann* [1988] I.R. 83 at 87–88. Like *Corrigan, Quirke* was a case involving category (iv) Discipline in the typology sketched at pp. 594–596. The facts were that after his event, in spite of being asked to do so by an athletics official, the applicant-athlete failed to return to the drug testing room to give the required sample and instead left the sports ground. A few days later he was asked to give a written explanation for this failure and offered an explanation which, according to Barr J., was "patently untenable and . . . unacceptable." However, there were two crucial points in the applicant's favour. The first was that he should have been made aware when being asked to undergo the drug test that he would be liable to suspension if he failed to take the test. The other point was that, at the later stage, the applicant did not know that a formal complaint was being made against him to the national committee of the respondent athletics board or that it was to this that he was being required to furnish an explanation.
60 (1978) 112 I.L.T.R. 9. The facts in *The State (Hegarty) v. Winters* [1956] I.R. 320 were similar to those of the *Killiney case*, save that in *Hegarty* the successful party had accompanied the decision-maker to the inspection, and, accordingly, the Supreme Court treated the case as an instance of the no-bias rule. On *Hegarty*, see p. 514.

the sewerage disposal facilities in the area of the proposed development were already overloaded. There was a direct conflict of evidence at the oral inquiry as to whether raw sewerage was to be found on the foreshore near the development. After the inquiry had been concluded, the inspector examined the foreshore on his own and included a record of his findings in his report to the Minister who was, at the time of the case, responsible for deciding planning appeals. In the High Court, Finlay P. invalidated the Minister's decision because it was based on evidence which had not been disclosed to the party disadvantaged by it, who thus had no opportunity to reply to it.

The second case is *The State (Polymark Ltd.) v. I.T.G.W.U.*[61] in which an employer had made a submission before the Labour Court that, in the circumstances of the particular case, the Court had no jurisdiction to entertain an appeal from the Equality Officer. In response to this submission, the Labour Court adjourned the case in order to seek legal advice from the registrar and, having received it, continued with the case. In the High Court, the applicant employer complained of the fact that his counsel before the Labour Court had not been made aware of the advice given or afforded an opportunity of commenting upon it. Blayney J. decided the case on the basis that even if this were correct he would, since no useful purpose would be served,[62] exercise his discretion against granting a remedy. However Blayney J. evidently felt that the applicant's contention was correct in principle. In a passage (which has however, been substantially glossed: see below), he stated:

> "It might be of assistance for the future, however, if I were to indicate what procedure the Labour Court could safely adopt if similar circumstances arise again. They should first inform the parties of their intention to ask the registrar for legal advice; then, having obtained the advice, they should, at a resumed hearing, inform the parties of the nature of the advice they had obtained and give the parties an opportunity of making submissions in regard to it, and finally, having heard the submissions, the members of the court should, on their own, without further reference to the registrar, arrive at their own conclusion on the issue."[63]

---

61 [1987] I.L.R.M. 357.
62 See pp. 731–734.
63 [1987] I.L.R.M. 357 at 363. But *cf.* the gloss put on this decision by the Supreme Court in *Georgopolous v. Beaumont Hospital Board*, unreported, Supreme Court, June 4, 1997. Note also the further gloss put on these principles in *Cronin v. Competition Authority*, unreported, Supreme Court, November 27, 1997. Where the Authority was supplied with confidential business information by an oil company whereupon it proceeded to issue a draft category licence under s.4(2) of the Competition Act 1991. The applicant complained that it was only then that he had been asked for his comments and that the Authority had cleary acted on the basis of the material submitted by the oil company to which he was not privy. Barrington J. stressed that the procedures adopted by the Authority had to have regard to the fact that it is required to make "extremely complex decisions" as to how best the policies of the competition legislation may be achieved. There was thus a "fallacy" underlying the applicant's fair procedures arguments:

> "This is not a case of litigation inter partes with the Competition Authority acting in the role of some kind of arbitrator. The Competition Authority is an administrative body which formulates it's competition policy in the light of the requirements of the common good, the provisions of the statute, and prevailing market conditions. To carry out this role properly it must have access to information and undertakings must be free to inform it of their business secrets, while at the same time being reassured that their confidence will be respected by the Authority."

Another authority on the same issue is *Kiely v. Minister for Social Welfare (No. 2)*[64] which arose after the appellant's husband had suffered an accident at work which caused severe burns and led eventually to depression. A few months later he died and the appellant, K, claimed a death benefit under the Social Welfare (Occupational Injuries) Act 1966. Her claim was heard by the deciding officer and, on appeal, the appeals officer in the Department of Social Welfare. Before the appeals officer, the principal issue – on which the medical expert giving evidence for K disagreed with the Minister for Social Welfare's medical adviser – was whether it was possible for a heart attack to have been caused by depression and, thus, to be connected with her husband's employment. This question was settled against K by the appeals officer. The first of the three grounds on which K succeeded before the Supreme Court was that during the interval between the hearing of the appeal and the notification of the decision nearly two months later, the medical assessor had written a letter to the appeals officer giving new evidence as to why depression could not cause a heart attack. This evidence included the bulletin of an international medical symposium and the practice of actuaries in assessing "life. mortality in relation to anxiety states." In explaining why this evidence had been obtained in breach of the rules of constitutional justice, Henchy J. stated briefly that the assessor's function is "to act as a medical dictionary and not as a medical report."[65]

These cases illustrate a difficulty which is likely to loom large in the future. It arises from a contrast of cultures: first, a large part of the *raison d'être* of specialised tribunals is that the tribunal has the ability and opportunity to accumulate a wealth of specialised knowledge, information and expertise. This indeed is said to be one of its advantages over a court. To some extent, therefore a tribunal's decision is the result not only of the evidence adduced by the parties at a particular hearing; it is also the product of the tribunal's own expertise, which has been brought to bear upon the evidence. However, this attitude collides with a rule which is central to all judicial or quasi-judicial adjudication, namely that a decision must be made in accordance only with evidence introduced at the hearing, tested by the opposing sides and forming part of the record. And thus, the categories of material of which judicial or official notice may be taken is severely limited. Outside Ireland, various tests have been proposed for resolving these two conflicting tensions.[66] First, a distinction has been made according to whether a tribunal is using its expertise as a substitute for evidence or only for the purpose of evaluating the evidence that has already been presented. This test, which of course involves a difficult question of degree, would seem to accord with the distinction drawn, in *Kiely (No. 2)* between

---

[64] [1977] I.R. 267. *Cf. Horan v. An Post*, unreported, High Court, January 18, 1991, pp. 9–11.

[65] A further example of the same broad situation occurred in the case of *Geraghty v. Minister for Local Government (No. 2)* [1976] I.R. 153. The relevant point here is that some of the information on which the decision regarding the plaintiff's planning appeal had been taken was material (reports on other appeals from the same geographical area) which the plaintiff had not seen and had not had the opportunity to comment upon.

[66] *cf.* de Smith's, *Judicial Review of Administrative Action* (4th ed., 1980), pp. 203–207 and the 5th ed. of the same book (1995) at pp. 444–447. The change from the fourth to the fifth editions in this authoritative work may be characterised as a shift in an "Irish-direction". But significantly, this appears to be due not to any Irish or recent English case law but, presumably, because of the new editors' views.

a medical dictionary and a medical report. However, it might be argued that the court misapplied its own test in *Kiely* in that a medical report is personal to a specific patient, whereas the issue in that case (whether depression is capable of causing a heart attack) was a general question which could have been appropriately dealt with in a medical dictionary. Another test, also used outside Ireland, distinguishes between the general accumulated experience of the decision-maker, which need not be shown to an applicant, and material obtained from an identifiable source. Comparing the Irish cases with this test, it seems clear that *Killiney and Ballybrack (No. 1)* and *Polymark* are in line with them, but it may be argued that the material relied on by the Minister and his department in *Geraghty (No. 2)*[67] or by the appeals officer in *Kiely (No. 2)* might have been classified as "accumulated experience." However, broadly speaking one can comment that in these cases a rather stringent standard was set, possibly because here as elsewhere the courts were subconsciously imposing upon the procedures of a tribunal the same mores which a court must observe in its own procedure.

There has, however, been a distinct change of direction in the most recent case in this area. This was *Georgopolous v. Beaumont Hospital Board*[68] which admittedly concerned what the courts characterised as the relatively informal procedure involved in terminating a contract of employment. One feature of the procedure about which the applicant complained was that the legal assessor, who was advising the lay Hospital Board, had given his advice in the absence of the applicant and without the advice being disclosed to him. Rejecting this argument in the High Court, Murphy J. quoted the passage from the *Polymark* which has already been rehearsed here and then went onto say:

> "I would respectfully agree with what Blayney J. was quoted as saying in that judgment. It seems to me that his views were based on the practice traditionally adopted by judges of the High Court of repeating for the benefit of counsel any advice, information or observation given to him by a registrar of the court . . . However, in the present case it is essential to bear in mind that the function of the board was to determine as a matter of fact whether the allegations made against their employee were well-founded. They were not determining any question of law nor would they have been competent to do so. The need for legal guidance was to ensure that a lay body was acquainted with what may be seen as the ever expanding requirements of the rules of natural and constitutional justice . . . Indeed one might expect something in the nature of a conference or informal seminar to brief the members of such a tribunal on the legal principles applicable to their functions. It seems to me inconceivable that a tribunal having obtained . . . such advice should be required to lay it before any parties . . . pleading before them."[69]

---

[67] See above, n. 65.

[68] [1994] 1 I.L.R.M. 58 (High Ct.); unreported, Supreme Court, June 4, 1997.

[69] *ibid.* at 62. There appears to have been no discussion of a distinct right of a party to be present at the hearing. *Cf.* Harris, O'Boyle and Warbrick, *Law of the European Convention on Human Rights* (1995).

In the Supreme Court, too, *Polymark* was distinguished rather unconvincingly and the plaintiff's argument rejected, on the basis that the Board had to determine a question of fact only; whereas the advice from the assessor concerned points of law. One could question the logic of this distinction in the light of the fact that there will certainly be times when the termination of a contract will involve points of law and the legal advice given must have been of some relevance to the issue decided. Accordingly, it may be realistic to regard this decision as giving broad support for the view suggested by way of comment earlier, namely that there are limits to the type of information or expertise which a tribunal is bound to share with a person affected.

3. Person Affected Must Be Equipped To Make The Best Possible Case

We turn now to deal with aspects of the operation of the *audi alteram partem* rule, which relate to the second category identified above, namely that in relation to all aspects (including for example where appropriate a plea in mitigation[70]) the person should have the necessary facilities to make the best possible case on his behalf.

Right to an oral hearing, right to summon witnesses and right to cross-examine

Plainly whilst these issues may need to be considered independently, there is often a substantial connection between them. In any case, with each of them, as with other aspects of the *audi alteram partem* rule it may be misleading to speak of a "right" since in such an amorphous area, entitlement to the advantage sought will depend on all the circumstances of the case.[71] On the question of whether they apply, de Smith states: "A fair 'hearing' does not necessarily mean that there must be an opportunity to be heard orally. In some situations it is sufficient if written representations are considered."[72]

---

[70] *e.g. Georgopolous v. Beaumont Hospital Board*, unreported, Supreme Court, June 4, 1997, at pp. 16–21 (citing *Graham v. The Racing Board*, unreported, High Court, November 22, 1983, p. 7). However, in *Georgopolous*, it was held that it sufficed that the plaintiff had had the opportunity to discuss the subject of "penalty" at the conclusion of the evidence on the substantive question of termination of the applicant's contract; albeit he was not permitted to address the Board on the question of "penalty" in a discrete hearing. This line of argument had earlier been rejected in the High Court by Murphy J. on the more basic ground that this was not a disciplinary tribunal, but a review by an employer of the conduct of his employee and, in consequence, a less stringent standard applied.

[71] See, *e.g.* the comments of Keane J. in *The State (Williams) v. Army Pensions Board* [1981] I.L.R.M. 379 at 382: "Whether [there must be an oral hearing] in any particular case must depend on the circumstances of that case. . . . The application in the present case was capable of being dealt with fairly . . . in the manner actually adopted by [the Board]." Webster J. made similar comments in relation to a prisoner's right to call witnesses and cross-examine, etc., before a board of prison visitors in *R. v. Home Secretary, ex p. Tarrant* [1985] Q.B. 251.

[72] de Smith, *op. cit.* above, n. 66, p. 437. See also Wade and Forsyth, *Administrative Law* (7th ed., 1994), p. 537. As far as appeals to An Bord Pleanála are concerned, it is clear that the Board has a discretion as to whether to allow an oral hearing save in the case of appeals specified by regulation: Local Government (Planning and Development) Act 1992, s.12. No such regulations have yet been made. See also, *Kiely v. Minister for Social Welfare (No. 2)* [1977] I.R. 267 at 278.

The case of *Re Haughey*,[73] which arose out of the Dáil Committee of Public Accounts investigation into the expenditure of the grant in aid for Northern Ireland relief, is instructive in the context of a right to call witnesses or to cross-examine opposing witnesses. During the course of the Committee's investigations, a senior Garda Officer made a number of serious allegations against Mr Haughey. These accusations lay at the heart of the Committee's investigation, so much so, the Court considered, that he might be regarded as being in an analogous position to a party in a court case, at any rate, so far as his good name was concerned. Emphasising this factor, Ó Dálaigh C.J., writing for the Supreme Court majority, in a much cited passage, held that the Committee ought to have granted Mr Haughey the following procedural safeguards:

"(a) that he should be furnished with a copy of the evidence which reflected on his good name; (b) that he should be allowed to cross-examine, by counsel, his accuser or accusers; (c) that he should be allowed to give rebutting evidence; and (d) that he should be permitted to address, again by counsel, the Committee in his own defence."[74]

A case on the other side of what it is suggested is the same line from that drawn in *Haughey* was *The State (Boyle) v. General Medical Services (Payment) Board*[75] which stemmed from an investigation which had established that the applicant doctor's claims for remuneration, under the "choice of doctor" scheme were excessive. Under the agreement on which the scheme was based, the applicant could, as he did, complain to an appeal committee. His appeal was rejected following an oral hearing. The committee based its decision on, *inter alia*, statistical data concerning the average number of home visits in the area in which the applicant practised. The applicant requested that the expert who had compiled the data should be made available for cross-examination before the committee. This request was refused. Keane J. held that this refusal did not constitute a violation of constitutional justice because when the applicant received a copy of the data he had not raised any specific issue as to its reliability, which required oral evidence in order to be resolved.

Flanagan v. University College, Dublin[76] is notable in a number of respects, among them, Barron J.'s assumption that the applicant was entitled to the rights under discussion here. The applicant in *Flanagan* was a student who had studied for a

---

73 [1971] I.R. 217.
74 *Ibid.* at 263. Failure to permit cross-examination was also held to be a breach of *audi alteram partem* in *Kiely v. Minister for Social Welfare* [1977] I.R. 287 where this right was granted to the other side. As Keane J. observed in *The State (Boyle) v. General Medical Services (Payment) Board* [1981] I.L.R.M. 14, *Kiely* turns on the lack of even-handedness displayed by the appeals officer, (in comparison with which see the European Convention doctrine of "equality of arms": Harris, O'Boyle and Warbrick, *op. cit.*, above, n.67, pp. 202, 208–209). Accordingly, it would be wrong to deduce any comprehensive right to cross-examine from the facts of *Kiely*. See also, *Turner v. Pilotage Committee of Dublin Pilotage Authority*, unreported, High Court, June 14, 1988, at pp. 2 and 5. citing *Re Haughey* which was also cited in *Gallagher v. Revenue Commissioners (No. 2)* [1995] 1 I.R. 55 at 62, 76–78 in holding that there is a "right to cross-examine witnesses as to facts which are essential to the establishment of the charges . . ."
75 [1981] I.L.R.M. 14. See too *Mooney v. An Post*, unreported, Supreme Court, March 20, 1997, discussed below at pp. 591–592. But *cf. R. v. Hull Prison Visitors, ex p. St. Germain (No. 2)* [1979] 1 W.L.R. 1401 and *Galvin v. Chief Appeals Officer* [1997] 3 I.R. 240.
76 [1988] I.R. 724. See also p. 521.

Diploma in Applied Social Science. She took honours in her written papers but the lecturer supervising her work suspected that she had copied parts of the essay, which was the other requirement of the Diploma. The matter was referred to the Registrar, as a breach of discipline. The Registrar wrote to the applicant asking her to appear before a committee of discipline but giving her no indication of the nature of the breach. The applicant made several attempts to find out from the Registrar what was alleged against her. Eventually some three weeks after the responsible lecturer had read her essay, she was told, over the telephone, about the allegation. The committee of discipline met six days later. Of the procedure which the committee should have followed at the hearing, Barron J. observed that a charge of plagiarism is the most serious breach of academic discipline and that the procedures should approach those of a court hearing. He stated:

> "In my view, the procedures must approach those of a court hearing. The applicant should have received in writing details of the precise change being made and the basic fact alleged to constitute the alleged offence . . . At the hearing itself, she should have been able to hear the evidence against her, to challenge that evidence on cross-examination, and to present her own evidence."[77]

Another case in which it seems to have been held by the Supreme Court that, in some circumstances, there is a right to cross-examine is *Gallagher v. Revenue Commissioners (No.2)*.[78] This decision arose out of the purported dismissal of an officer of customs and excise for allegedly deliberately undervaluing vehicles which had been imported illegally into the State, (a dismissal which had been before the courts on two other occasions).[79] The central fact in the case against the applicant was the value of the second-hand vehicles. Yet (notwithstanding vigorous requests from the applicant's legal advisers) the witnesses on this point were not called before the inquiry for cross-examination; all the evidence on the point was hearsay. The framework within which the decision on the point was set was that, to quote Hamilton C.J. in the Supreme Court:

> ". . . while tribunals exercising quasi-judicial functions, as the second named appellant was in this case, are given a certain latitude in the exercise of their functions and in determining the requirements of natural justice and fair procedures in the circumstances of the case, they may not act in such a way as to imperil a fair hearing or a fair result."[80]

---

[77] *Ibid.* at 731. As a result of this hearing, the committee decided to refer the matter of the applicant's guilt to an independent expert. This reference was held to be improper for a number of reasons. In the first place, whilst the committee secured the applicant's consent to this course of action, they did so on the basis that the independent assessor would be a university lecturer in human behaviour. However, the applicant claimed – and Barron J. appears to have accepted the claim – that the assessor did not fall within this category. Secondly, when the Registrar's officer purported to send on a copy of the assessor's report, a significant paragraph was omitted from it. Thirdly, the applicant's request for a postponement of the reconvened meeting of the disciplinary committee was refused.

[78] [1995] 1 I.R. 55.: ". . . without an oral hearing, it would be extremely difficult, if not impossible to arrive at a true judgment on the issues which arose in this case."

[79] [1991] I.L.RM. 632 (Blayney J.) (applicant entitled to transcript of his interview, legal representation, etc.); unreported judgment of O'Hanlon J. (delay) which is referred to at [1995] 1 I.L.R.M. 245 at 253.

[80] [1995] 1 I.R. 55 at 76. (Emphasis added.) Denham J. concurred with Hamilton C.J.

What then were "the circumstances of the case" and "[the] imperil[ment] of a fair result" which turned the decision here? It seems that these included, the gravity of the consequences for the applicant (dismissal for misconduct, in something like disgrace, after twenty years' service), and the fact that the issue involved (the price of a particular second-hand vehicle) was both the essence of the entire case, and assumed to be a matter of peculiar subjectivity and volatility. However it is significant, as somewhat qualifying the value of the case as a precedent that in his separate assenting judgment, O'Flaherty J. stated:

> ". . . while I appreciate that the essential case made on behalf of the respondent is that his legal representatives were not given an opportunity to cross-examine witnesses, the more fundamental defect in the proceedings is that no proper evidence at all of the value of the vehicles was led."[81]

The manner in which administrative authorities must exercise their discretion in favour of an oral hearing with cross-examination is further illustrated by *Galvin v. Chief Appeals Officer*.[82] In this case the applicant's entitlement to an old age pension rested in part on whether he had paid insurance contributions between 1948 and 1961. The Appeals Officer denied a request for an oral hearing, preferring to rely on the departmental records (which purported to show that no insurance contributions were made during this period), instead of the evidence to the contrary tendered by the accountant of the applicant's former employer. Costello P. agreed that there were no "hard and fast rules" determining whether constitutional justice required an oral hearing in every case:

> "The case . . . must be decided on the circumstances pertaining, the nature of the inquiry being undertaken by the decision-maker, the rules under which the decision-maker is acting and the subject-matter with which he is dealing and account should also be taken as to whether an oral hearing was requested. In this case there is no doubt that an important right was in issue (that is the applicant's right to a pension for life). The statute gives an express power to hold an oral hearing and to examine witness under oath; a request for an oral hearing was made."

Costello P. then drew attention to the cumulative effect of a number of considerations, including the inherent unreliability of records which were so old; a series of administrative blunders which had already been made in this case and the failure to assess the evidence tendered on behalf of the applicant. Taken together, these

---

81 [1995] 1 I.R. 55 at 87. One further feature of the case should be mentioned. The respondents relied rather heavily on the fact that they were without the statutory right to *subpoena* witnesses. The Court, however, was unimpressed by this line of argument because, on the facts, there was no evidence that, even without such powers, the respondents would have had any difficulty in securing the attendance of witnesses. More significant for the future is that the general tone of the judgment ([1995] 1 I.R. at 79 and 87) seems to have been of the view that, even had attendance been impossible, the proceedings would still have been flawed. See however the explicit passage from *R. v. Board of Visitors of Hull Prison ex. parte St. Germain* [1979] 1 W.L.R. 1401 at 1409 which is quoted with approval at 78–79. Notice, though, that the passage from *St. Germain* also states that a chairman may exercise his discretion to limit the number of witnesses if "the total number sought to be called is an attempt by the prisoner to render the hearing virtually impracticable."

82 [1997] 3 I.R. 240.

factors meant that "without an oral hearing it would be extremely difficult – if not impossible – to arrive at a true judgment on the issues which arose in this case."

This case was thus very different from *Boyle* where the inherent reliability of the statistical data to be used in the investigation was not at issue. Likewise, in *Mooney v. An Post*[83] the Supreme Court held that there was no issue of fact which required that the plaintiff be given an oral hearing before his dismissal as a postman. The plaintiff, when confronted with the evidence against him, remained silent. In these circumstances, said Barrington J. the plaintiff "had raised no issue of fact which needed to be referred to a civil tribunal."

Representation

Where there is an oral hearing, its practical value may depend on whether the individual is represented by an experienced, though not necessarily legally qualified, advocate. As against this, it will often happen that the advocate is a lawyer and it is often said that the involvement of lawyers has, in the long run, the effect of pro-tracting and complicating the proceedings, to no advantage.[84] However, in other jurisdictions the tide appears to be running in favour of a right to be represented.[85] In Ireland, the position is still in doubt. In *McGrath and O'Ruairc v. Trustees of Maynooth College*,[86] which involved the dismissal of two University lecturers, the Supreme Court said that there was a right to be represented by a lawyer though not, as the plaintiffs preferred, by their trade union representatives. But on the other hand, in two recent disciplinary cases, *Smullen* and *Gallagher*[87] a claim for repre-sentation was refused. This claim, did however, succeed in *Flanagan v. University College, Dublin* where, under the relevant procedural regulations, a student could only be represented by the Dean of Women's Studies and/or the President of the Students' Union, neither of whom the applicant knew. In *Flanagan*, with its grave consequences for the applicant and its rather nuanced evidence, the High Court regarded the offer of representation by these personages as inadequate. Barron J. rejected as "obviously fallacious"[88] the argument that since the applicant, who was a social worker, was educated, articulate and experienced in writing case reports and putting forward their contents to case conferences, she would be well equipped to make her own case. Barron J. also rejected the idea that plagiarism is essentially a simple matter: the three experts who had examined Miss Flanagan's thesis had each

---

83   Unreported, Supreme Court, March 20, 1997.
84   *Report of the Committee on Civil Legal Aid and Advice* (1978, Prl. 2574), p. 50.
85   *R. v. Home Secretary, ex p. Tarrant* [1985] Q.B. 251, and see de Smith, *op. cit.*, above, n.66, p. 213 and Jackson, *Natural Justice* (1979), pp. 73–79.
86   [1979] I.L.R.M. 166. See, too *Clancy v. I.R.F.U.* [1995] I.L.R.M. 189 at 200 (right to be legally represented before the I.R.F.U. committee to determine whether the applicant could play for a new club (a very brief discussion).
87   *The State (Gallagher) v. Governor of Portlaoise Prison*, unreported, High Court, May 18, 1977 (prison discipline); *The State (Smullen) v. Duffy* [1980] I.L.R.M. 46 (school expulsion). In *MacGrath v. Attorney General*, unreported, High Court, March 29, 1995, it was held that the provision of a law library for the use of a lay-person who represented himself was not one of the unspecified rights protected by Article 40.3.1º.
88   [1988] I.R. 732. *Flanagan* was followed in *Gallagher v. The Revenue Commissioners (No.1)* [1991] 2 I.R. 370, in which it was held (at 377–378) by Blayney J. that the disciplinary charges against the applicant were so serious as to warrant an entitlement to legal representation.

made different judgments on it. Of the two disciplinary cases alluded to, earlier in this paragraph, Barron J. distinguished the first, *Smullen* – and it is suggested he could equally well have distinguished *Gallagher* – on the ground that: "the procedures adopted were fair and that what the school did was reasonable having regard to its magisterial responsibility and its obligation to enforce and maintain discipline. No element of such responsibility or duty exists in the present case."[89] However, in *Corcoran v. Minister for Social Welfare*[90] – which arose out of a social welfare appeal before an appeals officer of the Department of Social Welfare – the contention that there was a right to representation was rejected (though, admittedly, representation had in fact been allowed).[91] Murphy J. made the following general statement:

"No precedent or authority has been produced for the general proposition that a lay tribunal exercising a quasi-judicial function must afford to the parties appearing before it an opportunity to procure legal advice and be represented by lawyers. Less still is there any authority for the proposition that the State would be bound to pay for such assistance. In so far as the nature of the issue before the tribunal is a material fact, in determining the procedures to be adopted it must be recognised in the present case that not merely is there an ample right of appeal to an aggrieved party but that there is an unlimited right to re-open the issue 'in the light of new evidence or of new facts.'"[92]

This passage has been anticipated or echoed in a number of other authorities.[93] In the light of this knotty case law, it seems that the best synthesis may be to say only that the deciding authority must consider whether in all the circumstances, (especially the seriousness of the consequences for the applicant) representation is necessary in the interests of justice.[94] For in Ireland, there has been no equivalent of the list (enunciated in *R. v. Secretary of State for the Home Department, ex p. Tarrant*[95]) the factors to be taken into account when a board of prison visitors is exercising its discretion to permit legal representation to a prisoner charged before it with offences against prison discipline. In *Tarrant*, this list, which might, subject to appropriate modifications, be applied in other contexts, included the following items:

"1. The seriousness of the charge and of the potential penalty . . . 2. Whether any points of law are likely to arise . . . 3. The capacity of a particular prisoner

---

[89] *Ibid.*

[90] [1991] 2 I.R. 175.

[91] *Haughey* and *The State (Healy) v. Donoghue* [1976] I.R. 325 were distinguished in *Corcoran* on the ground that in each a criminal charge was involved (though this may be doubted in the case of *Haughey*). And as to *Flanagan*, this case was distinguished apparently on the basis of a passage from *Flanagan*, ([1988] I.R. at 729–730), to the effect that the standard of constitutional justice depends upon all the circumstances, including the gravity of consequences for the applicant. In addition it was stated that: "the only matter in issue was whether the means of the applicant exceeded a particular figure and clearly this was information which was particularly within his own knowledge. ([1991] 2 I.R. at 183)."

[92] [1991] 2 I.R. 175 at 183.

[93] *O'Neill v. Iarnrod Éireann* [1991] E.L.R. 1; *Aziz v. Midland Health Board* [1995] E.L.R. 48; *Scariff v. Taylor* [1996] 2 I.L.R.M. 278 at 287, 289; *Galvin v. The Chief Appeals Officer* [1997] 3 I.R. 240.

[94] See *Tarrant* and *Enderby Town F.C. v. Football Association* [1971] Ch. 598.

[95] [1985] Q.B. 25, approved by the House of Lords in *Hone v. Maze Prison Board of Visitors* [1988] A.C. 379.

to present his own case ... 4. Procedural difficulties ... 5. The need for reasonable speed in making their adjudication ... 6. The need for fairness as between prisoners and as between prisoners and prison officers."[96]

Financial assistance to pay for representation?

Given that legal representation is necessary, the question then arises as to whether there is any obligation on the State or its agencies to provide any form of financial assistance towards payment for legal costs, at least in the case of an indigent person. Before turning briefly to the general principle in regard to this issue, one ought to clear out of the way three exceptional categories in which payment must be made. First, a statute may provide expressly for the payment of costs.[97] Secondly in a rather surprising case,[98] the legal costs of representation at an inquiry were held to be payable as damages, consequential on a negligent act by CIÉ. Thirdly in the case of a criminal trial (even in the absence of statute), there may be a constitutional right to legal assistance, depending on "the seriousness of the charge having regard to the person charged ... the nature of the penalty ... and his capacity ... to speak for and defend himself adequately."[99] It has been held, however, that this does not extend to "the earlier or ancillary stages of criminal proceedings".[100]

However, there is nothing in any of the case law cited as authority for these (exceptional) categories to suggest there is any general principle, applicable to administrative cases, on the basis of which legal costs may be claimed. And some of the authorities[101] actually state that any general principle is confined to criminal cases.

Public hearing

There has been hitherto little Irish authority on which the question of whether fair procedures dictates that an oral hearing must be held in public. The *zeitgeist* in favour of open government militates in favour of such a requirement; on the other

---

96 [1985] Q.B. 251. *In Re Morrison* [1991] N.I. 70 at 76, Carswell J. drew attention to the difficulties faced by prison governors "holding [disciplinary] adjudications in which often difficult legal concepts ... have to be dealt with [when] they have not the benefit of legal training ..."

97 See, *e.g.* p. 278 (Social Welfare); and pp. 303–306 (Tribunals of Inquiry). Note that the Civil Legal Aid Act 1995, s.27(2) (b) gives the Minister for Justice, Equality and Law Reform the power to extend the scope of the legal aid scheme to cover tribunals. *Cf. Employment Appeals Tribunal Sixteenth Annual Report* (1983, Pl. 2733): "while the procedures of the Tribunal were intended to be formal, speedy and inexpensive, the increasing involvement by the legal profession, particularly in claims under the Unfair Dismissals Act 1977, has tended to make hearings more formal, prolonged and costly, with an over-emphasis on legal procedures and technicalities" (p.4). According to the 1983 Report, 19.7 per cent of employees and 23.9 per cent of employers opted for legal representation. In the Twenty Fifth Annual Report (1992, P.L. 9986) the equivalent figures were employees: 18 per cent were represented by lawyers and 22 per cent by trade unions; employers: 19 per cent were represented by lawyers and 3 per cent by trade unions. (However the figures for employers are an under-estimate because more than one claim may be taken against the same employer.)

98 *Condon v. CIÉ*, unreported, High Court, November 22, 1984. See p. 306.

99 *The State (O) v. Daly* [1977] I.R. 312 at 315, *per* O'Higgins C.J. qualifying *The State (Healy) v. Donoghue* [1976] I.R. 325. The passage quoted is from *Daly.* See also *McSorley v. Governor of Mountjoy Prison* [1996] 2 I.L.R.M. 331 at 338, and *Kirwan v. Minister for Justice* [1994] 2 I.R. 417.

100 *The State (O) v. Daly* [1977] I.R. at 315.

101 *K Security Ltd v. Ireland*, unreported, High Court, July 15, 1977; *Condon* at pp. 17–19; *Daly* [1977] I.R. at 315.

hand, certainly in particular situations, there may be good reason to exclude from the hearing those with no interest (however defined) in the issue.[102] This issue did, however, arise in *Barry v. Medical Council*[103] where Costello P. appeared to suggest that the guarantee of fair procedures contained in Article 40.3 bestowed a qualified right to an open hearing, although the existence of a right of appeal to a court sitting in public "was a factor to be taken into account when determining whether the absence of public hearings before the [Fitness to Practice] Committee should be regarded as being unfair." In this case the Fitness to Practice Committee of the Medical Council ruled that it had discretion to hold public hearings, but determined that the present case should nonetheless be heard *in camera*, since otherwise "the most intimate private matters would be disclosed to public scrutiny should the hearings be public." Costello P. held that the Committee had exercised their discretion fairly in arriving at this conclusion, having regard, *inter alia*, to the complainants' constitutional right to privacy and the qualification which is itself contained in Article 6(1) of the Convention.[104]

Deciding without hearing

It frequently happens that the decision-making and information-gathering functions are divorced from each other, as for instance where the body in which a decision has been vested, either instructs its officials, or constitutes a sub-committee, to conduct interviews, examine records, etc. The question arises as to how far this process can go before it is held that the individuals affected have not been allowed a fair hearing because the decision maker has not itself heard the case. One context in which this situation has arisen, in Ireland,[105] is the decision as to a planning appeal or the confirmation of a compulsory purchase order, which is vested in Bord Pleanála or the Minister for the Environment, respectively. The decision often requires a hearing at the site, which is chaired by an inspector and is not attended by the Board or Minister. Nevertheless, it was agreed, before the statutory dispensation which presently operates,[106] in the *Murphy-Geraghty* line of cases,[107] that this procedure

---

[102] While Art.6(1) of the European Convention of Human Rights guarantees, *inter alia*, a "fair and public hearing", the case law of the European Court of Human Rights demonstrates (i) that there is no requirement that all stages of the proceedings should be held in public and (ii) that there is no breach of Art.6(1) if there is an appeal to an appellate court from a disciplinary tribunal which has sat in private, provided that the appellate court sits in public and has jurisdiction to determine questions of fact as well as law: see *Weber v. Switzerland* (1990) 12 E.H.R.R. 508 (*in camera* hearing of contempt charge held to violate Art.6(1)) and *Diennet v. France* (1996) 21 E.H.R.R. 554 (*in camera* hearing of disciplinary charge against doctor held to violate Art.6(1)). In *Campbell and Fell v. United Kingdom* (1985) 7 E.H.R.R. 165 it was held that to require the holding of prison disciplinary hearings in public would place disproportionate burdens on prison authorities. However, the Court ruled that Art.6(1) required that the authorities disclose the result of any such disciplinary adjudication.

[103] Unreported, High Court, February 11, 1997.

[104] Which, *inter alia*, permits the exclusion of the press where this is necessary for the protection "of the private lives of the parties".

[105] For the English law, see P. P. Craig, *Administrative Law* (3rd ed., 1994), p. 317.

[106] See Local Government (Planning and Development) Act 1983, s.11(6).

[107] *Murphy v. Dublin Corporation* [1972] I.R. 215. See, to like effect, *Murphy v. Dublin Corporation (No. 2)* [1976] I.R. 143; *Geraghty v. Minister for Local Government* [1976] I.R. 153. There were some differences between the judges, but this was on another point, namely, the operation of the *delegatus* principle. These cases are discussed at pp. 486–487.

is valid, provided that the inspector gives the Minister "if not a verbatim account . . . at least a fair and accurate account of what transpired and one which gives accurately to the Minister the evidence and the submissions of each party . . . "[108]

The decision of Carroll J. in *Genmark Pharma Ltd v. Minister for Health*[109] provides a good illustration of this point. The applicant had applied to the Minister for a product authorisation for a new pharmaceutical drug and the Minister fully referred the application to the National Drugs Advisory Board.[110] Carroll J. held that the Minister had infringed constitutional justice by adopting the procedures which he did:

> ". . . while the Minister was entitled to seek advice, he was not entitled to rely on advice in the form of conclusions without reference to the basic material on which those conclusions were based.[111] As the competent authority the Minister must be in a position to make his own evaluation of the advice received based on relevant documentation submitted. This he failed to do. Neither the documentation furnished by Genmark to the NDAB nor a reasonable summary of it was forwarded to the Minister. The advice he received did not even deal with a major point made by Genmark . . . namely, that [certain types of] clinical trials were neither possible nor necessary. The advice did not say why the absence of [these] clinical trials was fatal. While the Minister would be entitled to make up his own mind on this question whether he received advice on it or not, he would nonetheless have to give reasons why he rejected Genmark's arguments . . . [T]he advice did not relate specifically to the documentation so that the Minister could evaluate the advice at the same time as he evaluated the submissions of Genmark. The Minister should have been sent whatever documentation was relevant to enable him to evaluate the advice and the submissions."

Carroll J. also found that the Minister had relied on a ground which was contained in the Authority's advice and which had not been disclosed to the applicant. Relying on the authority of *Geraghty*, she held that the applicant just entitled to know not merely the main grounds of objection, but must be informed of all such grounds.

In *Hession v. Irish Land Commission*,[112] the respondent landowner's objection to the inclusion of his farmland on the Irish Land Commission's provisional list was heard before two lay Commissioners. However, the case was adjourned for two years. At the adjourned hearing, where one of the Commissioners had been replaced

---

[108]   *Murphy v. Dublin Corporation* [1972] I.R. 239.
[109]   Unreported, High Court, July 11, 1997.
[110]   Now the Irish Medicines Board.
[111]   Carroll J. cited *Flanagan v. University College, Dublin* [1988] I.R. 724 and *Jeffs v. New Zealand Dairy Production and Marketing Board* [1967] 1 A.C. 551 as authorities for this proposition.
[112]   [1978] I.R. 322. In *Re McNally's Application* [1985] N.I. 17 where a Prison Board had sat on an earlier occasion to determine whether a prisoner who faced serious disciplinary charges should be entitled to legal aid, but in order to decide that point it was found necessary to hear evidence from certain prison officers as to the extent of their injuries. At a later stage a differently composed panel heard the substantive case, and the applicant was adjudged guilty of these offences. On these facts, Gibson L.J. found that these procedures did not amount to a breach of natural justice. The reason was that the later proceedings were not simply a continuance of the earlier partly heard case, but were rather "a complete hearing of every aspect of the substantive issue".

by another Commissioner, the respondent's objection was rejected. The Supreme Court held that this result must have been based at least in part upon evidence given at the initial hearing, and accordingly the decision was void.[113] The case is unsatisfactory in that the court did not find whether there was any record (or if so, what quality of record) of the initial hearing before the reconstituted lay Commissioners or whether there was any other factor to distinguish the case from the *Murphy* and *Geraghty* line of authority, which was not even mentioned.

In the situation under discussion, there is often a close interaction between the *audi alteram partem* rule and the *delegatus non potest delegare* principle.[114] An instance is *O'Brien v. Bord na Móna*[115] which involved the compulsory acquisition of the plaintiff farmer's bogland. The plaintiff had submitted to one of the Board's officials that the Board need only take a leasehold interest, with the land reverting to him after all the turf had been removed. Because of the Board's long-established policy of acquiring the fee simple interest, the official did not even bother to transmit this information to the Board. The Supreme Court dealt first with the argument that there had been no breach of the *audi alteram* rule because the decision had been delegated to the official who had received the plaintiff's submission. It held that even had there been a delegation (though there was, on the facts, no sign of one) the decision would still have been invalid because determinations regarding compulsory acquisition are not capable of being delegated to officials. The court then turned to the alternative issue and held that the *audi alteram* rule had been broken by the official's failure to relay the plaintiff's submission to the board of Bord na Móna (in which the decision was vested).[116]

O'Brien was distinguished by Carroll J. in the High Court in *ESB v. Gormley*[117] which involved the placing of an electric line upon the defendant's land. The defendant relied, *inter alia*, upon the fact that her objections had not been relayed to the ESB Board. Carroll J. rejected this argument and distinguished *O'Brien* primarily because the line had already been finally decided by the Board before the defendant acquired the land; but also because – and this is a point of more general significance – it was permissible for the Board to delegate to its officials negotiations with landowners and decisions regarding the relatively minor issue of the position of intermediate pylons. Unfortunately, in none of these cases have any guidelines been given as to what conditions (*e.g.* as regards control, reporting etc.) must be satisfied in order to legitimate the delegation.[118]

A distinct situation in which this problem may arise is where the delegation has the effect of depriving some third party of the benefit of the *audi alteram partem*

---

113 See also, *Re McNally's Application* [1985] N.I. 17 at 22; *R. (Dobbyn) v. Belfast JJ.* [1917] 2 I.R. 297; *R. (Department of Agriculture) v. Londonderry JJ.* [1917] 2 I.R. 283.
114 On which, see pp. 481–485.
115 [1983] I.R. 255.
116 The court rejected the argument that since the plaintiff's argument would have been so unlikely to sway the Board, this breach did not matter (see further pp. 614–615). On a separate point the court's decision, at this stage, could also have been put on the ground that the Board's decision [against the plaintiff] would have been founded on an inflexible rule of policy: see pp. 668–675.
117 [1985] I.R. 129. Carroll J. was reversed, on other grounds, by the Supreme Court: see [1985] I.R. 144.
118 For an acceptable delegation of fact-collection and recommendation by a committee to an official, see *Mooney v. An Post* [1994] E.L.R. 103 at 118.

precept. A typical situation in which this may arise is the planning field: planning permission may be granted subject to a condition, which, in order to retain flexibility, depends upon agreement between the local planning authority and the developer. The condition might, for example, make the permission subject to the erection of a fence built to specifications to be agreed between the developer and the local planning authority. The essential point here is that any neighbour is denied the opportunity to learn of the content of this agreement and perhaps to object to it. Leaving aside the issue of whether the *audi alterem partem* precept applies at all at the initial stage of the planning process,[119] all one can say is that the question of whether the precept has to be observed is one of degree, in that it could be made to depend on the significance of the condition and of the discretion which has been left to the parties – in other words a form of the *de minimis* principle.

This seems to be one (though not the main) factor for the decision in *McNamara v. An Bord Pleanála*.[120] Here the relevant planning conditions (fixed by An Bord Pleanála in respect of the grant of permission for a waste dump) required certain matters – *inter alia* the details of a bird and vermin control scheme – to be settled by agreement between the developer and local planning authority. The contention that the applicant would be denied the opportunity to object to what had been agreed was rejected by Barr J. who stated :

> "There is no reason to believe that . . . the planning authority . . . will not co-operate with the applicant or any other interested party in the matter of submissions they may wish to make on functions delegated to the planning authority by the board and, if asked, will inform them of developments in that regard before decisions are taken."[121]

This passage appears to hold (reasonably convincingly) – that the right to make representations was satisfied in that it was open to the applicant, who *ex hypothesis* knew about the planning condition left to be settled, to feed in their comments to the local authority.[122]

Confirmation of a decision

It is a significant principle that an absence of constitutional justice at the initial decision-making stage is not cured by the provision of an appellate stage at which the rules are observed. The policy underlying the principle is discussed in Part 6 of this chapter. Here it is proposed to discuss a significant restriction on this principle. For it has recently come to be accepted, that where a "provisional" decision is taken without observing the *audi alteram* rule, this defect can be remedied if the person

---

[119] See pp. 544–545.

[120] [1996] 2 I.L.R.M. 339 at 357. See also *Houlihan v. An Bord Pleanála*, unreported, High Court, October 4, 1993 and *Boland v. An Bord Pleanála* [1996] 3 I.R. 435.

[121] [1996] 2 I.L.R.M. 339 at 362. The passage here uses the term delegation. Some of the conditions in the case involved delegation and some agreement. It seems to have been accepted that the principle was the same in either case.

[122] However, it would seem possible to construct an argument based on the right to object (under the terms of the Planning Code) requiring information to be lodged of the detail of the development. Such argument is not addressed in this passage. Possibly, an answer to such an argument would be the *de minimis* rule.

affected has the chance to put his side of the case before the decision is made permanent.[123] In short, the process can sometimes be characterised as a single decision, (as opposed to a discrete decision, followed by an appeal) for the purposes of the constitutional justice principles. The effect of this characterisation would be to avoid the principle explained at the start of the paragraph.

The first case to be examined is *The State (Duffy) v. Minister for Defence*[124] which arose out of the discharge of a petty officer from the Navy. The appellant, who was one of the few people in the history of the Navy to fail to get his engine-room artificer certificate, had been warned by his commanding officer that he was going to be discharged, to which he replied that he was "going to do something about this."[125] His commanding officer told him that he was free to do so and ensured that the decision was not implemented for seven days so that the applicant could make whatever representations he wished. In fact, none were made. Reversing D'Arcy J. in the High Court, Henchy J. for the Supreme Court drew a distinction between "the decision to proceed to discharge" and "the actual discharge" seven days later and held that the fact that the applicant could have made representations during this period of delay, constituted adequate compliance with the *audi alteram partem* rule. Henchy J. thus rejected (though without discussion) the possibility that the commanding officer might, at the final stage, be biased by loyalty to his own previous decision.[126]

Gammell v. Dublin County Council[127] involved an order prohibiting the erection of temporary dwellings which had been made under the Local Government (Sanitary Services) Act 1948, in respect of the plaintiff's caravan site, by the defendant council. The plaintiff was not aware of the inspection of her site by the local authority and health board experts on whose certificate the local authority relied in making the order. Following the procedure under the 1948 Act, a notice that the order had been made and that any person aggrieved had 14 days in which to apply to the Minister for the Environment, asking for the order to be annulled, was published in a newspaper circulating locally. On such an application the order could then be annulled or confirmed by the Minister. Carroll J. held that this opportunity to make

---

123 A somewhat similar, if more nuanced, position has been adopted by the Privy Council in *Calvin v. Carr* [1980] A.C. 574 at 592.

124 [1979] I.L.R.M. 65. (distinguished in *The State (Murphy) v. Kielt* [1984] I.R. 465 at 478; *The State (Murphy) v. Governor of St. Patrick's Institution* [1985] I.R. 141 at 147). For a similar case to *Duffy* see *The State (Donnelly) v. Minister for Defence*, unreported, High Court, October 8, 1979. In *The State (McCann) v. The Racing Board* [1983] I.L.R.M. 67 which involved the revocation of a course betting permit by the Board, Barron J. distinguished between the Board's "decid[ing] whether matters alleged justified . . . revocation" and "the ultimate decision of the Board . . . before the . . . revocation takes effect." The words quoted confirm the distinction drawn in *Duffy* and in the later case of *Gammell v. Dublin County Council* [1983] I.L.R.M. 413 discussed below. Other cases in which the situation under discussion might appear to arise, but was not mentioned by the court, are *The State (Boyle) v. General Medical Services (Payment) Board* [1981] I.L.R.M. 14 and *The State (Williams) v. Army Pensions Board* [1983] I.R. 308.

125 *cf.* "I will do such things, What they are yet I know not, but they shall be the terrors of the earth" – *King Lear*, Act II.

126 It is submitted in regard to both *Duffy* and *Donnelly* that it may be unrealistic to assume that, in a strict military hierarchy, a superior officer who has taken up the definite position that a subordinate ought to be dismissed will resile from that position because of arguments advanced by the subordinate.

127 [1983] I.L.R.M. 413.

representations to the Minister sufficed for compliance with the *audi alteram partem* rule (notwithstanding that the plaintiff had not seen the newspaper notice, a point to which we return in the next section).

Although Carroll J. did adopt a lengthy passage from the judgment in *Duffy* as part of her reasoning, there was an important point at which *Gammell* differed from *Duffy*, namely, that in *Gammell* the confirmation was to be given by a body other than the body which had taken the initial decision. This made the confirmation look more like an appeal and required the High Court to confront a question not mentioned in *Duffy*, namely how to distinguish the structure of the administrative process in *Gammell* from the *Ingle* and *Moran*[128] line of authority. Both *Ingle* and *Moran* had held that a failure to allow a person affected by a decision the right to make his case at the time of the initial decision would not be cured by the provision of an appellate stage at which this right was allowed. Carroll J. drew an important distinction in the following passage:

> "However, in this case we are not dealing with an order effective when made and an appeal therefrom to an appellate body. Under section 31 of the [1948] Act the order has no effect until the person aggrieved has been given an opportunity of stating reasons why it should not come into effect. There is no 'appeal' to the Minister from an operative order. There is machinery set up under the section whereby an aggrieved party can make representations why the order should not come into operation. If successful, the order is annulled by the Minister and it never becomes operative. This is very different to the *Ingle* case and the *Moran* case where the revocation of the licence became operative immediately and of necessity there had to be a time lag between the revocation and the determination of an appeal in the District Court. Is there any real distinction between machinery which provides for an order to be made with delayed effect giving an opportunity to interested parties to make representations for annulment which, if successful, will result in the order never becoming operative and machinery which gives an opportunity to interested parties to make representations why an order should not be made, which, if successful, will result in the order never being made. . . .
>
> The fact that the representations are to be made to the Minister and not to the body making the order does not seem to me to be invidious in any respect. In fact, even though the County Council would not appear to be inhibited from acting, it seems preferable that representation should be made to the Minister who can avoid the criticism which might be levelled at the County Council that they are judges in their own cause."[129]

---

[128] *Ingle v. O'Brien* (1975) 109 I.L.T.R. 4; *Moran v. Attorney General* [1976] I.R. 400. On these authorities, see pp. 615–616.
[129] [1983] I.L.R.M. 413 at 417–418.

This distinction,[130] can also be applied in other areas. Take, for instance, applications for planning permission:[131] considered in isolation, the procedure before a local planning authority might appear to violate the *audi alteram partem* rule in that (confining the discussion to the applicant for planning permission and not examining the position of objectors)[132] the applicant is not told of the authority's provisional thinking on his application, much less allowed any opportunity to make representations in regard to it. On the other hand, there is ample constitutional justice at the rehearing, on appeal, to An Bord Pleanála. The crucial question thus is whether the initial application stage is to be examined in isolation or whether it is to be considered together with the proceedings before An Bord Pleanála. In other words, is the structure of the decision-making system analogous to that involved in *Gammell*? It is submitted that the two systems are similar and thus that the planning application system does not violate the *audi alteram partem* rule. The key factor is that (as with the prohibition order) a local planning authority decision granting permission does not come into effect until the appeal has been heard or, if no appeal is taken, until the period for appealing has elapsed.[133] However, it must be admitted that this line of argument was not followed or even considered in *Frenchurch v. Wexford County Council.*[134]

It is suggested that a broadly similar approach was followed in a different field (courts-martial) in *Scariff v. Taylor*.[135] Here it was held that a failure of legal representation at the stage of informal investigation and taking of evidence – which was a preliminary to a court martial – did not imperil a fair hearing : for the accused was not placed in peril until the actual hearing of the court martial and the sworn evidence was not placed before the court martial on a plea of not guilty. Hence there is no breach of constitutional justice, although the appellant was not represented at this stage.

Most of the cases, so far, have concerned the question of whether observance of the *audi alteram partem* rule at a later stage makes up for a deficiency in the initial

---

130 For which some support may be found in *O'Brien v. Bord na Móna* [1983] I.R. 268. Here the plaintiff's case was that the body which had taken a provisional decision as regards a compulsory order would be biased, by the provisional decision, when it came to the stage of confirmation, and, consequently, that there should be an "appeal against the making of a compulsory acquisition order, or . . . confirmation by an external authority. . . ." ([1983] I.R. 255 at 281). It seems to have been assumed in both the High Court (which upheld the plaintiff's claims) and the Supreme Court (which, admittedly, rejected the plaintiff's case) that either confirmation or an appeal to an external authority would cure the defect arising from any bias in the original decision. There is some support here for the idea that an appeal may be treated as being equivalent to a confirmation for the purposes of constitutional justice. The same distinction was also drawn, in the context of Art. 34.1, in *Re Solicitors Act 1954 and D. a solicitor* (1961) 95 I.L.T.R. 60.
131 The actual planning situation should be considered in the light of the *Frenchurch Properties case* [1992] 2 I.R. 268 discussed at pp. 544–545 above. Notice also that it might be made a point of distinction between the *Gammell* and the planning situation that in the planning situation, it is the private individual rather that the public body (as in *Gammell*) which is denied permission to do something.
132 On which see *The State (Stanford) v. Dun Laoghaire Corporation*, unreported, Supreme Court, February 20, 1981.
133 Local Government (Planning and Development) Act 1963, s.26(9), as amended by s.20 of the Local Government (Planning and Development) Act 1983.
134 [1992] 2 I.R. 268 on which see pp. 544–545.
135 [1996] 2 I.L.R.M. 278. For the application of Art. 6(1) of the Convention to courts-martial, see *Findlay v. United Kingdom* (1997) 24 E.H.R.R. 221.

stage. The reverse question focuses on the later stage, as in the case of *Carroll v. Minister for Agriculture and Food*[136] which concerned the basic fairness of the procedure for testing cattle for "reactors". The applicant had submitted that the procedure did not incorporate any appeal mechanism and did not enable the applicant to challenge the test or have an independent re-test in the event of a disputed finding. Blayney J. rejected this argument, correctly, it is suggested.

Duty to give reasons[137]

It used to be the law that an administrative body was under no obligation to give reasons for its final[138] decision.[139] However, by today, as we shall see, this is no longer true in the case of an administrative body. (Rather surprisingly, the issue of whether there is an obligation on a court to give reasons for its judgment, appears not to have been raised.[140]) In Ireland (though not in England[141]) as often, at first, change was left to the judges (though certain specific statutory interventions should be noted, for example the duty to give reasons for a refusal of an application for planning permission or for any conditions attached to a grant of permission).[142] Over the past decade or so, the courts have developed a right to reasons, in certain circumstances by tapping a vein of constitutional justice. More recently an ever more far-reaching development is coming about through the Freedom of Information Act 1997, which comes into effect in 1998. Before turning to the Act, which is by far the most important source of law here, we shall briefly survey the pre-Act law, both because of its inherent interest and because it applies in the few areas, which the Act does not reach.

Pre-1997 Act Law The first case in this line of authority is *The State (Daly) v. Minister for Agriculture*[143] which dealt with the dismissal of a probationer civil servant under section 7 of the Civil Service Regulation Act 1956, as amended by

---

[136] [1991] 1 I.R. 230 at 235.

[137] See, de Smith, *op. cit.* above, n. 66, pp. 457–473; Wade and Forsyth, *op. cit.* above, n. 72, pp. 541–545, 942–945, 981–982; Craig, *Administrative Law* (3rd ed., 1994), pp. 310–316. For monographs on the law of England and other common law jurisdictions, see Flick, "Administrative Adjudications and the duty to give reasons" (1978) *Public Law* 16; Akehurst, "Statement of Reasons for Judicial and Administrative Reasons" (1970) 33 M.L.R. 154; Woolf, *Protection of the Public – A New Challenge* (The Hamlyn Lectures for 1989), pp. 92–97). Craig, "The Common Law, Reasons and Administrative Justice" [1994] C.L.J. 282 and literature cited at fn.2 thereof.

[138] As contrasted with the duty to give reasons for a provisional decision which may arise as part of the narrow *audi alteram partem* rule. For the question of an arbitrator's duty to give reasons see *Vogelaar v. Callaghan* [1996] 1 I.R. 88 at 93 and *Doyle v. Kildare County Council* [1995] 2 I.R. 424 at 431.

[139] *Kiely v. Minister for Social Welfare (No. 2)* [1977] I.R. 267 at 274; *The State (Cole) v. Labour Court* (1984) 3 *J.S.L.L.* 128 (though here there appears to have been a significant qualification: a party could "request the Court to give its decision in such a way that an appeal on a point of law could be taken.").

[140] See Wade and Forsyth, *op. cit.*, above, n.72, pp. 541–542.

[141] In England the Tribunals and Inquiries Act 1971, s.12(1) (*cf.* United States (Federal Administrative Procedure Act, s.8(b)) imposes a duty to give reasons upon a large number of tribunals.

[142] Local Government (Planning and Development) Act 1976, s.39(g). Other examples: Solicitors (Amendment) Act 1994, s.15(4)(e) (adjudicator in respect of complaints "shall give reasons . . . in every report to the Society."); S.I. No. 85 of 1994, reg 40(2), (4)(vii).

[143] [1987] I.R. 165.

section 3 of the Civil Service Regulation (Amendment) Act 1958. This provision states that where a civil servant is serving a probationary period, if the "appropriate authority is satisfied that he has failed to fulfil the conditions of probation . . ." the authority shall terminate the service of such civil servant. Here the applicant had been dismissed with no indication of the ground for his dismissal; nor had any been given during the hearing before the High Court. The State's strongest authority was *Broomfield v. Minister for Justice*[144] which concerned the dismissal of a civil servant, under the same statutory authority. In *Broomfield*, Costello J. had stated that in contrast with an office-holder, a probationer's service may be ended because: ". . . his employing authority may consider the probationer unsuited for permanent employment and, without any specific charge of any acts of misconduct, the employing authority keeps to himself the right not to appoint the probationer on a full-time basis."[145]

However, in *Daly*, Barron J. held that *Broomfield* had been implicitly overruled by Henchy J.'s observation in *The State (Lynch) v. Cooney*[146] that:

". . . [any] opinion formed by the Minister [under the statutory authority] must be one which is bona fide held and factually sustainable and not unreasonable. The court must ensure that the material upon which the Minister acted is capable of supporting his decision. Since the Minister has failed to disclose the material upon which he acted or the reasons for his action there is no matter from which the court can determine whether or not such material was capable of supporting his decision. Since the Minister continues to refuse to supply this material, it must be presumed that there was no such material.

In the result therefore the Minister was entitled to dispense with the services of the prosecutor without warning him that he proposed to act in that manner. However, once his decision was challenged, he was obliged to disclose to the prosecutor the material upon which he had acted and to give his reasons for so doing."

In *International Fishing Vessels Ltd v. Minister for the Marine*[147] what was at stake was the Minister's refusal to renew the applicant's sea-fishing boat licence. The applicant had breached a condition which had been attached to its previous licence and which provided that at least 75 per cent. of its crew should be either Irish citizens or nationals of an E.C. state. In response to a solicitor's letter asking for more detailed reasons, the Minister had refused "as a matter of policy" to give any reasons. Counsel for the Minister argued that while the Minister was obliged to act fairly, this did not include a duty to give reasons: however, Blayney J. followed *Creedon*[148] (although characterising the Minister's function as "not quasi-judicial") and *Daly* and held that the Minister was under a duty to give reasons.[149]

---

144 Unreported, High Court, April 10, 1981. (*Ex tempore*)
145 *Ibid.* at p. 5 of the judgment, quoted in *Daly* at [1987] I.R. at 170–171.
146 [1982] I.R. 337 at 361.
147 [1989] I.R. 149. For the sequel to this case, see *International Fishing Vessels Ltd v. Minister for the Marine (No. 2)* [1991] 2 I.R. 92.
148 *The State (Creedon) v. The Criminal Injuries Compensation Tribunal* [1989] I.R. 51. For a more detailed discussion of *Creedon*, see 2nd edition of this book at p. 459.
149 [1987] I.R. 329. For another appeal case, see *Golding v. The Labour Court* [1994] E. L. R. 153. See also, *Garda Representative Association v. Ireland* [1989] I.R. 193; *Pok Sun Shun v. Ireland* [1986]

The striking feature of these authorities is that in each case, the right to reasons was grounded in the fact that the decision for which reasons were sought was either reviewable or subject to appeal. (It is significant to take note here that Article 34.3.1° of the Constitution establishes a right to judicial review[150]; and that, in order to make this right efficacious, reasons must be provided.) In *Daly*, Barron J. stated: ". . . the Minister was entitled to dispense with the services of the applicant without warning him that he proposed to act in that manner. However, *once his decision was challenged*, he was obliged to disclose to the applicant the material and to give his reasons for so doing."[151]

This is a significant feature to which we must return after we have examined the more recent authorities, which might appear to disturb the even tenor of success for the applicant which had been established by the line of authorities exemplified above. In *H v. Director of Public Prosecutions*,[152] the first of these cases, it was probably a crucial point, that it was the D.P.P.[153] against whom the applicant sought an order. Secondly, in *Manning v. Shackleton*[154] the applicant sought to challenge a decision of a statutory arbitrator (appointed under the Acquisition of Land (Assessment of Compensation) Act 1919) whose award did not recite the reasons for the decision. Barron J. referred to the earlier authorities such as *International Fishing* and said:

"These cases indicate that the giving of reasons by a person or body required to act judicially may be compelled by this court when such reasons are necessary to determine whether such a power has been validly exercised. It is not an essential obligation and arises only when required to prevent an injustice or ensure that not only has justice been done but is seen to have been done. The absence of reasons in this award itself does not invalidate it. The question is, whether, if reasons are not now given, justice will neither be done nor be seen to be done."[155]

Barron J. concluded on the facts that, with regard to one aspect of the award, the applicant would suffer prejudice if reasons were not given. (Despite this, the passage

I.L.R.M. 593 at 599 (confining itself to cases where rights of appeal exist under statute); *Breen v. Minister for Defence* [1994] 2 I.R. 34 at 41.

[150] See p. 455. The classic statement of the considerations determining whether reasons must be given is to be found in *McCormack v. Garda Complaints Board* [1997] 2 I.L.R.M. 321 at 332–333, *per* Costello, P.

[151] [1987] I.R. 165 at 172 (Emphasis added.). See to similar effect, Finlay C.J. in *Creedon* at 54–55 and *International Fishing* [1989] I.R. 149 at 155 and *Anheuser Busch Inc. v. Controller of Patents, Design and Trade Marks* [1987] I.R. 329 at 331 (right of appeal) and Carroll J. in *Gavin v. Criminal Injuries Compensation Tribunal* [1997] 1 I.R. 132.

[152] [1994] 2 I.L.R.M. 285 at 290–291 (O'Flaherty J.). This reasoning was based on the premise that judicial review lies only in exceptional circumstances against the Director. It might also have been justified on the ground that to require the prosecuting authorities to give reasons for a failure to prosecute in a given case might well be unfair: see the comments of Costello P. in *McCormack v. Garda Síochána Complaints Board* [1997] 2 I.L.R.M. 321 at 334. Notice also Hogan's comment in Hadfield (ed.), *Judicial Review: A Thematic Approach* (1995), at p. 347.

[153] The Supreme Court stressed that as judicial review was only available in limited circumstances against the Director, the usual rationale for the granting of reasons – so that a potential applicant might know where he or she stood *vis-à-vis* an application for judicial review – did not apply. On this point see pp. 688–689.

[154] [1994] 1 I.R. 397.

[155] *Ibid.* at 403–404. This view was substantially endorsed by the Supreme Court [1996] 2 I.R. 85.

quoted appears to be leading up to a rejection – or, at least, a narrowing – of the requirement of reasons.)

Take finally *Rajah v. Royal College of Surgeons*.[156] Here the applicant student had failed both the end of session exams and the autumn re-sits. Exercising its discretion, under the appropriate regulations, the Academic Board of the respondent institution had declined to allow the applicant to repeat the year and re-sit the exams. No reasons were given for this decision and no effort had been made by the applicant to ascertain the reasons prior to the original application to the High Court. However Keane J. did not mention this last consideration. Instead he stated:

> "In general, bodies which are not courts but which exercise functions of a judicial or quasi-judicial nature determining legal rights and obligations must give reasons for their decisions, because of the requirements of constitutional and natural justice and in order to ensure that the superior courts may exercise their jurisdiction to enquire into and, if necessary, correct such decisions: see *The State (Creedon) v. Criminal Injuries Compensation Tribunal*. The requirement to give reasons may extend even further to purely administrative bodies, at least where their decisions affect legal rights and obligations: see *International Fishing Vessels Ltd* . . . A decision such as that of the respondents in the present case, however, was not, in my view, of a nature which necessitated the giving of reasons."[157]

One may take this passage – with its elliptical, concluding sentence – as implicitly characterising the Academic Board's decision as amounting to the refusal of a discretionary *privelegium*, the granting of which turned upon mixed academic-personal considerations. As such it was at the furthest pole from quasi-judicial decision[158] and hence attracted a lowly standard of constitutional justice. At the same time it might have been thought that, the earlier line of authorities might have been influential just because they spanned a very wide range of decisions in the field of public administration (public service employment; the Criminal Injuries Compensation Tribunal; trade licensing and; trade mark appeals).

In one way or another (for the *ratios*, *obiters* and absences of enthusiasm are rather various) these three recent authorities had partially undermined, if rather indefinitely, the solid foundation upon which the right to reasons[159] appeared to have been erected.

---

156 [1994] 1 I.R. 384. For further cases declining to require reasons. See *Tang v. Minister for Justice* [1996] 2 I.L.R.M 46 at 62 mentioned below at p. 599; *McCormack v. The Garda Síochána Complaints Board* [1997] 2 I.L.R.M. 321; *Maigueside Communications v. The Independent Radio and Television Commission*, unreported, High Court, July 18, 1997 (distinguishing between a situation in which one particular applicant is refused and a situation in which only one applicant is chosen); and *Flood v. Garda Síochána Complaints Board*, unreported, High Court, October 8, 1997.

157 *Ibid.* at 395. See also *R. v. Higher Education Funding Council ex p. I.D.S.* [1994] 1 W.L.R. 242 in which it was said Sedley J. that "where what is to be impugned is on the evidence no more than an informed exercise of academic judgment, fairness alone will not require reasons to be given."

158 For this dichotomy in the context of constitutional justice, see pp. 601–602. It should, however, be noted that in *Clancy v. I.R.F.U.* [1995] 1 I.L.R.M. 193, 200, *Rajah* was tersely followed without any of the sort of analysis attempted in the text.

159 In parenthesis, let us consider the theoretical question of the conceptual banner under which the right to reasons is to march. The first possibility was invoked in English Law, in the House of Lords

573

Freedom of Information Act 1997   The 1997 Act establishes a far-reaching duty to give reasons. The central provision is section 18(1) which states:

> "The head of a public body shall on application to him or her in that behalf, in writing or in such other form as may be determined, by a person who is affected by an act of the body and has a material interest in a matter affected by the act or to which it relates, not later than 4 weeks after the receipt of the application, cause a statement, in writing or in such other form as may be determined, to be given to the person –
> (a) of the reasons for the act, and
> (b) of any findings on any material issues of fact made for the purpose of the act."[160]

The key term here which has however, already been discussed[161] is "public body" because it is this term which determines the (substantial) scope of the Act. Accordingly, here we shall merely note that, where it applies, the Act goes beyond the previous obligation to give reasons which have been deduced (mainly) from constitutional justice, in four important respects. In the first place, the requirement that the reasons be required in order to facilitate a judicial review or appeal, canvassed above,[162] has no equivalent in the Act. Secondly, as we have also seen, the most recent cases evidence a tendency to restrict (admittedly, rather darkly) the type of decision and circumstances to which the right is attracted. There is no shadow of an equivalent in the Act.

Thirdly, take a decision which involves preferring one policy, situation, individual etc. to another; for example, the selection of one area of the country, rather

---

case of *R v. Secretary of State for Trade and Industry ex p. Lonrho* [1989] 1 W.L.R. 525. Here it was held that an absence of reasons for a decision not to refer a merger to the Monopolies and Mergers Commission was not *per se* unlawful. Rather, if all the known facts pointed overwhelmingly in favour of a different decision, the decision-maker who had given no reasons could not complain if the court drew the inference that he had no rational reason for his decision. In other words, failure to give reasons, as a defect, is a pensioner of substantive irrationality or unreasonableness.

Secondly, in a number of authorities including *Rajah* – in the passage quoted already – the right is put on the basis of "constitutional and natural justice" (which is the reason why it is included in the present chapter). And in *H*, no objection was taken to the fact that the reasons point was submitted as an alternative submission to a substantive reasonableness argument. In other words, no argument was made, on behalf of the D.P.P., that the applicant ought first to have sought reasons and then, only when these were not forthcoming, to have sought judicial review on substantive grounds. The conclusion from this omission – though admittedly too much should not be made of a point which was not argued – is that the duty to give reasons is a free-standing element of constitutional justice, rather than being conditional upon a refusal of reasons after judicial review had been invoked.

Thirdly, in *Breen v. Minister for Defence* [1994] 2 I.R. 32 at 41–42 (see further pp. 623–624) the duty to give reasons has apparently been associated with (to use a deliberately vague term) a public body's substantive duty to consider a matter fully, (on which see p. 676, n.241). Again, in certain circumstances – namely where there is an expectation regarding reasons – the doctrine of legitimate expectations (see Chapter 16) – may have a role to play. Finally, on a wide plane, there is a link between the right to reasons and the whole notion of open government. Thus as with many a developing area of law, the relationship between the duty to give reasons and other doctrines is not entirely settled. See also, Craig, [1994] C.L.J. at 300–301.

160   This obligation is foreshadowed in the *Devlin Report on Public Services Organisation Review* (Prl. 792) App. 1, p. 456.
161   See p. 495.
162   See p. 572. *Cf.* the comments of Finlay P. in *The State (Sweeney) v. Minister for Environment* [1979] I.L.R.M. 35.

than another for a grant scheme or why a particular candidate did not get a post in the public service.[163] In this category of decision, reasons have, classically, not been required on the ground that since it is always difficult to prove a negative, to impose such a duty on the responsible public body would be to impose too heavy a burden. However, in the case of the Act, the scope of the duty to supply reasons is defined, in section 18, by reference to an "act" and this is defined as "including a decision . . .". It may be, therefore, that there is no restriction (as there is in the case of constitutional justice) so that reasons will have to given for both negative and positive acts; as well as for policy and administrative decisions.

Finally, consider the main channel of the *audi alteram partem* principle. For this precept, of course, requires that, as part of the obligation to facilitate the person likely to be affected by a decision in making his case, certain types of information should be given to him.[164] Among this information will often be what might amount to the provisional reasons why it is anticipated that the issue may go against him. Where this is the case, it will frequently be clear that the reasons which finally motivated the deciding authority were the same as those mentioned or implied at the earlier stage of the decision-making process. Oddly enough, the link between the duty to give a person affected notice of the case against him and the duty to give reasons for the final decision has seldom, if ever, been authoritatively scrutinised in this jurisdiction.[165] The question is whether an adequate performance of the duty to give notice of the case against a person will, on the assumption that the reasons are the same at each stage, also satisfy the duty to give reasons at the final stage. The answer is that while this may be so in the case of the obligation to give reasons, grounded upon constitutional justice; it is unlikely to be so in the case of the Act

---

[163] Here one should note that one of the few exclusions in the Act is in respect of "decisions of the Civil Service Commissioners pursuant to section 17(1)(d) or (e) of the Civil Service Commissioners Act 1956 not to accept a person as qualified". This refers to the suitability of a candidate on the grounds of character (section 17(1)(d)) or "all other relevant respects" (section 17(1)(e)). But there are other grounds specified in section 17(1) as relevant in connection with the selection of candidates for appointment, namely knowledge and ability; age and health. And where selection or non-selection is based on one of these grounds, then it seems that the general principle reasserts itself.

[164] See pp. 541–546.

[165] One rare and slightly tantalising example of this line of thought being placed before a court appears to occur in the summary of counsel for the state's submission given in *International Fishing Vessels Ltd v. Minister for Marine* [1989] I.R. 149 at 154. "The Minister had made clear what material was before him. What the applicant was seeking was a formal statement by the Minister of his position." However, Blayney J.'s response to this argument is too general to advance the argument on this point.

What is possibly another (rather unclear) exception to the statement in the text that the present question has not arisen in a case occurred in *Doran v. Commissioner of An Garda Síochána.* [1994] 1 I.L.R.M. 303. The applicant's complaint was that he had not been given reasons for the Garda Review Board's decision (on family grounds) to transfer him to another station. However, O'Hanlon J. distinguished the line of authorities discussed in this section on the basis, *inter alios*, that (at 311) "the applicant was at all relevant stages *well aware*, in general terms, of the matters which were causing concern to his superior officers in the Garda Síochána." (At 309, O'Hanlon J. refers to the account of this area in the second edition of this work.) See also *International Fishing Vessels v. Minister for Marine (No.2)* [1991] 2 I.R. 92, 103. In this case the word "reasons" is used throughout judgments but it is not discussed here under the present rubric because the applicant's case is discussed (at 102 and 104) on the basis that had he received a full statement of reasons he might have made more effective representations, in other words, on the basis of *audi alterem partem simpliciter.*

just because of the way in which the obligation is formulated in section 18(1) of the Act, quoted above.

One question which obviously arises is this. After the Act comes into effect one year or, in the case of local authorities or health boards up to eighteen months after the date of its passing (April 10, 1997) – what vitality is left to the constitutional justice obligation to give reasons. In view of what has been said above, the answer is: very little. In fact, the only room left for a constitutional justice obligation seems two-fold. It is true that as mentioned earlier, there are other public bodies to which the duty applies, only as and when the necessary order is made. However, it must be said that in almost all of the cases decided so far, it has happened that the respondent has been within the category of public bodies already covered by the Act.

Finally, we ought briefly to examine the advantages and disadvantages of a duty to give reasons. Apart from the fact that the giving of reasons would facilitate any review or appeal, the advantages appear to be twofold. In the first place: "a decision is apt to be better if the reasons for it have to be set out in writing because the reasons are then more likely to have been properly thought out."[166] Secondly, reasons would give, to the person immediately affected and the public generally, confidence that the decision had been properly taken.

As regards the disadvantages of a duty to give reasons, an Australian authority has written:

> "At least two arguments have been advanced against the giving of reasons. First, the giving of reasons would impose additional administrative burdens and might well be an undue drain on the resources of an agency. Such burdens may even result in the giving of canned reasons. Secondly, reasons may hinder the manner in which a discretion is exercised and it may be thought that some discretions should be uncontrollable. But considerations of administrative expediency should not mitigate principles of fairness and few, if any, discretions should be uncontrollable."[167]

To judge by their pro-individual stance in other contexts, Irish judges are likely to sympathise with the comment contained in the final sentence of this extract and not to be much impressed by the first of the two arguments advanced in the passage. (On the other hand, (as mentioned earlier), in some situations the actual gains conferred by the imposition of a duty to give reasons at the final stage will not be significant.) Moreover, it may be the extensive duty to give reasons established in the strong form by the 1997 Act, will have significant consequential effects in such neighbouring fields as: estoppel, *res judicata*, the control of discretionary powers and the following of precedent in regard to administrative actions.

---

[166] *The Franks Report*, 1957 (Cmnd. 218), para. 98. Notice that Craig, above, n.134, *op. cit.* p. 283 adds the thought that the requirement of reasons will help to ensure that "the provision of reasons can be of real significance in ensuring that other objectives of administrative law are not frustrated. If, for example, we decide to grant consultation rights in certain areas, then a duty to furnish reasons will make it more difficult for the decision-maker merely to go through the motions of hearing interested parties without actually taking their views into account."

[167] Flick, above, n.137, *op. cit.* p. 19.

How extensive must the reasons be?

The next issue to be mentioned is the content of the duty to give reasons. In other words, how exact and comprehensive a statement of reasons is necessary in order to satisfy the duty? All we have to go on here is the scanty pre-Act law.[168] If one looks at the reasoning from Finlay C.J.'s judgment in *Creedon* ("the unsuccessful applicant . . . should be made aware in general and broad terms of the grounds"[169]), one would expect that the test should be whether the statement of reasons is sufficiently clear for the reasonable man; rather than whether it conforms to any formal requirements. And sure enough, Keane J. has remarked: ". . . the determination by the Labour Court need not . . . take any particular form: what is essential is that the manner in which it is expressed leaves no room for doubt as to the reasons which led to the decision, thus ensuring that neither the appellate nor the supervisory jurisdiction of this Court is frustrated by an inadequate indication of reasons".[170]

In the Supreme Court, too, a fairly relaxed attitude was taken in the case of *Faulker v. Minister for Industry and Commerce*.[171] Here the applicant had complained to the Labour Court that she has been the victim of sexual discrimination (as regards promotion in the civil service). All that the Labour Court gave by way of reasons for rejecting the applicant's claim was: "having examined in detail the claimant's assessment records, the Court is satisfied that the Department had reasonable grounds other than sex or marital status for her non-promotion in April 1989."[172] Ruling that this sufficed, O'Flaherty J. stated:

> "I would reiterate, what has been said on a number of occasions, that when reasons are required from administrative tribunals they should be required only to give the broad gist of the basis for their decisions. We do no service to the public in general, or to particular individuals, if we subject every decision of every administrative tribunal to minute analysis."[173]

---

[168] It has been held in the specialised context of reasons required by statute (Local Government (Planning and Development) Act 1976, s.39(9)) for planning decisions, that the reasons given in support of conditions attached to the grant of planning permission must be logically capable of justifying the imposition of that condition: *Killiney and Ballybrack Residents Assoc. Ltd v. Minister for Local Government (No. 2)* [1978] I.L.R.M. 78.

[169] [1988] I.R. 51 at 55.

[170] *Golding v. The Labour Court* [1994] E. L.R.153 at 159. On the particular facts of the case, the applicant failed to meet this standard with Keane J. stating (at 158):
". . . It is sufficient to say that, having regard to the specific incorporation in the determination by the Labour Court of the Equality Officer's recommendation and the letter of appeal and their unqualified acceptance that her conclusions were well founded, there is not the slightest difficulty in elaborating the reasons for the decision of the Labour Court which were clearly in substance the same as those which had led to the recommendation of the Equality Officer."

[171] [1997] E.L.R. 107.

[172] *Ibid.* at 110.

[173] [1997] E.L.R. 107 at 111. See also the similar comments of Murphy J. in the High Court [1993] E.L.R. 187 and also *Anisimova v. Minister for Justice*, unreported, Supreme Court, November 28, 1997 p. 600 and those of Keane J. in *Manning v. Shackelton* [1996] 3 I.R. 85. *A contra* Finlay C.J. in *North Western Health Board v. Martyn* [1987] I.R. 565 at 568 and 579. Keane J. stated in *Manning v. Shackelton* (at 97):
"It is obvious that, if arbitrators appointed under the Acquisition of Lands (Assessment of Compensation) Act 1919 were to be required to give a reasoned judgment on every case, the inevitable result would be a multiplicity of applications by dissatisfied claimants or acquiring

Findings of fact and materials available to public bodies

Closely related to the duty to give reasons are two other duties. The first of these is provided by the Freedom of Information Act 1997, the scope and (few) limitations of which have been noted in the preceding section. By section 18(1) of the 1997 Act:

> "The head of a public body shall, on application to him or her in that behalf, in writing . . . by a person who is affected by an act of the body . . . cause a statement, in writing or such other form as may be determined, to be given to the person –
>
> . . .
>
> (b) of any findings on any material issues of fact made for the purposes of the act."

Secondly, the overlapping and longer established contribution of constitutional justice is a requirement that a decision-making authority should, in order to facilitate judicial review of its decision, indicate to the person affected, the materials which were before it when the decision was taken. Indeed such a duty was initially mentioned, in the same breath as the duty to give reasons, in a passage from Henchy J.'s judgment in *Lynch* which has already been quoted.[174] It was also raised (on what might seem a rather inconclusive fashion) in the judgment of Finlay C.J. in *P. and F. Sharpe v. Dublin City and County Manager*.[175] The passage is as follows:

> "The necessity for the elected members in the case of any direction under section 4 [of the City and County Management (Amendment) Act 1955] concerning the granting or refusing of a planning permission to act in a judicial manner would *inter alia* involve an obligation to ensure that an adequate note was taken, not necessarily verbatim but of sufficient detail to permit a court upon review to be able to ascertain the material on which the decision had been reached."[176]

In *O'Keeffe v. An Bord Pleanála*,[177] Costello J. drew upon this passage from *Sharpe* as part of the basis for its finding that the Board's decision was procedurally void because *inter alia* of the Board's failure to keep minutes or to list the material before it. On the facts of the case, the Supreme Court (again speaking *per* Finlay C.J.)[178]

---

authorities which, although doubtless couched in the language of judicial review, would be in effect attempts to appeal from the award. Such a consequence would be inconsistent with the policy [of finality] underlying the arbitration procedure . . ."

While An Bord Pleanála is not required to provide a "discursive judgment", the necessity to provide grounds for a decision is not satisfied "by recourse to an uninformative, if technically correct formula": *O'Donoghue v. An Bord Pleanála* [1991] I.L.R.M. 750 at 757, *per* Murphy J.

Exceptionally, however, deciding authorities are statutorily required to give detailed reasons for their decision and in such cases generalised reasons are not enough: *Genmark Pharma Ltd v. Minister for Health*, unreported, High Court, July 11, 1997.

174 See p. 571.
175 [1989] I.L.R.M. 565. See also, *McLoughlin v. Minister for Social Welfare* [1958] I.R. 1; *Kiely v. Minister for Social Welfare (No. 1)* [1971] I.R. 21; *Kiely v. Minister for Social Welfare (No. 2)* [1977] I.R. 297; *McKinley v. Minister for Defence* [1988] I.R. 139, 142; *Thompson v. Minister for Social Welfare* [1989] I.R. 618.
176 [1989] I.L.R.M at 579.
177 [1993] 1 I.R. 39.
178 *Ibid.* On this point of distinction Finlay C.J. stated:

reversed the High Court and distinguished *Sharpe*. However in doing so it made a number of points, which may be significant for the development of the law. The most important of these is that it implied that there could in principle be an obligation on a public body to indicate the materials which were before it, so as to facilitate judicial review. However this was qualified in two respects. In the first place, the question of whether the mode by which this duty is discharged has to be by way of the provision of the minutes of a meeting or whether other means are acceptable depends upon the circumstances of the case. Secondly, the Chief Justice held that it is the applicant who bears the onus (in practice, a substantial difficulty) of establishing the nature of the material which was before the decision-maker, a matter which will be explored in the following chapter.[179] A related point is that before an applicant could complain of a want of material, he must have formally called upon the public body to supply the necessary information. This precondition was not satisfied in the instant case because:[180]

"... no request was made by letter, by any form of motion or by seeking any form of interlocutory order of any description by the plaintiff to the defendants to establish by affidavit or by other means the material which was before the Board before it reached its decision on the planning appeal."

A further example of a requirement that a public body should, in order to facilitate judicial review, record the material before it, arose in the unusual case of *Brennan v. Minister for Justice*.[181] As elaborated elsewhere, the main point in the case was a successful argument that the respondent had abused her power of granting pardons. In addition, in respect of the present point, Geoghegan J. stated:

"Although the exercise of the power by the minister need not be exercised in public as I indicated, it is constitutionally necessary, in my view, that all the evidence and information leading up to and the reasons for the exercise of the

---

"The requirement that a decision-making authority should keep minutes sufficient to allow proof of the material before it in the event of judicial review, which is contained in the decision of this Court in *Sharpe v. The Dublin City Manager*, must, I am satisfied, be read in its precise terms in the light of the body and the decision which was concerned in that case. In that case, what was at issue was the decision of the elected members meeting as the Dublin County Council. Such a meeting would of necessity involve the making of presentations, speeches, possibly the reading of documents by various members of the County Council. All that was available to the Court in that case was certain reports, which were submitted and apparently read into the proceedings of the County Council at the particular meeting with which the Court was concerned ... In order to obtain satisfactory proof of the material before the members when they resolved, as they did, to direct the granting of planning permission, it would have been necessary to establish what other material was before them and open for their consideration, and the only practical manner in which that could predictably be done would be by minutes of the meeting.

That decision should not be taken, in my view, to mean that minutes contemporaneously made of the meeting of members of a board or of a tribunal are a necessary or the only method of establishing the material that was before them.

In this case it would have been sufficient for this purpose if it were possible to establish the documents which in addition to the inspector's report and that of Mr. Enders were considered by the Board in the form of a list of the documents and the availability of copies of them to the Applicant in a judicial review."

179 See p. 645.
180 [1993] 1 I.R. 39.
181 [1995] 1 I.R. 612.

power be recorded. This is a logical consequence of the special nature of the power which would have been envisaged as to be exercised only in special cases. But for the exercise of any power, whether constitutional, statutory or otherwise, some accountability is essential. There has been a long established practice that the minister does not answer questions in Dáil Éireann relating to individual instances of the exercise of this power. That being so, the only way that the minister can in practice be made accountable for the proper exercise of the power is by means of judicial review in an appropriate case. But a proper judicial review would be frustrated unless there were stated reasons recorded for the exercise of the power together with all the information on which it was based."[182]

This is an area which is capable of considerable development in the future.

Delay[183]

Two leading British authorities agree in admitting delay by the public authority to the charmed circle of general factors which will vitiate a decision, but only on rather guarded terms. According to de Smith: "[the idea of substantive fairness] . . . includes a duty . . . not . . . to delay the making of a decision to the prejudice of fundamental rights."[184] Wade and Forsyth states: "Delay in performing a legal duty may also amount to an abuse which the law will remedy."[185]

It seems likely – though the case law does not permit one to be dogmatic about the point – that in Ireland, too, delay, of itself, is not a ground of invalidity unless a plaintiff can point to some prejudice which flows from it. This was the approach adopted in the *ex tempore* judgment of Gannon J. in *McGowan v. Wren*.[186] The facts were that in September 1985 a sworn inquiry, under the Garda disciplinary regulations, was held to examine allegations that the plaintiffs-Gardai had committed a breach of discipline (the date of which is not given in the report). Owing to certain irregularities in the documents before it, the inquiry was discontinued. Another fresh inquiry to examine the same allegation was fixed for September 1987. The plaintiffs then applied unsuccessfully to the High Court to quash the Garda Commissioner's decision to appoint the second Board of Inquiry. On the delay point, Gannon J. said:

---

182 *Ibid.* at 629.
183 For a court's discretion to refuse a remedy where the litigant delays, see pp. 722–730. A number of the Ombudsman's cases have involved delay: see p. 359.
184 de Smith, Woolf and Jowell, (5th ed. 1995), p. 584.
185 *Administrative Law*, p. 435. All but one of Wade's authorities are from the 1980s. These two English authorities also agree in categorising delay, or at any rate squeezing it in, under the rubric of abuse of discretionary power. It is suggested that it is inappropriate to confine this vitiating factor to the exercise of a discretion, thereby excluding (say) payment of a welfare benefit, hearing a planning appeal or court proceedings. It is suggested too that delay is a matter of procedure or at least process, as opposed to substance. Possibly the more appropriate rubric for it, in the Irish framework, is the additional territory annexed by constitutional justice beyond the bounds of natural justice. This matter of classification is not perhaps of first importance and has received no attention in the few Irish cases on delay.
186 [1988] I.L.R.M. 744. See, to like effect, *Gallagher v. The Revenue Commissioners (No. 1)* [1991] 2 I.R. 370 at 375–376, *per* Blayney J. (where a person is charged with the disciplinary offence of grave misconduct in the performance of his duty, the court may not restrain the proceedings on the ground of inordinate delay in conducting the hearing but the delay is relevant in assessing the plaintiff's defence and to the imposition of any disciplinary measures should the charges be made out). See, too, *Gallagher v. Revenue Commissioners (No.2)* [1995] 1 I.L.R.M. 241 at 245.

"[At the first inquiry board] no one had considered the applicants' side of the case but they [had] heard the case to be made against [them]. [The applicants] are not suggesting that they are failing in recollection since the alleged events occurred. If there is any disadvantage in the delay, it must lie in the presentation of the investigation and is not a disadvantage to the applicants. I do not think that there are any grounds in delay upon which the applicants may rely for the relief sought."[187]

Another claim based on delay succeeded in the rather extreme circumstances of *Flynn v. An Post*[188] (though without, it will be suggested, contradicting *McGowan*). The plaintiff had been suspended from duty without pay in May 1984 because he

---

[187] *Ibid.* at 745–746. In the context of *McGowan*, one ought to mention the High Court judgment in *McNeill v. Commissioner of An Garda Síochána* [1994] 2 I.R. 426, (the Supreme Court judgment focussed on a different point) which also arose out of disciplinary proceedings against a Gardaí. The central point in the case was that more than four years had elapsed between the date, when the alleged disciplinary offence (making false declarations in respect of the number of hours worked) was first brought to the applicant's attention, and the fixing of the date for the hearing of the formal inquiry. As to the first period of delay – of ten months – the High Court held that the respondent had been justified in not proceeding because criminal charges were pending against the applicant and, accordingly, to go ahead might have prejudiced the applicant or caused unnecessary expense. During the second period – eight months – the Commissioner had initiated action under one regulation but then was legally advised that his remedy lay under a different regulation. This was not an unconscionable delay, in the view of Morris J., since: ". . . it would be unreal to suggest that the Commissioner was not moving towards a resolution of this case during that period. . . ." (at 435). For the next seven months, matters proceeded steadily until January 1993 when the appropriate notices were served on the applicant. Then, nine days later, the Supreme Court gave judgment in *McGrath v. Commissioner of An Garda Síochána*, unreported, Supreme Court, January 26, 1993. This ruling necessitated the taking of legal advice and the revision of the charges. Fresh charges were served seven months later ("entirely reasonable" at 435) and, eventually, a date for hearing was scheduled in January, 1994.

The central part of the judgment included the observation, by way of contrast, that the approach to be adopted where delay occurs in the context of criminal proceedings was *sui generis*. Speaking in the context of the instant (non-criminal) case, the judge stated at p. 436:

"I am, accordingly, of the view that while four and a half years approximately have elapsed since the time when these matters were first brought to the notice of the applicant, the applicant has not established to my satisfaction that the respondents have been guilty of any conduct for which they could reasonably be criticised and, accordingly, I am satisfied that the case falls into the category of cases where the onus clearly rests upon the applicant to establish to the satisfaction of the court that prejudice, on the balance of probabilities, will arise in the conduct of his defence to the allegations made against him."

The judge thus laid down a two-stage test: first, could the conduct of the respondent public body reasonably be criticised; if not – as in the present case – can the applicant show prejudice (as he could not, on the facts of *McNeill*). The applicant had argued that he had been specifically prejudiced by the delay in that a member of the executive committee of the Garda Representative Association who had knowledge of the practice and procedures of the Gardaí in Donegal (where the applicant was stationed) had died three years after the investigation had commenced. However, the Court found that other members of the force (though not necessarily members of the Association) would have similar knowledge.

McNeill is a slightly troublesome case to reconcile with the earlier case law. For it, quotes *McGowan* with approval; distinguishes the position in regard to delay in criminal proceedings (summarised below) from that in the field of public administration; and, on its own facts, takes a lenient view of a four year delay. Yet, on the other hand, the passage just quoted clearly contemplates, more or less out of clear blue sky that delay could, even in the absence of prejudice to the applicant, be a ground for invalidating an administrative decision provided that "the respondents have been guilty of any conduct for which they could reasonably be criticised".

[188] [1987] I.R. 68. See also, *C. v. The Legal Aid Board* [1991] 2 I.R. 43 at 56 where Gannon J. granted a declaration that the Board was obliged to consider the applicant's claim for civil legal aid within

was suspected of stealing letters and parcels. He had remained suspended for nearly three years until the Supreme Court decision in the instant case, in 1987. He lived on social welfare benefits and a distress fund organised by his union. In July 1984 the Director of Public Prosecutions decided to prosecute the plaintiff on indictment. The solicitor for An Post, who was also acting for the D.P.P., then wrote to the plaintiff to say that An Post would not bring the disciplinary action against the plaintiff until the criminal trial was over. A significant fact in the case was that, at this and all other stages, the plaintiff wished to press ahead with the disciplinary investigation. However, McCarthy J., with whose judgment three of the other judges concurred, stated:

> "In the High Court [in the instant case] it was held that the plaintiff's right to silence might be lost or he might be otherwise prejudiced in the criminal trial if the investigation had proceeded. Without expressing any view as to the nature of an alleged right to silence, in my judgment, if an accused in a criminal proceeding wishes to embark upon a course which may damage him in the manner suggested, it is no function of his employer, who is not the prosecutor (although the confusion of the two is understandable because of the D.P.P.'s choice of solicitor) to protect him from the consequences of such a course. There may be circumstances in which it would be proper to postpone an investigation pending a criminal trial; I am unable to prescribe them in a case where an employee is suspended without pay and wants the investigation to proceed; in so far as the observations of Woolf J. in *Reg. v. British Broadcasting Corporation ex parte Lavelle* [1983] 1 W.L.R. 23 at p. 36 suggests that it is a matter of ordinary discretion, weighing in the balance of several relevant factors, I would not accept it as a correct statement of the law applicable in this country."[189]

The plaintiff's criminal trial, which resulted in his acquittal on all charges, was held in November 1985. The provision under which he was suspended, section 13 of the Civil Service Regulation Act 1956, simply states that: "A suspending authority may

---

a reasonable time. Likewise, in *Philips v. Medical Council* [1991] 2 I.R. 115 at 143, *per* Costello J. said that the Council was under a "statutory duty to determine the plaintiff's application [for registration] within a reasonable time. It . . . has no lawful excuse which justifies this failure. I think a reasonable time for the consideration of the application was three months." See also *Re Gallagher's Application (No. 2)* [1996] 3 I.R. 15 and *HMIL Ltd v. Minister for Agriculture*, unreported, High Court, February 8, 1996 (similar principles).

[189] *Ibid.* at 82. On the delay point, the dissenting judge, Henchy J. was broadly in agreement with the other judges. However, he did contemplate (at 76–77) that there might be circumstances in which although an employee waives his rights as defendant-to-be he could not necessarily plead delay (*e.g.* if a strike were likely if dismissal occurred before the trial).

For the purposes of the future development of the law, the delay point is the more important part of *Flynn*. However, the point on which majority members of the court departed from Henchy J. is also of some practical interest. This point arose out of the fact that, in July 1984, the plaintiff had initiated the present plenary proceedings, claiming, *inter alia*, a declaration that his suspension was *ultra vires*. This fact was the ground of Henchy J.'s dissent in *Flynn*, where he stated (at 77–78) that it was "reasonable and proper for An Post to postpone the inquiry, for it might have proved to be unnecessary, futile and in conflict with the jurisdiction of the High Court." Rejecting this argument, McCarthy J., effectively writing for the majority, stated (at 84): "that the matters about which the enquiry would be concerned were wholly removed from the matters under consideration in the action itself." This surely underestimates the respect that all other institutions are required to pay to courts and also the surprising turn which court cases often take.

suspend a civil servant. . . ." In the circumstances, McCarthy J. held that: "To construe section 13 of the Act of 1956 as authorising a suspending authority to suspend without pay an employee of the company for a period of eighteen months does not appear to me to be a reasonable construction of the section nor one permissible within the constitutional framework."[190]

McCarthy J. went on to hold that the suspension ceased to be valid in August 1984, which was the date when An Post should have been ready to proceed with the formal investigation if they had not postponed the proceedings until the criminal trial was concluded. Accordingly he made a declaration to that effect and a consequential order for the payment of the plaintiff's salary from August 1984 to date.

Flynn could be read as supporting the proposition that any unjustifiable delay renders a decision or procedure invalid.[191] Alternatively, it could be taken as confirming the narrower view hazarded at the start of this section, namely that delay only renders a decision invalid where the delay has caused prejudice to the applicant. On this latter analysis, the way in which the applicant in Flynn had been prejudiced is that his suspension had forced him to live without wages for a long period. *Flynn* was interpreted by Costello J. in this second sense and then distinguished, on the facts, in *Myers v. Commissioner of the Garda Síochána.*[192] The factual background to *Myers* was similar to that in *Flynn.* In *Myers,* the applicant's superiors had become concerned at the number of unexecuted warrants (to the aggregate value of £2,664) which had been issued in respect of District Court fines and held by the applicant for collection. As a result, in early 1984, summonses were issued against the applicant involving charges of embezzlement, false pretences and forgery. The applicant was not tried until November 1986 when he was either acquitted, in respect of all counts, or charges were withdrawn by the Director of Public Prosecutions. After the summonses had been issued and thereafter up to the date of the present proceedings, the applicant had been suspended, under the Garda Síochána (Discipline) Regulations 1971, for repeated periods of three months each. Soon after the applicant's acquittal, the procedure for an investigation into the alleged breaches of discipline, arising out of the matters on which he had been acquitted, was initiated.[193] The applicant's first claim, following *Flynn,* was that his continued suspension for over two years pending the outcome of the criminal prosecution was unconstitutionally unfair. This submission was rejected – and *Flynn* distinguished – on two grounds. In the first place, in *Myers* the applicant has been receiving suspension pay of two-thirds of

---

190 *Ibid.* at 83.
191 There may also be some support for this proposition in *O'Flynn v. The Mid Western Health Board* [1989] I.R. 429 at 439. The case involved complaints against medical practitioners participating in the general medical services scheme (see p. 366). Whilst not making any finding regarding delay in the instant case, Barr J. stated:
"... injustice might well result if there is unreasonable delay on the part of a health board in notifying a general medical practitioner of complaints made against him. He should be given an opportunity to investigate and answer such charges as soon as practicable after they have been made to the health board."
(*A contra: Cannon v. Minister for the Marine* [1991] I.L.R.M. 261 at 265–267, where counsel for the Minister conceded that a delay of six months was unreasonable. Barr J. raised possibility of damages but only provided that the delay had caused loss).
192 Unreported, High Court, January 22, 1988.
193 *cf.* "The longest river winds somewhere safe to sea". Tennyson's *The Brook.*

his basic salary; whereas the applicant in *Flynn* had received nothing from his employers. Secondly, (as mentioned) it was a cardinal point, in *Flynn*, that the suspended employee had demanded that an internal inquiry might have prejudiced his defence in the pending criminal prosecution. By contrast, in *Myers*, there was no request that an immediate disciplinary inquiry be held.[194]

Next, there is one case (with rather extreme facts), in which a plea of delay succeeded, although it probably involved too specialised an area for any worthwhile general principle to emerge. This is the case of *Van Nierop v. Commissioners for Public Works*[195] which involved a notice of compulsory acquisition and the ensuing notice to treat, under the Fishery Harbour Centres Act 1968. There had been about 15 years' delay between the first notice and the present action and it was conceded, even by the Commissioners, that this could mean that the notices ceased to be valid (even though no time limit was fixed by the Act). This appears to have been grounded on the basis of equity and/or the intention of the legislature.

In summary one could say that the majority of Irish cases have still taken the view that for delay to succeed, actual prejudice must be shown.[196] However, there is also some minority, judicial support[197] for the view that absence of justification for the delay by the public body will be significant, either as a supplementary factor or possibly even as a ground of invaliditity in its own right.

Different considerations plainly apply where something is said, regarding timeliness, in the Act or procedural rules, regulating the decision. An example is *McNeill v. The Commissioner of An Garda Síochána*[198] which concerned a delay of seven years in the holding of disciplinary proceedings against a Garda under the Garda Síochána (Discipline) Regulations 1989. Holding the disciplining void, Hamilton C.J. stated:

> "The use in the regulations of phrases 'as soon as practicable', 'as soon as may be' and 'without avoidable delay', clearly indicate the intention of the Minister for Justice, as expressed in the said regulations, that the alleged breaches of discipline by members of the Garda Síochána be dealt with expeditiously and as a matter of urgency".

---

[194] *Ibid.* at p. 6 of the judgment. In addition, the applicant in *Myers* had a second claim (of which there was no equivalent in *Flynn*). This related not to the suspension itself, but to the disciplinary proceedings which had been initiated after the termination of the criminal prosecution. The applicant sought an order to prohibit these proceedings, too, on the ground of delay. This failed on the basis that no arguments had been advanced to show that the delay in this case had caused such prejudice that a disciplinary inquiry would be unfair

[195] [1990] 2 I.R. 189. See, to similar effect, *Grace Grice v. Dudley Corporation* [1958] Ch. 329 at 339. *A contra: P.J. Smyth v. Dublin Corporation* 89 I.L.T.R. 1.

[196] Contrast the jurisprudence of the European Court of Human Rights which seems to focus on the issue of whether the delay is justifiable (for instance, by reference to some legitimate necessity of the bureaucracy); rather than on the issue of whether the individual has been prejudiced: Harris, O'Boyle and Warbrick, *op. cit.*, above, 69, pp. 222–230.

[197] See *Flynn* above and *McNeill* which is analysed, above, pp. 581–582.

[198] [1997] 1 I.R. 469, 482, *McNeill* was distinguished in *McAuley v. Chief Superintendent Keating*, unreported, High Court, July 8, 1997, another Garda discipline case in which the delay was only one year.

Delay in court cases

It would, thus, be premature to enunciate any general doctrine of delay in regard to administrative decisions. However, in what is conventionally regarded as the more important (to the individual) area of court cases, pleas of delay have been more successful.

It is well-established that in the criminal field,[199] the right to trial in due course of law includes in principle, the right to an expeditious trial,[200] whether the trial was a trial on indictment or in principle[201] summary proceedings. Delay in the context of criminal cases, has been grounded on Article 38.1 of the Constitution[202] and such delay lies outside the proper boundaries of the present book. Accordingly this topic will be mentioned only briefly here (as a basis of comparison). For this reason, we shall focus upon delay between the date of the alleged offence and the date of the hearing (and we shall not consider, for instance, the time limit – imposed by statute[203] in the case of summary prosecutions – between the date of the offence and the time when the complaint is laid). The general precept has been confirmed by three Supreme Court cases, decided in March-June, 1994[204] the gist of that although there is no clear rule for determining whether the lapse of time is excessive, a court should take into account the nature of the offence; the cause of the delay, and whether the defence will be prejudiced. In other words, the essential point of distinction between criminal and administrative law cases is that if a delay is excessive, prejudice appears to be only one of the factors which was to be taken into account and the others, on their own, may suffice to invalidate the conviction.

In two of these three cases – *Cahalane v. Murphy*[205] and *Hogan v. The President of the Circuit Court*[206] – a unanimous Supreme Court upheld the decision of the High Court that a lower court was correct in dismissing charges on the ground of

---

199 In the civil field, see the rather extreme case of, *O'Keefe v. Commissioners of Public Works*, unreported, Supreme Court, March 24, 1980. In this case, the plaintiff sought to bring an action for damages in respect of an industrial accident which had occurred some 24 years earlier. Although a plenary summons had been issued within the three-year limitation period, the plaintiff took no steps to proceed with the action until some 17 years later. During that period he had accepted lump sum compensation from the defendants in discharge of all liability under the Workmen's Compensation Acts. Henchy J. took the view that the plaintiff should be estopped from proceeding with his claim, as a hearing in these circumstances would be contrary to natural justice.
See, to similar effect, *O'Domhnaill v. Merrick* [1984] I.R. 151 at 157–158 and *Toal v. Duignan (No. 2)* [1991] I.L.R.M. 140 at 142–143; *Primar Plc v. Stokes Kennedy Crowley* [1996] 2 I.R. 459 at 475.
200 *The State (O'Connell) v. Fawsitt* [1986] I.R. 362 at 379.
201 *D.P.P. v. Byrne* [1994] 2 I.R. 236.
202 For a general survey of "due course of law" and its many facets, see Hogan and Whyte, *Kelly, The Irish Constitution* (3rd ed., 1994), pp. 572–623.
203 Petty Sessions (Ireland) Act 1851, s. 10(4). See also *Hogan v. The President of the Circuit Court* [1994] 2 I.R. 513 at 521 where Finlay C.J. expressly rejected the submission that in considering whether the right to an early trial had been infringed the court was confined to examining the date on which the accused had been charged and the date of the trial itself.
204 See to like effect, *EO'R v. D.P.P.* [1996] 2 I.L.R.M. 128.
205 [1994] 2 I.R. 262. The charges in this case arose out of an investigation conducted by officials from the Revenue and Customs authorities between 1986 and 1991 into an alleged scheme whereby an alcohol based animal rub manufactured by the applicant – and for which purpose he had access to large quantities of duty-free alcohol – was being treated and sold on to publicans as whiskey and vodka for human consumption, thereby resulting in large losses to the Revenue in unpaid excise duties.
206 [1994] 2 I.R. 513.

delay. In the remaining case, *D.P.P. v. Byrne*,[207] the Supreme Court, with the same composition, rejected by a majority of three to two a defence based on delay.[208] However the significant point is that here, too, the majority adopted the principle outlined earlier in the previous paragraph.

A final feature of this trio of cases which is of interest is that they held that in determining whether a delay is unreasonable, it is irrelevant that the delay (or some part of it) is attributable to a state authority (like the Revenue Commissioners) over which the prosecution had no control. It remains to be seen how, in an analogous case, this would transfer to the field of public administration.

Double jeopardy

One ought to note the final argument in *Myers* – namely, double jeopardy – which although it is not, strictly speaking, related to delay, can often arise in conjunction with it. On this point, Costello J. stated:

> "Nor have any submissions been advanced to support the claim . . . that the proposed inquiry is invalid because it would amount 'to double jeopardy' – for good reason, because the *Flynn* case clearly shows that the dismissal of criminal charges against an employee is not in itself a bar to subsequent disciplinary proceedings arising out of the same set of facts, and no special circumstances creating such a bar have been shown to exist in this case."[209]

Speaking at a high level of abstraction, the fate of this argument is in line with the finding in *McGowan* (the facts of which were mentioned above[210]) that the fact that one set of abortive disciplinary proceedings had already been initiated was no necessary reason for holding that a later set was invalid.

Waiver

The question of waiver, by the individual affected, is an important issue which has received even less attention in the context of the *audi alteram partem* rule than in other contexts.[211] The issue was treated briefly in *Carroll v. Minister for Agriculture and Food*[212] which arose when, following the statutory procedure, the local veterinary inspector declared one of the applicant's cows to be a reactor and his farm to be a restricted holding. Blayney J. held:

> ". . . The applicant's criticism of the manner in which Mr. Lynch [a veterinary surgeon] carried out the test is not really relevant. No such criticism had been

---

207 [1994] 2 I.R. 263.
208 The difference between the majority and the minority was that the majority held that the onus is on a defendant, if he seeks to have a case dismissed, to satisfy a court that there are grounds for doing so; the minority held that the onus is on the prosecution to justify a delay. This point was not raised in the later cases. In addition, the majority and minority disagreed on their characterisation of the facts, with the majority holding that the period of ten months between commission and trial did not amount to an unreasonable delay.
209 p. 7 of the judgment in *Myers*. For *Myers*, see pp. 583–584.
210 See pp. 580–581.
211 On the issue of waiver and *nemo iudex*, see pp. 536–537.
212 [1991] 1 I.R. 230.

made by the applicant at the time [when the local veterinary inspector] made his decision. Accordingly, [the Minister] was perfectly entitled to act on Mr Lynch's finding. There was no reason why he should have any doubt about its accuracy. There was no obligation on him to investigate how Mr. Lynch had carried out the test. The position might have been different if, before making his decision, the applicant had questioned the manner in which Mr. Lynch had carried out the test. In the absence of any such complaint it was perfectly normal for him to rely on Mr. Lynch's finding."[213]

To turn next to a point which will often arise: in *O'Brien v. Bord na Móna*,[214] the High and Supreme Court explicitly left open the possibility that waiver would only be deemed to have occurred on actual notice or following the sending of an individual, specific notification. (On the facts of *O'Brien*, this question did not arise since it was admitted that the plaintiff had received actual notice by way of the newspaper advertisement.) Again, in *Glover v. B.L.N. Ltd*[215] a case involving the removal of an office-holder whose office was founded on contract, Walsh J. explicitly left open the question, which did not arise on the facts of the case, of the extent to which the rules of natural justice could have been excluded by express provision in the contract. In *Flanagan*, it was stated that the plaintiff's "informed consent"[216] would have been required to validate the selection of an independent moderator to determine whether her thesis included plagiarism. However neither in *Flanagan* nor elsewhere has this phrase been defined.

We have already mentioned the case of *The State (D) v. Groarke*[217] in which the Supreme Court held that a District Judge's warrant for the removal of a child, who had allegedly been abused, to a "place of safety" (Childrens Act 1908, section 24(i) was procedurally flawed. The aspect of the case which is relevant for present purposes is that the prosecutor had failed to complain about these flaws. As to this omission, Finlay C.J. remarked:

"... If the proceedings in the District Court in this case were fully adversarial in character, then the absence of any application for a further adjournment; the absence of any complaint about the late delivery of medical or other professional reports and the failure to request the showing of the video on behalf of the prosecutors would almost certainly make these complaints

---

213 *Ibid.* at 234–235.
214 [1983] I.R. 255 at 276 (Keane J.) and 287 (Finlay P.). See also *Re Mountcharles's Estate* [1935] I.R. 163, where the only notice of the Land Commission decision which determined the ownership of mining rights was that published in *Iris Oifigiúil*. Finding that these procedures were in breach of *audi alteram partem*, Kennedy C.J. commented ironically ([1935] I.R. 166): "[T]he Land Commission purported to give themselves power to determine questions submitted by the Minister behind the backs of interested parties ... while the very fact of such "determination" is not brought to their notice unless they happen to be members of that comparatively small and very select class of persons, the regular readers of *Iris Oifigiúil*." In *Gammell v. Dublin County Council* [1983] I.L.R.M. 413 (for facts on which see pp. 567–568) no point was taken about the need to notify the plaintiff (See 2nd edition of this book at pp. 470–471.)
215 [1973] I.R. 388 at 425. See further, pp. 767–768. *Cf. The State (Boyle) v. General Medical Services (Payments) Board* [1981] I.L.R.M. 14 at 15.
216 [1989] I.L.R.M. 469 at 476.
217 [1988] I.R. 187 (High Ct.); [1990] I.R. 305 (Sup. Ct.). See p. 510, n.79.

unsustainable on behalf of the prosecutors. These proceedings were not, however, in the view of this Court, fully adversarial in nature, since a dominant issue in them which had to be investigated was the welfare of this child."[218]

This rather brief passage appears to be based on the view that waiver does not apply, at any rate at its full rigour, where more than two interests are involved in a decision. This is curious. In the first place, such multi-polarity is a common feature of decisions in the field of public administration. Secondly, surely it was the interest of the prosecutor in the case, rather than the welfare of the child, which pulled in favour of applying natural justice.[219]

4. Types of Decisions which Attract the Rules of Constitutional Justice

It is generally assumed that the two rules of natural justice are co-extensive in their application.[220] This assumption is questionable, given the differing nature and function of the rules. Bias is a particularly heinous defect likely to lead to a general erosion of confidence in the administrative system, whereas the failure to grant a hearing does not appear to be such a fundamental flaw. Reflecting this broader reach, the no-bias limb of constitutional justice shades off into the rule against exercise of discretionary power in bad faith,[221] with the result that the rule against bias applies in some form to almost all decisions by public authorities. In contrast, the *audi alteram partem* rule of its nature applies to a more limited range of decisions – essentially decisions raising issues of fact or law rather than matters of policy. Again, it has been stated that the rules of natural justice do not apply where this would defeat the object of the administrative power.[222] Of its nature, this restriction is more likely to apply to *audi alteram partem* than to the no-bias rule.[223] However, these caveats notwithstanding, both rules will generally apply to the situations described in this Part.

Let us now list the categories of decision which have been held – or, more usually, assumed – to attract the rules.

---

[218] [1990] 1 I.R. at 310–11.

[219] Unless one takes the view that the major objective of constitutional justice is the discovery of truth; on this see Part 5.

[220] Clarke, "Natural Justice: Substance or Shadow?" [1975] *Public Law* 27.

[221] See pp. 628–631. For a good example of where the wrongful exercise of discretionary power was regarded as tantamount to bias: see *The State (McGeough) v. Louth County Council* (1973) 107 I.L.T.R. 13.

[222] *O'Callaghan v. Commissioners of Public Works* (1985) I.L.R.M. 364.

[223] But *cf.* the comments of Keane J. in *Mooney v. An Post* [1994] E.L.R. 103 at 116: "The two great central principles *audi alteram partem* and *nemo iudex in causa sua* cannot be applied in a uniform fashion to every set of facts. To take the most obvious example, the *nemo iudex* requirement cannot be literally applied to every employer confronted with a decision as to whether or not he should dismiss a particular employee. If it were, an employer could never dismiss an employee, since he would always be an interested party in the decision." This observation is presumably an illustration of the necessity doctrine, on which see pp. 628–631.

(i) Public and private employment

Historically, there were two distinctions of crucial importance for employment law. Office-holders (or officers) were distinguished from employees (servants), and, secondly, the category of office-holders was divided into two classes according to whether the holder was dismissible at pleasure or whether he could only be removed for cause. It was only the office-holder removable for cause who enjoyed the protection of the natural justice principles.

It seems plain that the second distinction is no longer part of the law. In *Garvey v. Ireland*[224] the Commissioner of the Garda Sióchàna argued successfully that his summary dismissal from office by the Government was contrary to natural justice. Of the four judges who comprised the majority, O'Higgins C.J. (with whom Parke J. agreed) decided that the office was not held merely at pleasure, but also concluded that this distinction was no longer significant. Henchy and Griffin JJ. classified the office as one held at pleasure, yet found that the rules of natural justice applied to any decision to dismiss.

It seems, too, that the distinction between an office-holder and an employee has ceased to be significant in the present context;[225] though it may be worth explaining it briefly. The office is the legal form for a "superior" post (which was, in past centuries, even regarded as a property-right of the holder). An office is a position to which certain important duties are attached, usually of a more or less public character, with its holder likely to be better qualified and freer from day-to-day control than a servant. It thus plays a pivotal part in the administration of government, whether at central or local level, or sometimes in the administration of a company or other corporation. In addition: "[An office] is created by Act of the National Parliament, charter, statutory regulation, articles of association of a company or of a body corporate formed under the authority of a statute, deed of trust, grant or by prescription."[226] By contrast, the master-servant relationship is usually founded exclusively upon a contract. It should be stressed, though, that even an office-holder may – and usually does – have a contract, which fixes a great part of his conditions. Finally, a servant may occupy a temporary, personal post whilst an office: "must have a sufficient degree of continuance to admit of its being held by successful incumbents . . . it cannot be limited to the tenure of one man, for if it were so, it would lack that independent existence which to my mind the word 'office' imports."[227]

The continuing validity of the distinction between an officer and an employee in the context of the *audi alteram* rule was questioned by the Supreme Court in *Glover v. B.L.N. Ltd,*[228] which arose from the dismissal of a company director for alleged misconduct and was, thus, in the field of private law. The dismissal was invalidated as the plaintiff had not been given a fair hearing by the board of the

---

224 [1981] I.R. 75.
225 There are of course many other contexts in which the distinction is significant. The distinction still appears to have relevance as far as the court's power to order reinstatement in cases of wrongful dismissal is concerned (but *cf. Glover v. B.L.N. Ltd* [1973] I.R. 388 at 427) and also for tax purposes: *Edwards v. Clinch* [1982] A.C. 845.
226 *per* Kenny J. in *Glover v. B.L.N. Ltd* [1973] I.R 388 at 414.
227 *per* Lord Wilberforce in *Edwards v. Clinch* [1982] A.C. 845 at 860.
228 [1973] I.R. 388. See O'Reilly, "The Constitution and the Law of Contract" (1973) 8 Ir. Jur.(N.S.) 197.

company. In the High Court, Kenny J. adopted the traditional English view that the rules of natural justice apply to the removal of an office-holder but not a servant, and held that the rules applied in the instant case because the plaintiff was characterised as being an office-holder. However, Walsh J., writing on behalf of the Supreme Court majority, stated:

> "[O]nce the matter is governed by the terms of a contract between the parties, it is immaterial whether the employee concerned is deemed to be a servant or an officer [because] public policy and the dictates of constitutional justice require that statutes, regulations or agreements setting up machinery for taking decisions which may affect right or impose liabilities should be construed as providing for fair procedures."[229]

However, *Glover* left a number of loose ends. In the first place, the contract of service in the case included a clause which expressly stated that a hearing would take place prior to any dismissal for misconduct, thus making it possible for the court to impute a term to the effect that any such hearing or inquiry should be fairly conducted. Consequently the *excursus* into the broader reaches of constitutional justice was *obiter*. Secondly, Walsh J. explicitly left open the questions of the situation where the relationship between the parties was not grounded in either contract or statute and the extent to which the rules could be excluded by express agreement. Finally, and most significantly, the passage quoted depends upon the impregnation of contract law by constitutional principles.

Several High Court decisions[230] showed judicial reluctance to follow this innovatory approach. The judges in these cases were naturally pressed, by counsel for the plaintiff, with the authority of *Glover*. This case was distinguished by confining it to its own facts, namely where there was a term in the contract under which the officer/employee was entitled to the benefit of constitutional justice.

The guantlet, thus thrown down, was picked up by the Supreme Court in *Gunn v. Bord na Choláiste Náisiúnta Ealaine is Deartha*[231] which appears finally to have extirpated the distinction between an employee and and an office-holder and which *Gunn* has frequently been followed.[232] So much for authority. As regards principle

---

[229] [1973] I.R. 425 at 427. See, to like effect, the comments of McWilliam J. in *Garvey v. Ireland* [1981] I.R. 75 at 82.

[230] In addition to those to be mentioned in the text, these include: *Heneghan v. The Western Regional Fisheries Board* [1986] I.L.R.M. 225 at 228; *Connolly v. McConnell* [1983] I.R. 172 at 178.
Lupton v. Allied Irish Banks Ltd (1983) 2 J.I.S.S.L. 107; *N.E.E.T.U. v. McConnell* (1983) 2 J.I.S.S.L. 97 and *Connolly v. McConnell* [1983] I.R. 172. These authorities are critiqued in the 2nd edition of this book at pp. 273–274.

[231] [1990] 2 I.R. 168. At the same time, it must be said that there were two features of the case which slightly undermine its authority as a precedent. First, Walsh J. made it clear that on the facts in *Gunn* a disciplinary scheme *had* been incorporated in the relationship between the National College and its staff. Secondly, Walsh J. held that the plaintiff was, in any case, an office-holder by virtue of s.1(3). (The provision states that: "an officer of An Bord includes a member of the academic staff of the College.") McCarthy J. also reasoned that as the plaintiff was a member of the academic staff, consequently he must be an officer. Strictly speaking these factors may render what the Supreme Court had to say on the question of the officer-employee distinction obiter. On the other hand, the Court's statements on this matter were well-considered and intended to be followed.

[232] *e.g. O'Neill v. Beaumont Hospital Board* [1990] I.L.R.M. 419; *Cooney v. An Post*, unreported, High Court, April 6, 1990; *Hickey v. Eastern Health Board* [1991] 1 I.R. 208 at 211. See also the classic authority of *Maunsell v. Minister for Education* [1940] I.R. 213 in which this distinction was not mentioned.

too, it is submitted that the *Glover-Gunn* line represents the appropriate out-come. On policy grounds, the modern view is that all means of livelihood are so important to the person to whom they belong that dismissal should require a fair procedure. On the technical plane, the distinction between an office-holder and a servant is "abstruse and verging on the asinine or bizarre."[233] Indeed in *Gunn*, the Supreme Court reversed the High Court on the question of whether the plaintiff was an officer, without either court offering a very rigorous analysis of the problem. Moreover, it is usually the case that even with an office-holder, the bulk of the terms of employment are fixed by contract, rather than statute, deed of trust, etc., a factor which erodes the basis of the distinction.

To what extent must *Gunn* now be read in the light of the comments of Barrington J. in *Mooney v. An Post*?[234] The judge first paid homage to *Gunn* in these terms:

> "It appears to me that what the Court was saying [in *Gunn*] is that society is not divided into two classes, one of whom – office holders – is entitled to the protection of the principles of natural and constitutional justice and the other of whom – employees – is not. Dismissal . . . with possible loss of pensions rights and damage to one's good name may, in modern society, be disastrous for any citizen. These are circumstances in which any citizen, however humble, may be entitled to the protection of natural and constitutional justice."

Having drawn attention to the difficulties which attend the application of the principles of constitutional justice – especially the *nemo iudex* rule – to the employer/employee situation, Barrington J. continued:

> "If the contract or statute governing a person's employment contains procedure whereby the employment may be terminated it will usually be sufficient for the employee to show that he has complied with this procedure. If the contract or statute contains a provision whereby an employee is entitled to a hearing before an independent board or arbitrator before he can be dismissed then clearly that independent board or arbitrator must conduct the relevant proceedings with due respect to the principles of natural and constitutional justice."[235]

However, Barrington J. agreed that given the nature of the employee-employer relationship, it is inherently difficult in practice to employ these elaborate procedures where the contract or statute specified that the employee might be dismissed for misconduct but yet does not specify any particular procedure:

> "Certainly the employee . . . is entitled to the benefit of fair procedures, but what these demand will depend upon the terms of his employment and the circumstances. . . . Certainly the minimum he is entitled to is to be informed of the charge against him and to be given an opportunity to answer it and to make submissions."

---

[233] de Smith, (4th ed., 1980) *op. cit.* above, n.66, p. 228. The distinction appears to have a rather fitful existence in England: see de Smith, (5th ed., 1995) pp. 227–233; Wade and Forsyth, *op. cit.* above, n.72, pp. 566–568. For the distinction in the context of nurses, see *Western Health Board v. Quigley* [1982] I.L.R.M. 390 followed in *Hickey v. Eastern Health Board* [1991] 1 I.R. at 211.

[234] Unreported, Supreme Court, March 20, 1997.

[235] For a later application of these principles, see now *Maher v. Irish Permanent plc*, unreported, High Court, August 27, 1997.

On the facts, the plaintiff had been given every opportunity to make his case. However, the plaintiff had not raised any issue requiring an oral hearing before an independent adjudicator, so that the Court did not have to consider what the position would have been had that occurred. However Barrington J. appears to have suggested that this would not have been necessary.[236] On the one hand, *Mooney* appears to re-open the office-holder/employee distinction. On the other hand (and it is submitted – the better point of view) *Mooney* merely emphasises the general point, considered earlier, that the standard of constitutional justice varies depending upon the circumstances, including (and this admittedly is a development of the law) whether the relevant terms of employment provide for such independent adjudication.[237]

The grounds for applying the *audi alteram partem* principle in the general area (*i.e.* not just public) of employment[238] are plural (carrying the possibility of an overlap between more than one, in any given situation). As can be seen from the case law just summarised, in addition to the Constitution, there may be a contract with an express or (more usually) implied term establishing fair procedures. Also, there is the Unfair Dismissals Acts 1977–1993, for it is now accepted that a fair dismissal requires the observance of the rules of natural justice.[239] There are, however, two restrictions on the impact of these Acts. First, it is possible that the natural justice rules, derived as a gloss on the statute, may have a different content from that of common law/constitutional natural justice, in that for instance, under the Act, it is necessary to balance up procedural and substantive justice. Secondly, the Act's protection extends among public sector employees, to all employees of semi-state bodies (apart from AnCo trainees and apprentices) and to the servants (as opposed to officers) of local authorities, vocational education committees and health boards. However, about one-fifth of the working population, most of whom are in public employment, are expressly excluded from the Act's field of operation.[240] Most, but not all, of those excluded have some other form of procedural protection against dismissal. Thus, for instance, of those excluded: officers of local authorities have a special statutory fair dismissal system under the Local Government Act 1941;[241] members of the Defence Forces and of the Garda Síochána are office-holders and hence, certainly may only be removed in accordance with the principles of

---

236 Barrington J. commented:
    "It is necessary also to consider the position of An Post. They were not in a position to set up an independent tribunal with power to subpoena witness even had they wished to do so."
    But *cf. O'Neill v. Beaumont Hospital Board* [1990] I.LR.M. 419 at 428–431 where such independent proceedings were set up by consent.
237 On this point, see further: "margin of appreciation" at pp. 607–608.
238 See, generally, Forde, *Employment Law*, (1991), pp. 166–172 and pp. 295–300; Redmond, *Dismissal Law in Ireland* (1982), pp. 62–81. (Though note strangely that Forde at p.167 states that "the operation of the *Nemo iudex* . . . rule in this area is doubtful").
239 See, *e.g. Warner-Lambert v. Tormey*, UD 255/1978; *Hynes v. Frederick Inns* UD 172/1978 and in Redmond, *loc. cit.*, pp. 160–169; and in Madden and Kerr, *Unfair Dismissal Cases and Commentary* (1990), Chap. 6.
240 s.2(1). s.2(1)(*h*) actually excludes "a person employed by or under the State other than persons designated for the time being under s.17 of the Industrial Relations Act 1969." The qualification "other than . . . " catches some 8,000 people, mostly industrial civil servants.
241 ss.24 and 25. See 294 *Dáil Debates*, Col. 480 (November 23, 1976). For an example of the 1941 Act in operation, see *O'Mahony v. Arklow U.D.C.* [1965] I.R. 710.

constitutional justice[242] and relevant disciplinary regulations; and it seems likely that civil servants are in the same position.[243]

Finally, one should note that whilst the great majority of cases happen to have occurred in the public, rather than the private, field, even the constitutional obligation to observe fair procedures (not to mention that which is implicit in the Unfair Dismissals legislation) appears to apply in both of these employment fields (see, for example *Glover v. BLN*). However the distinction between public and private may be important, for instance, in regard to the form of proceedings.[244]

(ii) Membership of trade unions, professional bodies or clubs

As the relationship between the member and the institution concerned is often grounded ultimately in contract, one is again faced with the question of how the rules of constitutional justice may be interpolated. A conceptually satisfactory answer to this difficult question has yet to be given, but for the moment the courts are content to construe the contract of membership as containing an implied term that fair procedures will be observed.[245] Different considerations, of course, arise in the case of professional bodies exercising *statutory powers*, and there can be no question but that the rules of constitutional justice are applicable to the exercise of such powers.

As illustrated earlier in this and the previous chapter, the content and stringency of the rules of constitutional justice vary enormously depending on 'the circumstances'. Thus, for example, it is likely that the classification into quasi-judicial and administrative functions,[246] would mean that a less rigorous rule would apply in the present context, at least in regard to trade unions and clubs. It is clear, however, that disciplinary action by a trade union,[247] professional body[248] or club[249] cannot be conducted on a summary, *ex parte* basis and the courts have set aside disciplinary actions either because it did not observe the rules of natural justice or because the requirements of the association's own constitution or rules relating to notice had not been complied with.[250] This has been extended even to suspension from a sporting organisation provided that it "involv[ed] the imposition of a substantial sanction."[251] which was, in the case from which this quotation was taken, the disqualification of an international shot-putter from all competition, including the

---

[242] *The State (Gleeson) v. Minister for Defence* [1976] I.R. 280 at 294.
[243] The position of civil servants has already been dealt with at p. 90.
[244] See pp. 765–776
[245] *Fisher v. Keane* (1878) 11 Ch. D. 853; *Dawkins v. Antrobus* (1881) 17 Ch.D. 615; *Flynn v. Grt. N. Ry. Co.* (1955) 89 I.L.T.R. 46; *Doyle v. Croke*, unreported, High Court, May 6, 1988. See p. 499.
[246] See pp. 601–602.
[247] *Kilkenny v. Irish Engineering and Foundry Worker's Union* (1939) Ir Jur.Rep. 52; *N.E.E.T.U. v. McConnell* (1983) 2 J.I.S.L.L. 97; *Connolly v. McConnell* [1983] I.R. 172. See also, Kerr and Whyte, *Irish Trade Union Law* (1985), pp. 113–121.
[248] *Manning v. Incorporated Law Society for Ireland*, unreported, High Court, March 8, 1980; *Re M., a doctor* [1984] I.R. 479; *The State (Boyle) v. General Medical Services (Payment) Board* [1981] I.L.R.M. 14; *O'Donoghue v. Veterinary Council* [1975] I.R. 398; *K. v. An Bord Altranais* [1990] 2 I.R. 396.
[249] *Forde v. Fottrell* (1930) 64 I.L.T.R. 89; *Goggins v. Feeney* (1949) 83 I.L.T.R. 181; *Ahern v. Molyneux* [1965] Ir.Jur.Rep. 59; *Cotter v. Sullivan*, unreported, High Court, April 23, 1980.
[250] *Doyle v. Griffin* [1937] I.R. 93.
[251] *Quirke v. Bord Luthchleas na hÉireann* [1988] I.R. 83 at 88.

Olympic Games, for 18 months. Clauses in such constitutions or rules which provide for automatic forfeiture of membership are probably void as contrary to public policy.[252] This has been the conclusion of the English courts, and given that the Constitution may inform notions of public policy, such reasoning would also seem to apply *a fortiori* in this jurisdiction. A general exception (which is elaborated below)[253] is that the rules of constitutional justice usually do not apply to suspensions from membership for a temporary period.

(iii) Licensing and commercial regulation

The application of the rules of natural justice in this area stems from the desire to protect an individual's livelihood and business interests. The rules of constitutional justice have also been applied to: the revocation or suspension of a taxi driver's licence[254] or a betting permit for a bookmaker[255]; the licensing of agricultural marts[256]; the censorship of publications[257]; the granting of a liquor licence in substitution for demolished licensed premises[258]; the renewal of an annual fishing licence[259] and the granting of product authorisations for pharmaceutical drugs.[260]

(iv) Discipline

Consider two of the leading cases in this area. In the first, *The State (Gleeson) v. Minister for Defence*,[261] the applicant had been summarily dismissed from the Defence Forces following an incident involving a group of soldiers of which he was one. This discharge was quashed by the Supreme Court, as the applicant had not been given an opportunity to meet the case against him or of dealing with the reason for his discharge. By contrast, in *The State (Duffy) v. Minister for Defence*,[262] the applicant had been dismissed from the Navy on the ground of inefficiency. The applicant's argument founded on breach of constitutional justice was rejected and *Gleeson* distinguished because the applicant had been warned as to why his position was in danger and allowed an opportunity to reply. To take another example from

---

252   *Edwards v. S.O.G.A.T.* [1971] Ch. 354. But *cf. Moran v. Workers Union of Ireland* [1943] I.R. 485.
253   See pp. 606–607.
254   *Ingle v. O'Brien* (1975) 109 I.L.T.R. 7; *Moran v. Attorney General* [1976] I.R. 400.
255   *McDonald v. Bord na gCon* [1965] I.R. 217; *The State (Grahame) v. Racing Board*, unreported, High Court, November 22, 1983.
256   *East Donegal Co-Operative Ltd v. Attorney General* [1970] I.R. 317. See also, *Gammell v. Dublin County Council* [1983] I.L.R.M. 413 (licensing of temporary dwellings.)
257   *Irish Family Planning Association v. Ryan* [1979] I.R. 295.
258   *Jaggers Restaurant Ltd v. Ahearne* [1988] I.R. 308.
259   *Slevin v. Shannon Regional Fisheries Board* [1995] 1 I.R. 460.
260   *Genmark Pharma Ltd v. Minister for Health*, unreported, High Court, July 11, 1997.
261   [1976] I.R. 286. This decision has been applied in *Hogan v. Minister for Justice* [1976–1977] I.L.R.M. 184. and *The State (Furey) v. Minister for Defence* [1988] I.L.R.M. 89. See, too, *McDonough v. Minister for Defence* [1991] 2 I.R. 331. *McGrath v. Commissioner of An Garda Síochána (Nos 1 and 2)* [1990] I.L.R.M. 817; [1993] I.L.R.M. 38.
262   [1979] I.L.R.M. 165 on which, see p. 567. See also, *The State (McGarrity) v. Deputy Garda Commissioner* (1978) 112 I.L.T.R. 25 (no obligation to give hearing to recruit Garda who was discharged at the end of his probationary period); *Delaney v. Garvey*, unreported, High Court, March 14, 1978. *Sed quaere* whether *McGarrity* is applicable in the case of a recruit discharged at end of a probationary period on the grounds of misconduct, *Chief Constable of N. Wales Police v. Evans* [1982] 1 W.L.R. 1155; *O'Rourke v. Miller* (1985) 58 A.L.R. 269.

a rather different field: it has been long established that the rules apply to the local government auditors jurisdiction in the field of local government.[263]

One feature of interest in this general area is the doubt over the extent to which one former principle retains vitality, namely the notion that in a disciplined organisation the need for unquestioning obedience to the commands of a superior was regarded as outweighing the advantages of constitutional justice.[264] Even the question of what is a "disciplined organisation" for this purpose is not clear-cut; but it may reasonably be regarded as constituting a spectrum running from (at the top) the prisons and the Defence Forces taking in, next, the Gardaí, the fire services and schools and then tailing off at higher educational institutions. However, over-precision in this area would be very unrealistic. The most that can be said is that, while there is no longer anything like a firm rule, this notion still retains some vitality; it is a factor which, in certain circumstances, will influence certain judges. There is, for instance, High Court authority accepting the argument that special considerations apply in relation to the power of the state to dispense with the services of members of the Defence Forces, of the Garda Síochána and of the prison service "because it is of vital concern to the community as a whole that the members of these services should be completely trustworthy."[265] This factor played a part in *The State (Donnelly) v. Minister for Defence*.[266] In *Donnelly* the applicant had been discharged from the Defence Forces as he was considered to have been a security risk. Some of the incidents in which the applicant was allegedly involved – such as the theft of a machine gun – were so serious that his commanding officer considered that they would warrant a discharge if no satisfactory explanation was forthcoming. Finlay P. agreed that the fact that the disciplinary officer had drafted an application for Donnelly's discharge was "suspicious," but he was satisfied that this was simply a recommendation and that the matter would not have been carried any further if the applicant had given a satisfactory explanation of the incidents in question. Accordingly, Finlay P. ruled that there was a no bias or prejudgment of the issue on the part of the commanding officer. The judge also took the view that in the subsequent interviews the applicant had been given an adequate opportunity to make his own case. Nor was Finlay P. impressed by the argument that the applicant had never been convicted of any offences, whether under military law or the ordinary criminal law, since there was a "clear public necessity" that the military authorities should have the discretion to remove persons considered to be a security risk.

As against this, in *Garvey v. Ireland*, the Supreme Court majority firmly rejected the argument:

> ". . . [t]hat the confidential and sensitive relationship that must necessarily exist between the Government of the day and the head of the national police force requires that the statutory right to remove a Commissioner from office

---

263 *Downey v. O'Brien* [1994] 2 I.L.R.M. 130 at 150. See also pp. 210–211.
264 *R. v. Army Council, ex p. Ravenscroft* [1917] 2 K.B. 504; *Ex p. Fry* [1954] 1 W.L.R. 730. *cf.* "Theirs not to make reply, | Theirs not to reason why, | Theirs but to do and die." (Tennyson, *The Charge of the Light Brigade*.)
265 *The State (Jordan) v. Garda Commissioner* [1987] I.L.R.M. 107, *per* O'Hanlon J.
266 Unreported, High Court, October 9, 1979. See to similar effect, *The State (Jordan) v. Garda Commissioner* [1987] I.L.R.M. 107.

at any time should not be interpreted as being shackled by an obligation to give a reason for its exercise. . . ."[267]

A compromise on the application of constitutional justice in the field of discipline is to say that the rules apply but, at any rate where fundamental interests are not at stake, the standard may be relaxed in the case of a disciplinary body. For example, in *The State (Gallagher) v. Governor of Portlaoise Prison*[268] the applicant's privileges (such as associations with other prisoners and the receipt of letters) had been suspended following a hearing before the Governor when he had been found guilty of relatively minor disciplinary offences. Finlay P. rejected the argument that legal representation was required in this situation: Gallagher had been afforded an opportunity to speak on his own behalf and that sufficed. The judge also referred to the "partly magisterial" nature of the prison governor's functions and seemed to imply that it would be wrong for the courts to impose anything but the most rudimentary procedural standards in the context of prison discipline.[269]

The cases examined so far could, many of them, have been classified under an earlier heading since the sanction was dismissal. It is questionable whether the rules of natural justice apply at all where the punishment involved is the involuntary transfer of personnel. Such transfers are regarded as administrative decisions, and this fact when coupled with the public interest in maintaining the efficiency of the security forces, means that it would probably require something akin to mala fides before such an administrative decision could be successfully challenged.[270] Similarly, it has been held that natural justice does not require a hearing prior to the suspension of a member of the Garda Siochana in the interests of good administration, pending a fuller disciplinary hearing, even though financial loss may be caused as a result.[271] Again, one can say that a further point of distinction which is of particular relevance in discipline cases is that the procedural standards which must be met in cases involving alleged misconduct are higher than in the case of discharges on the grounds of inefficiency.[272]

---

[267] [1981] I.R. 75 at 102, *per* Henchy J. See, to rather similar effect, *Gallagher v. Corrigan*, unreported, High Court, February 1, 1988, p. 11.

[268] Unreported, High Court, May 18, 1977. See also, *The State (Gallagher) v. Governor of Portlaoise Prison*, High Court, April 25, 1983 in which, in regard to the withholding, by the Governor, of letters to bank managers, a politician, and the Registrars of the High Court and the Supreme Court, McMahon J. said: "I am satisfied that in dealing with the prisoner's letters, the Governor was not acting judicially and had no obligation to afford the prisoner a hearing. The Governor's decisions did not involve any disputed questions of fact and were based on his own views as to the requirements of security of the prison." Though note that in *Murtagh v. St. Emer's National School* [1991] 2 I.R. 482 in spite of the extreme facts, Barron J. appeared to accept that the rules applied to a three days' suspension (though it indicated that the court might exercise its discretion to refuse relief on the ground of the trivial nature of the complaint). However, see now p. 607, n.321.

[269] See, to similar effect, *The State (Smullen) v. Duffy* [1980] I.L.R.M. 46.

[270] *The State (Boyle) v. Governor of the Military Detention Barracks* [1980] I.L.R.M. 242; *The State (Smith & Fox) v. Governor of Military Detention Barracks* [1980] I.L.R.M. 208 (prison transfer cases); *Corliss v. Ireland*, unreported, High Court, July 23, 1984 (transfer of Garda). For *Reidy v. Minister for Agriculture*, unreported, High Court, June 1989, see pp. 90–92.

[271] *McHugh v. Garda Commissioner* [1985] I.L.R.M. 606 at 609–610. But this authority may be narrow in its scope: see *Ní Bheoláin v. Dublin V.E.C.*, unreported, High Court, January 28, 1983 (natural justice applies to suspension without pay), and *Flynn v. An Post* [1987] I.R. 68. This topic is examined in more detail at pp. 606–607.

[272] This point was not mentioned in *Duffy*. But in both *Gleeson* and *Collins v. County Cork V.E.C.*,

(v) *Temporary release and parole*

Two cases concerned the parole/release of prisoners, under the Prisoners (Temporary Release) Rules 1960.[273] In neither case was anything said about the notion, just examined, that constitutional justice should be applied in a less stringent form in certain types of disciplinary case. Possibly, the reason for this was that the fundamental right of liberty was involved. In the first of these cases, *The State (Murphy) v. Kielt*,[274] the prosecutor had, after serving four months, been released for the remainder of his sentence. The release was subject to certain conditions including keeping the peace and being of good behaviour during the period of his release. However, whilst on release, the prosecutor was arrested and charged with attempted murder. The Governor "probably acting in a common-sense manner,"[275] treated the arrest on this serious charge as automatically terminating the temporary release. The High Court and, on appeal, the Supreme Court held that this termination was invalid for failure to observe the *audi alteram partem* rule, especially bearing in mind that charges are frequently dropped or not proceeded with. McCarthy J. remarked that while the suspicion regarding the person arrested must be assumed to be based on reasonable grounds, nevertheless the prisoner should be allowed the opportunity of contesting those grounds. Griffin J. added that: "[the grant and termination of a temporary release] are clearly acts which are administrative in nature. An informal procedure is all that is required provided that such procedure is conducted fairly."[276]

By contrast, what had happened in *Ryan v. Governor of Limerick Prison*[277] was not that a release was terminated; but that no release was granted. In September 1988 the applicant had been granted a series of brief temporary releases, culminating in one from September 30 to October 7 which had been, accompanied by indications that his release might be definite, (*e.g.* information from a welfare officer that he would be making monthly reports on the applicant to the Department of Justice and that the applicant's wife should return her prisoner's allowance book since he had been released from prison.) However the applicant's release was not renewed after October 7 (because, so he was informed by the Governor, there had been a rise in the crime rate in Limerick). In one of the very few cases in which it has ever been held that the rules of constitutional justice did not apply, Murphy J. distinguished sharply between the termination of a release and the refusal of a release (as on the facts here). In the later case, no right to constitutional justice arose because "[t]he temporary release is a privilege or concession to which a person in custody has no

---

unreported, High Court, May 26, 1982 it was said that higher procedural standards were required where some specific act of misconduct or negligence is involved. See also *McDonough v. Minister for Defence* [1991] I.L.R.M. 115. In *Hickey v. The Eastern Health Board* [1991] 1 I.R. 208, it appears to have been held that the rules of constitutional justice did not apply in a case where the applicant had been selected as the person to be made redundant, by the non-renewal of a temporary, part-time contract, in circumstances where there were other staff-members who had entered employment after her; yet who were not selected for redundancy. It was a supporting point in *Hickey* (at p. 212) that the applicant had not been removed for misconduct.

[273] S.I. No. 167 of 1960.
[274] [1984] I.R. 458.
[275] *Ibid.* at 462.
[276] *Ibid.* at 472. See also *Sherlock v. Governor of Mountjoy Prison* [1991] 1 I.R. 451.
[277] [1988] I.R. 198.

right and indeed it has never been argued . . . that he should be heard in relation to any consideration given to the exercise of such a concession in his favour."[278]

(vi) Property and planning

Even at times and in jurisdictions where the bounds of natural justice have been narrowly set, there has never been any doubt that the rules of natural justice apply to state interference with property rights.[279] Thus, the rules have been applied to compulsory purchase orders, and land acquisition procedures; decisions of An Bord Pleanála[280] and even, on one occasion, local planning authorities[281]; the making of a preservation order by the Commissioners of Public Works[282] and the award of a broadcasting contract by the I.R.T.C.[283]

An interesting and novel application of the principles of constitutional justice is to be found in *The State (Philpott) v. Registrar of Titles*.[284] The applicant, who was the registered owner of certain freehold property, was informed that the respondent had entered an inhibition on the folio, which prevented all dealings with the land save with the consent of the respondent.[285] The applicant was engaged in the process

---

[278] *Ibid.* at 199. Murphy J. then went on to make a related point (at 198–199):
". . . a practice appears to have evolved of prison governors . . . granting temporary release for short periods. I think it reasonable to assume that this practice has been adopted by prison governors . . . to overcome or circumvent the problems identified in [*Murphy*]. By abbreviating the duration of temporary releases the prison governor sets himself the task of determining whether or not a fresh release should be granted rather than having to decide whether an existing one should be terminated. Obviously this procedure has the attraction that the former course does not involve any hearing or enquiry . . . whereas the latter does. . . . Because this procedural change has such a dramatic effect I felt it appropriate to consider whether it constituted such a device as amounted to an abuse of the applicant's constitutional rights in the present case. In my view the answer must be in the negative. The temporary release is a privilege or concession to which a person in custody has no right. The fact that the release may be renewed on a number of occasions and not renewed subsequently does not confer any additional or new right on the prisoner."

[279] *Re Mountcharles' Estate* [1934] I.R. 754; *Foley v. Irish Land Commission* [1952] I.R. 118; *Re Roscrea Meat Products Estate* [1958] I.R. 47; *The State (Costello) v. Irish Land Commission* [1959] I.R. 353; *Clarke v. Irish Land Commission* [1976] I.R. 375; *Nolan v. Irish Land Commission* [1981] I.R. 23; *The State (Hussey) v. Irish Land Commission* [1983] I.L.R.M. 407; *O'Brien v. Bord na Móna* [1983] I.R. 255. See also, *Irish Land Commission v. Hession* [1978] I.R. 322 (decision of Land Commission set aside where Commissioners acted on the basis of evidence not properly before them).

[280] *Killiney and Ballybrack Residents Assoc. v. Minister for Local Government* (No. 1) (1978) 112 I.L.T.R. 69. *Geraghty v. Minister for Local Government* [1976] I.R. 153; *The State (Genport Ltd) v. An Bord Pleanála* [1983] I.L.R.M. 12; *The State (Boyd) v. An Bord Pleanála*, unreported, High Court, February 18, 1983; *The State (C.I.É.) v. An Bord Pleanála*, unreported, Supreme Court, December 12, 1984; *The State (Hussey & Kenny) v. An Bord Pleanála*, unreported, Supreme Court, December 20, 1984 and *Frenchurch Properties Ltd v. Wexford County Council* [1992] 2 I.R. 268 (where Lynch J. said that generally a planning authority "is not obliged to enter into a dialogue . . . or to indicate in advance to an applicant the authority's thinking or views before deciding on the application"). However, the judgment goes on to qualify this remark.

[281] *Frenchurch Properties Ltd v. Wexford County Council* [1992] 2 I.R. 268. See pp. 00.

[282] *O'Callaghan v. Commissioners of Public Works* [1985] I.L.R.M. 364.

[283] *Dublin and County Broadcasting Ltd v. I.R.T.C.* unreported, High Court, May 12, 1989; *TV3 v. I.R.T.C.* [1994] 2 I.R. 439.

[284] [1986] I.L.R.M. 499. For another case on property rights, see *Clancy v. Ireland* [1988] I.R. 326 described at p. 607, n.318.

[285] Registration of Title Act 1964, s.120 provides that the State will pay compensation to persons who suffer loss by reason of official errors in registration or entries obtained by fraud or forgery. Section 121 of the Act enables the Registrar to take action by means of the entry of a caution to protect the state from possible claims.

of selling the lands in question when this inhibition had been entered without prior warning or notice. The Registrar had acted following correspondence with certain third parties in which the third parties claimed certain rights over the lands. Gannon J. ruled that because of the grave nature of the interference in the land, natural justice required that persons affected by the entry of an inhibition should be given prior notice and an opportunity to show cause why it should not be entered. The judge accepted that in order to protect the common fund, it would be "imprudent or impractical" to give the owner prior notice and a hearing in urgent cases. He held, however, that the instant case did not fall within this category and, accordingly, quashed the Registrar's decision. It is self-evident that this decision will be of great significance, not only to the Land Registry, but also for other systems of registration.[286]

(vii) Payments of grants, benefits and pensions

There used to be a notion (held, at any rate in Britain) that the rules of constitutional justice did not apply to *privelegia, i.e.* discretionary payments, such as grants, benefits or pensions, to which the applicant had no statutory entitlement. To judge by a steady line of case law[287] in which the point has not even been raised and the rules were applied, the Irish courts have no interest in this restriction (which might not be relevant anyway, since many of these benefits have now been made matters of statutory right).

(viii) Deportation and treatment of aliens

It seems to have been generally accepted[288] that the rules of constitutional justice apply in this context. Indeed, successive counsel for the State appear to have thought it not even worth running any argument grounded on deportation being inherently an area in which the Minister must be allowed a free hand.[289] Take for instance, *Tang v. Minister for Justice*[290] in which it was accepted by the Supreme Court that the usual "principles of natural and constitutional justice"[291] apply (though, on the

---

[286]   *e.g.* the registration of company charges under Pt. IV of the Companies Act 1963. See *R v. Registrar of Companies ex. parte Easal Commodities Ltd* [1986] Q.B. 1114 and Pye, "Certificate of Registration – An Impenetrable Shield No More?" (1985) 3 I.L.T. (N.S.) 213.

[287]   *The State (McConnell) v. Eastern Health Board* unreported, High Court, June 1, 1983. See also, *McLoughlin v. Minister for Social Welfare* [1958] I.R. 1; *Kiely v. Minister for Social Welfare* [1971] I.R. 21; *Kiely v. Minister for Social Welfare (No. 2)* [1977] I.R. 297; *McKinley v. Minister for Defence* [1988] I.R. 139 at 142; *The State (Hoolahan) v. Minister for Social Welfare*, unreported, High Court, July 23, 1986; *Thompson v. Minister for Social Welfare* [1989] I.R. 618; *Corcoran v. Minister for Social Welfare* [1991] 2 I.R. 175.

[288]   *Abdelkefi v. Minister for Justice* [1984] I.L.R.M. 138; *Ghneim v. Minister for Justice, Irish Times,* September 2, 1989 (although here there was also a large element of legitimate expectation). *A contra: Pok Sun Shum v. Ireland* [1986] I.L.R.M. 593 at 599 where Costello J. held that because of "the special control of aliens which every State must exercise" natural justice did not require the Minister for Justice to inform an applicant of the information on the files and give him an opportunity to comment before refusing a certificate of naturalisation under the provisions of the Irish Citizenship and Nationality Act 1956. The tenor of *Fajujonu v. Minister for Justice* [1990] I.L.R.M. 234 (see pp. 665–666) is all in favour of there being such a right although, on the facts of the case, the question did not arise.

[289]   See pp. 665–666.

[290]   [1996] 2 I.L.R.M. 46.

[291]   *Ibid.* at 63.

facts of the case, it seems to have been held, in regard to a refusal of permission to an alien to remain in the State, that a rather low standard would suffice).[292]

This is further borne out by the Supreme Court's subsequent decision in *Anisimova v. Minister for Justice*.[293] In this case an ethnic Russian had travelled from Moldova to the United Kingdom by air and had thence made her way to Ireland. The Minister declined to entertain her application for asylum on the ground that since the United Kingdom was the first safe country in which she had landed, she ought to have first applied for asylum in that jurisdiction. The Minister then informed the applicant that she could make submissions within a 21 day period against the making of a recommendation for a deportation order, but that such submissions could not be based on any asylum claim, as this was a matter for the British authorities. While the applicant accepted that the Minister was correct in her application of the "first safe country" rule,[294] she claimed that the question of whether she came within the term of this rule had not been adequately and appropriately considered, particularly as the Minister's letter inviting submissions on other grounds had indicated that a deportation order would otherwise be made. It was argued that the Minister had expressly "declined to entertain the . . . application for asylum or to hear the applicant in relation to such application or any aspect of it." Murphy J. rejected this "somewhat artificial interpretation of the relevant events", as he took the view that the Minister had adequately complied with constitutional justice:

> "Whilst it is certain that the Minister did not any time undertake a substantive inquiry into the applicant's status as a refugee what she did do is conduct a full and fair inquiry as to how the applicant had travelled from her country of origin to Ireland via the United Kingdom. These inquiries were fundamental to what is described as the 'preliminary issue' on an application for asylum. It is unreal to treat the threat of deportation of the applicant as a procedure separate from the preliminary issue and as if it were based on different facts."

(ix) Legitimate expectations

This is a recently developed ground on which to apply the rules. It will be described later in Chapter 16. Here, though, one should note as a striking example, of this category, *Slevin v. Shannon Regional Fisheries Board*.[295] This arose out of the refusal to renew an annual fishing licence which had been granted to the applicant for the previous twenty five years. Barron J. stated: ". . . it seems to me that if the Board

---

[292] *e.g.* Hamilton C.J. stated (at 62) that: "In the exercise by her [the civil servant] of the discretion of the Minister, it was open to her to refuse the application for such reasons. As the matter was within the discretion of the minister, there was no obligation on the Minister to give to the applicants the reasons why their application to remain in the State was being refused."

[293] Unreported, Supreme Court, November 28, 1997.

[294] The applicant did not dispute but that the "Von Arnim letter" (setting out this State's practice in relation to political asylum requests) was required to be read in the light of the "first safe country" rule and were qualified *pro tanto*, even though the letter made no reference to this vital qualification. For further discussion of the "Von Arnim letter", see *Fakih v. Minister for Justice* [1993] 2 I.R. 406 and *Gutrani v. Minister for Justice* [1993] 2 I.R. 427, discussed at pp. 868–869.

[295] [1995] 1 I.R. 460. Notice that the judgment does not actually use the phrase "legitimate expectations" but this appears to be the substance of the point.

wished to alter the stance which it had taken year by year by granting the licences, it ought to have informed the applicant why it was so doing."[296]

(x) Tribunals

It is an element in the definition of a Tribunal that irrespective of its subject-matter, it should follow a fairly formal procedure. It follows – indeed the point is almost circular – that a tribunal should observe the precepts of constitutional justice. Indeed as we have seen many of the cases on *e.g.* discipline involve tribunals. This matter was touched on in Chapter 6.

5. General Principles

Thus far, an attempt has been made to pigeon-hole most of the cases in which the constitutional justice principles have been said to apply. The next question is whether there is any general principle which would indicate the common ground shared by these cases and so assist a lawyer advising a client to predict whether the principles apply to new areas. The short answer is that the Irish courts have spent little time in looking for a guiding principle[297] and, in any case, such a search would be inherently unlikely to be successful. Formerly, the English courts invoked the quasi-judicial/ administrative distinction to try to solve this problem. At the root of this classification lay the feeling that it was only decisions which were analogous to those taken by judges in courts which attracted the rules of natural justice. The reason was that these rules are, in essence, similar to the rules of procedure and evidence applied in a court. Thus, the rules of natural justice applied to quasi-judicial, but not administrative, decisions. Straightaway, this raises the difficulty of deciding precisely which decisions of government administration were to be regarded as analogous to decisions by courts, *i.e.* quasi-judicial. In England, various tests had been used (sometimes separately, sometimes in combination). First, came the test to be applied by the deciding body to require the determination of contested facts and/or the application of some fairly precise standard, as opposed to the exercise of a discretion. Secondly, reliance was sometimes been placed on the "trappings of the court" test: for instance, had the body taking the decision the power to summon witnesses and administer oaths? Did it usually sit in public? In England, servitude to such classifications has now been stigmatised as a "heresy".[298]

The administrative/quasi-judicial function classification has been used fitfully in the Irish case law, principally, as we have seen,[299] in regard to the first rule of constitutional justice but also, occasionally, in regard to the second rule as, for

---

[296]   *Ibid.* at 465.
[297]   But see the comments of Barron J. in *Clarke v. Judge Hogan* [1995] 1 I.R. 310 at 313 ("what is done must be seen to be fair. What is fair in any given situation depends upon *the consequences for the person adversely affected by the exercise of the power*. Here it may not, in law, be a punishment, but it would certainly be perceived as being such.") (Emphasis added).
[298]   *R. v. Gaming Board ex p. Benaim and Khaida* [1970] 2 Q.B. 417 at 430. See, further, de Smith, (5th ed., 1995) *op. cit.* above, n.66, Appendix.
[299]   See pp. 732–734.

example, in *The State (Williams) v. Army Pensions Board*.[300] Here the Supreme Court classified the Board's decision as quasi-judicial because it was not exercising a discretion to award a widow's benefit, but was applying a fairly well-defined statutory test, namely, whether a person's death was due to disease arising during service with the United Nations. However, it is significant that, in *Williams*, Keane J. in the High Court differed from the Supreme Court in that he classified the relevant function as "administrative" yet then went on to say: ". . . [I]t is clear from an abundance of recent authority, that even purely administrative acts of persons such as [the Army Pensions Board and the Minister for Defence] may be affected by the requirements of natural and constitutional justice."[301]

Indeed generally, the decisions in this (as in other fields) have not in practice been much influenced by any general guideline. The noticeable point which emerges from the case law is that the rules have almost always been held to apply (although, it may be, with a lower standard) even in a case like *East Donegal Co-Operatives Ltd v. Attorney-General*[302] which involved a discretionary decision (to grant a licence). It is remarkable how seldom the respondent has even bothered to argue that the rules do not apply, confining himself instead to arguments about the content of constitutional justice. For example, the argument that a discretionary social welfare benefit is only a privilege[303] is not even mentioned in the judgments in the *Kiely cases*. The most useful test as to whether the rules apply, may be the simple one of whether any serious individual interest is directly affected by a government action. Apart from certain decisions of the D.P.P. and cases of waiver which have been dealt with elsewhere, the decisions which may be exempt from the rules may be put under the following seven heads:

(i) Legislation

It has just been stated that the rules apply where any individual interest is *directly* affected. But what is the position where legislative decisions are concerned? The fact that the principal type of legislation is an Act of Parliament, made by a body where all interests are supposedly represented and which is traditionally not subject to control by the courts during the process of legislation, has traditionally encouraged courts to avoid this area, even if it is delegated legislation which is at issue. (However, as a matter of practice rather than law, departments of state customarily consult interest groups about the content of draft bills). However, as was demonstrated in the leading case of *Listowel UDC v. McDonagh*,[304] the no-bias rule

---

[300] [1983] I.R. 308. For other examples, see *Re Roscrea Meat Products Estate* [1958] I.R. 47; *The State (Shannon Atlantic Fisheries Ltd) v. McPolin* [1976] I.R. 93 at 98; *Geraghty v. Minister for Local Government* [1976] I.R. 153; *Connolly v. McConnell* [1983] I.R. 172; *The State (Genport Ltd) v. An Bord Pleanála* [1983] I.L.R.M. 12; *The State (Gallagher) v. Governor of Portlaoise Prison*, unreported, High Court, April 25, 1983. In some cases the courts have not used the term quasi-judicial, but have spoken instead of "a duty to act judicially": *McDonald v. Bord na gCon* [1965] I.R. 217; *O'Brien v. Bord na Móna* [1983] I.R. 255. This is only a terminological difference.

[301] [1981] I.L.R.M. at 382. See, to similar effect, *Flanagan v. U.C.D.* [1988] I.R. 724 at 730 (University disciplinary committee "not a judicial body [but] under a duty to act judicially.")

[302] [1970] I.R. 317.

[303] On which, see p. 599.

[304] [1968] I.R. 312.

may apply to delegated legislation, albeit in the attenuated form of the rule against mala fides. The New Zealand courts have held that it is sufficient if the donees of the power to make delegated legislation approach the matter with an open mind (albeit they are not preculded from having a prior opinion) and genuinely satisfy themselves that the statutory criteria have been complied with.[305]

The position is even less clear in regard to the *audi alteram partem* rule. The rationale usually given for excluding legislative decisions from the scope of the rules is that the *audi alteram partem* rule, at any rate, is more appropriate where a compact range of facts is in issue – for example, in a dismissal case, whether an employee was dishonest – and less appropriate when a broader range of acts and divergent considerations, for example, the economy or some other national interest, is concerned. Traditionally, legislative decisions were taken as being beyond the reach of the rule.[306] This orthodoxy was confirmed by McMahon J. in the High Court in *Cassidy v. Minister for Industry and Commerce*[307] where he held, without discussion, that the rule did not apply to require consultation with a vintners' association before the making of a statutory instrument fixing maximum prices for the sale of intoxicating liquor in the Dundalk area.

On the other hand, in some cases involving delegated legislation, it has been decided or assumed (although again without any discussion of the difficulties) that the maker was under a duty to consult interested parties. For example, in *Burke v. Minister for Labour*[308] a Joint Labour Committee had fixed minimum wages for

---

[305] *Creednz Inc. v. Governor-General* [1981] 1 N.Z.L.R. 172.

[306] *Bates v. Lord Hailsham* [1972] 1 W.L.R. 1373; *Essex C.C. v. Minister for Housing* (1967) 66 L.G.R. 23.

[307] [1978] I.R. 297. This point was not dealt with by the Supreme Court who found for the plaintiff on another ground: see p. 638.

[308] [1979] I.R. 354. In *The State (Lynch) v. Cooney* [1982] I.R. 337 the Supreme Court appears to have accepted that the Minister could have been under a duty to consult with interested parties prior to the making of a banning order by way of statutory instrument under s.31 of the Broadcasting Authority Act 1960. However, the Minister's failure to do this was excused by the Supreme Court in view of the fact that, in the circumstances of the case there was no time to hear the other side. In *U.S. International Tobacco Co. Ltd v. Attorney General* [1990] 1 I.R. 394. Hamilton P. reserved the question of whether the plaintiff company (whose products were the subject of an *ultra vires* banning order under the Health Act 1947) were entitled to be heard in advance of the making of such a statutory instrument. In *Abrahamson v. Law Society of Ireland* [1996] 1 I.R. 403 the facts concerned the Society's omission (in circumstances detailed at pp. 874–875) to exercise its power to make regulations, under the Solicitors' Acts 1954–1994, so as to re-introduce a system of exemptions from certain entrance exams for law graduates. The crucial point here is that the decision was taken without consultation with any of the law students affected. McCracken J. held that there was no obligation to consult giving, as the reason, merely the impracticability of consulting several hundred persons. The present point was not raised explicitly nor was the possibility of canvassing some representative group.

In *HML Ltd v. Minister for Agriculture*, unreported, High Court, February 8, 1996, Barr J. held that the Minister had acted contrary to fair procedures when devising new rules for the operation of the export refunds scheme. In doing so, the Minister had created a quasi-legislative framework and accordingly:

"A series of rules, some of which had serious financial consequences for Hibernia were created by the Minister and put into effect without prior notice to the contractors concerned."

Again, this case should not be understood as laying down a general duty to abide by fair procedures when making such rules. Rather, it was simply that, as, confined class of persons would be severely affected by the making of such new rules, the Minister was under a duty to observe fair procedures and to consult beforehand.

persons working in the hotel industry by means of an order made under the Industrial Relations Act 1946. Employers were obliged under pain of criminal sanction to respect this order and to comply with its terms. The employers' representatives wished to adduce evidence as to the real cost to the employers of the board and lodging provided for their employees, but the Committee fixed minimum wages without regard to this evidence. The Supreme Court was of opinion that the Committee's refusal to admit such evidence rendered the order invalid. In the view of Henchy J.:

> "Where Parliament has delegated functions of this nature, it is to be necessarily inferred as part of the legislative intention that the body which makes the orders will exercise its functions, not only with constitutional propriety and due regard to natural justice, but also within the framework of the terms and objects of the relevant Act and with basic fairness, reasonableness and good faith. The absoluteness of the delegation is susceptible of unjust and tyrannous abuse unless its operation is thus confined; so it is entirely proper to ascribe to the Oireachtas (being the Parliament of a State which is constitutionally bound to protect, by its laws, its citizens from unjust attack) an intention that the delegated functions must be exercised within those limitations."[309]

It may be that *Burke* has not laid down any general principle: the order which was invalidated in that case and the other cases cited on the previous page only applied to a small narrowly-defined category of situations and may (just) be regarded as involving an administrative decision cast in the guise of delegated legislation. It is, perhaps, only in such unusual cases that the makers of delegated legislation are under a duty to observe the *audi alteram partem* rule.

(ii) Policy

In regard to the question of whether the *audi alteram partem* rule does or should apply, much the same issues are raised if the decision being taken involves policy rather than legislation (as might be expected since legislation is of course a special category of policy). Some of the underlying issues, which have been little discussed here, are teased out in the following passage by a British writer, Peter Cane, who began by summarising the work of Lon Fuller who had advanced the view that natural justice was not suitable for dealing with what Professor Fuller called "'polycentric' disputes, that is disputes requiring account to be taken of a large number of interlocking and interacting interests and considerations." Professor Cane stated:

> "Fuller gave several examples of polycentric problems: how to divide between two art galleries 'in equal shares' a collection of paintings left by will; the task of establishing levels of wages and prices in a centrally controlled economy; . . .
>
> The essential feature of the judicial process which makes it unsuitable to deal with polycentric problems is its bipolar and adversary nature. It is designed for one party to put forward a proposition which the other party

---

[309] [1979] I.R. 354 at 361–362.

denies or opposes. For example, the plaintiff asserts that he owns Blackacre and the defendant denies it; or the plaintiff asserts that he is entitled to compensation from the defendant and the latter denies it. None of Fuller's examples lends itself to being dealt with in this all-or-nothing way. For example one of the galleries might want the Picasso if it also gets the Cezanne but not the Turner; but it would not insist on the Picasso if it got the Turner; but would want both if it did not get the Cezanne. The other gallery might have an equally complex set of preferences, and the greater the number of works involved, the more complex the preference sets might become. Again, the workers in an industry might claim a wage increase of £X, and their employers might resist it and offer £Y; but the interests of another part of the economy might be affected in such a way by either proposal that neither is acceptable.

. . . A good example in the administrative law context of a polycentric problem is provided by a motorway inquiry. The ramifications of the decision whether to build a motorway or not are enormous. At stake are not only the interests of potential motorway users and of persons whose land might be compulsorily acquired to provide a path for the motorway; also involved are the inhabitants of villages and towns which will be relieved of through-traffic by the motorway; British Rail may have an interest in inhibiting the development of alternative means for the transport of goods; improved transport and communications facilities provided by the motorway may benefit some businesses at the expense of others; and motorways have, of course, serious environmental effects which lovers of the countryside and people who live near the proposed route will be anxious to avoid. Not only would accommodation and compromise between these various interests be desirable, but also it may be that the best solution would be some alternative to a motorway, or some alternative route not already considered. The complexity of the issues involved makes the model of bipolar adversary presentation of fixed positions by parties in conflict seem inappropriate to the sound resolution of the issues involved. And since the adversary model of dispute settlement is inappropriate, so too is a standard of the validity of particular decisions on such issues which rests on the rules of natural justice."[310]

A policy question may arise either in regard to a specific single case (as, for instance, in the example discussed in the passage on the paintings) or in regard to a potentially unlimited category of persons or situations which happen to come within the boundaries of the decision (as, for instance, the wages example). Nothing very much turns upon this distinction. (Indeed it is hard to decide within which category the motorway example falls.) However, what can perhaps be said is that cases within the second category look, and are, rather closer to legislation than individual decisions and thus, as a general principle, should be less likely to attract the rules of constitutional justice.

---

[310] *An Introduction to Administrative Law* (1985), pp. 100–101. Professor Fuller's article will be found at (1978) 92 Harv.L.Rev. 252.

However, in the case even of decisions of a deliberative body, as to policy, which do not have a direct effect on an individual, it seems, as mentioned in the previous chapter,[311] that some concept of fair procedures operates.

In regard to policy decisions which affect only individuals (as distinct from quasi-legislative actions) it seems that it is now too late in the day to argue that such decisions do not attract the rules. Even in regard to the deportation of a (non-European Community) alien, it seems that the *audi alteram partem* rule probably has to be followed.[312]

(iii) Suspension: person affected "not in peril"[313]

Generally speaking, the rules of constitutional justice do not apply to suspensions. For instance, in *Rochford v. Storey*,[314] the plaintiffs had been suspended from membership of a trade union sporting club following a dispute over the plaintiff's eligibility for membership. The suspensions had been imposed when the plaintiffs had failed to attend a meeting at which they had been requested to produce evidence of their entitlement to become full members of the club. Even though O'Hanlon J. concluded that natural justice was complied with when the plaintiffs had been put on notice by letter that the validity of their membership was in dispute, he was also of opinion that the decision to suspend did not attract the rules. The reason was that this was not a suspension inflicted by way of punishment; but rather a suspension made as a holding operation pending enquiries. The same distinction was adopted by Barr J. in *Quirke v. Bord Luthchleas na hÉireann*:[315]

> ". . . the suspension of a member by a body such as B.L.E. or a trade union or professional association may take two different forms. On the one hand, it may be imposed as a holding operation pending the investigation of a complaint. Such a suspension does not imply that there has been a finding of any misbehaviour or breach of rules by the suspended person, but merely that an allegation of some such impropriety or misconduct has been made against the member in question. On the other hand, a suspension may be imposed not as a holding operation pending the outcome of an inquiry, but as a penalty by way of punishment of a member who has been found guilty of misconduct or breach of rules. The importance of the distinction is that where a suspension is

---

[311] See pp. 497–500. See too, *Association of General Practitioners v. Minister for Health* [1995] 1 I.R. 382 at 388–392. Here it was held by O'Hanlon J. that where terms of employment for a group of doctors are being fixed, there is no obligation at common law or under the Constitution, on the defendant to consult with an organisation representing his employees. Something similar could be said of *Shanley v. Galway Corporation* [1995] 1 I.R. 396 at 407 which concerned an apparently general decision taken by the defendant in regard to an area which had been designated as a casual trading area under the Casual Trading Act 1980. (This decision was to the effect that there a condition prohibiting trading in food of any kind should be included in all such licences.) But see pp. 602–604 (on individual decisions).

[312] See pp. 599–600.

[313] *Scariff v. Taylor* [1996] 2 I.L.R.M. 278 at 287, *per* Hamilton C.J.

[314] Unreported, High Court, November 4, 1982. See also, *McHugh v. Garda Commissioner* [1985] I.L.R.M. 606.

[315] [1988] I.R. 83 at 87.

imposed by way of punishment, it follows that the body in question has found its member guilty of significant misconduct or breach of rules."

However, it has also been held that the rules would apply where the suspension would have the effect of interfering with the affected individual's livelihood or reputation, as where he is suspended without pay or where the suspension imputes grave misconduct.[316] In addition, as explained already,[317] there is an argument that fair procedure may also require that the final, substantive decision should be taken with as little delay as possible so that the person affected is not kept in suspense longer than is necessary.[318]

A case which although at first sight may seem dissimilar, yet which engages, it is suggested, the same principle is *Scariff v. Taylor*[319] (the facts in which have been rehearsed already). In this case the strongest point justifying the holding that there was no right to representation was that the accused would not be in actual peril until the hearing of the court martial.

(iv) Trivial cases

One of the most fundamental ideas in the law is that the courts, especially the High Court will not interfere where the individual interest affected by a decision is too trivial to warrant such attention (a notion expressed in the maxim, *de minimis non curat lex*). This principle would have an obvious application in opposing an attempt to invoke constitutional justice to control the operation of (say) a sports or social club. It has, however, not been much considered[320] in Irish law.[321]

(v) Margin of appreciation

As is demonstrated at several points in this chapter, the constitutional justice rules allow a considerable margin of appreciation and the courts have held that within these broad limits (and subject, of course, to any particular procedural regulations)

---

316 *Flynn v. An Post* [1987] I.R. 68; *Ní Bheoláin v. Dublin V.E.C.*, unreported, High Court, January 28, 1983; *Collins v. Cork V.E.C.*, unreported, Supreme Court, March 18, 1983; *The State (Donegal V.E.C.) v. Minister for Education* [1985] I.R. 56.

317 See p. 596.

318 *Clancy v. Ireland* [1988] I.R. 326 involved a situation which was analogous to temporary suspension. The case concerned the constitutionality of the Offences against the State (Amendment) Act 1985. The major feature which saved the Act from unconstitutionality was that this claim was to be brought in the High Court, where the claimant is, of course, entitled to a fair hearing. However the result in *Clancy* is also in line with the law on temporary suspension in that here too what was involved was a provisional interference – in this case with property rights – but before it could be made permanent, the owner was allowed a hearing.

319 [1996] 2 I.L.R.M. 278. See p. 569. The English authorities on this point are helpfully summarised in *Rees v. Cane* [1994] 2 A.C. 173, 189 per Lord Slynn.

320 It was not, for example, discussed in *Rochford v. Storey* – it would not, of course, have been relevant in *Quirke v. Bord Luthchleas na hÉireann* for the reason that what was involved in that case was the disqualification of an international athlete.

321 But see the comments of Hederman J. in *Murtagh v. Board of St. Emer's National School* [1991] 2 I.R. 482 at 488: "A three day suspension for an admitted breach of discipline would be no more revisable by the High Court than, for example, the ordering of a pupil . . . to write out lines. . . ." And *cf.* Morris J. in *Clancy v. I.R.F.U.* [1995] 1 I.L.R.M. 193 at 198–199 "the degree to which the plaintiff's present rights are encroached upon by the rule . . . is minimal – and in my view falls to be considered in the same manner as that adopted in *Chestvale*" But note that Morris J. was dealing with retrospectively.

it is for the deciding agency itself to exercise "a certain discretion as to the manner in which it conducts the proceedings."[322] However, following the general principles which govern the exercise of any discretion, substantive or procedural, such a discretion must be genuinely exercised and it must be exercised fairly and reasonably.[323] Another type of exemption which exists in England – but which is probably not part of Irish law – stems from the idea that where a tribunal or other public authority has formulated a comprehensive, detailed code of procedure, the onus on a person who seeks to establish that this code is inconsistent with natural justice is very heavy.[324] By contrast, in Ireland, constitutional justice is not just a general norm of statutory interpretation; it also, as has been seen, enjoys the support of Article 40.3 of the Constitution. One consequence of this is that the courts will readily inject the rules of constitutional justice into even a comprehensive procedural code.[325] Finally, McCarthy J. has remarked: "If the proceedings derive from statute, then, in the absence of any set of fixed procedures, the relevant authority must create and carry out the necessary procedures; if the set or fixed procedure is not comprehensive, the authority must supplement it in such a fashion as to ensure compliance with constitutional justice, for which proposition there is a wealth of authority".[326]

(vi) Countervailing factors

In a number of cases, some of which have already been described, countervailing factors have been said to justify a failure to observe the rules of constitutional justice (or, more correctly, just the *audi alteram partem* limb).[327] Examples of such countervailing policies include the fact that the rule would cause a delay or otherwise defeat the object of the public authority's action[328] or that it was impossible for the public authority to contact the person affected to elicit his representations.[329] A

---

[322] *The State (Boyle) v. General Medical Services (Payments) Board* [1981] I.L.R.M. 14 at 16, *per* Keane J. See also *The State (Genport Ltd)* [1983] I.L.R.M. 12 at 16; *Scariff v. Taylor* [1996] 2 I.L.R.M. 278 at 289, *per* Denham J.

[323] *Irish Family Planning Assoc. v. Ryan* [1979] I.R. 295. Note the significant differences in tone between O'Higgins C.J. (Sup. Ct.) and that of Hamilton J. (High Ct.).

[324] Evans, "Some Limits to the Scope of Natural Justice" (1973) 36 M.L.R. 439. There is some Irish support for this point of view, (see, *e.g. The State (Fagan) v. Governor of Mountjoy Prison*, unreported, High Court, March 6, 1978) but generally the courts will, if necessary, superimpose constitutional standards on the terms of a statute: see, *e.g. O'Domhnaill v. Merrick* [1984] I.R. 151 and *Toal v. Duignan* [1991] I.L.R.M. 140.

[325] See, *e.g. East Donegal Co-Operatives Ltd v. Attorney General* [1970] I.R. 317; *Kiely v. Minister for Social Welfare (No. 2)* [1977] I.R. 267; *McKeen v. Meath County Council* [1997] 1 I.R. 299..

[326] *The State (Irish Pharmaceutical Union) v. E.A.T.* [1987] I.L.R.M. 36 at 40. As authority, *O'Brien, Loftus* and *East Donegal* were cited.

[327] *e.g. The State (Donnelly) v. Minister for Defence*, unreported, High Court, October 9, 1979; *The State (Jordan) v. Garda Commissioner* [1987] I.L.R.M. 107 (need to maintain public confidence in integrity of members of Defence Forces and Gardai).

[328] *R. v. Gaming Board, ex p. Benaim and Khaida* [1970] 2 Q.B. 417 at 430–32 (Board did not have to quote "chapter and verse" nor did it have to disclose the source of its information, if it would be contrary to the public interest, nor did the reasons for refusal have to be given). See also the comments of Gannon J. in *The State (Philpott) v. Registrar of Titles* [1986] I.L.R.M. 499 at 507 ("unless the urgency of the circumstances otherwise requires, justice requires . . ."). However "mere administrative difficulties in securing the attendance of witnesses before a tribunal" do not warrant suspension of the rules: *Gallagher v. Revenue Commissioners (No. 2)* [1995] 1 I.R. at 79, *per* Hamilton C.J.

[329] *Irish Family Planning Assoc. Ltd v. Ryan* [1979] I.R. 295 at 313–314, *per* O'Higgins C.J.

graphic illustration occurred in *O'Callaghan v. Commissioners of Public Works*.[330] The plaintiff was a farmer who owned a 2,000-year-old promontory fort which had been listed as a "national monument" under the National Monuments Acts 1930–1954. Ignoring the order, he instructed an agricultural contractor to plough up the land near the fort. Soon the ploughing had to be temporarily abandoned. The reason for this was damage to the plough. However, the imminent resumption of the work led the Commissioners to Public Works to make a preservation order which extended the Commissioners' powers to protect the fort. The Supreme Court rejected the argument that the Commissioners ought to have allowed the plaintiff farmer an opportunity to put forward any objection he might have had to the making of the preservation order. O'Higgins C.J. said:

> "Here an emergency had been created by the plaintiff's own action in defiance of his legal obligations. If the Commissioners had hesitated in acting as they did, the monument which it was their duty to preserve would have been seriously damaged or destroyed. Further, it was not possible to contact the plaintiff, because his address was not then known and did not become known to the Commissioners until some time later."[331]

Again, in *The State (Lynch) v. Cooney* O'Higgins C.J. justified the Minister for Post and Telegraph's refusal to apply the *audi alteram partem* rule before making a regulation which, *inter alia*, banned the applicant from making a party political broadcast, on the ground that "the time was short and a decision was urgent. There was no opportunity for debate or parley and, indeed, to permit or seek such might, in the circumstances, have defeated the very object and purpose of the section."[332] Finally, in *Carroll v. Minister for Agriculture*,[333] in assessing the basic fairness of the procedure for testing cattle for "reactors", the great importance of the eradication of bovine tuberculosis in the public interest was taken into account. These authorities suggest that there is a reservoir of discretionary power to which the principles of constitutional justice do not apply, which is wider than any of the specific examples mentioned so far identified. If this reading is correct, it is obviously pregnant with considerable possibilities for the future. It is also noteworthy that the courts have chosen to create a distinct ground of exemption rather than simply to exercise their long-established discretion to refuse to grant relief.[334]

(vii) Private transactions and arrangements

As illustrated earlier,[335] there is no doubt that the constitutional justice precepts apply to cases of loss employment even in the private law field. This fact suggests

---

330 [1985] I.L.R.M. 364.
331 *Ibid.* at 373–374.
332 [1982] I.R. 337, 365. See also his comments in *Irish Family Planning Assoc. v. Ryan* [1979] I.R. 295 at 313. See too, *The State (Smullen) v. Duffy* [1980] I.L.R.M. 46.
333 [1991] 1 I.R. 230. At p. 235, Blayney J. stated: ". . . the cattle, beef and dairy industry in the country . . . account for over 70% of farm output and some 20% of Irish manufacturing output. The combined value of these exports in 1987 came to 2.3 billion pounds. The existence of bovine tuberculosis creates problems in that intra-community [sc. E.U.] trade in cattle or beef showing any signs whatsoever of bovine tuberculosis is prohibited."
334 On which see Part 5 of Chap. 13.
335 See pp. 589–593.

the question of whether constitutional justice applies generally to private law transactions and arrangements. A mechanism for its importation is readily available in the form of the well-established notion that constitutional justice can be regarded, in appropriate circumstances, as an implicit term in a contract and this could presumably, with equal logic, be extended to other purely private law transactions such as an instrument constituting a settlement. However, whilst this area is without much helpful (Irish or English) authority, judicial or academic, it is suggested that, absent exceptional areas such as the employment cases, constitutional justice does not apply in the private law arena. Take, for example, *Carna Foods Ltd v. Eagle Star*,[336] in which it was contended unsuccessfully that since the absence of reasons for the cancellation of their insurance cover made it virtually impossible for them to obtain alternative cover, it was contrary to constitutional justice for the insurer to cancel their cover without giving reasons. McCracken J. stated:

> ". . . where a decision is taken to exercise a function in the public realm, the person affected is entitled to know the reasons for the decision. This is because statutory powers must be determined and exercised reasonably. The plaintiffs here seek to extend this principle into the realm of private contractual relationships. To decide that any principle of natural justice or constitutional justice applies would be a serious interference in the contractual position of parties in a commercial contract and with very wide-ranging consequences. To take two examples, if a person applied for a job and was refused it, is he entitled to be told the reasons? Secondly, if a manufacturer decided to change his supplier of raw materials, is the supplier entitled to know the reasons? Surely not."[337]

It has also been stated, emphatically, in a Northern Irish case that: "As a matter of company law, the rules of natural justice have no application to the decision of the members in general meeting. Such members are free to vote as their own individual interests and inclinations may require."[338] Again, in *Hounslow L.B.C. v. Twickenham Garden Developments Ltd*,[339] a case in which an architect had given notice, under the normal term in a building contract, that the contractor had failed to proceed with the work regularly and diligently, the English High Court found that the principles of natural justice did not apply to an architect's notice. Megarry J. stated: "The

---

[336] [1995] 1 I.R. 526.

[337] *Ibid.* at 530–531. It is testimony to the plaintiffs' lack of faith in any line of argument founded on constitutional justice that when the case was appealed, unsuccessfully ([1997] 2 I.L.R.M. 499) their arguments were principally based not on constitutional justice, but on the private law grounds of implied terms and the Competition Act 1991. In *Zockoll Group Ltd v. Telecom Eireann*, unreported, High Court, November 28, 1997, a case concerning the withdrawal of telephone numbers, Kelly J. said that he was not persuaded that public law principles of fair procedures applied "to the commercial relationship which exists between the defendant and its customers," However, the judge went on to hold that as the defendant had not acted "fairly and reasonably" in withdrawing the numbers, the plaintiff was entitled to mandatory relief. This seems to amount to an application of the principles of constitutional justice by the back door.

[338] *Hawthorn v. Ulster Flying Club Ltd* [1986] N.I.J.B. 56 at 94. However, on the facts of the case, Murray J. held that the rules applied to a decision to expel a member; *a contra: Gaiman v. National Association for Mental Health* [1970] 2 All E.R. 362.

[339] [1970] 3 All E.R. 326.

principles of natural justice are of wide application and great importance but they must be confined within proper limits and not allowed to run wild."[340] This last quotation suggests that short shrift would be given to suggestions for instance that: objects of a power of appointment must be heard before the donee of the power chooses among them; that a testator should solicit representations from a fond relative whom he intends to "leave out" of the will; or that a tenant must be heard before a landlord issues a notice to quit. The essential point is that the imposition of a formalised fair procedure is thought to be more appropriate when one is dealing with a powerful public or quasi-public body than with a private company or individual. There is a further point supporting this observation: as mentioned at the very start of this chapter, there is an intimate connection between natural or constitutional justice and, on the other hand, substantive controls imposed upon a decision-maker, as regards for example, "reasonableness" (covered in the next chapter). If, as is the case, persons governed exclusively by private law are not subject to these substantive controls – may indeed be as whimsical or capricious as they wish – then it would be anomalous if they were to be subjected to constitutional justice.

6. Concluding Comment

It is useful to illustrate the difficulties inherent in constitutional justice by way of the *Kiely* saga. Mrs Kiely's claim for a widow's benefit was rejected by a deciding officer and, on appeal, by the appeals officer in the Department of Social Welfare. The appeals officer's decision was struck down, on appeal, by the High Court;[341] the case was reheard by a second appeals officer who decided against the claimant; this decision was struck down in the Supreme Court;[342] the question was then decided by a third appeals officer, who reached the same decision as his two colleagues, and this time there was no review so that the decision was effective. It might well be asked rhetorically: who benefited from this substantial expenditure of legal costs and court time? Nor is the *Kiely* saga unique. The law reports are replete with judicial statements, offered, as consolation prizes, in cases in which some administrative action has been condemned for violation of constitutional justice, to the effect that the public authority may repeat the process, even reaching the same conclusion, provided only that the proper procedure is followed on the subsequent occasion.[343]

Disadvantages and Advantages

Neither the advantages nor the disadvantages of constitutional justice have yet been researched empirically in Ireland.[344] However, it seems reasonable to make the following assumptions: first, that greater procedural complexity increases delay and

---

[340] *Ibid.* at 347.
[341] *Kiely v. Minister for Social Welfare* [1971] I.R. 21.
[342] *Kiely v. Minister for Social Welfare (No. 2)* [1977] I.R. 267.
[343] See, *e.g. Quirke v. Bord Luthchleas na hÉireann* [1988] I.R. 83 at 88, *per* Barr J.
[344] Empirical research on the impact of judicial review generally upon the practices of the bureaucracy has just begun in the U.K. (as part of the Public Law Project.)

expense;[345] secondly, that the rules promote excessive caution among public servants, particularly at the lower levels where the officials cannot reasonably be expected to be familiar with the novel, and sometimes rather artificial, requirements of constitutional justice.[346] To take the example of an official charged with the duty of awarding a licence: he will know that it is more likely that the refusal of a licence will be challenged by a disappointed applicant than that an erroneous award of a licence will be challenged by a competitor or other member of the public. In view of this, there is a pressure, which is contrary to the public interest, upon the administrator to grant the licence. One of the consequences of the constitutional justice rules is to increase this pressure by imposing something analogous to the procedures of a law court in the very different circumstances of a tribunal or public authority. A British Government lawyer has remarked that: "while presently public administration is honest there is a risk that, as a result of judicial review, people will go through a charade: applicants to put themselves in the best possible position and the authority to defend themselves."[347]

As against this, constitutional justice is taken to carry five advantages. In the first place, an impartial decision-maker and an opportunity for the person affected to put forward his comments both help to promote an "appropriate" result. (The decision may be too subjective to speak of the *correct result*). As Megarry J. remarked in a notable passage:

> "As everyone who has anything to do with the law well knows, the path of the law is strewn with examples of open and shut cases which, somehow, were not; of unanswerable charges which, in the event, were completely answered; of inexplicable conduct which was fully explained; of fixed and unalterable determinations that, by discussion, suffered a change."[348]

---

[345] For a rare judicial acknowledgement of these difficulties, see the comments of Megarry J. in *McInnes v. Onslow-Fane* [1978] 1 W.L.R. 1520.

[346] *cf.* the comments of Murphy J. in *Anisimova v. Minister for Justice*, unreported, Supreme Court, November 28, 1997:

"With hindsight the proceedings of any and every tribunal., however formal or exalted, may well admit of improvement but it is of the utmost importance, particularly in the context of natural and constitutional justice, to test the attainment of the basic standards by reference to substance and reality rather than technicalities or ingenuous argument. If that position were otherwise, people of business affairs and those engaged in domestic or social tribunals of every description called upon to apply this important principle would be forced to abdicate their functions to lawyers who could select more appropriate terminology and invoke forms and formulae which might defy criticism, but not necessarily achieve justice."

[347] Referred to in Woolf, *Protection of the Public – A New Challenge*, p. 18. In Cork, junior staff in the Department of Social Welfare are warned that they are "walking through a legal minefield."

[348] *John v. Rees* [1970] Ch. 345 at 402. The passage from which this extract is taken was quoted with approval in *Gallagher v. Revenue Commissioners (No.2)* [1995] 1 I.R. 55 at 82 (O'Flaherty J.). See also *Keady v. Garda Commissioner* [1992] 2 I.R. 197 at 213. See too, in *Dawson v. Irish Brokers Association*, unreported, Supreme Court, February 27, 1997 where the defendants argued that the expulsion of the plaintiffs as members of the association was valid, even though no hearing had been granted in the manner contemplated by the defendants' own rules. The defendants contended that the plaintiffs were so obdurate that a hearing "would have done no good". O'Flaherty J. rejected this submission in trenchant terms:

"The answer to that submission surely must be that the whole point of *audi alteram partem* is that once people get around a table and have dialogue, many matters that seem incapable of resolution are resolved. The labour relations field is certainly replete with examples of persons

A hearing means that the risk of injustice caused by acting on an *ex parte* view of the situation will have been obviated. Even if the facts or arguments adduced by the person affected do not cause the decision to be reversed, they may lead to its being varied and thus, for instance, it has been held, in cases involving disciplinary punishments, that there is a right to be heard in mitigation.[349] It has been said that ". . . the holder's office being such a crucial part of his life, basic fairness requires that he should not be sundered from it without first being given a meaningful opportunity of being heard, if only *ad misericordiam*."[350]

Secondly, the duty to give reasons for a public authority's proposed decision (which is included in the *audi alteram partem* rule) might disclose to the person affected that the decision was being taken on grounds, or in circumstances, which rendered it invalid in substance. In such a case, the rule would assist the person affected by giving him information which would enable him to launch an action for judicial review on substantive grounds or, perhaps, to refer the matter to the Ombudsman or a T.D. or to seek some other sanction.[351] The point was put eloquently in the following passage from Henchy J.'s judgment in *Garvey v. Ireland*:

"If, by maintaining an obscuring silence, a Government could render their act of dismissal impenetrable as to its reasons and unreviewable as to its method, an office-holder such as the plaintiff could have his livelihood snatched from him, his chosen career snuffed out, his pension prospects dashed and his reputation irretrievably tarnished, without any hope of redress, no matter how unjustified or unfair his dismissal might be. I doubt if it would be even contended that the statutory power of removal from office could validly be used to dismiss a person for an unconstitutional reason (for example, because of his race, creed or colour); yet if such were to happen, and suddenness and silence were to be allowed to curtain off the dismissal from judicial scrutiny, the dismissed person, far from getting the constitutionally guaranteed protection from unjust attack, would be abandoned to the consequence of an unjust, unconstitutional and ruinous decision."[352]

Next, it should be noted that this passage suggests that if the grounds on which the incumbent were removed had been authoritatively stated, this might have been less discreditable than what might otherwise have been suspected. Likewise, in *Hickey*

---

who have taken entrenched positions; who will not change – but who after a process of discussion and mediation and so forth, miraculously, do come to a different point of view. Often both parties to a dispute travel the same road to Damascus, even if on opposite sides of the road."

[349] *R. (Hennessy) v. Department of Education* [1980] N.I. 109; *The State (Grahame) v. Racing Board*, unreported, High Court, November 22, 1983. Compliance with this requirement does not necessarily entail a subsequent oral hearing: *Georgopoulos v. Beaumont Hospital Board*, unreported, Supreme Court, June 4, 1997.

[350] *Garvey v. Ireland* [1981] I.R. 75 at 102, *per* Henchy J. For an earlier Supreme Court decision denying that natural justice extends to *ad misericordiam* pleas, see *The State (Costello) v. Irish Land Commission* [1959] I.R. 353.

[351] On this point, in the context of reasons, see p. 572.

[352] [1981] I.R. 75 at 101. But *cf. McDonnell v. Ireland*, unreported, Supreme Court, July 23, 1997 where Keane J. said that he "would have [had] little difficulty in holding "that in the case of a civil servant convicted of membership of an illegal organisation "the Minister would have been entitled to take the view that removal from his post should be an automatic consequence of the conviction and that the form of hearing envisaged in *Garvey* would be a redundant exercise."

v. Eastern Health Board,[353] Finlay C.J. noted that where an applicant has been dismissed for misconduct, then he would be entitled "as a matter of natural justice, to a fair hearing . . . ".

Fourthly, it is a matter of satisfaction and dignity to the individual that he should have his say before a decision is taken against him by a governmental agency. (This is the equivalent, in the administrative sphere, of "the day in court"). In *R. (Smyth) v. Co. Antrim Coroner*[354] it was sought to quash the verdict returned by a coroner's jury on the grounds that, in breach of the relevant regulations, the coroner had failed to sum up the evidence to the jury. Quashing the verdict, Kelly J. conceded that another jury, hearing the same evidence and assisted by a proper and adequate summing up of it by the coroner, might come to exactly the same verdict; but held that the next-of-kin were entitled "to have their unhappiness tempered by the knowledge that such a verdict was reached by a considered and regular inquiry."[355]

Finally, an open consistent procedure in which the state agency taking the decision is seen to be impartial is necessary to maintain the confidence of the general public in the institutions of government. For example, in a case where the failure of a Joint Labour Committee to hear certain relevant evidence was found to be contrary to the principle of *audi alteram partem*, Henchy J. adverted to the dangers of the "no merits" argument: "even if such evidence would have made no difference, the Committee by rejecting it unheard and unconsidered, left themselves open to the imputation of bias, unfairness and prejudice."[356]

Does a failure to follow the rules matter, if the substantive result be correct?

The relative importance which is to be assigned to the disadvantages and to each of the distinct advantages is relevant in considering two policy questions. The first issue, which has divided the judiciary in a number of jurisdictions, and which has arisen mainly in the context of the *audi alteram partem* limb of constitutional justice, is whether a failure to follow the rules is fatal where it is clear that the case was correctly decided, albeit by way of a wrongful procedure.

In Ireland, diametrically opposing views have been given to this conundrum, though usually without much in the way of discussion or consideration of precedent. The dominant view is represented by the majority judges in *Glover v. B.L.N. Ltd*,[357] who brushed aside the submission that, if a hearing had been held, there was nothing the plaintiff could have said anyway, with Walsh J. remarking: "This proposition only has to be stated to be rejected. The obligation to give a fair hearing to the guilty is just as great as the obligation to give a fair hearing to the innocent."[358] And in *O'Brien v. Bord na Móna*,[359] Finlay P. stated on behalf of the Supreme Court that:

---

[353] [1991] 1 I.R. 208 at 212.
[354] [1980] N.I. 123.
[355] [1980] N.I. at 125. See to, similar effect, *John v. Rees* [1970] 1 Ch. at 402.
[356] *Burke v. Minister for Labour* [1979] I.R. 354 at 362. See also the comments of O'Donnell L.J. in *R. (Hennessy) v. Department of the Environment* [1980] N.I. 109.
[357] [1973] I.R. 388.
[358] *Ibid*. at 429.
[359] [1983] I.R. 255 at 266. See Coffey, "Procedural Curbs on Powers of Compulsory Acquisition"

"A necessity for the observance of natural justice in the process of compulsory acquisition of property is too fundamental and important to be supplied by proof that objections would have been rejected if they had been entertained."[360]

By contrast, the dissenting judge in *Glover*, Fitzgerald J., was equally strong and terse in the opposite sense. Again in *Corrigan v. Irish Land Commission*,[361] another case on compulsory acquisition of land, Henchy J. considered that there was an "overriding reason" why in the circumstances of this case the doctrine of estoppel by conduct should apply: the reason was that it was inconceivable on the facts "that a fresh hearing could have any result other than a finding adverse to the appellant."[362]

Even overlooking the preliminary difficulty of a court being sure that the applicant had an impossible case, this difference of views is difficult to resolve. The most that can be said is that a judge should be more likely to invalidate the decision impugned if he assigns importance to the advantages of "the day in court" and confidence in public administration and less likely to do so if he regards these advantages as trivial and outweighed by the disadvantages which were mentioned at the start of this Part. In addition, the more serious the consequences for the aggrieved party, the less likely the courts are to refuse relief.[363]

It is, of course, always possible for the court to avoid laying down any general principle and, instead, to determine the outcome of the case by refusing relief on discretionary grounds and this approach has often been adopted.[364]

Appeals

The second policy question arising in this area concerns the effect of an appeal. Where a decision is taken in breach of the rules of constitutional justice, is the defect cured, if there is a right of appeal and, on appeal, the rules are observed? It has been consistently held that an appeal does not cure the flaw in the original decision.[365]

(1984) 6 D.U.L.J. (N.S.) 152. For other authorities along the same lines, see *Maunsell v. Minister for Education* [1940] I.R. 213; *General Medical Council v. Spackman* [1943] A.C. 627; *Ridge v. Baldwin* [1964] A.C. 40; *The State (Crothers) v. Kelly* [1978] I.L.R.M. 167 and see generally Clark, "Natural Justice: Substance or Shadow?" (1975) *Public Law* 27.

[360] [1983] I.R. at 287.

[361] [1977] I.R. 317. See also, to like effect: *Ward v. Bradford Corporation* (1970) 70 L.G.R. 27; *Glynn v. Keele University* [1971] 1 W.L.R. 487; *Irish Family Planning Assoc. v. Ryan* [1979] I.R. 295 at 319; *R. (McPherson) v. Ministry of Education* [1980] N.I. 115n; *Cheall v. A.P.E.X.* [1983] 2 A.C. 109; and *Green v. South Eastern Health Board*, unreported, High Court (Barron J.) December 11, 1987. Note also the comments of Lord Denning in *R. v. Home Secretary, ex p. Mughal* [1974] Q.B. 313 at 325. "Only too often the people who have done wrong seek to invoke the rules of natural justice in order to avoid the consequences." But see *Gallagher v. Revenue Commissioners (No.2)* [1995] 1 I.R. 55 at 63 where Morris J. rejected the argument that the applicant was "merely using his entitlement to fair procedures as an obstacle to his having to face up to his responsibilities."

[362] [1977] I.R. 327.

[363] See, *e.g. R. (Hennessy) v. Department of the Environment* [1980] N.I. 109; *O'Brien v. Bord na Móna* [1983] I.R. 255.

[364] *Fulbrook v. Berkshire Magistrates' Courts* (1970) 69 L.G.R. 75; *Ward v. Bradford Corporation* (1971) 70 L.G.R. 27; *Glynn v. Keele University* [1971] 1 W.L.R. 487; *R. (McPherson) v. Department of Education* [1980] N.I. 115n. On the question of the discretionary character of the remedies, see further, pp. 000. The British judges appear to have taken the same view – that the rules apply however weak the applicant's case – as the Irish majority line: Craig, above, n.137, *op. cit.* pp. 301–302.

[365] *Leary v. National Union of Vehicle Builders* [1971] Ch. 34; *Ingle v. O'Brien* (1975) 109 I.L.T.R. 9; *Moran v. Attorney General* [1976] I.R. 400; *Irish Family Planning Assoc. v. Ryan* [1979] I.R. 295;

However, the significance of this ruling has been reduced by the gloss introduced, in *Gammell v. Dublin County Council*,[366] namely that certain categories of "appeal" can be treated as part of the initial decision.

McDonough v. Minister for Defence [1991] 2 I.R. 33 at 41. *A contra: The State (Stanbridge) v. Mahon* [1979] I.R. 217; *Calvin v. Carr* [1980] A.C. 574 and *The State (Collins) v. Ruane* [1984] I.R. 105 at 124, *per* Henchy J. and *Halal Meat Packers Ltd v. E.A.T.* [1990] I.L.R.M. 293 at 309. But see, *obiter, Bane v. The Garda Representation Association* [1997] 2 I.R. 449.
[366] [1983] I.L.R.M. 413. See further, pp. 567–568.

CHAPTER 12

CONTROL OF DISCRETIONARY POWERS

1. Discretionary Power

There is a distinction between decisions involving the resolution of disputed questions of fact coupled with the application of pre-existing law (or, at least, a guideline) and, on the other hand, those involving the exercise of discretionary power. The first type of decision is quintessentially the domain of a court or tribunal, though, often and on a quite random basis, it may be vested in a Minister or local authority.[1] The second type of decision – that is where a discretionary or policy function is being exercised – may be illustrated by the following examples:

> "On the application of . . . a person who proposes to carry on the business of a livestock mart . . . in such form . . . as the Minister [for Agriculture] may direct, the Minister may, at his discretion, grant or refuse to grant a licence authorising the carrying on of the business of a livestock mart . . ."[2]

> "A sanitary authority may by order prohibit the erection . . . of temporary dwellings on any land or water in their sanitary district if they are of opinion that such erection . . . would be prejudicial to public health . . .".[3]

In spite of the apparent *carte blanche* which expressions like ". . . may, at his discretion . . . 'or' . . . if they are of opinion . . ." appear to bestow, discretionary powers are subject to the general requirements requiring the decision-maker to observe both the *vires* of the parent statute (explained in Chapter 9) and also subject to certain additional controls which form the subject-matter of this chapter. These controls are grouped under the headings of: "Abuse (or excess) of discretionary powers", covered in Part 2; and "Failure to exercise a discretion" described in Part 4. In addition, certain glosses deriving in part from the Constitution which have made an appearance here and (and in slightly different vestments) in Britain, in the past few years, are described in Part 3, under the title, "New Doctrines". By way of conclusion to this chapter, Part 5 offers some comments on the broad question of whether any discretionary powers are unreviewable.

This is a difficult area, in practice if not in theory. In the first place, there is a distinction, in principle, between the exercise of a discretionary power and a statutory

---

[1] See above, pp. 258–259.
[2] Livestock Marts Act 1967, s.3(1) examined in *East Donegal Co-Operatives Ltd v. Attorney General* [1970] I.R. 317 described at p. 635.
[3] Local Government (Sanitary Services) Act 1948, s.31(1) involved in *Listowel U.D.C. v. McDonagh* [1968] I.R. 312 (see pp. 629–630) and *Corporation of Limerick v. Sheridan* (1956) 90 I.L.T.R. 59 (see p. 405 and p. 675).

duty[4] imposed on a public authority (breach of which sounds in damages) in that the latter attracts strict liability whereas the former is discretionary. In practice, there are types of statutory duty[5] which are so broad and vague that the judicial task of determining their extent, in order to decide whether there has been a breach, comes close to the exercise of determining the considerations which are relevant to the exercise of a discretionary power so as to decide whether there has been an abuse of power.

Secondly, the difficulty of delineating the law in this area is increased by the fact that:

> "The scope of review may be conditioned by a variety of factors: the wording of the discretionary power, the subject-matter to which it is related, the character of the authority to which it is entrusted, the purpose for which it is conferred, the particular circumstances in which it has in fact been exercised, the materials available to the court, and in the last analysis whether a court is of the opinion that judicial intervention would be in the public interest. . . . Broadly speaking, however, one can say that the courts will show special restraint in applying tests of legality where (i) a power is exercisable in 'emergency' conditions . . . ; or (iii) the 'policy content of the power is large and its exercise affects large numbers of people. Their reluctance to intervene is likely to diminish the more closely the wording and content of the power approximate to those of a discretion typically exercised by a tribunal.'"[6]

These daunting observations show how wary the reader should be of generalisations in this field.

Thirdly, the same broad set of rules have been applied to the control of discretionary powers set in a number of different contexts. For example, they have been applied variously to procedural[7] as well as substantive questions. In the nature of things, most of the cases to be described in this chapter concern substantive issues. However, in *Boyhan v. Beef Tribunal*[8] they were applied without demur, to the exercise

---

4 For breach of statutory duty, see pp. 816–818.
5 *e.g.* see *O'Reilly v. Limerick Corporation* [1989] I.L.R.M. 181 at 189–191.
6 de Smith, *Judicial Review of Administrative Action* (4th ed., 1980) pp. 281, 297. Item (ii) in Professor de Smith's catalogue refers to immigration, expulsion and deportation cases; it is omitted because seemingly it does not apply here; see *The State (Kugan) v. Station Sergeant, Fitzgibbon St.* [1986] I.L.R.M. 95 (p. 634).
7 Yet surely in this field, the discretion is confined by the Constitution: since it has been held that the (qualified) right to constitutional justice exists by virtue of Article 40.3.1°. See pp. 503–504. This passage is not to be found in the current edition of *Judicial Review of Administrative Action* (5th ed., 1995), the authors of which are now de Smith, Lord Woolf and Prof. Jowell. Save where otherwise indicated, subsequent references to de Smith are to the 5th edition of this classical work.
8 [1993] 1 I.R. 210 at 221. See likewise, *Kiberd v. Hamilton* [1992] 2 I.R. 257 where a newspaper had published details of a controversial Government proposal just before certain allegations relating to this matter were about to be considered by a Tribunal of Inquiry. The manner of publication suggested that it had been culled from the files supplied by a State agency to the Tribunal. When the newspaper refused to disclose their sources, the Tribunal – acting reasonably it was held – made an order requiring them to do so pursuant to section 4 of the Tribunals of Inquiry (Evidence)(Amendment) Act 1979. See also *Desmond v. Glackin (No. 2)* [1993] 2 I.R. 67 (Ministerial appointment of inspector under Companies Act 1990 valid where decision made bona fide, was not unreasonable and was factually sustainable). See also the seminal English case of *Padfield v. Minister of Agriculture* [1968] A.C. 997.

of the Chairman's decision (under the Tribunals of Inquiry (Evidence) Act, 1921) to grant representation at the proceedings of the Tribunal.

More surprisingly, the same set of rules has also been applied without much discussion to a discretion exercised by a court (even though such a discretion – "a judicial discretion" – has traditionally been considered *sui generis*.) Take, for example, in *Cumann Lúthchleas Gael Teo. v. Judge Windle*.[9] Here, the test applied to a District Judge exercise of statutory discretion as to whether an offence was a minor offence, fit to be tried summarily, was the familiar (to administrative lawyers) one of whether "it was irrational or was unsupported by the evidence before [the Judge]."[10] Even more surprisingly, as we shall see,[11] the rules relating to control of discretion have also been applied in the field of error of fact.

Again, it seems that the framework of control is not radically affected where its object is not a singular decision but rather delegated legislation, *i.e.* regulations, rules etc.[12] For example, in *Philips v. Medical Council*[13] the High Court considered whether rules for the registration of doctors, made by the respondent, under the Medical Practitioners Act 1978 were *ultra vires* the Act. Costello J. stated:

"The Oireachtas conferred on the Council a statutory rule-making power. It must exercise it according to certain well-established principles. As stated by Henchy, J. in *Cassidy v. Minister for Industry and Commerce* [1978] I.R. 297 at p. 310:–

'The general rule of law is that where Parliament has by statute delegated a power of subordinate legislation, the power must be exercised within the limitations of that power as they are expressed or necessarily implied in the statutory delegation. Otherwise it will be held to have been invalidly exercised for being *ultra vires*. And it is a necessary implication in such a statutory delegation that the power to issue subordinate legislation should be exercised reasonably.'

The concept of reasonableness appears in many areas of our law and is one which it is difficult to formulate with precision. Mr. Justice Henchy [in *Cassidy*] went on to quote with approval a passage from Diplock L.J. in *Mixnam's Properties Ltd v. Chertsey Urban District Council* [1964] 1 Q.B. 214 where in the context of the exercise of subordinate legislative powers the concept of reasonableness was helpfully developed. The quotation reads:

'Thus, the kind of unreasonableness which invalidates a by-law is not the antonym of "unreasonableness" in the sense of which that expression is used in the common law, but such manifest arbitrariness, injustice or partiality that a court would say: "Parliament never intended to give authority to make such rules; they are unreasonable and ultra vires".'"[14]

---

9 [1994] 1 I.R. 525.
10 *Ibid.* at 540–541.
11 See p. 648.
12 See *Philips v. Medical Council* [1991] 2 I.R. 115 at 139–42, *Clancy v. IRFU* [1995] 1 I.L.R.M. 193 at 198; *Donegal Fuel and Supply Co Ltd v. Londonderry Port and Harbour Commissioners* [1994] 1 I.R. 24 at 40; *McCann v. Minister for Education* [1997] 1 I.L.R.M. 1. See also case law summarised at pp. 56–57. For delegated legislation, see p. 30.
13 [1991] 2 I.R. 115.
14 *Ibid.* at 139–140.

This suggests that the rules regarding reasonableness in this context are similar to, though perhaps rather more stringent than those which apply where the action under review is singular rather than legislative in character. Nevertheless, in *Philips*, Costello J. went on to hold that a requirement, in the rules, that the seven years practice as a doctor necessary for registration had to be consecutive, amounted to "manifest injustice" and thus that the rules were *ultra vires*. However, one should emphasise that whilst such a strong formula as "manifest injustice" or "unduly and improperly harsh"[15] is occasionally used in the context of delegated legislation, there is as yet no case in which this language can be identified as influencing the outcome.

Traditionally a distinction has not been drawn between the following: whether the exercise of discretionary power is to settle a large policy which is likely to have wide repercussions, in a number of cases; or whether it is merely to make a judgment between two competing courses of action in an individual case. Thus the same formula has recently been applied in cases involving points of judgment in regard to individual decisions. For example: the chairman of the Garda Conciliation Council's ruling as to whether a particular change in conditions of work could be considered by the Council; the Garda Review Board's decision to penalise an erring member of the Gardaí; or the Irish Coursing Clubs's award of a greyhound trophy.[16]

2. Abuse of Discretionary Power

The classic exposition of the principles traditionally restraining abuse of power by public authorities (which principles, like the rules of natural justice, are cast in the mould of specialised rules of statutory interpretation) was given by Lord Greene in *Associated Provincial Picture Houses Ltd v. Wednesbury Corporation*[17]:

"When an executive discretion is entrusted by Parliament to a body such as the local authority in this case, what appears to be an exercise of that discretion can only be challenged in the courts in a strictly limited class of case. As I have said, it must always be remembered that the court is not a court of appeal. When discretion of this kind is granted the law recognises certain principles upon which that discretion must be exercised, but within the four corners of those principles the discretion, in my opinion, is an absolute one and cannot be questioned in any court of law. . . . I am not sure myself whether the permissible grounds of attack cannot be defined under a single head. It has been perhaps a little bit confusing to find a series of grounds set out. Bad faith, dishonesty – those, of course, stand by themselves – unreasonableness, attention given to extraneous

---

15 *Clancy v. IRFU* [1995] 1 I.L.R.M. at 198. Though see *Warnock v. Revenue Commissioners* [1986] I.L.R.M. 37 (summarised at p. 640) in which the test of "burdensome and oppressive" was used although this did not involved delegated legislation.

16 The three decisions alluded to are: *Garda Representative Association v. Ireland* [1989] I.L.R.M. 1 (High Ct.); [1994] 1 I.L.R.M. 81 at 88–90 (Sup. Ct.); *Stroker v. Doherty* [1991] 1 I.R. 23 and *Mathews v. Irish Coursing Club* [1993] 1 I.R. 346 examined at 645–646, 642–643 and 646, respectively. The same formula was applied in *Greaney v. Dublin Corporation* [1994] 3 I.R. 384 at 391 (*obiter*) (The applicant for a fire safety certificate had presented the requisite information in such a fashion that finding it would impose an unreasonable work-load on the official; accordingly application was rejected and the judicial review proceedings failed).

17 [1948] 1 K.B. 223, 230.

circumstances, disregard of public policy and things like that have all been referred to, according to the facts of individual cases, as being matters which are relevant to the question. If they cannot all be confined under one head, they at any rate, I think, overlap to a very great extent. For instance, we have heard in this case a great deal about the meaning of the word 'unreasonable.' . . . It has frequently been used and is frequently used as a general description of the things that must not be done. For instance, a person entrusted with a discretion must, so to speak, direct himself properly in law. He must call his own attention to the matters which he is bound to consider. He must exclude from his consideration matters which are irrelevant to what he has to consider. If he does not obey those rules, he may truly be said, and often is said, to be acting 'unreasonably.' Similarly, there may be something so absurd that no sensible person could ever dream that it lay within the powers of the authority. Warrington L.J. in *Short v. Poole Corporation*[18] gave the example of the red-haired teacher, dismissed because she had red hair. That is unreasonable in one sense. In another sense it is taking into consideration extraneous matters. It is so unreasonable that it might almost be described as being done in bad faith; and, in fact, all these things run into one another."

One crucial precept which emerges from this passage is that a court reviewing a discretionary action is not to substitute its own view of the merits for that of the public body in which the legislature has vested the decision. As has been said:

"Judicial review is concerned, not with the decision, but with the decision-making process. Unless that restriction on the power of the court is observed, the court will in my view, under the guise of preventing the abuse of power, be itself guilty of usurping power."[19]

An analogy can usefully be drawn between the reviewing court's position and that of an appeal court which is asked to upset a jury verdict: the question is not what the court itself would have done had it been taking the initial decision, but rather whether no reasonable public body could have reached such a decision. This is especially true where the applicant's contention would require the reviewing court to investigate disputed facts. Here, one should raise briefly the possibility that the availability of a statutory right of appeal ought to influence the rules for the control of the exercise of a discretionary power: the thinking might be that if there were an appeal, then there would be less need for control through the court on review and accordingly, the courts should only intervene in an extreme case. The suggestion seems to be undesireable since appeal and review have different functions and, furthermore, the appellate body will often have only a restricted jurisdiction. In view of these considerations, it seems more appropriate that the significance of any appeal would be considered under the heading of the court's discretion in sending a remedy.[20] The point has not

---

[18] [1926] Ch. 66, 90–91.
[19] *Chief Constable of the North Wales Police v. Evans* [1982] 1 W.L.R. 1155, 1173–74, *per* Lord Brightman quoted with approval by Griffin J. in *The State (Keegan) v. The Stardust Victims Compensation Tribunal* [1986] I.R. 642 at 661. This passage has been frequently quoted with approval: see, *e.g. Garda Representative Association v. Ireland* [1994] 1 I.L.R.M. 81 at 81–89, *per* Finlay C.J. and *Flood v. Garda Síochána Complaints Board*, unreported, High Court, October 8, 1997.
[20] See pp. 734–739.

yet been squarely addressed in a court, though in *Ferris v. Dublin County Council*[21] Finlay C.J. rejected a submission that a higher standard of reasonableness should be set for a public body if no appeal is provided.

Whilst Lord Greene's judgment in *Wednesbury* has been quoted extensively both because of its exemplary clarity and because of its influence for at least four decades in most parts of the common law world, it must be emphasised that the law has not stood still. The formulae set out in the judgment ("unreasonableness," "public policy," etc.) have proved sufficiently elastic to accommodate far-reaching changes in judicial outlook (though it should also be noted that they had to be stated so generally that their application in concrete cases often gives rise to controversy[22]). However, notwithstanding the incremental change permitted by the *Wednesbury* formula which has just been described, by the mid-Eighties it was thought by many lawyers that a more radical and explicit modification was required. The forms taken by this mood was two-fold. First there has been a re-statement of the *Wednesbury* formula, which is discussed at the end of this Part.[23] Secondly, there are some signs of a change of principle, which are examined in the next Part of this chapter, under the heading "New Doctrines." However, it should be emphasised that these changes will not affect the outcome in most cases and that, side by side with these developments, *Wednesbury* remains of substantial contemporary importance, as witness the number of modern cases which have found a niche within this, rather than the next Part. As indicated, in the lengthy passage quoted earlier from *Wednesbury*, abuse of power can be subdivided into different aspects – bad faith; taking into account irrelevant considerations; and unreasonableness – which yet overlap to a considerable degree. Before returning to survey these aspects *seriatim*,[24] certain general matters must first be briefly examined.

---

[21] Unreported, Supreme Court, Finlay, C.J., November 7, 1990. There appears to be support for a contrary view in *Clancy v. IRFU* [1995] 1 I.L.R.M. 193, 198 (where *Ferris* is not, however mentioned). Dealing with I.R.F.U. regulations dealing with clubs for which a player could play, Morris J. stated:

> "Even if this is to be regarded as 'retrospective legislation' the regulation contains provision for an appeal procedure to the IRFU. who would be obliged under its rules to deal with all such appeals on their merits. They would be required in a proper case to remove the prohibition against playing. This provision alters the complexion of a rule which might otherwise be open to criticism as being unduly and improperly harsh."

What Morris J. seems to have in mind here appears to be not a true appeal but some kind of equity jurisdiction.

[22] Take, for example, the outcome of *Wednesbury* itself. The defendant was a local authority which was empowered, under the Sunday Entertainments Act 1932, to grant licences for Sunday entertainment at the cinema subject to such conditions as it thought fit. The plaintiff picture-house owner was granted a licence but subject to the condition that no children under 15 be admitted to a Sunday performance with or without an adult. This condition was challenged. The challenge failed and the Court of Appeal evidently regarded it as a very feeble case. Given the wide social and religious difference between Britain in the 1940s (with its Lord's Day observance tendency) and Ireland in the 1990s (with its televisions and videos), the issue is difficult to discuss. However, there seems at least a possibility that the plaintiff would have succeeded had he come before a present-day Irish court with the same facts. The reason for this surmise is that given the existence of Sunday opening at all, it might appear by today's standard of "reasonablesness", an unreasonable exercise of discretion to do as the defendant had done, namely to operate a blanket ban, preventing any person below the age of 15, even if accompanied by an adult, from watching any film, however innocuous.

[23] See pp. 641–643.

[24] See pp. 628–641.

Determining the facts

Another general problem which often arises in cases in this area is the difficulty of establishing facts which are essential in order to ground a judicial review application, for example as to bad faith or, where these have not been divulged, the reasons on which a decision is based. The obvious sources of information include: the minutes of a decision-making meeting; affidavits of participants at such a meeting; or public statements made by the responsible authority. Again, as we saw in the previous chapter,[25] there is a duty to give reasons and, thus, in appropriate circumstances, a decision may be either struck down for failure to give reasons or, alternatively, a court may be prepared to assume the worst as regards the public authority's motivation and, so, to strike down for abuse of a discretionary power. Next, in a characteristic passage in *East Donegal Co-Operatives Ltd v. Attorney-General*, Walsh J. noted the existence of such devices as discovery and interrogatories and then issued the following warning: ". . . the resources of the Courts . . . are not so limited that they could facilitate . . . the concealment of an infringement of constitutional rights or the masking of injustice."[26]

Another recourse for an appellant, frustrated by an absence of hard information, is that if there is an absence of explanation or elucidation, a court is entitled to infer the worst from a discrepancy between the decision taken and the decision which could have been expected if the proper guidelines had been observed.[27] Thus, an obvious relationship between a court making such an inference and the duty to give reasons.

The absence of reasons was at least a strong supporting factor in the case of *Breen v. Minister for Defence*.[28] Here the facts were that the respondent Minister

---

[25] For the duty to state reasons, see pp. 570–577.

[26] [1970] I.R. 317 at 349.

[27] *The State (McGough) v. Louth County Council* (1973) 107 I.L.T.R. 13, 25; *Padfield v. Minister for Agriculture* [1968] A.C. 1032 at 1061. Note that the proposition stated in the text is probably not supported by *P. & F. Sharpe Ltd v. Dublin County Council* [1989] I.R. 701 (the facts of which are given at pp. 235 and 643). Here, rejecting, on behalf of the Supreme Court, the argument that the Council's decision was unreasonable Finlay C.J. stated: (at 718–719).

> "It appears to me that both in the High Court and in this Court there is a very great difficulty in reaching a conclusion as to what the material was which was before the elected members at the time of their two discussions concerning this resolution and was considered by them prior to deciding to pass the resolution . . .
>
> It seems likely that for this issue to have been satisfactorily determined in the High Court the procedure adopted in this particular application for judicial review of proceeding on affidavits only was incorrect and insufficient and that what would have been required was an oral hearing preceded by simple pleadings. If I were satisfied that it had been established that the only matters which were before the elected members when they passed this resolution were the reports of the county manager and his engineering staff, I would incline to the view that the resolution would be so unreasonable as to fall within the category dealt with in *State (Keegan) v. Stardust Compensation Tribunal* [1986] I.R. 642. I am not satisfied on the facts as found in this case that that was the only information before the elected members. I would, therefore, uphold the conclusion reached by the learned trial judge in the High Court that he was unable to decide on the information before him, and in this context the onus would appear to be on the appellants, that the decision was unreasonable."

In the last sentence, the Chief Justice implicitly rejects the notion that the decision should be regarded as invalid (or at least that there is a presumption that it is unreasonable) if given without reasons. Yet later on (at 581), Finlay C.J. states that the local authority is under a duty to state reasons.

[28] [1994] 2 I.R. 34. For another example; see *R. v. Civil Service Appeals Board, ex p. Cunningham* [1991] 4 All E.R. 910.

had exercised his statutory discretion to reduce the applicant's army pension because of the fact that the applicant had obtained civil damages for the injury which had led to the pension being awarded. The Minister's decision was based on the fact that the damages award was for £60,000. This failed to take into account such factors as: the applicant's legal costs; delay in receiving the award; expenditure by the applicant in reliance on receiving both the entire award and a pension. As a result of these deductions, the applicant had only ever been in possession of roughly half the award. Representations based on these points were put to the Minister, without effecting any change. The Supreme Court speaking, *per* O'Flaherty J., stated:

> "The respondent having carefully, as he said, considered the representations, nonetheless, has not stated how he reacted to the information that he received about the dire straits in which this unfortunate man found himself.
>
> I am far from saying that every administrative decision must be accompanied by elaborate reasons such as would be appropriate to a judgment but the citizen's sense of resentment and frustration can be readily understood in circumstances where he has presented what he thinks is a viable case and has been met simply by a blanket refusal to change by the administrative decision-maker. Unfortunately, the decision arrived at appears to fly in the face of what the justice of the case required . . .
>
> I would hold that the respondent's decision was unreasonable because the stark fact is that the applicant never received the sum of £60,000."[29]

In this regard it should also be noted that the courts probably have an inherent jurisdiction to compel an administrative body to give a full account of the manner in which it arrived at its decision.[30] In any event, a respondent opposing an application for judicial review is required by Ord. 84, r.22(4) to file a statement "setting out concisely the grounds for such opposition and, if any facts are relied on therein, an affidavit verifying such facts",[31] so that in an appropriate case the High Court could probably compel a respondent to file an affidavit containing a fuller explanation than a mere laconic denial of any impropriety or illegality.

Thus, in *R v. Lancashire County Council, ex p. Huddleston*[32] – a case where a local authority appeared to have given "cursory and inadequate" consideration to an application for a discretionary grant – Sir John Donaldson M.R. said:

> "In proceedings for judicial review, the applicant no doubt has an axe to grind. This should not be true of [a public body]. The analogy is not exact, but just as judges of the inferior courts when challenged on the exercise of their jurisdiction traditionally explain fully what they have done, but are not partisan

---

[29] [1994] 2 I.R. 34 at 41–42.

[30] *The State (Creedon) v. Criminal Injuries Compensation Tribunal* [1988] I.R. 51 at 54–55, *per* Finlay C.J. *Creedon* was distinguished by Murphy J. in *O'Donoghue v. An Bord Pleanála* [1991] I.L.R.M. 751 at 759.

[31] It may be noted that in *Creedon* (where the application had been made under the pre-1986 Rules) the Tribunal (in the words of Finlay C.J. at 53):

> ". . . did not show cause by filing any affidavit, and did not further elaborate the reason for its decision but simply asserted by a notice showing cause that it had acted within jurisdiction . . . and that there was evidence on which it reached and was entitled to reach its decision."

in their own defence, so should be the public authorities. It is not discreditable to get it wrong. What is discreditable is a reluctance to explain fully what has occurred and why. [The authority submitted] that it is for the applicant to make out his case for judicial review and that it is not for the respondent authority to do it for him. This, in my judgment, is only partially correct. Certainly it is for the applicant to satisfy the court of his entitlement to judicial review and it is for the respondent to resist his application, if it considers it to be unjustified. But it is a process which falls to be conducted with all the cards face upwards on the table and the vast majority of the cards will start in the authority's hands . . . [The] authorities assist neither themselves nor the courts, if their response is a blanket assertion of having acted in accordance with law or one which begs the question. If the issue is whether an authority took a particular factor into account, it will be a sufficient response to show that it did. But if the allegation is that a decision is prima facie irrational and that there are grounds for inquiring whether something immaterial may have been considered or something material omitted from consideration, it really does not help to assert baldly that all relevant matters and no irrelevant matters were taken into consideration without condescending to mention at least some of the principal factors on which the decision was based."[33]

A good example of this unhelpful administrative attitude leading to the quashing of a decision on unreasonableness grounds is provided by *Gavin v. Criminal Injuries Compensation Tribunal*.[34] In this case the Tribunal concluded that the applicant had suffered significant mental distress as a result of a notorious crime. However, in awarding him £100,000, it did not specify how much was attributable to (i) lost earnings and (ii) pain and suffering, despite the fact that the actuarial evidence before the Tribunal suggested that the applicant's loss of earnings alone was over £500,000. When the applicant sought a detailed breakdown of these figures, the Tribunal's Secretary formally replied that having considered all aspects of the appeal at the oral hearing, the Tribunal saw no reason to vary its original decision.[35] Although the Secretary had filed an affidavit setting out the reasons which she believed the Tribunal had taken into account, Carroll J. did not consider that this was an acceptable means of demonstrating how the Tribunal had arrived at its decision:

"It is for the Tribunal to speak for itself. The long history of trauma and delay which the applicant had suffered for years demanded a reasoned decision if he

---

32 [1986] 2 All E.R. 941.
33 *Ibid.* at 945–946. The concluding part of this passage is echoed in the words of O'Flaherty J. in *Breen v. Minister for Defence, supra*, pp. 673–674. *Cf.* the comments of McCarthy J. in *O'Keeffe v. An Bord Pleanála* [1993] 1 I.R. 39 at 80: ". . . there are administrative bodies that prove less than co-operative in telling the public or individual members of it the reasons for a particular decision."
34 [1997] 1 I.R. 132. See also *The State (McGeough) v. Louth County Council* (1973) 107 I.L.T.R. 13.
35 Rather interestingly, however, a memorandum which emerged on discovery revealed that the Tribunal Secretary had spoken to a civil servant in the Department of Justice about the case. The memorandum of that conversation recorded her as saying that:
"The Chairperson is adamant that the Tribunal is not obliged to explain its award in any individual case to the applicant . . . Were a response to be supplied to Mr. Gavin it would, in effect, be providing him with 'ammunition' for any [subsequent] Court case."
This memorandum not only illustrates the potential value of discovery, but also provides a graphic illustration of the concerns expressed by Sir John Donaldson M.R. in *Huddleston* and by McCarthy J. in *O'Keeffe*.

were not to get the full amount of his claim. Perhaps it would have been acceptable if the applicant were furnished by the Tribunal with reasons immediately when he asked for them. But since that did not happen in this case, I need not concern myself with that possibility. What is not acceptable is for the Secretary to purport to say what the Tribunal thought and what its reasons were."[36]

As the Tribunal had thus not adequately explained why it had taken the step of drastically reducing uncontradicted financial calculations, Carroll J. quashed its determination. This case may thus be regarded as one where the lack of adequate reasons led the court to conclude that the decision was unreasonable in law.

This factor was also present in *Brennan v. Minister for Justice*,[37] a case with admittedly special facts. In this case the applicant District Judge challenged the validity of the petitions system which was operated by the Minister.[38] A minor chord in Geoghegan J.'s judgment for the applicant was that it was "constitutionally necessary" that:

". . . all the evidence and information leading up to and the reasons for the exercise of the power be recorded. This is a logical consequence of the special nature of the power which would have been envisaged as to be exercised only in special cases. But for the exercise of any power . . . some accountability is essential. There has been a long established practice that the Minister does not answer questions in Dail Éireann relating to individual instances of the exercise of this power. That being so, the only way that the Minister can in practice be made accountable for the proper exercise of the power is by means of judicial review in an appropriate case. But a proper judicial review would be frustrated unless there were stated reasons recorded for the exercise of the power together with all the information on which they were based."[39]

Geoghegan J. accordingly granted a declaration that the Minister did not properly exercise her powers of remission in that "no purported exceptional circumstances or reasons for the decisions were recorded" such as would have justified her in modifying the decision of the District Judge.

Plurality of Purposes

The question of motive is, of course, a peculiarly difficult issue of fact. It is nowhere more difficult than where the administrative authority is moved by a number of different purposes (a not unlikely situation which is considered here because it could arise in regard to more than one of the sub-heads of abuse). Where an authority has sought to achieve unauthorised as well as authorised purposes, the question of what test should be used to determine the validity of its act has been characterised as "a legal porcupine which bristles with difficulties as soon as it is touched."[40] A

---

[36] [1997] 1 I.R. 132 at 142.
[37] [1995] 1 I.R. 612.
[38] For the major theme, see p. 62.
[39] [1995] 1 I.R. 612 at 629.
[40] de Smith, *op. cit.* above, n.7 p. 340.

straightforward example occurred in *Cassidy v. Minister for Industry and Commerce*[41] in which the plaintiff's case, on the present point, failed because, as Henchy J. stated:

> "The evidence forces me to the conclusion that the primary and dominant purpose of the Minister in making these orders was to eliminate unwarranted price increases (a proper purpose) and that, while he also had as his aim the return of the publicans to the voluntary practice of not making price increases without giving him prior notice (an improper purpose) that aim was merely subsidiary and consequential to the dominant and permitted purpose."[42]

The facts were on the other side of the same line in the Northern Irish case of *Re Murray's Application*.[43] This case involved a chief constable's power to transfer police officers and to change their duties. The proper purpose of this power, it was accepted, was to promote the efficiency of the police force. In the instant case, this was not the chief constable's only purpose and it was established that he was also pursuing an unauthorised purpose, namely that of disciplining the officers who were transferred and whose duties had been changed. Carswell J. held that the transfer order was invalid and adopted – admittedly in a case involving rather suspicious facts – the most stringent of the tests which have been employed elsewhere in the common law world. Whilst refusing to find that punishment was the predominant motive for the transfer, he held that it sufficed, if the applicant could establish that this was one of the chief constable's purposes.

The question of plurality of purposes has also arisen in the rather particular circumstances of criminal procedure. In *People (Director of Public Prosecutions) v. Howley*[44] the accused had been arrested under section 30 of the Offences against the State Act 1939 in respect of the offence of cattle maiming. This offence under the Malicious Damage Act 1861 is a scheduled offence under the 1939 Act and, hence, a suspect may be detained for a period of up to 48 hours if arrested under section 30.[45] However, the cattle-maiming incident had occurred over a year prior to the accused's arrest and he submitted – with good reason, it might be thought – that this was merely a colourable device to permit his detention in respect of the (non-scheduled) offence of murder. The accused was suspected of the murder of a young woman (which had taken place over a year before the cattle-maiming incident) and it was argued that in reality it was the murder which was uppermost in the mind of the Gardai when they arrested him. *Howley* is, incidentally, of interest in an entirely different and more general context, namely, whether criminal procedure is broadly subject to the same substantive principles of judicial review as are other administrative actions of organs of the state. One British commentator has said that "where a constable has exercised a statutory discretion, his action is now in principle

---

41 [1978] I.R. 297. See also, *Murphy v. Dublin Corporation* [1976] I.R. 143; *Hussey v. Irish Land Commission*, Supreme Court, December 13, 1984; *The State (Bouzagou) v. The Station Sergeant, Fitzgibbon St. Garda Station* [1986] I.L.R.M. 95.

42 *Ibid.* 308–309.

43 [1987] 12 N.I.J.B. 2.

44 [1989] I.L.R.M. 624.

45 For a fuller treatment of the arrest and scheduling powers under this section, see Hogan and Walker, *Political Violence and the Law in Ireland* (1989), pp. 192–200.

subject to challenge under public law"[46] and the correctness of this view in this jurisdiction (at least in relation to the discretionary powers of arrest conferred by section 30 of the 1939 Act) would appear to have been borne out by a series of judicial decisions.[47] Take for instance *The State (Bowes) v. Fitzpatrick.*[48] Here the applicant had been arrested under section 30, ostensibly in respect of the scheduled offence of malicious damage to a weapon. But this damage to the weapon had occurred in the course of a murder and Finlay P. had little difficulty in concluding that by reason of the predominant motive of the Gardai involved, the arrest of the applicant was not, bona fide:

In *Howley,* however, the Supreme Court seemed suspicious of this line of argument. Walsh J. referred "to the English administrative law decisions [on plurality of purposes] cited to the court" but thought them of little assistance:

> "While in similar circumstances a court here might well arrive at the same conclusion in such an instance the subject matter of those decisions is so totally different from the point before this Court that, in my view, they are of no assistance in this case. What is before this Court is a much more fundamental point, namely whether somebody has been deprived of his liberty in accordance with law or has been deprived of his liberty in circumstances which render unlawful the deprivation of liberty and that therefore he has been the victim of violation of his constitutional right to liberty. Either his detention is lawful or it is not. There is no intermediate position. There can be no question of competing or predominant issues which can determine that question."[49]

This appears to suggest that criminal procedure is to be treated as a thing apart from all other administrative actions on the basis that the most important constitutional right of all – liberty – is involved. This, of course, is a major conceptual question on which Walsh J.'s remarks represent the first, rather than the last, word. Moreover, it may be observed that it is not uncommon for fundamental rights – such as liberty – to be affected by administrative action and that judicial review offers a flexible instrument for reconciling individual rights of varying importance with the community interest, within a wide range of statutory régimes. It would seem undesirable to shun this relatively well-developed system of law and to seek to build an alternative specialised edifice for criminal procedure.

Bad faith (mala fides)

Fraud (frequently known as mala fides or bad faith) exists where a public body "intends to achieve an object other than that for which he believes the power to have been

---

46 Lustgarten, *The Governance of the Police* (1986), p. 68.
47 See, *e.g. People (D.P.P.) v. Quilligan* [1986] I.R. 495 at 507; *D.P.P. v. Gilmore* [1981] I.L.R.M. 102, 105 and *The State (Trimbole) v. Governor of Mountjoy Prison* [1985] I.R. 550.
48 [1989] I.L.R.M. 624 at 635. The passage from *Howley* also appears to suggest that the validity of an arrest must be capable of being objectively ascertained without any reference to the motives of the policemen concerned. But this can scarcely be correct, since it is trite law that any discretionary power (whether it be conferred by statute or the common law) can only be exercised for the purpose for which it is conferred and that an improper motive can invalidate what would otherwise be a valid exercise of that power.
49 [1978] I.L.R.M. 195 at 196.

conferred."[50] Thus bad faith includes, but is wider than, the concept of "malice" which should be used only where the repository of the discretionary power is motivated by personal animosity against a person or persons affected by it. In the other direction, bad faith may be distinguished from bias (covered in Part 2 of Chapter 10) in that bias may have an objective existence, without any element of consciousness similar to the *criminal* law concept of *mens rea*; whereas the essence of bad faith is dishonesty.[51]

Straightaway, two features emerge: first, cases in which bad faith is established are inevitably rare. Courts naturally shrink from labelling elected representatives and/or public officials as dishonest.[52] Moreover, public bodies are often made up of groups of people with differing levels of information about the subject-matter and with varying outlooks, motivations and political allegiances. Against this background, it will often be difficult to bring home a charge of bad faith because of the need to prove something akin to the criminal law concept of *mens rea*. Secondly, if a court concludes that a discretionary decision is the product of the consideration of irrelevant factors or is unreasonable, then it will be held invalid, even if there is no element of bad faith. Thus it will usually be otiose to try to establish bad faith. One exception to this observation would occur in an action where a plaintiff is suing for the as yet undeveloped tort of misfeasance of public office as bad faith is a necessary element of this tort.[53] Again, bad faith is regarded as particularly heinous so that the consequences of such a finding are more far-reaching than with other defects and this has an effect, for example, on the exercise of a court's discretion to send a remedy or the interpretation of a statutory clause purporting to exclude judicial review.[54] Another exception involves cases where the subject-matter of the power and other circumstances are such that exercise of the power is beyond the reach of judicial review, for "honest abuse of power," yet the courts would be prepared to intervene, it seems reasonable to suppose, if bad faith could be established.

Irish case law tends to bear out these general propositions. It is seldom that bad faith has been alleged before a court, never mind established. Take, for example, *The State (O'Mahony) v. South Cork Board of Public Health*[55] where the applicant was a tenant of the Board whose application to purchase the cottage in which she was living (as she was entitled to do under a statutory scheme) had been rejected by the respondent.[56] There had been bad blood between the parties for some time. According to Maguire P.:

---

[50] de Smith, above, n.7 *op. cit.* p. 554.

[51] Thus because of the finding of "pique" in *O'Mahony*, the case is put under the heading of bad faith; whereas there is no reason to regard the similar case of *McGeough* as involving dishonesty and it is accordingly classified as a case of bias (see p. 522). Little usually turns on this point of characterisation.

[52] See *Smith v. East Elloe U.D.C.* [1956] A.C. 736 at 767 quoted with approval in *Listowel U.D.C. v. McDonagh* [1968] I.R. 312 at 317 and *P. & F. Sharpe* at 570.

[53] See pp. 812–816 see also, *Roncarelli v. Dupleiss* (1959) 16 D.L.R. (2d) 689, 705; *Dunlop v. Woollahra M.C.* [1982] A.C. 158; *Bourgoin S.A. v. Ministry of Agriculture* [1986] Q.B. 716; *Pine Valley Developments Ltd v. Minister for Environment* [1987] I.R. 23.

[54] For the court's discretion and exclusion clauses, see further pp. 717–739 and pp. 454–458.

[55] For bad faith in extradition law, see, *e.g. The State (Hully) v. Hynes* (1966) 100 I.L.T.R. 145 (real purpose of securing prosecutor was to charge him with revenue offences); *Ellis v. O'Dea* [1990] I.L.R.M. 87, 93 (real purpose to make applicant available for interrogation: hypothetical remark).

[56] [1941] Ir. Jur. Rep. 79. For another case in which what looked like at least a prima facie case of bad faith received short shrift, see *The State (Divito) v. Arklow U.D.C.* [1986] I.L.R.M. 123. (Respondent

"The obligation to repair rested on the landlords. The applicant was active in carrying out repairs to the cottage and had sought to make the respondents responsible for the expense of repairs which she claimed to have done by reason of the default of the respondents. In this she was partially successful. Reading between the lines of the affidavits, it would appear that the Board was annoyed because she had taken on herself to do repairs to her cottage and more annoyed still because she had obtained a decree against them for £18 in respect of these repairs. . . . Mere pique at an unfavourable judgment in the High Court seems to me to be no justification for attempting to deprive the applicant of her legal rights."[57]

What is notable is that, although opining that the authority's decision had been taken through "mere pique," the High Court formally classified the case as one of taking extraneous considerations into account and "failure to consider the tenant's application."

However, about a year before *Cogley* was decided, the Supreme Court had made it clear in *Listowel U.D.C. v. McDonagh*[58] that *mala fides* is "a well recognised ground of challenge." By the Local Government (Sanitary Services) Act 1948 a sanitary authority is empowered: '[to] prohibit the erection . . . of temporary dwellings . . . if they are of opinion that such erection . . . would be prejudicial to public health . . ." Purporting to act under this power, Listowel U.D.C. made an order banning the construction of temporary dwellings on a number of named streets.

---

local authority passed a resolution under the Gaming and Lotteries Act 1956, the result of which was that anyone with premises in the relevant area was entitled to apply to the District Court for a gaming licence. The applicant applied unsuccessfully for a licence, his application being opposed by the local authority. Before he could reapply, the local authority revoked its resolution under the 1956 Act.) *The State (Cogley) v. Dublin Corporation* [1970] I.R. 244 is an even more striking case. The facts were these: the prosecutor's application for planning permission having been refused by the Corporation, he appealed successfully to the Minister for Local Government. The remaining stage of the planning procedure was to seek the planning authority's approval and this was granted by the assistant city manager. However, subsequently, the elected members of the Corporation, using their power under section 30 of the Local Government (Planning and Development) Act 1963, passed a resolution revoking the permission which had been granted by the Minister. The possibility of bad faith was raised, but rejected, with some *hateur*, by Teevan J. (at pp. 249–250).

"However, these features are no more than suspicions or, I should say, possible suspicions; and it would be very unjust to base any conclusion on them impugning the honour of the members of the Corporation in their approach to the very complex and anxious problems of town planning
 . . . .

Perhaps I have dwelt too much on this aspect of the case for, while the submission was put forward by the prosecutor's counsel, it was not developed to any appreciable extent – doubtless because he would have felt it unfair to do so in the absence of precise probative facts."

It is also notable that in what seemed a strong case, the High Court (O'Keefe P.) should at the initial stage of the proceedings, have taken the unusual course of refusing to grant the applicant even a conditional order and, so, obliging him to appeal to the Supreme Court before the substantive stage of the case could be heard by Teevan J.

57 [1941] Ir. Jur. Rep. 81–83.
58 [1968] I.R. 312 at 318. There is also a strong whiff of *mala fides* in *McDonough v. Minister for Defence* [1991] 2 I.R. 33 at 41 (action taken against applicant ostensibly for dangerous driving "was primarily due to his having sought advice from the legal officer") and in *Hoey v. Minister for Justice* [1994] 3 I.R. 329. Here, the applicants sought an order of mandamus directing the local authority to perform its statutory duty to repair the courthouse in Drogheda. Shortly after the mandamus proceedings were threatened, the Minister made orders purportedly regulating the transaction of the business of the Circuit Court and providing that Drogheda should no longer serve as a Circuit town, thereby relieving the authority of the duty to repair the courthouse. Lynch J. held that the orders were void, as their purpose was not "really to regulate sittings of the Circuit Court at all but rather as a defence to these mandamus proceedings and for that reason they are . . . void."

The defendant was convicted and fined 10 shillings for contravening this order. His principal line of defence was to argue that the order had not been made bona fide in that the sanitary authority did not genuinely hold the necessary opinion. The prosecution submitted that such an argument could only be heard in judicial view proceedings; they could not be argued in collateral proceedings,[59] such as, in the instant case, a criminal prosecution. The Supreme Court rejected this argument, holding that the defendant was free to adduce evidence before the Circuit Court (to which the case had gone on appeal) as to: what transpired at the council meeting which considered the passing of the by-law; what views were expressed by members and officials of the Council; and the veracity of the opinion they expressed. In the result, the Circuit Court found as a matter of fact, that the order had been made bona fide.[60]

Improper purposes and irrelevant considerations

"Improper purpose" in this context refers to the fact that, in enacting a statute, the legislature is assumed to have had a definable purpose(s) or object(s). True to the idea that they are implementing the mandate of the legislature, the courts seek to ensure that the power contained in the measure is used only for the "proper purpose." A simple example is afforded by *McDonough v. Minister for Defence*[61] which concerned the discipling of a naval driver by being "grounded", *i.e.* being barred from driving any vehicle other than the tractor – with a resultant loss of pay. Lavan J. held that the applicant's disqualification should have been considered not from the perspective of punishing the applicant but from the distinct perspective of what risks would be involved for the public in permitting the applicant to go on driving.[62]

---

59 On which see p. 798.
60 The applicants put in evidence a council memorandum entitled "The itinerant problem." However, nine councillors swore that they were concerned only with health matters and their evidence was accepted.
61 [1991] 2 I.R. 33 at 41. See to similar effect, *The People (D.P.P.) v. McCaughey*, Supreme Court, November 20, 1989, in the context of a punishment fixed by a court, for an offence of dangerous driving. On the general point, see *Cassidy v. Minister for Industry and Commerce* [1978] I.R. 297. See also two planning cases: in *The State (Fitzgerald) v. An Bord Pleanála* [1985] I.L.R.M. 117, the Supreme Court struck down the respondent's grant of planning permission to retain a building erected without permission. The reason given, by the board for its decision was its opinion that the degree of injury and departure from the original structure for which an earlier permission had been given was not such as to warrant the removal of the structure. The Supreme Court took the view that these were irrelevant factors. *Quaere* whether the Court's decision would have been different had the Court considered the argument that for Bord Pleanàla not to grant permission would have violated the doctrine of proportionality (on which, see pp. 655–663). Again, in *Flanagan v. Galway County Council* [1990] 2 I.R. 66, Blayney J. quashed a grant of planning permission which had been awarded because the councillors were swayed by the need to retain employment. *Flanagan* was followed in similar circumstances, by Blayney J., in *Griffin v. Galway County Council*, unreported, High Court, October 25, 1990.
62 [1978] I.R. 297, 310. See also, *Minister for Industry and Commerce v. White*, High Court, February 16, 1981. For other examples see *Corporation of Limerick v. Sheridan* (1956) 90 I.L.T.R. 59 at 63–64. (Section 31 of the Local Government (Sanitary Services) Act 1948, was being used, in effect, to constitute the Corporation as a licensing authority, although there were other sections in the 1948 Act which were specifically designed to do that.); *Latchford v. Minister for Industry and Commerce* [1950] I.R. 33 (disqualification from baking subsidy on ground of criminal conviction, which was held to be an irrelevant factor); *The State (Keller) v. Galway Co.Co.* [1958] I.R. 142 (disabled person's allowance refused on ground that applicant capable of doing any job when test was whether he could do job of same kind for which he would be suited, if he were not handicapped; for a somewhat similar case concerning a complaint before the Ombudsman, see: *The State (Melbarien Enterprises Ltd) v. Revenue Commissioners* [1986] I.L.R.M. 476, 482 (tax clearance certificate refused because a

With knowledge of the proper purpose (a difficulty to which we return *infra*) and making certain assumptions,[63] the court then deduces the considerations which the public authority should have in mind when it is exercising a discretionary power created by the measure. It follows, therefore, that there is an intimate relationship between the rules that relevant considerations must be taken into account and irrelevant considerations excluded and, on the other hand, the rule that the proper purpose must be observed when a discretionary power is being exercised. Accordingly, there seems to be little point in discussing the cases in separate compartments: 'pursuing an improper purpose' being distinguished from 'taking into account an irrlevant consideration' according to which label has been used in the judgment. Instead, our selection of specimen cases is arranged according to the criterion of whether or not the statute creating the discretionary power explicitly states its purpose or explicitly identifies the considerations which must be taken into account in exercising the discretion.[64] It must be admitted, however, that even where such guidelines exist, they may be insufficiently precise to settle specific cases beyond a doubt.

One example of a statutory power, the relevant factors in relation to which were fairly plainly indicated, was considered in *The State (Cussen) v. Brennan*.[65] This case arose out of the selection, by the Local Appointment Commissioners (of whom Mr. Brennan was one) of a consultant paediatrician. It was established that, as far as paediatrics was concerned, the L.A.C. had judged the applicant to be slightly ahead of his nearest rival but that the rival candidate's knowledge of the Irish language had tipped the balance in his favour. According to the relevant statutory provision (Health Act 1970, section 18), it was for the Minister for Health to lay down the qualifications for the job. The Minister had duly done this and a knowledge of Irish was not among the qualifications which he had specified. Consequently the L.A.C. had taken irrelevant considerations into account.[66] Another example[67] which was

---

company with connections with the applicant company owed arrears of tax): see p. 54, n.237; *Ambiorix Ltd v. Minister for the Environment (No. 2)* [1992] 2 I.R. 37, (in regard to the test of whether there was a "special need to promote urban renewal" in an area, Minister had taken into account relevant factors); *Maher v. An Bord Pleanála* [1993] 1 I.R. 439 (depreciation in value of property in vicinity of development amounted to a relevant planning factor) *Gutrani v. Minister for Justice* [1993] 2 I.R. 429 at 438–439 (deportation of alien); *Madigan v. RTÉ* [1994] 2 I.L.R.M. 472 at 477–479 (allocation of party political broadcasts); *Kweder v. Minister for Justice* [1996] 1 I.R. 381 (Minister improperly refused entry visa merely because the applicant had been deported from the United Kingdom and this fact *in itself* was held by Geoghegan J. to be an irrelevant consideration); *Keane v. An Bord Pleanála* [1997] 1 I.L.R.M. 508 (impact of development outside of the State held to be a relevant consideration in the planning process).

63 See pp. 635–637.

64 This ground of distinction is explored in Taylor, "Judicial Review of Improper Purposes and Irrelevant Consideration" (1976) Camb.L.J. 272, 277 who argues that "Where the reasons [for action envisaged by the legislature] are enumerated in the empowering provision the technique used in most reported cases under the rubric 'irrelevant factors' is appropriate. Where there is a discretion as to reasons, the 'improper purpose' is the one to be used." *A contra: Hanks v. Minister of Housing and Local Government* [1963] 1 Q.B. 999 at 1020.

65 [1981] I.R. 181.

66 However the court exercised its discretion not to send an order because of undue delay on the part of the applicant (see pp. 722–730). The Local Authorities (Officers and Employees) Act 1983, s.2 effectively reversed the legal rule established in *Cussen* by providing that the LAC may take into account a knowledge of the Irish language.

67 *R. v. Secretary of State for Foreign Affairs ex. p. The World Development Movement* [1995] 1 W.L.R. 386. See de Smith *op. cit.* above, n.7 pp. 335–336.

fairly straightforward in law (notwithstanding the political controversy which it occasioned) concerned the British Overseas Development and Cooperation Act 1980 which bestowed a power to grant overseas aid on the Foreign Secretary "for the purpose of promoting the economy of an [overseas] country . . ." It was clear that the project which had been funded under the Act, the Pergau Dam in Malaysia, was not economically sound. Nor did there exist a "developmental promotion purpose" within the Act. Accordingly the applicant succeeded.

The most sophisticated formulation of factors which are to guide the exercise of a discretionary (it may be better to style it "a semi-discretionary") power is to be found in the Planning Code. According to the Local Government (Planning and Development) Act 1963, section 26(1), a local planning authority in dealing with a planning application, is:

". . . [R]estricted to considering the proper planning and development of the area of the authority (including the preservation and improvement of the amenities thereof), regard being had to the provisions of the development plan, the provisions of any special amenity area relating to the said area and the matters referred to in subsection (2) of this section."

Subsection (2) then goes on to empower the planning authority "without prejudice to the generality" of subsection (1) to impose a number of specified conditions among them. The use made in practice of this significant statutory power has already been described.[68]

---

68 At pp. 236–237. What is very curious, in the present context, is the line of cases, which have appeared to subject development by a local authority to something like the standard statutory controls over development, notwithstanding s. 4(1) of the Local Government (Planning and Development) Act 1963 which plainly states that development by a local authority within its own territorial area is exempted development. The cases referred to have usually arisen from protests by neighbours against attempts by local authorities to construct halting sites for travelling people. In the first of these cases, *O'Leary v. Dublin County Council* [1988] I.R. 150, O'Hanlon J. held that such a "development" contravened the development plan (thereby violating s. 39(1) of the 1963 Act, which provides that a local planning authority may not contravene the development plan). Next, in *Wilkinson v. Dublin County Council* [1991] I.L.R.M. 605 at 609, Costello J. held that a site would not be developed as a halting site on the ground that, even on the assumption that it did not violate the development plan, it should still be prevented because it was not consistent with "the proper planning and development of the area". Thirdly, in *Ferris v. Dublin County Council*, unreported Supreme Court, November 7, 1990 (as in *Wilkinson*) the Court rejected the possibility that the proposed halting site violated the development plan; yet went on to examine the possibility that it would constitute "a bad planning decision" and eventually concluded that, while the temporary provision, which was proposed, would not be "unreasonable . . . as a matter of proper planning and development" (at p. 11), this would probably not be true of a permanent site. Finally, in *O'Reilly v. O'Sullivan*, unreported, Supreme Court, February 26, 1997, Keane J. upheld by reference to *O'Keeffe* principles the provision of a halting site on local authority land, even though it was clear from the evidence that a private developer would not have obtained permission for such a development on private lands.

There would seem to be no warrant for a court to fly in the face of an explicit statutory provision (as did the second and third of the cases, just summarised) and it is remarkable that there was little or no discussion on this point. A local authority's decision to establish a halting site on its own land involves the exercise of discretion in regard to its own common law property rights. Now it is certainly arguable that a court may exercise control over a local authority's discretion in regard to its common law (as contradistinguished from statutory) rights: see pp. 773–776. However, there is no reason why such control should mimic the planning law from whose scope the local authority had been excluded. Moreover, such controls should be based on a wider range of factors than are to be found in the planning-environment field and should include matters like the local authority's obligations to help all elements

Naturally, the question of which considerations are relevant (or vice-versa) will vary, depending upon the particular legislation under which statutory power being exercised was established. This point may give rise to problems where the same decision touches upon different sets of legislation. A common coincidence of this type was presented to the High Court in *Carty v. Dublin Corporation*.[69] Here, first, the local authority had refused planning approval on the grounds of the inadequacy of the sewage disposal system. Next, an Bord Pleanála upheld an appeal against decision. Finally, the local authority refused Building Bye-Law Approval on the ground that the proposals for foul drainage were not acceptable. The plaintiffs claimed that, in considering the application for Building Bye-Law Approval, the local authority was bound by the Board's decision that the sewage disposal was adequate. Accordingly, the decision to refuse approval was invalid and amounted to a breach of statutory duty, grounding in damages. Rejecting this claim, Costello P. stated:

> "A sanitary authority is bound to exercise its statutory functions reasonably. When an issue of fact arises before it which has also been raised before the planning board (for example whether the existing sewage system is adequate to take the drainage from a proposed development), this obligation will require it to have regard to the decision of the board and the evidence which led to that decision, in exercising its own discretion on the issue. But having done so it may reach a different conclusion in the exercise of its own discretion . . .
>
> . . .
>
> When the local authority, *acting as a sanitary authority* is considering an application for building bye-law approval it is exercising its discretion under an entirely different code. There is no statutory requirement that a sanitary authority is bound to exercise its discretion in the same way as the planning board (a creature of an entirely separate code) exercised its powers on an issue on which the board has adjudicated."

Thus far cases have been examined in which the relevant statute provided an explicit statement of the factors which the public authority must take into account. Let us consider the situation arising when even this limited assistance is not available. Take first, two deportation cases, with contrasting results but each involving the statutory power to refuse an immigrant leave to land. In the first case, *The State (Kugan) v. Station Sergeant, Fitzgibbon St. Garda Station*,[70] deportation arose from refusal of entry based on the applicant's inadequate knowledge of English. This, Egan J. held in effect, was an irrelevant factor. In the contrasting case, *The State (Bouzagou) v. Station Sergeant, Fitzgibbon St. Garda Station*,[71] a

---

of the community and the need to keep the roads free of insanitary, unofficial camp sites and other non-planning factors. These factors appear now to have been given greater weight by the Supreme Court in *O'Reilly v. O'Sullivan*, above.

Some of the cases under discussion above are discussed from the narrow, local government perspective at pp. 193, 234–235.

[69] Unreported, High Court, October 16, 1996. See, to similar effect, *Doupe v. Limerick Corporation* [1981] I.L.R.M. 456, (*Doupe* was also decided by Costello J. (as he then was).)

[70] [1986] I.L.R.M. 95.

[71] [1985] I.R. 426. See, to like effect, *Gilmore v. Mitchell*, unreported, High Court, April 18, 1988 (Court agreed that the locality in which a Garda is stationed may be a relevant factor in determining a charge of conduct likely to bring discredit on the force.)

decision to refuse entry on the ground that the immigration officer believed that the applicant would be unable to support himself was upheld. In these cases (not untypically) little explanation was given of the process of teasing out 'the relevant considerations' from the general tenor of the statute creating the discretionary power. Something of the difficulties entailed in this process emerges from the well-known case of *East Donegal Co-Operatives Ltd v. Attorney-General*,[72] in which the Supreme Court scrutinised the Livestock Marts Act 1967, in order to decide a claim by a group of agricultural mart owners that the Act was unconstitutional. The Act bestows considerable discretionary power on the Minister for Agriculture enabling him to control marts, through the grant (whether absolutely or subject to conditions) or the revocation, of licences. In spite of the wide discretionary language in which these powers are couched, Walsh J. stated that:

"The words of the Act, and in particularly the general words, cannot be read in isolation and their content is to be derived from their context. Therefore words or phrases which at first sight might appear to be wide and general may be cut down in their construction when examined against the objects of the Act which are to be derived from a study of the Act as a whole including the long title."

Specifically:

"The provisions of section 6 [of the 1967 Act] throw considerable light upon the purposes, objects and scope of the Act because they refer specifically to the power of the Minister for Agriculture and Fisheries being directed towards the proper conduct of the businesses concerned, the standards in relation to such places and to the provision of adequate and suitable accomodation and facilities for such auctions. Section 6 also provides for the making of regulations dealing with what might be referred to as the mechanics of sale such as book-keeping, accommodation, hygiene, etc. . . . The type of conditions which the Minister may impose [on the grant of a mart licence] would include the site of the mart so as to ensure that, for example, it was not too near a place of worship or a particular road traffic hazard, or conditions aimed at the restriction of the carrying on of business at certain hours or on certain days so as to prevent interference with the activities of persons not connected with the mart, or conditions which indeed might be designed to facilitate the carrying on of business at the particular mart by preventing it being carried on at times which, by reason of particular local conditions or activities, would be detrimental to the business itself and to the persons having stock for sale at the mart or to persons resorting there for the purpose of purchasing livestock."[73]

General policy assumptions

So far we have examined cases in which the "relevant considerations" or "proper purposes/objectives" have been deduced by the courts from a study of the particular statute. In addition, there are certain general policy assumptions which the courts bring to their task and which have become well-established in the case law.

---

[72] [1970] I.R. 317. See also, *Doupe v. Limerick Corporation* [1981] I.L.R.M. 456, 461, *per* Costello J. (as he then was).
[73] [1970] I.R. 317 at 341–343.

First, it has been said that: "Parliament does not intend to deprive the subject of his common law rights except by express words or necessary implication."[74] Thus, for example, there are rebuttable presumptions that a statute does not authorise either any interference with general property rights[75] or the imposition of any money charge.[76] However, these are matters which need not be considered since they have already been explored.[77]

Secondly, any financial cost to the public body is obviously a factor to be taken into account. (In the case of local authorities, this notion used to be grounded on the basis that local authorities were regarded as being somewhat in the position of "trustees" in relation to their ratepayers and, hence, as owing them a "fiduciary" duty to observe business-like principles in regard to the expenditure of money.) It has been relied upon, for example, in cases establishing that, (even before the era of Public Procurement Rules[78]) in deciding to which contractor to award a public works contract, a local authority is obliged to take at least some account of the prices of the various tenders submitted to it.[79] A recent case in which this principle was treated as axiomatic (though only in regard to a subsidiary point) is *Donegal Fuel and Supply Co. Ltd v. Londonderry Port and Harbour Commissioners*.[80] Here an argument that some bye-laws, which permitted the use of part only of a harbour, were consequently *ultra vires* was repulsed on the ground of cost. Costello J. stated:

> "The harbour commissioners have a statutory duty to raise income and to apply it in fulfilment, *inter alia*, of the powers to maintain and repair quays and piers. That income may not be sufficient to repair and maintain every part of their undertaking and the harbour commissioners must have a discretion as to how its income is to be used. This means that the statutes must be construed so as to permit them to discontinue, or reduce, the use of part of their undertakings should financial constraints so require. This is what has happened in this case. It seems to me that the harbour commissioners have not acted unreasonably in proposing to limit in the way proposed in the draft bye-laws the use of the pier of Carrickarory."[81]

Thirdly, again in the field of local government, there is also a rule that powers may only be exercised by a local authority for the good of its own territorial area. A straightforward example of this principle in action occurred in *Murphy v. Dublin Corporation (No. 2)*[82] which involved a compulsory purchase order made by the

---

74 de Smith, (4th ed., 1980), *op. cit.*, above, n.6 p. 99. This topic is now dealt with in de Smith, Woolf and Jowell, (5th ed., 1995), *op. cit.*, above, n. 7 pp. 588–589 under the rubric "Decisions infringing fundamental rights".

75 See, *e.g. Limerick Corporation v. Sheridan* (1956) 90 I.L.T.R. 59, 64.

76 *City Brick and Terra Cotta Co. Ltd v. Belfast Corporation* [1958] N.I. 44, 70. For the high constitutional principle that taxation may only be levied with the consent of the Dáil: see Morgan, *op. cit.* p. 117.

77 See pp. 405–412.

78 On which, see pp. 124–128.

79 See generally, *The State (Raftis) v. Leonard* [1960] I.R. 381; *Bromley L.B.C. v. G.L.C.* [1983] 1 A.C. 768; H. A. Street, *Law Relating to Local Government* (Dublin, 1954), pp. 1263–1264 and cases cited therein; Kelly, "Local Authority Contracts, Tenders and Mandamus" (1967) 2 Ir. Jur. (N.S.) 7.

80 [1994] 1 I.R. 24.

81 *Ibid.* at 40.

82 [1976] I.R. 143.

defendants. The Supreme Court struck down the order because it found that the Corporation had made it, in part at least,[83] in order to meet the needs of another housing authority, namely Dublin County Council. A further instance of what may be regarded as a judicial assumption about the general policy underlying certain types of discretionary powers occurred in *Re Cook's Application*.[84] This was a case brought by some Alliance Party councillors on Belfast City councillors in response to certain actions taken by the Unionist majority on the Council in opposition to the Anglo-Irish Agreement of 1985. The applicants' first line of argument was to claim that opposition to the Agreement was not a matter of local government and as such was *ultra vires*. This argument was rejected on the ground that the actions were *intra vires* the Council in that the working of the Agreement could affect functions, for example, transport, parks and recreation, which are either functions, or incidental to the functions, of the Council. The second set of arguments centered on the fact that one of the actions taken by the Council was to pass a resolution to refrain from almost all Council and Committee meetings and, instead, to delegate the Council's functions to the Town Clerk. Accepting the applicants' argument on this point, Lord Lowry C.J. stated:

> "The Council's decision was from the local government standpoint – and we emphasise those words (*the local government standpoint*) – the negation of all the principles according to which local government is carried on through discussion and debate among elected representatives, culminating in decisions on a wide variety of important matters. To say this is not to call in question the ability of the Town Clerk; but to leave all these matters to a paid official, no matter how competent, is simply not the way to carry on local government. It is in fact completely unreasonable in the *Wednesbury* sense . . . It is the activity of the elected representatives which is the essence of local government, as distinct from giving the whole matter into the hands of the Town Clerk to make all the decisions and transact all the business of which he is legally capable."[85]

Finally, it has been stated (as a make-weight, rather than a *ratio decidendi*) that it is permissible for a public authority to be influenced by "the declared wishes of responsible members of the community."[86]

Reasonableness

As Lord Greene pointed out in the extract from his judgment in *Wednesbury Corporation* – quoted *supra* – reasonableness can be used, widely, to cover almost all forms of abuse of power. Used more narrowly and, therefore, more usefully, it refers to a decision which departs so radically from the normal standards of cost,

---

[83] On plurality of purposes see also pp. 626–628.

[84] [1986] N.I. 242.

[85] *ibid.* at 277.

[86] *The State (Divito) v. Arklow U.D.C.* [1986] I.L.R.M. 123; *a contra: The State (McGeough) v. Louth County Council.* (1973) 107 I.L.T.R. 13, 17, 18, 26. The cases may be reconcilable on the basis that the council resolution in *McGeough* flew in the face of the statute's policy: see pp. 674–675. For the sometimes contradictory relationship between this factor and the rule against fettering a discretion, see *Bromley L.B.C. v. G.L.C.* [1983] 1 A.C. 768.

convenience, morality, respect for individual rights, etc. that no reasonable public authority could have come to it. In this sense, reasonableness was traditionally seldom used by the courts because it entails deciding questions of judgment in highly political areas, where courts prefer not to tread. An unreasonable decision is usually reached because the responsible public authority took into account irrelevant considerations, failed to take into account relevant considerations; or pursued an improper purpose.[87] Accordingly, it can usually be struck down on one of these grounds, thereby enabling a court to avoid the public controversy which may be stirred up if a court labels the decision of a public and, it may be an elected, body as unreasonable. However, these risks notwithstanding,[88] in recent years Irish courts have been less shy of this head.

Consider first *Cassidy v. Minister for Industry and Commerce*,[89] which arose out of the creation of a maximum prices order in respect of bars in Dundalk, by which the same maxima were fixed for drinks sold in both public and lounge bars. The chief reason given by the Supreme Court for striking down the order was unreasonableness. Having quoted *Mixnam's* case[90] with approval, Henchy J. went on to state:

"Applied here [this test] produces the conclusion that Parliament could not have intended that licences of lounge bars would be treated so oppressively and unfairly by maximum-price orders. If the Minister had made a maximum-price order which forbade hotel owners to sell drink in their hotels at prices higher than those fixed for public bars, it would be generally accepted that such an order would be oppressive and unfair. The capital outlay and overhead expenses necessarily involved in the residential and other features of hotels are such that to force their drink prices down to those chargeable in a public bar would in many cases be ruinously unfair . . . if the orders are construed as not distinguishing lounge bars in any way, and as forcing their prices down to those of public bars, they fail unreasonably to have regard to the fact that owners of lounge bars, like hoteliers, are entitled because of capital outlay and overhead expenses, to separate treatment in the matter of drink prices. . . ."[91]

---

[87] Notice, for example, the following extract from *O'Keeffe v. An Bord Pleanála* [1993] 1 I.R. 39 where Costello J. said (at p. 60):

"It seems to me that I am driven to the conclusion that the Board acted ultra vires because either (a) it took matters into consideration which, although, perhaps furnishing a rational explanation for its decision were not connected with considerations relating to the proper planning and development of the area, or alternatively, (b), it reached a conclusion which no reasonable planning authority applying the standards of reason and commonsense as laid down by the Supreme Court could have reached, namely that the proposed development was consistent with the proper planning and development of the area. It follows that its decision must be quashed."

The Supreme Court, of course, took a different view of the underlying facts.

[88] See McAuslan, "Administrative Law, Collective Consumption and Judicial Policy" (1983) 45 M.L.R. 1.

[89] [1978] I.R. 297. For other cases on unreasonableness see *Limerick Corporation v. Sheridan* (1956) 90 I.L.I.R. 59, 64; *Greaney v. Scully* [1981] I.L.R.M. 340; *Lawlor v. Minister for Agriculture* [1988] I.L.R.M. 400, 418; *Stroker v. Doherty* [1991] 1 I.R. 23; *Harvey v. Minister for Social Welfare* [1990] I.L.R.M. 185; *Belfast Corporation v. Daly* [1963] N.I. 78 and *Philips v. The Medical Council* [1991] 2 I.R. 115 (requirement that seven years practice as a doctor must be consecutive to entitle applicant to full registration under the Medical Practitioners Act 1978 held to involve "manifest injustice" (at 141)).

[90] See p. 619.

[91] [1978] I.R. 311.

Henchy J.'s judgment in *Cassidy* was invoked in *The State (Kenny) v. Minister for Social Welfare*,[92] a case which, like *Cassidy*, could be regarded as involving discrimination. The Social Welfare (Consolidation) Act 1981 provided that a welfare payment should be made to an "unmarried mother." The central point in the case was that this expression was defined, by the relevant regulations, to cover a woman "if, not being or *having been* a married woman, she is the mother of a child . . ." (Authors italics). The consequence of this was that whilst the effect of all parts of the legislation, taken as a whole, was that to draw a distinction: while mothers who were deserted wives, prisoner's wives, or unmarried were entitled to these payments, by contrast, mothers who had been married but whose marriage had been dissolved were excluded from this bounty. The applicant was a member of this latter category. Finding in her favour, Egan J. stated:

> "Could Parliament have intended that one single class of mother should be excluded from the same benefits as those to which other classes of mother would be entitled? Was it intended that such a mother should be punished together with her child or children because her marriage had been dissolved? I think not. To repeat the words of Henchy J. it would be "oppressive" and "unfair."[93]

Another example is provided by the decision of the Supreme Court in *Doyle v. An Taoiseach*[94] in which the plaintiffs successfully challenged the validity of a 2 per cent. levy on the price of live cattle established by a statutory instrument made under the Finance Act 1966. While the levy was intended to bring farmers into the tax net, it was the proprietors of slaughterhouses or, in the case of exported animals, exporters, who were made primarily liable for the levy. This anomaly had the result that the farmer escaped liability for the operation of the levy. Had the levy been payable at the time when an animal was sold for slaughter or for export, this unfairness could have been avoided. As Henchy J. put it:

> "But in the case of exporters, the sale price was not the value of the levy; it was the value of the animal at the pier-head. This value might be, and frequently was, higher than the sale price. The exporter, therefore, became directly liable for a levy of an amount which he could not recover in full from the farmer, because he could not identify the seller of the animal; or, even when he could, because it would not be practicable to seek to recover the full amount of the levy; or because it was

---

92 [1986] I.R. 693. Previous to this decision the Ombudsman had received complaints from a number of divorced women who had been refused a Deserted Wife's Allowance. In the then existing state of the law, he had been unable to make a finding of maladministration. However, as a result of *Kenny*, in cases where the divorce was recognised in Ireland, some of these women were able to claim Unmarried Mother's Allowance: see *Annual Report of the Ombudsman for 1987* (P1.5258), p. 20.

93 *Ibid*. at 696. See to like effect *McHugh v. Minister for Social Welfare* [1994] 2 I.R. 139. Here the offending regulation was directed at a person who was in receipt of an unmarried mother's benefit and who was unfit for work so that she could not in addition claim unemployment benefit. Such a person was to be barred from obtaining disability benefit, notwithstanding that, if she had been fit for employment, she could have claimed 50% of unemployment benefit. McCarthy J. stated (at 156): "I am unable to find any logic that can underlie such a regulation . . . [The Regulation is] illogical, arbitrary and unfair". Accordingly it was held *ultra vires*. Egan J. dissented (at 159): We are not concerned with matters of social policy . . . [This] apparent anomaly [is not] so patently unreasonable . . . that [the regulations] application is wrong in law.

94 [1986] I.L.R.M. 693.

not possible for the exporter to assess at the time of purchase what the amount of the levy would be when the animal would arrive at the pier-head."[95]

These anomalies led the Supreme Court to conclude that the relevant statutory instruments were void for unreasonableness. The results produced by these orders were so "untargeted, indiscriminate and unfair" and so removed from their primary policy which, as was admitted by the defendants, was to tax farmers that the delegated legislation must be deemed to have been made in excess "of the impliedly intended scope of the delegation."[96]

Plainly on the other side of the line was *McGabhann v. Incorporated Law Society of Ireland*[97] in which one of the issues was whether the respondents could impose, as a standard to be attained in an examination a pass mark of either 50 per cent. in each of five subjects or, in the case of a candidate who failed to achieve that standard in no more than two subjects, an aggregate pass mark of 250 marks in all five subjects. Rejecting an attack on the rules setting this standard, Blayney J. said:

"Could it be said that the committee, in laying down this standard, was guilty of *manifest arbitrariness, injustice or partiality?* In my opinion it could not. There was no arbitrariness or partiality about it because it was a fixed standard which applied equally to all the candidates taking the examination. Nor could it be said to be unjust. An absolute standard of 50 per cent. in each subject would have been very rigid. To permit a candidate to pass who had fallen below 50 per cent. in no more than two subjects was a reasonable modification to introduce and in order to ensure a certain overall standard there had to be some minimum aggregate specified. And for this aggregate to be unjust, it seems to me it would have to be shown that it was fixed excessively high. But such is not the case. The figure of 250 simply requires an average equal to the pass mark. I am satisfied therefore that the standard was not unreasonable and so was lawful."[98]

In *Warnock v. The Revenue Commissioners*[99] the plaintiff-accountants claimed that a notice issued by the Revenue Commissioners (under section 59 of the Finance Act 1974) to provide certain information regarding the accountants' clients' affairs was unduly "burdensome and oppressive" in that compliance would involve an excessive amount of the accountants' staff time. The claim failed on the facts, although Costello J. appears to have accepted that, in extreme enough circumstances, the claim would have succeeded.

Plainly cases like *Warnock* and *Doyle* may also be regarded as falling into what de Smith singles out as a distinct category namely: "oppressive decisions [in which] the focus is upon the end product of the decision; upon its effect on individuals (and not upon the process by which the decision was reached). Decisions may be impugned under this head because of the unnecessarily onerous impact they have on the rights or interests of persons affected by them."[100]

---

[95] *Ibid.* 714–715.
[96] *Ibid.*
[97] [1989] I.L.R.M. 854.
[98] *Ibid.* 862–863. (Emphasis Added)
[99] [1986] I.L.R.M. 37.
[100] de Smith, Woolf and Jowell, (5th ed., 1995), *op. cit.*, above, n.7 p. 552. See also, the doctrine of proportionality at pp. 655–663.

"Fundamentally at variance with reason and common sense . . ."

Recently, there has been some judicial discussion of the definition of "reasonableness," without, it is suggested, making any major change of substance in this segment of the law. The discussion was triggered by Lord Diplock's judgment in *Council of Civil Service Unions v. Minister for the Civil Service*[101] ("the *GCHQ* case") in which he proposed to rechristen reasonableness as "irrationality" and offered a redefinition (which will be quoted later). It is not clear whether (as appears likely from reading the judgment) Lord Diplock intended to impose a narrower definition than had prevailed hitherto. This point will be explored further in the following Part of this chapter. In any case, any such narrowing, like the wording of the redefinition, has been implicitly rejected by Henchy J. in *The State (Keegan) v. The Stardust Victims Compensation Tribunal*[102] (the facts of which have already been given and are not, in any case, relevant in appreciating the law in the case). Henchy J. (with whom the other members of the court agreed on this point) offered his own reformulation of *Wednesbury* reasonableness:

> "The *Wednesbury* test of unreasonableness or irrationality has been considered in a number of subsequent cases and has been qualified to some extent. For example, in *Council of Civil Service Unions v. Minister for the Civil Service*, Lord Diplock said of the *Wednesbury* test:
>
>> 'It applies to a decision which is so outrageous in its defiance of logic or of accepted moral standards that no sensible person who had applied his mind to the question to be decided could have arrived at it.'
>
> For my part, I would be slow to test unreasonableness by seeing if the decision accords with logic. Many examples could be given of reputable decisions and of substantive laws which reject logic in favour of other considerations. I think in any event that it is only a particular aspect of logic that could be applicable in testing the validity of a decision when it is subjected to judicial review on the ground of unreasonableness, namely, whether the conclusion reached in the decision can be said to flow from the premises. If it plainly does not, it stands to be condemned on the less technical and more understandable test of whether it is fundamentally at variance with reason and common sense.
>
> As to the suggestion that the unreasonableness of a decision should be decided by the extent to which it fails to accord with *accepted moral* standards, I would be equally slow to accept that criterion. The concept of accepted moral standards represents a vague, elusive and changing body of standards which in a pluralist society is sometimes difficult to ascertain and is sometimes inappropriate or irrelevant to the decision in question (as it is to the decision in question in this case). The ethical or moral postulates of our Constitution will, of course, make certain decisions invalid for being repugnant to the Constitution, but in most cases a decision falls to be quashed for unreasonableness, not because of the extent to which it has departed from accepted moral standards (or positive morality), but because it is indefensible for being in the teeth of plain reason and

---

[101] [1985] A.C. 374 at 410. For further discussion of this judgment, see pp. 649–651.
[102] [1986] I.R. 642.

common sense. I would myself consider that the test of unreasonableness or irrationality in judicial review lies in considering whether the impugned decision plainly and unambiguously flies in the face of fundamental reason and common sense. If it does, then the decision-maker should be held to have acted *ultra vires*; for the necessarily implied constitutional limitation of jurisdiction in all decision-making which affects rights or duties requires, *inter alia*, that the decision-maker must not flagrantly reject or disregard fundamental reason or common sense in reaching his decision."[103]

In commenting on this passage, it should be emphasised that reasonableness will not always be a matter merely of sensible reasoning; not infrequently there will have to be a component based on morals or values. Such a component can, as Henchy J. stated, be drawn from the Constitution, augmented by what he called "common sense,"[104] which can be taken to include community values. Henchy J.'s reformulation appears to offer a sensible and balanced approach and, not surprisingly, the *Keegan* formula has been quoted with approval, in a large number of recent Irish cases.[105] However it has to be emphasised again that whatever form of words is used, the fundamental problem remains, namely, to set a reasonable balance between permitting some latitude to a public body invested with a discretionary power and, on the other hand, preventing really abnormal exercises of discretion; and also to try to ensure that this balance does not vary too much from judge to judge. Take for example, *Stroker v. Doherty*,[106] which involved an unsuccessful attempt to overturn a decision of the Gardai disciplinary Appeal Board. The Board had affirmed a decision that the applicant had been guilty of a breach of discipline of bringing the Gardai into disrepute in that, when off duty in a public house, he had made lewd statements about his wife to an acquaintance. Here it was necessary for the Supreme Court to reverse the High Court. McCarthy J. quoted the *Keegan* formula and then stated:

"Applying that test to the circumstances of this case, I am not prepared to hold that the conclusion of the Appeal Board involved a rejection or disregard of

---

[103] *Ibid.* at 658. Finlay C.J. commented on the various formulations in this passage. In *O'Keeffe v. An Bord Pleanála* [1993] 1 I.R. 39 at 70:
> "I am satisfied that these three different methods of expressing the circumstances under which a court can intervene are not in any way inconsistent one with the other, but rather complement each other and constitute not only a correct but a comprehensive description of the circumstances under which a court may, according to our law, intervene in such a decision on the basis of unreasonableness or irrationality."

[104] *cf.* Oscar Wilde, "that uncommon thing called commonsense."

[105] *e.g. Breen v. Minister for Defence* [1994] 2 I.R. 34 at 42; *O'Keeffe v. Bord Pleanála* [1993] 1 I.R. 39; [1992] I.L.R.M. 237; *Ferris v. Dublin County Council*, unreported, Supreme Court, November 7, 1990, at pp. 9–10. See, too, *Garda Rep. Assoc. v. Ireland* [1994] 1 I.L.R.M. 81, 89; *Doran v. Commissioner of An Garda Síochána* [1994] 1 I.L.R.M. 303, 311; *Mathews v. Irish Coursing Club* [1993] 1 I.R. 346. *Ryan v. Compensation Tribunal* [1997] 1 I.L.R.M. 194 at 199. For reasonableness, in the context of arbitration, see *Greaney v. Dublin Corporation* [1994] 3 I.R. 384 at 389. See *Doyle v. Kildare County Council* [1995] 2 I.R. 424 at 430. Note that it has been remarked that in the context of arbitration: "making an error of fact or of law or inconsistency of reasoning do not constitute "misconduct" (Arbitration Act 1954, s.38) such as would empower a court to set aside the award." Forde, *Arbitration Law and Practice* (1994) p. 118.

[106] [1991] 1 I.R. 23. For a similar case to *Stroker*, with a similar outcome, see *Doran v. Commissioner of Garda Síochána* [1994] 1 I.L.R.M. 303 at 311–312.

fundamental reason or common sense. There are, no doubt, many who would consider the incident in question as tasteless and offensive but irrelevant to An Garda Siochana as such, whatever about its relevance to the individual Garda; there are some who would consider that what a Garda says off duty and in plain clothes is strictly his own business; there are others who would consider that, in a small country community, members of the Gardái should be setting an example of decent conduct. *Quot homines tot sententiae.*

It follows that the appeal in respect of this breach should be allowed."[107]

The result was that the Board's decision was not invalidated, illustrating the unexceptionable point that the reformulated test, just like the *Wednesbury* principle, permits a margin of appreciation to the public authority.

A Change of Course

However what is more striking is that in recent cases, the Supreme Court appears, for reasons of policy rather than anything to do with the *Keegan* reformulation, to have narrowed the grounds on which the exercise of discretionary power will be struck down. This slight, but definite, mood-swing against judicial review on the basis of unreasonableness or any of its sub-heads or successors occurred first in *P. & F. Sharpe v. Dublin City and County Manager*,[108] the facts in which have already been given. All that need be mentioned here is that one of the points at issue was the validity of a grant of planning permission by the elected councillors of a local authority. This had been made in the face of opposition from the local authority staff based on the ground that the development would be a danger to traffic. Rejecting the submission that the grant of planning permission was invalid, Finlay C.J. stated:

"If I were satisfied that it had been established that the only matters which were before the elected members when they passed this resolution were the reports of the county manager and his engineering staff, I would incline to the view that the resolution would be so unreasonable as to fall within the category dealt with in *State (Keegan) v. Stardust Compensation Tribunal* . . . I am not satisfied on the facts as found in this case that that was the only information before the elected members. I would, therefore, uphold the conclusion reached by the learned trial judge in the High Court that he was unable to decide on the information before him, and in this context the onus would appear to be on the appellants, that the decision was unreasonable."[109]

---

107 [1991] 1 I.R. 23 at 29. See, to similar effect, Griffin J. at 26.
108 [1989] I.R. 701. See further at p. 235. There is a very clear divergence in tone between, on the one hand *Sharpe* and *O'Donoghue v. An Bord Pleanála* [1991] I.L.R.M. 750 and, on the other hand *The State (Creedon) v. Criminal Injuries Compensation Tribunal* [1989] I.L.R.M. 104 (also a judgment of Finlay C.J., which is discussed in 2nd edition of this book at p. 460) and *O'Keeffe v. An Bord Pleanála*, [1993] 1 I.R. 39 (*cf.* the contrast between the judgment of Costello J. and the Supreme Court). For discussion of some of these divergences, see *O'Donoghue* at 756–760.
109 [1989] I.R. 701 at 718–719. Contrast O'Hanlon J. in the High Court of the same case (at 571) who in finding for the applicant, stated the the *Wednesbury* reasonableness ought to be formulated at a more stringent level against the public body.

The next case in this line of authority is *O'Keeffe v. An Bord Pleanála*.[110] Here the respondent had granted planning permission for the erection of a long wave radio transmitting station, including a 300 metre high mast. This permission had been given in the face of recommendations against the grant of permission, contained in reports, drawn up by the Board's inspector and a technical inspector, respectively. The reports emphasised the effects of electro-magnetic interference on an area of radius 7 kilometre around the development, in which 5,000 people lived. The outcome of the case is not especially significant since on the view of the facts, adopted by the Supreme Court,[111] there was ample evidence in the reports which justified the Board in rejecting the inspector's recommendations. Much more striking is the tone of the following passage, from Finlay C.J.'s judgment:

". . . the circumstances under which the court can intervene on *the basis of irrationality with the decisionmaker involved in an administrative function* are limited and rare. It is of importance and, I would think, of assistance to consider not only as was done by Henchy J. in [the *Stardust* case] the circumstances under which the court can and should intervene, but also in brief terms and not necessarily comprehensively, to consider the circumstances under which the court cannot intervene.

The Court cannot interfere with the decision of an administrative decision-making authority merely on the grounds that (a) it is satisfied that on the facts as found it would have raised different inferences and conclusions, or (b) it is satisfied that the case against the decision made by the authority was much stronger than the case for it.

These considerations, described by counsel on behalf of the appellants as the height of the fence against judicial intervention by way of review on the grounds of irrationality of decision, are of particular importance in relation to questions of the decisions of planning authorities.

Under the provisions of the Planning Acts the Legislature has unequivocally and firmly placed *questions of planning, questions of the balance between development and the environment and the proper convenience and amenities of an area* within the jurisdiction of the planning authorities and the Board which are expected to have special skill, competence and experience in planning questions. The court is not vested with that jurisdiction, nor is it expected to, nor can it, exercise discretion with regard to planning matters.

I am satisfied that in order for an applicant for judicial review to satisfy a court that the decision-making authority has acted irrationally in the sense which I have outlined above so that the court can intervene and quash its decision, it is necessary that the applicant should establish to the satisfaction of the court

---

[110] [1993] 1 I.R. 39. This line of authority was also followed and approved in *Garda Representative Association v. Ireland* [1994] 1 I.L.R.M. 81 at 88–90.

[111] It appears probable that *O'Keeffe* should be classified as a case in which the applicant's claim was, in substance, that there was no evidence by which to sustain essential facts rather than one in which the final decision was irrational. However the differences are rather nuancé and the Court certainly discussed it as if it were in the second category and, accordingly, it is classified as being in this category in the text.

that *the decision-making authority had before it no relevant material which* would support its decision.

As was indicated by this Court in *P & F Sharpe Ltd v. The Dublin City Manager* . . . the onus of establishing all that material is on the applicant for judicial review, and if he fails in that onus he must fail in his claim for review. Accordingly, on the first submission made by the appellants, on this issue on this appeal, I would hold with them and allow the appeal.

The entire substantive issue arising on the question of an irrational decision was fully argued, however, and I am not content to rest my decision in this important case on the question of *the plaintiff's failure to discharge the onus of proof alone*.

Having carefully considered the entire of the contents of the inspector's report in this case, which was something over 120 pages in length, and having considered the annexed report of Mr. Enders of the Irish Service and Technology Agency who was specially seconded to the inspector for the purpose of the oral hearing of the appeal, I am driven to the conclusion that in the recitals of evidence given before the inspector, which are contained in his report, *there is ample material on all the vital issues concerning this planning decision* which would justify the Board in rejecting the concluding recommendations made by their inspector, notwithstanding the strength and clarity of those recommendations."[112]

The consistency between *O'Keeffe* and *Sharpe* is noteworthy for whilst the passage from *O'Keeffe*, just quoted, depended in part upon the fact that the case concerned, to repeat, bodies "which are expected to have special skill, competence and experience in planning questions", *Sharpe* could not have been a more different case, as it involved a section 4 resolution by which some councillors had effectively overturned the decision reached by the professional experts of the local authority. Yet in each case, the fundamental ruling was that, however odd an administrative decision, it is the person wishing to upset the decision who bears the onus of adducing evidence regarding the material on which the body has grounded its decision. It also bears emphasis that, at a general policy level, there is a divergence between this ruling and the view, noted earlier, that it is the public body which bears the onus of giving reasons to justify an apparently irrational decision. Tending in the same direction as the point emphasised in the previous paragraph is the observation made towards the start of the passage quoted, that "the circumstances under which the court can intervene on the basis of irrationality . . . are limited and rare."[113]

The incantation of the eternal verity that a review is not an appeal – a plain signal that it is only in a strong case that the applicant can expect success – also occurred in *Stroker* (the facts of which were given earlier) and in *Garda Representative Association v. Ireland*.[114] In this case the applicants sought to quash a decision which

---

112 [1993] 1 I.R. 39 at 71–72. (Emphasis Added) See also *Littondale v. Wicklow County Council* [1996] 2 I.L.R.M. 519 at 534; *Schwestermann v. An Bord Pleanála* [1994] 3 I.R. 437 at 447; *Maher v. An Bord Pleanála* [1993] 1 I.R. 439; *Boyhan v. Beef Tribunal* [1993] 1 I.R. 217 at 221.

113 Contrast with this observation the passage from the High Court judgment in *P & F Sharpe Ltd* [1989] I.L.R.M. 565 at 571; [1989] I.R. 710 which is quoted in the 2nd edition of this book at pp. 506–507.

114 [1994] 1 I.L.R.M. 81, confirming the High Court (Murphy J.) at [1989] I.L.R.M. 1.

had been made by a civil service conciliation body regarding an aspect of Garda overtime. The Supreme Court (with Finlay C.J. again giving judgment) found that the decision was not manifestly unreasonable according to the *Stardust* formula.[115] The decision of Barr J. in *ACT Shipping Ltd v. Minister for Marine*[116] is along similar lines.

However, a number of contemporary cases attest to the fact that the doctrine of unreasonableness retains some vitality, in particular circumstances. One example is *Mathews v. Irish Coursing Club Ltd*[117] The respondents (who are given statutory responsibility for greyhound meetings) found that the winning dog at a coursing meeting had been drugged. Having found the owner of the winning dog guilty, the Club simply imposed a fine, but allowed her to keep the trophy. The owner of the runner-up dog was successful in his application to have this decision set aside as being unreasonable. O'Hanlon J. described this case as "one of the infrequent cases where the intervention of the court may legitimately be invoked to challenge the validity of a decision made by an administrative tribunal." In its desire to be lenient towards the owner of the drugged dog, the Club was "manifestly unjust in relation to the applicant's rights in the matter" and further lost sight of its statutory obligations.[118] Here, it is worth noting that the Club's decision would have affected what were close to being the legal right of an individual (the owner of the runner-up) and this could have been a particular factor impelling the Court to intervene to ensure that the innocent dog had its day.

A second example is the decision of Barr J. in *The La Lavia*[119] where he quashed as unreasonable the refusal of the Commissioners of Public Works to grant an excavation licence to a group of expert divers and marine historians who had

---

[115] It is, however, hard to know what to make of a distinction drawn in another part of the judgment ([1994] 1 I.L.R.M. at 89): for the courts to give to the plaintiff a declaration that the chaiman of the council had been incorrect in his interpretation, as distinct from declaring that his interpretation was void or invalid, would be, precisely, to conduct an appeal from his decision.

[116] [1995] 3 I.R. 406. A cargo vessel owned by the plaintiffs had been badly damaged in bad weather and was abandoned by its crew. The vessel was carrying heavy bulk oil and an attempt was made to salvage it while it was drifting some 300km. off the south-west Irish coast. The Minister, acting on the basis of professional advice, made an order refusing the ship entry into Irish territorial waters. The salvage efforts failed and the ship was ultimately scuttled. Barr J. refused to hold that the decision to refuse entry was unreasonable in law. The right of safe haven for a vessel in distress was "primarily humanitarian rather than economic" and in this case there was no risk to life. On the other hand, there was a very real risk of coastal pollution and widespread environmental damage if the stricken vessel had proceeded to an Irish harbour. Barr J. said that the *Stardust* and *O'Keeffe* decisions made it clear "that the courts should be loath to interfere . . . with *intra vires* administrative decisions on the merits, particularly where the decision-maker is acting within his own area of professional expertise" and that in this regard the plaintiffs had not overcome the "difficult onus of proof." Barr J., however, was anxious to stress that this case involved a review of a difficult decision based upon specialised expertise.

[117] [1993] 1 I.R. 346. Note, however that in regard to a different aspect of the case, O'Hanlon J. stated: "While one might quarrel with the decision to overrule the sub-committee and to relieve the notice party from the fine . . . and also to lift the suspension of the greyhound . . . , I would accept that this was a legitimate exercise of the discretion vested in the executive committee and should not be interfered with by the court."

[118] [1993] 1 I.R. at 358. For another example of a successful plea of unreasonableness, see *Carrigaline Co. Ltd v. Minister for Transport* [1997] 1 I.L.R.M. 241 at 297, on which see pp. 331–336.

[119] Unreported, High Court, 26 July, 1994. On the facts, the Supreme Court took a more indulgent view of the Commissioners' action: see [1996] 1. I.L.R.M. 194.

discovered certain wrecks from the Spanish Armada off the Sligo coast. The judge stigmatised this refusal as "extraordinary" and one "going far beyond petty bureaucracy" and reading between the lines of the judgment it seems that he concluded that the Commissioners were actuated by a sense of dislike of the group and that they were determined not to co-operate with them. Thus it may be that this case was regarded – albeit *sub silento* – as a case of *mala fides* and, accordingly the Rule of Law cried out for the applicant to be given a remedy.

In another instance, the justification may have been (though this was not mentioned in the judgment) that the particular interest threatened by the administrative decision was constitutionally protected.[120] This was *Kajli v. Minister for Justice*[121] in which the respondent's decision requiring illegal immigrants to be deported was held to be unreasonable in the circumstances, namely that it was probable that no other country would accept them so that they might be condemned to indefinite travel between various third countries. Thus it would seem that one of the most valuable and stringently-protected rights of all – liberty – was under threat.

It also seems clear that the standard of review on irrationality grounds can vary greatly from case to case. Thus, for example, in *Farrell v. Attorney General*[122] the Supreme Court quashed a decision of the Attorney General to direct a new inquest pursuant to section 24(1) of the Coroner's Act 1962 where he had reversed his own original decision not to direct such a fresh inquest. Keane J. held that the later decision to direct an inquest was "irrational", since there was no evidence whatever which might have constituted material justifying the reversal of the earlier decision that a new inquest was neither necessary nor desirable. If Keane J. is here suggesting that the mere fact that the Attorney had changed his mind on this issue is to be regarded as evidence of irrationality or unreasonableness, this seems a harsh conclusion indeed. After all, a willingness to change one's opinion is usually regarded as evidence of open-mindedness rather than irrationality. Besides, as this appears to have been a case on which eminently reasonable persons might take "a diametrically opposite view" with each other,[123] so that the characterisation of a mere change of mind as evidence of irrationality seems certainly at odds with the higher standard of review set forth in *O'Keeffe v. An Bord Pleanála*.[124]

At this point, one ought to interpolate that the passages just quoted[125] from *Sharpe* and *O'Keeffe* appear to conflate two streams of law which had thitherto been regarded as distinct. These two streams are: the law relating to the control of discretionary powers; and that concerning the extent to which the High Court, in review proceedings can consider whether the decision before it includes any factual or legal error, the latter issue having already been considered in Chapter 9.[126] Take the

---

120 See pp. 663–666.
121 Unreported, High Court, August 21, 1992.
122 Unreported, Supreme Court, November 21, 1997.
123 *cf.* the comments of Murphy J. in *O'Donoghue v. An Bord Pleanála* [1991] I.L.R.M. 750 at 759.
124 It may be, however, that the true basis of the decision was that – as had been advanced by Smyth J. in the High Court, unreported, January 30, 1997 – the Attorney could not advance any reasons as would objectively justify the necessity to hold a fresh inquest. But Keane J. appears to have decided this case on the distinctly different ground of irrationality.
125 See pp. 643–645.
126 See pp. 426–428.

lengthy passage from *O'Keeffe* just quoted. It is rather unclear whether the judgment is addressing: an argument that *Bord Pleanála* started from certain facts (which were not in controversy) but weighed them unreasonably; or alternatively, that the Board determined the facts wrongly. The phrases italicised in the earlier part of the passage suggest the first alternative; but the phrases italicised in the later part give support to the view that what was being considered was that the Board lacked material to justify its conclusion[127] on the facts – in other words, the second alternative. If both sets of argument were being considered, they should surely have been treated separately.[128]

A similar analysis could be made of the passage quoted earlier from *Sharpe*. Here the focus is on "the matters before the elected members", "the only information", "the information before [the judge]"; yet there is also a reference to *Keegan* which purports to be a decision on reasonableness.

Unfortunately, this conflation appears to have gained popular currency and become ingrained in the law. Take, for instance, *Dumbrell v. Governor of Mountjoy Prison*[129] in which the applicants (who were prisoners) were found guilty of certain disciplinary offences in the following circumstances. A prison officer inspected a recreation hall and found it to be in good order. The three applicants were subsequently admitted to the hall, but after they had departed, it was found that the snooker table had been damaged. All three denied the charge of malicious damage and there were no other witnesses. The Governor stated that "as they were the only prisoners to use the hall during the period of the damage, I concluded that they were responsible for the damage."

The Supreme Court quashed the decision as being unreasonable in law. Blayney J. agreed that the Governor was entitled to conclude that one of the three had damaged the table, but "there was no evidence on which he could find which of them had done it, nor was there any evidence on which he could conclude that all three had caused the damage." Since there was no such evidence, it "was not reasonable to find all three guilty of having damaged the table."[130]

In commenting on this sweeping together of the test for no evidence with the test for the control of discretionary powers, one must concede that even the traditional, separate tests had something substantial in common, namely that the law is slanted heavily against an applicant who is seeking to upset the decision of the tribunal or other public body. Nevertheless the classic tests did involve different

---

127 On this question, see further p. 638.
128 de Smith *op. cit.*, above, n.7, pp. 133 *et seq.* A similar criticism might be made of *Ryan v. Compensation Tribunal* [1997] 1 I.L.R.M. 194 at 198–199.
129 Unreported, Supreme Court, December 20, 1993. For other examples of this undesirable tendency, see *Ambiorix Ltd. v. Minister for the Environment* [1992] 2 I.R. 37, 49–51. *Schwestermann v. An Bord Pleanála* [1995] 1 I.L.R.M. 269, 277 and *Littondale Ltd v. Wicklow County Council* [1996] 2 I.L.R.M. 519 at 537. Two other cases (*The State (Creedon) v. Criminal Injuries Compensation Tribunal* [1988] I.R. 51 and *Hill v. Criminal Injuries Compensation Tribunal* [1990] I.L.R.M. 36) in which this test featured were not classic examples of "unreasonableness" in that in each, a tribunal administering a (non-statutory) scheme was involved and it appeared as if an error as to facts and calculations, rather than exercise of discretion, had been made. However, the concept of "irrationality" (which may apply to a broader range of decisions than "unreasonableness") might seem to be especially apt in regard to these cases.
130 The quotations are taken from pp. 3, 6 of the judgment.

standards, that for facts being the more stringent, reflecting the fact that different considerations were involved. And it is to be deprecated if the "no evidence" precept, traditionally used for facts (and summarised in the passage quoted above), is to be sub-sumed under the test for discretionary power, in this casual, unconsidered way.

However it should be should be noted that recently something like the distinction for which we are arguing was drawn upon in *P.L. v. An tÁrd Chláraitheoir.*[131] Here Kinlen J. distinguished between the determination of the Registrar General as to the meaning and interpretation of a point of law (relating to domicile in the context of a foreign divorce) and on the other hand the exercise of a discretion.

3. New Doctrines

New departure in Britain

Wednesbury was reported in 1948 and, in its pragmatism, diffidence and vagueness, it is very much a product of its time, which may be regarded as the pre-Renaissance era in judicial review of administrative action. It was to be expected then that the energetic judicial statesmen of the present generation of English judges would attempt at least a restatement of the *Wednesbury* principles and this duly came (along with much else) in the *GCHQ* case. Lord Diplock stated:

"Judicial review has I think developed to a stage today when without reiterating any analysis of the steps by which the development has come about, one can conveniently classify under three heads the grounds upon which administrative action is subject to control by judicial review. The first ground I would call 'illegality,' the second 'irrationality' and the third 'procedural impropriety.'"[132]

It is the second head – irrationality – which has captured the lion's share of the attention. Lord Diplock went on to say of it:

"By 'irrationality' I mean what can by now be succinctly referred to as '*Wednesbury*

---

[131] [1995] 2 I.L.R.M. 241 at 251–252. Notice though that here too *O'Keefe* appears to have classified as a "discretion" case rather than (as it is submitted, it should have been) a "facts" case. For another case distinguishing between discretion and legal, see *Radio Limerick One v. IRTC* [1997] 2 I.L.R.M. 1 at 23–24, *per* Keane J.

A similar situation to that in the *PL* case was approached by the High Court it is submitted in a less sure-footed way in *Keogh v. Galway Corporation* [1995] 2 I.L.R.M. 312 at 317–319. The basic issue in *Keogh* was whether there had been a "material alteration" of a draft development plan (Local Government (Planning and Development) Act 1963, s.21A). The case was decided (in the applicant's favour) on the basis of *Wednesbury* reasonableness and also (seemingly) on the ground that there had been a total failure to exercise a discretion. (on which, see Part 4). But surely the question of whether there is a "material alteration" involves making a determination as to the existence of an objective legal category, which should have been reviewed by reference to different rules from than those which apply to a discretion. Admittedly, the result in this particular case would have been the same.

It might seem that a similar criticism to that made of *Keogh* might be made of *Littondale Ltd v. Wicklow County Council* [1996] 2 I.L.R.M. 519 at 536. Here, however the concept involved was "substantial works" in the context of the extension of time to complete a development (Local Government (Planning and Development) Act 1982, s.4(1). And Laffoy J. implicitly rejected the argument that "substantial works"was merely an objective legal category.

[132] [1985] A.C. 410. For further analysis in the Irish context, see pp. 641–642.

unreasonableness' (*Associated Provincial Picture Houses Ltd v. Wednesbury Corporation* [1948] 1 K.B. 223). It applies to a decision which is so outrageous in its defiance of logic or of accepted moral standards that no sensible person who had applied his mind to the question to be decided could have arrived at it. Whether a decision falls within this category is a question that judges by their training and experience should be well equipped to answer, or else there would be something badly wrong with our judicial system. . . ."

There were two sets of responses to this reorganisation of judicial review along functional lines. The first, the Irish judicial reaction, has already been examined, in the previous Part[133]: to summarise it, in *Keegan*, Henchy J. appears to have regarded *GCHQ* as requiring a more extreme level of unreasonableness – irrationality than did the older *Wednesbury* test. However, the British academic fall-out from *GCHQ* was less literal and more wide-ranging.[134] This second response is worthy of examination here because, notwithstanding *Keegan*, as we shall see below, post-*GHCQ* developments may be of influence in the future tenor of Irish law. To appreciate the significance of *GCHQ* in Britain, one must recall that in Britain, (where the judges lack what an Irish judge (speaking extra-judicially) has called "the nice secure foothold" of a written Constitution) the major constitutional foundation is the "sovereignty of Parliament" doctrine. It is this dogma which has irspired the conceptual strait-jacket of the *ultra vires* doctrine within which, until *GCHQ*, all restrictions on administrative actions (save for error of law on the face of the record) had had to be accommodated. Thus all such restrictions had to be justified by reference to an imputed legislative intent. Against this background, it was more awkward for a court to invoke, as a controlling factor upon an administrative action, any factor which could not, however artificially, be justified by reference to the particular legislation involved. (It is true that there were some exceptions, examples of which were considered earlier under the head of "General Policy Assumptions.") Thus some British commentators emphasise the reclassification of the relevant law into "illegality" and "irrationality." They use the contrast between these two factors to deduce a rejection of the narrow bounds which had been attributed to the category of "irrationality" by Henchy J. in *Keegan*. They argue that, whilst "illegality" is concerned with the infidelity of an official action to a statutory purpose and, thus, is tied to the intention of the legislature, by contrast, "irrationality," now fortified by classification as an independent and distinct category, provides a device which emancipates a reviewing court to give greater weight to objectively significant considerations. Among these considerations are: bad administrative practice, such as unfairness or unjustifiable inconsistency; vagueness or lack of certainty in the effect of a decision or standard and unjustifiable violation of fundamental rights. The sources of such fundamental rights include the European

---

[133] See pp. 641–643.
[134] Jowell and Lester, "Beyond *Wednesbury*: Substantive Principles of Administrative Law" (1987) *Public Law* 368. See also, "Proportionality: Neither Novel Nor Dangerous" in Jowell and Oliver (eds.) *New Directions in Judicial Review* (Stevens, 1988); Boyron, "Proportionality in English Administrative Law: A Faulty Translation" (1992) 12 O.J.L.S. 237; Gearty, "Administrative Law in the 1980s" (1987) 9 D.U.L.J. (N.S.) 91; Allan, "Pragmatism and Theory in Public Law" (1988) 104 L.Q.R. 422; P. P. Craig, *Administrative Law* (3rd ed., 1994), pp. 411–421.
[135] On the European Convention, see p. 666.

Convention on Human Rights.[135] Another major feature of the new departure is that it represents a new way of articulating the boundary between the needs and interests of the public administrative body, and those of the private individual. Previously the way in which this had been expressed had pivoted around the public body on the one hand its interests and those of the public which it served; and on the other hand, the need for safeguards against abuse of its power. By today, there is more reference to the legitimate interests of the individual adversely affected by the decision. At first sight, this might appear to be merely a matter of whether one describes the same boundary from one side rather than another. However, in practice this new formulation is likely to have practical consequences: the articulation of individual rights ("a rights-based culture") for better or for worse, is likely to drag the boundary in their favour and against the public body and, often, the community as well.

There is a related point – the existence of more appropriate, comprehensive and precise principles by which to police the exercise of such principles would enable a court to give a better reasoned explanation as to why a decision was struck down or upheld. There would be less suspicion of judicial subjectivity than within the *Wednesbury* cocoon: a court would be better able than if it were wielding the blunt instrument of *Wednesbury*-reasonableness to articulate reasons which would repulse the accusation of (consciously or unconsciously) following its own beliefs. It seems that Irish courts, anyway, have seldom been concerned with the long-term dangers of such accusations; but they may, nevertheless, represent a danger of which account should be taken.

However, one should not overestimate the extent of the change, even if it had been universally accepted by the judiciary. For the *Wednesbury* catalogue (with its modern reformulation in *GCHQ* and *Keegan*),[136] boldly used, would catch most of the deficiences which come within the proposed new law. Reasonableness, for instance, would encompass unfairness, violation of fundamental rights, or lack of proportionality. The proposed head of unjustifiable discrimination could probably have been accommodated within "taking into account an irrelevant factor," or bad faith. Moreover and, in the case the hard questions about the proper balance between freedom and control in the context of the courts' supervision of administrative actions – questions of values or appreciation rather than technique – remain.[137]

Impact of the Constitution

For present purposes, of course, the major question raised by the preceding excursus is what relevance it has for Ireland. The answer, it is tentatively suggested, is that it is of substantial indirect relevance. It is not directly relevant because of the major distinction between the British and Irish Constitutions, namely that in Ireland the Constitution provides a reservoir of desiderata which the courts should take into account in addition to the parent legislation and, in some cases, even as overriding

---

[136] And one should note parenthetically that in England, to date, most of the enthusiasm for these new developments has come from academic commentators, who have analysed judgments in the light of the new learning, rather than from actual use of the new concepts by the judges: see the two articles by Professor Jowell and Lord Lester cited at p. 530, n. 95.

[137] For further criticism, see P. P. Craig, *op. cit.*, above, n.134, Chap. 11.

the parent legislation. Accordingly, it is suggested that for the Irish courts to take on board the new English law, in an undigested form, would be to obfuscate the law by adding a fifth wheel to the chariot and creating (when coupled with the traditional common law and the Constitution) a very weighty superstructure of concepts for the amount of case law which these concepts are designed to organise. However, on the other hand as we shall see, the Constitution, like every such instrument, is suggestive, rather than fully articulate and so leaves a great deal to judicial interpretation, and the new English teaching may be helpful at this point.[138]

Let us turn now to the four types of use which have been made of the Constitution in the judicial review of administrative acts or delegated legislation.

(i) Equality

The first aspect of the Constitution to be examined is Article 40.1 by which: "All citizens shall, as human persons, be held equal before the law [subject to certain specified exceptions]. . . ."[139] Various passages from *East Donegal* dealing with what may be called "common law abuse of power" have already been quoted. It is notable that, in *East Donegal*, the Supreme Court (Walsh J.) also deduced similar law from Article 40.1.[140] The frequent references to the judgment of the President of the High Court, in the following extract from Walsh J.'s judgment, arise from the fact that Walsh J. was addressing himself to arguments which had found favour in the High Court:

"The learned President of the High Court in his judgment considered that the plaintiffs' claim that the power of the Minister to attach conditions to licences and to amend or to revoke such conditions gave the Minister an uncontrolled discretion which, in the words of the President, 'could be so exercised within the limits of the legislation as to amount to a breach of the guarantee contained in Article 40, s.1, of the Constitution.' The President continued as follows: 'It becomes obvious at once that the attachment of conditions to licences is subject to no such safe-guards as are provided in the case of the refusal or revocation of a licence.' The President went on to say later in that portion of his judgment that 'The contrast with the provisions of section 3(6), and the following subsections is so marked that one is compelled to accept the contention of the plaintiffs that it was intended that the conditions might be arbitrarily imposed, and that such arbitrary imposition of conditions was carefully left free from review. In this respect I have concluded that the legislation *can* be operated within its lawful limits so as to differentiate between citizens in a manner which does not reflect differences of capacity, physical or moral or of social function

---

[138] No doubt, the English courts could also learn from considering Irish authorities in regard to a number of areas covered in this book, but in fact Irish authorities have seldom been cited in English courts.

[139] On which, see Forde, "Equality and the Constitution" (1982) 18 Ir. Jur. (n.s.) 295; Hogan and Whyte, *Kelly, The Irish Constitution* (3rd ed., 1994), pp. 446–466. For cases involving equality under E.U. law, see *Bloomer v. Incorporated Law Society of Ireland* [1995] 3 I.R. 14 (at 45–51) and *Re Colgan* [1997] 1 C.M.L.R. 53.

[140] Notice also that, in *East Donegal*, the Minister's power to exclude any particular business from the scope of the licensing system was held unconstitutional. In an inadequately explained passage at pp. 349–351, it is unclear whether this result is founded on Art. 40.1 or Art. 15.2.1°.

and accordingly this provision of the legislation, in my view, does offend against the provisions of the Constitution.' . . . It is quite true that conditions need not be uniform for all licences for the reasons already given in this judgment, and that in many cases, they are by their nature necessarily peculiar to an individual applicant. However, it is not valid to infer that the legislation, because it made provision for such a scheme of administration or imposition of conditions, authorised the exercise of that function in a manner amounting to a breach of a right guaranteed by the Constitution. The conditions must be of the character already indicated in this judgment and they must be related to the objects of the Act in the way already indicated."[141]

The question which arises now is this: given the existence of the well-developed common law rules, how does Article 40.1 strengthen the law in this area? To follow this issue, it must be appreciated that equality cannot exist in the abstract. There must be some yardstick by which to classify individuals, situations, etc., as equal or unequal. There are two ways of approaching this problem.

(1) "Equality" means equal treatment, taking as the standard for what constitutes equal cases, the objects of the statute (*supra*). *East Donegal* itself was an example of this type.[142] As is stated in the passage quoted, the conditions imposed could differ from licence-holder A to licence-holder B, provided that they were justifiable by reference to the object of the Act. Whilst this involves no radical advance on the common law, it does help to give a sharper focus to discrimination as a head of review and thus, for example, to smooth the passage of the doctrine of *proportionalité* (which is considered below) into Irish law.[143]

(2) There must be no arbitrary or unjustifiable discrimination even if this is explicitly authorised by the statute.

The difference between categories (1) and (2) is that in (1), the standard the court is applying is deduced from the statute; whereas in (2), the standard is based on what the court itself, independently of the statute, regards as arbitrary. The difficulty in (2) is thus to decide what constitutes arbitrary discrimination. All that can be said here is that it would certainly include discrimination on the grounds of political allegiance, race, sex, illegitimacy, or of being an itinerant and that we know, from the wording of Article 40.1 itself that the concept excludes, "enactments [which] have due regard to differences of capacity, physical and moral, and of social function."

So far as Article 40.1 represents an advance on the traditional law, covered in Part 2 it derives from head (2), specifically from the fact that the provision bans arbitrary administrative actions even where these are authorised by the parent statute. (Attention should be drawn, however, to the restrictive interpretation given to "as human beings" which has limited the scope of application of Article 40.1.[144]) There is no need here

---

141 [1970] I.R. at 347–348.
142 See also, *Cassidy v. Minister for Industry and Commerce* [1978] I.R. 297, where although Art. 40.1 is not mentioned explicitly, Henchy J. refers to "unfair, unequal and arbitrary treatment" and "discrimination", *The State (Keegan) v. Stardust Compensation Tribunal* [1986] I.R. 642 at 658 and *Purcell v. Attorney General* [1995] 3 I.R. 287 (discriminatory application of taxing statute held to *ultra vires*).
143 *cf. C.C.S.U. v. Minister for Civil Service* [1985] A.C. 374 at 410 (Lord Diplock).
144 The case law is in Kelly, *op. cit.*, above, n.139. Blaney J. had Art. 40.1 in mind in *Purcell v. Attorney-General* [1995] 3 I.R. 287 a case in which it was held to be invalid to enforce a taxing statute (Farm Tax Act 1985) against some only of the persons within its scope.

for a general survey of Article 40.1, since such a survey is the province of constitutional law.[145] Although such case-law as we have had so far in this field has consisted of attempts to strike down laws, there is no doubt that in principle, Article 40.1 could be invoked to invalidate administrative actions. Indeed its wording – "All citizens shall . . . be held equal before the law" – seems very apt for this. It is worthwhile, therefore, briefly to survey its possible use in the present field. One way in which to implement the equality doctrine would be as a ban on "over-inclusive" or under-inclusive administrative schemes or policies. It has been said that: "a [scheme] is over-inclusive where it imposes burdens on various groups, some of whom are not in fact within the 'mischief' the law was designed to combat; alternatively, where the law grants benefits *inter alia* to groups who in fact should not be beneficiaries in the light of the law's overriding." Similarly, "a [scheme] is under-inclusive where it imposes burdens on one group but not on another essentially similar group; or where, in allocating certain benefits, it grants them to some groups but not to others who, in the light of the law's objective, are in an essentially similar situation."[146]

It is easy to see how such concepts might be used in situation in which the applicant: had been refused a grant or a corporation house; had been dismissed from public service employment; had had conditions imposed on his licence etc – where others in the same case had not yet suffered these rebuffs. In fact, the equality doctrine has not been invoked in such areas,[147] in part because such cases may be classified under other rubrics, namely: a legitimate expectation that the applicant would be treated in the same way as other persons in the same position[148]; the ban on inflexible rules of policy considered in Part 4; or even *Wednesbury*-unreasonableness (since equality may be regarded as a more focussed and incisive version of unreasonableness). Furthermore, one should bear in mind the sage observation that an administrative scheme is not necessarily invalid merely because it results in unequal treatment of two individuals in similar positions.[149] Some allowance must be made for the practical needs of mass public administration so that there will inevitably be some individual situations which diverge considerably from the criterion taken as typical in the devising of the particular class. One critical question is obviously going to be whether the criterion is *basically* sound and relevant to the policy to be implemented by the scheme.

---

[145] See *e.g. Kelly, The Irish Constitution op. cit.*, above, n.139, pp. 712–743; Forde, *Constitutional Law of Ireland* (1987) Chap. XVI; Casey *Constitutional Law of Ireland* (2nd ed., 1992), Chap. 13.

[146] Forde, *loc. cit.* pp. 450 and 448 respectively.

[147] Even in *Cassidy v. Minister for Industry and Commerce* and the cases which followed it, in invoking "unfair, unequal and arbitrary treatment" and (implicitly) discrimination, no reference was made to Article 40.1. But see *Purcell v. Attorney General* [1995] 3 I.R. 287 at 293–294 *per* Blayney J. where the Constitution is implicitly referred to, though with no mention of Art. 40.1. ("The effect of the statutory instrument was to discriminate unfairly against the owners of farms in excess of 150 statute acres because the tax was imposed on them alone . . .").

[148] There is a substantial overlap between the equality doctrine and legitimate expectations (on which see Chap. 16). But the points of contrast include: (i) the fact that equality is grounded in the Constitution (on legitimate expectations and the Constitution, see pp. 887–888); (ii) the applicant's anticipation of equal treatment compared with other members of the same group is only one of several possible sources of a legitimate expectation.

[149] *Kelly, The Irish Constitution, op. cit.*, above n.139, p. 734.

The obverse of the proposition that similar cases should be treated in the same way is that dissimilar cases should be treated differently and this precept, too, is part of the equality doctrine. It may be illustrated by *Cox v. Ireland*[150] which, like the other case law in this area involved an attempt to strike down a law rather than an administrative act. Here, the central feature was section 34 of the Offences Against the State Act, 1939. This provided that where a person was convicted by the Special Criminal Court of a scheduled offence, if that person's employment was such that he was remunerated out of public funds (and the plaintiff here was a teacher) then he should be disqualified from holding that post for seven years. The plaintiff successfully attacked the constitutionality of this law. He submitted that bearing in mind that "the State must, in its laws, as far as practicable, in pursuing these objectives, continue to protect the constitutional rights of the citizen",[151] the law was "impermissibly wide and indiscriminate"[152] in two respects.

In the first place, "the scheduling of offences . . . under the categories of class, kind or under any particular enactment . . . involves the existence of widely varying seriousness within any individual scheduling."[153] Secondly, the punishment was imposed upon almost all public sector employees, *i.e.* a category of widely disparate groups, totalling about 200,000 people.

In addition, the Supreme Court, *per* Finlay C.J. drew attention to the fact that: "The ultimate factor triggering the operation of s. 34 in any particular case is the venue of the trial which results in the conviction for a scheduled offence. That venue is primarily selected by the fact that the offence is scheduled, and can only be avoided by a decision of the Attorney General or of the Director of Public Prosecutions, in respect of which the accused person has no right of representation".[154] This passage makes it sound as if this feature is a further deficiency in the law. However, since this feature does not disimprove the position of a person convicted but may in certain circumstances (*i.e.* if the discretion was exercised so that he or she was tried in a court other than the Special Criminal Court) improve it. It is better, therefore, to regard this feature of the scheme as affording a device by which – if it were properly operated (by the AG or DPP granting a "right of representation") – the over-inclusiveness of the category could be relieved and, hence, presumably, operated in a fashion which is constitutional. This observation recalls the fact that, as noted earlier, at the policy level, there is a good deal in common between the principle under discussion here – that like cases should be treated in a like fashion – and a doctrine to be discussed below,[155] namely that in implementing a rule of a public body should be alert to the possibility that an exception ought to be made in the case of situation before it.

(ii) Proportionality

Perhaps the most likely concrete use to which Article 40.1 might be put is as a vehicle for the introduction of the principle of proportionality, which offers, as we

---

[150] [1992] 2 I.R. 503. See too, *Lovett v. Minister for Education* [1997] 1 I.L.R.M. 89 at 101, *per* Kelly J.; *Heaney v. Ireland* [1997] 1 I.L.R.M. 117 at 127–128, *per* O'Flaherty J.
[151] [1992] 2 I.R. 503 at 523.
[152] *Ibid.* at 524.
[153] *Ibid.* at 523.
[154] *Ibid.* at 524.
[155] See pp. 668–671.

shall see, a refined and more focussed version of equality into Irish law. In parenthesis, one should mention that it appears to have entered English Law by virtue of the *GCHQ* case.[156] And it has long existed in Continental law.[157] In Germany, for example, the principle has been applied in cases involving the expulsion of foreigners who have been convicted of an offence. The expulsion of a person who had committed a violent crime was upheld[158]; but the expulsion of someone who had committed a traffic offence was quashed.[159] Again, in France, the *proportionalité* doctrine has given birth (in the planning and compulsory acquisition field) to *le bilan coût avantages* (a balance of costs and benefits). This stemmed from a compulsory acquisition case in which the Conseil d'Etat had stated that a Minister could not declare an acquisition to be in the public interest unless "the interference with private property, the financial cost, and where they arose, the attendant social inconveniences are not excessive having regard to the needs of the operation."[160] The doctrine plays a central part in the jurisprudence of both the European Court of Justice and the European Court of Human Rights. Thus, in a case before the former, an attack on a Council Regulation which made skimmed milk powder compulsory for the feeding of livestock (in order to reduce surpluses of the powder) succeeded because the powder cost three times the price of vegetable feeding stuffs.[161]

The reason for making the connection, in Irish law, between Article 40.1 and the doctrine of proportionality is that the idea of equal treatment before the law draws with it the idea that, if there are any differences in treatment, these are only justifiable if they bear some sensible proportion to differences in circumstances. And this is, in a nutshell, the principle of proportionality. In addition we ought to note that, apart from Article 40.1, wherever substantive rights given by the Constitution are concerned, some notion of proportionality is always involved. This arises from the fact that some constitutionally-authorised exemption from the right will usually also be at issue. In reconciling the two, it is always assumed that, in the circumstances of the particular case, there must be a balance between the significance of the purpose served by the law or administrative action and, on the other hand, the damage to the constitutional right which is caused. At this point, we ought to note two possible qualifications to the proportionality doctrine. First: is it confined to cases in which the validity of a law – as opposed to an administrative action – is being assailed? Certainly, as we shall see from the case law surveyed below, where the doctrine is being used

---

156 [1985] A.C. 410. However, the doctrine suffered something of a set-back, as a distinct ground of review in *R. v. Home Secretary ex p. Brind* [1990] 1 A.C. 696, 748–50, 762–63, 767, *N.A.L.G.O. v. Secretary of State for the Environment* (1992) T.L.R. 576.

157 See Jowell and Lester, "Proportionality: Neither Novel Nor Dangerous" in Jowell and Oliver (eds.) *New Directions in Judicial Review*, (1988) from which the examples given in this paragraph of the text are drawn.

158 B. VerwGE 59 105 and 112. For the development of this principle in German law, see Schwarze, *European Administrative Law* (1992), pp. 685–692.

159 60 B VerwGE 75.

160 *Ville Nouvelle Est C. E.* Mai 28, 1971. Rec. 410, Concl. Braibant.

161 Case 114/76 *Bela-Muhle Josef Bergmann v. Grows-Farm* [1977] E.C.R. 1211. See also, Case 66/82 *Fromonçais S.A. v. FORMA* [1983] E.C.R. 395 where the Court of Justice stated:
"In order to establish whether a provision of Community law is consonant with the principle of proportionality it is necessary to establish, in the first place, whether the means it employs to achieve its aim correspond to the importance of the aim and in the second place whether they are necessary for its achievement."

to protect constitutional right there seems to be no reason that these rights should not enjoy this protection in either context and this seems to have been assumed to be so in the few cases we have.[162] The other possible *caveat* is more likely: it is whether the doctrine is indeed confined to the protection of "constitutionally-protected rights" or "legally-protected rights". These expressions were used, and were the basis of the applicant's failure, in *McCann v. Minister for Education*[163] where her claim for incremental salary credits depended upon regulations which – and here is the important point – did not have a statutory basis. Unfortunately, both the expressions quoted ("constitutionally" and "legally-protected rights") are used in the judgment. The precise ratio is uncertain, although the phrase "constitutionally-protected rights" is used more frequently.

A recent application of what seems to be the proportionality doctrine (though there was no explicit reference to the doctrine) may be found in *Fajujonu v. Minister for Justice*,[164] the facts of which are given below, in which Walsh J. stated:

> "In my view, he [the Minister for Justice] would have to be satisfied, for stated reasons, that the interests of the common good of the people of Ireland and of the protection of the State and its society are so predominant and so overwhelming in the circumstances of the case that an action which can have the effect of breaking up this family [*sc.* deportation] is not so disproportionate to the aim sought to be achieved as to be unsustainable."

The scope of the case may be regarded as restricted in that it dealt with rights protected by the Constitution.

A case which is also of significance here – although it involved an appeal rather than a review – is the case of *Balkan Tours v. Minister for Communications*.[165] This case was an appeal to the High Court from the Minister's revocation of a tour operator's licence. The rather brief basis of Lynch J.'s decision was that "the revocation of the licences would cause damage to the plaintiffs which would be disproportionate to their default . . .".[166] Another example is *Heaney v. Ireland*[167]

---

162 In *McCann v. Minister for Education* [1997] 1 I.L.R.M. 1 at 11 and see pp. 56–57. Costello P. was prepared to make this assumption "for the purposes of this judgment". See also *Radio Limerick (one) Ltd v. Indendent Radio and Television Communication* [1997] 2 I.L.R.M. 1 at 20, *per* Keane J. (revocation of licence or privilege might be so disproportionate as to amount to "manifest unreasonableness").

163 [1997] 1 I.L.R.M. 1.

164 [1990] I.L.R.M. 242. For the facts, see pp. 665–666.

165 [1988] I.L.R.M. 101. Another example is *Hand v. Dublin Corporation* [1989] I.R. 26 at 31 and 32. Although Barron J.'s reasoning is sometimes unclear, the judgment does involve some discussion of the doctrine of proportionality in the context of judicial review. For analysis of *Hand*, see second edition, pp. 542–544. The Supreme Court judgment appears to agree very briefly with the view that the doctrine of proportionality could not have been relevant on the facts of *Hand*: [1991] I.R. 409 at 418.

166 [1988] I.L.R.M. 101 at 108.

167 [1994] 3 I.R. 593. For another successful proportionality claim heard by the same judge, see *Daly v. The Revenue Commissioners* [1995] 3 I.R. 1. Here the target of the successful lack of proportionality claim was s. 26 of the Finance Act, 1990, which introduced a so-called withholding tax, levied against certain self-employed professional persons. Notice that in this judgment proportionality was grounded not on Article 40.1 but on the substantive right to property. As to the facts and result of the case, Costello P. held (at 11) that:

which concerned the constitutionality of section 52 of the Offences Against the State Act 1939 which abrogates the right to silence of a person detained under Part VI of the Act. Costello J. held first that "once it is established that an asserted right is a constitutionally protected right the court must then go on to examine the validity of the restrictions imposed on its exercise . . .". The judge then continued:

"In considering whether a restriction on the exercise of rights is permitted by the Constitution the courts in this country and elsewhere have found it helpful to apply the text of proportionality, a test which contains the notions of minimal restraint on the exercise of protected rights and the exigencies of the common good in a democratic society. This is a test frequently adopted by the European Court of Human Rights (see, for example *Sunday Times v. United Kingdom* (1979) 2 EHRR 245) and has recently been formulated by the Supreme Court in Canada in the following terms. The objective of the impugned provision must be of sufficient importance to warrant overriding a constitutionally protected right. It must relate to concerns pressing and substantial in a free and democratic society. The means chosen must pass a proportionality test. They must:

(a) be rationally connected to the objective and not be arbitrary, unfair or based on irrational considerations,

(b) impair the right as little as possible, and

(c) be such that their effects on rights are proportional to the objective (*Chaulk v. R.* (1990) 3 SCR 1303, 1335–1336."[168]

"When, as in this case, an applicant claims that his constitutionally protected right to private property referred to in Article 40.3.2° has been infringed and that the State has failed in the obligation imposed on it by that Article to protect his property rights he has to show that those rights have been subject to 'an unjust attack'. He can do this by showing that the law which has restricted the exercise of his rights or otherwise infringed them has failed to pass a proportionality test – a concept which I considered in *Heaney v. Ireland* [1994] 3 I.R. 593 and which Mr. Justice Keane more recently considered in *Iarnród Éireann v. Ireland* [1995] 2 I.L.R.M. 161. Costello J. then went on to quote the test formulated by the Canadian Supreme Court, which he quoted in *Heaney* which is quoted above."

[168] [1994] 3 I.R. 593 at 607. The judge then went on to apply the text of proportionality in the instant case in the following passage (at 608–609):

"Quite clearly the section imposed a restriction on the right to silence of a suspect arrested under s.30. But I do not think that it can be said that these provisions are arbitrary or based on any irrational considerations. What falls for consideration, then, is whether these restrictions impair the suspect's rights as little as possible and are such that their effects are proportional to the objective which the section seeks to achieve.

In applying the test of proportionality the court is required to assess the detriment to the right-holder which the restriction on the exercise of the right will impose. In relation to the right to silence it will be recalled that the reason why the law protects a suspect in custody against self-incrimination is to minimise the risk that he may wrongfully confess to having committed a crime. Undoubtedly a law which requires a suspect to give information under pain of punishment if he refuses to do so will increase this risk but in assessing the consequences of the law it is both helpful and relevant to consider what other protections the law affords to minimise it . . . Recalling that the object which s.52 has been enacted to achieve, namely the investigation and punishment of serious subversive crime, and having regard to the legal protections which exists which will

Where it is applied, the proportionality doctrine could of course, lead to a more "intense" scrutiny than *Wednesbury*-reasonableness (especially as *Wednesbury* has been trammelled by the Supreme Court, in the past few years). Proportionality can arise in more than one form. It may call for a balance between the "ends" – i.e. the objective which it is intended (and likely?) to achieve by the particular exercise of a discretion – and, on the other hand the "means" which include the disadvantage to the applicant which ensues. Another form, which has not yet been adopted in Ireland, would be compare the costs of the method which has been adopted by the public body, to secure the objective, with the costs which would be entailed by some possible alternative method of achieving the same objective. With this exercise, it might be necessary to enter in the balance not only the respective costs to the individuals affected but also, as a set-off, those which would be incurred by the public body. All this evaluation and balancing would impose considerable demands upon a judge – demands which he might not be qualified either by experience or capacity, or by virture of the information available to him, to meet. A further consideration is that the very language of the proportionality test ("impair the right as little as possible", etc.,) tends to be oriented in favour of the individual. Certainly, if such test were to be operated in a mechanistic fashion by the judiciary, its effect might be to cast the onus on the decision-maker to demonstrate that the exercise of the discretionary power did not unnecessarily impact adversely on the applicant: a far cry, it might be thought, from the accommodating standard for reasonableness articulated in *O'Keeffe v. An Bord Pleanála*.[169]

One way of meeting this substantial theoretical and technical difficulty would be to confine the operation of the proportionality doctrine to certain particular and appropriate areas. The first and most obvious candidate would be those situations

---

minimise the risk involved in the operation of the section as outlined above . . . it seems to me that the restriction on the right to silence imposed by the section cannot be regarded as excessive and that it is proportionate to the objective which it is designed to achieve. It follows therefore that the section does not infringe Article 38 and is constitutionally valid."

The Supreme Court upheld this conclusion without, however, pronouncing on this precise test: [1996] 1 I.R. 580. Costello J.'s test in *Heaney* was, however, expressly applied by the Supreme Court in *Re Article 26 and the Employment Equality Bill 1997* [1997] E.L.R. 132.

[169] [1993] 1 I.R. 39. *Cf.* the comments of Keane J. in *Radio Limerick One Ltd v. Independent Radio and Television Commission* [1997] 2 I.L.R.M. 1 at 20 where he noted that in the celebrated article by Jowell and Lester, "Proportionality: Neither Novel nor Dangerous" in Jowell and Oliver (eds.), *New Directions in Judicial Review* (1988):

"The learned authors argued persuasively that the recognition of proportionality as a doctrine in administrative law would not permit intervention in the merits of the decisions of public officials to an extent greater than the *Wednesbury* test already allows. They urge, on the contrary, that its adoption, where appropriate, would be of assistance in eliminating the somewhat vaguer standards which would otherwise prevail in this area of the law."

Unfortunately, Keane J. did not find it necessary to pronounce judicially on the merits of this argument. A further complication is that there are different versions of the proportionality doctrine. Thus, in *Tuohy v. Courtney* [1994] 3 I.R. 1 Finlay C.J. clearly implied (at 47) that a law would only be found to be unconstitutional on proportionality grounds where "the balance contained in the impugned legislation is so contrary to reason and fairness as to constitute an unjust attack on some individual's consitutional rights." This version is clearly more accommodating to legislative discretion than the version set out by Costello J. in *Heaney*, although it must be stressed that Finlay C.J. expressly prefaced his remarks by observing that this was only applicable where the Oireachtas was engaged in balancing *competing* constitutional rights. Thus, perhaps, if the proportionality doctrine were to be applied as a ground of administrative law review, the *Tuohy v. Courtney* version of the doctrine might have to be preferred where competing rights were at stake.

in which it is with some constitutionally-protected, fundamental right *e.g.* the right to property or liberty that the exercise of discretion clashes. And certainly, as we have seen (although the present point has not been explicitly relied upon) most of the few Irish cases invoking proportionality have happened to involve laws rather than administrative actions which have been involved).

A second type of area in which the proportionality doctrine would seem peculiarly apt would be where applicant has been subjected to some punishment or penalty *e.g.* dismissal or revocation of a licence and it is claimed that this is disproportionate to the "offence" committed. Examples of this type include *Cox v. Ireland*[170] and *Lovett v. Minister for Education*.[171] The difficulty with this pragmatic analysis is that once the existence of this principle is admitted, there seems no reason why it should not be extended to all areas of administrative law.[172] This is illustrated by *Radio Limerick One Ltd v. Independent Radio and Television Commission*,[173] a case where the applicants unsuccessfully contended that the termination of their radio broadcasting contract for persistent breaches of the Radio and Television Act 1988 was disproportionate. While Keane J. was unwilling to commit himself to the principle that the doctrine could be invoked as a general basis for challenging administrative decisions, he continued:

> "... in some cases, at least, the disproportion between the gravity or otherwise of a breach of a condition attached to a statutory privilege and the permanent withdrawal of the privilege could be so gross as to render the revocation unreasonable within the *Wednesbury* or *Keegan* formulation. Thus, in the present case, if the amount of the advertising in the applicant's programmes had on two widely separated occasions exceeded the permitted statutory limit by a few seconds, the permanent revocation of the licence, with all that was entailed for the livelihood of those involved, would clearly be a reaction so disproportionate as to justify the court in setting it aside on the ground of manifest unreasonableness."[174]

Thus, while the Court expressly refrained from pronouncing on the applicability of the principle to administrative decisions, it did suggest that insofar as the principle

---

[170] [1992] 2 I.R. 503. For discussion of *Cox*, see p. 655.

[171] [1997] 2 I.L.R.M. 89. See p. 13. See also the comments of O'Flaherty J. in *Geoghegan v. Institute of Chartered Accountants in Ireland* [1995] 3 I.R. 86, 120 that a disciplinary punishment did not fit the offence and that "if there were a departure from the principle of proportionality the decision would be subject to review by the courts." For the express application of the principle of proportionality to sentencing, see *People (Director of Public Prosecutions) v. WC* [1994] 1 I.L.R.M. 321; *Meagher v. Judge O'Leary* [1998] 1 I.L.R.M. 321.

[172] As already noted, there has been some marked judicial reluctance to assume that this principle applies to the general remit of administrative law: see, e.g., the comments of Costello P. in *McCann v. Minister for Education* [1997] 1 I.L.R.M. 1, 11 and those of Laffoy J. in *O'Reilly v. O'Sullivan* unreported, High Court, July 25, 1996 (who expressly confined the application of the proportionality principle to infringements of constitutional rights). On the other hand, in *Re Gallagher's Application (No. 2)* [1996] 3 I.R. 10 at 63–65 Kelly J. expressly applied the principle of proportionality in considering the validity of an executive decision, albeit one which impacted on a constitutional right, *viz.*, liberty.

[173] [1997] 2 I.L.R.M. 1.

[174] *Ibid.* at 20. The judge added that given that the breaches were so persistent, it was "unnecessary to emphasise how remote that example is from what admittedly occurred in the present case."

applied, it must be regarded as a species of reasonableness. As the courts have already applied the principle in the context of potential infringements of constitutional rights by legislation, it seems difficult to see why this principle should not be applied to administrative decisions which impact on individual rights. Take note also that in *HMIL Ltd v. Minister for Agriculture and Food*[175] Barr J. concluded that the system of financial corrections which had been devised by the Minister constituted a disproportionate method of implementing an E.U. Regulation. The breaches in question were minor ones, yet they led to the penal forfeiture of securities. In this respect they infringed the doctrine of proportionality, "the essence of that doctrine" being that "where there is a breach of regulations the correction should be in accord with the gravity of the breach."

It is contended that the advantage of the proportionality doctrine is that it provides for a structured, rational and objective analysis of the impugned decision. (This is in marked contrast to what is – save in the clearest of cases – the inherently subjective nature of review on grounds of reasonableness.) However, it must not be supposed that the adoption of the proportionality principle solves all the problems in this area, since courts in differing jurisdictions purporting to apply this principle have reached widely differing conclusions on whether a given set of circumstances has given rise to a disproportionate interference with individual rights.

Consider, first, *Bhosphorus Hava Yollari Turizm Ve Tickaret Anonim Sirekti v. Minister for Transport*,[176] a case where the High Court quashed a decision of the Minister to impound, pursuant to Regulation No. 990/93 (the Serbian sanctions regulations), an aircraft which was about to leave from Dublin airport. The evidence showed that the aircraft, owned by Yugoslav Airlines, had been leased to a Turkish airline. The lease was entirely bona fide and Murphy J. struck down the Minister's action on grounds which may be regarded as involving the proportionality precept:

> "To impound an asset for the possession and enjoyment of which a wholly innocent party has paid a substantial sum of money simply because another party has a theoretical right to receive a nominal rent must be absurd . . . As long as the position is that no citizen of Serbia and Montenegro has any use or control over the aircraft in question or the opportunity to receive any income derived from it, then it would seem to me that the regulations have achieved their purpose fully and the impounding of the aircraft would constitute a wholly unwarranted intervention in the business of Bosphorus."[177]

While this case involved the application of European law (as opposed to domestic constitutional law), Murphy J.'s approach tends to illustrate the individualistic approach of the Irish judiciary to these questions. On appeal, the Supreme Court referred certain questions to the Court of Justice under Article 177.

In contrast with the views of Murphy J., the Court of Justice had no difficulty in concluding that the interference with the airline operator's property rights was proportionate:

---

[175] Unreported, High Court, February 8, 1996.
[176] [1994] 2 I.L.R.M. 551.
[177] *Ibid.* at 559–560.

"It is settled law that the fundamental rights invoked by *Bosphorous* are not absolute and their exercise may be subject to restrictions justified by objectives of general interest pursued by the Community . . . As compared with an objective of general interest so fundamental for the international community, which consists in putting an end to the state of war in the region and to the massive violations of human rights and humanitarian international law in the Republic of Bosnia-Herzegovina, the impounding of the aircraft in question, which is owned by an undertaking based in or operating from the Federal Republic of Yugoslavia, cannot be regarded as inappropriate or disproportionate."[178]

In the second case, *Air Canada v. United Kingdom*,[179] the European Court of Human Rights held that there had been no breach of Article 1 of the First Protocol of the European Convention on Human Rights[180] where an airline had to pay a substantial sum to customs authorities to avoid the forfeiture of a commercial aeroplane worth £60 million sterling, following the discovery on the plane of contraband drugs. The issue here was whether it was unfair attack on the property rights of innocent parties to penalise them for the wrongs of others. In a judgment, the reasoning of which seems rather terse, the Court simply held that the measures taken were proportionate having regard to the large quantities of drugs found because of the "general interest in combating international drug trafficking and the fact that customs laws often require harsh measures to make them effective."[181] Interestingly, Walsh J. dissented,[182] saying that the U.K. actions were disproportionate:

"[The plaintiffs] were the innocent and bona fide operators of an aircraft, worth many millions of pounds, on an international scheduled flight which was put at risk of forfeiture by the criminal actions of someone, unknown to the applicants and without recklessness on their part . . . Under the law of the United Kingdom . . . the innocence of the applicants does not affect the liability to forfeiture of the aircraft. In my opinion the provisións of Article 1 do not permit the action taken."[183]

In their own way, these two cases demonstrate the potentially individualistic emphasis of the Irish judiciary when it comes to assessing the proportionality of any interference with individual rights, thus re-inforcing the potentially individualistic emphasis of this doctrine, at least as applied by the Irish courts.

---

178   Case C–84/95 [1996] 3 C.M.L.R. 257 at 295.
179   (1995) 20 E.H.R.R. 150.
180   Which provides that:
     "Every natural or legal person is entitled to the peaceful enjoyment of his possessions. No one shall be deprived of his possessions except in the public interest and subject to the conditions provided for by law and by the general principles of international law.
       The preceding provisions shall not, however, in any way impair the right of a State to enforce such laws as it deems necessary to control the use of property in accordance with the general interest or to secure the payment of taxes or other contributions or penalties."
181   The Court seems to have been influenced by the fact (at 175) that this was "the latest in a long series of alleged security lapses".
182   There were also separate dissents from Martens and Pekannen JJ. The Court split by 5 votes to 4 in favour of the U.K.
183   (1995) 20 E.H.R.R. 150 at 179.

Finally, it remains to emphasise that (as has been demonstrated already) since additional proportionality is one of the general principles of Community law, the principle may be invoked to challenge the validity of Community measures or those domestic measures which implement Community law.[184] To take some examples, the right to free movement of workers (Article 48) is, like many other rights, subject to a public policy exception. The clearly established rule is that any derogation from this principle will only be sanctioned if the measure is the least restrictive possible in the circumstances.[185] In another type of case, *R v. Intervention Board, ex p. ED & F Man (Sugar) Ltd*[186] the applicant for an export licence was late – though by only four hours – in submitting the documentation to the Board and the subsequent forfeiture of a substantial security deposit was held to be disproportionate.[187]

Thus, the principle of proportionality has clearly won a place in Irish constitutional law and (probably) Irish administrative law by way of cases such as *Balkan Tours*, *Heaney* and *Daly*. While it has the advantage of objectivity, the precise relationship between this doctrine and review on grounds of reasonableness remains to be worked out, assuming, of course, that the principle can be relied on as far as "ordinary" administrative law cases (not involving breaches of constitutional rights) are concerned.

(iii) Specific values

The third way in which the Constitution can be used, is as a reservoir of specific values and desiderata. A capital example of this is *The State (Lynch) v. Cooney*.[188] The concrete question in this case was the validity of an order, made by the Minister for Posts and Telegraphs, at the time of the February 1982 General Election, directing RTE not to broadcast any programme, including a party political broadcast, inviting support for Provisional Sinn Fein. This order purported to be made under the Broadcasting Authority Act 1960, section 31, inserted by the Broadcasting Authority (Amendment) Act 1976. Under this section:

> "Where the Minister is of the opinion that the broadcasting of . . . any matter of a particular class would be likely to promote or incite to crime or would tend to undermine the authority of the State, he may by order direct the authority to refrain from broadcasting . . . any matter of the particular class, and the authority shall comply with the order."

---

184 See, *e.g.* Craig, *op. cit.*, above, n.134 pp. 411–421; Schwarze, *European Administrative Law* (1992), pp. 710–866 and de Burca, "The Principle of Proportionality and its Application in EC Law" [1993] Y.B.E.L. 105.

185 See, *e.g.* Case 14/74 *Van Duyn v. Home Office* [1974] E.C.R. 1337; Case 67/74) *Bonsignore v. Oberstadt-Direktor der Stadt Köln* [1975] E.C.R. 297; *Kweder v. Minister for Justice* [1996] 1 I.R. 381.

186 Case 181/84 [1985] E.C.R. 2889.

187 See also, *e.g.* Case 240/78 *Atlanta Amsterdam BV v. Produktschaap voor Vee en Vlees* [1979] E.C.R. 2137; *HMIL Ltd v. Minister for Agriculture and Food*, unreported, High Court, February 6, 1996.

188 [1982] I.R. 337. See Gearty (1982) 4 D.U.L.J. (N.S.) 95. In the High Court O'Hanlon J. had ruled that the section was unconstitutional as in his opinion it purported to confer a subjective discretionary power on the Minister which might be used to override the rights to free speech protected by Art. 40.6.1°. This reasoning is somewhat similar to that employed by Kenny J. in *Macauley v. Minister for Posts and Telegraphs* [1966] I.R. 345. Section 2(1) of the Ministers and Secretaries Act 1924 required that the Attorney General grant his *fiat* before an action could be commenced against a Minister of State. Kenny J. ruled that the power conferred by s.2(1) was not reviewable by the

The principal question was whether this section was unconstitutional for contravention of Article 40.6.1° which protects the right to free expression but also makes it subject to the objectively formulated exception that the State must "endeavour to ensure that organs of public opinion . . . shall not be used to undermine public order or morality. . . ."

On a literal reading, section 31 is extremely wide: absent bad faith, it would indeed give the Minister the power to determine his own *vires*. Following this interpretation, which had been applied in earlier Supreme Court authorities, the High Court held that it was unconstitutional because, in contrast with the exemption to Article 40.6.1° just quoted, the test for the existence of the power created by the section was subjective and, hence, virtually unreviewable. It is striking that the Supreme Court not only reversed the High Court but also disavowed two of its own previous decisions.[189] O'Higgins C.J. said ". . . any opinion formed [under section 31] must be one which is *bona fide* held and factually sustainable and not unreasonable".[190] He also stated:

> "The legislation deals with, amongst other things, the control of freedom of expression and free speech within the powers granted by [Art. 40.6.1°] of the Constitution. This provision enables the State, in certain instances, to control these rights and freedoms. . . . [It] is clearly the duty of the State to intervene to prevent broadcasts . . . which are aimed at [the overthrow of the State] . . . These, however, are objective determinations and obviously the fundamental rights of citizens to express freely their convictions and opinions cannot be curtailed or prevented on any irrational or capricious ground. It must be presumed that when the Oireachtas conferred these powers on the Minister it intended that they be exercised only in conformity with the Consitution.
>
> The Court is of the opinion that s.31, sub-s.1, of the Act of 1960, as amended, does not confer on the Minister the wide, unfettered and sweeping powers which have been alleged by the prosecutor. The Court is satisfied that the sub-section does not include review by the Courts and that any opinion formed by the Minister thereunder must be one which is *bona fide* held and factually sustainable and not unreasonable."[191]

His judgment was based on a particularly strong application of the presumption of constitutionality. Adopting this approach, the judge was able to read the wording of section 31 in an objective sense so bringing it into line with Article 40.6.1° and upholding the section's constitutionality.

The second and final stage in the Supreme Court's reasoning was to examine whether the order, made by the Minister, banning Sinn Féin from the air-waves was

---

courts, and, on that basis, he proceeded to invalidate the subsection as it impeded the citizen's right of access to the courts protected by Art. 40.3.

[189] O'Higgins C.J. said ([1982] I.R. 337 at 360): "While the opinion of the former Supreme Court expressed in 1940 (*Re Article 26 and the Offences against the State (Amendment) Bill 1940* [1940] I.R. 470) and 1957 (*Re O'Laighleis* [1960] I.R. 93) reflected what was then current judicial orthodoxy, judicial thinking has since undergone a change."

[190] [1982] I.R. 337 at 361. This passage was adopted in *Ó Cléirigh v. Minister for Agriculture* [1996] 2 I.L.R.M. 12 at 15. However, it is submitted that in *Ó Cléirigh*, it is clear from the context, that the words ". . . as such cannot be impugned" were a slip.

[191] [1982] I.R. 337 at 361.

intra vires the reduced power created by the court's reading of section 31. Having examined evidence of the organisation's policy – "to disestablish both States, North and South" – the Court held that the Minister was fully justified – indeed, Henchy J. stated that it would have been "perverse" not to hold the opinion prescribed by section 31. Accordingly the order was held to be *intra vires*.

In addition, there have been a number of immigration or deportation cases in which Articles 41 and 42 of the Constitution (The Family and Education) have been invoked. In three cases which came before the High Court – *The State (Bouzagou) v. Fitzgibbon St. Garda Station*[192]; *Pok Sun Shum v. Ireland*[193]; and *Osheku v. Ireland*[194] the plaintiffs sought unsuccessfully to rely on Articles 41 and 42 as grounds for restraining the Minister for Justice from exercising his discretion to deport (*Pok Sun Shun* and *Osheku*) or to refuse entry to (*Bouzagou*) an alien. In the case of deportation, the Minister's discretion is ample, being conditioned upon whether "he deems it to be conducive to the public good [to deport]."[195] (The relevant wording was fairly similar in *Bouzagou*). In each case, the alien was married to an Irish citizen (though in *Bouzagou* at least, this point was not critical since it was said that the rights recognised by Articles 41 and 42 are not confined to citizens). In each case, the plaintiff's broad submission was made that, as a result of the Constitution, the Irish citizen was entitled to the society of her spouse or parent within the State and that this constitutional right effectively restricted the Minister's discretion. For present purposes, it is significant that, in each case, the High Court appears to have accepted that, if the rights bestowed by Articles 41 and 42 were absolute, the submission would have succeeded on the ground that the Minister's order was unconstitutional. These submissions failed as a result of the view taken of the extent of the constitutional right (something which is, only of incidental interest here). The decision in each case was based on the notion that there is an exception to the rights of the family under Article 41, for as Gannon J. said in *Osheku*: ". . . it is in the interest of the common good of a State that it should have control of the entry of aliens, their departure, and their activities and duration of stay within the State . . ."[196]

However, in a fourth case, *Fajujonu v. Minister for Justice*[197] – admittedly, in somewhat different factual circumstances – the Supreme Court sounded a different emphasis from that of the High Court. The facts of *Fajujonu* were that the first two applicants were aliens, a husband and wife, who had some years previously come to reside in Ireland. The third applicant was their daughter who had been born in Ireland and was, therefore, an Irish citizen. The family had lived illegally within the State and, in these proceedings, they sought an order that the first applicant – the father – should not be deported. Deportation would have meant that the daughter would be faced with the dilemma of either being compulsorily separated from her parents, in breach of her constitutional family rights, or, alternatively, being forced

---

[192] [1986] I.L.R.M. 98.
[193] [1986] I.L.R.M. 593.
[194] [1987] I.L.R.M. 330.
[195] Aliens Order 1946, (S.R. and O. No. 395 of 1946) as amended by the Aliens (Amendment) Order, (S.I. No. 128 of 1975).
[196] [1987] I.L.R.M. 342.
[197] [1990] I.L.R.M. 234.

to leave the State of which she was a citizen. It was significant – and a point of contrast with the High Court cases – that although the parents were illegal immigrants, they had otherwise done nothing wrong. The resolution of the matter reached by the Supreme Court (which could well be regarded as a warning shot across the Minister for Justice's bows) was that the Minister should only deport the first applicant if he were "satisfied that for good and sufficient reason the 'common good' required it."[198]

A further constitutional right which has been drawn upon in the present context is that there must be no religious discrimination and, in particular, that the State, in providing aid for schools, must not "discriminate" between schools.[199]

Nor is this just a matter of fundamental rights *per se*: other constitutional provisions may also be relevant. A straightforward example is Article 15.2.1 (the Oreachtas has "the sole and exclusive power of making laws. . . .") As explained in more detail above, this was used in *Cooke v. Walsh*[200] to strike down regulations made by the Minister of Health, which purported to exclude persons, otherwise entitled under the Health Act 1970, to free medical services from such entitlement, where their injuries were sustained as a result of a road accident and where they were entitled to compensation for their injuries.

In parenthesis, one should note that, in addition to the Constitution a further reservoir of individual rights, against which to test the actions of public bodies, may be available, namely the European Convention on Human Rights.[201] The question for present purposes, is of course whether and, in what sense, these are a part of Irish domestic law. One bar to this importation is Article 29.6 of the Constitution which states that no international agreement can be a part of domestic law unless by way of act of the Oireachtas.[202] However there may be ways around this.[203] One of these is the possibility of importation as an accoutrement of European Union law. Another lies in the fact that what is under (brief) discussion here is not the use of the Convention to countermand a positive domestic law but rather its use, as a factor, by which to limit a discretionary power. In this limited form, the European Convention is ever increasingly employed in the U.K.[204] Perhaps the topic is of less interest here because of the presence of a written Constitution, powered by a forceful judiciary. In any case, this reservoir remains largely untapped in this jurisdiction.

---

[198]   *Ibid* at 239.

[199]   See, *e.g. Quinn's Supermarket v. Attorney General* [1972] I.R. 1; *Mulloy v. Minister for Education* [1975] I.R. 88; *M. v. An Bord Uchtála* [1975] I.R. 81.

[200]   [1984] I.L.R.M. 208. See, further, pp. 11–12.

[201]   In *Kavanagh v. Ireland* [1996] 1 I.R. 321 it was submitted that the Convention is part of domestic law by virtue of Article 29.4.4° of the Constitution and Title 1 of Article F of the Treaty on European Union which provides: "The Union shall respect fundamental rights, as guaranteed by the European Convention . . .". However since Laffoy J. considered that the applicant had not established any breach of the Convention, she did not find it necessary to determine the point. For use of the European Convention, see also *Re Curran and McCann's Application* [1985] N.I. 261.).

[202]   See Casey, *Constitutional Law of Ireland* (2nd ed., 1992), pp. 160–164.

[203]   Casey notes, at p. 163, that the European Covention has been used (*O'Leary v. A.G.* [1991] I.L.R.M. 454 and *State (Healy) v. Donoghue* [1976] I.R. 325, 351) as evidence to support a conclusion that a particular constitutional right is implicit in the Constitution. There is also a presumption that Irish law conforms with the convention: *Ó'Domhnaill v. Merrick* [1984] I.R. 151; *Desmond v. Glackin (No. 1)* [1993] 3 I.R. 1. For the present status of the Convention in Irish law, see *Doyle v. Garda Commissioner* [1998] 1 I.L.R.M. 229.

[204]   See, *e.g.*, *R. v. Ministry of Defence, ex. p. Smith* [1996] 1 All E.R. 257.

(iv) Common law judicial review refounded

This way of drawing upon the Constitution consists simply of refounding upon it the traditional common law power of judicial review for: reasonableness, taking irrelevant considerations into account, etc. – and, so, giving them a higher status. The instances in which the legislature will actually try to uproot the courts' power of judicial review – and hence in which the statute is held unconstitutional – are few. Accordingly the major practical value of this development is that it encourages the judges to be somewhat bolder in reviewing administrative actions than if they were dependent upon the presumed intention of the legislature.[205] The major statement[206] of this source of judicial review is to be found in Henchy J.'s separate, assenting judgment in *The State (Lynch) v. Cooney*. We have already mentioned *Lynch* in the context of the other judges' *ratio*, which was grounded on the specific constitutional provision establishing free speech, which was under attack in that case. Henchy J.'s judgment took a wider view based on personal rights (moreover from the expansiveness of the thinking, it is possible that it is not confined to personal rights which are protected by the Constitution). The seminal passage is as follows:

"I conceive the present state of evolution of administrative law in the Courts on this topic to be that when a statute confers on a non-judicial person or body a decision-making power affecting personal rights, conditional on that person or body reaching a prescribed opinion or conclusion based on a subjective assessment, a person who shows that a personal right of his has been breached or is liable to be breached by a decision purporting to be made in exercise of that power has standing to seek, and the High Court jurisdiction to give, a ruling as to whether the pre-condition for the valid exercise of the power has been complied with in a way that brings the decision within the express or necessarily implied, range of the power conferred by the statute. It is to be presumed that when it conferred the power, Parliament intended the power to be exercised only in a manner that would be in conformity with the Constitution and within the limitations of the power as they are to be gathered from the statutory scheme or design. This means, amongst other things, not only that the power must be exercised in good faith, but that the opinion or other subjective conclusion set as a precondition for the valid exercise of the power must be reached by a route that does not make the exercise unlawful–such as by misinterpreting the law, or by misapplying it through taking into consideration irrelevant matters of fact, or through ignoring relevant matters. Otherwise, the exercise of the power will be held to be invalid for being *ultra vires*."[207]

---

[205] This book is largely concerned with the interpretation of legislation (to ascertain whether administrative actions come within legislation). However, irrationality has also been used in the interpretation of the Constitution itself *e.g.* as to constitutional duties, in interpreting the duty to provide remuneration for judges which is not irrational (*McMenamin v. Ireland* [1996] 3 I.R. 100 at 112–113); or in interpreting the balance between constitutional rights and exemptions to them (*Blake v. Attorney General* [1982] I.R. 117; *Brennan v. Attorney General* [1984] I.L.R.M. 355).

[206] See also, *Garvey v. Ireland* [1981] I.R. 75 at 97; *The State (Daly) v. Minister for Agriculture* [1987] I.R. 165 at 172 (Barron J.)

[207] [1982] I.R. 337 at 380–381. See also, *D.P.P. v. Gilmore* [1981] I.L.R.M. 102 at 105 (Henchy J.).

The passage appears to give a constitutional foundation to the restatement of the general common law which is contained in the final two sentences. The decision in the case may be taken as involving a rejection of the plain words of a statute for it is significant that the passage just quoted must (as mentioned in the earlier discussion of *Lynch*) be read in the context of a statutory formula which used the words "if the Minister is satisfied . . .". This is certainly in line with recent developments, even in Britain, where the judges do not have the aid and comfort of a written constitution.[208]

4. Failure to Exercise a Discretion

Whereas "Abuse of discretion" (examined in Part 2) refers to a wrongly-exercised discretion, failure to exercise a discretion means that a public body vested with a discretionary power has incapacitated itself from being able to exercise its discretion at all. More specifically, there are at least seven ways in which this undesirable result may be brought about, namely: by delegating the decision to another body; by acting on the dictation of another body; by some previous agreement, representation, etc.; by a general blanket policy in the area; by taking the decision over such a broad area that all elements of it cannot have been adequately scrutinised; by "rubber-stamping" a decision; or by failing to acknowledge that there is any discretion to be exercised. The first two heads have already been discussed in Parts 12 and 14 of Chapter 9, since they apply generally to all types of decision and are not peculiar to discretionary powers. The third head will be examined in Parts 2 and 3 of Chapter 16. Accordingly here we shall deal only with the remaining four ways in which a body may disable itself from exercising its discretion freely and fully.

Adhering to an inflexible policy rule[209]

Various dangers attend on a discretionary power, for instance, the danger of being, or seeming, arbitrary, partial or inconsistent. (And it should be noted that while – oddly – there is no separate category of 'inconsistency' in traditional judicial review, the phenomenon falls readily under such other rubrics as: unreasonableness; discrimination (under Art. 40.1); bias; or even bad faith. In some situations, legitimate expectations law might be apt.). One way – and it might seem an eminently reasonable way – of avoiding the danger of a public administrator being arbitrary, is to proclaim and follow some precise and rational policy-rule in the exercise of the discretion. Such a solution carries its own difficulty, namely that, to the extent that the rule is rigidly followed, it emphasises a single policy and shuts out consideration

---

[208] Henchy J. quoted de Smith's *Judicial Review of Administrative Action* (4th ed., 1980), p. 326 with approval: "[T]he courts will not readily be deterred by subjectively worded statutory formulae from determining whether acts done avowedly in pursuance of statutory powers bear an adequate relationship to the purposes prescribed by the statute" ([1982] I.R. 337 at 380). The law has come a long way since decisions such as *Liversidge v. Anderson* [1942] A.C. 206 where an objectively worded statutory provision was read in a subjective fashion by the majority. For in *Lynch*, a subjectively-worded statutory provision was read in an objective sense.

[209] See Galligan, (1976) *Public Law* 332.

of all others and thus neutralises the discretion which it was the intention of the legislature to create. Thus, on some pure plane, one would expect that where a discretionary decision is taken in accordance with a rule, it would therefore be invalid. On the other hand, common sense suggests that, in view of the desirability of avoiding arbitrariness and the other defects mentioned, the law should lean far over to accommodate such rules of practice. The result of these conflicting tensions is that there is a principle banning policy rules, but it is subject to a fairly wide exception.

One straightforward illustrations of the principle occurred *in Re N, a solicitor*.[210] Here the applicant had fallen into some difficulties in running his practice, and he subsequently failed to apply for a practising certificate. The Incorporated Law Society had a rule of practice that, in such circumstances, an applicant is bound to spend a year as an assistant solicitor in a solicitor's office before being considered for a full practising certificate and thus when N did apply for a certificate, he was refused a full certificate. Finlay P. held that the rule unduly fettered the discretion of the Society, and prevented full consideration of the merits of the applicant's case. While the Society was entitled to have a policy, it could not be applied to all cases in an inflexible manner. Finlay P. accordingly reversed the order made by the Society, saying that the Society may have paid insufficient regard "to the likely effect on a prospective employer of an applicant of the age of this applicant seeking employment and not carrying a full unqualified certificate."

Consider next the judgment of Kelly J. in *Mishra v. Minister for Justice*.[211] In this case a foreign doctor applied to the Minister for a certificate of naturalisation, but this was refused by reference to a general policy not to naturalise persons who would be unemployable in their chosen profession and who would immigrate on having obtained Irish citizenship. Although the statutory discretion in question was expressed to be "absolute",[212] Kelly J. held that the Minister had to abide by the principles of fair procedures. The judge stated:

> "[There is nothing] which forbids the Minister upon whom the discretionary power under s.15 is conferred to guide the implementation of that discretion by means of a policy or set of rules. However, care must be taken to ensure that the application of this policy or rules does not disable the Minister from exercising her discretion in individual cases. In other words, the use of a policy or a set of fixed rules must not fetter the discretion which is conferred by the

---

210 Unreported, High Court, June 30, 1980. See also, *Rice v. Dublin Corporation* [1947] I.R. 425, 455–456; *East Donegal v. Attorney General* [1970] I.R. 317, 344; *Norris v. Attorney General* [1984] I.R. 36, 81 (McCarthy J.), *M. C. v. Legal Aid Board* [1991] 2 I.R. 43; *Frenchchurch Properties Ltd v. Wexford County Council* [1992] 2 I.R. 268 at 282–283. A statutory body cannot fetter its discretion by contract: see, *e.g. Gilheaney v. Revenue Commissioners* [1996] E.L.R. 25 (discussed at p. 96) and *Birkdale District Electricity Supply Co. Ltd v. Corporation of Southport* [1926] A.C. 335.

211 [1996] 1 I.R. 189. See also *Devitt v. Minister for Education* [1989] I.L.R.M. 639 at 649, *per* Lardner J. ("No doubt in relation to the exercise of this statutory discretion the Minister may adopt general rules or guidelines", but he may not do in a manner which limits "the scope of the discretion entrusted to him or to disable him himself from the full exercise of it.") See further *C.R. v. An Bord Uchtála* [1994] 1 I.L.R.M. 217.

212 Irish Nationality and Citizenship Act 1956 Act, s.15 (as inserted by s.4 of the Irish Nationality and Citizenship Act 1986). Instances of where the discretion is expressed to be "absolute" are nowadays relatively rare, probably because the Oireachtas has discovered that this use of this language does not immunise the decision-maker from judicial review, a point illustrated by *Mishra* itself.

Act. Neither, in my view, must the application of those rules produce a result which is fundamentally at variance with the evidence placed before the Minister by an applicant."[213]

Kelly J. quashed the Minister's decision, since there was no evidence that he intended to immigrate. The situation was quite the contrary. The plaintiff had solemnly declared that he intended to reside here. Accordingly, for "the making of an assumption adverse to him concerning his future intention" fundamental fairness required "at least that he be given an opportunity to clarify his position."[214] By way of comparing *Mishra* with *N.*, the following comments may be made. In the first place, the second and third sentences in the passage quoted above, commencing with the words: "However care must be taken", re-state the principle on which *N.* was decided and which is mainly under discussion in this section. However, the fourth sentence – which was the *ratio* in *Mishra* – concerned a slightly different point. It was not to a substantive rule or policy, but with what it could be characterised with a "rule of evidence" and this though distinct, plainly have a good deal in common, namely concern that the public body exercises its discretion freely.

It is significant – from the perspective of efficient public administration (something with which adminstrative law occasionally concerns itself) – that the opening sentence of the passage quoted above from *Mishra* acknowledges that it is permissible for a public body to guide the implementation of its discretion by means of a policy or a set of rules? The same idea has been expressed in the following classic passage from *R. v. Port of London, ex p. Kynoch*:

"There are on the one hand cases where a tribunal in the honest exercise of its discretion has adopted a policy, and without refusing to hear an applicant intimates to him what its policy is, and that after hearing him it will in accordance with its policy decide against him, *unless there is something exceptional in his case.* . . . On the other hand there are cases where the tribunal has passed a rule or come to a determination not to hear any application of a particular character by whomsoever made. There is a wide distinction to be drawn between the two classes."[215]

It can thus be seen that, in England, at least, the exception has substantially diluted the principle banning "a policy-rule." A similar exception probably exists in Ireland. Let us consider this passage in the context of the following issue. Where limited resources, like corporation houses, are being distributed, the system often adopted is to give credit to those whose name has been longest on the waiting list. The question arises whether such a waiting list is valid, a question which was relevant, though it

---

[213] [1996] 1 I.R. 189 at 205. See also *The State (Kershaw) v. Eastern Health Board* [1985] I.L.R.M. 235 where Finlay P. held that a ministerial circular which purported "to exclude absolutely" a health board's discretion to consider whether an applicant's means were sufficient for her needs was invalid. For the question of why the case did not engage the principle against "acting under dictation", see p. 000. See also *Attorney General (Tilley) v. Wandsworth L.B.C.* [1981] 1 W.L.R. 854.

[214] *Ibid.* at 206. *cf.* the similarities of this reasoning on the fair procedures issue with that of Lynch J. in *Frenchurch Properties Ltd v. Wexford County Council* [1992] 2 I.R. 268.

[215] [1919] 1 K.B. 176 at 184. See also, *British Oxygen v. Board of Trade* [1971] A.C. 610 and *Re Findlay* [1985] A.C. 318.

was not directly addressed, in *McDonald v. Dublin Corporation*[216] and *McNamee v. Buncrana U.D.C.*[217]

In *McDonald*, the Supreme Court, *per* O'Higgins C.J. had held that where a person is in need of housing, there is a duty on the relevant housing authority at least to consider whether their needs outweigh those of other applicants even if the other applicants have been waiting longer. However, especially when *McDonald* is read in the light of O'Higgins C.J.'s later comment in *McNamee* on his judgment in *McDonald*, it seems that the idea of the waiting list is not entirely condemned. O'Higgins C.J. said in *McNamee*: "It was not intended to suggest [in *McDonald*] that a housing authority need not have regard as a matter of priority to those in its functional area who have been resident or domiciled there for a particular period of time."[218]

On this interpretation, what was being said in *McDonald* (which involved rather an extreme case) was only that in a strong enough case – that is, strong in the context of the purposes of the Housing Act 1966 – the housing authority must be prepared to override the dictates of the waiting list; and not that the waiting list may always, or even usually, be ignored. In short, a policy rule was permitted. On this analysis, there is a good deal in common between *McDonald-McNamee* and the precept permitting a policy rule acknowledged in *Mishra* or *Kynoch*.

One can reconcile *McNamee* with *N* on the basis that the latter two cases involved situations which were so exceptional that the Law Society should have been prepared at least to consider a departure from their usual rule of practice. Thus, on any view of this issue, there may be instances where an apparent fettering of discretion may be found to be objectively justifiable, especially where the decision retains an element of flexibility. Thus, in *Association of General Practitioners Ltd v. Minister for Health*[219] O'Hanlon J. upheld the validity of an agreement whereby the Minister had recognised one single organisation as the body for consultation and representation in respect of claims for doctors was "a reasonable and permissable one", having regard especially to the fact that no other representative body had yet come forward. While to some extent the Minister had fettered his discretion in so acting, this was:

> "quite defensible having regard to the importance of securing uniformity in terms and conditions of employment for all [participating] doctors, so far as it was possible to do so."[220]

O'Hanlon J. further stressed that the agreement was for a comparatively short duration, which left scope for coping with "unexpected and unforseen developments." If there were to be, for example, a mass exodus from the recognised organisation to the plaintiff, the Minister would have the necessary flexibility to recognise the new organisation, as the existing agreement was subject to review at regular intervals.

---

[216] Unreported, Supreme Court, July 23, 1980. For other issues in *McDonald*, see p. 243.
[217] [1983] I.R. 213.
[218] *Ibid.* 220.
[219] [1995] 1 I.R. 382.
[220] *Ibid.* at 393.

Recently, there have been two firm statements of the precept (admittedly by the same judge) in the important context of licensing. One of these[221] was the High Court case of *Carrigaline Community Television Co. Ltd v. Minister for Transport*[222] which concerned the legality of the Minister's decision to grant licences, under the Wireless Telegraphy (Television Programme Retransmission) Regulations 1989, for the MMDS system to the exclusion – and this is the important point – of any other form of re-transmission system. Holding this decision unlawful, Keane J. stated:

> "The cumulative effect of all these factors was a decision by the Minister to reject the plaintiffs' application without any detailed investigation of the question as to whether it was a feasible method of meeting an existing public demand for the U.K. programme services. It was the view of the Minister's officials, and one which prevailed with successive occupants of the office of the Minister, that the political pressure for the reception of the U.K. programme services could be met, without undertaking any lengthy examination of the plaintiffs', and other similar schemes, by opting for the grant of the MMDS licences on a basis which excluded the granting of licences for any other form of scheme.
>
> Such a decision might well be regarded as according with reason and common sense. As I have noted, however, those are not the only criteria by which the validity of the minister's decision falls to be assessed. His paramount duty remained to consider all the proposals before him for the use of the air waves in a fair and impartial manner. He was not entitled effectively to foreclose such a consideration of any applications, including the plaintiffs, by determining in advance, as he did, that one form of retransmission alone would be permitted and that franchises would be granted for it to the exclusion of any other system. I am satisfied that that was not a valid exercise of the power vested in the Minister."[223]

Given the usefulness (mentioned earlier), to both an administrator and interested parties of having some policy-rule, it may seem that this case represents a rather "strong" application of the precept in favour of a free exercise of discretion. One should add, therefore, by way of possible explanation, that the feeling emerges from the judgment that the grounds inspiring this particular policy-rule were rather flimsy and out-dated.

To hark back to a topic mentioned earlier,[224] a policy-rule will often take the form of a circular (or other administrative rule) which has been made in order to canalise a statutory discretion and to indicate, to those affected, how the public body issuing circular intends to exercise its discretion.[225] A typical example is a circular

---

[221] The other is *O'Neill v. Minister for Agriculture* [1997] 2 I.L.R.M. 435 on which see pp. 329–336.

[222] [1997] 1 I.L.R.M. 241. See further, pp. 46–47, 331–336.

[223] *Ibid.* at 296–297.

[224] See pp. 56–57.

[225] In some cases the circular will be issued by one body purporting to direct another public body, as to how it should exercise its discretion (for example circulars issued by the Minister for the Environment or Education to local authorities or VECs, respectively). In such a situation, the distinct precept of 'acting on the dictation of another body' (on which, see pp. 489–492) is engaged, in addition to the principle discussed in the text.

indicating that a grant will be paid if, but only if, certain conditions are satisfied. Analytically, this will amount to an indication (indeed, a legitimate expectation may even be created) as to how a discretion is going to be exercised in a series of individual decisions. This rather common situation received some attention in *McCann v. Minister for Education.*[226] Here the Minister had created by circular an administrative system for the payment of incremental salaries to secondary teachers. It was claimed that the Minister had erred in law in refusing an application for the recognition of past incremental service when the Minister decided that, as the application did not satisfy the requirements for credit specified by the circular, the applicant was not entitled to such credit. It was claimed that the Minister had, in effect, fettered her discretion by treating the rules as if they had statutory force and that she had failed to evaluate the application on the merits instead of by reference to the circular. Costello P. rejected this submission, stating :

> "It is in no way improper for those rules to make provision (a) for teachers who will qualify for such salaries and (b) for the conditions under which the different rules of incremental salary will be paid. If this is so, then it cannot be wrong for the Minister to apply such rules when considering an application in an individual case for payment of incremental salary . . .
>
> I think it is correct to regard the Minister as 'fettering her discretion' by so doing. She is not exercising a power conferred by statute which must be exercised in the manner Parliament prescribes. She is administering funds allocated to her by Parliament in accordance with rules which she or her predecessors had validly made."[227]

Two comments may be made on this passage. In the first place, the first two sentences fly in the face of the generally understood law in this area, (unjustifiable though it may be) which has just been rehearsed, namely that an administrator should always consider whether in an exceptional case, the particular policy rule should not be applied. The second point (which is stated in the final two sentences of the extract ("She is not exercising a power . . .")) suggests that Costello P. might be understood to be qualifying the generally understood law, in a significant way. He appears to distinguish between two situations: first, where a Minister is 'exercising a [statutory] power', in which cases, presumably, the general law applies; and secondly, where there is no substantive statutory power governing the Minister and she is simply distributing moneys committed to her in the Appropriation Act. In this latter case, it seems that the general rule does not apply.[228]

The present area of law may be one of those upon which the duty to give reasons may apply. This emerged, in Irish law,[229] in the Supreme Court case of *Breen v.*

---

226 [1997] 1 I.L.R.M. 1.

227 *Ibid.*, at 10. The case is discussed at pp. 56–57.

228 One rather dated justification for this might be that the rule is, according to the classical teaching, like the other principles of judicial review of administrative acts, grounded in a presumption regarding 'the intentions of the legislature'. Thus where the legislature is not involved, in the sense of there being no substantive statute, then there is no need to worry about its intention.

229 See also *R. v. Civil Service Appeal Board ex p. Cunningham* [1991] 4 All E.R. 310 at 319 in which the Court of Appeal stated that the Civil Service Appeal Board should be required to state its reasons "sufficient to show that they were directing their mind . . ."

Minister for Defence.[230] The applicant had been a private in the army who had been involved in a motor accident, as a result of which he had sustained serious injuries. Accordingly, he was granted a pension. Later, he sued the State for damages for personal injuries. In these circumstances, the Minister has a statutory discretion to reduce the pension and did so, in the instant case, by reducing the pension to nothing. The applicant's main argument was that, in exercising his discretion, the respondent had failed to take into account the applicant's individual circumstances. Amongst a number of closely-related arguments, the applicant also appears to have won the Court's support for a submission based on the notion of a duty to give reasons to justify adherence to a policy rule by a decision-maker. Speaking for the Court, O'Flaherty J. stated:

> "The respondent having carefully, as he said, considered the representations, nonetheless, has not stated how he reacted to the information that he received about the dire straits in which this unfortunate man found himself.
>
> I am far from saying that every administrative decision must be accompanied by elaborate reasons such as would be appropriate to a judgment but the citizen's sense of resentment and frustration can be readily understood in circumstances where he has presented what he thinks is a viable case and has been met simply *by a blanket refusal to change* by the administrative decision-maker. Unfortunately, the decision arrived at appears to fly in the face of what the justice of the case required."[231]

There remains a further related point, which focuses on the content of the policy-rule: in spite of any possible relaxation of the principle banning policy rules, it must surely follow from the law explained in Part 2 of this chapter, that for a policy rule to be permissible, its content must not fly in the face of the policies envisaged by the relevant statute. An example of these two principles coming together is afforded by the multi-faceted case of *The State (McGeough) v. Lough County Council*[232] in which the applicant complained successfully of a county manager's refusal to give his consent, required under the Labourers Act 1936, to the sale of the applicant's labourer's cottage. This refusal was motivated, in part, by a general resolution passed by the Council expressing disfavour of any such sale. Leaving aside the fact that the decision was vested not in the Council, but in the county manager,[233] one of the

---

[230] [1994] 2 I.R. 34.

[231] *Ibid.* at 41–42.

[232] (1973) 107 I.L.T.R. 13 at 19. See also the passage quoted earlier from *Mishra v. Minister for Justice* [1996] 1 I.R. 189 at 205. Note also in *Duff v. Minister for Agriculture* [1997] 2 I.R. 22 (discussed further at pp. 843–844) O'Flaherty J. characterised (at 74–75) the Minister's failure, by reason of a mistake of law, to exercise a discretion to provide a milk quota for development farmers as analogous to what had occurred in *McGeough* in that in both instances a public personage had debarred themselves – albeit for different reasons – from exercising a statutory discretion:

> "In this case, the Minister, through his mistake of law, put himself in a position where he could not come to exercise a discretion. In the one case, the County Manager acted deliberately; the Minister's mistake was inadvertent, but the result looked at objectively is the same: the persons entitled to expect that a discretion might be exercised in their favour are unable to get the benefit of that to which they had a legitimate expectation."

[233] For "acting under the dictation of another body," see *McGeough* (1973) 107 I.L.T.R. 13, 19 and see generally pp. 489–492.

grounds on which the applicant succeeded was as follows: the purpose of the 1936 Act was taken to be that the owner of a cottage should be allowed to sell it save in the exceptional cases in which the manager's consent was withheld, whereas the council resolution purported to ban sales in any circumstances whatsoever. The resolution was thus "wholly improper as an attempt on [the Council's] part to amend the statutory conditions on which purchasers hold their cottages."[234]

(ii) Failing to address the specific issue[235]

Consider a discretionary power taking the following form: "If it appears to the Minister that [a particular state of affairs is so] then the Minister may exercise [such a power in connection with that state of affairs]." What the rule presently under discussion means is that the Minister will only be regarded as having properly exercised his discretion, if he has genuinely considered whether the requisite state of affairs exists in relation to all the sectors which are affected by his exercise of the power. Thus, if the power is exercised over a very broad area, a court is liable to say that the Minister cannot be sure that the requisite state of affairs genuinely exists in relation to the entire area caught by the Minister's decision. Two examples[236] of this rule in operation in modern Irish law may be cited of which the first is *Limerick Corporation v. Sheridan*.[237] To summarise the facts: the relevant statutory provision allowed the Corporation to prohibit temporary dwellings on any land where their "erection would be prejudicial to public health." The Corporation made an order affecting almost the entire area of the county borough. One of the grounds on which the order was struck down was that the area covered was so large that the court thought it unlikely that the Corporation could have formed the requisite opinion with respect to *all* parts of the land caught by the order.

The second example is the case of *Roche v. Minister for Industry and Commerce*[238] which concerned a mineral acquisition order made by the Minister in respect of "all minerals . . . under the land described in the Schedule to this Order . . ." The order was made under the Minerals Development Act 1940, section 14(1) by which:

"Whenever it appears to the Minister that there are minerals on or under any land and that such minerals are not being worked . . . and the Minister is of opinion that it is desirable in the public interest, with a view to the exploitation of such minerals, that the working of such minerals should be controlled by the State, the Minister . . . may by order . . . compulsorily acquire such minerals."

Dealing with the rule we are illustrating, Henchy J. said, in *Roche*:

". . . [T]he Minister must make an appraisal of the situation in the light of the particular mineral substances which he invoked . . . and must consider whether it is desirable in the public interest, with a view to their exploitation, that the

---

234 (1973) 107 I.L.T.R. 18, 20, 24–26, 28.
235 This rubric and that adopted in items (iii) and (iv) seems not to be used in the British textbooks.
236 For another example, see *The State (Minister for Local Government) v. Ennis U.D.C.* [1939] I.R. 258 at 260.
237 (1956) 90 I.L.T.R. 59. See pp. 405–406.
238 [1978] I.R. 149.

working of them should be controlled by the State . . . the acquisition orders in question here [are] bad for they are blanket orders to cover "all minerals" under the land . . . and thereby show a want of the discrimination and appraisal necessary on the part of the Minster to comply with the . . . prerequisites set out in the subsection."[239]

(iii) 'Rubber-stamping'

The rubric 'rubber-stamping' (coined by the present writers) covers the straight-forward notion that a discretionary power must be exercised in substance and not merely in form. One illustration is provided by a case which has already been mentioned in Chapter 3, namely *Inspector of Taxes' Association v. Minister for the Public Service*.[240] Up to 1960 a staff association known as the Association of Inspectors of Taxes represented Inspectors of Taxes (Technical). In 1960 the expansion of the PAYE scheme to cover all employees necessitated the appointment of extra staff to the Revenue Commissioners. A number of additional Inspectors of Taxes were appointed, who: possessed no technical qualifications; were not granted a commission by the Minister, and were designated "Inspectors of Taxes (Clerical)." However, the Minister refused to create a separate personnel grade for these new Inspectors so that the two categories of Inspector occupied the same grade. The significance of this was that the plaintiff Association had been formed in 1980 to represent the interests of Inspectors of Taxes (Technical) only and not the Inspector of Taxes (Clerical). The Association sought recognition from the Minister for the Public Service in order to be allowed to participate in the public service Conciliation and Arbitration Scheme. The Minister (and this is the critical point, which was not challenged in the case) had a policy of recognising a staff association only if it permitted entry to all the members of a particular grade. Accordingly, the Association's claim for recognition turned on the success of their submission to the Minister that there should be separate gradings for Technical and Clerical Inspectors. When this argument was rejected, the Association challenged the decision on the ground that the Minister had not really examined the possibility of regrading, but instead had merely looked back to the refusal by the Minister for Finance (the predecessor of the Minister for the Public Service) in 1960, of an earlier request that a distinct grade for Clerical Inspectors be established. Rejecting this argument, on the facts, but apparently accepting its correctness in law Finlay C.J. held that before taking the 1980 decision: "[The Minister had gone] in detail into the existing situation in 1980 of the various categories of Inspectors of Taxes; the work that they carried out; and the material factors which might be appropriate if a re-grading of them had been contemplated." Finlay C.J. concluded that the Minister had come to a considered decision on the application to re-grade, and that decision could not be attacked as unreasonable.

What is probably a further illustration of this notion can be drawn from *Fajujonu v. Minister for Justice*,[241] the facts of which have already been given. Here the appeal

---

[239] *Ibid.* at 156.
[240] [1986] I.L.R.M. 296. See pp. 99–101.
[241] [1990] I.L.R.M. 234. See also pp. 665–666. See also, *The State (Thornhill) v. Minster for Defence* [1986] I.R. 1 at 12 (followed *McKinley v. Minister for Defence* [1988] I.R. 139 and also in *Breen*

was formally dismissed, but, at the same time, the Supreme Court enunciated some definitive views as to how they expected the Minister to treat the Fajujonu family in the future. Finlay C.J. stated:

"[T]here is not any finding [of fact] that the existence of important family rights in the children of this marriage have been ignored. . . . Neither, however, is there a finding nor any evidence, it would appear to me, to support a finding of a careful consideration of those rights and a particular importance attached to them by reason of their constitutional origin. In any event the position of the family itself, the exercise by it of its rights to remain as a family unit and the exigencies of the common good which may be affected by the continued residence in the State of the first and second-named plaintiffs, are all matters which must of necessity, have been subject to at least the possibility, of very substantial change since this matter was investigated in 1984.

. . . I am, however, satisfied also that if, having had due regard to those considerations and having conducted such inquiry as may be appropriate as to the facts and factors now affecting the whole situation in a fair and proper manner, the Minister is satisfied that for good and sufficient reason the common good requires that the residence of these parents within the State should be terminated . . . that this is an order he is entitled to make pursuant to the Act of 1935."[242]

This passage can be taken as an example of the idea under discussion, namely that a discretionary power must be scrupulously exercised, especially where constitutional rights are involved.

(iv) Failing to acknowledge that there is any discretion to exercise

It seems likely that this is a more common category than yet appears from the decided cases (possibly because it is difficult to distinguish from the last category). A typical example is *Sherwin v. Minister for the Environment.*[243] The background to the case was that the Referendum Act 1994, section 26 provides that at a

---

v. Minister for Defence [1994] 2. I.R. 34 at 41–41. See also *Rederij Kennemerland N.V. v. Attorney General* [1989] I.L.R.M. 821 at 839 *per* Gannon J. who observed that the Commissioner did no more than "provide by his presence and signature the formal appearances of compliances with the statutory requirements." This issue has also been considered in a series of search warrant cases. Thus, in *The People (Director of Public Prosecutions) v. Kenny* [1990] 2 I.R. 110 at 117 McCarthy J. ruled that a search warrant was invalid:

"There was no evidence that the Peace Commissioner inquired into the basis of the Garda's suspicions. On the contrary, on the evidence adduced at the trial the only conclusion is that the Peace Commissioner . . . acted purely on the say-so of [the police]. In doing so, he failed to exercise any discretion; he failed to carry out his function under the section and, accordingly, the warrant was invalid."

See also *Byrne v. Grey* [1988] I.R. 31; *R v. Maidstone Crown Court, ex p. Waitt* [1988] Crim. L.R. 384; *R v. Southwark Crown Court, ex p. Sorsky Defries* [1996] Crim. L.R. 195 (far-reaching search warrant should not "be allowed to go through on the nod"); *Hanahoe v. District Judge Hussey*, unreported, High Court, November 14, 1997. See also *Genmark Pharma Ltd v. Minister for Health*, unreported, July 11, 1997 (where Carroll J. held that it was the Minister who had made a product authorisation and did not improperly defer to the views of National Drugs Advisory Board).

242 *Ibid.* at 238–239.
243 Unreported, High Court, March 11, 1997. (The Minister appears not to have taken the point that s. 164 may have been unconstitutional by virtue of Art. 15.21° on which see pp. 10–12). See, to analogous effect, *Abrahamson v. Law Society of Ireland* [1996] 2 I.L.R.M. 481 at 499–500.

Referendum, all personation agents and agents who assist at the count are to be nominated by a member of the Oireachtas yet, in the case of the Fifteenth Amendment of the Constitution (No. 2) Bill (to remove the divorce ban) each of the parties represented in the Oireachtas were pro-divorce. The plaintiff who was an anti-divorce activist wrote to the Minister asking him to use his discretion under section 164(1) to make adaptations or modifications by ministerial order where there is "an emergency or special difficulty". The essence of the letter in reply was that "the Minister has no power to alter [section 26] by regulations". Notwithstanding that the referendum was long over, at the time of the case, Costello P. ruled that "the Minister had misconstrued the section" and went on to make a declaration that "the Minister has jurisdiction to consider whether there exists circumstances of special difficulty . . . [and if he so decides] to modify section 26 . . ."[244]

5. Are There Unreviewable Discretionary Powers?

Writing in 1966, Professor Kelly stated that:

". . . provided an authority entrusted with administrative discretion keeps inside its *vires* and (where appropriate) commits no open breach of natural justice it may act as foolishly, unreasonably or even unfairly as it likes and the Courts cannot (or at any rate will not) interfere."[245]

Commenting on this statement only five years later, the same writer made *amende honorable*:

"In the light of four subsequent Irish decisions, it is clear that this point of view, whatever justification it may have had in 1966, does not now correctly state Irish law on the matter; . . . the Courts have, within the last three years, explicitly marked out bridgeheads from which the exercise of statutory discretion can be controlled on more penetrating criteria than mere *vires* (as traditionally understood) or natural justice."[246]

The preceding parts of this chapter consist largely of an account of the break-out from these bridgeheads.

The islands of immunity from judicial review which continue to remain above the waterline are few and each of them has to be justified by cogent reasons. Before going on to examine these exceptional areas, it is appropriate to describe some illustrations of the general proposition, namely that the tide of judicial review has been steadily rising.

---

[244] Both quotations from *Sherwin* p. 22.

[245] Kelly, "Administrative Discretion and the Courts" (1966) 1 Ir. Jur. (N.S.), 209, 210. Note, however, such cases as *The State (McGeough) v. Louth C.C.* (1973) 107 I.L.T.R. 13 which was decided in 1956 but not reported until 1973, and *The State (O'Mahoney) v. South Cork Board of Public Health* [1941] Ir. Jur. Rep. 79.

[246] Kelly, "Judicial Review of Administrative Action: New Irish Trends" (1971) 6 Ir. Jur. (N.S.) 40. The four subsequent Irish decisions referred to were: *Listowel U.D.C. v. McDonagh* [1968] I.R. 312; *Central Dublin Development Assoc. v. Attorney General* (1975) 109 I.L.T.R. 69; *Kiely v. Minister for Social Welfare* [1971] I.R. 21 and *East Donegal Co-Operatives Ltd v. Att.-Gen.* [1970] I.R. 317.

The Constitution

There are a number of instances founded in the Constitution, of judicial intervention, in situations which might previously have been thought to present non-justiciable issues. These may be dealt with very briefly since they often concern high policy and really belong in the realm of constitutional law.[247] One group involves the proceedings of the Oireachtas or the process of amending the Constitution, by way of referendum. Despite the separation of powers and (in the case of the proceedings of the Oireachtas) the provisions of the Constitution dealing with parliamentary privilege, the courts have been prepared to intervene in these areas. Certain well known examples may be mentioned. First, in In *Re Haughey*[248] it is striking that the Supreme Court was prepared to consider whether the Dáil Public Accounts Committee had transgressed the boundaries fixed for it by the Dáil Standing Orders (though without explicitly considering the question of whether the court was empowered to intervene in the internal proceedings of the Oireachtas).[249] Secondly, in *Re Article 26 and the Emergency Powers Bill 1976*,[250] the Supreme Court expressly reserved for consideration the question of whether it had jurisdiction to review a declaration of emergency passed by both Houses of the Oireachtas, despite the fact that, to judge by the clear words and purpose of Article 28.3.3°, it was intended that the Oireachtas should have the final say on this question.

As mentioned, one line of cases[251] concerned the various actions, taken by the Government in referendum campaigns, to encourage the passage of the proposal. In various court cases, at High and Supreme Court level, the view had been steadily, if slightly vaguely expressed that this was an area in which courts either had no jurisdiction or should not exercise it.[252] This line of previous authority climaxed in *McKenna v. An Taoiseach (No. 2)*[253] in the High Court. The substance of this decision arose from the fact that the Government was funding only one side in the Divorce Referendum. This, it was contended, violated various of the plaintiff's constitutional rights, among them the right to a fair referendum procedure. However the plaintiff claim failed at a preliminary point, with the High Court (Keane J.) taking the line of authority against a court's intervention in the political process to its furthest extent and holding that: "For the courts to review decisions in this area

---

[247] See *Kelly, The Irish Constitution, op. cit.* above, n. 139, pp. 135–148; 1124–1130; Morgan, *The Separation of Powers in the Irish Constitution* (1997), Chap 11.I.

[248] [1971] I.R. 217. See also the abortive *Norris* proceedings described at p. 507, n.66.

[249] For an affirmation of the traditional rule that the courts will not scrutinise the internal workings of Parliament, see *O'Crowley v. Minister for Finance* [1935] I.R. 536 and *O'Malley v. An Ceann Comhairle* [1997] 1 I.R. 428 (refusing the applicant liberty to seek judicial review of a decision of the respondent to disallow a Dáil question). However, *O'Malley* does not seem to have been a very strong case in the light of the facts that: (i) no explicit provision of the Constitution was alleged to have been violated; (ii) no purpose would be served by a court order in respect of a question which had been disallowed eight years earlier.

[250] [1977] I.R. 159. See Morgan, "The Emergency Powers Bill Reference – II" (1979)14 Ir. Jur. (N.S.) 252 at 256–262.

[251] See too, *Dudley v. An Taoiseach* [1994] 2 I.L.R.M. 322 (leave to institute judicial review granted against government on fact of its failure to hold a bye-election within a reasonable period). But *cf. O'Malley v. An Ceann Comhairle* [1997] 1 I.R. 428 (no judicial review of the Dáil's internal affairs).

[252] On which see *Kelly, The Irish Constitution, op. cit.* above n.139, pp. 1129–30; Morgan, *The Separation of Powers in the Irish Constitution*, op. cit., above, n.247, Chap 11.1

[253] [1995] 2 I.R. 10.

679

by the Government or Dáil Éireann would be for them to assume a role which is exclusively entrusted to those organs of state, and one which the courts are conspicuously ill-equipped to undertake." Keane J. buttressed this conclusion by a reference to the 'political question'doctrine.[254] This refers to a residual category of issues – some, but not all, having a strongly political flavour – which the U.S. courts have decided, for various historical or policy reasons, to treat as non-justiciable.

The striking point, for present purposes, is that, against this background, the Supreme Court (by a majority) reversed the High Court on this point and, consequently, found for the plaintiff. Although the Court did not explicitly address the point which had succeeded in the High Court and in earlier cases, its views came across fairly clearly. Giving the leading judgment, Hamilton C.J. included, in a section headed: "Jurisdiction of the Court", lengthy quotations from the High Court judgment and from one of the earlier decisions.[255] Immediately, there follows the comment: "These statements are based on the concept of the separation of powers . . ."[256] Next, the learned judge quotes from earlier judgments the thrust of which is that the Separation of Powers must give way to the Supremacy of the Constitution.[257] He concludes that: "the exercise by the Government of the executive power of the State is subject to the provision of the Constitution."[258] Conspicuous by its absence here is any concession to the notion of the "political question" (which had found favour earlier) namely that there are some areas which, though they may involve a violation of the Constitution, are of such a character that they are not appropriate for judicial resolution.[259]

In regard to the tension between either the separation of powers[260] or the notion of the "political question" and, on the other hand the Supremacy of the Constitution,

---

[254] *Ibid.* at p. 18–19. According to the U.S. *locus classicus* on the subject, *Baker v. Carr* (1962) 369 U.S. 186, 217, *per* Brennan J. a political question arises where one or more of the following situations exist:

"a textually demonstrable constitutional commitment of the issue to a coordinate political department; or a lack of judicially discoverable and manageable standards for resolving it; the impossibility of deciding without an initial policy determination of a kind clearly for non-judicial discretion; the impossibility of a court's undertaking independent resolution without expressing a lack of the respect due to coordinate branches of government; . . . the potentiality of embarrassment from multifarious pronouncements by various departments on one question."

Keane J. stated (at 19) that: "each of [the *Baker*] criteria, with the exception of the penultimate one [support the view that] the question in this case is clearly one for resolution by the legislative and executive arms of Government and not by the judicial arm." This seems to go rather far.

[255] [1995] 2 I.R. 20 at 39, referring to *Crotty v. An Taoiseach* [1987] I.R. 713 and *McKenna v. An Taoiseach (No. 1)* [1995] 2 I.R. 1. See Sherlock, "Constitutional Change, Referenda and the courts in Ireland" (1997) *Public Law* 125.

[256] [1995] 2 I.R. 10 at 39.

[257] *Crotty v. An Taoiseach* [1987] I.R. at 722–723, on which see Morgan, *The Separation of Powers in the Irish Constitution, op. cit.*, above, n.247, Chap. 3.V.

[258] [1995] 2 I.R. at 40.

[259] Of the judges other than Hamilton C.J., Blayney J. ([1995] 2 I.R. at 50) stated that he agreed with the Chief Justice. Denham J. made a statement (at 51) similar to that of Hamilton C.J. The other judges do not allude to the matter. However, even the dissenting judge (Egan J.) did not ground his decision on the point canvassed in the text; but rather on the absence of any explicit constitutional provision barring expenditure.

[260] On broad separation of powers principles, it has sometimes been said that the courts will refrain from interfering with the process of legislation: *O'Crowley v. Minister for Finance* [1935] I.R. 536; *Halpin v. Attorney General* [1936] I.R. 226; *Wireless Dealers Assoc. v. Fair Trade Commission,* unreported, Supreme Court, March 7, 1956; *Roche v. Ireland,* unreported, High Court, June 16,

it is the supremacy doctrine, which has prevailed. As Walsh J. stated in *Crotty v. An Taoiseach* "to the judicial organ of government alone is given the power to decide if there has been a breach of constitutional restraints."[261] The strength of this principle – and also, the lack of judicial interest in any political question doctrine – was demonstrated again in *Crotty* itself. The plaintiff had sought a declaration and injunction restraining the Government from ratifying the Single European Act (SEA) which was a treaty, signed by members of the European Community (E.C.), the criticial parts of which provided for improved co-operation in the sphere of foreign policy. The plaintiff's argument was that since Article 29.4 vests the Government with the power to conduct foreign affairs, it is not open to the State to fetter the Government's authority by a treaty which would oblige it to make foreign policy with a greater measure of co-operation with other Member States of the EC. The aspect of this multi-faceted case, which is relevant here, is that neither the majority nor the dissenting judges so much as adverted to the "political question" doctrine.[262] It might have been thought that such an argument would have been apt; not only were foreign affairs involved, but the basis of *Crotty* was the hobgoblin of sovereignty and its alleged erosion. In a world of highly qualified sovereigns, this is an issue *par excellence* of political judgment.

Plainly the issue of the constitutionality of a major act of foreign policy is at a considerable remove from the normal province of administrative law. However, it seems fair to extrapolate from the fact that there is no place for the political question, even in what might be thought to be such a natural situation as that disclosed in *Crotty*, to the proposition that it is unlikely to find a welcome in any of the more usual actions controlled by administrative law.

A further example is provided by *Brennan v. Minister for Justice*,[263] which consisted of a successful application of judicial review in respect of the Minister's powers of remission or commutation of punishments imposed in a criminal court. The facts, admittedly were rather extreme: in 1993 (to take a typical year), approximately 4 000 petitions had been made to the Minister for remission or commutation and some change had been made in well over half of these cases. These powers – historically an aspect of the Prerogative – are presently established by Article 13.6 of the Constitution; but largely exercised by the Minister for Justice under the Criminal Justice Act 1951, section 23. It was held that there had been an abuse of the Minister's statutory power.[264]

1983 and *Finn v. Attorney General* [1983] I.R. 154. Yet judicial intervention will be forthcoming if the constitutionally required stages of law-making have not been carried out: *R. (O'Brien) v. Governor of the North Dublin Military Barracks* [1924] 1 I.R. 32; *Victoria v. Commonwealth* (1975) 7 A.L.R. 1; *Western Australia v. Commonwealth* (1975) 7 A.L.R. 159.

261 [1987] I.R. 713. See also (on the constitutional aspect of the case) Hogan, "The Supreme Court and the Single European Act" (1987) 22 Ir. Jur. 55.

262 The same point could be illustrated by the absence of any reference to the "political question" doctrine in *McGimpsey v. Ireland* [1988] I.R. 565 (H.C.); [1990] 1 I.R. 110 (S.C.). Note, however, that in the High Court, Barrington J. appears to have employed a species of the "political question" doctrine in order to defeat a subsidiary part of the plaintiff's claim. Thus, for example, the plaintiffs complained about the failure to consult the unionist community in Northern Ireland regarding the Anglo-Irish Agreement, but Barrington J. observed (at 592) that this appeared to be "essentially a political matter and not for a court of law."

263 [1995] 1 I.R. 612.

264 Geoghegan J. stated (at 628–629):

The striking point, for present purposes, is that, in this case, the possibility that there was any kind of jurisdictional bar on judicial review in respect of the exercise of the Minister's powers of remission or commutation by virtue of these powers was not even considered worthy of discussion.

One of the few clear constitutional exclusions of the courts is to be found in Article 13.8° which states that the President shall not be answerable to: "any court for the exercise and performance of the powers and functions of his office."[265]

Non-Constitutional cases

Outside the realm of the Constitution, one should notice that in *Inspector of Taxes v. Minister for the Public Service*[266] the Supreme Court stated that a decision of the Minister in regard to grading, which affects the salary and career prospects of certain civil servants, is, like any other administrative action, open to review. Other decisions indicate that the exercise of certain prosecutorial discretions may be subject to review. Thus in *The State (O'Callaghan) v. O'hUadaigh*[267] Finlay P. accepted that the power of the Director of Public Prosecutions to enter a *nolle prosequi* was reviewable and in *Norris v. Attorney-General*[268] McCarthy J. suggested that a positive decision not to prosecute in respect of all crimes of a particular nature would be unlawful, and, by implication, subject to review. In *The State (McCormack) v. Curran*[269] Walsh J. stated that it was: "The common law duty of a policeman to

---

"I am quite satisfied that Article 13, s. 6 of the Constitution was never intended to create a parallel or alternative system of justice to that provided for by Article 34. Yet that is precisely what is happening in these cases. There is no evidence that the Minister found exceptional or unusual circumstances to justify her modifying the judge's order. The kind of points put forward either by the petitioning TD or by the Garda superintendent in his respective reports or by the petitioner himself are all points which either were or could have been put before the judge when he was considering sentence. There was nothing in any of the reports before the minister to indicate that that was not done and, if so, that it could not have been done. I am not necessarily suggesting that the Minister can only exercise her power if there is a change of circumstances following on the District Judge's order. Indeed, I think it would be unwise to attempt any definition of what precisely the exceptional circumstances would have to justify remission of a fine. I think that in very exceptional cases a Minister might be able to exercise his or her power in circumstances where he or she believed the judge's decision was wholly unsupportable. . . .

 But in general it would seem to me that having regard to the clear provisions of the Constitution relating to the courts, the power under Article 13, s. 6 must have been intended to be exercised sparingly. Indeed, this is reinforced by the fact that the power is, by the Constitution itself, vested only in the President. But the Article enables the power to be also vested in some other authority if it is conferred by law. That authority need not necessarily even be a Minister answerable to Dáil Éireann."

265 This is presumably the basis for the view, expressed more than once, by President Robinson, or her spokesperson, that the office of President is "self-regulating". For comment, on this surprising claim see Mee, "The changing nature of the Presidency: The President and the Government should be Friends" (1996) 14 I.L.R. 2.

266 [1986] I.L.R.M. 296 *contra*, unreported, High Court, March 24, 1983, p. 31. See pp. 549–550.

267 [1977] I.R. 42. In *Raymond v. Attorney General* [1982] Q.B. 839 at 847 Shaw L.J. observed that "Unless [the D.P.P.'s decision] is manifestly such that it could not be honestly and reasonably arrived at, it cannot . . . be impugned." *Cf.* also *Flynn v. D.P.P.* [1986] I.L.R.M. 290. Note that in *The State (Killian) v. Attorney General* (1958) 92 I.L.T.R. 182 the former Supreme Court ruled that the entry of a *nolle prosequi* by the Attorney-General could not be subject to judicial review. The exact precedential status of this decision in the light of *O'Callaghan* and *Flynn* is unclear.
 For cases on the D.P.P.'s authority to order a transfer to the Special Criminal Court, see pp. 686–690.

268 [1984] I.R. 36 at 81.

269 [1987] I.L.R.M. 225 at 239. See Finlay C.J.'s variation at 236.

bring criminals to justice and a refusal by a policeman on notice not to pursue a criminal [would be] a common law misdemeanour." It is also by now well established that it is open to a judge to overrule governmental claims to the non-disclosure of evidence before a court.[270] In England, the Divisional Court has set aside a decision not to prosecute, taken by the D.P.P., on the ground that the decision was unreasonable in that it failed to have regard to a material consideration.[271]

As explained already, the dominant judicial view would appear to be that all discretionary powers are reviewable. This may be illustrated in the general administration context by *Duff v. Minister for Agriculture.*[272] Here the plaintiffs were a group of small farmers. The State on its own behalf and as agent for the European Commission approved their plans to develop their farms (which included borrowing money) on the basis that there would be an expanded quota for the sale of their milk. However, subsequently the plaintiffs were not allocated any "reference quantity" to enable them to fulfil their development plan. They claimed damages to compensate them for this loss.

The plaintiff's claim failed before Murphy J. in the High Court who relied upon the older, more cautious approach to judicial review. He stated:

"The Regulations deliberately chose to confer a discretion which though not absolute . . . does not appear to have been restricted by any identifiable objective or in any purposeful fashion. I can only infer that the discretion was granted to each Member State to be exercised in accordance with the national policy of that State rather than the attainment of particular objectives within the Council Regulations.

Even leaving aside any question of the application of the doctrine of the separation of powers it seems to me impossible for the Courts to review decisions based on questions of national policy. To do so would involve the State disclosing publicly details of highly confidential national and international planning and strategy and even if that were done some yardstick would have to be found by which the Courts could be invited to say that such policies were irrational. I do not think that the first of these propositions is desirable or that the second is possible . . . [There is] difficulty in evaluating conduct which may have repercussions in so many different ways and in so many different places. Political decisions of a policy nature are inherently far removed from the relatively compact arguments concerning the legal or constitutional rights of parties to litigation before the Courts.

Accordingly, I take the view that whilst the Minister's discretion was not unfettered and was not capable of being exercised in an arbitrary fashion it was a decision based on national policy for which the Minister like all politicians in a democratic society is answerable politically and not to the Courts of Law established under the Constitution unless the policy infringes the

---

270 See Chap. 14. It bears noting that while this result was grounded on Art. 34.1 of the Constitution by the Supreme Court, in *Murphy v. Dublin Corporation* [1972] I.R. 215, the High Court in the same case had laid down the same principle (at 227) using the standard common law rules for the control of a discretionary power.

271 *R. v. D.P.P. ex p. C.* [1995] Cr.App.R 136.

272 [1997] 2 I.R. 22.

constitutional rights of the citizen or is shown to involve the abuse of a fiduciary function which is not the case."[273]

For present purposes, the striking point about these sentiments is their rarity. The High Court decision was reversed in the Supreme Court and the approach taken in the passage was not adopted, for instance, even by the minority judges who would have upheld the High Court's decision. The minority judges relied mainly on the more conventional basis that the Minister's decision did not defy "fundamental reason and common sense".[274]

The power of the courts to review prison disciplinary decisions appears to be taken as almost axiomatic. Thus, in *Gallagher v. Corrigan*[275] Blayney J. readily accepted, *obiter*, that judicial review would lie to control disciplinary decisions taken by prison authorities, whether it be in respect of prisoners or prison officers:

"There is obviously a considerable difference between the Governor's exercising discipline over prisoners and his exercising discipline over his officers, but it seems to me that it would be anomalous . . . that prisoners should be entitled to the protection of the rules of natural and constitutional justice, but that prison officers should not . . . The Governor in exercising his powers of discipline over prison officers is also discharging a function which is partly magisterial and partly of a judicial or decision-making character, with the consequence that he must comply with the rules of natural and constitutional justice."[276]

Indeed, apart from the cases involving the exercise of a prosecutorial discretion, which are considered, *infra*, the only case in which the power of review has been seriously doubted or undermined is *The State (Sheehan) v. Government of Ireland*,[277] where the applicant sought judicial review of the Government's failure to bring into force section 60(1) of the Civil Liability Act 1961, which abolishes the common law rule that a highway authority cannot be held liable for non-feasance or non-repair of the public highway. Section 60(7) provided that no commencement order could be made for a date prior to April 1, 1967, and in the High Court Costello J. held that the Government's discretion as to when it was to be brought into force was not open-ended, but rather subject to review:

"Whilst no time limit is imposed, and to that extent some discretion in the exercise of the power is given to the Government, it seems to me that if Parliament intended (as I think it clearly did) that the law should be reformed, it did not intend to confer a discretion which would permit that intention to be frustrated. This means that the discretion given by s.60(7) is a limited one, and that it should be construed as requiring the Government to make an order within

---

273 [1997] 2 I.R. 22 at 43–44. For the facts in the case and the divergence between the minority and the majority, see p. 829, n.147.

274 *ibid.* at 103, *per* Keane J. Note though, that Keane J. also remarked that: "Ultimately [the Minister's decision] had to be made by a Minister responsible to Dáil Éireann and to the people in the electoral process." See also similar comments of the other dissenting judge, Hamilton C.J. at 70–71.

275 Unreported, High Court, February 1, 1988. For equivalent British authorities, see *R. v. Governor of Maze Prison ex. parte McKiernan* [1986] N.I. 385; *Leech v. Deputy Governor of Parkhurst Prison* [1988] A.C. 533.

276 *Ibid.* pp. 12–13 of the judgment.

277 [1987] I.R. 550. See Hogan, "Judicial Review of an Executive Discretion" (1987) 9 D.U.L.J. 91.

a reasonable time after the 1st April 1967. Obviously a reasonable time has long since passed and, in my opinion, the Government is shown to have failed to carry out its statutory duty."[278]

The Supreme Court, however, took a different view of this matter. Henchy J. held that the subsection conferred on the Government what, in effect, is an unreviewable discretionary power:

"The use of 'shall' and 'may,' both in the subsection and in the section as a whole, point to the conclusion that the radical law-reform embodied in the section was not intended to come into effect before the 1st April 1967 and thereafter only on such day as *may* be fixed by the Government. Not, be it noted, on such date as *shall* be fixed by the Government. Limiting words such as 'as soon as may be' or 'as soon as convenient,' which are to be found in comparable statutory provisions, are markedly absent.". . .

[The] important law reform to be effected by the section was not to take effect unless and until the Government became satisfied that, in the light of factors such as the necessary deployment of financial and other resources, the postulated reform would come into effect. The discretion vested in the Government to bring the section into operation on a date after 1st April 1967 *was not limited in any way as to time or otherwise."*[279]

These passages would seem to suggest that the Oireachtas may, if it sees fit to do so, invest the Government (or a Minister or an administrative agency) with an unreviewable discretionary power, provided that the statutory language is sufficiently clear.[280]

---

278 *Ibid.* at 556.
279 *Ibid.* at 561. But surely, the invocation (in the early part of this passage) of what amounts to the *expressio unius* principle seems misplaced in this statutory context. It was clearly intended that the Government should be given a discretion in the matter, but the use of the word "may" for this purpose probably results from the use of a convenient statutory formula to which no special significance should be attached.

In opposition to Henchy J.'s judgment: see the comments (at 563) of McCarthy J.'s dissenting judgment; Bennion, *Statutory Interpretation* (1984) p. 416; and Hodgson J. in *R. v. Secretary of State for the Environment ex. p. Greater London Council, The Times*, Dec. 2, 1983.

More comment on *Sheehan* will be found in the second edition of this book at pp. 70–72. *Sheehan* is distinguishable from *R. v. Home Secretary ex parte. Fire Brigades Union* [1995] 2 A.C. 513, which concerned the Criminal Justice Act 1988, section 171 of which reads: "this Act shall come into force on such date as the Secretary of State may appoint." No day was ever appointed. Instead, the Secretary of State announced that the scheme contained in the Act should be replaced by a non-statutory scheme. The English courts made rather heavy weather of the case (see (1996) 112 L.Q.R. 177), in which judicial review of this scheme was sought. The House of Lords eventually held, by a majority of 3:2 that in the words of Lord Lloyd, the section quoted earlier conferred a power on the Secretary of State "to say when but not whether" and, accordingly, in introducing a plainly inconsistent scheme (the point at which the case differed from *Sheehan*) the Secretary of State had abused this power.

280 The same (or similar) formulae as that in the 1961 Act are still in use today. For example: s.2 of the Air Pollution Act 1987; s.2 of the Labour Services Act 1987; s.27(4) of the National Monuments (Amendment) Act 1987 and s.1(2) of the Safety, Health and Welfare (Off-Shore Installations) Act 1987 all provide that the relevant Minister "may" make an order bringing the Act into force.

However, notice that despite this point of distinction, in the note from the L.Q.R. mentioned in n.279, the writer Mr Justice Thomas, a New Zealand judge, remarked in an observation which is relevant to *Sheehan*: ". . . a more positive perception of the judicial function might have led their Lordships to conclude that the Secretary of State was under a legal duty to bring the relevant provisions into force as soon as he considered it possible or practical to do so."

Yet this would seem to fly in the fact of the fundamental tenor of our modern administrative law.

Quite apart from exceptional cases such as *Sheehan*, attempts have been made – though, it must be said, only rarely and then not in recent statutes – to put certain powers or decisions beyond the courts' power of review by the use of appropriately-worded statutory formulae. One example is section 22 of the Voluntary Health Insurance Act 1957 by which the Minister for Health "may, *in his absolute discretion* grant or refuse to grant to any person a . . . health insurance licence." Another example is afforded by section 34 of the Offences Against the State Act 1939 by which, save in capital cases, the Government "may, *at their absolute discretion*, at any time remit in whole or in part or modify (by way of mitigation only) or defer any punishment imposed by a Special Criminal Court." (Authors' italics) It is suggested that, especially since, as explained above, judicial review has now been given a constitutional pedestal, its removal could not be effected by any statutory formulae.[281]

The question of whether a court would regard the statutory language as precluding judicial review would depend more on the nature of the subject-matter and other circumstances than the wording of the provision. Thus, to take the health insurance licence example just quoted, there seems scant chance that a court would treat itself as debarred from the area of insurance licensing. The same might not be true of the remission of punishment example in view of its historical links with security issues (a matter which is examined below).

Security and Prosecution Cases

In some cases an immunity from judicial review may be regarded as having been implicitly conferred by the Constitution. This argument seems to be the only satisfactory explanation of the line of cases which holds that the power of the Director of Public Prosecutions to order the transfer of trials to the Special Criminal Court is only reviewable on straitened grounds. (One should notice the divergence between this line and the cases, considered earlier,[282] holding or asserting that the D.P.P.'s power to enter a *nolle prosequi* or not to prosecute crimes of a particular type is reviewable.) Article 38.3.1° expressly permits the creation of such courts, and vests the Oireachtas with a plenary legislative power to regulate their "constitution, powers, jurisdiction and procedure." The Offences against the State Act 1939 now vests the Director of Public Prosecutions with power to order the trial of accused persons before the Special Criminal Court once he is satisfied that in his opinion the ordinary courts are inadequate "to secure the effective administration of justice and the preservation of public peace and order in relation to the trial of such person on such a charge."[283] In the first pair of cases in this area, the High Court ruled in *Savage v. D.P.P.*[284] (Finlay P.) and *Judge v. D.P.P.* (Carroll J.)[285]

---

[281] In a sense, the "absolute discretion" is an indirect attempt to create an ouster clause. On this, see pp. 458–460.

[282] See pp. 682–683.

[283] For an account of the relevant provisions, see Casey, *The Irish Law Officers: Roles and Responsibilities of the Attorney General and Director of Public Prosecutions* (1996), pp. 300–311.

[284] [1982] I.L.R.M. 385 at 389. See also, *Re McCurtain* [1941] I.R. 83.

[285] [1984] I.L.R.M. 224. The Supreme Court had earlier reserved this question: see *Re Article 26 and*

that once the D.P.P. bona fide holds that opinion, then the matter is not subject to any further review.

Both cases stress the security difficulties which made it impractical for the Director of Public Prosecutions to disclose the reasons.[286] In *Judge* Carroll J. was unimpressed by the argument that such an investigation might be held *in camera*, presumably because she considered that even an *in camera* investigation would involve the danger of a "leak" of highly sensitive information. By contrast, in *The State (Lynch) v. Cooney*[287] – another "security" case but of a rather different type – the Supreme Court was willing to review a banning order issued by the Minister for Posts under the Broadcasting Acts. This discrepancy between *Judge* and *Lynch* is probably explicable by reference to the differing nature of the decision under review and of the range of information on which it would probably turn. In regard to the prosecution of terrorist offenders, much of this information is likely to be confidential, whereas the decision in *Lynch*, involving the public impact of Sinn Féin policies upon the Irish television audience, would be less likely to involve such sensitive material. But in any event, the utilitarian basis of *Savage* and *Judge*, coupled with a desire not to discommode the prosecuting authorities in such a sensitive matter, is out of line with the general judicial trend in favour of review.[288]

The next relevant case is that of *The State (McCormack) v. Curran*.[289] The facts in *McCormack* have already been given.[290] Here it is relevant only to say that the case arose out of the applicant's attempt to oblige the Director of Public Prosecutions to prosecute him in Ireland in order to frustrate a criminal prosecution which was pending against him in Belfast Crown Court. The question was whether the Director of Public Prosecution's discretion to prosecute was open to review. Barr J. rejected this submission, and, following *Savage*, held that the exercise of discretion was unreviewable. However, in the Supreme Court, (not uncharacteristically) no reference was made to any authorities and, instead, Finlay C.J. stated, with no preliminary discussion:

"In regard to the DPP I reject also the submission that he has only got a discretion as to whether to prosecute or not to prosecute in any particular case related

---

the *Criminal Law (Jurisdiction) Bill 1975* [1977] I.R. 129; *The State (Littlejohn) v. Governor of Mountjoy Prison*, unreported, Supreme Court, March 18, 1976.

286   See, *e.g.* the comments of Finlay P. in *Savage* at 389:
"If the contention made [by] the plaintiffs was correct . . . it would be necessary for the Director in order to uphold the certificate he issued and for the Special Criminal Court to have jurisdiction over the case which on his certificate has been sent forward for trial by it to reveal in open court in litigation at the instance of the accused person himself all the information, knowledge and facts upon which he formed his opinion. This would obviously, as a practical matter, entirely make impossible the operation of Part V of the Act of 1939 for the trial of any non-scheduled offence by the Special Criminal Court whilst it is established and in existence. The revealing of such information in open court under conditions under which persons are seeking to overthrow the established organs of the State would be a security impossibility and to interpret section 46(2) of the Act of 1939 so as to make that necessary would be to vitiate the entire purpose of that subsection."

287   [1982] I.R. 337.

288   The decisions in *Savage* and *Judge* have both come in for considerable criticism: see Byrne (1981) 16 Ir. Jur. (N.S.) 86; (1984) 6 D.U.L.J. (N.S.) 177 and Pye (1985) 3 I.L.T. (N.S.) 65.

289   [1987] I.L.R.M.225.

290   See p. 491, n.486.

exclusively to the probative value of the evidence laid before him. Again, I am satisfied that there are many other factors which may be appropriate and proper for him to take into consideration. I do not consider that it would be wise or helpful to seek to list them in any exclusive way. If, of course, it can be demonstrated that he reaches a decision *mala fide* or influenced by an improper motive or improper policy then his decision would be reviewable by a court. To that extent I reject the contention again made on behalf of this respondent that his decisions were not as a matter of public policy ever reviewable by a court."[291]

Two comments may be made in regard to *McCormack*. First, contrasting the situation in *McCormack* with that in *Savage* and *Judge*, it may be observed that *McCormack* was a more likely candidate for a policy holding that there should be a bar on judicial review, because, in addition to the security element (which was common to all three cases) there was an international dimension which included a comparison of the possibilities of prosecuting cases in Belfast as against Dublin. If in an area such as this, the ban against judicial review could be lifted though in a very restricted way, there can be few other areas in which it can, consistently, be retained.

However, secondly and more importantly, it seems likely from the guarded language of the Supreme Court's formulations in *McCormack* that what was contemplated was not the full sweep of judicial review which applies generally to discretionary powers, but rather a power of review which was restricted to something akin to mala fides. That this may be so appears from the Chief Justice's reference to "a decision *mala fides* or . . . improper motive or improper policy" and Walsh J.'s use of the rather extreme term "perverse."[292]

What one might call the doctrine of the D.P.P.'s partial-immunity from judicial review has also been upheld in two recent cases. In *H. v. D.P.P.*,[293] it was confirmed in the (admittedly rather extreme) circumstances of a mother's unsuccessful attempt to obtain an order directing the D.P.P. to bring proceedings for sexual abuse against their son. Furthermore, the Supreme Court held[294] that it followed from this partial immunity (in the light of the grounding of the duty to give reasons[295]) that the D.P.P. was generally not obliged to give reasons for a decision not to prosecute (or,

---

[291] [1987] I.L.R.M. 237. See too Walsh J. at 239.

[292] This, certainly, was the view taken by Lynch J. in *Foley v. Director of Public Prosecutions, Irish Times Law Reports*, September 25, 1989, yet another case on the Director of Public Prosecution's power to order the transfer of trials to the Special Criminal Court. Here Lynch J. was reported as stating:

". . . while there might seem to be a slight conflict between the judgment of Mr. Justice Finlay, as President of the High Court, in *Savage*'s case and his judgment as Chief Justice in *McCormack*'s case it seems that in reality the latter was a development of the former and an expansion of it.

. . . the net result of the judgments in these cases was that the decision of the Director of Public Prosecutions in issuing certificates under the Offences Against the State Act 1939 was not reviewable, unless the applicant had established a prima facie case of some irregularity of a serious nature [*e.g. mala fides*] such as to amount to some impropriety of some sort or other. The onus of establishing such an irregularity must rest on the applicant."

[293] [1994] 2 I.R. 589. See also *Flood v. Garda Síochána Complaints Board* [1997] 3 I.R. 321.

[294] *Ibid.* at 603, *per* O'Flaherty J. and 606–607 *per* Denham J.

[295] See p. 572.

presumably, though there has been no case on this point) a decision to prosecute. Again, in *Kavanagh v. Ireland*,[296] the Supreme Court declined to grant a number of orders in relation to the applicant's trial before the Special Criminal Court including a declaration that there was no basis for the D.P.P. or the Government being of the opinion that the ordinary criminal courts are inadequate to secure the effective administration of justice (such being the appropriate statutory tests to be applied at different stages by the D.P.P. and the government). Following the general trend in this area, Barrington J. summarised the legislation and then stated:

> "Provided these powers have been exercised in a *bona fide* manner the ordinary courts have no function in relation to them. There is a certain logic in this as the question under consideration is the adequacy or otherwise of the ordinary courts to secure the effective administration of justice and the preservation of public peace and order.
>
> The question of whether the ordinary Courts are or are not adequate to secure the effective administration of justice and the preservation of public peace and order is primarily a political question, and, for that reason, is left to the legislature and the executive. The fact that the control intended is primarily a political control is underlined by s. 35, sub-s. 5 which provides that it shall be lawful for Dáil Éireann, at anytime where Part V of the Act is in force, to pass a resolution annulling the proclamation by virtue of which Part V was brought into force . . ."[297]

The judgment of the only other judge to give a written judgment – Keane J. – is to like effect, though it is, if anything, stronger than that of Barrington J. The reasoning of Keane J. in the following passage, is of particular interest in the context of the earlier discussion of 'the political question':

> "Sovereignty resides in the people alone and the exclusive vesting in the judicial arm of the power to declare unlawful the actions of the Government or the Oireachtas is simply part of the system of checks and balances essential to the operation of the separation of powers. It follows that, where the Constitution has unequivocally assigned to either the Government or the Oireachtas a power to be exercised exclusively by them, judicial restraint of an unusual order is called for before the courts intervene. That is also no more than a recognition that, while all three organs of State derive their powers from the people, the Government and the Oireachtas are accountable, directly and indirectly, to the people in the electoral process."[298]

---

[296] [1996] 1 I.R. 321. Nothing was said in the High or the Supreme Court about the fact that the applicant had been charged in the S.C.C. on 20 July, 1994 about five weeks before the first Northern Irish ceasefire came into effect or that the case was heard in the High Court several months later. For the High Court discussion, see [1996] 1 I.L.R.M. at 336–337, *per* Laffoy J.

[297] [1996] 1 I.R. at 350. See also at 360.

[298] *Ibid.* at 362–363. See also *Ward v. Government of Ireland*, unreported, Supreme Court, December 18, 1997 (similar principles applied by Lynch and Barron JJ. in rejecting further challenge to the jurisdiction of Special Criminal Court).

In short, it seems that, if a court were to exercise a power of review in security cases of this type (and this has not happened yet) it would only be in the most extreme cases.[299]

Another area which, unusually, does involve something of the same wide and difficult range of policy factors as these cases, is section 2 of the Extradition (Amendment) Act 1987 (which established a new section 44B of the Extradition Act 1965). This provision now requires the Attorney-General to direct that a particular warrant shall not be indorsed unless:

> ". . . the Attorney General, having considered such information as he deems appropriate, is of opinion that:
>
> (a) there is a clear intention to prosecute . . . the person named or described in the warrant concerned for the offence specified therein . . . and
>
> (b) such intention is founded on the existence of sufficient evidence."

The obvious question which arises from this provision is whether the Attorney-General's decision is subject to review. The effect of the gloss on *McCormack* introduced in *Foley* may be that the Attorney-General would be obliged to disclose, in open court, the material on which he had reached his decision (subject to any claim for executive privilege) if, but only if, the applicant had succeeded in establishing a prima facie case as to *mala fides* or improper motive.[300]

---

[299] See the graduated scale of review applied in the prison transfer cases: *The State (Smith and Fox) v. Governor of the Curragh Military Barracks* [1980] I.L.R.M. 208; *The State (Boyle) v. Governor of the Curragh Military Barracks* [1980] I.L.R.M. 242.

[300] One detailed point which should be noted is that this material would anyway have to be disclosed at the trial in the U.K. of the person to be sent back. This is a distinguishing point from *Savage, Judge* and *Foley* (although not *McCormack*) where the question to be determined by the Director of Public Prosecutions was rather different from that which would emerge in open court at the applicant's trial. This might be a point of distinction from these authorities.

CHAPTER 13

APPLICATION FOR JUDICIAL REVIEW

1. Introduction

Prior to October 1986 a person aggrieved by a decision of an administrative body or lower court was obliged to choose between a variety of remedies open to him. In addition to the principal State side orders of certiorari, prohibition and mandamus,[1] the private law remedies of the declaration and injunction could also have been invoked. These two sets of remedies differed in the scope of their application, depending on the nature of the decision, defect or public body involved. Writing in 1966, Griffith and Street commented as follows:

> "The remedies, for no practical reason are plural; some of them cannot be used if another remedy is available; the lines between them are imprecise and shifting [and] the judges employ vague concepts (which they do not define) in marking the boundaries of each remedy."[2]

Before the new Rules of the Superior Courts came into force in October 1986,[3] if an applicant sought the wrong remedy, no relief could be granted to him because he had asked for the improper order.[4] Under the *ancien régime*, the former state side orders could be awarded in lieu of each other, but were not interchangeable with the private law remedies. What this meant, in practice, was that if an applicant had sought, say, certiorari, but the court was of the view that mandamus was more appropriate, then the latter remedy could be awarded. However, if on an application for certiorari it transpired that the applicant had a good case on the merits, yet the restrictions on

---

[1] The other State side orders are habeas corpus (or an application for an inquiry under Art. 40.4.2°, as it is more properly described) and *quo warranto*. The remedy of habeas corpus falls outside the scope of this book, but see *Kelly, The Irish Constitution* (3rd ed., 1994) pp. 895–912. *Quo warranto* proceedings are now virtually obsolete, and there has been only one reported case involving *quo warranto* since 1922: *The State (Lycester) v. Hegarty* (1941) 75 I.L.T.R. 121, where the powers of the Master of the High Court in such proceedings are discussed. The modern practice is to seek a declaration that an office-holder has been invalidly appointed rather than to proceed by way of *quo warranto*: see *Glynn v. Roscommon County Council* (1959) 93 I.L.T.R. 149. Proceedings by way of *quo warranto* must now be brought as an application for judicial review: see R.S.C. – 1986, Ord. 84, r. 18(1)

[2] Griffith and Street, *Principles of Administrative Law* (1966), p. 236.

[3] S.I. No. 15 of 1986. These Rules come into force on October 1, 1986. For an account of the previous State side practice, see Law Reform Commission Working Paper No. 8, *Judicial Review of Administrative Action: The Problem of Remedies* (1979) and Graham, "Judicial Review: Where to Reform" (1984) 6 D.U.L.J. (N.S.) 25. (Mr Edgar Graham was a most gifted young academic lawyer and politician who was murdered by the IRA in December 1983.) The new Rules very largely follow the scheme of reform as proposed by the Law Reform Commission in their working paper.

[4] As, for example, happened in cases such as *The State (Colquhoun) v. D'Arcy* [1936] I.R. 641 and *O'Doherty v. Attorney General* [1941] I.R. 569.

the scope of certiorari were such that it was not available, then no alternative remedy such as a declaration or damages could be awarded. In such a situation the litigant would be required to brace himself for a fresh set of plenary proceedings, where the wider remedy of the declaration might be available. To take the converse example, the circumstances could be such that a litigant might initiate proceedings by way of plenary summons for a declaration, only to be turned away with the bitter-sweet news that although he had a good case on the merits, yet since one of the State side orders would have been available, he should have sought that order: the rationale for such a decision was that since the State side orders were the specialised form of proceedings for a public law matter, the normally private law remedies of a declaration or injunction should only have been sought if no State side order was apt for the case. Such blots on the legal system occurred but rarely. However, the very possibility of a catastrophe of this type, especially when coupled with the vagaries of the field of operation of the former State side orders, which might appeal more to one judge rather than another, increased even further the usual hazards of litigation.

The principal innovatory feature of the new judicial review procedure is the creation of a new comprehensive procedure (known as an "application for judicial review") which enables an aggrieved party to test the legality of administrative action in the High Court. The major objective behind the creation of this new procedure is to obviate the possibility that a good case on the merits will be lost because of the wrong choice of remedy. This result is achieved because, now, irrespective of the remedies claimed in the pleadings, "the Court may grant any relief mentioned in [Order 84, rule 18] which it considers appropriate."[5]

In the light of this, the question arises, does it ever matter which order is awarded? The answer is that it will be worth the applicant's time to argue for one order rather than another in only a few cases. First, as a matter of procedure, considered below, the time limits in the case of certiorari are more generous than for the other remedies.[6] Secondly, due to the wording of Order 84, rule 20(7)(a) of the Rules of the Superior Courts 1986, it seems possible for an applicant to obtain a form of interlocutory relief on an *ex parte* basis where certiorari (or prohibition) is sought, whereas this is not true if a declaration is sought.[7] Finally, as the declaration is not a coercive remedy, there may well be circumstances in which a coercive remedy is required in order, *e.g.* to expunge a conviction[8] and other (probably more numerous) circumstances in which the declaratory remedy will be preferred.[9]

---

[5] R.S.C. 1986, Ord. 84, r.19.

[6] Six months as compared with three months. For a suggestion that the time limit provisions might be *ultra vires*, see p. 694.

[7] R.S.C. 1986, Ord. 84, r. 20 (7) (b) provides that where other relief is sought, the Court may "at any time grant in the proceedings such interim relief as could be granted in an action begun by plenary summons." However, as an interpretation of Ord. 84., r.(7)(a) which allows the Court to grant what amounts to an interlocutory injunction on an *ex parte* basis might well be *ultra vires* the powers of the Rules Committee, it may be that there will not prove to be any great difference between r. 7(a) and r. 7(b) and, in the absence of any authoritative ruling on this question, the sub-rule has been applied unevenly in practice.

[8] *cf.* the words of Lord Goddard in *Pyx Granite Ltd v. Ministry of Housing and Local Government* [1960] A.C. 260 at 290:
"I know of no authority for saying that if an order or decision can be attacked by certiorari the court is debarred from granting a declaration in an appropriate case. The remedies are not mutually

Beyond this, there seems to be very little to choose – in terms of practical consequences, as opposed to *amour propre* – between one remedy and another. Accordingly, while such a course would have been beyond the competence of the Superior Courts Rules Committee, it may be asked: would anything have been lost if the six traditional remedies had been replaced by a single comprehensive remedy (which might have been called, like the principal remedy for judicial review in the United States Federal Courts, the "petition for review")? The answer would seem to be in the negative, although some may have feared that if the traditional orders were amputated, some violence might have been done to the substantive law of judicial review (which originally developed in the interstices of the prerogative writs) and possibly also to the law on standing and discretion.

In addition to the major change of authorising the Court to grant what it considered the "correct" order even though a different order had been sought, the 1986 Rules also made provision for such matters as time limits;[10] *locus standi;*[11] discovery and interrogatories[12] and interim relief,[13] matters which are elaborated below. The Rules also establish for the first time a right to claim damages in combination with an application for one of the public law remedies.[14]

Given the far-reaching dimensions of the changes brought about by Order 84, it remains to be seen whether these changes can truly be said to be *intra vires* the Superior Court Rules Committee. The Committee is confined to making rules dealing with "pleading and practice and procedure generally"[15] and the precaution has been taken in other jurisdictions to put precisely the sort of change effected by Order 84 on a statutory footing.[16] Nevertheless, it has been powerfully argued that the changes effected by Order 84 are, in fact, *intra vires*:

> "Taking care not to abolish quo warranto, Ord. 84 does not seem to have made any substantive change in the definition, content, or application of the remedies available on an application for judicial review."[17]

---

exclusive, though no doubt there are some orders, notably, convictions before justices, where the only appropriate remedy is certiorari."

9   For the courts' preference for granting declaratory relief rather than certiorari as a matter of "politeness" to the public body concerned, see below, p. 701.

10 R.S.C. 1986 Ord. 84, r. 21(1) imposes a general time limit of three months (six months where the relief claimed is certiorari) from the date "when grounds for the application first arose." The court has a discretion to extend these time limits. See below, pp. 725–730.

11 *Ibid.*, Ord. 84, r. 20(4) provides that the High Court shall not grant leave unless it considers that the applicant has a "sufficient interest" in the matter to which the application relates. See pp. 739–751.

12 *Ibid.*, Ord. 84, r. 20(7). See p. 709.

13 *Ibid.*, Ord. 84, r. 20(7). See pp. 710–712.

14 See below, pp. 799–800. Of course, it was always the law that a plaintiff seeking declaratory and injunctive relief by means of a plenary hearing could also seek damages.

15 Courts of Justice Act 1924, s.36, (as applied by ss.14 and 48 of the Courts (Supplemental Provisions) Act 1961).

16 See, *e.g.* Judicature (Northern Ireland) Act 1978, ss.18–21 and Supreme Court Act 1981, s.31 (England and Wales). The Law Reform Commission in their Working Paper No. 8 *Judicial Review of Administrative Action: The Problem of Remedies* (1979) also recommended (p. 79) that these changes be made by means of legislation.

17 Collins & O'Reilly, *Civil Proceedings and the State in Ireland* (1989), p. 76. It might be queried, however, whether the appropriate test is whether the 1986 Rules effected any change. For the basic issue arising from Article 15.2.1° is the relationship between the content of the parent statute and the subordinate legislation (in this case, Order 84) and, in particular, whether the subordinate legislation

Yet the correctness of this view may turn on the manner in which Order 84 is interpreted in practice.[18] Or, to put it another way, the fact that the Order 84 changes lack a statutory backing may induce the courts to take a narrower view of them than might otherwise be the case. Three examples may be given.

First, it would not seem to be open to the Committee to prescribe via the new Order 84 (whether expressly or by implication) an exclusive procedure as far as applications for judicial review are concerned. The right to challenge an administrative decision in the High Court by means of plenary summons is a substantive right which may not be taken away save by clear statutory language.[19]

Secondly, the time limits imposed by Order 84, rule 21 are very short – six months in the case of certiorari and three months in other cases (although the High Court has power to extend these time limits where there is "good reason" to do so). In contrast, the ordinary time limit for declaratory actions prescribed by the Statute of Limitations 1957 is six years. In the first place, as a matter of common law *ultra vires*, it must be doubtful whether it was open to the Committee to prescribe by Rule of Court what might in effect amount to a radically different limitation period, for a limitation period of this character is arguably not a matter of practice and procedure at all. Moreover, in view of Article 15.2.1° of the Constitution, if the applicant's right of access to the courts is to be curbed, it would seem that this substantive right can only be taken away in circumstances where the Oireachtas has legislated to that effect[20] or, at the very least, that there is legislation containing such principle or policy as would permit the Rules Committee to introduce such a time-limit.[21] Finally, the justification for different time-limits (three months and six months respectively) in the case of the broadly similar remedies of declaration and certiorari is by no means self-evident. Might it not be argued that the validity of such differing time-limits could be challenged on grounds of lack of reasonableness and rationality?

Thirdly, the power contained in Order 84, rule 26(5) to remit the matter to the original court, tribunal or authority in the wake of an order of certiorari also seems questionable. It is true that in many cases, the effect of an order will be to quash

---

authorises a principle not to be found in the parent statute. It does not matter whether any novel principle comes from current subordinate legislation or its predecessor. Notice, too, the comments of Lord Denning in *O'Reilly v. Mackman* [1983] 2 A.C. 237 at 256:

"When the Rules Committee made R.S.C., Ord. 53 some of us on the Committee had doubts about whether some of it was not *ultra vires*, but we took the risk because it was so desirable."

[18] Of course, it is not as yet completely clear as to whether Ord. 84 has, in fact, prescribed such an exclusive procedure, although the judgment of Costello J. in *O'Donnell v. Dún Laoghaire Corporation* (No. 2) [1991] I.L.R.M. 301, suggests strongly that it does not. However, it may be surmised that the absence of legislation will make the Irish courts much more reluctant to adopt the *O'Reilly v. Mackman* [1983] 2 A.C. 237 approach (see below pp. 792–797). As to whether Ord. 84, r.20(7)(a) has altered substantive law (and is thus *ultra vires*) as far the granting of substantive relief is concerned: see pp. 710–712.

[19] See the comments of Lord Simonds in *Pyx Granite Co. Ltd v. Ministry of Housing and Local Government* [1960] A.C. 260 at 286 and Lord Lowry in *Roy v. Kensington and Chelsea Family Practitioner* [1992] 1 All E.R. 705 at 728–729. Article 34.3.1° of the Constitution might also be relevant, if it were considered that the procedures specified for the application to the High Court were too restrictive. See pp. 454–460.

[20] *cf.* the reasoning of the Supreme Court in *Murphy v. Greene* [1990] 2 I.R. 566 which by implication stresses the need for legislation to curb the right of access to the courts.

[21] *cf.* the reasoning in *Harvey v. Minister for Social Welfare* [1990] 2 I.R. 232 and *Meagher v. Minister for Agriculture & Food* [1994] 1 I.R. 329.

the decision and, in those circumstances, there will generally be no objection in law to the recommencement of proceedings before that body.[22] In many cases, however, Order 84, rule 26(5) will operate in the same manner as an order for retrial. However, the power to order a retrial is generally held to be a matter of substantive law and this would seem to cast doubts on the *vires* of this particular change.[23]

Judicial review does not apply to the Superior Courts.

One important limitation to the scope of judicial review ought to be immediately stated: it is not available to review a decision of a Superior Court of record.[24] Thus, decisions of the High Court, Court of Criminal Appeal and the Supreme Court cannot be reviewed by means of judicial review. The High Court's power of judicial review is an inherent one which is designed to ensure that inferior courts,[25] tribunals,[26] university visitors[27] and other bodies exercising public functions do not exceed their jurisdiction. However, judicial review will lie to quash decisions of officers such

---

[22]   See *Bord na Móna v. An Bord Pleanála* [1985] I.R. 260 where Keane J. found certain conditions attached to a planning permission by a local authority and confirmed by An Bord Pleanála to be invalid with the result that the permission fell in its entirety. The possibility of a remittal back to An Bord Pleanála to allow them to make a fresh order on the appeal was canvassed during the course of the hearing, but Keane J. said that (at 211) "it was accepted that there was *no statutory basis for such a course*" (emphasis added). *Cf.* however the comments of Finlay C.J. on this point in *Sheehan v. Reilly* [1993] 2 I.R. 81, 92–93, discussed below at p. 713, n.117.

[23]   A definitive analysis of this complex question may be found in Costello, "Certiorari followed by remittal" (1993) I.C.L.J. 145. It should be noted that Costello is of the view that as the 1986 Rules did not effect any change in the substantive law, the provisions of Ord. 84, r. 26(5) are *intra vires*. However, it may be said in response that the appropriate question is whether a statutory instrument introduces a principle which is not contained in an Act of the Oireachtas

[24]   "The High Court, whether sitting as the Central Criminal Court or otherwise, is not an inferior court subject to coercive orders such as mandamus," *per* Henchy J. in *People (D.P.P.) v. Quilligan (No. 2)* [1989] I.R. 46 at 57. In *Blackall v. Grehan* [1995] 3 I.R. 208 the applicant sought to quash an order of the Circuit Court which had been affirmed by the High Court following a circuit appeal and which by virtue of s.39 of the Courts of Justice Act 1936 had been rendered final and not appealable. The applicants claimed that as the Circuit Court lacked jurisdiction, the High Court's order was equally amenable to challenge by by means of judicial review. Egan J. said that under these circumstances the applicants should have sought a judicial review of the Circuit Court instead of appealing to the High Court and that they were now "seeking judicial review in respect of an order of the High Court and this is something to which they are not entitled". See also, *Re A Company* [1981] A.C. 374.

[25]   The Special Criminal Court ranks as an inferior court for this purpose, despite that fact that in recent years it has been the practice for a High Court judge to preside over that Court. There have been numerous examples of applications for judicial review of decisions of the Special Criminal Court, but in no case has it been argued that judicial review will not lie to quash its decisions. For an example of where a decision of the Special Criminal Court was quashed by certiorari, see *The State (D.P.P.) v. Special Criminal Court*, unreported, High Court, Barrington J., May 18, 1983.

[26]   Judicial review will, of course, also lie where a High Court judge is presiding over a tribunal, where he is not sitting as a High Court judge as such: *Baldwin & Francis Ltd v. Patents Appeal Tribunal* [1959] A.C. 663. Thus, for example, in *Attorney General v. Hamilton (No.1)* [1993] 2 I.R. 250 the Supreme Court granted a declaration by way of judicial review to the effect that Hamilton P. had, in his capacity as Chairman of the Beef Tribunal (a tribunal of inquiry set up under the Tribunal of Inquiries Acts, 1921–1979) erred in law in receiving certain evidence that, if admitted, would have breached the absolute cabinet confidentiality provided for in Art. 28.4 of the Constitution. Note, however, that in *Attorney General v. Hamilton (No. 2)* [1993] 3 I.R. 227, (a subsequent application for judicial review of the Beef Tribunal) both Finlay C.J. and O'Flaherty J. expressly reserved the question of whether in the former's words, "judicial review is an appropriate remedy for parties who have been aggrieved by rulings made by a tribunal of inquiry."

[27]   *Page v. Hull University Visitor* [1993] 1 A.C. 682; *R. v. Visitors to the Inns of Court, ex p. Calder* [1994] 3 Q.B. 1.

as the Master of the High Court[28] or a Taxing Master,[29] as it has been held that the High Court is not thereby making an order against itself or any other "Superior Court", but rather against an officer "attached" to the High Court.

2. Distinctive Features of Particular Remedies

It was traditionally the case – and remains so to some extent – that for an issue to be amenable to judicial review, two sets of conditions must be satisfied. In the first place, it must be a matter of public law, a topic to which we return at length below in Chapter 14.1 and 2. Secondly, each of the orders has its own characteristics. Whilst some of the law in relation to these is artificial or even antiquarian and is probably of little significance in an age impatient of technicalities, it is still worth mentioning some of this law, whether for reasons of historical context or of possible contemporary significance. It may be convenient to deal first with rules which are common to the three former state side orders, certiorari, prohibition and mandamus.

"Determining questions affecting the rights of subjects"

It was traditionally understood that these three public law remedies shared certain restrictive features. For instance, they would only lie to review something in the nature of a decision. It was not required to have to been absolutely final, but there are cases which held that a requirement that the decision be approved by another person or body prevents the orders from issuing.[30] Allied to this was the notion that the public law remedies would not lie to a body whose sole function was to make a recommendation, and that the impugned determination had to affect rights or impose liabilities.[31] The modern tendency, however, is to eschew a rigid classification of whether a determination is "binding" "conclusive" or whether the "legal rights" of the citizen have been affected. The courts are apt to examine whether the applicant has suffered a real or possible prejudice and to see whether he has a sufficient interest in the matter. In addition, the courts have declared themselves prepared to review decisions in cases involving questions of so-called "soft" law (*e.g.*, decisions based on application of administrative circulars and guidelines) where questions of legal rights (at least in the strict sense of that term) may not necessarily arise.[32]

---

[28]   *Elwyn (Cottons) Ltd v. Master of the High Court* [1989] I.R. 14 (mandamus lies to compel the Master of the High Court to grant protective measures under the Jurisdiction of Courts and Enforcement of Judgments (European Communities) Act 1988).

[29]   *The State (Gallagher, Shatter & Co.) v. de Valera*, unreported, High Court, Costello J., December 9, 1983 (certiorari lies to quash decision of the Taxing Master as to costs). While this decision was reversed on its facts by the Supreme Court ([1987] I.L.R.M. 1), there was no suggestion that judicial review would not lie to quash his decision. Certiorari was also granted in *The State (Gallagher, Shatter & Co.) v. de Valera (No. 2)* [1991] 2 I.R. 198. But *cf. Re Weir and Higgins' Application* [1988] N.I. 338.

[30]   *Re Local Government Board, ex p. Kingstown Commissioners* (1886) 18 L.R. Ir. 509; *R. v. St. Lawrence's Hospital, ex p. Pritchard* [1953] 1 W.L.R. 1158.

[31]   *The State (St. Stephen's Green Club) v. Labour Court* [1961] I.R. 85; and the comments of Murnaghan J. in *The State (Pharmaceutical Society) v. Fair Trade Commission* (1965) 99 I.L.T.R. 24 at 31–32 (no prohibition to respondent body as it could not affect individual rights or liabilities).

[32]   See generally above, pp. 53–57.

Take *MacPhartaláin v. Commissioners of Public Works*,[33] where the applicants were land owners who challenged a decision of the Commissioners to designate certain lands as areas of scientific interest and importance. The Commissioners contended that the act of designation was not judicially reviewable, since no decision had been taken affecting the lands. This was not accepted by the Supreme Court, as Finlay C.J. drew attention to the fact that the act of designation constituted an impediment to the development of the lands.[34] As the applicants had never been given any opportunity of making representations in advance of this decision, the Court had no hestitation in quashing it. Cases such as *MacPhartaláin* show that the concept of the "determination of rights" is loosely construed. It could not have been said in the former case that a preliminary report in and of itself affects legal rights or imposes liabilities. But the critical factor is often whether the applicants were prejudiced in the contested determination, and whether they would obtain a real benefit if the determination was quashed.[35]

"Having the duty to act judicially"

Related to the requirement that for the remedy to be appropriate, legal rights must be at issue was the precept that the administrative body had to be under a duty to act judicially[36] before such remedies could be granted. Nowadays this requirement (insofar as it still exists) does not in practice greatly restrict the scope of certiorari or prohibition. First, the duty to act judicially is implied where there is a power to affect rights or impose liabilities.[37] Moreover even in cases where there is no duty

---

33 [1994] 3 I.R. 353. See also *The State (Shannon Atlantic Fisheries Ltd) v. McPolin* [1976] I.R. 93 (High Court has power to quash the report of a statutory inquiry even where the time limit for a criminal prosecution on foot of such a report has expired). Of course, not every decision which potentially affects individual rights is amenable to judicial review; in *B v. An Bord uchtála* [1997] 1 I.L.R.M. 15 Murphy J. said that "the mere expression of an opinion by the Board, as opposed to the adjudication on an [adoption] application was not susceptible of judicial review or a declaration made in lieu of certiorari".

34 The applicants' prospects of obtaining a grant for afforestation – and, hence, the value of the lands – was diminished as a result of the designation.

35 This has been the attitude taken in cases such as *The State (Hayes) v. Criminal Injuries Compensation Board* [1982] I.L.R.M. 210 (certiorari lies to review decisions of extra-statutory body) and *The State (Melbarien Enterprises Ltd) v. Revenue Commissioners* [1985] I.R. 706 (certiorari lies to review refusal to grant tax clearance certificate, *i.e.* a purely administrative decision not taken pursuant to statutory power).

36 *The State (Crowley) v. Irish Land Commission* [1951] I.R. 250. O'Higgins C.J. appeared to insist upon this requirement in *The State (Abenglen Properties Ltd) v. Dublin Corporation* [1984] I.R. 381 at 392, as did Hamilton P. in *Byrne v. Grey* [1988] I.R. 31 at 40; Barr J. in *Egan v. Minister for Defence*, unreported, High Court, November 24, 1988 and Finlay C.J. in *MacPhartaláin v. Commissioners of Public Works* [1994] 3 I.R. 353. It may be observed that the applicants succeeded in each of the Irish cases just mentioned, save in *Abenglen* where the failure was unrelated to the choice of remedy. Note too that in *O'Reilly v. Mackman* [1983] 2 A.C. 237, the House of Lords ruled that the duty to act judicially was no longer to be required in the case of applications for certiorari or prohibition.

37 *Ridge v. Baldwin* [1964] A.C. 40; *R. v. Hillingdon B.C., ex p. Royco Homes Ltd* [1974] Q.B. 720; *The State (Conlan) v. Military Service Pensions Referee* [1947] I.R. 264 (certiorari does not lie to review ministerial decision to request respondent referee to review the grant of a military service pension, as Minister under no duty to act judicially) is one of the very few cases in which the applicant has failed to satisfy this requirement. It also appears that certiorari cannot be used to mount a direct challenge to the validity of a statute or delegated legislation, as no duty to act judicially arises in the case of the exercise of a legislative function: *Re Local Government Board, ex p. Kingstown Commissioners* (1886) 18 L.R. Ir. 509. Of course, certiorari can be used to mount an indirect collateral

to act judicially, mandamus will issue and this reflects the fact that until nearly the end of the nineteenth century, mandamus was used to enforce administrative and ministerial duties of every description.[38]

Notwithstanding this qualification, certiorari traditionally enjoyed one distinct procedural advantage over and above the other remedies. It would lie to review not only *ultra vires* decisions, but it would also quash for error on the face of the record.[39]

Certiorari, Prohibition and Mandamus: the distinctions

The demarcation lines between these three remedies are, broadly speaking, as follows. Certiorari lies to quash a decision of a public body which has been arrived at in excess of jurisdiction[40] or where the error appears on the face of the record, whereas prohibition is sought to restrain that body from doing something which would be in excess of its jurisdiction. There is no real difference in principle between the two remedies, save that prohibition may be invoked at an earlier stage. The difference is thus almost exclusively one of tense. By contrast, the principal function of mandamus arises where a public body has failed to take action. Its purpose is to secure the performance of a public duty imposed on a public body either by statute or by common law.[41]

Special features of mandamus

Mandamus is, technically, a recognised statutory remedy in that section 28(8) of the Supreme Court of Judicature (Ireland) Act 1877 permits an interlocutory order of mandamus to be granted in all cases "where it is just and convenient to do so". Thus, unlike certiorari and prohibition, it was theoretically possible to obtain interim relief in mandamus cases even prior to the Rules of the Superior Courts 1986, although the facility does not seem to have been ever availed of in practice. Curiously enough,

---

challenge to the validity of such legislation: see Hogan, "Challenging the Validity of an Act of the Oireachtas by way of Certiorari"(1982) 4 D.U.L.J.130 (N.S.).

[38] Wade and Forsyth, *Administrative Law* (1994) pp. 645–647.

[39] See above pp. 430–434. It is curious that the power to quash for error on the face of the record is nowadays so rarely invoked. But *cf. Bannon v. Employment Appeals Tribunal* [1993] 1 I.R. 500 for a good modern illustration of the utility of this jurisdiction.

[40] There are some instances where the right to apply for certiorari is conferred by statute. Such legislation is principally to be found in 19th century local government statutes. Thus, s.12 of the Local Government (Ireland) Act 1871 gives persons aggrieved a right to apply to the High Court for certiorari to quash a charge or surcharge. In *Downey v. O'Brien* [1994] 2 I.L.R.M. 130, Costello J. held (at 135), following an earlier decision of a Divisional High Court in The *State (Raftis) v. Leonard* [1960] I.R. 381 to like effect, that s.12 certiorari proceedings did not constitute an appeal by way of re-hearing, but that, unlike ordinary certiorari proceedings, the court may come:
   "to a different conclusion on the evidence which was before the auditor and is not confined merely to considering whether there was evidence to support his findings of fact."

[41] "The person or body against whom the order is sought must be shown to have neglected to perform some public duty imposed on him or them by law": *Minister for Labour v. Grace* [1993] 2 I.R. 53 at 55, *per* O'Hanlon J. Prior to the enactment of the Judicature Acts, the courts regularly granted mandamus compelling private persons and bodies to perform duties imposed by statute (*e.g.* compelling secretaries of companies to make statutory returns), but it seems safe to say that mandamus "now belong essentially to public law" and no longer serves this function: see Wade and Forsyth, *op.cit.* above, n. 38 p. 646 and see also Harding, *Public Duties and Public Law* (1989) pp. 86–97.

the Rules of the Superior Courts have always assimilated the practice and procedure of mandamus applications to that of interpleader actions, and this feature of mandamus is retained in the new Order 84, rule 25(2). Consequently, discovery and interrogatories have always been available in applications for mandamus, and, in a suitable case, the applicant is entitled to a jury trial.[42] Any applicant for mandamus must first call on the administrative body concerned to do its duty, and this must have been refused,[43] although there is nowadays some room for doubt whether this "formalistic approach" would be adopted in every case.[44] The requirement that there be "a demand and refusal" has much to commend it: it makes sense that the administrative body concerned be given the chance to mend its hand before the aggrieved citizen resorts to litigation. But the courts do not insist upon this requirement where it is unsuitable[45] or where the refusal can be inferred from the circumstances.[46]

In addition to its central remit to enforce a duty which had not been discharged, in the more formal atmosphere which existed before 1986, mandamus was sometimes pressed into service to perform another less obvious function. In cases where the impugned order was classified as being administrative (as opposed to judicial)[47] in character, certiorari was not available and mandamus was granted in its place. The rationale was that in such cases no valid decision was deemed to exist, so that mandamus could lie to command the decision-maker to arrive at a decision. This practice was known as "certiorarified mandamus" and it was developed at a time when it was thought that certiorari would not lie in respect of purely administrative decisions. It was thought to be necessarily implicit in the grant of mandamus – that is, an order to the deciding official to determine the matter according to law – that

---

42 R.S.C. 1986, Ord. 36, r. 7 (which applies to interpleader and, consequently, to mandamus proceedings) allows the court to order a jury trial where there is a contested issue of fact. The last reported occasion on which a jury trial on an issue of fact in a mandamus application appears to have been ordered is *The State (Modern Homes (Ire.) Ltd) v. Dublin Corporation* [1953] I.R. 202.

43 "It is an established rule that the prosecutor must make a specific demand for the performance of the public duty in question, and it must be shown that this demand has been refused, or has been followed by conduct which the Court considers as tantamount to a refusal," *per* Fitzgibbon J. in *R. (Butler) v. Navan U.D.C.* [1926] I.R. 466 at 470–471. See also *R. (Hewson) v. Wicklow County Council* [1908] 2 I.R. 101 and *The State (Modern Homes (Ire.) Ltd) v. Dublin Corporation* [1953] I.R. 202 (refusal of applicant's demand inferred where respondents "made positive decisions to continue with existing law").

44 Lewis, *Judicial Remedies in Public Law* (1991) comments (p. 171): "There is old authority requiring the applicant to have made an express demand for the authority to act and for the authority to have been refused. In modern times the formalistic approach is unlikely to be required." De Smith, Woolf and Jowell, *Judicial Review of Administrative Action* (5th, ed., 1995) observe doubtfully (p. 700) that: "It is preferable for the applicant to be able to show that he demanded performance of the duty and that performance has been refused by the authority obliged to discharge it."

45 *R. v. Hanley Revising Barrister* [1912] 3 K.B. 518.

46 Thus, in *Point Exhibition Co. Ltd v. Revenue Commissioners* [1993] 2 I.R. 551 at 555 Geoghegan J. said that:
    "... the applicant was entitled to a decision one way or the other within a reasonable time. The respondents quite obviously did not make such decision within any time span that could be regarded as reasonable. Accordingly, the applicant is entitled to treat the delay as a refusal and to seek an order of mandamus directing the granting of the licence."
    See also *The State (Modern Homes (Ire.) Ltd) v. Dublin Corporation* [1953] I.R. 202.

47 This form of mandamus was formerly held not to lie where the decision-making authority is exercising judicial (or quasi-judicial) functions. See: *R. (Spain) v. Income Tax Commissioners* [1934] I.R. 27; *R. (Clonmel Lunatic Asylum) v. Considine* [1917] 2 I.R. 1; *The State (Keller) v. Galway County Council* [1958] I.R. 142.

the impugned decision was a nullity. Because of the procedural improvements effected by the new Rules, where certiorari is not appropriate, then a declaration (which is now available in the same proceedings) may now be granted. Accordingly, this form of certiorarified mandamus is probably now obsolete, as the technical distinctions which gave rise to this form of mandamus appear to have vanished from the realities of contemporary judicial review practice.

Mandamus is, of course, the most appropriate remedy where the enforcement of a statutory duty is sought. The statutory duty in question must, however, be "clearly and unambiguously expressed in the statute,"[48] or, for that matter, in the Constitution[49] before mandamus will issue.

Declaration and injunction

Although it is not a purely public law remedy, the declaratory action has come to occupy a special place, as a safety net, in our public law, chiefly because of the restrictions which hitherto restricted the scope of the former state-side orders. Indeed, it bears stating that a declaration would cover the ground of all of these remedies: it would apply to decisions taken, those to be taken or those which ought to have been taken. Furthermore, it would go beyond this territory to cover – up to a limit patrolled by the rules, covered below[50] as to ripeness and standing – anticipated or hypothetical decisions or acts in the field of public law.

The declaratory action is of comparatively modern vintage, for the common law viewed non-coercive remedies with disfavour. As far as Ireland is concerned, the declaratory action has its origins in the Chancery (Ireland) Act 1867, section 155 of which stated that no action should be open to the objection that a merely declaratory decree or order was sought thereby, and that it should be possible for the court to make binding declarations of right whether any consequential relief is or could be claimed or not.[51] The wording of section 155 is substantially reproduced in Order 19, rule 29 of the Rules of the Superior Courts. The power of the High Court to grant an injunction has a similar source, namely section 28(8) of the Supreme

---

[48] *The State (Sheehan) v. Government of Ireland* [1987] I.R. 550 at 562 *per* Henchy J. In *Minister for Labour v. Grace* [1993] 2 I.R. 53 at 55 O'Hanlon J. said that for mandamus to issue for the enforcement of a statutory right:
> "it must appear that the statute in question imposes a duty, the performance or non-performance of which is not a matter of discretion, and if a power or discretion only, as distinct from a duty, exists, an order of mandamus will not be granted by the court."

In *C v. Legal Aid Board* [1991] 2 I.R. 43 at 54 Gannon J. said that mandamus should not issue unless "by its execution an effective, and frequently an immediate, purpose can be achieved by way of remedy for a wrong done".

[49] *Delap v. An tAire Dlí agus Cirt*, unreported, High Court, July 13, 1990; *Dudley v. An Taoiseach* [1994] 2 I.L.R.M. 321 ("arguable case" that Government under "constitutional obligation" to move the writ for a by-election after a "reasonable time has elapsed from the vacancy arising") and *F.N. v. Minister for Health* [1995] 2 I.L.R.M. 297.

[50] See below at pp. 756–758.

[51] It may be noted that in *Guaranty Trust Co. of N.Y. v. Hannay & Co.* [1915] 2 K.B. 536 at 568, Bankes L.J. asserted that the courts had always possessed a residual jurisdiction to grant declaratory judgments. This statement was made, however, in the context of an action to have Rules of Court permitting the granting of declarations declared *ultra vires*. Naturally the Rules would have been *ultra vires* if they did not amount to procedural improvements of a jurisdiction which already existed.

Court of Judicature (Ireland) Act 1877,[52] which enabled the court to grant this remedy in all cases where it appeared just and convenient to do so. Despite the generality of the language used, this subsection did not extend the reach of the injunction to claims for which no remedy had previously existed either at law or in equity, nor were the principles governing the grant of an injunction substantially altered.[53] As the specialist public law remedies of prohibition and mandamus often fulfill the role which might otherwise be discharged by the injunction, applications for injunctions in public law are not very common.

Demarcation between former state side orders and equitable orders

A border-line may be drawn between the three former state side orders and the two orders which originated in the Courts of Equity, as to both their scope and their impact. As regards impact, a major feature is that a declaratory judgment merely declares the rights or the legal position of the parties to an action.[54] This is a matter of some significance in practice. A declaratory judgment is not of itself coercive, although the litigant may safely assume that public bodies will respect and obey such a judgment. Thus, as a matter of, as it were, politeness, the court will often simply grant a declaration in defiance of the precept that certiorari is the proper remedy.[55] By contrast the effect of certiorari is positively to quash the impugned decision or order. Other distinctions between the three orders which originated in the state side proceedings and the two which originated in equity are relatively minor.[56]

There is also a difference in scope between the two sets of remedies. Before 1986, even in public law cases, a declaration or an injunction could only be commenced by plenary summons. However, under the new regime if the respondent is a public body, a declaration or an injunction may be sought through an application for judicial review. Nevertheless some element of apartheid remains. Order 84, rule 18(1) of the Rules of the Superior Court states that:

> "An application for an order of certiorari [etc.] shall be made by way of application of judicial review."

By contrast, Order 84, rule 18(2) provides:

---

52 As applied to the present High Court by s.8(2) of the Courts (Supplemental Provisions) Act 1961. Section 28(8) of the 1877 Act only refers in terms to the granting of an interlocutory order, but this subsection encompasses the grant of a final order: *Beddow v. Beddow* (1878) 9 Ch.D. 89 at 93, *per* Jessel M.R.

53 *cf.* the comments of Brett L.J. in *North London Railway. Co. v. Great Northern Railway Co.* (1883) 11 Q.B.D. 30 at 36–37: ". . . if no court had the power of issuing an injunction before the Judicature Act, no part of the High Court has power to issue an injunction now." It is true that in *Moore v. Attorney General* [1927] I.R. 569 at 580 Murnaghan J. observed that the 1877 Act "extends the principles upon which the jurisdiction was formerly exercised by the Court of Chancery", but "the better view would seem to be that the legislation did not confer any additional jurisdiction on the court": Delany, *Equity and the Law of Trusts in Ireland* (1995) p. 371. The view of Brett L.J. has, moreover, been followed by the House of Lords: *Gouriet v. Union of Post Office Workers* [1978] A.C. 435; *The Siskina* [1987] A.C. 210; *South Carolina Insurance Co. v. Assurance Maatschappij 'de Zeven Provincien' NV* [1987] A.C. 24.

54 See generally, Woolf and Zamir, *The Declaratory Judgment* (1993).

55 See, *e.g. Attorney General v. Hamilton* (No.1) [1993] 2 I.R. 250 and *B v. An Bord Úchtála* [1997] 1 I.L.R.M. 15.

56 See above, p. 700.

701

"An application for a declaration or an injunction may be made by way of an application for judicial review, and on such an application the Court may grant the declaration or injunction claimed if it considers that, having regard to —

(a) the nature of the matters in respect of which relief may be granted by way of an order of mandamus, prohibition, certiorari or quo warranto

(b) the nature of the persons and bodies against whom relief may be granted by way of such order, and

(c) all the circumstances of the case,

it would be just and convenient for the declaration or injunction to be granted on an application for judicial review."[57]

It is difficult in the absence of any relevant case law to interpret these provisions. However, it seems reasonably clear that the former state side orders still retain their pre-1986 premier position in that a declaration or injunction is only to be granted where there is some good reason under rule 18(2)(a), (b) or (c). (This, of course, stems from the fact that the state side orders were the specialist remedies, whereas declaration and injunction were merely pressed into service, where necessary, in order to make up for the technical limitations borne by these three remedies.) Paragraphs (a) and (b) seem to direct the court to take into account the limitations of the former state side orders so far as the nature of the "matters" (*i.e.* function and defect in its exercise) or bodies, respectively, are concerned. And the wording of paragraph (c) would certainly be wide enough to embrace the fact that it is often considered politic to grant a declaratory remedy against a public body.

Is a declaration (or injunction) an independent remedy?

The next question to be considered also arises from the traditional principle that the remedies of declaration and injunction are merely ancilliary to the specialist public law remedies of certiorari, prohibition and mandamus. The notion that the declaration and injunction are merely ancilliary has been thought to lead to the conclusion that they may be granted only in the situation where certiorari (or one of the other specialist remedies) would in principle have been available, yet, by reason of some special feature of the case and the deficiencies of certiorari, was not granted. This point might be of considerable practical significance in a situation in which a circular, stautory instrument or even an Act of the Oireachtas had been made which the applicant feared would damage his interests, but where no concrete decision against him had yet been taken. In this situation, it might well be argued by the defendant

---

57 *Pandion Haliaetus Ltd v. Revenue Commissioners* [1987] I.R. 309 provides a good example of the operation of Ord. 84, r. 18(2) in practice. Here the applicant company sought repayment of a substantial sum which had been withheld by the Revenue Commissioners on the ground that the company was involved in a "sham" tax avoidance scheme. Blayney J. rejected that contention and held that the company was entitled to a repayment of this sum. The Revenue Commissioners had taken the position that even if this were so, Pandion should appeal the Inspector of Taxes' determination. Pandion, in response, had contended on the basis of an earlier determination by an Inspector of Taxes that it was entitled to a repayment and that an appeal would, accordingly, be pointless. Blayney J. accepted this latter submission and observed that Pandion had "no method of enforcing repayment apart from claiming the declaration sought". Accordingly, Blayney J. held that it was "just and convenient" within the meaning of Ord. 84, r. 18(2) that a declaration in respect of the payments due should be granted by him to resolve the deadlock.

that even in principle, certiorari would not have been available because of the lack of a concrete decision. No doubt prudence suggests that belt and braces will be used and that in such circumstances the pleadings will seek to construct a "decision" upon which a certiorari could plausibly be granted but where declaratory relief is the real objective.[58] As such subterfuges may sometimes fail, the question may therefore directly arise: can a declaration be granted by way of judicial review in circumstances in which certiorari is in principle not available?

Whilst the point remains an open one[59] it is suggested that since 1986 there are two reasons why the answer should be in the affirmative. On an ordinary reading of Order 84, rule 18(2) there is nothing to suggest that any additional condition, which has not been expressly mentioned in the sub-rule itself, should be imposed upon the applicant. Secondly, as a matter of principle and policy, the thrust of the 1986 changes was to eliminate difficulties arising from the limitiations on the former state side orders. This was done by importing the possibility of granting a declaration to make good the deficiencies of the former state side orders. In the light of these circumstances, surely the declaration would not be straitened by such an additional condition. This may be buttressed by noting that if the contention that a declaration could only be granted if a certiorari were in principle also available were correct, then the litigant would be driven to seek a declaration by means of plenary proceedings – a form of *O'Reilly v. Mackman* in reverse. If this result were correct, then the effect would be to substantially reduce the scope of the 1986 reforms.

This interpretation of the corresponding provisions of Order 53 of the English Rules of the Supreme Court was accepted as correct by the House of Lords in the seminal decision of *Equal Opportunities Commission v. Secretary of State for Employment*.[60] In this case the EOC sought to quash by way of judicial review a 'decision' of the Employment Secretary in which in a letter addressed to the applicants he had "declined to accept" that the United Kingdom was in breach of its obligations under Community law by failing to provide part-time workers with the same benefits in relation to redundancy and unfair dismissal. The House of Lords first ruled that the Employment Secretary had made no "decision" that could be quashed,[61] but held that the applicants could nonetheless seek a declaration that the legislation did not comply with Community law by way of judicial review. Lord Browne-Wilkinson gave three reasons for this conclusion, two[62] of which are relevant in an Irish context:

---

58 *cf. McMenamin v. Ireland* [1994] 2 I.L.R.M. 368 where the "decision" in question was said to have been the refusal on the part of the Minister for Justice to sponsor new legislation which would have revised certain judicial pension entitlements. Geoghegan J. ultimately granted the applicant a declaration by way of judicial review. See also *Cox v. Ireland* [1992] 2 I.R. 503, below, n.64. In *B v. An Bord Úchtála* [1997] 1 I.L.R.M. 15 Murphy J. said that a mere statement of opinion on the part of an administrative body would not be amenable to certiorari.

59 In *Kenny v. Revenue Commissioners* [1996] 3 I.R. 315, Costello P. appeared to reserve the question of whether the High Court had jurisdiction "to make a declaratory order under Ord. 84, r. 18(2) even though an order of certiorari is not sought in the application and, if sought, would not be granted".

60 [1995] 1 A.C. 1.

61 *Ibid.* at 26, *per* Lord Keith:
      "[T]hat letter does not constitute a decision. It does no more than state the Secretary of State's view that the threshold provision [of the legislation] regarding redundancy pay and compensation for unfair dismissal are justifiable and in conformity with Community law."

62 The other reason was that, if it were otherwise, a person seeking a declaration as to public law rights would be left without a remedy. He could not, by reason of the *O'Reilly v. Mackman* rule, proceed by

> "Order 53, r.1(2) does not say that a declaration is only to be made in lieu of a prerogative order. All it requires is that the court should have regard to 'the nature of the matters in respect of which' prerogative orders can be made . . . Finally, the terms of Ord. 15, r.16 itself indicate the same result. Judicial review proceedings under Ord. 53 are 'proceedings'. Therefore the effect of Ord. 15, r.16 is that the court in judicial review proceedings for a declaration can make a declaratory order 'whether or not any consequential relief . . . *could* be claimed'."[63]

It would seem, therefore, that if the reasoning contained in the *Equal Opportunities Commission* decision were to be followed by the Irish courts (and there is nothing to suggest that it should not be) there is no longer any reason why a litigant whose principal aim is to challenge the validity of legislation should not directly do so by means of judicial review. In other words, it would no longer be necessary – as has happened on occasion heretofore – for an applicant to seek certiorari to quash a particular decision, while seeking a declaration of the invalidity of a statutory provision as ancilliary relief.[64]

A conceptually distinct problem – which might, however, arise in the same factual situation (such as where there was no concrete decision having been taken against the applicant) – is that the raising of the issue might be regarded as premature (or not 'ripe')[65] or that the applicant is lacking in standing.[66]

3. Judicial Review Procedure

Applications for judicial review: the grant of leave

The procedure in relation to applications for certiorari, prohibition and mandamus is governed by Order 84, rule 18(1) which provides that:

---

way of ordinary action and he could not proceed by way of judicial review in the absence of a "decision" which was capable of being quashed by certiorari. This reason does not apply in this jurisdiction: see *O'Donnell v. Dun Laoghaire Corporation (No. 2)* [1991] I.L.R.M. 301, see pp. 790–794.

[63] *Equal Opportunities Commission v. Secretary of State for Employment* [1995] 1 A.C. 1 at 36. Order 84, r. 18(2) is the Irish equivalent of Ord. 53, r. 1(2) of the English Rules. An analysis of the Irish Rules confirms the applicability in this jurisdiction of Lord Browne–Wilkinson's final point. Order 19, r. 29 provides that:

> "No action or pleading shall be open to objection on the ground that a merely declaratory judgment or order is sought thereby, and the Court may, if it thinks fit, make binding declarations of right whether any consequential relief is or could be claimed."

The word "action" clearly includes judicial review proceedings in that Ord. 125 defines "action" as meaning:

> ". . . a civil proceeding commenced by originating summons or in such other manner as may be prescribed by these Rules . . ."

[64] In *Cox v. Ireland* [1992] 2 I.R. 503 the plaintiff challenged the 'decision' of certain civil servants to apply the provision of s.34 of the Offences against the State Act 1939 to his circumstances, while also challenging the validity of the section. The Supreme Court ruled that the civil servants in question had not made a 'decision' in that (*per* Finlay C.J. at 521) the two defendants "had no alternative but to apply the provisions of s.34 to the case of the plaintiff" until the provisions in question were declared unconstitutional. The Court nonetheless granted a declaration by way of judicial review that the section in question was unconstitutional.

[65] See below pp. 756–758.

[66] See below pp. 739–755.

"An application for an order of certiorari, mandamus, prohibition or quo warranto shall be made by way of application for judicial review in accordance with the provisions of this Order."

Order 84, rule 20(1) requires that no application for judicial review shall be made unless the prior leave of the court has been obtained.[67] An application for leave must be made by motion *ex parte* by a notice containing, *inter alia*, details of the relief sought and the grounds on which it is sought, and an affidavit verifying the facts relied on.[68] Leave will not be granted unless the applicant has a "sufficient interest in the matter" to which the application relates.[69] If the court grants leave, it may impose such terms as to costs as it thinks fit, and may require an undertaking as to damages.[70]

Amending the grant of leave

The court may permit an application for leave to be amended on such terms (if any) as it think fit.[71] The principles on which the courts will grant such leave to amend have not yet been fully explored. However, in *McCormack v. Garda Síochána Complaints Board*[72] Costello P. observed that

". . . only in exceptional circumstances would liberty to amend a grounding statement to be made because the court's jurisdiction to entertain the application is based on and limited by the order granting leave. But when facts come to light which could not be known at the time when leave was obtained and when the amendment would not prejudice the respondents, then it seems a proper exercise of the court's power of amendment to permit the amendment rather than require that the new grounds be litigated in fresh proceedings."[73]

This test seems too strict. It is true that the court's jurisdiction is contingent on the order granting leave. But as the Rules of Court themselves expressly envisage that the grounding statement can be amended, perhaps the better way of approaching the matter would be to ask whether the court which granted leave would also have granted leave on the fresh grounds. If the answer to this question is in the affirmative, then the court of trial should also in principle (subject to questions of prejudice, delay etc.) grant leave to amend.

---

67 R.S.C. 1986, Ord. 84, r. 20(1). For an excellent account of practice and procedure in this area see Collins and O'Reilly, *op. cit.* above, n.17, pp. 82–93.
68 Ord. 84, r. 20(2). It is not always essential that the grounding affidavit be sworn by the applicant, but where the facts in issue are in controversy the applicant cannot seek to avoid cross-examination by arranging for an affidavit to be sworn by some other person (such as his solicitor): see *Probets v. Glackin* [1993] 3 I.R. 134. Moreover, the court is entitled to refuse relief on discretionary grounds if material facts are suppressed in the affidavit: *R. (Bryson) v. Lisnaskea Guardians* [1918] 2 I.R. 258; *The State (Nicolaou) v. An Bord Úchtála* [1966] I.R. 567; *Cork Corporation v. O'Connell* [1982] I.L.R.M. 505 and *G v. Director of Public Prosecutions* [1994] 1 I.R. 374 at 378, *per* Finlay C.J.
69 R.S.C. 1986, Ord. 84, r. 20(4). This matter is considered further at pp. 739–740.
70 R.S.C. 1986, Ord. 84, r. 20(6).
71 R.S.C. 1986, Ord. 84, r. 23(2). The grant of leave to amend can be done at the hearing of the action or at "the hearing of the motion or summons" or, at an earlier stage of the proceedings: see *Mulloy v. Governor of Limerick Prison*, unreported, Supreme Court, July 14, 1991, disapproving of earlier dicta of Blayney J. to the contrary in *Ahern v. Minister for Industry and Commerce (No.2)* [1990] 1 I.R. 55.
72 [1997] 2 I.L.R.M. 321.
73 *Ibid.* at 326.

It is important to note that special considerations apply in the case of judicial review applications governed by statutory time limits, such as section 82(3B) of the Local Government (Planning and Development) Act 1963 and section 85(8) of the Environmental Protection Agency Act 1992. For the object of such legislation is to ensure, *inter alia*, that the respondent is made "aware that the validity of [any] such decision is being questioned and aware of the basis for such questioning so that they may prepare their response to such proceedings expeditiously"[74] Accordingly, the courts will not permit an amendment, outside of the statutory limits, of the original grounds on which leave was granted, save, perhaps, where the amendment sought was *de minimis* in the context of the original grounds or (possibly) where no prejudice would be caused to the existing parties or to any potential parties who might have had an interest in the litigation[75] Thus, for example, as the application in *Ní Eilí v. Environmental Protection Agency*[76] was for an amendment which would have amounted to "an additional and entirely new case" after the two month period prescribed by the 1992 Act had expired, it is scarcely surprising that Kelly J. refused the applicant leave to amend. However, this does not mean that the applicant is precluded "from introducing evidence after expiration of the two-month limitation period in further support or amplification of the grounds of objection relied on, provided that such grounds are specified in the original documentation which has been served on all relevant parties within time".[77]

The requirement as to leave[78]

The requirement as to leave is a most important feature of the judicial review procedure. It serves as a "filtering device"[79] and guards against unmeritorious claims that a particular decision is invalid.[80] This two-stage procedure also means that the High Court no longer has power to grant an absolute order of certiorari, prohibition or mandamus following an *ex parte* application.[81] The requirement for leave was

---

[74] *Ní Eilí v. Environmental Protection Agency* [1997] 2 I.L.R.M. 458 at 464, *per* Kelly J.
[75] See *Keane v. An Bord Pleanála* unreported, High Court, June 20, 1995; *McNamara v. An Bord Pleanála* [1996] 2 I.L.R.M. 339 and *Ní Eilí v. Environmental Protection Agency* [1997] 2 I.L.R.M. 458.
[76] [1997] 2 I.L.R.M. 458.
[77] *McNamara v. An Bord Pleanála* [1996] 2 I.L.R.M. 339 at 352, *per* Barr J.
[78] See generally, Bradley, "Leave – A Necessary Protection for a Judicial Review Application" (1996) 14 I.L.T. 158; Le Suer and Sunkin, "Applications for Judicial Review; The Requirement of Leave" (1992) *Public Law* 102 and Hadfield, "Judicial Review in Northern Ireland: A Primer" (1991) 42 N.I.L.Q. 332.
[79] This was one of the principal reasons given by the House of Lords in *O'Reilly v. Mackman* [1983] 2 A.C. 237 as to why challenges to administrative action brought by plenary summons (as in the case of a declaration or injunction), and which thus circumvent the requirement for leave, should be struck out as an abuse of process.
[80] *G. v. Director Public Prosecutions* [1994] 1 I.R. 374; *O'Reilly v. Cassidy (No.1)* [1995] 1 I.L.R.M. 306. See also the comments of Lord Diplock in *R v. Inland Revenue Commissioners, ex p. National Federation of Self-Employed and Small Businesses Ltd* [1982] A.C. 617 at 643–4. In *Keane v. An Bord Pleanála*, unreported, High Court, June 20, 1995, Murphy J. described the burden which the applicant must discharge at this stage as "modest".
[81] See R.S.C. 1962, Ord. 84, rr. 9, 28 and 38. This power was exercised in unusual cases where no proper defence to the granting of an absolute order *ex parte* could be made out: see *The State (Attorney General) v. Coghlan*, unreported, High Court, May 10, 1974 and *Re Zwann's Application* [1981] I.R. 395.

comprehensively examined by the Supreme Court in *G. v. Director of Public Prosecutions*.[82] In this case the applicant sought an order of prohibition preventing his trial on a number of sex abuse charges on the ground of undue delay. Lavan J. had initially refused leave to apply for judicial review on the ground that indictable offences did not attract a specific time limit, but leave was granted on appeal by the Supreme Court. The following passage from the judgment of Finlay C.J. – wherein he set out the tests to be applied in considering whether leave should be granted – is of such importance that it deserves to be quoted in full:

> "An applicant must satisfy the court in a prima facie manner by the facts set out in the affidavit and submissions made in support of his application of the following matters:
>
> (a) That he has a sufficient interest in the matter to which the application relates to comply with rule 20(4).
>
> (b) That the facts averred in the affidavit would be sufficient, if proved, to support a statable ground for the form of relief sought by judicial review.
>
> (c) That on those facts an arguable case in law can be made that the applicant is entitled to the relief which he seeks.
>
> (d) That the application has been made promptly and in any event within the three months or six months time limits provided for in Order 84., r.21(1), or that the Court is satisfied that there is a good reason for extending this time limit . . .[83]
>
> (e) That the only effective remedy. on the facts established by the applicant, which the applicant would obtain would be an order by way of judicial review or, if there be an alternate remedy, that the application by way of judicial review is, on all the facts of the case, a more appropriate method of procedure."[84]

Finlay C.J. added that the above conditions were not "exhaustive" and he specifically drew attention to the discretionary character of the judicial review remedies. Applying those tests, he considered that leave should be granted, as the question of whether mere lapse of time created a presumption of prejudice was an "arguable" issue which could only be determined following a full hearing.[85]

---

82   [1994] 1 I.R. 374.

83   For the issue of delay, see pp. 725–729.

84   [1994] 1 I.R. 374 at 377–378. In *Kenny v. Revenue Commissioners*, [1996] 3 I.R. 315 Costello P. refused leave even where he assumed that the applicant had an arguable case, on the ground that it had not been shown that he had the requisite *locus standi* and that there was a more appropriate remedy available to him.

85   Similar principles were applied by the Supreme Court in *O'Reilly v. Cassidy (No. 1)* [1995] 1 I.L.R.M. 306. Here a Circuit Court judge had allowed an appeal against the renewal of a liquor licence, but controversy had arisen when comments were made about the fact that the judge's daughter had appeared for the objectors. Keane J. refused leave, but an appeal against this refusal was allowed by the Supreme Court, with both Finlay C.J. and O'Flaherty J. observing that the possible bias issue raised an arguable ground that deserved to proceed to full hearing. An interesting feature of both *G.* and *O'Reilly* is that the applicants in both cases, having been refused leave at first instance were granted leave on appeal and ultimately both succeeded at the full hearing of judicial review applications. For the sequel to *O'Reilly*, see *O'Reilly v. Cassidy (No. 2)* [1995] 1 I.L.R.M. 311.

Has a disappointed applicant the right to go from judge to judge?

The requirement for leave corresponds to the former practice on the state side whereby the applicant was required to seek a conditional order. If a conditional order were granted, an application was brought by motion to make the order absolute and the respondent was required to show cause why it should not be made absolute.[86] But if the applicant were refused a conditional order, he had the right to go around all the High Court judges in pursuit of his remedy.[87] It would seem that even under the 1986 Rules an applicant who is refused leave may still move from judge to judge to apply for judicial review, although the absence of clear contemporary authority makes it difficult to offer a firm view on this issue.

Appealing or setting aside the grant of leave

This might be argued on the ground that the grant of leave too, constitutes a decision of the High Court which may be appealed to the Supreme Court by virtue of Article 34.4.3°.[88] But is it also the case that a putative respondent could appeal the grant of leave? The existence of such a right of appeal is more doubtful and not supported by present practice. In this regard we may note the the the comments of McCarthy J. in *The State (Hughes) v. O'Hanrahan*[89] where he doubted though without giving any reason whether anyone (other than the applicants) can appeal against an order *ex parte*. The proper course of action for a respondent who objects to the grant of leave would seem to be to bring a motion seeking to have it set aside. The existence of such a jurisdiction was recognised by Carswell J. in *Re Savage's Application*.[90] While recognising that the burden on a respondent who moved the Court to have the grant of leave set aside was a "heavy one", nevertheless:

> "If on mature consideration of the facts, and with the benefit of the arguments presented to me by both sides, I now accept that there is not an arguable case on the facts, then I think that I should set aside the grant of leave."[91]

In effect, therefore, this jurisdiction to set aside is but an example in this particular context of a more general power to strike out on the ground that the proccedings are "clearly unsustainable".[92] If anything, however, this jurisdiction to set aside must be even more sparingly exercised, in that the granting of leave by the High Court

---

[86] R.S.C. 1962, Ord. 84, rr. 9, 25 and 37.

[87] This occurred in *The State (Richardson) v. Governor of Mountjoy Prison* [1980] I.L.R.M. 82, where Barrington J. granted the applicant leave following the initial refusal of leave by Keane J. In *The State (Dowling) v. Kingston* [1937] I.R. 699, dealing with the somewhat analagous case of habeas corpus applications, Murnaghan J. clearly contemplated that the disappointed applicant had the right to move from judge to judge to seek an *ex parte* order.

[88] The existence of such a right of appeal is also clearly envisaged by R.S.C. Order 58, r. 13 which provides that where an applicant has been refused leave by the High Court "an application for a similar purpose may be made to the Supreme Court *ex parte* within four days from the date of the refusal, or within such enlarged time as the Supreme Court may allow".

[89] [1986] I.L.R.M. 218 at 221.

[90] [1991] N.I. 103.

[91] *Ibid.* at 107.

[92] *O'Neill v. Ryan* [1993] I.L.R.M. 557 at 561, *per* Blayney J. See also *Sun Fat Chan v. Osseous Ltd* [1992] 1 I.R. 425 and *D.K. v. A.K.* [1993] I.L.R.M. 710.

presupposes – in a way that the mere issuing of a plenary summons does not – that the case is at least an arguable one.

Enlargement of procedural facilities

Before the 1986 reforms, it was said of certiorari, prohibition and mandamus that they afford a:

> "speedy and effective remedy to a person aggrieved by a clear excess of jurisdiction by an inferior tribunal. But they are not designed to raise issues of fact for the High Court to determine de novo."[93]

As a result, prior to 1986 applicants often encountered formidable procedural difficulties in cases turning on disputed facts. One way to surmount these difficulties was to apply to cross-examine deponents on their affidavits, and this practice received the approval of the Supreme Court.[94] However, while discovery was available,[95] there was no procedure for serving interrogatories, or for obtaining interlocutory relief pending the determination of the application. It was for these reasons that where issues of fact were raised in a challenge to the validity of administrative action, litigants tended to proceed by way of plenary hearing and seek an injunction or a declaration.[96] These procedural restrictions have now been removed. One may now apply for discovery or interrogatories,[97] and granting of leave to apply for judicial review will generally[98] operate as a stay of the proceedings to which the application relates. The court may also direct that the application for judicial review shall be made by plenary summons, instead of by originating notice of motion.[99] Any such notice of motion must be served on all persons directly affected within 14 days after the grant of leave, or within "such other period as the court may direct".[100] In default of service, the stay of proceedings shall lapse.[101]

---

93 *R. v. Fulham Rent Tribunal, ex p. Zerek* [1951] 2 K.B. 1 at 11, *per* Devlin J.
94 *The State (Furey) v. Minister for Defence* [1989] I.L.R.M. 89.
95 Ord. 31 R.S.C. 1962, gave the court power to order discovery "in any cause or matter" and there was no objection to the use of this power in state side applications: *The State (McGarrity) v. Deputy Garda Commissioner* (1978) 112 I.L.T.R. 25.
96 See the comments of Henchy J. in *M. v. An Bord Úchtála* [1977] I.R. 287 at 297. The use of the plenary procedure in the wake of the new Rules does not per se amount to an abuse of process: but the principles pertaining to delay, etc., as far as judicial review proceedings will apply, mutatis mutandis, to plenary actions: see *O'Donnell v. Dun Laoghaire Corporation* [1991] I.L.R.M. 301.
97 R.S.C. 1986, Ord. 84, r. 25
98 R.S.C. 1986, Ord. 84, r. 20(7)(a) provides that upon an application for judicial review by way of certiorari or prohibition, the grant of leave will, if the court so directs, operate as a stay of the proceedings until the determination of the application or until further order. If other relief is sought, Ord. 84, r. 20(7)(b) empowers the court to grant such interim relief "as could be granted in an action begun by plenary summons". On the Court's power to grant a stay, see *R. v. Inspectorate of Pollution, ex p. Greenpeace Ltd* [1994] 4 All E.R. 321 and below, pp. 710–712.
99 The court also has a power, upon an application for prohibition or quo warranto, to direct a plenary hearing with directions as to pleadings, discovery, etc.: see R.S.C. 1986, Ord. 84, r. 26(7) Where liberty is granted to proceed by way of plenary summons, then "the action should be presented by the plaintiff on oral evidence unless the court directs by order a hearing on affidavit or accepts from the parties an expressly agreed statement of the facts": *per* Finlay C.J. in *O'Keeffe v An Bord Pleanála* [1993] 1 I.R. 39 at 78–79.
100 R.S.C. 1986, Ord. 84, r. 22(1). The High Court had previously held that under the terms of the pre-1986 Rules it lacked such a jurisdiction to extend time in similar circumstances: see *The State (Fitzsimons) v. Kearney* [1981] I.R. 406.
101 R.S.C. 1986, Ord. 84, r. 22(3). In the case of a motion on notice, it shall be returnable for the first available motion day after the expiry of 10 days from the date of service, unless the court otherwise

Any respondent who intends to oppose the application for judicial review by way of notice of opposition[102] must file in the Central Office a statement setting out concisely the grounds for such opposition and, if any facts are relied on, an affidavit verifying such facts.[103] A copy of such statement or affidavit must be served on all parties[104] within seven days from the date of service of the notice of motion, or such other period as the court may direct.[105] In practice, this seven-day period has proved to be unrealistic and applications to extend time for the filing of a notice of opposition are very common. In *Butler v. Ruane*[106] McCarthy J. held that such an order could be made ex parte, although he thought that in some cases, the judge hearing the application for an extension:

> "[W]ould, if the circumstances so require, refuse to grant the order sought *ex parte* and direct that the motion be brought on notice."[107]

The power to stay

Order 84, rule 20(7) of the Rules of the Superior Courts 1986 provides that:

> "Where leave to apply for judicial review is granted then –
>
> (a) if the relief sought is an order of prohibition or certiorari and the Court so directs, the grant shall operate as a stay of the proceedings[108] to which the

---

directs. An affidavit of service must be filed prior to the hearing of the motion or summons: see Ord. 84, r. 22(5).

[102] If the court has directed that the application for judicial review be made by way of plenary summons under R.S.C. 1986, Ord. 84, r. 22(1), the respondent will presumably conduct his defence as if in a plenary action. There is, however, no specific provision for this in the Rules (save in the case of applications for prohibition or quo warranto, for which see Ord. 84, r. 26(7)).

[103] R.S.C. 1986, Ord. 84, r. 22(4). Where leave is granted on certain grounds only, then the appropriate practice for the respondent is to file a statement of opposition directed solely to those grounds, while "ignoring those grounds upon which leave had not been granted": *H. v. Director of Public Prosecutions* [1994] 2 I.R. 589 at 607, *per* Denham J.

[104] This includes notice parties, *i.e.* persons likely to be affected adversely by the granting of the relief sought. In very exceptional cases a notice party may apply to the Court to be joined as a notice party simply for the purpose of clearing his good name: see *Fitzpatrick v. Garda Commissioner, Irish Times*, July 2, 1996. It appears that the court has no jurisdiction to grant declaratory orders (or, it would seem, any other relief under Ord. 84) *as against notice parties* who are not joined as respondents: see the dicta of Costello P. in *Kenny v. Revenue Commissioners* [1996] 3 I.R. 315. See also *R. v. Rent Officer, ex p. Muldoon* [1996] 3 All E.R. 498.

[105] The latest judicial review Practice Direction (which appeared in the *Legal Diary*, February 26, 1993) provides that:
> "Practitioners are requested to lodge with the Registrar seven days in advance of the hearing of the notice of motion for judicial review a bound book containing the following documents: (i) copy notice of motion; (ii) copy order granting leave to make application for judicial review; (iii) copy grounding statement (notice of application); (iv) copy verifying affidavit; (v) copy exhibits; (vi) copy exhibits; (vii) copy affidavits verifying statement of opposition (if any); (viii) affidavit of personal service of motion, statement, affidavit and order giving leave on all parties to be served (O. 84, r. 22(5)); and (ix) in applications for order of certiorari copy of order/decision subject of appliation verified by affidavit (if not already exhibited above)(see O. 84, r. 26(2))."

[106] [1989] I.L.R.M. 159.

[107] *Ibid.* at 161.

[108] The corresponding phrase in the English Rules has been described as meaning "a stay of the process by which the decision challenged has been reached, including the decision itself": *R v. Secretary of State for Education, ex p. Avon C.C.* [1991] 1 Q.B. 558 at 560, *per* Glidewell L.J.

application relates until the determination of the application or until the Court otherwise orders;

(b) if any other relief is sought, the Court may at any time grant in the proceedings such interim relief as could be granted in an action begun by plenary summons."

The effect of Order 84, rule 20(7)(a) would seem to be that the High Court is empowered to grant the equivalent of an interlocutory injunction after a purely *ex parte* hearing. This would appear to be the natural construction of the sub-rule and it has been so interpreted in practice.[109] Is it accurate, however, to equate the granting of a stay with an interlocutory injunction? In *R. v. Secretary of State for Education, ex p. Avon CC*[110] Glidewell L.J. thought the two could not be so equated:

"[A stay] is not properly described as an injunction, which is an order directed at a party to litigation, not to the court or to a decision-making body. Of course, in some respects an application for judicial review appears to have similarities to civil proceedings between two opposing parties, in which an injunction may be ordered by the court at the suit of one party directed to the other. When correctly analysed, however, the apparent similarity disappears . . . [The decision-maker] is not in any true sense an opposing party, any more than an inferior court whose decision is challenged is an opposing party. Thus the distinction between an injunction and a stay arises out of the difference between the positions of the persons or bodies concerned."[111]

Yet it may be doubted whether this theoretical distinction between a stay and injunction can be consistently maintained, a point illustrated by *R. v. Pollution Inspectorate, ex p. Greenpeace Ltd.*[112] Here the applicant sought a stay on the respondent's decision to grant an authorisation permitting British Nuclear Fuels plc to complete a certain testing system. Scott L.J. observed that:

"[I]f the real purpose of interlocutory relief in a judicial review case is to prevent executive action by a third party being carried out pursuant to the decision under attack, the more suitable procedure would be to have the third

---

[109] As pointed out by Collins and O'Reilly, *op. cit.* above, n. 17, p. 92, practice varies in this regard, but the granting of a stay under Ord. 84, r. 20(7)(a) at leave stage pending the hearing of the application is quite common. In *Murphy v. Turf Club* [1989] I.R. 171 at 173 Barr J. refers to the fact that he stayed the suspension of the applicant's training licence for a nine-day period following the granting of leave to apply for certiorari. This would seem to suggest an attempt to assimilate the practice regarding the granting of stays to that of the normal practice with injunctions. Note also that in *Garda Representative Association v. Ireland*, unreported, Supreme Court, December 18, 1987, Finlay C.J. said in an *ex tempore* judgment that the ordinary principles governing interlocutory injunction applied to the granting of interlocutory relief under Ord. 84, r. 20(7)(b). In *Fitzpatrick v. Garda Commissioner (No. 2)* [1996] E.L.R. 244 Kelly J. noted that all counsel in the case had accepted that the *Garda Representative Association* case was authority for the proposition that "an application for judicial review is identical to those which apply in ordinary civil litigation." However, it may be that these words apply only to Ord. 84, r. 20(7)(b) and that the different wording of Ord. 84, r. 20(7)(a) will compel the courts to arrive at a different result.

[110] [1991] 1 Q.B. 558.

[111] *Ibid. cf.* the views of Sir John Donaldson M.R. in *R. v. Lancashire CC, ex p. Huddelston* [1986] 2 All E.R. 941 at 945.

[112] [1994] 4 All E.R. 321.

party in question joined and then to seek an interlocutory injunction against that party, rather than to seek a stay of the decision. If, however, the purpose is pursued, as it has been in the present case, by an application for a stay of the decision rather than by an interlocutory injunction against the third party, the courts should . . . look to the substance rather than the form, and apply the same principles to the application as would have been applicable had the application been for an interlocutory injunction."[113]

If, therefore, one may treat in most instances the grant of a stay as the practical equivalent of an injunction and if Order 84, rule 20 (7) on its true construction authorises what amounts to the grant of an interlocutory injunction on an *ex parte* basis, then doubts must arise as to whether this sub-rule is *intra vires*, since such a change would significantly alter the substantive law pertaining to interlocutory relief. The normal practice with regard to interlocutory injunctions is, of course, that interim relief (which generally lasts for a matter of days at most) may be granted on an *ex parte* basis, but thereafter the plaintiff must apply on notice for an interlocutory injunction[114] and, indeed, this practice is expressly preserved as far as relief under Order 84, rule 20(7)(b) is concerned.[115] However, under Order 84, rule 20(7)(a), the applicant who seeks certiorari or prohibition is entitled to a stay (where the High Court so directs) until the hearing of the application or until the court otherwise orders. As already noted, such a stay is in practice equivalent to an interlocutory injunction and the onus would thus be on the respondents to bring a motion to have such an order discharged. This, of course, reverses the burden of proof by placing the onus on the respondents. It also means that applicants seeking certiorari or prohibition have a distinct procedural advantage in contrast to cases where only an injunction is sought. This again is an undesirable departure, inasmuch as one of the intentions behind the Order 84 procedure was to equalise the status of each individual remedy.

Remittal

One innovatory feature of the 1986 Rules is Order 84, rule 26(4) which provides:

"Where the relief sought is an order of certiorari and the Court is satisfied that there are grounds for quashing the decision to which the application

---

113   *Ibid.* at 327.

114   See Keane, *Equity and the Law of Trusts and the Republic of Ireland* (1988), para. 15.27.

115   It is not, of course, possible to obtain an interlocutory order of mandamus or a declaration, but the court has power to grant interim relief by way of injunction where mandamus or a declaration is the substantive relief sought. For a case (with unusual facts) where an interim Mareva injunction was granted on an application for mandamus, see *Elwyn (Cottons) Ltd v. Pearle Designs Ltd* [1989] I.R. 9 at 13, *per* Carroll J. and *Elwyn (Cottons) Ltd v. Master of the High Court* [1989] I.R. 14 at 15. In certain very unusual cases a declaration may be granted in interlocutory proceedings: *International General Electric Co. of New York Ltd v. Commissioners of Customs and Excise* [1962] Ch. 784; *Clarke v. Chadburn* [1985] 1 All E.R. 211. But, as Upjohn L.J. observed (at 789) in the *General Electric* case, this jurisdiction (which amounts to a form of summary judgment) is to be "sparingly exercised" and, moreover, if such relief is granted in interlocutory proceedings "it finally determines and declares the rights of the parties and it is not open to further review save on appeal". Upjohn L.J. added (at 790) that he could not see "how there could be such an animal" as an interim declaratory order "which does not finally determine the rights of the parties".

relates, the Court may, in addition to quashing it, remit the matter to the Court, tribunal or authority concerned with a direction to reconsider it and reach a decision in accordance with the findings of the Court."

This is clearly a provision of utility which can obviate the need for an order of mandamus or, indeed, spare the parties the cost of instituting fresh proceedings. An example of this last type of advantage category may be demonstrated, by way of contrast, with the facts of the 1984 case of *Bord na Móna v. Galway County Council*.[116] Keane J. quashed a planning permission granted by An Bord Pleanála on appeal because of the existence of an invalid condition. Keane J. held that he had no jurisdiction to remit the matter to An Bord Pleanála and so the applicant for planning permission (who, after all, had won the action) was obliged to apply afresh to the local planning authority. Under the 1986 Rules, the matter could simply have been remitted to An Bord Pleanála without further ado. However, there is no statutory grounding for this power and, again, it may be questioned as to whether this new rule is *intra vires* the powers of the Superior Court Rules Committee.[117]

The first reported case in which this power appears to have been exercised is *Comerford v. O'Malley*.[118] Under the Casual Trading Act 1980 an appeal may be taken to the Circuit Court against the making of bye-laws by a local authority under that Act. The respondent Circuit judge did approve the order and bye-laws in question, but Egan J. found that some of the bye-laws were *ultra vires* the Act. Egan J. found that he had no power to vary the Circuit judge's decision by excluding the *ultra vires* bye-laws because to do so would be to assume functions reserved to the Circuit Court. However, apparently acting under Order 84, rule 26(4), he felt able to remit the matter directly to the Circuit Court instead of leaving it to be commenced again at the local authority level. This power was also exercised by Blayney J. adopted in *Ahern v. Kerry County Council*[119] where having quashed a resolution to adopt certain expenditure on the ground that the estimates were not properly considered by the local authority in accordance with section 10 of the City and

---

[116] [1985] I.R. 205.
[117] See above, pp.694–695. *Cf.* the comments of Finlay C.J. in *Sheehan v. Reilly* [1993] 2 I.R. 81 at 92–3:
> "Neither [Ord. 84, r. 26(4)] nor any rule similar to it was contained in the Rules of the Superior Courts, 1962. It must first clearly be stated that this rule which, on the face of it, gives to the court a discretion as to whether or not to remit a matter in which an order has been quashed for further consideration cannot, having regard to the limitations of the powers vested in the rule-making authority pursuant to the Courts of Justice Acts be the grant of any new or different power that is not already vested in the court by statute or by virtue of inherent jurisdiction."

In his insightful article on this topic, "Certiorari Followed by Remittal" (1993) 2 *Irish Criminal Law Journal* 145 Costello has argued powerfully that the rule is not *ultra vires* in that a form of remittal has always existed as part of the High Court's inherent jurisdiction. But if the historical practice suggests that a rudimentary form of remittal existed in the early part of the last century, it took the form of certiorari to quash and mandamus to re-hear the matter, a practice which, as Costello himself notes, continued spasmodically into this century. At all events, the historical evidence does not unequivocally support the proposition that the present form of remittal always existed as part of the court's inherent jurisdiction. Moreover, the power to re-prosecute (which is what the power to remit in criminal cases effectively is) has been held not to be a matter of mere procedure and beyond the capacity of the Rules Committee to regulate by mere rule of court: see the comments of Henchy J. in *People (D.P.P.) v. Qulligan* (No. 2) [1989] I.R. 46 at 54–55.
[118] [1987] I.L.R.M. 595.
[119] [1988] I.L.R.M. 392.

County Management (Amendment) Act 1955, he remitted the matter to the County Council in accordance with Order 84, rule 26(4). This approach is also evident in the judgment of Carroll J. in *Hurley v. Motor Insurer's Bureau of Ireland*,[120] a case where the respondent had rejected the applicant's claim for reasons which were imprecise and unclear. Its decision was quashed and the matter was remitted to it for reconsideration in the light of her judgment. On the other hand, there must be findings of the court which make it meaningful for the power to remit to be exercised. Thus, in *Murphy v. Wallace*,[121] once Barron J. found that the statutory powers relating to penal warrants which had been granted to Revenue Commissioners were unconstitutional, he considered it pointless to attempt to exercise his power to remit.[122]

Criminal cases   There are now four leading decisions governing remittal in criminal matters. In the first of these, *Sheehan v. Reilly*,[123] the applicant had, due to an apparent oversight, already completed his sentence some time before the High Court finally ordered his release. The application for release under Article 40.4 of the Constitution had been, for some reason, adjourned for a six-week period before the final order for release was made, even though – according to the Supreme Court – the illegal character of the detention ought to have been apparent at the date of the first application, thus compounding the prisoner's ordeal. The Supreme Court in those circumstances declined to exercise its discretion in favour of a re-trial, since, in the words of Finlay C.J.:

> ". . . having regard to the fact that he was detained for a substantial period thereafter, and that instead of securing the rights to which he was entitled under Article 40 he instead, at a delayed time, succeeded in quashing the order which, on its face, appears to be invalid, that it would not be just or fair that he should be again charged with [and] possibly convicted of and punished for this offence."[124]

In effect *Sheehan's* case decided that an applicant should not suffer by reason of prosecution or judicial errors, a point confirmed by another Supreme Court judgment

---

[120]   [1993] I.L.R.M. 886. See also *Matthews v. Irish Coursing Club Ltd* [1993] 1 I.R. 346 (where O'Hanlon J. remitted the issue of penalty to the respondents who, he held, had imposed an unreasonably light penalty on the owner of a winning greyhound who was found to have consumed illegal substances) and *Hoburn Homes Ltd v. An Bord Pleanála* [1993] I.L.R.M. 368 (where Denham J. held that as one of the three conditions advanced by An Bord Pleanála for refusing permission was *ultra vires*, the decision should be remitted to that extent only for reconsideration by An Bord Pleanála. Normally, there would be no need for such an order where (as here) the other two reasons could independently justify the refusal. However, the significant point is that the *ultra vires* condition bore heavily on the applicant's potential right to compensation under the Local Government (Planning and Development) Acts 1963–1990). See also *Devrajan v. Ballagh* [1993] 3 I.R. 377 and *O'Shea v. Garda Commissioner* [1994] 2 I.R. 408 (dismissal of Garda adjudged to have been in breach of rules of natural justice; issue remitted to respondent for fresh decision "having heard submissions from the applicant".)

[121]   [1993] 3 I.R. 138.

[122]   *Ibid.* at 146, *per* Barron J.: "There are no findings of the court which would enable the District [Judge] to reconsider the matter of the issue of the penal warrants."

[123]   [1993] 2 I.R. 81. See also *Singh v. Ruane* [1990] I.L.R.M. 62; *Director of Public Prosecutions v. Johnston* [1988] I.L.R.M. 747; and *Dawson v. Hamill (No. 2)* [1991] 1 I.R. 213.

[124]   [1993] 2 I.R. 81 at 93. See also *Director of Public Prosecutions v. Judge Kelly* [1997] 1 I.R. 405 (order of remittal should not be made where the fairness of a fresh trial might be imperilled by the absence of a key witness).

delivered on the same day: *Sweeney v. Brophy*.[125] Here the applicant had been convicted of common assault following what Hederman J. described as "a totally unsatisfactory trial". The Supreme Court found that in the circumstances the applicant was entitled to plead *autrefois acquit* so that no question of a re-trial would arise. Hederman J. added that even if there had been power to order a re-trial, it would have been inappropriate to exercise this power in the present case, given that the applicant had "endured enough" and the prosecution was partially responsible for what had occured in the course of the original re-trial. On the other hand, it seems that the courts will exercise their powers of remittal where it appears that the applicant would not be seriously prejudiced by a re-trial. Thus, in *Grennan v. Kirby*[126] Murphy J. remitted the case to the District Court having quashed a conviction in circumstances where the judge had wrongly refused to grant the applicant an adjournment, saying that the conviction was a nullity and "presented no barrier to the prosecution now proceeding in the District Court".[127] Finally, in *Bowes v. Devally*[128] Geoghegan J. ruled that a forfeiture order which had been imposed consequent upon a conviction for possession of drugs was invalid. Given that the Supreme Court had previously ruled that a sentence was not severable,[129] Geoghegan J. felt that he had no alternative but to quash the sentence in its entirety. However, the judge held that it was "manifestly" a case where the power of remittal should be exercised.[130]

Costs

While the costs of proceedings lie in the discretion of the court, these will usually follow the event.[131] There is, however, also a general judicial reluctance to award costs against an impecunious applicant in judicial review proceedings, even where no important point of principle is at issue. In some cases raising general points of importance, the courts have even been prepared to award costs to the losing applicant.[132]

---

[125]   [1993] 2 I.R. 202. See also *Dawson v. Hamill (No. 2)* [1991] 1 I.R. 213 and *Dineen v. Delap* [1994] 2 I.R. 228.

[126]   [1994] 2 I.L.R.M. 199.

[127]   *Ibid.* at 203. This question is further considered in the context of which errors affect jursidiction: see above pp. 417–430.

[128]   [1995] 1 I.R. 315.

[129]   *The State (Kiernan) v. deBúrca* [1963] I.R. 348.

[130]   *Ibid.* at 319, where Geoghegan J. added:
   "This does not mean that the Circuit Court should re-hear the matter. The Circuit Court has already done so and [the judge] has made a perfectly valid decision in relation to both conviction and sentence apart from forfeiture. All that is required now is for the [Circuit judge] to make a new order varying the order of the District Court by removing the order for forfeiture but otherwise affirming the District Court order."

[131]   R.S.C. 1986, Ord. 99, r. 1(1). No court fees are payable in judicial review proceedings involving certiorari and mandamus: see Supreme Court and High Court (Fees) Order 1982 (S.I. No. 43 of 1982) para. 8. The provisions of the Attorney General's scheme involving legal aid, in certain types of judicial review proceedings, may also apply: see Collins and O'Reilly, *op. cit.* above, n.17, p. 53.

[132]   *T.F. v. Ireland* [1995] 1 I.R. 321. In *McKenna v. An Taoiseach (No. 2)* [1995] 2 I.R. 10 the plaintiff sought to restrain the Government from spending IR£0.5m. on promotional literature advocating a "Yes" vote in the referendum on divorce. In the High Court Keane J. refused to award costs against her (although he was not persuaded by her constitutional argument) saying that "the point raised was undoubtedly one of exceptional public importance" and that "constitutional challenges of that nature brought by private citizens in a responsible manner clearly should not be discouraged". Of course, as is well known, the plaintiff was ultimately to appeal with success to the Supreme Court against this judgment.

And this attitude usually pulls in the same direction as a preference to award costs against, rather than in favour of, a public body.

The applicant will also generally be entitled to the costs of the initial *ex parte* application for judicial review, even where the respondent does not contest the actual making of the order. This emerges from *Ó' Murchú v. Cláraitheoir na gCuideachtaí*,[133] where the applicant had obtained leave to apply for an order of mandamus against the Registrar of Companies and the Minister for Industry and Commerce. The Minister had promulgated a statutory instrument under the Companies Acts 1963 to 1983, but, at the date of the application, an Irish language copy of that instrument was not available. Although the applicant had demanded a copy it only became available shortly after the order granting leave had been made and the question then arose as to whether the applicant was entitled to the initial costs of her application. O'Hanlon J. held that as she had a constitutional right to conduct her affairs in Irish if she wished, it was "reasonable for her to commence these proceedings in order to obtain the relief she sought from the High Court"[134] and, accordingly, he granted her the costs of the original *ex parte* application.

To the rule that costs will generally follow the event, there is, however, a most important exception. No order for costs may be made against a respondent who is a member of the judiciary in judicial review proceedings where the error was made bona fide and the application was unopposed. This long-standing rule was reaffirmed by the Supreme Court in *McIlwraith v. Fawsitt*.[135] The respondent Circuit Court judge had extended time for the hearing of an appeal by the applicant's employers from the Employment Appeals Tribunal and in doing so, he exceeded his jurisdiction. The applicant obtained leave to seek certiorari to quash the order. However, matters did not proceed any further since the main dispute, as between the applicant and his employers, was settled before the judicial review proceedings came on. The Supreme Court held that the applicant was not entitled to the costs of the initial *ex parte* application, with Finlay C.J. saying that:

> "[U]nder no circumstances should the High Court upon application to it for judicial review with regard to either a decision of a District Justice or of a Circuit Court judge award costs to a successful applicant in a case where there is no question of impropriety or *mala fide* on the part of the judge concerned and where he has not sought to defend an order which apparently is invalid. For that reason, I am satisfied that the practice which I understood to have been usual in the High Court of adding as a further respondent in judicial review proceedings the other contesting party so as to create *a legitimus contradictor* for any issue that may arise in the event that the Circuit Court judge or District Justice concerned does not seek to defend the order should be universally followed."[136]

---

133 Unreported, High Court, O'Hanlon J., June 20, 1988.
134 *Ibid*. This part of the judgment reads in the original (at p. 4):
   "agus go raibh sé reasúnta na himeachta seo do chur ar bun d'fhonn faoiseamh do lorg ón Ard-Chúirt."
135 [1990] I.L.R.M. 1. Finlay C.J. expressly followed the decision of the former Supreme Court in *The State (Prendergast) v. Rochford*, unreported, Supreme Court, July 1, 1952. In that case, Maguire C.J. in turn had followed the decision of Palles C.B. in *R. (King) v. Londonderry JJ*. (1912) 46 I.L.T.R. 105. For other pre-1922 examples of this practice, see *Hynes v. Clare JJ*. (1911) 45 I.L.T.R. 76 (costs awarded where contumacy on part of justices) and *R. (Roche) v. Clare JJ*. (1912) 46 I.L.T.R. 80.
136 [1990] I.L.R.M. 1 at 4.

It is hard to see why members of the judiciary should stand in this privileged position as regards costs and the older authorities supporting this proposition echo an era when Crown (and later State) immunity reigned supreme. Nevertheless, it should be possible for an applicant to circumvent the restrictive nature of this rule by adding a further respondent, such as (where appropriate) Ireland, the Attorney General or the Director of Public Prosecutions, as was suggested by Finlay C.J.

4. The Discretionary Nature of the Remedies

General attitudes to the exercise of discretion

This is an area which, unfortunately, has become clouded in confusion. The public law remedies, including the declaration and injunction are all – and equally – discretionary remedies. However, it is clear that this discretion is to be exercised on settled principles, regardless of the form of proceedings.[137] In general, the court will grant relief in respect of *ultra vires* administrative action in the absence of good reason to the contrary. In the past, relief was said to issue *ex debito justitiae* (*i.e.* almost as a matter of right) in such circumstances.[138] It was true that the applicant's right to relief might be lost on account of his delay, bad conduct, etc., but, generally speaking, this would only happen where to grant relief would prejudice the rights or interests of the administrative body concerned or third parties.[139] This rule is, however, now generally regarded as too inflexible and restrictive of the extent of the courts' discretion in relation to the granting of relief and it has been said that the court must be satisfied "not only as to matters such as default in the performance of a public duty and jurisdictional error, but also that it would be just and proper in all the circumstances to grant [relief]."[140]

A good example of the modern move away from the traditional rules regarding the exercise of discretion is provided by the Supreme Court's decision in *The State (Abenglen Properties Ltd) v. Dublin Corporation,*[141] a case which, admittedly, pre-

---

137 See the comments of Henchy J. in *The State (Nicoloau) v. An Bord Úchtála* [1966] I.R. 567 at 618 and in *M. v. An Bord Úchtála* [1977] I.R. 287 at 297.

138 *R. (Bridgeman) v. Drury* [1894] 2 I.R. 489; *R. (Kildare C.C.) v. Commissioner for Valuation* [1901] 2 I.R. 215; *The State (Kerry C.C.) v. Minister for Local Government* [1933] I.R. 517; *The State (Doyle) v. Carr* [1970] I.R. 87; and *M. v. An Bord Úchtála* [1977] I.R. 287 (judgment of Henchy J.) A "person aggrieved" (on which see below, pp. 740–741) was defined as someone whose legal rights or interests were affected by the impugned order: *R. v. Thames Magistrates' Court, ex p. Greenbaum* (1957) 55 L.G.R. 129; *The State (Toft) v. Galway Corporation* [1981] I.L.R.M. 439.

139 As happened in cases such as *The State (Cussen) v. Brennan* [1981] I.R. 181 (applicant's delay caused third parties to change position in the belief that he would not challenge *ultra vires* appointment; held, it would now be unfair to third parties to grant applicant the relief sought) and *Minister for Education v. Letterkenny Regional Technical College* [1995] 1 I.L.R.M. 438. See also *R. v. Monopolies Commission, ex p. Argyll plc* [1986] 1 W.L.R. 793.

140 *The State (Cussen) v. Brennan* [1981] I.R. 181, *per* Henchy J. See also *Minister for Education v. Letterkenny RTC* [1995] 1 I.L.R.M. 438 may now be considered. In *G. v. Director of Public Prosecutions* [1994] 1 I.R. 374 at 378 Finlay C.J. commented that "judicial review in many instances is an entirely discretionary remedy which may well include, amongst other things, consideration of whether the matter concerned is one of importance or triviality and also as to whether the applicant has shown good faith in the making of an *ex parte* application".

141 [1984] I.R. 384. See Hogan, "Remoulding Certiorari: A Critique of *The State (Abenglen Properties Ltd) v. Dublin Corporation"* (1982) 17 Ir. Jur. 32 (N.S.); Jackson, "Certiorari, Alternative Remedies

sented exceptional facts. This case presented a challenge to the validity of certain conditions attached to the grant of planning permission. Relief was refused on the grounds that the applicants had failed to exhaust alternative remedies and that an order of certiorari would serve no useful purpose in the circumstances of the case. But Henchy J. for the majority appeared to go further when he stated that the grant of certiorari in civil cases was purely discretionary. However, in *The State (Furey) v. Minister for Defence*,[142] a majority of the Supreme Court reverted to the more orthodox position by stating that a person aggrieved by *ultra vires* administrative action was entitled to relief *ex debito justitiae*. It was not enough to show, for example, that there had been undue delay on the part of the applicant. McCarthy J.'s judgment implies that the respondents would have to establish that it would now be unfair to them or third parties or that there were other exceptional circumstances present in the case before the court would be justified in refusing relief. Although the difference between *Abenglen* and *Furey* is largely one of emphasis, the *Furey* decision did appear to indicate a return to traditional principles on the part of the Supreme Court.

Subsequently, however, there have been a number of Supreme Court dicta and High Court decisions which suggest that the grant of relief should be purely discretionary.[143] However, it may be significant that in each of the High Court cases the applicant sought to raise unmeritorious technical points. In *Connors v. Delap*,[144] for example the applicant sought to challenge a conviction for driving a motor vehicle without insurance on the ground that the summons issued by the District Court clerk was defective.[145] Lynch J. pointed out that the reason why the applicant had failed to answer the summons and appear before the District Court was because

---

and Judicial Discretion" (1983) 5 D.U.L.J. 100 (N.S) and Collins, "Ex Debito Justitiae" (1988) 10 D.U.L.J. 130 (N.S.). For a very thoughtful analysis of the issue of discretion, see Bingham, "Should Public Law Remedies be Discretionary?" (1991) *Public Law* 64.

[142] [1988] I.L.R.M. 87. Note that in *The State (R. F. Gallagher, Shatter & Co.) v. de Valera*, unreported, High Court, December 9, 1983, Costello J. stated that the test laid down by Henchy J. in *Abenglen Properties* was that while "aggrieved persons are entitled to certiorari only on a discretionary basis, if the requirements of justice and fairness justified the making of the order, then it should be made".

[143] *Duff v. Mangan* [1994] 1 I.L.R.M. 91 at 101 *per* Denham J. and *G. v. Director of of Public Prosecutions* [1994] 1 I.R. 374 at 378 (where Finlay C.J. noted that judicial review "in many instances is an entirely discretionary remedy"(emphasis added)). Note also the interesting manner in which Keane J. attempted to sum up the present state of the law (with apparent approval from the Supreme Court) in *Barry v. Fitzpatrick* [1996] 1 I.L.R.M. 512 at 516:

> ". . . the relief for judicial review is a discretionary remedy and where the application is without merit the court may refuse to grant the reliefs sought, unless, as in the extreme circumstances of the *The State (Vozza) v. O'Floinn* [1957] I.R. 227 where, despite the lack of merit or conduct which might otherwise disentitle the applicant to the reliefs sought, there is a clear violation of his constitutional rights in respect of a conviction or (in the confined circumstances defined by Henchy J. in *The State (Abenglen Properties Ltd) v. Dublin Corporation* [1984] I.R. 381) the cases in which certiorari is said to issue *ex debito justitiae* and the matter ceases to be a matter of discretion."

[144] [1988] I.L.R.M. 93.

[145] This argument was based on the decision of the Supreme Court in *The State (Clarke) v. Roche* [1986] I.R. 619. In this case the Supreme Court held, *inter alia*, that s.10 of the Petty Sessions (Ireland) Act 1851 required that a District Court clerk or Peace Commissioner should personally consider and adjudicate upon an application for a summons under that Act. This in practice meant that all computer summonses were invalid, since there had not been an individual adjudication prior to the issue of the summonses. This decision gave rise to a veritable flood of applications for judicial review and necessitated the immediate passage of the Courts (No. 3) Act 1986 (for commentary, see Hogan [1986] I.C.L.S.A. 33/01 – 33/09).

"he did not wish to face up to charges to which he knew he had no defence". Accordingly, he did not think that certiorari should issue to quash a conviction based on a technically defective summons:

> "If I were to make an order of certiorari in favour of the applicant based on the technical points on which he relies, it would clearly deprive the people of Ireland of the just retribution to which they are entitled in respect of the crime committed by the applicant.Certiorari is a discretionary remedy. In the present case the applicant has no merits on the substance of the case and is also late in bringing his application."[146]

These views would appear clearly to be incompatible with *Furey*. It would seem that yet another pronouncement by the Supreme Court on this question will be necessary before the matter can be regarded as having been authoritatively decided one way or the other.

Although the grounds on which relief may be denied are not closed, we may now separately examine[147] the discretionary bars[148] to relief which are most frequently encountered.

(i) Lack of good faith and general conduct of the applicant

All applications for judicial review require the utmost good faith and full disclosure of all material facts on the part of the applicant.[149] This is because the initial application is *ex parte*,[150] because there is usually no oral evidence and because of the generally weighty issues raised by the application. Accordingly, relief may be withheld where the applicant has been guilty of gross exaggeration in his affidavits or where relevant evidence has been suppressed.[151] For example, in *The State (Vozza) v. O'Floinn*,[152] the applicant (who was of Italian origin) sought to quash his conviction for larceny on the grounds that he had not been informed of his right to jury trial and, secondly, that he did not understand the court procedure. A Divisional

---

[146] *Ibid.* at 97–98. See also *White v. Hussey* [1989] I.L.R.M. 109.

[147] See the comments of Byrne and Binchy, *Annual Review of Irish Law 1988* (1989), pp. 32–33 that "in recent years discretionary grounds for refusing relief have become more widespread in Irish law".

[148] At common law it was clear that the Attorney-General could not be refused relief on discretionary grounds (such as delay): see, *e.g. Re an Application for Certiorari* [1965] N.I. 67. Murnaghan J. made a similar observation in *The State (Kerry County Council) v. Minister for Local Government* [1933] I.R. 517 at 546. But, as Lord McDermott L.C.J. explained (at 70–71) in *Re an Application for Certiorari* [1965] N.I. 67, this rule was derived from the fact that the Attorney General had a privileged position as representing the Crown. In view of this rationale and the general reasoning in *Howard v. Commissioners for Public Works* [1994] 1 I.R. 101 (see below pp. 933–935), not to speak of the injustice which might be caused to an individual litigant if discretionary bars such as delay could not be pleaded against the Attorney General, it must be doubtful whether such a rule has survived the enactment of the Constitution. Note that in *Director of Public Prosecutions v. Macklin* [1989] I.L.R.M. 113 the Director of Public Prosecutions was denied certiorari on discretionary grounds, but the point was not canvassed before Lardner J.

[149] *Cork Corporation v. O'Connell* [1982] I.L.R.M. 505.

[150] Save now in the case of applications to quash decisions of planning authorities and An Bord Pleanála.

[151] *R. v. Kensington I.T.C.* [1917] 1 K.B. 486; *R. (Bryson) v. Lisnaskea Guardians* [1918] 2 I.R. 258; *The State (Vozza) v. O'Floinn* [1957] I.R. 227; *The State (Nicolaou) v. An Bord Úchtála* [1966] I.R. 567 at 610 (Henchy J.); *Cork Corporation v. O'Connell* [1982] I.L.R.M. 505 at 508, *per* Griffin J.; and *G. v. Director of Public Prosecutions* [1994] 1 I.R. 374 at 378, *per* Finlay C.J.

[152] [1957] I.R. 227.

High Court refused to quash the conviction, on the grounds that the applicant had disentitled himself to relief by reason of his "grossly exaggerated and unrealistic" affidavits. In the Supreme Court, Kingsmill Moore J. agreed that Vozza had probably "exaggerated his capacity not to understand English", but doubted whether he was able fully to understand court procedure. Moreover, Vozza had not suppressed facts in respect of not being informed about his right to jury trial and so there were no grounds for refusing him relief on this basis. There was also the consideration that the application sought to quash a criminal conviction, so that the relief was to be granted *ex debito justitiae*. A similar argument regarding lack of good faith was rejected by the Supreme Court in *The State (Furey) v. Minister for Defence*.[153] Here the applicant had failed to reveal certain minor disciplinary offences when seeking to quash his dismissal from the Defence Forces, but McCarthy J. was prepared to ignore this lack of candour in the circumstances, especially as the Defence Forces themselves had wrongly classified his record as "unsatisfactory" instead of "fair".

The court will also have regard to the general conduct of the applicant[154]; the reasons for the application[155] and whether the granting of relief would cause hardship to innocent third parties.[156] Thus, in *Ahern v. Minister for Industry and Commerce (No. 2)*[157] the applicant was placed on compulsory sick leave following his

---

[153] [1988] I.L.R.M. 89. See also *Taxback Ltd v. Revenue Commissioners*, unreported, High Court, January 21, 1997, another case involving a certain lack of candour. McCracken J. nonetheless granted the relief claimed, possibly because this was a case in which there had been a suggestion that innocent third parties – for whom the applicant was acting – might have been prejudiced if the application were not granted. McCracken J. went on to say that while in the circumstances this was not a ground for dismissing the application, "it was a matter that I intend to deal with when it comes to the question of costs."

No such special considerations were present in *Re O'Neill* [1990] 3 N.I.J.B. 1, where Murray L.J. refused to quash a decision of the N.I. Housing Executive that the applicant was intentionally homeless on the ground that, *inter alia*, she had misled the Executive and the Court. He added (at 33–34):
"Against this background . . . the Court should be very slow to help an applicant who, instead of being completely frank and honest with the Executive about her situation, creates difficulties for the Executive in the ascertainment of the true facts by misstatements which inevitably must hinder their investigations and their ascertainments of those facts."

[154] *Ex parte Fry* [1954] 1 W.L.R. 730; *Fulbrook v. Berkshire Magistrates' Court* (1970) 69 L.G.R. 75; *Condon v. Minister for Agriculture*, unreported, High Court, October 12, 1990; *Murtagh v. Board of Governors of St. Emer's National School* [1991] 1 I.R. 482.

[155] *The State (Abenglen Properties Ltd) v. Dublin Corporation* [1984] I.R. 384 (attempt to obtain benefit "not contemplated" by the planning code); *The State (Conlon Construction Co. Ltd) v. Cork County Council*, unreported, High Court, July 31, 1975; *R. (Burns) v. Tyrone JJ.* [1961] N.I. 167; *R. v. Monopolies Commission, ex p. Argyll plc* [1986] 1 W.L.R. 763 (rival company attempting to obtain advantage from procedural defect in Commission's ruling).

[156] See, *e.g. Minister for Education v. Letterkenny RTC* [1995] 1 I.L.R.M. 438 (unfair to quash statutory appointment where successful candidate had resigned from his earlier post to take up that appointment); *The State (Cussen) v. Brennan* [1981] I.R. 181 (similar principle); *Brennan v. Minister for Justice* [1995] 2 I.L.R.M. 206 (unfair to quash ministerial decision remitting a court fine where the petitioners had sought the mitigation of the fine in accordance with long-standing practice and where the granting of declaratory relief would have been more appropriate) and *Kenny v. Revenue Commissioners* [1996] 3 I.R. 315 (granting of relief would simply delay other proceedings in which the applicant was a defendant and where the granting of judicial review was not necessary to protect his rights).

[157] Unreported, High Court, July 29, 1990. See also *Connolly v. Collector of Custom and Excise*, unreported, High Court, October 5, 1992 where Blayney J. hinted that he would have refused, on discretionary grounds, to grant mandamus compelling the respondent to award a seven-day publican's licence having regard "to the very extraordinary conduct of the applicant in totally ignoring the licensing laws for almost six years before bringing this application".

"unreasonable refusal to see a psychiatrist". Blayney J. held that this decision was invalid, but refused to quash the decision because of the applicant's unreasonable behaviour, which was compounded by his persistent allegations (which Blayney J. found to be wholly unfounded) that his superiors were not acting bona fide. An innovative (but entirely justifiable) approach to the exercise of discretion may be found in *Brennan v. Minister for Justice*.[158] Here Geoghegan J. declined on discretionary grounds to quash ministerial decisions which he found had improperly remitted certain fines and penalties which had been imposed by the applicant District Court judge. The convicted persons had applied to the Minister for remission of the penalties in accordance with long-standing practice and Geoghegan J. felt that it would be unfair to deprive them of the benefit of the decision in their own case, particularly as their cases had been selected on a more or less random basis in order to test the legality of a more general practice and as the declaratory relief actually granted was sufficient to clarify the law.

Nevertheless, the discretion to refuse relief on this ground where a proper case has been made out is sparingly exercised. *Re Hogan's Application*[159] is a good example of this judicial attitude. Here Carswell J. found that the applicant (who was a Sinn Féin councillor) had been invalidly excluded from her council seat and that a council resolution to that effect was *ultra vires*. Carswell J. was invited to refuse to grant relief on the ground that:

> "[I]t ill behoves an active Sinn Féin supporter to come to court and ask it to order a council to resume meeting and proceed with ordinary democratic processes [and that the applicant] was seeking relief of a political nature on behalf of one faction seeking to take political advantage over another."[160]

The judge, however, declined to refuse relief on this ground:

> "[The applicant] and her party may well desire to see their political opponents discomfited, but this is not the only case where this may follow as the result of a legitimate application for judicial review. Notwithstanding the known aims and policies of Sinn Féin, its members are not debarred by law from standing for election and taking their seats as district councillors. It would in consequence be wrong in my judgment to bar the applicant, because she is a member of Sinn Féin, from seeking redress against a council which is in breach of statutory duty when she has made out a proper case to be granted it."[161]

A further example of this approach may be found in *Carrigaline Community Television Ltd v. Minister for Communications*.[162] In this case the plaintiffs, who had for many years operated an unlicensed cable television system challenged the grant of an exclusive licence to another rival company. Having found that the Minister had wrongly

---

[158] [1995] 2 I.L.R.M. 206.
[159] (1985) 5 N.I.J.B. 81.
[160] *Ibid.* at 101.
[161] *Ibid.* at 102. See also *Flynn and O'Flaherty Properties Ltd v. Dublin Corporation* [1997] 2 I.R. 560 (the High Court should not refuse to grant a declaration on discretionary grounds that the applicant had obtained a default planning permission simply because of a "lack of judicial enthusiasm" for default permissions of this kind).
[162] [1997] 1 I.L.R.M. 241.

refused to entertain the plaintiff's application for such a licence, Keane J. then rejected the suggestion that the plaintiffs' illegal activities disentitled them to relief. The Minister had acquiesced in their illegal activities by declining to prosecute[163] and Keane J. explained that while the courts could not "condone or excuse" that illegal conduct, it should not seek "to punish the offender by depriving him of his constitutional rights". Again while the "salutary maxim" of *ex turpi causa non oritur actio* and the principle that he who comes to equity must come with clean hands "retain their ancient vigour in the law", they should not be allowed "to work a greater injustice by depriving citizens of the right to natural justice and fair procedures".

(ii) Delay

General principles Order 84, rule 21(1) of the Rules of the Superior Courts 1986 provides that all applications for judicial review "shall be made promptly" and in any event within three months from the date when the grounds for the application first arose, or six months when the relief sought is certiorari.[164] The court has a discretion to extend these time limits where "there is a good reason"[165] for doing so. The decision of the Superior Court Rules Committee to impose such relatively short time limits was somewhat surprising given that the Law Reform Commission had recommended that the issue of delay should be left entirely to the discretion of the court. Nevertheless, there is always the discretion to extend time of which substantial use has been made, as we shall see.

Prior to the adoption of the 1986 Rules, the general attitude of the courts had been to ask whether the delay had been such as to affect prejudicially the rights of third parties. In cases where there was prejudice, periods of as short as four months had been held to disentitle the applicant to relief "to which he was otherwise entitled *ex debito justitiae*" where such delay prejudiced the rights of third parties.[166] On the other side of the line, delay of itself is not a ground for refusing relief, where the applicant has suffered a "public wrong" at the hands of the State or its agents.

---

[163] *Ibid.* at 300. "The person responsible under the law for initiating such prosecutions was the Minister. One can only view with scepticism the suggestion that there were technical or procedural difficulties in initiating such prosecutions. The reality is that the authorities were unwilling to incur the odium of instituting prosecutions against people who were seen as a providing a community service which would not otherwise be available . . .".

[164] It is not clear why the rule should be six months in the case of certiorari, as opposed to three months in the case of the other remedies. One possibility is that it is because historically it was always certiorari which was involved in criminal cases and because certiorari is still the premier remedy in the field of public law. In the majority of cases the applicant will be seeking certiorari, so that the six months will be the "target date" within which the application will have to be made. The distinction between the permitted time limits is nonetheless difficult to justify.

[165] However, where the appropriate time limit prescribed by R.S.C. 1986, Ord. 84, r. 21(1) has expired, then, *per* Hederman J. in *O'Flynn v. Mid-Western Health Board* [1991] 2 I.R. 223 at 236:
". . . the judge should be furnished with the reasons for the delay in the grounding affidavit and he should decide whether there are grounds for excusing the delay. Even if leave is granted at the *ex parte* stage, nonetheless, when the trial judge comes to hear the matter he must adjudicate upon whether the delay was reasonable and such as may be excused or not."

[166] *The State (Cussen) v. Brennan* [1981] I.R. 181 (delay in challenging a particular appointment had led successful applicant to change position, so that it would be unfair to grant the relief claimed); *R. (Rainey) v. Belfast Recorder* (1937) 71 I.L.T.R. 272; *Minister for Education v. Letterkenny Regional Technical College* [1995] 1 I.L.R.M. 438. But *cf. M v. An Bord Úchtála* [1977] I.R. 287 (where the Supreme Court invalidated an adoption order despite a delay of over three years and where the child had spent all of its sentient life with the adoptive parents).

This emerged from the Supreme Court's decision in 1984 in *The State (Furey) v. Minister for Defence*.[167] Although these certiorari proceedings were not commenced until more than four years from the date of the applicant's dismissal from the Defence Forces,[168] the Court granted the order sought, as the applicant had been unaware of his right to challenge the validity of the dismissal as being contrary to the rules of natural justice. McCarthy J. said moreover that he could see no reason:

> "[W]hy delay, however long, should, of itself, disentitle to certiorari any applicant for that remedy who can demonstrate that a public wrong has been done to him – that, for instance, a conviction has been obtained without jurisdiction, or that otherwise the State has wronged him and that wrong continues to mark or mar his life."[169]

As far as criminal cases are concerned, the general principle prior to 1986 appeared to be that the applicant cannot be precluded by his delay from challenging a conviction made in excess of jurisdiction or which is bad on its face[170] but this principle applied to convictions only and not to orders of return for trial.[171] It had also been doubted whether even gross laches would prevent an order of prohibition from issuing to restrain an inferior court from proceeding with a criminal trial where it had no jurisdiction.[172] Thus, presumably the fact that the applicant had suffered a "public wrong" – *e.g.* invalid dismissal from State employment, or conviction imposed without jurisdiction – would still now of itself be a "good reason" for the High Court to extend the time limits contained in Order 84, rule 21(1).

Effect of the 1986 Rules   In some cases, the 1986 Rules have brought about a stricter judicial attitude[173] to the issue of delay and it may be convenient if some of the legal issues arising from the Rules are separately examined.

(a) The obligation to apply "promptly"   There is some slight authority for the view that an applicant who has not moved "promptly" for judicial review may find that he is out of time, even where the application has been brought within the six months' time limit. Thus, contemporary English practice demonstrates that there

---

167   [1988] I.L.R.M. 89. See Hogan, "Natural and Constitutional Justice: Adieu to Laissez-Faire" (1984) 19 Ir. Jur. 309 (N.S.).

168   See also *The State Gleeson v. Minister for Defence* [1976] I.R. 280.

169   [1988] I.L.R.M. 100. McCarthy J. distinguished *The State (Cussen) v. Brennan* [1981] I.R. 181 on the basis that in *Furey* (unlike *Cussen*) the granting of certiorari would not prejudice third party rights. See also, *The State (Director of Public Prosecution) v. Ó hUadáigh*, unreported, High Court, January 30, 1984; *The State (Murphy) v. Kielt* [1984] I.R. 458 (delay on the part of applicant for certiorari not such as to prejudice respondent or other third party); *The State (Gleeson) v. Martin* [1985] I.L.R.M. 578.

170   *The State (Kelly) v. District Justice for Bandon* [1947] I.R. 258; *The State (Furey) v. Minister for Defence* [1988] I.L.R.M. 88. But *cf.* the comments of Henchy J. to the contrary in *The State (Abenglen Properties Ltd v. Dublin Corporation* [1984] I.R. 384 at 403.

171   *The State (Walsh) v. Maguire* [1979] I.R. 372; *The State (Coveney) v. Special Criminal Court* [1982] I.L.R.M. 284. *Cf.* the comments of McCarthy J. in *O'Flynn v. Mid-Western Health Board* [1991] 2 I.R. 223 at 239 to the effect that the *ex debito justitiae* only applies to final orders affecting rights and not where the decision is "merely a step in the process".

172   *The State (Coveney) v. Special Criminal Court* [1982] I.L.R.M. 284 at 289, *per* Finlay P.

173   See Hogan, "Time Limits and Judicial Review Applications" (1988) 82 *Gaz. of the Incorporated Law Society of Ireland* 237 and Collins and O'Reilly, *op. cit.* above, n.17, pp. 93–96.

may be cases where it will be incumbent on the applicant to move with great speed, especially where the challenge is to the award of licences to third parties[174] or where the impugned decision effects large scale administrative changes affecting many interests.[175] One of the few Irish cases where this point appears to have considered is *Eurocontainer Shipping plc v. Minister for Marine*,[176] where a more lenient attitude was taken. Here the validity of an international tonnage certificate which had been awarded by the respondent in respect of a particular vessel had been challenged. The application had been brought just within six months of the decision and it was contended that it had not been brought "promptly" within the meaning of the Rules. Barr J. rejected this submission on several grounds. It had been reasonable for the applicant to wait to have had operational experience of the tonnage measurement for the vessel. Secondly, applying the principles of McCarthy J.'s judgment in *Furey*, there was no reason why delay in and of itself should defeat the application and, finally, the respondent had not been inconvenienced by the delay and there was no evidence of any prejudice to third parties.

It is true that in two other reported cases – *Director of Public Prosecutions v. Macklin*[177] and *Director of Public Prosecutions v. Judge Kelly*[178] – this point was successfully taken. In the former case the applicant sought to have certain orders of a District Court judge quashed. Lardner J. accepted that the respondent had acted *ultra vires*, but pointed to the fact that the Director had not acted "promptly" within the meaning of Order 84, rule 21(1) inasmuch as he had delayed almost six months in making the application. As there was no explanation for this delay, Lardner J. refused to grant the orders of certiorari sought. However, this decision is probably best explained by the fact that this was a case in which the objective on the part of the notice party was to prevent a re-trial and the law always leans in favour of an accused. Similar considerations underlay the second case where the Director had sought to quash a ruling of a trial judge to direct the jury to acquit the notice party of sexual offences charges. The application for leave was made within four days of the end of the six month period, but by this stage the notice party had to face trial

---

[174] In *R. v. Independent Television Commission, ex p. TVNi Ltd, The Times*, December 30, 1991, the English Court of Appeal held that the applicant who sought to challenge the award of a broadcasting licence had not moved promptly. The potential licences had been nominated in mid-October and the final award was made seven weeks later. The applicant had not availed of the opportunity to apply during that seven-week "window" and, accordingly, had delayed unduly. Lord Donaldson M.R. emphasised that:

"In these matters people must act with the utmost promptitude because so many third parties are affected by the decision and are entitled to act on it unless they have clear and prompt notice that the decision is challenged."

[175] Lindsay, "Delay in Judicial Review Cases" (1995) *Public Law* 417 refers (at p. 423) to an unreported 1993 English High Court decision, *R v. Home Secretary, ex p. Prison Officers' Association*, where Otton J. refused leave on the ground of lack of promptness, even though the challenge was made one month after a decision to implement a different system of transferring remand prisoners to a particular area. The Association had advance knowledge of the likely changes and had "ample opportunity" to apply on receipt of the decision-letter. Furthermore, third party rights were at stake: agency nurses had been employed, court transport arrangements made and rotas of prison officers had been fixed. *Cf. The State (Cussen) v. Brennan* [1981] I.R. 181 and *Minister for Education v. Letterkenny Regional Technical College* [1995] 1 I.L.R.M. 438.

[176] Unreported, High Court, December 11, 1992.

[177] [1989] I.L.R.M. 113.

[178] [1997] 1 I.R. 405.

on serious charges on five seperate occasions (due to the unavailability of a key prosecution witness). In these circumstances Laffoy J. held that the Director had not applied sufficiently promptly for judicial review, particularly as she considered that the notice party's constitutional right to a trial with reasonable expedition would have been infringed if the acquittal were now to be quashed.

(b) Extensions of time for "good reason"   If an applicant who, although within time, has not been prompt in seeking judicial review may be required to explain this delay, the same is true, *a fortiori*, of cases where the delay has been greater than six months, provided, of course, that the issue is raised by the respondent.[179] Accordingly, where the appropriate time-limit prescribed by Order 84, rule 21(1) has expired, then, as Hederman J. said in *O'Flynn v. Mid-Western Health Board*[180]:

> ". . . the judge should be furnished with the reasons for the delay in the grounding affidavit and he should decide whether there are grounds for excusing the delay. Even if leave is granted at the ex parte stage, nonetheless, when the trial judge comes to hear the matter he must adjudicate upon whether the delay was reasonable and such as may be excused or not."[181]

Nevertheless, the prescribed time limits are not applied rigidly and the power to extend time is, generally speaking, liberally employed, provided that the delay can be explained and there is no evidence of prejudice to third parties. As McCarthy J. in *O'Flynn v. Mid-Western Health Board*:

> "There is ample ground for saying that both in principle and in precedent, an application for judicial review should not fail merely because it is out of time. In principle, it is right to relieve against delay in challenging an administrative decision where the delay has not prejudiced third parties."[182]

As Costello J. explained in *O'Donnell v. Dún Laoghaire Corporation (No. 2)*,[183] the phrase "good reasons" is one:

> "Of wide import which it would be futile to attempt to define precisely. However, in considering whether or not there are good reasons for extending the time, I think it is clear that the test must be an objective one and the court should not extend the time merely because an aggrieved plaintiff believed that he or she was justified in delaying the institution of proceedings. What the plaintiff has to show (and I think the onus under Ord. 84, r. 21 is on the plaintiff) is that there are reasons which both explain the delay and afford a justifiable excuse for the delay."[184]

---

[179] *Director of Public Prosecutions v. McMenamin*, unreported, High Court, March 23, 1996 (respondents not permitted to raise delay issue when it was not raised in the notice of opposition).

[180] [1991] 2 I.R. 223.

[181] *Ibid.* at 236.

[182] *Ibid.* at 239. Nevertheless, as McCarthy J. himself pointed out in *O'Flynn* that these considerations only apply where "the impugned decision has an immediate effect on rights and is not merely a step in the process". For a similar approach, see the judgment of Lord Lowry L.C.J. for the Northern Irish Court of Appeal in *Re Coleman's Application* [1988] N.I. 205.

[183] [1991] I.L.R.M. 301.

[184] *Ibid.* at 315.

The English Court of Appeal and House of Lords in *R. v. Dairy Quota Tribunal, ex p. Caswell*[185] took a fairly stringent attitude to this question. The applicants were farmers who were required to pay super-levy charges following a misconstruction of the relevant regulations in their case by the Dairy Quota Tribunal. However, they had delayed by up to two years in applying for judicial review. Thus, despite the applicant's success on the merits of the case, the Court of Appeal refused to quash the Tribunal's decision because of the undue delay. Lloyd L.J. said that it was not open to an applicant who was outside the three-month limit to argue that there was no undue delay. The Court could, of course, grant the applicant an extension if there was "good reason" to do so, such as where he had a good case on the merits. But even then, the Court is obliged to consider whether the granting of relief would substantially prejudice the rights of third parties or "would be detrimental to good administration".[186] Lloyd L.J. held that the delay would be prejudicial to good administration, since a substantial number of applicants during a five-year period might thereby be entitled to re-apply for an additional quota if the Caswells were to succeed in obtaining relief. Although these views were endorsed by Lord Goff in the House of Lords, this seems an unduly harsh attitude to take and quite unnecessarily overprotective of public authorities.

Even in this jurisdiction, delay beyond the six months' period may be fatal to the applicant's chances of success if it is unexplained. This point is well illustrated by the Supreme Court's decision in *O'Flynn v. Mid-Western Health Board*[187] where the applicants had waited some eight months before applying for judicial review of a decision to establish a committee investigating certain complaints against the applicant medical practitioners. As the application was made just two days before the Committee was due to sit, it was held that the application had been unduly delayed. This decision must be viewed in the light of its particular facts and is best regarded as an authority for the proposition that the courts will look with disfavour on eleventh hour applications for prohibition to restrain the work of an administrative tribunal.[188]

This judicial attitude is echoed in a series of other decisions. In *Connors v. Delap*,[189] Lynch J. considered that he should exercise his discretion against an applicant who was relying on a technical point and who had waited some 18 months before challenging his District Court conviction. This approach was followed by Barr J.

---

[185] [1989] 1 W.L.R. 1089 (CA); [1990] 2 A.C. 738 (HL).

[186] It is important to emphasise that this decision largely turned on an interpretation of s.31(6) of the English Supreme Court Act 1981 which has no Irish counterpart. This subsection empowers the courts to refuse relief by way of judicial review where "this would be likely to cause substantial hardship to, or substantially prejudice the rights of, any person or would be detrimental to good administration". The absence of a similar provision in this country means that the English decisions on delay and the exercise of discretion must be viewed with some circumspection: see the comments of Costello J. in *O'Donnell v. Dún Laoghaire Corporation (No. 2)* [1991] I.L.R.M. 315 at 318–319.

[187] [1991] 2 I.R. 223. See also *Healy v. Fingal County Council*, unreported, High Court, January 17, 1997.

[188] *Ibid. cf.* the comments of Hederman J. at 236:
"Various administrative bodies have their own procedures, but they are required to engage, just as courts do, in the pursuit of justice. I would deprecate eleventh hour attempts to render nugatory their efforts. Members of such tribunals are bound to feel a sense of frustration if hearings are arranged, everything regarding procedure agreed in advance and then they are met with an order of the High Court prohibiting them from going any further."

[189] [1989] I.L.R.M. 93.

in refusing relief in *White v. Hussey*,[190] where again the defect in the conviction was of a technical character and the delay approached 14 months. The question of undue delay was again considered by Barr J. in *Solan v. Director of Public Prosecutions*.[191] Here the applicant sought to challenge District Court convictions imposed some 18 months previously. Barr J. could not accept that, in view of the decision in *Furey*, certiorari should issue *ex debito justitiae*. There were, he thought, three reasons why this case fell outside the ambit of McCarthy J.'s reasoning:

> "First, in *Furey's* case the applicant put before the court in evidence a detailed explanation for his delay in seeking relief by way of judicial review, whereas no evidence whatever has been given by or on behalf of Mr. Solan to justify his delay in that regard. In the absence of evidence explaining delay, there is no basis on which the court can exercise its discretion to grant an extension of time for making the applications. Secondly, Mr. Furey's application was regarded as having substantial merit per se, whereas there is no evidence to suggest that Mr. Solan may not have been properly convicted on the merits. Thirdly, Mr. Furey's only remedy was by way of judicial review [whereas Mr. Solan may appeal to the Circuit Court]."[192]

Despite these differences the fact remains that the applicant's conviction was invalid; yet mere lapse of time was enough to shut out his application for certiorari. Decisions such as *Connors* and *Solan* show a move away from the long-standing principle that a person aggrieved by an *ultra vires* decision is entitled to a quashing order *ex debito justitiae*. Indeed, part of the problem stems from the fact that the Superior Court Rules Committee elected to follow the more restrictive approach as to delay adopted in England.[193] It would have been preferable instead to follow the recommendations of the Law Reform Commission who thought there should be no fixed time limits and that the question of delay should be a matter for the discretion of the court, subject always to the doctrine of laches.[194]

However, where excusing circumstances have been found, periods of delay beyond the six months have generally been overlooked in the absence of prejudice to the respondents. In *Murphy v. Minister for Social Welfare*[195] Blayney J. was prepared to extend time in circumstances where an appeals officer had erred in law

---

190 [1989] I.L.R.M. 109.
191 [1989] I.L.R.M. 491. See Collins, "Ex Debito Justitiae" (1988) 10 D.U.L.J. 130 (N.S.) for a critique of these decisons.
192 [1989] I.L.R.M. 491 at 493–494.
193 But, of course, as has already been emphasised (see above, p. 726, n.186), Ord. 53, r. 4 of the English Rules (which deals with delay) follows s.31(6) of the Supreme Court Act 1981. In contrast, there is no statutory parallel to s.31(6) in this jurisdiction.
194 At p.81 of the Working Paper No. 8, *Judicial Review of Administrative Action: The Problem of Remedies*.
195 [1987] I.R. 295. See also *Murphy v. District Justice Wallace* [1993] 2 I.R. 138 (where the applicant was held to be justified in waiting for a decision by the prosecution as to how they would continue in the wake of another High Court decision before taking any steps by way of seeking judicial review); *Bane v. Garda Representative Association* [1997] 2 I.R. 449 (similar principle) and *O'Leary v. Cork County Council* [1994] 1 I.R. 59 (where O'Hanlon J. acknowledged that while the application "may be technically out of time" – as some seven months had elapsed – he was prepared to grant the necessary extension of the period within which the application could be brought as the delay "had not been inordinate".)

in determining that the applicant was not in insurable employment, despite the fact that there had been a delay of up to 15 months in seeking relief. There was no evidence that the respondent was prejudiced by the delay and, rather like the facts of *Furey*, the applicant had entered into correspondence with the respondents with a view to making alternative arrangements with respect to his pension contributions. The same judge took a similar view in *Corrigan v. Gallagher*.[196] Here the increments of several prison officers had been forfeited, following related decisions of the prison authorities and the Minister for Justice that the officers had been negligent in the performance of their duties. While the challenge to the Minister's decision had been brought within the six months' period, the applicants were out of time by some two weeks in respect of the decision of the prison authorities. Blayney J. considered that the decisions in question had been arrived at in breach of the *audi alteram partem* rule and granted the orders of certiorari sought. He thought that there was "good reason" within the meaning of Order 84, rule 21(1) to extend the time. Both decisions were interlinked and it:

> ". . . would not seem reasonable, given that the decisions implementing the recommendations of the sanctions could be attacked, to refuse to allow to be attacked also the decision [of the prison authorities] recommending the sanction, particularly as the applications in regard to those decisions were only two weeks outside the six-month period."[197]

Blayney J. also drew attention to the fact that the applicants may have been misled in certain respects by the respondents, a factor contributing further to the delay. This trend was powerfully reinforced by the judgment of Costello J. in *O'Donnell v. Dún Laoghaire Corporation (No. 2)*.[198] In 1989 the plaintiff commenced a plenary action whereby he sought to challenge water charges imposed by the Corporation between 1983 and 1985 and it was argued that relief should be denied on discretionary grounds because of this delay. Costello J. firstly held that there were "good reasons" within the meaning of Order 84. rule 21 for the plaintiff delaying until June 1988, since prior to that date, the plaintiff:

> ". . . did not undertake the burden of instituting proceedings because he believed that the legality issue could be adjudicated upon in proceedings instituted by the Corporation either against him or other householders who, he was aware, had raised the validity of the orders in other proceedings."[199]

After June 1988, the defendants began to turn off the water supply of the houses of persons (including the plaintiff) who had failed to pay the disputed water charges. However, during the 1988–1989 period, the plaintiff enlisted the support of no less than three public representatives in an effort to settle this dispute. Costello J., applying the principles of *Furey*, said that this constituted a "reasonable explanation" for this further delay, adding that:

---

[196] Unreported, High Court, February 2, 1988.
[197] At pp. 21–22 of his judgment. See also, *Byrne v. Grey* [1988] I.R. 31 and *Berkeley v. Edwards* [1988] I.R. 217.
[198] [1991] I.L.R.M. 301.
[199] *Ibid.* at 316.

"No third parties have acquired rights which it would be unjust to injure by making the declaratory order the plaintiff seeks. Whilst it is true that the declaratory order may cause the defendants' administrative and, perhaps, financial problems, I do not think that they are such as to justify the court refusing the plaintiff relief to which otherwise he would be entitled."[200]

This judgment, together with those of Blayney J. in *Murphy* and *Corrigan*, are more in harmony with the principles laid down in *Furey* than are the views of Lynch J. and Barr J. in cases such as *Connors*, *White* and *Solan*. It may be that while the new Order 84, rule 21 originally caused some members of the High Court to adopt a stricter approach to delay, the subsequent cases appear to suggest a return to the *Furey* principles, despite the wording of the rule.

(c) Delay causing administrative inconvenience The question of whether relief should be refused because a delayed application (even though there may be a reasonable explanation for it) might lead to administrative inconvenience has not yet been fully explored in this jurisdiction. To some extent, this issue is bound up with questions of prejudice to third parties and the retroactive consequences of a decision of invalidity.[201] To date, however, the courts appear largely unimpressed by pleas of administrative inconvenience in the absence of established or potential prejudice to third parties.[202]

(d) Delay and the special position of Community Law It remains to advert to the special position of delay and Community law. In *Emmott v. Minister for Social Welfare*[203] the European Court of Justice held that for so long as a directive had not been properly transposed into domestic law, individuals were unable to ascertain the full extent of their rights. In such circumstances, the Court ruled that the Minister could not invoke the six months time limit prescribed by Order 84, rule 21 to defeat the applicant's judicial review application, which application had sought to invoke

---

200 *Ibid.* at 318. See also *Re Coleman's Application* [1988] N.I. 205 where a delayed application for judicial review was brought as a preliminary to an action against members of a juvenile court for damages for wrongful arrest and false imprisonment. Lord Lowry L.C.J. rejected the suggestion that the undue delay might prejudice the position of the magistrates, as there was no reason to suppose that the Lord Chancellor would not invoke his statutory powers to meet the expenses incurred by a magistrate in the execution of his office.

201 *cf. Duff v. Minister for Agriculture and Food* [1997] 2 I.R. 22, a case where the validity of the distribution by the Minister in 1984 of the entire national milk quota was at issue. Murphy J. noted that counsel for the applicant had "fairly, properly and . . . necessarily" conceded that "the status quo ante could not be restored" and that the Minister "made the decision to distribute the entire national quota [to the farming community] and having done so could not possibly recall it."

202 In *O'Flynn v. Mid-Western Health Board* [1991] 2 I.R. 223 McCarthy J. would not have refused relief simply because the delay caused (admittedly minor) administrative prejudice. Costello J. had taken a similar attitude in *O'Donnell v. Dun Laoghaire Corporation (No. 2)* [1991] I.L.R.M. 301, where he said that the fact that the invalidation of this decision to make certain water charges might cause the defendant "administrative and, perhaps, financial problems" they were not such "as to justify the court refusing the plaintiff relief to which otherwise he would be entitled." There is a hint in this comment that had the administrative inconvenience in question been more substantial, a different attitude might have been taken. *Cf.* the comments of O'Higgins C.J. in *The State (Byrne) v. Frawley* [1978] I.R. 326 and Henchy J. in *Murphy v. Attorney General* [1982] I.R. 241 in the context of retroactive invalidity.

203 Case–208/90, [1991] E.C.R. I–4269.

individual rights conferred by the directive. It should be noted, however, that subsequent decisions have ensured that *Emmott* "does not have the wide general application which it appears to have on first reading",[204] inasmuch as Member States are entitled to rely on a limitation period – as opposed to the jurisdictional bar rejected in *Emmott* – limiting the period of years prior to the bringing of the claim in respect of which the damages were payable.[205]

(iii) Acquiescence and waiver

The courts will not allow the creation of a wholly new jurisdiction through acquiescence or waiver.[206] Nevertheless, where the position is reversed, *i.e.* where the acquiescence and waiver is that of the applicant he may be disentitled to relief. In *R. (Kildare County Council) v. Commissioner of Valuation*[207] the applicant appealed to the County Court against a valuation revision. It was only when the decision of the County Court proved not to be as favourable as expected that the applicant claimed that the County Court had no jurisdiction in the matter. The Court of Appeal ruled that, even assuming that the County Court had acted without jurisdiction, relief should be refused on discretionary grounds. Holmes L.J. said that he found it difficult to conceive of a "stronger case of estoppel by conduct".[208] Similarly in *The State (Byrne) v. Frawley*[209] the applicant's failure to raise certain alleged irregularities in his trial when appealing to the Court of Criminal Appeal was found to be prima facie evidence of acquiescence. Participation (or continued participation) in proceedings may constitute acquiescence where the party seeking to challenge the decision was aware of the full facts and failed to take objection to the composition or procedure of the tribunal.[210] The right to object to an irregularity of procedure or breach of natural justice may also be lost by waiver.[211]

---

[204] *Tate v. Minister for Social Welfare* [1995] 1 I.L.R.M. 507 at 529, *per* Carroll J.

[205] Case C–338/91, *Steenhorst-Neerings* [1993] E.C.R. I–5475; Case C–410/92, *Johnson v. Chief Adjudication Officer* [1994] E.C.R. I–5483; and *Tate v. Minister for Social Welfare* [1995] 1 I.L.R.M. 507.

[206] *Corrigan v. Irish Land Commission* [1977] I.R. 317 at 325, *per* Henchy J.; *The State (Byrne) v. Frawley* [1978] I.R. 326 at 342, *per* O'Higgins C.J. See above pp. 453–454.

[207] [1901] 2 I.R. 215. See also *R. (Mathews) v. Petticrew* (1886) 18 L.R. Ir. 342; *The State (McKay) v. Cork Circuit Judge* [1937] I.R. 650 and *R. (Doris) v. Ministry for Health* [1954] N.I. 79.

[208] The *Kildare* case was distinguished by Barron J. in *Browne v. An Bord Pleanála* [1991] 2 I.R. 209. In the latter case the applicants had appealed to An Bord Pleanála and then subsequently sought judicial review of that decision, but the judge was unimpressed by arguments based on estoppel and waiver, saying (at 214):
> "Undoubtedly, the lengthy appeal before the [Board] could have been avoided if the applicants had sought and obtained an order of prohibition on the basis of lack of jurisdiction. But the applicants never led anyone to believe that they would not do so, if their appeal was unsuccessful . . .".

[209] [1978] I.R. 326.

[210] *The State (Cronin) v. Circuit Judge for Western Circuit* [1937] I.R. 44; *The State (Redmond) v. Wexford Corporation* [1946] I.R. 409. But the principle does not apply where the applicant is unaware of the full facts, or has been taken by surprise: *R. (Harrington) v. Clare JJ.* [1918] 2 I.R. 116; *The State (McDonagh) v. Sheerin* [1981] I.L.R.M. 149; *The State (Cole) v. Labour Court* (1984) 3 J.I.S.L.L. 128.

[211] *Corrigan v. Irish Land Commission* [1977] I.R. 317. See above, pp. 453–454. But failure to attend the hearing of a tribunal whose jurisdiction and composition have been clearly disputed does not constitute a waiver: *Bane v. Garda Representative Association* [1997] 2 I.R. 449.

(iv) Where no useful and legitimate purpose would be served

The court will not make an order which cannot now be implemented or which would be either futile[212] or illegal.[213] Nor will relief be granted where this would simply cause further delay[214] or would confer no practical benefit on the applicant[215] or where no legitimate purpose would be served.[216] There have been several heterogeneous examples of where relief on this ground has been refused and which may be cited for purposes of illustration.

In *H. v. Director of Public Prosecutions*[217] Barron J. refused to grant an order of mandamus compelling the Director of Public Prosecutions to reconsider a decision,[218] he had taken five years previously not to prosecute certain members of the applicant's family in respect of alleged sexual offences against her son, since he was not persuaded that it would have been in the infant's interests to pursue this matter, "particularly after such a lapse of time". In *The State (Abenglen Properties Ltd) v. Dublin Corporation*[219] the Supreme Court refused to quash the granting of a planning permission when it became clear that the applicants could not obtain the default planning permission which they had sought. In *Farrell v. Farelly*,[220]

---

212 *Minister for Labour v. Grace* [1993] 2 I.R. 53 (where O'Hanlon J. refused to grant mandamus in circumstances where this would have been a "meaningless exercise"). *Ryan v. Compensation Tribunal* [1997] I.L.R.M. 194 (where Costello P. refused to quash a decision awarding compensation which (it was claimed) failed to include a sum for home help payments as the law had since been changed to impose on health boards a statutory duty to provide such a service free of charge).

213 *Kenny Homes & Co. Ltd v. Galway City and County Manager* [1995] 1 I.R. 178 (no mandamus to compel City Manager to comply with an invalid resolution)

214 *Fulbrook v. Berkshire Magistrates' Court* (1970) 69 L.G.R. 85; *The State (Walshe) v. Maguire* [1979] I.R. 372 and *R v. Monopolies Commission, ex p. Argyll plc* [1986] 1 W.L.R. 763, where Sir John Donaldson emphasised (at 774) the need for "speed of decision, particularly in the financial field." This principle is similarly illustrated by *A. v. Eastern Health Board*, unreported, High Court, November 28, 1997. Here Geoghegan J. refused to quash a District Court order permitting a pregnant minor (who was the subject of a care order) to travel to the United Kingdom in order to have an abortion, despite an inadvertent breach of fair procedures on the part of the District Judge when she refused to grant counsel for the parents (who opposed the abortion) a short adjournment to enable him obtain assistance from a psychiatrist so that he could cross-examine several expert witnesses more effectively. While Geoghegan J. accepted than in an ordinary case the order might be quashed and remitted to the District Court because of the wrongful refusal of that adjournment, he declined to do so, on discretionary grounds, saying that he was quite satisfied:

"... that in all the circumstances of this case, including the nature of the hearing which did in fact take place and the absolute urgency for finality and the firm belief that even if such adjournment had been granted it would have made no difference to the order made ... that as a matter of discretion I ought not to quash [it]."

215 *Heavey v. Pilotage Committee of the Dublin Pilotage Authority*, unreported, High Court, May 7, 1992 (quashing of Committee decision not necessary for the protection of the applicant's rights and applicant could re-apply for to the Committee for a favourable decision in view of altered circumstances.)

216 An unusual case such as *Director of Public Prosecutions v. Judge Kelly* [1997] 1 I.R. 405 probably fits within this category. In this case the Director had sought to quash a ruling of a trial judge to direct the jury to acquit the notice party of sexual offences charges. While Laffoy J. agreed that the trial judge had acted *ultra vires* in making such an order, she nonetheless refused on discretionary grounds to quash the order, as the non-availability of a key witness had the "potential of being highly prejudicial to the notice party" and materially affected "his ability to defend himself".

217 [1994] 2 I.R. 589.

218 On the question of whether judicial review will lie for this purpose: see above, pp. 668–669.

219 [1984] I.R. 384. See also *The State (Doyle) v. Carr* [1970] I.R. 87 and *R. (Campbell College) v. Department of Education* [1982] N.I. 123.

220 [1988] I.R. 201.

O'Hanlon J. held that even if the search warrants, issued by a Peace Commissioner under section 42 of the Larceny Act 1916 and used to search the applicant's house, were invalid, he would refuse certiorari. The reason was that both the applicants had subsequently been convicted and the quashing of the warrants would serve no useful purpose, as this would not have affected the admissibility of the evidence. And in another search warrant case, *Byrne v. Grey*,[221] Hamilton P. refused to grant relief where the sole object of the quashing order was to secure the exclusion of evidence obtained on foot of that search. Such exclusion was for the court of trial and the court should not grant relief by way of judicial review where this would be to anticipate the rulings of the trial court.

The courts have sometimes recognised in this context that it may serve a useful purpose to grant relief in order to clear an applicant's name. Thus, in *The State (Furey) v. Minister for Defence*[222] certiorari was granted to quash an ignominious dismissal from the Defence Forces. Even though the applicant's probationary period had long since expired, McCarthy J. rejected the argument that a quashing order would serve no useful purpose on the grounds that an order would allow him to vindicate his reputation.[223] However, the decision of the Supreme Court in *Barry v. Fitzpatrick*[224] suggests a different approach. Here the applicant had been remanded in custody beyond the statutory eight day period without his consent. While the Court agreed that the remands were bad in law, a majority held that as the order was spent, no useful purpose would be served by quashing same. The difference between *Furey* and *Barry* is one of degree, but the fact remains that in the latter case the Court refused to quash an order which related to the applicant's constitutional right to liberty.

Relief will not be granted if the purpose is not regarded as legitimate. This ground of refusal is more difficult to identify, but there have been cases where the courts have held that they will not facilitate a litigant who seeks relief for an unmeritorious or ulterior purpose. There are elements of such thinking in *Abenglen Properties* and also in the judgment of Henchy J. in *The State (Doyle) v. Carr*.[225] Here the applicant established that the District Court order providing for a transfer of a publican's licence on an interim basis was invalid. However, the publican had long since acquired a perfectly valid full licence and this of itself was a ground for refusing to quash an order which was now spent. However, reading between the lines of the

---

[221] [1988] I.R. 31.

[222] [1988] I.L.R.M. 89.

[223] This proposition is also illustrated by the judgment of Barron J. in *Clarke v. Hogan* [1995] 1 I.R. 310, a case where a binding over order was found to have been made in breach of the rules of natural justice. Even though the order was probably spent and was, strictly speaking, not a punishment Barron J. held that:

"if the procedure relating to the making of the order is not in accordance with the constitutional guarantee [of fair procedures] it seems to me that the court should not refuse to exercise its discretion [to quash the order]."

Likewise, in *Bane v. Garda Representative Association* [1997] 2 I.R. 449. Kelly J. quashed certain disciplinary penalties which had been imposed on them by the Association, despite the fact they had "departed from the GRA and had no intention of ever rejoining." The record of the Association nonetheless contained "findings of guilt concerning serious misconduct on their part", so that, just as in *Furey* they were entitled to an order which would vindicate their reputation.

[224] [1996] 1 I.L.R.M. 512.

[225] [1970] I.R. 69. See also, *Kilkenny v. IEFWU* [1939] Ir. Jur. Rep. 52.

judgment of Henchy J., it may be that relief was also refused because it appeared that the application was simply a strategem designed sought to discomfit a business rival. Another example is, perhaps, provided by *Re McGlinchey's Application*[226] where Lowry L.C.J. refused to quash an extradition order which was long since spent. It was plain that the quashing of the order at this remove would not provide the applicant with any legal advantage for the purpose of proceedings in Northern Ireland, but the applicant argued that this might assist him in pending criminal proceedings in the Republic. Lord Lowry, however, thought that it would be improper to grant relief as this might be thought "to interfere with proceedings in another jurisdiction." This principle was applied in a rather different context by Hutton L.C.J. in *Re Russell's Application*,[227] where mandamus compelling the prison authorities to comply with certain features of the Northern Ireland prison rules was refused, since to do so in the circumstances might have endangered prison security. Hutton L.C.J. felt that it was proper on discretionary grounds to refuse to grant this relief and that he was entitled for this purpose to have regard to the potentially harmful consequences which might flow from the granting of relief. This reasoning seems dubious, inasmuch as the exercise of discretion in this manner does not seem consistent with the rule of law.

There is some English authority for the proposition that mandamus will not be granted if the respondent has not the resources to carry out its functions or where it is doing its best to perform its functions within a limited budget.[228] But this line of authority must be viewed with care in the light of Lynch J.'s judgment in *Hoey v. Minister for Justice*[229] and that of Carroll J. in *Brady v. Cavan County Council*.[230] In the *Hoey* case, the respondents pleaded that excessive expense justified the Minister in failing to provide local authorities with sufficient resources to fulfill their statutory duties under the Courthouses (Provision and Maintenance) Act 1935, but Lynch J. was unimpressed by this:

"It is not open to the Executive by arrangements made with the local authority or by promises made to the local authority to relieve such local authority from the obligations expressly imposed upon it by the Act of 1935. . . . If the Executive wishes to limit or reduce such obligations, the Executive must introduce the appropriate legislation to the Oireachtas and must persuade the Oireachtas to enact the same."[231]

In the *Brady* case, the applicants sought mandamus to compel Cavan County Council to repair a certain road. Carroll J. first held that the local authority was under a duty to repair the road and it was common case that this road (along, indeed, with many others within the authority's functional area) was in a poor state of repair.

---

[226] [1987] 3 N.I.J.B. 1.
[227] [1990] N.I. 188.
[228] *R. v. Bristol Corporation, ex p. Hendy* [1974] 1 W.L.R. 498.
[229] [1994] 3 I.R. 329.
[230] [1997] 1 I.L.R.M. 390.
[231] [1994] 3 I.R. 329 at 343. See also *F.N. v. Minister for Education* [1995] 2 I.L.R.M. 297 at 303 (where Geoghegan J. said that the State was under constitutional obligation to provide suitable methods of treatment for the applicant unless this would be so "impractical or so prohibitively expensive as would come within any notional limit on the State's constitutional obligations").

She continued:

> "The Oireachtas having imposed and continued a statutory obligation on a
> local authority to maintain roads, must, as long as that obligation remains
> unqualified, make it possible for the local authorities to perform its statutory
> duties . . . This is not a case of telling the government how it must spend
> money. It is a case of the Oireachtas having imposed a statutory duty on local
> authorities, being required to provide means of carrying out that duty."[232]

Carroll J. refused to withhold relief on discretionary grounds:

> "It is not impossible for the County Council to carry out its statutory duties
> *vis-à-vis* the applicants. The objection raised by the county council is that the
> applicants will get precedence over other similarly disadvantaged residents
> in County Cavan. That may well be so. But the fact is that they have applied
> to the court for relief and they are entitled to it. The flood gates are a problem
> for another day unless the statutory duties are amended."[233]

However, Carroll J. granted the Council a six month stay on the order to give it time
to comply with the terms of the judgment. There are other examples of a similar
judicial attitude.

Thus, in *Hoey*[234] Lynch J. placed a stay on an order of mandamus directing the
Minister to perform her statutory duty to keep a particular court house in good repair
to enable the necessary repair work to be performed in the interim period. The
judgment of Barrington J. in *The State (Richardson) v. Governor of Mountjoy
Prison*[235] evinced a similar attitude. In this case the judge concluded that the hygiene
facilities provided in the womens' section of Mountjoy Prison were so inadequate
that the State had failed in its constitutional duty to vindicate the applicant prisoner's
right to bodily integrity. Nevertheless, the judge granted a short adjournment to
allow the recommendations for the improvement of facilities to be implemented.[236]

(v) Availability of alternate remedies

The existence of an alternative remedy does not of itself debar an application for
judicial review. The question is essentially one for the discretion of the court and
regard will be had to the adequacy of the alternate remedy[237] and to all the circum-

---

232 [1997] 1 I.L.R.M. 390 at 400.
233 *Ibid.*
234 [1994] 3 I.R. 329. See also the companion case of *Keane v. Minister for Justice* [1993] 3 I.R. 347
and *R. v. Greater London Council, ex p. Blackburn* [1976] 1 W.L.R. 550.
235 [1980] I.L.R.M. 82. See also *F.N. v. Minister for Education* [1995] 2 I.L.R.M. 297 (same principle).
236 Another interesting example is furnished by the decision of Costello J. in *The State (Sheehan) v.
Government of Ireland* [1987] I.R. 550, where he gave the Government five months to make an
order bringing into force s.60(1) of the Civil Liability Act 1961. His decision was, however, reversed
by the Supreme Court. A similar approach was taken by O'Hanlon J. in his judgment in *Delap v.
An tAire Dlí agus Cirt*, unreported, High Court, July 13, 1990, where he held that the respondents
had failed in their constitutional duty to provide an official version in Irish of the Rules of the
Superior Courts. O'Hanlon J. declined to make an immediate order of mandamus, but adjourned
the application for a four month period given that the official translation service was confident that
the Irish version would shortly be available.
237 *The State (Stanbridge) v. Mahon* [1979] I.R. 214; *The State (Glover) v. McCarthy* [1981] I.L.R.M.
47; *The State (Pheasantry Ltd) v. Donnelly* [1982] I.L.R.M. 512; *Aprile v. Naas U.D.C.*, unreported,

stances of the case.[238] In *The State (Abenglen Properties Ltd) v. Dublin Corporation*[239] the Supreme Court had appeared to lean in favour of the "exhaustion of remedies" requirement. The applicant company had sought certiorari to quash certain conditions attached by the respondent to the grant of planning permission, thus by-passing the possible appeal to An Bord Pleanála which the relevant legislation made available for them. It was said that the applicants were entitled to a ruling by the High Court as to the *vires* of these conditions and that the legality of the conditions was not within the capacity of An Bord Pleanála. While it appears that the applicant's evident desire to obtain a benefit "not contemplated by the planning code" may have coloured the court's attitude, Henchy J. also stated that where the Oireachtas had provided "a self-contained administrative scheme",[240] the courts should not intervene by way of judicial review where – as in the instant case – the statutory appellate procedure was adequate to meet the complaint on which the application was grounded.[241]

This approach has been followed in a series of cases. Thus, in *Nova Colour Graphic Supplies Ltd v. Employment Appeals Tribunal*[242] Barron J. held that as the issues arising out of an unfair dismissal case would be reheard *de novo* by the Circuit

---

High Court, November 22, 1983; *The State (Redmond) v. Delap*, unreported, High Court, July 31, 1984; *The State (Abenglen Properties Ltd) v. Dublin Corporation* [1984] I.R. 384; *The State (McInerney Properties Ltd) v. Dublin C.C.* [1985] I.L.R.M. 513; *Creedon v. Dublin Corporation* [1984] I.R. 427; *The State (Wilson) v. Neilan* [1985] I.R. 89 and *Duff v. Mangan* [1994] 1 I.L.R.M. 91.

238 Thus, in *Bane v. Garda Representative Association* [1997] 2 I.R. 449, Kelly J. quashed certain disciplinary penalties on the ground that there had been clear departures from the rule against bias. Although the applicants had not exhausted the domestic appeal mechanism provided by the Association's rules, this did not debar them from obtaining relief:

"While there may be cases where a lack of natural justice in the tribunal of first instance might be cured by a sufficiency of natural justice in the appellated tribunal, but I do not believe this to be one of them. I am of the view that the relationship between the parties was so soured that the failure on the part of the applicants to exercise their right of internal appeal was not conducted such as would debar them from obtaining an order of certiorari."

See also *The State (Litzouw) v. Johnson* [1981] I.L.R.M. 273; *Duff v. Mangan* [1994] 1 I.L.R.M. 91.

239 [1984] I.R. 384.

240 *Ibid.* at 405. The applicants had sought to have the planning permission with its oppressive conditions quashed. Once that order was secured, they then proposed to argue that the planning authority had made "no decision" within the time limits envisaged by the Local Government (Planning and Development) Act 1963 and then claim entitlement to a default planning permission under s. 26(4)(a)(iii) so that they would obtain the permission they had originally sought, shorn of any conditions. Henchy J. described this process of reasoning as "totally unacceptable": *ibid.* at 400. See the same judge's views in *The State (Collins) v. Ruane* [1984] I.R. 151, where he indicated that a person convicted in the District Court should normally appeal to the Circuit Court before applying for judicial review, even where the complaint was that natural justice had been breached at first instance.

241 See also the judgment of Costello P. in *Kenny v. Revenue Commissioners* [1996] 3 I.R. 315. Here the applicant sought to challenge a stamp duty adjudication (which was favourable to a notice party to the proceedings) made by the Revenue Commissioners by means of judicial review. The notice party was suing the applicant on foot of a promissory note and the latter claimed that the instruments in question should have attracted a far greater stamp duty. Costello P. ruled that the issue of the adjudication should more properly be raised in the existing proceedings:

". . . if a defendant is sued on instruments which he claims are liable to stamp duty and claims that they are inadmissible in evidence on the ground that they . . . have been inadequately stamped those issues should be determined in those proceedings and he should not be permitted to institute further proceedings which are not necessary to protect his interests and which will certainly delay a final adjudication on the plaintiff's claim."

242 [1987] I.R. 426. A similar view was taken by Carroll J. in *Memorex World Trade Córpn. v. Employment Appeals Tribunal* [1990] 2 I.R. 184 but *cf. Mythen v. Employment Appeals Tribunal* [1990] 1 I.R. 98, discussed below.

Court (where the applicant's appeal was pending), this procedure was more appropriate than an application for judicial review. A similar view was taken by Costello J. in *O'Connor v. Kerry County Council*,[243] where the applicant had challenged the validity of an enforcement notice served under the Local Government (Planning and Development) Act 1963. Costello J. refused the relief sought, saying that an appeal to An Bord Pleanála was a more appropriate remedy than judicial review. Essentially, the same policy was applied in a different situation in *Byrne v. Grey*[244] in which Hamilton P. refused to grant certiorari to quash an invalid search warrant on the grounds that the real object of the application was to seek to exclude certain evidence and the ruling on admissibility was best left to the court of trial. Accordingly, relief was refused on discretionary grounds. The approach adopted in *Abenglen* is also the view taken – both traditionally and in trenchantly worded recent cases – in England[245] and Northern Ireland.[246]

However the approach taken in *Abenglen* and subsequent cases has now been put in doubt as a result of the Supreme Court's decision in *P. & F. Sharpe Ltd v. Dublin City and County Manager*.[247] The applicant sought permission to build an access road on to a new dual carriageway, but the respondent indicated that, for reasons of traffic safety, he was unwilling to accede to this request. He further declined to comply with a resolution passed under section 4 of the City and County Management (Amendment) Act 1955 on the grounds that it was unlawful. The applicants sought an order of mandamus compelling the respondents to comply with the resolution. The Supreme Court refused to grant an order of mandamus on the grounds that the resolution in question was a nullity, but did grant certiorari to quash the respondent's refusal to grant permission for the access road. The respondents had argued that as the applicants had commenced an appeal to An Bord Pleanála against the decision to refuse permission, they should be confined to that remedy and certiorari should be refused on discretionary grounds. Finlay C.J. did not accept this contention:

> "The powers of An Bord Pleanála on the making of an appeal to it would be entirely confined to the consideration of the matters before it on the basis of proper planning and development of the area and it would have no jurisdiction

---

[243] [1989] I.L.R.M. 660. See also *Donegal Fuel and Supply Co. Ltd v. Londonderry Harbour Commissioners* [1994] 1 I.R. 24 (an objector to draft bye-laws is required to exhaust his statutory remedies before "seeking the aid of the court in relation to them.")

[244] [1988] I.R. 31.

[245] "Judicial review will not be granted" said May L.J. "save in the most exceptional circumstances": *R. v. Chief Constable of Merseyside Police, ex p. Calveley* [1986] Q.B. 424 at 435. In *R. v. Inland Revenue Commissioners, ex p. Preston* [1985] A.C. 835 at 862 Lord Templeman stated bluntly that "judicial review should not be granted where an alternative remedy is available". *R v. Birmingham City Council, ex p. Ferrero Ltd* [1993] 1 All E.R. 530 (where Taylor L.J. said that the High Court must ask itself in considering this question what is the real issue to be determined and whether the appeal procedure was suitable to determine it).

[246] See *Re Philip's Application*, unreported, Northern Irish High Court, January 18, 1995 (civil servant had two other perfectly suitable appellate remedies open to him to redress his claim that he was wrongly dismissed and Carswell L.J. held that even if he were of the view that judicial review would lie, relief would be refused on discretionary grounds).

[247] [1989] I.R. 701. See also *Tennyson v. Dún Laoghaire Corporation* [1991] 2 I.R. 527 (applicants who had lodged an appeal to an Bord Pleanála which was still pending were not confined to that remedy and were entitled to seek judicial review) and *Healy v. Dublin County Council*, unreported, High Court, April 29, 1993.

to consider the question of the validity, from a legal point of view, of the purported decision by the county manager. It would not, therefore, be just for the [applicants] to be deprived of their right to have that decision quashed for want of validity."[248]

This, however, is precisely the argument which had been advanced by the applicants in *Abenglen* who had sought an authoritative ruling from the High Court as to the validity (as opposed to the merits) of the conditions attached by the planning authority. By contrast, in *P. & F. Sharpe* the issue related to the reasonableness of the local authority's decision and was thus even closer to the merits than the pure *ultra vires* issue raised in *Abenglen*. In addition, the argument against granting relief in *P. & F. Sharpe* was stronger than in *Abenglen*, inasmuch as the applicants had also concurrently sought to appeal to An Bord Pleanála in addition to commencing judicial review proceedings; whereas in *Abenglen* an appeal was available, but not actually exercised. It used to be trite law that a relief would not be granted where an alternative remedy has been invoked and is pending[249] or where an applicant has deliberately pursued an alternate remedy in the belief that this course of action was in his best interests.[250] The advantages, in terms of consistency and orderly decision-making among state organs are obvious and it is suggested that this facet, at least, of the rather unconsidered finding in *Sharpe* will not be followed. One difficulty arising from *P. & F. Sharpe* is that the law as to appellate remedies is still left uncertain inasmuch as Finlay C.J. purported to distinguish (as opposed to overrule) this aspect of *Abenglen*.

The *Sharpe* approach was, nevertheless, apparently followed in *Mythen v. Employment Appeals Tribunal*[251] where Barrington J. quashed a decision of the respondents on the ground that it had misapplied the Transfer of Undertakings Directive 77/187/EEC. Barrington J. did not think that certiorari could be refused on the ground that the applicant should have appealed to the Circuit Court:

"[T]he Tribunal erred as to its jurisdiction in refusing to entertain the applicant's claim. The applicant is entitled to have the matter investigated by a judge of first instance [and this] is particularly true in a case such as the present where there is an allegation of victimisation and where the date of the agreement to sell the business, the date of the expiration of the applicant's

---

[248] *Ibid.* at 721.
[249] "Certiorari will not lie regarding a matter which is pending before an appellate court": *Duff v. Mangan* [1994] 1 I.L.R.M. 91 at 96, *per* Denham J. See also *The State (Roche) v. Delap* [1980] I.R. 170; *The State (Wilson) v. Neilan* [1985] I.R. 89. But *cf. The State (Cunningham) v. O'Floinn* [1960] I.R. 198. Note that Ord. 84, r. 20 (5) provides that where certiorari is sought to quash an order which may be the subject of an appeal, the court may adjourn the application for leave until the "appeal is determined or the time for appealing has expired".
[250] *The State (Conlon Construction Co. Ltd) v. Cork County Council*, unreported, High Court, July 31, 1975. But the mere fact that alternative remedies have been invoked does not of itself preclude an application for judicial review when the pursuit of these alternative remedies proves to be unsuccessful: *The State (Ryan) v. Revenue Commissioners* [1934] I.R. 1; *The State (Vozza) v. O'Floinn* [1957] I.R. 227; *The State (N.C.E. Ltd) v. Dublin County Council* [1979] I.L.R.M. 249 and *Duff v. Mangan* [1994] 1 I.L.R.M. 91.
[251] [1990] 1 I.R. 98.

employment and the date and circumstances of the selection of workers to be made redundant may all be interrelated and of vital importance."[252]

It is interesting to note that Barrington J. described the substantive issue raised by the applicant as "a very important and difficult point".[253] This more relaxed attitude may also be discerned in the judgment of Denham J. in *Duff v. Mangan*.[254] In these proceedings, a District Judge proceeded to convict the applicant of road traffic offences, despite the prosecution's failure to prove that the complaint had been made within time. The conviction was appealed to the Circuit Court, but when his solicitor's request for a further adjournment was refused, the appeal was struck out. While Denham J. agreed that the right of appeal to the Circuit Court provided an adequate alternate remedy and that certiorari was a discretionary remedy which the courts "will grant cautiously when there is an adequate alternative remedy which has been inadequately prosecuted", it was appropriate nonetheless to quash the conviction.[255]

A distinct point is that there is a strong, though not unanimous, line of authority that the exhaustion requirement will not now be insisted upon where the complaint relates to a breach of constitutional justice.[256] This is perhaps partly because of the particularly grievous nature of the error. On the other hand, it must be borne in mind that certiorari "is not appropriate to a routine mishap which may befall any trial" and that the correct remedy in such circumstances is by way of appeal.[257]

Upon these divergent authorities, three comments may be offered. In the first place, the two lines of authority are presumably grounded on different policy views in that the *Abenglen* line takes the view that if the applicant had a fair, full trial on the merits available to him, on appeal, then he has little to complain about. The

---

[252] *Ibid*. at 108–109. This view can scarcely be reconciled with the approach of Barron J. in *Nova Colour Graphic Supplies* nor that of Carroll J. in *Memorex*. However Lynch J. adopted similar views in *Gill v. Connellen* [1987] I.R. 541.

[253] In *C.R. v. An Bord Úchtála* [1993] 3 I.R. 535 Morris J. quashed a decision of the respondent as it had not considered the application on the merits. The judge considered that it was more appropriate to adopt this procedure and to remit the matter to the Adoption Board, rather than insisting that the applicant exhaust his statutory remedies under s. 22(5) of the Adoption Act 1952. The latter application "would of necessity involve delay and expense and, given the applicant's state of health, it is entirely undesirable". In addition, the applicant was entitled to have his application "determined and properly determined by either one of the tribunals identified in the Act, *i.e.* the Board or the court" and he was entitled "to look to each of them to properly perform its function".

[254] [1994] 1 I.L.R.M. 91. See also *McGoldrick v. An Bord Pleanála* [1997] 1 I.R. 500.

[255] One consideration underlying this decision appears to have been that this issue had arisen at the time when, in Denham J.'s words, the "question of the complaint grounding the summons was the subject of considerable litigation", so that it would have been wrong to preclude the applicant from seeking judicial review in respect of this vital legal issue.

[256] A view adopted in the following authorities: *Leary v. National Union of Vehicle Builders* [1971] Ch. 34; *Ingle v. O'Brien* (1975) 109 I.L.T.R. 6; *Moran v. Attorney General* [1976] I.R. 400; *Irish Family Planning Assoc. Ltd v. Ryan* [1979] I.R. 295; *The State (Grahame) v. Racing Board*, High Court, November 22, 1983. *A contra*, the decisions in *Memorex* and *Ruane*. In *Bane v. Garda Representative Association* [1997] 2 I.R. 449. Kelly J. acknowledged that there might be cases where a lack of natural justice at first instance might be cured by a sufficiency of natural justice in the appellate tribunal, but in the present case "the relationship between the parties was so soured" that it would have been pointless to insist on the exhaustion requirement. See further at p. 735, n. 238.

[257] *Sweeney v. Brophy* [1993] 2 I.R. 202 at 211, *per* Hederman J.; *Grennan v. Kirby* [1994] 2 I.L.R.M. 199 at 202, *per* Murphy J. These principles were applied by Laffoy J. in *Maher v. O'Donnell* [1995] 3 I.R. 530 when she said that the non-attendance of a witness whom an accused expected to attend a trial, but whose attendance he did not arrange for, which "should be sought to be remedied by way of appeal, not by way of certiorari".

alternative, *Sharpe* view is that the applicant is entitled to a proper decision at the initial stage without being put to the trauma, delay and expense of an appeal. The second comment is to suggest that a partial reconciliation may be made between the two views by focusing on the basic assumption of whether the appeal does indeed put the applicant in as good a position as he would have been in, had the initial decision been intra vires and valid. The adequacy of the alternative remedy is a matter mentioned in the introductory remarks to this Part and its significance is attested in many authorities. Something of this approach is adopted in the passage from *Mythen* just quoted. It is stated even more explicitly in *Gill v. Connellan*,[258] a case where the applicant was convicted in the District Court in circumstances where his solicitor was not afforded an adequate opportunity to make legal submissions. While Lynch J. accepted that, as a general rule, the proper course was to exhaust appellate remedies, the present case was different:

> "Neither the facts nor the law have been adequately heard in the District Court. On appeal to the Circuit Court, therefore, the appeal could hardly be said to be by way of rehearing – the case would more truly be heard for the first time. The applicant and his solicitor would be deprived of the possible advantages of having gone over the whole facts and law and of having heard the submissions and cross-examination by the prosecuting Superintendent in the District Court."[259]

The third comment, in contrast to the first two, approaches the question not from the perspective of the individual but from the general interest of the legal system in ensuring that public bodies remain within their appointed bounds. From this perspective, it would seem that the availability of an alternate remedy militates in favour of the court exercising its discretion to grant relief. Finally, it may be said that since the appellate body involved in both *Abenglen* and *Sharpe* was the same (An Bord Pleanála), these two cases seem hardly capable of being reconciled. However it may be that some consistency can be built upon a reasonable principle by considering, in the context of a given case and the alleged blemish, exactly how comprehensive and appropriate is the right of appeal which was provided.

5. *Locus Standi*

The current law on *locus standi* is currently in a state of flux. The modern tendency of the courts in common law countries is to move away from a technical approach to *locus standi* towards a rationalisation of standing requirements based on considerations relating to the general administration of justice, and the separation of powers.[260] Further proof that the current trend is away from the technical approach to standing is supplied by recent dicta to the effect that the standing rules are merely

---

[258] [1987] I.R. 541.
[259] *Ibid.* at 548.
[260] See the judgment of Henchy J. in *Cahill v. Sutton* [1980] I.R. 269. For a perceptive analysis of this case and subsequent developments, see Sherlock, "Understanding Standing: Locus Standi in Irish Constitutional Law" (1987) *Public Law* 345.

rules of practice (which may be relaxed if there are "weighty countervailing considerations" justifying a departure from the ordinary rules), and that these requirements are the same regardless of the form of the proceedings.[261] As a most practical matter, it should be noted that (apart from *Cahill v. Sutton*[262] and a few other exceptional cases [263]) in no major recent case has the applicant failed on the basis of standing, and, as shall see, there is contemporary case law in which even traces of conventional standing requirements are difficult to discern. Following the 1986 reforms, Order 84, rule 20(4) now provides that leave to apply for judicial review shall not be granted unless the applicant "has a sufficient interest in the matter to which the application relates." As noted below, the effect of a similar change in the English Rules of Court has been stated to permit an *actio popularis* (or "citizen's action") in suitable cases.[264] It seems probable (from the judicial silence on the point) that the change in the Irish rules has not had a similar, or indeed any, effect.

The traditional standing rules

At common law, the standing rules varied depending on the character of the remedies. The public law remedies of certiorari and prohibition always contained an element of the *actio popularis*, as the purpose of these remedies was not merely to avoid injustice inter partes, but also to maintain order in the legal system.[265] In theory it was thus open to anyone – even a stranger to the proceedings – to apply for certiorari or prohibition. In practice, however, relief was hardly even given to anyone other than a "person aggrieved".[266]

A stricter approach was taken in the case of the declaration and the injunction, and here standing rules reflected the fact that these remedies were derived from private law. An applicant was required to show the existence of a legal right or other

---

[261] *Cahill v. Sutton* [1980] I.R. 269 at 285, *per* Henchy J.; *The State (Lynch) v. Cooney* [1982] I.R. 33 at 369, *per* Walsh J.

[262] [1980] I.R. 269.

[263] See *Bargaintown Ltd v. Dublin Corporation* [1993] I.L.R.M. 890, described at pp. 749–750. Other examples include *Chambers v. An Bord Pleanála* [1992] 1 I.R. 134 (discussed at pp. 748–749) (where the High Court it was held that the applicant had no *locus standi*, a conclusion reversed by the Supreme Court on appeal); *Shannon v. District Judge McGuinness*, unreported, High Court, March 20, 1997 (prosecution witnesses had no *locus standi* to quash the dismissal of a summons brought by the Director of Public Prosecutions) and *Riordan v. An Taoiseach*, unreported, High Court, November 14, 1997 (discussed at p. 753, n. 323) (plaintiff had no standing to impugn the appointment of judges to tribunals and commissions, although this conclusion may have been overtaken by the Supreme Court's decision in the separate case of *Riordan v. An Tánaiste*, unreported, November 28, 1997).

[264] Wade and Forsyth, *Administrative Law* (1994), p. 712.

[265] Yardley, "Certiorari and the Problem of Locus Standi" (1955) 71 L.Q.R. 388; "Prohibition and Mandamus and the Problem of Locus Standi" (1957) 73 L.Q.R. 534. The *locus standi* requirements for mandamus have always been somewhat stricter than in the case of the other public law remedies: *R. v. Lewisham Guardians* [1897] 1 Q.B. 498 (existence of specific legal right); *R. (I.U.D.W.C.) v. Rathmines U.D.C.* [1928] I.R. 260 (where Hanna J. said that an applicant must demonstrate that a "legal right" was infringed and where O'Byrne J. said that a "specific interest in performance of duty" was required.). But for a less restrictive approach, see *The State (Modern Homes (Ire.) Ltd) v. Dublin Corporation* [1953] I.R. 202; *The State (A.C.C. Ltd) v. Navan U.D.C.*, unreported, High Court, February 22, 1980.

[266] In cases such as *The State (Kerry County Council) v. Minister for Local Government* [1933] I.R. 517; *The State (Doyle) v. Carr* [1970] I.R. 87 and *The State (Toft) v. Galway Corporation* [1981] I.L.R.M. 439, certiorari was refused to applicants who were not "persons aggrieved".

cognisable interest which was affected or threatened.[267] An example of this restrictive approach is provided by *Irish Permanent Building Society Ltd v. Caldwell (No. 1)*,[268] where the plaintiffs had challenged the decision of the Registrar of Building Societies to register a new building society. The defendants brought a motion seeking to have the plaintiffs' claim struck out on the grounds that they had not claimed that they suffered or would suffer peculiar injury as a result of this allegedly invalid decision. Although Keane J. refused to strike out the claim on the grounds that the matter deserved "full and unhurried consideration", he did hint strongly that the infringement, or threatened infringement, of some legal right or interest was a prerequisite in declaratory proceedings of this nature.[269]

However the law, in respect of both sets of remedies, has long moved away from the stricter, technical requirement of a legal right and towards the notion that the applicant should have suffered some prejudice going beyond that felt by most other members of the community. That this is so was stated in the major Supreme Court case of *Cahill v. Sutton*,[270] which confirmed and articulated an existing trend, rather than marking a new departure.

Preliminary points

However, before returning to explore this central issue further, we should attempt to clear away three preliminary points. In the first place, whatever about the historical position set out in the previous paragraph, the standing requirements are now the same whether the court is dealing with the three remedies which originated on the State side or the two which originated in the Courts of Equity. That this is so had been accepted even before the new system was introduced.[271] It has surely been put beyond any doubt by the advent of the new regime. The policy of the new Rules is to achieve uniformity between the remedies. This is confirmed by the fact that Order 84, rule 20(4) (which provides that the court "shall not grant leave unless it considers that the applicant has a sufficient interest in the matter") applies to all of the remedies, irrespective of the form of the proceedings. This must mean that the *locus standi* requirements do not vary from remedy to remedy.

Secondly, it has now been stated judicially on several occasions, that the standing requirements are the same, even though the application for judicial review involves the constitutionality of a law or an executive or administrative action, rather than merely the vires of an administrative action with no such constitutional issues.[272]

---

267 *Weir v. Fermanagh C.C.* [1913] 1 I.R. 193; *Gregory v. Camden L.B.C.* [1966] 1 W.L.R. 899; *Gouriet v. U.P.O.W.* [1978] A.C. 435.

268 [1979] I.L.R.M. 273. But *cf. Martin v. Dublin Corporation*, unreported, High Court, November 14, 1977.

269 The plaintiffs subsequently amended their pleadings to include a claim that they had suffered loss and damage: see *Irish Permanent Building Society v. Caldwell (No. 2)* [1981] I.L.R.M. 242. Keane J.'s view must now be taken to have been superseded by the judgment of the Supreme Court in *Society for the Protection of Unborn Children (Ire.) Ltd v. Coogan* [1989] I.R. 734.

270 [1980] I.R. 269.

271 See, *e.g. The State (Lynch) v. Cooney* [1982] I.R. 337 at 369, *per* Walsh J. See also, *Irish Permanent Building Society v. Caldwell (No. 2)* [1981] I.L.R.M. 242.

272 *The State (Sheehan) v. Government of Ireland* [1987] I.R. 550 at 557, *per* Costello J. (who thought that it was "to be expected" that the test in each case "should be formulated somewhat differently"); *Duggan v. An Taoiseach* [1989] I.L.R.M. 710 at 725, *per* Hamilton P. However, *Society for the*

It is significant that whereas *Cahill v. Sutton* was a case involving the constitutionality of a law, yet the principle it laid down has been widely followed in cases falling within each of the other two categories.

The third and final preliminary point is the fact that the issue of standing is distinct from that of the merits or strength of an applicant's case. This orthodoxy would hardly be worth stating were it not for the fact that in Britain the House of Lords has seized upon the analogous changes to Order 84 as a ground for rejecting the traditional view: *Inland Revenue Commissioners v. National Federation of Self-Employed and Small Businesses Ltd.*[273] This case concerned an application for judicial review of the respondent's decision to grant an amnesty to a group of printing workers who for many years had defrauded the Inland Revenue and evaded tax. The House of Lords ruled that it could not be shown that the Revenue had acted *ultra vires* in granting such an amnesty, and, accordingly, it could not be said that the Federation had a "sufficient interest" in the application. If, however, there were grounds for thinking that the Revenue had acted improperly, then the Federation would have had standing to complain. The approach taken in this case, or, at any rate, in the more radical judgments of Lords Diplock and Scarman, appears to merge the hitherto distinct concepts of standing and merits by creating a two-stage process. At the leave stage, it is only the hopeless or meddlesome applicants who may be rejected on this ground. At the substantive hearing, the issue of standing has to be considered in the light of the nature of the powers and duties of the public authority and the character of the alleged illegality. In addition, the House of Lords – or some members thereof – seems to have gone so far as to hold that "the more important the issue and the stronger the merits of the application, the more ready will the courts be to grant leave notwithstanding the limited personal involvement of the individual".[274]

There is no reason to expect the Irish courts to draw upon Order 84, (which does expressly require "a sufficient interest") in order to follow this rather surprising English authority.[275] Every case has treated the issue of standing independently

---

Protection of Unborn Children (Ireland) Ltd v. Coogan [1989] I.R. 734 both Finlay C.J. (at 742) and Walsh J. (at 746) gives some cause to suggest that the standing requirements may be stricter where it is a law, rather than an administrative or executive action, whose constitutionality is at stake. Humphreys and O'Dowd, "Locus Standi to Enforce the Constitution" (1990) 3 I.L.T. 14 at 15 suggest that the fact that the courts cannot fill the statutory vacuum created by the invalidation of legislation argues in favour of stricter standing rules in cases challenging the constitutionality of legislation.

[273] [1982] A.C. 617. The "broad and flexible" approach to standing suggested by this case (see de Smith, Woolf and Jowell, *op. cit.*, above, n.44 p. 117) has been followed in the majority of subsequent English decisions. See, *e.g. R v. Department of Transport, ex p. Presvac Engineering Ltd* (1992) 4 Admin L.R. 121 (rival company has standing to challenge validity of statutory certificate granted to competitor); *R v. General Council of the Bar ex p. Percival* [1991] 1 Q.B. 212 (complainant regarding alleged unprofessional conduct has standing to seek judicial review re Bar Council inquiry); *R v. HM Inspectorate of Pollution, ex p. Greenpeace Ltd (No. 2)* [1994] 4 All E.R. 239; *R v. Secretary of State of Foreign Affairs, ex p. World Development Movement Ltd* [1995] 1 W.L.R. 386 (bona fide pressure groups have standing). But *cf. Holmes v. Checkland, The Times,* April 15, 1987; *R v. Secretary of State for the Environment ex p. Rose Theatre Ltd* [1990] 1 Q.B. 504. In the latter case Schiemann J. stated that it was not the function of the courts "to be there for every individual who was interested in having the legality of an administrative decision litigated".

[274] de Smith, Woolf and Jowell, *op. cit.*, above, n.44 p. 118.

[275] But *cf.* the comments of Costello P. in *Kenny v. Revenue Commissioners* [1996] 3 I.R. 315 where he said (at 318) that a taxpayer has "no locus standi to challenge administrative decisions, including adjudications, made by the Revenue Commissioners relating to the duties and tax payable by another

from the merits.[276] In this jurisdiction (the position is, as we shall see, less clear) a standing rule is retained and in *Cahill*, the reasoning was based on the need to safeguard the proper administration of justice (against the officious man of straw); to prevent the abuse of the power of judicial review; and to uphold the principle of the separation of powers. In addition, it was said in *Cahill* that a case brought by a litigant with no direct interest would tend to lack in Henchy J.'s words "the force and urgency of reality".[277] It has also been said that a standing rule is "constitutionally inspired but not constitutionally compelled".[278] It is among a package of devices which enable a judge to refuse to address the merits of a constitutional claim. At base then, the content of a standing rule depends upon a judge's view of the proper place of judicial review in a constitutional policy.

Cahill v. Sutton

The decision of the Supreme Court in *Cahill v. Sutton* was the first modern Irish case thoroughly to address the issue of *locus standi*. It involved a medical negligence claim in which the plaintiff was time barred under the Statute of Limitations 1957, section 11(2)(b). The plaintiff challenged the section on the ground that it contained no exception to protect the right to litigate of an injured person who had only become aware of the facts on which his claim was based after the period of limitation had expired. The essential point for present purposes was that the plaintiff was not herself such a person since at all material times she was aware of all the facts necessary to ground her claim. In sum, said Henchy J.:

> "the plaintiff is seeking to be allowed to conjure up, invoke and champion the putative constitutional rights of a hypothetical third party, so that the provisions of s.11, subs. 2(b), may be declared unconstitutional on the basis of that constitutional jus tertii – thus allowing the plaintiff to march through the resulting gap in the statute."[279]

Only two of the five unanimous judges who heard *Cahill* gave substantive judgments. The tenor of O'Higgins C.J.'s fairly brief judgment and Henchy J.'s judgment are in accord. However, as Henchy J. gave the more elaborate consideration to the standing topic, which was the main point, it is his treatment which is generally

---

taxpayer". This may be true so far as it goes, but it could scarcely be suggested that a taxpayer has no standing to challenge unfair preferential treatment accorded by the Revenue Commissioners to another taxpayer. This, it will be recalled, was the gravamen of the complaint in the *Self-Employed* case.

276 *Cahill v. Sutton* 1980] I.R. 269; *The State (Lynch) v. Cooney* [1982] I.R. 337 and *Norris v. Attorney General* [1984] I.R. 36. But note that in *Lynch* Walsh J. said (at 369):
  "[Rules of standing] must be flexible so as to be individually applicable to the particular facts of any given case. Such a question cannot be regarded as a preliminary point unless there is an admission of all the facts necessary to decide the issue. In the absence of any admission in any case where the point is raised, it is necessary for the court to enter into a sufficient examination of the facts and, having heard them, to decide whether or not a sufficient interest has been established."

277 [1980] I.R. 269 at 282–283. Though note that in *Norris v. Attorney General* [1984] I.R. 36 at 91 McCarthy J. remarked apropos of what might be termed the "busybody" basis of *Cahill* "from 1937–1980, I doubt if the court records reveal many, or even any, instances of such officious interference".

278 Sherlock, *loc. cit.*, pp. 266–269, where these ideas are developed.

279 [1980] I.R. 269 at 280.

regarded as the more authoritative. In holding that Ms. Cahill had no standing to make the only argument which could assist her, Henchy J. stated:

> "[An applicant] must show that the impact of the impugned law on his personal situation discloses an injury or prejudice which he has either suffered or is in imminent danger of suffering.
>
> This rule, however, being but a rule of practice must, like all such rules, be subject to expansion, exception or qualification when the justice of the case so requires. Since the paramount consideration in the exercise of the jurisdiction of the Courts to review legislation in the light of the Constitution is to ensure that persons entitled to the benefit of a constitutional right will not be prejudiced through being wrongfully deprived of it, there will be cases where the want of the normal locus standi on the part of the person questioning the constitutionality of the statute may be overlooked if, in the circumstances of the case, there is a transcendent need to assert against the statute the constitutional provision that has been invoked. For example, while the challenger may lack the personal standing normally required, those prejudicially affected by the impugned statute may not be in a position to assert adequately, or in time, their constitutional rights. In such a case the court might decide to ignore the want of normal personal standing on the part of the litigant before it. Likewise, the absence of a prejudice or injury peculiar to the challenger might be overlooked, in the discretion of the court, if the impugned provision is directed at or operable against a grouping which includes the challenger, or with whom the challenger may be said to have a common interest – particularly in cases where, because of the nature of the subject-matter, it is difficult to segregate those affected from those not affected by the challenged provision."[280]

Two comments may be made on this passage. First, what may be taken as the general rule, which is contained in the first paragraph, describes the plaintiff's title to sue as "injury or prejudice." Later in the judgment, it was said that he must "stand in real or imminent danger of being adversely affected." These formulations are, of course, much broader than the traditional standard (at any rate for the remedies of declaration or injunction). Secondly, Henchy J. acknowledged that the rule was flexible and embraced a number of exceptions "when the justice of the case so requires." Given the entire range of public cases which the standing rule must accommodate, it is inevitable that the rule should be broad and flexible.[281]

Post-Cahill cases

The question is: how has *Cahill* fared in subsequent cases? It is certainly true that it has been quoted with approval in almost every case on standing.[282] This formal

---

[280] *Ibid.* at 284–285. In *Tuohy v. Courtney* [1994] 3 I.R. 1 at 42 a case with facts roughly similar to *Cahill v. Sutton* (save that the plaintiff in that case did not attempt to raise a *jus tertii*) the Supreme Court held that, in the words of Finlay C.J., there was "clear evidence" of the existence of the plaintiff's *locus standi*.

[281] *The State (Lynch) v. Cooney* [1982] I.R. 337 at 369, *per* Walsh J.

[282] A notable exception being *Norris v. Attorney General* [1984] I.R. 36 at 91 where McCarthy J. described *Cahill* as a case "he was bound reluctantly to follow".

obeisance, of course, does not necessarily mean that it has been influential upon later judgments. In the post-*Cahill* era, the few cases in which the rules of standing have prevented an issue from being examined on the merits are cases in which the claim may be regarded as opportunist and unmeritorious.[283] Of course, this is no bad thing. But it does make it difficult to assess the impact of *Cahill*. It is suggested, nevertheless, that the following review of recent case law in this area demonstrates that (with the possible exception of *ESB v. Gormley*[284]) the cases accord reasonably well with the flexible *Cahill* principles.

The first significant decision after *Cahill* was *The State (Lynch) v. Cooney*[285] in which the question of *locus standi* arose in the context of a ministerial ban made under the provisions of section 31 of the Broadcasting (Authority) Act 1960. The ministerial order purported to prevent Radio Telefís Éireann from broadcasting a party political broadcast on behalf of Sinn Féin which, under RTÉ's guidelines, agreed with all the major parties, for the allocation of party political broadcasts, was entitled to one such broadcast. The Supreme Court was unanimously of the view that the organisation's representatives had sufficient interest to challenge the validity of the ban in certiorari proceedings. As Walsh J. put it, irrespective of whether the applicants had a "right" or a mere "privilege", they had suffered a loss and had been affected in a material way. According to O'Higgins C.J.:

> "In such circumstances the respondent and his party were deprived of a benefit lawfully accorded to them in the first instance and, in my view, were entitled to complain if the deprivation were unlawful."[286]

The more difficult question, of course, would have been if the applicant had not been a member of the political party affected but a mere voter, arguing that he had been unlawfully denied his opportunity to hear all points of view in the forthcoming election. Case law reviewed later[287] suggests – though almost invariably with the result that the plaintiff had standing – that such a claim would not have been turned away simply on the ground that the applicant was no worse off than the other two million or so electors, provided the application was bona fide and there was no other more obvious plaintiff. As against this, however, the point may be made that there would have been more obvious plaintiffs in the person of party officials or members.

The majority of the subsequent decisions have involved a straightforward application of the *Cahill* principle. In *The State (King) v. Minister for Justice*[288] (which

---

283   See Sherlock, *loc. cit.*, p. 264.

284   [1985] I.R. 129.

285   [1982] I.R. 337.

286   *Ibid.* at 362–363.

287   As suggested by the judgments in cases such as *Crotty v. An Taoiseach* [1987] I.R. 713; *Society for the Protection of Unborn Children (Ireland) Ltd v. Coogan* [1989] I.R. 734; *McGimpsey v. Ireland* [1990] 1 I.R. 110; *Iarnród Éireann v. Ireland* [1995] 2 I.L.R.M. 161 and *McKenna v. An Taoiseach* [1995] 2 I.R. 10.

288   [1984] I.R. 169. In both *Keane v. Minister for Justice* [1994] 3 I.R. 329 and *Hoey v. Minister for Justice* [1994] 3 I.R. 329 local solicitors successfully applied for orders of mandamus compelling the Minister to exercise her statutory powers under the 1935 Act to repair certain courthouses, but no issue of *locus standi* arose in either case. Note that in *Brennan v. Minister for Justice* [1995] 1 I.R. 612, Geoghegan J. held that the applicant District Judge had sufficient *locus standi* to challenge the validity of the exercise by the Minister of her statutory powers under the Criminal Justice Act

actually pre-dates *Cahill*) the applicants obtained an order of mandamus commanding the Minister to exercise his statutory powers, under the Courthouses (Provision and Maintenance) Act 1935 to renew and repair Waterford Courthouse. Rather surprisingly, Doyle J. rejected the argument that the applicants (one of whom was President of the Waterford Law Society) had standing as representatives of the Society which Doyle J. noted was "an unincorporated body whose membership includes most, if not all, of the solicitors practising in the city and county of Waterford". However, Doyle J. went on to hold that the applicants had standing in their own right:

> "Both gentlemen carry on an extensive practice in the Waterford court and may, therefore, be regarded as having a particular personal interest in the provision of proper court accommodation to enable them to earn their livelihood."[289]

In *Ahern v. Kerry County Council*[290] Blayney J. held that the applicant had standing in his capacity as a member of the Council to challenge the validity of a resolution to adopt estimates. Here, perhaps, it was assumed that, absent some special qualfication – such as membership of the Council or being a ratepayer[291] – an ordinary private individual would lack the necessary locus standi to challenge the validity of estimates adopted by the County Council.[292]

In *The State (Sheehan) v. Government of Ireland*[293] the applicant sought an order compelling the Government to bring into force section 60(1) of the Civil Liability Act 1961 which abolishes the non-feasance rule with prospective effect. Mr. Sheehan had been injured by tripping on a pavement and, anticipating that his claim might be defeated by the non-feasance rule, commenced mandamus proceedings. His standing to do so was strenuously contested by the respondents, on the basis that as the section only has prospective force, it could avail the applicant nothing even if it were brought into effect.

1951 whereby she commuted certain fines and punishments which imposed had been imposed by the respondent in his judicial capacity.

[289] *Ibid.* at 175. As far as the wider issue concerning the right of organisations and consumer groups to bring legal proceedings on behalf of its members, see Cousins, "The Protection of Collective Rights before the Irish Courts" (1993) 14 I.L.T. 110 and 134.

[290] [1988] I.L.R.M. 392. Blayney J. followed the decision of the Northern Irish Court of Appeal in *Re Cooke's Application* [1986] N.I. 242.

[291] Some difficulty in connection with the category of ratepayer standing arises from the fact that it is now only business rates which are actually levied: see pp. 211–213. However, the technique by which domestic rates were abolished is that the rating authority "shall make an allowance to the person so rated by them and such allowance shall equal in amount the rate in the pound and accordingly the rate so made shall be abated": Local Government (Financial Provisions) Act 1978, s. 3(1). S. 17 further provides that:

"A person shall not be regarded as not being a ratepayer within the meaning, or for the purposes, of any enactment by reason only of the making to him of an allowance under this Act."

This oblique technique which creates non-rate paying rate payers has been regarded as necessary to retain rateable valuations for such secondary purposes as determining Circuit Court jurisdiction or rate-payer standing. Perhaps the better solution would have been to allow any local residents standing in an action against his or her local authority, where they have a genuine interest in the outcome and not simply because they happen to be ratepayers: see the comments of Morris J. in *Bargaintown Ltd v. Dublin Corporation* [1993] I.L.R.M. 890 at 895. *Cf.* the words of Lord Denning in *R. v. Greater London Council, ex p. Blackburn* [1976] 1 W.L.R. 550.

[292] Another example of this approach is afforded by the decision of Hamilton P. in *Duggan v. An Taoiseach* [1989] I.L.R.M. 710 at 724–725, an authority which is analysed in the 2nd edition of this book at pp. 617–618.

[293] [1987] I.R. 550.

In the High Court, Costello J. applied the standard test in mandamus proceedings: has it been established that the applicant suffered prejudice to an extent greater than the members of the public? (The judge considered that while this test was "formulated somewhat differently" than the *Cahill v. Sutton* principles, it was "not very different".)[294] Costello J. went on to hold that the applicant had satisfied this test, despite the fact that the making of the order would not relieve the prejudice in his own case:

> "He has an interest in the operation of the Act which is not just that which all citizens have in the enforcement of the law. He is an aggrieved citizen who may have suffered the loss of a substantial amount of money due to the Government's failure to carry out its duties. It seems to me that this gives him a special interest in the matter, and that the court's rules of standing should not shut out a complainant with such an interest from asking that the court's supervisory functions be exercised. Secondly, it was pointed out that should Mr. Sheehan be able to establish that the Corporation has been guilty of non-feasance but not of misfeasance with the result that his claim against the Corporation fails, then an action for damages would lie against the Government for its failure to carry out its statutory function. Whilst expressing no concluded view on the force of this contention, it is obviously not a frivolous or insubstantial one. It is clear therefore that Mr. Sheehan has an interest (which other members of the public do not share) . . .[295]

One may characterise these two points by saying, of the first, that it amounts to extending the law somewhat by recognising that the applicant had a "special interest", albeit not in the conventional material sense, but because he had a legitimate reason for being aggrieved, namely, the fact that he could not be compensated for his injuries. The second reason, although for some reason offered more tentatively by Costello J., is well in line with the present law. It amounts to saying that the applicant has an interest, namely that success might facilitate him in bringing an action for breach of statutory duty.

On appeal, a majority of the Supreme Court rejected the applicant's case on other grounds. However, McCarthy J. in his dissent agreed with Costello J.'s conclusion on *locus standi*, as otherwise no private individual would have had standing to maintain the proceedings.[296] This may be regarded as a reason either for according standing to the applicant on more or less the same basis as the exceptional constitutional cases referred to later, or more logically, for modifying the strict common

---

[294] *Ibid.* at 557. Costello J. added that:
"[T]he test in *Cahill v. Sutton* (where prejudice to the personal situation of the plaintiff would be sufficient) is not very different to that in *The State (Modern Homes (Ire.) Ltd v. Dublin Corporation* (in which prejudice to an extent greater than to the members of the public was required) and I think that I am entitled to follow the earlier judgment and consider whether the [applicant] herein has a `sufficient interest' in the performance by the Government of its duty under the Act of 1961 to justify his claim in these proceedings."

[295] *Ibid.* at 558. Costello J. also cautioned that:
". . . our courts should now look with considerable caution on earlier [*sc.* pre-*National Federation of Self-Employed and Small Businesses*] authorities which have now been discarded by the House of Lords and which may have formed the basis of earlier decisions in this country."

[296] On appeal, Henchy J. did observe (at 560), however, that the applicant was "lacking in that special interest in the outcome of the mandamus proceedings." This comment might be thought to imply that Costello J. was wrong to hold that the applicant had the necessary standing to maintain the proceedings.

law rules as to the need for relator proceedings, as has now occurred in *Society for the Protection of Unborn Children (Ireland) Ltd v. Coogan*.[297]

The decision of the Supreme Court in *E.S.B. v. Gormley*[298] represents a more problematic application of the principles in *Cahill v. Sutton*. Here the defendant was allowed to challenge the validity of a planning permission on the grounds that the advertisement indicating an intention to apply for permission (which is required by section 26(1) of the Local Government (Planning and Development) Act 1963), was defective. It had been argued that as the defendant had acquired the lands after the planning permission had been granted, she was not prejudiced or affected by this irregularity.

This argument was accepted by Carroll J. in the High Court, but rejected in the Supreme Court, where Finlay C.J. stated:

> "[*locus standi*] does not depend upon the person making such challenge being able to demonstrate that the non-compliance directly affected him or her. Such a challenge can properly be made by any person who is affected by the permission granted and if made, and if non-compliance is established, then the permission is invalid not by reason of prejudice or disadvantage to the person challenging it but by reason of a want of power and jurisdiction in the planning authority to exercise their right of granting or refusing permission."[299]

There are parts of this passage (notably the first sentence and the second part of the second sentence) which appear to contradict *Cahill* and to justify the summary in the head note in the *Irish Reports*: "as a member of the public who was affected by the planning permission granted, the defendant was entitled to challenge the validity of that permission". However, perhaps it is more correct to read this passage in the light of the facts of the case, namely that Mrs Gormley was peculiarly affected by the fact that she had bought the land from P., who was the land-owner at the time the advertisement appeared. Plainly, even on the narrowest view, P. would have had standing as the land-owner. Had the application for planning permission been properly advertised, P. might have objected and permission not been granted. This would have been very much in the defendant's interest and, accordingly, Mrs Gormley as his successor in title was entitled to complain that the application had not been properly advertised. Even in private law, there are many situations in which a land-owner is affected by burdens or benefits, which were annexed to the land during the time of his predecessor in title, and it does not seem an unreasonable extension of *Cahill* to adopt a similar view in public law.

The concept of prejudice

Two other contemporary decisions illustrate the concept of prejudice as it relates to *locus standi*. In *Chambers v. An Bord Pleanála*[300] the applicant was a member

---

[297] [1989] I.R. 734. For an interesting account of this case, see Humphreys and O'Dowd, "Locus Standi to Enforce the Constitution" (1990) 8 I.L.T. 14.
[298] [1985] I.R. 129.
[299] *Ibid*. at 157.
[300] [1992] 1 I.R. 134.

of an environmental pressure group that had opposed the granting of planning permission for the erection of a pharmaceutical manufacturing facility. When permission was granted following an oral hearing before An Bord Pleanála, the plaintiffs (who were husband and wife) sought to set aside that decision. In the High Court, Lavan J. held that the plaintiffs lacked *locus standi* for this purpose, on the particular and rather novel ground that they had not actually participated as an objector at an earlier stage. The Supreme Court took a different view, with Egan J. holding that it was reasonable for the plaintiffs to allow the pressure group (of which they were members) to deal with the oral hearing. There was no question but that the plaintiffs did have standing in their own right. One of the plaintiffs was an asthmatic, both lived near the proposed site and both had indirectly participated in the appeal via membership of the pressure group in question. This conclusion would seem plainly in line with *Cahill v. Sutton*. Possibly different considerations would arise had the plaintiffs lived in a different part of the State remote from the proposed factory and opposed the decision for purely ideological reasons.[301] Although the Court did not have to address this wider issue, the rationale underlying the exceptional constitutional cases which afford a generous degree of standing to such public-spirited "ideological" plaintffs would seem no less applicable to such a case, especially if there was no other obvious plaintiff at hand who could show that he personally would suffer in a special way from the proposed development.

The interesting case of *Bargaintown Ltd v. Dublin Corporation*[302] raises novel standing questions. Here the applicant held the sub-lease of certain premises from Mr Foster. Mr Foster in turn held the head-lease in the premises from the respondents and when the head lease expired, he applied to the Circuit Court for a reversionary lease. Although the respondents were well aware of the applicant's desire to buy out the premises, the proceedings were compromised with an agreement to sell the fee simple to Foster. The applicant then sought to challenge this disposal of the property on the ground, in effect, that since the respondent had failed to consult with it prior to completing the sale, it had acted unreasonably in law in failing to seek the highest possible purchase price for the property.

It is noteworthy that Morris J. first rejected the suggestion that the applicant had standing simply *qua* ratepayer, a view which represents long-established law, at any rate in Britain.[303] Nor did he accept that, on the facts, it was aggrieved by the decision not to consider it as a potential buyer:

"On my understanding of the law, this does not bring the applicant sufficiently far so as to confer on it a sufficient interest to maintain these proceedings. It does not establish an 'injury or prejudice' as stated in *Cahill v. Sutton*. It does

---

[301] Although the plaintiffs' opposition in *Chambers* seems to have been at least partly motivated by such concerns.

[302] [1993] I.L.R.M. 890.

[303] See de Smith, Woolf and Jowell, *op. cit.*, above, n.44 pp.133–34 and p. 746, n.291, Morris J. stated at (895):
"The applicant comes before the court in its capacity as a ratepayer who has a financial interest in the manner in which the Corporation conducts its affairs in relation to the disposal of the property. This would leave the applicant in no better position than many thousands of thousands of business houses in the city and if this were its only claim to be entitled to bring these proceedings, then in my view it would clearly fail."

not establish that any interest, which it might have, had been adversely affected by the sale, as referred to in *Duggan v. An Taoiseach*, nor does it establish that it has or may suffer a substantial amount of money as referred to in *The State (Sheehan) v. Government of Ireland*. The furthest that the applicant can go in this case is to establish that it is bitterly disappointed by the fact that the Corporation failed to give it an opportunity to make a bid for the fee simple. The reality of the position is that the applicant is now in no worse position than it was before the sale of the fee simple to the notice party. It is in precisely the same position."[304]

With its implicit assumption that *locus standi* requires a pre-existing legal interest, this case appears to represent an unsupportable throw-back to an earlier era. It is probable, however, that the judge was influenced, at some level, by the fact that the local authority was exercising not a statutory power, but rather its rights *qua* private land-owner.[305]

These fears have been ameliorated by the same judge's later decision in *Lancefort Ltd v. An Bord Pleanála*.[306] In this case Morris J. had to consider whether a limited company which had been formed by a group of dedicated conservationists had *locus standi* to challenge a decision to grant planning permission. Although it had been argued that as the company (which had limited assets) had only been formed after the date of the grant of the permission in order to afford "the true applicants a shield against an award of costs", Morris J. was clearly impressed by the bona fides of the company's promoters.[307] He proceeded to hold that the applicant company did have the requisite standing and that the present case fell within one of the exceptions to *Cahill v. Sutton:*

> "In the present case a decision has been taken by a number of conscientious concerned persons to seek the protection of the court through a limited company . . . To rule that the company had no *locus standi* would have the effect of depriving these persons of access to the courts. I am of the view that they have demonstrated their *bona fide* interest in these proceedings by the work and effort which they have given in the past to this project . . . I think that it would be improper to rely upon the rule of *locus standi* to deprive them of the opportunity of access to the courts and I believe that there are, in the words of Henchy J., [in *Cahill v. Sutton*] weighty countervailing considerations justifying the departure from the rule."[308]

---

[304] [1993] I.L.R.M. 890 at 896.
[305] For this distinction, see pp. 773–776.
[306] [1997] 2 I.L.R.M. 508.
[307] Morris J. described them (at 513) as:
". . . genuinely and honestly concerned and have devoted significant effort in the past for the protection of listed and historical buildings and have a legitimate concern for the historical building heritage of Dublin and throughout the country . . . [T]his group has worked tirelessly and frequently without pay towards this end. Mr. Smith, a prominent member of An Taisce . . . was the person to whom An Taisce delegated the function of opposing this development. I do not accept that Mr. Smith or any of his associates fall within the category of persons contemplated by Henchy J. in *Cahill v. Sutton* [1980] I.R. 269 which he described at p. 284 as 'the crank, the obstructionist, the meddlesome, the perverse [and] the officious man of straw,'"
[308] *Ibid.* at 515–516.

This judgment clearly takes a liberal view of standing requirements and provides considerable support for bona fide interest groups who wish to impugn administrative decisions of concern to them. To that extent, it is in harmony with the preponderance of authority which either expressly or by implication have allowed standing in the case of corporate bodies.[309]

Exceptional constitutional cases

We must now turn to a series of major constitutional cases which have been regarded as constituting special cases justifying an exception to the *Cahill* principles. This attitude was confirmed by the Supreme Court in *Society for the Protection of Unborn Children (Ireland) Ltd v. Coogan*.[310] Here the plaintiff Society sought an injunction restraining the dissemination of a student handbook containing information on abortion services, claiming that this booklet infringed Article 40.3.3°. Finlay C.J. first observed that the plaintiffs merely sought to restrain what it claimed was a threatened breach of the Constitution by the defendants. The test in such a case was:

> "[T]hat of a bona fide concern and interest, interest being used in the sense of proximity or an objective interest. To ascertain whether such bona fide concern and interest exist in a particular case it is of special importance to consider the nature of the constitutional right sought to be protected. In this case, the right is the right to life of an unborn child in its mother's womb. The threat to that constitutional right which it is sought to avoid is the death of the child. In respect of such a threat, there can never be a victim or potential victim who can sue."[311]

In *Cahill*, Henchy J. had stated that, by way of exception to the general rule, a litigant could have standing even though "he lack[ed] the personal standing normally required if those prejudicially affected by the impugned statute [are] not in a position to assert adequately their constitutional rights."[312] As observed by the Supreme Court in *Coogan*; what clearer case could be found of a "being" not capable of asserting its constitutional right than that of a foetus whose mother was contemplating an abortion? As Walsh J. said:

---

[309] See, *e.g. Society of Protection of Unborn Children (Ire.) Ltd v. Grogan* [1989] I.R. 734; *Iarnród Éireann v. Ireland* [1996] 3 I.R. 321; *East Wicklow Community Conservation Ltd v. Wicklow County Council* [1996] 3 I.R. 175 (although the standing issue did not feature in the latter case). *Malahide Community Council Ltd v. Fingal County Council* [1997] 3 I.R. 383 is the only case where a discordant note was struck. Here Lynch J. said that he could not see how a limited company "lacking the five senses of human persons" could be affected by planning decisions, "except by increasing of diminishing its asset value if it owns lands or buildings favourably or unfavourably affected by such decisions". Thus, "in the absence of economic interests it seems to me that a limited company is not an appropriate body to litigate matters arising from the [Planning] Acts". Lynch J.'s comments were purely *obiter* and the fact that another member of the three-judge Supreme Court – Hamilton C.J. – was prompted expressly to reserve his position on this question suggests that this restrictive view of corporate and interest-group standing will not find a ready acceptance.

[310] [1989] I.R. 734.

[311] *Ibid.* at 742.

[312] [1980] I.R. 269. These cases should be regarded as qualifying the primary *Cahill v. Sutton* rules, rather than as retreating from them. As Walsh J. remarked in *Coogan* ([1989] I.R. 734 at 746) the decision in *Cahill* is not "of such sweeping application as is sometimes thought."

"When the unborn life is threatened by the parent or parents with the encouragement or assistance of other persons, there is an obvious need for somebody to assert the interest of the unborn. In the present case the plaintiffs have shown a genuine interest in the protection of unborn life and it was reasonable on their part to raise the issue as representing the interest of unborn lives."[313]

In *Crotty v. An Taoiseach*,[314] where the plaintiff had challenged the validity of the ratification of the Single European Act, the Supreme Court found for him on the standing issue. If the Single European Act were to be ratified, it would affect every citizen and, accordingly, the plaintiff had *locus standi* "to challenge the Act notwithstanding his failure to prove the threat of any special injury or prejudice to him, as distinct from any other citizen, arising from the Act".[315] This approach was followed by Barrington J. in the High Court in *McGimpsey v. Ireland*,[316] where the constitutionality of the Anglo-Irish Agreement was at issue. He found that the plaintiffs had standing to challenge the Agreement as they "were patently sincere and serious people who have raised an important constitutional issue which affects them and thousands of others on both sides of the border"[317] a view subsequently accepted (although with some reservations) by the Supreme Court on appeal.

This view is also apparent in the judgment of Keane J. in *McKenna v. An Taoiseach (No. 2)*,[318] a case where the plaintiff ultimately succeeeded before the Supreme Court in establishing that the use of public monies in advocating a "Yes" vote at a referendum was unconstitutional. Her standing to make this claim had been put at issue before the High Court, but Keane J. had no doubt but that this claim came within the afore-mentioned category of exceptional constitutional cases.[319] A similar view was taken in *Riordan v. An Tánaiste*,[320] where a private citizen had sought an order restraining the Tánaiste from acting in a manner which he claimed infringed Article 28.6.3° of the Constitution.[321] Budd J. held that as the plaintiff was a "citizen with a genuine and sincere interest in the political life of the

---

[313] [1989] I.R. 734 at 747.
[314] [1987] I.R. 713.
[315] *Ibid.* at 766. *Cf.* the decision of English Divisional High Court in *R v. Foreign Secretary, ex p. Rees-Mogg* [1994] Q.B. 552 where the applicant (who wished to restrain the ratification of the Maastricht Treaty by the U.K. Government) was granted standing because of his "sincere concern for constitutional issues."
[316] [1988] I.R. 567 (High Ct.); [1990]1 I.R. 110 (Sup. Ct.).
[317] *Ibid.* at 580.
[318] [1995] 2 I.R. 10.
[319] On this point Keane J. said (at 15):
"It is clear that the present proceedings belong to a category of cases in which a challenge to the constitutionality of legislation or other acts is unlikely to emerge if the specific criteria enunciated by the Supreme Court in *Cahill v. Sutton* [1980] I.R. 269 are applied. It is clear from the observations of Finlay C.J. in *Crotty v. An Taoiseach* [1987] I.R. 773 that a broader approach should be adopted in cases of this nature and I have no hesitation in concluding that the plaintiff was entitled to institute and maintain the present proceedings."
The issue of standing does not appear to have been dealt with on appeal (possibly because the State considered that it was not worth raising) and it is, of course, implicit in the Supreme Court judgments that Ms McKenna had the requisite standing.
[320] [1995] 3 I.R. 62 (High Ct.); unreported, Supreme Court, November 25, 1997.
[321] Art. 28.6.3° provides that the Tánaiste should "act for or in the place of the Taoiseach during the temporary absence of the Taoiseach." The applicant contended that this provision was infringed when both the Taoiseach and the Tánaiste were simultaneously absent from the State. Budd J. rejected this

country", he was entitled to take proceedings restraining the Government from acting in a manner which he contended was unconstitutional.[322] This view was endorsed by the Supreme Court on appeal. Thus, Keane J. considered that if there had been a breach of Article 28.6.3°,[323] it would be unrealistic to expect the Attorney General to commence the appropriate proceedings. It followed that:

". . . the High Court would have to afford *locus standi* to any concerned citizen who instituted the relevant proceedings or accept that the courts were powerless to deal with an admitted and serious failure by a high constitutional officer to perform his or her duty. It is clear that in such circumstances, the only course open to the High Court would be to afford *locus standi* to such a citizen."

It is to the credit of the Irish courts that they have consistently taken a broader view of *locus standi* requirements in this type of constitutional case than have their American counterparts.[324]

In comparing these recent decisions on standing with the *Cahill v. Sutton* principles, one may group *Coogan* with *Crotty, McGimpsey , McKenna* and *Riordan* since each involves examples of what Henchy J. in *Cahill* called a "transcendent need to assert against the statute the constitutional provisions".[325] This is clearly a very broad exemption, since it cannot be every constitutional point which warrants a suspension of the normal standing rules. The great question which will now be briefly examined, is what common threads may be discerned running through the

---

claim on the merits, saying (at 85) that it authorised the Tánaiste to assume the functions of the Taoiseach when the latter was "absent" in the sense of being temporarily unable to fulfill his functions: "either through illness, incapacity, or his being incommunicado, whether at home or abroad. It follows from this that as long as the Taoiseach is not himself absent in this specific sense during this time, he is complying with his constitutional duty, regardless of whether he happens to be within the geographical confines of the State or not."

[322] Budd J. said (at 75) that: "A citizen is entitled to take appropriate steps to ensure that the Constitution, as the fundamental law of the State, is observed by those in high office." See also, *Martin v. Dublin Corporation*, unreported, High Court, November 14, 1978, where Costello J. granted an interlocutory injunction to restrain building operations on a site which the plaintiff, a distinguished Professor of Medieval History, claimed was a national monument. The Corporation had argued that the plaintiff lacked *locus standi*, but Costello J. disagreed, saying that he thought that, at the trial of the action, the plaintiff would be able to establish that the general approach of the courts in constitutional cases should be followed in cases where a citizen claimed that a public body was not carrying out the law.

[323] The State apparently accepted that if a duty fell to be performed by the Taoiseach and both he and the Tánaiste were out of the country, he or the Tánaiste would be obliged to return in order to perform the duty. In Keane J.'s view the difficulty for the plaintiff was that he had been unable to point to "any instance where both constitutional officers were out of the country and a duty fell to be performed by the Taoiseach in the State", so that the obstacle in his way was not "any alleged lack of standing: it is simply that the occasion which might give him such standing has not arisen." In short, this was a case of ripeness, considered at pp. 756–758. While the principal judgment in this case was given by O'Flaherty J. (who dealt with the merits and did not find it necessary to address the standing issue), the other Supreme Court judges agreed with both judgments. It may be noted that in a separate case, *Riordan v. An Taoiseach*, unreported, High Court, November 14, 1997, Costello P. held that the plaintiff had no standing to challenge the constitutionality of the appointment of Ms. Justice Carroll as Chairperson of the Commission of Nursing. This judgment was delivered two weeks before the Supreme Court's judgment in the separate *Riordan* case and Costello P's rather restrictive attitude to the standing issue seems to have been overtaken by the Supreme Court's subsequent decision.

[324] See, *e.g. Schlesinger v. Reservists to Stop the War* 418 U.S. 208 (1974) and *Valley Forge Christian College v. Americans United for the Separation of Church and State* 454 U.S. 464 (1982).

[325] [1980] I.R. 269 at 285.

cases under review. It may be suggested that the following requirements are necessary to bring a case within this exception to the usual *Cahill* principles.

First, it must be reasonable to assume that there is no one who has standing in the classic sense of being directly and materially affected by the allegedly unconstitutional law or the administrative action which is said to be invalid. As Walsh J. remarked in *Coogan*:

> "[E]ven in cases where it is sought to invalidate a legislative provision the Court will, where the circumstances warrant it, permit a person whose personal interest is not directly or indirectly, presently, or in the future, threatened, to maintain proceedings if the circumstances are such that the public interest warrants it. In this context, the public interest must be taken in the widest sense."[326]

This was expressly recognised by Keane J. in *Iarnród Éireann v. Ireland*[327] where he acknowledged that the courts were more likely to accord a generous view of standing where "the nature of the constitutional challenge is such that a plaintiff will not emerge whose interests may be said to be either immediately or prospectively affected in a manner specific to him or her."[328] This exceptional head of standing is more likely to arise in cases where it is said that there has been a breach of constitutional provisions setting out the powers and functions of the State, rather than raising individual constitutional rights: *Crotty, McGimpsey, McKenna* and *Riordan* clearly fall into this category.[329]

The other requirement is that the litigants should have a serious concern with the matter, the formula used in *McGimpsey* being "patently sincere and serious" and in Coogan "bona fide concern and interest."[330] Again, in *Iarnród Éireann*, Keane J. stated: "... it cannot be said that, because every citizen has an interest in ensuring that the Constitution is observed, everyone is entitled to invoke its provisions, irrespective of actual or threatened injury to him or her resulting from the operation of the impugned statute." The assumption here is that if that dreaded figure, the meddlesome and crank litigant, is not to be excluded by the test of material interest, then he must be excluded in some other way. One way in which the seriousness of the litigant might be shown would be if the litigant were, or were a member of, a representative association, as in the Coogan case. Another possibility is that, as mentioned in McGimpsey, there should be a large number of persons affected by the action or law, of which

---

[326] [1989] I.R. 734 at 746–747.

[327] [1995] 2 I.L.R.M. 161.

[328] *Ibid.* at 189. At the same reference, Keane J. distinguished cases like *Cahill* and *East Donegal* from cases like *Crotty* on the basis that in *East Donegal* "it is probable that a plaintiff will emerge of whom it can be said that he or she is affected by the legislation . . . in a manner peculiar to him or her."

[329] As Keane J. said in *Iarnród Éireann* (at 189): "Such claims typically arise in the context of purported changes to the structure of government itself or its relationship to other sovereign governments." Other examples are afforded by cases such as *O'Donovan v. Attorney General* [1961] I.R. 114 and *O'Malley v. An Taoiseach* [1990] I.L.R.M. 460 (both cases where the issue of whether there had been a fair distribution of Dáil seats was raised) where a similarly liberal approach to standing appears to have been adopted.

[330] In *Riordan v. An Tánaiste* the applicant was described by Budd J. as somebody who had "shown an active interest in the Government of the country." He had also stood for election on a number of occasions and had previously made representations to the Government concerning the alleged breach of Article 28.6.3°. of the Constitution.

complaint was made. It remains to be seen whether it is essential that a large section of the population must be affected or whether, as seems more probable, this is merely one type of evidence of the seriousness of the litigant's case.

Jus tertii

One further difficulty which was raised by the Supreme Court in *McGimpsey* pertains to the relationship of the plaintiffs not only to the law or act of which they complain; but also to the character of the flaw which they perceive in it. Plainly, as distinguished members of the Official Unionist party of Northern Ireland, the plaintiffs had standing in the narrow sense as they were concerned about the signing of the Anglo-Irish Agreement. The difficulty lies in the particular constitutional argument on which they principally relied, *viz.* the jurisdictional claim in respect of Northern Ireland contained in Articles 2 and 3 of the Constitution which, as Unionists, they naturally found offensive. Although the Supreme Court decided that their case should be heard on the merits, Finlay C.J. had considerable reservations as to whether a claim of this kind could be entertained:

> "As a general proposition, it would appear to me that one would have to entertain considerable doubt as to whether any citizen would have the locus standi to challenge the constitutional validity of an act of the executive or of a statute of the Oireachtas, for the specific and sole purpose of achieving an objective directly contrary to the purpose of the constitutional provisions invoked."[331]

Indeed, one might observe that the McGimpseys' relation to Articles 2 and 3 was roughly analogous to that between Mrs Cahill and the defect which she wished to rely upon in the Statute of Limitations. This in turn raises the question of the distinction between *locus standi* and *jus tertii*.

In turning to a definition, one should note that the concept of *jus tertii* has not yet been treated judicially as a separate category. The distinction between the two concepts is that *locus standi* involves the litigant's status in relation to the administrative action (or law) and its consequences, whilst *jus tertii* refers to his position *vis-à-vis* the particular defect in the administrative action or law, of which complaint is made and, in particular, whether it is competent for him to rely on the rights of a third party in order to advance his argument. Strictly speaking, as is acknowledged in Henchy J.'s judgment in that case, *Cahill*, like *McGimpsey*, was a *jus tertii* case in that the plaintiff was certainly affected by the law; but not by the particular infirmity of which she complained. Another example is the plaintiff's argument in *Norris v. Attorney-General*,[332] that since the sections of the Offences

---

[331] [1990] 1 I.R. 110. McCarthy J., however, thought (at 123) that "one does not determine *locus standi* by motive, but rather by objective assessment of rights and the means of protecting them". He was, however, minded to deny the plaintiffs standing on the ground that only citizens could challenge an agreement of this kind. Similar sentiments are to be found in the judgment of Gannon J. in *Rederei Kennermerland N.V. v. Attorney General* [1989] I.L.R.M. 821. *Cf.* the position of the plaintiff in *McKenna v. An Taoiseach (No. 2)* [1995] 2 I.R. 10 who was in favour of the adoption of the Fifteenth Amendment of the Constitution Bill, 1995, but who opposed the funding of this measure by the Government.

[332] [1984] I.R. 36.

Against the Person Act 1861 applied, *inter alia*, to married persons, they constituted a violation of marital privacy. The High Court and Supreme Court agreed that the plaintiff had general standing to attack the constitutionality of the impugned provisions. However, since his evidence showed that he would never marry, the courts declined to permit him to rely on arguments based on marital privacy. The exception was the dissenting judge, McCarthy J., who defined *locus standi* narrowly as "the status to maintain the action and not the right to advance arguments of a particular kind, unrelated to the facts of the case."[333] He held that once *locus standi* (in the narrow sense in which he defined it) had been established, there was no restriction on the type of arguments which could be adduced to support a litigant's case. However, this is an idiosyncratic view. In other cases, no distinction has been drawn between situations which, strictly speaking, involve a *jus tertii* and those which involve *locus standi* in the narrow sense, both categories being lumped together under the broad head of locus standi. Moreover, the important point is that whichever category was involved a similar test has been applied (save in *McGimpsey*) the litigant is required to have an "interest" in both the administrative action (and its consequences) and in the particular defect of which he complains.

Ripeness

There is another theoretical distinction which need only be examined briefly since its existence, independent of standing, has only recently been examined by the courts. This is the requirement of ripeness, by which a litigant whose interest is likely to be affected by an administrative action or law may not initiate proceedings until the threat has actually materialised or until the public body in question has taken concrete steps. In short, he may not take action in respect of an abstraction or a hypothesis.

This issue (which necessarily is usually associated with the declaratory remedy) arose in *Blythe v. Attorney-General (No. 2)*.[334] Here the plaintiffs had formed an organisation known as "The League of Youth" but, anticipating an executive ban, sought a declaration to the effect that the organisation was a lawful one. Johnston J. held that the making of a declaratory order lay in the discretion of the court and that jurisdiction must be exercised "judicially" and "cautiously". He added that: "It is only binding declarations that can be made. That must mean a declaration that is binding upon someone else who can, and who, in the opinion of the Court, ought to be bound."[335] The present case was premature and Johnston J. considered that the case was not a proper one for the exercise of his discretion. In view of the fact that the plaintiffs appeared to have a genuine apprehension that such a ban might be imposed, this seems an unduly narrow approach to take. The issue of ripeness also arose in *East Donegal Co-operative Ltd v. Attorney General*.[336] where it was, in fact, discussed under the heading of *locus standi*. The plaintiffs were mart-owners who sought a declaration that the Livestock Marts Act 1967 which had established a

---

[333] For further examples, see *L'Henryenat v. Ireland* [1983] I.R. 193 and *Madigan v. Attorney General* [1986] I.L.R.M. 136.

[334] [1936] I.R. 549.

[335] *Ibid.* at 554.

[336] [1970] I.R. 317. The issue also arose in *Riordan v. An Tánaiste*, unreported, Supreme Court, November 25, 1997, discussed at pp. 752–753.

licensing system for marts was unconstitutional. They clearly had the necessary *locus standi* (in the strict sense of the term) to challenge this regime, but the key issue was whether they had taken the action prematurely. Their licences had not been revoked, nor had the conduct of their business otherwise been interfered with. The Supreme Court, however, concluded that the plaintiffs did have a genuine apprehension that their business activities might be interfered with and that, accordingly, the action was not premature. The rationale for this decision was later expressed by Walsh J. in the following terms:

> "This Court in *East Donegal* expressly rejected the contention that it was necessary for a plaintiff to show that the provisions of the legislation impugned applied not only to the activities in which he was currently engaged but that their application has 'affected his interests adversely'. This decides that a person does not to have to wait to be injured. Once again, the question of sufficiency of interest will depend upon the circumstances of the case and upon what appears to be the extent or nature of the impact of the impugned law on the [applicant's] position."[337]

Similarly, Henchy J. in *Cahill* referred to "an injury or prejudice which he has either suffered or is in imminent danger of suffering."[338] As with *jus tertii* and *locus standi*, the courts have adopted the sensible view with regard to ripeness that sufficiency of interest is such a loose, expansive category that there is no value in attempting to draw demarcation lines around it.

The issue of ripeness has also arisen in a number of cases where the applicant has sought to anticipate a certain course of conduct. This point is well illustrated by *Phillips v. Medical Council*,[339] a case where the respondent's Fitness to Practice Committee had decided that there were prima facie grounds to warrant a statutory investigation into the conduct of certain doctors. To this end, the Committee commissioned a report from an independent expert and when his draft report appeared to exonerate the applicant in respect of any question of professional misconduct, the latter sought various orders by means of judicial review. In effect, the applicant sought to compel the Committee to discontinue the inquiry, but Carroll J. refused this relief on the ground that the application was premature:

> "Judicial review does not exist to direct procedure in advance but to make sure that bodies which have made decisions susceptible of review have carried out their duties in accordance with the law and in conformity with natural and constitutional justice. Since the High Court cannot anticipate or direct what the findings of the Committee will be, the application for an order of prohibition against holding the inquiry on the grounds that it must of necessity be a nullity must also fail."[340]

---

[337] *The State (Lynch) v. Cooney* [1982] I.R. 337 at 371. See also, *Curtis v. Attorney General* [1985] I.R. 458 at 462 where Carroll J. said that: "It is not necessary that a determination adversely affecting rights must first be made before a constitutional challenge can be started. It is sufficient if there is a reasonable apprehension of such determination."

[338] [1980] I.R. 269, 286.

[339] [1991] 2 I.R. 115.

[340] *Ibid.* at 475. For a similar approach, see *Clune v. Director of Public Prosecutions* [1981] I.L.R.M. 17 (High Court cannot anticipate that District Court will not fairly adjudicate pending criminal

This attitude is also evident in the judgment of Costello J. in *Donegal Fuel & Supply Co. Ltd v. Londonderry Harbour Commissioners*,[341] a case where the applicants had sought judicial review to prevent the Minister for the Marine from approving certain bye-laws which they claimed were *ultra vires*. Costello J. dismissed the application, saying that even if it were shown that the draft bye laws were *ultra vires* the Minister's powers or unreasonable, "the court cannot assume that they would be adopted by the Minister" and that such an objector is required to exhaust his statutory remedies before seeking judicial review. This may be too narrow a view. After all, and notwithstanding any question of the operation of the presumption of validity or constitutionality, the question of *vires* is a matter for the courts and not for the Minister.[342] If an applicant can clearly demonstrate that the proposed course of action would be *ultra vires*, should not the courts be prepared to intervene in advance, at least in clear cases?

6. Relator Actions

The Attorney-General may sue *ex officio* to enforce the law, and no special injury need be shown in such proceedings.[343] The Attorney General may also sue at the relation (*i.e.* at the instance) of some members of the public in order to stop a breach of the law. The use of the relator action enables a private individual to sue where he might otherwise not have the necessary *locus standi*. In effect, the relator action is a form of *actio popularis*, which is subject to the control of the Attorney General and is part of his ancient role as *parens patriae*. However, the Attorney General is at all times the plaintiff in a relator action:

> "It has been settled beyond the possibility of question that the Attorney General alone is plaintiff. It is true that he generally permits the relator to select a solicitor to conduct the case; but such person is not the solicitor of the relator, but of the Attorney General, who remains *dominus litis* throughout the proceedings."[344]

Nevertheless, where an undertaking as to damages has been given by the relator, the relator alone will be liable on foot of that undertaking.[345] The grant of the

---

charges). On the other hand, there may be cases where for sound, practical reasons, the courts will not regard the application as premature. Thus, in *Minister for Finance v. Flynn*, unreported, High Court, February 9, 1996, Carroll J. rejected the submission that an application for judicial review of a decision of the Taxing Master which interpreted part of a costs order which had been made by the *Beef Tribunal* was premature: "[As] the same point is going to come up in many taxations, it is an appropriate case to consider an application for judicial review as it would be a waste of time and money if the Taxing Master proceeded to tax costs on an erroneous interpretation of the order."

[341] [1994] 1 I.R. 24.

[342] *cf. P. & F. Sharpe Ltd v. Dublin City and County Manager* [1989] I.R. 701. This was the approach of the English Court of Appeal in *R. v. H.M. Treasury, ex p. Smedley* [1985] 1 Q.B. 657 (court could grant declaration as to draft order in Council requiring parliamentary approval, because judicial views on *vires* of the measure might be of assistance to parliament as well as to the parties). See also *R. v. Electricity Commissioner, ex p. London Electricity Joint Committee Co. Ltd* [1924] 1 K.B. 171.

[343] *Attorney General (O'Duffy) v. Appleton* [1907] 1 I.R. 252; *Attorney General v. Paperlink Ltd* [1984] I.L.R.M. 373; *Attorney General v. X.* [1992] 1 I.R. 1.

[344] *Attorney General (Humphreys) v. Governors of Erasmus Smith's Schools* [1910] 1 I.R. 325 at 331, *per* Cherry LJ (as Attorney General alone is plaintiff, relator (who was not a barrister) not entitled to appear personally to argue case).

[345] *Attorney General (Martin) v. Dublin Corporation* [1983] I.L.R.M. 254.

Attorney General's consent (or *fiat*) to the relator action simply means that the relator has been conferred with the necessary standing in order to permit him to litigate an arguable case, and does not necessarily imply approval of the proceedings.

Because of the traditional stringency of the standing rule, until relatively recent times, the Attorney General was regarded, in certain circumstances, as enjoying an exclusive role in the enforcement of public rights.[346] The decision in *Irish Permanent Building Society Ltd v. Caldwell (No. 1)*[347] which has been mentioned, above, supplies a good example of this.[348] In this case, Keane J. hinted very strongly that the plaintiff would have to be able to show that the decision infringed some private right which it enjoyed[349] as the protection of public rights was the exclusive preserve of the Attorney General, or a plaintiff suing at his relation:

> "I cannot detect any fundamental difference between the law in this country and [the law as stated in England in *Gouriet*]. It is at least arguable that the limitations recognised by the common law on the right of a private citizen to assert a right, public in its nature, without the intervention of the Attorney General, were not in any way affected by the enactment of the present Constitution."[350]

However, the obverse of the widening of standing rules in the context of high constitutional matters established by cases such as *Crotty*, *McGimpsey* and *Coogan* is the termination of the Attorney's traditional monopoly to enforce public rights. In other words, if the standing rules are widened, there is less need to call upon the Attorney General. And it is clear from recent cases that the traditional views expressed in *Caldwell* no longer hold sway at least where fundamental constitutional rights are concerned.

The first of the modern cases to be considered is *Attorney General (Society for the Protection of Unborn Children (Ireland) Ltd) v. Open-Door Counselling Ltd.*[351] Here the plaintiff who had originally commenced proceedings without the intervention of the Attorney General sought to restrain the defendants' counselling activities which, it was claimed, provided active assistance for women seeking to avail of abortion facilities in Great Britain, contrary to Article 40.3.3° of the Constitution. The Attorney General was subsequently joined at the close of pleadings. It was clear that the plaintiff had *locus standi ex relatione* the Attorney General, but, in a

---

[346] *Moore v. Attorney General for Irish Free State* [1930] I.R. 471; *Gouriet v. Union of Post Office Workers* [1978] A.C. 435; *Irish Permanent Building Society Ltd v. Caldwell (No. 1)* [1979] I.L.R.M. 273 and see Casey, *The Irish Law Officers* (1996), pp. 157–167. The Attorney General still retains this exclusive role in the United Kingdom: see De Smith, Woolf and Jowell, *op. cit.*, above, n.44, pp. 146–154.

[347] [1979] I.L.R.M. 273.

[348] See p. 741, n.269.

[349] The plaintiffs subsequently amended their pleadings and averred that the registration of the rival building society had caused them loss and damage: *Irish Permanent Building Society Ltd v. Caldwell (No. 2)* [1981] I.L.R.M. 242. *Cf. Gouriet*, above, n.346.

[350] [1981] I.L.R.M. 242 at 275–276. This view must now be regarded as having been superseded by the judgment of the Supreme Court in *Society for the Protection of Unborn Children (Ireland) Ltd v. Coogan* [1989] I.R. 734 and, indeed, by Keane J.'s own comments in *Riordan v. An Tánaiste*, unreported, Supreme Court, November 25, 1997 (See above pp. 752–753).

[351] [1988] I.R. 593.

subsequent judgment, Hamilton P. was required to decide the issue of the costs incurred – and here is the practical point – prior to the joining of the Attorney General. This in turn raised the question of whether the Society would independently have had standing without the benefit of the Attorney General's intervention. Hamilton P. ruled that it was not necessary for the Society to have obtained the *fiat*:

> "[H]aving regard to the obvious fact that the unborn themselves cannot seek the protection of the court, the obligation which rests on all organs of government to support the right to life of the unborn must and should be extended to all persons, artificial and real. In bringing these proceedings, the Society was fulfilling this obligation and I have no doubt but that they had *locus standi* to maintain these proceedings."[352]

This question was even more directly at issue in a subsequent case involving the Society: *Society for the Protection of Unborn Children (Ireland) Ltd v. Coogan*.[353] Here the Society sought to restrain the dissemination of a student publication containing information on abortion services which again was said to infringe Article 40.3.3°. On this occasion the Society had not invoked the Attorney-General's protection, but Carroll J. ruled in a very short, *ex tempore* judgment that, without his *fiat*, the Society had no *locus standi* to maintain the proceedings.[354]

The Supreme Court, however, took a different view. Finlay C.J. said that the contention that only the Attorney General could sue to protect a constitutional right of this nature would represent "a major curtailment of the duty and power of the courts to defend and uphold the Constitution."[355] The Society had the requisite standing, as it had a bona fide and legitimate interest in the outcome of the proceedings. In a powerful concurring judgment, Walsh J. first observed that:

> "The question at issue in the present case is not one of a public right in the classical sense (and I do not subscribe to the view that only the Attorney General can sue in respect of such public rights) but it is a very unique private right which there is a public interest in preserving.It is a right guaranteed by public law, as it is part of the fundamental law of the State by reason of being incorporated into the Constitution. In my view, every member of the public has an interest in seeing that the fundamental law of the State is not defeated."[356]

---

[352] Hamilton P. said in the High Court, *ibid.* at 604.
"The public interests are committed to the care of the Attorney General. He is entitled to sue to restrain the commission of an unlawful act, to protect and vindicate a right acknowledged by the Constitution and to prevent the corruption of public morals. I am satisfied that the Attorney General has the *locus standi* to maintain these proceedings and that when the Attorney General sues with a relator, the relator need have no personal interest in the subject except his interest as a member of the public: see *Attorney General v. Logan* [1891] 2 Q.B. 100."

[353] [1989] I.R. 734.

[354] She said that (*ibid.* at 737): "The plaintiff has assumed the self-appointed role of policing the Supreme Court judgment. In my opinion, it has no right to seek undertakings from citizens and it is the Attorney General who is the proper party to move in such a case." The tone of this judgment is most remarkable.

[355] *Ibid.* at 742.

[356] *Ibid* at 748. Griffin J. reserved the question of the role of the Attorney General and "on the extent or limits" of *Cahill v. Sutton* [1980] I.R. 269, but agreed that the Society had standing, as they had a "bona fide interest and concern for the unborn."

It was equally clear that the Attorney General enjoyed no exclusive right to vindicate these constitutional rights:

"[T]he Attorney General by virtue of his constitutional office also has cast upon him in the appropriate case the duty of defending the Constitution and vindicating the rights conferred or guaranteed by it. He has therefore a sufficient interest at all times to represent the public interest in the protection of the right in question in this case, but not the exclusive right to move in the matter."[357]

Walsh J. also drew attention to the fact that the Attorney General might, wearing his other hat as Government legal adviser, be required to defend the actions of either the executive or the Oireachtas:

"If some Department of State or some public health authority with the approval, if not the encouragement, of the executive power, were to engage in activities which this Court in the Open Door Counselling case restrained as being a violation of the Constitution, it would be an intolerable situation if the defence or vindication of constitutional rights was to be confined to the very officer of State who had been entrusted with the task of defending such impugned activities."[358]

It is clear from the judgment of Walsh J. that these observations are of general application and the decision in *Coogan* does not turn on the constitutional nature of the rights protected by Article 40.3.3°.

Indeed, O'Hanlon J. appeared to arrive at a similar conclusion in *Parsons v. Kavanagh*[359] where the plaintiff had sought an injunction to restrain the actions of the defendants who were apparently engaged in operating a bus service in competition with her, without having obtained the necessary licence under the Road Transport Act 1932. Although the 1932 Act was passed for the benefit of the public rather than individual licence holders, the plaintiff was entitled to an injunction restraining "unlawful activity which impaired in a significant manner the exercise of her constitutional right to her living by lawful means".[360] This view was also endorsed

---

[357] *Ibid* at 743.

[358] *Ibid* at 744. Barrington J. had also drawn attention to this possible anomaly in *Irish Permanent Building Society v. Caldwell (No. 2)* [1981] I.L.R.M. 242. The Attorney General had refused his *fiat* to the plaintiffs, yet, following discovery of documents, they learned that the Attorney General had actually advised the defendants as to the conduct of the litigation. McCarthy J. also adverted to this in *The State (Sheehan) v. Government of Ireland* [1987] I.R. 550, where the applicant had sought mandamus to compel the Government to bring into force s. 60(1) of the Civil Liability Act 1961. Dealing with the argument that the applicant had no standing and that only the Attorney-General could assert such a right, McCarthy J. said (at 562–563):

"If the prosecutor, or another in like position, does not have *locus standi*, then who has? In theory, the Attorney General could assert the public right and seek the relief claimed; in practice, this has no reality. The Attorney General is legal adviser to the Government and presumably, has advised the Government that it is not under the legal obligation for which the prosecutor contends."

See also the comments to like effect of Keane J. in *Riordan v. An Tánaiste*, unreported, Supreme Court, November 25, 1997, above pp. 752–753.

[359] [1990] I.L.R.M. 560.

[360] *Ibid.* at 567. See also *M.M. D.S. Television v. South East Deflector Association Ltd*, unreported, High Court, April 8, 1997 (injunction granted to restrain competitor from engaging in illegal activities.)

by the Supreme Court in *Lovett v. Gogan*[361] – a case which also concerned an attempt by one licensed transport undertaking to obtain an injunction restraining the illegal activities of a competitor – where Finlay C.J. stated that the "true position" was that such a plaintiff was "entitled to such an injunction if he can establish that it is the only way of protecting him from the threatened invasion of his constitutional rights".[362]

A discordant note was subsequently struck by the Supreme Court in *Incorporated Law Society v. Carroll*[363] in holding (though without mentioning *Kavanagh* or *Grogan*) that the plaintiff society had no standing to seek an injunction restraining a defendant from engaging in what was alleged to be unlicensed practice as a solicitor. Here Blayney J. observed that the Law Society did not have standing and consequently that the enforcement of such public rights was a matter for the Attorney General alone. Leaving aside the fact that this decision goes against the trend of cases such as *Coogan*, it seems curious, in the wake of *Lovett v. Grogan,* that an individual solicitor would appear to have the requisite *locus standi* to seek an injunction restraining an unqualified person acting in competition against him, while the statutory body responsible for regulating the profession in question has been held to have no such standing to enforce the law.

At all events, these decisions (with the exception of *Carroll*) establish that the relaxing of the standing rules has had the result that the Attorney General is now seldom left with an exclusive right to assert the public interest. It is on the basis of this proviso that these cases may be reconciled with the *Cahill v. Sutton* principles. Moreover, there are explicit judicial statements to suggest that the Attorney General does not enjoy an exclusive function to enforce the law, even where constitutional rights are not at stake. In *Coogan*, Walsh J. said that he did not "subscribe to the view" that the Attorney General enjoyed an exclusive right to enforce public rights.[364] A similar view was hinted at by McCarthy J. in *Attorney General (McGarry) v. Sligo County Council*,[365] where the plaintiffs had obtained the *fiat* of the Attorney General in proceedings whereby they sought to restrain the defendant from constructing a refuse dump in the vicinity of a national monument. While the issue did not arise for consideration, McCarthy J. said that he must not be taken as "supporting or otherwise" the view of McWilliam J. in the High Court "that it was necessary to bring these proceedings as a relator action".[366]

The minority view in *Coogan* is worth noting, since both Carroll J. in the High Court and McCarthy J. in the Supreme Court expressed concern at the prospect of

---

[361] [1995] 3 I.R. 132.

[362] *Ibid.* at 142. This was found to be necessary on the facts, having regard to the minimal penalties provided for in the 1932 Act, as otherwise the plaintiff's constitutional right to earn his livelihood by lawful means would have been interfered with. On the other hand, in *O'Connor v. Williams* [1996] 2 I.L.R.M. 382 Barron J. refused to grant an injunction to taxi-drivers restraining the illegal activities of hackney-drivers on the ground that the penalties were substantial and that the "criminal law is sufficiently strong to prevent the damage at present been caused to the plaintiffs".

[363] [1995] 3 I.R. 145.

[364] [1989] I.R. 734 at 743.

[365] [1991] 1 I.R. 99 (decided in 1989).

[366] *Ibid.* at 114. These comments do not square readily with his subsequent comments (quoted at p. 763) in *Coogan*. The question of whether an interested member of the public required the *fiat* of the Attorney General to sue in respect of a charities matter was expressly reserved by the Supreme Court in *Connolly v. Byrne*, unreported, January 23, 1997.

private individuals or pressure groups being equipped to police the activities of other private persons by commencing litigation which is founded on some political, ideological or religious motivation, rather than some personal grievance which is justiciable at law. Accordingly, McCarthy J. in his dissenting judgment sought to restate the traditional rule that ordinarily it is the Attorney General, as the defender of public rights, who can enforce public rights. However, he addressed the concerns voiced by the majority judges by proposing two exceptions to the general rule:

> "If the Government, through the legislature or otherwise, were to act so as to breach [Art. 40.3.3°], it must a priori be open to any citizen to call the judicial organ of government in aid. If the feared breach is through the act of some other person or body, immediacy may require personal initiation of the suit. The only requirement in either case would be a *bona fide* intent."[367]

Finally, two queries may be raised with regard to the Attorney's decision to grant or not grant his consent to a relator action. However, this may be done very briefly, for, if, as has just been argued, the standing rules in regard to constitutional and public matters have been substantially relaxed, then the Attorney's decision in this field is of less significance than formerly. The first query is whether, as is the case in England, the Attorney's decision to grant his consent is immune from judicial review. One can illustrate this by noting that despite our relatively relaxed standing rules, there is still a rule regarding standing and, accordingly, cases may occur from time to time which do not come within the existing *Cahill v. Sutton* exceptions and where the intervention of the Attorney General may still be required. Could Ms Cahill, for example, have either sought or compelled the Attorney General to intervene on her behalf to argue the constitutionality of section 11(2)(b) of the Statute of Limitations 1957? The answer may be that, in practice, the majority of such cases which fall outside the exceptions will not involve fundamental constitutional issues and are unlikely to be situations in which the Attorney General will feel impelled to intervene. However one can at least pose the question of whether, in an extreme enough case, judicial review proceedings would lie. In 1980 Professor Casey argued that it was open to the Irish courts to hold that the Attorney General's consent was no more unfettered than that of a Minister, and that if the Attorney General's consent was unreviewable, this will be "a situation unique in Irish law".[368] As things stand, it is not possible to predict with full confidence what attitude Irish courts will take to the question of the reviewability (or otherwise) of the Attorney General's decision. Although this is a matter which must await judicial resolution, the probability is that the courts will follow the approach which they have adopted in the case of review of the Director of Public Prosecutions, namely, that the courts will interfere only

---

367 *Ibid.* at 751.
368 *The Office of the Attorney General in Ireland* (1980), p. 154. At the equivalent point in the 2nd. ed. (p. 166), Professor Casey says that the issue is "not clear". Professor Casey rested his argument on cases such as *East Donegal Co-operatives Ltd v. Attorney General* [1970] I.R. 317 which stress that all exercises of administrative discretion should, in principle, be open to review. Contrast *Macauley v. Minister for Posts and Telegraphs* [1966] I.R. 345 at 346, where Kenny J. opined that the Attorney General "is free to grant or withhold his *fiat* for any reason and if he decides to withhold it, no proceedings to review his decision can successfully be brought in the Courts." See also the discussion in Chap. 12 (pp. 678–690). "Are there unreviewable discretionary powers?"

where he reaches a decision "mala fide or influenced by an improper motive or improper policy".[369]

The second question is whether relator proceedings have survived the enactment of the Constitution. In relation to this a number of disparate points arise. For instance, as we have seen, the issue of standing is primarily a question for the courts and the standing requirements have been formulated with the interests of the proper administration of justice in mind. Thus, on the one hand, the courts will not allow unrestricted standing (as this might lead to a possible abuse of the judicial power). Accordingly, a procedure whereby a non-judicial personage such as the Attorney General could effectively confer standing on a plaintiff might appear to be an unconstitutional interference with the administration of justice. To take the opposite case: what if the Attorney refused to confer standing? The very fact that the Attorney General is supposed to act judicially and weigh up evidence before deciding to grant his *fiat* might lead one to suppose that he was exercising judicial powers which are not of a limited nature, contrary to Article 34.1 (although it may be noted that analogous arguments have been rejected by the courts in the context of the Attorney's functions under the Extradition (Amendment) Act 1987.[370]) However, as against this, in the days of a strict standing rule, it was the judges themselves who imposed such limitation. An Attorney General who refused to assist a litigant, with no individual interest, to circumvent a strict standing rule, could hardly be said to be interfering with the administration of justice by the courts.[371]

---

[369] *The State (McCormack) v. Curran* [1987] I.L.R.M. 225 at 237, *per* Finlay C.J. See also *H. v. Director of Public Prosecutions* [1994] 2 I.R. 589. Note also the comments of Professor Casey, *The Irish Law Officers* (1996) pp. 166–167:

"But even if the Attorney's decision was susceptible of review in principle, the most probable ground of review would seem to be irrationality; and the Supreme Court's approach to this matter [in *O'Keeffe v. An Bord Pleanála* [1993] 1 I.R. 39] would not promise success to the applicant." But it might also be argued that the *O'Keeffe* principles do not necessarily apply to the Attorney's decision to refuse to grant his *fiat*, inasmuch as such a decision does not involve the inter-action of complex questions of policy and administrative expertise. It was these factors which seem to have influenced the Supreme Court to allow such administrative tribunals a large "margin of appreciation" in cases in which decisions of such bodies are challenged on grounds of reasonableness.

[370] *Wheeler v. Culligan* [1989] I.R. 344.

[371] Compare a remark by Walsh J. in *Coogan*, which concerned a statutory rather than a judge-made rule: "There must be some doubt on the question of whether any statute could validly seek to exclude members of the public from calling in aid the judicial power in defence of the public interest in the vindication of constitutional rights." [1989] I.R. 734 at 745–746. *Cf. Macauley v. Minister for Posts and Telegraphs* [1966] I.R. 345.

CHAPTER 14

THE SCOPE OF PUBLIC LAW

1. The Public/Private Divide in Irish Law

The expression public law is best defined simply by comparison with private law. Thus, whilst private law governs relations between private individuals (*e.g.* contract, tort, property law) by contrast, public law comprises rules which are particular to the relations between a public body and, on the other hand, private individuals or companies.[1] One should note, though that the ordinary private law of, say, contract also applies in appropriate contexts to public bodies: a point which is developed below. Public law is more or less synonymous with administrative law but is used here in preference to administrative law because a wide, conceptual point is under consideration.

In France, this public–private divide has been a fundamental of the control of the organs of public administration in the civil law jurisdictions, since the time of Napoleon. In contrast, the common law with its dislike of special régimes reacted (in the case of Dicey, with asperity) against this segregation. However, with the attempts in England and elsewhere in the common law world (in the 1970s and 1980s) to put the supervision of public administration upon a systematic and reformed basis, some element of demarcation beyond that required by the English prerogative writs seemed, to many people, to be inevitable.

One ought to emphasise that the public–private law dichotomy may be applied to either (or both): the body which is exercising a function; and the function being exercised. We shall return to this distinction which is often overlooked, later. For the moment, let us note that the public–private dichotomy (in whichever of the two forms just identified) can arise in a number of contexts. For example, we have already noted, in the case of the Ombudsman that the bodies within his bailiwick are specified in his constituent statute and are public in nature. There is thus no possibility of arguing that he could entertain a complaint against (say) the Law Society of Ireland.[2] Other contexts in which public–private divide applies include the bodies which are subject to the new legitimate expectations precept[3] and those which enjoy the privilege against disclosure, on public policy grounds, of confidential evidence before a court.[4]

---

1 For a more elaborate treatment of the distinction between public and private law, see pp. 767–771.
2 However, it must be noted that so long as a body is on the Ombudsman's statutory list, the argument has not been make that complaints are excluded on the basis that private law is involved see pp. 342–343.
3 This forms the background to cases such as *Eogan v. University College, Dublin* [1996] 2 I.L.R.M. 132. See generally at pp. 878–879.
4 See below, pp. 946–947.

However, far and away the main forum in which the dichotomy may arise is the field of judicial review of administrative action. In this field, perhaps even more than any other, Irish law has developed at a considerable angle to English law. The reason is that: while the dictates of the principles underlying the common law system are, broadly speaking, the same here as in England; yet, as we shall see, the judges have frequently turned a blind eye to the consequences of the public–private divide (especially so in the case of public functions rather than public bodies) whilst spasmodically acknowledging its existence. It is quite likely, however, that in the future, Irish law will move somewhat closer to the general common law theory. Accordingly, we have thought it appropriate (if possibly premature) to dignify the present subject matter with a separate chapter, an arrangement which also carries the advantage of ameliorating the curse of interminable length hanging over the previous chapter. At the same time, the fluidity in Irish practice has provided us with good reason to notice, by way of contrast, some of the anomalies and infelicities to which the theory can lead. However, it is inevitable that this chapter should be long on areas of doubt and difficulty, and short on simple certainties.

Another complicating factor lies in the fact that even, so far as judicial review is concerned, the public-private divide may arise in the following four distinct contexts:

(a) We have already covered the central topics in the judicial review of administrative action, the substantial bloc of law being covered in Chapters 9 to 12 and most of the procedural-machinery law in Chapter 13 ("The Application for Judicial Review"). However, we have left over from Chapter 13 until this chapter, the basic question of which bodies and what activities fall within the specialised régime of the application for judicial review. Before the reformation in procedure, described in Chapter 13, the general understanding was that in seeking to challenge decisions of certain types of entity on the fringe of the public body category (*e.g.* trade unions and universities), a litigant could not proceed by way of State side order (the fore-runner of the contemporary application for judicial review application), but could proceed by the less convenient method of plenary proceedings for a declaration or injunction. Thus, the advent of the application for judicial review, with the declaration and injunction within its empire, raises the question of whether trade unions or universities were more or less automatically brought within its sweep. In addition, there remains the related question, already mentioned briefly, of whether its scope extends to an impeccably public law entity (*e.g.* the Minister for the Environment) when exercising a private law function.

(b) As explained in the previous chapter, the possibility of agitating a public law matter by way of a declaration or injunction granted in the course of plenary proceedings sprung up because of the often arbitrary restrictions upon the scope of certiorari, prohibition, etc. In the Brave New World, in which a declaration or injunction is available in an application for judicial review, a question arises which is, in a sense, the inverse of that canvassed in (a). That question is whether in the case of issues which could have been heard by way of judicial review, a litigant may instead apply for a declaration or injunction, in plenary proceedings.

(c) In some cases, of which the strongest example is dismissal from employment, the significance of the distinction between public and private law lies in the fact that the remedy available is often in practice more potent where the issue is properly characterised as coming within the scope of public law. Depending upon the character of the circumstances (identity of employer; nature of employment relationship; type of defect in the dismissal), the employee may be able bring the case into the field of public law. If he can do so, then it will usually be open to him to secure a remedy establishing that the dismissal was invalid so that, as a matter of law, he retains his post: (whether this is done by way of an application for judicial review; or by obtaining a declaration or an injunction in plenary proceedings is of lesser importance). By contrast, an employee who is confined to a private law remedy, is generally restricted to damages (usually of a limited amount, under the Unfair Dismissals Acts 1977–1993).[5] In practice, this may make a hugely significant – even spectacular – difference.[6]

(d) Bearing in mind the existence of two separate forms of procedure, the question arises whether, in the case of a matter which could not have been heard by way of judicial review, because either the respondent body or the function being exercised fell outside the scope of the application for judicial review, does it follow that none of the substantive judicial review principles (*ultra vires*, constitutional justice, legitimate expectations,[7] reasonableness, etc.) may be applied? One straightforward answer would be in the affirmative, on the basis that if a case is private in nature for one purpose (*i.e.* and therefore does not come within the scope of an Order 84 judicial review application) so should it be for the purpose of substantive judicial review principles. The alternative view would be that the considerations which justify the conclusion that a particular matter may not proceed by way of judicial review are rather different from those which apply in the case of the substantive principles of judicial review.

Topics (c) and (d) have not yet received much judicial or academic attention. However, there is more to be said about topics (a) and (b) and this elaboration will form the subject-matter of sections 2 and 3 following. In the present part, it remains to consider, generally, the public – private law divide.

We may start by taking a fresh look at *Glover v. BLN Ltd*,[8] a case where the Supreme Court held that the rules of *audi alteram partem* applied in the indisputably private law context of the dismissal of a company director. Walsh J. justified the

---

5 The Employment Appeals Tribunal has power to order the re-instatement or re-engagement of the employee in question, but, in practice, these remedies are rarely granted. This is especially true of the former remdy.

6 Note, *e.g.* the sequel to *Garvey v. Ireland* [1981] I.R. 75, a case where the dismissal of the plaintiff as Garda Commissioner was held – admittedly in plenary proceedings – to have been invalid and void. The plaintiff subsequently obtained damages (see *Garvey v. Ireland (No. 2)* [1979] I.L.R.M. 266 and the Garda Síochána Act 1979 was enacted retrospectively to validate the actions of the person who had been purporting to act as Garda Commissioner.

7 Thus, it seems implicit in Shanley J.'s judgment in *Eogan v. University College, Dublin* [1996] 2 I.L.R.M. 132 that if the decision of the respondent was not amenable to judicial review (which he held it was) then the public law doctrine of legitimate expectations would have had no application.

8 [1973] I.R. 388.

application of these rules to the facts of this case on the basis that "the dictates of constitutional justice" require that "statutes, regulations or agreements setting up machinery for taking decisions which may affect rights or impose liabilities should be construed as providing for fair procedures".[9]

This passage expresses the strong view that constitutional justice applied, notwithstanding the fact that a private law entity and function was involved. The other step – the one which is relevant here – seems, it is suggested, to have been assumed. It is that given that judicial review proceedings were plainly not applicable just because the circumstances related to private law; yet given that it had been decided that constitutional justice should apply, it was nevertheless assumed to follow that constitutional justice had to be applied in plenary proceedings.[10] It may also be the case that constitutional justice is to be regarded as especially significant and, consequently, to be applied especially widely. This significance is illustrated by the fact that, in contrast to, *e.g.* unreasonableness or legitimate expectations, it has now been endowed with its own special place in the Constitution.

The great question remains of what would happen if, in a similar contemporary case, the plaintiff were to argue that his dismissal as company director was disproportionate or unreasonable in law: would the courts be willing to apply such principles (which have hitherto been confined to public law) to the facts of a private law case? The case law in this area is mixed and very tentative, but one must greatly doubt whether, save, perhaps, in special circumstances, the Irish courts would, if pressed, be willing to import the full range of public law doctrines into private law.

An example of the first line of authority is *Doyle v. Kildare County Council*,[11] a case where the plaintiffs appealed against an arbitration award made consequent upon a compulsory land acquisition on the ground that the sum awarded was so low as to be "unreasonable, irrational or perverse". While Flood J. rejected this claim on the facts, he was prepared to do so by reference to standard administrative law principles of reasonableness.[12] An echo of this approach may also be found in a passing comment of O'Flaherty J. (with whom Blaney J. agreed) in *Geoghegan v. Institute of Chartered Accountants*,[13] where the question was whether a disciplinary decision of the Institute was amenable to judicial review. While the Supreme Court was divided on this issue,[14] O'Flaherty J. doubted that judicial review would lie. However, he added, nonetheless that "if there were a departure from the principle of proportionality the decision would be subject to review by the courts" meaning presumably review in plenary proceedings.[15]

---

[9] *Ibid.* at 427.
[10] See also, *e.g.* cases such as *McGrath and O'Ruairc v. Trustees of Maynooth College* [1979] I.L.R.M. 166; *Gunn v. Bord na Choláiste Náisiúnta Ealaine is Deartha* [1990] 2 I.R. 168 and *Georgopulous v. Beaumont Hospital Board*, unreported, Supreme Court, June 4, 1997. These are all cases where the courts held that constitutional justice applied to disciplinary proceedings otherwise governed by private law.
[11] [1996] 1 I.L.R.M. 252.
[12] For example, he cited *The State (Keegan) v. Stardust Victims' Compensation Tribunal* [1986] I.R. 652 and *P & F Sharpe Ltd v. Dublin City and County Manager* [1989] I.R. 701. The Supreme Court affirmed this part of his finding without comment.
[13] [1995] 3 I.R. 86.
[14] See pp. 783–784.
[15] *Ibid.* at 120.

The alternative line of authority is represented by *Rajah v. College of Surgeons*[16] Keane J. had to consider the submission that an academic appeals board was obliged to state its reasons for its decision. In the first place, he rejected the submission that judicial review would lie. However there was another distinct ground on which the applicant would also fail. Keane J. stated:

> "I have already found that the respondents are not a body the decisions of which are amenable to judicial review. I do not think that they should be regarded as under an obligation to give reasons for all their decisions. In general, bodies which are not courts but which exercise functions of a judicial or quasi-judicial nature determining legal rights and obligations must give reasons for their decisions . . . The requirement to give reasons may extend even further to purely administrative bodies, at least where their decisions affect legal rights and obligations . . . A decision such as that of the respondents in the present case, however, was not . . . of a nature which necessitated the giving of reasons."[17]

While Keane J. did not expressly say so, it seems implicit in his judgment that the reason was he also considered it inappropiate to apply public law doctrines to determine a private law case. Here, therefore, there seems to have been a holding that the relevant substantive judicial review principles did not apply.

This question was further considered by McCracken J. in *Carna Foods Ltd v. Eagle Star Insurance Co. (Ireland) Ltd*,[18] a case which concerned the question of whether a private insurer was obliged to give reasons in respect of the non-renewal of a insurance contract. This was a case mounted by way of plenary proceedings. However, the basis of the rejection of the plaintiff's claim was not this, but rather the fact that the case concerned private contractual relationships. The judge concluded that the *Glover* principles did not apply, as, in contrast to that case, "there was no procedure or machinery" for the determination of rights and liabilities and, like *Rajah*, the "decision of an insurance company to cancel or refuse insurance could not be said to be a function of a judicial or quasi-judicial nature". And suppose that the contract had provided for some form of adjudication on the renewal issue, would it have been open to the plaintiff to contend that the failure to renew was, for example, unreasonable in law?

In many ways, the best way of posing this question is to ask whether abuses of private power should be subject to public law controls. It is noteworthy that in *R v. Jockey Club, ex p. Aga Khan*[19] Hoffmann L.J. observed that:

> "private power may affect the public interest and the livelihoods of many individuals. But that does not subject it to the rules of public law. If control is needed, it must be found in the law of contract, the doctrine of restraint of trade . . . . Articles 85 and 86 of the EEC Treaty and all the other instruments available in law for curbing the excesses of private power."[20]

---

16 [1994] 1 I.R. 384.
17 *Ibid.* at 395. See p. 573.
18 [1995] 1 I.R. 526. This issue was not addressed by the Supreme Court on appeal: [1997] 2 I.R. 193.
19 [1993] 2 All ER 853.
20 *Ibid.* at 875.

It is true that, in certain circumstances, competition law can sometimes provide an effective remedy and, moreover, the reasoning in such cases sometimes parallels that applicable to public law. A good example here is provided by *Donovan v. Electricity Supply Board*,[21] a case which concerned the membership rules of an electrical trade association. The ESB decided that it would only permit electricity connection on premises where a certificate of compliance from a member of the trade association was produced, or, in the case of an unregistered contractor, a certificate from an inspector employed by the association. Costello J. held that the membership rules in their original form had anti-competitive effects because:

> ". . . the imprecision of criteria for enrolment, the lack of objective standards for registration, the arbitrary power to refuse enrolment, the absence of any appeal procedure [all] imposed unjustified restrictions on enrolment on the register."[22]

This is obviously an area with potential for growth. Perhaps the best solution would be if contract law and competition law were to evolve in tandem to provide new controls of abuses of private law which would parallel – while remaining distinct from – similar developments in the field of public law.

There are a number of historical/political developments which have stretched public law from its pristine (and possibly unrealistic) simplicity to the uncertainties and anomalies of today. The first of these is that the scope of governmental power has increased so much that there are few islands of private right against which it does not, at least potentially, lap. For example, private property may be compulsorily acquired and even if it is not, there are restrictions upon what may be done with it. Again, in the dirigiste State, governmental controls – through licensing, compulsory contractual terms,[23] grants – can make such a big impact on activities within the private sector that it is difficult to know where one stops and the other begins.

Secondly, governmental power is articulated by a variety of forms. A utility, for instance, may be operated in the form of: a Department of State; a state-sponsored body; or a private company in which the State may have a share-holding. Again, a private company with a monopoly or a trade union with a closed shop may dispose of a reservoir of power greater than many State organs.

It is a useful base-line to note that because of the nature and history of judicial review most of the actions to which it was traditionally directed, were actions (purportedly) authorised by statute and discharged by bodies constituted by statute. Plainly there are two types of restriction here.[24] In the first place, as regards the body

---

21 [1994] 2 I.R. 305. But see *Carna Foods v. Eagle Star* [1995] 1 I.R. 526 at 532.
22 *Ibid* at 324.
23 Thus, *e.g.* holders of sound broadcasting licences under the Radio and Television Act 1988 are required to enter into contracts with the Independent Radio and Television Commission and s.14 of this Act specifies the conditions attaching to such contracts. Another example is provided by Health (Community Pharmacy Contractor Agreement) Regulations, 1996 (S.I. No. 152 of 1996) which regulates aspects of the contract entered into between health boards and the proprietors of community pharmacies to enable the latter to provide pharmacy services under the Health Act 1970.
24 The topical importance of public law in England has led to a lot of academic writing on the subject. See, e.g., de Smith, Woolf and Jowell, *Judicial Review of Administrative Action* (5th ed.,1995) chap. 3; Craig, *Administrative Law*, (3rd ed., 1994) chap. 15; Wade and Forsyth, *Administrative Law* (7th

involved, the High Court could only exercise public law powers of control over a body which was grounded upon statute, statutory instrument or prerogative. Secondly, as to the particular function being discharged control could only be exercised when the body was using statutory, as opposed to common law, powers. It remains to enlarge upon each of these two points, considering whether they are still correct.

Which bodies are within the scope of public law?: "Public bodies"

It used to be thought that such bodies had to be constituted by statute and irrespective of the particular function being discharged in the case, broadly speaking, to serve a "public" function. The classification of functions as "public" was, at base, ideological and historical, rather than legal. Where the first condition – "constituted by statute" – was satisfied then it almost always happened that so, too, was the public function requirement. What was problematic was the question of non-statutory bodies whose character, status and functions were, in some way, "public". The authority of such bodies might be based on "custom" or the agreement of the parties affected. As we shall see in a moment, even less straightforward systems of legal support developed. Where such bodies had a significant effect upon the community, the realistic argument came to be made that public law should "move on from the *ultra vires* rule to a concern for the protection of individuals, and for the control of power, rather than powers, or *vires*".[25]

It is symptomatic of the activist temper of Irish law and its traditional lack of sympathy with technical doctrine[26] that in *The State (Hayes) v. Criminal Injuries Compensation Tribunal*,[27] it was actually conceded that the standard substantive and procedural rules of judicial review applied to the Tribunal. However, it can also be said that this was an appropriate concession: for although the Tribunal was non-statutory in status, it was a body with a public character, set up by executive act to administer moneys voted by the Oireachtas, according to an extra-statutory published scheme, while following a quasi-judicial procedure.

Another instructive decision is that of *R. v. Panel on Take-overs and Mergers, ex p. Datafin plc*,[28] concerned a self-regulating unincorporated association which devised and operated the City Code on Take-overs, a non-statutory scheme.[29] The Court of Appeal held that certiorari would issue to such a body (though, in the instant case, it exercised its discretion not to make an order). The kernel of the court's reasoning has been well summarised as follows:

---

ed., 1994) chap. 18; Woolf, "Public Law – Private Law: Why the Divide?" [1986] *Public Law* 220; Oliver, "Is the *Ultra Vires* Rule the Basis of Judicial Review?" [1987] *Public Law* 543; Beatson, 'Public' and 'Private' in English Administrative Law" (1987) 103 L.Q.R. 34; Tanney, "Procedural Exclusivity in Administrative Law" [1994] *Public Law* 51; Fredman and Morris, "The Costs of Exclusivity: Public and Private re-examined" [1994] *Public Law* 69; and Emery, "Public Law or Private Law? – The Limits of Procedural Exclusivity" [1995] *Public Law* 450.

25 Oliver, *ibid.* at p. 543.

26 However, in view of the large number of contemporary Irish authorities on this technical distinction between public law and private law, this traditional approach may be changing.

27 [1982] I.L.R.M. 210 at 211. See the analagous English case of *R. v. Criminal Injuries Compensation Board, ex p. Lain* [1967] 2 Q.B. 864, where this issue is much discussed.

28 [1987] Q.B. 815.

29 The Irish Takeover Panel has been established by statute and it is interesting to note that its decisions may only be challenged by means of judicial review: see Irish Takeover Panel Act 1997, ss. 3 and 13.

"While the court excluded from judicial review and 'publicness' bodies whose sole source of power was a consensual submission, it pointed out that the power of self-regulatory bodies such as the Panel is not exclusively consensual. Rather it is a system whereby a group of people acting in concert use their collective power to force themselves and others to comply with a code of conduct of their own devising. But the existence of de facto power was insufficient in itself to make the Panel 'public' and amenable to judicial review. What was vital was that (a) the decision that there should be a central but non-statutory regulatory body for takeovers was a government decision and, (b) the non-statutory system was buttressed by a periphery of statutory powers and penalties which assume that the Panel is the centrepiece of the regulatory system. The test is thus whether de facto power is underpinned by either a government decision to have regulation by a non-statutory body or by statutory support or, as in the *Take-over Panel* case, by both."[30]

Two points bear emphasis. In the first place, it will often happen that even where (as in the case of the (British) Take-over Panel) there is an element, real or artificial, of consensus, nevertheless the body's activities will have an effect on those outside the consensus (*e.g.* shareholders, employees, customers). Secondly, it happened that in the two cases just mentioned there was an organisational link between the body and the Government. What is to happen if this link is absent yet the body is performing governmental-type functions, such as, for example, the regulation of a sport or of some important community activity. In short, here one has a private body with public functions as opposed to the reverse which is discussed elsewhere.[31] Of bodies like the Gaelic Athletic Association and Bord Lúthchleas na hÉireann[32] it has been said, in England, that: "If they did not exist, the government might have to invent them."[33] Does it follow from this that they ought to be regarded as subject to public law, even though there is no element of Government control? As a matter of policy, this question depends at a fundamental level upon whether one views judicial review as being primarily concerned to protect the rights of the individual or to discipline the agencies of the State. Traditionally, it has been regarded as the latter.

Some clarity might be brought to the law in this confusing area, if the concepts underlying the judgment of the Court of Justice in *Foster v. British Gas*[34] were to be borrowed by the Irish courts. In this case the Court of Justice was required to determine whether a particular state-owned company was an "emanation of the

---

[30] Beatson, *op.cit.* above, n. 24, pp. 50–51.
[31] See p. 782.
[32] The Irish Athletics Board.
[33] *cf.* the comments of Hoffmann L.J. in *R v. Jockey Club, ex p. Aga Khan* [1993] 2 All E.R. 853 at 875: "The fact that certain functions of the Jockey Club could be exercised by a statutory body and that they are so exercised in some other countries does not make them governmental functions in England." The functions discharged by the Jockey Club in England are now discharged in Ireland by a statutory body, the Racing Regulatory Body established by the Irish Horseracing Industy Act 1994. For a similar approach to that found in *Aga Khan*, see also *R v. Chief Rabbi, ex p. Wachmann* [1992] 1 W.L.R. 1306 (judicial review does not lie in respect of the Chief Rabbi's disciplinary function); *R v. Jockey Club, ex p. RAM Racecourses Ltd* [1993] 2 All E.R. 225 (fixture allocation functions of Jockey Club not available for judicial review) and *R. v. Football Association Ltd, ex p. Football League Ltd* [1993] 2 All E.R. 833 (similar principle).
[34] Case C–188/89 [1990] E.C.R. I–3313.

State" for the purposes of being bound by the terms of a directly effective E.U. Directive.[35] The test applied by the Court was in the following terms:

> "The Court has held in a series of cases that unconditional and sufficiently precise provisions of a Directive could be relied on against organisations or bodies which were subject to the authority or control of the State or had special powers beyond those which result from the normal rules applicable to relations between individuals."[36]

While it is true that this judgment must suffer the particular criticism as far as the present (domestic) context is concerned that the extent of the State – and, consequently, the horizontal effect of directives – can vary according to the diverse national rules concerning the State ownership in the economy,[37] nevertheless the conceptual analysis offered by this judgment is a useful one. We have noted that in cases such as *Geoghegan v. Institute of Chartered Accountants*[38] some judges were prepared to hold[39] that a decision of a self-regulatory professional association to take disciplinary action against a member was not governed by public law, even though that association's disciplinary rules had been approved by the Government. By contrast, in *R. v. Pharmaceutical Society ex p. API*[40] the Court of Justice held that a similar independent professional association was bound by Article 30 of the Treaty of Rome, because its activities and powers went beyond those of a typical private organisation.[41] If this useful analysis were to be employed in future cases it would mean that the Irish courts would have constructed a more realistic assesment of the extent of public law than the unduly formalistic attitude taken in some (but by no means all) cases.

Sources and character of power: statutory rather than common law

So far, the nature of the body has been discussed. The other question concerns the particular power which it is exercising. For while public law deals only with public bodies, it is also true that public bodies are sometimes governed by private law, in such fields as property, contract and tort. As has been said: "Like public figures, at least in theory, public bodies are entitled to have a private life."[42] This is certainly a long-established doctrine. It links up with the Diceyan view that, save in exceptional cases when there is some specific reason to justify the contrary, public bodies

---

[35] See generally, Craig and De Burca, *EC Law, Text Cases and Materials* (1995) pp. 184–189 and Curtin, "The Province of Government: Delimiting the Direct Effect of Directives in the Common Law Context" (1990) 15 E.L. Rev. 195.

[36] At para. 18 of the judgment.

[37] This point is illustrated by some of the post-*Foster* decisions such as Case C–419/92, *Scholz v. Universitaria di Cagliari* [1994] E.C.R. I–505 which proceeded on the common ground that the University of Cagliari was an "emanation of the State". However, as White notes in "Equality in the Canteen" (1994) 19 E.L. Rev. 308, whether other universities are to be treated as emanations of the State will depend on the funding and organisation of the institution concerned.

[38] [1995] 3 I.R. 86.

[39] See pp. 783–784.

[40] Joined Cases 266–267/87 [1989] E.C.R. 1295.

[41] For a similar approach, see also *SAT Fluggesellschaft mbH v. Eurocontrol,* Case C–364/92 [1994] E.C.R. I–43.

[42] Woolf, *op.cit.* above, n. 24, p. 223.

should be subject to the same law as private individuals. When Dicey enunciated this influential principle, he did so, by way of contrast against his (erroneous) portrayal of the *droit administratif* which, supposedly, set a rather low standard by which to control the Executive. Now, paradoxically, what is happening is that the law has developed to such an extent that it frequently offers a more stringent control over public bodies than over private bodies. One area in which this has occurred is the area of legitimate expectations. Here, within a few years, principles have developed which, to a varying degree, have superseded the normal rules on the formation of a contract and contractual dealing, where it is a public authority which is the defendant.[43]

This is, however, a particular area. If we return to the general principle, we find that in relation to it, the traditional teaching was that the private law activities of public bodies were to be regulated by private law in more or less the same way as in the case of private individuals or companies. In this jurisdiction, as we shall presently see,[44] this traditional principle has been articulated and sometimes followed. But, in addition, where public bodies are involved, there have been instances of private law cases litigated by way of judicial review and, even, examples of substantive judicial review precepts being applied to private law cases.

It is submitted that these developments are unfortunate and that the traditional principle ought to be retained. Consider the alternative. In the first place, it would introduce uncertainty into a fairly settled area if, as features of some new public law of contract (perhaps derived from the notion of mala fides) public authorities were made subject – to take a few hypothetical examples – to a particularly stringent doctrine of undue influence or remoteness of damage; or a duty of full disclosure (analagous to that which presently exists in regard to contracts *uberrimae fidei*). Secondly, such changes would be unfair to public authorities. For, while it is one thing to say, as Dicey did, that public authorities should not be above the law; it is another to state that public authorities should be at a disadvantage. In a constitutional democracy, public authorities should be – and to a substantial degree, are – merely embodiments of community interests and it would be wrong to suggest that – certainly, at least, as far as their financial dealings are concerned – they should be put in a different position from private parties.

There is, of course, a case to be made for saying that, in exceptional circumstances, public authorities should be subject to an exceptionally strict régime such that they should be governed in their common law activities by special principles of public law as well as the ordinary private law. This argument focuses upon the

---

[43] See pp. 858–900, and see also, *e.g.* the readiness of the High Court in both *Deane v. Voluntary Health Insurance Board (No. 2)*, unreported, High Court, April 22, 1993 and *Zockoll Group v. Bord Telecom Éireann*, unreported, High Court, November 28, 1997 to conclude that public bodies exercising quasi-monopoly powers had acted unreasonably in law in dealing with particular customers (see pp. 181–182. It is noteworthy that in both instances there had been no actual finding that the undertakings concerned had abused their dominant position, but were instead found liable by reference to standard public law principles. Interestingly, in *Zockoll*, Kelly J. doubted whether the public law principles of natural justice would apply to the withdrawal of telephone service, but he nonetheless held that the withdrawal of certain telephone numbers amounted in the circumstances of that case to an unreasonable exercise of statutory powers.

[44] On this point see pp. 775–776.

fact that public authorities dispose of huge reservoirs of economic power by way, largely, of making contracts and do so, moreover, in some sense, as a trustee for the community. They should not be free, therefore, to abuse the power which freedom of contract gives in order, for instance, either: to achieve policy objectives which would normally be effected by the exercise of the discretionary powers (a point to which we return below); or to alter the commercial or social ecology for others. An example of the second exception is most likely to arise in monopoly or near-monopoly conditions and the application of this principle in such conditions has been accepted, at any rate on the authority of a powerful *obiter dictum* in *McCord v. ESB*.[45] The subject of the *obiter dictum* (in these plenary proceedings seeking damages for breach of contract) was the ESB's standard form contract for the supply of electricity of which Henchy J. stated:

> ". . . judicial self-control requires that I withhold adverse comments on certain terms of the contract, such as that which purports to give contractual force to the idea that notices of intended disconnection may be taken as having been delivered on the weekday following the day they were posted; or on even the final term of the contract by which 'the Board reserves to itself the right to add to, alter or amend any of the foregoing terms and conditions, as it may think fit.'"[46]

Commenting on this legal artefact, Henchy J. said:

> "[The] contract made between the plaintiff and Board (incorporating the General Conditions Relating to Supply) is what is nowadays called a contract of adhesion: it is a standardized mass contract which must be entered into, on a take it or leave it basis, by the occupier of every premises in which electricity is to be used. The would-be consumer has no standing to ask that a single iota of the draft contract presented to him be changed before he signs it. He must lump it or leave it. But, because for reasons that are too obvious to enumerate, he cannot do without electricity, he is invariably forced by necessity into signing the contract, regardless of the fact that he may consider some of its terms arbitrary, or oppressive, or demonstrably unfair. He is compelled, from a position of weakness and necessity vis-à-vis a monopolist supplier of a vital commodity, to enter into what falls into the classification of a contract . . . The real facts show that such an approach is largely based on legal fictions. When a monopoly supplier of a vital public utility – which is what the Board is – forces on all its consumers a common form of contract, reserving to itself sweeping powers, including the power to vary the document unilaterally as it may think fit, such an instrument has less affinity with a freely negotiated interpersonal contract than with a set of bye-laws or with any other form of autonomic legislation. As such, its terms may have to be construed not simply as contractual elements but as components of a piece of delegated legislation, the validity of which will depend on whether it has kept within

---

[45] [1980] I.L.R.M. 153.
[46] *Ibid.* at 161.

the express or implied confines of the statutory delegation and, even if it has, whether the delegation granted or assumed is now consistent with the provisions of the Constitution of 1937.

. . .

However, having regard to my conclusion that the contractual powers of the Board are in the nature of delegated legislation, and because a statute replacing the powers conferred on the Board by the 1927 Act [Electricity (Supply) Act 1927] may result from this case, it might not be out of place to refer to what was laid down by this Court in the following passage in its judgment in *Cityview Press Ltd v. An Chomhairle Oiliúna"*.[47]

The judge then went on to quote the well-known passage concerning the impact of Article 15.2.1° of the Constitution upon the type of delegated legislation which is permissible. Even if the law does not go as far as to invoke this subsection of the Constitution, it seems reasonable to assume (from the tenor of the passage and the words "keep[ing] within the express or implied confines of the statutory delegation") that the normal common law controls which apply to delegated legislation – reasonableness, etc. – would also operate in the present case. Indeed, O'Higgins C.J. stated in *McCord*: "these General Conditions emanating as they do exclusively from the appellant must be construed strictly and must be operated fairly and reasonably".[48] Could the Supreme Court judgments in *McCord* be used as the basis for a test to determine when the contractual terms of a public body ought to be subject to judicial review? The test would presumably be along the lines of whether the case was one of (to quote from the judgment of Henchy J.) : ". . . a monopoly supplier of a vital public utility [is forcing] on its customers a common form of contract, reserving to itself sweeping powers . . .". Yet this test evokes the obvious objection that private suppliers of services and goods are sometimes *de facto* monopolists and almost invariably fix their own terms.

Let us turn now to an other exceptional area in which it is suggested that public law principles should apply to the making of contracts or the ownership of property, namely where these powers are used to implement some public policy, distinct from the usual commercial objectives which motivate any private person in entering a contract. One possible example relates to the administrative practice whereby persons tendering for or supplying services for the Government or other state agencies are required to present a tax clearance certificate. The programme implementing this policy is often without statutory means of support. It is, however, underpinned by a substantial sanction, as, in practice, no person can obtain a government contract without the benefit of such a certificate.[49]

---

[47] *Ibid.* at 161–162. The *Cityview Press* case is reported at [1980] I.R. 317. It is discussed below, at p. 11.

[48] [1980] I.L.R.M. 153 at 155.

[49] For cases in which public law principles were applied to a local authority's rôle as landlord under the private law Landlord and Tenant Act, 1931 s. 57 (2)(a), see *Rice v. Dublin Corporation* [1947] I.R. 425 at 455–456 discussed in the 2nd. ed. pp. 326–327 and *Wilkinson v. Dublin Co. Co.* [1991] I.L.R.M. 605 at 611.

2. The Limits of the Application for Judicial Review

As noted in the previous chapter, there are two sets of limitations upon the scope of applications for judicial review. The first of these (which was formerly of greater significance than it is today) is based on the characteristics of the remedies themselves. It has already been covered in chapter 13.2. The second requirement namely that the issue should be public in nature, is now dealt with by outlining the Irish case law in this issue, the more abstract discussion having already been covered in Part I of this chapter.

It may be useful, first of all, to set the scene by inquiring why in the light of the safeguards built into the application for judicial review procedure notwithstanding[50] any properly advised litigant might even want to argue his way on to the path of judicial review, if the apparently easier road offered by plenary proceedings were open to him. The answer is that, depending on the circumstances, there may be definite advantages to be gained from following that which might seem, at first sight, to be the rockier road. Judicial review proceedings are speedier and less expensive than the plenary procedure. Proceeding by way of judicial review may offer an applicant certain tactical advantages deriving from the fact that a High Court judge will determine at an early stage whether the case is sufficiently stateable to merit the grant of leave and, if leave is granted, this to a limited extent may have the effect of disadvantaging a potential respondent.[51]

The first Irish case in which this question was discussed after the coming into force of the new Rules is *Murtagh v. Board of Governors of St. Emer's School*,[52]

---

[50] For which see above pp. 706–707.

[51] This may be especially true in cases where the grant of leave attracts wide publicity in cases and where both sides are competing for media attention. *Cf.* the comments of O'Hanlon J. in *Desmond v. Glackin* [1993] 1 I.R. 1 at 9:

"Although the [judicial review] application was made *ex parte* it was not to be expected that it would escape the notice of the media when the interest of the public in the affair had already been whetted to an inordinate extent. The application was made in open court and reached the ears of the newsmen, giving rise to a flurry of activity on their part . . . Press reports of orders made by the courts on *ex parte* applications, where only one side has been heard, and more particularly the headlines which accompany such reports, often convey the wrong impression that some issue between the parties has been finally determined. I consider that there is a real risk that the general public will be deceived as to the nature of the relief granted unless such applications are reported in a very accurate manner."

See also Murphy J.'s telling comments in *Geoghegan v. Institute of Chartered Accountants in Ireland* [1995] 3 I.R. 86 at 101:

"In Ireland one suspects that judicial review is preferred as being a more expeditious and, perhaps, more glamorous remedy. The fact that there is an early hearing in the sense that there is an immediate application for leave to institute the proceedings is at least superficially attractive. It is no doubt a comfort to the party initiating proceedings to see the matter appear in a court list at an early date if only for that limited purpose rather than endure what must seem the interminable delay involved in statements of claim, defences, particulars, interrogatories and discovery."

See also the comments of Budd J. in *C.B. v. Director of Public Prosecutions*, unreported, High Court, October 9, 1995, regarding the publicity which applications for judicial review often generate.

[52] [1991] 1 I.R. 482. The Supreme Court subsequently dismissed the applicant's appeal against Barron J.'s judgment. No clear *ratio* emerges from that judgment, but the Court appears to have taken the view that, even assuming judicial review did lie, relief should be denied on discretionary grounds. Hederman J. clearly took the view that judicial review did not lie, as the punishment in question was

where Barron J. said that Order 84 was "intended to avoid submissions that the moving party had adopted the wrong procedure".[53] In this case, certiorari had been sought to quash a minor disciplinary punishment imposed on a schoolboy attending national school. The respondents raised the issue as to whether certiorari would lie, but Barron J. found for the applicant on this point. Stressing that the body whose decision it is sought to quash "must be discharging a function of a public nature affecting private rights" and must also be under a duty "to act fairly in arriving at the decision", Barron J. said that the questions of discipline in national schools were not in the private domain:

> "The school is a national school under the Department of Education. Rules formulated by the Department with the concurrence of the Minister for Finance govern every aspect of its existence. This includes school discipline. The provisions for discipline [in the respondents' school] are no different in character from any other of the Rules governing these schools. They are not consensual in nature. Nor do they become so because, where different schools may have adopted different codes of discipline, one school rather than another is chosen. In each case, the parameters of the code are governed by the Rules."[54]

Barron J.'s analysis of the public law element of the Rules for the National Schools is undoubtedly correct. And yet this public law–private law demarcation can give rise to serious anomalies. For example, does it follow from this demarcation that a declaratory action by way of plenary summons should be the only remedy available to a student expelled from university for serious misconduct, since this disciplinary jurisdiction is consensual and probably does not have its origins in public law? The gravity of this punishment of expulsion from university vastly exceeds that imposed in *Murtagh*, so it would be strange if the expeditious and cheaper remedy of judicial review were available in the latter case only.[55]

---

governed by private law; McCarthy J. reserved his position and O'Flaherty J. said (at 490) that the proceedings "should have been dismissed as quite inappropriate for judicial review", without, however, indicating whether judicial review could ever lie in respect of such a punishment. See also, *The State (Smullen) v. Duffy* [1980] I.L.R.M. 46 where a similar point does not appear to have been argued. Note that in England it has been held (correctly, it is submitted) that judicial review will lie to quash the decision of a local authority which, acting as an appeals committee, had upheld the permanent expulsion of a student from a private school: *R v. Cardinal Newman's School, Birmingham, ex p. S., The Times*, December 26, 1997. Note, however, that decisions of the Educational Committee of the Law Society have been held to be amenable to judicial review, since such decisions were taken pursuant to the Solicitors Act 1954 and the statutory instruments made thereunder: see *Gilmer v. Incorporated Law Society of Ireland* [1989] I.L.R.M. 590 and *MacGabhann v. Incorporated Law Society of Ireland* [1989] I.L.R.M. 854.

53 *Ibid.* at 486.
54 *Ibid.*
55 Compare this with the decision of Murphy J. in *Ó hUallacháin v. Burke* [1988] I.L.R.M. 693 which concerned the administration of a secondary school governed by a deed of trust. Did certiorari lie to quash a decision of the school management to limit the intake of pupils on the ground that the imposition of such a quota was unreasonable in law? Murphy J. not only held that the quota was not unreasonable in the circumstances of the case, but expressed considerable doubts as to whether judicial review would lie. While he refrained from expressing a final view of the "serious questions" as to jurisdiction which arose, he distinguished (at 702) *The State (Hayes) v. Criminal Injuries Compensation Board* [1982] I.L.R.M. 210 (in which it had been conceded by the State that the High Court had jurisdiction to review the operation of an extra-statutory tribunal) on the ground that:

Just as in England, there is now much uncertainty regarding the proper scope of judicial review. In one of the first cases where the point arose in the wake of the new Rules, *Murphy v. Turf Club*,[56] the applicant sought to challenge by way of judicial review a decision of the Turf Club not to renew a trainer's licence on the ground that the decision had been arrived at in breach of fair procedures.[57] While the Turf Club enjoys certain statutory powers,[58] these powers were held by Barr J. to be immaterial in this context as the Turf Board's disciplinary jurisdiction in respect of trainers was derived from contract. In the event, the applicant could not proceed by way of judicial review, but could only proceed in the ordinary way for breach of contract. As Barr J. said:

> "I have no doubt that the relationship between the applicant and the [Turf Club] derives from contract . . . and the [latter's] duty to regulate the sport of horse-racing in Ireland, though having a public dimension, is not a public duty as envisaged by the Court of Appeal in *R. v. Take-Over Panel, ex p. Datafin Plc*[59] and in purporting to revoke the applicant's training licence the respondent was not exercising a public law function. On the contrary, its decision was that of a domestic tribunal exercising a regulatory function over the applicant, being an interested person who had voluntarily submitted to its jurisdiction."[60]

"I doubt whether one can validly equate the deed of trust in the present case with the publications of a ministerial scheme . . . The deed of trust is a binding legal instrument which can be invoked and enforced at the behest of the parties thereto and indeed it would fall to the Attorney General to enforce the obligation imposed on trust deeds insofar as those duties relate or consist of a charity for the advancement of education. The relationship of course between the board of management and the principal and the other staff of the college or indeed between the students and the board of management are matters of comment and matters to be determined in accordance with private law.

56 [1989] I.R. 172

57 The applicant would seem to have had a good case on the merits. Inspectors called to the applicant's stables and, as a result of their complaints, the licence was revoked without any form of hearing some two days later: see *ibid.* at 172.

58 Such as the power to exclude certain persons from race-meetings: Racing and Racecourses Act 1945, s.39.

59 [1987] Q.B. 815. In *Bowes v. Motor Insurers' Bureau of Ireland* [1989] I.R. 225 Finlay C.J. said (at 228) that decisions of the Board (which is an extra-statutory body charged with the administering the agreement made between the insurance companies and the Minister for the Environment) "could only be reviewed by the courts . . . in accordance with the principles of judicial review". This short passage would suggest that decisions of the Board under this agreement are governed by principles of public law and that, accordingly, such decisions of the Board can be challenged by way of judicial review. This suggestion was taken up by Carroll J. in her judgment in *Hurley v. Motor Insurers' Bureau of Ireland* [1993] I.L.R.M. 886 when she quashed a decision which she found to be unreasonable and irrational.

60 Above, n. 56 at 174–175. In view of the fact that the Turf Club's disciplinary functions have now been subsumed into the functions of the Racing Regulatory Body established by Part III of the Irish Horseracing Industry Act 1994 and since the latter body is now obliged by s.45(2) of that Act to provide for an appeals procedure to be conducted in a "fair and impartial manner", one may expect that *Murphy v. Turf Club* would now be decided differently today in the light of the altered statutory background. *Murphy* was distinguished by the Supreme Court in *Walsh v. Irish Red Cross Society Ltd* [1997] 2 I.R. 479, where the issue was whether a person who had been expelled from the Society could challenge that expulsion by means of judicial review. Blayney J. noted that the Society has been established by the Irish Red Cross Act 1938 and a statutory instrument made pursuant to that Act. Given that the statutory instrument provided that all Irish citizens had the right to become

This passage prompts a number of observations. First, it illustrates the fact that the Turf Club can be amenable to judicial review in respect of some of its functions (for example, excluding the members of the public from racecourses) and not for others. This is not simply a matter of procedure, as indicated above in Part I: if judicial review does not lie then it is probable that the decision itself could only have been challenged on the private law ground that the Turf Club was in breach of contract as opposed to the wider public grounds based on reasonableness, irrationality and so forth (although this is not definitive as can be seen from Part I),[61] which deals with the public/private divide in the context of the substance of judicial review. Secondly, is it not altogether unrealistic to regard the Turf Club's jurisdiction as "voluntary" given that it enjoys a monopoly in respect of the granting of a horse-trainer's licence?[62] Thirdly, the *Murphy* judgment fails to take account of the argument that in reality the Turf Club was exercising a quasi-governmental function.

The private law/public law boundary has also been explored in a series of subsequent decisions and the following cases may be taken as representative. The first two of these, *O'Neill v. Íarnrod Éireann*[63] and *Beirne v. Garda Commissioner*[64] illustrate from different perspectives the issues which arise in applications for judicial review in respect of what essentially are employment matters. In the former case the respondent-employer had dismissed the applicant–employee in circumstances which amounted, so Barr J. found in the High Court, to a breach of the duty to observe fair procedures. Barr J. held, however, that the applicant was not entitled to apply for judicial review since the relationship between the applicant and the respondent was founded in a contractual relationship of master and servant.

In the Supreme Court in *O'Neill*, counsel for the applicant relied on cases such as *Murtagh, Ryan v. VIP Taxi Co-operative Society Ltd*[65] and *Flanagan v. University*

---

members of the Society on payment of the appropriate fee, Blayney J. said that he was satisified that "membership of the Society is not consensual" and that an examination of the statutory background, "the manner in which the Society was established, its structure and rules" demonstrated that "membership of the Society is not governed by private law, but is in the public domain." *Walsh* was applied by Kelly J. in *Bane v. Garda Representative Association* [1997] 2 I.R. 449, discussed at p. 785.

61 See above pp. 771–773.
62 It is true that in the not dissimilar *Aga Khan* case, *R v. Jockey Club, ex p. Aga Khan* [1993] 2 All E.R. 853 at 873 Farquharson L.J. dismissed this objection with these pithy remarks:

"Mr. Kentridge has referred to the lack of reality in describing such a relationship as consensual. The fact is that if the applicant wished to race his horses in this country he had no choice but to submit to the Jockey Club's jurisdiction. This may be true but nobody is obliged to race his horses in this country and it does not destroy the element of consensuality."

But *cf.* the comments of Pannick, "Who is subject to judicial review and in respect of what?" (1992) *Public Law* 1 where the author argued that the "source of power" test should no longer be conclusive on the issue of whether judicial review should lie, but that instead the courts should ask themselves whether (at p. 3):

"the respondent body has such a de facto monopoly over public life that an individual has no effective choice but to comply with their rules, regulations and decisions in order to operate in that area."

63 [1991] I.L.R.M. 129.
64 [1993] I.L.R.M. 1. See generally, Delany, "The Scope of Judicial Review – A Question of the Source or Nature of Powers" (1993) 11 I.L.T. 12.
65 *Irish Times*, April 10, 1989. In this case Lardner J. had quashed by certiorari an internal disciplinary decision of a taxi company on the ground that fair procedures had not been observed, but the question of whether judicial review would lie does not appear to have been argued.

College Dublin.[66] On appeal, the Supreme Court nevertheless upheld the approach of the High Court. Hederman J. stated: "I am satisfied that relief sought under Order 84 lies only against public authorities in respect of the duties conferred upon them by law [*sc.* statute][67]." And, addressing the argument that the judicial review procedure applied in the instant case just because constitutional justice was involved, Hederman J. added that "a constitutional issue of justice and fairness which may arise between private parties can only be determined by ordinary court procedure. See, for example, *Glover v. B.L.N. Ltd*".[68] Finlay C.J. expressed similar reservations.[69] Here, be it noted, is an example of a practice adverted to earlier, namely the conflation of a case on the nature of the body under review with a case on the source of the power under review.

The authority of *O'Neill v. Íarnrod Éireann* is weakened by the fact that the judgments were delivered in the context of an *ex parte* appeal and that, as a result of this, a majority of the Court considered that it would be incorrect to cut out the applicant at this preliminary stage from his opportunity of relief by way of judicial review. Nevertheless, there is no doubting the strength or unanimity of the views expressed.

In *Beirne v. Garda Commissioner*[70] the applicant was a probationer Garda who was dismissed for alleged misconduct. All members of the Supreme Court were agreed that fair procedures had not been observed and a majority of the Court held that such a decision was amenable to challenge by way of judicial review. Finlay C.J. laid down the following test:

> "The principle which, in general, excludes from the ambit of judicial review decisions made in the realm of private law by persons or tribunals whose authority derives from contract is . . . confined to cases or instances where the duty being performed by the decision-making authority is manifestly a private duty and where his right to make it derived from contract or solely from consent or the agreement of the parties affected. Where the duty being carried out by a decision-making authority, as occurs in this case, is of a nature which might ordinarily be seen as coming within the public domain, that decision can only be excluded from the reach of jurisdiction in judicial review if it can be shown that it solely and exclusively derived from an individual contract made in private law."[71]

---

[66] [1989] I.R. 172.
[67] *O'Neill v. Íarnrod Éireann* [1991] I.L.R.M. 129 at 133.
[68] *Ibid.*
[69] He had previously expressed similar reservations in *O'Neill v. Beaumont Hospital Board* [1990] I.L.R.M. 419. This issue has also caused difficulties for courts in both England and Northern Ireland. There is authority for the proposition that disputes concerning civil service contracts are governed solely by private law: see *R. v. Lord Chancellor's Department, ex p. Nangle* [1992] 1 All E.R. 897. On the other hand, there is also impressive authority for the proposition that judicial review will lie where the issue had "characteristics which imported the element of public law, rather than to focus upon the classification of the civil servant's employment or office": see *per* Carswell L.J. in *Re Philip's Application*, unreported, Northern Irish High Court, January 18, 1995. As the dispute in that case had not come before any statutory tribunal or similar body and as the impugned decision had not been one of "general application" and had not involved "any matter of public policy or turned on interpretation of legal powers", Carswell L.J. held that, in these circumstances, judicial review did not lie.
[70] [1993] I.L.R.M. 1.
[71] *Ibid.* at 2.

While it was true that the applicant's terms of employment provided that the Commissioner might dismiss him for misconduct, this jurisdiction was not one "which is solely or purely or even mainly derived from contract" but it is "a clear jurisdiction necessarily vested in the Commissioner by reason of the office which he holds and the statutory powers which are attached to it". In the circumstances, the decision was amenable to judicial review.

The principles in *Beirne* were applied in an unusual manner by Barr J. in *Browne v. Dundalk UDC*.[72] Here the representatives of the Sinn Féin party had contracted to hire a hall for their annual conference from the respondents. When the elected councillors learnt of this development, they passed a resolution recommending that the town clerk rescind the contract. The town clerk then sought to rescind the contract and the applicants sought judicial review of that decision. At the hearing it was not seriously disputed that the respondents were in breach of contract. While the applicants could well have sought specific performance of the contract, Barr J. held that judicial review would lie:

> "In the instant case there is no doubt that the hiring of the town hall to the applicant by the town clerk with the authority of the county manager constituted a valid administrative contract in private law made on behalf of the local authority. *Prima facie*, therefore, it is outside the realm of judicial review."[73]

However, applying the *Beirne* test, Barr J. held that there was an element in the purported recission of the contract which was not derived "solely and exclusively" from the contract itself:

> "I am satisfied that there is a crucial element in the transaction which brings it into the realm of public law and subject to judicial review . . . . The resolution of the council was successful in procuring the unlawful rescission of the hiring contract by the town clerk acting on behalf of the local authority. As the council's resolution was in terms politically motivated, it was clearly in the public domain."[74]

This is a most interesting example of political motives being regarded as being sufficient to give a particular case a public law dimension. While it might be tempting to treat this case as being purely private law in character, it might be conceded that the political motivation rendered the Council's decision unreasonable in the administrative law sense of that term and, accordingly, possibly amenable to quashing by way of judicial review.[75] It is notable, too, that in this case, substantive private law (contract law) was administered by way of public law proceedings (a reversal of the possibility canvassed above in Part 1 of this chapter[76]).

---

72 [1993] I.L.R.M. 328.
73 *Ibid.*, at 333–334.
74 *Ibid.* at 334. But *cf.* the judgment of Barr J. in *Healy v. Fingal County Council*, unreported, High Court, January 17, 1997 (deduction from councillor's expenses by way of equitable set-off held not to be within scope of judicial review).
75 *cf. Re Cook's Application* [1986] N.I. 242.
76 See above, p. 772.

On the other hand, *Rajah v. Royal College of Surgeons in Ireland*[77] is a decision which is on the other side of the line. Here the question was whether decisions taken by the respondents with regard to the exclusion of medical students from its College were amenable to judicial review. Keane J. held that they were not, since the decisions in question derived not from public law, "but from the contract which came into being when the applicant became a student in the College". The fact that RCSI derived its existence in law "from a charter or Act of Parliament is not a sufficient ground for bringing matters relating to the conduct and academic standing of its students within the ambit of judicial review".[78]

Murphy J. took a similar view in the case of *Geoghegan v. Institute of Chartered Accountants*.[79] Here the applicant was facing disciplinary charges and sought judicial review seeking to prohibit the Institute from proceeding with these charges. Although the evidence demonstrated that the Insitiute had been created by charter and supplemented by private Act of the Oireachtas and, furthermore, that the Institute's disciplinary code had been submitted to the Government for its approval, Murphy J. held that its decisions were not amenable to judicial review. In his view, the decisions in question were purely private decisions governed by consent and not amenable to judicial review. This is questionable, since the evidence showed that the disciplinary code in question had been agreed as appropriate in the absence of legislation.[80] On appeal, the Supreme Court appears to have been evenly divided on this question.[81] O'Flaherty J. (with whom Blayney J. agreed) declared that he was "inclined to agree" with Murphy J. and found support for this proposition in the judgment of the Divisional High Court in *The State (Colquhoun) v. D'Arcy*.[82] However, he qualified his remarks by adding that:

---

[77] [1994] 1 I.R. 384. *Cf.* in contrast the comments of Sedley J. in *R v. Manchester Metropolitan University, ex p. Nolan, The Independent,* July 15, 1993, where he said that as the respondent University was a "public institution discharging public functions and having no visitor, it is subject to judicial review of its decision on the normal grounds." See Carroll, "Enforcing Student's Rights in Irish and English Law" (1994) 12 I. L.T. 259.

[78] *Rajah, ibid.* at 394. *Cf.* the comments of Kelly L.J. in *Malone v. Queen's University, Belfast* [1988] N.I. 67 at 82 where he said that the fact that a University had been established by way of royal charter was "so remote and indirect that it can not realistically be said to bring in any significant element of public law." Similar arguments did not, however, sway Shanley J. in a similar (but, perhaps, distinguishable) case: *Eogan v. University College, Dublin* [1996] 2 I.L.R.M. 132. See below at pp. 784–785.

[79] [1995] 3 I.R. 86.

[80] But compare the approach of the English Court of Appeal in *R. v. Take-over Panel, ex p. Datafin* [1987] 1 All E.R. 564 and *R. v. Visitors of Inns of Courts, ex p. Calder* [1993] Q.B. 1. On the other hand, in *R. v. Jockey Club, ex p. Aga Khan* [1993] 2 All E.R. 853 the English Court of Appeal held that decisions of the Jockey Club were not amenable to judicial review, even though the Court accepted that "if the Jockey Club did not regulate this activity the government would probably be driven to create a public body to do so".

[81] O'Flaherty J. (with whom Blayney J. concurred) said in *Geoghegan v. Institute of Chartered Accountants* [1995] 3 I.R. 86 at 121 that he was "inclined to agree" with the judgment of Murphy J. (although he later emphasised that the "actual form of procedure used" was of "secondary importance"). Both Egan and Denham JJ. delivered separate judgments indicating their disagreement with Murphy J. on this question. Hamilton C.J. expressly reserved his position on this question.

[82] [1936] I.R. 641. In this case a Divisional High Court held that a canonical disciplinary inquiry was not amenable to review by certiorari. While the result was correct, some of the comments of the Court regarding the scope of certiorari would now be regarded as dated. It seems curious that O'Flaherty J. should look to this decision – which, it must be recalled, was decided at a time well before the development of modern administrative law – in order to determine the parameters of the present scope of judicial review.

". . . the actual *form* of procedure used to judicially review an action by a body entrusted with great power which can affect the livelihood of persons is of secondary importance. It may be that the most appropriate procedure in any given case is the one that gets the case on quickest . . .".[83]

On the other hand Denham J. was clearly of the view that judicial review would lie in respect of decisions of the Institute. She enumerated six separate factors which she thought pointed towards this conclusion:

"(1) This case relates to a major profession . . . with a special connection to the judicial organ of Government . . .

(2) The original source of the powers of the Institute is the Charter – through that and the legislation . . . the Institute has a nexus with two branches of the Government of the State.

(3) The functions of the Institute and its members come within the public domain of the State.

(4) The method by which the contractual relationship between the Institute and the [member] was created is an important factor as it was necessary for the individual to agree in a 'form' contract to the disciplinary process to gain entrance to membership of the Institute.

(5) The consequences of the domestic tribunal's decision may be very serious for a member.

(6) The proceedings before the disciplinary tribunal must be fair and in accordance with the principles of natural justice . . . . [84]"

This latter approach seems more compelling. After all, the *Geoghegan* case concerned the exercise of powers in relation to a regulated profession with statutory links to the administration of justice. In effect, the disciplinary procedures in question were agreed with the Government in lieu of legislation and against that background it would seem pure formalism to suggest that judicial review should not lie.[85]

At all events, in the first decision on this point delivered in the wake of *Geoghegan, Eogan v. University College, Dublin*,[86] Shanley J. clearly indicated his preference for the views of Denham J. This case concerned a claim brought on behalf of a retired professor that a new policy of refusing to extend tenure beyond the age of 65 years infringed his legitimate expectations. The College Stautes

---

[83] *Geoghegan v. Institute of Chartered Accountants* [1995] 3 I.R. 86 at 121. In *Rafferty v. Bus Éireann* [1997] 2 I.R. 424, Kelly J. said (correctly, it is submitted) that he was by "no means certain" that the "quickest procedure" argument represented the correct criterion and he noted that these comments of O'Flaherty J. were merely *obiter dicta*.

[84] [1995] 3 I.R 86 at 130–131.

[85] See generally Costello, "The Identification of Organisations Subject to Judicial Review" (1995) 17 D.U.L.J. 89 (N.S.). If O'Flaherty J. is correct, it would seem to mean that other extra-statutory bodies established under a "standard form contract" basis – such as the Barristers' Professional Conduct Tribunal – would not be amenable to judicial review. Note, however, that in persuasively argued judgments, the English Court of Appeal took a different view: see *R. v. Visitors to the Inns of Court, ex p. Calder* [1994] Q.B. 1.

[86] [1996] 2 I.L.R.M. 132.

permitted serving professors to continue in office to the age of 70, providing that this was recommended by the Governing Body with the consent of the University Senate. Shanley J. drew attention to the fact that the statutes in question had been made pursuant to the Irish Universities Act 1908 and that by section 5(2) of that Act, the statutes were required to be laid before both Houses of the Oireachtas. In the circumstances, as he was satisfied that as the decision to appoint and not to continue in office "were decisions taken in substance pursuant to the statutory regime flowing from the 1908 Act", Shanley J. held that this decision in question could be challenged by means of judicial review.[87]

A similar preference was evinced by Kelly J. in *Rafferty v. Bus Éireann*[88], where the applicants challenged by way of judicial route a decision of the respondent to alter their terms of employment in a manner which (they claimed) infringed section 14 of the Transport (Reorganisation of Coras Iompair Éireann) Act 1986. Kelly J. applied the factors identified by Denham J. in *Geoghegan* in concluding that the respondent's decision could be challenged by way of judicial review.[89] Kelly J. again applied these same criteria in *Bane v. Garda Representative Association*,[90] a case where the applicants had challenged by way of judicial review certain disciplinary actions which had been taken against them by the Association. In holding that the decisions were amenable to judicial review, Kelly J. drew attention to the fact that a number of the *Geoghegan* criteria were also present in this case. Thus, while the law is still in a state of flux, it seems that clear weight of judicial authority on this point favours the more liberal approach advanced by Denham J. in *Geoghegan*.

Does judicial review lie in respect of companies and other private law bodies exercising public law powers?

A related question which has yet to be authoritatively answered is whether private law bodies discharging public law powers are amenable to judicial review. The decision in *Geoghegan* may provide an example of this, but, perhaps, the problem might more clearly arise if, say, new legislation were to authorise the Minister for Justice to allow prisons to be run by private security firms. In principle, it would

---

87 The strict *ratio decidendi* of this decision appears to be authority for the proposition that only decisions made pursuant to the UCD statutes are amenable to judicial review and that, perhaps, different considerations would arise if the applicant had held a non-tenured post which was not governed by the statutes: see, *e.g. Re Malone's Application* [1988] N.I. 67. See also *O'Connor v. Nenagh UDC*, unreported, High Court, July 16, 1996.

88 [1997] 2 I.R. 424. See, however, *Healy v. Fingal County Council*, unreported, High Court, January 17, 1997 where the applicant was a local councillor who had challenged the validity of an order made by a county manager deducting sums due to the Council. Barr J. held that as the Council was deducting the sums by way of equitable set-off, the applicant could not proceed by way of judicial review.

89 He observed that:
"Whilst the contracts of employment which form the subject of this action may originally have been private ones between employee and employer (albeit a public employer), they have been altered by statute and are given an express statutory protection which is not the case in an ordinary private contract. I am of the view that the relationship between the parties here is not derived solely from a private law contract."

90 [1997] 2 I.R. 449.

seem that judicial review would lie in such an instance to quash an unlawful disciplinary punishment, notwithstanding the fact that the power would have been exercised by or on behalf of a private security firm. A contemporary instance of where such public law powers have been conferred on what is, in form, a private body is provided by the Irish Aviation Authority Act 1993. The Irish Aviation Authority is cast as a private company,[91] but it may exercise quite far-reaching regulatory, licensing and related functions, including the power to detain aircraft.[92] Furthermore, it is "owned" and financed by the State. It would seem inconceivable that the owner of an airplane who claimed that its detention was unlawful would not have a remedy by way of judicial review against the Authority, its status as a private company notwithstanding.[93]

The unsatisfactory nature of the public law/private law divide

The uncertainty created by the wealth of case law on this vexed subject is, for several reasons, scarcely satisfactory. As Carswell J. succintly put it in a Northern Irish context:

> "It does not seem to me consistent with the development of the law since the fusion of law and equity that the claimant's choice of remedy should be made to possess such a degree of importance; and it seems to me quite undesirable that litigants should be subjected unnecessarily to the hazards of having to make a correct guess in which court to pursue their claims."[94]

This uncertainty, perhaps, gives added weight to the question (which it is often salutary to ask about questions of doctrine), namely: does it matter and, if so, why?[95]

---

[91] However, this rather disguises the essential nature of the company, since shareholders who are not Ministers of the Government are required to hold their shares in trust for the Minister for Finance: see s.24 of the 1993 Act. See generally, Hoy, "Annotation to The Irish Aviation Authority Act 1993" [1993] I.C.L.S.A. 29–01. The Irish Takeover Panel is another example of what in reality is a public law body, even though in form it is a public company formed and registered under the Companies Acts 1963–1990: see Irish Takeover Panel Act 1997, s.3(1). The public law character of the Panel is underscored by the fact that its decisions can only be challenged by means of judicial review: see s.13(1) of the 1997 Act.

[92] Thus, by virtue of s.67 of the Irish Aviation Authority Act 1993, the company may exercise powers of detention (formerly exercised by the Minister) in respect of aircraft who have not paid certain aerodrome and route charges.

[93] In *Matthews v. Irish Coursing Club Ltd* [1993] 1 I.R. 346 O'Hanlon J. granted an order of certiorari quashing a decision of the respondent company. The company had been given certain statutory responsibilities under the Greyhound Industry Act 1958 and O'Hanlon J. observed (at 354) that it had been accepted that "the decision made by the respondent was an exercise of its discretionary powers as a body established by statute and having important public duties to perform".

[94] *Re Carroll* [1988] N.I. 152 at 165.

[95] Thus, in *Geoghegan v. Institute of Chartered Accountants in Ireland* [1995] 3 I.R. 86, O'Flaherty J. suggested (at 121) that the distinction was only of "secondary importance" and that in the case of a challenge to "an action by a body entrusted with great powers", it may be that "the most appropriate procedure in any given case is the one that gets the case on quickest". It may be noted that these remarks followed an earlier statement by the judge (at 120) indicating that the Institute was governed by the substantive rules of public law (fair procedures, proportionality, etc.) But if this is so, there would appear to be something of an internal contradiction in this reasoning. If the Institute's disciplinary functions are governed by the substantive rules of public law, then – if one makes the assumption that the same definition of the public/private border applies in the two contexts (on which see above pp. 738–784) – there seems little reason to suggest that the judicial review procedure should not lie, even though O'Flaherty J. said that he inclined to the view that a challenge to a decision of the Institute should not be brought by way of judicial review.

We can answer this question briefly by underscoring considerations which have been mentioned earlier in this section and the more theoretical Part 1 of this chapter. First, we will consider the significance of the public/private divide, in the context, of the application of the substantive principles of judicial review. If one takes the view that, for example the requirement of reasonableness should not be imposed promiscuously on all transactions and functions even if a public body or what may seem to be a public body is involved, then it would seem inevitable that some such borderline should be observed. Take, secondly, the question of the scope of the application for judicial review. Here a variety of different judicial approaches is manifest. At first sight, there may be much to be said for the view that quickest is best, especially given the fact that the classic view for differentiation – namely, the safeguards built into the application for judicial review to protect the position of the public bodies – is *ex hypothesis* of little significance, given that a properly advised applicant has decided to embark on the judicial review route.

However, other factors remain relevant. First, if an application for judicial review is being entertained it is unthinkable that the substantive principles of judicial review would not be applied. In this way the issue raised earlier concerning the applicability of these substantive principles would have been automatically settled simply by permitting the judicial review application to proceed. Secondly, since there are substantial advantages – notably expedition[96] – in the judicial review route. It is axiomatic that there must be some principled criterion to determine which type of litigant should have the chance of these advantages. It is accepted even in the most expansive of judicial authorities that the criterion should be grounded upon the notion that the State's action in the public law field has a peculiarly significant effect upon the community. The conclusion would seem to follow that there has to be some concept of a public/private divide in order to ensure that only certain types of cases enjoy this special procedure.

At the same time great care needs to be taken in defining this borderline. Does it, for example, make any sense to distinguish between the decisions of, say, different educational institutions on the basis of their legal origin? The essential point is that in each case they wield a substantial degree of educational power over the individual and often do so, on what is, in practice, close to a monopoly basis. On this view, it seems preferable, first, that they should all be subject to the same form of supervision by the courts, and, secondly, that that form should be an application for judicial review.[97]

---

[96] See generally Chap. 13.

[97] This is a vexed question. In *Flanagan v. University College, Dublin* [1988] I.R. 724 certiorari was granted to quash such a disciplinary punishment and the procedural issue of whether judicial review would lie was not raised. The issue might also have been addressed in *Kenny v. Kelly* [1988] I.R. 457 (a judicial review case involving UCD admissions policy), but this procedural objection was only raised at the hearing and Barron J. said that, at this stage, it was too late to raise this point.

There have been some English cases where certiorari was said to lie to quash a punishment of this kind (*e.g. R. v. Aston University Senate, ex p. Roffey* [1969] 2 Q.B. 538), but this was doubted by Russell L.J. in *Herring v. Templeman* [1973] 3 All E.R. 569 at 585. There was a suggestion in *R. v. Disciplinary Committee of the Jockey Club, ex p. Massingberd-Mundy* [1993] 2 All E.R. 207 that the fact that the Jockey Club was established by Royal Charter might be enough to make it amenable to judicial review. Perhaps the fact that both the University of Dublin and the constituent colleges of the National University of Ireland were established by Royal Charter (in the latter case by charter under the Irish Universities Act 1908) might be sufficient for this purpose. However, in *Malone v.*

When, however one turns from the question of what is a public body to the issue of whether a particular power is to be classified as "public" and hence, subject to judicial review, there may be (as was argued above in Part 1 of this chapter) a genuine basis for a more discriminating attitude. Such an attitude would, as was done in *O'Neill v. Íarnrod Éireann*, regard statutory powers as exceptional, far-reaching and, therefore, "public" and, so, to be treated differently from a contract of employment (or any other commercial contract) on the basis that a contract of employment with a public body should be treated in the same way as a contract with a private employer.[98]

3. Can a Public Law Issue be Litigated by Way of Plenary Proceedings?

It is to be noted that unlike Order 84, rule 18(1) of the Rules of the Superior Courts (which, of course, relates to the purely public law remedies of certiorari, prohibition and mandamus), rule 18(2) is couched in discretionary language. ("An application for a declaration may be made by way of an application for judicial review.") It might appear that the litigant is given a choice: he may apply for a declaration or an injunction by way of an application for judicial review or he may, as in the pre-1986 era, commence the proceedings by way of plenary summons. But the litigant's choice is not an unrestricted one; in the first place, it would seem likely that the application for judicial review is only available where the proceedings relate to the exercise of public law powers by a public body. The issue here has previously been discussed in the case of the specialist public law remedies, certiorari, prohibition and mandamus and one might presume that the solution would be the same in the case of the declaration and injunction, for the reason that the policy implications are similar.

But in regard to the declaration and injunction, there is a further question which of its nature could only arise in the case of these two remedies for the reason that they are available on a plenary summons. It is really the reverse problem to that

---

Queen's University, Belfast [1988] N.I. 67 at 82 these facts were said by Kelly L.J. to be "so remote and indirect that it can not realistically be said to bring in any significant element of public law", an approach echoed by the judgment of Keane J. in *Rajah v. Royal College of Surgeons in Ireland* [1994] 1 I.R. 384. Yet a further approach is evident in the judgment of Shanley J. in *Eogan v. University College, Dublin* [1996] 2 I.L.R.M. 132 where he held that decisions of the University taken pursuant to its internal statutes which were promulgated under the Irish Universities Act 1908 were amenable to judicial review. In any event, it is undesirable that the availability of judicial review should turn on such fine points.

[98] By way of contrast, see the approach of the Court of Justice to the analogous question of the extent of the State in the context of European Community law. In *Foster v. British Gas plc*, Case C–188/89, [1990] E.C.R. I–3313 the Court held that the "direct effect" doctrine might be invoked by employees of State companies "which were subject to the authority or control of the State or had special powers beyond those which result from the normal rules applicable to relations between individuals". On the other hand, the English Court of Appeal has held that it does not suffice for this purpose that the body in question is ultimately owned by the State: see *Doughty v. Rolls Royce plc* [1992] 1 C.M.L.R. 1045. On this topic, see Curtin, "The Province of Government: Delimiting the Direct Effect of Directives in the Common Law Context" (1990) 15 E.L. Rev. 195 and above pp. 772–773.

which has been encountered in Part 2 of this chapter. It is this: where declaration or injunction is sought to be raised in a public law matter is the party aggrieved confined to an application by way of judicial review or may he or she litigate the case by way of plenary summons? Before addressing this issue further, it may be convenient to elaborate it and (for the sake of comparison) the reverse issue, by way of examples:

> A local authority fails to honour its contractual obligation to purchase certain products from X Company Ltd. X Company Ltd seeks a declaration that the local authority are in breach of contract. X Company Ltd cannot proceed by way of an application for judicial review, for although the respondent is a public body, the matter does not relate to the exercise of the authority's public law functions, but is governed by ordinary principles of contract. X Company Ltd must commence declaratory proceedings by way of plenary summons. If the company proceeds by way of an application for judicial review, the court may, instead of refusing the application, order the proceedings to continue as if they had been begun by plenary summons.

Secondly, consider the converse case, *i.e.* where public functions are involved:

> A local authority refuses to grant Y a licence under the Casual Trading Act 1980. Y seeks a declaration that this refusal is invalid. Since Y's claim relates to the exercise of public law powers by a public body, then of course, the declaratory action may proceed by way of an application for judicial review. It appears that in this jurisdiction, Y may, alternatively, commence the proceedings by way of plenary summons, save that, in exceptional cases, questions of an abuse of process may arise where the litigant's motivation is to circumvent the stricter time limits and other safeguards provided for in Order 84 by proceedings by way of plenary summons.

Let us now enlarge on the subject-matter illustrated by the second example. It should be noted that there is no converse power to that contained in Order 84, rule 26(5) whereby proceedings, commenced by way of judicial review, may be ordered to continue as if they had begun by way of plenary summons.[99] It is not immediately obvious why the courts should not have been given the power to "convert" an action

---

[99] In *R. v. East Berkshire Health Authority, ex p. Walsh* [1985] Q.B. 152 at 166 Sir John Donaldson M.R. described the equivalent English rule in the following terms:

> "This is an anti-technicality rule. It is designed to preserve the position of an applicant for relief who finds that the basis of that relief is private law rather than public law. It is not designed to allow him to amend and to claim different relief."

In that case the applicant had sought certiorari and had made only passing references to declaratory relief. The Court of Appeal refused to allow him to amend his claim and proceed as if the proceedings had begun by way of plenary summons. This attitude is probably too restrictive as far as practice in this jurisdiction is concerned. Ord. 84, r. 26(5) has often been invoked to enable judicial review cases presenting complex legal and factual issues to proceed by way of plenary summons. It is true that the position in *Walsh* was somewhat different in that the entire basis of his claim was held to be outside the equivalent of Ord. 84, as opposed to the majority of cases where this rule is invoked where it is considered more convenient having regard to the facts of the case to allow the matter to proceed by way of plenary summons. Nevertheless, it is difficult to envisage the Irish courts taking such narrow view of an anti-technicality rule.

commenced by way of plenary summons into an application for judicial review. It may be that, were such a power to exist, it would facilitate litigants who wished to circumvent the inherent restrictions in the Order 84 procedure (the need for leave, strict time limits, etc.) by commencing their action by way of plenary summons and for these reasons, the Superior Court Rules Committee deliberately elected to allow conversion in one direction only. If this is so, this would be another powerful argument in favour of the approach favoured by the English courts (and described below), namely that Order 84 creates a special self-contained procedure for challenging administrative decisions and that, as a general rule, any challenges to such a decision must be brought in this fashion. It is to this important issue that we now turn.

Procedural exclusivity and the decision in O'Reilly v. Mackman

The English law on this point was established by *O'Reilly v. Mackman*[100] in which certain prisoners commenced declaratory proceedings by plenary summons against a prison board of visitors. They sought declarations to the effect that the board of visitors had acted contrary to natural justice and that disciplinary punishments imposed by them were invalid. As this complaint was likely to raise many disputed issues of fact, it was decided to proceed by way of plenary action rather than by way of an application for judicial review. The House of Lords held that the actions should be struck out as an abuse of process.

In a judgment "full of synthesising power"[101] Lord Diplock pointed out that whereas formerly the courts had, by concession, encouraged the use of the declaration and injunction in public law cases in order to permit litigants to avoid the procedural limitations of scope which then attached to the purely public law remedies of certiorari, prohibition and mandamus, this concession should now be withdrawn in view of the removal of those procedural defects by the new Rules of Court. More importantly, the new judicial review procedures contained certain safeguards designed to protect public bodies from vexatious and unmeritorious claims. An applicant for judicial review must obtain leave from the High Court, and conditions may be attached to the grant of leave. The applicant must, from the outset, put his case on affidavit, and cannot rely on merely unsworn allegations in the pleadings. What is of special importance is that there is such a short time-limit. This means that the judicial review procedure provides for a speedy and expeditious determination of the validity of administrative action, in contrast to the delays that may be caused in the case of an action commenced by plenary summons. Such delays would be particularly unwelcome in such diverse areas as extradition, planning and adoption. As Lord Diplock explained:

> "So to delay the judge's decision [as to whether to grant leave] would defeat the public policy that underlies the grant of those protections: viz. the need, in the interest of good administration and of third parties who may be

---

[100] 1983] 2 A.C. 237. For largely critical comment see Wade, "Procedure and Prerogative in Public Law" (1985) 101 L.Q.R. 180. Many will agree with Professor Jolowicz's observation that *O'Reilly v. Mackman* represented a "singularly unfortunate step back to the technicalities of a by-gone age": see "The Forms of Action Disinterred" (1983) Camb. L.J. 15, 1

[101] Wade, *ibid.* at p. 186.

indirectly affected by the decision, for speedy certainty as to whether it has the effect of a decision which is valid in public law. An action for a declaration and an injunction need not be commenced until the very end of the limitation period and the plaintiffs are not required to support their allegations by evidence on oath until the actual trial. The period of uncertainty as to the validity of a decision that has been challenged or allegations that may eventually turn out to be baseless or unsupported by evidence on oath, may thus be strung out for a very lengthy period. Unless such an act can be struck out summarily at the outset as an abuse of the process of the court, the whole purpose of the public policy to which the change [in the Rules] was directed would be defeated."[102]

Given the similarities between the two systems of judicial review in both Ireland and England, a cogent argument might be made in favour of the application of the reasoning in *O'Reilly* in Ireland, especially in view of the fact that any other result would mean that the safeguards now contained in Order 84, which are designed to protect public authorities, could be circumvented by the use of an alternative procedure.

Nevertheless, even if it is difficult to take issue with the principle underlying Lord Diplock's reasoning, its practical operation has wreaked havoc ever since. A whole new process of characterisation of claims has become necessary and the decision in *O'Reilly* has been made subject to numerous exceptions.[103] It may even be said that the whole object of the reforms has been defeated by the decision. The new rules were designed to ease the path of public law litigants and to ensure that a meritorious application was not lost by reason of the wrong choice of remedy. In Britain, however, many litigants have found in the wake of *O'Reilly v. Mackman* that their applications for judicial review have been struck out by reason of the wrong choice of proceedings.[104] In fact, this result is actually now more frequent than ever was the case prior to the introduction of the new Rules in England in 1977, when the procedural reforms, designed to avoid precisely this result, came into force. Furthermore, judicial unhappiness with this decision is growing and there are signs that the entire issue may have to be re-considered by the House of Lords.[105] In summary, to import to operate the *O'Reilly* gloss in Ireland would entail drawing a demarcation line between public and private law and thus admitting by the back door the curse of characterisation which had just been ceremoniously expelled at

---

102   *O'Reilly v. Mackman* [1983] 2 A.C. 237 at 284.
103   The judicially-created exceptions include the following:
  – where there is no objection: *Gillick v. West Norfolk Area Health Authority* [1986] A.C. 112,
  – where the invalidity arises by way of defence: *Davy v. Spelthorne B.C.* [1984] A.C. 264; *R v. Reading Crown Court, ex p. Hutchinson* [1987] Q.B. 384,
  – where the Ord. 53 procedure is not well suited to the nature of the dispute: *Mercury Ltd v. Director General of Telecommunications* [1996] 1 W.L.R. 48,
  – where the issues arise collaterally in a claim for the infringement of a right of the plaintiff arising under private law: *Wandsworth L.B.C. v. Winder* [1985] A.C. 461; *Roy v. Kensington and Chelsea and Westminister FPC* [1992] 1 A.C. 624.
104   The procedural complexities arising from the *O'Reilly v. Mackman* are well summarised by Wade and Forsyth, *op. cit.*, above, n.24 pp. 686–695.
105   In *Equal Opportunities Commission v. Secretary of State* [1995] 1 A.C. 1 Lord Lowry commented (at 34) that he had never "been entirely happy with the wide procedural restriction for which *O'Reilly v. Mackman* is an authority, and I hope that that case will one day be the subject of your Lordships' further consideration." See also his speech in *Roy v. Kensington and Chelsea and Westminster Family Practitioner Committee* [1992] 1 A.C. 624.

the front door. Moreover, it does not appear that, under the pre-1986 Rules, public authorities were, in fact, unduly troubled by the prospect of having to defend actions for declarations or injunctions commenced by plenary summons.[106] Finally, in those special cases where speed of decision and certainty are considered to be of critical importance, the Oireachtas may intervene by statute and legislate for a form of *O'Reilly v. Mackman* rule, as has now been done in a number of special instances most notably by the Local Government (Planning and Development) Act 1992, which is considered below.

The rejection of O'Reilly v. Mackman *in Ireland*

The courts in this jurisdiction have shown no enthusiasm for *O'Reilly v. Mackman*: there have been several important actions where the applicant commenced a public law claim by way of plenary summons, yet this fact went unremarked.[107] Barron J. has commented (albeit in the context of whether certiorari would lie in a matter allegedly private in nature) that the object of Order 84 was "intended to avoid submissions that the moving party had adopted the wrong procedure",[108] a view which argues strongly against the adoption of *O'Reilly v. Mackman*. However, it was not until the judgment of Costello J. in *O'Donnell v. Dún Laoghaire Corporation*[109] that the matter received full consideration by an Irish court. Here the plaintiffs successfully established that certain water charges imposed by the defendants some years previously were invalid. It was argued that it was an abuse of process for the plaintiffs to proceed by way of plenary action, especially since the action had been commenced outside the three months time-limit prescribed by Order 84, rule 21(1).

In *O'Donnell* Costello J. explained that he could not follow the House of Lords' decision in *O'Reilly v. Mackman* because:

> "Firstly, as a matter of construction, I cannot construe the new rules as meaning that in matters of public law, O.84 provides an exclusive remedy in cases where the aggrieved party wishes to obtain a declaratory order and that such a person abuses the courts' processes by applying for such an order by plenary action. Secondly, I do not think that the court is at liberty to apply policy considerations and conclude that the public interest requires that the court should construe its jurisdiction granted by the new rules in the restrictive way suggested . . .".[110]

However Costello J. then went on to address and, to some degree, adopt the policy underlying *O'Reilly*. He held that the safeguards contained in Ord. 84 should be

---

[106] In *M v. An Bord Uchtála* [1977] I.R. 713 the Supreme Court saw no obstacle to the plaintiff's choice of declaration in preference to certiorari to quash a decision of the adoption board. See also the comments of Lord Slynn in *Mercury Ltd v. Director General of Telecommunications* [1996] 1 W.L.R. 48.

[107] These cases are too numerous to mention, but notable examples include *Crotty v. An Taoiseach* [1987] I.R. 713 (challenge to the validity of ratification of the Single European Act); *McGimpsey v. Ireland* [1988] I.R. 567 (challenge to the Anglo-Irish Agreement) and *McKenna v. An Taoiseach* (No. 2) [1995] 2 I.R. 10 (challenge to validity of government spending on divorce referendum).

[108] *Murtagh v. Board of Governors of St. Emer's School* [1991] 2 I.R. 482 at 486.

[109] [1991] I.L.R.M. 301.

[110] *Ibid.* at 314. A further consideration is that Ord. 84 has not been given statutory backing – there is no Irish counterpart to s. 31 of the Supreme Court Act 1981 – and in the absence of equivalent statutory provisions, the Superior Court Rules Committee would probably have been acting *ultra vires* had it

applied, *mutatis mutandis*, to actions against public authorities commenced by plenary summons (writ of summons):

"[I]n considering the effects of delay in a plenary action there are now persuasive reasons for adopting the principles enshrined in O. 84, r.21 relating to delay in applications for judicial review, so that if the plenary action is not brought within the three months [[111]] from the date on which the cause of action arose the court would normally refuse relief unless it is satisfied that had the claim been brought under O. 84, time would have been extended."[112]

Because he felt that the Order 84 safeguards could be applied to plenary actions against public authorities, Costello J. concluded that:

"The apprehended use of plenary actions as a device to defeat the protections given by Ord. 84 is not a real danger and does not justify the court in concluding that the proceedings by plenary action for declaratory relief must be an abuse of process."[113]

Apart from the different legal cultures prevailing in both jurisdictions - Irish judges seem to have a distaste for technical arguments of this kind – the fact that a majority of constitutional actions have been begun by plenary proceedings and not by judicial review must also have influenced this conclusion. In many of these cases the plaintiff simply attacks the constitutionality of the impugned legislation and there is no administrative law "decision" which lends itself to being quashed.[114]

The approach of Costello J. is a very sensible one and is certainly preferable to the inherent difficulties posed by *O'Reilly v. Mackman*. It is also in accord with the usual tenor of Irish decisions which is anti-technicality and, often, sympathetic to applicants. Yet the judgment does not address all of Lord Diplock's objections: what, for example, of the plaintiff who side-steps the requirement to obtain leave to apply for judicial review and simply commences a plenary action, as, in certain circumstances, this might amount to an abuse of process? This dichotomy will remain for so long as the Rules of the Superior Courts contain in-built special advantages for public authorities, since for so long as these safeguards remain, some litigants will seek to circumvent them by resorting to plenary actions.[115]

---

purported to prescribe an exclusive procedure for challenging the validity of an administrative decision.

111 In this case the plaintiff had sought a declaration that a decision to levy certain services charges was invalid. The time limit in such instances is three months: Order 84, r. 21(1). If the plaintiff had sought certiorari, the time limit would have been six months. It is not easy to discern why the different remedies should themselves have differing time limits .

112 *O'Donnell v. Dún Laoghaire Corporation* [1991] I.L.R.M. 301 at 314. For the reasons why despite the delay, on the facts in *O'Donnell*, the plaintiffs succeeded, see pp. 728–729. *O'Donnell* was followed by Kelly J. in *Landers v. Garda Síochána Complaints Board* [1997] 3 I.R. 347.

113 *Ibid.* 315. See also *O'Connor v. Nenagh UDC*, unreported, High Court, July 16, 1996, a case where the applicant challenged the validity of a certificate granted by the respondent in 1994 to a prospective purchaser of a supermarket to the effect that it was not aware of any non-compliance with the terms of an earlier planning permission granted in 1974. Geoghegan J. refused to entertain the application for judicial review on the ground that this was in reality an indirect means of challenging the validity of the earlier planning permission and an attempt to circumvent time limits for such a challenge which had long expired. See, too, *Cavern Systems Ltd v. Clontarf Residents' Association* [1984] I.L.R.M. 23 on pp. 794–795.

114 But *cf.* now *Equal Opportunities Commission v. Secretary of State for Employment* [1995] 1 A.C. 1.

115 *cf.* the speech of Lord Lowry in *Roy v. Kensignton and Chelsea FPC* [1992] 1 A.C. 634.

One answer to the problem just posed might be to apply parallel reasoning to that of Costello J. and to say that if the time limit contained in Order 84 could be applied to plenary actions, so too could the jurisdiction to exclude a weak case.[116] More significantly, though, is the basic problem, namely, that special safeguards for public authorities have only been provided in the case of public law. Thus, it might be thought that the radical transplant surgery which was performed by Costello J. (so far, be it noted, without any imprimatur from the Supreme Court) in respect of plenary actions would apply only in the case of public law. If this is correct, then the problem of characterisation would remain (though it has been somewhat contained). Furthermore, the Irish solution does not mean (as in England) that a public law action fails automatically if it is brought in plenary proceedings; rather that it fails only if it is deemed to constitute an abuse of process (the operation of which concept may also cause uncertainty).

One way of systematising the sort of compromise which appears to have been reached in Irish law would be to establish a single comprehensive form of action in all cases, irrespective of whether they involve public or private law. The speed and other advantages attaching to the present system of judicial review could have been preserved if the Rules of Court had provided for a special summary procedure (perhaps along the lines of the present special summons procedure with affidavit evidence and expedited hearings) in cases involving public authorities, with power to transfer the case to plenary hearing where this was warranted by the complexity of the facts or legal issues at stake. Finally, as we have already noted, there is the possibility of legislation prescribing special procedures for certain types of judicial review applications, *e.g.* in planning matters, to which we now turn.

Legislating for O'Reilly v. Mackman: *the 1992 Planning Act*

Despite the practical difficulties which *O'Reilly v. Mackman* has caused the courts in the United Kingdom and Costello J.'s studied refusal to follow this decision, it would have to be recognised that there are certain circumstances where the avoidance of the judicial review procedure could give rise to an abuse of process. The main objection to *O'Reilly* lies in the fact that the House of Lords apparently insisted that every public law matter must be commenced by way of judicial review.

Planning law is one area where the possibility of such an abuse is manifest. This is well illustrated by the decision of Costello J. in 1983 in *Cavern Systems Dublin Ltd v. Clontarf Residents Association*[117] where a residents association had issued plenary proceedings challenging the grant of a planning permission – be it noted – within the two month statutory time limit. The association did not, however, serve the summons on the planning authority within that period, but claimed that it was entitled to do so at any time within the 12 months prescribed by Rules of Court.[118]

---

[116] One difficulty with this suggestion is that, unlike under the Order 84 procedure, there is no mechanism whereby a plaintiff can, ordinarily speaking, be required to obtain leave to commence a civil action by plenary summons. It is true that the courts possess a jurisdiction both under Ord. 19, r. 26 and by virtue of their own inherent jurisdiction to grant a summary judgment against a plaintiff where the case is frivolous or vexatious or doomed to fail (see, *e.g. O'Neill v. Ryan* [1993] I.L.R.M. 557), but the onus lies on the defendant to bring a motion to have the proceedings struck out and it is clear that this is relief which will only be granted in exceptional cases.

[117] [1984] I.L.R.M. 24.

[118] Now Ord. 8, r. 1 of the Rules of the Superior Courts 1986 (S.I. No. 15 of 1986).

Costello J. held that, in the absence of a compelling reason, the omission to serve the summons within the two month statutory period prescribed for planning cases was an abuse of process, as otherwise "the objector will have consciously rendered the [statutory time limit] useless and have flouted parliament's will".[119]

What is interesting is that, perhaps, because of the situation disclosed in cases such as *Clontarf Residents*, the Oireachtas has now expressly legislated for a form of the *O'Reilly v. Mackman* rule in planning matters.[120] Section 82(3A) of the Local Government (Planning and Development) Act 1963 (as inserted by section 19(3) of the Local Government (Planning and Development) Act 1992) now provides as follows:

> "(3A) A person shall not question the validity of a [planning permission or planning decision] otherwise than by way of application for judicial review under Order 84 of the Rules of the Superior Courts . . .
>
> . . .
>
> (3B)(a) An application for leave to apply for judicial review [under Order 84] shall —
> (i) be made within the period of two months commencing on the date on which the decision is given, and
> (ii) be made by motion on notice . . . to [all interested parties]."[121]

If this section did not contain the express prohibition on proceeding otherwise than by way of the Order 84 judicial review procedure, this would have been the very type of case calling for the application of an *O'Reilly v. Mackman* type rule or an *O'Donnell*-type exercise of the court's power to restrain an abuse. For the section provides for a special time limit[122] and the requirement as to leave is more stringent than in the case of judicial review in non-planning matters.[123] These safeguards are

---

119 *Clontarf Residents* [1984] I.L.R.M. 24 at 29–30. See also *O'Connor v. Nenagh UDC*, unreported High Court, July 16, 1996.

120 This formula has proved popular with the Oireachtas: see, *e.g.* Transport (Dublin Light Rail) Act 1996, s.12 (no challenge to decision of ministerial inquiry save by means of judicial review); Irish Takeover Panel Act 1997, s.13 (no challenge to decisions of Irish Takeover Panel save by means of judicial review).

121 The details of the parties who must be served are set out in s. 82 (3B)(a)(ii) and include (depending on the circumstances) the planning authority, An Bord Pleanála and the developer.

122 The application must be moved within two months s.82 (3B)(a)(i) of the 1963 Act, and time cannot be extended. In contrast, other applications for judicial review must be moved within six months and time can be extended where there is good reason to do so: R.S.C. Ord. 84, r.20(1). It suffices that the application is actually made within the time period, even if the original application is adjourned to a date outside of the time period: *Tennyson v. Dun Laoghaire Corporation* [1991] 2 I.R. 527. If the two-month period expires on a Saturday or Sunday or a public holiday, "time is extended until the first opportunity at which such application could have been made", see *Max Developments Ltd v. An Bord Pleanála* [1994] 2 I.R. 121 at 124, *per* Flood J. In *Keane v. An Bord Pleanála*, unreported, High Court, June 20, 1995, Murphy J. refused to sanction an amendment to the statement of grounds of an applicant challenging the validity of a planning permission, as to do so "would be to permit the applicant to bring the amended case outside the time limit prescribed by the 1992 Act". This was also the view of Barr J. in *McNamara v. An Bord Pleanála (No. 2)* [1996] 2 I.L.R.M. 339 where he stressed that the respondents were entitled to know within the two month period not only that the permission was being challanged but "also the specific grounds on which the challenge was based".

123 Section 82(3B)(a) of the 1963 Act provides that leave to challenge the validity of a planning decision shall not be granted "unless the High Court is satisfied that there are substantial grounds for

designed to ensure that development projects are not held up pending lengthy legal challenges which have little prospect of eventual success.[124] As Finlay C.J. said in *KSK Enterprises Ltd v. An Bord Pleanála*:

> ". . . it is clear that the intention of the legislature was greatly to confine the opportunity of persons to impugn by way of judicial review decisions made by the planning authorities and, in particular, one must assume that it was intended that a person who has obtained a planning permission should at a very short interval after the date of such decision in the absence of a judicial review be entirely legally protected against subsequent challenge to the

---

contending that the decision is invalid or ought to be quashed". This requirement is clearly more onerous than in the case of the ordinary application for leave. As for the meaning of the phrase "substantial grounds", see *Scott v. An Bord Pleanála* [1995] 1 I.L.R.M. 424 (where Egan J. equated this phrase with "reasonable grounds"; *Byrne v. Wicklow County Council*, unreported High Court, November 3, 1994; *Boland v. An Bord Pleanála* [1996] 3 I.R. 435; *Mulhall v. An Bord Pleanála, Irish Times*, June 10, 1996; *Blessington & District Community Council Ltd v. Wicklow County Council* [1997] 1 I.R. 273; *RGDATA Ltd v. An Bord Pleanála*, unreported, High Court, April 8, 1997; *Drogheda Port Co. v. Louth County Council*, unreported, High Court, April 11, 1997; *Lancefort Ltd v. An Bord Pleanála* [1997] 2 I.L.R.M. 508 and *Hynes v. An Bord Pleanála*, unreported, High Court, December 10, 1997. In *Lancefort* Marvis J. said (at 516) that "a ground cannot be 'substantial' if it cannot succeed."A further gloss was put on this phrase by Carroll J. in *McNamara v. An Bord Pleanála* (No. 1) [1995] 2 I.L.R.M. 125 when she described "substantial grounds" as being "reasonable", "arguable" and "weighty" and "it must not be trivial or tenuous." In *Keane v. An Bord Pleanála*, unreported High Court, June 20, 1995, where the applicant sought leave on both planning and non-planning grounds, Murphy J. contrasted the test applicable under the 1992 Act with the "modest" standard required in applications for leave in ordinary (*i.e.* non-planning) judicial review cases. *Cf.* the comments of Denham J. in *G. v. Director of Public Prosecutions* [1994] 1 I.R. 374 at 381 where she said that an applicant for judicial review (in a non-planning case) was merely required to show that at the leave stage that he had "an arguable case in law", although she conceded that on the actual application for judicial review "an applicant has an altogether heavier burden of proof to discharge".

The constitutionality of the absolute nature of the two-months time limit may be open to challenge. While accepting the public interest in ensuring that developers are not frustrated by lengthy delays in the planning system (see *KSK Enterprises Ltd v. An Bord Pleanála* [1994] 2 I.R. 128, it might be argued that the unqualified and absolute nature of the time limit constitutes a disproportionate attack on an applicant's property rights and right to litigate: see, *e.g. Brady v. Donegal County Council* [1989] I.L.R.M. 282. Note that both the Transport (Dublin Light Rail) Act 1997 and the Irish Takeover Panel Act 1997 contain saving clauses. S. 12(2)(b) of the Light Rail Act provides that the court has power to extend two-month time limit where it considers that there is "good and sufficient reason for extending the period within which the application shall be made". S.13(5) of the Takeover Panel Act allows for an extension of time where the failure to make the application "was not due to any neglect or default of [the applicant] or any person acting on his or behalf" and the extension of time "would not result in an injustice being done to any other person concerned in this matter", with the court being expressly directed to consider the possible consequences to third parties in this regard.

124 This policy is further under-scored by s. 82(3B)(b)(i) of the Local Government (Planning and Development) Act 1963 (as inserted by s.19(3) of the 1992 Act) which provides that the decision of the High Court on the application for leave to apply for judicial review or the judicial review application itself shall be final unless leave to appeal is granted by the High Court. Such leave is not to be granted unless the High Court certifies that its decisions "involves a point of law of exceptional public importance and that it is desirable in the public interest that an appeal should be taken to the Supreme Court". Once leave to appeal is granted, the Supreme Court is not confined to the point certified: see *Scott v. An Bord Pleanála* [1995] 1 I.L.R.M. 424. S. 82(3B)(b)(ii) contains a saver (required by Art. 34.4.4° of the Constitution) excepting from this statutory ouster determinations of the High Court involving a question as to the validity of a law having regard to the provisions of the Constitution. However, no appeal will lie to Supreme Court against the decision of the High Court to refuse to grant leave to appeal pursuant to s.82(3B)(b)(i) of the 1963 Act: see *Irish Asphalt Ltd v. An Bord Pleanála* [1997] 1 I.L.R.M. 81.

decision that was made and therefore presumably left in a position to act with safety upon the basis of that decision."[125]

In such circumstances, it would make little sense if an applicant could circumvent these particular statutory requirements by resorting to plenary proceedings where a declaration of invalidity could be sought without the need for leave and where the plaintiff's case would not have had to be put on affidavit. These considerations do not apply, however, to *every* type of administrative law proceedings. There is thus a strong argument to be made that *O'Reilly v. Mackman* should be made the exception and not the rule and that, if it is considered desirable that particular types of cases must be commenced by way of judicial review proceedings, any such innovation should be created by statute and not by the courts.[126]

Public law element is collateral

The discussion thus far has focussed upon a situation in which the applicant has sought a declaration in plenary proceedings, when he might have applied for a declaration by way of application for judicial review – in other words, the circumstances are such that the proceedings are exclusively or primarily public law in character. However, the situation in which the public law element is subordinate and arises as a collateral issue in a criminal prosecution or a civil law action needs to be considered.

A typical example of the former is *Listowel UDC v. McDonagh*[127] in which an accused was permitted to raise the defence to a prosecution for violating bye laws was that the bye laws were *ultra vires*. A typical example of the latter situation is *Cooper v. Wandsworth LBC*[128] in which the plaintiff sued for trespass to land. The local

---

125 [1994] 2 I.R. 128 at 135. See generally Macken, "How high the Hurdle? The Arcon Case and Judicial Review of Planning Decisions" (1995) 13 I.L.T. 78 (N.S.).
126 There is already a strong hint of this in the speech of Lord Lowry in *Roy v. Kensington and Chelsea and Westminister Family Practitioner Committee* [1992] 1 A.C. 624 at 653 when he said that he much preferred the "broad approach" to *O'Reilly v. Mackman*. By this he meant that the rule "did not apply generally against bringing actions to vindicate private rights in all circumstances in which those actions involved a challenge to a public law act or decision, but that it merely required the aggrieved person to proceed by way of judicial review only when private law rights were not at stake". Lord Lowry added that he much preferred the broad approach "which is both traditionally orthodox and consistent with the *Pyx Granite* principle [1960] A.C. 260. . . . It would also , if adopted, have the practical merit of getting rid of a procedural minefield . . .". For similar comments made by him in *Equal Opportunities Commission v. Secretary of State for Employment* [1995] 1 A.C. 1, see above p. 791, n.105. Likewise, in *Rye v. Sheffield City Council* [1997] 4 All E.R. 747, the English Court of Appeal gave guidelines with a view to stopping what Lord Woolf M.R. described (at 754) "this constant unprofitable litigation over the divide between public and private law proceedings." In essence, the guidelines suggest that proceedings begun by ordinary action should not be struck out if, had "the case, been brought by way of judicial review when the action was commenced, it is clear leave would have been granted." Lord Woolf M.R. then continued by saying that if the court would have granted leave (at 755):
  "then that is at least an indication that there has been no harm to the interests judicial review is designed to protect. In addition the court should consider by which procedure the case could be appropriately tried. If the answer is that an ordinary action is equally or more appropriate than an application for judicial review that again should be an indication that the action should not be struck out."
127 [1968] I.R. 312.
128 (1863) 14 C.B. 180 (N.S.).

authority's defence was founded upon a compulsory purchase order and the public law element was the validity of the compulsory purchase order. The question is whether there is any reason why such cases – or, at any rate, the public law element in such cases – have to be taken by way of judicial review. In England, such a contention would have some (albeit somewhat controversial) authority to support it.[129]

In this jurisdiction, the preponderance of authority is generally against this principle, save that there have been judicial suggestions to the effect that in cases where the impugned order is challenged collaterally, the deciding authority ought to be given the opportunity of defending the validity of its own order.[130]

In the first place, as a matter of principle, one should note that, as explained earlier, it has been held that a litigant who applies for a declaration in plenary proceedings is not necessarily barred because he could have gone by way of application for judicial review. And if the legal system has, so to speak, swallowed a camel, why strain at a gnat? It is also notable that a substantial minority of contemporary Irish administrative law decisions have, in fact, been cases of the type under consideration here, *i.e.* those litigated by way of plenary proceedings or criminal prosecution. Yet, in almost of all of them, the point was not even raised. One of the few exceptions to this observation is *Listowel UDC v. McDonagh* (a pre–1986 decision), where the Supreme Court fully, if somewhat impatiently, addressed the issue and ruled that there was no reason to require the accused to agitate the public law point in separate judicial review proceedings and then to have it adopted in the criminal prosecution. Indeed, there have been some cases – see, *e.g. Byrne v. Grey*[131] – where the courts have declined to entertain a judicial review application on the ground that the ultimate issue raised (in that case, the admissibility of evidence obtained pursuant to a search warrant which was said to be invalid) was best dealt with by the court of trial.

---

[129] The situation in England is rather complicated but in *Director of Public Prosecutions v. Bugg* [1993] Q.B. 473 it was held that magistrates hearing a prosecution for breach of bye-laws could entertain a challenge to the validity of bye-laws only on grounds of "substantive invalidity" (*i.e.* where the byelaws were on their face outside the scope of their powers or patently unreasonable). A challenge, however, on the ground of "procedural invalidity" was not normally an appropriate matter to be investigated in a magistrates' court such an investigation generally required evidence in proceedings to which the makers of the bye-laws would not be a party. (See also *Boddington v. British Transport Police, The Times*, July 23, 1996). See generally, Emery, "The *Vires* Defence – *Ultra Vires* as a Defence to Criminal or Civil Proceedings" (1992) Camb. L.J. 308; Feldman, "Collateral Challenge and Judicial Review: the Boundary Disputes Continues" [1993] P.L. 37 and Craig, *op. cit* above, n.24, pp. 552–562.

[130] In *Faulkner v. Minister for Industry and Commerce* [1997] E.L.R. 107 where O'Flaherty J. hinted that it was for this reason that a challenge to a decision of the Labour Court for an alleged breach of the requirement to state reasons should not have been by way of appeal on a point of law where the Labour Court was not a party, but rather by way of judicial review where the Labour Court would have been a respondent to such proceedings. See also to like effect the same judge's comments in *McSorley v. Governor of Mountjoy Prison* [1997] 2 I.R. 258. Note also the comments of Finlay P. in *Re Comhaltas Ceolteoirí Éireann*, unreported, High Court, December 5, 1977 where he held that the validity of a decision of a planning authority could not be challenged in the course of a case-stated from the District Court, since "it would be contrary to natural justice for a court to be called upon to adjudicate on the validity of the acts of the planning authority in a case to which they were not a party."

[131] [1988] I.R. 31.

CHAPTER 15

DAMAGES

1. Damages and Judicial Review

Prior to the introduction of the new Rules of the Superior Courts in 1986[1] it was not possible to combine a claim for damages with an application for a State side order, (although such a claim could be combined with an application for a declaration or injunction in plenary proceedings). If damages were sought, it was necessary to commence separate proceedings.[2] It may be surmised that prior to the procedural changes effected by the new Rules in 1986 many litigants were content to secure the invalidation of the impugned administrative act, and were not prepared to commence separate proceedings in order to press their claim for damages. The new Rules of the Superior Courts seek to rectify this procedural anomaly by providing for a new unified judicial review procedure. The new Order 84, rule 24 empowers the court to grant damages in addition to, or in lieu of, a State side order, or a declaration or an injunction. Order 84, rule 24 provides as follows:

> "(1) On an application for judicial review the Court may, subject to paragraph (2), award damages to an applicant if
>
> > (a) he has included in the statement in support of his application for leave under [Order 84, rule 20(3)] a claim for damages arising for any matter to which the application relates, and
> > (b) the Court is satisfied that, if the claim had been made in a civil action against any respondent or respondents begun by the applicant at the time of making this application, he would have been awarded damages."

The effect of these changes has been to make it easier for applicants to recover damages in respect of wrongful administrative action and such claims are now made with increasing frequency.

One practical problem which is likely to arise is whether it is possible to proceed via the Order 84 procedure where the applicant's claim is solely for damages. The strict language of Order 84, rule 24(1)(a) would seem to suggest a negative answer to this query, as the wording of this rule appears to imply that the court's jurisdiction to award damages presupposes the independent existence of an application for judicial review. In other words, the remedy of damages is only ancilliary to the

---

[1] S.I. No. 15 of 1986.
[2] Law Reform Commission, *Judicial Review of Administrative Action*, Working Paper No. 8 – 1979 (December 1979) pp. 4–5.

principal remedies of certiorari, prohibition, declaration, etc., and this would seem to imply that the judicial review procedure should not be availed of where damages are the principal remedy sought by the applicant. Yet this construction of Order 84, rule 24(1)(a) would seem to give rise to its own difficulties.

Assume that an applicant wishes to claim damages by way of an application for judicial review for false imprisonment and breach of constitutional rights following an unlawful arrest under section 30 of the Offences against the State Act 1939, on the ground that the extension order authorising a further 24 hours detention was unlawful.[3] It is, of course, open to him to proceed by way of plenary summons, but let us assume for reasons of speed and convenience he elects to seek damages by way of judicial review. The applicant will certainly encounter procedural difficulties if he merely seeks damages, but with a view to circumventing these problems, he may be advised to apply for an order of certiorari quashing the extension order. Such an application for certiorari is not vexatious or spurious if the applicant genuinely wishes to demonstrate the invalidity of this extension order. But what if the application for certiorari is included simply to ward off possible procedural difficulties? In such a case, are the courts to bar the applicant's path and direct that he proceed by way of plenary summons rather than on an application for judicial review?

A further difficulty is illustrated by the English case of *R. v. Home Secretary, ex p. Dew*.[4] Here a prisoner sought mandamus to compel the prison authorities to provide him with adequate medical treatment and damages for negligence. After the initial *ex parte* application had been made, the prison authorities undertook to provide the required medical treatment so that the applicant was left with his claim for damages. In those circumstances, Neill J. ruled that as the claim for damages did not arise from public law, it could not proceed and he struck out the judicial review proceedings.

It would be undesirable if the equivalent rule in this jurisdiction were to be interpreted so narrowly In particular, the question of whether an ancilliary claim for damages arises from public or private law may throw up formidable issues of characterisation. Thus, an action for trespass would generally be classified as private law, but how do matters stand if the claim is combined with a public law cause of action, such as a claim for breach of constitutional rights? Perhaps the best way of approaching the problem is to say that, provided that the claim for damages by way of judicial review is bona fide, the courts should entertain it.

---

[3] Order 19, r. 5 provides in relevant part that:
   "In all cases alleging a wrong within the meaning of the Civil Liability Acts 1961–1964, particulars of such wrong, any personal injuries suffered and any items of special damage shall be set out in the statement of claim or counterclaim and particulars of any contributory negligence shall be set out in the defence."
   Order 19, r. 7 deals with particulars. In effect, this means that all claims for damages in an application for judicial review must be fully pleaded in a manner analogous to that required in a plenary hearing. In *Duggan v. An Taoiseach* [1989] I.L.R.M. 710 at 731 Hamilton P. required that the plaintiffs "submit a statement of claim setting forth the loss which they alleged they have and are likely to suffer" before a judge of the High Court could assess the damages to which they were entitled by reason of a breach of their legitimate expectations.
[4] [1987] 1 W.L.R. 881. *Cf.* the comments of de Smith, Woolf & Jowell, *Judicial Review of Administrative Action* (1995) p. 200 where this decision is described as "unduly restrictive" and one which "requires reconsideration".

2. Common Law Defences to Actions in Tort

As a general proposition, it is true to say that neither the State nor any other public authority enjoys any special position in the law of torts. The general law – trespass, negligence, nuisance, breach of statutory duty, etc., – applies in substantially the same way as to a private person.[5] This is an important aspect of the rule of law and damages actions are an effective means of securing judicial protection against unlawful administrative action.

Most of the special immunities and exemptions for public bodies, which are considered presently, are statutory in origin. However, one wide common law principle is the rule that where a statute authorises the doing of a particular act, then no action will lie at the suit of any person if the inevitable consequence of the act is to cause damage, provided, of course, that it is done without negligence.[6] The most common application of this principle is where public bodies are authorised to commit what might otherwise be a nuisance.

One case in which this principle was considered is *Kelly v. Dublin County Council*.[7] Here, the defendant local authority had made use of a vacant site beside the plaintiff's cottage for the purpose of storing vehicles and materials used in an extensive road construction project. The plaintiffs claimed that these activities amounted to an actionable nuisance, but the defendants argued that they enjoyed statutory protection under the Local Government Act 1925. O'Hanlon J. found that the activities in question amounted to a nuisance. Next, as to the question of the defence under examination here, he held that while the 1925 Act afforded protection to the defendant's road construction work, it did not extend to the provision and use of a depot for vehicles and materials.[8] In the alternative, O'Hanlon J. held that the defendants had not shown that the nuisance was an inevitable result of the exercise of the statutory powers for there was no evidence to show that the Council had no reasonable alternative but to use this particular site.

Take next a case in which negligence was involved. In *Red Cow Service Station Ltd v. Murphy International Ltd and Bord Gáis Éireann*[9] it was held that, while under section 27(1)(d) of the Gas Act 1976 Bord Gáis Éireann has the power to dig or break or interfere with any road, if they acted negligently, *e.g.* broke a telephone cable and caused damage to the plaintiff beyond what was essential and necessary, they could not claim the protection of the Act. The 1976 Act provides a particular remedy and method of computation for any loss caused by the operation of the Act.

---

5   This passage was cited with approval by Blayney J. in *Emerald Meats Ltd v. Minister for Agriculture* [1997] 2 I.L.R.M. 275 at 295.
6   *Allen v. Gulf Oil Refining Ltd* [1981] A.C. 1001.
7   Unreported, High Court, O'Hanlon J. February 21, 1986.
8   Although it might well have been contended that as these ancilliary works were necessarily implied by the terms of the 1925 Act, the immunity should have also extended to them.
9   (1985) 3 I.L.T. (N.S.) 15. In *Collins v. Gypsum Industries Ltd* [1975] I.R. 331, the plaintiffs had claimed damages for personal injuries under the Mineral Development Act 1940. The Supreme Court held, however, that the 1940 Act provided for a scheme of compensation in respect of damage to land caused by mining operations and it did not extend to personal injuries. The proper forum for pursuing such a claim for personal injuries was that provided by the ordinary courts. See also, *Tate & Lyle Food Distribution Co. Ltd v. Greater London Council* [1983] 2 A.C. 509.

However, in *Allen v. Gulf Oil Refining Ltd*[10] a private Act of Parliament had authorised the defendant to construct a refinery but it did not specifically authorise the operation of the refinery. Some neighbours complained of excessive smell, vibration and noise and sued in nuisance. Nevertheless, the House of Lords ruled that the operation of the refinery was authorised at least by necessary implication; and as a result the plaintiffs had no remedy in so far as the nuisance complained of was the inevitable result of the authorised operation. But for reasons explained below, it is difficult to believe that an Irish court would reach the same conclusion were it faced with a case on similar facts."[11]

3. Rules of Immunity for Particular Sectors

There are, however, in addition, special rules creating immunity for particular areas of governmental action. As these exceptions (which, apart from the first one, are statutory in origin) are heterogeneous, they may be considered separately.

(i) *Roads*

The principle that a local authority is not liable for an injury to a user of the highway caused by a hole in the road resulting from failure to repair can be traced back to *Russell v. The Men Dwelling in the County of Devon*.[12] The basis of this immunity is that at common law the duty of repairing highways fell on the community, (though by virtue of a statute of 1614,[13] this duty was imposed on the parish). Because the inhabitants were not a corporation they could not be sued collectively and therefore no action lay against them in respect of their failure to carry out their duty. By contrast, in the case of misfeasance, someone has acted and the local authority who employed that person may be liable.[14] Despite the changes wrought by the Local Government (Ireland) Act 1898 – most notably the imposition, by section 82, on every county and district council of the duty of keeping the road in good condition and repair – the position remained the same.[15] The distinction between non-feasance and misfeasance has been judicially described as both "unsatisfactory"[16] and "anomalous",[17] but was regarded as sufficiently well-established to warrant its abrogation by statute. Section 60(1) of the Civil Liability Act 1961 provides that:

---

[10] [1981] A.C. 1001.
[11] See pp. 827–829.
[12] (1788) 2 T.R. 667.
[13] 11, 12 & 13 Jac. 1, c. 7 (Ir.), following the lines of the 1555 English statute (2 & 3 Ph. & M., c. 8).
[14] Notice Wade, *Administrative Law*, (7th ed., 1994), p. 782 gives a somewhat different account.
[15] *Harbinson v. Armagh County Council* [1902] 2 I.R. 538. The reasons for this restrictive approach were explained by Johnson J. (at 560–561):
   "To create such a liability a legislative enactment in express and affirmative terms is necessary, which should show that the Legislature in transferring the duty to this corporate body intended to change the nature and extent of their liability. I do not find anything in these enactments which shows any intention of the Legislature to impose on the corporate county council or on the ratepayers whom they represent a new liability which did not previously exist at common law or by statute, for non-feasance."
[16] *Kelly v. Mayo County Council* [1964] I.R. 315 at 324, *per* Kingsmill Moore J.
[17] *O'Brien v. Waterford County Council* [1926] I.R. 1 at 8, *per* Murnaghan J.

"A local authority shall be liable for damages caused as a result of their failure to maintain adequately a public road." Section 60(7), however, provides that the section is to come into operation on such day, not earlier than April 1, 1967, as might be fixed by order of the Government.

Since no such order has yet been made Costello J. held in *The State (Sheehan) v. Government of Ireland*[18] that the Government had failed in its statutory duty and made an order of mandamus directed against the Government compelling them to bring section 60 of the 1961 Act into effect. A majority of the Supreme Court, however, took a different view, with Henchy J. holding in effect that the discretion vested in the Government was unreviewable.[19]

In addition, the Oireachtas now seems determined to maintain this immunity, as section 19(4) and (5) of the Roads Act 1993 provide that:

"(4) No action or other proceedings shall lie or be maintainable against—

(a) the [National Roads] Authority,
(b) a committee performing functions delegated to it by the Authority,
(c) a road authority performing functions on behalf of the Authority,
(d) a body providing services to the Authority,

for the recovery of damages in respect of injury to persons, damage to property or other loss alleged to have been caused or contributed to by a failure of the Authority to perform or to comply with any of the functions conferred on it.

(5) (a) The Authority shall not be liable for damages caused as a result of any failure to maintain a national road.[20]

(b) In paragraph (a), 'damage' includes loss of property, loss of life and personal injury."

It is nonetheless possible, despite the result in *Sheehan*, that, given recent developments in the general law of civil liability,[21] the Supreme Court would react favourably to arguments that road authorities are not immune from liability in respect

---

18 [1987] I.R. 550. This case is further discussed at pp. 684–686.

19 *Ibid.* at 561. Note that in Northern Ireland the law was changed by the Roads (Liability of Road Authorities for Neglect) Act (Northern Ireland) 1966. Section 1(1) of this Act abrogated any rule of law which operated to exempt road authorities from liability for non-repair of roads. The law was further amended by the Roads (Northern Ireland) Order 1980, art. 8(1), which imposes an express duty on the Department of Environment to maintain all roads and to provide such maintenance compounds as it think fit. In *McKernan v. McGeown and Department of the Environment* [1983] N.I. 167, Gibson L.J. said, however, that there was no difference between the nature and extent of liability under the 1966 Act and the 1980 Order. As to liability under the 1966 Act, see *Lagan v. Department of the Environment* [1978] N.I. 120. For some limitations in the scope of the 1980 Order, see *Devenney v. Department of Environment* [1986] N.I. 7 and *Neill v. Department of Environment for Northern Ireland* [1990] N.I. 84.

20 "National road" is defined by s.2 of the 1993 Act as meaning a "public road or a proposed public road which is classified as a national road under section 10". In effect, the National Roads Authority has assumed responsibility for all major roads and local roads remain the responsibility of local authorities: see s.13 of the 1993 Act.

21 In *Forsyth v. Evans* [1980] N.I. 230, Kelly J. said that he was attracted "to the view that the neighbour principle of *Donoghue v. Stevenson* [1932] A.C. 562 might be applied having regard to modern day conditions and their extensive user". He was satisfied that there was "a sufficient relationship of proximity or neighbourhood" between a highway authority and the drivers and passengers of motor vehicles on highways. He considered, however, that there were sufficient considerations of public

of negligent non-feasance[22] and, if necessary, would hold that section 19(5)(a) of the 1993 Act is unconstitutional.

Since *Purtill v. Athlone U.D.C.*,[23] the Irish courts have steadily recognised the existence of a duty of care in situations where formerly it had been held that the defendant was exempt from responsibility (*e.g.* liability of occupier to trespasser,[24] liability of builder to second purchaser,[25] liability of animal owners[26]) and the rule would seem to be at variance with the march of the modern law of negligence at common law. As regards the immunity which the 1993 Act seeks to provide, might not a plaintiff injured in an accident due to failure to repair a hole in a road and unable to recover compensation because either of the common law principle or section 19(5)(a) of the 1993 Act, claim that the State has failed to vindicate, as required by Article 40.3 of the Constitution, his right to bodily integrity and the right to litigate a justiciable controversy? It is significant that such a claim would appear to be merely the invocation, in the context of a local authority, of the principles established in *Byrne v. Ireland*.[27]

(ii) *Treatment of the mentally ill*

Leave of the High Court is required where it is sought to institute civil proceedings against a health board in respect of acts purporting to have been done in pursuance of the Mental Treatment Act 1945.[28] Section 260(1) of the 1945 Act, which provides for the requirement of leave, goes on to state that such leave shall only be granted where the High Court is satisfied that there are substantial grounds for contending that the person against whom the proceedings are to be brought acted in bad faith or without reasonable care. The meaning of "substantial grounds" was considered by the Supreme Court in *O'Dowd v. North Western Health Board*,[29] where O'Higgins C.J. said that the section did no more than require the applicant:

> "To discharge the same onus of proof as he would be required to discharge in pursuing a claim for damages for a tort outside the Act, but to discharge it at an earlier point in time."[30]

---

    policy which justified the non-extension of the neighbour principle in this situation. (The case concerned the Department of the Environment's failure to minimise the hazards of weather on road surfaces.) Implicit support for the rationale of this decision is to be found in *Stovin v. Wise* [1996] 3 All E.R. 801 and *Convery v. Dublin County Council* [1996] 3 I.R. 153.

22 A water authority has been held to owe a duty of care to pedestrians using a footpath on a public highway in respect of water installations installed by it: *Ferguson v. Department of Environment* [1990] N.I. 247; and a local authority has been found guilty of a breach of a statutory duty where a pedestrian fell into an exposed gully, even though the road in question had not been taken in charge at the time: *Merriman v. Dublin Corporation* [1992] 1 I.R. 129.

23 [1968] I.R. 205.

24 *McNamara v. ESB* [1975] I.R. 1.

25 *Ward v. McMaster* [1985] I.R. 29. See Kerr (1985) 7 D.U.L.J. (N.S.) 109.

26 *Gillick v. O'Reilly* [1984] I.L.R.M. 402.

27 [1972] I.R. 241. See further, the comments of Barrington J. in *Duff v. Minister for Agriculture* [1997] 2 I.R. 22 whereby he appeared to suggest that Art. 40.3 imposed a duty on the judiciary to provide a remedy for a wrongful administrative act causing loss and damage.

28 Although the 1945 Act was described as a comprehensive statute providing for the treatment of mental disturbance and the care of persons suffering therefrom (see *Re Phillip Clarke* [1950] I.R. 235), it is generally recognised that new, fresh legislation is urgently needed.

29 [1983] I.L.R.M. 186.

30 *Ibid.* at 190.

In this case, a majority of the Supreme Court held that a mental patient who had been discharged after only six days of custody had not established "substantial grounds" within the meaning of section 260. It was true that the initial medical diagnosis was that the plaintiff was unlikely to recover within six months, but both O'Higgins C.J. and Griffin J. considered that, on the facts, there was nothing to suggest that this diagnosis had been incorrect or had been arrived at in a negligent fashion.

This question was further considered by the Supreme Court in *Murphy v. Greene*[31] where the Court stressed that as section 260 represented a curtailment of the constitutional right of every individual to have access to the courts, it must be strictly construed. Finlay C.J. nevertheless concluded that, this constitutional principle notwithstanding, the phrase "substantial grounds" meant "something more than probable or prima facie grounds".[32]

(iii) *Postal and telecommunications services*

Special provision is also made by section 64 of the Postal and Telecommunications Services Act 1983[33] which provides that An Post shall be immune from all liability in respect of any loss or damage suffered by a person in the use of a postal service by reason of (i) failure or delay in providing, operating or maintaining a postal service, or, (ii) failure, interruption, suspension or restriction of a postal service. Similarly, members of staff are immune from civil liability except at the suit of An Post itself in respect of any such loss or damage. Section 88 of the 1983 Act provides a similar immunity to Bord Telecom Éireann in respect of loss or damage suffered by reason of failure, etc., of a telecommunications service or any error or omission in a directory published by Bord Telecom itself or any telegrams or telex messages transmitted by the company.[34]

(iv) *Special Criminal Court*

Article 38.3 of the Constitution allows for the establishment of special courts where the ordinary courts "are inadequate to secure the effective administration of justice and the preservation of public peace and order". Part V of the Offences against the State Act 1939 regulates, *inter alia*, the composition, practice and procedure of the

---

[31] [1990] 2 I.R. 566.

[32] *Ibid.* at 573. In the present case a doctor had, following an emergency call, wrongly diagnosed the plaintiff (who was not his patient and who was drunk and disorderly on the evening in question) as suffering from mental illness and had him committed to an institution. The Court nonetheless concluded that the plaintiff had not satisfied the test contained in section 260 and refused him leave to commence the proceedings. See also *O'Reilly v. Moroney* [1992] 2 I.R. 145; *Bailey v. Gallagher* [1996] 2 I.L.R.M. 433; *Croke v. Smith*, Supreme Court, July 31, 1996 and *Melly v. Moran*, unreported, High Court, June 18, 1997. For a general discussion of the law in this area, see Cooney and O'Neill, *Psychiatric Detention: Civil Commitment in Ireland* (1997).

[33] On this provision in the context of the Ombudsman, see above pp. 375–378.

[34] The British Post Office enjoys a similar immunity which is of long standing and now contained in the British Telecommunications Act 1981, s.29. For cases where the Post Office has been permitted to avail of these generous statutory immunities, see *Triefus & Co. Ltd v. Post Office* [1957] Q.B. 353; *Stephen Harold & Co. Ltd v. Post Office* [1977] 1 W.L.R. 1171 and *American Express Co. v. British Airports Board* [1983] 1 W.L.R. 701. A similar immunity which was enjoyed by British Telecom was repealed by the Telecommunications Act 1984. Wade and Forsyth, *Administrative Law* (7th ed., 1994) p. 173 sees "no good reason" for such immunities and thinks it surprising that they "are still tolerated".

Special Criminal Court. Since the ordinary constitutional guarantees do not apply to this Court and in view of its extraordinary nature, it is, perhaps, not surprising that section 53(1) of the 1939 Act should provide *ex abundante cautela*[35] that:

> "No action, prosecution, or other proceeding, civil or criminal, shall lie against any member of a Special Criminal Court in respect of any order made, conviction or sentence pronounced, or other thing done by that Court or in respect of anything done by such member in the course of the performance of his duties or the exercise of his powers as a member of that Court, whether such thing was or was not necessary to the performance of such duties or the exercise of such powers."

Section 53(2) confers an immunity from defamation in respect of anything "written or said by [a witness] in giving evidence before a Special Criminal Court" and section 53(3) provides for a complete immunity in respect of anything done by a registrar, clerk or servant of the court in the performance of their duties, irrespective of "whether such thing was or was not necessary to the performance of such duties".

(v) *Defence Forces*

Section 111 of the Defence Act 1954 provides that, where any action is commenced against any person for any act done in pursuance, execution or intended execution of the Act or in respect of any alleged neglect or default in the execution of the Act, the action must be brought in the High Court and must be instituted within six months of the act, neglect or default complained of. This provision is modelled on the Public Authorities (Protection) Act 1893 which provided that any action, prosecution or proceeding against any person for any act done in pursuance, execution or intended execution of any, *inter alia*, public duty or authority should not lie or be instituted unless it was commenced within six months after the act, neglect or default complained of. The 1893 Act, however, was repealed by the Public Authorities (Judicial Proceedings) Act 1954 and actions against public authorities, other than the Defence Forces, are now subject to the general provisions of the Statute of Limitations 1957. In *Ryan v. Ireland*[36] the Supreme Court held that section 111 had no relevance to a case where it was alleged that officers of the Defence Forces had been guilty of common law negligence in the performance of their duties.

(vi) *Fire services*

A complete immunity is given by section 36 of the Fire Services Act 1981[37] to fire and sanitary authorities who are discharging their fire safety, fire fighting and fire protection functions under this Act. Section 36 provides:

---

[35] The Special Criminal Court would in any case presumably benefit from the common law immunity attaching to judicial acts (*cf. Deighnan v. Ireland* [1995] 2 I.R. 56), assuming, of course, that such an immunity has survived the enactment of the Constitution: see below pp. 921–924. For a full discussion of the jurisdiction and work of the Special Criminal Court, see Hogan and Walker, *Political Violence and the Law in Ireland* (1989) pp. 227–244 and *Kelly, The Irish Constitution* (3rd ed., 1994), pp. 645–649.

[36] [1989] I.R. 177.

[37] This immunity was originally contained in s.5(2) of the Fire Brigade Act 1940 (which was repealed and replaced by the Fire Services Act 1981) and the reasons for the immunity were given as follows

"No action or other proceeding shall lie or be maintainable against the Minister, or against a fire authority or a sanitary authority or any officer or servant of, or person engaged by, any such authority for recovery of damages in respect of injury to persons or property alleged to have been caused or contributed to by the failure to comply with any functions conferred by this Act."

(vii) *Police and prosecuting authorities*

The question of whether the police and prosecuting authorities enjoy an immunity in respect of actions brought by either suspects or victims of crime is one which does not appear to have been judicially decided in this jurisdiction prior to Costello P.'s judgment in *W. v. Ireland (No.2)*.[38] In other jurisdictions the courts have held that prosecuting authorities enjoy either a complete immunity on policy grounds[39] or else a more limited immunity which does not exclude liability for deliberate misfeasance or malicious prosecutions.[40] In England, wide-ranging immunities have been upheld in the case of investigations by social workers responsible for child-care[41]; police investigations[42] and prosecuting authorities.[43] In *W.*, Costello P. held that the Attorney General enjoyed an immunity from suit in negligence in respect

---

by the Parliamentary Secretary for Local Government at the Committee Stage of the Bill: 78 *Dáil Debates* Col. 7145 (February 21, 1940).

"If damage caused by the outbreak of a particular fire could be made the basis of a claim against the local authority, it is considered that public funds might be liable to be applied towards compensation which can at present be obtained only on the basis of a contractual arrangement between a private person and an insurance company."

The English Court of Appeal has held that while a fire brigade was not, merely by attending at and fighting a fire, under a duty of care to the owners of the premises damages or destroyed by the fire, it would be liable where a danger created by its own negligence caused extra damage, unless it could be shown that the extra damage would have occurred in any event: *Capital and Counties Plc v. Hampshire County Council* [1997] 2 All E.R. 865.

38 [1997] 2 I.R. 142. In this case the plaintiffs (who were victims of child sexual abuse) had sued the state in respect of the emotional distress which had been caused to them by the failure to extradite promptly a notorious sex offender.

39 *Imbler v. Pachtmann* 424 U.S. 409 (1976); *Elguzouli-Daf v. Metropolitan Police Commissioner* [1995] Q.B. 335; *Olutu v. Home Office* [1997] 1 All E.R. 485. (Although *Olutu* is really a breach of statutory duty action, the public policy reasons for immunity are never far from the surface). The reasons given by Powell J. in *Imbler* include arguments based on public trust and diversion from duties. In relation to the former argument he observed that: "The public trust of the prosecutor's office would suffer if he were constrained in making every decision by the consequences in terms of his own liability in a suit for damages" and in relation to the "diversion" argument he noted that if the prosecutor "could be made to answer in court each time such a person charged him with wrongdoing, his energy and attention would be diverted from the pressing duty of enforcing the criminal law".

40 *Nelles v. Ontario* 60 D.L.R. (4th) 609 (1989). The comments (at 641) of Lamer J. (who delivered the majority judgment) would probably have an instinctive appeal for their Irish counterparts:

"The fundamental flaw with an absolute immunity for prosecutors is that the wrongdoer cannot be held accountable by the victim through the legal process . . . Granting an absolute immunity to prosecutors is akin to granting a licence to subvert individual rights. Not only does absolute immunity negate a private right of action, but . . . it may be that it would effectively bar the seeking of a remedy pursuant to s. 24(1) of the Canadian Charter of Rights and Freedoms . . .".

41 *X v. Bedfordshire County Council* [1995] 3 All E.R. 353.

42 *Hill v. Chief Constable for W. Yorkshire* [1989] A.C. 53; *Alexandrou v. Oxford* [1993] 4 All E.R. 328; *Osman v. Ferguson* [1993] 4 All E.R. 344.

43 *Elguzouli-Daf v. Metopolitan Police Commissioner* [1995] Q.B. 335.

of the discharge of his statutory functions under section 2 of the Extradition (Amendment) Act 1987.[44] Even if there were sufficient proximity between the parties to give rise to a duty of care,[45] there were compelling public policy reasons why such a duty of care should not be imposed. If such a duty were imposed on the Attorney (or, for that matter, other prosecuting authorities) there was an unacceptable risk of a conflict between "the proper exercise of his public function with the common law duty of care to the victim which might result in an improper exercise of his statutory functions".

(vii) *Regulatory authorities*

Nearly all regulatory legislation enacted in recent times provides that the regulatory agency and its members enjoy either an absolute or qualified immunity. Two representative examples may be given. Section 61 of the Safety, Health and Welfare at Work Act 1989 provides that:

> "No action or other proceedings shall lie or be maintainable against the Authority or an enforcing agency . . . for the recovery of damages in respect of any injury to persons, damage to property or other loss alleged to have been caused or contributed to by a failure to perform or to comply with any of the functions imposed on the said Authority or enforcing agency . . .".[46]

Section 53 of the Investment Intermediaries Act 1995 is more typical in that it provides a qualified immunity where the regulatory authority acts in good faith:

> "A supervisory authority or any employee or officer of a supervisory authority . . . shall not be liable in damages for anything done or omitted in the discharge or purported discharge of any of its functions under this Act unless it is shown that the act or omission was in bad faith."

Similar qualified immunities are provided in other contemporary legislation[47] and it may be thought that the qualified immunity is more likely to be in accord with the (qualified) guarantee of rights conferred by the Constitution than is the absolute immunity contained in the 1989 Act.[48]

---

[44] Section 2 of the 1987 Act requires the Attorney General not to endorse a particular extradition warrant from the United Kingdom for execution unless he is satisfied that it is backed by sufficient evidence and that there is an intention to prosecute in respect of such evidence.

[45] And Costello P. in *W.* thought that there was not, saying that s.2:

"... conferred a public professional function on the Attorney General which created no relationship of any sort between him and the victims of the crimes referred to in the warrants he was considering. This is in striking contrast to the statutory provisions of the Housing Act 1966 which were designed to assist a class of persons and which the Supreme Court held in *Ward v. McMaster* [1988] I.R. 337 conferred a special relationship between them and the housing authority which resulted in the imposition of a common law duty of care."

[46] See also Environmental Protection Agency Act 1992, s.15 for a similar, absolute immunity of this type.

[47] See, *e.g.* Stock Exchange Act 1995, s.53(1); Irish Takeover Panel Act 1997, s.17

[48] For a very useful discussion of the constitutionality of this section, see Byrne, [1989] I.C.L.S.A. 7–01 *et seq.*

4. Constitutionality of Statutory Rules of Immunity

The issue of whether it is competent for the Oireachtas to establish special rules of immunity or even to confer complete immunity from suit is something which has never been directly judicially considered. This issue clearly arises in the wake of *Byrne v. Ireland*,[49] where the Supreme Court invalidated the common law rule whereby the State was deemed to be immune from suit. The Court held that: (i) none of the prerogatives which had hitherto attached to the Crown had survived the enactment of the Constitution[50]; and (ii) any such immunity would be inconsistent with the plaintiff's constitutional rights to have access to the courts and to recover damages in respect of a legal wrong. As Budd J. observed, the constitutional rights given to citizens "would be quite meaningless, in so far as suing the State is concerned, unless they were in some way enforceable against the State".[51] This decision has had enormous repercussions. Not only did it abolish at one fell swoop a long-standing immunity of the State and thus raised doubts about the constitutionality of other immunities conferred by statute,[52] but it raised the prospect of the "constitutionalisation" of the entire law of torts, at least as far as actions against the State and public officials were concerned.[53]

As indicated, the Supreme Court's decision in *Byrne* would seem to suggest that such immunities are constitutionally vulnerable, as being inconsistent with the State's obligation under Article 40.3 to defend and vindicate individual personal rights. This is reinforced by *Ryan v. Ireland*[54] where the Supreme Court held that common law immunities relieving the Defence Forces from liability in respect of injuries to soldiers engaged on active service were unconstitutional.

If such is the case, then surely a shadow must hang over the validity of section 36 of the Fire Services Act 1981, at least in so far as it precludes a fireman from suing a fire authority in respect of the negligent discharge of their statutory duties under the 1981 Act. It is difficult to see how such an immunity could survive if an

---

[49] [1972] I.R. 241.
[50] See generally, Kelly, *op.cit.* above, n.35, pp. 1134–1155; Kelly, "Hidden Treasure and the Constitution" (1988) 10 D.U.L.J. (N.S.) 1; and Lenihan, "Royal Prerogatives and the Constitution" (1989) 24 Ir. Jur. (N.S.) 1. This case is further discussed below at pp. 905–908.
[51] [1972] I.R. 241 at 292.
[52] *e.g.* the immunities provided in the Postal and Telecommunications Services Act 1983 for An Post (s.64) and Telecom Éireann (s.88) in respect of actions for loss and damage arising out of the postal and telecommunications systems respectively. Note that in *Ryan v. Ireland* [1989] I.R. 177 at 183 the Supreme Court held that insofar as the common law provided for an immunity from suit in respect of an action for negligence taken by a soldier on active service, such a rule had not survived the enactment of the Constitution "since it would be inconsistent with the guarantees by the State to respect, defend and vindicate the rights of the citizen contained in Article 40.3 of the Constitution". However, the State has been held not to be liable (whether vicariously or otherwise) in respect of the actions of a judge "because no action is maintainable for anything said or done by a trial judge in the exercise of a jurisdiction which belongs to and is exercisable by him": *Deighnan v. Ireland* [1995] 2 I.R. 56 at 62, *per* Flood J.
[53] See Cooney and Kerr, "Constitutional Aspects of Irish Tort Law" (1991) 13 D.U.L.J. (N.S.) 1. But the Supreme Court has subsequently indicated that there are limits to this development: *McDonnell v. Ireland,* unreported, Supreme Court, July 23, 1997 discussed below at pp. 824–827. As Barrington J. said in that case, "constitutional rights should not be regarded as wild cards which can be played at any time to defeat all existing rules."
[54] [1989] I.R. 177.

analagous common law immunity enjoyed by the Defence Forces has been condemned as unconstitutional. And while it is easy to understand the legislative intention to favour the rescue services and to ensure that they will not be hampered by the threat of legal action, the absolute nature of this immunity seems hard to justify. Again, what of the fire authority which through some gross act of negligence on its part, failed to answer a distress call? Certainly major constitutional issues would be raised should the authority seek to fall back in such circumstances on the provisions of section 36 of the 1981 Act in order to defend itself against an action for negligence.[55]

One way of justifying such immunities might be to adopt the reasoning in *Pine Valley Developments Ltd v. Minister for Environment*[56] and say that, the personal rights guarantees contained in Article 40.3 are not absolute and that the Oireachtas has to balance the common good against them and that in some instances no action will lie for negligence or breach of duty. Such an immunity might, therefore, be justified on the basis of public policy grounds either in order to protect persons performing an essential social service (such as firemen) or some implied constitutional value (such as the independence of persons performing judicial or quasi-judicial functions).

This conclusion is strongly suggested by Costello P. in *W. v. Ireland (No. 2)*[57] where an immunity in negligence in respect of the Attorney General's prosecutorial functions was upheld. Costello P. distinguished *Ryan v. Ireland* on the basis that this was not a decision in which an issue "relating to immunity from suit on public policy grounds arose". Nor was this case an authority for the proposition that:

> ". . . in no case could the law confer immunity from suit on a constitutional officer and . . . the Irish courts have recognised the validity of such a rule in relation to judges carrying out their judicial functions. Laws may limit the exercise of protected rights and in each case when the claim is raised it is a question for the court to decide where, in the interests of the common good, the balance should lie."

This last sentence echoes the potential future application of the proportionality doctrine in this area of immunity and quasi-immunity.[58] If such a doctrine were to be so applied, one possible compromise might be for the courts to hold that not all special rules of immunity or quasi-immunity are *per se* unconstitutional where such quasi-immunities were objectively justified, but a complete and absolute immunity (such as that contained in sections 64 and 88 of the Postal and Telecommunications Services Act 1983) would nonetheless seem susceptible to a successful constitutional challenge.

---

[55] Of course, it might be contended, quite irrespective of section 36 of the 1981 Act, that a fire authority owes no common law duty of care to respond to an emergency call. On this point, see *Capital and Counties plc v. Hampshire County Council* [1997] 2 All E.R. 865 (see above, n. 37).

[56] [1987] I.R. 23.

[57] [1997] 2 I.R. 142. For the facts of this case, see below, p. 824.

[58] For contemporary applications of this doctrine, see *Daly v. Revenue Commissioners* [1995] 3 I.R. 1 and *Heaney v. Ireland* [1997] 1 I.L.R.M. 117.

5. Governmental Liability and Judicial Control of Administrative Action

It is a cardinal principle – mentioned at the start of this chapter – that there is no direct relationship between the power of the court to annul an administrative act and liability to pay damages or monetary compensation. When a court annuls an administrative act on procedural grounds, that decision is deemed to be *ultra vires* and void *ab initio*. However, it does not follow that a declaration of invalidity of an administrative decision in and of itself gives rise to a cause of action in damages. It seems that an invalid administrative act will sound in damages only if:

(i) it happens also to constitute the commission of a recognised tort, such as false imprisonment, trespass or negligence;

(ii) where the invalid act was motivated by malice or the authority knew that it did not have the power which it purports to exercise, i.e. the tort of misfeasance of public office;

(iii) there is a breach of statutory duty; or

(iv) the invalid act amounts to an infringement of a personal constitutional right or a breach of the plaintiff's legitimate expectations.[59]

It remains to consider each of these categories.

(i) *The commission of a recognised tort*

There are many heterogeneous examples of cases where either the State or public officials have been found liable for recognised torts such as false imprisonment, trespass, nuisance[60] or negligence[61], following a finding that the relevant decisions in question have been found to be *ultra vires*.

In *Gildea v. Hipwell*,[62] for example, the Governor of Sligo Prison was held liable in damages for false imprisonment for wrongfully detaining the plaintiff pursuant to an invalid arrest warrant. Likewise in *Walsh v. Ireland*[63] the State was held

---

[59] In *Duff v. Minister for Agriculture and Food* [1997] 2 I.R. 22 the Minister was held liable in damages for breach of legitimate expectations. See also below, pp. 843–844.

[60] See, *e.g. Kelly v. Dublin County Council*, unreported, High Court, February 1986; *Gillingham B.C. v. Medway (Chatham) Dock Co. Ltd* [1992] 3 All E.R. 923.

[61] *Siney v. Dublin Corporation* [1980] I.R. 400; *Ward v. McMaster* [1988] I.R. 337.

[62] [1942] I.R. 489. The question arises as to whether the prison governor could now rely on the *Pine Valley* defence, *viz.* that he was discharging a public duty in good faith without notice of the invalidity. On balance it would seem that he could not, since in the absence of a valid warrant, the plaintiff would have been falsely detained and liability in such circumstances is strict and not in any way contingent on the knowledge of the detainer.

[63] Unreported, Supreme Court, November 30, 1994. See also *McGowan v. Farrell, Irish Times*, February 15, 1975 and *McIntyre v. Lewis* [1991] 1 I.R. 121. In the *Walsh* case the defendants sought unsuccessfully to rely on the provisions of s.50 of the Constabulary (Ireland) Act 1836 which provides that:
"... when any action shall be brought against any constable for any act done in obedience to the warrant of any magistrate, such constable shall not be responsible for any irregularity in the issuing of such warrant, or for any want of jurisdiction in the magistrate issuing the same, and such constable may plead the general issue and give such warrant in evidence; and upon producing such warrant and proving that the signature thereto is the handwriting of the person whose name shall appear subscribed thereto, and that such person is reputed to be and acts as a magistrate of such county or district (as the case may be), and that the act or acts complied of were done in

vicariously liable for false imprisonment, following the wrongful arrest of the plaintiff by members of the Garda Síochána who did not realise that the wrong person had, in fact, been arrested by them. And in *Farrell v. Minister for Agriculture and Food*[64] the Minister was held liable in trespass when, with the mantle of statutory regulations assumed to be valid[65] around him "[he] constrained the plaintiff to bring his herd to be slaughtered" and, thus, wrongfully and directly interfered with the plaintiff's right to possession of his chattels. There are also numerous examples where either an individual garda[66] or the State itself have been liable for wrongful arrest.[67] Strangely enough, there do not appear to be any reported cases of either the State or public officials being found liable in trespass, but presumably such officials would be liable in trespass where they searched a dwelling on foot of an invalid search warrant.

Liability in negligence is dealt with elsewhere.[68]

(ii) *Misfeasance of public office*

Quite independently of any developments on the constitutional front, Irish law recognises the tort of "misfeasance in public office", although, up to recent times, there were few authorities directly in point. The tort of misfeasance in public office is committed where an act is performed by a public official, either maliciously, or with actual knowledge that it is committed without jurisdiction, and is so done with the known consequence that it would injure the plaintiff.[69] Two cases

---

obedience to such warrant, the jury who shall try the said issue shall find a verdict for the constable, and such constable shall recover his cost of suit."

See also *Hanahoe v. District Judge Hussey*, unreported, High Court, November 14, 1997, a case where details of a highly sensitive Garda search of solicitors' offices were improperly "leaked" to the media in advance by an individual member of the Garda Síochána. Kinlen J. held that this amounted to negligence in the execution of the warrant and held the State vicariously liable. However, Kinlen J. refused to hold that the State was liable for this apparent misfeasance of office on the part of the (unidentified) Garda in question, as the evidence was that "secrecy and discretion were fully impressed on the [search team] as part of their obligations," so that any such misconduct "would be wholly outside the scope of his employment."

[64] Unreported, High Court, October 11, 1995.

[65] Carroll J. held that the regulations were, in fact, invalid.

[66] See, *e.g. Lynch v. Fitzgerald* [1938] I.R. 382 where a detective was held personally liable in an action under the Fatal Accident Act 1846.

[67] *Walsh v. Ireland*, unreported, Supreme Court, November 30, 1994.

[68] At pp. 829–845.

[69] This passage was approved by Keane J. in *McDonnell v. Ireland*, unreported, Supreme Court, July 23, 1997. It is difficult to improve on the following definition of the tort given by Smith J. in *Farrington v. Thompson* (1959) V.R. 286 at 293:

"[I]f a public official does an act which, to his knowledge, amounts to an abuse of his office, and he thereby causes damage to another person, then an action in tort for misfeasance of public office will lie at the suit of that other person."

See also, *Roncarelli v. Duplessis* (1959) 16 D.L.R. (2d) 689 and *David v. Abdul Cader* [1963] 1 W.L.R. 834. For an example of malice in the sense of pique, spite or improper purpose, see *Elliott v. Chief Constable of Wiltshire*, *The Times*, December 5, 1996. Here it was alleged that a police officer had improperly disclosed details of previous convictions held on a police computer in order to procure the plaintiff's dismissal as a journalist who had been examining allegations of police misconduct. Scott V.-C. held that if these allegations were proved, they would constitute the tort of misfeasance. *In Hanahoe v. District Judge Hussey*, unreported, High Court, November 14, 1997, Kinlen J. appeared to accept that the actions of an individual Garda who "leaked" details of a highly sensitive Garda search of solicitors' offices in advance to the media amounted to misfeasance of office. However, he found that

which deal with related questions are *Johnston v. Meldon*[70] and *O'Conghaile v. Wallace.*[71]

In *Johnston* the plaintiff, who had been convicted by magistrates of a statutory offence of unlawful fishing, was fined and imprisoned, in default of payment of the fine. The plaintiff had set up a defence of a bona fide claim to fish where he did, and had raised an issue as to the ownership of the fisheries where the acts complained of had taken place. The conviction was accordingly quashed on the grounds that the plaintiff had raised a question of title which the magistrates had no jurisdiction to decide. However, the Court of Exchequer held that, absent malice, the plaintiff's claim for false imprisonment must fail even though the conviction had been quashed. The magistrates had fallen into legal error in the course of an adjudication in respect of a matter which they had authority to decide, but this of itself was not actionable. But the Court implied that the result might have been different if the magistrates had actual knowledge of the irregularity. This principle was confirmed by the Supreme Court in *O'Conghaile v. Wallace,* where Fitzgibbon J. stated that where a public official acts in good faith on foot of an order of a court or tribunal of competent jurisdiction, he is protected against an action for damages in respect of anything done by him before that order is quashed for procedural impropriety. Again, the Court intimated that different considerations would arise if the official had actual knowledge of the irregularity, or where the court or tribunal which made the order was not one of competent jurisdiction.[72]

Despite the fact that the tort of misfeasance is now pleaded with increasing frequency, its precise contours remain uncertain. What does appear to be clear is that something akin to malice (in the legal sense of that term) must be proved in order to establish liability for misfeasance of public office.

The modern jurisprudence appears to bear out this conclusion.[73] In the first of these cases, *Corliss v. Ireland,*[74] the plaintiffs, who were detective police officers, sued for defamation and the question arose as to whether the pleadings disclosed a reasonable cause of action. The defamation was said to have arisen by reason of

---

such misconduct was clearly outside the scope of employment of the member in question, so that the State could not be made vicariously liable.

[70] (1891) 30 L.R. Ir. 13.
[71] [1938] I.R. 526.
[72] *Ibid.* at 555. Fitzgibbon J. observed that:
   "There is, however, authority for the proposition that officers are supposed, or presumed, to know the general jurisdiction of the tribunals whose orders they are bound to prepare or execute, and that they may be liable in trespass if they prepare or execute an order which shows upon its face that it is outside the general jurisdiction of the tribunal which professed to make it."
[73] Though note that in *Deane v. Voluntary Health Insurance Board (No. 2)*, unreported, Supreme Court, July 28, 1994, the Court appeared to suggest that a public body might be liable for misfeasance of public office if its statutory powers were merely exercised "unreasonably and unfairly" in a manner which caused loss and damage: see below, p. 816. For a more orthodox approach, see the judgment of Kenny J. in *McDonald v. Bord na gCon (No. 3)*, unreported, High Court, January 13, 1966. In *Three Rivers DC v. Bank of England (No. 3)* [1996] 3 All E.R. 558 at 582 Clarke J. said (quoting with approval from the judgment of Deane J. in *Northern Territory v. Mengel* (1994–5) 185 C.L.R. 307) that:
   "Malice, in the sense of an intention to injure the plaintiff or a person in a class of which the plaintiff is a member are alternative, not cumulative, ingredients of the tort. To act with such knowledge is to act in a sufficient sense maliciously."
[74] Unreported, High Court, July 23, 1984.

the fact that the plaintiffs had been transferred by the Garda Commissioner under section 8(1) of the Police Forces Amalgamation Act 1923 from the Crimes Section of the Technical Bureau of the Garda Síochána to alternative duties, thereby giving rise to the implication that they were not fit for their original duties. Hamilton J. held that if it could be established that the transfer order was malicious – as opposed merely to establishing that it was invalid – then liability in damages could arise. The onus of proof was on the plaintiffs, but he added that:

> "Want of probable cause and malice are not necessarily unrelated and independent. The absence of just cause may go to prove malice, and similarly, the presence of oblique or dishonest motives may go to show the absence of probable cause. Malice may be inferred from recklessness and the circumstances from which it may be inferred need not be extrinsic to the circumstances in which the act is done or to the manner of doing it."[75]

The Supreme Court also confirmed in *Pine Valley Developments Ltd v. Minister for the Environment*[76] that liability could arise where an *ultra vires* decision was coupled with malice. In this case, the Minister for the Environment had granted on appeal a planning permission which the Supreme Court had held to be *ultra vires*.[77] This resulted in an estimated loss of some IR£1.5 million to the plaintiffs, who then commenced proceedings claiming damages as against the Minister. While the *ultra vires* act of itself did not give rise to liability, Finlay C.J. agreed that the presence of malice or knowledge of the lack of *vires* would give rise to liability in damages. The question of misfeasance, however, did not arise on the facts, for the evidence showed that the Minister had acted on the basis of legal advice prior to granting the planning permission. Accordingly, his actions could not possibly:

> "constitute such a gross abuse of power or wholly unreasonable exercise of power as to lead to an inference that he was aware that he was exercising a power which he did not possess. The only evidence led in this case quite clearly indicates to the contrary, and that the Minister was of the belief that he was exercising a power which he possessed."[78]

---

[75] *Ibid.* at pp. 16–17 of the judgment, quoting from the Lord Justice Clerk in *Robertson v. Keith* [1936] S.C. 36 at 37. See also *Calveley v. Chief Constable of Merseyside Police* [1989] A.C. 1228 at 1240 where the House of Lords agreed that had the plaintiff been suspended "maliciously in the sense indicated, this would certainly be capable of constituting the tort of misfeasance in public office." Lord Bridge had earlier said (*ibid.*) that the tort of misfeasance must at least:
> "involve an act done in the exercise or purported exercise by the public officer of some power or authority with which he is clothed by virtue of the office he holds which is done in bad faith or (possibly) without reasonable cause."

[76] [1987] I.R. 23. In his judgment, Henchy J. expressly approved of the reasoning in two then leading English authorities: *Dunlop v. Woollahra Municipal Council* [1982] A.C. 158 and *Burgoin S.A. v. Ministry of Agriculture* [1986] Q.B. 716.

[77] *The State (Pine Valley Developments Ltd) v. Dublin County Council* [1984] I.R. 407. The Supreme Court held that the Minister had no power to contravene the planning authority's development plan when exercising his statutory powers of appeal in planning cases.

[78] *Pine Valley Developments Ltd v. Minister for the Enviroment* [1987] I.R. 23 at 36. See also *Farrell v. Minister for Agriculture and Food*, unreported, High Court, October 11, 1995, where Carroll J. held that the Minister had wrongfully removed cattle pursuant to an invalid regulation. She ruled that while the defendant was liable in trespass, there was no liability in misfeasance because when

Similar principles have been applied in relation to the exercise of governmental power in other jurisdictions.[79]

Though each of these cases tend in the same direction, it is worth noting that in none of them were the motives necessary to establish an action for misfeasance of public office found to exist. As a practical matter it is manifest that this would be a most difficult case to establish[80] and there appear to be only two Irish cases where liability under this heading was established. In *Re "The La Lavia"*[81] Barr J. awarded damages in misfeasance against the Office of Public Works following the quashing of a preservation order which had been made in respect of a maritime wreck, saying:

> "I am satisfied that the officials who were responsible for the making of the order knew, or strongly suspected, that there was no statutory authority under [the National Monuments Act 1930] for making it. It seems to me that the circumstances fall within the principle laid down by the Supreme Court in *Pine Valley Developments Ltd v. Minister for Environment* that where it did not possess the power which it purported to exercise, it is answerable in damages to a person who is injured by the exercise of the power."[82]

---

so acting the Minister did not know that the regulations were *ultra vires*. See also *C. W. Shipping Co. v. Limerick Harbour Commissioners* [1989] I.L.R.M. 416 (similar principle); *O'Donnell v. Dun Laoghaire Corporation* [1991] I.L.R.M. 301 (wrongful suspension of water supply to plaintiff's home, but no liability as no recognised tort thereby committed and actions not motivated by malice); *Bloomer v. Incorporated Law Society of Ireland* [1995] 3 I.R. 14 (no liability for misfeasance in respect of invalid statutory instrument, as the Society acted "in good faith and reasonably in all the circumstances").

79 The Court of Justice of the European Communities takes a similar view in cases arising under Art. 215 of the Treaty of Rome. Mere illegality causing loss is not, of itself, enough, as liability will only arise "exceptionally" in cases "in which the institution concerned has manifestly and gravely disregarded the limits on the exercise of its powers": Joined Cases 116 & 127/77 *G.R. Amylum N.V. & Tunnel Refineries Ltd v. Council & Commission* [1979] E.C.R. 3497. Analogous principles have been established by the U.S. Supreme Court: see, *e.g.* the comments of Powell J. in *Harlow v. Fitzgerald* 457 U.S. 800 at 814–815 (1982):
> "Government officials performing discretionary functions generally are shielded from liability for civil damages in so far as their conduct does not violate clearly established statutory or constitutional rights of which a reasonable person would have known."

80 In *Northern Territory v. Mengel* (1994–5) 185 C.L.R. 307 the High Court of Australia suggested (without having to decide the point) an even more stringent requirement for proof of the mental element of misfeasance by requiring proof of intentional infliction of harm. The Court equated (at 347) this tort with those torts such as *Wilkinson v. Downton* [1897] 2 Q.B. 57 "which impose liablity on private individuals for the intentional infliction of harm". The following passage from the concurring judgment of Brennan J. (at 357) seems a better approach:
> "Misfeasance in public office consist of a purported exercise of some power or authority by a public officer otherwise than in an honest attempt to perform the functions of his or her office whereby loss is caused to a plaintiff. Malice, knowledge and reckless indifference are states of mind that stamp on a purported but invalid exercise of power the character of abuse of or misfeasance in public office. If the impugned conduct then causes injury, the cause of action is complete."

In *Three Rivers DC v. Bank of England (No. 3)* [1996] 3 All E.R. 558 at 582 Clarke J. said:
> "The tort of misfeasance in public office is concerned with a deliberate and dishonest wrongful abuse of the powers given to a public officer. It is not to be equated with torts based on an intention to injure, although, as suggested by the majority in *Mengel*, it has some similarities to them."

81 Unreported, High Court, July 26, 1994.
82 This approach corresponds to the test advanced (at 582) by Clarke J. in *Three Rivers*:
> "For the purposes of the requirement that the [public] officer knows that he has no power to do the act complained of, it is sufficient that the officer has actual knowledge that the act complained of was unlawful, or, in circumstances in which he believes or suspects that the act is beyond his

In *Deane v. Voluntary Health Insurance Board (No. 2)*[83] the Supreme Court held that the V.H.I. had wrongfully exercised its statutory powers in withdrawing insurance cover from a hospital. Blayney J. observed:

> "[In the High Court, Keane J.] did not categorise the tort constituted by the VHI exercising their powers unreasonably and unfairly, but if he had done so, the probability is that having regard to its ingredients he would have classified it as misfeasance in public office . . .".

(iii) *Breach of statutory duty*

A plaintiff may also seek damages in respect of breach of statutory duty, a cause of action, which although certainly not peculiar to public bodies is likely to arise in this area. Given that a showing of negligence has no bearing on the question of whether a plaintiff is entitled to succeed, the imposition of liability for breach of statutory duty is really another form of strict liability. The major problem in this area is whether breach of the statute gives rise to a private right of action. Very occasionally the statute will state explicitly that breach of the statute does[84] or does not[85] do so. Generally, however, the statute will be silent on the matter, and the courts will engage in the fictitious exercise of imputing legislative intent in order to determine whether breach of the statute will give rise to a civil action.[86]

If the duty is owed to the public at large, then no action for breach of that duty will lie. Thus, in *Pine Valley Developments Ltd v. Minister for the Environment*[87] the Supreme Court held no action for breach of statutory duty would lie against the defendant Minister who had granted a planning permission (which was subsequently found to be invalid) to the plaintiffs. Finlay C.J. said:

> "The Minister in making his purported decision to grant outline planning permission was exercising a decision-making function vested in him for the discharge of a public purpose or duty. The statutory duty thus arising must, however, in law, be clearly distinguished from duties imposed by statute on persons or bodies for the specific protection of the rights of individuals which

---

powers, that he does not ascertain whether or not that is so, or fails to take such steps as would be taken by an honest and reasonable man to ascertain the true position.

For the purposes of the requirement that the officer knows that his act will probably injure the plaintiff or a person in a class of which the plaintiff is a member it is sufficient if the officer has actual knowledge that his act will probably damage the plaintiff or such a person or, in circumstances in which he believes or suspects that his act will probably damage the plaintiff or such a person, if he does not ascertain whether or not that is so, or fails to make such inquiries as an honest and reasonable man would make as to the probability of such damage."

[83] Unreported, Supreme Court, July 28, 1994. (This judgment is reported in O'Connor, *Competition Law Source Book* (1996) Vol. 2, p. 1099 (High Ct.), p. 1145 (Sup. Ct.)).

[84] See, *e.g.* Competition Act 1991, s.6; Electoral Act 1992, s.159.

[85] Examples include Landlord and Tenant (Ground Rents) (No. 2) Act 1978, s.24(3) (no action shall lie against Registrar of Titles in relation to his duty to hear applications to vest the fee simple in dwellinghouses in an order "which is consistent with the efficient discharge of any of his functions as Registrar of Titles"); Postal and Telecommunication Services Act 1983, s.15(2); Litter Pollution Act 1997, s.14 (no action for damages by reason of failure of local authority to exercise their statutory functions).

[86] See generally, McMahon and Binchy, *The Irish Law of Torts* (2nd ed., 1990) pp. 373–388.

[87] [1987] I.R. 23.

are deemed to be absolute and breach of which may lead to an action for damages."[88]

On the other side of the line was *Moyne v. Londonderry Port and Harbour Commissioners*[89] where Costello J. found that the breach of the statutory duties imposed on the defendants by the provisions of the Londonderry Port and Harbour Act 1854 to keep certain harbours open gave rise to an action for damages at the suit of members of the public living in the locality:

> "[It] is clear that the statute with which this case is concerned is strikingly different from that class of statutes which the courts held concerned a duty to the public only. Here it cannot reasonably be argued that the duty to maintain the pier was imposed for the benefit of the Irish public generally. The benefit which was being afforded by the pier was being conferred primarily on a definable class of persons, namely those living in the clearly defined geographical area of the Inishowen peninsula, and particularly those living and working on its eastern seaboard."[90]

If a plaintiff is found to have suffered loss and damage by reason of a breach of statutory duty, he is entitled to recover general damages as well as special damages in respect of that loss.[91]

Before considering the separate question of actions for breaches of constitutional rights, it must be noted that these settled common law rules of statutory interpretation have yielded in some instances to over-riding constitutional considerations.[92] Thus,

---

[88] *Ibid.* at 36. See also *Walsh v. Kilkenny County Council* [1978] I.L.R.M. 1; *Siney v. Dublin Corporation* [1980] I.R. 400; and *Bloomer v. Incorporated Law Society of Ireland* [1995] 3 I.R. 14 for a similar approach. In effect, cases such as *Walsh* and *Siney* are examples of where the plaintiffs could not show that they came within the class of persons intended to be benefited by the imposition of the statutory duty. But *cf. O'Neill v. Clare County Council* [1983] I.L.R.M. 141 (planning authority liable in damages in respect of wilful refusal to grant planning permission in circumstances where they were statutorily obliged to do so); *Bakht v. Medical Council* [1990] 1 I.R. 515 (where the plaintiff was awarded IR£12,500 damages in respect of his loss of earnings for one year during which period he could not practise medicine by reason of the wrongful failure of the Medical Council to adopt the necessary registration rules under the Medical Practitioners Act 1978); and *Emerald Meats Ltd v. Minister for Agriculture and Food* [1997] 2 I.L.R.M. 275 (Minister liable in damages for what was "in effect" a breach of statutory duty imposed by an E.C. Regulation).

[89] [1986] I.R. 299.

[90] *Ibid.* at 314. See also *Waterford Harbour Commissioners v. British Railway Board* [1979] I.L.R.M. 296 where the Supreme Court held that the provisions of s.70 of the Fishguard and Rosslare Railways and Harbours Act 1898 (which imposed an obligation on the defendants to maintain a shipping service from Waterford to Fishguard in Wales) enabled the plaintiff harbour authority to maintain an action for breach of statutory duty when this service was terminated. As O'Higgins C.J. observed (at 341), the statutory provision in question was intended to benefit not only the general public but had also been enacted for the protection and benefit of the harbour authority. But *cf. John C. Doherty Timber Ltd v. Drogheda Harbour Commissioners* [1993] 1 I.R. 315 (no duty owed to users of quayside).

[91] *Emerald Meats Ltd v. Minister for Agriculture and Food* [1997] 2 I.L.R.M. 275. In the words of Blayney J. (at 295): "Since 'general damage' is damage which the law implies in every infringement of an absolute right and special damage means particular damage beyond general damage, it is difficult to see how the Minister could be liable for the former and not for the latter."

[92] In the case of what amounts to a breach of statutory duty imposed by Community law, the *Francovich* doctrine (on which see further at pp. 845–849) requires, in the words of Blayney J. in *Emerald Meats Ltd v. Minister for Agriculture and Food* [1997] 2 I.L.R.M. 275, that the courts must uphold the right

---

in *Parsons v. Kavanagh*[93] the plaintiff was a licensed bus operator who faced competition on the same bus route from an unlicensed competitor. O'Hanlon J. first rejected the contention that the Road Transport Acts 1932–1933 were to be construed as statutes passed for the benefit of a limited class of the public, namely, licensed operators under the terms of the Acts. For O'Hanlon J. felt that earlier authorities (such as in *Cutler v. Wandsworth Stadium Ltd*[94]) – which would dictate that the plaintiff would have had no cause of action – would have to yield to constitutional considerations:

> "The right to earn one's living by any lawful means was recognised by Kenny J. in *Murtagh Properties Ltd v. Cleary*[95] [where] he granted an injunction to restrain picketing of licensed premises on the basis that it amounted to an unlawful interference with the constitutional right of the bar maids employed therein to earn their livelihood . . . The Supreme Court in *Byrne v. Ireland*[96] was primarily concerned with the enforceability of civil claims against the State in situations where a right of action would arise against a private individual but the judgments also stress that rights derived from the Constitution must be safeguarded by remedies to be provided by the courts."[97]

O'Hanlon J. then concluded that:

> "The constitutional right to earn one's livelihood by any lawful means carries with it the entitlement to be protected against any unlawful activity on the part of another person which materially impairs or infringes that right."[98]

In the event, therefore, as the defendant had thus engaged in unlawful activity which significantly impaired the plaintiff's exercise of her constitutional right to earn a livelihood, O'Hanlon J. granted an injunction restraining the defendant from carrying on business as an unlicensed operator. In future, therefore, the answer to the question of whether breach of statutory duty gives rise to an action in damages may depend not on the presumed legislative intent as ascertained by a construction of the relevant statutory provisions, but rather on the issue of whether the absence of such a remedy would infringe the constitutional rights of the plaintiff.

---

to award damages from a Member State "for the breach of an obligation imposed on it by Community law".

[93] [1990] I.L.R.M. 560.

[94] [1949] A.C. 398.

[95] [1972] I.R. 330.

[96] [1972] I.R. 241.

[97] [1990] I.L.R.M. 560 at 566. This result had already been anticipated by Barrington J. in *Irish Permanent Building Society v. Caldwell (No. 2)* [1981] I.L.R.M. 242 at 254 where the judge rejected the suggestion that the "parliamentary intent" test could determine whether a particular plaintiff could recover damages for breach of statutory duty:

> "But in our jurisdiction the citizen would appear to have a remedy, by virtue of the provisions of Article 40.3, if he has or may suffer damage as a result of a breach of the law in circumstances which amount to an injustice."

[98] *Ibid.* See also *Lovett v. Gogan* [1995] 3 I.R. 132 (a case with very similar facts), where this approach was expressly affirmed by the Supreme Court.

(iv) *Breach of constitutional rights*

We turn now to the more general use of the Constitution in the area of damages. Article 40.3.1° provides that the State "guarantees in its laws to respect, and, as far as practicable, by its laws to defend and vindicate the personal rights of the citizen." The willingness of the courts to countenance a re-shaping of remedies in the light of the Constitution is nowhere more evident than in the context of the law of torts.[99] It must be observed, first of all, that the Constitution in general and Article 40.3.1° in particular may be used in either of two ways. The first, which has already been described above in Part 4 of this chapter, is as a device to render invalid some illegitimate defence whether established by statute or common law, on which a public body could otherwise rely. The other type of use of the Constitution is as a basis to establish (positively) some cause of action which would not otherwise exist. This section concentrates on the second usage, although, given the nature of the material, a certain degree of overlap is inevitable.

In regard to the use of the Constitution to establish new causes of action, there are essentially two schools of thought and the courts have not yet really confronted, still less chosen between, these two schools of thought.[100] The first is that the Constitution gives the courts a general licence to engage in an entire re-balancing exercise of the competing rights involved so as to shape the existing contours of tort law[101] (and, where necessary, to create entirely new torts[102]) in the light of constitutional considerations. The second and more conservative view is that the courts are entitled to intervene "only where there has been a failure to implement or, where the implementation relied on is plainly inadequate to effectuate the constitutional guarantee in question."[103]

---

[99] The best analysis of this problem is found in Binchy, "Constitutional Remedies and the Law of Torts" in O'Reilly (ed.), Human Rights and Constitutional Law: Essays in Honour of Brian Walsh (1992) pp. 201–225. See generally *Kelly, The Irish Constitution op. cit.* above, n.35 pp. 707–708.

[100] See, now, however, the comprehensive judgments of Costello P. in *W. v. Ireland (No. 2)* [1997] 2 I.R. 142 and in *McDonnell v. Ireland*, unreported, Supreme Court, July 23, 1997.

[101] See, *e.g. Byrne v. Ireland* [1972] I.R. 241 (state immunity from suit inconsistent with constitutional obligation to vindicate legal and constitutional rights); *Ryan v. Ireland* [1989] I.R. 177 (any common law rule preventing soldiers suing the State for negligence would be unconstitutional) and *McKinley v. Minister for Defence* [1992] 2 I.R. 333 (common law rule confining loss of consortium actions to husbands only would infringe equality guarantee in Article 40.1 and, hence, the cause of action must be extended so as to permit wives to sue for loss of consortium).

[102] See, *e.g. Kennedy v. Ireland* [1987] I.R. 587 (state liable in damages for improper invasion of plaintiff's privacy); *Healy v. Minister for Defence*, unreported, High Court, July 7, 1994 (soldier could recover damages for breach of constitutional right to fair procedures); *Lovett v. Gogan* [1995] 3 I.R. 132 at 142 (plaintiff entitled to sue for invasion of constitutional right to earn a livelihood); *Walsh v. Ireland*, unreported, Supreme Court, November 30, 1994 (where Hamilton C.J. described the wrongful arrest of the plaintiff as "a breach of his constitutional right to liberty and to his good name" and that the courts were thereby obliged to vindicate that right by means of a substantial award of damages).

[103] *Hanrahan v. Merck, Sharp and Dohme (Ireland) Ltd* [1988] I.L.R.M. 629 at 636, *per* Henchy J.; and *Murphy v. Ireland* [1996] 2 I.L.R.M. 461 at 467, *per* Carroll J. However, in *McDonnell v. Ireland*, unreported, Supreme Court, July 23, 1997, Keane J. said of Henchy J.'s comments in *Hanrahan* that there was nothing in this passage.

". . . to suggest that where a plaintiff is obliged to have recourse to an action for breach of a constitutional right, because the existing corpus of tort law affords him no remedy, or an inadequate remedy, that action cannot in turn be described as an action in tort, albeit a tort not hitherto recognised by the law, within the meaning of, and for the purpose of, the [Statute of Limitations 1957.]"

One may begin with the leading statement of Walsh J. in *Meskell v. CIÉ*:

> "It has been said on a number of occasions in this Court . . . that a right guaranteed by the Constitution or granted by the Constitution can be protected by action or enforced by action even though such action may not fit into any of the ordinary forms of action in either common law or equity and that the constitutional right carries within it, its own right to a remedy or for the enforcement of it. Therefore, if a person has suffered damage by virtue of a breach of a constitutional right, that person is entitled to seek redress against the person or persons who have infringed that right."[104]

This statement of principle has been subsequently widely approved[105] and has formed the basis for the courts' preparedness to depart from the conventional limitations of the law of administrative law remedies, at least where existing common law or statutory remedies were either inadequate or non-existent.[106]

In fact, ever since the decision in *Meskell* there have been quite a number of cases where damages have been awarded for breach of constitutional rights in

---

Note, however, the comments of Barrington J. in the same case (discussed below at pp. 825–826) which effectively endorse the views of Henchy J.

Henchy J. subsequently expressed a similar view in *Hynes-O'Sullivan v. O'Driscoll* [1988] I.R. 436 at 450 where he said that any re-formulation of the law of qualified privilege "must reflect a due balancing of the constitutional right of freedom of expression and the constitutional protection of every citizen's good name" but that the "articulation of public policy on such a matter would seem to be primarily a matter for the Legislature". There is more than a hint of this in *Walsh v. Family Planning Services Ltd* [1992] 1 I.R. 496 at 522 where McCarthy J. cautioned against using the personal rights guarantees in Article 40 "to elevate the status of a trifling cause of action" (here, a technical assault), implying that the plaintiff should be left to his remedy in tort. See also the comments of Barron J. in *Sweeney v. Duggan* [1991] 2 I.R. 274 at 285 to the effect that Art. 40.3 involved "no more than a guarantee of a just law of negligence"; those of Carroll J. to same effect in *Murphy v. Ireland* [1996] 2 I.L.R.M. 461 and the elaborate reasoning of Costello P. in *W. v. Ireland (No. 2)* [1997] 2 I.R. 142.

104 [1973] I.R. 121 at 121. Other courts have taken a similar view. Thus, in *Bivens v. Six Unknown Federal Narcotic Agents* 403 U.S. 388 (1971) Brennan J. said that "where federally protected rights have been invaded, it has been the rule from the beginning that courts will be alert to adjust their remedies so as to grant the necessary relief." More recently, in *Simpson v. Attorney General* [1994] 3 N.Z.L.R. 667 the New Zealand Court of Appeal expressly followed *Meskell* when the Court held that an infringement of the New Zealand Bill of Rights gave rise to a cause of action. The following comments of Hardie Boys J. (at 702) are of interest:

> "The New Zealand Bill of Rights Act, if it is to be no more than an empty statement, is a commitment by the Crown that those who are in the three branches of the Government exercise its functions, powers and duties and will observe the rights that the Bill affirms. It is, I consider, implicit in that commitment, indeed essential to its worth, that the Courts are not only to observe the Bill in the discharge of their own duties but are able to grant appropriate and effective remedies where rights have been infringed. I see no reason to think that this should depend on the terms of a written constitution. Enjoyment of the basic human rights are the entitlement of every citizen, and their protection the obligation of every civilised state. They are inherent in and are essential to the structure of society. They do not depend on the legal or constitutional form in which they are declared. The reasoning that has led the Privy Council and the Courts of Ireland and India to the conclusions reached in the cases to which I have referred . . . is in my opinion equally valid to the New Zealand Bill of Rights Act if it is to have life and meaning."

105 See, *e.g. Lovett v. Gogan* [1995] 3 I.R. 132 at 142, *per* Finlay C.J.

106 Although in *W. v. Ireland (No. 2)* [1997] 2 I.R. 142, Costello P. was of the view that in every case where *Meskell*-type damages were awarded, no remedy had existed under existing law and that none of these cases "decided that an action for damages for breach of a guaranteed right would lie in cases where the existing law protected the right".

circumstances where no cause of action would lie at common law. In *Kearney v. Ireland*[107] a prisoner was awarded (admittedly nominal) damages against the State for breach of his constitutional right to communicate when his mail was stopped by reason by industrial action taken by prisoner officers. In *Kennedy v. Ireland*[108] substantial damages[109] were awarded where Hamilton P. concluded that agents of the State had deliberately engaged in irregular phone-tapping of the plaintiff journalists' telephones. This was an actionable violation of the plaintiffs' constitutional right to privacy, even if such an action would not have sounded at common law.

In *Conway v. Irish National Teachers' Organisation*[110] the Supreme Court, drawing here on Article 42, awarded exemplary damages for breach of the plaintiff's constitutional right to education. The Court found that the defendant union had recklessly engaged in industrial action which had left a class in a small village bereft of education for six months. The Court concluded, having regard to the supreme importance of the right to education, that the defendants were aware of the importance of that right and that the breach was an intended, as distinct from inadvertent, breach of that right.

In *McHugh v. Commissioner of An Garda Síochána*,[111] the Supreme Court held that the protection afforded to the plaintiff's property rights by Article 40.3.2.° required that the State compensate him in respect of the legal costs which he incurred as a result of a statutory disciplinary inquiry which, it subsequently transpired, was invalid.

Finally, in *Healy v. Minister for Defence*[112], a case where an army officer was adjudged to have been unfairly overlooked for promotion, Barron J. held that the plaintiff was entitled to rely on the constitutional guarantee of fair procedures and could sue for damages in respect of such breach.[113]

A further example of the interaction of traditional tort rules and constitutional principles is supplied by *Re the "La Lavia"*.[114] In this multi-faceted case Barr J. found that the Commissioners of Public Works had made an order restraining the finders of the wrecks of ships from the Spanish Armada from conducting an inspection of the wrecks in circumstances where the Commissioners either knew

---

[107] [1986] I.R. 116.
[108] [1987] I.R. 587. See Hogan, "Free Speech, Privacy and the Press in Ireland" (1987) *Public Law* 509.
[109] Totalling IR £50,000 to the three separate plaintiffs, Hamilton P. said (*ibid.* at 594) that in assessing damages he had had regard to the fact that the infringement "was carried out deliberately, consciously and without justification by the executive organ of the State which is under a constitutional obligation to respect, vindicate and defend that right."
[110] [1991] 2 I.R. 305.
[111] [1986] I.R. 116.
[112] Unreported, High Court, July 7, 1994.
[113] However, Barron J. refused to award exemplary damages. Applying the principles contained in *Conway v. Irish National Teachers' Organisation* [1991] 2 I.R. 205, he held that not every breach of constitutional rights attracted the award of exemplary damages and the facts of the present case did not establish "any conscious and wilful disregard of the plaintiff's constitutional rights". *Cf. Pettigrew v. Northern Irish Office* [1990] N.I. 179 where exemplary damages were awarded to prisoners bitten by dogs controlled by prison officers. Hutton L.C.J. held that as the prison officers had deliberately refrained from restraining the dogs it was appropriate to award exemplary damages since it constituted "oppressive conduct by servants of the government."
[114] Unreported, High Court, July 26, 1994. The Supreme Court reversed Barr J. solely on the facts: [1996] 1 I.L.R.M. 194.

"or had good reason to suspect that it did not have such power".[115] Barr J. declined to hold that the plaintiffs were entitled to damages for breach of their constitutionally protected property rights, as he had already found that they had no salvage rights in respect of the wrecks. The implication, however, is that, had such salvage rights been established in law, the plaintiffs would have been entitled to damages on a strict liability basis for breach of their property rights by reason of the illegal administrative action in question.

It will be immediately appreciated – especially having regard to the large number of individual rights which merit constitutional protection and the relative frequency with which these rights are infringed both by the State or private individuals[116] – that these developments could readily lead to the complete circumvention of the traditional restrictions imposed by the law of torts (for example, limitations requiring proof of negligence and so forth).[117] Accordingly, it might not be altogether surprising if, in order to avoid the creation of an alternative system of quasi-tort law by resort to the action for breach of constitutional rights as its main vehicle, we were to witness some form of judicial checks on the emergence of such a strict liability system.[118] In particular, it may be that the courts will move away from the present strict liability system in actions for breach of constitutional rights in favour of some *via media* requiring proof of fault or knowledge of illegality.[119]

---

[115] See also *Pine Valley Developments Ltd v. Minister for Environment* [1987] I.R. 23 (no liability for misfeasance, as Minister at all times acted pursuant to legal advice, even if that advice later proved to be mistaken); *Duff v. Minister for Agriculture* [1997] 2 I.R. 22 (similar principle) (High Ct.); *Heavey v. Pilotage Committee of the Dublin Pilotage Authority*, unreported, High Court, May 7, 1992 (suggestion that the Committee purported to exercise a power they knew they did not have rejected on the facts); and *Deane v. Voluntary Health Insurance Board (No. 2)*, unreported, Supreme Court, July 28, 1994 (defendants liable under rubric of misfeasance for wrongful abuse of statutory power).

[116] A plaintiff may, of course, recover damages in an appropriate case against a *private* defendant, for "uniquely the Irish Constitution confers a right of action for breach of constitutional rights against persons other than the State and its officials": *PH v. John Murphy & Sons Ltd* [1987] I.R. 621 at 626, *per* Costello J.

[117] See, *e.g.* the comments of Henchy J. in *Hanrahan* and *Hynes-O'Sullivan*, above, p. 819.

[118] *cf.* the comments of Binchy, *op.cit.*, above, n. 99, pp. 214–215:
"In cases where a court holds that a defendant was not under a duty of care relative to the plaintiff, it is doing more than merely relieving the defendant of liability: it is holding that broad considerations of social and economic policy warrant the establishment of immunity in these circumstances . . . Of course, the determination in negligence proceedings that the case is one involving immunity from liability on the basis of an absence of a duty of care can, and should, have no *necessary* implication that a similar determination should apply in the context of infringement of constitutional rights; but the public policy considerations leading to such a determination would in most instances have required the court to address the constitutional dimension, at least tacitly. A decision not to impose a duty of care in negligence is not lightly taken, without regard to the probable aftershocks throughout the legal system."

[119] There is already a hint of this in some judgments: see, *e.g. Moyne v. Londonderry Port and Harbour Commissioners* [1986] I.R. 299, where Costello J. said (without elaborating) that the infliction of pecuniary loss by a State agent in the course of an illegal act did not of itself establish an infringement of the constitutional right to earn a livelihood. In this regard the Irish courts might well be influenced by the attitude taken by the Court of Justice in the *Factortame* and *Brasserie du Pêcheur* litigation with regard to State liability for infringement of the Treaty of Rome (discussed below at pp. 845–849). As against this, it should be noted that: (i) in (the admittedly very different) context of the exclusion of unconstitutionally obtained evidence, liability is strict and there is no good faith exception: *The People (D.P.P.) v. Kenny* [1990] 2 I.R. 110; and (ii) the decision in *Moyne* might have to be re-assessed in the light of the comments of Barrington J. in *Duff v. Minister for Agriculture and Food* [1997] 2 I.R. 22.

Thus, consistently with this strand of judicial thinking, it appears that a plea of breach of constitutional rights cannot be used to circumvent the inherent limitations of the law of torts or the quasi-immunities enjoyed by persons discharging public office, if these limitations or immunities are in themselves justifiable by reference to accepted constitutional values. This emerges from the Supreme Court's decision in *Pine Valley Developments Ltd v. Minister for the Environment*,[120] and that of Costello P. in *W. v. Ireland*. In the former case the plaintiffs sued for damages in respect of a breach of their property rights following a ruling by the Supreme Court that a planning permission granted to them by the defendant Minister was invalid. However, Finlay C.J. observed that:

> ". . . the State may have to balance its protection of the right as against other obligations arising from regard for the common good."[121]

The Chief Justice continued:

> "I am satisfied that it would be reasonable to regard as a requirement of the common good an immunity to persons in whom are vested statutory powers of decision from claims for compensation where they act *bona fide* and without negligence. Such an immunity would contribute to the efficient and decisive exercise of such statutory powers and would, it seems to me, tend to avoid indecisiveness and delay, which might otherwise be involved."[122]

And while the reasoning of Henchy J. in his concurring judgment contained a slightly different emphasis, he added that:

> ". . . the exemption of the State from liability in damages is not alone not an unconstitutionality but is in harmony with the due operation of the organs of government established under the Constitution."[123]

In effect, the Court appears to have created a quasi-immunity in favour of persons discharging public duties affecting the rights or liberties of others, thus effectively emasculating the potential scope of liability for breach of constitutional rights in this area. But why should this be so? Finlay C.J. said that, were it otherwise, this would lead to "an inevitable paralysis of the capacity for decisive action in the administration of public office".[124] But this reasoning seems contrary to modern

---

[120] [1987] I.R. 23.
[121] *Ibid.* at 38, quoting from the judgment of O'Higgins C.J. in *Moynihan v. Greensmyth* [1977] I.R. 56 at 71.
[122] *Ibid.*
[123] *Ibid.* at 43.
[124] *Ibid.* at 38. It is interesting to note that Lord Keith also expressed similar sentiments in *Rowling v. Takaro Properties Ltd* [1988] A.C. 473 where he said (at 502) that:
> "It is to be hoped that, as a general rule, imposition of liability in negligence will lead to a higher standard of care in the performance of the relevant type of act; but sometimes not only may this not be so, but the imposition of liability may lead to harmful consequences. [A] danger may exist in cases such as the present, because, once it became known that liability in negligence may be imposed on the ground that a minister has misconstrued a statute and so acted ultra vires, the cautious civil servant may go to extreme lengths in ensuring that legal advice or even the opinion of the court, is obtained before decisions are taken, thereby leading to unnecessary delay in a considerable number of cases."

principles of liability. In most other areas of tort law, the imposition of higher standards is viewed as salutary and practically every immunity from liability has disappeared.[125]

In *W. v. Ireland (No. 2)*, the plaintiff claimed that the Attorney General had infringed her constitutional right to bodily integrity by not processing with sufficient expedition the extradition of a sex offender who had abused her. Costello P. first held that the Attorney General enjoyed a common law immunity in respect of the negligence claim. The question then arose as to whether the plaintiff could, in effect, circumvent the limitations of the law of tort by pursuing the claim for breach of constitutional rights. Costello P. held that she could not as:

"... the law of torts which is applicable in this case was not ineffective to protect the plaintiff's constitutionally guaranteed rights. It does not follow that because a plaintiff does not recover damages under the applicable law (in this case, the law of torts) that it must be ineffective in protecting guaranteed rights. It is necessary to consider why the plaintiff's claim failed ... [T]he applicable principles of the law of torts established that there was neither a duty owed to the plaintiff by the defendant under the law of torts or the Constitution to process the extradition warrants speedily and so by applying the principles of the law of torts the plaintiff was not deprived of a remedy to which she was entitled under the Constitution."

Of course, it is implicit in this analysis that the limitations inherent in the common law and statute are in themselves constitutionally justifiable. Attractive though Costello P.'s reasoning is, it carries with it the danger that the courts will too readily assume that judge-made law dealing with the law of wrongs created in some instances centuries before the Constitution was enacted adequately protects constitutional rights. The Supreme Court was equivocal on this issue in *McDonnell v. Ireland*.[126] In this case the plaintiff had forfeited his civil service post in 1974 pursuant to section 34 of the Offences against the State Act 1939 following his conviction for membership of an illegal organisation. This provision was found to be unconstitutional in separate proceedings in 1991[127] and it was only then that the plaintiff brought an action claiming damages for breach of constitutional rights. However, the Supreme Court held that insofar as he had a cause of action under the Constitution it

---

See also *John Munroe (Acrylics) Ltd v. London Fire Authority* [1996] 4 All E.R. 318 where Rougier J. refused to hold that a fire authority owed a general duty of care in respect of the manner in which they attended to their fire-fighting duties, in part because he feared that the imposition of such a duty would lead to "defensive fire-fighting".

[125] Take, for instance, the principles of liability in general and professional negligence in particular. In *Roche v. Peilow* [1985] I.R. 232 the Supreme Court held that a solicitor was guilty of professional negligence, even though he had not departed from what was then accepted conveyancing practice, because he ought to have realised (*per* Henchy J. at 254) "that the practice in question was fraught with danger for his client and was readily avoidable or remediable". The thinking here is that the imposition of such liability will have a salutary effect on professional standards and will ensure that solicitors (and other professionals) are sufficiently careful in the discharge of their duties. Yet cases such as *Pine Valley* and *Takaro Properties* show no willingness to accept that the potential imposition of such liability for negligent administrative errors might have a similar effect on administrators and others discharging public functions or quasi-judicial duties.

[126] Unreported, Supreme Court, July 23, 1997.

[127] *Cox v. Ireland* [1992] 2 I.R. 503.

was nonetheless statute-barred, since this form of action was an action in tort, at least for the purposes of the Statute of Limitations.[128] Nor could it be suggested that there was any policy reason why a different limitation period should not apply to actions for breach of constitutional rights.[129] On the wider issue of policy, slightly different views were expressed by both Barrington and Keane JJ. The latter hinted that the Constitution might yet have a large impact on the law of torts[130], whereas the former appears to have espoused the approach of Henchy J. in *Hanrahan v. Merck, Sharp & Dohme* when he said:

> "The general problem of resolving how constitutional rights are to be balanced against each other and reconciled with the exigencies of the common good, is, in the first instance, a matter for the legislature. It is only when the legislature has failed in its constitutional duty to defend or vindicate a particlar constitutional right pursuant . . . that this Court . . . will feel obliged to fashion its own remedy. If, however, a practical method of defending or vindicating the right already exists, at common law or by statute, there will be no need for this Court to interfere.
>
> There is no doubt that constitutional rights do not need recognition by the legislature or by common law to be effective. If necessary, the courts will define them and fashion a remedy for their breach . . . But, at the same time,

---

[128] Thus, referring to *Kennedy v. Ireland* [1987] I.R. 587 Keane J. acknowledged that:
"even in the absence of a written constitution, such a novel growth might, for all one knows, have flourished steadily in this jurisdiction. The fact that it did so in the form of an action for infringement of a constitutional right does not prevent it . . . from being classified as a civil wrong: indeed, I do not know of any other category to which it could be assigned. Specifically, it can be classified as a civil wrong which is not a breach of contract but which is remediable by an action for unliquidated damages and/or an injunction."
Both Barrington and Barron JJ. expressed some reserve on this point, with the former saying that it was not necessary to decide for the purpose of this case whether "all breaches of constitutional right are torts within the meaning of the Statute of Limitations. No doubt the terms have been used as interchangeable by judges when the distinction was not of any great importance."

[129] Keane J. observed:
"Whatever may be the position with regard to other possible defences, no one has been able to identify in this case any ground for supposing that an action for breach of a constitutional right which has all the indicia of an action in tort should have a different limitation period from that applicable to actions in tort generally – or, indeed, no limitation period at all – other than its origin in the Constitution itself, which is a classically circular argument."
Keane J. then cited the policy reasons underlying the Statutes of Limitation identified by Finlay C.J. in *Tuohy v. Courtney* [1994] 3 I.R. 1, adding:
"I can see no reason why an actress sunbathing in her back garden whose privacy is intruded upon by a long-range camera should defer proceedings until her old age to provide herself with a nest egg, while a young man or woman rendered a paraplegic by a drunken motorist must be cut off from suing after three years. The policy reasons identified [in *Tuohy v. Courtney*] are applicable to actions such as the present as much as to actions founded on tort in the conventional sense."

[130] Keane J. commented that:
"It may, of course, be the case that in considering whether other features of the general corpus of tort law apply to actions in protection of constitutional rights, questions may arise which are not relevant in these proceedings. Professor William Binchy in an interesting essay ("Constitutional Remedies and the Law of Torts" *Human Rights and Constitutional Law: Essays in Honour of Brian Walsh* (1992)) has suggested that significant differences may arise in some contexts given that, as he argues, the English law of tort was traditionally concerned with providing redress of wrongs, whereas the Constitution is essentially concerned with the protection of rights. Again, however, it is unnecessary to embark on those uncharted seas."

constitutional rights should not be regarded as wild cards which can be played at any time to defeat all existing rules. If the general law provides an adequate cause of action to vindicate a constitutional right it appears to me that the injured party cannot ask the Court to devise a new and different cause of action. Thus, the Constitution guarantees the citizen's right to his or her good name but the cause of action to defend his or her good name is the action for defamation with all its incidents including the time limit within which the action must be commenced."

This passage suggests that while the Constitution will continue to influence the development of the law of torts, its role will not be a radical one. And yet it may be predicted that these observations of Barrington J. will not be accepted in future cases without qualification. If, for example, the statutory time limit for defamation actions was peculiarly unfair or oppressive, would not a plaintiff be entitled to challenge as unconstitutional this incident of the existing tort, on the ground that the Oireachtas had thereby failed to vindicate the constitutional right to good name?[131] It must, moreover, be doubtful if the Oireachtas could ever in effect coerce a plaintiff who sues for damages for the infringement of a constitutional right to accept the limitations of an existing common law cause of action, unless these limitations were inherently fair, proportionate and adequately vindicated the constitutional right in question. Despite the elaborate nature of the analysis in both *W* and *McDonnell*, a fresh reappraisal of the relationship between the Constitution and the law of torts and the extent to which the Oireachtas can create new immunities or quasi-immunities would nonetheless seem to be called for.

Finally, the constitutional right in question is one which must be personal to the individual. In *Greene v. Minister for Agriculture*[132] Murphy J. held that the Minister had infringed Article 41.3.1°. (which provides that the State "pledges to protect the institution of marriage, on which the family is founded and to protect it against attack") by implementing the provisions of a European Community directive dealing with headage payment grants in a manner which discriminated against married couples. Murphy J. said that as the breach was that of a general pledge contained in the Constitution and did not relate to a personal constitutional right (such as, for example the right to liberty), the plaintiffs could not recover.[133] While the desire to

---

131 *cf. McKinley v. Minister for Defence* [1992] 2 I.R. 333 where the Supreme Court held that the common law rule which confined the cause of action for loss of consortium to husbands alone contravened Article 40.1. A majority of the Court "rescued" the tort by extending it on a gender-neutral basis. The point remains that the Court condemned on constitutional grounds an inherent limitation of the existing loss of consortium action.

132 [1990] 2 I.R. 17. The case concerned the manner in which the Minister had implemented Directive 75/286/EEC. The Minister had provided that farmers and their spouses whose off-farm income exceeded a certain maximum were precluded from obtaining certain headage payment grants. Murphy J. held that by including the off-farm income of spouses (but not, *e.g.* the off-farm income earned by the common law wife of the applicant farmer) the Minister had violated the constitutional guarantee to protect the family as contained in Art. 41.3.1°.

133 Thus, Murphy J. could say in *Greene* (at 28):
"The plaintiffs in the present case, unlike those in *Pine Valley*, cannot establish the infringement of a personal constitutional right. The only right which they can assert successfully is the general right of the citizens to the performance by the State of its obligation 'to guard with special care the institution of marriage.' Whilst I accept that citizens are entitled to ensure that that duty is honoured,

---

draw the line at some point is, perhaps, understandable, it introduces a new element of characterisation and one which is rather reminiscent of the line which has been drawn by the common law in the context of breach of statutory duty and which has now been to some degree uprooted by reliance on the Constitution.[134] Take, as an example of this difficulty, Article 44.2.3°:

> "The State shall not impose any disabilities or make any discrimination on the ground of religious profession, belief or status."

This is clearly a general pledge, but it would also appear to confer a personal right so as to entitle a person aggrieved by a breach thereof to damages in respect of that breach.

6. Statutory Right to Compensation

We have seen that, at common law, there is no general right to obtain compensation or damages in respect of administrative decisions which have been properly taken within jurisdiction. However, tortious acts apart, right to compensation in respect of certain administrative decisions has often been granted by way of specific statute. Such a statutory right arises, for example, where land has been acquired by an administrative body[135] or where the value of land has been reduced by certain types of planning decisions. Naturally, if the damage which materialises is not within the scope of the statutory claim, then no compensation may be recovered on this score; though it may well happen that an alternative action will lie in tort.[136] There are many administrative decisions which affect legal rights or interests in respect of which no statutory right to compensation exists: for example, the power of a local authority to require measures to be taken to prevent water pollution[137] or to order the demolition of a dangerous house[138] fall into this category. It would be out of place to provide a full list of administrative decisions in respect of which no compensation is payable[139] but the general principle on which the Oireachtas appears

---

the duty cast on the State does not create a corresponding right in the individual citizen so that a breach of the duty would necessarily constitute an infringement of any right of his."
Note, however, that in *Murphy v. Attorney General* [1982] I.R. 241 the Supreme Court regarded Art. 41.3.1° as creating individual rights on which married couples could rely.

134 See above, pp. 816–818.
135 See generally McDermott and Woulfe, *Compulsory Purchase and Compensation in Ireland: Law and Practice* (1992).
136 *Red Cow Service Station Ltd v. Bord Gáis Éireann* (1985) 3 I.L.T. (N.S.) 15. In *Collins v. Gypsum Industries Ltd* [1975] I.R. 321, the plaintiffs had claimed damages for personal injuries under the Mineral Development Act 1940. The Supreme Court held, however, that the 1940 Act provided for a scheme of compensation in respect of damage to land caused by mining operations and it did not extend to personal injuries. The proper forum for pursuing such a claim for personal injuries was that provided by the ordinary courts. See also, *Tate & Lyle Food Distribution Co. Ltd v. Greater London Council* [1983] 2 A.C. 509.
137 Local Government (Water Pollution) Act 1977.
138 Local Government (Sanitary Services) Act 1964.
139 Examples include the Local Government (Planning and Development) Acts 1963–1990 (no compensation payable for, by today, most types of planning refusals); the National Monuments Acts 1930–1994 (no compensation for reduction in land values caused by imposition of preservation order on national monuments).

to operate is that no provision for compensation is made in respect of administrative decisions which can be objectively shown to be in the public interest unless this would impose an undue burden on the individual citizen.

These principles may have to be re-examined in the light of the provisions of Article 40.3 and Article 43 of the Constitution. Article 40.3 requires the State by its laws to protect "as best it may from unjust attack" and in the case "of injustice done" to vindicate the property rights of every citizen. Article 43, while protecting the institution of private property rights permits the delimitation of such rights "with a view to reconciling their exercise with the exigencies of the common good".[140] The interpretation of these separate provisions is fraught with uncertainty, but the following propositions can be put forward with some confidence:

1. Article 40.3 protects individual rights over particular items of real and personal property, while Article 43 deals with the institution of private property.[141]
2. If the action of the state authorities can be justified by reference to Article 43, then such action cannot by definition be regarded as an "unjust attack" on the individual's property rights as protected by Article 40.3.[142]
3. It is for the courts to say whether the delimitation of property rights is actually required by social justice and the exigencies of the common good, *i.e.* whether this general regulation of particular property rights can be justified under Article 43.[143]
4. The courts will test the validity of any such interference with property rights by reference to the principle of proportionality.[144]

While the case law is in the course of development, it will be seen that the relevant legislation dealing with the right to compensation may have to be reassessed in the light of cases such as *Electricity Supply Board v. Gormley*,[145] where the Supreme Court held that, where a statutory scheme of compensation was established to compensate landowners for an interference with their land, the property rights guarantees contained in Articles 40.3 and 43 of the Constitution required that such legislation provide for assessment of compensation by an independent arbitrator.

In particular, it must be doubted whether general techniques of statutory interpretation are applicable in the light of such constitutional provisions. The general principle established by the English courts is that no action will lie in respect of acts done under lawful authority; nor will a public authority be liable in tort where the injury complained of is the inevitable consequence of that which has been legislatively ordained. In *Allen v. Gulf Oil Refining Ltd*,[146] the House of Lords applied these principles to hold that as the construction of a particular oil refinery

---

140 See generally, *Kelly, The Irish Constitution, op. cit.* above, n.35, pp. 1061–1091; Casey, *Constitutional Law in Ireland* (2nd ed., 1992) pp. 531–551.
141 *Blake v. Attorney General* [1982] I.R. 117.
142 *Dreher v. Irish Land Commission* [1984] I.L.R.M. 94; *O'Callaghan v. Commissioners of Public Works* [1985] I.L.R.M. 364; *Lawlor v. Minister for Agriculture* [1990] 1 I.R. 356.
143 *Buckley v. Attorney General* [1950] I.R. 64; *Electricity Supply Company v. Gormley* [1985] I.R. 129.
144 *Tuohy v. Courtney* [1994] 3 I.R. 1; *Daly v. Revenue Commissioners* [1995] 3 I.R. 1.
145 [1985] I.R. 129.
146 [1981] A.C. 1001. See also *Kelly v. Dublin County Council*, unreported, High Court, February 21, 1986 (Council liable for damages caused by storing of vehicles in neighbouring depot, as nuisance not shown to have been the "inevitable result of the exercise of statutory powers") .

was authorised by legislation, that Act had – at least by necessary implication – authorised the operation of the refinery – and that neighbours who complained of the smell, noise and vibration had no cause of action as the nuisance complained of was the inevitable consequence of the operation of the refinery.

It is difficult to believe that an Irish court would reach the same conclusion were it faced with a case with similar facts.[147] If the statute plainly extinguished neighbouring landowners' rights to sue in respect of such nuisance, an Irish court would probably rule that such provisions amounted to an unconstitutional attack[148] on the plaintiff's rights to sue in tort,[149] (which itself is a species of the property right protected by Article 40.3) or to recover compensation in respect of this state interference with their property rights.

Alternatively, if the statute was silent on the matter, an Irish court, applying the presumption of constitutionality, would probably rule that as there was no overt legislative intention to act in an unconstitutional fashion, it must be presumed that the legislature did not intend to deprive the plaintiffs of their right to sue in respect of the nuisance caused by the operation of the refinery. In short, cases such as *Gormley* show that there may have to be a complete reappraisal of the general principles of law governing the citizen's right to recover damages or compensation in respect of administrative decisions which injuriously affect his property rights. It is true that a great many statutes already confer a right to compensation, but even where no such express right has been granted the effect of Articles 40.3 and 43 of the Constitution is probably such as to oblige the courts to imply such a right, or, at the very least, judicially create the right to sue the administrative body concerned in tort.

7. Liability for the Negligent Exercise of Discretionary Public Powers

One may summarise this area of the law by saying that public authorities are subject to broadly the same common law of tortious liability as private individuals or companies. They (or their servants or agents) must (to take examples of what may

---

147 There is more than a hint of this in *Duff v. Minister for Agriculture* [1997] 2 I.R. 22 where a majority of the Supreme Court held that the plaintiff farmers should be compensated following a mistake of law on the part of the Minister. The basis for this conclusion is not entirely clear, but Barrington J. appeared to ground this finding on the basis of Art. 40.3.2°:

"... this Court would be doing less than its duty if it failed to vindicate their right to compensation in the circumstances of this case. It may not now be practicable for this Court or for the Minister to give them the outlet for the sale of their milk which they were led by State agencies to believe that they would get but this Court can, at least, award them compensation for their loss".

While it is, of course, true that the facts of *Duff* were very different to those of *Allen*, the key point is that there is a strong hint that Art. 40.3 effectively requires *ubi jus, ibi remedium* where a wrongful act has caused a private wrong, unless, perhaps, there are compelling policy reasons which make such a course of redress impossible.

148 Unless, of course, it could be said that such interference was justified by considerations pertaining to the common good, such as to result in no violation of their constitutional rights.

149 On the ground that otherwise existing tort law would be "plainly inadequate" (to use the language of Henchy J. in *Hanrahan v. Merck, Sharp and Dohme Ltd* [1988] I.L.R.M. 629 at 636) to vindicate the landowner's constitutional rights.

be called straightforward, operational torts): drive carefully; observe the appropriate duties of an employer or occupier; or, if they dig a trench, ensure that it is guarded so that no one will fall into it. The only public law issue which arises in relation to such issues is a matter discussed in Parts 2–4, namely: whether as a result of some special rule, a defence is available to a public authority which would not be available to a private individual. The issue to be discussed next namely, liability for the negligent exercise of a statutory discretionary power, is not about operational torts, but about a function peculiar to public authorities, which calls for special discussion.

Before discussing the law however, it is as well to identify the policy features, which make the shaping of the law in this area so different and difficult and explain why it is so unsatisfactory. In the first place, as a matter of tort law, the damage caused by invalid administrative action will usually result in pure economic loss, without any physical damage. Secondly, often, as we shall presently see, the complaint will be that a public body has failed to prevent some third party from inflicting loss on the complainant which the plaintiff claims has been broken. Thus the obligation would be a duty to take positive action. Here are two grounds on each of which general tort law has been slow to impose liability.[150] Thirdly and, even more significantly, from the perspective of administrative law, we have already noted in the context of the abuse of discretionary powers,[151] there is the major policy premise that a decision assigned to a public body should not be assigned to the judiciary. Furthermore, as has already been stated,[152] just because there is an unlawful exercise of discretionary powers,[153] it does not follow that any tort has been committed. Next, it may be thought that the imposition of discipline through the courts on a public body may have a chilling effect on the quality of the decisions of administrators,[154] who must be allowed a "margin of appreciation" to balance divergent factors, including economy, public resources and fairness to all members of the community and not just the plaintiff. And this is at least as true where the discipline concerned is liability in tort rather than a finding of invalidity.

The issue as to what extent public bodies may be liable for the negligent exercise of their discretionary powers, as contrasted with a mere operational decision or action, is one which has beset the courts of the common law world for the last 20 years or so, but especially since the decision of the House of Lords in *Anns v. Merton L.B.C.*[155] In this case, a block of flats developed cracks because, apparently, it had been built on inadequate foundations. The question of whether the local authority could be liable in negligence for its failure to exercise their discretionary statutory power to inspect the foundations was among the preliminary issues raised.[156] Lord

---

[150] On this, see de Smith, Woolf and Jowell, *op. cit.* above n.4, pp. 774–782.

[151] See above, pp. 641–649.

[152] See p. 811.

[153] See Chap. 12.

[154] This reasoning was very much to the fore in the judgment of Finlay C.J. in *Pine Valley Developments Ltd v. Minister for Environment* [1987] I.R. 23 and that of Costello P. in *W. v. Ireland (No.2)* [1997] 2 I.R. 142.

[155] [1978] A.C. 726.

[156] The Council inspector had apparently acted *ultra vires* in the discretion vested in him by not ensuring that the plans and foundations were in accordance with the building byelaws. The assumed facts (*Anns* was tried on a preliminary point of law) were consistent with his having been negligent either in not inspecting the foundations or in the manner in which the inspection was actually carried out.

Wilberforce set out what has come to be known as the "two-tier test".[157] The first requirement was that there could not be liability for the negligent exercise of a discretionary power "unless the act complained of lies outside the ambit of the power", *i.e.* a showing of *ultra vires* was a prerequisite to liability for the negligent exercise (or non-exercise) of a discretionary public power. This requirement was included in order to accommodate the fact that as the legislature saw fit to invest the public body with a discretionary power, it presumably intended to allow it some margin of appreciation. Once *ultra vires* was established, then in principle, a plaintiff could sue, provided he could satisfy the normal requirements of the tort of negligence. At this point the second stage of Lord Wilberforce's test came into play and the fact that the subject-matter of the case involved a discretionary power rather than an operational matter was again significant. For the more operational the power may be, the easier it is to superimpose a common law duty of care since liability is determined in accordance with the ordinary law of negligence.[158] By contrast, in the case of a discretionary power, the question of the persons to whom a duty of care is owed is much more open-ended and it is more difficult to establish in the case of any particular plaintiff.

Considerable doubts had been expressed in several important English and Privy Council[159] decisions about Lord Wilberforce's duty of care formula before that case was finally overruled.[160] These doubts appear to cast a cloud over the entirety of the reasoning in *Anns*, including those aspects of Lord Wilberforce's judgment which deal exclusively with liability arising from the negligent exercise of discretionary power. In certain contexts, the courts have been reluctant to hold that public authorities owe the general public a duty of care[161] and, even in the case of

---

157   *Ibid.* at 753–758. Somewhat confusingly, Lord Wilberforce also enunciated a separate "two-tier" test based on proximity and public policy considerations in relation to liability in negligence generally. This test is distinct from the special two-tier test of liability which he sought to apply in the area of negligent exercise of discretionary powers.

158   Lord Wilberforce referred to *Indian Towing Co. v. U.S.* 350 U.S. 61 (1955) where a decision to build a lighthouse was classified as a "policy" decision, but the failure to keep the lighthouse in working order was described as "operational negligence". And while Blayney J. did not employ this terminology in *Burke v. Dublin Corporation* [1990] 1 I.R. 18, he did appear to differentiate as far as liability was concerned between the Corporation's decision to purchase a new and cheaper form of heating system for certain tenants (a form of policy decision) and the actual maintenance of the system in good working order (an operational matter). But *cf.* the comments of Costello J. in *Ward v. McMaster* [1985] I.R. 29 at 47 where he described the policy/operational distinction as one of "degree" and "certainly one which may be difficult to make with precision in many cases". These comments presciently anticipated later developments for in *Stovin v. Wise* [1996] 3 All E.R. 801 Lord Hoffmann, speaking for a majority of the House of Lords, described this distinction as "inadequate" and this part of the *Anns* reasoning must also be regarded as having been overruled.

159   *Yuen Kun Yeu v. Attorney General of Hong Kong* [1988] A.C. 175; *Rowling v. Takaro Properties Ltd* [1988] A.C. 473; *Caparo Industries plc v. Dickman* [1990] 2 A. C. 605.

160   In *Murphy v. Brentwood DC* [1991] 1 A. C. 398.

161   This is true of attempts to impose a duty of care upon regulators: see, *e.g. Pine Valley Developments Ltd v. Minister for Environment* [1987] I.R. 23; *Yuen Kun Yeu v. Attorney General for Hong Kong* [1988] A.C. 175; *McMahon v. Ireland* [1988] I.L.R.M. 610. The English courts have also consistently refused to countenance the suggestion that the law-enforcement agencies owe victims or potential victims of crime a duty of care: see, *e.g. Hill v. Chief Constable of West Yorkshire* [1989] A.C. 53; *Alexandrou v. Oxford* [1993] 4 All E.R. 328; *Osman v. Ferguson* [1993] 4 All E.R. 344; *X v. Bedfordshire County Council* [1995] 2 A.C. 633; See also *Skinner v. Secretary of State for Transport, The Times*, January 3, 1995 where it was held, *per* Edwards J., that "in their ordinary function of

ultra vires acts, the courts are unwilling to impose liability where these public functions have been discharged in good faith.[162] Secondly, it is now evident that the question of whether a duty of care is to be imposed on the public body for the negligent exercise of a discretionary power depends, at least in part, upon the relevant statutory context.[163] This, in turn, has tended to assimilate the test for negligence to that of liability for breach of statutory duty, namely was the plaintiff a member of the class of persons which the statute was designed to protect? Finally, it must be borne in mind in any analysis of the case law that the different approaches to this problem and the judicial pronouncements thereon cannot always be reconciled.[164] In this respect, there is a similarity between this area and contemporary developments in the general law of negligence[165] where, for instance, the recent economic loss cases have reduced the law in this area to an uncertain state (not uncommon at a time of change) and, in turn, have tended to cast considerable doubt on Lord Wilberforce's expansive judgment in *Anns*.

It bears remarking, finally, that though nearly all the cases presently to be considered may certainly be classified under the rubric of negligent exercise of discretionary power, yet they almost all fall within a rather small sub-field of this area, namely the regulation of private, commercial activity such as building and planning matters. This means that apart from exceptional cases such as *McMahon v. Ireland*,[166] the wider aspects of a potentially vast field remain uncharted by judicial decision or even, to a large extent, academic comment. We have not yet gone much beyond the range of policy decisions similar to those which may arise in the private law field where, for instance: a hospital's policy is not to adopt a particular surgical technique; or a stock-broker's policy is not to buy a share in a particular type of undertaking. Thus, we have not yet encountered cases raising broader issues such as, for example situations in which: a victim of a motor-accident claims that this accident was caused by the highway authority's failure to improve a junction[167]; or a trader argues that the decision to turn the road on which his shop is located into a one-way street was negligent, thereby causing him financial loss; or, to go even further, where an exporter claims that the Government's decision to withdraw export credit insurance for a particular project because of the uncertain political and financial climate in the foreign country for which the goods were destined was negligently

---

watching, listening and co-ordinating search and rescue, the coastguard owes no legally enforceable duty of care to any member of the sea-going public, even in an emergency".

162 See, *e.g.* the decisions in *Pine Valley; McMahon; Rowling v. Takaro Properties Ltd* [1988] A.C. 473; *Jones v. Department of Employment* [1989] Q.B. 1.

163 This was the approach adopted by the House of Lords in *Governors of Peabody Donation Fund v. Sir Lindsay Parkinson & Co. Ltd* [1985] A.C. 210 and *Stovin v. Wise* [1996] 3 All E.R. 801 and by McCarthy J. in *Sunderland v. McGreavey* [1990] I.L.R.M. 658 and by Keane J. in *Convery v. Dublin County Council* [1996] 3 I.R. 153.

164 A fact readily acknowledged by Henchy J. in *Ward v. McMaster* [1988] I.R. 337 at 341. Thus, in *Convery v. Dublin Co. Council* [1996] 3 I.R. 153 Keane J. held that *Weir v. Dun Laoghaire Corporation* [1983] I.R. 242 must be regarded as having been reversed *sub silentio* by *Sunderland v. McGreavey* [1990] I.L.R.M. 658, since both decisions were "clearly irreconcilable".

165 See, *e.g. Murphy v. Brentwood D.C.* [1991] 1 A.C. 398.

166 [1988] I.L.R.M. 610.

167 This, however, formed the basis for the (unsuccessful) action in *Stovin v. Wise* [1996] 3 All E.R. 801.

arrived at. Clearly, the plaintiff in each such example would face an up-hill task to establish liability. Not only would the courts be reluctant to impose a duty of care on the public authority in question, but they might elect to reject such claims by a heavy emphasis on the *ultra vires* test or some other modern re-formulation of the *Anns* conditions. Nevertheless, it seems likely that claims of this kind will, at least, be presented with increasing frequency over the next decade.

Since an understanding of the developments in other common law jurisdictions following the decision in *Anns* is essential in any consideration of this issue, it will be convenient if we first assess the response in those jurisdictions to *Anns* before analysing the more recent Irish decisions.

The retreat from Anns *in England*

While, in the immediate aftermath of *Anns*, Lord Wilberforce's judgment was acclaimed as a masterly analysis of liability in negligence in general and that of public authorities in particular, it was quickly felt that *Anns* had unduly widened the scope of public authority liability. In one of the decisions which seems to have followed *Anns*, *Acrecrest Ltd v. W.S. Hattrell & Partners*,[168] the English Court of Appeal held that a local authority owed a duty of care in the exercise of its statutory supervision functions to a building developer. Accordingly, it held the authority liable for financial loss where an inspector had failed to insist on sufficiently deep foundations, even though there was no question of any apprehended injury to the health or safety of the developer. However, in *Peabody Donation Fund v. Sir Lindsay Parkinson & Co.*,[169] the House of Lords held that *Acrecrest* was wrongly decided and that the Court of Appeal had misapplied *Anns*. The facts of *Peabody* were very similar to those of *Acrecrest*. The plaintiffs had engaged in a large-scale building project and they were obliged by statute to deposit drainage plans with the defendant local authority. The local authority approved plans which had been drawn up by the plaintiffs' architects. Later it transpired that the plans were defective and the plaintiffs incurred substantial losses as a result. It was claimed that the local authority should have activated their statutory enforcement powers and that they were accordingly negligent in failing to ensure that the plaintiffs adhered to their original plans.

The House of Lords rejected the claim. Lord Keith accepted that the plaintiffs' loss was a reasonably foreseeable consequence of the local authority's inaction. Nevertheless, he held that in the light of the purpose of the statutory powers, no duty of care was owed to the plaintiffs by the local authority. The purpose of the enforcement powers was to safeguard the occupiers of houses within the authority's functional area and to protect the public interest; they were not designed to protect developers such as the plaintiff from the economic loss which they might suffer as a result of their own failure to comply with the relevant building regulations. Lord Keith added that there had been "a tendency in some recent cases" to treat passages from Lord Wilberforce's judgment in *Anns* "as being themselves of a definitive character" but he observed that this was "a temptation which should be resisted".

---

[168] [1983] Q.B. 260.
[169] [1985] A.C. 210.

A duty of care should only be imposed where "it was just and reasonable to do so"[170] and a mere relationship of proximity between the parties did not of itself suffice. Further evidence of judicial discomfort with *Anns* is evidenced by the fact that Lord Keith made no mention of the *ultra vires* test as a prerequisite to liability.[171]

In *Yuen Kun Yeu v. Attorney General for Hong Kong*[172] the Privy Council emphasised that the *Anns* test of itself was no longer a safe guide on the question of the very existence of a duty of care. Here, the plaintiffs had lost substantial sums of money following the collapse of a deposit-taking company. It was said that the authorities had been negligent in failing to exercise their statutory powers in order to safeguard the interests of the depositors with the company. Lord Keith said first that the *Anns* test had been "elevated to a degree of importance greater than it merits and greater perhaps than its author intended".[173] He proceeded by emphasising that foreseeability of harm did not of itself have the effect of bringing into being "a relationship apt to give rise to a duty of care". Here the commissioner of deposit-taking companies had no day-to-day control over the management of any company and it might be:

> "[a] very delicate choice whether the best course was to deregister a company forthwith or to allow it to continue in business with some hope that, after appropriate measures by the management, its financial position would improve."[174]

Lord Fraser concluded that, in the circumstances, there was no "special relationship" between the commissioner and those "unascertained members of the public who might in future become exposed to the risk of financial loss through depositing money with the company" as to give rise to a duty of care.

Finally, in *Stovin v. Wise*[175] (a case which was unusual in that it did haul out into the deeper waters of policy formation and expenditure) the House of Lords discarded Lord Wilberforce's "policy/operational" distinction as "inadequate". In this case a

---

[170] *Ibid.* at 241.

[171] This trend was continued by cases such as *Investors in Industry Commercial Properties Ltd v. South Bedfordshire D.C.* [1986] Q.B. 1034 and *Curran v. Northern Ireland Co-Ownership Housing Association Ltd* [1987] A.C. 718. In the former case, the English Court of Appeal held that the original owner was normally owed no duty of care by the local authority since he himself was under a duty to comply with the building laws. In any case, even if the owner was not personally negligent, it would be neither "just nor reasonable" to impose liability on a local authority. In *Curran*, the plaintiffs had purchased their house with the assistance of a mortgage from the Northern Ireland Housing Executive, a statutory authority responsible for the provision of housing accommodation and the general improvement of the housing stock. An extension to the house had been constructed, also with the benefit of a grant from the Housing Executive. The House of Lords decided that the Executive did not owe the plaintiffs a duty of care, saying that a contrary conclusion would be "bizarre". As Lord Bridge explained (at 728), insofar as there was any statutory duty on the Executive: "the purpose of imposing any such duty is for the protection of the public revenue, not of the recipients of the grant".

[172] [1988] 1 A.C. 175. By contrast with the result in this case, see the British Parliamentary Commissioner of Administration's handling of the *Barlow Clowes* complaint: (1991) *Public Law* at pp. 192 and 408.

[173] *Ibid.* at 191. Indeed, the wider "two-tier" test for liability in negligence generally enunciated by Lord Wilberforce in *Anns* has now been overruled by the House of Lords; *Murphy v. Brentwood D.C.* [1991] 1 A.C. 398 and *Caparo Industries plc v. Dickman* [1990] 2 A.C. 605. But McCarthy J. has said ([1988] I.R. 337 at 347) in *Ward v. McMaster* that he would not seek "to dilute the words of Lord Wilberforce".

[174] [1988] 1 A.C. 175 at 195.

[175] [1996] 3 All E.R. 801.

plaintiff was injured when his motor cycle collided with a car where the view from the plaintiff's perspective was obscured by an earth bank on railway land adjacent to the road. The local authority was aware that the presence of the earth bank made the junction dangerous and was taking steps to remove it, but nothing had been done by the date of the accident. Lord Hoffmann gave two reasons for his conclusion that the Council could not be made liable for the failure to improve the junction. First, the attitude of the council was perfectly reasonable, since the focus of their attention was on the many other sites "which already had much higher accident records".[176] It followed that the question of whether anything should be done about the junction was

> ". . . at all times firmly within the area of the council's discretion. As they were not under a public law duty to do the work, the first condition for the imposition of a duty of care was not satisfied."[177]

Even if that condition had been satisfied, Lord Hoffmann reasoned that it would be wrong to impose liability since there had been no element of reliance on the part of the plaintiff on the Council having improved the junction.[178]

It is clear, therefore, that the reasoning in *Anns* has been almost completely disowned. The English courts have been reluctant to impose liability in the case of "discretionary" (as opposed to "operational") decisions[179] and, in any event, liability will only be imposed where this is "just and reasonable". As we shall see, the Irish courts have taken a rather different road and arrived at a rather different destination.

The approach of the Irish Courts

A wide variety of approaches has been taken by the Irish courts to this question over the last decade and so it is difficult to ascertain any fixed pattern as far as judicial reasoning is concerned. In the first major case of its kind *Siney v. Dublin Corporation*,[180] the plaintiff had been allocated a flat by the defendant. It transpired that it was unfit for human habitation. However, it is not clear whether the inspection was taken pursuant to the authority's statutory powers or its statutory duties. If, as seems likely, the inspection was taken pursuant to a statutory power, then according

---

[176] *Ibid.* at 832.
[177] *Ibid.*
[178] He added (*ibid.* at 832):
"Everyone could see that it was still the same. Mr. Stovin was not arbitrarily denied a benefit which was routinely provided to others . . . It is not without significance that the Canadian cases in which a duty of care has been held to exist have all involved routine inspection and maintenance rather than improvements."
The Canadian cases mentioned in Lord Hoffmann's judgment include *Barratt v. District of North Vancouver* [1980] 2 S.C.R. 418 (frequency of road inspections was a matter of policy and could not form the basis of a charge of negligence); *Just v. British Columbia* [1989] 2 S.C.R. 1228 (frequency of inspections was an operational matter which could form the basis of a charge of negligence); *Brown v. British Columbia* [1994] 1 S.C.R. 420 (road department's decision to continue infrequent summer schedule of road inspections into November was a matter of policy).
[179] Insofar as this distinction has still survived *Stovin v. Wise.*
[180] [1980] I.R. 400. See also, *Coleman v. Dundalk U.D.C.*, unreported, Supreme Court, July 17, 1987; *Burke v. Dublin Corporation* [1990] 1 I.R. 18 and *Howard v. Dublin Corporation* [1996] 2 I.R. 325. For an account of *Siney* see, Clark and Kerr, "Council Housing, Implied Terms and Negligence – A Critique of *Siney v. Dublin Corporation*" (1980) 15 Ir. Jur. (N.S.) 32.

to the *Anns* test, it would have been necessary to show that the authority's inspectors acted "outside any delegated discretion either as to the making of an inspection or as to the manner in which the inspection was made".[181] But although *Anns* was referred to with approval, no mention was made of the *ultra vires* requirement. And so, in finding that the local authority was negligent, the Supreme Court appears to have applied the standard common law principles of liability – the neighbourhood principle enunciated in *Donoghue v. Stevenson*.[182]

Although the next major decision of the Supreme Court – *Weir v. Dún Laoghaire Corporation*[183] – has now been overruled[184], the reasoning still merits an analysis. Here, the plaintiff had tripped and fallen on a public road as a result of a difference in road levels caused by the construction of a bus lay-by. No warning of this difference in level had been given although the entire tarmacadam roadway had appeared level. There was thus clear evidence of negligence on the part of those engaged in constructing the lay-by. The local authority had granted planning permission to a development company to build a shopping centre nearby and it had been a condition of this permission that the bus lay-by be built. Thus, the lay-by was constructed with the "knowledge and approval" of the defendant local authority.

A majority of the Supreme Court ruled that the local authority was liable in negligence. O'Higgins C.J. appeared to emphasise the fact that the local authority had insisted on the construction of the lay-by, and that the work was carried on with the knowledge and approval of the local authority in their capacity both as planning authority and highway authority. The tenor of this remarkable judgment suggests that because the local authority insisted on the condition, it must have in a sense "authorised" the work with the result that the construction company came to be regarded as the local authority's servants or agents.[185]

Weir was a completely unsatisfactory decision because it ignored, *inter alia*, the public law nature of a local authority's powers and functions. Just as in *Siney*, no mention was made of the *ultra vires* requirement and no authorities were referred to in the judgments of the Supreme Court. It is also interesting to note that the result in *Weir* is the exact opposite to that arrived at by the House of Lords in *Peabody*. In both cases building developers sought to escape the consequences of their own negligence (or that of their agents) by claiming that a local authority was negligent in not activating its statutory powers. In direct contrast to the result in *Peabody*, the Supreme Court in *Weir* appeared to have held that a local authority owes a duty of care in the discharge of its statutory functions to the grantee of a planning permission to protect him from the consequences of his own negligence. Perhaps the only surprising feature of this judgment lies not in the fact that it has since been overruled, but that such a wholly indefensible proposition was ever endorsed by the Supreme Court.

---

[181] Clarke and Kerr, *ibid.* p. 51.
[182] [1932] A.C. 1.
[183] [1983] I.R. 242.
[184] In *Convery v. Dublin County Council* [1996] 3 I.R. 153 Keane J. said that *Weir* was "clearly irreconcilable" with the subsequent decision in *Sunderland v. McGreavey*.
[185] Griffin J.'s trenchant dissent protested against such an extension of liability on the ground that it was "warranted neither by principle nor authority."

The judgment of Costello J. in *Ward v. McMaster*[186] represents a more considered approach to this problem. In this case the plaintiff had purchased a new house which turned out to be grossly sub-standard structurally and a health risk. Proceedings were then instituted against the builder and the local authority. There were two aspects of the claim against the local authority. The plaintiff had applied to the council for a loan of IR£12,000 under the provisions of the Housing Act 1966 to enable him to purchase the house.[187] The council sent a valuer who reported that it was in good repair and that its market value was IR£25,000. The plaintiff alleged that this valuation was negligently carried out and that the council was vicariously liable.

Costello J. found that the valuer had no professional qualification relating to building construction and was employed simply to place a market value on the property. The standard of care required of him was merely that of an ordinary skilled auctioneer and he had not been negligent. The plaintiff successfully alleged, however, that the council was directly liable in that it had broken the common law duty of care owed to him in carrying out its statutory functions. The council had a statutory power under the 1966 Act to grant a loan to the plaintiff and a statutory duty by virtue of the relevant regulations to inspect the property before granting a loan. In carrying out the inspection, a duty to act with care arose, a duty which was broken by authorising an inspection by someone who lacked the necessary qualification to ascertain reasonably discoverable defects. Costello J. had no doubt, on the authority of cases such as *Anns* and *Siney*, that a common law duty of care based on the principle established in *Donoghue v. Stevenson* might exist when statutory functions were being performed. Following a review of the relevant authorities including *Peabody*, Costello J. concluded that the relevant principles in cases of this kind were as follows:

> "(a) When deciding whether a local authority exercising statutory functions is under a common law duty of care the court must firstly ascertain whether a relationship of proximity existed between the parties such that in the reasonable contemplation of the authority carelessness on their part might cause loss. But all the circumstances of the case must in addition be considered, including the statutory provisions under which the authority is acting. Of particular significance in this connection is the purpose for which the statutory powers were conferred and whether or not the plaintiff is in the class of persons which the statute was designed to assist.
>
> (b) It is material in all cases for the court in reaching its decision on the existence and scope of the alleged duty to consider whether it is just and reasonable that a common law duty of care as alleged should in all the circumstances exist."[188]

Applying these principles to the facts as found, Costello J. concluded that, although the plaintiff did not expressly inform any member of the council's staff, he was relying on their valuation. Further, although the council carried out the

---

[186] [1985] I.R. 29 (High Ct.).
[187] s.39 of the Housing Act 1966 provides that a local authority may lend money to a person for the purpose of acquiring or constructing a house.
[188] [1985] I.R. 29 at 49–50.

valuation for its own purposes and to comply with its statutory obligations, the council ought to have been aware that it was probable that the plaintiff, a person of limited means, would not have gone to the expense of having the house examined by a professionally qualified person and would have relied on the inspection which he knew would be carried out for the purpose of the loan application. There was therefore a sufficient relationship of proximity and there was nothing in the dealings between the parties which restricted or limited the duties in any way. In particular, no warning against relying on the proposed valuation was given. As to the scope of the duty, Costello J. concluded that the council should have ensured that the person carrying out the valuation would be competent to discover reasonably ascertainable defects which would materially affect its market value.

The judge did not attempt to draw any sharp distinction between "powers" and "duties" for the purposes of liability. He also declined to pay too much regard to the distinction drawn by Lord Wilberforce in *Anns* between "discretionary" and "operational" decisions, concluding that the matter was essentially a question of whether it was "just and reasonable" in the circumstances that a common law duty of care as alleged should exist. The council appealed to the Supreme Court against the finding of liability, but prior to the hearing of that appeal, there are two other important decisions of the High Court which merit consideration.

In *Sunderland v. McGreavey*[189] the plaintiffs had purchased a house from a builder and owner of the site. When the house proved to be hopelessly defective and unfit for human habitation due to flooding and a defective drainage system, the plaintiffs sued the local authority on the ground that it was the authority which had granted both planning and retention permission for the house, and as such they owed him a duty of care. Lardner J. followed the reasoning of Costello J. in *Ward v. McMaster*, first examining the statutory background to the exercise of the authority's statutory functions:

> "[The relevant provisions of the Planning Acts] are intended to assist in the implementation of the proper development of the planning authority's area in accordance with the development plan. They do not seem to be concerned with such matters as the specification or design of particular septic tanks or soak-away areas which might appropriately be the subject of local authority building regulations, nor I think are they concerned with the protection of individual houses against flooding due to a locally high-water table."[190]

Lardner J. also had regard to factors such as that the local authority had not adopted building regulations and the way in which the plaintiff's claim against the local authority was framed by reference to:

> ". . . the erection of a dwellinghouse in an area allegedly liable to flooding and with a drainage system which was incapable of function, I have come to the conclusion that, in regard to the matters complained of by the plaintiffs, a relationship of proximity did not exist between Louth County Council and the plaintiffs; that the purposes for which these powers are conferred are quite

---

[189] [1987] I.R. 372 (High Ct.).
[190] *Ibid.* at 389.

different and distinct from and did not comprehend the subject-matter of the plaintiffs' complaints which more properly fall within the appropriate area of building regulations. In all the circumstances, I conclude that in considering whether to grant the original planning permission and the ultimate permission for the retention of the dwelling house Louth County Council did not owe the plaintiffs a common law duty of care in regard to the matters complained of and that to hold otherwise would not be just or reasonable in the circumstances."[191]

Quite irrespective of the test one might care to apply to the facts of such a case (be it the *Anns* formulation or the "just and reasonable" test), Lardner J.'s decision would seem to be correct. Clearly, any decision bearing on the question of planning permission is largely a question of planning policy and a decision to grant planning permission cannot in any sense be taken as warranting the soundness of any subsequent construction on the site.

The judgment of Blayney J. in *McMahon v. Ireland*[192] is along similar lines. As in the Privy Council decision in *Yuen Kun Yeu* (considered above) the plaintiff had lost money following the collapse of a deposit-taking institution which, taking advantage of an exemption in the Central Bank Act 1971 which it then enjoyed, had carried on a form of banking business. It was claimed that both the Ministers for Finance and Industry and Commerce, on the one hand, and the Registrar of Friendly Societies, on the other, were negligent in failing to ensure that the legislation was amended so as to end this particular exemption. Blayney J. found that neither Minister was responsible for the initial exemption; nor did they owe the plaintiff a duty of care to bring a Bill before the Oireachtas to seek to have the 1971 Act amended. Blayney J. considered that the position of the Registrar of Friendly Societies was analogous, in principle, and in several points of detail, to that of the commissioner of deposit-taking companies in *Yuen Kun Yeu*. It should, however, be noted that what was involved in *Yuen Kun Yeu* was merely the failure to exercise a discretionary power. By contrast, in *McMahon* the plaintiff had to go to the length of arguing that the Minister should have sought to persuade the Oireachtas to bring forward amending legislation. In any case, Blayney J. in *McMahon* followed the reasoning of the Privy Council in *Yuen Kun Yeu* and held that the Registrar owed the plaintiffs no duty of care. And while Blayney J. did not expressly say so, *McMahon* stands out from the other negligence cases which have arisen (mostly in the planning or building field) in that it involved a public authority decision which was plainly at the discretionary end of the spectrum. It is in regard to this type of policy decision that liability in negligence is most difficult to establish.

In 1988, the entire question was exhaustively examined by the Supreme Court when delivering judgment on the appeal from Costello J. in *Ward v. McMaster.*[193]

---

191 [1987] I.R. 372 at 390.
192 [1988] I.R.L.M. 610. See, McGrath (1987) 9 D.U.L.J. (N.S.) 163. But the Oireachtas is clearly taking no chances, for s.17(9) of the Building Societies Act 1989 now provides as follows:
   "The grant of an authorisation to a society by or under this section shall not constitute a warranty as to the solvency of the society to which it is granted and the State or the Central Bank shall not be liable in respect of any losses incurred through the insolvency of a society to which an authorisation is deemed granted under this section or granted by the Bank."
193 [1988] I.R. 337.

Henchy J. (with whom Finlay C.J. and Griffin J. concurred) considered that while the council were plainly in breach of their public duty, it was for the plaintiffs to show that there was sufficient proximity between the parties to give rise to a duty of care. This they had done:

> "The consequences to the plaintiff of a failure on their part to value the house properly should have been anticipated by the council in view of factors such as that, in order to qualify for the loan, the plaintiff had to show that he was unable to obtain the loan from a commercial agency and that his circumstances were such that he would otherwise need to be re-housed by the council. A borrower of that degree of indigence could not have been reasonably expected to incur the further expense of getting a structural survey of the house done."[194]

McCarthy J. (with whom Finlay C.J. (again) and Walsh J. concurred) spoke in similar language, but stressed that he would not "seek to dilute the words of Lord Wilberforce" in *Anns*. McCarthy J. said that whilst Costello J. had rested his conclusion on the "fair and reasonable test", he preferred to express the duty as arising from the "proximity of the parties, the foreseeability of the damage and the absence of any compelling exemption based on public policy".[195] While McCarthy J. did not rule out the possibility of public policy issues providing a defence, he considered that "such a consideration must be a very powerful one" if it is to be used to deny "an injured party his right to redress at the expense of the person or body that injured him".[196] On the critical issue of whether there was sufficient proximity between the parties, McCarthy J. said:

> "This proximity had its origin in the Housing Act 1966 and the consequent loan scheme. This Act imposed a statutory duty upon the County Council and it was in the carrying out of that statutory duty that the alleged negligence took place. It is a simple application of the principle of *Donoghue v. Stevenson*, confirmed in *Anns* and implicit in *Siney*, that the relationship between the party and the plaintiff and the County Council created a duty to take reasonable care arising from the public duty of the County Council under the statute. The statute did not create a private duty, but such arose from the relationship between the parties."[197]

---

[194] *Ibid.* at 342.
[195] *Ibid.* at 349. See also *Burke v. Dublin Corporation* [1991] 1 I.R. 314 and *Howard v. Dublin Corporation* [1996] 2 I.R. 235 (discussed below at p. 842). In other cases, however, no proximity has been found to exist. Thus, in *Cotter v. Minister for Agriculture*, unreported, Supreme Court, April 1, 1993, O'Flaherty J. concluded that there was no proximity between the Minister and certain farmers giving rise to a duty of care in circumstances where the latter had arranged for a contractor to carry out certain drainage works while the Minister had simply arranged to pay them a grant in respect of these works.
[196] [1988] I.R. 337 at 347.
[197] *Ibid.* at 351. There have been some subsequent attempts to highlight the special facts of this case. Thus, in *Cotter v. Minister for Agriculture*, unreported, Supreme Court, April 1, 1993 O'Flaherty J. observed that in *Ward* the Court took "an especial account of the indigency of the plaintiffs in that case, together with the obligation that rested on the local authority not to do anything to encourage the existence of houses that would be unfit for human habitation which, in turn, would have been contrary to the relevant housing legislation." In *Convery v. Dublin County Council* [1996] 3 I.R. 153 Keane J. stressed that it was the relative lack of means of the plaintiffs in *Ward, i.e.* the

Moreover, the loss was reasonably foreseeable, as it did not require "much imag-ination" on the part of the officers of the council to contemplate that a purchaser under the scheme would both lack the personal means of having an expert exam-ination and "might well think" that the very circumstances of the council investing its money in the house was "a badge of quality".

In 1990, in *Sunderland v. McGreavey*[198] the Supreme Court agreed with Lardner J.'s analysis and dismissed the plaintiff's appeal. In holding that planning authorities did not owe purchasers or occupiers a duty of care to ensure that a particular dwelling was structurally sound and suitable for human habitation, McCarthy J. distinguished between cases such as *Siney* and *Ward* on the one hand and the present case on the other:

> "The fundamental difference between what may be called planning and housing legislation is that the first is regulatory or licensing according to the requirements of the proper planning and development, but the second is a provision in a social context for those who are unable to provide for them-selves. If they are unable to provide for themselves, then the duty on the provider reaches the role that would be taken by professional advisers engaged on behalf of the beneficiary. This is in marked contrast to the watchdog role that is created under the Planning Act, a watchdog role that is for the benefit of the public at large."[199]

If the plaintiff's argument were correct, McCarthy J. continued, it would mean that planning authorities and An Bord Pleanála would be under a duty of care to inspect dwelling houses before deciding to grant permission. These potential consequences were mentioned not "*in terrorem*", but rather to seek to identify "on a reasonable approach the intention of the legislature in enacting the relevant parts of the 1963 Act". The judge concluded that:

> "The Act in conferring statutory powers on planning authorities imposed on them a duty towards the public at large. In my view, in conferring these powers, the Oireachtas did not include a purpose of protecting persons who occupy buildings erected in the functional area of planning authorities from the sort of damage which the plaintiffs suffered. That being so, the Council, in the exercise of those powers, owed no duty of care at common law to the plaintiffs."[200]

---

fact that they "belonged to a particular category of persons for whose benefit the powers and duties of the housing authority" under the Housing Act 1966 was of "critical importance in determining whether they owed him a duty of care in the exercise of those powers and duties". On the other hand, in *Hanahoe v. District Judge Hussey*, unreported, High Court, November 14, 1997, Kinlen J. accepted that the actions of an (unidentifiable) individual Garda who "leaked" details of a highly sensitive Garda search of solicitors' offices in advance to the media amounted to negligence. As it was readily foreseeable that such actions would cause the plaintiffs' loss and damage, the plaintiffs could bring themselves within the passages of the judgment of McCarthy J. in *Ward v. McMaster* which have just been quoted in the text.

198 [1990] I.L.R.M. 658.
199 *Ibid.* at 658.
200 *Ibid.*

It may be remarked in passing that in determining the liability of the planning authority McCarthy J. appears to have employed a test grounded on the intention of the legislature in determining the liability of the planning authority. This approach is very similar to that employed by Lord Fraser in *Peabody Donation Fund v. Sir Lindsay Parkinson & Co.*[201] and is in marked contrast to the "two-tier" test which was accepted in McCarthy J.'s own judgment in *Ward v. McMaster*.

Finally, three recent cases have emphasised the limited circumstances in which a plaintiff can successfully sue in respect of the manner in which discretionary powers have been exercised. In the first of these, *Howard v. Dublin Corporation*[202] Lavan J. held that the Corporation owed the plaintiffs a duty of care (which, he found on the facts, had not been breached) in respect of loans which they made to certain indigent defendants under statutory powers conferred by section 40(1)(a) of the Housing Act 1966:

> "The defendants would be in breach of their statutory duty under s.40(1)(a) were they to make loans which rendered houses unfit for human habitation by the installation of a seriously defective heating system. Breach of this public law duty could give rise to a private law action in negligence in circumstances where a relationship of proximity exists. Just such a relationship of proximity exists here given the specific objectives of the Housing Acts and the straitened circumstances of the legislation's beneficiaries."[203]

In *Convery v. Dublin County Council*[204], which centred around a major policy decision,[205] the plaintiff sought an injunction to compel the Council to take action to abate the huge increase of traffic volumes which had "caused a serious interference with the normal amenities of life in a residential area as a result of a volume of traffic which is greatly in excess of the design capacities of the roads". Keane J. held that the action in negligence must fail, since the Council did not owe the plaintiff any duty of care:

> "The powers and duties of the County Council as planning authority and roads authority are vested in them in order to ensure the proper planning and development of their area and the provision and maintenance of an appropriate road network in that area. While the exercise of those powers and duties can be regulated by the High Court by means of the judicial review process so as to ensure that they are exercised only in accordance with law, the plaintiff does not belong to any category of persons to whom the Council, in the exercise of those powers, owed a duty of care at common law."[206]

---

[201] [1985] A.C. 210.

[202] [1996] 2 I.R. 235.

[203] *Ibid.* at 239. It may be noted that s.22(1) of the Housing (Miscellaneous Provisions) Act 1992 now provides that:
"The granting of assistance by the Minister or a housing authority in respect of a house shall not imply any warranty on the part of the Minister or the authority, as the case may be, in relation to the state of repair or condition of the house or its fitness for human habitation."
The loans at issue in *Howard* pre-dated the enactment of this provision.

[204] [1996] 3 I.R. 153.

[205] For comment on this, see p. 844.

[206] *Ibid.* at 174.

In *Duff v. Minister for Agriculture*[207] Murphy J. rejected a claim that agricultural advisers employed by the Minister had failed to give the plaintiff farmers competent professional advice in relation to the pending implications of the super levy régime when preparing the development plans for their farms, but acknowledged that in such a case, had the advisers been negligent, the Minister would have been vicariously liable in the ordinary way. On appeal, the question centred on whether the Minister might be liable in damages in respect of his failure to allocate a milk quota to the development farmers whom he had promised to assist. The minority appears to have characterised the situation as involving a policy decision which the Minister had taken reasonably.[208] By contrast, and it is suggested, more realistically, the majority[209] drew a distinction between the Minister's decision to help the plaintiffs (which was a policy decision but one which had been taken in the plaintiffs' favour) and the unlawful means by which he sought to implement that decision.

The critical reasoning is in the following extract from Barrington J.'s judgment:

> "As previously stated, the plaintiffs could have had no legitimate expectation that the law would not be changed. Neither could they have any right that the Minister would exercise his discretion under Article 3 of Regulation (EEC) No. 857/84. But once the Minister had decided to give them a reference quantity out of the national quota the Minister had a duty, and they had a right to expect, that the Minister would implement this decision in a lawful manner. The Minister, in breach of his duty and of their rights, attempted to implement his decision in a manner which was unlawful. As a result the plaintiffs did not obtain the special reference quantities to which they were entitled and have, in consequence, suffered damage and loss.
>
> The trouble is that the method which the Minister chose to provide for the development farmers was unlawful. He chose this method due to a mistake of law on his part. When he discovered his mistake, in the autumn of 1984, the situation had changed because the national quota had been divided up without making provision for the national reserve out of which the development farmers could receive their quota. It was now too late, or the Minister felt it was too late, to retrieve the situation . . . If, as appears to be the case, the plaintiffs have suffered loss and damage as a result of the Minister's mistake of law, it appears to me to be just and proper in the circumstances of this case, that the Minister should pay them compensation."[210]

This important passage is a little unclear. It seems likely though that the claim based on legitimate expectations was rejected on the ground that a legitimate expectation cannot prevail against the exercise of a statutory power, still less a change of law.[211] Rather the plaintiffs appear to have succeeded on the ground of something like a

---

[207] [1997] 2 I.R. 22.
[208] O'Flaherty, Blayney and Barrington JJ.; Hamilton C.J. and Keane J. dissented.
[209] See p. 22 and p. 875, n. 82.
[210] [1997] 2 I.R. 22 at 77–78 (Blayney J. agreed with Barrington J.), the third member of the majority, O'Flaherty J. formulated the point somewhat differently. O'Flaherty J. did use, to some degree, the phrase "legitimate expectation" and also drew explicitly on the notion of restitution, on which see below pp. 850–857.
[211] On this aspect of legitimate expectations, see below pp. 860–875; 883–887.

negligent error of law in that the Minister had misunderstood the E.C. Directive which he was applying. This may be classified as a special case of operational negligence as opposed to the negligent exercise of a discretionary power. The only point on which it might be faulted is to query whether the sort of public policy defence which won the day for the State in *Pine Valley Developments Ltd v. Minister for Environment*[212] applied here.

So far as the results in the cases outlined here[213] are concerned, the following summary may be offered. One case (in which the plaintiff lost) – *McMahon* – involved decisions which were close to the discretionary end of the spectrum. There have been few cases in this area in any jurisdiction and very few have been successful. Two other cases – *Sunderland* and *Convery* – were manifestly a rather forlorn attempt on the part of the plaintiffs in each case to ascribe liability to the local authority. In other cases – *Siney, Ward* and *Duff* – the plaintiff won and it is significant that *Ward* involved a similar situation to that resolved by the House of Lords in *Curran* in favour of the local authority. Such results – in which the tenor of the Irish decisions is often in contrast not only with British but with other foreign decisions – display the Irish courts' marked preference for the individual plaintiff. In any area where any test is bound to include a large margin of judicial appreciation, previous results may be a better guide to future decisions than any stated formula.

However, in as much as formulae do afford a predictable guide, it is worth noting that the only attempts at such a formulation occurred in *Ward v. McMaster*. In the High Court, Costello J. declined to pay too much regard to the distinction between "discretionary" and "operational" decisions. In the Supreme Court, while not seeking to dilute the *Anns* formula, McCarthy J. was plainly more concerned with that facet of the *Anns* test which emphasises the potential duty of care to the individual. McCarthy J. did also, however, examine the other limb of the *Anns* test, namely the *ultra vires* requirement which does provide some protection for the public authority. Counsel for the Council had put his argument grounded on this limb thus:

> "The omission held to be culpable arose from a decision of policy or discretion which was not open to question by the courts in an action such as this. It was, it is said, a policy decision within the discretion of the County Council not to have any inspection other than that which produced a valuer's certificate: to carry out inspections in every instance through an engineer or like qualified person would greatly reduce the amount of money available in loans with consequent damage to the true purpose of the Housing Act."[214]

---

212 [1987] I.R. 23. See further above at pp. 823–824.

213 See also, *Ryan v. Ireland (No. 2)*, unreported, High Court, October 19, 1989 (the sequel to *Ryan v. Ireland* [1989] I.R. 177) where Barr J. found that officers of the Defence Forces had been negligent at an "operational level" in not taking adequate steps to protect Irish troops serving with the UN forces in the Lebanon from the possibility of attack by militia groups. The plaintiff was awarded £198,354 in damages.

214 [1988] I.R. 337 at 346. What is striking about the decision in *Ward* is that there was scant mention of a consideration regarded as central by the House of Lords in *Curran v. Northern Ireland Housing Executive* [1987] A.C. 718, a case with similar facts. Addressing the contention that the Housing Executive owed the plaintiff borrower a duty of care, Lord Bridge remarked that any duty imposed on the Executive was:
  "[T]o satisfy themselves that the grant-aided works have been properly executed, it seems to me clear that the purpose of imposing any such duty is for the protection of the public revenue, not the recipients of the grant or their successors in title."

McCarthy J., however, could not accept this submission:

> "The monetary argument does not bear critical examination. The County Council would not be required to have an engineering inspection in any case in which the relevant house is newly built since procedures for grants involve inspections at the material times with regard to such things as foundations etc., whilst the house is being built. Likewise, houses of significant age would not require inspections to deal with defects arising from subsidence; visual inspection by a relatively unqualified person would be quite adequate to disclose such defects. In any event, I see no bar to the County Council expressly excluding any representations to be inferred from the fact that it sanctions a particular loan. Having regard to this conclusion, it is not necessary for me to express an opinion as to whether or not so-called policy considerations are, in that context, free from review in the Courts in an action of this kind."[215]

This passage shows the Supreme Court as just leaving open the possibility that, in an appropriate case, it might be proper to take into account the discretion accorded by the Oireachtas to the public authority.[216] This view might possibly be recognised either by making policy considerations effectively – to borrow McCarthy J.'s phrase – "free from review", or through the use of some other device, such as the *ultra vires* requirement employed by Lord Wilberforce in *Anns*. It may also be significant that subsequent decisions – such as *Cotter* and *Convery* – have sought to stress the special facts of *Ward* and have been wary of employing McCarthy J.'s open-ended formula in a manner that might impose new liabilities on public authorities.

8. Liability of the State for Breach of E.C. Law

A related question is the liability of the State for breach of Community law. In the seminal decision of *Francovich v. Italy*[217] the Court of Justice of the European Communities held that a Member State might be liable in damages in respect of loss and damage which was directly caused by the State's failure to implement a directive which conferred directly enforceable rights. The Court further indicated that a plaintiff's entitlement to damages must be determined in accordance with national procedural rules, which must not be less favourable than those relating to similar domestic claims and must not be framed so as to make it virtually impossible or excessively difficult to obtain compensation. The peculiar difficulties associated with this topic arise from the fact that just because a particular Directive has either not been implemented at all or transposed inadequately into national law, the courts lack precise guidance as regards the contents of the obligation which has been breached. In addition, the attendant procedural law (*e.g.* measure of damages, limitation periods etc.) has to be worked up from scratch.

---

[215] *Ibid.* at 346–347.
[216] Note that in *Graham v. Minister for Environment*, unreported, High Court, May 1, 1996, Morris J. held that although a returning officer had wrongly denied the plaintiff the right to vote, there was no negligence as the officer had acted diligently and within the limits of her statutory discretion.
[217] Case C–6/90, [1991] E.C.R. I–5357.

Some of these issues were explored by Carroll J. in her judgment in *Tate v. Minister for Social Welfare*,[218] a case arising from the State's failure adequately to transpose the Equality Directive 7/79/EEC into national law. Carroll J. rejected the submission that the plaintiffs' claim for damages by reason of the failure to implement the Directive derived from the Constitution[219] and also held that the concept "of the duty of care taken from the common law of negligence has no bearing on the legal issues in the case". Rather the plaintiffs entitlement to sue "was a wrong arising from Community law which has domestic effect" and was a "breach of duty to implement the Directive and it approximates to a breach of constitutional duty". However the Minister's defense succeeded: Carroll J. concluded that the six-year limitation period contained in section 11 of the Statute of Limitations Act 1957 applied to actions seeking damages for breaches of Community law. Just as the word "tort" in the section captured breaches of statutory duty and breaches of constitutional rights, so also "the word 'tort' is sufficiently wide to cover breaches of the obligations of the State under Community law".[220] It is noteworthy that Carroll J. regarded this cause of action as an autonomous one arising under the Community law, and not necessarily conforming to any of the established domestic causes of action. On the other hand, in *Emerald Meats Ltd v. Minister for Agriculture and Food* [221] Blayney J. held that a breach of a duty imposed on the Minister by an E.C. Regulation was "in effect" a breach of a statutory duty and held that the State was accordingly liable in damages by virtue of standard *Francovich* principles.

The entire question of liability was reconsidered by the Court of Justice in a series of cases with complex reasoning decided in 1996. In the first of these, *Brasserie du Pêcheur SA v. Germany*[222], a French brewery sought damages from the German State in respect of the operation of beer purity laws[223] which, during the period of their operation, had prevented them from importing their beer into Germany. Here, the Court first re-affirmed the general *Francovich* principles to the effect that Member States "were obliged to make good damage caused to individuals by breaches of Community law attributable to the State",[224] even where (as here) the national legislature was responsible for the breach in question.

---

[218] [1995] 1 I.R. 418.

[219] On this point, Carroll J. said (*ibid*. at 435–436) "The function of [Art. 29.4.5° of the Constitution] was to allow the body of European Community law to have effect in Ireland in spite of any provision in the Constitution. It did not confer any new constitutional right; rather its tendency is to qualify those rights."

[220] This reasoning was affirmed by the Supreme Court in *McDonnell v. Ireland*, unreported, July 23, 1997 (see at pp. 824–826). Note that in *Schmidt v. Home Secretary of the United Kingdom* [1995] 1 I.L.R.M. 301 at 305 Geoghegan J. held that for the purpose of Art. 5(3) of the Brussels Convention on Jurisdiction and Enforcement of Judgments, "breaches of constitutional rights and actionable breaches of Community law are 'matters relating to tort' within the meaning of Article 5 . . . ".

[221] [1997] 2 I.L.R.M. 275. See also *Coppinger v. Waterford County Council*, unreported, High Court, March 18, 1996.

[222] Case C–46/93 [1996] 2 C.M.L.R. 889. It was heard together with Case C–48/93 *R v. Transport Secretary, ex p. Factortame Ltd* [1996] 2 C.M.L.R. 889 ("Factortame III"). There is already a huge volume of literature on the implications of these decisions: see, *e.g.* Van Gerven (1995) 32 C.M.L.Rev. 679; L. Neville Brown, "State Liability to Individuals in Damages: An Emerging Doctrine of EC Law" (1996) 31 Ir. Jur. (N.S.) 7; Gravells, "State Liability in damages for breach of European Community law" [1996] *Public Law* 567 and Craig, "Once More unto the Breach: The Community, the State and Damages Liability" (1997) 113 *Law Quarterly Review* 67.

[223] The laws in question had been declared to be contrary to Art. 30 of the Treaty of Rome in Case 178/84 Case C–46/93 *Brasserie du Pêcheur SA* [1987] E.C.R. 1227.

[224] *Commission v. Germany* [1996] 1 C.M.L.R. 889 at 987.

The Court then went on to consider the question of liability where the breach was caused by legislative acts. Here, the Court drew a distinction between a situation where the national legislature's discretion was heavily circumscribed – such as where it failed to implement a directive within the given period prescribed by the directive[225] – and a case where a Member State acts in a field where it has a wide discretion comparable to that of the Community institutions in implementing Community policies. In this second category:

"... the conditions under which it may incur liability must, in principle, be the same as those under which the Community institutions incur liability in a comparable situation."[226]

The Court then explained the nature of these conditions:

"The strict approach taken towards the liability of the Community in the exercise of its legislative activities is due to two considerations. First, even where the legality of measures is subject to judicial review, exercise of the legislative function must not be hindered by the prospect of actions for damages whenever the general interest of the Community requires legislative measures to be adopted which may adversely affect individual interests. Second, in a legislative context characterised by the exercise of a wide discretion, which is essential for implementing a Community policy, the Community cannot incur liability unless the institution concerned has manifestly and gravely disregarded the limits on the exercise of its powers."[227]

Applying these principles to the facts of the case, the Court first concluded that, in the absence of harmonisation, the German legislature enjoyed a wide discretion in the matter. It then applied the *Francovich* tests: infringing a Community rule intended to confer individual rights; serious breach; and, thirdly, a direct causal link between the breach of the obligation resting on the State and the damage sustained by the injured parties. The first test was clearly satisfied in the case of Article 30 and the question of the causal link specified in the third test was a matter for the national courts themselves. The Court laid down general principles governing the second key ("serious breach of Community law") condition:

"... the decisive test for finding that a breach of Community law is sufficiently serious is whether the Member State or the Community institution concerned manifestly and gravely disregarded the limits on its discretion. The factors which the competent court may take into consideration include the

---

225 In the subsequent case of *Dillenkofer v. Germany* Joined Cases C–178 and 188–190/94 [1996] 3 C.M.L.R. 469 (a case arising out of damages claims arising from Germany's failure to implement the Package Holidays Directive 90/314/EEC within the prescribed time) the Court of Justice ruled that:
   "Failure to take any measure to transpose a directive in order to achieve the result it prescribes within the period laid down for that purpose constitutes per se a serious breach of Community law and consequently gives rise to a right of reparation for individuals suffering injury if the result prescribed by the directive entails the grant to individuals of rights whose content is identifiable and a causal link exists between the breach of the State's obligation and the loss and damage suffered."
226 Joined Cases C–46 and 48/93 [1996] 1 C.M.L.R. 889 at 989.
227 *Ibid.* at 988, citing Joined Cases 83 & 94/76 and 4, 15 & 40/77, *HNL v. Council* [1978] E.C.R. 1209.

clarity and precision of the rule breached, the measure of discretion left to the national or Community authorities, whether the infringement and the damage caused was intentional or involuntary, whether any error of law was excusable or inexcusable, the fact that the position taken by a Community institution may have contributed to the omission and the adoption or retention of national measures or practices contrary to Community law. On any view, a breach of Community law will be sufficiently serious if it has persisted despite a judgment finding the infringement in question to be established, or a preliminary ruling or the settled case law of the Court on the matter from which it is clear that the conduct in question constituted an infringement."[228]

While the ultimate finding on liability was a matter for the national courts, the Court then gave guidance in the cases under consideration. It doubted, for example, whether the German breach was an excusable error, "since the incompatability of such rules with Article 30 was manifest in the light of earlier decision of the Court".[229] For comparison, one should note that in the case of *Factortame* – which concerned British legislation regarding the registration of fishing trawlers, which had imposed nationality restrictions – the Court held that the national courts might take into account factors such as:

". . . the legal disputes relating to the particular features of common fisheries policy, the attitude of the Commission, which made its position known to the United Kingdom in good time, and the assessments as to the state of certainty of Community law made by the national courts in the interim proceedings brought by individuals affected by the Merchant Shipping Act [1988]."[230]

Subject to these considerations, the questions of liability fell then to be determined by national law, subject to the requirements that the conditions laid down should not be less favourable than those relating to similar domestic claims and that the restrictions must not be such as in practice to make it excessively difficult to obtain such reparation. In *Factortame III* the Court concluded that the condition required by English law, which demands proof of misfeasance in public office, was not acceptable as a pre-condition to liability, since "such an abuse of power [was] inconceivable on the part of the legislature".[231]

---

[228] [1996] 1 C.M.L.R. 889 at 990. It is worth noting that the Court expressly rejected (at 993) the suggestion that the obligation to make reparation for loss and damage "cannot, however, depend upon a condition based on any concept of fault going beyond that of a sufficiently serious breach of Community law" as the imposition "of such a supplementary condition would be tantamount to calling into question the right to reparation founded on the Community legal order".

[229] *Ibid.* citing Case 120/78 *Rewe-Zentral* [1979] E.C.R. 649 ("Cassis de Dijon") and Case 193/80 *Commission v. Italy* [1981] E.C.R. 3019 ("vinegar"). In contrast, the position with regard to the prohibition on the use of additives "was significantly less conclusive" until the Court's judgment in *Commission v. Germany*, where that prohibition was held to be contrary to Art. 30.

[230] [1996] 1 C.M.L.R. 889 at 991. Not surprisingly, the English Courts subsequently held that the trawler owners were entitled to damages for "manifest and grave" breaches of E.C. Law: *R. v. Transport Secretary, ex p. Factortame Ltd (No. 5), The Times*, September 11, 1997.

[231] *Ibid* at 992. It is clear from this decision that the earlier leading English authority on State liability for breach of Community law, *Bourgoin SA v. Ministry of Agriculture, Fisheries and Food* [1986] 1 Q.B. 716 – which had insisted on proof of misfeasance as a pre-condition to liability for breach of Community law – must no longer be regarded as good law.

The parameters of *Brasserie du Pêcheur* were further illustrated by two subsequent decisions. In the first of these, *R. v. HM Treasury, ex p. British Telecommunications plc*,[232] the British authorities had erred in law in the manner in which they had transposed a directive No. 90/531 governing public procurement in telecommunications sector into domestic law.[233] However, on this occasion, the Court of Justice held that this breach had not been sufficiently serious to give rise to liability on the part of the United Kingdom:

> "In the present case, Article 8(1) is imprecisely worded and was reasonably capable of bearing, as well as the construction applied to it by the Court in this judgment, the interpretation given to it by the United Kingdom in good faith and on the basis of arguments which are not entirely devoid of substance. That interpretation, which was also shared by other Member States, was not manifestly contrary to the wording of the directive or to the objective pursued by it.
>
> Moreover, no guidance was available to the United Kingdom from case law of the Court as to the interpretation of the provision at issue, nor did the Commission raise the matter when the 1992 Regulations were adopted."[234]

The second case provides an example falling on the other side of the line. In *R. v. Ministry of Agriculture, Fisheries and Food, ex p. Hedley Lomas (Ireland) Ltd*[235] the British authorities had wrongly refused the applicants an export licence for the export of live sheep to Spain, despite the fact that such trade had been harmonised by Directive 74/577. Here there had been a clear breach of rights which both Article 34 of the Treaty of Rome and the Directive had sought to protect, and this had caused damage. Thus the first and third conditions specified in *Brasserie du Pêcheur* were satisfied. As far as the second condition (serious breach) was concerned, the Court strongly hinted that a breach of the Directive was enough to establish liability:

> "As regards the second condition, where, at the time when it committed the infringement, the Member State in question was not called upon to make legislative choices and had only considerably reduced, or even no, discretion, the mere infringement of Community law may be sufficient to establish the existence of a sufficiently serious breach."[236]

9. Liability in Contract

Neither the State nor public authorities enjoy any immunity in respect of the ordinary law of contract. It is true that certain principles of administrative law operate to

---

[232] Case C–392/93 [1996] 2 C.M.L.R. 217.
[233] The British authorities had determined which of the telecommunications services were to be exempted in the manner required by Art. 8(1) of the directive. The Court held that this decision was one for the telecommunications entities themselves.
[234] Case C–392/93 [1996] 2 C.M.L.R. 217 at 245.
[235] Case C–5/94 [1996] 2 C.M.L.R. 391.
[236] *Ibid.* at 448.

restrict the power of public bodies to enter into legally binding contracts – thus public bodies may not contract so as to fetter their discretionary powers[237] or, if they exceed their statutory *vires*, do they create an estoppel?[238] However, there are no other special rules applicable to contracts entered into by public bodies. These matters are considered, as indicated, in other chapters of the book.

10. Liability in Restitution

The law of restitution[239] has recently emerged in the common law world as a third head of the private law of obligations, "separate from both contract and tort".[240] The principle against unjust enrichment,[241] by which "a person who has been unjustly enriched at the expense of another is required to make restitution to that other",[242] lies at the heart of the law of restitution.

Local authorities and public bodies can sue and be sued in restitution in much the same way as they can sue and be sued in contract and tort and in the 1990s, there has been an increasing number of such cases, in part because of the special restrictions in the law of contract, as it affects public authorities, which have just been noted. Thus, for example, if they have rendered or received a benefit under mistake, or duress, or for a consideration which has failed,[243] an action in restitution will lie. This is especially so where they have been party to an invalid contract. For example, in *Hazell v. Hammersmith and Fulham Council*,[244] the House of Lords held that certain contracts under which English local authorities had borrowed from banks to invest in interest rate swaps were *ultra vires* the local authorities. In Irish

---

[237] See, *e.g. Gilheaney v. Revenue Commissioners* [1996] E.L.R. 25 and below p. 863.

[238] See below p. 863.

[239] See generally, Birks, *An Introduction to the Law of Restitution* (1989); Burrows, *The Law of Restitution* (1993); Goff and Jones, *The Law of Restitution* (4th ed., 1993).

[240] *Dublin Corporation v. Building and Allied Trade Union* [1996] 1 I.R. 468 at 483 *per* Keane J., on which see O'Dell "Restitution and *Res Judicata* in the Irish Supreme Court" (1997) 113 L.Q.R. 245.

[241] O'Dell "The Principle Against Unjust Enrichment" (1993) 15 D.U.L.J. (N.S.) 27.

[242] Article 1, *Restatement of the Law, Restitution* (1937).

[243] These are the examples of causes of action in restitution given by Keane J in *Dublin Corporation v. Building and Allied Trade Union* [1996] 1 I.R. 484: "the law, as it has been developed, has avoided the dangers of 'palm-tree justice' by identifying whether the case belongs in a specific category which justifies so describing the enrichment: possible instances are money paid under duress, or as a result of a mistake of fact or law or accompanied by a total failure of consideration". In *O'Rourke v. Revenue Commissioners* [1996] 2 I.R. 1 the same judge added that, as in other common law jurisdictions, "the doctrine has been developed incrementally on a case by case basis, so as to ensure that a vague and uncharted area of the law in which 'palm tree' justice flourishes is not judicially encouraged." To similar effect is the approach of the High Court of Australia in *Pavey and Matthews v. Paul* (1987) 162 C.L.R. 221 and of the Supreme Court of Canada in *Peel v. Canada and Ontario* (1993) 98 D.L.R. (4th) 140.

[244] [1992] 2 A.C. 1. *Westdeutsche Landesbank v. Islington L. B. C.* [1994] 4 All E. R. 890 (Hobhouse J. and C. A.). When the matter reached the House of Lords ([1996] A.C. 669), such an obligation to make restitution at common law was no longer an issue, and the judgments of their Lordships are largely confined to the question of whether there was a parallel equitable obligation, which would therefore found a jurisdiction to award compound interest. A similar approach to the *vires* of statutory corporations has been taken at Irish law: see, *e.g. Huntsgrove Developments v. Meath Co. Co.* [1994] 2 I.L.R.M. 36; *Keane v. An Bord Pleanála* [1997] 1 I. R. 184.

law, it is clear that the banks would have been entitled to restitution of the money so lent.[245]

Another important public law example (discussed below) of this principle arises where a rate-payer or taxpayer pays such rates or taxes pursuant to a statute which is unconstitutional, or to a statutory instrument which is *ultra vires*, or pursuant to an invalid or perhaps even simply overstated demand, and the rate-payer or taxpayer seeks to recover the amount so paid. Either mistake or duress will readily supply such a plaintiff with a cause of action.

Mistake

As to mistake, "if a person pays money to another under a mistake of fact which *causes* him to make the payment, he is *prima facie* entitled to recover it as money paid under a mistake of fact".[246] Thus, in *Dolan v. Neligan*,[247] the plaintiff had paid customs duty on imported drink, and then challenged the basis of assessment under the procedure laid down by section 30 of the Customs Consolidation Act 1876. He succeeded. In this action, commenced by plenary summons, he sought restitution of the overpayments, *inter alia*, on the grounds that they were mistaken payments. In the High Court, Kenny J. held that the plaintiff had paid the duty on the basis of a mistake, and that such a mistake was a mistake of law.

The general rule here had been that money paid under a mistake of law – as opposed to mistake of fact – is not recoverable.[248] The rigour of this rule was tempered by the fact that a mistake of law has sometimes been characterised as a mistake of fact. Furthermore, the courts will often hold that the payment is not a voluntary one, and thus recoverable, if the parties were not on equal terms, and the defendants were responsible for the mistake. Thus, in *Dolan v. Neligan*, in the High Court, Kenny J. stated, *obiter* that:

> "the moneys were paid under a mistake of law about the interpretation of the Finance Acts, but it does not follow that they cannot be recovered. The statement that money paid under a mistake of law cannot be recovered is, I think, an inaccurate simplification of a complex problem . . . I am satisfied that money paid by one person because of a mistake of law can be recovered by him if the cause of the mistake were the statements about the law made to

---

245 *Re P.M.P.A. Garage (Longmile) Ltd (No. 2)* [1992] 1 I.R. 332; [1992] I.L.R.M. 349 (High Ct. *per* Murphy J.) on which see O'Dell "Estoppel and *Ultra Vires* Contracts" (1992) 14 D.U.L.J. (N.S.) 123; *P.M.P.A. v. P.M.P.S.* unreported, High Court, Murphy J., June 27, 1994. See also *O'Hehir v. Cahill* (1912) 47 I.L.T.R. 274; *O'Hehir v. Kane* (1912) 47 I.L.T.R. 277; *Re Irish Provident Assurance Company Ltd* [1913] 1 I.R. 353. See now the Netting of Financial Contracts Act 1995, s.4(1).

246 *Barclays Bank v. Simms* [1980] Q.B. 677 at 694, *per* Goff J. (emphasis added). To like effect is the Irish decision of *National Bank v. O'Connor* (1969) 103 I.L.T.R. 73. See also *David Securities v. Commonwealth Bank of Australia* (1992) 175 C.L.R. 353.

247 [1967] I.R. 247.

248 Thus, in *O'Rourke v. Revenue Commissioners (No. 2)* [1996] 2 I.R. 1 Keane J. found that the overpayments of tax had been clearly made "under a mistake of law, without any protest by the plaintiff" and in circumstances where there had been no compulsion or duress. Keane J. commented that in those circumstances it would, "until the recent decision of the House of Lords in *Woolwich Building Society v. Inland Revenue Commissioners* [1993] 1 A.C. 70 have been the received wisdom in Ireland and in England that such monies were irrecoverable".

him by the party receiving the money, or if the parties were not on equal terms at the time when the payment was made. . . . The payment of . . . duty . . . was caused by the error made by [the defendants]: they were solely responsible for the mistake and they ought to have known better. . . . the plaintiff would, in my opinion, be entitled to recover the moneys overpaid by him because they were paid under a mistake of law caused entirely by the defendant."[249]

In the event, however, Kenny J. held that such arguments should have been made in the proceedings under the Customs Consolidation Act 1876, and dismissed the plaintiff's claim; the Supreme Court found a remedy under that Act, and did not need to address the position at common law. Nevertheless, the Supreme Court has subsequently confirmed Kenny J.'s analysis.[250] Moreover more recently, this mistake of law bar has been abolished in Canada[251] and Australia.[252] Although some relatively recent High Court cases have mentioned the mistake of law bar,[253] its decline has proceeded apace in the Irish courts,[254] and Henchy J. in the Supreme Court in *Pine Valley Developments Ltd v. Minister for Environment* held that "so much of the purchase price as was attributable to the planning permission was paid under a mistake of law, but in my opinion it would be recoverable no less than if it had been paid under a mistake of fact".[255] Thus, in the now leading Irish case on restitution, Keane J. in the Supreme Court in *Dublin Corporation v. Building and Allied Trade Union*[256] accepted a cause of action based on "a mistake of fact *or law*".[257] Likewise, in *Air Canada v. British Colombia*[258] certain airlines had paid taxes to the defendant states in respect of fuel purchased at airports, and then challenged the constitutionality of the taxing statute. The statute was held unconstitutional, and the airlines sought the recovery of the overpaid tax on the grounds of mistake. In the Supreme Court of Canada, the defence of mistake of law failed. La Forest J.[259] held

---

[249] [1967] I.R. 247 at 259–260. See also the comments of Keane J. in *O'Rourke v. Revenue Commissioners (No. 2)* [1996] 2 I.R. 1.

[250] *Rogers v. Louth Co. Co.* [1981] I.R. 265 at 271 *per* Griffin J.; *Cp. East Cork Foods v. O'Dwyer Steel* [1978] I.R. 103 at 108–109, *per* Henchy J.

[251] *Air Canada v. British Colombia* (1989) 59 D.L.R. (4th) 161.

[252] *David Securities v. Commonwealth Bank of Australia* (1992) 175 C.L.R. 353. See also *Commissioner of State Revenue v. Royal Insurance* (1995) 69 A.L.J.R. 51.

[253] *Doolan v. Murray*, unreported, High Court, December 21, 1993, Keane J; *Carbury Milk Products v. Minister for Agriculture* (1993) *Irish Tax Reports* 492.

[254] Cases like *Dolan, East Cork Foods*, and *Rogers* demonstrated an impatience with the rule and a desire to get around it or to abrogate it. In *Dublin Corporation v. Trinity College Dublin* [1985] I.L.R.M. 84 (High Ct.); [1985] I.L.R.M. 283 (Sup. Ct.) in an action to recover overpaid rates, Hamilton J. in the High Court allowed recovery of money paid under a mistake of law, saying that (at 286) "where money is paid, whether under a mistake of fact or law, justice requires that such money should be recoverable if the law so permits". The Supreme Court overruled Hamilton J. on the interpretation of the relevant statute and did not reach the mistake issue.

[255] [1987] I.R. 23 at 42.

[256] [1996] 1 I.R. 468. In this case the plaintiff sought to recover on a restitutionary basis compensation awarded to the defendants by an arbitrator. The award was designed to compensate the defendants for the demolition of a building which was never reinstated by them. The Supreme Court held that as the matter was now *res judicata* and the award was now made final by the Arbitration Acts, 1954–1980, this issue could not be reopened by reliance on the doctrine of restitution.

[257] *Ibid.* at 484. (Emphasis added.)

[258] *Air Canada v. British Colombia* (1989) 59 D.L.R. (4th) 161.

[259] Lamer and L'Hereux-Dube JJ. concurring; Wilson J. expressed to similar effect: (1989) 59 D.L.R. (4th) 161 at 169.

"In my view the distinction between mistake of fact and mistake of law should play no part in the law of Restitution. Both species of mistake, if one can be distinguished from the other, should, in an appropriate case, be considered as factors which can make an enrichment at the plaintiff's expense 'unjust' . . ."[260]

This is also borne out by the very important judgment of Keane J. in *O'Rourke v. Revenue Commissioners (No. 2).*[261] Here, the plaintiff was one of some ninety social welfare branch managers who had wrongly paid income tax under Schedule E as opposed to Schedule D. Following a High Court ruling brought by another branch manager, it became clear that the plaintiff was entitled to a refund of taxes which he duly received. The question then arose as to whether he would be entitled to interest on these sums. Keane J. had no doubt but that he was:

"If, however, the plaintiff was entitled as a matter of law to these sums [of income tax], then it would seem to follow inevitably that the defendants were unjustly enriched at the expense of the plaintiff and that the plaintiff is entitled to be paid a sum which fairly represents the extent of that unjust enrichment."[262]

Keane J. went on then to apply with approval the reasoning in the *Woolwich* case:

"It seems to me that, if the law as laid down in [the *Woolwich* case] is applicable in Ireland the tax overpaid by the plaintiff was recoverable as a matter of right. It would follow automatically from that conclusion that the plaintiff was entitled to interest so as to compensate him for the unjust enrichment effected at his expense by the defendants. I do not consider that any meaningful distinction can be drawn in this context between the tax paid under a regulation subsequently found *ultra vires*, as in the *Woolwich* case, and excessive amounts paid by a taxpayer because the taxing authority has misconstrued a relevant statute or regulation, which is the position here. Lord Goff in the *Woolwich* case, while not deciding the point, indicated his view that it was not a significant distinction and Lord Jauncey, in the course of his dissenting opinion, dismissed it as a distinction without a difference. I would respectfully agree with those views. Similarly, while the fact that the plaintiff clearly permitted the sums to be deducted from his payments without protest is clearly of significance in [the context of possible defences], it is clear . . . that the majority decision in the *Woolwich* case was founded on a wider principle, *i.e.*, that the money was paid for no consideration."[263]

In the light of this judgment it can be safely stated that the mistake of fact/mistake of law distinction has more or less completely collapsed.

Duress

As to duress, where a public official, by virtue of an office which enables him to demand and enforce a charge, demands and receives payments of moneys which

---

[260] (1989) 59 D.L.R. (4th) 161 at 192; citing with approval the judgment of Dickson J. (dissenting) in the earlier *Hydro Electric Commision of Nepean v. Ontario Hydro* (1982) 132 D.L.R. (3d.) 193.

[261] [1996] 2 I.R. 1.

[262] *Ibid.* at 9.

[263] *Ibid.* at 13.

are not due, the courts have held that such public bodies are liable to make restitution where the money has been had and received by such a body *colore officii* (duress by colour of office)[264], the duress in the circumstances being the express or implied threat by the office holder to impose a sanction upon the payer in the event of non-payment. Thus, in *Rogers v. Louth Co. Co.*[265] the Supreme Court held that the plaintiff was entitled to recover an excessive sum demanded *colore officii* by the defendants as the price of the redemption of an annuity due to them under the provisions of the Housing Act 1966.[266] The Court held that the payment was not a "voluntary" one, for as Griffin J. explained:

> "The parties were not on equal terms. The defendants had the power if they thought fit, to withhold payment for the redemption of the annuity; they were prepared to allow the plaintiff to redeem it but only on the conditions imposed by them, which included exacting a payment in excess of that permitted by statute. The plaintiff [had no] reason to think that she was not liable to pay the sum demanded by the defendant for the redemption of the annuity. . . .[267]

Thus, a taxpayer who has paid taxes pursuant to an unconstitutional taxing statute can recover such taxes as money paid under duress *colore oficii*. In *Murphy v. Attorney General*,[268] Henchy J., for the Supreme Court, held that the payments were "involuntary",[269] and "recoverable as money exacted *colore officii*"[270] since such payments "are regarded by the law as being made under duress".[271] There was, therefore, on the facts, a cause of action. However, in considering potential defences to the Government's *prima facie* liability to make such restitution, Henchy J. observed that it "is one of the first principles of the law of restitution on the ground of unjust enrichment"[272] that there be a defence of change of position.[273] By this defence, a defendant, who received the money in good faith and thereafter spent it, may, in certain circumstances, by virtue of that expenditure, defeat a plaintiff's claim. In respect of those taxpayers who had objected to the government's receipt by commencing proceedings, the government's receipt was not bona fide, and the government were

---

264 On this type of duress, see Burrows "Public Authorities, *Ultra Vires* and Restitution", Essay 3 in Burrows (ed.) *Essays in the Law of Restitution* (Oxford, 1991) p. 39 at p. 41 *et seq.* In *Dolan v. Neligan* [1967] I.R. 247 the plaintiff had never accepted that duty was payable in respect of certain goods and only paid the duty because, in the words of Kenny J. (at 252), "the gun was to my head".
265 [1981] I.R. 265
266 The plaintiff was the personal representative of the deceased. A cottage had previously been vested in the deceased in fee simple free from incumbrances, but subject to an annual annuity due to the defendants.
267 [1981] I.R. 265 at 271. See also *Dolan v. Nelligan* [1967] I.R. 247.
268 [1982] I.R. 241.
269 [1982] I.R. 241 at 317.
270 *Ibid.*
271 *Ibid.* at 316, citing *Mason v. New South Wales* (1959) 102 C.L.R. 108 at 141 *per* Windeyer J., in turn citing *Sargood Bros. v. The Commonwealth* (1910) 11 C.L.R. 258 at 276 *per* O'Connor J. Griffin J. (*ibid.* at 331) and Parke J. (*ibid.* at 336) agreed with this reasoning, and Kenny J. (in partial dissent, *ibid.* at pp 335–336) also approved *Mason* and *Sargood*. See also *Bell Bros. Property Ltd v. Shire of Serpentine Jarrahdale* (1969) 121 C.L.R. 137.
272 [1982] I.R. 241 at 319.
273 A defence which is also available in Australia (*David Securities v. Commonwealth Bank of Australia* (1992) 175 C.L.R. 353), Canada (*Storthoaks v. Mobil Oil Canada* (1975) 55 D.L.R. (3d) 1) and England (*Lipkin Gorman v. Karpnale* [1991] 2 A.C. 548).

under a duty to make restitution to such taxpayers; by contrast, in respect of those taxpayers who had not objected to the government's receipt, that receipt was bona fide, and the defence of change of position provided the government with a defence to such taxpayer's claims in restitution.[274] The State had been led to believe, by the protracted absence of a claim to the contrary, that it was legally and constitutionally entitled to spend the taxes thus collected. In the view of Henchy J.:

> "[T]he position had become so altered, the logistics of reparation so weighted and distorted by factors such as inflation and interest, the *prima facie* right of the taxpayers to be recouped so devalued by the fact that, as members of the community . . . they had benefited from the taxes thus collected, that it would be inequitable, unjust and unreal to expect the State to make full restitution."[275]

It is important, however, not to read such sentiments as seeking to appropriate to the courts a general pragmatic power simply to have regard to what might be styled the justice of the case.[276] It is true that Henchy J. did say that:

> "[o]ver the centuries the law has come to realise, in one degree or another, that factors such as prescription . . . , waiver, estoppel, laches, a statute of limitation, res judicata or other matters . . . may debar a person from obtaining redress in courts for injury, pecuniary or otherwise, which would be justiciable and redressable if such considerations had not intervened".[277]

Nonetheless, all the matters there listed are recognised defences, and Henchy J.'s decision was to the effect that the recognised defence of change of position in the law of restitution provided the goverment with a partial (if ultimately significant) defence to their *prima facie* liability to make restitution.

The true *ratio* of this part of Henchy J.'s judgment in *Murphy* is that there are limits to the extent of these defences. This is borne out by the judgment of Keane J. in *O'Rourke v. Revenue Commissioners (No. 2)*.[278] In this case Keane J. was required to consider whether the remarks of Henchy J. served to operate as a bar to restitutionary relief on the part of some ninety social welfare branch managers. Keane J. held that they did not and he emphasised the limited class of persons involved:

---

274 See, for example, the reading of *Murphy* offered by Budd J. in the High Court in *Dublin Corporation v. Building and Allied Trade Union* [1996] 1 I.R. 468. This issue was not dealt with in the Supreme Court: see [1996] 1 I.R. 468.

275 [1982] I.R. 241 at 302. Compare such policy considerations with the special policy of fiscal chaos underpinning the defence of passing on in *Air Canada v British Columbia* (1989) 59 D.L.R. (4th) 161 at 191–194 *per* La Forest J. However, that defence was in turn doubted by Wilson J. in the same case, and not accepted by the House of Lords in *Woolwich v. I.R.C. (No. 2)* [1993] A.C. 70 or the High Court of Australia in *Commissioner of State Revenue v. Royal Insurance* (1995) 69 A.L.J.R. 51. See also Case 199/82 *State Finance Administration v. San Giorgio SpA* [1983] E.C.R. 501 also rejecting such a defence of "passing on".

276 See the discussion of *Cotter and McDermott v. Minister for Social Welfare (No. 2)* [1990] 2 C.M.L.R. 94 and 141 (Hamilton P.) and [1991] 3 C.M.L.R. 507 (E.C.J.) in Whyte and O'Dell "Welfare, Women and Unjust Enrichment" (1991) 20 I.L.J. 304 and in O'Dell "A Tragedy in Five Acts. Behind the Scenes in *Cotter and McDermott (No. 2)*" (1992) 2 I.S.L.R. 34. On the sequel to these cases, see *Tate v. Minister for Social Welfare* [1995] 1 I.R. 418 at on which see O'Dell [1995] *Restitution Law Review* p. 220.

277 [1982] I.R. 241 at 314. In *Dublin Corporation v. Building and Allied Trade Union* [1996] 1 I.R. 468, Keane J. pointed to this reference to *res judicata* and concluded that it provided a policy to preclude restitution on the facts before him.

278 [1996] 2 I.R. 1. For the facts of this case, see above at p. 853.

"The consequences in fiscal terms of such unravelling [in *Murphy*] of every taxpayer's accounts need not be emphasised. . . .

The contrast with the present case is clear. Here the Court is concerned with eighty to ninety social welfare branch managers and the retrospective fiscal adjustments are of minimal significance in comparison to what was involved in [*Murphy*'s case]. The conclusion of the majority in the latter case – that restitution would be 'inequitable, unjust and unreal' – is not necessarily applicable to the circumstances of this case.

. . .

It is an important feature of *Murphy*'s case, moreover, that the relevant provisions of the income tax code were struck down as unconstitutional. Hence, as Henchy J. also pointed out, the only way in which the significant imbalance in the State's finances that would be the result of all the affected taxpayers being recouped could be corrected would be by imposing additional taxation on new cohorts of taxpayers, thereby compounding the resultant inequities and injustice. In contrast, in such a case as the present, not merely are the numbers affected so relatively small as to render the distortion of the State's finances minimal and legitimately outweighed by the injustice to the plaintiff of having his money withheld from him: the State is in a position to ensure by legislation, if it is so minded, that taxpayers who find themselves in a similar position may have their common law right of recovery constrained by statutory provisions of the nature referred to by Lord Slynn in the *Woolwich* case."[279]

Keane J. thus held (by implication, at least) that since the class of affected tax payers was confined to some ninety persons and the sums involved were so relatively small, the State could not legitimately plead change of circumstances by way of defence. The strong implication, of course – and expressly borne out by *Murphy* – is that such a defence *would* have been available had the sums involved been collectively so significant as to have adversely affected the State's fiscal position.

---

[279] *Ibid.* at 17–18. But the constitutionality of any such legislation would be surely open to doubt if it effectively made such sums irrecoverable. This would appear to constitute a disproportionate interference with property rights (*cf. Daly v. Revenue Commissioners* [1995] 3 I.R. 1) in the absence of a peculiarly compelling justification for such legislation. Note, however, that in the aftermath of the *Woolwich* litigation the United Kingdom enacted legislation – Finance Act 1991, s.53 – which validated retrospectively the tax regulations which had been declared to be *ultra vires*, save in respect of building societies which had commended proceedings before 1986 (a condition which only *Woolwich* could meet). In *National and Provincial Building Society v. United Kingdom* (1998) 24 E.H.R.R. 127 the European Court of Human Rights held that there had been no breach of either Article 1 of the First Protocol (property rights) or Article 6(1) (fair procedures in civil litigation) of the Convention on the part of the United Kingdom in enacting this legislation, despite the fact that it rendered the pending claims to restitution of other building societies "unwinnable". The Court thus concluded that in the particular circumstances of the case:

"including the presence of compelling public interest considerations militating in favour of legislative intervention and the fact that the dispute between the Treasury and the applicants took place in the tax sector in an area where recourse to retrospective tax legislation was not confined to the United Kingdom, the Court concluded that the applicant societies could not justifiably complain that they were denied a right of access to a court for a judicial determination on their rights."

Other causes of action in restitution

According to Keane J. in *Dublin Corporation v. Building and Allied Trade Union*,[280] the principle against unjust enrichment

> "explains why the law recognises, in a variety of distinct categories of cases, an obligation on the part of the defendant to make fair and just restitution for a benefit derived at the expense of the plaintiff and assists in the determination, by the ordinary process of legal reasoning, of the question of whether the law should, in justice, recognise the obligation in a new and developing category of case."[281]

The House of Lords in *Woolwich Building Society v. I.R.C. (No. 2)*[282] seems to have done just that; the Woolwich paid taxes on foot of a statutory instrument which was then held to be *ultra vires*. Lord Goff for the majority of the House of Lords held that money paid by a citizen to a public authority in the form of taxes or other levies paid pursuant to an *ultra vires* demand by the authority is *prima facie* recoverable by the citizen as of right. Prior to this decision there had been strong academic support for the proposition that, apart at all from the causes of action in mistake and duress described above, the law already recognised such a claim of right.[283] Lord Goff, however, considered that although such a principle was not directly supported by the authorities, the House could and should reformulate the law in accordance with that principle. As we have just seen, this principle has now been accepted as a matter of Irish law by the judgment of Keane J. in *O'Rourke v. Revenue Commissioners (No. 2)*.[284]

In conclusion, therefore, the recently emerged law of restitution imposes obligations upon those who have been unjustly enriched to make restitution to those at whose expense they have been so unjustly enriched. It is a principle upon which local authorities and public bodies can both sue and be sued. In particular, to the extent that such a body has received levies, taxes or rates, on foot of a mistake or duress, or simply *ultra vires*, they are required to make restitution of such a receipt, according to the principles and defences of the law of restitution.

---

[280] [1996] 1 I.R. 468.

[281] *ibid.* at 483 approving the decision of Deane J. in the High Court of Australia in *Pavey & Matthews v. Paul* (1987) 162 C.L.R. 221 at 256. See also the similar approach of the Supreme Court of Canada in *Peel v. Canada and Ontario* (1993) 98 D.L.R. (4th) 140.

[282] [1993] A.C. 70. See Birks "'When Money is Paid in Pursuance of a Void Authority . . .' – A Duty to Repay?" (1992) *Public Law* 580; Beatson "Restitution of Taxes, Levies and Other Imposts: Defining the Extent of the *Woolwich* Principle" (1993) 109 L.Q.R. 401; McKendrick "Restitution of Unlawfully Demanded Tax" [1993] L.M.C.L.Q. 88; Virgo "The Law of Taxation is not an Island – Overpaid Taxes and the Law of Restitution" (1993) *British Tax Review* 442.

[283] Birks "Restitution From the Executive: A Tercentary Footnote to the Bill of Rights" in Finn (ed.) *Essays on Restitution* (Sydney, 1990) p. 164.

[284] [1996] 2 I.R. 1. *Cf. Dolan v. Neligan* [1967] I.R. 247 at 243–254, *per* Kenny J.

CHAPTER 16

LEGITIMATE EXPECTATIONS AND ESTOPPEL

1. Introduction

When the first edition of this book was published in 1986, the principle of legitimate expectations scarcely received a mention. Yet this principle, which was to receive the imprimatur of the Supreme Court in its decision in *Webb v. Ireland*[1] in December 1987, has launched a host of subsequent cases. Apart from the doctrine of proportionality, there is, perhaps, no other principle which has so rapidly given rise to so much litigation or which has so quickly become embedded in the fabric of the legal system. Recently, however, the tide appears to be turning and there have been increasing signs of judicial unease with some of the potentially more far-reaching aspects of this doctrine.[2] This in turn has meant that some of the case law is not always readily reconcilable.[3]

Besides its native roots in estoppel and cognate equitable concepts,[4] the principle may also be traced to German administrative law ("*Vertrauensschutz*")[5] and has been

---

[1] [1988] I.R. 353. There has been a considerable amount of academic writing on this topic, see, *e.g.* Baldwin and Horne, "Expectations in a Joyless Landscape" (1986) 49 M.L.R. 685; Forsyth, "The Provenance and Protection of Legitimate Expectations" (1988) Camb.L.J. 238; Delany, "The Doctrine of Legitimate Expectations in Irish Law" (1990) 12 D.U.L.J. 1 (N.S.) "The Doctrine of Legitimate Expectations: Recent Developments" (1993) 11 I.L.T. 192 (N.S.) and "The Future of the Doctrine at Legitimate Expectations in Irish Administrative Law" (1997) 32 *Irish Jurist* 217; Craig, "Legitimate Expectations: A Conceptual Analysis" (1992) 108 L.Q.R. 79 and "Substantive Legitimate Expectations in Domestic and Community Law" (1996) Camb. L.J. 289; Singh, "Making Legitimate Use of Legitimate Expectations" (1994) 144 N.L.J. 289; and Brady, "Aspiring Students, Retiring Professors and the Doctrine of Legitimate Expectation" (1996) 31 Ir. Jur. (N.S.) 133.

[2] See, *e.g.* the judgment of Costello J. in *Tara Prospecting Ltd v. Minister for Energy* [1993] I.L.R.M. 771. In *Association of General Practitioners Ltd. v. Minister for Health* [1995] 1 I.R. 382 at 393–394 O'Hanlon J. said that if the plea of legitimate expectations were "allowed its head", it could "introduce an unwelcome element of uncertainty into well-defined law concerning rights of property, right of contract and other matters".

[3] A point noted by McCracken J. in *Abrahamson v. Law Society of Ireland*, [1996] 1 I.R. 403 at 422; ". . . I find it very difficult to reconcile some of these decisions, although it is only to be expected that in an evolving concept that there will be contradictory judgments".

[4] *cf.* the comments of Brady, *op.cit.* above, n.1 at p. 133
  "Further evidence of equity's vital role in the modern legal system is afforded by the recent emergence of the now widely used doctrine·of legitimate expectation which has a close affinity to the long established doctrine of estoppel."

[5] Literally, "protection of confidence". But this literal translation is apt to be misleading, since it might appear to correspond with the equitable doctrine of breach of confidence and the words "legitimate expectations" are used instead. The use of the noun *Vertrauen* in this context implies that a trust or confidence will be honoured or protected by a public body, thus conveying the idea that principles of good administration require that a public body should honour its promises and undertakings. See generally, Usher, "The Influence of National Concepts on Decisions of the European Court" (1976) 1 E.L. Rev. 359; Forsyth, and Delany, *op. cit.* above, n.1.

recognised as a general principle of law by the European Court of Justice.[6] The principle appears to have been subsequently transplanted into our legal system via judgments of the Court of Justice and the House of Lords.[7] Lord Mackenzie Stuart's statement may be as true of Ireland as it is of England:

> "Can one here [in *GCHQ*] detect the influence of Community law or at least some of the Member States? It is at least possible to suggest that the answer is yes. The concept of recognising that a failure to respect legitimate expectations may give rise, in public law, to a remedy is a novelty in English law which lacks discernible English parentage. To find the true ancestry one does not have to go far beyond the channel."[8]

It is likely, therefore, that developments in the administrative law of the European Communities will have a considerable influence on the future progress of this principle in this jurisdiction.

It will be readily appreciated that the doctrine of legitimate expectations has very close affinities with that of promissory estoppel and, indeed, there are judicial dicta to the effect that these doctrines are more or less interchangeable.[9] While these dicta probably go too far and do not recognise important differences between the two principles, nevertheless they show the close relationship between them. In any event, the courts have shown an increasing willingness to hold a public authority to an earlier promise, representation or practice, irrespective of which of the doctrines the decision

---

6   See, *e.g.* Case 81/72 *Commission v. Council (Staff Salaries)* [1973] E.C.R. 575; Case 2/75, *EVGF v. Mackprang* [1975] E.C.R. 607; Case C–350/88, *Delacre v. Commission* [1990] E.C.R. I–395; and Weatherill and Beaumont, *EC Law* (1993) pp. 223–225. The classic case is now, of course, Case 120/86, *Mulder v. Minister van Landbouwen en Visserij* [1988] E.C.R. 2321 where the Court of Justice held that a milk producer who had been encouraged by provisions of a Community Regulation to suspend the marketing of milk for a limited period could not, following the expiry of that period, be subjected to new restrictions which specifically prejudiced him as far as future milk production was concerned. See generally on this issue, Sharpston, "Legitimate Expectations and Economic Reality" (1990) 15 E.L. Rev. 103.

7   Most notably *Attorney General of Hong Kong v. Ng Yuen Shiu* [1983] 2 A.C. 629 and *Council of Civil Service Unions v. Minister for the Public Service* ("the GCHQ case") [1985] A.C. 319. In *Wiley v. Revenue Commissioners* [1994] 2 I.R. 160 O'Flaherty J. referred with approval to both the *Staff Salaries* case and *Ng Yuen Shiu* saying (at 172–173): "But I do not believe that they go father than our experience and do not extend the boundaries of this remedy to a point which has not already been established in our jurisprudence."

8   Mackenzie Stuart, "Recent Developments in English Administrative Law – The Impact of Europe?" in Capotorti (ed.), *Du Droit International au Droit de L'Integration, Liber amicorum P. Pescatore* (1987) p. 417. Note also the comments of Murphy J. in *Duff v. Minister for Agriculture* [1997] 2 I.R. 22 at 41–42:
> "There has been a notable evolution in administrative law in the State over the past thiry years. No doubt membership of the European Community and closer ties with those countries having a civil as opposed to a common law system will accelerate further the changes in this regard."
The adoption by the Irish courts of the principles of proportionality and legitimate expectations appears to have been influenced by this European jurisprudence, see, *e.g.* the comments of Hamilton P. in *Carbury Milk Products Ltd v. Minister for Agriculture* (1988–1993) 4 Irish Tax Reports 492.

9   See, *e.g.* the comments of Finlay C.J. in *Webb v. Ireland* [1988] I.R. 353 at 384, those of Murphy J. in *Garda Representative Association v. Ireland* [1989] I.R. 193 and those of O'Hanlon J. in *Association of General Practitioners Ltd v. Minister of Health* [1995] 1 I.R. 382. In November 1986 (*i.e.* over a year prior to the Supreme Court's decision in *Webb*) Murphy J. refused to accept that the doctrine of legitimate expectations formed part of our law: see *Goldrick v. Dublin Corporation* (1987) 6 J.I.S.L.L. 156.

is grounded upon. We shall postpone our comparison of the two doctrines until section 9 of this chapter, by which stage the case law in this field will have been surveyed.

Legitimate expectations only apply to public bodies[10]

The field of operation of the legitimate expectations doctrine is one which has to date been imperfectly explored. However, it seems clear that the legitimate expectations doctrine is one which is exclusively public law in character.[11] While the doctrine has obvious affinities with promissory estoppel, it may be doubted whether the element of detrimental reliance is necessary.[12] In other words, legitimate expectations are protected in the interests of safeguarding the citizen against haphazard and unfair changes in administrative policy and practice.[13] If this is the true rationale for the doctrine, then, clearly, there would be no basis for extending the ambit of legitimate expectations to private law. As it happens, most claims involving the principle of legitimate expectations have been brought by way of application for judicial review, but there seems no reason in principle why such a claim could not be advanced in plenary proceedings so long as the respondent is governed by public law.[14]

2. Legitimate Expectations, Estoppel and the *Ultra Vires* Principle

One significant feature which the two doctrines share is that they are each potentially in conflict with the major principle of public law, namely the *ultra vires* rule: a public authority cannot give itself a jurisdiction it does not possess. It cannot do this by a mistaken conclusion as to the extent of its own powers and neither can it do so by creating an estoppel or a legitimate expectation.[15]

The leading Irish authority in which the plea of *ultra vires* prevailed over an argument founded upon estoppel is *Re Green Dale Building Co.*[16] The significant point here is that under the Housing Act 1966, a notice to treat in relation to land purchases may only be served after the compulsory purchase order has become

---

[10] In *Kenny v. Kelly* [1988] I.R. 547 the issue arose as to whether a university is a "public body" for the purpose, *inter alia*, of invoking the legitimate expectations doctrine (the facts are discussed below at p. 864). Barron J. held that the respondents had not disputed the applicant's entitlement to proceed by way of judicial review in sufficient time and went on to treat University College, Dublin as a "public body" for the purposes of this case. But the matter appears to have been put beyond doubt by the elaborate judgment of Shanley J. in *Eogan v. University College, Dublin* [1996] 2 I.L.R.M. 302 where he held that a decision of the Governing Body pursuant to the internal statutes of the University was amenable to judicial review, so that in this instance, at least, an applicant could invoke the legitimate expectations doctrine.

[11] See, *e.g. O'Reilly v. Mackman* [1983] 2 A.C. 237; *Council of Civil Service Unions v. Minister for Public Service* [1985] A.C. 319; *Duggan v. An Taoiseach* [1989] I.L.R.M. 713; and *Eogan v. University College Dublin* [1996] 2 I.L.R.M. 302.

[12] This point is further analysed at below pp. 881–883.

[13] See below pp. 865–869.

[14] As happened in cases such as *Webb v. Ireland* [1988] I.R. 353.

[15] Nor, in principle, at any rate, can this be done by the applicant's own consent or waiver: See pp. 865–869.

[16] [1977] I.R. 256.

operative and a C.P.O. does not become operative pending the determination of proceedings which challenge its validity.[17] In this case, a notice to treat was served by a local authority in 1972 but this notice was invalid as proceedings had already been commenced by a third party challenging the validity of the compulsory purchase order on which the notice depended. That order did, however, take effect in 1975, after the third-party proceedings had been dismissed. At this point, the housing authority immediately served a second notice to treat. However, the value of Green Dale's land was less in 1975 than it had been in 1972 and so the company wished to rely on the first notice to treat. Thus, they contended that the authority should be estopped from relying on the invalidity of this first notice because:

1. the authority had implicitly represented that it had been validly served; and

2. the company had, relying on the validity of that representation, acted to their detriment by treating the lands as sterile from 1972, and by submitting to an abortive arbitration to assess the compensation payable.

The Supreme Court rejected the submission that the doctrine of promissory estoppel could have any application in cases of this nature. Henchy J. reasoned that it would entirely destroy the doctrine of *ultra vires* if the donee of a statutory power could extend his power by creating an estoppel. The judge noted that the company was seeking to estop the local authority from asserting that it had acted in breach of an express or implied prohibition or restriction of function in a statute. To permit an estoppel in these circumstances would require the court acting to defy the will of the Oireachtas as set out in the statute.[18]

This point had been made earlier by Kenny J. in *Re Parke Davis & Co.'s T.M. Application.*[19] Here the Controller of Trade Marks had refused to register the mark in respect of particular pharmaceutical products in Part A of the Register on the grounds of lack of distinctiveness. It was contended that because the Controller had previously registered a particular mark (belonging to an entirely different company) of this nature in Part A, he was estopped from raising the distinctiveness argument. This was firmly rejected by Kenny J.:

---

17 Housing Act 1966, s.79(1).
18 *Green Dale* was followed in *Dublin Corporation v. McGrath* [1978] I.L.R.M. 208. In *Morris v. Garvey* [1983] I.R. 319 the Supreme Court ordered the demolition of an unauthorised development in proceedings taken pursuant to s.27 of the Local Government (Planning and Development) Act 1976, despite the fact that the respondent had been assured by a planning official that the planning permission was not necessary in respect of the development. Henchy J. commented thus (at 324–325):
    "If he wished to retain the unpermitted walls, the respondent should have applied for a fresh development permission—thus enabling the applicant, or any member of the public to raise such objection as might be thought warranted. In such circumstances the opinion of a planning official— no matter how genuinely given—cannot be allowed to defeat the rights of the public . . . "
The reasoning in *Green Dale* was also followed by Lardner J. in *Devitt v. Minister for Education* [1989] I.L.R.M. 639 in holding that a representation made in an administrative circular could not estop the respondent Minister in the performance of her statutory functions and similar views were expressed by Blayney J. in *Power v. Minister for Social Welfare* [1987] I.R. 307 and by Costello J. in *Nolan v. Minister for Environment* [1989] I.R. 357 and in *Galvin v. Chief Appeals Officer* [1997] 3 I.R. 240.
19 [1976] F.S.R. 195.

"The Controller is a public official on whom many duties are imposed by the Trade Marks Act 1963: one of those is to ensure that all marks which are put on the register gets this privilege by complying with the law. He also has a discretion to refuse to accept a mark if he thinks it undesirable that it should be on the register. He cannot be estopped by anything which his predecessors or he might have done from exercising his judgment on each application."[20]

Thus, it is clear that previous decisions of the Controller cannot create an estoppel and it would seem that similar arguments would nowadays be deployed to defeat a claim based on legitimate expectations.

More often it is not (as in *Green Dale* or *Parke Davis*) an implicit assurance, but rather an express agreement or representation on which the plaintiff seeks to ground a claim to an estoppel or a legitimate expectation. The defendant public authority then replies by arguing that it would be *ultra vires* to fetter its discretionary power by an agreement of any kind. In some cases, the reverse happens: the agreement is honoured and it is some third party who seeks judicial review of the action honouring the agreement by claiming that it is ultra vires because it is not a free exercise of a discretionary power.[21]

For a classic example of the first type of case, in which the Crown (in Irish terms, the State) was allowed to break an explicit agreement, deliberately made, consider *Redereiaktiebolaget Amphitrite v. The King.*[22] Here, certain neutral shipowners sued on foot of an undertaking given by the British Government that if a particular ship was sent to the United Kingdom laden with a particular cargo, she would not be detained under the blockade regulations then in force. Rowlatt J. dismissed their petition of right, on the ground that:

"[I]t is not competent for the Government to fetter its future executive action which must necessarily be determined by the needs of the community when the question arises. It cannot by contract hamper its freedom of action in matters which concern the welfare of the State."[23]

This reasoning was followed by FitzGibbon J. in *Kenny v. Cosgrave*[24] where the plaintiff sought to rely on a promise made to him by W. T. Cosgrave, then President of the Executive Council. Mr Cosgrave apparently represented to him that if the plaintiff (who was a builder) refused to compromise with his striking employees, then the Executive Council would reimburse him for any losses thereby incurred by him. The plaintiff acted on this assurance to his detriment, and duly sued Mr Cosgrave, personally. Because he chose to sue Mr Cosgrave,[25] his action was struck out, as disclosing no reasonable cause of action. However, the relevant point here

---

[20] *Ibid.* at 197.

[21] See, *e.g. Stringer v. Minister for Housing and Local Government* [1970] 1 W.L.R. 1281; *Bromley L.B.C. v. Greater London Council* [1983] 1 A.C. 768.

[22] [1921] 3 K.B. 300. *Amphitrite* has been referred to as their Lordships' contribution to the war effort.

[23] *Ibid.* But even applying modern legitimate expectations doctrines it is not clear that the result would have been different, especially if the British Government could have demonstrated a change of circumstances which, viewed objectively, might reasonably have justified resiling from earlier assuances. See, *e.g.* the "change of circumstances" cases discussed at pp. 877–879.

[24] [1926] I.R. 517.

[25] On this point see below, pp. 918–919.

is that even if the action had been brought against the Executive Council, it would have been bound to fail on the ground that the Government cannot fetter its future executive action.[26]

There is no doubt but that if the *ultra vires* principle is strictly applied, it is capable of causing considerable injustice and, incidentally, largely stifling the legitimate expectation–estoppel doctrine at birth in the public law field. As will be demonstrated by the survey of the case law in section 3 of this chapter, the law in this area remains immature and in particular no satisfactory accommodation has been found between the conflicting tensions of the *ultra vires* principle and the legitimate expectation–estoppel doctrine. Indeed, the determination as to which tension is to prevail tends to vary from judge to judge. One compromise which seems to be in the ascendancy is to confine the legitimate expectation–estoppel doctrine to procedural rights, at least where what is at issue concerns the exercise of discretionary powers under statute to procedural rights only.[27]

Another stopping point, which was accepted *obiter* by Henchy J. in *Re Green Dale Building Co.*,[28] would be an exception which debarred a public authority from relying on a mere irregularity which it ought in fairness to have overlooked, but any such exceptions have been confined to technicalities.[29] Henchy J. did not explain why technicalities represented an exception to the rule. It might be an example of the application of the *de minimis* principle. But perhaps the exception represents a wider principle which would allow an estoppel in respect of *ultra vires* action where the injustice to the plaintiff was not outweighed by any tangible public benefit.[30] Indeed, the very fact that a public body sees fit to resile from an earlier promise might itself amount to an abuse of discretionary powers and, hence, itself amount to an *ultra vires* act. Such a balancing of interests would surely be acceptable given that the object of the *ultra vires* rule is to protect the public interest.[31] It could also be said that the mere fact that the public authority has acted *ultra vires* should not of itself be decisive, and that regard must be had to other considerations.[32]

---

[26] *Kenny v. Cosgrave* [1926] I.R. 517 at 523–528. Notice too: "It is a long established principle of administrative law that a public authority cannot by contract disable itself from exercising a discretionary power conferred on it by the legislature": *Gilheaney v. Revenue Commissioners* [1996] E.L.R. 25 at 37, *per* Costello P. See also *Ayr Harbour Trustees v. Osward* 8 App. Cas. 623 (harbour trustees could not validly enter into a contract which purported to bind them and their successors not to exercise a statutory power); *Ransom v. Surbiton Borough Council* [1949] Ch. 180 (planning authority cannot contract not to revoke a planning permission) and *Corry (Williams) & Son Ltd v. London Corporation* [1951] 2 K.B. 476 (port authority cannot contract to exercise in the future a statutory power to make bye-laws in a certain way).

[27] *Wiley v. Revenue Commissioners* [1994] 2 I.R. 190; *Hempenstall v. Minister for Environment* [1993] I.L.R.M. 318; *Tara Prospecting Ltd v. Minister for Energy* [1993] I.L.R.M. 771 and *Gilheaney v. Revenue Commissioners* [1996] E.L.R. 25. See further below, pp. 869–875.

[28] [1977] I.R. 257 at 264.

[29] See, *e.g. Wells v. Minister for Housing and Local Government* [1967] 1 W.L.R. 1000; *Lever Finance Ltd v. Westminster* L.B.C. [1971] 1 Q.B. 222. But even these authorities are considered doubtful in light of more recent developments, see *Western Fish Products Ltd v. Penwith District Council* [1981] 2 All E.R. 204 and *Rootkin v. Kent County Council* [1981] 1 W.L.R. 1186.

[30] Craig, *Administrative Law* (1994) p. 663–671.

[31] The courts regularly engage in such reasoning when considering whether to invalidate past administrative decisions: see, *e.g. Murphy v. Attorney General* [1982] I.R. 241.

[32] Craig, *op. cit.* above, n.30, p. 659–661.

It has also been suggested that a public body should be bound by *ultra vires* representations by its authorised agents when that body is acting in a proprietary rather than in a governmental or administrative capacity.[33] This proposition has a certain superficial attractiveness, but its application involves the difficulty of characterising between a function as governmental rather than proprietary, a distinction which it is not easy to draw.

There is another feature which often arises in this area. What if a representation is made which is beyond the powers of the official who gave the assurance but which is not actually *ultra vires* the public body itself. In this situation the doctrine of estoppel might be allowed to apply. Such an approach would have obvious affinities with the "internal management rule" in company law[34] and appears to have been adopted – albeit without elaborate discussion – by Barron J. in *Kenny v. Kelly*.[35] Here the applicant had sought a deferral of a place offered to her by University College, Dublin. An administrative official informed the applicant's father that her request for a deferral for one year had been granted. As it happened, the official who had communicated that information had misconstrued her instructions, but, of course, the granting of such a deferral was not *ultra vires* the respondents. Barron J. held that this representation was binding, since if the official had misrepresented her instructions, this "does not entitle the respondent to deny her apparent authority to bind the respondent".[36]

Nevertheless, this approach would be of assistance only in a limited class of cases. In *Dublin Corporation v. McGrath*,[37] for example, the defendant submitted that the planning authority was estopped from denying the existence of planning permission in respect of an unauthorised structure. It appeared that an agent of the authority had given verbal permission for the construction of a garage which was subsequently erected by the defendant. The plea of estoppel failed, for, as McMahon J. observed, not only did the agent not have power to make such a representation, but such a representation was also *ultra vires* the planning authority itself.

If the courts propose to adhere rigidly to this "jurisdictional principle", then there is much to be said for compensating individuals who have relied to their detriment on an *ultra vires* representation.[38] It may be that the eventual solution

---

33 *Ibid.*
34 See Ussher, *Irish Company Law* (1986) pp. 152–153.
35 [1988] I.R. 547.
36 *Ibid.* at 462. *cf.* the views of Costello J. in *Nolan v. Minister for Environment* [1989] I.R. 357 who did not think that the Minister could be bound by the views expressed by a local authority engineer in the course of a planning inquiry.
37 [1978] I.L.R.M. 208.
38 This theme is developed by Craig, *op.cit.* above, n.30, p. 863. *cf.* the decision of the European Court of Human Rights in *Pine Valley Developments Ltd v. Ireland* (1992) 14 E.H.R.R. 319 where the failure of the Oireachtas to cater for the situation of the applicants when enacting legislation which sought to validate certain *ultra vires* planning permissions granted by the Minister for Local Government was held to constitute an unfair discrimination contrary to Article 14 of the Convention when taken together with Article 1 of the First Protocol. Note, however, that the Court was not persuaded that the failure to provide compensation following the invalidation of the planning permission in and of itself constituted a disproportionate interference with property rights (at 319):
     "The applicants were engaged on a commercial venture which, by its very nature, involved an element of risk and they were aware not only of the zoning plan but also of the opposition of the local authority, Dublin County Council, to any departure from it. This being so, the Court does

which the courts will adopt is to find the public authority liable under the principle of *Hedley Byrne & Co. Ltd v. Heller & Partners Ltd*,[39] *i.e.* liability in negligence for careless misrepresentations resulting in pure financial loss to the misrepresentee, even though no contractual or recognised fiduciary relationship between the parties exists. In addition, such cases would seem to come within the ambit of the Ombudsman's power.[40]

3. Legitimate Expectations and Estoppel: Seminal Cases

The impetus for the present developments in the law has largely come from the decision of the House of Lords in *Council of Civil Service Unions v. Minister for the Public Service* ("the *GCHQ case*") and that of the Supreme Court in *Webb v. Ireland*.[41]

In the former case, the majority of employees working at Government Communications Headquarters, a highly sensitive defence establishment, belonged to a trade union. There was a long-standing practice whereby all matters pertaining to the terms and conditions of employment were the subject of prior consultation between the management and the unions. The British Government, fearing that industrial action at GCHQ was impairing defence readiness, unilaterally revised the conditions of employment for GCHQ employees by providing that they would no longer be eligible to join any trade union other than a departmental staff association recognised by the director of GCHQ.

The speeches of Lords Fraser and Diplock were notable for the fact that they were willing to classify the practice of the consultation as a legitimate expectation enjoyed by the GCHQ employees and to hold that, in principle, the rules of natural justice had to be complied with when such an expectation was not going to be honoured. Lord Fraser said:

> "Legitimate, or reasonable, expectation may arise either from an express promise given on behalf of a public authority or from the existence of a regular practice which the claimant can reasonably expect to continue."[42]

---

not consider that the annulment of the permission without any remedial action being taken in their favour can be regaded as a disproportionate measure."

39 [1964] A.C. 465.

40 The Ombudsman Act 1980, s.4(2), provides, *inter alia*, that the Ombudsman may investigate any action where it appears to him that the action was, or may have been, taken as "the result of negligence or carelessness": see below, p. 358.

41 [1985] A.C. 374 and [1988] I.R. 353 respectively. This is not the first time that the phrase "legitimate expectations" has been used by the English courts, but *GCHQ* is regarded as the first major case in which the concept received the seal of approval of the House of Lords. Lord Denning had used this phrase in contrasting a legitimate expectation with a "mere privilege" in *Schmidt v. Home Secretary* [1969] 2 Ch. 149 (an aliens' expulsion case). Forsyth, *op. cit.*, above, n.1, comments that Lord Denning informed him in a private letter that he felt sure that the concept of legitimate expectations "came out of my own head and not from any continental or other source". The phrase was also used in a number of prison cases where prisoners sought to challenge loss of remission (*R. v. Hull Prison Board, ex p. St. Germain (No. 2)* [1979] 1 W.L.R. 1041 and *O'Reilly v. Mackman* [1983] 2 A.C. 237) and in cases where it was said that a public body should adhere to a settled procedure (*R. v. Liverpool Corporation ex p. Liverpool Taxi Fleet Operators' Association* [1972] 2 Q.B. 299; *Att.–Gen. of Hong Kong v. Ng Yuen Shiu* [1983] 2 A.C. 629.

42 *GCHQ* [1985] A.C. 374 at 401.

Lord Diplock added:

> "[The] civil servants employed at GCHQ who were members of national trade unions had, at best, a legitimate expectation that they would continue to enjoy the benefits of such membership and of representation by those trade unions in any consultations and negotiations with representatives of the management of that government department as to changes in any term of their employment. So, but again prima facie only, they were entitled, as a matter of public policy under the head of 'procedural impropriety', before administrative action was taken on a decision to withdraw that benefit, to have communicated to the national trade unions by which they had theretofore been represented the reason for such withdrawal, and for such unions to be given an opportunity to comment on it."[43]

Lord Diplock went on to hold that, on the facts of the instant case, this prima facie right to consultation had to yield to the interests of national security. The British Government had decided to take action unilaterally, just because advance notice to the unions might very well lead to the kind of industrial action which the decision barring trade union membership to GCHQ employees was designed to prevent. It is worth noting, in passing, that as this case only involved a legitimate expectation that a particular procedure would be followed, it has been largely superseded by other subsequent developments.

On one line of authority, the legitimate expectations doctrine is confined, where a statutory discretion is concerned, to establishing procedural rights. One form which this may take – and the only one which it has taken thus far in Ireland in the case of statutory powers[44] – is that a public body is obliged to honour a commitment which it has given that some particular procedure must be followed. The alternative – and less straightforward form – is illustrated in *GCHQ*. It is that even though the public body is free to resile from the commitment given (at least where there is a change of circumstances), it can do so only *after* it has given the person affected by this reversal *some* form of hearing.[45]

A further impetus was provided by the decision of the Supreme Court in *Webb v. Ireland*.[46] The plaintiffs were the finders of a hoard of treasure containing exceptionally valuable specimens of early Christian art. These articles were handed over for safe-keeping to the Director of the National Museum who assured the plaintiffs that they would be honourably treated. The plaintiffs' claim for recovery of the treasure failed, but they succeeded in their claim that they had a legitimate expectation that they would be honourably treated and that the State had failed to honour that assurance. Finlay C.J. put the matter thus:

---

43 *Ibid.* at 412.
44 See, *e.g. Fakih v. Minister for Justice* [1993] 2 I.R . 406; *Navan Tanker Services Ltd v. Meath County Council*, unreported, High Court, December 13, 1996 and *Anisimova v. Minister for Justice*, unreported, Supreme Court, November 28, 1997.
45 See, *e.g. Eogan v. University College Dublin* [1996] 2 I.L.R.M. 302 (Professor Eogan had acquired an expectation that he would be allowed to continue in office until the age of 70, but it was held that this expectation was defeated by a change of circumstances necessitating an earlier retirement age and where the applicant had been given every opportunity to make submissions).
46 [1988] I.R. 353. For an interesting account of some of the issues which arose in this multi-faceted case, see Kelly, "Hidden Treasure and the Constitution" (1988) 10 D.U.L.J. 5 (N.S.).

"It would appear that the doctrine of 'legitimate expectations', sometimes described as 'reasonable expectations' has not in those terms been the subject of any decisions of our courts. However, the doctrine connoted by such expressions is but an aspect of the well-recognised concept of promissory estoppel whereby a promise or representation as to intention may in certain circumstances be held binding on the representor or promisor. The nature and extent of that doctrine in circumstances such as those of this case has been expressed as follows by Lord Denning M.R. in *Amalgamated Property Co. v. Texas Bank*:

> 'When the parties to a transaction proceed on the basis of an underlying assumption – either of law or of fact – whether due to misrepresentation or mistake makes no difference – on which they have conducted the dealings between them – neither of them will be allowed to go back on that assumption when it would be unfair or unjust to allow him to do so. If one of them does seek to go back on it, the courts will give the other such remedy as the equity of the case demands.'"[47]

The plaintiffs had argued that the long-standing practice of the National Museum of paying rewards to finders of such treasure was enough to create a legitimate expectation to fair compensation in their favour, but Finlay C.J. did not find it necessary to rule on this point. In his view:

> "[T]he plaintiff's claim for compensation rests solidly on the fact that the assurance given to Mr. Webb that he would be honourably treated (which should be held to mean that he would be reasonably rewarded) was an integral part of the transaction whereby he deposited the hoard in the National Museum. It would be inequitable and unjust if the State were to be allowed to repudiate that assurance and give only a meagre and disproportionate award."[48]

Thus analysed, the *Webb* decision would seem to have been an instance of a generous application of the doctrine of promissory estoppel, rather than presaging a radical new development in the law. Moreover, this judgment was given in the context of a case in which no statutory powers of the State were involved and, accordingly, where there was no potential conflict between the plaintiff's legitimate expectations and the doctrine that the exercise of statutory powers may not be fettered by estoppel, a point which has deservedly received attention in the subsequent case law.[49] It is also worth noting that the rights at issue in *Webb* were

---

47 *Ibid.* at 384. The quotation from Lord Denning is at [1982] Q.B. 84 at 122.
48 *Ibid.* at 679. This principle was applied in somewhat similar circumstances by Barr J. in *Re the "La Lavia"*, unreported, High Court, July 26, 1994. Here the plaintiffs had discovered three vessels from the Spanish Armada and Barr J. said that in the circumstances they had acquired a legitimate expectation that they would be treatedly honourably: "The general tenor of negotiations . . . created a legitimate expectation in the minds of the [plaintiffs] that they would be fairly treated by the State and would receive a reasonable reward for the discovery which they made." Note, however, that the Supreme Court took a different view of these facts: [1996] 1 I.L.R.M. 194.
49 See, *e.g.* the comments of O'Flaherty J. in *Wiley v. Revenue Commissioners* [1994] 2 I.R. 160 (see below, pp. 870–871) and those of Costello J. in *Tara Prospecting Ltd v. Minister for Energy* [1993] I.L.R.M. 771.

substantive rights, whereas the legitimate expectation recognised in *GCHQ* was procedural only (as emerges clearly from the passage quoted earlier from Lord Diplock's judgment) – the right to advance consultation before withdrawing the right to belong to a trade union.

In any event, the decision in *Webb* has given rise to a host of subsequent case law and, as might be expected from an area of law in an inchoate stage of development, many doctrinal questions have yet to be adequately resolved. While the subsequent case law has been fitful and somewhat inconsistent, the principle is nonetheless well established. The major difference between Irish and European law in this regard would appear to be that, many Irish judges very largely confine the application of the principle of legitimate expectations to the sphere of *procedural* as distinct from substantive rights, at least where the granting of *substantive* rights would conflict with the principle that the donor of a statutory power may not fetter by estoppel his freedom of action.[50]

Procedural commitments

Two recent decisions illustrate the use of legitimate expectations to require a public body to honour a procedural commitment. In *Fakih v. Minister for Justice*[51] a number of Lebanese immigrants had illegally arrived in Ireland. Their applications for refugee status were summarily rejected and they were refused permission to enter the State. They asserted that their applications should have been dealt with on the basis of procedures privately agreed between the Irish Minister for Justice and the United Nations High Commissioner for Refugees in 1985 prior to the making of any deportation order.[52] Unlike *Webb*, there was no question that the applicants had received any promise or representation that they would be treated in this fashion before they arrived in Ireland, so that the issue of advance knowledge, still less acting to one's detriment – an essential feature of the promissory estoppel doctrine – simply did not arise.

O'Hanlon J. nevertheless held that the applicants had acquired a legitimate expectation that they would be dealt with according to the terms of the 1985 agreement and he quoted the following passage from the speech of Lord Fraser in *Attorney General of Hong Kong v. Ng Yuen Shiu*[53] with approval:

> "The justification [for the principle of legitimate expectations] is primarily that, when a public authority has promised to follow a certain procedure, it is in the interest of good administration that it should act fairly and should implement its promise, so long as the implementation does not interfere with its statutory duty."[54]

---

[50] In *Wiley v. Revenue Commissioners* [1994] 2 I.R. 160, O'Flaherty J. described (at 172) *Webb's* case as one involving a claim for substantive relief based upon a legitimate expectation. But *Webb* did not involve any potential clash with the exercise of a statutory power.

[51] [1993] 2 I.R. 406.

[52] The agreement set out the steps (such as personal interviews, etc.) that would be taken by immigration officers in respect of applications for refugee status.

[53] [1983] 2 A.C. 629.

[54] *Ibid.* at 638.

O'Hanlon J. then continued by saying:

> "As the law has developed it has come to be applied in situations where the conventional plea of estoppel by conduct might not be available since the party seeking to rely on the plea of legitimate expectation may not be able to establish that he has been induced by the conduct of the other party to act to his own detriment."[55]

The judge, therefore, concluded that the applicants had acquired a legitimate expectation that their request for asylum would be dealt with in accordance with the 1985 procedures, even though, of course, they could have had no knowledge of these arrangements prior to their arrival in the State. This, perhaps, is not so much an example of a legitimate expectation – since expectation is usually dependent on prior knowledge – but rather an application of the principle that it is in the interests of good and orderly administration that, in the absence of good reasons to the contrary, an administrator should be bound by agreed procedures.

This precise issue surfaced again in a subsequent immigration case, *Gutrani v. Minister for Justice*.[56] On this occasion the Minister agreed not to deport an illegal immigrant save in accordance with the terms of the 1985 scheme and this concession was adjudged to have been properly made by the Supreme Court. McCarthy J. commented:

> "Having established such a scheme, however informally so, he would appear to be bound to apply it to appropriate cases, and his decision would be subject to judicial review. It does not appear to me to depend on any principle of legitimate or reasonable expectation; it is, simply, the procedure which the Minister has undertaken to enforce."[57]

4. The Development of the Legitimate Expectations Doctrine and Associated Difficulties

The next five decisions illustrate the failure of a legitimate expectations claim and the assertion of the more conventional and orthodox common law perspective in the field of substantive rights: *Egan v. Minister for Defence*[58]; *Wiley v. The Revenue*

---

55   [1993] 2 I.R. 406 at 424. Note, however, that in *Re "La Lavia"* [1996] 1 I.L.R.M. 194 – a case which, like *Webb*, involved the practice of paying rewards for archaeological finds – O'Flaherty J. rejected (at 200) a plea of legitimate expectations on the ground that no promise "was held out to the respondents at any time by the servants of the State in such a manner as would bind the State. Indeed, the whole idea of a promise is that it has to make an impression on the mind of the promisee". However, the Court acknowledged that there might be circumstances (although it did not have to decide the point) where the practice "was so well established and regular that the expectation of a reward was, therefore, so well-founded that the court should give effect to it".

56   [1993] 2 I.R. 427.

57   *Ibid.*, 436. See also the judgment of Carroll J. in *Navan Tanker Services Ltd v. Meath County Council*, unreported, High Court, December 13, 1996 (applicant had acquired a legitimate expectation that its application for a licence would be dealt with in accordance with fair procedures).

58   Unreported, High Court, November 24, 1988.

Commissioners[59]; *Tara Prospecting v. Minister for Energy*[60]; *Gilheaney v. Revenue Commissioners;*[61] and *Abrahamson v. Law Society of Ireland.*[62]

In the *Egan* case, the applicant was an aircraft pilot with the Air Corps, but because of the large number of such pilots who were leaving the Defence Forces in order to fly with commercial airlines, the Minister refused him permission to retire prematurely. It was claimed that the applicant had a legitimate expectation that such permission would be granted, but Barr J. could not accept this:

> "Even if I were to proceed from the premise that in 1966 when the applicant joined the army, there was a long-established and universally recognised practice that officers of five years' standing and upwards who apply to the Minister for permission to retire early were duly given leave to do so and that that practice continued until mid-1988, it would not derogate from the Minister's statutory right to refuse permission on reasonable grounds in any particular case. Such a practice, however firmly entrenched it may have been in the life of the permanent Defence Forces, did not amount to an implied promise or representation (as envisaged by Finlay C.J. in *Webb v. Ireland*) made by the Minister to the officer corps that permission to retire would be granted in each and every case."

In the *Wiley* case the applicant was a partially disabled driver who, pursuant to a statutory scheme, obtained on separate occasions in 1983 and 1985 substantial repayments of excise duty otherwise due on motor vehicles. In 1986, the Revenue Commissioners, conscious that a scheme designed for the benefit of wholly disabled drivers had been availed of by ineligible persons, introduced more stringent evidential requirements so as to ensure that the statutory requirements were met. The applicant was not aware of this when he purchased a new motor vehicle in 1987 and he subsequently found that the medical certificates as to the extent of his partial disability were not accepted. He then claimed that he had acquired a legitimate expectation that the pre-1986 arrangements should be continued in his case, or, failing that, that "if there was to be a change in the requirements of the Revenue Commissioners, he should have been told in advance of his purchase of a new motor car".[63]

It is scarcely surprising that this application was rejected by the Supreme Court.[64] The views of O'Flaherty J. may be taken as representative of the Court's attitude:

> "It will be clear immediately that acceptance of this submission would involve a radical enlargement of the scope of legitimate expectations. It would involve the courts saying to the administration that it was not entitled to set more

---

[59] [1993] I.L.R.M. 482.
[60] [1993] I.L.R.M. 771.
[61] [1996] E.L.R. 25.
[62] [1996] 1 I.R. 403.
[63] *Wiley v. The Revenue Commissioner* [1994] 2.I.R. 160.
[64] The Court of Justice would scarcely have taken a different view, for as was said in Case C–350/88, *Delacre v. Commission* [1990] E.C.R. I–395 at 462: "Traders cannot have a legitimate expectation that an existing situation which is capable of being altered by the Community institutions in the exercise of their discretionary powers will be maintained."

stringent standards so that it might discharge its statutory obligations, without giving notice to anyone who might have benefited in the past from a more relaxed set of rules. Stated thus, I believe that it would involve the courts in an unwarranted system of interference with the actions of administrators."[65]

This reasoning can probably be best explained as being based not on the principle that legitimate expectations may not operate to fetter the exercise of discretionary powers, but rather on the associated and, if anything, more stringent precept that legitimate expectations may not be invoked in defiance of "statutory obligations" (to quote O'Flaherty J.). What is interesting nevertheless is that while O'Flaherty J. rejected the claim on the facts, he was nonetheless prepared to envisage further expansions of the doctrine and he also signified his willingness in this regard to draw on the jurisprudence of the Court of Justice in this area.[66]

In the *Tara Prospecting* case the applicant companies had been awarded mining prospecting licences under the Minerals Development Act 1940 in 1981 and 1984. The companies found some gold deposits in the areas covered by their licences and they re-applied for a renewal of their prospecting licences. These licences were granted, but large areas of territory included in the earlier licences were excluded. The Minister justified this exclusion on environmental, cultural and religious grounds.[67] The applicants challenged this aspect of the decision on the ground that it violated the principle of legitimate expectations: they asserted that the Minister had represented that their licences would be renewed in full if the prospecting had proved to be successful.

Following a review of leading English[68] and Australian[69] authorities, Costello J. concluded that (as mentioned above in section 2 of this chapter) in cases involving the exercise of statutory powers the doctrine of legitimate expectations was limited

---

65   *Wiley v. The Revenue Commissioners* [1994] 2 I.R. 160 at 174.
66   See, above, n.5.
67   Some of the lands were particularly scenic. One licence had also included Croagh Patrick, a traditional place of pilgramage.
68   Including *R. v. Liverpool Corporation, ex p. Liverpool Taxi Fleet Operators' Association* [1972] 2 Q.B. 299; *Re Westminister County Council* [1986] A.C. 668.
69   Costello J. quoted extensively from the judgment of the Australian High Court in *Attorney General for New South Wales v. Quin* (1990) 170 C.L.R. 1. In this case a former magistrate claimed that the Attorney General's failure to recommend him for appointment to a local court constituted a breach of his legitimate expectations. Brennan J. held that the doctrine of legitimate expectations could not apply to the present claim, since the applicant was seeking a *substantive* rather than a *procedural* right (*i.e.* a judicial appointment). If the law were otherwise, it would mean (at 39–40) that:
> "A legitimate expectation not amounting to a legal right would be enforceable as though it were, and changes in government policy, even when sanctioned by the ballot box, could be sterilised by expectations which the superseded policy had enlivened."

This issue also surfaced in a curious manner in the confidence debate in the Dáil in November 1994 arising out of the appointment of the then Attorney General as President of the High Court. The then Taoiseach (Mr A. Reynolds, T.D.) had asserted that by convention the Attorney had first claim on any judicial vacancy and that this convention was in the nature of a condition of employment of the Attorney General. This contention was, it is submitted, convincingly countered by the Tánaiste (Mr R. Spring, T.D.) speaking in the same debate: (447 *Dáil Debates,* Col. 352, November 16, 1994) :
> "Our Constitution reserves the right of appointment of members of the judiciary to the President of Ireland, acting on the advice of the Government . . . Any promise of 'condition of employment' which guaranteed an appointment to the judiciary, thereby pre-empting the free and unfettered decision of the Government in the matter, would clearly have to be null and void . . . ".

to procedural matters. In other cases, the doctrine might exceptionally (as in the *Webb* case) include substantive rights, but such cases really represented an application of the principles of promissiory estoppel rather than legitimate expectations as such. He summarised his conclusions on the present state of the law as follows

"(1) There is a duty on a minister who is exercising a discretionary power which may affect rights or interests to adopt fair procedures in the exercise of the power. Where a member of the public has a legitimate expectation arising from the minister's words and/or conduct that (a) he will be given a hearing before a decision adverse to his interests will be taken or (b) that he will obtain a benefit from the exercise of the power then the Minister also has a duty to act fairly towards him and this may involve a duty to give him a fair hearing before a decision adverse to his interests is taken. There would then arise a co-relative right to a fair hearing which, if denied, will justify the court in quashing the decision.

(2) The existence of a legitimate expectation that a benefit will be conferred does not in itself give rise to any legal or equitable right to the benefit itself which can be [judicially] enforced. However, in cases involving public authorities, other than cases involving the exercise of statutory discretionary powers, an equitable right to the benefit may arise from the application of the principles of promissory estoppel to which effect will be given by appropriate court order.

(3) In cases involving the exercise of a discretionary statutory power the only legitimate expectation relating to the conferring of the benefit that can be inferred from words or conduct is a conditional one, namely, that a benefit will be conferred provided that at the time that the Minister considers that it is a proper exercise of the statutory power in the light of current policy to grant it. Such a conditional expectation cannot give rise to the benefit should it later be refused by the Minister in the public interest.

(4) In cases involving the exercise of a discretionary statutory power in which an explicit assurance has been given which gives rise to an expectation that a benefit will be conferred no enforceable equitable or legal right to the benefit can arise. No promissory estoppel can arise because the Minister cannot estop either himself or his successors from exercising a discretionary power in the manner prescribed by Parliament at the time it is exercised."[70]

---

[70] *Tara Prospecting v. Minister for Energy* [1993] I.L.R.M. 771 at 789. This passage was approved and followed by Morris J. in *Dempsey v. Minister for Justice* [1994] 1 I.L.R.M. 401. Here a prisoner claimed that he had acquired a legitimate expectation that he would not be transferred from one prison (with a more favourable regime) to another (with a less favourable regime). The claim failed on the facts, but Morris J. added that even if this were not so, the claim would be bound to fail as a matter of law. The Minister was given very broad statutory powers in relation to the transfer of prisoners and she could not be estopped in the exercise of such powers. See also to like effect the comments of Lardner J. in *Devitt v. Minister for Education* [1989] I.L.R.M. 639 at 651 and those of Morris J. in *John M.P. Greaney Ltd . v. Dublin Corporation* [1994] 3 I.R. 384 at 392–393 and (in an English context) those of Laws J. in *R. v. Secretary of State for Transport, ex p. Richmond upon Thames London BC* [1994] 1 W.L.R. 74.

On the facts Costello J. agreed that the applicants could reasonably have expected that if prospecting was successful, their licences would be renewed until such time as they were in a position to apply for a mining lease:

> "But this expectation could only be a conditional one as the Minister was exercising a discretionary power and the applicants should have been aware that the renewal of the licence was conditional on the Minister concluding at the time of renewal that renewal was in the public interest. This was the only 'legitimate expectation' that the applicants could entertain. As the Minister concluded that the renewal of licences was not in the public interest no enforceable right to them could possibly arise."[71]

Costello P. returned to this theme in *Gilheaney v. Revenue Commissioners*.[72] Here an Executive Officer applied for the post of press officer (which has Higher Executive Officer status) with the Revenue Commissioners. He was not immediately successful, but was placed on a panel for future promotions. The post was subsequently filled by the transfer of another officer of H.E.O. status, and not by the promotion of an E.O. officer. The applicant claimed that this infringed the principle of legitimate expectations, but Costello P. ruled that to give effect to this claim would run counter to the Government's power under section 17 of the Civil Service Regulation Act 1956 to fix the conditions governing the promotion of civil servants and also to vary arrangements made to give effect to such conditions:

> "This power cannot be fettered in the way suggested. No doubt the applicant had an expectation that he would be appointed to the vacancy that arose as

---

[71] *Ibid.* at 789. *cf.* the very similar test enunciated by Stuart-Smith L.J. in *R. v. Jockey Club, ex p. RAM Racecourses Ltd* [1993] 2 All E.R. 225 at 236–237. Costello J. had previously expressed similar sentiments in *Hempenstall v. Minister for the Environnment* [1994] 2 I.R. 20. In this case the Minister had rescinded a previous moratorium on the grant of new taxi licences in the light of a new departmental report on the subject. Costello J. held (*Hempenstall* at 32) that no plea of legitimate expectations could prevail in such circumstances:

> "It seems to me that the law should not trammel the exercise by a Minister of his statutory functions even if, in the light of new information and advice, he exercises them in a manner contrary to an earlier statement of intent."

For a less doctrinaire approach to this question, see the judgment of Sedley J. in *R. v. Ministry for Agriculture, Fisheries and Foods, ex p. Hamble (Offshore) Fisheries Ltd* [1995] 2 All E.R. 714 where he said that the test was whether the individual's expectation "of different treatment has a legitimacy which in fairness [defeats] the policy choice which threatens to frustrate it".

[72] [1996] E.L.R. 25.

[73] Craig, "Substantive Legitimate Expectations in Domestic and Community Law" [1996] Camb. L.J. 289 comments (at p. 311) that the reasoning behind the traditional "draconian doctrine" is unconvincing and argues – correctly, it is submitted – that cases such as Case 120/86 *Mulder v. Minister van Landbouw en Visserij* [1988] E.C.R. 2321 (see below, p. 875) demonstrate that if is often necessary "to balance the public interest in legality and the private interest in legal certainty". In this regard, it may be noted that in *Fusco v. O'Dea*, unreported High Court, June 28, 1995, Geoghegan J. held that it would be "unjust, oppressive or invidious" within the meaning of s.50(2)(b) of the Extradition Act 1965 to deliver up an accused for extradition when he had been impliedly led to believe that his case would be dealt with under the Criminal Law (Jurisdiction) Act 1976 (and in respect of which he served a sentence in this State). He had also changed his position on foot of these implied representations. While this case is, doubtless, a particular one which was decided in the context of a special statutory provision, there are nonetheless traces of "substantive" legitimate expections (*i.e.* in this instance, not to be extradited) which effectively prevailed against a statutory power (*i.e.* the power to order to order the extradition of suspects) lurking in this decision.

873

he was next in line on the panel for promotion . . . But he could not have had a 'legitimate expectation' because no restriction on the section 17 powers is permissible."

And yet one wonders whether this principle can – or, at any rate, ought – to be stated in such absolute terms. While it is undoubtedly important in the public interest that public authorities should remain the maximum freedom of movement and should not be fettered by estoppel, the rigid application of this principle may clash with other public values – reasonableness, fairness, proportionality – which it is also important to safeguard.[73] This point is illustrated by an earlier decision of Costello J., *Philips v. Medical Council.*[74] In this case a foreign doctor had sought registration under the terms of rules promulgated in September 1980. While that application was pending, the Council adopted new rules which it then sought to apply to the plaintiff's case. Costello J. would not, however, permit this:

> "The parties in this case had treated the September 1980 rules as those governing the plaintiff's application. The plaintiff had a reasonable expectation that his application would be determined in accordance with them. It would . . . be grossly unfair to allow the Council to recind the rules when an application was pending under these and adopt new ones which effectively made it impossible for the plaintiff to be registered."[75]

Philips thus illustrates that there must be at least some category of case where the strict application of the orthodox principles later applied in cases such as *Tara Prospecting* and *Gilheaney* must yield to other considerations in order to avoid a real injustice in a particular case. Moreover, there is a world of a difference between allowing a legitimate expectation to prevail against the exercise of a statutory power in cases where the exercise of that power is largely personal in its consequences to the applicant or a potentially small number of persons (as in *Philips*) and cases where this would retard the capacity of the Government or adminstrators to make new policy decisions affecting the community at large (as in *Tara Prospecting*).

Consider, finally, *Abrahamson v. Law Society of Ireland.*[76] In this case the respondent Society had published a booklet stating that a person with a law degree from certain law schools in the Republic of Ireland would be exempt from the need to pass the entrance examination in specified core legal subjects. Subsequently – and following the decision of Laffoy J. in *Bloomer v. Law Society of Ireland*[77] – the respondent changed certain regulations which had been made under the Solicitors Acts 1954–1994, so that, henceforth, all law students were required to take the entrance examinations. In *Abrahamson*, it was held that the students had acquired

---

[74] [1991] 2 I.R. 115.

[75] *Ibid.* at 138. In *Abrahamson v. Law Society of Ireland* [1996] 1 I.R. 403, McCracken J. hinted that *Philips* must be regarded as an example of the furthest which the courts have gone in permitting a plea of legitimate expectations to prevail in a case presenting a possible clash with the exercise of a statutory power and suggested (at 496) that this case "must now be considered in the light of certain other decisions in which the courts have refused to interfere with the exercise of a statutory discretion". The "certain other cases" instanced by McCracken J. included *Wiley, Hempenstall* and *Tara Prospecting*.

[76] [1996] 2 I.L.R.M. 481.

[77] [1995] 3 I.R. 14.

a legitimate expectation that the original regulations[78] would remain in force long enough to be taken advantage of by even first year law students. Next, however, McCracken J. ruled that since the original regulation had been held to be *ultra vires* in the *Bloomer* case, it would not be lawful to direct the Law Society to consider granting exemptions on the basis of it.[79] However, the matter did not end there, since under a different regulation, the Society had a discretion to grant exemptions which could have been exercised in the applicant's favour. McCracken J. nonetheless held that he could not direct the Law Society to do so, since this would amount to an interference by the Court with the exercise of a statutory discretion. Nevertheless, the upshot of the case was ultimately favourable to the applicants. The Court's emphasis on the Society's discretion, together with certain judicial hints (including a suggestion that a claim for damages might lie) appears to have prompted the Law Society to exercise its discretion in favour of the applicants and it did so. Had it not done so, it is likely that there would have been further proceedings to review the distinct issue of reasonabless in law of its failure so to act.

These decisions – representing as they do the distilled wisdom and experience of the Irish courts with regard to the legitimate expectations doctrine – makes an interesting contrast with the celebrated judgment of the Court of Justice in *Mulder v. Minister van Landbouw en Visserij*.[80] Here the European Court of Justice found parts of Community milk marketing regulations to be invalid on the ground that it violated the applicants' legitimate expectations. Certain milk producers had opted out of milk production for a five-year period in return for payment of a premium by the Community. At the end of this period, the applicants found themselves unable to resume milk production because the subsequent milk quota regulations did not take account of their special position.[81] The Court said that where a producer:

> ". . . has been encouraged by a Community measure to suspend marketing for a limited period in the general interest and against payment of a premium he may legitimately expect not to be subject, upon the expiry of his undertaking, to restrictions which specifically affect him precisely because he availed himself of the possibilities offered by the Community provisions."[82]

---

[78] Solicitors Acts, 1954 and 1960 (Apprenticeship and Education) Regulations 1991, (S.I. No. 9 of 1991).

[79] This is the distinction between *Bloomer* and *Philips*, since the *vires* of the rules relied on the plaintiff in the latter case had never been put in issue by any third party.

[80] Case 120/86, [1988] E.C.R. 2321.

[81] The milk quota regulations were based on milk production by producers in reference years. The gravemen of the plaintiffs' complaint was that they had been prevented under the terms of their undertaking from producing milk in those years.

[82] *Ibid.* at 2352. At the same time it is important to stress that the Court of Justice has placed sensible limitations on the scope of the legitimate expectations doctrine. In particular, it is plain that, absent exceptional circumstances, changes in a statutory regime governing matters such as licensing, trading conditions, etc., will rarely give rise to a successful plea of legitimate expectations. As the Court said in Case C–63/93, *Duff v. Minister for Agriculture and Food* [1996] E.C.R. I–539 the principle of legitimate expectations in Community law:

> ". . . is the corollary of the principle of legal certainty, which requires that legal rules be clear and precise, and aims to ensure that situations and legal relationships governed by Community law remain foreseeable. It is settled case-law that in the sphere of the common organisation of the markets, whose purpose involves constant adjustments to meet changes in the economic situation, economic agents cannot legitimately expect that they will not be subject to restrictions

It would seem unlikely – at least to judge by reference to *Tara Prospecting* and *Gilheaney* – that the Irish courts would have approached the *Mulder* problem in the same way. *Mulder* is a legitimate expectations case involving substantive rights and the exercise of statutory powers (in this instance, the allocation of milk quotas), but both *Tara Prospecting* and *Gilheaney* appear to insist that in the context of statutory powers, the principle of legitimate expectations must yield to the over-riding principle that the discharge of such powers may not be fettered by estoppel.

There has been at least one Irish case raising issues of legitimate expections under both domestic and European law. In *Carbury Milk Products Ltd v. Minister for Agriculture*,[83] the plaintiffs had manufactured a certain type of milk product which they submitted to the defendants. The defendants classified the product as a milk protein product for Common Customs Tariff Classification purposes and this meant that the company was entitled to export refunds for third country sales. On the strength of this classification the plaintiffs entered into contracts with third parties based outside the European Community in the expectation that such export refunds would be payable.[84] Some two years later, however, the defendants realised that, through no fault of the plaintiffs, an error had been made: the product was, in fact, to be classified as a whey powder which did not attract export refunds. The plaintiffs then claimed an entitlement to export refunds for the two years during which the product had been wrongly classified as being entitled to such payments. Hamilton P., in a judgment which provides a good example of the inter-action of promissory estoppel and legitimate expectations under both Irish and European law, held that in these circumstances the Minister was estopped from denying the plaintiffs entitlement to the export refunds.

Whether one classifies this case as an example of promissory estoppel or legitimate expectations, it is plain that the company deserved to succeed in their claim. As other cases demonstrate, the Irish courts have no difficulty in such circumstances in drawing on European concepts of legitimate expectations in order to bolster a conclusion that a plaintiff was entitled to relief where it had been misled into altering its position to its detriment by a representation by an agent of the State. Difficulties arise, however, where the effect of the legitimate expectation would be to fetter the exercise of a statutory power by a Minister or other statutory body.

In comparing – and attempting to reconcile – *Wiley*, *Egan*, *Tara Prospecting*, *Gilheaney*, *Abrahamson*, etc., with *Carbury Milk* – it may be helpful to draw the following distinction (although, it should be noted, that it has not been adverted to in any of the Irish cases). This distinction is between an expectation which arises because the public body had on the occasion when the expectation was created, made a misstatement of law which was then later corrected; and on the other hand, one which arises because a public body indicates that it is going to exercise a

---

arising out of future rules of market or structural policy . . . [T]he principle of legitimate expectations may be invoked as against Community rules only to the extent that the Community itself has previously created a situation which can give rise to a legitimate expectation.."

[83] (1988–1993) 4 Irish Tax Reports 492.

[84] Hamilton P. found (at 543) that the prices fixed by the plaintiffs for these contracts "were based on their entitlement to such refunds and that were it not for such classification they would have exported their product to and developed a market for such product in EEC countries".

statutory discretionary power in one sense and then, subsequently exercises it in a different fashion. These two situations may appear similar when viewed from the perspective of the disappointed individual; but from the view point of the public body, they may involve entirely different considerations. Thus, it may be that they should be treated differently.

To elaborate, take first the case of a public body changing the way in which it exercises its discretionary power. Here the principle (which may be used to justify decisions such as *Tara Prospecting, Gilheaney* and *Eogan*) that a public body should not be fettered in the exercise of its discretionary power is engaged. The traditional view underlying this principle has this merit, *i.e.* the notion that since a public body is responsible to the entire community, it should, in principle, be free to change its policy, without any countervailing pressure of court action to bar it from doing so.

The second situation is where an error as to law[85] is made by the public body. Where, as sometimes is the case, this is the result of negligence it would be reasonable – as a matter of general principle – that (in contrast to the first situation) compensation ought to be paid on the same basis as in private law cases of negligent misstatement. The *caveat* "as a matter of general principle" indicates that there are substantial qualifications which may prevent the general principle from operating. For example, there may be public policy factors which would create the reason for an exemption, as for instance that the decision was quasi-judicial in nature.[86] Again, it would be appropriate to consider whether the misrepresentee ought to have relied upon what the public body said or did (or failed to say or do), a point well illustrated by *Carbury Milk*. In *Carbury Milk* the classification of the plaintiff's milk product depended in part on the legal definition but also in part – and here is the important point – upon the classification by the defendant Minister (rather than depending exclusively upon the general law, which it was open to anyone to discover). One could reasonably regard the Minister's initial misclassification as being negligent rather than as being influenced by a change of policy. This category – an error as to law – would also seem to cover the cases which are discussed below in section 8 of this chapter, under the heading "Advance Rulings, etc., from the Revenue Commissioners and legitimate expectations " and, so it may be, on the basis of the distinction just discussed, that in an appropriate case from this field, a claimant, grounding himself on legitimate expectation, would be successful.

Reasons justifying a change of position

Even quite apart from what has already been said about not fettering a discretion, the public body is probably entitled to resile from its previous practice or

---

85 A somewhat analagous point arose in *Philips v. Medical Council* [1991] 2 I.R. 115. This case concerned the non-registration of the plaintiff by the Medical Council under the Medical Practitioners Act 1978. (On this case, see also above, p. 874.) To justify its refusal to register the plaintiff, the Council sought to rely on Rules made in August 1980 under the Act. However, Costello J. held that the Council was estopped from relying upon these Rules just because, following the plaintiff's request, they had sent him a copy of Rules with a different content which had been made in September 1980. Accordingly, it was held that the Council had made a representation that the plaintiff could rely on the September 1980 Rules.

86 The decision in *Wiley* might conceivably be an example of this (as well, of course, as the other grounds of justification mentioned earlier).

representation where there actually exist in the particular case objective reasons which justify this change of position. At most, then, the effect of the doctrine of legitimate expectations is only to protect the citizen against an arbitrary change of position by a public authority.

This very point had been made in the *GCHQ* case itself, where objective considerations of national security were found to justify a departure from previous practice. Similarly, the judgment of Barr J. in *Egan v. Minister for Defence*[87] provides another illustration of these principles. Here the plaintiff was an officer in the Air Corps who sought the Minister's permission (as is required by the Defence Act 1954) for early retirement (in order to take up a position with a private airline). Barr J. found that there was, in fact, no settled practice giving rise to a legitimate expectation on the part of the plaintiff. Significantly, however, Barr J. added that even if the Minister had departed from previous practice, this would not have been either unfair or unjust in the circumstances:

> "The criterion is whether the Minister's decision is reasonable having regard to the circumstances of the particular case. He is entitled to take account of special circumstances such as those which occurred in 1988 when, within a short period of time, he was faced with numerous applications for early retirement from the Air Corps. This created a new situation, and, in the interest of maintaining a viable Air Corps, he was entitled to deal with the matter as he did."[88]

A good example of this point[89] is also provided by *Eogan v. University College, Dublin*.[90] The evidence in this case established that academic staff at UCD traditionally enjoyed the benefit of staying in office until aged 70,[91] but this practice was changed in 1987 and extensions in office were no longer sanctioned in order to "achieve a reduction in the age profile of academic staff in UCD and to make financial savings". While Shanley J. agreed that Professor Eogan had acquired a legitimate expectation in relation to the retirement age, this simply entitled him to comment on the proposed change and he had been given every opportunity of doing so. Furthermore, as UCD had rational grounds for altering its prior practice, it was held to be entitled to do so.[92]

---

[87] Unreported, High Court, November 24, 1988.

[88] *Ibid.* at pp. 15–16 of the judgment. A similar claim was made in *The State (Rajan) v. Minister for Industry and Commerce* [1988] I.L.R.M. 231, 242 to the effect that established disciplinary practices were not followed in the applicant's case and that his legitimate expectations were accordingly violated, This claim was found by Barron J. not to arise on the facts of the case.

[89] See also *R. v. Health Secretary, ex p. US Tobacco International Inc.* [1992] 1 Q.B. 353 and *Re Findlay* [1985] A.C. 318.

[90] [1996] 2 I.L.R.M. 302.

[91] The College statutes provide that all professors in good standing shall continue in office until 65, but might continue in office until 70, provided "that this further continuance in office is recommended to the Senate of the University by the Governing Body with the approval of the President and is sanctioned by the Senate annually."

[92] A legitimate expectation can probably also be defeated by operation of law, a point illustrated by *Abrahamson v. Law Society of Ireland* [1996] 1 I.R. 403. In this case, certain law students were held to have acquired a legitimate expectation that they would be exempted from the necessity to sit certain examinations. However, that expectation was itself founded on a regulation which was found to be invalid by the High Court in *Bloomer v. Incorporated Law Society of Ireland* [1995] 3 I.R. 14

Accordingly,these authorities demonstrate that a public body is entitled to change its position where new factors or objective alterations in circumstances will justify it in so doing and this remains true even though the private citizen had a legitimate expectation that the public body would adhere to the previous practice.

What conduct or practice gives rise to an expectation or estoppel?

It is self-evident that an expectation or an estoppel may be grounded upon an explicit statement of the person who is seeking to rely upon it.[93] However, the facts seldom present themselves in such a convenient form. More commonly, the question which is posed is whether some conduct or settled practice will suffice. In *Webb*, for example, Finlay C.J. did not find it necessary to decide whether the long-standing practice adopted by the National Museum of paying *ex gratia* sums to the finders of treasure trove could of itself give rise to a legitimate expectation which would be enforceable against the State.[94] The question has subsequently arisen as to whether a regular practice, of itself, can give rise to a legitimate expectation, as suggested by Lord Fraser in the *GCHQ* case.

In *Egan v. Minister for Defence*,[95] the plaintiff – who was an officer in the air corps – sought early retirement in order to take up a civillian post. When the Minister refused, the plaintiff claimed that he had acquired a legitimate expectation that the request would be granted, as in the past, similar requests had virtually always been granted. Barr J. was emphatic that a long-standing practice could not suffice:

> "Even if I were to proceed from the premise . . . that . . . there was a long established and universally recognised practice that officers of five years standing and upwards who applied to the Minister for permission to retire early were duly given leave to do so and that that practice continued until mid–1988, it would not derogate from the Minister's statutory right to refuse permission on reasonable grounds in a particular case. Such a practice, however firmly entrenched it may have been in the life of the permanent defence force, did not amount to an implied promise or representation (as envisaged by the Chief Justice in *Webb v. Ireland*) made by the Minister to the officer corps . . . that permission to retire would be granted in every case as of course."[96]

---

and in these special circumstances McCracken J. felt that he was precluded from granting the students the substantive relief which they sought.

93 "For [the doctrine of legitimate expectations] to operate, I would have to be satisfied that an unqualified assurance was given to the applicant which formed an integral part of the transaction upon which the applicant made his application" or, alternatively, that the practice was "so well established and regular" that the courts should give effect to it: *John M.P. Greaney Ltd v. Dublin Corporation* [1994] 3 I.R. 384 at 392, *per* Morris J.

94 This point was also reserved by the Supreme Court in another finder's case, *"Re La Lavia"* [1996] 1 I.R. 403, but the judgment of O'Flaherty J. in that case contains a strong hint that the Court would have been prepared to hold that a well-established and regular practice could give rise to a legitimate expectation.

95 Unreported, High Court, November 24, 1988.

96 At p. 15 of the judgment. This passage from *Egan* was quoted with approval by McGuinness J. in *Maigueside Communications Ltd v. Independent Radio and Television Commission (No.2)*, unreported, High Court, July 18, 1997, a case where the unsuccessful applicant for a radio licence claimed that

This very question was also considered by Blayney J. in *Wiley v. Revenue Commissioners.*[97] The respondents operated a scheme whereby disabled drivers could obtain a refund of excise duty and value added tax levied on motor vehicles where it was established that the owner was disabled and that the vehicle was otherwise exempt for road tax under section 43(1) of the Finance Act 1968. This statutory exemption was granted where the driver could show that he was disabled to the extent that he was "wholly, or almost wholly, without the use of each of his legs". The applicant had certain physical disabilities which prevented him driving an ordinary motor car, but it was conceded his disability did not correspond to the criteria which would entitle him to a refund or exemption. Nevertheless, on two occasions the applicant applied for, and was granted, a refund of excise duty and VAT. By the time of the applicant's third application for a refund, the respondents had altered their practice in that they required not only a certificate of exemption from road tax, but also a copy of the medical certificate on which the road tax exemption was granted. As the medical certificate disclosed that the applicant did not satisfy the exemption criteria, his application was refused.

As we have seen, the present question was not the major issue at stake in *Wiley*. However, it is worth noting that Blayney J. stated that "the doing of something on two occasions only could not constitute a practice".

A further example of conduct giving rise to a legitimate expectation is supplied by *Ghneim v. Minister for Justice,*[98] a case decided by the same judge. Here the applicant was a Libyan national who had illegally remained in Ireland beyond the time period stipulated by his entry visa. He had, however, applied in March 1988 for permission to stay to complete his studies in Ireland and, at the date of the hearing in September 1989, this request was still under consideration. Hamilton P. went so far as to hold that this delay in informing the applicant of a decision in his case was such that he had developed a reasonable expectation that his request that he be permitted to complete his studies would be granted. Hamilton P. accordingly granted an injunction restraining the Minister from taking steps to force the applicant to leave the jurisdiction until the latter had a reasonable time to complete his studies.[99]

A related and straightforward point is that to succeed in a legitimate expectation claim, the applicant must be able to bring himself within the scope or terms (as it were) of the expectation. This point was brought out in *Cannon v. Minister for Marine.*[100] Here the applicant had applied in 1986 for a licence for a particular boat

---

it had acquired a legitimate expectation that all such applicants would be afforded an oral hearing. McGuinness J. could not accept this argument, saying that even if "the commission had at all times previously granted oral hearings to every applicant, that does not in itself create a legitimate expectation that all future competitions will be run in the same way."

97 [1989] I.R. 350 (High Ct.); [1994] 2 I.R. 160 (Sup. Ct.). In *Association of General Practitioners Ltd v. Minister for Health* [1995] 1 I.R. 382 O'Hanlon J. rejected the plaintiff's plea of legitimate expectations as he could find no evidence on the facts that the Minister or his representatives had "in the past, by words actions or conduct, done anything which could reasonably give rise to an expectation on the part of, or giving a right of audience to, the plaintiffs . . . ". A similar conclusion arrived at on the facts by Shanley J. in *Murphy v. Minister for the Marine*, unreported, High Court,, April 11, 1997.

98 *The Irish Times*, September 2, 1989.

99 Which Hamilton P. considered as being 12 months from the date of the hearing.

100 [1991] 1 I.R. 82.

which he hoped to purchase and the licence was duly granted. It then transpired that he could not afford that particular boat. The Minister then allowed the applicant, on a concessionary basis, an opportunity to purchase another vessel of similar size and indicated that he would also grant a licence in respect of such a vessel. The applicant delayed for a two-year period before he contemplated purchasing such a vessel, but was then refused a licence. Barr J. acknowledged that the applicant had acquired an expectation that the licence would be granted, but this could not be regarded as a legitimate one:

> "I am satisfied that neither party ever envisaged that the Minister's concession was intended to be open-ended. I apprehend that when it was made both parties assumed that it was to apply for a reasonable period to enable the applicant to find a suitable alternative vessel. There is no evidence to suggest that either party contemplated that it might take upwards of two years to do so."[101]

Is an assurance or representation of itself enough to give rise to a legitimate expectation?

There have been some High Court decision which hold that a mere representation of itself will not give rise to a legitimate expectation, as there must be something approaching reliance or change of circumstances so as to make it unfair or inequitable for the representor to renege on an assurance.

In the first of these cases, *Garda Representative Association v. Ireland*[102] the plaintiffs sought to rely on an assurance given by the Minister for Justice in the Dáil that certain overtime payments would not be abolished without consultation with the representative associations. Murphy J. held that this could not form the basis of a legitimate expectation, "as there [was] no evidence that the plaintiffs relied upon the Minister's statement".

And in *Cosgrove v. Legal Aid Board*,[103] the applicant argued that she had acquired a legitimate expectation by reason of the general representations made concerning the legal aid scheme that the Board would deal promptly with her application for assistance. While Gannon J. acknowledged that while the "existence of the scheme and the nature of its purpose and its availability" may have given rise to expectations, she had not acquired a legitimate expectation in this regard since there was no evidence that she had acted to her detriment. This approach seems somewhat unadventurous, representing an unwillingness on the part of at least some High Court judges to recognise the principle of legitimate expectations as being anything more than a species of the doctrine of promissory estoppel. This is one of the few cases in which an applicant has failed because of "no reliance", and indeed in a significant number of cases in which the applicant succeeded there appears to have been no reliance. However, in the most recent examination of this aspect of legitimate

---

101 *Ibid.* at 88.
102 [1989] I.L.R.M. 1 (High Ct.). This question did not feature on appeal to the Supreme Court which focussed on the reasonableness issue: see [1994] 1 I.L.R.M. 81.
103 [1991] 2 I.R. 43.

expectations in *Abrahamson v. Law Society of Ireland*,[104] McCracken J. expressly doubted whether detrimental reliance was necessary in a true legitimate expectations (as distinct from promissory estoppel) case.[105]

Must the promise have been communicated to the applicant?

There is also a line of authority to the effect that the claim for breach of legitimate expectation will not arise where the promise made by the representor was never communicated to the applicant. A further point is that any such representation must be unqualified and unambiguous. This point was made by Lardner J. in *Devitt v. Minister for Education*[106] where the plaintiff had submitted that since the Minister had allowed the applicant to apply for a permanent teaching post, she could not turn around and appoint the applicant to a mere temporary post. In the absence of an "unqualified assurance" (such as had been given in *Webb*), Lardner J. did not think that the applicant had acquired a legitimate expectation that she would be appointed to a permanent position:

> "There are really only two matters alleged as involving the Minister. [First] the fact that an inspector of the Department of Education sat on the board which interviewed the applicant and [secondly] the letter from the Department in reply to the applicant's inquiry as to the point of the salary scale at which the applicant had left her previous teaching appointment and would re-enter it if appointed. None of these matters appear to involve any assurance by the Minister of the kind contended for by the applicant."[107]

Thus, in *Nolan v. Minister for Environment*[108] Costello J. held that the applicant could not rely on an alleged representation in a letter sent to her local residents' association in the absence of evidence that this representation was communicated to her at the relevant time. Likewise, in *Re "La Lavia"*[109] O'Flaherty J. rejected the plea of legitimate expectations in the absence of an explicit representation causing the applicants to act to their reliance, as the "whole idea of a promise is that it has to make an impression on the mind of the promisee".[110] It should be noted, however, that in that case O'Flaherty J. left open the possibility that a regular practice might in and of itself establish an entitlement to a legitimate expectation.

Yet in *Fakih v. Minister for Justice*[111] the applicants (who were Lebanese asylum seekers) were held to be entitled to rely on the terms of (an admittedly solemn) commitments given regarding the treatment of asylum seekers contained in a letter

---

[104] [1996] 1 I.R. 403

[105] This matter is considered above, pp. 874–875.

[106] [1989] I.L.R.M. 636.

[107] *Ibid.* at 650–651. In *John M.P. Greaney Ltd v. Dublin Corporation* [1994] 3 I.R. 384 Morris J. held (at 392) that a legitimate expectations plea failed on the facts as "nothing in the nature of a firm assurance was ever given to the first applicant as an integral part of the transaction under which it lodged the application."

[108] [1989] I.R. 357.

[109] [1996] 1 I.L.R.M. 194.

[110] *Ibid.* at 200. Note that in *Devitt v. Minister for Education* [1989] I.L.R.M. 639, Lardner J. held that the applicant could not rely on the terms of a memorandum issued by the Minister to local authorities, since it had never been intended to communicate this information to the public at large.

[111] [1993] 2 I.R. 406. See also pp. 868–869.

written by the Minister to the United Nations High Commissioner for Refugees, but in respect of which the applicants could have had no advance knowledge prior to their illegal entry into the State. Perhaps the case law can be reconciled on the basis that in the latter case the Minister had intended to lay down binding procedures applicable to all appropriate cases, whereas the documents in *Nolan* and *Devitt* were in the nature of internal memoranda which were not expressed to be for the benefit of the public at large.

When is an expectation "legitimate"?

The major reason why the plaintiff failed in *Wiley* was Blayney J.'s finding that it was necessary for the applicant to show not only that he had an expectation that he would receive the refund; but also that such an expectation was a legitimate one:

> "I am prepared to accept that [the applicant] had an expectation that he would get a refund. This arose from the fact that he had got such a refund on two previous occasions. But I am unable to accept that his expectation could be said to be a legitimate expectation. It did not derive from his having been eligible under the scheme to get the refund since it is now conceded that he was not. [I]t is only [where the applicant] considered that he was entitled to the refund that he could have a legitimate expectation of getting it again. Otherwise, at best, all he could have believed was that he had a good chance of getting it because he had got it twice before. And no doubt that would have been a reasonable belief. But it fell far short of being a legitimate expectation. Such expectation as he had could only have been the result of a failure to appreciate what any reasonable person ought to have known [about the relevant criteria] and for that reason could not in my opinion constitute a legitimate expectation. And, of course, if he did in fact know what it seems to me he ought to have known, there could be no question of his having any real expectation, let alone a legitimate one."[112]

5. Legitimate Expectations Cannot Prevail Against Legislation

There are other limits to the scope of legitimate expectations. The principles discussed above in sections 2 and 3 of this chapter would seem to require that the doctrine could not be invoked – save, perhaps, in very special cases such as *Phillips v. Medical Council*[113] – to limit the scope of a statutory power. *A fortiori* – and this is the subject of the present part – it cannot surely be invoked to prevent the enactment or enforcement of legislation.[114] This point is illustrated by *Pesca Valentia Ltd v.*

---

[112] *Wiley v. The Revenue Commissioner* [1989] I.R. 350 at 355. See also *Donohue v. Revenue Commissioners* [1993] 1 I.R. 172 where Blayney J. found that a revenue official either knew or ought to have been aware that his assignment to a particular post would terminate after seven years, so that, on the facts, no question of a legitimate expectation ever arose.

[113] [1991] 2 I.R. 115.

[114] *cf.* the comments of Lord Diplock in *Hughes v. Department of Health and Social Security* [1985] A.C. 776 at 788 to the effect that the liberty to change administrative policy was "inherent in our

Minister for Fisheries[115] where it was argued that the conduct of certain semi-sponsored agencies such as the Industrial Development Authority gave rise to a legitimate expectation on the part of the plaintiffs that no fundamental legislative changes would be made affecting their right to fish.[116] Keane J. rejected this contention:

> "[W]hile the plaintiffs were undoubtedly encouraged in their project by semi-state bodies, they were not given any assurance that the law regulating fishing would never be altered so as adversely to affect them nor, if such an assurance had been given, could any legal rights have grown from it. *No such 'estoppel' could conceivably operate so as to prevent the Oireachtas from legislating or the executive from implementing the legislation when enacted.*"[117]

Keane J. was, probably, here drawing on two fundamental constitutional principles, each of which may be regarded, at some level, as stemming from the separation of powers and the rule of law. The first of these is that the executive arm of government (or, any other third party, *e.g.* as in the instant case, a state-sponsored body) cannot commit the legislature as to the laws it will or will not make. Secondly – and here we come to a doctrine which is analogous to the precept that one cannot fetter a discretionary power – the legislature's power of law-making cannot be fettered probably even by the Oireachtas itself (though an attempt to do this would be rather unlikely). This is inherent in the nature of the organs of government. It is also implicit, in particular, in Article 15.2.1° ("The sole and exclusive power of making of making laws . . . is hereby vested in the Oireachtas").

Another illustration of this is provided by *Nova Media Services Ltd v. Minister for Posts and Telegraphs*[118] Here the plaintiffs operated an illegal radio station without a licence. When their equipment was seized by officials from the Department, the plaintiffs sought an interlocutory injunction restraining the defendant from interfering with their broadcasting activities pending the outcome of a challenge to the constitutional validity of the broadcasting legislation. The plaintiff argued that the official inaction and tacit co-operation from the Minister, public representatives and State agencies had encouraged them "to enter into and to expand the particular business in which they are now engaged". Murphy J. expressed sympathy with their dilemma, but said that:

---

constitutional form of government". For a particularly graphic example, see *R . v. Secretary of State for Health, ex p. US Tobacco International Ltd* [1992] 1 Q.B. 353.

[115] [1990] 2 I.R. 305.

[116] See also the *U.S. Tobacco Case*, above n.114.

[117] *Ibid.* at 323. (emphasis added). See also *Hempenstall v. Minister for the Environment* [1994] 2 I.R. 20 at 32, *per* Costello J. (no legitimate expectation or promissory estoppel to prevent the Minister from making new regulations). This was also echoed by Laffoy J. in *Kavanagh v. Government of Ireland* [1996] 1 I.R. 321. Here the plaintiff claimed that representations made on behalf of the Government at a hearing before the United Nations Human Rights Committee in 1993 meant that only persons associated with subversive actions connected with Northern Ireland could be returned for trial in the Special Criminal Court. This contention was, however, rejected by Laffoy J. She observed that the effect of a proclamation was governed by the provisions of the Offences against the State Act 1939 and that no "representation or utterance by a representative of the State can alter the effect of a law enacted by the Oireachtas". The Supreme Court took a similar view when dismissing the appeal.

[118] [1984] I.L.R.M. 161.

"If the position is that persons in authority are prepared to make use of and co-operate with illegal radio broadcasts, it is not surprising that the owners of those stations should assume that they have an immunity from the law or that, at the very least, the law would not be enforced against them. However, the effect of a statute is clear. It does not wither away from lack of use and it cannot be repealed, waived or abandoned, even by the express decision or agreement of the Executive or any administrator and still less by an explicit representation by public representatives or State agencies."[119]

It should be emphasised that what was involved here was not a commitment to exercise a discretionary power in a particular way but rather a promise to ignore a statute, moreover a statute creating a criminal offence. Seen in this light, the outcome was altogether unsurprising.

At first sight, *Duggan v. An Taoiseach*[120] appears to have been a legitimate expectations case and was, indeed, decided on that basis. It is suggested, however, that it can be better explained as an illustration of the wider principle under discussion here, namely, that the executive cannot change the law. In *Duggan* the appplicant civil servants challenged a decision of the Government to transfer them from the Farm Tax Office to another department following the purported suspension of the operation of the Farm Tax Act 1985. It was held by Hamilton P., in the first place, that because of the unusual nature of the applicants' transfer to the Farm Tax Office, and because the Office was established for a specific purpose and for a limited period, they could not have had any expectation that they would be allowed to remain in those posts on a permanent basis. Secondly, however, the applicants did have a legitimate expectation that they would continue in the post to which they had been appointed in an acting capacity until the work of the Office was either completed or "terminated in accordance with law ". Hamilton P., thus, held that the unlawful decision of the Government to suspend the operation of the Farm Tax Office constituted an infringement of the applicant's legitimate expectations, for it should be emphasised that a central feature of the case was that the 1985 Act imposed an obligation on the Government to pursue the work on which the civil servants were engaged in the office. Although the terminology of legitimate expectations was prominent in *Duggan*, there was in fact no need to invoke this principle. As Hamilton P. himself explained, the work of the Farm Tax Office was to continue until it had been "terminated in accordance with law".[121] Thus, it appears that the basic principle of the case is that the Government is subject to the law and cannot, of itself, change the law (in this case, the Farm Tax Act 1985).

Yet, there have been at least two other cases in which the courts have apparently been prepared to allow a legitimate expectation to prevail against a statute. The first of these is *Waterford Harbour Commissioners v. British Railway Board*[122] where the Supreme Court effectively held that a statutory provision had been allowed to fall into disuse. The facts were that the defendants were under a statutory duty

---

119 [1984] I.L.R.M. 161 at 169.
120 [1989] I.L.R.M. 710.
121 *Ibid.* at 728.
122 [1979] I.L.R.M. 296.

imposed by section 70 of the Fishguard and Rosslare Railways and Harbours Act 1898 to provide a daily steamer service between Waterford and the Welsh coast. Political considerations, changed commercial trends and the advent of war all combined to undermine the viability of the provision of a daily service. The parties reached an agreement in 1939 by which the defendants agreed to provide a thrice-weekly service while the plaintiffs undertook not to sue for damages for breach of statutory duty. When the defendants gave notice of intention to discontinue the service in 1977, the plaintiffs sued for damages for breach of statutory duty and for breach of contract. A majority of the Supreme Court held that while the plaintiffs could sue for breach of contract, they were now estopped from pursuing the claim for breach of statutory duty, since by their conduct they had led the defendants to believe that their statutory obligations were "moribund or dead". Henchy J. added:

> "Thus, so far as the plaintiffs were concerned, from 1939 to 1977, section 70 had been allowed to become a dead letter. In the circumstances, the plaintiffs are estopped from reverting to the position they were in when they could justifiably have said that section 70 should be complied with."[123]

In respect of this surprising passage, the following three points of criticism or limitation may be adduced. First, this rare pre-*Webb* example of a successful plea of legitimate expectation was founded not upon practice but upon a formal agreement not to sue for damages, which had been renewed on several occasions over a 40-year period. Secondly, notwithstanding the language used in the passage quoted, the same result could have been reached by a holding that these particular parties had reached an agreement by which the plaintiffs promised not to enforce their statutory rights, *i.e.* in effect, an out of court settlement. This is a fairly common arrangement, at any rate as between private parties and there appears no reason why it should be different where the defendant is a public body. It is altogether different from a commitment either to change or not to change the law. By "law" we mean an Act of the Oireachtas. (The reason for making this definitional point is that we assume that the position in regard to the making of a statutory instrument adopted by the case law, seems to be the same as for the exercise of any other statutory discretionary power so that there are no distinctive features requiring discussion here.) Finally, the language of the judgment notwithstanding ("dead letter"), *Waterford Harbour* is not a case of desuetude and thus, following on from the second point, there was nothing to stop a person who was not a party to the agreement – for instance, the Attorney General – from enforcing the statutory rights in question.

The other controversial case is *Conroy v. Garda Commissioner*.[124] The facts were that the plaintiff had been injured in the course of his duties as a member of the Garda Síochána. He duly commenced proceedings under the Garda Síochána (Compensation) Acts. It was agreed between the parties that the case for compensation would be heard on the following basis: that the plaintiff would retire from the Gardaí on a 100 per cent disability pension and Finlay P. duly made his award to the plaintiff. It was subsequently determined that the plaintiff was entitled only

---

123 [1979] I.L.R.M. 296 at 353.
124 [1989] I.R. 140.

to a 66 per cent pension and fresh proceedings were then commenced claiming that he had now a legitimate expectation that he would receive a 100 per cent disability pension.

Hamilton P. first dealt with the estoppel argument and rejected the contention that the plaintiff could be awarded a full disability pension by agreement:

> "[T]he payment of a special pension is governed by the statutes, statutory orders and regulations relating to the pensions of members of An Garda Síochána and the procedures therein set forth must be followed. Consequently, I am satisfied that it was not open to the respondent in the Garda Síochána (Compensation) Act proceedings, or any person acting on his behalf to enter into an enforceable agreement with the applicant to grant him a special pension on the basis of 100 per cent disability and that no enforceable agreement with regard thereto was entered into."[125]

Despite the failure of the estoppel argument, the plaintiff had nonetheless acquired a legitimate expectation that he would receive a full pension. The reason was that the sum awarded by Finlay P. in the earlier compensation proceedings would almost certainly have been greater had he but known that the plaintiff would only have received a 66 per cent pension. According to Hamilton P.:

> "The matter was dealt with by [Finlay P.] on the basis that the plaintiff would be entitled to and would be awarded a special pension based on 100 per cent disability. The actuarial evidence before him was based on this assumption and counsel appearing on behalf of the Minister for the Public Service did not object to this or in any way suggest that the plaintiff would not be awarded a special pension based on 100 per cent disability. In the events which have happened the plaintiff in those proceeding had, in my opinion, a legitimate expectation or reasonable expectation that he would have been awarded a 100 per cent disability pension."[126]

Thus, on one view, an estoppel was allowed to prevail against the terms of a statutory provision. This flies in the face of the well-established orthodoxy, restated in cases *Nova Media Services*[127] and *Pesca Valentia*[128] – that a statutory provision cannot be allowed – in the words of Murphy J. in *Nova Media Services* – to be "repealed, waived or abandoned" by decision or agreement. Accordingly, it may be best to classify *Conroy* as a case where the plaintiff was compensated – via the legitimate expectations doctrine – for the innocent misrepresentation made by the Minister for the Public Service at the time of the earlier case. This basis also has the merit of reconciling the two passages, just quoted, with each other.

Unconstitutionality?

Can the provisions of the Constitution be used to buttress some version of the legitimate expectation doctrine, in however attenuated a form? If this were the case,

---

125   *Ibid.* at 144.
126   *Ibid.* at 147.
127   [1984] I.L.R.M. 161.
128   [1990] 2 I.R. 305.

this version might be drawn upon not only as against the Oireachtas, (a point which would be relevant to the group of cases just analysed) and against the executive where it was the executive which had dishonoured some expectation and was seeking to rely on the precept against fettering discretionary powers. Since this line of argument has yet to be determined by the courts, it is worth testing it by reference to hypothetical cases.

One particular point of difficulty arising in this context concerns the precise source in the Constitution of this possible version of the doctrine. In the first place, depending upon the strength of the commitment entered into, by the applicant, in reliance on the expectation, it might be possible to argue that a change of law amounted to an illegitimate interference with property rights, contrary to Article 40.3.2° and Article 43. Take, as an example, legislative reductions in the tax allowance bestowed on those who had entered into a long-term loan commitment in order to purchase a house. A home-owner might wish to argue that he had entered into a loan contract to borrow money and repay it, over a 20-year period, and had done this in reliance on the tax regime remaining the same as at the time when he had entered this contract, which was long before such a change was contemplated. The home owner would probably argue – plausibly – that a contract is a form of property right. However, it seems overwhelmingly likely that a submission along these lines would fail on two grounds, namely: (i) that there was no direct interference with the contract, but only a substantial alteration in the surrounding taxation regime;[129] (ii) more significantly, there *should* be no such expectation: given the vicissitudes of public finance (including uncertainties of both income and expenditure), would any reasonable person suppose that the Oireachtas could be committing itself to follow a fixed policy in this field?

It is true that argument (i) would not exist in the case of those who have invested on the strength of direct legislative assurances – *e.g.* the 10-year tax rebates afforded in the case of approved investments in designated areas under the Urban Renewal Act 1986. However, in this example – the more basic objection – argument (ii) would persist: it would be a very strong thing to argue that the Oireachtas was restricted in its reaction to the needs of State economic policy.

Take, next, an example of a situation in which neither argument (i) nor (because so few people are involved) argument (ii) would exist. Suppose the Government were to give an unequivocal promise to an individual (or an ascertainable group of individuals) working in the Irish public service that if they go to work for some international organisation, an arrangement would be made to ensure that their pensions would be worth the same as if they had continued to work in the public service here. Assuming that no such arrangement were made and assuming too that no specific legislation were necessary, it seems probable[130] that, in such an extreme case, the employees could succeed against the executive on the basis of common

---

[129] *cf. Kerry Co-Operative v. An Bord Báinne* [1990] I.L.R.M. 642, where Costello J. held in the context of the rights of a shareholder in a registered society, that although the contract was a type of constitutional property right, there was no implied term in the contract between the shareholder and the society that the fractional interest of the company's share capital, which it represented, would remain constant.

[130] See, *e.g. Webb v. Ireland* [1988] I.R. 353 *Staunton v. St. Lawrence's Hospital,* unreported, High Court, February 21, 1986.

law legitimate expectations (*i.e.* with no constitutional contribution) legitimate – always provided that no change of law is required.

However, if by contrast, a legislative change were required in this context, then the first of the employees' legal difficulties would be that there is no specific provision in the Constitution – such as the property rights – to sustain their case. Nevertheless, in other areas, the courts have been prepared to hold, even without a specific constitutional provision, that the State must behave in a conventionally constitutional manner.[131] Likewise, here the courts might be prepared to rely on some notion of the rule of law, including a requirement of fair and reliable dealing by the State which could be conjured from the general structure and assumptions of the Constitution, including Article 40.1 (equality before the law) and the capacious Article 40.3.1° (unenumerated rights). If this were done, the only remaining difficulty would lie in the fact that the type of situation under discussion (and many of the others which could have been hypothesised) would require a court to make an order directing the Oireachtas to bring in a specified law. This is a rather considerable, if not insuperable, obstacle, the precise difficulties of which are discussed, in another context, below.[132]

6. Summary

In view of the roller-coaster course taken by the law over the past decade and also by way of attempting to give some guidance for the future, it may be useful at this point to attempt a brief stock-taking:

1. Notwithstanding the language actually used in the case, it might be more realistic to explain *Webb* as essentially a private law case which may be sustained on the basis of promissory estoppel, without any necessity to haul out into the broader reaches of legitimate expectations. It has also been argued that the *Waterford Harbour* case[133] may also be regarded as a private law case.

2. One distinct area exists where the applicant is seeking to rely upon a legitimate expectation relating not to the law as it was or was said to be; but rather as to a change of law (or abstention from change) which has allegedly been promised. Subject to any possibility of constitutional intervention,[134] the legitimate expectations doctrine can certainly not be invoked in this context: see *Pesca Valentia*.[135] Related to this is the notion that even the executive must obey the law: see *Duggan*.[136]

3. Where procedural rights are concerned, it seems clear from cases like *Fakih v. Minister for Justice*[137] and *Gutrani*,[138] supported by similar cases in other jurisdictions, that the doctrine can be invoked to require the observance of such rights.

---

131 See, *e.g. Byrne v. Ireland* [1972] I.R. 241; *McKenna v. An Taoiseach* (No.2) [1995] 2 I.R. 10.
132 But *cf.* the rather ambiguous approach taken by the Supreme Court in *McMenamin v. Ireland* [1996] 3 I.R. 100 on the precise issue of whether the Courts could actually direct the Oireachtas to legislate in respect of a particular matter.
133 [1979] I.L.R.M. 296.
134 See pp. 887–888.
135 [1985] I.R. 193.
136 [1989] I.L.R.M. 710.
137 [1993] 2 I.R. 406. See also *Navan Tanker Services Ltd v. Meath County Council*, unreported, High Court, December 13, 1996.
138 [1993] 2 I.R. 427.

4. Earlier,[139] we referred to a distinction which might be drawn between a misrepresentation which arises because a law had, at the initial point, been misunderstood by some public authority and, on the other hand, one occurring where there is a statutory discretion which had been exercised differently at the initial and the later stages. In fact, most of the Irish cases so far have been of this latter type. And in a large number of cases of this type – *Nova Media*,[140] *Tara Prospecting*,[141] *Gilheany*,[142] *Egan*,[143] *Devitt*,[144] *Abrahamson*,[145] and probably *Wiley*,[146] – the traditional teaching that the executive cannot fetter its statutory discretion has re-asserted itself, in preference to the legitimate expectations doctrine. There are only two decisions (to be described in the following part) in which the two lines of policy have been in conflict, and where the legitimate expectations doctrine has prevailed. One of these, *Latchford v. Minister for Industry and Commerce*[147] is now a rather old case, in which the countervailing precept of not fettering executive discretion was not even mentioned. *Staunton v. St. Lawrence's Hospital*[148] was a similar type of case and it is probably significant that neither case concerned the exercise of a *statutory* power and that, in each, the basis of the legitimate expectation was a circular.

5. The first category, mentioned in paragraph 4 above, concerned a misunderstanding or misapplication, of the law, which had been communicated to the applicant and thus, it was claimed, gave rise to a legitimate expectation. It may, for policy reasons explained in the discussion of *Carbury Products*,[149] be apt to single out cases in this category and to treat them differently from cases involving the exercise of a statutory discretion.

6. A fixed and settled practice may of itself give rise to a legitimate expectation: see, *e.g. Webb* (semble) and *Eogan v. University College, Dublin*.[150]

7. A public body will be permitted to resile from an earlier commitment or settled practice if this is justified by a change of position: see, *e.g. Egan*, *Eogan* and *Abrahamson*.

7. Administrative Circulars and Legitimate Expectations

The cases disclose that one of the most common ways in which legitimate expectations have been created is by way of an administrative circular. An early

---

[139] See above pp. 886–887.
[140] [1984] I.L.R.M. 161.
[141] [1993] I.L.R.M. 771.
[142] [1996] E.L.R. 25.
[143] Unreported, High Court, November 24, 1988.
[144] [1989] I.L.R.M. 639.
[145] [1996] 1 I.R. 403.
[146] [1994] 2 I.R. 160.
[147] [1950] I.R. 33.
[148] Unreported, High Court, February 21, 1986. See below, pp. 891–892.
[149] See p. 876.
[150] [1996] 2 I.L.R.M. 302. But *cf.* the comments of Barr J. in *Egan* and McGuinness J. in *Maigueside Communications Ltd v. IRTC*, unreported, High Court, July 17, 1997.

example of this is provided by *Latchford v. Minister for Industry and Commerce*,[151] which concerned a ministerial scheme providing for the payment of subsidies to bakers. This published scheme contained certain conditions, with all of which the plaintiffs had complied. The Minister refused to sanction the payment of the subsidy on the ground that the plaintiffs had been convicted of an offence relating to the sale of bread. The published conditions, however, did not disqualify a claimant on this ground. The Supreme Court accordingly made a declaration that the Minister was not entitled to withhold payment of the subsidy, with Murnaghan J. commenting:

"After having made and published the conditions on which the payment of subsidy would be made, the Minister can alter these conditions from time to time; but until altered or withdrawn, the conditions apply, and persons who have complied with the conditions are entitled to claim that they have qualified for payment of the subsidy."[152]

This is a classic example of where an administrative circular may be said to have created legitimate expectations, although, of course, the Supreme Court did not use this language as such. It is worth noting, however, that the scheme in *Latchford* appeared to be an ad hoc, non-statutory administrative one. If, however, one changes the facts of *Latchford* slightly, the possible limitations of this decision become evident. Assume that the Minister had been vested with a statutory power to grant the subsidy "in suitable cases" and that the conditions for the award of the subsidy had been duly published by administrative circular. Even in a case where the plaintiff had complied with every prescribed detail (and duly changed position to his detriment in the process), the line of authority described in section 4 of this chapter, if observed suggests that a plea of legitimate expectations would be unavailing, since this would cut across the exercise of a discretionary power.

Another instance is provided by *Staunton v. St. Lawrence's Hospital*,[153] where the defendants had acted on foot of a Departmental circular issued by the Department of Health and arranged for the payment of special salary increases to certain consultants. The Department subsequently sought to issue a new circular revoking these special increases, but by this stage the hospital had entered into a new contract with the plaintiff which provided for these special payments. The hospital then claimed the cost of these additional payments from the State. It was common case that there was no statutory obligation or discretion imposed on the Minister for Health to make the reimbursements claimed by the hospital. Nevertheless, Lardner J. concluded that the State was bound by the terms of the original circular:

"When the hospital acted in accordance with, and in reliance upon its terms, clause 12 [of the circular] gave rise to a contractual obligation which bound the Minister to adjust the hospital's financial allocation to the extent that was

---

151 [1950] I.R. 33.
152 *Ibid.* at 40–41. In *Anisimova v. Minister for Justice*, unreported, Supreme Court, November 28, 1997 Murphy J. suggested that earlier decisions such as *Fakih v. Minister for Justice* [1993] 2 I.R. 406 and *Gutrani v. Minister for Justice* [1993] 2 I.R. 427 were best explained not so much by reference to the doctrine of legitimate expectations, but rather by the principle identified in *Latchford*, *i.e.* that the Minister was bound by the terms of the scheme which he had himself established.
153 Unreported, High Court, February 21, 1986.

necessary to cover the additional cost incurred by the hospital in respect of the common contract made with the plaintiff."[154]

While this case may also be readily classified as one of legitimate expectations arising from reliance upon the terms of an administrative circular, it could be regarded as a case of promissory estoppel. The hospital had acted, to its detriment, upon a representation made by the Department and was allowed to use the estoppel not merely as a "shield", but also as a cause of action in itself to recover the moneys in question from the State.

But suppose that in *Latchford* the scheme had been superimposed on a statutory provision which had provided that the Minister may pay the subsidy in such circumstances "as he deems fit and proper". It is at this point that the doctrine of legitimate expectations runs up against the principle (discussed above in section 2) that there can be no estoppel in respect of the exercise of statutory powers. One way of explaining why, in *Latchford* and *Staunton* the doctrine of legitimate expectations triumphed is that in these cases the expectation arose from a circular and circulars are – and are intended to – taken seriously by administrators and citizenry, few of whom readily appreciate the difference between a law and a circular. However, an argument concerning the impact of legitimate expectations derived from a circular failed in *Devitt v. Minister for Education.*[155] In this case, the applicant had been appointed to a permanent teaching post by the County Dublin Vocational Education Committee. Under section 23 of the Vocational Education Act 1930, an application for a full-time position was to be made in the first instance to the appropriate Vocational Education Committee. The Committee's appointment was, in turn, subject to the Minister's approval. A ministerial circular entitled Memorandum V7 issued in 1967 appeared to indicate that the Minister would abide by the Committee's decision, provided the person in question was duly qualified and there was satisfactory evidence of age, health and character. In this case, the Minister – in an apparent effort to reduce the number of teaching posts created by Vocational Education Committees – invoked her powers under section 23(2) of the 1930 Act and refused to give her consent to the appointment. It was argued that the Minister was confined to the matters referred to in the circular and could not invoke other matters in seeking to exercise her discretion. Lardner J. could not accept this submission:

---

[154] *Ibid.* at pp. 9–10 of the judgment. In *Donohue v. Revenue Commissioners* [1993] 1 I.R. 172 Blayney J. suggested that had the defendants refused to pay certain allowances specified in a circular as payable to certain of its employees in a circular that the applicant would have been entitled to sue in order to recover them.

[155] [1989] I.L.R.M. 639. Compare this reasoning with that of the English Court of Appeal in *R. v. Home Secretary, ex p. Khan* [1985] 1 All E.R. 40 where it was held that the Home Secretary was bound to follow the procedures set out in a circular issued by him concerning the entry of children into the United Kingdom for adoption purposes. He was not entitled to depart from those procedures without affording those affected an opportunity to be heard. Lardner J. considered that *Khan* was distinguishable on the grounds: (i) that the circular had not been issued to the general public; and (ii) the legitimate expectation contended for would be incompatible with the Minister's statutory duty. But surely the significant point of distinction is that *Khan* (like *Fakih v. Minister for Justice* [1993] 2 I.R. 406) was a case involving legitimate expectations in relation to the procedures to be followed, whereas the legitimate expectation at issue in *Devitt* concerned substantive grounds (the number of available teaching positions).

"No doubt in relation to the exercise of this statutory discretion the Minister may adopt general rules or procedures to guide herself or to notify other concerned parties as to the manner in which he will exercise his discretion provided that they are relevant to the exercise of his powers and are reasonable. But he is not in my view entitled by such rules or procedures to limit the scope of the discretion entrusted to him or disable himself from the full exercise of it. Nor in my judgment may such a practice be relied upon by the applicant as estopping a Minister from the full exercise of the discretion vested in her by the Act."[156]

8. Advance Rulings, etc., from the Revenue Commissioners and Legitimate Expectations

The administration of our tax laws would also seem likely to prove a fertile source of legitimate expectation claims. For it is a significant feature of tax practice in this jurisdiction that the Revenue Commissioners will sometimes give what have come to be known as "advance rulings"[157] on tax planning schemes, *i.e.* indicate their position in advance on whether a particular scheme will avoid a tax liability.[158] A second practice exists whereby the Revenue Commissioners will grant extra-statutory concessions to mitigate the rigour of the revenue code, although (in contrast to the practice prevailing in the United Kingdom) such concessions are not published. The reason for this refusal to publish is that the Revenue Commissioners

---

[156] *Ibid.* at 649.

[157] The term "advance ruling" was defined by the Commission on Taxation in their *Fifth Report* (p. 47) as "a statement by the Revenue Commissioners on how they will interpret legislative provisions in a given situation". In contrast, in *Pandion Haliaetus Ltd v. Revenue Commissioners* [1987] I.R. 309, Blayney J. appeared to be less enamoured of the term, saying (at 317) that there was no justification for attributing "the connotation of a final irreversible decision", as this term "advance ruling" was "not a term of art". The English courts have taken a more forthright view of this question, even though, in practice, the tax-payer has usually failed on the ground of lack of full disclosure: see *R . v. Inland Revenue Commissioners, ex p. Preston* [1985] A.C. 835; *R. v. Inland Revenue Commissioners, ex p. MFK Ltd* [1990] 1 All E.R. 91; and *Matrix Securities Ltd v. Inland Revenue Commissioners* [1994] 1 All E.R. 769 (both cases where the tax-payer failed by reason of the absence of full disclosure). In the former case Bingham L.J. observed (at 110): "No doubt a statement formally published by the Revenue to the world at large might safely be regarded as binding, subject to its terms, in any case clearly falling within them."

[158] Reardon, "The Operation of the Revenue Commissioners in Relation to Inland Revenue Matters" (Unpublished LL.M. thesis, University College, Cork, 1989) comments as follows (pp. 123–124):
    "There is no general clearance or rulings procedure for transactions. The only exceptions are cases in which incentive reliefs for projects with which the Industrial Development Authority or another State agency is associated: see the White Paper, "Industrial Policy" (July, 1984), para. 8.5. The policy behind this exception is to attract foreign industry and investment to Ireland. So the general rule is that the Revenue Commissioners do not give advance rulings which are binding on Inspectors of Taxes when the latter come to compute tax liability, grant exemptions, reliefs or allowances or issue notices of assessment in individual cases. The reasons for this were outlined by the Revenue Commissioners to the Commission on Taxation (see *Fifth Report*, at para. 3.9) as follows:
    (i) the volume of work to which this would give rise would be enormous;
    (ii) the facts put before the Revenue Commissioners are often inconsistent with the final position;
    (iii) the Revenue Commissioners could be liable for damages if the courts overturned their opinion; and
    (iv) they do not wish to facilitate tax avoidance."

assert that extra-statutory concessions exist on an individual basis and that general concessions are not allowed and, therefore, do not exist. The Commission on Taxation in its *Fifth Report* expressed dissatisfaction with this attitude, saying that if the interpretation of a particular piece of legislation amounts to the granting of an extra-statutory concession, then the same interpretation should apply in all similar situations.[159] Finally, there are occasional statements of practice by the Revenue Commissioners, indicating generally what attitude they will take in regard to the interpretation and application of certain legislation. The Commission on Taxation concluded that the Revenue Commissioners were reticent to acknowledge the existence of these practices. Hard information on Revenue practice was difficult to come by and, in addition, the decentralisation of the Office of the Revenue Commissioners meant that there were inconsistencies in the operation of such practices.[160]

There would seem to be room for the operation of the doctrine of legitimate expectations in any of these three areas so as to prevent the Revenue officials from reneging on prior representations or from unilaterally altering settled practices or from treating similarly situated taxpayers in an inconsistent fashion. However, as in other areas, this doctrine must be reconciled with the conflicting principle that the Revenue Commissioners, like other public officials, cannot be estopped in the exercise of their statutory powers.[161]

This entire matter was considered by the House of Lords in *R. v. Inland Revenue Commissioners, ex p. Preston.*[162] The applicant had engaged in a series of sophisticated tax avoidance manoeuvres which had attracted the attention of the respondents. In 1978, the applicant arranged a settlement of his tax affairs, but as part of this arrangement, he was required to provide full information concerning certain share dealings. It subsequently transpired that the information supplied was, in Lord Templeman's words, "woefully inadequate" and in 1982, the respondents decided to reopen the earlier settlement. Was this a breach of the applicant's legitimate expectations or otherwise an abuse of power?

Significantly, Lord Templeman agreed that, in principle, judicial review would lie in a case of this sort where the Commissioners had sought unilaterally to renege on an earlier representation:

> "In principle, I see no reason why the appellant should not be entitled to judicial review of a decision taken by the commissioners if that decision is unfair to the appellant because the conduct of the commissioners is equivalent to a breach of contract or breach of representation. Such a decision falls within the ambit of an abuse of power for which in the present case judicial review is the sole remedy and an appropriate remedy."[163]

---

[159] *Ibid.* at para. 3.18.

[160] *Ibid.* at paras. 3.6 and 3.7.

[161] In *Matrix Securities Ltd v. Inland Revenue Commissioners* [1994] 1 All E.R. 769 Lord Griffiths stressed (at 781) that it would be wrong "to hold the Revenue to the mistaken clearance and allow the scheme to go ahead at a cost of some £38m. of lost revenue to the national exchequer", saying that it was one thing to hold the Revenue "to a clearance that has been acted on in good faith", but quite another not "to permit the correction of an error before it has been acted on".

[162] [1985] A.C. 835.

[163] *Ibid.* at 864–865. See also *R v. Inland Revenue Commissioners, ex p. MFK Ltd* [1990] 1 All E.R. 91 and *Matrix Securities Ltd v. Inland Revenue Commissioners* [1994] 1 All E.R. 769.

However, on the facts of the particular case, the claim failed because the applicant had not kept his side of the bargain: he had not disclosed relevant information in the manner requested by the respondents, so that it was not now unfair for the respondents to reopen earlier transactions.

A similar conclusion was arrived at on the facts by Blayney J. in *Pandion Haliaetus Ltd v. Revenue Commissioners*.[164] Here the Revenue Commissioners were asked for, and gave, their views on the tax implications of certain patent licensing transactions. However, as had happened in *Preston*, the judge was satisfied that the respondents had not been given full details of the schemes as actually adopted by the applicant companies, so that the applicants could not rely on official correspondence "as being binding rulings or expressions of opinion in relation to the tax implications of the scheme". However, what is more significant is that the judge went on to doubt whether such "advance rulings" could be binding:

> "[The applicant's case] assumes that when the Revenue Commissioners give a taxpayer an opinion on some query submitted to them, the taxpayer's Inspector is bound by that opinion and must act in accordance with it. I cannot see any legal basis for this. The Revenue Commissioners are not the agents of the Inspector of Taxes. And they would have to be his agents, acting with his authority, if their opinion was to bind him. [N]either can be identified with the other. Accordingly, an Inspector is not bound by a prior opinion expressed to the taxpayer by the Revenue Commissioners. So, in the present case, even if the Revenue Commissioners had expressed opinions beforehand on the actual transaction which took place, it does not follow that the Inspector would have been bound by that opinion."[165]

Even making allowance for the fact that *Pandion Haliaetus* was decided a few months before *Webb*, this approach (which, in any event, skirts the main issue under discussion here – the conflict between a taxation statute and an assurance given by the Revenue Commissioners) seems nonetheless unduly narrow and formalistic. Even if there is no formal relationship of agency between the Commissioners and an individual inspector, this fact would not appear to be crucial. There was, after all, no formal relationship of agency between the Director of the National Museum and the State in *Webb*, yet the former's "unqualified assurance" was sufficient to bind the latter. It would seem quite wrong and unfair if a similar assurance given by the Commissioners could, without further justification, be unilaterally reneged upon by an individual inspector and, in this respect, the wider view adopted by Lord Templeman in *Preston* is to be preferred.[166] One might link this observation with the distinction drawn earlier[167] between the exercise of a statutory discretion and the interpretation of a statutory provision. What is involved in Revenue Commissioners assurances is usually closer to the latter.

---

[164] [1987] I.R. 307.
[165] *Ibid*. at 318.
[166] A better example of the immunity under discussion might be the view that the Director of Public Prosecutions could not be estopped from prosecuting in an individual case by reason of an immunity purportedly granted by the Government.
[167] See above, pp. 864–865.

9. The Distinction Between Legitimate Expectations and Promissory Estoppel

In practice, these two principles may be regarded as convergent. So, for example, in *Kenny v. Kelly*[168] the applicant had been given an assurance that she could defer taking up a place at the Arts Faculty in University College, Dublin until the following academic year. Barron J. held that "whichever legal approach is adopted", the respondents were precluded by both the doctrine of legitimate expectations and that of promissory estoppel from reneging on that assurance. Barron J. added that:

> "The principle of promissory estoppel upon which [*Webb*] was based applies equally in the present case. The promise of a deferral was in effect a promise not to require the applicant to register and pay the balance of her fees in 1986, but a promise to permit her to do so instead in 1987. Such a promise to delay the enforcement of legal rights is of the essence of the doctrine of promissory estoppel as it has developed."[169]

There have been other judicial assertions which have gone so far as to state that the doctrine of legitimate expectations does not really represent an advance on the principle of promissory estoppel. In *Webb v. Ireland*,[170] Finlay C.J. said that:

> "It would appear that the doctrine of 'legitimate expectation' has not in those terms been the subject of any decision of our courts. However, the doctrine connoted by such expressions is but an aspect of the well recognised equitable concept of promissory estoppel whereby a promise or representation as to intention may in certain circumstances be held to be binding on the representor or promisor."[171]

Barr J. referred to this passage in *Cannon v. Minister for the Marine*[172] and added:

> "An analysis of the foregoing statement of the law establishes that the concept of legitimate expectation being derived from an equitable doctrine, must be reviewed in the light of equitable principles. The test is whether in all the circumstances it would be unfair or unjust to allow a party to resile from a position created or adopted by him which at the time gave rise to a legitimate expectation in the mind of another that that situation would continue and might be acted upon by him to his advantage."[173]

This more conservative view was echoed by Murphy J. in his judgment in *Garda Representative Association v. Ireland*,[174] where he said that the Supreme Court in

---

[168] [1988] I.R. 457.
[169] *Ibid.* at 463.
[170] [1988] I.R. 353.
[171] *Ibid.* at 384. This view was also endorsed by the Supreme Court in *Re "La Lavia"* [1996] 1 I.L.R.M. 194, although the Court did appear to acknowledge that there might be instances where the legitimate expectations doctrine might extend beyond the confines of promissory estoppel.
[172] [1991] I.L.R.M. 261.
[173] *Ibid.* at 266.
[174] [1989] I.R. 193.

Webb had been "reluctant to recognise this doctrine [of promissory estoppel] as a new and separate doctrine within our legal system."[175]

However, despite the fact that both principles have appeared to work in parallel in cases such as *Webb, Garda Representative Association* and *Kenny*, there would appear to be some important doctrinal differences which have yet to be fully explored fully explored by the courts. This was acknowledged by McCracken J. in *Abrahamson v. Law Society of Ireland*[176] when he said:

> "While there is no doubt that the doctrine of legitimate expectation is similar too and probably founded upon the equitable concept of promissory estoppel . . . it has in fact been extended well beyond the bounds of that doctrine. Promissory estoppel is largely defensive in its nature . . . Its use is basically to ensure that a person who has made a representation that they will not exercise some legitimate right is in fact bound by that expectation and cannot exercise the right. Furthermore, it is usually, although not exclusively, related to matters of private right rather than public law."[177]

In this case, the students in question had clearly relied on the representations which were given to them by the Law Society, thus giving rise to a legitimate expectation which was at least partially defeated by a subsequent change in circumstances.[178] McCracken J. also added that, unlike promissory estoppel, damages can be awarded for breach of a legitimate expectation.[179]

The following analysis of these doctrinal differences between the principles of promissory estoppel and legitimate expectations is, accordingly, tentatively advanced.

1. Strictly speaking, the principle of promissory estoppel can only apply to suspend or vary the legal rights already existing between the parties by virtue of a contractual or other similar relationship. This contractual element was clearly present in cases such as *Kenny v. Kelly*. Even in cases such as *Webb* (where there was, admittedly, no such contractual relationship) the relationship of bailor/bailee between the parties was sufficient to allow – on even the most orthodox view of the law – for the application of the promissory estoppel doctrine. Such a relationship is not, however, essential for legitimate expectations, as is evidenced by cases where the plaintiff has sought to rely on the settled practices of a public body or representations made by it to the public in general and not necessarily to particular individuals.

2. There must be an element of reliance or acting to one's detriment in order to give rise to a promissory estoppel. This would not seem to be essential in the

---

175 *Ibid.* at 203.
176 [1996] 1 I.R. 431.
177 *Ibid.*, 418–419.
178 See above pp. 874–875. McCracken J. also doubted that it was, in fact, necessary for the students to demonstrate detrimental reliance in order to give rise to the legitimate expectation.
179 McCracken J. instanced *Duggan v. An Taoiseach* [1989] I.L.R.M. 710 as establishing the principle that damages may be awarded for breach of a legitimate expectation. Indeed, *Cannon v. Minister for Marine* [1991] I.L.R.M. 261 and the *Abrahamson* case itself may be said to provide further examples of this principle, as in the latter case, McCracken J. declared his willingness, should this have proved necessary, to award damages if a breach of legitimate expectation were established.

case of legitimate expectations, which, focussing upon the behaviour of the decision-maker holds that the interests of consistency, good administration and equal treatment (it may be that Article 40.1 of the Constitution will some day be invoked here) may, in an appropriate case, of themselves require – without any element of reliance – that the decision-maker abide by its previous practice or representation. This point was made by the Privy Council in *Attorney General of Hong Kong v. Ng. Yuen Shiu*[180] where the representation made to the illegal immigrants was held to be enforceable for this reason, even though all the elements required to found a promissory estoppel were not have been present in such a case. To take another example: suppose the Government were formally to undertake to release certain prisoners if they, in turn, undertook to renounce violence? In this example, there is no contractual or analogous relationship between the parties and it would be difficult to say that the prisoners acted to their detriment (in the sense that "detriment" is traditionally understood by the law of contract) so as to give rise to a promissory estoppel. However, in an appropriate case (a rather considerable restriction),[181] the courts could well hold such a promise to be legally binding by virtue of the doctrine of legitimate expectations?[182] The Irish courts have yet, however, to address this important issue.

3. There is another reason why a claim of legitimate expectation applies to a wider category of cases than does a plea of estoppel. It arises from the fact that, of its nature, estoppel operates only if the author of the misrepresentation is himself involved in the case usually, it happens, as the defendant. By contrast, with a legitimate expectation, the author of the misrepresentation, who created the expectation, may be a third party to the case. In most of the decided cases, this factor made no difference since it happened that the author of the misrepresentation was a party to the case. However, there is a decision in which it might have been of significance. This is the *Pandion Haliaetus* case, the facts of which have just been described earlier.[183] Here, it appears from the language of the passage quoted that Blayney J. analysed the situation as involving a plea of estoppel with legitimate expectation not being considered. On this analysis, he went on to reject the plaintiff's argument on the basis that the representation was given by the Revenue Commissioners, a separate entity from the Inspector of Taxes, who was the defendant in the case.

---

[180] [1983] 2 A.C. 629.

[181] Of course, one excludes from consideration, on public policy grounds, cases where the Government acted under duress or threats, such as where a promise to release a prisoner was made following a hostage-taking incident or kidnapping. But, equally, notice that any argument founded on the possible notion that the power of pardon is not subject to judicial review has now been exploded: see above pp. 681–682.

[182] In 1957 the Government made such a promise to internees who were interned under the Offences against the State (Amendment) Act 1940 in return for an undertaking not to engage in violent or unconstitutional activity. Interestingly enough, in *Lawless v. Ireland* (No. 3) (1978) 1 E.H.R.R. 15 at 34 (decided in 1961) the European Court of Human Rights made the following *obiter* observations:
"In a democratic country such as Ireland, the existence of this guarantee of release given publicly by the Government constituted a legal obligation on the Government to release all persons who have the undertaking."

[183] See p. 895.

4. By contrast, the next point of difference would seem to make it easier to establish a plea of estoppel. For if a public body makes an unambiguous representation to a private individual who then alters his position such as to give rise to a promissory estoppel, then it would seem to be irrelevant that, subsequently, new factors have come to light since then which would, objectively speaking, justify the body in question in changing its position or resiling from its representation.[184] The same would not, however, seem to be true of legitimate expectations. For example, had the defendants in *Egan v. Minister for Defence*[185] made a representation to the plaintiff which had given to a promissory estoppel, then it would have been no answer for the Minister to say that new factors had subsequently emerged which justified him in resiling from that promise. However, as we have seen, Barr J. was of the view that, even if there were a practice giving rise to a legitimate expectation, new factors (such as the increasing depletion of Air Corps personnel) would have justified the Minister in departing from that practice. Similar thinking is to be found in the speeches of the House of Lords in *GCHQ*, where new supervening national security considerations were found to justify a departure from the previous practice giving rise to a legitimate expectation.

5. It is quite clear that the doctrine of legitimate expectations is a principle whose operation is confined to the public law sphere and that it cannot be invoked in a purely private law dispute, even if the defendant were a public authority. This point does not appear to have expressly considered in this jurisdiction,[186] but it seems to follow from the first principles summarised in the preceding paragraphs, particularly from the principle, examined in paragraph 2, *viz.* that the principle of legitimate expectations contains an additional element over and above that of promissory estoppel, namely, that it is in the interests of fairness and good administration that a public body should not lightly or arbitrarily resile from a previous representation. By contrast, and subject only to the doctrine of promissory estoppel, a private citizen or undertaking is, in general, free to be as arbitrary as he pleases in his dealings.[187] Lord Diplock was very much alive to this private law/public law dichotomy in *O'Reilly v. Mackman*,[188] where the plaintiff prisoners challenged a disciplinary decision forfeiting remission of sentence:

---

[184] As opposed to circumstances which were known to at least one of the parties at the date of the transaction which is said to give rise to the promissory estoppel: see, *e.g. D. & C. Builders Ltd v. Rees* [1966] 2 Q.B. 617. Here the defendants (who were fully aware of the plaintiffs' precarious financial position) had unfairly extracted a promise from them to accept a smaller sum in respect of certain debts. The English Court of Appeal found that, in the circumstances, it would not be inequitable for the plaintiffs to go back on their promise and they could sue for the balance of the debts. The decision would almost certainly have gone the other way if the defendants could have shown: (i) that their precarious financial situation had arisen after the original promise had been made; and (ii) they had altered their circumstances in reliance on that promise.

[185] Unreported, High Court, November 24. 1988.

[186] However, this seems implicit in the judgment of Shanley J. in *Eogan v. University College Dublin* [1996] 2 I.L.R.M. 302. Moreover, in *Duggan v. An Taoiseach* [1989] I.L.R.M. 710 Hamilton P. said that in appropriate cases, the courts will protect a legitimate expection "by judicial review as a matter of public law".

[187] Of course, commercial undertakings are subject to numerous restraints – ranging from the Employment Equality Act 1977 to the Competition Acts 1991–1996 – which seek to curtail arbitrary and unfair labour and trade practices. The general point nonetheless holds true.

[188] [1983] 2 A.C. 237.

"So far as private law is concerned, all that each appellant had was a legitimate expectation, based upon his knowledge of what is the general practice, that he would be granted the maximum remission. In public law, as distinguished from private law, however, such legitimate expectation gave to each appellant a sufficient interest to challenge the legality of the adverse disciplinary award made against him by the board."[189]

10. *Res Judicata* and *Functus Officio*

One particular specialised species of estoppel is *res judicata*. The doctrine of *res judicata*, in relation to the judgment of a court, has been defined in the following manner by Holmes L.J.:

"A judgment not appealed from binds the parties and privies for all time by what appears on its face; and if it can be shown that, in the course of the action that resulted in the judgment, a certain definite material issue not set forth in the judgment itself was raised by the parties and determined judicially or by consent, it would be contrary to public policy to allow the same parties to re-agitate the same matter in subsequent legal proceedings."[190]

The two aspects of *res judicata* are contained in this passage. First, a "cause of action" estoppel precludes the same parties from relitigating an action which has been finally determined by a court of competent jurisdiction – this is *res judicata* "in its most essential form".[191] Secondly, an "issue estoppel" (or "constructive *res judicata*") prevents the parties to the earlier proceedings litigating an essential feature – "a certain definite material issue" – of the earlier decision.[192] In addition, however, a judgment *in rem* binds not only the parties to the litigation, but conclusively determines the status of a particular *res* or thing.[193]

A particular feature of this broad and difficult area of the law is that the doctrine of *res judicata* has hitherto had a limited application in regard to administrative decisions.[194] Such decisions rarely fulfil the required probanda for *res judicata*: they do not deal with matters of status[195] and generally do not involve a *lis* between private individuals.[196] More fundamentally, a rigid application of the doctrine might conflict with two essential principles of administrative law: that jurisdiction cannot be created by estoppel, and that statutory powers and duties may not be fettered.[197]

---

[189] [1983] 2 A.C. 237 at 275.
[190] *Irish Land Commission v. Ryan* [1900] 2 I.R. 565 at 584. For a general discussion of this topic see Spencer Bower, Turner, *Res Judicata* (1969).
[191] Spencer Bower, Turner, *ibid.* p. 149.
[192] *D. v. C.* [1984] I.L.R.M. 173; *Hoystead v. Federal Taxation Commissioner* [1926] A.C. 155.
[193] See, *e.g. Abrahamson v. Law Society of Ireland* [1996] 1 I.R. 403 (earlier finding by High Court that part of a particular statutory instrument was invalid on the ground that it discriminated on grounds of nationality, contrary to Art. 6 of the E.C. Treaty operated as a judgment *in rem* and was thus generally binding, even though other parties may not have been parties to the earlier action.)
[194] Ganz, "Estoppel and Res Judicata in Administrative Law" [1965] *Public Law* 237.
[195] *McMahon v. Leahy* [1984] I.R. 525 (prior extradition order).
[196] *R v. Fulham Tribunal, ex p. Zerek* [1951] 2 K.B. 1 at 11, *per* Devlin J.
[197] *Bradshaw v. M'Mullan* [1920] 2 I.R. 412 (prior court settlement contrary to Local Government (Ireland) Act 1898; plea of *res judicata* failed as one cannot give "judicial effect to a transaction

Subject to all these qualifications, the doctrine of *res judicata* is not confined to courts of law but may also apply in certain circumstances to tribunals and administrative authorities with powers to make binding determinations.[198]

That *res judicata* can only have a limited application in administrative law is well illustrated by a series of important decisions concerning rating and taxation. In *Society of Medical Officers of Health v. Hope*[199] a medical society successfully claimed before a Lands Tribunal that it was entitled to an exemption from rates. Some years later, a fresh valuation list was drawn up. Upon a further attempt being made to assess the society, *res judicata* was pleaded before the Lands Tribunal. Although it was conceded that there had been no material change of circumstances, the House of Lords ruled that no such estoppel arose. Emphasis was placed on the limited nature of the tribunal's jurisdiction, with Lord Radcliffe observing that the tribunal's jurisdiction was to decide the liability of a person "for a defined and terminable period". Put another way, the tribunal had a public duty to make a correct assessment on the rate-payer on each occasion, and no estoppel could be raised to prevent the tribunal from carrying out its duties under the statute.

A similar conclusion was reached by a majority of the Supreme Court in *Kildare County Council v. Keogh* where the facts were essentially similar to those in *Hope*.[200] Walsh J. pointed out that the doctrine of *res judicata* was inapplicable to rating cases, as the question of liability for rates for one year was always to be treated as inherently a different question to that of liability for another year, even though "there might be an identity on the question of law involved". These principles were applied in *Clare County Council v. Mahon*.[201] Here the defendants had claimed that the plaintiffs were bound by a prior Circuit Court judgment in which a claim made in respect of unpaid water charges was dismissed on the ground that the defendants were entitled to the benefit of a charitable trust which had effectively relieved them from the obligation to pay such rates. Carroll J. held that no issue estoppel arose, inasmuch as the Circuit Court had no jurisdiction to make a binding *in rem* declaration regarding the existence of a charitable trust. She added:

---

which the statute expressly forbids" (Lord Shaw)). See also the comments of Walsh J. in *Kildare County Council v. Keogh* [1971] I.R. 330 at 343: "It would be contrary to public policy that an erroneous construction of a statute should be perpetuated so as to decide successive claims between the same parties" and the judgment of Carroll J. in *Dublin County Council v. Mahon* [1995] 3 I.R. 193. However, this rationale has been rejected by Lord Bridge in *Thrasyvoulou v. Secretary of State for Environment* [1990] 2 A.C. 273.

198 *Athlone Woollen Mills Ltd v. Athlone U.D.C.* [1950] I.R. 1; *Thrasyvoulou v. Secretary of State for Environment* [1990] 2 A.C. 273 and *Crown Estate Commrs. v. Dorset County Council* [1990] 1 Ch. 297.

199 [1960] A.C. 551.

200 [1971] I.R. 330, following the Privy Council decision in *Caffoor v. Colombo Income Tax Commissioner* [1961] A.C. 584 where it was held that a tribunal's determination that a certain trust was charitable was conclusive only for the relevant year of assessment. The doctrine of *res judicata* did not prevent the tribunal from reopening this question in any subsequent years. But in England, Millett J. has said that these tax and rating cases should be regarded as *sui generis* and anomalous and should not be regarded as detracting from the possible application of *res judicata* to administrative law in an appropriate case: *Crown Estate Commissioners v. Dorset County Council* [1990] 1 Ch. 297 at 312.

201 [1995] 3 I.R. 193.

"Regarding issue estoppel, the claim for water rates belongs to a special category where no estoppel arises as between one year and the next . . . There can be no estoppel which would preclude the plaintiff from pursuing its statutory duty or from arguing the interpretation of a centre."[202]

It is sometimes sought to explain away the first two of these decisions (*Hope* and *Keogh*) by saying that the initial decision was "administrative" as opposed to "judicial".[203] But such technical arguments are unconvincing, for *res judicata* may operate once a tribunal has power to determine an issue and such argument would hardly explain away *Mahon*. The true principle is, as Lord Keith pointed out in *Hope's* case, that no estoppel can prevent a public body from carrying out its public duty. This principle was recognised by O'Hanlon J. in *Aprile v. Naas U.D.C.*[204] where he declined to apply the doctrine of *res judicata* to a decision of a planning authority. In that case the applicant had applied for retention permission in respect of an amusement centre. This application was refused by the respondent planning authority on the grounds that the proposed amusement centre would constitute a traffic hazard, and as such would be contrary to the proper planning and development of the area. The applicant took steps to deal with these objections, and he made a further application for permission. Once again, the application was refused, but on this occasion the planning authority gave new grounds for the refusal.

O'Hanlon J. held that the doctrine of *res judicata* was inapplicable in the circumstances of the case. In his view, no estoppel could operate to prevent the authority from carrying out its statutory duty:

"If a fresh application is later made in relation to the development of the same lands, there is an obligation on the planning authority, whenever it is called upon to deal with the application, to consider it *de novo* and to have regard to all aspects of the proper planning and development of the area as of that time, in granting or refusing the application."

However, in a major decision, *Thrasyvoulou v. Secretary of State for the Environment*,[205] the House of Lords has confirmed that while the principle of *res judicata* does not apply to the refusal of planning permission – since such a refusal does not serve to create a legal right to such permission in favour of the applicant – the converse is not true.[206] In other words, adjudicative decisions which have been resolved in favour of the private citizen can, in an appropriate statutory context, attract the doctrine of *res judicata*. As Lord Bridge explained, the public policy behind *res judicata* was of such fundamental importance that its application could not be confined to private law litigation:

---

202 *Ibid.* at 207.
203 Ganz, *op. cit.* above, n.194, deals with these arguments, and rebuts them in a convincing fashion.
204 Unreported, High Court, O'Hanlon J., November 22, 1983. But *cf. Dublin County Council v. Tallaght Blocks Co. Ltd*, unreported, Supreme Court, May 17, 1983, where Hederman J. stated that where a developer applied for planning permission in respect of an unauthorised structure and was refused, he could not later be heard to argue that permission for the development was not required.
205 [1990] 2 A.C. 273.
206 Lord Bridge rationalised this apparent dichotomy in the following terms (*ibid.* at 290):

"In principle, [*res judicata*] must apply equally to adjudications in the field of public law. In relation to *adjudications subject to a comprehensive self-contained statutory code*, the presumption, in my opinion, must be that where the statute has created a specific jurisdiction for the determination of any issue which establishes the existence of a legal right, the principle of *res judicata* applies to give finality to that determination unless an intention to exclude that principle can properly be inferred as a matter of construction of the relevant statutory provisions."[207]

Lord Bridge acknowledged that a statutory body could not, by estoppel, fetter the exercise of its statutory powers, but said that the principles underlying *res judicata* were so different from that which underlie estoppel by representation that the authorities on estoppel in public law had "no relevance" for this purpose.

If Lord Bridge's analysis is followed in this jurisdiction, this would seem to leave room for a much greater application of the doctrine of *res judicata* in administrative cases than had hitherto been thought possible.[208] The potential application of this principle to decisions of administrative bodies exercising limited judicial powers under cover of Article 37 is obvious, provided, of course, that such decisions create legal rights in favour of the applicant (such as by granting a licence or permission) and this principle may be applied more widely to all administrative adjudications involving a decision in the nature of a *lis*. It might mean, for example, that planning authorities which had granted outline planning permission would be bound by the principle of that earlier decision when it came to considering the grant of a full planning permission. This, perhaps, would only be as it should be, since it would be most unfair that administrative bodies should be allowed to resile from the implications of a previous adjudication in favour of an individual citizen.

The *res judicata* doctrine must not be confused with the situation where the decision-taker has become *functus officio*. If a public authority has statutory power to determine some question its decision will generally be final and irrevocable.[209]

"A decision to grant planning permission creates, of course, rights which such a grant confers. But a decision to withhold planning permission resolves no issue of legal right whatever. It is no more than a decision that in existing circumstances and in light of existing planning policies the development in question is not one which it would be appropriate to permit. Consequently, in my view, such a decision cannot give rise to an estoppel *per rem judicatam*."

[207] *Ibid.* at 289 (emphasis added). See also, to the like effect, *Crown Estate Commissioners v. Dorset County Council* [1990] 1 Ch. 297.

[208] It is only in very exceptional circumstances (such as that disclosed in the *Athlone Woollen Mills* case) that the doctrine of *res judicata* has been applied to decisions of planning authorities in this jurisdiction. In *Littondale Ltd v. Wicklow County Council* [1996] 2 I.L.R.M. 519, Laffoy J. stressed that in the *Athlone Woollen Mills* case the respondent planning authority relied on the *res judicata* doctrine "in circumstances in which it had declined to make a decision on the second appliation". In *Littondale* the authority accepted and adjudicated upon the second planning appliation, gave different reasons for its refusal and informed the applicant of its decision. Laffoy J. held that in such circumstances the respondent was estopped from relying on the plea of *res judicata*. However, in *The State (Kenny and Hussey) v. An Bord Pleanála*, unreported, Supreme Court, December 20, 1984, McCarthy J. observed that while he did not have to determine whether *res judicata* applied to planning decisions, he found it difficult to see how a planning authority could be permitted "to come to a different view when circumstances do not change". For a similar approach, see *O'Dea v. Minister for Local Government* (1957) 91 I.L.T.R. 169.

[209] Of course, there are some examples of where the decision-maker is expressly given the statutory power to alter his original decision. Thus, s.248(1)(a) of the Social Welfare (Consolidation) Act

This is not because of the operation of *res judicata*, but rather because the authority lacks jurisdiction to alter its original decision and has become *functus officio*.[210]

11. Judicial review and *res judicata*

We turn now to a different focus of attention: we are concerned not with the original decision taken by a public authority, but with the situation in which such a decision has been subject to judicial review. The question is whether the High (or Supreme) Court decision in the judicial review proceedings attracts the *res judicata* doctrine. It would seem that, up to recently at any rate, *res judicata* was inapplicable in cases where the public law remedies of certiorari, prohibition and mandamus had been refused (as opposed to being granted). These remedies were primarily regarded as being concerned with the maintenance of order in the legal system. It was argued that they did not purport finally to determine the private rights of the parties *inter se*, and it was said that the court was merely required to decide "whether there had been a plain excess of jurisdiction or not."[211] Therefore, where the High Court or Supreme Court had, for example, refused to quash a decision of the Rent Tribunal in certiorari proceedings in a case where it had been argued that it lacked jurisdiction, it would still have been open to the landlord to argue in subsequent civil proceedings that in fact no tenancy had existed and that the Rent Tribunal acted *ultra vires* in assuming jurisdiction. The fact that neither the High Court nor Supreme Court was prepared to quash this order could not be conclusive of the jurisdictional issue, which could then be tried *de novo* on oral evidence before the court which was seised of the landlord's application for (say) possession.

The basis for this principle was that the High Court could not readily assess the conflicting evidence simply on the basis of the affidavits tendered in the old form of State side proceedings. (It is just for this reason that *res judicata* does apply where relief was refused following a plenary hearing in the case of an application for a declaration, injunction or damages). But it would seem that this rationale had been undermined by the new Order 84, rule 25(1) of the Rules of the Superior Courts, 1986, which allows the court to conduct an oral hearing (including cross-examination of deponents on their affidavits) in an application for judicial review. If the court can thus inquire and determine *de novo* on oral evidence whether the facts giving rise to the tribunal's jurisdiction exist, can there be any sound reason why the refusal of certiorari, prohibition or mandamus should not attract the rule of *res judicata*?

1993 now provides that a deciding officer may, at any time, revise a decision of a deciding officer if it appears to him that:

> "the decision was erroneous in the light of new evidence or of new facts which have been brought to his notice since the date on which it was given or by reason of some mistake having been made in relation to the law or the facts, or if it appears to him that there has been any relevant change of circumstances since the decision was given . . . ".

210 *Re 56 Denton Road* [1952] 2 All E.R. 799. See also, *Re Lynham's Estate* [1928] I.R. 127.
211 *R. v. Fulham Rent Tribunal, ex p. Zerek* [1951] 2 K.B. 1 at 13, *per* Devlin J.

CHAPTER 17

THE STATE IN LITIGATION

1. Patrimony of the Prerogative

In the United Kingdom, the prerogative has been said to embrace "those rights and capacities which the King alone enjoys in contradistinction to others".[1] In the United Kingdom many of the former prerogative rights have been uprooted, qualified or superseded by statute, or shrivelled by desuetude.[2] Nevertheless, the prerogative still covers a diverse bundle of rights, powers, privileges, etc., most of which are exercised by the Crown on the advice of the responsible ministers.[3]

In Ireland, by contrast, the former prerogative had been largely superseded in that much of the ground which the prerogative covers in the United Kingdom is regulated by the Constitution or, to a lesser extent, by statute.[4] Thus, for instance, when the President appoints or removes Ministers or dissolves the Dáil, she does so on the authority of Articles 13.1 and 13.2 and 28.9.4°, respectively. Again, the prerogative of mercy has been overtaken by the right of pardon and remission of punishment vested in the President by Article 13.6; whilst the prerogative to declare war is now grounded in Article 28.3.1° (which reserves this right to the Dáil). In the case of certain of the other prerogatives, their content is such as actually to conflict with the Constitution. In the leading case of *Byrne v. Ireland*[5] where the plaintiff had been injured when she fell into a trench dug by or, more probably, on the authority of the Minister for Posts and Telegraphs, the State sought to defend itself by calling in aid the supposed prerogative of immunity from tort action. However,

---

[1] Blackstone, *Commentaries*, Vol.1, p. 239. See also, Wade, "Procedure and Prerogative in Public Law'" (1985) 101 L.Q.R. 180.

[2] Wade and Forsyth, *Administrative Law* (1994) comment, at pp. 247–248 that:
"Prerogative powers may also, it seems, be atrophied by mere disuse. Thus the Crown used to employ the prerogative writ ne exeat regno to prevent a person leaving the country; but the courts have held for many years that this remedy is granted only to a creditor for the restraint of an absconding debtor."
See *Felton v. Callis* [1969] 1 Q.B. 200.

[3] On the prerogative generally, see de Smith, *Constitutional and Administrative Law* (3rd ed.,1977) and Wade and Forsyth, *op.cit.*, above, n.2, pp. 247–249.

[4] Thus, for example, the High Court's jurisdiction in wardship cases is now expressly conferred by s.9(1) of the Courts (Supplemental Provisions) Act 1961. That jurisdiction had formerly "been recognised as forming part of the royal prerogative, as a high duty in the Sovereign as *parens patriae*": see *per* Lord Ashbourne C. in *Re Birch* 29 L.R. Ir. 274 at 275 and the statutory devolution of that former prerogative jurisdiction to the present High Court is discussed by Blayney J. in his judgment in *Re a Ward of Court* [1995] 2 I.L.R.M. 401. It might, of course, be contended that this subsection simply (but erroneously) recognises the existence of a substantive jurisdiction which, in its pre–1922 prerogative form has ceased to exist and that this jurisdiction is now derived from a combination of constitutional provisions such as Articles 34.3.1°, 40.3, 41 and 42.

[5] [1972] I.R. 241.

the Supreme Court held this prerogative to be unconstitutional. According to the narrower alternative ratio (the other ratio is covered below) the reason for this was that this immunity interfered unjustifiably with the right to litigate a justiciable controversy (under Article 40.3.1°). Another example of a prerogative whose contents are in conflict with the Constitution is provided by a series of cases which held that, since the Central Fund of the Irish Exchequer does not have the character of a royal fund, it cannot attract the prerogative of priority of debts due to the State in case of an insolvency.[6] Again the prerogative of the Crown to enforce payment of a judgment debtor by securing the arrest and imprisonment of the debtor is scarcely compatible with Article 40.4.1°.[7]

Pre-*Byrne*, it had, however been accepted[8] – although without much discussion – that, save for cases, where it had been superseded by, or was in conflict with, the Constitution or a statute, the prerogative had managed to navigate the rapids of 1922 and 1937. In short, it had been assumed that there was nothing in the nature or source of the prerogative to prevent its continued existence, as it continues to exist, for instance, in such former-colony Republics as Zambia. However, *Byrne v. Ireland* – which was subsequently confirmed by the Supreme Court in *Webb v. Ireland*[9] and *Howard v. Commissioners of Public Works*[10] – gave the quietus to that notion.[11]

Nevertheless, since the prerogative represents such an important stage in the evolution of the law covered in the remainder of this chapter, a brief summary of these developments remains relevant.

The view that the prerogative had survived the enactment of the Constitution of the Irish Free State in 1922 was based, in the first instance, upon Article 49.1 of the Constitution which provides that:

> "All powers, functions, rights and prerogatives whatsoever exercisable in or in respect of Saorstát Éireann immediately before the 11th day of December, 1936, whether in virture of the Constitution then in force or otherwise, by the authority in which the executive power of Saorstát Éireann was then vested are hereby declared to belong to the people."

---

6. *Re P.C., an Arranging Debtor* [1939] I.R. 306; *Re Irish Mutual Insurance Association Ltd* [1955] I.R. 176.

7. In *The State (Coombes) v. Furlong*, unreported High Court, February 1, 1963, Davitt P. appeared to doubt whether this particular prerogative had survived "the constitutional changes of 1922 and 1937".

8. In *Cooper v. Attorney General* [1935] I.R. 425 at 440 Johnson J. had said that "the prerogative rights of the Crown were carried over as part of the law of the Irish Free State by Article 73 of the [1922] Constitution". See also, *Re Mahony, a Bankrupt* [1926] I.R. 202; *Galway County Council v. Minister for Finance* [1931] I.R. 215; and *Re Irish Mutual Employers Association Ltd* [1955] I.R. 176 for similar expressions of judicial opinion.

9. [1988] I.R. 353. For criticism of this decision, see Kelly, "Hidden Treasure and the Constitution" (1988) 10 D.U.L.J. 5 (N.S.); Gwynn Morgan, "Constitutional Interpretation" (1988) 10 D.U.L.J. 24 (N.S.); Lenihan, "Royal Prerogatives and the Constitution" (1989) 24 Ir. Jur. 1 (N.S.) and Costello, "The Expulsion of Prerogative Doctrine from Irish Law: Quantifying and Remedying the Loss of the Royal Prerogative" (1997) 32 Ir. Jur. 145.

10. [1994] 1 I.R. 101. See Hogan, "The Mullaghmore Case" (1993) 15 D.U.L.J. 243 (N.S.).

11. Although, *cf.* the judgment of O'Flaherty J. in *Geoghegan v. Institute of Chartered Accountants in Ireland*, [1995] 3 I.R. 86, which advocates "a more gradual approach in regard to the place of the royal prerogative in our constitutional scheme of things".

This provision makes the inquiry turn on the antecedent question of whether the prerogative existed in Saorstát Éireann before December 11, 1936. The significance of this date lies in the fact that it was the day when the Irish Free State Constitution was amended to extirpate the King (formerly the head of state in whom all executive authority was vested under Articles 41, 51, 55, 60 and 68 of the Irish Free State Constitution). Prior to *Byrne*, it had been assumed that the presence of the King drew with it the prerogative. This argument was rejected by the majority in *Byrne*. In response to the argument just summarised, it was said that the King's powers could be confined to those actually specified in the 1922 Constitution: there was no necessary reason why they had to be identical with those which the Crown enjoyed in the United Kingdom or in pre-Independence Ireland. There is, however a different argument for saying that the prerogative survived the establishment of the State: "[The prerogative] was part of the common law which was applied to the Irish Free State by Article 73".[12] In response to this argument, the kernel of the Court's argument is contained in the following extract from Walsh J.'s judgment:

> "the basis of the Crown prerogative(s) in English law was that the King was the personification of the State. Article 2 of the Constitution of the Irish Free State declared that all the powers of government and all authority, legislative, executive and judicial, in Ireland were derived from the people of Ireland and that the same should be exercised in the Irish Free State through the organisations established by or under and in accord with that Constitution. The basis of the prerogative of the English Crown was quite inconsistent with the declaration contained in that Article. The King enjoyed a personal pre-eminence; perfection was ascribed to him."[13]

(Article 2 is not reproduced separately here since it is quoted practically verbatim in the above extract. The article is substantially reproduced in Article 6.1 of the present Constitution.)

This passage merits two observations. First, it might have seemed more realistic to regard Article 2 as a statement of political principle, in other words as a generalised warning to Irish Governments that they held their power "on trust" for the People along the lines of the generally accepted Lockeian, "social contract" theory of limited government; and also as a warning to the British Crown that as governmental authority came ultimately from the People, it was not for the British to start trying to take power away from the Irish Free State or to interfere with it in any way.

Secondly, leaving aside this criticism, the effect of Article 2 is to stipulate (i) that all powers of government flow in some sense from the People and, (ii) that these powers may only be exercised by the independent Irish organs of government. As to the content of the powers of government, little is said. In view of this, Article 2 could have been interpreted as not affecting the content of these powers but rather as relocating the basis of State authority from the King to the people and as shifting the mode of its exercise from the King to the organs established by the Irish Constitution.

---

12 *Cork County Council v. Commissioners of Public Works* [1945] I.R. 561 at 578, *per* O'Byrne J.
13 [1972] I.R. 241 at 272.

At a broader level, Professor Kelly has criticised not so much the reasoning, as the conclusion, in *Byrne*. He summarises his views, characteristically cogently, in the following passage:

". . . the statutory usage of the Irish Free State, positive and negative, together with the opinions of judges who played a part in drafting its Constitution, together with the record of what actually was done in those years in such matters as pardons, passports, and precedence of counsel, suggest that the Crown and its prerogative were understood to have survived into the newly independent Irish State, as part of the common law, under Article 73, so far as such survival was not, in letter or in spirit, inconsistent with some specific dimension of the new Constitution. I think that for us today, 50 or 60 years later, to take the line that our fathers and grandfathers in legal and official life quite misunderstood the nature of the machine they were not only operating but had also in fact constructed is to adopt an unreal and intellectually unamiable position."[14]

Irrespective of such criticisms, however, it now seems clear – subject to some judicial hints that aspects of *Byrne* and *Webb* will have to be re-considered – that the prerogative is not part of the Irish constitutional legal scene. This means, it might be thought, that the State is without certain pockets of legitimate authority the need for which is likely to arise unexpectedly or in an emergency, when there might be no time for the passage of legislation. Examples (drawn from English Law) include the rules: permitting the seizure or destruction of private property, in time of war or imminent danger (albeit on payment of compensation); affording a significant component in martial law; and enabling the State to create corporations, without statutory authority.[15]

The question of the continued existence of the prerogative of treasure trove came up for consideration by the Supreme Court in *Webb v. Ireland*. The plaintiffs in this case were the finders of an exceptionally valuable hoard of early Christian objects who had handed over the artefacts to the National Museum for safe-keeping.[16] They were dissatisfied with the IR£10,000 compensation offered to them by the State and commenced proceedings seeking the delivery up by the State of these objects. The State pleaded that it was not a mere bailee, but that by reason of the prerogative of treasure trove, it had acquired a superior title to that of the plaintiffs.

The Supreme Court, affirming the reasoning of Walsh J. in *Byrne*, held that none of the royal prerogatives had survived the enactment of the Constitution. Nor was it possible, said Finlay C.J., to distinguish between the prerogative of sovereign immunity "which could be traced to the royal dignity of the King" and a prerogative of treasure trove which it was stated:

---

[14] Kelly, *loc. cit.* above, n. 9, p. 14. In *Geoghegan v. Institute of Chartered Acountants*, above, n. 11, O'Flaherty J. referred to this article and said (at 118) that: "Doubtless, in any future debate [this] essay which favours a more gradual approach in regard to the place of the royal prerogative in our constitutional scheme of things will provide of immense value."

[15] Wade and Forsyth, *op. cit.* above, n. 2, pp. 247–249 and Costello, *op. cit.* above, n.9, pp. 147–164.

[16] The find was described by Blayney J. as "one of the most significant discoveries of early Christian art ever made". The hoard was valued by him in a separate judgment at IR£5,536,000.

". . . [C]ould be traced or related not to the dignity of his person, but to his position as sovereign or ruler. Such a distinction does not alter the view that I have expressed with regard to the effect of the provisions of the Constitution of 1922, and appears to me to ignore the essential point which is that by virtue of the provisions of the Constitution of 1922 what was being created was a brand new sovereign State and that the function, power or position of the King in that sovereign State was such only as was vested in him by that Constitution and by the State created by it."[17]

This meant that no part of the prerogative had survived and, indeed, it was on this basis that the plaintiffs had succeeded before Blayney J. in the High Court. This result was, however, avoided in the Supreme Court by the use of rather surprising reasoning. Finlay C.J. nevertheless went on to hold that the State did enjoy a right to a modern form of the treasure trove prerogative by virtue of Article 5, which proclaims that: "Ireland is a sovereign, democratic State."[18] Finlay C.J. stated:

". . . [O]ne of the most important national assets belonging to the people is their heritage and knowledge of its true origins and the buildings and objects which constitute keys to their ancient history. If this be so, then it would appear to me to follow that a necessary ingredient of sovereignty in a modern state and certainly in this State, having regard to the terms of the Constitution, with an emphasis on its historical origins and a constant concern for the common good is and should be an ownership by the State of objects which constitute antiquities of importance and which have no known owner."[19]

This trend was subsequently continued by the Supreme Court's decision in *Howard v. Commissioners of Public Works.*[20] Here a majority of the court confirmed that none of the former Crown prerogatives had survived the enactment of the Constitution and that as the former rule whereby it was presumed that the State was not bound by the application of statute could not be divorced from its prerogative origins, it too had failed to survive the enactment of the Constitution.

---

17 *Webb v. Ireland* [1988] I.R. 353 at 382. In *The "La Lavia"* [1996] 1 I.L.R.M. 194 (a case concerning the payment by the State of a reward to salvors of a maritime wreck) Denham J. drew attention to one consequence of the *Webb* decision when she observed at 201–202 that since the prerogative right to treasure trove had not survived the enactment of the Constitution, the:

"'rights' of the State were thereafter to be found in the Constitution. If one side of the coin (treasure trove) did not survive [after] 1922, would the other side (reward) survive on its own? It would appear logical that both sides of the coin would cease to continue. The question then is whether [that] constitutional basis would envisage a reward system . . .".

This, perhaps, is to take the non-surivival of the prerogative to its logical extremes. *Cf.* now the more tempered approach advocated by O'Flaherty J. in *Geoghegan v. Institute of Chartered Accountants* [1995] 3 I.R. 86.

18 Morgan, *op. cit.* above, n. 9, predicts that the "broadness and vagueness of the concept of sovereignty [contained in Art. 5] make it likely to be used as an aid when the post-1922 existence of other former prerogatives comes before the Courts".

19 *Webb v. Ireland* [1988] I.R. 353 at 383. But it is not easy to see why the State's ownership of such artefacts should be deemed to be an inherent feature of the State's sovereignty. As an alternative *ratio* a majority of the Court (Finlay C.J., Henchy and Griffin JJ.) held that the phrase "all royalties" contained in Art. 10.3 was broad enough to include artefacts, such as the Derrynaflan chalice. Walsh and McCarthy JJ. dissented strongly from this latter conclusion, with the former saying (at 393) that the word "royalties" was to be construed as referring to "the sums paid or payable for the use or exploration of the natural resources."

20 [1994] 1 I.R. 101.

The Geoghegan *case: some signs of retrenchment*

The first hint that the Supreme Court might be prepared to draw back from the absolutist position it had taken in cases such as *Webb* and *Howard* may be found in the judgment of O'Flaherty J. in *Geoghegan v. Institute of Chartered Accountants.*[21] In this case, an accountant who facing disciplinary charges before a disciplinary panel established by the Institute – which was itself a charter body established by exercise of the prerogative prior to 1922 – raised the question of whether such bodies had actually survived the enactment of the Constitution. While the court appears implicitly to have acknowledged that the former prerogative power to establish a corporation by letters patent or by charter had not survived the enactment of the Constitution, O'Flaherty J. was decidely unimpressed by the argument that bodies validly established prior to that date had also ceased to have existence:

> ". . . If we were to attempt to declare that the charter did not exist since the establishment of the State, it would mean that in a suit brought by a person for the purpose of safeguarding his professional qualification we would be declaring that he had no qualification to safeguard because the Institute to which he thought that he belonged had no legal existence. I believe that it would be wrong even to entertain the possibility of such a nonsensical result."[22]

O'Flaherty J. – who incidentally had been the only dissenter in *Howard* on the question of whether the State exemption from statute had survived – then went on to hint that aspects of *Byrne* and *Webb* might need to be re-considered:

> "As regards the decisions in *Byrne* and *Webb* since each was concerned with a single question in respect of the royal preprogative . . . . it may be that if in a future case a wider question is raised concerning the royal prerogative the parameters of the judgments in these cases may need to be delineated. Doubtless, in any future debate Professor John M. Kelly's essay which favours a more gradual approach in regard to the place of the royal prerogative in our constitutional scheme of things . . . will prove of immense value."[23]

This must be regarded as a clear manifestation of judicial concern about the formidable legal and practical difficulties that would result in the straightforward disappearance of the prerogative. It is, however, scarcely accurate for O'Flaherty J. to describe *Byrne* and *Webb* as simply presenting issues as to the survival of individual prerogatives, since the entire thrust of these cases was that none of the prerogatives rights had survived the enactment of the Constitution.

Conclusions

Subject to these potential hints contained in *Geoghegan*, the net effect of the trilogy of cases, *Byrne*, *Webb* and *Howard*, therefore, while confirming that none of the

---

[21] [1995] 3 I.R. 86.

[22] *Ibid.* at 118. Blaney J. agreed with O'Flaherty J. and the other members of the Supreme Court reserved their positions on this issue.

[23] *Ibid.* The essay in question is "Hidden Treasure and the Constitution" (1988) 10 D.U.L.J. 5 (N.S.), see above, n. 9.

prerogative rights have survived at common law, is to allow the State to assert the equivalent of such prerogative rights, provided that such rights can be shown to derive expressly or impliedly from the Constitution. And although this argument was not accepted by the majority in *Howard*, the rule whereby the State is presumed to be exempt from the application of statute might have been rationalised on the basis that although it was: "[S]ometimes called a prerogative right is, in fact, nothing more than a reservation, or exception, introduced for the public benefit, and equally applicable to all governments".[24]

These remarks were anticipated in the case of public interest immunity (or "executive privilege") from disclosure of documents as early as 1925 by Meredith J. in *Leen v. President of the Executive Council*.[25] Dealing with the suggestion that only the Crown could claim executive privilege, Meredith J. remarked:

"[This privilege] appears to me to be broad based upon the public interest. This privilege has roots in the general conception of State interests and the functions of Courts of Justice, which make it independent of the particular type of constitution under the body of law which recognises that principle is administered."[26]

A narrower and more convincing example of the same phenomenon – the relocation of a former prerogative on a more acceptable basis – concerns the right to a passport. Whilst this has its origin in the prerogative,[27] it seems likely that the present administrative arrangements would be upheld as a means of giving effect to the citizen's constitutional right to travel abroad.[28]

In any event, the general effect of *Byrne*, *Webb* and *Howard* is that whilst the prerogative has been formally expelled, certain former prerogatives may yet be

---

[24] *Byrne v. Ireland*, above, n. 5, at 287, *per* Walsh J., quoting from the judgment of Story J. in *United States v. Hoar* (1821) 26 Fed.Cas. 329.

[25] [1926] I.R. 456.

[26] *Ibid.* at 463.

[27] This is certainly the position in England: "[T]here is no doubt that passports are issued under the royal prerogative in the discretion of the Secretary of State," *per* O'Connor L.J. in *R. v. Foreign Secretary, ex p. Everett* [1989] Q.B. 811 at 817. Finlay P. took a similar view in *The State (M.) v. Minister for Foreign Affairs* [1979] I.R. 73 at 76 where he said that the "granting or withholding of a passport does not appear to have been of statutory origin but would appear to have derived originally from the Crown prerogative".

[28] As recognised in *The State (M.) v. Minister for Foreign Affairs, ibid; Lennon v. Ganly* [1981] I.L.R.M. 84; *P.I. v. Ireland* [1989] I.L.R.M. 810; and *Attorney General v. X.* [1992] 1 I.R. 1: see Kelly, *op.cit.,* above, n.9, pp. 67–69; 777–778. In this regard it seems very doubtful if the former prerogative writ of *ne exeat regno* has survived in any form, The writ is nowadays used in the United Kingdom solely as a means of restraining absconding debtors leaving the jurisdiction (*Felton v. Callis* [1969] 1 Q.B. 200.), but quite irrespective of *Byrne*, *Webb* and *Howard*, such a restraining jurisdiction would seem quite at odds with the constitutional guarantees of liberrty and the right to travel. *Cf.* Bankruptcy Act 1988, s.124 which makes it an offence (carrying a maximum penalty of IR£500) for an absconding debtor to leave the State, but does not actually make provision for such a restraining order. It may be that a creditor would have standing to seek an injunction restraining the debtor from breaching the criminal law (see *Lovett v. Gogan* [1995] 3 I.R. 132), but the court would presumably uphold the constitutional right to travel. Section 23(1) of the 1988 Act gives the High Court actual power to arrest an absconding bankrupt who is about to leave the State. This latter section would also presumably encounter some possible constitutional objections, but perhaps might be upheld as a necessary ancillary to the due administration of justice: see *Tam Hing Yee v. Wu Tai Wai* [1992] L.R.C. (Const.) 596 (where the Hong Kong Court of Appeal upheld such an order on administration of justice grounds).

indirectly admitted to the post-1922 polity. For this to occur, such prerogatives must comply with two conditions. The first of these, has always existed. It is a rational and relatively predictable condition, namely, that the prerogative should not conflict with the Constitution. The effect of *Byrne, Webb* and *Howard* is to add a second – and, it is suggested – a vague and unnecessary condition. This has been articulated by reference to such subjective factors as the public interest (*Leen*); legislative intention (*Byrne*); and sovereignty (*Webb*).

2. The State as Juristic Person

In holding in *Byrne v. Ireland* that the State could be sued in tort, the Supreme Court necessarily confirmed that the State had legal personality. It is true that the significance of this is reduced to some extent by the fact that most central government functions are vested in Ministers who have been designated as corporations sole by the Ministers and Secretaries Act 1924. In addition, Article 28.2 makes a grant of the executive power of the State to the Government, a body which is legally distinct from a Minister. However, this constitutional provision is carefully made "subject to the provisions of this Constitution" which suggests that the State retains in itself executive power for some purposes and this alone would be a ground on which to suggest that the State has some legal personality. It is also significant that it is the State and not the responsible Minister who is vicariously responsible for a tort committed by a civil servant (since it is the State which employs a civil servant), although the position in contract is less clear. The significance of this is that this common law responsibility is among the reasons why the State's legal personality is an important matter.

However, one further preliminary point which is of importance arises from the fact that in Britain two alternative means of defining the prerogative have been adopted. The first is to restrict the prerogative to those powers which are unique to the Crown. The alternative and wider approach is to treat the prerogative as embracing "every power of the Crown which is non-statutory".[29] If the latter approach is adopted,[30] certain difficulties are presented by reason of the Supreme Court's decisions to the effect that the prerogative did not survive the constitutional changes after 1922, namely, that the State would be lacking in even the legal personality and

---

[29] Dicey, *Law of the Constitution* (10th ed., 1959), p. 425, quoted by Wade, "Procedure and Prerogative in Public Law" (1985) 101 L.Q.R. 180 at 191. See also, Wade and Forsyth, *op. cit.*, above, n. 2, pp. 248–249. To Sir William Wade belongs the credit for pointing out the difficulties with the second approach.

[30] In Ireland the prerogative was defined by Kennedy C.J. in *In Re K., An Arranging Debtor* [1927] I.R. 260 at 270 as: "the residue of discretionary or arbitrary power which at any given time is legally left in the hands of the Crown". Similar views are to be found in *R. v. Criminal Injuries Compensation Tribunal, ex p. Lain* [1967] 2 Q.B. 864 at 881, *per* Diplock L.J. and *Council of Civil Service Unions v. Minister for the Public Service* [1985] A.C. 374. Note, however, that in *R. v. Panel on Take-Overs ex p. Datafin plc* [1987] Q.B. 815 at 848 Lloyd L.J. accepted the narrower definition of the prerogative urged by Sir William Wade. It may be of interest that in *M.F. v. Legal Aid Board* [1993] I.L.R.M. 797 Finlay C.J. said that the Board had been established by "executive act" of the Government, *i.e.* perhaps implying that Art. 28 of the Constitiution provided sufficient authority for this decision. This view avoids any difficulties associated with the prerogative.

attributes which are possessed by the ordinary artificial legal person, since, if one utilises the second definition, this very personality would derive from the prerogative.[31] Such a suggestion, however, would serve only to confuse the character of the Irish State with that of the United Kingdom. In the United Kingdom it is the Crown, a corporation sole, whose character and capacities were initially determined by the prerogative, which acts as the State. In Ireland, the State is the creation of the people and designed according to the (admittedly rather vague) specifications of the Constitution.[32] The most that could ever have been claimed for the prerogative in Ireland is that, entering the polity via the bridges of Article 73 of the 1922 Constitution and Article 49.1 of the present Constitution, it might have contributed certain auxiliary rights and privileges to the capabilities of the State, rather than actually establishing it and shaping it. However, as we have seen as a result of *Byrne*, *Webb* and *Howard* it has now been determined that the prerogative did not survive beyond 1922.

It seems clear, therefore, that the State's legal personality is independent of the prerogative and not in any sense contigent on its survival. The question then is whether the State has all the usual powers of a legal person to sue and be sued; establish companies; expend money and generally bear similar legal rights and duties to those of an ordinary artificial person. These are now matters to be determined by the Constitution, as interpreted by case law. However, it is true that:

> "[T]he Constitution gives no express answer [to the question of the State's legal personality], nor to questions about the State's legal capacities or privileges. These answers must be elaborated from the narrow base of Article 5, with the help of some other indications."[33]

Nor does statute offer any real assistance, for the only statutory provisions even to allude to this matter are sections 10 and 11 of the State Property Act 1954, which confer extensive powers on the Minister for Finance in relation to the sale, exchange, transfer and leasing of State lands. And insofar as the 1954 Act says anything about the present issue, it implies a lack of confidence about the State's capacity to hold, lease and convey real property. The 1954 Act was, however, passed in an era long before *Byrne v. Ireland* and the rapid modern development of constitutional thought and the useage of statute could, in any event, be scarcely conclusive on the issue.

In fact, it is a different line of argument, which has found favour in the few cases on this topic. This argument is grounded in the rights and duties, on the high constitutional plane, with which the Constitution endows the State. These include: the capacity to own natural resources, lands, minerals and waters (Article 10); the power to commit itself to international agreements and international organisations (Article 29.4 and 5); the duty to provide for free primary education (Article 42.4) as well, of course, as the State's liability in tort, which was stated in *Byrne* to be founded on Article 40.3. Surely it would be strange, indeed, if the State were not also endowed with an adequate legal personality on the mundane level of making grants,

---

[31] *Halsbury's Laws of England* (4th ed.), para. 931.
[32] *Byrne v. Ireland* [1972] I.R. 241.
[33] Hogan and Whyte, *Kelly, The Irish Constitution* (3rd ed., 1994), p. 26.

entering contracts, etc., to equip it to implement these rights and bear these duties?[34] This line of thought finds expression in the following example of judicial statesmanship taken from the judgment of Kingsmill Moore J. in *Comyn v. Attorney General*:[35]

> "There is at least one point on which general agreement may be found, namely, the practical necessity of endowing the State with some form of legal personality. Ultimately, the nature and attributes of the State must be found in the wording of the Constitution. It is, however, not unreasonable to assume that those who framed, and those who debated, the Constitution were familiar with current opinions as to the nature of the State. The Constitution has told us a great deal about the State, its organisation, its rights, its obligations and its attributes; but still it has not attempted to define its juristic nature. Is it a corporation? Is it, as has been suggested, an unincorporated association? Is it neither of these, but a legal persona of a new type and sui generis? These questions may provide much food for discussion in future cases. It is not necessary, and it would be dangerous, to attempt a full or final answer. For the purposes of this case, all that is necessary is to find that the State is conceived of as a juristic person or entity having as one of its many attributes the capacity to hold property. It may; or may not, be a corporation. It may be a conception entirely new to English and Irish law; but I hold that it is a juristic person and can hold property."[36]

Thus, if – as has been judicially confirmed – the State is a juristic person (whether in virtue of Article 5 or otherwise), then it would seem to follow that the State must thereby enjoy the ordinary legal capacity of an artificial person. Accordingly, the State's right to make contracts, establish companies, etc., would seem to be derived from this juristic status and the non-survival of the prerogative has no bearing on the issue.

3. Liability of the State and Ministers

The purpose of this part to outline the relationship between the State, ministers and the civil service as these have been created (the word is used advisedly as some artificiality is involved here) by the courts in the context of tort and contract litigation.

There are two bases to the central executive organ's capacity to sue and to be sued, and the relationship between these two bases has not yet been clarified. The first basis is the Ministers and Secretaries Act 1924 section 2(1) of which provides:

> "Each of the Ministers, heads of the respective departments of State shall be a corporation sole under his style or name aforesaidand shall have perpetual succession and an official seal and may sue and be sued."

---

[34] Casey, *Constitutional Law of Ireland* (1992), pp. 102–193.
[35] [1950] I.R. 142.
[36] *Ibid.* at 160–161.

The purposes of making each of the Ministers a corporation sole have been explained as follows by Sullivan P. in *Carolan v. Minister for Defence*[37] (a case in which the plaintiff claimed damages for personal injuries sustained through the alleged negligence of a soldier driving an Army lorry):

"1. to secure continuity of title and obviate the need for the transfer of State property, rights and obligations from a Minister to his successor;

2. to secure that persons contracting with the Government through any of its Departments should have the ordinary remedy of action available in case of breach of contract;

3. to enable a Minister to be sued in his corporate capacity for a wrongful act done by him as such Minister or by his orders and directions. I cannot think that the legislature intended to go further and create by this section a liability in each Minister for all the wrongful acts or defaults of all the persons employed in his Department."[38]

Comment is unnecessary on the first of these functions; the third is considered below and the second will be examined immediately.

Contract

The second function mentioned in the quotation enables the Minister to be sued in contract in the ordinary way, rather than, as formerly, having to proceed by way of the Petition of Right (Ireland) Act 1873. At common law, the existence of the prerogative ensured that neither the Crown nor its servants could be sued upon a contract.[39]

As in private law, it is, of course, a precondition of the Minister's liability that the contract was actually made by a person (usually a civil servant) who could be regarded as the agent of the Minister. The question of agency featured in *Grenham v. Minister for Defence*[40] in which Hanna J. held that army officers, who had commandeered motor vehicles for military purposes during the Civil War, were not agents of the Minister so as to make him liable on the contract. However, because of the unusual facts of the case and the brevity of the judgment, Grenham cannot be regarded as having significant precedential value. This case does raise the more general question of whether an action arising out of a contract made by a civil servant should be brought against the State or against the Minister for the Department in which the civil servant worked. It would seem that the contract should be brought against the Minister and this is buttressed by the fact that government

---

[37] [1927] I.R. 62.

[38] *Ibid.* at 69.

[39] As Phillimore J. said in *Graham v. Public Works Commissioners* [1901] 2 K.B. 781 at 789–790:
"The Crown cannot be sued; and that being so, neither can the subject take action indirectly against the Crown by suing a servant of the Crown upon a contract made by the servant as agent of the Crown."
But even at common law it was clear that certain public officials could, in Phillimore J.'s words, be designated "as agents of the Crown but with a power of contracting as principals" (*i.e.* not merely as agents).

[40] [1926] I.R. 54.

contracts are always made in the name of the appropriate Minister. In effect, the Minister is – to adapt Phillimore J.'s formulation – an agent of the State but with the power of contracting as principal. Moreover, the fact that a civil servant, is, in law, a servant of the State, rather than the Minister does not prevent him from also being the agent of his Minister (whose alter ego he is always said to be in the conventional and slightly imprecise usage). While, the question is not of great significance, so long as it remains unresolved, the prudent plaintiff will join both the State and the relevant Minister as defendants.

Tort

Byrne v. Ireland[41] is the basis of liability in tort. Until *Byrne v. Ireland*, the general rule was that neither the State nor any of its organs could be liable for an action in tort. Historically, the British Crown was immune from actions in tort (whether directly or vicariously, through the behaviour of Crown servants),[42] both because of the principle that the King could do no wrong and because of the King's disability to command himself to appear before his own courts. In tort, in contrast to contract, this relic persisted into the twentieth century. In *Carolan v. Minister for Defence*, Sullivan P. held that section 2 of the Minister and Secretaries Act 1924 was intended not to alter the position because its objective was only to allow:

> "a Minister to be sued in his corporate capacity for a wrongful act done by him as such Minister, or by his orders or directions, I cannot think that the Legislature intended to go further, and create by this section a liability in each Minister for all wrongful acts or defaults of all the persons employed in his Department."[43]

The evident injustice of this situation was ameliorated in particular areas by statute. For instance, section 59 of the Civil Liability Act 1961 provides that where a wrong is committed through the use of a motor vehicle belonging to the State, and driven by a person acting in the course of his employment, then the Minister for Finance is liable.[44] Further legislative reform to abolish the general principle of state immunity[45] (as had happened elsewhere) was promised.[46] In addition, there was a scheme of *ex gratia* payments but this could not be regarded as a satisfactory substitute for all action against the State.

However, the most far-reaching developments were to come via the judiciary. In 1965, in *Macauley v. Minister for Posts and Telegraphs*,[47] Kenny J. said that in

---

[41] [1972] I.R. 241.

[42] See, *e.g. Murphy v. Soady* [1903] 2 I.R. 213, where the Commissioners of Public Works were permitted to invoke Crown immunity to defeat an action for negligence.

[43] [1927] I.R. 62 at 69. In fact, the Dáil Debates reveals that the intention was to abolish the State's immunity. See the comments of the Attorney General (Hugh Kennedy, subsequently Chief Justice) at 5 *Dáil Debates* Col. 1498 (December 16, 1923) cited in Hogan and Whyte, *Kelly: The Irish Constitution* (3rd ed., 1994), p. 1145.

[44] For other legislative interventions, see Osborough, "The Demise of the State's Immunity in Tort" (1973) 8 Ir. Jur. 274 (N.S.), pp. 278–279.

[45] See Osborough, *ibid.* at pp. 281–282 referring to s.64 of the Workman's Compensation Act 1934; the Garda Síochána Acts 1941–1945, and ss.3, 100 and 118 of the Factories Act 1955.

[46] Programme of Law Reform (January 1962), p. 7. See also, 215 *Dáil Debates* Col. 1858 (May 20, 1965).

[47] [1966] I.R. 345.

his view the State could be sued "whenever this is necessary to vindicate or assert the rights of a citizen." Accordingly, the requirement in section 2(1) of the Ministers and Secretaries Act 1924 (which required the fiat of the Attorney General before proceedings could be instituted against the Minister) was held to be unconstitutional. Finally, in *Byrne v. Ireland*, as already mentioned, the Supreme Court ruled that the doctrine of sovereign or state immunity had not survived the enactment of the Constitution of Ireland. Both Walsh and Budd JJ. (who delivered the majority judgments) held first that the prerogative, of which state immunity was a part, had not survived the enactment of the Constitution. Secondly and specifically, in respect of state immunity itself, it was held that, even if the State were internally sovereign, this did not necessarily mean that it was immune from actions before its own courts and, indeed, such result was expressly excluded by certain provisions of the Constitution. For instance, Article 42.4 declares that the State is to provide for free primary education. This sub-article carried the necessary implication that if the State failed in this obligation, it could be sued in respect of such continued default. Similarly, Article 40.3 guarantees, the citizen right of access to the courts and the right to sue in respect of a justiciable controversy. Moreover, it was emphasised that there was a critical difference between the State in Ireland and the Crown in the United Kingdom which sufficed to explain why the former was liable in tort while at common law, the Crown was above the law. The difference is that whereas in the United Kingdom the Crown personifies the State and is the sovereign authority, in Ireland it is the people, and not the State, who are sovereign.

In *Byrne*, it had not been open to the plaintiff to sue the Minister, since *Carolan v. Minister for Defence*[48] had decided that both the Minister and civil servants were fellow employees of the State. The judgments in *Byrne* confirmed this rule and, consequently, a Minister cannot be made vicariously liable for the tortious acts of civil servants in his Department. As Walsh J. explained:

"All persons employed in the various Departments of the Government and the other Departments of State, whether they be in the civil service or not, are in the service of the State and the State is liable for damages done by such person in carrying out the affairs of the State so long as that person is acting within the terms of his employment."[49]

Unfortunately, *Byrne*, like many another epoch-making authority, leaves many questions unanswered. First, it would seem probable that this decision has not effected an implied repeal of the earlier statutory provisions which granted limited statutory rights to sue specified Ministers. For example, in the case of a person injured by the negligent use of a vehicle used in the service of the State, the aggrieved party may still either sue the Minister for Finance by virtue of the Civil Liability Act 1961,[50] or the State itself under the principle enunciated in *Byrne*. Secondly, is it possible to enact legislation which would modify the effects of the *Byrne* decision?

---

[48] [1927] I.R. 62.
[49] *Byrne v. Ireland* [1972] I.R. 241 at 285–286.
[50] Originally Road Traffic Act 1933, s.116. The Minister for Finance is not, however, liable where the State employee is not acting within the course of his employment: *Murray v. Minister for Finance*, unreported Supreme Court, April 22, 1982 (off-duty policeman).

Such legislation might provide, for example, that injured parties could only sue the Minister for Finance, and not the State, or that a special limitation period would apply to actions against the State. Such alternative arrangements would not unfairly impinge on a person's right to litigate a justiciable controversey. But, equally, it is doubtful whether legislation which sought to tamper with the principle enunciated in *Byrne* – such as legislation placing an upper limit on the quantum of damages recoverable in actions against the State or which precluded recovery in respect of certain types of economic loss which were otherwise recoverable – would survive constitutional challenge.

The major query raised by *Byrne* is the relationship between the new liability which the case created and the existing basis for suing the central state authority (*i.e.* the right to sue Ministers of State created by section 2 of the 1924 Act). Reference has already been made to one question raised by *Byrne*, namely, whether breach of contract actions should be brought against the State or the responsible Minister. A similar question arises in relation to tort actions. In the first place; as stated already, it is quite clear that where the tort was actually committed by a civil servant, the Minister cannot usually be held to be responsible.

However, Sullivan P. in *Carolan v. Minister for Defence* acknowledged that one of the functions of section 2 was to enable the Minister to be sued "in his corporate capacity for a wrongful act done by him as Minister, or by his orders or directions."[51] What this probably means is that the Minister cannot be held vicariously liable for the torts of his civil servants, but this does not affect his direct liability in tort. There is an important distinction between the direct liability of a Minister for the acts of his civil servants and vicarious liability for the torts committed by them. If a plaintiff contends that the Minister ordered or authorised the civil servant to commit the action complained of, or that the Minister was careless in selecting or supervising the employee, then this is an allegation of direct or personal liability on the part of the Minister and the action can proceed under section 2(1) of the 1924 Act.[52] On the other hand, vicarious liability arises when the law attaches liability to the employer for the employee's torts even where the employer is not personally at fault. For this more usual category of liability, as already mentioned, the appropriate defendant is the State.

Personal responsibility of Minister or public servant

It ought to be emphasised that the cardinal and historical principle that, if the plaintiff prefers, the responsible public servant or ministerial incumbent may be sued in tort personally, (rather than of the State or the Minister as corporation sole), remains correct. Thus, in *Lynch v. Fitzgerald* [53] the detectives who had unlawfully killed the son of the plaintiff during the course of suppressing a riot were found to be personally liable in an action under the Fatal Accidents Act 1846.

---

[51] [1927] I.R. 62 at 68–69.

[52] In cases of direct liability, it is the Minister's negligence which is the basis of the action and it is not crucial that the employee in question was negligent. On this general question, see McMahon & Binchy, *Irish Law of Torts* (2nd ed., 1990), pp. 748–761.

[53] [1938] I.R. 382. This case was, of course, decided in the pre-*Byrne* era and so the State was still assumed to be immune from suit. And, for the reasons set out in *Carolan's* case, the plaintiff could not sue the Minister for Justice, as the Minister and the detectives were both fellow servants of the

It is, likewise, worth emphasising that the Minister, *qua* corporation sole[54] is a separate legal entity from the incumbent at any particular time. *Sheil v. Attorney General*[55] is a good illustration of this principle. The plaintiff had been a train-bearer to the former Master of the Rolls, and upon the abolition of that judicial office in 1924, he was granted a declaration against the Attorney General to the effect that he was entitled to compensation under Article 10 of the Anglo-Irish Treaty 1921, to be paid out of monies voted by the Oireachtas. Costs of the action were awarded against the Attorney General. However, it was against Mr John Costello personally, the then holder of the office, that the plaintiff sought to enforce this part of the judgment. The original judgment was then rectified to make it clear that the costs, as well as the compensation, were also entitled to come from funds appropriated by the Oireachtas.

By contrast, in contract there is no personal liability. In *Kenny v. Cosgrave*[56] the President of the Executive Council had told an employer whose workers were on strike that it was essential that the strikers' demands be resisted. The President promised that the Executive Council would also indemnify him against any financial loss which resulted from this resistance. The action failed before the Supreme Court on a number of grounds, which included the fact that Mr Cosgrave had been sued personally and neither a Minister nor a civil servant can be held personally liable on a State contract.

Vicarious liability of the State

Irrespective of the fact that public servants will seldom be sued personally,[57] their formal liability is of obvious importance since (just as with any other employer) the State's liability is usually vicarious and is thus contingent upon proof of the employee's individual liability, usually in negligence. Public officials, while not as such carrying on a business or profession, necessarily hold themselves out as having special knowledge and authority in their field of activity. If they make a decision or give specific advice regarding the application of departmental or Governmental policy, in circumstances where they should know that their advice will be relied on, it would be consistent with general principles of negligence for the Irish courts to hold that they are under a duty to be reasonably careful. Nevertheless, assuming that such a duty of care does exist, it would seem that liability under this heading will be difficult to establish not least because of the various special defences which Ministers and other public officials have sometimes been held to enjoy. In *Pine*

State and thus the doctrine of *respondeat superior* could not apply. See also, *Gildea v. Hipwell* [1942] I.R. 489 (prison governor personally liable for false imprisonment) and *Liversidge v. Anderson* [1942] A.C. 206 at 210–211 (action for false imprisonment against British Home Secretary). In the case of *Kennedy v. Ireland* [1987] I.R. 587 (where the plaintiff journalists telephones had been unlawfully intercepted on the instructions of the Minister for Justice), the plaintiffs choose not to sue the Minister personally.

54 On this point, see pp. 914–915.
55 (1928) 62 I.L.T.S.J. 199 (referred to in Casey, *The Office of the Attorney General in Ireland* (1st ed., 1980), pp. 161–162).
56 [1926] I.R. 517. See further at pp. 862–863.
57 There have been examples of where the State has indemnified civil servants in such instances.

Valley Developments Ltd. v. Minister for the Environment[58] the Supreme Court held that the defendant Minister must be acquitted of negligence where he had acted on the basis of legal advice. The plaintiffs had suffered considerable financial loss as a result of the invalidation of a planning permission which had been granted to them by the defendant. The evidence showed, however, that the Minister's legal advisers believed that he had power to grant such permission and the Court held that, in such circumstances, no liability could attach. As Finlay C.J. said:

> "If a Minister of State, granted as a *persona designata* a specific duty and function to make decisions under a statutory code (as occurs in this case), exercises his decision *bona fide*, having obtained and followed the legal advice of the permanent legal advisers attached to his department, I can not see how he could be said to have been negligent if the law eventually proves to be otherwise than they have advised him and if by reason of that, he makes an order which is invalid or *ultra vires*."[59]

The Supreme Court was, however, less than clear as to the precise extent of a Minister's duty in general. Henchy J. (with whom Griffin and Lardner JJ. agreed) expressly stated that the Minister's duty was to give "his decision with the care and circumspection to be expected from a reasonably careful Minister". But Finlay C.J. (Hederman J. concurring), with whom Griffin and Lardner JJ. also agreed, appeared to enumerate a different test, referring with approval to a dictum of Lord Moulton in *Everett v. Griffiths*[60] to the effect that the Minister's duty was merely to make a decision honestly and in good faith.[61]

A further query which this case leaves unanswered, of course, is what is the position if the legal advice tendered to the Minister had been negligent? This, of course, was not the case in *Pine Valley*, because the advice then given to the Minister represented the common understanding of the legal profession at the time when it was given. However, had these facts been otherwise, and assuming that the negligent advice had been given by a civil servant (as opposed to a private practitioner), there would appear in principle to be no reason why the State should not have been made vicariously liable for the negligent advice.[62]

This matter was also considered by Blayney J. in *McMahon v. Ireland*.[63] Here the suggestion was that the Minister for Finance and the Minister for Industry and

---

[58] [1987] I.R. 23.
[59] *Ibid.* at 35
[60] [1921] A.C. 631 at 695.
[61] [1987] I.R. 23 at 38. *Cf. Jones v. Department of Environment* [1989] Q.B. 1 where the English Court of Appeal held that a social security officer did not owe a claimant a common law duty of care in calculating social security entitlements. Glidewell L.J. said (at 22) that, as a matter of general principle:
> "[I]f a government department or officer, charged with the making of decisions whether certain payments should be made, is subject to a statutory right of appeals against his decisions, he owes no duty of care in private law. Misfeasance apart, he is only susceptible in public law to judicial review or to the right of appeal provided by the statute under which he makes his decision."
[62] See *Cotter v. Minister for Agriculture*, unreported, High Court, November 15, 1991 (Minister liable for negligent advice given by his officials, but claim failed on the facts) and *Duff v. Minister for Agriculture* [1997] 2 I.R. 22 (similar principle, but the claim in negligence failed on the facts).
[63] [1988] I.L.R.M. 610. See MacGrath (1987) 9 D.U.L.J. 163 (N.S.).

Commerce were negligent in allowing an under–capitalised friendly society (which ultimately became insolvent, leaving unsecured and unpaid creditors) to continue in operation what in effect was a banking business outside the control of the Central Bank.[64] Blayney J. found that there was no cause of action *vis-à-vis* the Ministers:

> "Neither [Minister] was responsible for the initial exemption [from the scope of the Central Bank Acts] of which the plaintiff complains. It was contained in a statute enacted by the Oireachtas. And it could not be contended that either Minister owed the plaintiff a duty of care to have the Central Bank Act amended so as to prevent industrial provident societies from taking deposits."[65]

Blayney J. thus appears to have demonstrated a willingness to test the ministerial activity by reference to standard principles of negligence. However, he concluded his judgment by saying that the principles of quasi-immunity enjoyed by persons discharging quasi-judicial functions which were recognised by *Pine Valley* would have been applicable to the present case and would, in any event, have been enough to defeat the plaintiff's claim.[66]

4. Vicarious Liability of the State for Actions of Judges, Gardaí, Prison Officers and the Defence Forces

The question of just who is a servant of the State for the purposes of liability as a result of the decision in *Byrne* remains to be considered. This, in practice often arises together with the question of special defences, for in some cases, the servants will enjoy an immunity or quasi-immunity (usually statutory in origin) in their own right. However, the topic of statutory defences has already been covered in Part 2 of Chapter 15, save in the case of judges, whose immunity if it exists derives from the Constitution.

(i) *Judges*

Clearly the judiciary are not civil servants nor employees of the Government, but there is no reason why they should not be regarded as servants of the State for the purposes of vicarious liability, since the courts are organs of the State. At common law, judges enjoyed immunity from suit in respect in judicial acts.[67] It may be asked whether this common law immunity is compatible with constitutional principles and has survived the decision in *Byrne*. The immunity is founded on public policy. As Lord Salmon explained in *Sutcliffe v. Thackrah*:

---

[64] Friendly societies had been exempted from the requirement to hold banking licences under the Central Bank Act 1971.

[65] [1988] I.L.R.M. 610 at 612.

[66] While Blayney J. only applied the *Pine Valley* principles in the case of the claim against the Registrar of Friendly Societies (who, it was said, had been negligent in failing to take action under s.16 of the Industrial and Provident Societies (Amendment) Act 1978 to direct the company to cease accepting deposits), it is implicit in his judgment that he would have been prepared to apply these principles to the case of the two Ministers had this been required.

[67] See generally, Olowofoyeku, *Suing Judges: A Study of Judicial Immunity* (1993).

"It is well settled that judges, barristers, solicitors, jurors and witnesses enjoy an absolute immunity in respect of any civil action being brought against them in respect of anything they say or do in court during the course of the trial. The law recognises that, on the balance of convenience, public policy demands that they shall have such an immunity. It is of great public importance that they shall all perform their functions free from fear that disgruntled and possibly impecunious persons who have lost their cause or been convicted may subsequently harass them with litigation."[68]

Indeed, as Murnaghan J. observed in the High Court in *Byrne v. Ireland*, any other conclusion might lead to obvious difficulties:

"It would be very invidious if the High Court had to entertain an action against the State based on an allegation against the Supreme Court."[69]

Thus, at common law, judges, acting in their judicial capacity, are not liable in tort. Moreover, the defence of absolute privilege attaches to all statements made by judges during judicial proceedings.[70] This immunity might be considered to be vulnerable to challenge, on *Byrne* – type grounds, as the State is required by Article 40.3 of the Constitution, by its laws, to defend and vindicate the personal rights of the citizen, which include the right to litigate a justiciable controversy and to recover damages to in respect of a tortious act.[71] As against this, the most fundamental rule of constitutional interpretation is that the Constitution must be read as a whole and that its several provisions "must not be looked at in isolation, but be treated as interlocking parts of the general constitutional scheme."[72] Immunity from suit in respect of judicial acts would appear to be latent in Articles 34 and 35, which guarantee the administration of justice by judges and judicial independence.[73] Given that the courts lean against an interpretation which perverts "any of the fundamental purposes of the Constituton", it is probable that the constitutional right to litigate a justiciable controversy will have to give way to this judicial immunity from suit and such a possibility is accommodated in Article 40.3.1° by the words "so far as it is practicable".[74] This is strongly suggested by the reasoning of the Supreme Court

---

[68] [1974] A.C. 727 at 757.

[69] [1972] I.R. 241 at 253.

[70] *Tughan v. Craig* [1918] 1 I.R. 245; *Macauley v. Wyse-Power* (1943) 77 I.L.T.R. 61; *Coyle v. Roe, The Irish Times*, June 28, 1984 and *Deighan v. Ireland* [1995] 2 I.R. 56. In *Attorney General v. Hamilton (No.1)* [1993] 2 I.R. 250 at 285 McCarthy J. commented that:

   "At common law acts done or words spoken by a judge in his judicial capacity are absolutely privileged. That common law rule has never been tested within the constitutional framework, although the common law rule has been enforced."

[71] *O'Brien v. Keogh* [1972] I.R. 142 and Hogan and Whyte, *Kelly, op.cit.*, above, n.43, pp. 770–773.

[72] *Tormey v. Ireland* [1985] I.R. 289 at 296, *per* Henchy J.

[73] This was the view taken by the U.S. Supreme Court in *Pierson v. Ray* 386 U.S. 547 (1967). As Warren C.J. explained (at 533), the possibility of a damages action "would contribute not to principled and fearless decision-making, but to intimidation". Nevertheless, other forms of remedial relief may be granted as against a judge where this is "constitutionally required and necessary or to prevent irreparable harm": *Pulliam v. Allen* 466 U.S. 539, *per* Blackmun J.

[74] *Ibid.* This point was recognised by Murphy J. in *Looney v. Bank of Ireland* [1996] 1 I.R. 157 in upholding the validity of common law rules conferring absolute privilege on witnesses giving evidence in court. The judge observed that in this instance the constitutional interest in the fair

in *Pine Valley Developments Ltd v. Minister for the Environment*.[75] If persons discharging a quasi-judicial function enjoy an immunity from suit provided that they act "negligently and bona fide",[76] then *a fortiori* persons discharging judicial functions should enjoy a complete immunity from suit in respect of acts done in the course of their judicial duties, as their judicial independence would otherwise be compromised.

However, it might be suggested the requirements of judicial independence could be solved by the executive indemnifying individual members of the judiciary as has been suggested in the different context of an order for costs.[77] This suggestion might be extended to ensure that the judiciary would be indemnified against an order for damages. This would tend to preserve the independence of the judiciary, while ensuring that the personal rights of the individual to litigate a justiciable controversy were adequately respected. On the other hand, considerations pertaining to public confidence, judicial esteem and the very propriety of stigmatizing another judicial decision as negligent may make it unlikely that this suggestion will ever be accepted. This view is partly borne out by the judgment of Flood J. in *Deighnan v. Ireland*[78] where the traditional common law rule was re-iterated without any concessions to modern constitutional thinking. Moreover. Flood J. stoutly rejected the possibility of vicarious liability,[79] adding that the decision in *Maharaj v. Attorney General of Trinidad and Tobago (No. 2)*[80] – where the Privy Council had allowed an advocate who had been wrongly imprisoned for contempt of court to sue the State of Trinidad for damages for breach of his constitutional right to liberty – had turned on a specific provision of s.6(1) of the Constitution of Trinidad and Tobago and "no such corresponding provision exists in Ireland or in our Constitution."[81] Yet this response may be thought to have dealt less than fully with this submission. Subject to an argument regarding the countervailing constitutional considerations mentioned above, why should a plaintiff not be entitled to recover damages for a wrong done

---

administration of justice took precedence over the constitutional right to a good name, saying that the privilege:

"derives from the necessity of affording to witnesses the opportunity of giving their evidence fairly and freely . . . It derives from the very nature of the judicial process and the independent judiciary created by our Constitution."

75 [1987] I.R. 23.

76 *Ibid.* at 38, *per* Finlay C.J.

77 A suggestion made by Finlay C.J. in *MacIlwraith v. Fawsitt* [1990] I.L.R.M. 1. See pp. 716–717.

78 [1995] 2 I.R. 56. The plaintiff claimed that Costello J. had erred in previously convicting the plaintiff of contempt of court and he accordingly sought to sue Ireland, the Minister for Justice and the Minister for Finance on the ground that they were vicariously liable for the allegedly tortious act of the judge.

79 ". . . it follows that if the trial judge is not liable in damages for any erroneous decision made by him, the juridical body 'Ireland' cannot in any circumstances be rendered liable if the only basis upon which such a proposition could be founded is vicarious liability. Vicarious liability cannot arise unless there is primarily liability. Again vicarious liability is a concept related to the law of torts and it is certainly arguable whether the events in this case could ever be regarded as a tort."

80 [1979] A.C. 385.

81 [1995] 2 I.R. 56 at 63. But, in fact, in this respect, s.6(1) of the Trinidadian Constitution does no more than guarantee redress for breach of constitutional rights. So far from this provision having no Irish equivalent, Article 40.3 of the Irish Constitution seems to be even more emphatic in respect of the duties and obligations cast on the State in defence of the personal rights of citizens.

to him by an agent of the State when it has been done in the exercise of the judicial power of the State?

(ii) *The police and prison officers*

It is now clear that both the Gardaí and prison officers are servants of the State. The State has thus been held responsible under the doctrine of *respondeat superior* for the wrongful acts of Gardaí and prison officers acting within the scope of their employment in accordance with the principles enunciated in *Byrne*. This emerges from a number of recent cases. For example, in *Dowman v. Ireland*[82] the State was held to be vicariously liable for the tort of false imprisonment following an unlawful arrest effected by members of the Garda. In *McIntyre v. Lewis*[83] the State was held vicariously liable for assault, false imprisonment and malicious prosecutions committed by Gardaí in the course of their employment.

This matter was also considered by Costello J. in *Kearney v. Minister for Justice*,[84] which concerned the liability of the State for constitutional wrongs committed by prison officers. In this case, the plaintiff's mail was stopped by reason of unofficial action taken by prison officials. Costello J. held that although these actions did not amount to a tort at common law, they did constitute a breach of the plaintiff's constitutional right to communicate. On the question of the State's vicarious liability, the judge had this to say:

> "The wrong that was committed in this case was an unjustified infringement of a constitutional right, not a tort; and it was committed by a servant of the State and, accordingly, Ireland can be sued in respect of it: see *Byrne v. Ireland*. The State is clearly liable for such a wrong when it can be shown that had the wrong been a tort, vicarious liability would attach to the State. The wrongful act in this case was obviously connected with the functions for which the prison officers or officers who committed it were employed, and even though the act was not authorised I cannot hold that it was performed outside the scope of his or their employment. The plaintiff is therefore entitled to be awarded damages against the State."[85]

This reasoning would appear to apply, *mutatis mutandis*, to the Gardaí and ensure that the State is vicariously liable for torts or constitutional wrongs committed by members of the force within the scope of their employment and, indeed, *Walsh v. Ireland*[86] provides direct authority for this proposition. Here the plaintiff had been wrongly arrested by members of the Garda Síochána following what Hamilton C.J. described as a "clear case of mistaken identity". The Chief Justice said that the arrest of the plaintiff was nonetheless unlawful and that:

---

[82] [1986] I.L.R.M. 111.
[83] [1991] 1 I.R. 121.
[84] [1986] I.R. 116.
[85] *Ibid.* at 122. *Cf. McHugh v. Garda Commissioner* [1986] I.R. 228 where Finlay C.J. accepted (at 233) that Ireland was vicariously liable for a breach of constitutional rights committed by the Garda Commissioner.
[86] Unreported, Supreme Court, November 30, 1994.

"was effected by members of the Garda Síochána acting in pursuance of their duties on behalf of the State, that such arrest was a breach of the constitutional right of the [plaintiff] to his personal liberty and a failure by the organs of State to defend and vindicate such right and that the defendants are liable in respect thereof."

The Supreme Court rejected a defence based on section 50 of the Constabulary (Ireland) Act 1836[87] since no action had been brought against the Gardaí who had actually effected the arrest. Moreover, the arrest had not been effected "in obedience to the warrant", since the wrong person had actually been arrested.

(iii) *Members of the Defence Forces*

Members of the Defence Forces are regarded as servants of the State for the purposes of the *Byrne* decision, and in the series of cases which followed this decision, the State did not attempt to dispute this point. However, in *Ryan v. Ireland*,[88] the Supreme Court was given the opportunity of considering the liability of the State in respect of tortious acts committed by officers while engaged in active service. The plaintiff was a member of the Irish contingent which formed part of the United Nations International Force serving in the Lebanon. In April 1979 a member of Christian Militia had been shot dead outside an Irish Army post and it appears that the militia were determined to seek revenge on the members of the Irish contingent. Although there were clear signals that such an attack was being planned, the plaintiff was ordered to take a rest in a portacabin shelter which had not been sandbagged. His position was attacked after he had gone to sleep and he was seriously injured by a mortar which struck his portacabin. There was evidence of negligent preparations to meet the attack and the Supreme Court was asked to consider:

(i) whether at common law the State enjoyed an immunity from suit in respect of negligent acts committed by serving officers on active service; and

(ii) if the answer to this was in the affirmative, whether such an immunity was consistent with the provisions of the Constitution.

Dealing with the first question, Finlay C.J. observed that Article 28.3 of the Constitution gives the Oireachtas extensive powers to deal with war and the preservation of the State in time of war and that the Constitution may not be invoked

---

[87] Which provides that:
 "... when any action shall be brought against any constable for any act done in obedience to the verdict of any magistrate, such constable shall not be responsible for any irregularity in issuing the warrant, or for any want of jurisdiction in the magistrate issuing the same, and such constable may plead the general issue and give such warrant and providing that the signature thereto is the handwriting of the person whose name shall appear subscribed thereto, and that such person is reputed to be and acts as a magistrate . . . and that the act or acts complained of were done in obedience to such warrant, the jury who shall try the said issue shall find a verdict for such constable, and such constable shall recover his cost of suit."

[88] [1989] I.R. 177. See also *Healy v. Minister for Defence*, unreported, High Court, July 7, 1994 (damages awarded to member of the Defence Forces for breach of constitutional right to fair procedures).

to invalidate "legislation expressed to be for such purpose". He concluded that these provisions made it impossible to accept:

> "the application of a common law doctrine arising from necessity to ensure the safety of the State during a period of war or armed rebellion which has the effect of abrogating constitutional rights. In so far, therefore, as the principle apparently supporting some of the decisions to which we have been referred is the question of the dominant priority in regard to the defence of the State, such decisions would not appear to be applicable and cannot be applied to the question of service with the United Nations force. I, therefore, conclude that an immunity from suit, or the negation of any duty of care to, a serving soldier in respect of operations consisting of armed conflict or hostilities has not been established as part of our common law."[89]

And, as to the second question, even if such an immunity had existed at common law, it would not have survived the enactment of the Constitution:

> "I conclude that in the blanket form which has been contended for [such an immunity] would be inconsistent with the guarantees by the State to respect, defend and vindicate the rights of the citizens contained in Article 40.3.1° and Article 40.3.2° of the Constitution."[90]

5. Procedural Aspects of Litigation Involving the State

(i) *Litigation involving the State and Government*

The procedural aspects of suing the State were considered by the Supreme Court in *Byrne v. Ireland*.[91] The State's power or right to defend itself is one which can be exercised only by or on the authority of Government (by virtue of the provisions of Article 28.2 of the Constitution). Walsh J. said that, if it was the Attorney General's opinion that the Government should authorise the defence by the State of the claim brought against it, then the defence was a matter of public interest and was properly financed out of public monies. If the Government did not wish to authorise the defence then the Attorney General would not defend the case and in that case the correct procedure would be to sue the State and to join the Attorney General in order to effect service upon the Attorney General for both parties. (It is not at all clear why it is necessary to join the Attorney General). If the claim should succeed, judgment would be against the State and not against the Attorney General because the Attorney General had only been joined in a representative capacity as the law officer of State designated by the Constitution.[92] As a result, Ireland must be joined as a defendant in any proceedings where there is a claim for either a liquidated or unliquidated sum and it does not for this purpose suffice merely to

---

[89] *Ibid.* at 182.
[90] *Ibid.* at 182–183.
[91] [1972] I.R. 24.
[92] *Ibid.* at 289. See also *Sheil v. Attorney General* (1928) 62 I.L.T.S.J. 199.

nominate the Attorney General as the defendant.[93]

So far we have spoken of the State as defendant, but there is no reason why the State may not sue as plaintiff in its own right. One such case is *Ireland v. Mulvey*,[94] where the State commenced proceedings against the defendants claiming that it had title over an eight-century cross by virtue of Article 5 of the Constitution. Hamilton P. granted Ireland an interlocutory injunction restraining the defendants from removing the cross from the jurisdiction.

A related question which sometimes arises is whether the Government, as distinct from the State, can sue and be sued and whether it has legal personality for this purpose. A practice has emerged whereby all the individual members of the Government have been sued in cases involving the actions of the Government: see, *e.g. Crotty v. An Taoiseach*[95]; *McKenna v. An Taoiseach (No. 2)*.[96] However, in *The State (Sheehan) v. Government of Ireland*[97] the Government was sued as such and no objection was taken to that course of action. It may, of course, be said that in *Sheehan's* case the complaint related to the failure to perform a specific duty which had imposed on the Government by statute and that different considerations may arise as to the propriety of suing the Government in cases (such as, perhaps, a breach of contract action) where no such statutory (or, indeed, constitutional)[98] obligation has been imposed directly on the Government. Nevertheless, in view of the fact that the Government has been vested with specific constitutional and statutory functions, it seems reasonably clear (even if the matter is not completely beyond doubt) that it is a juristic person with legal capacity and may sue and be sued.

(ii) *Enforcement of judgments*

The Supreme Court in *Byrne v. Ireland* did not consider how a decree for the plaintiff would be executed or enforced. Walsh J. however, did comment that "an order for mandamus to compel compliance with the judgment would be an appropriate step and not without precedent".[99] Budd J. said that he took it for granted that the necessary monies to meet the decree would be provided. "That would only be what would be normally expected in a State governed according to the rule of law and there would seem to be no reason to believe that the State would not honour its legal obligations."[100] If it had been necessary to come to a final decision on this point,

---

93   *Murphy v. Attorney General* [1982] I.R. 241 at 315–316, *per* Henchy J.
94   *The Irish Times*, November 11, 1989. See also *Ireland v. Kelly* [1992] I.L.R.M. 582 (State claiming to be entitled to act as executor of an estate where executor had been convicted of murder). See, too, the case brought by the Minister for Justice against the Garda Representatives Association, *The Irish Times*, September 14, 1996.
95   [1987] I.R. 713.
96   [1995] 2 I.R. 10.
97   [1987] I.R. 550. See also *Lang v. Government of Ireland* [1993] E.L.R. 234 and *Kavanagh v. Government of Ireland* [1996] 1 I.R. 321.
98   In *Dudley v. An Taoiseach* [1994] 2 I.L.R.M. 321 Geoghegan J. granted liberty to the applicant to seek judicial review against the Government in respect of its failure to fulfill an alleged constitutional obligation (holding a bye-election within a reasonable period of time). Yet the judge refused leave to apply for judicial review in respect of Dáil Éireann, on the ground that the courts "cannot mandamus the body of members of the Dáil as such to vote in a particular way on a particular motion". This, however, is not quite the same thing as saying that Dáil Éireann is not a juristic person without legal capacity.
99   [1972] I.R. 241 at 289.

he thought that "the ordinary procedure of execution by way of levy or enforcement by mandamus would both seem to be appropriate."[101]

(iii) *Mandamus*

At common law the writ of mandamus did not lie against a Minister of the Crown and in Northern Ireland it has been held that an application for mandamus against the Minister for Home Affairs was unsustainable.[102] In the Republic, however, this immunity has not survived and in *The State (King) v. Minister for Justice*[103] Doyle J. granted an order of mandamus commanding the Minister to exercise the statutory duties imposed on him by section 6(1) of the Courthouses (Provisions and Mainte-nance) Act 1935, namely, to direct the Commissioners of Public Works in Ireland to execute such repairs and to do such other work as may be necessary or proper to put the court accommodation at Waterford into proper repair and condition. Doyle J. relied on the majority decision of the Supreme Court in *Byrne v. Ireland* in holding that the survival of such an immunity would be inconsistent with the general tenor of the Constitution in that there "is no power, institution, or person in the land free of the law save where such immunity is expressed, or provided for, in the Constitution itself".[104] This view was also accepted as correct by Costello J. in *The State (Sheehan) v. Government of Ireland*,[105] where counsel for the Government had submitted that mandamus would not lie against the Government. Costello J. thought that this submission was based on the proposition that:

> "In English law since a prerogative order emanates from the Crown it cannot lie against the Crown. But there is no analogy between the law of Ireland and England on this topic. An order of mandamus made now by an Irish court is not a prerogative writ of mandamus which, before the establishment of the State, was the means by which the courts enforced observance of statutory duties and under the Constitution the Government which it establishes is not the successor to the Crown. There is no constitutional reason, therefore, which would prohibit the making of an order of mandamus against the Government."[106]

---

[100] *Ibid.* at 307. In *Hoey v. Minister for Justice* [1994] 3 I.R. 329 at 350, Lynch J. said that a contention that lack of resources prevented a Minister from carrying out her statutory duty to repair a courthouse imposed by s.6(1) of the Courthouses (Provision and Maintenance) Act 1935 was based upon "a misconception of the powers, duties and functions of the executive in regard to the implementation of legislation enacted by the Oireachtas". If the statutory duties in question proved to be excessively costly and "the executive wishes to limit or reduce such obligations, the executive must introduce the appropriate legislation to the Oireachtas and persuade the Oireachtas to enact the same". However, note the comments of Geoghegan J. in *Dudley v. An Taoiseach*: see above, n.98.

[101] *Ibid.*

[102] *R. (Diamond and Fleming) v. Warnock* [1946] N.I. 171.

[103] [1984] I.R. 169. A Minister can be found guilty of contempt of court: see *Desmond v. Glackin (No.1)* [1993] 3 I.R. 1. It is interesting that there was no suggestion in this case that the Minister enjoyed any vestigial immunity in this regard. This contrasts with the position in the United Kingdom, where it was not until the decision in *M v. Home Office* [1993] 3 W.L.R. 433 that the "principle that Crown officers do not partake of the Crown's immunity is re-instated", but even then "in the last analysis the House of Lords' judgment contains an inconsistency about enforcement": see Wade and Forsyth, *Administrative Law* (1994), p. 587.

[104] *Ibid. at* 176, quoting from the judgment of Walsh J. in *Byrne v. Ireland* [1972] I.R. 241 at 281.

[105] [1987] I.R. 550.

[106] *Ibid.* at 555. In *Dudley v. An Taoiseach* [1994] 2 I.L.R.M. 321 the applicant sought leave to challenge

Accordingly, therefore, any vestigial immunity which might hitherto have attached in respect of mandamus to Ministers, the Government or even, it would seem, Ireland itself, has now been judicially removed. As against this, however, there remains the awkward fact (see below) that the Supreme Court has refused to grant an injunction against the State. There is very little policy justification for distinguishing between an order of mandamus and an injunction in this context and, accordingly, the matter cannot be regarded as absolutely beyond doubt.

(iv) *Injunctions*

The Supreme Court has ruled, in *Pesca Valentia Ltd. v. Minister for Fisheries*[107] that it is not appropriate that any injunction should ever be given against Ireland. Instead, the practice is to grant injunctions against the relevant Minister. No reasons were given for this conclusion by Finlay C.J. in his judgment in *Pesca Valentia*[108] and this immunity would seem difficult to justify. If Ireland can be liable for damages, why should it enjoy an immunity for another form of remedy, such as an injunction? This is especially so, given that it now seems that mandamus (a very similar form of remedy to an injunction) will lie against Ireland.

The second situation in which there may, in certain cirumstances, be difficulty about the grant of an injunction is where it is sought in order to restrain the operation of an Act of the Oireachtas or to prevent a threatened breach of a constitutional right,[109] pending the outcome of the full hearing. In *Pesca Valentia*, the Supreme Court held that the duty of the courts to protect persons against the invasion of their constitutional rights or against unconstitutional action meant that there must exist a jurisdiction to restrain, in an appropriate case, the operation of a statutory provision pending a challenge to its validity. As Finlay C.J. observed:

> "It would seem wholly inconsistent with that duty if the Court were to be without power in an appropriate case to restrain by injunction an action against a person which found its authority in a statutory provision which might eventually be held to be invalid having regard to the Constitution."[110]

---

the failure on the part of the Government and the Dáil to hold a bye-election in compliance with what (was contended were) constitutional requirements. Geoghegan J., following *Sheehan*, granted leave to apply for judicial review in respect of the Government's alleged failure to comply with constitutional obligations but refused to grant leave in respect of the Dáil because (at 324):

> "No enforceable order can be made by the courts as against Dáil Éireann as such. Dáil Éireann can only give the direction if the majority of the members vote for the motion but the courts cannot *mandamus* the body of members of the Dáil as such to vote in a particular way on a particular motion."

107 [1985] I.R. 193.
108 *Ibid.* at 202.
109 See, *e.g. X v. Flynn, The Irish Times*, May 20, 1994 (interlocutory injunction granted to restrain threatened infringement of the plaintiff's constitutional right to privacy by newspaper reporters). *Cf. M v. Drury* [1994] 2 I.R. 8 where a similar application failed on the merits. In *Colmey v. Pinewood Development Ltd* [1994] 3 I.R. 360 Carroll J. refused to grant an interlocutory injunction restraining a District Judge from exercising jurisdiction in ejectment proccedings pending a constitutional challenge, but the merits of the main action were described by her as "prima facie . . . extremely weak."
110 [1985] I.R. 193 at 201.

The Chief Justice continued by hinting that this power would be more readily exercised where a penal statute was under challenge. Accordingly, the Supreme Court granted an injunction restraining the prosecution of the plaintiff company under the Fisheries (Amendment) Act 1983 pending the outcome of a constitutional challenge. A spectacular example of the exercise of this power may be found in *Crotty v. An Taoiseach*[111] where Barrington J., who was subsequently upheld by the Supreme Court, granted an injunction restraining the Government from ratifying the Single European Act pending the outcome of the plaintiff's constitutional challenge to the validity of such a ratification.

In the last decade the *Pesca Valentia* principles have weathered somewhat unevenly. In *Cooke v. Minister for Communications*,[112] with no apparent consideration of *Pesca Valentia*, the Supreme Court refused to grant an injunction to the proprietor of an unlicensed radio station restraining the Minister from invoking his statutory powers to direct the termination of electricity and telecommunications supplies, pending a challenge as to the constitutional propriety of the Independent Radio and Television Act 1988, which established such a licensing regime. Walsh J. said that:

"Where an existing statute rendered an activity illegal, the court would not by injunction restrain the imposition of preventive measures authorised by the statute, even where a challenge to the constitutional validity of the said statute was pending."

In *Carrigaline Community Television v. Minister for Transport (No. 1)*,[113] however, an interlocutory injunction was granted restraining the Minister invoking his powers under the Wireless Telegraphy Act 1926 to prevent the continued operation of an unlicensed television transmission service pending a challenge to the validity of the Minister's decision to refuse the plaintiffs a licence for this purpose.[114]

In *Grange Developments Ltd. v. Dublin County Council (No. 4)*[115] Murphy J. refused to grant an injunction staying the enforcement of an arbitrator's award of compensation in favour of the plaintiffs under the Local Government (Planning and Development) Act 1963, pending a challenge to the validity of the compensa-tion provisions of that Act. Murphy J. agreed that an injunction to restrain the operation of contested statutory provisions could be granted in an appropriate case, but he thought

---

[111] [1987] I.R. 713.
[112] *Irish Times Law Report*, February 20, 1989. See also, the comments of Murphy J. in *Nova Media Services Ltd v. Minister for Posts and Telegraphs* [1984] I.L.R.M. 161 at 169 (a case with facts similar to those in *Cooke*):
"In principle it may be that in certain circumstances the courts might in the proper exercise of their discretion refuse to grant an injunction to secure compliance with a statutory provision by members of the public pending a decision by the courts as to the constitutionality of the particular statute, but it would only be in the most extraordinary circumstances that the courts would intervene to prevent the Minister or the Government agencies from exercising a function conferred upon him or them by the express terms of a statute made for the control of a public resource and for the benefit of the public good."
[113] [1994] 2 I.R. 359.
[114] Costello J. applied the *Pesca Valentia* principles, saying (at 367) that the plaintiff had been carrying on an unlicensed service for nine years, during which time no prosecution had been instituted. It was accordingly entitled to have its challenge to the validity of the licence determined in advance of any future criminal prosecution.
[115] [1989] I.R. 337.

that such relief should only be granted in exceptional cases. The present case did not fit into that category, as the County Council could not show that they would suffer irreparable loss. The sum of money paid by way of compensation was readily ascertainable and was repayable in the event of the impugned provisions being declared unconstitutional.

(v) *Miscellaneous*

At common law the Crown enjoyed a variety of procedural privileges derived from the prerogative.[116] Thus, neither laches nor delay could be imputed to the Crown[117] and the courts would not deny relief on discretionary grounds to the Attorney General.[118] In addition the courts did not require the Attorney General to tender an undertaking as to damages where he sought an injunction to enforce the law.[119] The absence of recent case law on these issues (which stems from the fact that they come into play mainly if the State were the plaintiff) makes it difficult to offer any firm views. However, in principle, it would seem that these rules, derived as they are from the prerogative,[120] are unlikely to have survived for the benefit of the State. This is especially so, given that the entire tenor of *Byrne v. Ireland*[121] is such as to suggest that the State should stand on an equal footing with all other litigants and should not enjoy procedural privileges not available to the private litigant.

---

116   Halsbury, *Laws of England* (4th ed.), para. 931.

117   *Re an Application for Certiorari* [1965] N.I. 67.

118   *The State (Kerry County Council) v. Minister for Local Government* [1933] I.R. 517 at 546, *per* Murnaghan J. Quite apart from other constitutional considerations arising from the nature of the prerogative origins of this rule, etc., this rule could hardly have survived (at least in its unqualified form) into a modern era. Undue delay on the part of the Attorney General in applying for, *e.g.* an order of certiorari or an injunction might cause a defendant great hardship where, for example, the defendant had altered his position in reliance on the validity of the order in question. A rule of practice which ordained that the court should not have regard to such potential consequences for the defendant would scarcely seem compatible with the constitutional guarantees of fair procedures or equality.

119   *Hoffman-La Roche & Co. A.G. v. Trade Secretary* [1975] A.C. 295. The House of Lords held that the rule that an injunction could not be required of the Crown where it was sued in a proprietary capacity had been abolished by the Crown Proceedings Act 1947, but the privileged position of the Crown in cases where it was seeking an injunction to enforce the law remained unaffected by this legislative change. It is likely that a similar distinction would be adopted by the Irish courts, even in the absence of any equivalent legislation.

120   It may be that the rule whereby the Attorney General is not required to tender an undertaking in damages in cases where an injunction to enforce the law is sought should not properly be regarded as a prerogative right emanating from the Crown, but rather a rule properly regarded as subsisting for the public benefit. As Lord Goff explained in *Kirklees BC v. Wickes Building Supplies Ltd* [1993] A.C. 227 at 274 the "old Crown privilege" had been dismantled and there was in its place "a principle upon which, in certain limited circumstances, the court has a discretion whether or not to require an undertaking from the Crown as a law enforcer." The principle "appears to be related not to the Crown but to the Crown when performing a particular function." Note, however, that in *Howard v. Commissiners of Public Works* [1994] 1 I.R. 101 a majority of the Supreme Court rejected a similar argument in the case of the presumption that the State was not bound by the application of statute, with both Finlay C.J. and Denham J. stressing that the rule could not be divorced from its prerogative origins. Moreover, a defendant who suffered loss and damage might justifiably assert that the absence of an undertaking as to damages amounted to an invasion of his property rights as guaranteed by Art. 40.3.2°.

121   [1972] I.R. 241.

6. State Exemption from Statute

As usually stated, this exemption meant that the State was not "bound" (*i.e.* affected to its disadvantage) by a statute unless it is referred to either expressly or by necessary implication. An early example is provided by *Galway County Council v. Minister for Finance*[122] where one of the issues was whether the defendant Minister was free to set off as against the plaintiff's claim, an overpayment which he had made to them eight years earlier. The County Council submitted in reply that the Minister's claim was not statute-barred. Johnson J. was unimpressed by this argument:

> "[T]he Minister relies on prerogative rights and contends that the sub-section has no applicability to a claim such as the present, there being no indication in the subsection that it was the intention of the Legislature to bind the Crown or the State. There has been no doubt and it has not been argued in the present case to the contrary, that the prerogative and prerogative right can be relied upon by the Irish Free State, and is part of the law of the land, I can see nothing in [the subsection] that suggests that it was intended to have any applicability to the Crown or the State and, I think, therefore, that the defendant is entitled to rely on this set-off."[123]

In *Irish Land Commission v. Ruane*[124] the High Court applied the rule that the exemption may be excluded by necessary implication. The statutory provision in question in that case, the Increase of Rent and Mortgage Interest (Restriction) Act 1923, restricted the right of the landlord to recover possession unless "the dwelling house is reasonably required for the purpose of the execution of the duties of any Government Department or any local authority or statutory undertaking." Both Johnston and Gavan Duffy JJ. appear to have assumed[125] that this provision only applied where the Department, local authority or statutory undertaking was the landlord, and, accordingly, that the provision would be redundant if it were excluded in the case of State property. However, in *Fitzsimons v. Menkin*,[126] a majority of the Supreme Court ruled that the provision was of general application, and would apply even in the case of a private landlord. Although such a situation would seem likely to be rare, the Supreme Court held in the later case of *Cork County Council v. Commissioners of Public Works*[127] that this change of interpretation destroyed the premise on which the judgment in *Ruane* was founded, and meant that, in the usual way, the State was exempt from the application of the 1923 Act. The question of

---

[122] [1931] I.R. 215.

[123] *Ibid.*, 232. See now s.3(1) of the Statute of Limitations 1957, which provides that the Statute shall apply to "proceedings by or against a State authority in the same manner as if that State authority were a private individual." See also, 318 *Dáil Debates* 240–247 (February 20, 1980) (restriction on application to State of Landlord and Tenant (Amendment) Act 1980, though see also Landlord and Tenant (Amendment) Act 1984, s.14). Note that from time to time even contemporary statues expressly stipulate that the State will be bound: see, *e.g.* Environmental Protection Agency Act 1992, s.3(5) which provides that this Act applied "to activities operated by or in the charge of the State."

[124] [1938] I.R. 148.

[125] Certainly this was the view that was taken of their judgments by the Supreme Court in *Cork County Council v. Commissioners of Public Works* [1945] I.R. 561.

[126] [1938] I.R. 805.

[127] [1945] I.R. 561.

whether the State was bound by another statute, the Local Government (Rates on Small Dwellings) Act 1928, which made provision for the rating of the owners of dwellings below a specified rateable value, in lieu of the occupiers, also arose in the *Cork County Council* case. A majority of the Supreme Court rejected the argument that it was a necessary implication in the construction of the Act that it should be held to bind the State merely because, in the words of O'Byrne J., "the opposite construction would have the effect of leaving certain houses free from liability".[128] The Court accordingly held the houses owned by the defendant Commissioners were exempt from rates.

All three members of the Supreme Court accepted that the exemption of the State from the application of statutes had survived the enactment of the Constitution. However, there are clear hints in the judgments of O'Byrne and Black JJ. that this exemption could be rationalised in terms of a principle of statutory construction rather than a privilege derived from concepts of a regal personality.[129]

The combined weight of these authorities – despite the fact that some of the comments might properly have been regarded as merely *obiter* – all suggested that the traditional rule had survived the enactment of the Constitution. It is true that these decisions had largely rested on the supposition that the prerogative had survived the enactment of the Constitution, but even in *Byrne v. Ireland*[130] – where that supposition was said to have been erroneous – Walsh J. was prepared to contemplate the survival of this common law presumption on the ground that:

"And though this [exemption] is sometimes called a prerogative right, it is in fact nothing more than a reservation, or exception, introduced for the public benefit, and equally applicable to all governments."[131]

This approach was rejected by a majority of the Supreme Court in *Howard v. Commissioners of Public Works*.[132] In this case the defendants had proposed the construction of visitors' centres in three area of outstanding scenic beauty. These proposals had proved to be very controversial and the legality of the Commissioner's actions were challenged in the courts. Quite apart from the more specific question of whether the Commissioners, as a body corporate, had any power to construct interpretative centres,[133] the major question was whether these proposals required

---

128   *Ibid.* at 581. In *Howard v. Commissioners of Public Works* [1994] 1 I.R. 101 at 136 Finlay C.J. said that O'Byrne J.'s judgment "must be considered as *obiter*, even to the core of his decision and certainly does not form part of the other decisions reached on that issue in the Court, both of which proceeded upon an acceptance of the succession under the Constitution of the State to the Crown prerogative."

129   Thus, Black J. observed [1945] I.R. 561 at 587: "Much time was devoted to discussing the true nature of this right and to combating the supposition that so far as it still exists, it is inseparable from the institution of kingship. If that were so, one would not expect to find such a right recognised for over a century by the Courts of the United States of America where the institution of kingship has no existence."

130   [1972] I.R. 241.

131   *Ibid.* at 278, quoting Story J. in *United States v. Hoar* (1821) 2 Mason 311 at 313. The U.S. Supreme Court has accepted the survival of this rule of statutory construction, despite its origins as a Crown prerogative: *Guaranty Trust Co. v. United States* 304 U.S. 126 (1938); *United States v. Nardone* 338 U.S. 303 (1939).

132   [1994] 1 I.R. 101. See generally, Hogan, "The Mullaghmore Case" (1993) 15 D.U.L.J. 243 (N.S.). This decision had been presciently anticipated in Keane, "The 1963 Planning Act – Twenty Years On" (1983) 5 D.U.L.J. 92.

133   See pp. 395 and 404 above.

planning permission. It was common case that these proposals would have required planning permission had the Commissioners been a private body and this raised the more fundamental question of whether the traditional rule presuming that the State was not bound by statute had survived the enactment of the Constitution.

A majority[134] of the Supreme Court concluded that the rule had not survived the enactment of the Constitution. In the view of the majority, the rule could not be divorced from its historical origins. Both Finlay C.J. and Denham J. quoted from recent British authority to demonstrate this point, including the following passage from the judgment of Diplock L.J. in *B.B.C. v. Johns*:

> "The question is, thus, one of construction of statutes. Since laws are made by rulers for subjects, a general expression in a statute such as 'any person' is descriptive of those upon whom the statute imposes obligation or restraints is not to be read as including the ruler himself."[135]

Denham J. considered that the "enlightening phrase" in this passage was the reference to "since laws are made by rulers for subjects". In her view, this demonstrated that the rule was so deeply rooted in the prerogative and "the Crown as personification of the State" that it was insperable from that concept. It is, of course, correct to note that the British courts have even very recently re-affirmed the rule in those terms,[136] but this should not prove to be decisive for the Irish courts.

The consequences of the Howard *decision*

Even if the Supreme Court was wrong to condemn the rule as simply an outcrop of the now vanished prerogative, the fact remains that the rule (because of its discriminatory content) is unlikely to persist in a modern world, as is clear from other jurisdictions.[137]

---

[134] Finlay C.J., Blayney, Egan and Denham JJ. O'Flaherty J. dissented.

[135] [1965] Ch. 32 at 78–79. This passage was expressly approved by the House of Lords in *The Lord Advocate v. Dumbarton BC* [1990] 2 A.C. 580 where the rule that the Crown was not bound by a statute unless expressly named or by necessary implication was re-affirmed.

[136] In the *Dumbarton* case, *ibid.*

[137] The rule has been abandoned in India. As Subba Rao C.J. explained in *State of West Bengal v. Corporation of Calcutta* [1967] A.I.R. 997 at 1007–8:

> "There are many reasons why the said rule of construction is inconsistent with and incongruous in the present set-up. We have no Crown: the archaic rule based on the prerogative and perfection of the Crown has no relevance to a democratic republic: it is inconsistent with the rule of law based on the doctrine of equality. It introduces conflicts and discrimination. The normal construction, namely, that the general Act applies to citizens as well as to States unless it expressly or by necessary implication exempts the State from its operation, steers clear of all the said anomalies. It prima facie applies to all States and subjects alike, a construction consistent with the philosophy of equality enshrined in our Constitution. This natural approach avoids the archaic rule and moves with the modern trends. This will not cause hardship to the State. The State can make an Act, if it chooses, providing for its exemption from its operation."

The rule has also been relaxed in Australia. As Mason C.J. explained in *Bropho v. Western Australia* (1990) 171 C.L.R. 1 at 21–2:

> ". . . Once it has been accepted that a legislative intention to bind the Crown may be disclosed notwithstanding that it could not be said that that intention was 'manifest from the terms' of the statute or would otherwise be 'wholly frustrated', fundamental principle precludes confinement of the general words which the Legislature has used in a way which will defeat that intention."

A related question concerns the capacity of the Oireachtas to exempt the State and state bodies from the scope of any legislation. Both Finlay C.J. and Denham J.[138] expressly contemplated the enactment of legislative exceptions of this kind. The Local Government (Planning and Development) Act 1993 – which was enacted in the wake of the *Howard* decision – provides an example of such a specifically tailored exception. The Act provides that, subject to certain exceptions in favour of certain developments associated with or for the purposes of "public safety or order, the administration of justice or national security or defence",[139] the planning laws shall henceforth apply to all State development. It is possible that there are limits to this form of exception and legislation which sought to confer unjustified and disproportionate advantages on State bodies by, *e.g.* creating certain immunities or exceptions in their favour might be open to challenge on constitutional grounds other than the non-importation of the prerogative.[140]

7. Privilege Against the Disclosure of Official Documents

Historical antecedents

It was formerly the law that Ministers could not be compelled by court order to produce documents for inspection or even to disclose the existence of a document. This applied in all litigation, irrespective of whether the Minister or the State were actually a party to it. All that was necessary for the exercise of this privilege was an affidavit claiming it, signed by the responsible Minister or one of his senior civil servants. There were, plainly, two elements to this privilege:

(i) There was a public interest in maintaining the confidentiality of certain official documents; and

(ii) It was for the responsible Minister, and not the court, to decide whether this interest outweighed the public interest in the fair administration of justice.

As has been remarked, "the newly independent State, having shaken off the yolk of the Crown, embraced with enthusiasm many of its privileges".[141] The privilege was

---

138 As Denham J. said, [1994] 1 I.R. 101 at 160 ". . . the Oireachtas may legislate including or excluding the application of an Act to the executive in accordance with constitutional parameters."

139 See s.2(1)(a) of the Act. Article 156 of the Local Government (Planning and Development) Regulations 1994 (S.I. No. 86 of 1994) now provides that certain specified developments (including Garda barracks, prisons, courthouses, certain classes of Government buildings etc.) are to be regarded as exempted development for planning purposes: see Scannell, *Environmental and Planning Law in Ireland* (1994) at 160–161.

140 The most probable line of attack would be where some person's right to litigate a justiciable controversy were unjustifiably curtailed, a point canvassed at pp. 454–460. In this regard, see the comments of Henchy J. in *Dillane v. Ireland* [1980] I.L.R.M. 167 upholding the validity of Rule 67 of the District Court Rules 1948 which exempts Gardaí from possible exposure to costs following a unuccessful prosecution. There was here a clear suggestion that had the Rule gone further and conferrred a wider immunity than was strictly necessary that it would have been open to challenge on both Article 40.1 and Article 40.3 grounds.

141 Russell, "A Privilege of the State" (1967) 2 Ir. Jur. 88 (N.S.). This prescient article reviewed the former law and predicted its demise. For a fine analysis of the development of the law in the United Kingdom, see Jacob, "From privileged Crown to interested public" (1993) *Public Law* 121.

invoked to protect: communications between the Executive Council and the Shaw Commission which investigated the destruction of Ballyheigue Castle;[142] advices and minutes given to the Minister for Local Government in regard to the Electoral (Amendment) Act 1959[143] and, in a prosecution for "showing for gain an indecent and profane performance" the instructions, given by their superiors, to the detectives who watched the play.[144]

The modern law: the Murphy *and* Ambiorix *decisions*

The law was authoritatively changed in *Murphy v. Dublin Corporation*,[145] a case which arose in the wake of objections raised by the plaintiff to a proposed compulsory purchase order in respect of his lands. A public inquiry was held in accordance with the usual procedure, and the planning inspector sent a report of the proceedings to the Minister. In dealing with the Minister's claim for privilege in respect of the report, Walsh J. stated:

> "Under the Constitution the administration of justice is committed solely to the judiciary in the exercise of their powers . . . Power to compel the attendance of witnesses and the production of evidence is an inherent part of the judicial power of government of the State and is the ultimate safeguard of justice in the State. The proper exercise of the three powers of government . . . is in the public interest. There may be occasions when the different aspects of the public interest 'pull in contrary directions' . . . If the conflict arises during the exercise of judicial power then, in my view, it is the judicial power which will decide which public interest shall prevail. This does not mean that the court will always decide that the interest of the litigant shall prevail. It is for the court to decide which is the superior interest in the circumstances of the particular case and to determine the matter accordingly."[146]

The courts thus still retain a discretion to preserve the confidential nature of official documents in the public interest, but this matter may not be constitutionally remitted to a non-judicial personage.[147] The courts will,of course, be reluctant to overrule official claims for privilege, especially in sensitive areas concerning the security or safety of the State.[148] But as Walsh J. remarked:

---

142 *Leen v. President of the Executive Council* [1926] I.R. 456.

143 *O'Donovan v. Minister for Local Government* [1961] I.R. 114.

144 *Attorney General v. Simpson* [1959] I.R. 335. In *Kenny v. Minister for Defence* (1942) Ir. Jur.Rep. 81 (an action in contract concerning the construction of army huts), Maguire P. observed that the Minister was entitled to claim privilege in respect of "documents of a confidential nature". A prison governor was allowed to claim privilege in respect of confidential information concerning a planned prison escape: see *The State (Comerford) v. Governor of Mountjoy Prison* [1981] I.L.R.M. 86.

145 [1972] I.R. 215. For discussion of this important decision and the subsequent case of *Geraghty v. Minister for Environment* [1975] I.R. 300, see Casey, "Inadmissibility of evidence on grounds of public interest" (1977) D.U.L.J. 11 (N.S.). For an analysis of the modern English law on this subject, see Brown, "Public Interest Immunity" [1994] *Public Law* 579.

146 *Ibid.*, at 233–234.

147 In contrast, note the late Professor de Smith's view that judges are poorly equipped to hold the balance: de Smith, *Judicial Review of Administrative Action* (4th ed, 1980) pp. 74–75.

148 See, *e.g. Comerford's* case, [1981] I.L.R.M. 86 and *People v. Ferguson*, unreported, Court of Criminal Appeal, October 27, 1975. *Cf.* the comments of Costello J. in *Director of Consumer Affairs v. Sugar Distributors Ltd* [1991] 1 I.R. 225 at 227: "The Court is required to balance the need to protect the privacy of the public service against [the] need to avoid a possible injustice to litigants."

"It may well be that it would be rare or infrequent for a court after its own examination, to arrive at a different conclusion from that expressed by the Minister, but that is a far remove from accepting without question the judgment of the Minister."[149]

In 1991 the Supreme Court emphatically upheld the *Murphy* principles in *Ambiorix Ltd v. Minister for Environment (No. 1)*[150] and rejected the suggestion that the earlier decision had been wrongly decided.[151] In this case the plaintiffs claimed that the designation of certain lands under the provisions of the Urban Renewal Act 1986[152] was *ultra vires*. To that end they sought discovery of certain memoranda for Government and other Cabinet documents which dealt with these issues. The defendants resisted discovery on class rather than content grounds, namely, that the discovery of these documents might prejudice the "necessary requirements of confidentiality of cabinet, Government and ministerial communications and discussions" and the "confidentiality and the collective responsibility of the Government."[153] Finlay C.J. summarised the effect of the *Murphy* principles and then stated that:

"(a) The Executive cannot prevent the judicial power from examining documents which are relevant to an issue in a civil trial for the purpose of deciding whether they must be produced.

(b) There is no obligation on the judicial power to examine any particular document before deciding that it is exempt from production and it can and will in many instances uphold a claim of privilege merely on the basis of a description of its nature and contents which it (the judicial power) accepts.

(c) There cannot, accordingly, be a generally applicable class or category of documents exempted from production by reason of the rank in the public service of the person creating them or the position of the individual or body intended to use them."[154]

---

149 [1972] I.R. 215 at 236. McWilliam J. made a similar point in *Hunt v. Roscommon Vocational Education Committee*, unreported, High Court, May 1, 1981, where the substantive action involved a claim for wrongful dismissal by a former headmaster of a vocational school. The Minister for Education claimed privilege in respect of documents containing the opinions expressed by individual civil servants on the case. The judge observed that the claim for privilege depended on whether there was "a likelihood of injury to the State or the public service by the production of the documents". This interest had to be balanced against that of the fair administration of justice, and the task of the court was to decide as between the merits of these competing interests. As far as the instant case was concerned, there was no suggestion that disclosure of the documents would be detrimental to the public interest. Nor was it any answer to say that the civil service administration might be adversely affected if there was an appreciation by officers of the Department that their memoranda might subsequently be read out in court. See also, *Geraghty v. Minister for Local Government* [1975] I.R. 300; *Folens and Co. v. Minister for Education* [1981] I.L.R.M. 121; and *Incorporated Law Society of Ireland v. Minister for Justice* [1987] I.L.R.M. 42.

150 [1992] 1 I.R. 277.

151 Thus, McCarthy J. observed *ibid.* at 289 that "to depart, as we are invited to do, from the reasoning and the decision in *Murphy v. Dublin Corporation* would be to lessen or impair judicial sovereignty in the administration of justice."

152 The owners of the properties in question would have obtained certain tax and other fiscal advantages by reason of this designation.

153 [1992] 1 I.R. 277 at 280. Note that in *Gormley v. Ireland* [1993] 2 I.R. 75 at 78 Murphy J. permitted discovery of what were "unquestionably confidential, sensitive documents recording for the greater part submissions and advices by senior civil servants to Ministers and indeed to the Government."

154 [1992] 1 I.R. 277 at 283–284.

Finlay C.J. emphasised that these principles stemmed directly from the constitutional requirements ordaining the separation of powers, so that they did not require justification "in relation to any particular consequence which any other approach might have". The Chief Justice nonetheless drew attention to the practical consequences which might follow if a privilege of this kind "were accepted as a general standard" as it might mean that:

> "the right of any individual citizen to challenge a decision made by the Government or a Minister of the Government, on the basis that it was made without material which supported it or having regard to the consideration of material which was wholly irrelevant to it could never be mounted."[155]

A consistent line of authorities has been established which has assumed that responsible ministers and civil servants will not be deterred by the prospect that their confidential deliberations will ultimately be disclosed by discovery in the course of civil litigation. Public interest immunity has frequently been claimed on the ground that the public servants concerned might henceforth be less than candid if the documents in question were required to be disclosed.[156] With the particular exception of *Hamilton (No.1)* (considered below), the courts have, by and large, been less than sympathetic to this argument.[157] In *Fitzpatrick v. Independent Newspapers plc*[158] Costello J. held that documents pertaining to a statutory inquiry carried out by Bord na gCon were not privileged, as he could not see "how the production of these particular documents would be adverse to the public interest" or how "their production would injure the proper functioning of the service which the Board is required by statute to provide". This trend was continued by both Lardner J. in *Ahern v. Minister for Industry & Commerce*[159] and Blayney J. in *P.M.P.S. Ltd v. P.M.P.A. Ltd.*[160] In *Ahern*, the applicant was an established officer in the Patent

---

[155] *Ibid.* at 285. In his concurring judgment McCarthy J. drew attention (at 289) to the fact that the plaintiffs had claimed that the tax concessions granted to one of the defendants were based on invalid considerations:
> "the exact nature of which must be contained in the documents for which privilege is claimed. Yet it is said that the plaintiffs are to be denied inspection of at least some of these documents. They would thus be precluded from identifying the strength of their case."

[156] In *Ambiorix Ltd v. Minister for Environment* [1992] 1 I.R. 277 the argument was put thus (at 281) by a senior official from the Department of the Taoiseach when it was averred that the production of government memoranda would not be in the public interest as "officials might tend where possible to make their comments or suggestions or recommendations orally rather in a written format, and such a tendency would not be in the interest of the public or in the efficiency of the public service." On "class grounds" see p. 944.

[157] In *Ambiorix Ltd v. Minister for Environment (No.1)* ibid at 287 McCarthy J. referred to the post-*Murphy* case law and said that it provided "an empirical answer to the statements made on affidavit by several deponents that 'the disclosure of such documents would tend to hinder the free communication necessary for such government for the proper running of the public service." Likewise in *Breathnach v. Ireland (No.3)* [1993] 2 I.R. 458 at 472–472 Keane J. observed that in civil proceedings "the desirability of preserving confidentiality in case of communications between members of the executive has been significantly eroded as a proper factor to be taken into account by the courts". Keane J. acknowledged, however, that the necessity to preserve confidentiality may be greater in criminal matters: see [1993] 2 I.R. at 473. See also the comments of Lord Keith in *Burmah Oil Co. Ltd v. Bank of England* [1980] A.C. 1090.

[158] [1988] I.R. 132.

[159] Unreported, High Court, March 4, 1988.

[160] [1990] 1 I.R. 284.

Office who sought judicial review to challenge certain disciplinary action taken by the Minister. The respondent objected to the production of confidential reports prepared by the applicant's immediate superiors on the grounds that:

"[D]isclosure of them would considerably interfere with the day-to-day running of a Civil Service Department and would breach fundamental concepts of confidentiality which pertain to the ability of officers to report on the conduct of officers they supervise."[161]

Lardner J. could not accept these submissions, as the reports in question were prepared simply with the particular applicant in mind. As the reports were highly relevant to the applicant's case and as Lardner J. was not satisfied that production of the reports would have the consequences feared by the respondent, he accordingly disallowed the claim of privilege. In *P.M.P.S. Ltd v. P.M.P.A. Ltd*, the liquidator of a friendly society sought discovery of documents pertaining to an investigation carried out on behalf of the Registrar prior to the collapse of the society in question. Blayney J. rejected the argument that the inspector's functions and civil service morale would be undermined if privilege could not be claimed:

"Nobody interrogated by the inspector could be under any illusion that information obtained by him would be confidential. Nor can I accept either that responsible civil servants would be any less likely to speak with the Registrar if the memorandum was disclosed to the liquidator."[162]

Not surprisingly, the force of this argument is even further eroded where it is evident that the material in question will, anyway, be made available to the public or otherwise enter the public domain.[163]

The Cabinet Confidentiality case and the 17th Amendment of the Constitution

The Supreme Court's decision in *Attorney General v. Hamilton (No.1)*[164] arose in unusual circumstances. One of the issues which the Tribunal of Inquiry into the Beef industry had been required to examine concerned allegations regarding the operation of the statutory export credit insurance scheme. There was a conflict of evidence as to whether the Government at a particular meeting had decided, in respect of beef exports to the Iraqi market, to confine the allocation of this very valuable insurance to two named companies. When Mr Ray Burke TD, a former Minister for Industry and Commerce, appeared to give evidence before the Tribunal, counsel for the Attorney General objected, on grounds of cabinet confidentiality, to a line of questioning which sought to establish what had transpired at the Government

---

161 At p. 3 of the judgment.
162 [1990] 1 I.R. 284 at 287. See also *Silver Hill Duckling Co. Ltd v. Minister for Agriculture* [1987] I.R. 289 (no privilege for minutes of E.C. standing veterinary committee) and *Duff v. Minister for Agriculture (No. 1)* [1992] 1 I.R. 198 (no privilege for confidential briefing documents prepared for E.C. Council meeting).
163 *Rooney v. Skeffington* [1997] 1 I.R. 22; *McDaid v. Minister for Marine* [1994] 3 I.R. 321.
164 [1993] 2 I.R. 250. See generally, Hogan, "The Cabinet Confidentiality Case" (1993) 8 *Irish Political Studies* 131; and Hogan and Whyte, *Kelly, op.cit.*, above, n.43, pp. 250–258.

meeting in question. When the Tribunal overruled the objection, the Attorney General sought judicial review of that decision.

O'Hanlon J. was unimpressed by this argument, stressing that it was inconsistent with the principles underlying *Murphy v. Dublin Corporation*,[165] while also drawing attention to what he considered to be the unacceptable corollaries of the Attorney General's submission.[166] A majority of the Supreme Court, however, upheld this submission. Finlay C.J. first ruled that the *Murphy* and *Ambiorix* principles had no application to the present case:

". . . the principles laid down in these two cases derive, on consideration of the judgments in them, so clearly and unambiguously from the question of the exercise of the judicial power, that they cannot be, automatically, principles applicable to the question of the evidence adduced before the Tribunal of Inquiry."[167]

The essential premise of the majority was that absolute confidentiality was a corollary of the principle of collective responsibility provided for in Article 28.4 of the Constitution:

"It is clear from the very nature of the collective responsibility of the Government that discussions among its members at their formal meetings must be confidential, otherwise its decisions are liable to be fatally weakened by disclosure of dissenting views . . . If it were permissible to compel in any circumstances the disclosure of the contents of discussions which take place at Government meetings the executive role of the Government as envisaged by the Constitution, perhaps, even de-stabilised."[168]

The insistence that the confidentiality which certainly flows from Article 28.4 must be absolute seems unpersuasive and would, if strictly applied, lead to striking anomalies. In the first place, it seems odd that government papers and documents of a highly confidential character may be discovered in the course of civil litigation,

---

[165] [1972] I.R. 215.
[166] As he said [1993] 2 I.R. 250 at 258–259:
   "It has not been unknown in the history of government in other countries for totally corrupt governments to come to power and for the members to enrich themselves dishonestly at the cost of the public purse. Were such a situation to arise at some unforeseen future time in our own country and were the information to leak out of discussions at cabinet level at which such a nefarious plot was being considered, the legal submissions now advanced . . . would prevent any future Tribunal of Inquiry appointed by the Houses of the Oireachtas from obtaining the informnation it needed to establish guilt where guilt existed. I do not consider that our Constitution has failed to protect the public interest in the manner suggested. It would hardly be a model of its kind if it were so deficient in such an important respect."
   In *O'Brien v. Ireland* [1995] 1 I.L.R.M. 22 O'Hanlon J. subsequently observed (at 29):
   "The effect of the [*Cabinet Confidentiality*] decision appears to be that a complete prohibition on disclosure exists in such a case, without the courts being left with 'any scope to decide where necessary between conflicting claims based on the public interest between compelling production of documents and exempting from the publication' (as referred to in the *Ambiorix* case)."
[167] [1993] 2 I.R. 250 at 270.
[168] *Ibid.* at 275, *per* Hederman J. Finlay C.J. also spoke (at p. 266) of the "necessity for full, free and frank discussion between members of the Government prior to the making of decisions, something which would appear to be an inevitable adjunct to the obligation to meet collectively and to act collectively."

whereas discussions at Government meetings are inadmissible before a Tribunal of Inquiry.[169] For if the declared objective of the absolute confidentiality rule is to protect the workings of Government, then this rule is subverted if highly confidential documentation revealing the thought processes of individual Ministers may be discovered in civil litigation.[170] Thus, the most that can be said by way of support for the majority in *Hamilton (No.1)* is that it sets a particularly heavy premium on the Government's presenting a united phalanx to Dáil and public. By contrast, the *Murphy/Ambiorix* line of authority sets a heavy premium on the administration of justice before a court.

The *ratio* in *Hamilton (No.1)* was unpopular, not least because it was feared that it might interfere with the operation of future tribunals of inquiry. Accordingly, at a time when two separate Tribunals of Inquiry had been established,[171] it was in effect partially reversed by the Seventeenth Amendment of the Constitution Act 1997 which inserted the following provision, as the new Article 28.4.3°[172] of the Constitution:

> "The confidentiality of discussions at meetings of the Government shall be respected in all circumstances, save only where the High Court determines that disclosure should be made in respect of a particular matter –
>
> i.   in the interests of the administration of justice by a Court, or
>
> ii. by virtue of an overriding public interest, pursuant to an application in that behalf by a tribunal appointed by the Government or a Minister of the Government on the authority of the Houses of the Oireachtas to inquire into matters stated by them to be of public importance."

There are three features to this provision. First, as already mentioned, it reverses the effect of *Hamilton (No.1)*, but only on the basis that it is for the High Court to determine whether "disclosure should be made . . . by virtue of an overriding public interest". Secondly, it makes plain a point, on which some doubt had arisen,[173] namely that where court proceedings (as opposed to a tribunal) were concerned, the *Murphy* and *Ambiorix* line of authority governs the question, even though discussions at a Government meeting are in question. Here one should emphasise that, as with the first precept, it is the High Court[174] which must be involved, irrespective of whether the disclosure has arisen in the course of proceedings before a different court. Thirdly, the new Article 28.4.3° – which states that the confidentiality

---

169 Byrne and Binchy, *Annual Review of Irish Law 1992* comment (at p. 216) that "undoubtedly, the majority decision is difficult to reconcile with the existing case law, particularly the general thrust of the discovery cases".

170 Byrne and Binchy, *ibid.*, conclude (at p. 217) that "the precise circumstances [of the case] were, apparently, highly influential to the outcome", *i.e.* implying that this decision will not in practice prove to be an authority for the propositions that might seem logically to flow from the decision of the majority.

171 See p. 296.

172 The existing Article 28.4.3° (dealing with the presentation of the estimates) has now been re-numbered as Article 28.4.4°.

173 See Hogan and Whyte, *Kelly, The Irish Constitution, op. cit.*, above n.33, 381–383; Morgan, *The Separation of Powers in the Irish Constiution*, pp. 161–162.

174 Although Article 28.4.3° refers only to the High Court, an appeal would seem to lie to the Supreme Court by virtue of Article 34.4.3°.

of Government meetings be respected "in *all* circumstances" – contains a remarkably strong statement of the confidentiality precept and certain (potentially unwelcome) consequences would appear to follow. It would seem to bar a Minister who is resigning from the Government because he was not prepared to bear collective responsibility for a particular policy or decision from recounting relevant details from the Government meeting.[175] It would even appear to prevent a Minister from informing his senior civil servants of what happened at a particular Government meeting. It might also interfere with publication of ministerial biographies and other historical memoirs where this recounted the background to the decisions of a Government, however ancient the episodes involved.[176] And here one should recall that Ireland has been called "a minor country, with a major country's history."

Examples of the privilege against disclosure being upheld

There have been instances of where the privilege has been upheld. In *O'Mahony v. Ireland*[177] the plaintiff, who was a soldier with the Irish UN contingent in the Lebanon, claimed damages for negligence against the State. It was said that Irish army officers had permitted him and his two colleagues to be placed under the control of an officer who was not a member of the UN interim force, thereby causing him to fall into the hands of the irregular Christian Militia. His colleagues were killed and he was seriously injured as a result. A separate court of inquiry was conducted by the Irish Defence Forces and by the UN force itself. Barrington J. upheld the claim of public interest privilege. It was not unreasonable for the Minister for Defence to provide that the court of inquiry organised by the Defence Forces should be confidential:

> "having regard to the nature of the work which a court of inquiry could do and the possible security implications. The privilege, therefore, was properly claimed."

Again, with regard to the UN inquiry, Barrington J. said that the report had been passed on to the Irish Government in circumstances of confidentiality:

> "The Government had taken the view that it was under a duty to preserve the confidence. This was a reasonable attitude and the privilege was properly claimed."[178]

---

175   *cf.* the full disclosures which were made to the Dáil and to the public detailing the precise sequence of events which took place at the Government meeting of November 9, 1994 leading to the appointment of a new President of the High Court.
176   Thus, for example, de Vere White, *Kevin O'Higgins* (1986) contains an account (pp. 256–257) of the fateful Government meeting during the Civil War in December 1922 which led to the summary execution of four prisoners by way of reprisal for the murder of Deputy Sean Hales.
177   *The Irish Times*, July 28, 1989.
178   This decision was followed by O'Hanlon J. in *O'Brien v. Ireland* [1995] 1 I.L.R.M. 22. The plaintiff claimed that her husband had been killed while on UN duty in the Lebanon by reason of the negligence of the defendants. O'Hanlon J. held that the defendants could successfully plead privilege in relation to the contents of an official UN inquiry, as such diplomatic documents were inviolable under international law and, further, as their production might jeopardise the security of the Irish and other contingents who were still based in the Lebanon. But *cf. Dublin Meatpackers Ltd v. Ireland, The Irish Times*, April 13, 1989 (no privilege for diplomatic exchanges with U.K. officials concerning operation of beef slaughtering scheme). *W. v. Ireland (No. 1)* [1997] 2 I.R. 133 (similar principle re details of foreign extradition request).

Thus here that privilege appears to have been extended – not unreasonably – to apply to documents emanating from third parties which the Government regards under a duty to keep confidential.

The procedure for adjudication on pleas of privilege and onus of proof

The procedure to be followed in adjudicating upon a claim for privilege is a most important matter. In the first place, where a document is relevant, the burden of proving that it is privileged rests on the State.[179] It may be possible for the court to decide the claim without an inspection. As Finlay C.J. said in *Ambiorix Ltd v. Minister for Environment (No.1)*:

"There is no obligation on the judicial power to examine any particular document before deciding that it is exempt from production, and it can and will in many instances uphold a claim of privilege in respect of a document merely on the basis of a description of its nature and contents which it (the judicial power) accepts."[180]

However, even before any inspection is ordered, the affidavit must be clear and must sustain at least a prima facie case that the documents are privileged and, in fact, a surprisingly large number of claims have failed at this stage. In one case McWilliam J. complained that to ask the court "to examine all these documents under the circumstances of the present case seems to me to be getting very close to asking the Court to prepare the affadavit of discovery."[181] However, in some cases it will be necessary for the court to inspect the documents, possibly *in camera*, in order to decide whether to order discovery.[182]

---

[179] Once the relevance of the documents in question has been established, the "burden of satisying the court that a particular document ought not to be produced lies upon the party, or the person, who makes such a claim": per Walsh J. in *Murphy v. Dublin Corporation* [1972] I.R. 215 at 235. See also *Breathnach v. Ireland (No.3)* [1993] 2 I.R. 458. English practice appears to differ in this regard, in that it is for the party seeking to overcome the public interest immunity claim "to demonstrate the existence of a counter-acting interest calling for the disclosure of the particular documents involved": *Evans v. Chief Constable of Surrey* [1988] 1 Q.B. 588 at 593, *per* Wood J.

[180] [1992] 1 I.R. 277 at 284. See also *Murphy v. Dublin Corporation* [1972] I.R. 215 at 234–235 and *Breathnach v. Ireland (No.3) ibid.* at 469. In some instances inspection by the court will be required. An example of this is provided by *Director of Consumer Affairs v. Sugar Distributors Ltd* [1991] 1 I.R. 225, where Costello J. said (at 229) that the public interest required that documents which formed the basis of a complaint to the Director that the provisions of the Restrictive Practices Acts had been breached should not be disclosed unless the court concluded following inspection of the documents that "the documents might tend to show that the defendant had not committed the wrongful acts alleged against him." In *W. v. Ireland* [1997] 2 I.R. 133 Geoghegan J. said that on the facts of that case it would have been impossible for him to determine whether the documents in question were privileged on public interest grounds without having looked at the documents in question.

[181] *Hunt v. Roscommon VEC*, unreported, High Court, May 1, 1981. See also *Murphy v. Dublin Corporation* [1972] I.R. 215 at 237.

[182] *cf.* the comments of Keane J. in *Skeffington v. Rooney* [1997] 1 I.R. 22 at 35:
"The reluctance of the courts in England to examine documents in respect of which a claim has been made by a public official that they belong to a class which has been recognised as privileged (usually because it is said that it was 'necessary for the proper functioning of the public service' that they be withheld) has not been shared by Irish courts . . . On occasions these issues can be resolved by the judge by reference to the description of the documents contained in the affidavit of discovery. More frequently it will involve an examination of some or all of the disputed documents. In any event the procedure to be adopted must depend to some extent upon the circumstances of each case and the nature and extent of the disputed documents."

There are a number of further points which require further elaboration.

(a) No "class" grounds. There is one significant point on which modern Irish law would appear to differ from that prevailing in Britain. In Britain, the courts are still prepared, in certain circumstances, to allow privilege in respect of a document not only on the grounds of its own particular content, but also on the grounds that it belongs to a class of documents, some or most of whose members will have a confidential content. The thinking underlying "class privilege" is that official documents of certain categories are so sensitive that they would not be fearlessly and candidly written if there were any possibility that they might be made public.[183] The concept of privilege on class grounds was, however, rejected by the Supreme Court in *Murphy* and especially in *Ambiorix* as inconsistent with the principle of judicial independence enshrined in Article 34.1. A good example of the "no class" principle is illustrated by *W. v. Ireland*,[184] a case where the plaintiff was suing the State for loss and damage arising from what was said to have been the failure of the State to secure the expeditious extradition of a particular suspect. To this end the plaintiff sought discovery of certain documents which had been supplied by the Office of the U.K. Attorney General to the Irish Attorney General. While Geoghegan J. accepted that these documents were supplied in confidence and that it was in the public interest that this confidence should be upheld, he referred to what Walsh J. had said in *Murphy* and rejected a claim for privilege based on class grounds. On the facts, Geoghegan J. held in favour of disclosure, largely because the criminal proceedings had long been disposed of and it was difficult to see any particular reason "why the U.K. Government would be concerned about the production of the particular documents" in question.

(b) Criminal proceedings. In *Murphy*, Walsh J. had been careful to refrain from expressing any opinion as to the scope of executive privilege in criminal proceedings. This very point which was at issue in *D.P.P. (Hanley) v. Holly*[185] where, at a hearing in the District Court of a charge of unlawful assault, the defence called upon the investigating Garda to produce his report of the incident. Privilege was claimed by the State, and this claim was upheld by the District Judge.

Keane J. held that this conclusion was incorrect. In the light of the principles enunciated by Walsh J. in *Murphy*, he was satisfied that a general claim of privilege in the case of police communications failed "because as a class their admission would be against the public interest is no longer sustainable". To succeed it would have been necessary for the Garda authorities to advance a specific ground of possible damage to the public interest which might result from the disclosure of such documents, although Keane J. remarked that in the circumstances of the case it seemed "highly unlikely that any such ground exists".[186] In contrast, in *People v.*

---

183 *Burmah Oil Co. v. Bank of England* [1980] A.C. 1090.
184 [1997] 2 I.R. 133.
185 [1984] I.L.R.M. 149. See O'Connor, "The Privilege of Non-Disclosure and Informers" (1980) 15 Ir. Jur. 111 (N.S.).
186 Keane J. regarded *Attorney General v. Simpson* [1959] I.R. 105 as having been implicitly overruled by *Murphy v. Dublin Corporation* [1972] I.R. 215. See also *People v. Ferguson*, unreported, Court

Eccles[187] the Court of Criminal Appeal upheld a privilege claim in circumstances which were markedly different from those in *Holly's* case. It ruled that, in the exceptional circumstances of the case, the disclosure of confidential Garda information would have been contrary to the public interest. The defendants were charged with capital murder (and other serious offences). They had been arrested under section 30 of the Offences against the State Act 1939, and an extension order had been served on them permitting their detention for up to 48 hours. The Chief Superintendent who had caused the extension order to be served on the defendants claimed that he had received information which suggested that one of the defendants should be detained for a further 24 hour period. The Chief Superintendent claimed privilege when asked to reveal the source of this information. Hederman J. ruled that the Special Criminal Court was correct to uphold the claim of privilege:

"The Chief Superintendent was entitled to claim privilege in respect of both the source, and the nature of the source, of the sensitive, confidential information he received in respect of the applicant. Normally a member of the Garda Síochána cannot claim privilege in respect of information received from a fellow member of the force simply by virtue of its being such a communication. The circumstances in this case, however, were exceptional. [Privilege was claimed] on the ground that 'it would be dangerous to identify whether the source was civilian or police.' This he was clearly entitled to do."[188]

The principles governing discovery of confidential police documentation were re-stated by Keane J. in a comprehensive judgment in *Breathneach v. Ireland (No. 3)*.[189] He first endorsed his earlier judgment in *Holly* and emphasised that no "class" claim of privilege could arise simply by reason of the fact that these were Garda documents. He then addressed the factors to be considered in the balancing process:

". . . the court . . . is required to balance the public interest in the proper administration of justice against the public interest reflected in the grounds put forward for non-disclosure in the present case . . . It is only where the first public interest outweighs the second public interest that an inspection should be undertaken or disclosure should be ordered. In considering the first public interest, it is necessary to determine to what extent, if any, the relevant documents may advance the plaintiff's case or damage the defendant's case or fairly lead to an enquiry which may produce either of these consequences . . . [T]here may be documents the very nature of which is such that inspection is not necessary to determine on which side the scales come down. Thus, information supplied

---

of Criminal Appeal, October 27, 1975 (where a similar view was taken) and *Gormley v. Ireland* [1993] 2 I.R. 75 (where Murphy J. refused to order the discovery of "highly confidential" Garda documentation, "the disclosure of which might be significantly detrimental to the public interest").

[187] (1986) 3 Frewen 36. See also *The People (Director of Public Prosecutions) v. Reddan* [1995] 3 I.R. 560 (where Blayney J. held that privilege was properly claimed where there was a reasonable basis for the conclusion that the Garda source would be in danger if his identity were revealed).

[188] *Ibid.* at 63. *Cf. Burke v. Central Independent Television PLC* [1994] 2 I.R. 61, a case with unusual facts where the Supreme Court upheld a claim of privilege of non-disclosure by a journalist on the ground that the discovery of the documentation might put at risk the lives of others, including undercover police officers.

[189] [1993] 2 I.R. 448.

in confidence to the gardai should not in general be disclosed or at least not in cases like the present where the innocence of an accused person is not in issue. . . . Again, there may be material the disclosure of which would be of assistance to criminals by revealing methods of detection or combating crime, a consideration of particular importance today when criminal activity tends to be highly organised and professional. There may be cases involving the security of the State, where even disclosure of the existence of the document should not be allowed. None of these factors – and there may, of course, well be others which have not occurred to me – which would remove the necessity of even inspecting the documents is present in this case."[190]

The judge concluded that, on the facts, the documents were likely to be of some assistance to the plaintiff in his malicious prosecution claim and this consideration overcame the competing public interest in maintaining the confidentiality of the documents in question. Dealing with a different form of privilege which, it might be thought, however, could often arise from the same situation as the privilege under discussion here, Keane J. continued by rejecting the suggestion that the documentation in question could attract legal professional privilege on the ground that the dominant purpose for its preparation was contemplated or pending litigation.[191] The documentation in question consisted of Garda files concerning an investigation into a train robbery, which had been submitted to the Director of Public Prosecutions so that a decision could be taken regarding a possible prosecution.

(c) Extension of privilege to all public interest cases. In *Murphy's* case, Walsh J. emphasised the point that "executive privilege only applied to a Minister who was exercising "the executive powers of government of the State". If this observation is taken at its face value, it would appear narrowly to restrict the immunity to Ministers exercising their executive powers under Article 28 of the Constitution.[192] But if the immunity has now (in fact, since *Leen's* case in 1926) been severed from the prerogative, and put on the basis of public interest, it seems arbitrary and unnecessary to confine the immunity in this narrow fashion. The evidence tends to suggest that the immunity is not so confined. For example, in *The State (Williams) v. Army Pensions Board*,[193] Henchy J. assumed that privilege could be claimed, in a suitable case, in respect of the Board's documents. Again, in *Geraghty v. Dublin Corporation*,[194] the immunity was allowed to protect some of the documents for

---

[190] *Ibid.* at 469.
[191] Keane J. observed that such documentation would be generated in every case where the commission of a crime was suspected, adding that (at 472):
> "The fact that the documents in question may . . . be submitted by the investigating gardaí to the Director of Public Prosecutions in order to obtain his decision as to whether a prosecution should be instituted could not possibly give that material the same status as, to take, an obvious example, a medical report obtained by a plaintiff in a personal injuries action solely for the purposes of his claim."

[192] As opposed to when the Minister has acted merely as a *persona designata*, as in *Murphy v. Dublin Corporation*.
[193] [1983] I.R. 308. In *Skeffington v. Rooney* [1997] 1 I.R. 22 Keane J. similarly ruled that the Garda Síochána Complaints Board would be entitled to claim public interest immunity in respect of materials supplied to it in confidence.
[194] [1975] I.R. 300.

which it was claimed, although that case involved a Minister hearing a planning appeal, and thus taking a quasi-judicial – as opposed to executive – function. In *D. v. National Society for the Prevention of Cruelty to Children*,[195] the House of Lords held that the defendant body (a private, charitable body which did, however, enjoy official status to the extent of being an "authorised person" for the purpose of bringing child care proceedings under the relevant English legislation) was entitled to claim immunity on the grounds of public interest in respect of members of the public who had given information to them concerning child abuse.

On the other hand, a somewhat discordant note was struck by Costello J. in *Buckley v. Incorporated Law Society of Ireland*,[196] a case where the defendant body had claimed privilege in respect of complaints which had been made by members of the public about a particular solicitor. Costello J. agreed that while the Law Society undoubtedly "carries out important statutory duties in the public interest", it was also clear that the Society "was not part of the public service and so cannot claim to refuse inspection on the ground of 'executive privilege' which is granted in the public interest." The judge, nevertheless, went on to uphold the substance of the claim of privilege on the ground of the "informer's privilege", namely that it would be contrary to the public interest if the Society were to reveal the identity of complainants.[197]

This approach of Costello J. seems too narrow. After all, the "informer's privilege" is in reality but one example of a wider public interest privilege which is designed to ensure to promote the effectiveness of administration. The privilege has thus outgrown its historical roots and should not simply be confined to Ministers and civil servants discharging the executive power of the State.[198]

(d) **Informer privilege.** A peculiarly important aspect of this doctrine is that of informer privilege. The courts have recognised that the public interest will generally require that the identity of informants must be protected from disclosure. This is not just confined to criminal proceedings, but is nowadays extended to a variety of statutory bodies and agencies, such as, for example, the Director of Consumer Affairs,[199] the Garda Síochána Complaints Board[200] and the Law Society of Ireland.[201] The

---

[195] [1978] A.C. 171.

[196] [1994] 2 I.R. 44.

[197] Costello J. accepted, *ibid.* at 51 counsel's argument that if it were known that:
"documents relating to complaints to the [Society] may be disclosed at some future time, persons with legitimate complaints may be discouraged by the fear of public disclosure of their private affairs from coming forward, thus reducing the effectiveness of the [Society's] supervisory role."

[198] Indeed, in the somewhat analogous case of *Director of Consumer Affairs v. Sugar Distributors Ltd* [1991] 1 I.R. 225 (where the Director was seeking an order restraining the defendants from engaging in certain alleged anti-competitive practices) Costello J. held that the Director was entitled to claim public interest privilege in respect of information supplied to him in confidence by complainants, even though there could be no suggestion that the Director was discharging part of the executive power of the State. (Here, too, the judge independently justified his decision on the "informer's privilege" ground).

[199] *Director of Consumer Affairs v. Sugar Distributors Ltd, ibid.* In *The State (Comerford) v. Governor of Mountjoy Prison* [1981] I.L.R.M. 86 a prison governor was allowed to claim privilege in respect of confidential information concerning a planned prison escape.

[200] *Skeffington v. Rooney* [1997] 1 I.R. 22.

[201] *Buckley v. Incorporated Law Society of Ireland* [1994] 2 I.R. 44. See also *D. v. National Society*

immunity from disclosure under this head is not absolute and the courts may be prepared to permit disclosure if this will "tend to show that the defendant had not committed the wrongful acts alleged against him"[202] or where it has not been demonstrated that confidentiality was an essential feature of the complaints procedure operated by the statutory body in question.[203]

(e) Does the right to a fair hearing require the disclosure of documents?

The dictates of constitutional justice will often require the disclosure of relevant evidence, and this is especially so where the decision-maker is exercising quasi-judicial functions. In *O'Leary v. Minister for Industry and Commerce*[204] a bridge in the neighbourhood of the plaintiff's farm had been submerged by the Electricity Supply Board in the course of the construction of a hydro-electric scheme. The Board was required by the relevant legislation to build a new bridge unless the defendant Minister determined that in the circumstances this was not necessary. Privilege was claimed in respect of memoranda and other communications exchanged between the Board and the Minister Ó Dálaigh C.J. observed that the Minister had been cast in a quasi-judicial role and that he was required to make "an objective finding in effect as between the parties". The communications of the Board to the Minister were not those of an adviser in relation to the discharge of a statutory duty, but were rather "the representations of a party with an interest". The *audi alteram partem* principle therefore required that such circumstances be disclosed.[205]

A related point is that very often the public authority in question will have in its possession all the relevant documentation and that without access to such

---

202 *for Protection of Cruelty to Children* [1978] A.C. 171 (child protection society entitled to claim privilege in respect of the identity of persons reporting instances of maltreatment of children).

202 *Director of Consumer Affairs v. Sugar Distributors Ltd* [1991] 1 I.R. 225 at 229, *per* Costello J.

203 *cf.* the comments of Keane J. in *Skeffington v. Rooney* [1997] 1 I.R. 22 at 38 a case where the Garda Síochána Complaints Board claimed privilege in respect of statements made to them with respect to a particular complaint:

"... the documents in question were broadly similar to what one might find in the 'book of evidence' in a criminal trial on indictment and that there was nothing in any of the statements of a confidential nature or which suggested that the statements had been made on a confidential basis."

In *Church v. Garda Commissioner*, unreported, High Court, March 18, 1997, Costello P. upheld the validity of a direction to two detectives which had been given by the Commissioner requiring them to disclose the identity of an informant who was suspected of having made a malicious complaint. Costello P. distinguished cases such as *Sugar Distributors* on the ground that they involved decisions on "the law of evidence relating to privilege from non-disclosure in civil proceedings" and had no application when considering whether or not the Commissioner had acted *ultra vires* in making the impugned order.

See also *R v. Chief Constable, ex p. Wiley* [1994] 3 All E.R. 420, where the House of Lords took a similar view of the discoverability of documents generated by an investigation into alleged police misbehaviour. See further Ganz, "Matrix Churchill and Public Interest Immunity" (1993) 56 M.L.R. 564 and "Matrix Churchill and Public Interest Immunity: A Postscript" (1995) 58 M.L.R. 417.

204 [1966] I.R. 676.

205 Non-disclosure of documents was also found to breach the *audi alteram partem* rule in *Geraghty v. Minister for Local Government* [1975] I.R. 300 and *The State (Williams) v. Army Pensions Board* [1983] I.R. 308. On the other hand, in *Haussmann v. Minister for the Marine* [1991] I.L.R.M. 382 Blayney J. held on the special facts of that case that production of an inspector's report into a marine tragedy was not necessary to enable the widow of a victim to participate adequately in a statutory inquiry as the witness statements and other evidence "which had been furnished to her contain[ed] all the information" that would be necessary to enable her so to participate and that, accordingly, the failure to make discovery was not a breach of fair procedures.

documentation the applicant could not hope to be able to make out his case.[206] This very point was made by McCarthy J. in *Ambiorix Ltd v. Minister for Environment*,[207] a case where the plaintiffs claimed that the Minister had acted on improper considerations in designating certain lands which would then benefit from certain urban renewal tax concessions:

"The Constitution guarantees fair procedures in the administration of justice; discovery of documents is part of those procedures. The plaintiffs here allege a case of unfair competition, contending that tax concessions made to the fifth defendant were based on invalid considerations, the exact nature of which must be contained in the documents for which privilege is claimed. Yet, it is said that the plaintiffs are to be denied inspection of at least some of these documents. They would thus be precluded from identifying the strength of their case. It is accurately described as a 'Catch 22' situation."[208]

However, the rule will not always require that such disclosure of relevant documents be made: there will be situations where the constitutional guarantee of fair procedures, which, of course, is not absolute, may have to yield to the need to preserve confidential information.[209] In sum, even where the adjudicating agency is a tribunal (or other non-judicial personage), there is a positive, although qualified, obligation to disclose in the form of the right to a fair hearing, arising from constitutional justice (grounded in Article 40.3.1.°) Where a court is involved, this general precept would still apply. However, the main argument, which has been under discussion in most of this Part, is founded upon Article 34.1 and a court's prerogative to ensure that justice is administered fairly. The difference is probably not significant and, in any case, has yet to receive judicial consideration.

(f) Does the Constitution places limits on the power of the Oireachtas to create new categories of statutory privilege? The extent to which the Oireachtas is free to create new forms of statutory public interest privilege is not entirely clear and has received scant judicial consideration. There are a number of diverse examples of such statutory privileges, including an immunity from disclosure for officials of

---

206 *cf.* the comments of Sir John Donaldson MR in *R v. Lancashire CC, ex p. Huddleston* [1986] 2 All E.R. 941:
  "[Counsel for the respondent] says that it is for the applicant to make out his case for judicial review and that it is not for respondent authority to do it for him. This, in my judgment, is only partially correct. Certainly it is for the applicant to satisfy the court of his entitlement to judicial review and it is for the respondent to resist his application, if he considers it to be unjustified. But it is a process which falls to be conducted with all the cards face upwards on the table and the vast majority of the cards will start in the authority's hands."

207 [1992] 1 I.R. 277.

208 *Ibid.* at 289. See also the comments of Finlay C.J. to like effect at 285 and *O'Keeffe v. An Bord Pleanála* [1993] 1 I.R. 39.

209 Thus, in *The State (Williams) v. Army Pensions Board* [1983] I.R. 308 the respondent Board's failure to disclose certain medical evidence in their possession was found to be a breach of constitutional justice. Henchy J. observed that there might well be other cases where for reasons such as "State security or other considerations of public policy," the Board might be privileged from disclosing, or making full disclosure of, the evidence before them.

the Central Bank[210]; the archives of United Nations[211]; findings and recommendations of military courts of inquiry[212] and records of An Bord Uchtála[213] Of course, it does not suffice for this purpose merely because the officials or employees are statutorily prohibited from disclosing confidential information.[214] Here we are examining a different question from that considered earlier in this Part in two respects. First, the source of the privilege is statutory rather than the common law prerogative (however presently defined). Secondly, the content of the privilege is, in some cases, defined by reasonably precise statutory rules (which it is for a court to apply) rather than allowing the judiciary a complete free hand, guided only by general principle and case law. In *O'Brien v. Ireland*[215] O'Hanlon J. adverted to this issue, saying that neither *Murphy* or *Ambiorix*:

> "was intended to convey that the power of the legislature to intervene and confer the privilege of exemption from production on specified categories of documentary or other evidence was curtailed or restricted in any way, save insofar as any legislation enacted must not conflict with the overriding provisions of the Constitution."[216]

This, of course, leaves open the questions of what provisions of the Constitution would be engaged and also what types of "curtail[ment] or restrict[ion]" would be termed. However, it might be that legislation which, for example, purported to create a statutory privilege from immunity in all instances of litigation against the State or some commercial State body (such as Aer Lingus or the ESB) would presumably be open to challenge on the grounds that it infringed the right of access to the courts (Articles 34.1 and 40.3.1°) or equality (Article 40.1). Again legislation which attempted to bar all evidence against the State unless it were corroborated by at least two persons might be questionable on the basis that it violated the guarantee of fair procedures and (possibly) that it usurped the judicial function by excluding categories of otherwise admissible and relevant evidence.[217]

An interesting contemporary example of such a statutory provision – which is an exception to what was said earlier regarding the content of a privilege being defined precisely – is supplied by section 10(3) of Interception of Postal Packets

---

[210] Central Bank Act 1989, s.16 (see *Cully v. Central Bank Ltd* [1984] I.L.R.M. 683, where the statutory predecessor to this section was discussed by O'Hanlon J.)

[211] Diplomatic Relations and Immunities Act 1967, s.9

[212] Rules of Procedure (Defence Forces) 1954 (S.I. No. 243 of 1954), Article 121. See *O'Brien v. Ireland* [1995] 1 I.L.R.M. 22.

[213] Adoption Act, 1976, s.8. See generally *P.B. v. A.L.* [1996] 1 I.L.R.M. 154.

[214] As Keane J. said in *Skeffington v. Rooney* [1997] 1 I.R. 22 at 37 such a provision:
> "... is not in any sense a prohibition on the production to a court in the interests of justice of documents in the Board's possession which are relevant to proceedings before that court. If the Oireachtas had intended to confer a privilege or immunity on such documents, it would have used language similar to that contained in the other statutes ... [referred to in *O'Brien* and *P.B.*]"

[215] [1995] 1 I.L.R.M. 22.

[216] *Ibid.* at 29.

[217] *cf. S. v. S.* [1983] I.R. 68 (where a common law rule which prevented either husband or wife giving evidence as to the true paternity of a child born to a woman in marriage was held by O'Hanlon J. to be inconsistent with the constitutional guarantee of basic fairness of procedures, as it was calculated "to defeat the due and proper administration of justice").

and Telecommunications (Regulation) Act 1993. This subsection provides that in civil proceedings alleging an unlawful interception without proper authorisation of telecommunications or postal messages, a court must first determine whether such an interception has taken place as alleged and unless this has been affirmatively determined, no discovery can be made which would tend to disclose the existence of an official authorisation or any related matter. It is said that without such a safeguard, any person "wanting to find out whether his telephone had been tapped" might start proceedings with a view to compelling an official in Bord Telecom or An Post "to say whether there had been an interception".[218] Nevertheless, while the public interest in protecting the integrity of an official interception system must be very great, the constitutionality of such a far-reaching exclusion clause must, in the light of cases such as *Murphy* and *Ambiorix* be open to question. In addition, without the benefit of discovery, a plaintiff who was the victim of an unlawful interception could not easily establish this fact. Here is the very type of "Catch-22" situation which, as we have already seen, was stigmatised by McCarthy J. in *Ambiorix* as a breach of fair procedures.

(g) **May any public interest immunity be waived?** As we have already noted, public interest immunity was formerly regarded as a feature of Crown immunity which might, therefore, be waived if the responsible Minister saw fit. In the United Kingdom, this view has been increasingly questioned. If the public interest is now the basis for the non-disclosure of otherwise relevant documents, then "individuals should be unable to waive it for their own purposes".[219] It may be, of course, that with changing circumstances the balance may alter, even with regard to a particular document so that the public interest may not, after all, require non-disclosure, but this is "not strictly a question of waiver, but of public interest immunity ceasing to attach to a statement if particular circumstances exist".[220] There seems to be no direct Irish authority on the point, but this view of the law would appear to have been endorsed – though only by analogy – by Finlay C.J. in (admittedly obiter) remarks in *Attorney General v. Hamilton (No.1)*[221] where he described the principle of cabinet confidentiality as:

". . . a constitutional right which, in my view, goes to the fundamental machinery of government, and is, therefore, not capable of being waived by any individual member of government, nor in my view, are the details and contents of discussions at meetings of the Government capable of being made public, for the purpose of this Inquiry, by a decision of any succeeding Government."[222]

---

218 424 *Dáil Debates* Col. 1201, *per* the Minister for Justice (Mr. P. Flynn TD).
219 *Hehir v. Commissioner of Police of the Metropolis* [1982] 1 W.L.R. 715 at 722, *per* Lawton L.J. This passage was approved by Lord Woolf in *R v. Chief Constable, ex p. Wiley* [1994] 3 All E.R. 420 at 440, who, however, added the following divergent comments:
". . . an ordinary individual is in a different position from a public body since it is the public in whose interests immunity is conferred and a public body may be in a position to represent the public."
220 *Hehir v. Commissioner of Police of the Metropolis* [1982] 1 W.L.R. 715 at 723, *per* Brightman L.J.
221 [1993] 2 I.R. 250. This question was not addressed by the other two member of the majority, Hederman and O'Flaherty JJ.
222 *Ibid.* at 272.

On this view, the Government could not "waive" the privilege and authorise the disclosure. The logical corollary of this argument is that documents revealing Government discussions should not be disclosed under the thirty year rule. This almost occurred in 1992 when civil servants were reported to have withheld certain documents (which were due for release under the thirty year rule) on this ground. The Taoiseach intervened and ordered the release of the documents, saying that the operation of the thirty-year rule had not been specifically considered by the Supreme Court in the *Cabinet Confidentiality* case.[223] This case, of course, concerned the very special instance of cabinet confidentiality as ordained by Article 28.2 of the Constitution and it is understandable that a constitutional imperative of this kind could not be waived. Having regard to the exceptional character of this case and its underlying facts, different considerations would necessarily seem to apply to other documents not falling within this special rubric, in that the public interest with regard to disclosure may necessrily shift and change. At the same time, if the court has determined that the public interest requires that certain documents should not be disclosed, principle might suggest that an individual Minister or other respondent could not "waive" the privilege and authorise the disclosure.

8. Obligations Conditional on the Dáil's Approval

It was formerly considered that the voting of funds by Parliament was a condition precedent to the validity of contracts to which the State is a party. This view, which is founded on the basic constitutional principle that the consent of Parliament is necessary for the expenditure of public monies, derives principally from the old case of *Churchward v. R.* and, in particular from an unnecessarily wide statement in that case from Shea J.[224] The wide propositions suggested in *Churchward's* case was rejected in *New South Wales v. Bardolph*.[225] It has now been accepted that the result in *Churchward* depended on the peculiar fact of the case, namely that the contract in the case expressly provided that payment, for the carriage of mails between Dover and the Continent were to be made out of monies voted by Paliament and no such monies were voted. Thus, in other jurisdictions, *Churchward* is now regarded as an authority only for the unexceptionable proposition that a contract[226] may be expressly made subject to parliamentary appropriation, whether by statute, constitutional provision or, as in *Churchward*, by express words or (as we shall see, may be the case in this jurisdiction) by constitutional provision.[227]

In Ireland, the unreconstructed *Churchward* doctrine was explicitly relied upon just after independence in the case of *Kenny v. Cosgrave*.[228] Here the President of

---

223   *The Irish Times*, January 3, 1993.
224   (1865) LR 1 Q.B. 173.
225   (1934) 52 C.L.R. 455.
226   And not just, of course, contracts. See, for example, in *Conroy v. Minister for Defence* [1934] I.R. 679 (Supreme Court granted a declaration that the Minister was bound to take steps for the payment of a pension to the plaintiff).
227   See generally, Hogg, *Liability of the Crown in Australia, New Zealand and the United Kingdom* (Melbourne, 1971), Chap. 5; Turpin, *Government Contracts* (1972), Chap. 1 and Street, *Governmental Liability* (1953), Chap. 3.
228   [1926] I.R. 517.

the Executive Council had told an employer whose workers were on strike that it was essential that the employer resist the demands and had promised that the Executive Council would indemnify him against any financial loss which ensued from this resistance. The promise was not honoured and the plaintiff sued for damages. Even on the assumption that there was a contract between the plaintiff and the Executive Council, his claim was rejected on the grounds that the Executive Council could not "make a binding contract to pay public money without the authority of the Oireachtas [sc. given in advance]." The authority of the decision is, however, weakened by the fact that Fitzgibbon J. speaking for the Supreme Court, also rested his decision on the doctrine that the Government may not make a contract which fetters its discretionary power[229] and apparently failed to perceive that he was dealing with separate rules.[230]

There are several reasons why it would appear that *Kenny* would not be followed (by the Supreme Court, at least) in a modern climate. In the first place, the doctrine seems at odds with modern develoments in the doctrine of legitimate expectations.[231]

Again, there is a wealth of authority against *Kenny*. *Bardolph's* case has already been briefly noted. The Irish authorities commence with *Leyden v. Attorney General*[232] which was decided just before *Kenny*. The plaintiff, in *Leyden*, sought certain declarations in respect of his salary under a contract employing him as a teacher. His claim was resisted by the defendants on the grounds that a contract with a government department was involved, for the payment of which no grant had been made by the Oireachtas. In granting the orders sought, the Supreme Court distinguished *Churchward* on the ground that the remedy sought was only a declaration of the plaintiff's rights. However, Murnaghan J. also observed that: "[*Churchward's*] doctrine will require a careful scrutiny before it is given such a wide application as was here contended for."[233] *Maunsell v. Minister for Education*[234] was a case similar to *Leyden* (save that no contract was involved) in that a teacher was suing for a declaration of his right to salary based on the Rules and Regulations of the Commissioners of National Education in Ireland. In *Maunsell* Gavan Duffy J. rejected an argument based on the *Churchward* doctrine with some hauteur founding himself, in part, on Article 34.3.1°, which gives the High Court full original jurisdiction:

"Finally, I am solemnly assured that I can give no relief to the plaintiff because the Executive cannot bind itself in law by a promise to pay, I cannot entertain

---

229   See further pp. 668–675.
230   [1926] I.R. 517 at 528, where Fitzgibbon J. cited *Rederiaktiebolaget Amphitritie v. The King* [1921] 3 K.B. 500 in support of the proposition that the Government could not by contract fetter its discretion to act in the public interest as it saw fit.
231   See Chap. 16.
232   [1926] I.R. 334.
233   *Ibid.* at 367. See also, *Attorney General v. Great Southern Ry. Co.* [1925] A.C. 754, a case with an Irish connection, discussed by Street, *op. cit.* above, n.227, pp. 88–89.
234   [1940] I.R. 213. Certain other cases such as *Kildare County Council v. Minister for Finance* [1931] I.R. 215 and *Latchford v. Minister for Industry and Commerce* [1950] I.R. 33, involved (it was claimed) a statutory debt in respect of which funds had already been approved by the Oireachtas (by an Appropriation Act or in some other way) and thus did not raise the problem examined in the text.

any suggestion that a public servant, the conditions of whose remuneration are in dispute is precluded from invoking the jurisdiction of the High Court to declare his rights until an Appropriation Act has been enacted providing his Department with money to pay him, however necessary it may be to prove that such an Act has been passed before an order for payment is made."[235]

The final qualifying clause in this passage[236] recalls the doctrine which is now generally accepted in Britain and elsewhere in the Commonwealth: namely, that whilst parliamentary appropriation is not necessary to the validity of a contract, before the monies can actually be paid, there must be properly authorised funds available. This point is not peculiar to contract, for there are many cases (such as actions in tort) where the problem of enforcing an action against the State could also theoretically arise. The question is, of course, most unlikely ever to arise in practice since it may be assumed that the State will fulfil its legal obligations. Where a monetary judgment against the State is concerned, a specific parliamentary vote will not usually be necessary to meet the judgment, as there will usually be an appropriate existing vote from which the money can be taken (provided, of course, that the Dáil has not expressly forbidden this). And even if there is no such vote, it may be assumed that the Government would bring the necessary supplementary estimate before the Dáil, and that the Dáil would pass it.

In view, however, of the question's inherent constitutional interest, the question of what would happen if the Dáil failed to vote the necessary funds to meet the State's obligations may briefly be examined. In Britain, the common law rule that no form of execution was available against the Crown was an aspect of the prerogative, and founded on the fiction that the King could do not wrong.[237] It is plain from *Byrne* that this doctrine did not survive in Ireland. There is, however, another fundamental constitutional principle which might appear to be a barrier in the case of damages: Articles 11 and 17.2 of the Constitution make it clear that all State expenditure must be authorised by the Dáil.[238] There is, accordingly, some authority for the proposition that any form of enforcement which required a monetary payment would constitute an interference with this principle.[239] Take, for example, *Conroy*

---

[235] *Ibid.* at 236–237.

[236] See also, to like effect, *Leyden v. Attorney General* [1926] I.R. 334.

[237] Wade and Forsyth, *op.cit.*, above, n.2, p. 822.

[238] See also, the comments of Gannon J. in *K. Security Ltd v. Ireland*, unreported, High Court, July 15, 1977. However, to take the opposite case, just because certain expenditure has been authorised by the Dáil does not mean that the contract in question is necessarily *intra vires*. In *Howard v. Commissioners of Public Works* [1994] 1 I.R. 101 monies had been voted by the Dáil for the construction of certain visitors' centres by the Commissioners. The construction of these projects was found by Costello J. to have been *ultra vires* the Commissioners' powers (see pp. 395 and 404) and he then continued (at 116):
> ". . . the grant by this statute to a statutory body like the Commissioners of money to defray the charges of the services it is providing does not empower it to provide services which are not within its statutory powers as ascertained from the enactments relating to the statutory body . . . [T]hat approval by a majority of members of Dáil Éireann of expenditure by the Commissioners on the visitors' centre . . . must have been based on the belief that such expenditure could lawfully have been undertaken by the Commissioners. If, as I think is the case, this expenditure is outside the Commissioners' statutory powers then the resolution of approval cannot have the effect of bringing it within them.".

[239] It is also just possible that any enforcement involving monetary payment would be held to constitute an interference with the business of the Oireachtas, and would run up against Art. 15 (parliamentary

---

954

v. Minister for Defence,[240] in which the Supreme Court granted a declaration that the Minister was bound to take steps for the payment of a pension to the plaintiff, and that under the terms of the Military Service (Pensions) Act 1924, he had no authority to question the plaintiff's entitlement. The Act had stipulated that no person could receive a military service pension unless money for this purpose had been voted by the Oireachtas. This meant, according to Kennedy C.J., that it was the duty of the Minister for Defence to submit the particulars of the pensions granted by him to the Oireachtas "so that the moneys [could] be voted accordingly if the Oireachtas so please[d]". It should be noted that even in this traditional authority the Minister was put under an obligation to execute his part of the parliamentary process, but, secondly, that the Oireachtas was free to do it as it "please[d]."

A variant of this problem has arisen in more recent times in a series of cases dealing with delapidated courthouses where the State has sought to argue that certain orders or decrees should not be made by reason of the insufficiency of resources. In *Hoey v. Minister for Justice*[241] the applicant, who had demonstrated that the Minister was in breach of her duty under the Courthouses (Provision and Maintenance) Act 1935 to repair the courthouses in question, was met with the objection that the Minister had insufficient funds for this purpose. Lynch J. rejected this submission as based "upon a misconception of the powers, duties and functions of the Executive in regard to the implementation of legislation enated by the Oireachtas." The judge added that if these statutory obligations were now regarded as burdensome, "the Executive must introduce the appropriate legislation to the Oireachtas and persuade the Oireachtas to enact the same."[242] If it appears that this attitude involves a disregard of the prerogatives of the Oireachtas (and especially the Dáil) with regard to the supply of funds and, indeed, general separation of powers principles, it may be said that such an attitude has been fairly consistently adopted by the judges in other (non financial) areas in which the autonomy of the Dáil might appear to be engaged.[243]

Finally, it may be noted that in *McC. v. Eastern Health Board*[244] the Supreme Court took a slightly different view of this question in comparison to that taken by Lynch J. in *Hoey.* This case concerned the alleged failure of a health board to process foreign adoption requests as "soon as practicable" as required by section 5 of the Adoption Act 1991. In the present case, the evidence established, in the words of Keane J., that the delays were the result:

---

privilege). However as parliamentary privilege is so much less extensive in Ireland than in Britain, this seems unlikely.

240 [1934] I.R. 679.

241 [1994] 3 I.R. 329. See also *Keane v. Minister for Justice* [1994] 3 I.R. 347.

242 *Ibid.* at 343. That is not say that budgetary considerations are of no relevance in this context, as the courts may, on discretionary grounds, place a stay on the order for relief in order to give the Minister time to comply with the order in question: see pp. 733–734.

243 See, *e.g.* Hogan and Whyte, *Kelly, op. cit.,* above, n. 33, pp. 170–176.

244 [1996] 2 I.R. 296.

". . . of the considerable increase in the number of such applications in the functional area of the [health board], the imposition of new statutory responsibilities in the area of child care on the [health board] and the shortage generally of qualified and experienced personnel capable of carrying out the necessary assessments."[245]

Keane J. distinguished *Hoey* and held for the respondent on the basis that in that case the Minister had given the local authorities an unlawful direction not to provide any court accommodation in the town in question. However, *McC.* clearly indicates that the courts will not assume that statutory bodies have – or must be given – unlimited resources in order that they may fully discharge their statutory obligations.

---

[245] [1996] 2 I.R. 296 at 311.

INDEX

Compiled by Julitta Clancy, Registered Indexer